The Wiley Blackwell
Handbook of
Transpersonal Psychology

In summary, this volume succeeds in accomplishing a lot. It clearly provides an update on the accomplishments of transpersonal psychology. It also raises issues of profound importance both for the discipline of transpersonal psychology and for the broader field. It will serve as a useful reference for a comprehensive overview of the entire discipline for years to come. Anyone who claims to be a scholar of the entire field of psychology must read it.

PsycCRITIQUES

This book is a great source of up to date information, and a great contribution to our understanding of this important area of work.

ACPNL Magazine

The new *Handbook of Transpersonal Psychology* is a necessity today. Many transpersonal psychologists and psychotherapists have been waiting for such a comprehensive work. Congratulations to Harris Friedman and Glenn Hartelius. May this book contribute to an increasingly adventurous, creative and vibrant universe.

Ingo B. Jahrsetz, President, The European Transpersonal Association

The *Handbook of Transpersonal Psychology* is an outstanding, comprehensive overview of the field. It is a valuable resource for professional transpersonal practioners, and an excellent introduction for those who are new to this wide-ranging discipline.

Frances Vaughan, PhD. Psychologist, author of Shadows of the Sacred: Seeing Through Spiritual Illusions

Finally, the vast literature on transpersonal psychology has been collected in what is clearly the essential handbook for psychologists and others who have either too apologetically endorsed or too critically rejected what undoubtedly will define psychology in the future. If you are not a transpersonal psychologist now, you will be after exploring this handbook. No longer can one dismiss the range of topics confronted by transpersonal psychologists nor demand methodological restraints that refuse to confront the realities transpersonal psychologists explore. This is a marvelous handbook- critical, expansive, and like much of what transpersonal psychologists study, sublime.

Ralph W. Hood Jr., University of Tennessee, Chattanooga

The Wiley Blackwell Handbook of Transpersonal Psychology

Edited by

Harris L. Friedman
University of Florida

Glenn Hartelius
Sofia University, Palo Alto, CA

WILEY Blackwell

This edition first published 2015
© 2013 John Wiley & Sons, Ltd

Edition history: The Wiley Blackwell Handbook of Transpersonal Psychology, edited by
Harris L. Friedman and Glenn Hartelius, John Wiley & Sons, Ltd (hardback, 2013)

Registered Office
John Wiley & Sons Ltd, The Atrium, Southern Gate, Chichester, West Sussex, PO19 8SQ, UK

Editorial Offices
350 Main Street, Malden, MA 02148-5020, USA
9600 Garsington Road, Oxford, OX4 2DQ, UK
The Atrium, Southern Gate, Chichester, West Sussex, PO19 8SQ, UK

For details of our global editorial offices, for customer services, and for information about how to apply
for permission to reuse the copyright material in this book please see our website at
www.wiley.com/wiley blackwell.

The right of Harris L. Friedman and Glenn Hartelius to be identified as the authors of the editorial
material in this work has been asserted in accordance with the UK Copyright, Designs and Patents
Act 1988.

Library of Congress Cataloging-in-Publication Data

The Wiley Blackwell handbook of transpersonal psychology / [edited by] Harris L. Friedman,
Glenn Hartelius.
    pages cm
  Includes bibliographical references and index.
    ISBN 978-1-119-96755-2 (cloth)   ISBN 978-1-119-05029-2 (paper)
  1. Transpersonal psychology–Handbooks, manuals, etc.   I. Friedman, Harris L. editor of
compilation.   II. Hartelius, Glenn editor of compilation.
  BF204.7.W55 2013
  150.19_87–dc23

                                                                              2013012018

A catalogue record for this book is available from the British Library.

Cover image: © Getty Images / Raul Touzon

Typeset in 10/12.5pt Galliard by SPi Publisher Services, Pondicherry, India

1   2015

Dedicated to the Memory of Earl Clement Brown (1928–2002)

Contents

Notes on Contributors

Rosemarie Anderson, PhD, is Professor of Psychology at Sofia University. She has written extensively on Intuitive Inquiry, Embodied Writing, the Body Insight Scale, and psychospiritual development. Her current interests focus on feminine mysteries as reflected in mythology and sacred geography. She, along with William Braud, co-authored two books on transpersonal research methods.

Julie Beischel, PhD, Co-Founder and Director of Research at the Windbridge Institute, served as Co-Director of the VERITAS Research Program at the University of Arizona. Her research has been published in peer-reviewed journals including *Journal of Parapsychology, Journal of Scientific Exploration, Transpersonal Psychology Review, Australian Journal of Parapsychology,* and *Explore: The Journal of Science and Healing.*

Kim A. Bella, PhD, is currently adjunct professor of psychology and sociology at Bristol Community College in southeastern Massachusetts. Dr. Bella's research interests and expertise include the exploration and intersection of creativity, nutrition, and mental health. Dr. Bella also maintains a clinical practice specializing in transpersonally oriented expressive arts and other therapeutic techniques.

William Braud, PhD, was Professor Emeritus at Sofia University and died in May, 2012. He wrote extensively in transpersonal psychology, parapsychology, exceptional human experience, and consciousness studies. His website, http://incl usivepsychology.com, includes an archive of many of his publications. Along with Rosemarie Anderson, he co-authored two books on transpersonal research methods.

Christine Brooks, PhD, is Associate Professor and Chair of the Residential MA and PhD programs in Transpersonal Psychology at Sofia University. She is a member of the Advisory Board of the Center for the Sacred Feminine and the Chair of the Diversity Action Team at Sofia. Her scholarship focuses on issues of diversity in transpersonal psychology and related fields and exploring the potential for social transformation and social justice from a transpersonal perspective.

Jeanine M. Canty, PhD, is Associate Professor at Naropa University in Boulder, CO. Her teaching intersects the natural world, justice, contemplative practice, and transformative learning. Teaching in the Environmental Studies and Environmental Leadership programs, her courses include Ecopsychology, Deep Ecology, Multicultural Perspectives for Environmental Leaders, and an 8-day Wilderness solo.

Katherine E. Coder, PhD, is a community and transpersonal psychologist who counsels, consults, teaches, writes, and builds communities of healing and transformation. She serves as an adjunct faculty member at the University of Miami. Her research interests include mystic activism, holistic wellbeing interventions, and innovative models of social change.

Allan Combs, PhD, is a transpersonal psychologist, consciousness researcher, neuropsychologist, and systems theorist. He holds appointments at the California Institute of Integral Studies where he is the Director of the *Center for the Study of Consciousness*, and at Saybrook University. He is author of over 200 publications on transpersonal psychology and consciousness.

Brant Cortright, PhD, is a professor at the California Institute of Integral Studies. He is the author of *Integral Psychology: Yoga, Growth and Opening the Heart* and *Psychotherapy and Spirit: Theory and Practice in Transpersonal Psychotherapy* (SUNY Press). He is a licensed clinical psychologist with a private practice in San Francisco.

Michael Daniels, PhD, is Editor of *Transpersonal Psychology Review*. He was formerly program leader for the MSc in Consciousness and Transpersonal Psychology at Liverpool John Moores University. His numerous publications in transpersonal psychology include two books: *Self-Discovery the Jungian Way* (Routledge, 1992), and *Shadow, Self, Spirit* (Imprint Academic, 2005).

John V. Davis, PhD, is a professor at Naropa University and author of *The Diamond Approach: An Introduction to the Teachings of A.H. Almaas* (Shambhala). He is an ordained Diamond Approach teacher and a staff member of the School of Lost Borders, where he trains wilderness rites of passage guides.

Daniel Deslauriers, PhD, is professor in the Transformative Studies Doctorate at the California Institute of Integral Studies. He is co-author of Integral Dreaming (SUNY Press) and co-founder of the Montreal Center for the Study of Dreams.

James Fadiman, (BA, Harvard, PhD, Stanford) has taught at Brandeis, San Francisco State, and Stanford, and co-founded the Institute for Transpersonal Psyhcology, now Sofia University. His most recent book is *The Psychedelic Explorer's Guide: Safe, Therapeutic and Sacred Journeys*. He has been a management consultant, Director of Noetics, and president of two natural resource companies.

Jorge N. Ferrer, PhD, is professor of East-West Psychology at the California Institute of Integral Studies, San Francisco. He is the author of *Revisioning Transpersonal Theory: A Participatory Vision of Human Spirituality* (SUNY Press, 2002) and coeditor of *The Participatory Turn: Spirituality, Mysticism, Religious Studies* (SUNY Press, 2008).

Eric FitzMedrud, PhD, is Core Faculty in the PsyD in Clinical Psychology residential program at Sofia University. He also serves and the Clinical Director of Sofia

University's Community Center for Health & Wellness and in private practice in Palo Alto, California.

Kendra Ford, MA, is a doctoral candidate in Transpersonal Psychology and adjunct faculty at Sofia University in Palo Alto, California. She has a background in mental health casework and advocacy and is currently devoted to raising awareness of feminist issues through transpersonal psychology, spiritualized social justice, research, education, and art.

Cheryl Fracasso, PhD, is pursuing licensure as a marriage and family therapist at Antioch University Seattle. She holds a PhD in psychology from Saybrook University, and serves as faculty at University of Phoenix. She works as an Advisory Board Member for the *NeuroQuantology* journal and the American Center for the Integration of Spiritually Transformative Experiences (ACISTE).

Harris L. Friedman, Ph.D. is Research Professor of Psychology (Retired, University of Florida), Professor Emeritus (Saybrook University), and a clinical and organizational psychologist. He serves as Senior Editor of the *International Journal of Transpersonal Studies*, Associate Editor of *The Humanistic Psychologist*, and has published extensively in transpersonal psychology.

Albert P. Garcia-Romeu is a postdoctoral fellow at Johns Hopkins University School of Medicine, where he is currently researching the effects of psychedelic compounds in human subjects, with a focus on psilocybin as a potential treatment for addiction. He received his doctorate at the Institute of Transpersonal Psychology where he studied the measurement and experience of self-transcendence in healthy adults.

Bruce Greyson, MD, is the Chester Carlson Professor of Psychiatry and Neurobehavioral Sciences and Director of the Division of Perceptual Studies at the University of Virginia School of Medicine. He is a Distinguished Life Fellow of the American Psychiatric Association, and former editor of the *Journal of Near-Death Studies.*

Stanislav Grof, MD, is one of the founders and chief theoreticians of transpersonal psychology, and the founding president of the International Transpersonal Association, with over fifty years experience in research involving psychotherapy and nonordinary states of consciousness. He was formerly Chief of Psychiatric Research at the Maryland Psychiatric Research Center, Assistant Professor of Psychiatry at Johns Hopkins University School of Medicine, and scholar-in-residence at Esalen Institute. He is the author of numerous books on transpersonal topics.

Glenn Hartelius, PhD, serves on core faculty at Sofia University in Palo Alto, CA. He is editor of the *International Journal of Transpersonal Studies*, and Secretary of the International Transpersonal Association. He teaches meditation and attentional training skills internationally, and has published in the fields of transpersonal psychology and consciousness studies.

Arthur Hastings, PhD, is executive professor and Director of the William James Center for Consciousness Studies at Sofia University, Palo Alto, CA, in the Transpersonal Psychology Program. His specialties are states of consciousness, exceptional human experiences, and theory. He is also known for his work with healing bereavement.

Lisa Herman is Director Creative Expression and Executive Core Faculty at Sofia University, Core Faculty at Meridian University and Adjunct Faculty at ISIS-Canada. She is a Registered Expressive Arts Therapist and a licensed Marriage and Family Therapist and Clinical Supervisor, as well as a novelist and performance artist.

Anne Huffman, PhD, is a faculty member at Sofia University. Her research interests include spirituality, transpersonal studies, LGBT issues, diversity, and generational research. She maintains a private practice in spiritual guidance. She worked closely with Dr. Robert Frager to create and develop the MA in Spiritual Guidance program at Sofia University.

Harvey J. Irwin, PhD, has an international reputation in parapsychological research. His publications include over a hundred papers in academic journals and four books, including the highly praised and widely used text *An Introduction to Parapsychology.* He is Honorary Research Fellow at the School of Psychology in the University of New England, Australia, where he taught for over 30 years.

Zvi Ish-Shalom, PhD, is Assistant Professor of Religious Studies at Naropa University in Boulder, CO. His areas of research and teaching include kabbalah, hasidism, comparative mysticism, psychology of religious experience, and embodied forms of spiritual practice. He is also an ordained rabbi, a certified Rolfer and a student of the Diamond Approach.

Don Hanlon Johnson, PhD, is a professor of Somatics in the School of Professional Psychology and Health at California Institute of Integral Studies, and founder of the first graduate degree program in the field of somatic psychotherapy. He is author of four books, four collections, and several articles focused on the role of investigations and practical cultivation of direct bodily experience in the organization of the personal world and the social order.

Jacob Kaminker, PhD, is Core Faculty in the Holistic Counseling Program at John F. Kennedy University. He is Associate Managing Editor for the *International Journal of Transpersonal Studies* and sits on the Board of the International Expressive Arts Therapy Association. His work is in the areas of spiritual diversity issues in clinical practice, mysticism, parapsychology, dreams, and imagination.

Andrew Kornfeld is recent graduate of the University of California at Santa Cruz, Andrew Kornfeld obtained dual degrees in Neuroscience and Psychology. While at school, Andrew co-founded the Brain, Mind, and Consciousness Society, which explores the connections between the physical, biological, and social sciences.

B. Les Lancaster, PhD, is Emeritus Professor of Transpersonal Psychology at Liverpool John Moores University, UK, Honorary Research Fellow in the Centre for Jewish Studies at Manchester University, and Dean (Transpersonal Psychology), Professional Development Foundation/Middlesex University. He is currently Chair of the Transpersonal Psychology Section of the British Psychological Society.

Charles D. Laughlin, PhD, is an emeritus professor, Department of Anthropology, Carleton University, Ottawa, Ontario, Canada. He is co-author of *Brain, Symbol and Experience: Toward a Neurophenomenology of Human Consciousness, The Spectrum of*

Ritual, and the author of *Communing with the Gods: Consciousness, Culture and the Dreaming Brain.* He is a mature contemplative who was a Tibetan Buddhist monk for six years, and a practitioner of Husserlian transcendental phenomenology.

G. Frank Lawlis, PhD, has focused upon clinical and research methods of the spirit-mind-body, since he received his doctorate in psychology from Texas Tech University. He is a Fellow of the American Psychological Association. He is oversight adviser of the Dr. Phil Show and Director of Testing, American Mensa.

David Lukoff, PhD, is a Professor of Psychology at Sofia University in Palo Alto, CA, Co-president of the Association for Transpersonal Psychology, and a licensed psychologist in California. His work focuses on spiritual issues and mental health. He is author of 80 articles and chapters, and is co-author of the *Diagnotic and Statistical Manual -IV*'s category, Religious or Spiritual Problem.

Douglas A. MacDonald, PhD, is an Associate Professor of Psychology at the University of Detroit Mercy and part-time faculty at Saybrook University. He has been doing research in the area of spirituality for the past 20 years with primary emphasis on measurement and assessment. He is involved in an editorial capacity with a number of scholarly journals.

Fabrice Nye, PhD, graduated from the Institute of Transpersonal Psychology, and practices clinical psychology as a postdoctoral fellow at the Community Center for Health and Wellness, in Palo Alto, California. He did his doctoral research on stress reduction.

Genie Palmer, PhD, is an associate professor and executive core faculty member at Sofia University where she teaches courses in transpersonal research skills and methods. Her areas of research and writing include impacts of exceptional human experiences and exploration of various states of consciousness (epiphany, peak, and mystical experiences).

James D. Pappas, PhD, is a registered clinical psychologist. He practices East-West therapeutic approaches that include mindfulness, compassion, acceptance, cognitive-behavioural, and somatic experiencing. Dr. Pappas has taught numerous university courses, conducted research in transpersonal assessment as well as on primary and secondary trauma. He is developing Philotimo Publishing for mindfulness and compassion based literature.

Thomas B. Roberts, PhD, is an emeritus professor in the Honors Program at Northern Illinois University, Thomas Roberts has taught a course on psychedelics since 1981. His major publications are *Psychedelic Medicine* (2-vols. with Michael Winkelman), *Spiritual Growth with Entheogens,* and *The Psychedelic Future of the Mind.* He originated the celebration of Bicycle Day.

Adam J. Rock, PhD, holds posts at the International Transpersonal Association, the Australian Institute of Parapsychological Research (President), the *International Journal of Transpersonal Studies, Anthropology of Consciousness,* and the *Australian Journal of Parapsychology.* He has published dozens of academic journals articles as well as numerous books.

Vitor Rodrigues, PhD in Psychology, author of 12 books, and psychotherapist, was the President of the European Transpersonal Association (EUROTAS) 2005-2009. He taught at Portuguese universities during 17 years. He uses Regression Therapy, Hypnosis, Meditation, Guided Imagery, and Psychic Defence techniques, according to clients' needs. He delivers lectures, workshops and courses in Portugal and throughout Europe in the same areas.

Donald Rothberg, PhD, is on the Teachers Council at Spirit Rock Meditation Center in California and formerly taught at the University of Kentucky, Kenyon College, and Saybrook Graduate School. He writes and teaches on meditation, spirituality and psychology, and socially engaged spirituality. He is the author of *The Engaged Spiritual Life* and the co-editor of *Ken Wilber in Dialogue*.

Geffen Rothe, MA, holds a degree from Institute of Transpersonal Psychology (Sophia University). Owner and Director of Well-Defined Solutions, her company provides business consultation services internationally. Her passion is empowering individuals and companies to pursue profitable professional practices that honor the path of conscious, compassionate living, both individually and collectively.

Nancy Rowe, PhD, is an Associate Professor and Chair of the Master of Transpersonal Psychology program at Sofia University. She brings experience in expressive arts therapy, spiritual guidance, and teacher education to her teaching, professional contribution, retreat/seminar facilitation, curriculum development/program design, and writing. Her research focuses on transformative learning, earth-centered spirituality, and creativity.

Paul J. Roy, PhD, is Provost of Sofia University. Over the last 17 years, he has been director of the University's counseling center, clinical faculty director, and Dean of the On-Campus Programs. He is a licensed psychologist and spiritual guide. He has authored a book, and several book chapters, and articles in the areas of clinical psychology, peace psychology, and spirituality.

Ilene A. Serlin, PhD, BC-DMT, psychologist and registered dance/movement therapist in San Francisco and Marin, is past-president of the San Francisco Psychological Association, a Fellow of the American Psychological Association (APA), and past-president of the APA's Division of Humanistic Psychology. She has taught at Saybrook, Lesley University, University of California Los Angeles, the New York Gestalt Institute, the C.G. Jung Institute in Zurich, and is editor of *Whole Person Healthcare* (2007, 3 vol., Praeger).

Shauna L. Shapiro, PhD, is Associate Professor of Counseling Psychology at Santa Clara University and an internationally recognized expert in mindfulness. She has conducted extensive clinical research investigating the effects of mindfulness and published over 70 peer-reviewed journal articles in addition to co-authoring the critically acclaimed professional text, *The Art and Science of Mindfulness*.

Lance Storm, PhD, is the author of the books *The Enigma of Numbers* (2008) and *A Parapsychological Investigation of the Theory of Psychopraxia* (2010). He also has published numerous peer-reviewed journal articles, and edited/co-edited several scholarly volumes. He has been awarded the Parapsychological Association's Outstanding Research Contribution Award and the Frances P. Bolton Fellowship.

Charles T. Tart, PhD, is Executive Faculty at Sofia University and Professor Emeritus of Psychology at University of California Davis. Internationally known for research with altered states, transpersonal psychology, and parapsychology, his books include *Altered States of Consciousness* and *Transpersonal Psychologies*, while his latest is *The End of Materialism: How Evidence of the Paranormal is Bringing Science and Spirit Together*.

Theodore Usatynski, MA, is the author of *Instinctual Intelligence* and director of Instinctual Intelligence Consulting, LLC. He holds Graduate degrees from Harvard and Naropa universities. His professional training includes the Sensorimotor Psychotherapy Institute Treatment for Trauma Program and he is a student of the Diamond Approach.

Alan G. Vaughan, PhD, JD, is a member of the core faculty and director of the graduate psychology programs in Jungian studies at Saybrook University. He is in private practice as a clinical-consulting psychologist and Jungian analyst. He is on the International Editorial Board of the *Jung Journal of Culture & Psyche*.

Jenny Wade, PhD, is a transpersonal theorist and researcher specializing in consciousness studies and change. A professor at Sofia University and organization development expert, her research ranges from the esoteric, such as ancient northern European paganism, to proprietary intellectual property developed for clients, such as the predictors of outstanding organization performance.

Harald Walach, PhD, is Director of the Institute of Transcultural Health Sciences at the European University Viadrina in Frankfurt (Oder), Germany, where he also coordinates a postgraduate training program for doctors in complementary medicine and cultural studies. He holds a double Ph.D. in Clinical Psychology, and History and Theory of Science, and has authored more than 100 peer reviewed papers, several books and numerous book chapters.

Kathleen Wall, PhD, is Associate Professor at Sofia University Palo Alto, California and a contributor to The Spirituality and Health Institute, Santa Clara University, California. She is an author on several publications about spiritually integrated psychological practices. She co-developed Psycho-Spiritual Integrative Therapy (PSIT) and leads research and trainings on PSIT.

Roger Walsh, MD, PhD, DHL, is professor of psychiatry, philosophy, and anthropology at the University of California at Irvine. His publications include *Essential Spirituality: The Seven Central Practices* and *The World of Shamanism*. He has also coedited the books *Paths Beyond Ego: The Transpersonal Vision*, *Higher Wisdom*, and most recently *The World's Great Wisdom*.

Ian E. Wickramasekera II, PsyD, is a Professor of Clinical Psychology at the University of the Rockies in Colorado Springs, CO. He is a Past-President of the American Psychological Association's Society of Psychological Hypnosis (Division 30). He has a lifelong fascination with topics such as Affective Neuroscience, Bon-Buddhism, Empathy, Hypnosis, Integrative Medicine, and Lucid Dreaming.

Michael J. Winkelman, PhD, pioneered cross-cultural, biological and evolutionary models of shamanism (*Shamans, Priests and Witches* 1992; *Shamanism a Biopsychosocial Paradigm of Consciousness and Healing 2010*). He retired from the School of Human Evolution and Social Change at Arizona State University in 2009 and currently resides in central Brazil.

Foreword

Stanley Krippner

Frequently, I am asked to make recommendations for people wanting to become acquainted with the considerable literature in transpersonal psychology. However, there has been no contemporary singular source to which to refer them—the last effort to compile such a reference into one volume was the *Textbook of Transpersonal Psychiatry and Psychology* (Scotton, Chinen, & Battista, 1996), which is now nearly two decades old. Consequently, this handbook fills an important niche that will be useful for all who want an overview of the area, as it combines within one resource a variety of perspectives and topics that collectively serve to outline and define transpersonal psychology.

Many have attempted to define transpersonal psychology. In fact, few fields have exerted as much effort in defining itself. Hartelius, Caplan, and Rardin (2007) examined 160 definitions from the first 35 years of the field's existence, and found three major themes. First, transpersonal psychology is commonly defined as one that examines states of consciousness and stages of human development that go beyond the bounds of the self as normally defined, as well as the aspirations and paths of practice directed at transcending the conventional "I." It is also defined as an integrative or holistic approach that considers not just the intellect, but the whole embodied person situated in local and global community, ecosystem, and cosmos. Additionally, it considers the dynamics of human transformation, both individually and collectively.

My approach to defining the transpersonal refers to experiences that lead to the impression of a more complete encounter with "reality" in which the sense of identity extends beyond ordinary limits to encompass broader, deeper, and wider aspects of life (Krippner, 2002), similar to Friedman's (1983) construct of self-expansiveness. I see this as dependent upon both the experients' consciousness and its cultural context. Transpersonal psychology, as one of several varieties of transpersonal study, is informed by science and provides a paradigm that integrates the entirety of human activity and experience, from the most pathological to the most sublime. In understanding transpersonal psychology as a science, I have found William James' (1912/1976) "radical empiricism" useful, which he defined as follows: "To be radical, an empiricism must neither admit into its constructions any element that is not directly experienced, nor exclude from them any element that is directly experienced" (p. 22). However, science is not the only approach to understanding the transpersonal, as there are many other epistemologies or "ways of knowing," such as relying on the body, feelings, intuition, and transpersonal-anomalous experiences, which all can provide access to experiential realms that conventional science has not yet acknowledged, much less appreciated (e.g., Anderson & Braud, 2011). One area in which transpersonal psychology has a particular opportunity is in working to develop new connections between these ways of knowing and the tradition of science—as in, for example, attempting to operationalize Tart's (1972) suggestion that it may be possible to develop state-specific sciences.

The chapters in this handbook cover a wide range of viewpoints that together illuminate transpersonal psychology. Many in the founding generation of the field are approaching retirement; a few have retired or passed from the ranks. This work brings together the scholarship of many of the senior scholars still within the field and pairs it with the impulse and energy of emerging scholars—often within the same chapter. In this way it represents not only a distillation of the wisdom of those who formed the field, but also the sharing of the mantle with a new generation who will carry transpersonal psychology forward.

This important volume serves as a milestone for transpersonal psychology as a discipline coming of age. It reflects its many successes, as well as points to areas in which considerable work is still required. Within the ranks of those who consider themselves transpersonal psychologists is great diversity, as not all perspectives are in accord with each other, but collectively they address the whole gamut that makes for transpersonal psychology, which can be seen as they are brought together here. Transpersonal psychology owes appreciation to the efforts of Harris Friedman and Glenn Hartelius who, as editors of this handbook, have drawn together a rich collection of chapters, which can now serve as the starting place for those who want to become acquainted with its diversity. More than ever before, a transpersonal view that can integrate not only the field of psychology, but that can also provide an inspiring framework for understanding humanity's essential connection to the cosmos, is needed for human adaptation and flourishing. This handbook furthers that effort.

References

Anderson, R., & Braud, W. (2011). Transforming self and others through research: Transpersonal research methods and skills for the human sciences and humanities. Albany, NY: State University of New York Press.

Friedman, H. (1983). The Self-Expansiveness Level Form: A conceptualization and measurement of a transpersonal construct. *Journal of Transpersonal Psychology, 15,* 37-50.

Hartelius, G., Caplan, M., & Rardin, M.-A. (2007). Transpersonal psychology: Defining the past, divining the future. *The Humanistic Psychologist, 35*(2), 135-160.

James, W. (1976). Essays in radical empiricism. Cambridge, MA: Harvard University Press. (Original work published 1912)

Krippner, S. (2002). Dancing with the trickster: Notes for a transpersonal autobiography. *International Journal of Transpersonal Studies, 21*, 1-18. Retrieved from http://www.stan leykrippner.com/papers/autobiogood.htm

Scotton, B., Chinen, A., & Battista, J. (Eds.). (1996). Textbook of transpersonal psychiatry and psychology. New York, NY: Basic Books.

Tart, C. T. (1972). States of consciousness and state-specific sciences. *Science, 176*, 1203-1210.

Acknowledgments

The editors wish to acknowledge the many transpersonal scholars who participated in the visioning and writing of this volume. Their generosity with time and effort is what made this work possible. In addition to a number of the authors who provided feedback on the scope of this Handbook, and to whom we are grateful for that service, we also wish to thank Søren Brier, Paul Cunningham, Jan Fisher, Harry Hunt, Akbar Husain, Ingo Jahrsetz, Charlotte Lewis (since passed), Olga Louchakova, Mark McCaslin, Sangeetha Menon, Ron Pilato, Stuart Sovatsky, and Frances Vaughan for their responses that helped to shape this volume. In addition, thanks go to Cheryl Fracasso for editorial and administrative assistance.

Special appreciation and acknowledgment are due to Anne Friedman and Michaela Aizer, the editors' partners. It is in some ways inconsiderate to acknowledge spouses only for their support, which evokes traditional patriarchal dynamics. However, our partners have been this and much more, contributing significantly to the shaping and balancing of how we each come to the concepts of this field. They deserve credit as well as appreciation.

Transpersonal psychology is an approach that emphasizes, among other things, the interconnectedness of individuals—the fact that in growth and transformation and creative expression, we do nothing alone. We have had the privilege to serve as editors, but without the participation of our colleagues and our partners, this volume could not have come to fruition.

Editors' Introduction

The Promise (and Some Perils) of Transpersonal Psychology

Harris L. Friedman and Glenn Hartelius

As a term, *transpersonal psychology* is a juxtaposition of three disparate ideas contained within its linguistic components: *psychology*, *personal*, and *trans*. As a psychology, it is focused on the scientific understanding of, and applications for working with, the individual, commonly seen as an isolated nexus of affect, cognition, and behavior embodied within a unitary biological encasement distinct from its environ (see Friedman, 2002). Clearly the notion of an individual, whose attributes can be mechanistically dissected should be exhumed for a more holistic understanding, as its components of affect, cognition, and behavior are no more separate in the individual than is its biological aspect separate from its many interconnected contexts. Humans isolated from their matrices of support, such as physical necessities like air and social necessities like succorance as a baby, would surely not survive. Further, that which differentiates an individual from other individuals, as well as that which lends some degree of continuity to an individual over time and across space, is the usual defining *personal* aspects of the individual, or the personality. Although the study of personality is a core subdiscipline of psychology, it lacks consensual understanding, despite that many competing perspectives have long attempted to construct unifying views of the person (John, Robins, & Pervin, 2008). These concerns engage with various tensions, such as understanding intrapersonal (including developmentally across time), interpersonal (including socially and culturally across space), and biological differences, which all serve as backdrop to that which is personal within humans. This is aptly reflected in the famous quote by Murray and Kluckhohn (1953), "EVERY *MAN* is in certain respects. a. *like all* other *men*, b. *like* some other men, c. *like no* other *man*" (n.p.). Then, throwing the prefix *trans*, most often seen as meaning *beyond*, into this mixture provides even further basis for confusion. This prefix, when attached to the personal, implies somewhat of a disqualifier, referencing that the personal is incomplete. It introduces an enigma, as in, exactly who is the person that might require going beyond and what is the beyond where the person might be going. In transpersonal psychology, this beyond has typically related to experiencing (or seeking to experience) so-called higher states of consciousness and possible spiritual realms, which both presumably go beyond the personal. In another meaning of the prefix, however, trans can also refer to a bridge, perhaps betwixt and between the person, that spans the boundaries dividing the person from the world of others and things, and even from transcendent possibilities that can be construed as super-personal or supernatural (as in the possible spirits implied by the term spirituality (Lindeman, Blomqvist, & Takada, 2012). Then there is the extreme possibility of that about which cannot be spoken cogently, the ultimate mysteries that can be described perhaps as God or non-duality, or in other ways that do not define but merely serve as a place marker for whatever might be ineffable. So, to coherently discuss transpersonal psychology when the notion of the individual as isolated within conventional understandings in psychology is obviously flawed, what constitutes the personality is ambiguous, and to what the prefix trans refers is inadequately specified together pose a triple conundrum.

One of us (Hartelius, Caplan, & Rardin, 2007) summarized previously published transpersonal definitions into basic themes via content analysis. The first focuses on the self as beyond ordinary ego separateness, recognizing the complex interconnectedness of self with all, including the cosmos as a whole. The second focuses on integrative approaches through employing the most inclusive framework to comprehend self, emphasizing spiritual and transcendent qualities. The third focuses on transformation, applying transpersonal perspective to individual and systems change processes. All three themes reinforce each other mutually as evolving parts of the definition.

Another way to understand transpersonal psychology is historically, as it emerged as a part of psychology during a time of turmoil when old structures were breaking down and new ones were not yet available for their replacement. Its immediate precursor, the humanistic psychology movement, stemmed from rebellious psychologists who rejected the two then-prevailing forces in psychology, psychoanalysis and behaviorism, and created a so-called third force focused on honoring human beings in a more holistic way. For some, however, the humanistic rebellion was still inadequate, resulting in rejection of the limitations of a humanistic perspective focused around the person as a whole but still relatively isolated entity, and moved toward embracing a wider and deeper, rather than human-centered, vantage that embedded the person within the largest aspects of the cosmos. These pioneering founders were unhappy with the extent of the revolution fomented by humanistic psychology, and sought more, but what this more is remains unclear. As such, transpersonal psychology is still a work in progress and, after more than half a century, it continues to search for its identity.

A major concern in transpersonal psychology thus involves definitional issues. Perhaps it is not yet adequately defined because it has not attained sufficient maturity, as it awaits a new paradigm that remains to be discovered or constructed, a prerequisite to its definition becoming better articulated. Alternately, perhaps by dealing with the most overarching perspective that humans might strive to attain, transpersonal psychology can never be summarized in any pithy way, similar to how a map can never completely capture the territory it attempts to portray.

What can be said generally about transpersonal psychology as an approach is that it supports the use of systematic scientific methodology, but critiques the insertion of modernist metaphysical assumptions about the mind-independent nature of the world (cf. Braud & Anderson, 1998; Anderson & Braud, 2011; Tart, 2004). It asserts, by contrast, that scientific method can be applied to research questions that reflect other types of assumptive frames, such as phenomenological, postmodern, traditionalist, feminist, and participatory frames, among others. Good research requires that the methodology be appropriate to the object of study. For example, one obviously does not immerse salt crystals in water in order to examine their structure for, since salt crystals dissolve in water, the methodology thwarts the objective of the inquiry. Something similar may be true of assumptive frames, for when reports of exceptional human experiences and capacities are placed within modernist assumptions about the nature of reality, they may appear to be delusional beliefs or anomalies that make no rational sense.

Modern Western philosophy, following Descartes, supposes mind and matter to be separate in some fundamental way, which in psychology has led to a practical denial of the personal mind as anything more than a brain-based biological information-processing system that, for some unknown reason, seems to be aware of itself (cf. Grof, 1983). This might be adequate were it not for the vast body of contemporary and historical reports of human experiences and capacities that are difficult to explain in satisfactory ways within such a context. These encounters at times transform the lives of individuals and change the course of entire societies; they inspire questions about the adequacy of what the modern West supposes to be the nature of reality.

Parapsychological research, investigating these experiences and capacities as anomalies within a modernist frame, has produced substantial evidence that such phenomena may not just be delusional reports. In this process, parapsychological researchers have advanced the rigor of scientific methodology by developing innovations, such as double-blind research. If the research evidence supporting such anomalies is valid, it would suggest that reality may be bigger and deeper than what modernism describes.

If Western notions of reality are to be expanded, then it may be that these anomalous exceptional human experiences and capacities—some of which are well supported by empirical evidence—offer clues about the ways in which modernist assumptions are deficient. Yet if a modernist metaphysic is imposed on research (cf. Mahner, 2012), then those very aspects of the phenomena will necessarily be discounted *a priori*, and the knowledge that might be generated from them will be lost. Evidence challenging the *de facto* metaphysical assumptions that tend to accompany science is disallowed on the grounds that it challenges those assumptions—rather like a judge who refuses to consider a motion to recuse him- or herself. Under the impetus to do good science, this actually constitutes resistance to critical examination of a metaphysical position.

Transpersonal scholars support further pursuit of research that extends the boundaries of knowledge and how it is produced, including the study of phenomena that may not adhere to the limits of reality suggested by a modernist metaphysic. Yet a transpersonal approach typically goes farther than merely considering anomalies within a reductive philosophical frame: it seeks out other carefully-constructed and critically-evaluated assumptive frames that may be more effective at producing a useful understanding of non-ordinary phenomena.

One example of a non-reductive frame of reference is phenomenology, which engages in the description of phenomenal experience without subjecting its veridicality to scrutiny based on particular presuppositions about reality. Another example is the traditionalist frame, which proposes, for example, a Buddhist psychology or a yoga psychology; a variant on this is the perennialist frame, which holds that various spiritual epistemologies reflect hidden but ontologically real aspects of the cosmos expressed in culture-specific ways. A postmodern frame, though diverse in its expressions, typically holds that the division of the world into objects of perception is a function of the perceivers, and does not reflect inherent properties of the world. Feminist and participatory approaches tend to emphasize the intersubjective nature of reality, and the researcher as being a participant in a living, relational process; subjectivity here is taken as foundational to reality, not a quality set over against an objective domain.

A transpersonal approach, then, pursues its study of psychology or other aspects of the humanities, within multiple frames of reference—within the field this is sometimes referred to as multiple ways of knowing (e.g., Braud, 2006). Transpersonalism critiques much of standard science for imposing a metaphysical frame while claiming to be strictly empirical; at the same time, it accepts the fact that a modernist frame is a simple and pragmatic one that can support a wide range of research topics. In this critique the transpersonal field finds touchpoints with postmodern scholarship, whose methods the field also utilizes. Yet there is also a contrast with some expressions of postmodernism, in that many transpersonal scholars are not ready to cede more scientifically-oriented fields such as psychology to strictly reductive approaches, or to relinquish the ontological reality of experiential phenomena.

A transpersonal approach is not in any sense anti-realist; a critique of the metaphysical assumption of a mind-independent reality does not necessarily imply an embrace of magical thinking. There are many ways to characterize the relationship between mind and nature other than strict dualism or uncritical fusion. Transpersonal psychology has the opportunity to participate in the development of this leading-edge aspect of inquiry, not only philosophically, but also empirically through the pursuit of research questions and methodologies that are congruent with alternate ways of considering reality.

Much of our desire to produce this handbook stemmed from our struggles to adequately define the discipline of transpersonal psychology. As editors, we do not always agree upon the best strategy although, as authors and co-authors of a few specific chapters in the handbook, we share our own approaches to definitional issues. However, as editors of the overall volume, we are interested in staying near the data provided by the many who have joined us this handbook through their writings. Rather than trying to abstract basic themes or other commonalities from this diverse collection of chapters, our hope is that by presenting various views, the panoply of approaches and content subsumed under transpersonal psychology can speak self-evidently. Ken Wilber, the well-known philosopher who once was a leader in, but no longer identifies with, the transpersonal movement, once quipped to one of us (personal communication to Friedman, circa 2002), "every year there is a contest to define transpersonal, and every year no one wins." Perhaps this book taken as a whole, not in piecemeal fashion, might or at least place in the contest for this particular year.

Our volume commences with a dedication, expressing some of the travails experienced by one of us (Friedman) in attempting to do dissertation research on transpersonal psychology within a mainstream doctoral program, a situation that has changed little after many decades. This is followed by "A Brand from the Burning: Defining Transpersonal Psychology," by one of us (Hartelius) and two co-authors, Geffen Rothe and Paul Roy. This initial chapter sets the tone for what follows, as it attempts to simplify the numerous definitions to something that can be shared on a brief elevator ride when someone quizzically asks, what exactly is transpersonal psychology? A further definitional attempt stems from a historical perspective, as Michael Daniels writes on the "Traditional Roots, History, and Evolution of the Transpersonal Perspective." This is followed by "The Call to a Spiritual Psychology: Should Transpersonal Psychology Convert?" by both of us, and James Pappas. In this chapter, we (and Pappas) try to engage with what makes transpersonal psychology, which is so little understood (often even by its own adherents), worth retaining, as much of its content overlaps with spiritual psychology. It is noted that, when transpersonal psychology was founded, the term spiritual was taboo in psychology, whereas now it has widespread acceptance, so it is reasonable to ask why the field should hold onto a less well-known and controversial term. Finally in this section, Harald Walach offers "Criticisms of Transpersonal Psychology and Beyond—The Future of Transpersonal Psychology: A Science and Culture of Consciousness," as a reflection of some of the meta-issues and possible dangers of transpersonal psychology—representing the sort of self-criticism that is mandatory within a responsible discipline. Together these four chapters constitute the *Introduction to Transpersonal Psychology* section of this volume.

The next section, *Transpersonal Theories*, takes on the heart of what transpersonal psychology movement offers, its theoretical perspective. Stanislav Grof, one of the most influential founders of transpersonal psychology, presents a very personal piece titled, "Revision and Revisioning of Psychology: Legacy from Half a Century of Consciousness Research," which sets the tone by sharing his involvement since the onset of the movement, as well as his unique theoretical perspective. Albert Garcia-Romeu and Charles T. Tart, also one of the pioneering luminaries in the transpersonal movement, focus on "Altered States of Consciousness and Transpersonal Psychology." They present the notion that ordinarily experienced consciousness states are but a sample of many potential states, and so-called higher states are the essence of how many view the main focus of transpersonal psychology. Alan Vaughan's chapter, "Jung, Analytical Psychology, and Transpersonal Psychology," follows with an introduction to the work of Jung, one of the major precursors to the movement and still a source of contemporary inspiration and creativity. Brant Cortright next presents "Integral Psychology," focusing on synthesizing Eastern and Western psychospiritual perspectives relying on the insights of Sri Aurobindo, another transpersonal luminary. Alan Combs then writes "Transcend and Include: Ken Wilber's Contribution to Transpersonal Psychology," sharing the complex worldview of another of the main contributors to transpersonal psychology. One of us (Hartelius) along with Jorge N. Ferrer presents "Transpersonal Philosophy: The Participatory Turn," further articulating a relatively recent approach to avoiding some of the dilemmas of earlier frames within transpersonal psychology. Following this, one of us (Friedman) writes on the importance of using conventional science within transpersonal psychology, illustrating with "Self-Expansiveness Theory" as one scientific approach. Last in this section on transpersonal theories, Les Lancaster writes on "Neuroscience and the Transpersonal," which deepens the connection of transpersonal psychology with science.

The following section focuses on *Transpersonal Methodologies*. Rosemarie Anderson and William Braud provide an overview of the unique methodological challenges in their chapter, "Transpersonal Research and Future Directions." Charles Laughlin and Adam Rock share a uniquely transpersonal research perspective in "Neurophenomenology: Enhancing the Experimental and Cross-Cultural Study of Brain and Experience." Next, Douglas A. MacDonald and one of us (Friedman) present "Quantitative Assessment of Transpersonal and Spiritual Constructs" as a way of using conventional psychological methods applied to nonconventional transpersonal material. One of us (Friedman) then discusses the "The Role of Science in Transpersonal Psychology: The Advantages of Middle-Range Theory." Rounding out this section, Douglas A. MacDonald writes on the "Philosophical Underpinnings of Transpersonal Psychology as a Science."

The next section focuses on *Transpersonal Experiences*, starting with Genie Palmer and Arthur Hastings, who write on "Exceptional Human Experiences," which have always been a central focus of transpersonal psychology. One type of exceptional experience that has particularly captivated the transpersonal movement is the topic of the chapter by James Fadiman and Andrew Kornfield titled "Psychedelic-Induced Experiences." Another type of exceptional experience that has been important in much of transpersonal discourse is the topic of the chapter by Cheryl Fracasso and Bruce Greyson, as well as one of us (Friedman) titled "Near-Death Experiences and Transpersonal Psychology: Focus on Helping Near-Death Experiencers." This is followed by Jenny Wade's chapter on "Transpersonal Sexual Experiences," which are often triggers to profound experiences of a transpersonal nature. Concluding this section is the chapter by Adam Rock, Lance Storm, Harvey J. Irwin, and Julie Beischel on "Parapsychology."

The following section focuses on *Transpersonal Approaches to Transformation, Healing, and Wellness*. Jacob Kaminker and David Lukoff write on "Transpersonal Perspectives on Mental Health and Mental Illness," which has been another central concern of transpersonal psychology. Douglas A. MacDonald, Roger Walsh, and Shauna Shapiro present a chapter on "Meditation: Empirical Research and Future Directions," which also has been the focus of much of transpersonal work. Similarly, Thomas B. Roberts and Michael Winkelman write on "Psychedelic Induced Transpersonal Experiences, Therapies, and Their Implications for Transpersonal Psychology," which has also been a major focus for transpersonal psychology. Don Hanlon Johnson presents a chapter on "Transpersonal Dimensions of Somatic Therapies," which constitute a variety of practices that are not always identified as transpersonal psychology, but which have close ties in many traditions to achieving transpersonal experiences. Ian Wickramasekera II writes on "Hypnotherapy and Transpersonal Psychology: Answering the Call Within," as hypnosis also has long been a way recognized in the West, as well as in other traditions, to enter transpersonal states. Daniel Deslauriers presents on "Dreaming and Transpersonal Psychology," as dreamwork is another avenue long used to understand and work with transpersonal experiences. Kim Bella and Ilene Serlin write on "Expressive and Creative Arts Therapies" as yet another avenue to enter extraordinary states for healing purposes. Kathleen Wall, Fabrice Nye, and Eric Fitzmedrud present on "Psychospiritual Integrative Practices," which they have been researching to facilitate positive change from a transpersonal perspective. John Davis, Theodore J. Usatynski, and Zvi Ish-Shalom write on the "Diamond Approach" of A. H. Almaas, another major figure in transpersonal psychology. Last in this section,

Vitor Rodrigues and one of us (Friedman) write on "Transpersonal Psychotherapy," which has always been an important concern of the transpersonal movement. Together chapters in this section provide a glimpse of many of the ways in which transpersonal psychology is applied.

The final section of this volume is on *Transpersonal Studies,* which relates transpersonal psychology in a broader way to various disciplines and perspectives. John Davis writes on "Ecopsychology and Transpersonal Psychology," as a core aspect of the movement has been focused on going beyond a human perspective to one more interrelated to other life forms and the earth. Christine Brooks, Kendra Ford, and Anne Huffman write on "Feminist and Cultural Contributions to Transpersonal Psychology," as the voices of women and people of color have often been under-represented in the movement. Donald Rothberg and Katherine Coder continue this theme by writing on "Widening Circles: The Emergence of Transpersonal Social Engagement," as transpersonal psychology has often neglected engagement in our world by focusing primarily on the "inner" psychospiritual development of individuals, often excluding attention both to social relationships and to the ways that the social dimension is internalized in the individual. Similarly, Frank Lawlis focuses on "Modern Miracles from Ancient Medicine: Transpersonal Medicine Approaches," giving recognition to indigenous and ancient contributions to healing. Next, Lisa Herman focuses on "Transpersonal Experience and the Arts: From the Chauvet Cave to Occupy Wall Street" to give yet another perspective complementing transpersonal psychology. Last in this section, Nancy Rowe and William Braud focus on one of the major modern institutions in "Transpersonal Education."

Our introduction started, as the book itself did, with definitional issues, many of which are unresolved in the open horizons of transpersonal psychology and in its collective searching and researching for the beyond and across. Our hope is that this collection, although it may not be able to reduce the complexity of what transpersonal psychology is to an easily graspable essence, can as a whole overview the area in a way that well reflects many of its facets.

We also need to acknowledge that there are many gaps in this coverage, as this handbook is incomplete in a variety of ways. For one, we are concerned about how transpersonal psychology can be misused, and we think of numerous cases of guru abuse and spiritual bypass, as well as how powerful ideas can be co-opted for evil as well as used for good. Even the extreme examples, such as the totalitarian Nazi atrocities being linked to what can be seen as transpersonal ideology, always lurks as background shadow. There is an adage that any medicine capable of healing is also capable of harming, and its potency can be employed for either, or perhaps both, good and evil. So too for transpersonal psychology, as we see it offering opportunities for both liberation and bondage.

Another area we have not included due to lack of space is the relationship between transpersonal psychology and numerous religious traditions that offer transpersonal psychological insights, often surpassing in depth and breadth what contemporary transpersonal psychology presents as paltry in comparison. For this reason, studying transpersonal psychology for those seeking such experiences is no substitute for engaging in traditions that, in some cases, have been refined over millennia. However, practicing within a tradition always comes with baggage, and some aspects of this may not be desirable from contemporary perspectives, such as by foisting meta-physical concepts that might seem outdated in view of modern science or imposing values, such as subjugation of women or defilement of the body, which are anathema to modern sensibilities. In this regard, transpersonal psychology, like the study of comparative religion, provides a way to look critically at traditions, while gaining what can be gleaned from them in a profound way. Consequently, we think it crucial that transpersonal psychology learn from the great spiritual traditions, but never accept them uncritically as a whole and, especially, that it never become a religion.

There are many areas of transpersonal psychology that have not been included in this volume, but which are germane and warrant mention. We think of the rich tran-scendentalist traditions in the West, and the many syncretistic movements, such as theosophy that attempted to merge East and West, as areas neglected in this hand-book. We also think of the implications of transpersonal psychology on organizations and management for which there is an emerging literature (e.g., Law, Lancaster, & DiGiovanni, 2010), as well as on reconciling divisiveness. Among the many challenges to peace in the world are conflicts arising from differing worldviews that seem irrec-oncilable but, perhaps can be reconciled by an overarching perspective, such as can be offered by transpersonal psychology.

Last, deserving mention is the struggle with foundational issues that transpersonal psychology brings to the forefront, including by questioning what is knowable (i.e., ontology), how it can be known (i.e., epistemology), and most fundamentally by questioning who is the knower (i.e., the self) as inseparable from the process and product of knowing. The ontological position of transpersonal psychology challenges naïve materialism that reduces all to matter and equates consciousness with brain activ-ity. The epistemological position of transpersonal psychology seeks alternate ways of knowing, such as through exploring how varying consciousness states affect knowl-edge. And, even more fundamental, transpersonal psychology radically explores the knower, which is a mystery rather than a tacit given. Transpersonal psychology ques-tions these, and other, foundational assumptions that underlie both traditional world-views and conventional scientific dogma, opening to uncharted possibilities about ourselves and the world. In this sense, transpersonal psychology is still enshrouded with mystery, as a stretching toward what is not yet known rationally or empirically, but is known to be of great importance.

By tackling such questions, transpersonal psychology pioneered study in many marginalized areas. Interestingly, mainstream psychology has grown considerably since the advent of transpersonal psychology, and has embraced many of the posi-tions transpersonal psychology first explored. For example, studying consciousness is now legitimate, but it was taboo when transpersonal psychology first explored it. Likewise, transpersonal psychology seriously explored spiritual claims from East-ern and indigenous tradition with respect, while mainstream psychology tended to denigrate other cultures, and this respect for other cultures anticipated the multicul-turalism now common within mainstream psychology. Transpersonal psychology also challenged limitations in rigid scientific methods, and led in the paradigm shift in which the hegemony of quantitative approaches are now gradually yielding to alterna-tives, such as qualitative and mixed-method approaches, in psychology. In these, and many other, ways, transpersonal psychology has been at the forefront, channeling the mainstream into positive directions.

However, much of what transpersonal psychology offers has not yet been accepted by the mainstream. For example, the proposal for state-specific sciences, in which research may be conducted under alternate states of consciousness (Tart, 1975), is still too radical for the mainstream of psychology. However, these approaches may be the only valid ways to study humans under some conditions, such as related to exceptional experiences not easily comprehensible within a Western cultural framework. Many traditional meditation systems use practices that take great time and effort to master for exploring higher consciousness, and these practices have often been cumulatively refined through consensual internal observations that have been shared and tested over millennia within their cultural contexts. These constitute valid empirical data, but using a different approach to science than employed in the West. Considering that typical Western studies of meditation start by teaching beginners to meditate in ways that involve only short-term training, and contrast this to the millennia of cumulative cultural knowledge derived from authentic spiritual traditions that are practiced over a lifetime. Consequently, alternate methods for studying these types of extraordinary phenomena, which are both complex and subtle, may be more appropriate than the superficial applications used by conventional science. In this regard, transpersonal psychology has pioneered human science methods involving radically altered assumptions about ontology and epistemology, as well as about the self as knower, but has much still to learn from various traditions. It also has its advantages over traditions, as it is free to follow its own programs of inquiry without constraints from any fixed belief system.

Transpersonal psychology also has its advantages over the psychology of religion. For example, it takes its data from diverse spiritual traditions, which differs it from the psychology of religion that is primarily derivative from the monotheistic Judeo-Christian traditions. The psychology of religion also focuses more on studying external variables, such as demographics, and less on studying experience. That mainstream psychology of religion retains much of its parochial cultural baggage, positions transpersonal psychology well in offering creative ways to escape many such cultural traps. However, it is also important to note that transpersonal psychology is subject to its own cultural traps by often being over enthusiastic about so-called exotic traditions, sometimes embracing them whole and "going native" (Friedman, 2009). In this sense, although it is important to both learn from authentic traditions but to also retain a scientific, although construed broadly, approach.

As a handbook that is published at one point in time and space, these limitations notwithstanding, our hope is that this volume will serve the purpose of clarifying and promoting the worth of transpersonal psychology. Our belief is that transpersonal psychology is more than an esoteric approach to concerns that lack practicality but, rather, it provides a source to meld deep insights that can be empirically and broadly defined, tested, and implemented for facilitating humankind's adaptation in needed ways that respect and benefit all.

References

Anderson, R., & Braud, W. (2011). Transforming self and others through research: *Transpersonal research methods and skills for the human sciences and humanities.* Albany, NY: State University of New York Press.

Braud, W. (2006). Educating the "more" in holistic transpersonal higher education: A 30+ year perspective on the approach of the Institute of Transpersonal Psychology. *Journal of Transpersonal Psychology, 38*(2), 133-158.

Braud, W., & Anderson, R. (1998). *Transpersonal research methods for the social sciences: Honoring human experience.* Thousand Oaks, CA: Sage.

Friedman, H. (2002). Transpersonal psychology as a scientific field. *International Journal of Transpersonal Studies, 21,* 175-187.

Friedman, H. (2009). Xenophilia as a cultural trap: Bridging the gap between transpersonal psychology and religious/spiritual traditions. *International Journal of Transpersonal Studies, 28,* 107-111.

Grof, S. (1983). East and West: Ancient wisdom and modern science. *Journal of Transpersonal Psychology, 15*(1), 13-36.

Hartelius, G., Caplan, M., & Rardin, M. (2007). Transpersonal psychology: Defining the past, divining the future. *The Humanistic Psychologist, 35*(2), 1-26.

John, O., Robins, R., & Pervin, L. (2008). *Handbook of personality: Theory and research* (3rd ed.). New York, NY: Guilford Press.

Law, H. C., Lancaster, L., & DiGiovanni (2010). A wider role for coaching psychology - applying transpersonal coaching psychology. *The Coaching Psychologist, 6*(1), 22-31.

Lindeman, M., Blomqvist, S., & Takada, M. (2012). Distinguishing spirituality from other constructs: Not a matter of well-being but of belief in supernatural spirits. *Journal of Nervous and Mental Disease, 200*(2), 167-173.

Mahner, M. (2012). The role of metaphysical naturalism in science. *Science & Education, 21*(10), 1437-1459.

Murray, H., & Kluckhohn, C. (1953). *Personality in nature, society, and culture.* Retrieved from www.panarchy.org/kluckhohn/personality.1953.html

Tart, C. T. (1975). *States of consciousness.* New York: E. P. Dutton.

Tart, C. T. (2004). On the scientific foundations of transpersonal psychology: Contributions from parapsychology (Forum). *Journal of Transpersonal Psychology, 36*(1), 66-90.

Part I

Introduction to
Transpersonal Psychology

1

A Brand from the Burning

Defining Transpersonal Psychology

Glenn Hartelius, Geffen Rothe, and Paul J. Roy

Transpersonal psychology stands to benefit from simple definitions that can serve efforts to create a practical, durable, worldwide awareness of the field. Although it is perhaps the most developed academic discipline still aligned with the cultural forces that inspired the personal growth industry, the alternative health field, the popular spirituality movement, and the vision of ecological sustainability, transpersonal psychology has little name recognition within these circles. Further refinement of the field's identity might support a process of *rebranding* the field, so that it can serve as a more effective and recognized participant in the vast cultural momentum it has helped to precipitate.

There are few disciplines in which the very nature and definition of the field of study are in question. Biology is the study of living organisms, while literature is the scholarly examination of written works deemed worthy of deeper consideration. In most cases, the name of the field provides an easily understood synopsis of its content area: economics, law, engineering, astrophysics. Even within psychology, subdisciplines are readily identifiable by their names: counseling psychology, military psychology, experimental psychology. Transpersonal psychology has not had the luxury of a readily understood name or area of study, and has struggled to define itself in clear and articulate ways.

This situation has come about because the transpersonal project, of which transpersonal psychology is a part, is no simple undertaking, and no modest effort merely to add to psychology by including human spirituality. Rather, it is an ambitious effort to redefine ourselves as humans and the world as we know it. It is a project that sets out to understand the cosmos in ways that are not constrained by either the sometimes-heavy hand of religious tradition or the objectifying eye of science. Instead, the transpersonal approach seeks a new vision, one in which both human science and human spirituality can be honored. For this reason, any satisfying definition of the

The Wiley Blackwell Handbook of Transpersonal Psychology, First Edition.
Edited by Harris L. Friedman and Glenn Hartelius.
© 2013 John Wiley & Sons, Ltd. Published 2015 by John Wiley & Sons, Ltd.

field of transpersonal psychology needs to do more than describe its topic area: it must also convey the shifted vision within which this subject matter is considered.

The literature of transpersonal psychology contains scores of efforts to define the field, including, during the past 20 years, several systematic efforts to review published definitions with the goal of arriving at a more comprehensive synopsis (Hartelius, Caplan, & Rardin, 2007; Lajoie & Shapiro, 1992; Shapiro, Lee, & Gross, 2002). Yet even the most recent and detailed of these failures to produce a definition that approaches the succinct clarity with which most other fields of psychology are named. In this chapter, we argue that the results of earlier studies need to be further distilled into a concise, easily understood descriptor of transpersonal psychology, and we offer three characterizing terms—*psychology of self-expansiveness, whole-person psychology,* and *psychology of transformative process*—as well as a short-phrase definition that combines facets of these into what may be a somewhat comprehensive overview of the stance of field.

In addition to the characterizations of the field we have listed, evidence will be presented for several positive trends within transpersonal psychology that support its viability as a global discipline. Based on analyses of the primary journals within the field, it appears that there are long-term trends toward greater use of empirical studies and quantitative research methods, increased inclusion of academic voices from beyond North America, and expanded representation of women scholars.

Defining the Field

The first formal definition of transpersonal psychology was published by Sutich in 1968, and served as the basis for the Statement of Purpose that appeared in various iterations in the *Journal of Transpersonal Psychology* from 1969 until 1983 (Lajoie, Shapiro, & Roberts, 1991). This definition focused mainly on higher human needs, values, states, and potentials. Lajoie and Shapiro (1992) presented 40 definitions of transpersonal psychology published between 1968 and 1991. Based on thematic analysis, the authors suggested that transpersonal psychology studied "humanity's highest potential," and "unitive, spiritual, and transcendent states of consciousness" (p. 91). Shapiro et al. (2002) offered an additional 80 definitions published between 1991 and 2002, and concluded that the most frequent themes pertained to ego transcendence and spirituality, in line with the Lajoie and Shapiro definition of a decade earlier. Based on this work, transpersonal psychology appeared to be concerned primarily with a human potential to go beyond the ego and achieve higher states of consciousness.

A careful reanalysis of 160 definitions of transpersonal psychology published from 1968 to 2003, including most of those cited above, found that this focus on self-transcendence through elevated states of mind was only one of three themes present in descriptions of the field (Hartelius et al., 2007). Rather than counting themes within the definitions, which risks that the themes recognized by the researchers will be biased toward those already formulated, this reappraisal divided the corpus of definitions into meaning units, and then allowed themes to emerge in patterns of relationship discovered through repeated engagement with those units. These findings pointed to a wider understanding of the field than had been offered by previous analyses of definitions, a view that was found to be in significant harmony with a 1980 effort by Boucouvalas to compile a comprehensive outline of the field from leading scholars.

According to Hartelius et al. (2007), the definitions studied could be classified into three themes: transpersonal psychology as a beyond-ego psychology, as an integrative/holistic psychology, and as a psychology of transformation. As a beyond-ego psychology, it focuses on experiences that are transpersonal in content. It includes exceptional human experiences stemming from intentional practices such as shamanism and meditation, as well as occurrences that arise from various forms of mysticism, psi phenomena, near-death, and out-of-body experiences, which do not necessarily require intentional practices. These can lead to various experiences, such as transcendent, peak, and unitive, and also to a variety of stages or qualities that can be seen as beyond-ego, such as compassion and altruism. These latter are related to developmental levels of optimal human potential, including higher consciousness, advanced ego maturity, and elevated values, meaning, and purpose reflecting such a potential. At the inception of transpersonal psychology, this beyond-ego aspect was a dominant focus of the field, as reflected in the fact that a thematic analysis of the articles in the first five volumes of the *Journal of Transpersonal Psychology* (*JTP*; 1969-1973; $n = 40$) showed that 100% contained elements related to this theme. Some decades later (1999-2003; $n = 46$), 93% of articles in the *JTP* still reflected this aspect of the field.

As an integrative/holistic pursuit, transpersonal psychology examines the phenomena of psyche as elements that belong not merely to the ego, but to larger contexts as well: the living body in its entirety, the therapeutic relationship, the social and ecological situation, or the greater-than-human matrix of existence (Hartelius et al., 2007). It also refers to transpersonal as a psychology that embraces wider contexts through holistic, multicultural, integrative, or integral approaches. This theme appeared in only 25% of articles in *JTP* during its early years (1969-1973), but was included in fully 78% of articles published 1999-2003. The significantly increased frequency of this aspect within papers published by *JTP* suggests that this way of defining and using transpersonal psychology has become significantly more common as the field has matured.

As an approach to transformation, transpersonal psychology studies psychospiritual development beyond conventional sexual and cognitive maturity, self-actualization, and other forms of transformative growth (Hartelius et al., 2007). Here the transpersonal is not merely the *content* of a beyond-ego psychology, nor just the widened *context* of a whole-person psychology, but also the force or *catalyst* that drives human development toward its greater potentials. In addition, from this vantage transpersonal psychology considers how its findings might apply to ethical thinking and behavior, compassionate social action, service to humanity, or the transformation of such areas as psychotherapy, education, business, and so on. This facet developed much as the prior theme, growing from a presence in only 28% of *JTP* articles between 1969 and 1973 to representation in 74% of articles during the years 1999-2003.

These three themes were found to represent 91% of the total meaning units identified in the corpus of 160 definitions ($n = 1395$), and 100% of the meaning units with content related to the topic area of transpersonal psychology ($n = 1270$; Hartelius et al., 2007). Based on this analysis, Hartelius et al. offered the following definition of the field:

> Transpersonal psychology: An approach to psychology that 1) studies phenomena beyond the ego as context for 2) an integrative/holistic psychology; this provides a framework for 3) understanding and cultivating human transformation. (p. 145)

As perhaps the most succinct and comprehensive empirically based definition of the field to that date, this effort demonstrated that the field is in fact a coherent enterprise, and offered substantive response to critics who suggested that the field was dead due in part to its inability to define itself (e.g., Wilber, 2000).

Although this definition and the analysis that informed it seem to have achieved a step forward in the refinement of the identity of transpersonal psychology, the result is still slightly unwieldy and obscure in comparison with more lucid descriptions that can be articulated in other subdisciplines of psychology (such as educational psychology or psychology of religion). Of course, these also have their own significant inconsistencies and discord, but to most observers the general thrust of such subdisciplines is less confusing than that of transpersonal psychology. To refer to the field in terms of three separate aspects, each requiring its own explanation, does not provide a readily grasped sense of transpersonal psychology. An efficient descriptor should ideally capture a more central component of vision, so that the three definitional themes can be understood as facets of this element, expressed in simple, clear language.

Rebranding Transpersonal Psychology

Branding is the process of creating a name that identifies and differentiates a product in the mind of the public, and *brand equity* (here referred to as *brand*) is the reputation that the product develops (Clifton et al., 2009). Building a brand involves not only creating awareness of a particular product, but also presenting it in terms that demonstrate its relevance to people's lives and is resonant with their personal values and aspirations (Bedbury & Fenichell, 2002). While branding is more commonly associated with commercial than academic enterprises, it is also coming to be recognized as an aspect of successful scholarly disciplines (Moore, 2010).

As an example, the brand of paleoanthropology—the once rather obscure discipline that studies prehistoric humans—has benefitted significantly from the popular fictional works written by Jean M. Auel (Ruddick, 2009). Although criticized by some as factually inadequate (Fagan, 1987) and described by others as romanticist (Stableford, 1995) or controversial extensions of fact (Ruddick, 2009), Auel has succeeded in transforming the genre of prehistoric fiction by weaving the scientific findings of paleoanthropology into prehistoric tales to which contemporary readers—especially women, the main readers of fiction—could relate. In this way, Auel increased the field's "brand *relevance* and brand *resonance*" (Bedbury & Fenichell, 2002, p. 3). Now with more than 45 million copies of her books in print (Collett-White, 2011), Auel has arguably made the discipline of paleoanthropology vastly more visible and comprehensible within many parts of Western culture.

In contrast, transpersonal psychology is an example of a field with a branding challenge. The approach has been criticized for being unscientific (Kurtz, 1991; Shermer, 2002), antiscientific, unrealistic, asocial, authoritarian, absolutist, dogmatic, dangerous (Ellis, 1986, 1989), psychologically unsound (Ellis & Yeager, 1989; May, 1986), and unable to adequately define itself (Wilber, 2000) or its methodology (Friedman, 2002). While many of these criticisms have received vigorous responses (Cunningham, 2007; Hartelius et al., 2007; Wilber, 1989), it is clear that the field has not been highly successful in conveying to a broader audience the deep significance its proponents believe that it holds.

Although it may be impossible to reduce transpersonal psychology accurately to a single short-phrase definition that will satisfy all scholars within the field, this chapter examines three succinct characterizations, each of which spans the three definitional themes from the perspective of one of those themes. The first defines the field as a psychology of self-expansiveness, the second as a whole-person, transformative approach to human existence that includes psychology as part of a broader scope of study, and the third as a psychology of transformative process. A definition is by nature selective and reductive, therefore these three are offered as perhaps incrementally closer to one that may serve the branding of the field both within academic circles and broader society, and are preliminary to the discussion of a short-phrase definition that attempts to represent them all.

A Psychology of Self-Expansiveness

Humanistic psychology arose in the 1950s in response to the then-prevalent behavioral and psychoanalytic approaches, based on the critique that these psychologies offered a limited and illness-focused view of the human psyche—one that left out health, growth, human potential, empathy, inner meaning, purpose, and experience (Jourard, 1966; Rogers, 1963a). The behaviors visible from outside, or the drives arising from unconscious levels, were of significance only as they related to a whole person engaged in creating themselves through the present-moment processes of living. What transpersonal psychology added to this was the notion that the whole person included more—included their relationships with values, visions, and experiences that took them beyond the boundaries of their individual sense of self (Maslow, 1968, 1969).

In its early years, transpersonal psychology functioned primarily as a psychology of these "farther reaches of human nature" (Maslow, 1969, p. 1) understood as states of consciousness, stages of development, practices, and aspirations relating to aspects of the self that are beyond the personal ego (Hartelius et al., 2007). Friedman's (1981, 1983, this volume) construct of self-expansiveness, although rooted in this traditional understanding of the field, is also relevant to the definitions that frame it as a holistic/integrative enterprise, and as a psychology of transformation (Hartelius et al., 2007). Considered as a psychology of self-expansiveness:

> Transpersonal psychology studies the self conceived not only as isolated individual bound to the here-and-now of the present, but capable of expanding to include others, nature, or all of space and time, or of embodying some larger aspect of the world. These shifted boundaries may be reflected as non-ordinary states of consciousness.

From this perspective, the altered states of consciousness that characterize spiritual, mystical, and transcendent experience are not delusional distortions, but can be understood as perceptions and experiences associated with a self that seems expanded beyond its conventional limits.[1] That is, the boundary between me and not-me is shifted inward and outward, as well as forward and backwards in time, and, from that shifted stance, the aspirant or mystic apprehends the world as something quite different—sometimes ecstatically or terrifyingly different—than it appears to be from the ordinary sense of self. This application clearly represents the topic area and perspective of early transpersonal psychology, which understood itself to be examining the capacity of the self to move beyond conventional ego boundaries.

According to Friedman (this volume), this view of the self is based in William James' (1890) insight that boundaries used to define the individual are simply arbitrary limitations on a potentially all-encompassing Self. The notion that the self is capable of expanding beyond conventional boundaries implies that self is relationally interconnected with community and world. Significantly, experiences of an expanded self often bring the sense that self, other, and/or world are interconnected in just this way. This is exactly the domain of transpersonal psychology defined as an integrative/holistic approach—the second of the three main definitional themes described by Hartelius et al. (2007).

These experiences of expanding beyond an ordinary sense of self are sought not so much for their novelty (although this undoubtedly happens) as for their "healing and heuristic potential" (Grof, 2003, p. 52)—their ability to foster an experience of meaning, purpose, and belonging in the world. A psychology of self-expansiveness is therefore engaged not only with these experiences, but with their transformative capacities—which is the focus of the third major way of defining transpersonal psychology (Hartelius et al., 2007). While it describes the capacity for self-concept or identity to become more expansive, the construct of self-expansiveness does not explicitly include any dynamic principles to account for transformation. However, it is implicit that more expansiveness in the sense of self is desirable, provided that it is accompanied by appropriate maturity and personal integration.

Despite its modest reflection of transformative process, the construct of self-expansiveness has the advantage of being amenable to scientific measurement. In addition, in this volume Friedman proposes that self-expansiveness can do more than define a core concept within transpersonal psychology: He suggests that it can be employed as a way to understand the relationship between various psychotherapies, from the perspective that different approaches to psychotherapy operate at different levels of self-expansiveness. For example, cognitive-behavioral therapy might be seen as functioning at a lower level of self-expansiveness than a transpersonal or Jungian psychotherapy.

A Whole-Person Psychology/Multi-disciplinary Orientation

If the self is capable of expanding beyond its conventional boundaries, and if a transpersonal psychology studies those aspects that are beyond the ordinary experience of self, this suggests the need for understanding the whole person in a sense that includes not only body and mind, but also relationship and situatedness in the world. One of the authors, Paul Roy, has spent years in leadership of the largest transpersonal institution (Sofia University, formerly the Institute of Transpersonal Psychology). Over much of his time immersed in the field, he has worked on crafting a definition of the field situated within the holistic/integrative theme, but spanning also its other dimensions. His definition is as follows:

> Transpersonal studies is a whole-person, transformative approach to human existence and human experience that includes the spiritual and transcendent as well as the social and community dimensions of human life, all within the context of the global eco-system in which we live.

Note that this definition is not of transpersonal psychology, but transpersonal studies as an approach to something broader than psychology: a holistic perspective that examines human life in the context of an interconnected world. If one attempts a whole-person psychology, it soon becomes clear that the psyche is not a discrete thing functioning in isolation from body, community, or environment, but a local aspect of an interconnected whole (Hartelius, 2006)—a whole that must be engaged in order to understand any of its facets. Transpersonal is then necessarily more than a psychology; it must also be a multidisciplinary scholarly *orientation* (Boucouvalas, 1999)—an orientation that has been called transpersonal studies (Wilber, 1995a; Friedman, 2002).

The interdisciplinary nature of the field was identified by Boucouvalas (1980) as part of her work to outline the early field. By this time a transpersonal anthropology already existed (Schwartz, 2000), and it became clear that a transpersonal approach might also be applied in other areas of scholarship, such as sociology (Walsh, 1993), social engagement (Rothberg & Coder, this volume), education (Rowe & Braud, this volume), medicine (Lawlis, this volume), business (Schott, 1992), law (Scoglio, 1998), art (Herman, this volume), literature (Kalaidjian, 1991), philosophy (Hartelius & Ferrer, this volume; Wilber, 1995a), ecology (Fox, 1990), and so forth. These are in addition to resonant areas of study more closely related to psychology: somatic psychology, which examines the body as it is lived (see Johnson, this volume); ecopsychology, which considers the way in which the individual psyche is interrelated to nature (see Davis & Canty, this volume); and cultural psychology (Brooks, Huffman, & Ford, this volume).

The whole-person, transformative approach brings such a wide-angle lens that it easily includes consideration of those experiences in which one expands beyond the normal sense of self, and on the transformative potentials of these and other experiences—thus addressing the other main themes used to define transpersonal psychology. Although the transpersonal approach is sweeping in scope, the reach for grand theory (e.g., Wilber, 1995b, 1996, 1998) has by now been moderated with calls for understanding each facet in its own context (Hartelius & Ferrer, this volume), and for the development of mid-range theory (Friedman, this volume). In addition, as will be presented in a later section, the emphasis in the field on empirical work appears to be slowly increasing. This suggests that there may be two dynamics at play in the development of the transpersonal orientation: a widened scope of inquiry, coupled with a more focused approach on specific inquiry.

A Psychology of Transformative Process

Transformation as process is specifically distinct from the states and stages of transformation first considered within the field, and implies more than simple progress from one developmental stage to another. An early pointer in this direction was Vaughan (1979), who proposed that transpersonal psychotherapy consisted of content, context, and process. Within this setting, she suggested that content pointed to client experiences that went beyond the ordinary limits of ego and personality, and context was represented by the therapist's values, beliefs, and intentions. Process, for Vaughan, consisted not merely of moving from one stage to another within a fixed landscape, but of a shift in the self engaged in that movement. Early in the journey the self seeks to gain power relative to its surroundings, because it understands itself as distinct from the world. Later, a quite different sort of self realizes that it exists "as a web of mutually conditioned relationships and that one is absolutely connected with all of existence" (Vaughan, 1979, p. 106).

Transformative process is a journey in which there is not simply movement from one place or stage to another, but in which the landscape, the destination, and the journeyer shift and change as part of that movement. One might say that

> transpersonal as a psychology of transformative process understands the individual mind, human communities, and the cosmos itself to be interconnected living systems in constant engagement with creative self-expression and self-invention.

Transformative process is a term that evokes not merely psychological self-actualization (Maslow, 1943, 1958) that drives toward the highest human potential (Vaughan, 1982), but also a philosophy and cosmology that understand the world as living process purposefully evolving toward a meaningful end (Neville, 2007), even though that end may not be distinct from the process itself. In psychology, this type of transformative process has also been called individuation (Jung, 1939, 1969), psychosynthesis (Assagioli, 1965), the formative tendency (Rogers, 1978, 1980), an actualizing tendency (Rogers, 1963b), autopoiesis (Maturana & Varela, 1980), holotropic (Grof, 1998, 2003), and the evolution of consciousness (Combs, 1995; Wilber, 1979), among other terms. Yet these principles have often been considered cosmological as well as psychological: Rogers (1978) imagined the formative tendency as a property of the universe in which individuals also participated; Maturana and Varela (1980) saw autopoiesis as characterizing all living systems; and Wilber (1979) and Combs (1995) understood the personal evolution of consciousness as microcosmic reflections of an impulse that drives the cosmos. In philosophy, this is the domain of process thinkers who imagine the universe as an ongoing process of becoming (Ferrer, 2008; Gendlin, 1997; Whitehead, 1979). The individual is understood as a participant in this larger transformative process.

A process view differs radically from the philosophical heritage of the West, for it posits that reality is not made of discrete things, but of processes of change (Whitehead, 1979). "Things" are processes in temporary states of greater stability. The scrambled eggs I had this morning were not scrambled eggs yesterday, are not scrambled eggs once they are eaten, and will not remain scrambled eggs even if they are not eaten.

Although this unstable condition allows for no certainty, the process itself can be trusted (Gendlin, 2006). This view has much in common with the Advaita Vedantin teaching that the nature of created reality is illusory (Whitfield, 2009). This non-dual school of Hinduism offers the traditional story of a clay pot, which in the past was unshaped clay, and in the future will be shards; therefore, the notion that there is some enduring "thing" that is a clay pot is illusory. It is only the ultimate divine source of these forms and of their constant transformation, Brahman, who according to this tradition can be trusted. It should be noted that, unlike Aurobindo (1990) who held to a view of historical spiritual evolution toward a divine ultimate, Advaita Vedanta does not see spiritual significance in any process of change.

Under this rubric, the exceptional human experiences examined in the field's role as a beyond-ego psychology can be understood as *markers of transformative process.* It is when such phenomena are seen as tokens of humanity's largely untapped potentials, rather than mere oddities, that they gain the meaning and significance that transpersonal psychologists ascribe to them. It is arguably the absence of this notion of transformative process within much of mainstream psychology that accounts for the general dismissal of this category of human experience. In other words, the element of transformative process is not only congruent with transpersonal as a beyond-ego psychology, it provides an essential context that elevates beyond-ego phenomena to the importance they have consistently held within the field.

Likewise, transpersonal psychology may be seen as an integrative/holistic psychology because it understands the human mind as interwoven with the fabric of body, community, and world—all four of these inextricably linked within a *matrix of transformative process.* In other words, the cosmos is not made up of lifeless, rule-following particles within the vast loneliness of space, but rather is an interconnected living system in the constant activity of relationship. In the words of Berry (1996), "the universe is a communion of subjects rather than a collection of objects" (n.p.). Mind and nature are not separate (Bateson, 1979), but different facets of intertwined, self-organizing process (cf. Maturana & Varela, 1980; Whitehead, 1979), each implicit within the other (cf. Gendlin, 1997). It is because mind is considered within the context of reality as an interconnected process *matrix* that a more holistic approach becomes essential to transpersonal psychology; it is because reality is understood as *transformative* process that transpersonal psychology understands itself to be in relationship with the great spiritual traditions of the world, seeking to integrate Eastern, Western, indigenous, mystical, and scientific insights into a broad, inclusive, and effective human psychology.

Thirdly, transpersonal psychology can be understood as a psychology of transformation, one that studies humans as participating *members of transformative process.* If the world is an interconnected and evolving whole, then individuals are empowered and embedded agents of that process—capable of striving to cultivate mindfully personal, interpersonal, and societal change in line with such higher human values and aspirations as compassion, discernment, and appreciation of differences (Institute of Transpersonal Psychology, 2011).

In order to further illustrate these three aspects of transformative process, it may be helpful to situate them within transpersonal theory. Grof (2003) has identified what he has called *holotropic states,* non-ordinary states that promote healing and personal transformation. Such states might serve similar functions when invoked in group settings, a practice that has been documented in both Western and non-Western cultures (cf. Hunt, 2010), as well as perhaps supporting an alignment of human society with larger evolutionary forces (Grof, 2000). Holotropic states have been equated with the range of spiritual or mystical states known from a variety of cultures and traditions, and are associated with the cultivation of intuition, extrasensory perception, creative inspiration, experiences of communion with others, with nature, or with more-than-human presences, sometimes yielding insight or psycho-emotional healing (Grof, 2003). Their dynamic has been characterized as self-expansive—that is, one in which the ego is diminished as the self comes to identify with greater expanses of reality (cf. Friedman, 1981, 1983). Holotropic states are exemplary of those that serve as markers of transformative process. They are roughly comparable to the altered states that, as Tart (1975, 2008) has suggested, may yield valuable, state-specific knowledge not available in more ordinary states of mind.

Ferrer (2002, 2008) has called for situating the study of spiritual experience and development within *participatory philosophy*. In participatory thought—and there cannot, by definition, be any single authoritative participatory view—reality is an ever-shifting, self-transforming matrix of relational process. Within this interconnected movement, all persons and communities who journey toward wholeness and spiritual fulfillment, do so from their own unique location. Their path is not so much navigation of some predefined spiritual landscape as it is negotiation of an ongoing relationship with larger presences of life. Dialogue with others and with differing traditions can add perspective, but any generalities that may be drawn must be held lightly because they are mere abstractions from a dynamic and ever-evolving intersubjective process that has no permanent structure.

Aurobindo (1990), Gebser (1972, 1949/1986), and Wilber (Combs, 1995, this volume) have understood individuals and society to be in the grip of evolutionary forces that carry them toward a divine ultimate. *Transformation of consciousness* is not merely developmental maturation, but a process in which the very identity of the participating subject (individual or collective) is radically reorganized as it comes under the influence of higher forces. In the views of these scholars, traditions may vary in their outward form, but the progression of organizing patterns is invariant, the evolutionary spiritual path toward the singular divine clearly defined (cf. Schuon, 1953/1984).

In Washburn's (1995) model, the ego emerges from what he called the Dynamic Ground, the creative source of the psyche. The journey of transformation involves the ego's journey outward as it pushes for individuation from the Dynamic Ground, and, having achieved a degree of integrity, its return into intimate relationship with its source. Psychodynamic theory, within which he situated himself, has described the outward journey; for Washburn it is spiritual traditions that point to and cultivate renewal through return to a deeply reconfigured relationship with the Dynamic Ground. He characterized the process of personal transformation, then, as an evolving relationship with the matrix that birthed and sustains it.

In varying ways, each of these theoretical approaches reflects facets of transformative process. Some emphasize the process of *transformation*, others more clearly reflect *process* as the context and substance of transformation. Some, such as Wilber and Aurobindo, have see transformation as an *ascending* process of evolution in which development is cumulative; others, such as Grof and Washburn, have imagined transformation as *descending*, as returning to recover aspects of self lost in earlier stages of growth (Daniels, 2005). What they have in common is the view of humans as agents of evolution in an interdependent and evolving world.

Transpersonal psychology, along with humanistic psychology, arose in response to psychologies that reduced the person to their simplest actions, their basest motivations, and their most material structures: bio-machines in a purposeless physical wasteland. In contrast, a transpersonal approach sees certain non-ordinary states as evidence that humans participate in an interconnected whole, evolving purposefully toward unseen but sometimes deeply felt ultimates. It is the sensed presence of this process, whether expressed in the language of science or spirituality, which infuses life with felt meaning. Healing interventions such as psychotherapy then become focused on aligning the personal desire for wholeness with this larger evolutionary current.

Rebranding the Field

These three characterizations of the field, each carrying a different emphasis and each resonant with a different aspect of the themes found within historical definitions of transpersonal psychology, may be of service in presenting this approach more clearly and compellingly to a broader audience. In addition, better descriptions may serve as building blocks toward a short-phrase definition that can perhaps begin to bridge the field to the popular movements for which it has relevance. Before considering such a definition, it should be noted that each of the depictions offered here has its own particular virtues.

For example, defining transpersonal as a psychology of self-expansiveness, while it may also require explanation, carries the benefit of being a scientifically accessible method as well as a praxis. This definition focuses on what is unique about the topic area of the field, and does so in a way that is compatible with mainstream scholarship. The expansion of self-concept to include the body fits well with the alternative health field; expansion to identify with the natural world can promote healthy environmental values (Hoot & Friedman, 2011), and expanding one's sense of self to include the whole of the cosmos is consistent with the vision of some contemporary spirituality movements.

Describing transpersonal as a whole-person, transformative approach conveys the unique vision and values of transpersonal psychology in a simple and effective way. In addition, this definition points to the fact that the individual is interconnected with community, and both are woven into the world. This naturally suggests the larger scholarly orientation of transpersonal studies, which can bring a holistic lens to many topics beyond psychology as well. Interest in the whole person has resonance with the personal growth industry, which promotes cultivating a balanced life; it is also consistent with the alternative health field's emphasis on treating the whole person. Whole-person transformation is in harmony with some popular notions of spirituality, and consideration of one's intimate connection with the world may promote ecological sustainability.

Considering transpersonal as a psychology of transformative process emphasizes its interest in personal and social transformation that promotes self-actualization and compassionate service to humanity. This also points to its alignment with new philoso-phies that seek to move beyond modern and postmodern thought, toward process-based models and sciences. The emphasis on transformation resonates directly with the core of the personal growth and popular spirituality industries. When healing is understood as a transformative process of making whole, it also finds connection with complementary and alternative health concepts, and can be applied broadly to healing the earth, as well as to its many inhabitants.

A summary definition. The rich connotations of each of these strands provides an opportunity to imagine how they might be woven together into an easily accessible short-phrase definition. Here is one such attempt:

> Transpersonal psychology is a transformative psychology of the whole person in intimate relationship with a diverse, interconnected and evolving world; it pays special attention to self-expansive states as well as to spiritual, mystical, and other exceptional human experiences that gain meaning in such a context.

From the peak experiences that first intrigued Maslow (1968), to Grof's (1973) research with psychedelics, to spiritual (e.g., Daniels, 2005), mystical (e.g., Lukoff & Lu, 1988), exceptional (Palmer & Braud, 2002) and other beyond-ego experiences (Walsh & Vaughan, 1993), transpersonal scholars have typically held that many of these encounters may represent an engagement with some profound aspect of real-ity (cf. Ferrer, 2008), one that may have life-changing effects (e.g., Doblin, 1991). Transpersonal psychology typically assumes that there is an intimacy between the indi-vidual and the larger world, an interconnectedness that, when directly experienced, can be transformative.

Yet if true, such intimacy between self and world has potential implications for more than the psychospiritual development of the individual. If true, then perhaps the world is not rule-following bits of matter, but a self-organizing living system in which humans participate (Maturana & Varela, 1980). Mind and nature are not separate (Bateson, 1979), but woven of the same fabric, co-participants in complementary forces of creative evolution (Hartelius & Ferrer, this volume). In this view the affective connections that connect the individual to the world also bind us to each other in a shared destiny, making the welfare of each person the concern of all.

This definition robustly represents the holistic/integrative and transformational definitional themes found by Hartelius et al. (2007), as well as the characterizations of transpersonal psychology as a transformative, whole-person approach and as a psy-chology of transformative process. It gives less emphasis to the traditional terminology of the field, which often focuses more specifically on non-ordinary experiences. How-ever, we would argue that the latter approach limits the field to a specialty topic area, rather than opening it as an approach to scholarship. Furthermore, without an interpretive context that allows transpersonal experiences to hold the significance that transpersonal scholars ascribe to them, such experiences cannot be more than novelties and anomalies.

Transpersonal psychology will likely always require some explanation in order to be grasped. However, a succinct definition that addresses all three aspects of the field,

[handwritten marginal note: my belief nearly exactly]

along with more developed characterizations of those aspects, may be of service in making it more comprehensible to a wider population. Toward this same end, the following section presents findings of research on how certain aspects of transpersonal psychology have developed over time.

Trends within Transpersonal Psychology

The field is defined not only by how it is described, but by how it takes shape. Following are studies that offer evidence for three trends within transpersonal psychology: a steady increase in empirical research broadly and in quantitative studies specifically, consistent movement toward greater inclusion of work by scholars outside of North America, and growing participation by women scholars. The three studies presented here are based on reviews of the two indexed journals containing the term transpersonal in the name: the *Journal of Transpersonal Psychology* (*JTP*), and the *International Journal of Transpersonal Studies* (*IJTS*).

Study 1

As with humanistic psychology, transpersonal psychology has generally been more engaged in clarifying its theoretical constructs than it has been in empirical work. In order to look at the role of empirical work within transpersonal psychology over time, a review was conducted of each article published in *JTP* from its founding in 1969 through 2009, and in *IJTS* from its first issue in 1981 through 2009.

Method. Articles in the two target journals were differentiated from editorials and reviews, and were then identified as either theoretical or empirical; the latter were further labeled as either quantitative, qualitative, or mixed-methods studies.

Results and discussion. Results from the first year of *JTP*'s publication (1969) were analyzed separately, and the remainder compiled by decade—1970 to 1979, 1980 to 1989, and so forth—in order to track any change in the percentage of empirical articles published within the field in the easily comprehensible increment of calendrical decades.

Of all content articles published in either *JTP* or *IJTS* between 1969 and 2009 ($n = 654$), 13% were identified as empirical. Both journals demonstrated a tendency toward a greater number of empirical articles over time, though *JTP* had a somewhat larger percentage of empirical papers than *IJTS*. Taken together as representing a significant portion of the professional literature within the field, the role of empirical studies can be seen as increasing steadily over time: As a percentage of the total, empirical papers were 0% of those published in 1969 ($n = 10$), 4% of those published between 1970 and 1979 ($n = 87$), 12% of those published between 1980 to 1989 ($n = 175$), 15% of those published between 1990 and 1999 ($n = 185$), and 17% of those published between 2000 and 2009 ($n = 197$). This suggests that empirical studies, although still strongly in the minority, are slowly gaining importance within transpersonal psychology.

Of empirical papers published in *JTP* or *IJTS* from inception through 2009 (*n* = 85), most (57%) were qualitative; quantitative studies represented 31% of empirical studies, and mixed methods just 11%. Over time the percentage of qualitative articles fluctuated but demonstrated no clear trend; mixed methods declined from 43% of empirical articles during the 1970s to just 6% between 2000 and 2009, and quantitative papers increased from 14% in the 1970s to 39% in the 2000s. Although this study suggests that the field has a long-standing appreciation of qualitative research, it also offers evidence that quantitative research is gradually gaining favor as well.

Study 2

Transpersonal psychology was founded in Northern California, and even today a large number of scholars within the field work in North America. To determine the role that scholars from other parts of the world play within the field, a review was conducted over the same sample of literature examined in Study 1: all content articles published in *JTP* or *IJTS* from their respective dates of founding through 2009.

Method. The geographical location for each author of the articles identified in Study 1 was used to assign that author to one of seven geographical regions: North America, Latin America, Europe, Middle East, Africa, Asia, and Australasia. Each paper was assigned the value *n* = 1, so that each author on a paper by multiple authors was assigned an appropriate fraction of the value of that paper.

Results and discussion. Results generally showed an increase in participation by non-North American authors over time within the target journals. Of papers published in the 1970s (*n* = 87), 100% were by authors in North America; this figure decreased to 70% of papers published in the 1980s (*n* = 175) and 1990s (*n* = 185), and 65% of those published in the 2000s (*n* = 197). As an international journal, *IJTS* consistently had a larger representation of authors from outside North American than *JTP*. The percentage of North American authors published in *IJTS* actually increased from 36% in the 1980s to 52% in the 2000s, likely reflecting in part the fact that the journal headquarters moved from Australia (1981-1992) to Hawaii (1993-2002), and then to the U.S. mainland (2003-present). Taken together, however, these results clearly suggest a trend toward greater participation by non-North American authors in the core literature of the field. Inconsistent with this trend are results from the year 1969, showing 90% North American authorship; however, the presence of a single non-North American author had a disproportional impact on this small sample (*n* = 10).

Trends within the non-North American authors include a significant increase in participation by European authors in the target journals over time, from 0% presence in articles published in the 1970s (*n* = 87) to 20% of those published in the 2000s (*n* = 197). At the same time, authorship by Australasian authors decreased from a high of 26% of papers published in the 1980s (*n* = 175) to just 5% of those published in the 2000s. The large representation of Australasian authors in the 1980s can likely be attributed to the founding of the *Australian Journal of Transpersonal Psychology* in

Australia in 1981, and the decline to its transformation into the Hawaii-based *IJTS* in 1993.

Of the total number of papers published by *JTP* and *IJTS* during the period studied ($n = 654$), just 4% were authored by scholars in Latin America, the Middle East, Africa, and Asia combined. This suggests that transpersonal psychology currently has much greater impact in first-world nations, and that its scholarship still needs to be enriched by voices from many more cultures and societies around the world.

Study 3

In their 2007 paper, Hartelius et al. (2007) found that during the first 20 years of the field's existence, women authors accounted for only 12% of articles published in *JTP*; the percentage of women authors in that journal increased to 25% during 1998 to 2003. The current study updates this earlier work, and, as with Studies 1 and 2, examines both *JTP* and *IJTS* from each publication's first volume through 2009.

Method. A list of author names was compiled for each relevant year of publication of the target journals. Gender was determined as in the earlier study: through familiarity with the gender of the author, through web searches referring to the author by personal pronoun, and where necessary through searches to determine the gender typically associated with a particular given name. Each article was assigned the value $n = 1$, and for papers by multiple authors each author was assigned an appropriate fraction of that value.

Results and discussion. The results of this study were generally consistent with those of the earlier study that examined only authors published in *JTP*, and only sampled certain years. The current study reviewed all years up to and including 2009. Considering the year 1969 separately, the percentage of women authors in this small sample ($n = 10$) was 0. In the 1970s, 14% of total papers published ($n = 87$) were women; this increased to 18% of articles published in the 1980s ($n = 175$), 19% of those published in the 1990s ($n = 185$), and 23% of those published in the 2000s ($n = 197$).

The largest increase in women authors, decade-over-decade, occurred in *JTP* between the 1990s and the 2000s; women authorship increased from 21% of papers published in that journal during the 1990s ($n = 93$) to 33% of those published in the 2000s ($n = 93$). This shift coincided with another positive step toward gender diversity within the field: the selection of the first woman editor of *JTP* in 2000.

Conclusion

Transpersonal psychology has taken on an extraordinarily complex challenge. Some scholars see this challenge as attempting to study exceptional human experiences using current scientific methods in a careful way that reduces those phenomena in as minimal a way as possible. Others work to understand the world carefully and critically through the shifted lens of a transpersonal vision that understands the intimate interweaving of all life, and search for ways to extend scientific work that may be compatible with this stance—embracing scientific methods, but rejecting the often-accompanying philosophy that assumes life to be constructed of rule-following particles (cf. Grof, 1983).

Whatever the research strategy, what holds transpersonal psychology together is a shared vision of the world as a vibrant, alive, and intelligent community. Whether it is the insights of the unconscious mind, the wisdom of the body, the cultural repositories built up within human culture, or the adaptive capacities of the ecosystem, a transpersonal approach understands that it needs to engage in inquiry with respect and humility if it is to win a deeper knowledge of the living processes that ripple through the world.

Note

1. Friedman's (1981, 1983, this volume) construct focuses on self-concept rather than on self-as-experienced, as the latter is notably difficult to measure, it appears to make the assumption that self-concept will be informed by self-experience—a strategic move that allows an intangible to be measured based on its reflection within cognitive beliefs.

References

Assagioli, R. (1965). *Psychosynthesis: A collection of basic writings.* New York, NY: Psychosynthesis Research Foundation.

Aurobindo, Sri. (1990). *The psychic being: Soul: Its nature, mission, evolution.* Wilmot, WI: Lotus Light.

Bateson, G. (1979). *Mind and nature: A necessary unity* (Advances in systems theory, complexity, and the human sciences). New York, NY: Hampton Press.

Bedbury, S., & Fenichell, S. (2002). *A new brand world: 8 principles for achieving brand leadership in the 21st century.* New York, NY: Viking/Penguin Putnam.

Berry, T. (1996). Ethics and ecology. Paper presented to the Harvard Seminar on Environmental Values (April 9). Retrieved from www.csco.ca

Boucouvalas, M. (1980). Transpersonal psychology: An outline of the field. *Journal of Transpersonal Psychology, 12*(1), 37-46.

Boucouvalas, M. (1999). Following the movement: From transpersonal psychology to a multidisciplinary transpersonal orientation. *Journal of Transpersonal Psychology, 31*(1), 27-39.

Brooks, C., Ford, K., & Huffman, A. (this volume). Feminist and cultural contributions to transpersonal psychology (Chapter 34).

Clifton, R., Ahmad, S., Allen, T., Anholt, S., Barwise, P., Blackett, T., ... Smith, S. (2009). *Brands and branding.* New York, NY: Bloomberg Press.

Collett-White, M. (2011, March 29). Jean Auel concludes prehistoric saga with 6th book. *Reuters: UK Edition.* Retrieved at http://uk.reuters.com/article/2011/03/29/arts-jeanauel-earthschildren-idUKLDE72R1KB20110329

Combs, A. (1995). *The radiance of being: Complexity, chaos, and the evolution of consciousness.* St. Paul, MN: Paragon House.

Combs, A. (this volume). Transcend and include: Ken Wilber's contribution to transpersonal psychology (Chapter 9).

Cunningham, P. (2007). The challenges, prospects, and promise of transpersonal psychology. *International Journal of Transpersonal Studies, 26*(1), 41-55.

Daniels, M. (2005). *Shadow, self, spirit: Essays in transpersonal psychology.* Exeter, UK: Imprint Academic.

Davis, J. V., & Canty, J. M. (this volume). Ecopsychology and transpersonal psychology (Chapter 33).

Doblin, R. (1991). Pahnke's "Good Friday Experiment": A long-term follow-up and methodological critique. *Journal of Transpersonal Psychology, 23*(1), 1-28.

Ellis, A. (1986). Fanaticism that may lead to a nuclear holocaust: The contributions of scientific counseling and psychotherapy. *Journal of Counseling and Development, 65*(3), 146-151.

Ellis, A. (1989). Dangers of transpersonal psychology: A reply to Ken Wilber. *Journal of Counseling and Development, 67*(6), 336-337.

Ellis, A., & Yeager, R. J. (1989). *Why some therapies don't work: The dangers of transpersonal psychology.* Amherst, NY: Prometheus Books.

Fagan, B. M. (1987). Life with Ayla and her friends: Jean Auel and the new phenomenon of Ice Age fiction. *Scientific American, 256*(6), 132-135.

Ferrer, J. N. (2002). *Revisioning transpersonal theory: A participatory vision of human spirituality.* Albany, NY: State University of New York Press.

Ferrer, J. N. (2008). Spiritual knowing as participatory enaction: An answer to the question of religious pluralism. In J. N. Ferrer & J. H. Sherman (Eds.), *The participatory turn: Spirituality, mysticism, religious studies* (pp. 135-169). Albany, NY: State University of New York Press.

Fox, W. (1990). Transpersonal ecology: "Psychologizing" ecophilosophy. *Journal of Transpersonal Psychology, 22*(1), 59-96.

Friedman, H. (1981). *The Self-Expansiveness Level Form: A conceptualization and measurement of a transpersonal construct.* Ann Arbor, MI: Dissertation Abstracts International. (UMI No. 8117150)

Friedman, H. (1983). The Self-Expansiveness Level Form: A conceptualization and measurement of a transpersonal construct. *Journal of Transpersonal Psychology, 15*, 37-50.

Friedman, H. (2002). Transpersonal psychology as a scientific field. *International Journal of Transpersonal Studies, 21*, 175-187.

Friedman, H. (this volume). The role of science in transpersonal psychology: The advantages of middle-range theory (Chapter 16).

Friedman, H. (this volume). Transpersonal self-expansiveness as a scientific construct (Chapter 11).

Gebser, J. (1972). Foundations of the aperspectival world. *Main Currents, 29*, 2.

Gebser, J. (1986). *The ever-present origin.* (N. Barstad and A. Mickunas, Trans.). Athens, OH: Ohio University Press. (Original work published 1949)

Gendlin, E. T. (1997). *A process model.* Spring Valley, NY: Focusing Institute.

Gendlin, E. T. (2006, November). *In having one shape, the truth is more, but it isn't a shape.* Keynote address, Psychology of Trust and Feeling Conference, Stony Brook University, New York.

Grof, S. (1973). Theoretical and empirical basis of transpersonal psychology and psychotherapy: Observations from LSD research. *Journal of Transpersonal Psychology, 5*(1), 15-53.

Grof, S. (1983). East and West: Ancient wisdom and modern science. *Journal of Transpersonal Psychology, 15*(1), 13-36.

Grof, S. (1998). Human nature and the nature of reality: Conceptual challenges from consciousness research. *Journal of Psychoactive Drugs, 30*(4), 343-357.

Grof, S. (2000). *Psychology of the future: Lessons from modern consciousness research*. Albany, NY: State University of New York Press.

Grof, S. (2003). Implications of modern consciousness research for psychology: Holotropic experiences and their healing and heuristic potential. *The Humanistic Psychologist*, *31*(2-3), 50-85.

Hartelius, G. (2006). All that glisters is not gold: Heterophenomenology and transpersonal theory. *Journal of Consciousness Studies*, *13*(6), 81-95.

Hartelius, G., Caplan, M., & Rardin, M.-A. (2007). Transpersonal psychology: Defining the past, divining the future. *The Humanistic Psychologist*, *35*(2), 135-160.

Hartelius, G., & Ferrer, J. N. (this volume). Transpersonal philosophy: The participatory turn (Chapter 10).

Herman, L. (this volume). Transpersonal experience and the arts: From Chauvet Cave to Occupy Wall Street (Chapter 37).

Hoot, R. E., & Friedman, H. (2011). Connectedness and environmental behavior: Sense of interconnectedness and pro-environmental behavior. *International Journal of Transpersonal Studies*, *30*(1-2), 89-100.

Hunt, H. (2010). Consciousness and society: Societal aspects and implications of transpersonal psychology. *International Journal of Transpersonal Studies*, *29*(1), 20-30.

Institute of Transpersonal Psychology. (2011). *Catalog*. Palo Alto, CA: Author.

James, W. (1890). *The principles of psychology*. New York, NY: Henry Holt.

Johnson, D. H. (this volume). Transpersonal dimensions of somatic therapies (Chapter 26).

Jourard, S. (1966). The "awareness of potentialities" syndrome. *Journal of Humanistic Psychology*, *6*(2), 139-140.

Jung, C. G. (1939). *The integration of the personality*. Oxford, UK: Farrar & Rinehart.

Jung, C. G. (1969). *The collected works of C. G. Jung* (Vol. 9, Part 1, The archetypes and the collective unconscious; 2nd ed.). Princeton, NJ: Princeton University Press.

Kalaidjian, W. (1991). Transpersonal poetics: Language writing and the historical avant-gardes in postmodern culture. *American Literary History*, *3*(2), 319-336.

Kurtz, P. (1991). *The transcendental temptation*. Buffalo, NY: Prometheus Books.

Lajoie, D., & Shapiro, S. I. (1992). Definitions of transpersonal psychology: The first twenty-three years. *Journal of Transpersonal Psychology*, *24*(1), 79-98.

Lajoie, D., Shapiro, S. I., & Roberts, T. B. (1991). A historical analysis of the statement of purpose in *The Journal of Transpersonal Psychology*. *Journal of Transpersonal Psychology*, *23*(2), 175-182.

Lawlis, G. F. (this volume). Modern miracles from ancient medicine: Transpersonal medicine approaches (Chapter 36).

Lukoff, D., & Lu, F. G. (1988). Transpersonal psychology research review topic: Mystical experience. *Journal of Transpersonal Psychology*, *20*(2), 161-184.

Maslow, A. H. (1943). A theory of human motivation. *Psychological Review*, *50*(4), 370-396.

Maslow, A. H. (1958). A dynamic theory of human motivation. In A. H. Maslow (Ed.), *Understanding human motivation* (pp. 26-47). Cleveland, OH: Howard Allen.

Maslow, A. H. (1968). *Toward a psychology of being* (2nd ed.). New York, NY: Van Nostrand Reinhold.

Maslow, A. H. (1969). The farther reaches of human nature. *Journal of Transpersonal Psychology*, *1*(1), 1-10.

Maturana, H., & Varela, F. (1980). Autopoiesis and cognition: The realization of the living, In R. S. Cohen & M. W. Wartofsky (Eds.), *Boston studies in the philosophy of science*, (Vol 42). Dordrecht, The Netherlands: D. Reidel.

May, R. (1986). Transpersonal or transcendental? *The Humanistic Psychologist*, *19*, 87-90.

Moore, R. M. (2010). The rising tide: "Branding" in the academic marketplace. *Change: The Magazine of Higher Learning, 36*(3), 56-61.

Neville, B. (2007). What kind of universe? Rogers, Whitehead and transformative process. *Person-Centered & Experiential Therapies, 6*(4), 271-285.

Palmer, G., & Braud, W. (2002). Exceptional human experiences, disclosure, and a more inclusive view of physical, psychological, and spiritual well-being. *Journal of Transpersonal Psychology, 34*(1), 29-61.

Rogers, C. R. (1963a). *Actualizing tendency in relation to "motives" and to consciousness.* Lincoln, NB: University of Nebraska Press.

Rogers, C. R. (1963b). Toward a science of the person. *Journal of Humanistic Psychology, 3*(2), 72-92.

Rogers, C. R. (1978). The formative tendency. *Journal of Humanistic Psychology, 18*(1), 23-26.

Rogers, C. R. (1980). *A way of being.* New York, NY: Houghton-Mifflin.

Rothberg, D., & Coder, K. E. (this volume). Widening circles: The emergence of transpersonal social engagement (Chapter 35).

Rowe, N., & Braud, W. (this volume). Transpersonal education (Chapter 38).

Ruddick, N. (2009). *Fire in the stone: Prehistoric fiction from Charles Darwin to Jean M. Auel.* Middletown, CT: Wesleyan University Press.

Schott, R. L. (1992). Abraham Maslow, humanistic psychology and organization leadership: A Jungian perspective. *Journal of Humanistic Psychology, 32*(1), 106-120.

Schuon, F. (1984). *The transcendent unity of religions.* Wheaton, IL: Theosophical Publishing House. (Original work published 1953)

Schwartz, S. A. (2000). *Boulders in the stream: The lineage and founding of the Society for the Anthropology of Consciousness.* Society for the Anthropology of Consciousness/American Anthropological Association. Retrieved from www.sacaaa.org/history.asp

Scoglio, S. (1998). *Transforming privacy: A transpersonal philosophy of rights.* Westport, CT: Praeger.

Shapiro, S. I., Lee, G. W., & Gross, P. L. (2002). The essence of transpersonal psychology. *International Journal of Transpersonal Studies, 21*, 19-32.

Shermer, M. (2002). *Why people believe weird things.* New York, NY: Henry Holt.

Stableford, B. (1995). Origin of man. In J. Clute & P. Nicholls (Eds.), *The encyclopedia of fiction* (pp. 894-895). New York, NY: St. Martin's Press.

Sutich, A. J. (1968). Transpersonal psychology: An emerging force. *Journal of Humanistic Psychology, 8*(1), 77-78.

Tart, C. T. (1975). *States of consciousness.* New York, NY: Dutton.

Tart, C. T. (2008). Accessing state-specific transpersonal knowledge: Inducing altered states. *Journal of Transpersonal Psychology, 40*(2), 137-154.

Vaughan, F. (1979). Transpersonal psychotherapy: Context, content, and process. *Journal of Transpersonal Psychology, 11*(2), 101-110.

Vaughan, F. E. (1982). The transpersonal perspective: A personal overview. *Journal of Transpersonal Psychology, 14*(1), 37-45.

Walsh, R. (1993). The transpersonal movement: A history and state of the art. *Journal of Transpersonal Psychology, 25*(2), 123-139.

Walsh, R., & Vaughan, F. (1993). *Paths beyond ego (the transpersonal vision).* New York, NY: Jeremy P. Tarcher/Putnam.

Washburn, M. (1995). *The ego and the dynamic ground: A transpersonal theory of human development* (2nd ed., Rev.). Albany, NY: State University of New York Press.

Whitehead, A. N. (1979). *Process and reality: An essay in cosmology* (corrected ed.; D. R. Griffin & D. W. Sherburne, Eds.). New York, NY: Free Press.

Whitfield, C. (2009). *The Jungian myth and Advaita Vedanta*. Chennai, Tamil Nadu, India: Arsha Vidya.

Wilber, K. (1979). A developmental view of consciousness. *Journal of Transpersonal Psychology, 11*(1), 1-21.

Wilber, K. (1989). Let's nuke the transpersonalists: A response to Albert Ellis. *Journal of Counseling and Development, 67*(1), 332-335.

Wilber, K. (1995a). An informal overview of transpersonal studies. *Journal of Transpersonal Psychology, 27*(2), 107-129.

Wilber, K. (1995b). *Sex, ecology, spirituality: The spirit of evolution*. Boston, MA: Shambhala.

Wilber, K. (1996). *A brief history of everything*. Boston, MA: Shambhala.

Wilber, K. (1998). *The marriage of sense and soul: Integrating science and religion*. Boston, MA: Shambhala.

Wilber, K. (2000). Waves, streams, states and self—A summary of my psychological model (Or, outline of an integral psychology). Appendix C: The death of psychology and the birth of the integral. Retrieved from http://wilber.shambhala.com/html/books/psych_model/psych_model1.cfm/xid,7345/yid,3040482

2

Traditional Roots, History, and Evolution of the Transpersonal Perspective

Michael Daniels

The Transpersonal and Transpersonal Psychology

The word *transpersonal* (beyond or through the personal) refers to experiences, processes, and events in which the usual self-conscious awareness is transcended and in which there is a sense of connection to, or participation with, a larger, more meaningful reality (Daniels, 2005). The transpersonal is often equated with the domain of spirituality and religious experience although it also encompasses non-religious forms of self-transcending participation such as may be experienced in profound human relationships, or from the realization of the essential connection of humans to nature. Although these other phenomena could also be understood as expressions of human spirituality, the term transpersonal is often preferred because it avoids many of the metaphysical and religious preconceptions that generally accompany any discussion of spirituality (Daniels, 2005; Walsh & Vaughan, 1993). Central to the transpersonal perspective is the assumption that transpersonal phenomena involve a fundamental *transformation* of normal egoic existence to some ultimately more satisfying or valuable condition. In other words, there is a strong normative, soteriological or salvific agenda to the transpersonal (Caplan, Hartelius, & Rardin, 2003; Daniels, 2005; Ferrer, 2002, 2011; Hartelius, Caplan, & Rardin, 2007).

Transpersonal psychology is a branch of psychology that specializes in the investigation of transpersonal phenomena and associated forms of psychological and social transformation. Partly because the transpersonal encompasses more than the phenomena of religion, transpersonal psychology is not the same as the *psychology of religion* (cf. Fontana, 2003; Hood, Hill, & Spilka, 2009; Wulff, 1997). Also, although the psychology of religion tends to focus on the empirical *description* and psychological *analysis* of religious experience and behavior, transpersonal psychology is an explicitly *normative* discipline. In other words, transpersonal psychology directly and proactively addresses and promotes the need for human transformation.

The Wiley Blackwell Handbook of Transpersonal Psychology, First Edition.
Edited by Harris L. Friedman and Glenn Hartelius.
© 2013 John Wiley & Sons, Ltd. Published 2015 by John Wiley & Sons, Ltd.

A danger inherent in any normative approach is that it can become *ideological* in the sense of promoting a system of belief and practice for which there may be little or no verifiable evidence or rational justification (Daniels, 2011). Emphasizing this danger, some have dismissed transpersonal psychology as merely another new-age superstition, fad or cult, set on peddling its own brand of faith (e.g., Ellis & Yeager, 1989). Others from within the discipline (e.g., Daniels, 2011; Friedman, 2002, 2005) have sought to minimize the dangers of ideological bias and of myth-mongering through transpersonal psychology's clear commitment to a *scientific* approach to knowledge and research. Such a perspective seeks to distinguish the formal discipline of transpersonal psychology (based on strict, though necessarily broad, scientific protocols) from various nonscientific *transpersonal psychologies* (Daniels, 2011) such as Buddhist psychology, Kabbalistic psychology, and astrological psychology, as well as from other approaches within the broader *transpersonal movement* or field of *transpersonal studies* that do not adopt psychological modes of explanation (cf. Boucouvalas, 1999; Daniels, 2005, 2011; Friedman, 2002; Walsh & Vaughan, 1993). These other approaches include theology, philosophy, religious studies, folk traditions and New Age thought, as well as transpersonal research within such disciplines as anthropology, neuroscience, pharmacology, economics, political science, and sociology.

Identifying transpersonal psychology as a scientific discipline should not be confused with *scientism,* that is, the positivist attempt to reduce all phenomena to a materialistic, mechanistic, or strictly rational explanation. Transpersonal phenomena are inherently subtle and elusive and the preferred mode of explanation in transpersonal psychology is therefore *hermeneutic* (emphasizing understanding and interpretation) requiring psychological rather than physical or physiological constructs and models (Daniels, 2005). In other words, transpersonal psychology focuses on explicating the human meaning of transpersonal phenomena, which it aims to achieve using psychological discourse. This does not mean that transpersonal psychologists cannot learn from studies in brain science that examine the neurological correlates of transpersonal experiences, but that knowledge of brain processes cannot explain the subjective qualities (*qualia*) of such experiences, nor their meaning and significance to the person (cf. Lancaster, 2004; Velmans, 2000).

The normative, soteriological agenda of transpersonal psychology means that it is best considered as an *applied* rather than pure science. Transpersonal psychologists are concerned not only with *understanding* transpersonal phenomena and their associated process of transformation, but also with their *realization*. In this respect transpersonal psychology represents a value-laden and responsible *moral science of action* rather than a value-free and determinist *natural science of behavior* (Shotter, 1975). This implies that transpersonal psychology should be orientated not only to investigating, but also to bringing about the kinds of transformation it examines—in the researcher, in other individuals, in the wider community and, ultimately, at the global, possibly even cosmic, level.

Origins of Transpersonal Psychology

Although the term transpersonal is a relatively recent coinage (Hastings, 1999), transpersonal phenomena have been known and studied for millennia, not least by spiritual practitioners, mystics, and theologians. It is possible to understand some religious approaches (especially, perhaps, Buddhist theory and practice) as being early forms of scientific transpersonal psychology, but in general most religious approaches to transpersonal understanding rest upon the authority of tradition rather than of direct knowing, the value of belief rather than inquiry, and an understanding that is based on mythological and metaphysical rather than psychological concepts (Daniels, 2005, 2011).

Modern *transpersonal psychology* has its clearest origins in the work of the eminent American psychologist William James (1842-1910), not coincidentally also the first person known to have used the English term, trans-personal, in a 1905 Harvard course syllabus (Taylor, 1996a). His 1901-1902 Gifford Lectures on Natural Religion at the University of Edinburgh (published in 1902 as *The Varieties of Religious Experience*) investigated the religious questions through a psychological analysis of religious phenomena. Such experience, James (1912) argued, is the legitimate subject matter of scientific psychology and may be investigated using a "radical empiricism" that encompasses the observation of internal mental states and processes (see also Taylor, 1996b).

William James was also an important pioneer of psychical research which he saw as central to understanding many religious questions, such as whether the human personality may survive bodily death (Murphy & Ballou, 1961). His interest in religious experiences was also informed by his acquaintance with the mystical doctrines of Emanuel Swedenborg, American Transcendentalism, Theosophy, Christian mysticism, Sufism, Buddhism, Vedanta, and Yoga (Taylor, 1996b), as well as by his own experiments (e.g., James, 1882, 1898) with the psychoactive nitrous oxide (laughing gas). Largely as a result of these drug-induced experiences (Nelson, 2002), James (1902/1960) was led to conclude that:

> Our normal waking consciousness, rational consciousness as we call it, is but one special type of consciousness, whilst all about it, parted from it by the filmiest of screens, there lie potential forms of consciousness entirely different. (p. 373-374)

The same year that James was delivering his Gifford Lectures (1901) also saw the publication of a seminal book about exalted and joyous episodes of *Cosmic Consciousness* (experiences of deep connection to the Universe as a living, ordered Presence) written by the Canadian psychiatrist Richard M. Bucke (1837-1902; Bucke, 1901/2001). Bucke, who was friend and biographer of Walt Whitman, believed that cosmic consciousness provided direct experiential confirmation of Whitman's conception of "My Soul" (the Oversoul or universal spirit of the American Transcendentalists) and that the origin of all religion lies in this universal experience. Bucke was therefore an early advocate (as were the Theosophists) of the doctrine of the *perennial philosophy* (Huxley, 1947),[1] that is, the belief that all religions share a common experiential and doctrinal deep structure that recognizes the essential divinity of the human soul.

Psychological theory in the early 20th century was dominated by the psychoanalytic movement. Sigmund Freud himself took an uncompromisingly reductionist approach to religious and spiritual experience, viewing the religious impulse as a manifestation of unconscious conflicts and unhealthy psychological projections. In contrast, the Swiss analytical psychologist C. G. Jung (1875-1961), at one time a close associate and colleague of Freud, became highly critical of Freud's dismissal of spiritual experience as essentially an expression of neurosis. Jung's own spiritual and psychic experiences, and his dramatic mythic encounter with the unconscious following his split with Freud in 1913 (Jung, 2009), profoundly influenced his psychological development and thinking. As a result, he came to view the spiritual impulse as the manifestation and projection of essentially healthy *archetypes* (universal patterns of experience) that exist within humankind's transpersonal (überpersonlich) *collective unconscious*. In Jung's analytical psychology (e.g., Jung, 1966, 1967, 1969, 1991; see also Jacobi, 1968; Storr, 1991) the fundamental goal of human life is *individuation*—essentially a psychospiritual quest for full humanness and psychological integration, representing the realization of the archetype of the Self. Jung believed that the psyche has a natural growth-orientated tendency (the *transcendent function*) that creatively seeks to resolve oppositions and to unify unconscious and conscious contents. The process of individuation could therefore be facilitated by encouraging the transcendent function through working creatively and imaginatively with dream images, symbols, and myths that represent the process of psychospiritual transformation.

Another important influence from the psychoanalytic movement was the work of the Italian psychiatrist Roberto Assagioli (1888-1974). As with Jung, Assagioli had a lifelong interest in spirituality, mysticism and the occult. A student of raja yoga and also of the esoteric theosophist teacher Alice Bailey (Firman & Gila, 2002), Assagioli developed a theoretical and practical system of therapy and psychological development called *psychosynthesis* (Assagioli, 1993), which explicitly incorporates the spiritual dimensions of human experience in its attempt to integrate the discoveries of psychoanalysis with those of the spiritual traditions. Assagioli argued that Jung's concept of the collective unconscious does not adequately distinguish between "higher," "middle," and "lower" realms of the unconscious (pp. 17-18). For Assagioli, psychological development involves the exploration and integration (synthesis) of all three realms, but especially the higher unconscious, which he saw as the source of mystical experiences, higher intuitions and aspirations, moral imperatives, altruism, compassion, genius, and illumination (Assagioli, 1991, 1993; Firman & Gila, 2002). Psychosynthesis advocates various practical techniques, including meditation and visualization, as aids to transpersonal exploration and integration. In working with the higher unconscious, and in learning to understand one's higher nature and purpose, Assagioli (e.g., 1991, 1993) believed that a person contacts and expresses the Higher Self (Transpersonal Self, or Spiritual Self), equivalent to the *Atman* (universal Self or Soul of the Hindu *Upanishads*). As a result, one moves beyond *personal psychosynthesis* (the achievement of a well-integrated personality, centered on the personal ego) to spiritual or *transpersonal psychosynthesis* (the synthesis of personal ego with the Higher Self).

While the psychoanalytic movement prevailed in Europe in the early and middle 20th century, American psychology at this time became dominated by the behaviorism of Edward Thorndike, John B. Watson, and, latterly, B. F. Skinner. In its focus on animal and human *behavior,* behaviorism ignored inner, spiritual experience and attached no special significance to religious behavior. Consequently, behaviorism was seen as irrelevant by those interested in the areas of spirituality and inner psychological development. It was in reaction to the perceived reductionism and blinkered perspective of behaviorism (and also that of Freudian psychoanalysis) that the so-named *Third Force* of *humanistic psychology* emerged in the US in the mid 20th century, through the pioneering work of Abraham Maslow (1908-1970; e.g., 1954/1970, 1962/1968) in academic psychology and Carl Rogers (1902-1987; e.g., Rogers, 1951, 1961/2004) in psychotherapy and counseling. Humanistic psychology was formally established with the launch of the *Journal of Humanistic Psychology* in 1961, and the formation of the Association for Humanistic Psychology (AHP) the following year. With roots in humanism, phenomenology, and existentialism, humanistic psychology emphasizes and seeks to promote human rationality, agency, positive inner experience, mental health, and the full realization of individual potential (self-actualization). It also aims to reinstate interest in the kinds of "higher" human experiences that are generally ignored or neglected by mainstream psychology. These include love, empathy, creativity, intuition, mystical experience, altruism, and compassion. Maslow's own research on what he termed self-actualizing people (Maslow 1962/1968, 1954/1970, 1973), found that many report experiences of transcendence, including peak or ecstatic moments of self-forgetting, as well as a strong "metamotivational" desire to actualize universal transcendent values, such as justice, unity, beauty, and perfection. Himself an atheist, although one who recognized the reality of spiritual experiences and motives, Maslow interpreted these transcendent and transformational phenomena as expressions of our universal (biological) human nature (Daniels, 2005). Carl Rogers similarly expressed a strictly humanistic (biological-psychological-existential) rather than religious or metaphysical interpretation of the impulse towards happiness, goodness, and fulfillment. Indeed Rogers saw religion (especially the Protestant tradition with which he was most familiar) as exerting a powerful negative influence on human well-being (Rogers, 1961/2004).

The tensions that are expressed in the work of Maslow and Rogers, resulting from recognizing the importance of spiritual motives and experience while simultaneously adopting a biological-humanist-existential perspective, remain largely unresolved. Although some within the humanistic movement have attempted to dissociate themselves from what they see as the encroachment of religious and spiritual ideas into humanistic psychology (e.g., Schneider, 1987), others have consistently sought to consolidate and promote spiritual concerns. Indeed it was the desire to focus more specifically on spiritual matters that led to the initial suggestion that a *Fourth Force* in psychology was needed (Grof, 2008; Hastings, 1999), perhaps with the intention of leaving the Third Force of humanistic psychology to cater for those pursuing strictly existential and psychotherapeutic concerns. As a result, in the late 1960s, Maslow, together with his colleagues Stan Grof, Anthony Sutich, Miles Vich, and others, proposed the term *transpersonal psychology* for this Fourth Force. To help realize such a force, the *Journal of Transpersonal Psychology* was launched in 1969, under the editorship of Anthony Sutich, and, in 1972, the parent Association for Transpersonal Psychology (ATP) was established, holding its first conferences the following year (Grof, 2008; Sutich, 1969, 1976; Vich, 1990; Walsh, 1993). However, despite the concern expressed by some to demarcate humanistic from transpersonal psychology, such a clear separation has never happened. For example, the *Journal of Humanistic Psychology* continues to publish articles on transpersonal topics while AHP and ATP regularly co-sponsor many events. In 2007, AHP and ATP held a joint event to celebrate and reinforce their connection, and the two sister organizations now offer joint professional membership at a reduced rate (*AHP Perspective,* 2007/2008, p. 3).

Social and cultural developments in the 1960s also influenced the direction taken by transpersonal psychology. These included the widespread use of psychedelic drugs among the affluent youth of America and Europe. Although this was often little more than a recreational activity or a way of confirming an anti-establishment alternative lifestyle and identity, LSD, mescaline, and other hallucinogens were viewed by some as facilitating valid states of spiritual consciousness. As early as 1954, the British writer Aldous Huxley argued in *The Doors of Perception* that mescaline could be a valuable aid in expanding human consciousness. Also in the 1950s and 1960s, the Czech psychiatrist Stan Grof pioneered the clinical use of LSD, for example in treating alcoholism and drug addiction. Grof (e.g., 2000) has called the LSD experience *holotropic* (oriented towards wholeness) and his research suggests that by accessing and working through holotropic experiences, people are able to achieve greater self-understanding and psychological healing. Grof also found that, especially with higher doses of LSD, people would often report a rich and extraordinary variety of transpersonal experiences in which the sense of time, space, and self, as well as the normal distinction between mind and matter, became drastically altered. Just as William James had concluded from his experiences with nitrous oxide, Grof believed that LSD enabled people to experience transpersonal realities normally hidden from everyday consciousness. In the 1970s, after LSD use had become federally prohibited in the USA, Grof discovered that holotropic and transpersonal experiences could be induced using a technique he developed with his wife Christina. Called *Holotropic Breathwork^{TM},* it involved lengthy sessions of altered breathing combined with loud evocative music and body work (Grof, 2000).

Perhaps the most important contribution made by Grof's psychedelic-holotropic approach to understanding transpersonal experiences is his recognition of their extraordinary range, richness, and variety. Transpersonal experiences include, but are not limited to, cosmic consciousness, or to other traditional categories of mystical or religious experience. In many cases, they may have no obvious spiritual quality—as, for example, in consciousness of cellular structures, or experiences of other times and places—and may include the full gamut of paranormal phenomena (Grof, 1988, 2000).

For many people, however, *spirituality* continues to be the hallmark of the transpersonal. In the 1960s, at the same time as the psychedelic movement peaked, there was also an explosion of interest among Americans and Europeans in Eastern religions—notably Hinduism and Buddhism—and in Eastern forms of meditation. Much of this interest had been sparked by the Beat Generation writers of the 1950s, including Jack Kerouac, Allen Ginsberg, and William Burroughs, whose own radical ideas of social and spiritual liberation had been influenced by the European romantic poets, by American Transcendentalism, and by Zen Buddhism. The British philosopher and writer Alan Watts also created significant Western interest in Eastern philosophies (especially Buddhism) through his books *The Way of Zen* (1957) and *Psychotherapy East and West* (1961). Following Watts's lead, Eastern teachings came to be seen by many Westerners as both practical and psychologically sophisticated, and as promising the kind of direct spiritual experience and potential for psychological growth they perceived as absent from traditional Western religions. These philosophies were not only absorbed into the popular counterculture of the time, but also increasingly came to dominate academic transpersonal psychology through the influence of such writers and teachers as Sri Aurobindo (e.g., 1970, 1990), Ram Dass (e.g., 1971), and Chögyam Trungpa (e.g., 1973). Although Hinduism and Buddhism have had the clearest impact on theory and research in transpersonal psychology, other religious-mystical teachings have also been absorbed, including Kabbalah, Christian mysticism, Gurdjieffian philosophy, Shamanism, Sufism, Taoism, Theosophy, and neopaganism (Daniels, 2005).

Developments in Transpersonal Psychology

From the early 1960s, meditation and other methods of personal transformation, among them encounter groups, Yoga, psychodrama, Gestalt therapy, Holotropic Breathwork™ and body work, came to be taught at avant-garde "growth centers" such as the Esalen Institute (www.esalen.org) that was established by Michael Murphy and Richard Price at Big Sur, California, in 1962 (Goldman, 2012). These centers soon became the focus of what has been called the *human potential movement*—a diffuse, rich, eclectic mix of transformational approaches and technologies that, in many ways, represents the practical and experientially orientated wing of humanistic and transpersonal psychology. Esalen, in particular, especially in its early days, attracted a formidable team of presenters, including Gregory Bateson, Joseph Campbell, Buckminster Fuller, Stan Grof, Aldous Huxley, Timothy Leary, George Leonard, Abraham Maslow, Fritz Perls, J. B. Rhine, Carl Rogers, Will Schutz, Paul Tillich, and Alan Watts.

Serious academic and professional interest in the transpersonal became more formally established with the development of specialist humanistic-transpersonal graduate schools and therapeutic training programs. This had begun as early as 1951, with the founding by Louis Gainsborough of the American Academy of Asian Studies in San Francisco and the appointment of Alan Watts and Haridas Chaudhuri as professors (Subbiondo, 2011). Chaudhuri was a Bengali integral philosopher and former associate of the renowned Indian teacher of integral yoga, Sri Aurobindo (1872-1950). In 1968, Chaudhuri relaunched the Academy as the California Institute of Asian Studies (CIAS) and in 1980 the school changed its name to the California Institute of Integral Studies (CIIS; CIIS, n.d.; Subbiondo, 2011). It currently offers a wide range of accredited educational programs in transpersonal and related areas. Research or graduate training programs in transpersonal psychology have since been developed by a number of other educational institutions, including, the Institute for Transpersonal Psychology (now Sofia University), John F. Kennedy University, Naropa University, and Saybrook University in the USA and, Liverpool John Moores University, University of Chichester, and the University of Northampton in the UK. In addition, transpersonally based psychotherapeutic training is offered by an increasing number of privately run centers, including those taking a Jungian, psychosynthesis, Buddhist, or integral perspective.

A number of academic journals (as well as more popular periodicals) now specialize in publishing research in transpersonal psychology. These include the *Journal of Humanistic Psychology, Journal of Transpersonal Psychology, International Journal of Transpersonal Studies, ReVision, Transpersonal Psychology Review* (the Journal of the British Psychological Society Transpersonal Psychology Section), and *Journal of Transpersonal Research*. Additionally, transpersonal psychology research often appears in journals of such related disciplines as religious studies, parapsychology, consciousness studies, counseling and psychotherapy, clinical psychology, psychiatry, and positive psychology, as well as in more specialist journals, for example those dedicated to dream research or near-death studies. A few publishing houses also specialize in books on transpersonal psychology. Notable among these are SUNY Press and Shambhala Publications.

Since its formal inception in 1969, research and theory in transpersonal psychology has focused on certain key areas of interest:

a Defining the nature and role of transpersonal psychology more carefully, including its relationship to other disciplines (e.g., Caplan et al., 2003; Daniels, 2005; Ferrer, 2002; Hartelius et al., 2007; Lajoie & Shapiro, 1992; Walsh & Vaughan, 1993).
b The characterization and development of epistemologies and research methodologies that are appropriate to transpersonal psychology's normative agenda and subject matter (e.g., Anderson & Braud, 2011; Braud & Anderson, 1998; Ferrer, 2002).
c Empirical research on transpersonal consciousness (e.g., Murphy & Donovan, 1997; Tart, 1990).
d The creation and evaluation of theoretical models of transpersonal states, processes, and events (e.g., Ferrer, 2002; Washburn, 1994, 1995; Wilber, 1977, 1995, 2000, 2006).
e The development and assessment of transpersonal approaches to psychotherapy, counseling, and psychiatry (e.g., Boorstein, 1996; Cortright, 1997; Sperry & Shafranske, 2004).
f The development of effective methods and practical guidance for individuals and groups seeking to explore the transpersonal (e.g., Ferrer, 2003; Leonard & Murphy, 1995; Murphy, 1992; Wilber, Patten, Leonard, & Morelli, 2008).

With much self-perceived success in these areas, transpersonal psychology has also sought acknowledgement and acceptance from the psychological establishment. One important motivation for this has been the expectation that research funding, which has been difficult to obtain for transpersonal topics, might then be more readily secured. Attempts to have transpersonal psychology accepted as a separate Division within the American Psychological Association have, to date, been unsuccessful, although various aspects of transpersonal psychology are represented in other APA divisions, principally Division 32: Society for Humanistic Psychology, and Division 36: Society for the Psychology of Religion and Spirituality. However, in 1996, the British Psychological Society became the first professional psychological association to approve the formation of an academic section in Transpersonal Psychology (www.transpersonalpsychology.org.uk).

Perspectives in Transpersonal Psychology:
An Historical Analysis

The question of exactly how to understand and define the transpersonal and spiritual continues to occupy transpersonal psychologists (Cunningham, 2007; Daniels, 2005; Fontana, 2003; Hartelius et al., 2007). Currently there is no universally accepted position within the field and this may account, at least in part, for the difficulties that have been encountered in obtaining full recognition for transpersonal psychology from the psychological establishment. Rather, four distinct perspectives may be identified (cf. Lancaster, 2004).[2]

- **The religious perspective**. The transpersonal and spiritual are seen in terms of our relationship to a divine reality that transcends mundane existence (e.g., God, Brahman, Supreme Being, Sachchidananda, Dharma, Tao, Great Spirit).
- **The psychological perspective**. Transpersonal experience and behavior are seen as expressions of underlying psychological processes. This perspective encompasses, for example, social psychological, cognitive, psychodynamic, and neurotheological approaches.
- **The humanistic/existential/feminist perspective**. Spirituality is seen as a funda-mental aspect of human experience through which one develops more profound and authentic understandings and relationships with the self and other people.
- **The ecological perspective**. This focuses on one's spiritual connection to, and ethical responsibility towards, the natural world (life, other species, Gaia, cosmos).

One way of considering these different perspectives is to relate them to important historical developments in human thinking about the self and the spiritual. Various writers have proposed that a fundamental change in human consciousness occurred in the period between c. 800 BCE and c. 200 BCE (e.g., Armstrong, 2006; Hick, 1989; Jaspers, 1949/1977; Jaynes, 1993; Tarnas, 1991; see also Daniels, 2005, 2009). Because this period involved a profound *turning point* (or revolution) in humans' understanding of themselves and their relationship with both nature and the super-natural, it has been called the *axial* period (after Jaspers, 1949/1977). The axial period thus represents a watershed separating what may be termed the *pre-axial* period (before c. 900 BCE) and the *post-axial* period (approximately corresponding to the Common Era). Because post-axial understanding reflects insights that first appeared in the axial period, some writers (e.g., Armstrong, 2006) do not make a clear distinction between the axial and post-axial eras.

Pre-axial religion is characterized by animistic, shamanistic, and mythic beliefs and practices based on the perceived interpenetration and codependence of the spiritual (supernatural), natural, and human worlds. Pre-axial societies emphasize the impor-tance of communal living in harmony with nature and the spirits. The function of religion is seen as maintaining the natural, human, and supernatural order and there-fore religious practices are essentially restorative in purpose (involving ritual, sacrifice, magic, and petitionary prayer). Most notably, pre-axial religion has no clear concept of progress or evolution. Change (as observed in the tides, seasons, astronomical movements, and animal migrations) is understood to be a cyclical process in which the cycles are themselves ordered and regular. When unpredictable changes occur (e.g., earthquakes, epidemics, famines), these are understood to represent a disturbance in the world order that is caused either by the breaking of taboos within the community, or by malicious magical attacks from outside. Here the religious leader of the community (the shaman, priest, or priestess) is charged with identifying the offender within, or the enemy outwith, and ensuring that appropriate measures are taken to appease the offended spirits, or to defend against and repulse any magical attack. It is important also to note that in pre-axial societies there is no clear (modern) concept of *individuality,* or of a separate personal self. Each person in the community has their assigned roles to fulfill and all are collectively responsible for ensuring the continued survival and well-being of the community.

During the pre-axial period, certain key religious ideas predominated. Firstly, there seems to have been an important emphasis on the feminine principle (fertility, motherhood, nurturing) although whether, at any time in prehistory, this amounted to a universal cult of the Goddess in the way suggested by some (e.g., Gimbutas, 1982) is a matter of debate. Consistent with this feminine emphasis on fertility, care and nurturance, the world is seen as a web of interconnection and interdependency. It is also itself sacred because it is infused with, and dependent upon, its relation with the spiritual realm. Pre-axial religion is therefore essentially life-affirming in its outlook, rejoicing in sensory experience, pleasure, natural growth, wellness, and fullness.

All this changed radically during the axial period, beginning around 800 BCE when Iron Age cultures were becoming established in the Near East, Europe, India, China, and Japan. The axial (Iron Age) period saw the development of new metal-working technologies that coincided with fundamental changes in agriculture, social systems, artistic expression, and religious beliefs and practices. These, in turn, may be seen as expressing a "Great Transformation" in human consciousness (Armstrong, 2006) most clearly exemplified by the philosophies of the Jewish Prophets (c. 800-400 BCE), Buddha (c. 563-483 BCE), Confucius (551-479 BCE), Lao Tse (traditionally a contemporary of Confucius), Socrates (c. 469-399 BCE) and Kapila (no dates, traditionally the founder of *Samkhya* philosophy within Hinduism).

The axial philosophies saw human beings in a new relationship to the Divine, to nature, and to society. In particular, the notions of *progress* and *conquest* became foundational. In their most developed forms, these notions were allied to a further emphasis on *individuality*. In this way progress and conquest came to be seen as an *individual heroic quest for salvation and perfection*—an idea that makes little sense from a pre-axial perspective. Conquest also came to be seen as involving the rising above, control, and subjugation of the individual's physical (animal) desires and imperfections through the cultivation of supposedly higher intellectual and spiritual qualities (rationality, self-knowledge, discipline, dispassion, ethical awareness, compassion, and empathy). Also, crucially, such self-development was seen as involving a process of struggle and *suffering* (Armstrong, 2006).

With its emphasis on the individual conquering hero it is not surprising that axial philosophy was sometimes used during this period (and later) to justify social and political conquest and the subjugation (and suffering) of others. It may also be noted that (with its Iron Age origins) axial philosophies idealize and appeal to what were almost certainly perceived at the time (and often since) as essentially *masculine* virtues of strength, courage, control, rationality, dispassion, and military-style discipline.

These changes in human (or perhaps men's) consciousness led to a fundamental alteration in the perception of the nature and function of religion as well as to corresponding adjustments to social systems and the mythologies that support them. Some of the important changes are summarized in Table 2.1.

As Karen Armstrong (2006) has brilliantly shown, axial themes lie at the heart of all the major modern (post-axial) World religions. These include the Abrahamic religions (Judaism, Christianity, Islam), Buddhism, Hinduism (especially Vedanta and Samkhya), Confucianism, Taoism, Jainism, Sikhism, and Zoroastrianism. Because these religions dominate modern thinking about spirituality, it is unsurprising that axial and post-axial themes also predominate within transpersonal psychology, as seen in the persisting emphasis on meditation, spiritual discipline, enlightenment, formless consciousness, spiritual "masters," levels and stages of attainment, transcendence, and the realization of the "higher self."

Table 2.1   Social, Mythological and Religious Elements in Pre-Axial and Axial Thought

Pre-axial	Axial
Tribal Society; Community	Patriarchy; Aristocracy
Sharing; Communal goods	Possession; Personal property
Co-dependence	Individuality
Heterarchy	Hierarchy
Social function	Heroic quest
Taboo; Custom	Rule; Law
Social conformity	Personal discipline
Mutual control	Individual control
Co-dependents	Masters (human and "ascended")
Sustenance	Perfection
Stasis	Progress
Healers; Shamans	Sages; Saints
Magic	Mysticism
Mind-body union	Mind-body split
Realism	Idealism
Non-rational knowing	Rational knowing
Many Spirits (polytheism)	One Spirit (monotheism)
Many Ways	The (One) Path
Beneficent Goddess	Ruling God
Female exemplar	Male exemplar
Mother	Father
Healing	Salvation
Passion	Dispassion (Compassion)
Ease; Enjoyment	Struggle; Suffering
Immanence	Transcendence
Fullness	Emptiness
Visionary experience	Formless enlightenment

Although the different post-axial religions vary in their specific views of the Divine (for example the Abrahamic religions believe in the existence of a single supreme Deity, whereas most forms of Buddhism reject a theistic conception), there are certain common ontological assumptions made by most, if not all, major post-axial religions. For this reason it may be possible to identify an underlying perennial post-axial philosophy (cf. Huxley, 1947). Central to this common post-axial ontology is the view that the only true reality is Spirit and that, ultimately, Spirit is one. Furthermore, Spirit is understood as the prior cause (creator) of the manifest world, implying that the world known to sensory experience is a dependent, secondary reality. This, in turn, leads to the assumption that two ontological realities exist. First, there is the absolute, prior, Reality of Spirit; second, there is the relative, dependent, reality (and experience) of the phenomenal world.

Three Vectors of Transpersonal Development

These ontological assumptions neatly support the soteriological (salvific) agenda of much post-axial religion whereby the path to spiritual salvation is one of refining (perfecting) human consciousness, from a prior state of ordinary, relative, gross, material, or sensory awareness towards the ultimate realization of absolute consciousness and union with Spirit. This soteriological agenda indicates what Ken Wilber (e.g., 1995, 1996) has termed an *ascending current* in transpersonal thought (see also, Daniels, 2005). This ascending current advocates a spiritual path of transcendence (of the relative, manifest world) in the achievement of "higher" (absolute) spiritual consciousness. As such it represents an other-worldly perspective in which the purpose of life is to disidentify with ordinary, sensory experience of the phenomenal world (*prakriti* in Samkhya philosophy), and to identify with the transcendental, absolute reality of spiritual consciousness (*purusha* in Samkhya philosophy). Moreover, taking the essentially *individualistic* position implied in axial and post-axial thought, this path of spiritual transformation through the refining of consciousness is seen as something to be undertaken by each individual in a personal (heroic) quest for absolute perfection that involves the conquest of unsatisfactory, relative, illusory experience.[3]

There is, however, another soteriological position that can be identified in post-axial thinking which Wilber (e.g., 1995, 1996) has called the *descending current*, representing a more this-worldly, immanent perspective. Here the axial emphases on progress, evolution, salvation, and transformation are applied to the manifest world of human experience. Hence the focus is less on individual achievement of transcendent states of spiritual consciousness, and more on the achievement of positive change in the world, on the development of empathy and compassion towards others, and on the path of service. From the perspective of the descending current, the manifest world (although, at present, corrupt or even evil) is seen as itself perfectible through active spiritually motivated interventions (both individual and collective).

In certain respects, the post-axial descending current may be seen as continuing some important pre-axial concerns (for example, with community, mutuality, and immanent spirituality) and thus as representing a more developmental, less revolutionary, post-axial perspective than that of the ascending current. Wilber (1995,

1996) has argued, for example, that in many of its early expressions, the change in religious and philosophical thinking that occurred during the axial and post-axial period represented an effective *integration* of the ascending and descending currents. Thus one may point to the Buddha's focus on both personal enlightenment and compassion for others, or Plato's ideas on both taming the passions and on social justice, or Confucius's ideas about the importance of both personal discipline and the maintenance of social order. According to Wilber (1995, 1996), it was sometime later in history that the ascending and descending currents began to diverge, eventually resulting in one-dimensional or "flatland" philosophical and religious approaches that are "merely Ascending" or "merely Descending" (e.g., Wilber, 1995, p. 341; 1996, pp. 11-12, 243ff.). Thus, for example, Gnosticism and, later, Catharism may be seen as merely ascending perspectives, whereas the nature romantics and scientific materialists represent different versions of a merely descending current. For Wilber, these one-dimensional perspectives have themselves driven many of the ideological wars between ascenders and descenders that have been witnessed in the past several centuries and which continue to rumble on into the present (e.g., those between religion and science, or between established and indigenous religions, or between humanist-existentialist and transpersonal perspectives). The solution to these unproductive wars, according to Wilber, is to work towards the development of religious and philosophical perspectives that are capable of reintegrating the ascending and descending currents. Indeed this is one important aspect of Wilber's own integral agenda, as represented by the work of his think tank, the Integral Institute (see, e.g., Wilber, 2006; http://integralinstitute.org).

Although Wilber's distinction between ascending and descending spiritual currents is a useful guide in many respects, there are certain difficulties with this formulation, particularly when considering the descending current. Firstly, the term descending could be seen as somewhat derogatory. Indeed the term is often used by Wilber to imply an inferior theoretical position, for example in his characterization of many descenders as "retro-Romantics" (Wilber, 1995, 1996). Secondly, the descending current often appears overly inclusive, for example in the way that it may embrace Jungian, psychedelic-holotropic, feminist, and ecological approaches to the transpersonal (Daniels, 2009). Finally, the meaning of the term descending is left essentially unclear and imprecise. What kind of descent is meant? Descent to what?

I have argued (Daniels, 2009) that the usual identification of descending currents actually conflates two fundamentally distinct soteriological positions. These may be characterized as:

1   the depth psychological perspective;
2   the relational participatory perspective.

The depth psychological perspective essentially argues that transpersonal development involves the exploration and integration of unconscious material that may be characterized as spiritual. As such, this approach is exemplified by the theories of Assagioli (1991, 1993), Firman & Gila (1997), Grof (e.g., 1988, 2000), Jung (e.g., 1966, 1967, 1969, 1991), Hillman (1977), Washburn (e.g., 1994, 1995), and Smith (2003), as well as in the practices and interpretations of some neopagans (Adler, 2006).

In contrast, the relational, participatory approach argues that transpersonal development involves realizing and expressing a spiritual connection to others and the
world. Fundamental to this approach is the importance of moving beyond an egocentric concern with one's own individuation or personal spiritual development towards
full participation with, commitment to, and responsibility for, other people, other
species, and the world at large. Such relational, participatory thinking is exemplified
in indigenous spiritualities (e.g., Harner, 1980; Kremer, 1998), feminist spirituality
(e.g., Brooks, 2010; Chittister, 1998; Starhawk, 1999; Wright, 1995, 1998), transpersonal ecology (e.g., Fox, 1995; Naess, 1973), relational spiritualities (e.g., Achterberg
& Rothberg, 1998; Wade, 2004; Welwood, 1991), and Ferrer's (e.g., 2002, 2011;
Ferrer & Sherman, 2008) participatory vision (emancipation from self-centeredness,
cocreative participation).

Because of the clear differences between the depth psychological and the relational
participatory perspectives, I have proposed (Daniels, 2009) that the term descending
should be restricted to the depth psychological approach (because this unequivocally
implies descent into the depths of the unconscious). To contrast with this, I suggest
that the relational participatory approach is better described using the metaphor of
extending because it implies expansion of the boundaries of moral and spiritual concern
outwards, from a purely self-referential stance to one that encompasses other people
and the larger political, economic, and ecological systems (cf. Friedman's, 1983,
concept of self-expansiveness).

The implication of this distinction is that one may identify *three* soteriological
approaches, that is, the ascending, descending, and extending, each expressing a
different set of values and perspectives (Table 2.2). Although (after Wilber) these
approaches may be termed *currents*, it may be more appropriate to view them as
dynamic vectors in transpersonal development, rather than as separate and discrete
streams (Daniels, 2009). In this way the possibility of combining and integrating
these directional forces becomes more explicit, avoiding the assumption that people
may tend to swim in only one stream.

Table 2.2 Three Vectors in Transpersonal Development

	Ascending	*Descending*	*Extending*
Metaphor	Height	Depth	Breadth
Keyword	Enlightenment	Individuation	Participation
Key virtues	Wisdom; Faith	Integration; Hope (confidence)	Compassion; Charity (love)
Tradition	Religion	Psychology	Humanism
Realm of exploration	Higher mind; "Superconscious"	Unconscious; Dynamic ground	People; World
Ego as	"Lower" self	Partial psychic system	Egocentrism; Anthropocentrism
Transcending	"Lower" nature	Psychic divisions	Self-centeredness
Union of	Self and Divine	Conscious and unconscious	Self and Other

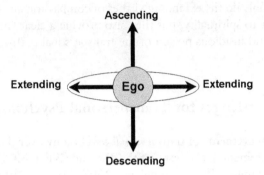

Figure 2.1   Three vectors of ego-transcendence.

As can be seen from Table 2.2, each of these vectors advocates a different path of ego-transcendence (widely considered to be the hallmark of transpersonal develop-ment). In this respect, the three vectors clearly express the major directions in which we may move beyond egocentrism (Figure 2.1).

Towards an Integral Perspective

The assumption behind this vector model is that a truly *integral* transpersonal perspec-tive needs to recognize and incorporate all three soteriological vectors. Furthermore, the vector model can perhaps also be used as a study guide to assess the degree to which particular transpersonal approaches approximate such an integral perspective (see Daniels, 2009, for a suggested analysis). Although many transpersonal approaches implicitly recognize aspects of all three vectors, only a few are explicitly all-vector (inte-gral) in their understanding, even if they continue to place emphasis on one or two specific vectors. Among these integral perspectives one should certainly include the approaches of Assagioli, Aurobindo, Ferrer, Grof, Washburn, and Wilber. Yet although these perspectives may, to varying degrees, *conceptually* recognize all three vectors in transpersonal development, the important question remains whether any of them is capable of supporting a truly all-vector, integral soteriology (practice). In this regard, the Integral Yoga of Aurobindo (1970, 1990; also Chaudhuri, 1965), the Integral Life Practice of Wilber (Wilber, et al., 2008) the Integral Transformative Practice of Leonard and Murphy (1995) and the Holistic Integration of Albareda and Romero (Ferrer, 2003) may all be seen as important developments.

In my opinion, for transpersonal theory and practice to be truly all-vector, it needs to incorporate (and be able to balance) the ascending, descending, and extending perspectives and soteriologies. In this way an all-vector approach may promote the essential transpersonal work of overcoming egocentrism through facilitating (1) wis-dom and faith (ascending), (2) psychological integration and hope (descending), and (3) compassion and charity (extending). However, although the virtues expressed by each vector are important, and all should be cultivated in an integral practice, a strong case could be made to consider the virtues of the extending vector to be pre-eminent.

For example, not only do the extending virtues of compassion and charity imply a real and practical point to spirituality, but they also provide a clear and effective antidote to that common and insidious poison of the transpersonal path—spiritual narcissism (cf. Walach, 2008).

Challenges for Transpersonal Psychology

Given the clear achievements of transpersonal psychology over the past decades it is, perhaps, an overstatement to suggest that the discipline is in crisis. However, problems and challenges certainly exist (Cunningham, 2007; Daniels, 2011). These manifest both within and outwith the discipline. Internally, transpersonal psychology remains factional and often conflicted. Outwardly it is relatively isolated from mainstream psychology, as well as from such cognate approaches as consciousness studies, psychology of religion, and positive psychology. External funding for research or for graduate training in transpersonal areas is hard to secure. Sadly, academic programs in transpersonal psychology are not always well-supported by parent institutions and, in some cases, have been closed. Other than private psychotherapeutic practice or personal coaching, career opportunities for transpersonal psychologists are relatively limited. It can be difficult, especially in the public sector, for individuals to incorporate transpersonal interests and activities within an academic career or within applied professions such as clinical, occupational, or educational psychology.

Meeting the external challenges will not be easy, particularly in the current global economic and political climate. But progress might be made through greater attention to some of the attitudes and assumptions that may be holding the field back, or holding it *within* what may be a sandbox largely of its own making (cf. Marien, 1983). In particular, I would make an urgent plea for less parochialism, less preciousness, less certainty, and less narcissism in transpersonal psychology. In their place, I would like to see more curiosity, more "Don't Know Mind," more speculation, more women's voices, more dialogue, and more *research*.

A related aspect of Marien's (1983) critique of the "sandbox syndrome" is the oft-perceived absence of real-world relevance in much contemporary humanistic and transpersonal psychology—itself somewhat paradoxical given the self-proclaimed mission towards human betterment. To a large extent this lack of social and political relevance may reflect the ascending-individualistic-narcissistic agenda that has dominated transpersonal psychology for so long, for example in the emphasis that continues to be placed upon exploring states of consciousness, and upon levels of individual spiritual achievement (cf. Ferrer, 2002).

Moving out of this sandbox is therefore vital if transpersonal psychology is to prosper and to be relevant. To do this, what is needed is both the vision and the courage to realize that, in addition to its many important professional applications (for example in clinical, educational, and organizational contexts), transpersonal psychology potentially has so much to offer (and receive) in the dialogue with other disciplines, as well as by fuller participation in the larger social-political sphere (cf. Rothberg, 2008). Transpersonal psychology may yet have a significant role to play in helping to promote inter-faith dialogue, religious tolerance, and mutual understanding, as well as in seeking to tackle the wider social problems such as alienation, "moral decline," rampant materialism, and ecological destruction.

Notes

1. I understand the participatory approach of Ferrer (e.g., 2002) to incorporate all four of these perspectives.
2. As Huxley (1947) noted, these ontological assumptions may be identified most clearly in Buddhism, Vedanta, and Samkhya (in the East) and Gnosticism, Neoplatonism, and Jewish and Christian mysticism (in the West).
3. In some cases, for example in Gnosticism, this soteriological agenda is further justified on the grounds that the manifest, material world is corrupt and evil.

References

Achterberg, J., & Rothberg, D. (1998). Relationship as spiritual practice. In D. Rothberg & S. Kelly (Eds.), *Ken Wilber in dialogue: Conversations with leading transpersonal thinkers* (pp. 261-274). Wheaton, IL: Quest Books.

Adler, M. (2006). *Drawing down the moon: Witches, druids, goddess-worshippers, and other pagans in America* (Rev. ed.). New York, NY: Penguin.

AHP Perspective (2007/2008, December/January). ATP and AHP got married in San Francisco. *AHP Perspective*, p. 3.

Anderson, R., & Braud, W. (2011). *Transforming self and others through research: Transpersonal research methods and skills for the human sciences and humanities*. Albany, NY: State University of New York Press.

Armstrong, K. (2006). *The great transformation: The world in the time of Buddha, Socrates, Confucius and Jeremiah*. London, UK: Atlantic Books.

Assagioli, R. (1991). *Transpersonal development: The dimension beyond psychosynthesis*. London, UK: HarperCollins.

Assagioli, R. (1993). *Psychosynthesis: The definitive guide to the principles and techniques of psychosynthesis*. London, UK: Thorsons.

Aurobindo, Sri (1970). *The life divine*. Pondicherry: Sri Aurobindo Ashram. (Original work published 1939-1940)

Aurobindo, Sri (1990). *The synthesis of yoga* (6th ed.). Silver Lake, WI: Lotus Light Publications. (Original work published 1948-1955)

Boorstein, S. (Ed.). (1996). *Transpersonal psychotherapy* (2nd ed.). Albany, NY: State University of New York Press.

Boucouvalas, M. (1999). Following the movement: From transpersonal psychology to a multidisciplinary transpersonal orientation. *Journal of Transpersonal Psychology, 31*(1), 27-39.

Braud, W. G., & Anderson, R. (1998). *Transpersonal research methods for the social sciences: Honoring human experience*. Thousand Oaks, CA: Sage.

Brooks, C. (2010). Unidentified allies: Intersections of feminist and transpersonal thought and potential contributions to social change. *International Journal of Transpersonal Studies, 29*(2), 33-57.

Bucke, R. M. (2001). *Cosmic consciousness: A study on the evolution of the human mind*. Bedford, MA: Applewood Books. (Original work published 1901)

California Institute of Integral Studies (n.d.). History of CIIS. Retrieved from http://www.ciis. edu/About_CIIS/CIIS_at_a_Glance/History_of_CIIS.html

Caplan, M., Hartelius, G., & Rardin, M.A. (2003). Contemporary viewpoints on transpersonal psychology. *Journal of Transpersonal Psychology, 35*(2), 143-162.

Chaudhuri, H. (1965). *Integral yoga: The concept of harmonious and creative living.* London, UK: George Allen & Unwin.

Chittister, J. D. (1998). *Heart of flesh: A feminist spirituality for women and men.* Grand Rapids, MI: Eerdmans/Novalis.

Cortright, B. (1997). *Psychotherapy and spirit: Theory and practice in transpersonal psychotherapy.* Albany, NY: State University of New York Press.

Cunningham, P. F. (2007). The challenges, prospects, and promise of transpersonal psychology. *International Journal of Transpersonal Studies, 26,* 41-55.

Daniels, M. (2005). *Shadow, self, spirit: Essays in transpersonal psychology.* Exeter, UK & Charlottesville, VA: Imprint Academic.

Daniels, M. (2009). Perspectives and vectors in transpersonal development. *Transpersonal Psychology Review, 13*(1), 87-99.

Daniels, M. (2011, September 17). Retrospective and challenges for transpersonal psychology. Keynote paper presented at the British Psychological Society Transpersonal Psychology Section 15th Annual Conference, Cober Hill, Scarborough. Retrieved from http://www.youtube.com/watch?v=FBidl7xfHl8

Ellis, A., & Yeager, R. J. (1989). *Why some therapies don't work: The dangers of transpersonal psychology.* New York, NY: Prometheus Books.

Ferrer, J. N. (2002). *Revisioning transpersonal theory: A participatory vision of human spirituality.* Albany, NY: State University of New York Press.

Ferrer, J. N. (2003). Integral transformative practice: A participatory perspective. *Journal of Transpersonal Psychology, 35*(1), 21-42.

Ferrer, J. N. (2011). Participatory spirituality and transpersonal theory: A ten-year retrospective. *Journal of Transpersonal Psychology, 43*(1), 1-34.

Ferrer, J. N., & Sherman, J. H. (2008). *The participatory turn: Spirituality, mysticism, religious studies.* Albany, NY: State University of New York Press.

Firman, J., & Gila, A. (1997). *The primal wound. A transpersonal view of trauma, addiction, and growth.* Albany, NY: State University of New York Press.

Firman, J., & Gila, A. (2002). *Psychosynthesis: A psychology of the spirit.* Albany, NY: State University of New York Press.

Fontana, D. (2003). *Psychology, religion, and spirituality.* Leicester, UK: BPS Blackwell.

Fox, W. (1995). *Toward a transpersonal ecology.* Albany, NY: State University of New York Press.

Friedman, H. (1983). The Self-Expansiveness Level Form: A conceptualization and measurement of a transpersonal construct. *Journal of Transpersonal Psychology, 15*(1), 37-50.

Friedman, H. (2002). Transpersonal psychology as a scientific field. *International Journal of Transpersonal Studies, 21,* 175-187.

Friedman, H. (2005). Problems of romanticism in transpersonal psychology: A case study of Aikido. *The Humanistic Psychologist, 33*(1), 3-24.

Gimbutas, M. (1982). *The goddesses and gods of old Europe: Myths and cult images* (Rev. ed.). Berkeley, CA: University of California Press.

Goldman, M. (2012). *The American soul rush: Esalen and the rise of spiritual privilege.* New York, NY: New York University Press.

Grof, S. (1988). *The adventure of self-discovery.* Albany, NY: State University of New York Press.

Grof, S. (2000). *Psychology of the future: Lessons from modern consciousness research.* Albany, NY: State University of New York Press.

Grof, S. (2008). Brief history of transpersonal psychology. *International Journal of Transpersonal Studies, 27,* 46-54.

Harner, M. (1980). *The way of the shaman.* New York, NY: Harper & Row.

Hartelius, G., Caplan, M., & Rardin, M. A. (2007). Transpersonal psychology: Defining the past, divining the future. *The Humanistic Psychologist, 35*(2), 1-26.

Hastings, A. (1999). Transpersonal psychology: The fourth force. In D. Moss (Ed.), *Humanistic and transpersonal psychology: A historical and biographical sourcebook* (pp. 192-208). Westport, CN: Greenwood Press.

Hick, J. (1989). *An interpretation of religion: Human responses to the transcendent.* Basingstoke, Hampshire, UK & New York, NY: Palgrave.

Hillman, J. (1977). *Re-visioning psychology.* New York, NY: Harper Perennial.

Hood, R. W., Jr., Hill, P. C., & Spilka, B. (2009). *The psychology of religion: An empirical approach* (4th ed.). New York, NY: Guilford Press.

Huxley, A. (1947). *The perennial philosophy.* London, UK: Chatto & Windus.

Huxley, A. (1954). *The doors of perception.* New York, NY: Harper.

Jacobi, J. (1968). *The psychology of C. G. Jung: An introduction with illustrations* (7th ed.) London, UK: Routledge & Kegan Paul.

James, W. (1882). The subjective effects of nitrous oxide. *Mind, 7,* n.p. Retrieved from http://www.erowid.org/chemicals/nitrous/nitrous_article1.shtml

James, W. (1898). Consciousness under nitrous oxide. *Psychological Review, 5,* 194-196.

James, W. (1912). *Essays in radical empiricism.* New York, NY: Longmans, Green.

James, W. (1960). *The varieties of religious experience: A study of human nature.* London, UK: Fontana. (Original work published 1902)

Jaspers, K. (1977). *The origin and goal of history.* Westport, CT: Greenwood Press. (Original work published 1949 [German])

Jaynes, J. (1993). *The origin of consciousness in the breakdown of the bicameral mind.* London, UK: Penguin Books.

Jung, C. G. (1966). *Collected works of C. G. Jung* (2nd ed.; R. F. C. Hull, Trans.). In *Two essays on analytical psychology* (Vol. 7). London, UK: Routledge. (Original works published 1917, 1928 [German])

Jung, C. G. (1967). *Collected works of C. G. Jung* (2nd ed.; R. F. C. Hull, Trans.). In *Symbols of transformation* (Vol. 5). London, UK: Routledge. (Original work published 1912 as *Psychology of the unconscious: A study of the transformations and symbolisms of the libido, a contribution to the history of the evolution of thought* [German])

Jung, C. G. (1969). *Collected works of C. G. Jung* (2nd ed.; R. F. C. Hull, Trans.). In *Psychology and religion: West and East* (Vol. 11). London, UK: Routledge. (Original work published 1938 [German])

Jung, C. G. (1991). *Collected works of C. G. Jung* (2nd ed.; R. F. C. Hull, Trans.). In Part 2. *Aion: Researches into the phenomonology of the self* (Vol. 9). London, UK: Routledge. (Original work published 1951 [German])

Jung, C. G. (2009). *The red book: Liber novus* (S. Shamdasani, Ed. & Trans.). New York, NY: Norton. (German with English translation)

Kremer, J. W. (1998). The shadow of evolutionary thinking. In D. Rothberg & S. Kelly (Eds.), *Ken Wilber in dialogue: Conversations with leading transpersonal thinkers* (pp. 239-258). Wheaton, IL: Quest Books.

Lajoie, D. H., & Shapiro, S. I. (1992). Definitions of transpersonal psychology: The first twenty-three years. *Journal of Transpersonal Psychology, 24*(1), 79-98.

Lancaster, B. L. (2004). *Approaches to consciousness: The marriage of science and mysticism.* Basingstoke, Hampshire, UK, & New York, NY: Palgrave MacMillan.

Leonard, G., & Murphy, M. (1995). *The life we are given: A long-term program for realizing the potential of body, mind, heart, and soul.* New York, NY: Jeremy P. Tarcher/Putnam.

Marien, M. (1983). The transformation as sandbox syndrome. *Journal of Humanistic Psychology, 23*(1), 7-15.

Maslow, A. H. (1968). *Toward a psychology of being* (2nd ed.). Princeton, NJ: Van Nostrand. (Original work published 1962)

Maslow, A. H. (1970). *Motivation and personality* (2nd ed.). New York, NY: Harper & Row. (Original work published 1954)

Maslow, A. H. (1973). *The farther reaches of human nature.* Harmondsworth, Middlesex, UK: Penguin.

Murphy, G., & Ballou, R. O. (1961). *William James on psychical research.* London, UK: Chatto & Windus.

Murphy, M. (1992). *The future of the body: Explorations into the further evolution of human nature.* New York, NY: Jeremy P. Tarcher/Putnam.

Murphy, M., & Donovan, S. (1997). *The physical and psychological effects of meditation: A review of contemporary research with a comprehensive bibliography, 1931-1996* (2nd ed.). Petaluma, CA.: Institute of Noetic Sciences.

Naess, A. (1973). The shallow and the deep, long range ecology movement: A summary. *Inquiry, 16*, 95-100.

Nelson, C. A. P. (2002). The artificial mystic state of mind: WJ, Benjamin Paul Blood, and the nitrous-oxide variety of religious experience. *Streams of William James, 4*(3), 23-31.

Ram Dass (1971). *Be here now.* San Cristobal, NM: Lama Foundation.

Rogers, C. R. (1951). *Client-centered therapy: Its current practice, implications and theory.* London, UK: Constable.

Rogers, C. R. (2004). *On becoming a person: A therapist's view of psychotherapy.* London, UK: Constable & Robinson. (Original work published 1961)

Rothberg, D. (2008). Connecting inner and outer transformation: Toward an expanded model of Buddhist practice. In J. N. Ferrer & J. H. Sherman (Eds.), *The participatory turn: Spirituality, mysticism, religious studies* (pp. 349-370). Albany, NY: State University of New York Press.

Schneider, K. J. (1987). The deified self: A "centaur" response to Wilber and the transpersonal movement. *Journal of Humanistic Psychology, 27*(2), 196-216.

Shotter, J. (1975). *Images of man in psychological research.* London, UK: Methuen.

Smith, H. (2003). *Cleansing the doors of perception: The religious significance of entheogenic plants and chemicals* (3rd ed.). Boulder, CO: Sentient Publications.

Sperry, L., & Shafranske, E. P. (2004). *Spiritually oriented psychotherapy.* Washington, DC: American Psychological Association.

Starhawk. (1999). *The spiral dance: A rebirth of the ancient religion of the Great Goddess* (20th anniversary ed.). New York, NY: HarperCollins.

Storr, A. (1991). *Jung.* New York, NY: Routledge.

Subbiondo, J. L. (2011). CIIS and American higher education. *Integral Review, 7*(1), 11-16.

Sutich, A. J. (1969). Some considerations regarding transpersonal psychology. *Journal of Transpersonal Psychology, 1*(1), 11-20.

Sutich, A. J. (1976). The emergence of the transpersonal orientation. *Journal of Transpersonal Psychology, 8*(1), 5-19.

Tarnas, R. (1991). *The passion of the Western mind: Understanding the ideas that have shaped our world view.* New York, NY: Crown.

Tart, C. T. (Ed.). (1990). *Altered states of consciousness* (3rd rev. ed.). New York, NY: Harper.

Taylor, E. (1996a). William James and transpersonal psychiatry. In. B. W. Scotton, A. B. Chinen, & J. R. Battista (Eds.), *Textbook of transpersonal psychiatry and psychology* (pp. 21-28). New York, NY: Basic Books.

Taylor, E. (1996b). *William James on consciousness beyond the margin*. Princeton, NJ: Princeton University Press.

Trungpa, C. (1973). *Cutting through spiritual materialism*. Boston, MA: Shambhala.

Velmans, M. (2000). *Understanding consciousness*. London, UK: Routledge.

Vich, M. A. (1990). The origins and growth of transpersonal psychology. *Journal of Humanistic Psychology, 30*(2), 47-50.

Wade, J. (2004). *Transcendent sex: When lovemaking opens the veil*. New York, NY: Simon & Schuster/Pocket.

Walach, H. (2008). Narcissism: The shadow of transpersonal psychology. *Transpersonal Psychology Review, 12*(2), 47-59.

Walsh, R., & Vaughan, F. (1993). On transpersonal definitions. *Journal of Transpersonal Psychology, 25*(2), 199-207.

Walsh, R. N. (1993). The transpersonal movement: A history and state of the art. *Journal of Transpersonal Psychology, 25*(3), 123-139.

Washburn, M. (1994). *Transpersonal psychology in psychoanalytic perspective*. Albany, NY: State University New York Press.

Washburn, M. (1995). *The ego and the dynamic ground* (Rev. ed.). Albany, NY: State University of New York Press.

Watts, A. (1957). *The way of Zen*. London, UK: Thames & Hudson.

Watts, A. (1961). *Psychotherapy East and West*. New York, NY: Pantheon Books.

Welwood, J. (1991). *Journey of the heart: Intimate relationship and the path of love*. London, UK: Mandala.

Wilber, K. (1977). *The spectrum of consciousness*. Wheaton, IL: Quest Books.

Wilber, K. (1995). *Sex, ecology, spirituality: The spirit of evolution*. Boston, MA: Shambhala.

Wilber, K. (1996). *A brief history of everything*. Dublin, Ireland: Gill & MacMillan.

Wilber, K. (2000). *Integral psychology: Consciousness, spirit, psychology, therapy*. Boston, MA: Shambhala.

Wilber, K. (2006). *Integral spirituality*. Boston, MA: Integral Books.

Wilber, K., Patten, T., Leonard, A., & Morelli, M. (2008). *Integral life practice: A 21st-century blueprint for physical health, emotional balance, mental clarity and spiritual awakening*. Boston, MA: Integral Books.

Wright, P. (1995). Bringing women's voices to transpersonal psychology. *ReVision, 17*(3), 3-10.

Wright, P. A. (1998). Gender issues in Ken Wilber's transpersonal theory. In D. Rothberg & S. Kelly (Eds.), *Ken Wilber in dialogue: Conversations with leading transpersonal thinkers* (pp. 207-236). Wheaton, IL: Quest Books.

Wulff, D. H. (1997). *Psychology of religion: Classic and contemporary* (2nd ed.). New York, NY: John Wiley & Sons, Ltd.

3

The Calling to a Spiritual Psychology

Should Transpersonal Psychology Convert?

Glenn Hartelius, Harris L. Friedman, and James D. Pappas

Transpersonal psychology was founded by an early group of humanistic psychologists who were dissatisfied with both conventional psychology (the then-prevailing forces of behaviorism and psychoanalysis), as well as the limitations of a person-centered psychology that ignored placing human beings within a cosmic perspective. In the search for an appropriate name for this new endeavor, the term *spirituality* was rejected by its founders for a variety of reasons, including the fact that this term was seen as too controversial. At the same time, "from its inception but under coded names, transpersonal psychology has been concerned with the spiritual dimension of human experience" (Helminiak, 2008, p. 161). This is in some tension with psychology, which as a scientific discipline has largely based its legitimacy through distancing itself from religion and spirituality, limiting its scope to what can be narrowly known through empiricism. Transpersonal psychology, seen as a subdiscipline of psychology, sought a replacement for the term spirituality as its Identifier. The more obscure term, *transpersonal,* was intentionally selected for reasons that include the absence of the metaphysical baggage and prejudice that spirituality carried. However, in recent years, the term spirituality has not only become acceptable, but it has experienced a renaissance within conventional psychology (e.g., Miller & Thoresen, 2003). At the same time, transpersonal psychology has come to be seen by some as a relic of the 1960s and the excesses of those heady times (e.g., psychedelic exploration; Friedman, 2006); for many others the term simply carries no meaning. In an ironic twist, the conditions prompting the initial effort to distance the field from the stigma associated with spirituality have been reversed, so that the term transpersonal, when it is recognized, now suffers from the very prejudices that led to its being embraced, while the originally taboo term spirituality has ascended into widespread acceptance.

This has led some to abandon the term transpersonal in favor of the now more acceptable term spirituality. For example, Sofia University, which until recently

The Wiley Blackwell Handbook of Transpersonal Psychology, First Edition.
Edited by Harris L. Friedman and Glenn Hartelius.
© 2013 John Wiley & Sons, Ltd. Published 2015 by John Wiley & Sons, Ltd.

was named the Institute of Transpersonal Psychology, retains the term transpersonal in its tagline rather than in its title. Although it still offers a Doctor of Philosophy (Ph.D.) program in transpersonal psychology, its companion Doctor of Psychology program (Psy.D.) makes no mention of transpersonal psychology. Instead, it describes itself as being a program that "integrates nondenominational spirituality and an understanding of world religious beliefs and practices into the training to be a clinical psychologist" (see http://www.sofia.edu/academics/resphd/clinical.php). In addition, the Association for Transpersonal Psychology (ATP), the first major transpersonal association, along with Sofia University, have over the past few years been cosponsoring a "Spirituality & Psychology Conference" (see http://www.itp.edu/conference2012/index.php), in which the term transpersonal simply does not appear. ATP, along with the transpersonal journal it sponsors (*Journal of Transpersonal Psychology*), has begun to seriously consider adopting the term spiritual, rather than (or in addition to) the term transpersonal for use in titling its organization and associated journal (David Lukoff, personal communication, ca. 2008). Some luminary figures in the subfield, such as Wilber (2000), have severed their connections with transpersonal psychology.

At the same time, spirituality is gaining traction in various areas of psychology. Calls for a spiritual psychology, or psychology of spirituality, have been increasing for at least the past twenty years (e.g., Benner, 1989), and in the early 21st century these appear to have greatly accelerated (Helminiak, 2001a, 2001b, 2005, 2008; Miovic, 2004; Sperry & Mansager, 2007; Steinfeld, 2000). Some authors have referred to spiritual psychology as if it were already a separate entity (e.g., Helminiak, 2005, 2008; Miovic, 2004; Steinfeld, 2000). There is also growing recognition of the importance of addressing spiritual issues within psychotherapies (e.g., Avants, Beitel, & Margolin, 2005; Bienenfeld & Yager, 2007; Bolletino, 2001; Lukoff & Lu, 2005; Mansager, 2002; Pargament & Saunders, 2007) and medical therapies (e.g., Ai, Seymour, Tice, Kronfol, & Bolling, 2009; Johnstone & Yoon, 2009; Koenig, 2010). In addition, there have been a plethora of professional papers written on spiritual psychology (e.g., Kapuscinski & Masters, 2010; Pargament & Sweeney, 2011), and even books published within the more conservative mainstream psychology presses, such as that of the American Psychological Association (e.g., Plante, 2009; Sperry & Shafranske, 2005), which until recently would have soundly rejected works on this subject. Perhaps most emblematic of this growing acceptance, the psychology of religion has recently changed the name of its division within the American Psychological Association to include spirituality (DeAngelis, 2008), effectively laying claim to that territory.

This raises an obvious question: Is transpersonal psychology essentially spiritual psychology under a more obscure—and now less marketable—name? If it is the meaning underlying the name, and not the name itself, which should be important, why cling to the name transpersonal? Aversion to the term spirituality has dissipated and spirituality, now seen favorably within psychology, is flourishing (Helminiak, 2005); at the same time, transpersonal might be perceived as suffering from disfavor, or waning interest, or both. Such an act of conversion might make transpersonal psychology easier to define and its mission simpler to understand, thus solving some of the identity challenges it has continually faced (Hartelius, Caplan, & Rardin, 2007). While better filling a contemporary need, it might also avoid current prejudices against the term transpersonal in some mainstream publishing companies, where manuscripts bearing this word may be turned down, and in mainstream universities, where applicants associated with the subdiscipline may not be hired or may be refused tenure.

For those who consider themselves strongly aligned with transpersonal psychology, this situation can be seen as a crisis of identity. The rapid acceptance of spirituality within the larger field of psychology may be the death knell for transpersonal psychology as an identified subdiscipline of psychology; alternately, it may provide opportunities for transpersonal psychology, which has been involved in the study of human spirituality since its inception. In a recent paper, one of the authors of this chapter has argued that "It's Premature to Write the Obituary for Humanistic Psychology" (Friedman, 2011), but whether the obituary for transpersonal psychology is now due can be considered an open question. Our hope is that the present volume evidences there is still much vibrancy left in the term transpersonal, and there remains great potential for transpersonal psychology to adapt and flourish while retaining its name.

The Intertwining of Transpersonal Psychology and Spirituality

The content area of transpersonal psychology has undeniably been linked to the study of spirituality. Spirituality is explicitly contained within many definitions of transpersonal psychology (e.g., Lajoie & Shapiro, 1992). A review conducted for this chapter of data collected earlier by Hartelius et al. (2007) showed that the term spiritual, as well as its various cognates, appeared in 109 of the160 definitions of transpersonal psychology collected for that study. In addition, much of the value that transpersonal psychology has contributed to conventional psychological thought has been through use of the term spirituality. For example, one of its key contributions involves reframing some psychological emergencies as being spiritual, rather than psychopathological, crises (Grof & Grof, 1989). This major breakthrough to the mainstream mental health establishment introduced the category of Religious or Spiritual Problem into the American Psychiatric Association's Diagnostic and Statistical Manual. Although it was championed by those holding transpersonal views (Turner, Lukoff, Barnhouse, & Lu, 1995), the term transpersonal was not used. Likewise, one of the most popular and fastest growing areas of research within contemporary psychology focuses on meditation, particularly the variant known as mindfulness. Meditation research was pioneered by transpersonal psychologists, yet the term transpersonal is hardly ever mentioned in the currently burgeoning literature on that topic (MacDonald, Walsh, & Shapiro, this volume).

What is a Spiritual Psychology?

To address whether transpersonal psychology is really only spiritual psychology under another name, there first has to be clarification about the conceptual domain of spirituality as it is currently used in psychology. Because the acceptable use of the term spirituality within psychology is rather recent, and is still evolving, we begin with distinguishing spirituality from religion.

The Religious Conceptual Domain

Religion can be understood as a method for publicly and privately expressing a set of beliefs, values, symbols, behaviors, and practices relating to what is considered sacred. Religious expressions are typically culturally based and commonly institutionalized. Even when only held privately, they rest on shared social understandings that may have been internalized. Richards and Bergin (2000) suggested that being religious is consistent with beliefs, feelings, and practices that are most commonly expressed "institutionally and denominationally as well as personally," and religious expressions are inclined to be "denominational, external, cognitive, behavioral, ritualistic, and public" (p. 5).

In regards to cultural ascriptions of religion, these involve procedures and techniques by which individuals have traditionally expressed their relation to the sacred. In the major world religions, they are usually guided by ideologies expressed by alleged charismatic founders, such as Buddhism's *Four Noble Truths* attributed to meditative discoveries by Siddhartha Gautama and Christianity's *New Testament* attributed to revelations associated with Jesus Christ. The instrumental element of religion in such a context is the "bond" or "connection" that exists between an individual and the sacred through some form of expression, whether an external practice, such as a method of prayer, or an internal, but socially-shared, belief system. Moreover, it is often a source that unites individuals through community and, in such a sense, binds individuals together as well as to the sacred, such as Buddhism's *sangha* and Christianity's church. This is consistent with its etymology from the Latin *religio*, which is based on the term *ligo* meaning "to bind" and is suggestive of a "bond between humanity and some greater-than-human-power" (National Institute for Healthcare Research, 1998, p. 15). It is also consistent with the similar expression in Sanskrit, *yoga*, which also means "to bind" or, more literally, to yoke.

Substantive aspects of religion. Contemporary views of religion, such as those offered by Zinnbauer, Pargament, and Scott (1999), often divide the concept into *substantive* (i.e., what religion represents, such as in terms of a motivational source) and *functional* aspects (i.e., what religion does, such as in terms of providing a support system). The *substantive* quality is observed in participation in religious activities, such as structured prayer, meditation, worship, chanting, or ritual, which constitute an individual's external religious expression (i.e., religiosity or religiousness) and usually is anchored in a shared cultural understanding. This is congruent with Spiro's (1966) suggestion that religion seen in this context is an "institution consisting of culturally patterned interaction with culturally postulated superhuman beings" (p. 96). However, in some cases, such as Buddhism, the sacred can alternatively be as seen as an individual's relatedness to a sacred, but impersonal, aspect that is typically not deified (although some Buddhist sects essentially deify the Buddha and other divinities, while other sects within Buddhism recognize deities only as non-ultimate beings). Religion in this sense is an *institutional process* whereby factors, such as social ritual (e.g., attending an institutionalized place of worship and prayer), assign an individual to a role encompassing a system of beliefs, attitudes, and practices. Notwithstanding that these rituals do not directly represent the extent of an individual's internal devotion or other depth indicators of religiousness, such behaviors reveal an individual's involvement in a methodological and ideological consensus of religion. Wulff (2003) emphasized this point by arguing that religion is "nothing more than narrow, dogmatic beliefs and obligatory religious observances" (p. 47). This conceptualization of religion, in terms of an individual's devotion limited to cultural-bound institutions, may be viewed as primarily motivated by external factors, among them living up to community expectations and opportunities for personal gain, even when experienced or practiced in isolation.

Notions of this sort have antecedents in the pioneering work of Allport (1950), who was the first to investigate religion from a psychometric perspective in order to differentiate between religion as a means-to-an-end and as an end-in-itself. Although he initially used the terms *immature religious sentiment* and *mature religious sentiment*, he changed them to *extrinsic* and *intrinsic religious orientation*, respectively, to study the prevalence of religious bigotry and prejudice in churchgoers and non-churchgoers. An immature religious sentiment may be associated with magical thinking (e.g., how Christian children are often socialized to view Santa Claus in the West), the use of supplicatory prayer (e.g., to gain personal favors from a deity), or thinking of a tribal nature (e.g., ethnocentric religious beliefs leading to feelings of superiority of an in-group). In contrast, a mature religious sentiment may be motivated by a genuine purpose to serve an individual's religion, specifically as the "value underlying all things desirable for its own sake" (Allport, 1961, p. 301). For Allport, the major difference between immature religion and mature religion is that the former was representative of an individual's self-centered, or perhaps family, tribal, or other socially limited motives, while the latter is suggestive of an individual's more universal, or master motives. In other words, self-centered motives indicate a self-serving purpose as the externalized aspects of religion, while master motives signify a faith-serving intention as the internalized aspects of religion.

In relationship to these distinctions, Allport (1961) differentiated between *extrinsically* and *intrinsically oriented* religious individuals, the former being religiously motivated as a means to achieving material gain, and the latter being religiously motivated for its own sake. According to Allport, much of religious sentiment is extrinsic, and an extrinsic approach to religion may undermine the deeper meaning of religious expression, namely relatedness to the sacred. Consequently, extrinsically oriented religious individuals may or may not embrace the so-called intended function of religion (Allport, 1966) and may even hold rigid parochial and fundamentalist notions that some single religion is the only true religion. This is likely related to the fact that such persons may tend to pursue religion primarily for utilitarian concerns (Burris, 1994), such as gaining personal or social rewards (Genia, 1993). In contrast, intrinsically oriented religious individuals may emphasize the unifying character of religion, because they are motivated by an authentic need to live religion rather than to use it as an instrumental means (Allport, 1966). The intrinsically oriented individual may also abandon aggrandizement, prejudice, and hatred to find deeper meanings through humility, compassion, and love. The master motive of such a person is to live religion to its fullest, internalizing purpose and faith, among other religious expressions. However, intrinsically oriented individuals can also be fundamentalist in the sense that they may be so deeply devoted to their own religion that they cannot respect other religions. It can even make them more likely to attempt to manipulate others to conform to their own religious orientation, perhaps even leading to deceptiveness (Burris, 1994).

Functional aspects of religion. The functional quality of religion addresses concerns about ontological (e.g., pertaining to the very nature of existence, being, reality, and the sacred) and epistemological (e.g., pertaining to understanding purpose, meaning, and fulfillment) issues. It also deals with the various effects of religion on societies, such as increasing group cohesiveness. If these functional aspects are left unaddressed, for example, in a religious practice based only on adhering to externalized institutionalized expressions (e.g., beliefs and practices that do not connect deeply with individuals" sense of the sacred), individuals can experience the frustration of unmet ontological and epistemological needs. Accordingly, Pargament (1997) argued that:

> This approach to religion [captures] the sense that religion is something more than a set of concepts and practices; rather, it has to do with life's most profound issues. It also opens up the study of religion to diverse traditions and innovative approaches, for no individual, group, or culture is spared the confrontations with ultimacy. (pp. 27-28)

Thus, externalized aspects of religion may not provide the important felt-sense of meaning as its internalized aspects, especially in a modern secularized context in which religious institutions may be appear empty.

The Spiritual Conceptual Domain

It is important to note that, traditionally, spirituality and religion were inextricably intertwined, but with the growth of multiculturalism, as well as other contemporary forces, these traditional connections have become increasingly weakened, and sometimes severed. For example, in homogenous cultures, people obtained spiritual fulfillment through religious institutions that were accepted as consensually valid, whereas in heterogeneous cultures in which multiple religions compete, there is more opportunity for people to separate the religious domain from their own sense of spirituality. This is resulting in a reconceptualization of religion and spirituality as different, as the two are increasingly separated within the contemporary West. Specifically, the category of religion may include aspects of spirituality, but there can be religion without spirituality, as religion also encompasses various sociocultural phenomena not specifically related to spirituality, such as compliance with institutional norms (e.g., church attendance for the purpose of socializing). These non-spiritual aspects of religion are often called religiosity, referring to the outer trappings of religion that may be devoid of their inner meaning. Spirituality, in turn, is not wholly contained within the domain of religion, as many can find spiritual fulfillment in non-religious ways, among them through communing with nature or engaging in practices outside of institutional guidelines. Individual meditation apart from a religious structure would be an example of this. The fact that these two closely related terms are not identical pertains to some imprecision in the use of the term spiritual—a fact that has been pointed out by many authors (e.g., Pedersen, Lonner, Draguns, & Trimble, 2007; Stifoss-Hanssen, 1999; Zinnbauer, Pargament, Cole et al., 1997).

Clarifying the conceptual domains of spirituality, and how it is related to that of religion, simplifies the task of situating spiritual psychology in order to compare it to transpersonal psychology. One fruitful approach to clarification is MacDonald's (2000) empirical effort to take diverse measures of different aspects of spirituality and refine them into common factors. However, this effort only defined what researchers are calling spirituality currently, and does not necessarily elucidate a better meaning for the concept, the usage of which is rapidly changing. In this regard, Pargament (1999) stated the following:

> The meanings of religion and spirituality appear to be evolving. Religion is moving from a broadband construct—one that includes both the institutional and the individual, and the good and the bad—to a narrowband institutional construct that restricts and inhibits human potential. Spirituality, on the other hand, is becoming differentiated from religion as an individual expression that speaks to the greatest of human capacities. (p. 3)

Koenig (2010) recently defined what he means when using the term spirituality from a psychology of religion perspective:

> To me, spirituality is distinguished from all other things—humanism, values, morals, and mental health—by its connection to the sacred, the transcendent. The transcendent is that which is outside of the self, and yet also within the self—and in Western traditions is called God, Allah, HaShem, or a Higher Power, and in Eastern traditions is called Ultimate Truth or Reality, Vishnu, Krishna, or Buddha. Spirituality is intimately connected to the supernatural and religion, although also extends beyond religion. Spirituality includes a search for the transcendent . . . (pp. 116-117)

Greer and Roof (1992) discussed how some may become their own religious authorities by listening to their "own little voice" instead of only following "institutional authorities" (p. 346). This type of religion veers into something perhaps better represented by the term spirituality. The context for such a quality may be embedded in a religious way of being that is not consistent with any parochial religious orientation but, rather, is a synthesis of organized and personal contemplations that develop an individual's unique religious worldview. In other words, although individuals may be affiliated with some particular religion, they are not necessarily limited to sanctioned methods and instead may develop their own way of living their religion or, alternatively, expressing their spirituality. This may include dealing with what might be called existential issues (e.g., a lack of purpose, meaning, and hope that can impede coping with such issues as mortality and isolation) through forming personalized religious connections to a sense of the sacred.

Defining the Spiritual in Non-Religious Ways

Connectedness to something sacred within a Western context is easily reduced to being understood only in theocentric ways, but if spirituality is truly a universal human phenomenon, then it must encompass more than deity-centered traditions (Helminiak, 2008). Historically, the term spiritual has antecedents in the ecclesiastical language of Judeo-Christian literature that describes an animating and supernatural force that has relevance to a divine figure, God. This has evolved from its etymological roots in Greek (*pneuma*) and Latin (*spiritus*), which mean breath or life or, perhaps better, life breathing force. In Western psychology, spirituality often refers to a personalized religion or the "subjective side of religious experience" (Hill & Pargament, 2003, p. 64), but usually is still seen as in relationship to God, or at least to some notion of higher power, because this term has been nested within the predominant Western Judeo-Christian tradition. Hence the term spirituality has been intertwined with prevailing religious concepts, if not religious practices. Theocentric approaches pervade most psychology of religion in the West, even when focused on spirituality. It thus reduces spirituality to its definition within a particular cultural context, excluding those who experience their interconnectedness to the cosmos in other ways, or those who declare themselves at once spiritual and yet atheistic or agnostic (Smith, 2001).

A Broader Version of Spirituality

The term spirituality is evolving to encompass more than connection to a deity or a designated sacred other. Instead, for some it may be the experience of communion with others, or connection with community or nature, or even a sense of interconnectedness with the world in its entirety that is perceived as sacred (Stifoss-Hanssen, 1999). This sense of interconnection is more than existential succor for, as the experienced frame of existence expands from isolated individual to interrelated community and cosmos, a process of transformation ensues. This interlinking of the sense of self with its context, which is both far broader and more enduring than tying it to any parochial vision, is a transpersonal process, perhaps similar to what Friedman (1983; Pappas & Friedman, 2007) called self-expansiveness. These views are consistent with those of Walsh and Vaughan (1993), who emphasized that transpersonal psychology is based on an expansion of the sense of self "beyond (*trans*) the individual or personal to encompass wider aspects of humankind, life *psyche,* and cosmos" (p. 3).

Spirituality, as the term is often used in the West, appears to point toward a functional, intrinsic, personally experienced connection with something sacred or higher, and also increasingly with something broader and more enduring, as well as the resulting transformative effects of both. Although organized religion may still be seen as one way of expressing an individual's spirituality (Spaeth, 2000), it is by no means the only way. An increasingly secularized version of spirituality is emerging, one that does not necessarily rely on supernatural notions and can be more detached from vestiges of institutional religion and other predominantly culturally mediated approaches.

It is clear that, while the terms religious and spiritual have considerable overlap, it is nevertheless possible to distinguish them (Stifoss-Hanssen, 1999; Zinnbauer, Pargament, Cole et al., 1997). Historically in the West, this has not always been the case. Prior to "the rise of secularism in [the 20th] century, and a popular disillusion-ment with religious institutions as a hindrance to personal experiences of the sacred," the two terms were virtually synonymous (Zinnbauer, Pargament, Cole et al., 1997, p. 550; see also Turner et al., 1995). However, again the meaning of these two terms appears to be diverging gradually as the spiritual needs of individuals and communities change.

This trend is apparent in North America where individuals increasingly self-identify as spiritual rather than religious (Saucier & Skrzypinska, 2006), supported by research in the US (Hout & Fischer, 2002), as well as in accord with findings in Canada (Pappas, 2003). Richards and Bergin (2000) summarized their distinction between the religious and the spiritual in this way:

> If a religious practice or experience (e.g., saying a prayer, engaging in ritual, reading a scripture) helps a person feel more closeness and connection with God or transcendent spiritual influences, then that practice or experience is also spiritual in nature. Without it, the practice or experience may be a religious one, but is not a spiritual one. (p. 5)

While spirituality and religiosity overlap and both may be salutary, they may operate in quite different ways in promoting positive outcomes, such as health (e.g., religious affiliation may offer social support, while individual spirituality may not). Wink, Dillon, and Fay (2005) found that spirituality, when felt (i.e., as a sacred connection to God, a higher power, or nature) and practiced (i.e., through personalized prayer, Eastern meditation, centering, or journeying) outside of religious institutions, was associated with autonomous or healthy narcissism, namely "personal independence, high self-aspirations, and resistance to social pressures" (p. 154). According to their study, spirituality tends to be associated with ego strength or autonomy rather than ego fragility or hypersensitivity.

A psychology of spirituality would thus seem to focus on both direct experiences of connection with something sacred and a sense of self as interconnected with the larger world, as well as the integrative and transformative effect of such experiences. In this regard, there seem to be two distinct spiritual psychologies, one of which focuses on interconnectedness in a more secular fashion and seems quite similar to what transper-sonal psychology is fundamentally about. For example, a study of 160 definitions of transpersonal psychology published over a period of some 35 years found that its con-tent consisted of three main themes: (1) a beyond-ego psychology, namely the study of phenomena in which the individual experiences or aspires to personal experience of something higher than the ego-based self; (2) an integrative/holistic psychology, which is the study of the human individual as part of an interconnected cosmos; and (3) transformative psychology, or the study of how humans attain to their higher potentials, both individually and collectively (Hartelius et al., 2007). These themes are highly consistent with prominent features of an interconnected and secular spir-ituality, but quite different from a version of spirituality that is intimately connected with any particular religious tradition. This also relates to the way that Krippner and Sulla (2000, p. 67) delineated between spiritual and transpersonal experiences, deny-ing they are synonyms and limiting transpersonal experiences to those in which "one's sense of identity appears to extend beyond its ordinary limits." In this regard, transpersonal psychology and approaches to spiritual psychology that redefine spirituality in ways that deal with interconnectedness or other naturalistic concepts (and that do not involve spirits or other supernatural beliefs) would be strongly aligned, perhaps even synonymous, with transpersonal psychology.

The Value Added by the Term Transpersonal

Considering that the term transpersonal psychology was selected historically to avoid prejudice that might be engendered by use of the term spirituality, and given that this latter term now might offer tremendous marketing and other advantages over the term transpersonal, what justification might there be for retaining the term transpersonal psychology? If there is justification for keeping this term, how should spiritual and transpersonal psychology be positioned with respect to each other?

Problems with Introducing the Term Spirituality within Psychology

One approach is to consider problems that might arise from the use of the term spirituality within psychology. Moberg (2002) argued that spirituality is divisively defined and interpreted based upon competing ideologies, while Belzen (2009) pointed out various hidden agendas in those promoting a psychology of spirituality. In other words, spiritual psychologies may have a dark side, and some who promote them might be attempting to insert their own religious agendas and ideologies into the scientific abode of psychology. Indeed, for those who hold faith-based and other non-scientific beliefs, part of the appeal of using the term spiritual in psychology is based on the fact that it can refer to the supernatural—in the literal sense of honoring some presence or force separate from the natural order of the cosmos. Spiritual psychologies of this sort are clearly distinct from transpersonal psychology, and although appealing to this group might broaden the base of interest in psychology, it would surely cause serious problems in the long run; those approaches to spiritual psychology that are more secular and less supernatural are more aligned with transpersonal psychology.

One illustration of a potential current problem with the use of the term spirituality in psychology involves the discipline's educational institutions. There are now six American Psychological Association (APA) accredited clinical or counseling psychology doctoral programs within the US that are explicitly Christian in orientation, including Azusa Pacific University, Biola University, Fuller Theological Seminary, George Fox University, Regent University, and Wheaton College (Narramore, n.d.). These emphasize integrating psychology with Biblical scriptures in learning to practice psychology from a Christian perspective, as well as fostering what is referred to as the spiritual growth of their students. These clearly religious programs subtly couch themselves as spiritual, and have somehow thereby managed to obtain legitimacy through APA-approval. While some scholars point to the urgent need for professional psychology look more closely at the role of spirituality within psychology training programs (e.g., Hage, 2006), little is known about this profound change in the profession. Although there has been some research on the training effectiveness of these Christian programs, little is known about the overall consequences of allowing this approach within the field (e.g., Walker, Gorsuch, Tan, & Otis, 2008).

This is new territory for the discipline of psychology, which heretofore has scrupulously eschewed combining religious and spiritual approaches within psychology as a science or as a praxis. We think training and practice that focuses on gaining multicultural sensitivity to diverse spiritual issues is warranted, as long as these are grounded in science and not simply faith. However, it is essential that no singular religious authority, such as Christian scripture, should be accepted as the basis for psychological training and practice. Indeed, the problem reaches well beyond these six programs, as there are many other parochial universities offering professional psychology programs in the US, and these often involve at least some restrictive, if not outright repressive, contexts. For example, programs sponsored within Catholic universities may deem certain practices as heretical (e.g., use of birth control and pro-choice stances) based on religious grounds, and tacitly, if not explicitly, forbid open discussions of their relative benefits and deficits. Comingling religion and spirituality within psychology poses many unsolved dilemmas: There are dangers in allowing psychology to embrace any parochial religious stance as being psychological per se, as this would inevitably privilege some views and disadvantage others. Overall, we see no scientific justification that can be provided to support Christian theology's application within psychology as a scientific discipline and profession. Having the dual usages of the term spirituality has opened doors to accepting the misapplication of religion under the guise of spirituality, as reflected in this proliferation of these parochial schools that amalgamate science and religion in indiscriminate ways.

Although transpersonal scholars tend to favor Eastern approaches over Christianity, this concern remains relevant. Buddhism, for example, has often been characterized as a science, yet it holds to various faith-based positions (e.g., belief in karmic reincarnation), which places it outside of psychology as a science (see Friedman, 2009, 2010). To uncritically accept Buddhist teachings as scientific when the tradition does not follow the various tenets of science would be a serious category error. The concern also applies more broadly to how transpersonal psychology endeavors to situate the study of the entire human being within a context generally congruent with perspectives held by a variety of religious and spiritual traditions. It is crucial that this not involve accepting any such tradition as being a valid psychology per se but, rather, considering these traditions within a broader scientific or scholarly context.

We hold that it is fitting that transpersonal psychology aspire to address the profound questions arising within spirituality in a scientific vein more suitable for a multicultural world, but not by embracing any singular spiritual tradition as underpinning its approach (e.g., Friedman, 2002). In this sense, transpersonal psychology is free to critique both Christian and Buddhist perspectives, as well as all religious and spiritual views. It can also learn from them and further them through scientific approaches broadly construed, without being limited to them.

In addition, defining spirituality as involving the supernatural (e.g., Koenig, 2010) poses a problem because psychology as a science can only deal with what is natural, albeit in a very open and broad way (Friedman, 2002). The very term spirituality connotes spirits, which unavoidably implies nonmaterial entities (e.g., deities) that are outside of the framework of empiricism that defines, and limits, scientific efforts.

Friedman (2002, this volume) has argued that psychology as a science can only be applied to natural, not supernatural, concerns, so this approach to spirituality positions it within one type of Cartesian divide, namely separating matter from spirit. One way that spiritual psychology can avoid the various dilemmas associated with studying and applying spirituality would be to keep its focus on the complex of behaviors, beliefs, and feelings related to spirituality, as well as acknowledging that spirituality itself cannot be directly accessed in a scientific way. This is the strategy explicitly used by MacDonald (2000, this volume) in his transpersonal approach to researching the "expressions" of spirituality, while avoiding any claim to be studying spirituality itself. One of us (Friedman, 1983, this volume) also uses a comparable strategy in his ongoing transpersonal psychology research. In addition, together MacDonald and Friedman (2001) have also outlined how a coherent scientific research program on spirituality can be conceptualized and pursued from a philosophical and methodological vantage.

This position does not negate the possibility of increasing the scope of science through the development of post-Cartesian frames and methods that can better handle the phenomenology of spiritual and mystical experience. However, such approaches are still in early stages of development and will need to demonstrate their value before they can be widely adopted. This course is the strategy that one of us (Hartelius, 2006, 2009; Hartelius & Ferrer, this volume) is actively pursuing.

Finally, we think it important to challenge the notion that including spirituality within psychology provides something that is only positive, resulting in some of that term's market appeal. This is contradicted by such concepts as awe, which include both connotations of terror in facing overwhelming aspects of the universe as well as positive emotions (Bonner & Friedman, 2011). Similarly, spirituality is often confounded with wellness, as if its value is to reduce the incidence of illness rather than to point to its more profound implications (Migdal & MacDonald, in press). Spirituality also contains a number of concepts that may not be very palatable within mainstream psychology if examined more closely. MacDonald's (2000) empirical approach to measures of spirituality arrived at five common factors. One of these is controversial, namely referring to parapsychological dimensions of spirituality. Of course, all religious traditions have their extraordinary aspects (e.g., the Catholic criteria of miracles required to elevate an individual to sainthood, the Hindu notion of siddhis, the shamanic notions of visiting the spirit world). Given that mainstream psychology is often uncomfortable with parapsychology, however, this dimension does potentially complicate the psychological consideration of spirituality as something only attractive, as many adherents to Western Judeo-Christian religions would likely be unhappy to deem their tradition's miracles as parapsychological phenomena.

Clarifying the Relationship between Spiritual and Transpersonal Psychology

This leads to the need to clarify the relationship between spiritual and transpersonal psychology. If these are merely synonyms, then holding onto the term could just be stubborn adherence to tradition. Admittedly, all three of us writing this chapter are fond of the term and would lament seeing its use abandoned, but this alone is not grounds to retain it. Alternatively, if sufficient value can be seen in retaining the term, then that would answer the central question addressed in this chapter, namely should the term spiritual psychology replace transpersonal psychology? For one, we think there are hazards in using the term spirituality that can be avoided by using the term transpersonal instead, as illustrated by the co-opting of APA-approved training programs by parochial traditions.

However, in a more positive vein, we see transpersonal psychology as including spirituality without being reduced to it. Equating these two would greatly diminish the transpersonal approach and excise a significant aspect of its vision. The transpersonal movement seeks to draw on both science and spirituality to forge a new vision of psyche and cosmos, one that suffers neither from the parochialism inherent in some religious and spiritual traditions, nor from the limitations of a narrowly applied natural science philosophy not well suited to what Maslow (1969a) called the farther reaches of human nature. Within such a shifted context, novel approaches to psychology, and perhaps other disciplines as well, can form (Walsh, 1993; Walsh & Vaughan, 1993). On the other hand, if transpersonal psychology were to take on the identity of spiritual psychology, it would be accepting a place within an academic and political framework that assigns marginal ontological status to both spiritual and religious experience, despite the success of spirituality in the current milieu. Instead, transpersonal psychology offers opportunities to not merely look backwards at religious and spiritual traditions, a term that itself refers backwards in history, but rather to look forward to innovative ways to explore creating new approaches, as well as their applications. A spiritual psychology has small chance of challenging the current state of affairs, while the transpersonal project has a more radical mission that is both broader and deeper than this. When Maslow (1969b) wrote the impassioned essay that launched the *Journal of Transpersonal Psychology*, he wrote as a scientist who embraced the scientific method, yet who saw that this very method could be used to challenge the objectivist philosophy and values on which science was built. He wrote as a humanist who had glimpsed a vision of humankind that filled but also overflowed the tradition of humanism, reuniting it with the great rivers of spiritual and mystical wisdom. Maslow announced a revolution, a profound shift in the modernist foundations of science and society. This same revolution is in full swing, under a thousand different names; it is brewing within transpersonalism, ecopsychology, somatic psychology, feminism, alternative medicine, and a hundred other disciplines. To reduce transpersonal psychology to something that merely looks backward toward traditions would abnegate this potential.

It has been over forty years since the founding of transpersonal psychology. Given the magnitude of its vision and the profundity of the revolution that it proposes, the fact that transpersonal psychology has not been widely embraced in so short a period of time should come as little surprise and less disappointment. The transpersonal vision of psychology challenges the philosophical foundations of modern science and postmodern society even as it retains a critical lens on the assumptions underlying the claims of the spiritual traditions that it honors and investigates. Transpersonal psychology offers a platform that aligns with the critical thinking and methodological carefulness of science without subscribing to scientism, that "perversion of science . . .

into a parochial ideology" (Friedman, 2002, p. 178). It can pursue a "new image of man [humankind]" (Maslow, 1969b, p. 6) from a foundation than is rigorous without being confined by modernism or eroded by postmodernism, and optimistic without being restricted by the structures of traditions, whether called religious or spiritual, or carried off by naïve romanticism (Friedman, 2002). In contrast with some versions of spirituality embraced by mainstream psychology, which appeals to the traditional— especially when it is related to specific religious traditions—the transpersonal vision is forward-looking and in the process of continual refinement.

Conclusion

The widespread acceptance of the study of spirituality is a valuable addition to psychology and one that may help psychotherapists deal more wisely and compassionately with clients who struggle with spiritual issues, as well as open up new avenues for theory, research, and praxis. In this regard, wherever it might be situated within the discipline of psychology, it is a welcome addition. It is important, however, that it not be presented in an idealized form in which its shadow is ignored. Potential abuses, such as through co-opting spirituality to further hidden agendas of proselytizing traditions, need to be avoided, and its full scope, including its capacity to be terrifyingly awful as well as inspiringly awesome (e.g., Bonner & Friedman, 2011) must be recognized, as spirituality is no mere bromide, but the deepest and most profound issue that can be imagined. We believe that spiritual approaches within psychology would best be situated within a transpersonal perspective to handle these issues with integrity, whether through a conventionally driven scientific approach (e.g., Friedman, 1983) or a possibly revitalized post-Cartesian approach (Hartelius, 2009). Either version of transpersonal psychology provides an appropriate and supportive home for an interest area of spiritual psychology. The primary characteristics of spiritual psychology, as defined in approaches to spirituality emphasizing secular and non-supernatural interconnectedness, fit extremely well with the three main definitional themes identified within transpersonal psychology (Hartelius et al., 2007).

Consequently, we conclude that spirituality should be developed as an area of study within, or closely linked with, the transpersonal field, rather than as a wholly separate discipline. For example, a closely related discipline of spiritual psychology might find a place within the larger domain of transpersonal studies, especially insofar as some of the approaches to spirituality involve supernatural notions that place it beyond the reach of conventional science. However abandoning the term transpersonal psychology to be replaced with the terms spiritual psychology or psychology of spirituality seems a tremendous loss. Transpersonal psychology allows a way to deal with a continuum of non-transcendent, yet still transpersonal, experiences that go beyond the individual and that can be scientifically studied (Friedman, this volume), as well as provides a potential way to frame transcendent experiences related to what is seen as spiritual in many traditions. This can be done by studying their expressions (MacDonald, 2000) as fruits that grow from them, without ontologically accepting these events as real in any consensual way. It also provides a way to deal with a variety of other issues in ways that lead us to conclude resoundingly that it is premature to write the obituary for transpersonal psychology, as the term may get some further good use if transpersonal psychology is developed properly.

References

Ai, A. L., Seymour, E. M., Tice, T. N., Kronfol, Z., & Bolling, S. F. (2009). Spiritual struggle related to plasma interleukin-6 prior to cardiac surgery. *Psychology of Religion and Spirituality, 1*(2), 112-128.

Allport, G. (1950). *The individual and his religion: A psychological interpretation.* New York, NY: Macmillan.

Allport, G. (1961). *Pattern and growth in personality.* New York, NY: Holt, Rinehart, and Winston.

Allport, G. (1966). The religious context of prejudice. *Journal for the Scientific Study of Religion, 5,* 447-457.

Avants, S. K., Beitel, M., & Margolin, A. (2005). Making the shift from "addict self" to "spiritual self": Results from a Stage I study of spiritual self-schema (3-S) therapy for the treatment of addiction and HIV risk behavior. *Mental Health, Religion, and Culture, 8,* 167-177.

Belzen, J. (2009). Studying the specificity of spirituality: Lessons from the psychology of religion. *Mental Health, Religion & Culture, 12*(3), 205-222.

Benner, D. G. (1989). Toward a psychology of spirituality: Implications for personality and psychotherapy. *Journal of Psychology and Christianity, 8*(1), 19-30.

Bienenfeld, D., & Yager, J. (2007). Issues of spirituality and religion in psychotherapy supervision. *The Israel Journal of Psychiatry and Related Sciences, 44*(3), 178-186.

Bolletino, R. C. (2001). A model of spirituality for psychotherapy and other fields of mind-body medicine. *Advances in Mind-body Medicine, 17*(2), 90-107.

Bonner, E., & Friedman, H. (2011). A conceptual clarification of the experience of awe: An interpretative phenomenological analysis. *The Humanistic Psychologist, 39,* 222-235.

Burris, C. (1994). Curvilinearity and religious types: A second look at intrinsic, extrinsic, and quest relations. *International Journal for the Psychology of Religion, 4,* 254-260.

DeAngelis, T. (2008). Div. 36 brings spirituality into research and practice: Growth and change within the division mirrors society's evolving thoughts about religion. *Monitor on Psychology, 39*(11), 60.

Friedman, H (1983). The Self-Expansiveness Level Form: A conceptualization and measurement of a transpersonal construct. *Journal of Transpersonal Psychology, 15,* 1-14.

Friedman, H. (2002). Transpersonal psychology as a scientific field. *International Journal of Transpersonal Studies, 21,* 175-187.

Friedman, H. (2006). The renewal of psychedelic research: Implications for humanistic and transpersonal psychology. *The Humanistic Psychologist, 34*(1), 39-58.

Friedman, H. (2009). Xenophilia as a cultural trap: Bridging the gap between transpersonal psychology and religious/spiritual traditions. *International Journal of Transpersonal Studies, 28,* 107-111.

Friedman, H. (2010). Is Buddhism a psychology? Commentary on romanticism in "Mindfulness in Psychology." *The Humanistic Psychologist, 38,* 184-189.

Friedman, H. (2011). It's premature to write the obituary for humanistic psychology. *Journal of Humanistic Psychology, 51*(4) 424-427.

Friedman, H. (this volume). Transpersonal self-expansiveness as a scientific construct (Chapter 11).

Genia, V. (1993). A psychometric evaluation of the Allport-Ross I / E scales in a religiously heterogeneous sample. *Journal for the Scientific Study of Religion, 32*, 284-290.

Greer, B., & Roof, W. (1992). "Desperately seeking Sheila:" Locating religious privatism in American society. *Journal for the Scientific Study of Religion, 31*, 346-352.

Grof, S., & Grof, C. (1989). *Spiritual emergency: When personal transformation becomes a crisis.* New York, NY: Jeremy P. Tarcher.

Hage, S. (2006). A closer look at the role of spirituality in psychology training programs. *Professional Psychology: Research and Practice, 37*(3), 303-310.

Hartelius, G. (2006). All that glisters is not gold: Heterophenomenology and transpersonal theory. *Journal of Consciousness Studies, 13*(6), 81-95.

Hartelius, G. (2009). Participatory empiricism: Toward a phenomenological-empirical science for human psychology. *Dissertation Abstracts International* 70(07) 0392B (UMI #3367157).

Hartelius, G., Caplan, M., & Rardin, M. A. (2007). Transpersonal psychology: Defining the past, divining the future. *Humanistic Psychologist, 35*(2), 1-26.

Helminiak, D. A. (2001a). Rejoinder and clarifications on Helminiak's (2001) "Treating spiritual issues in secular psychotherapy." *Counseling and Values, 45*(2), 237-251.

Helminiak, D. A. (2001b). Treating spiritual issues in secular psychotherapy. *Counseling and Values, 45*(2), 163-189.

Helminiak, D. A. (2005). A down-to-earth approach to the psychology of spirituality a century after James's *Varieties. The Humanist Psychologist, 33*(2), 69-86.

Helminiak, D. A. (2008). Confounding the divine and the spiritual: Challenges to a psychology of spirituality. *Pastoral Psychology, 57*, 161-182.

Hill, C., & Pargament, K. (2003). Advances in the conceptualization and measurement of religion and spirituality. *American Psychologist, 58*, 64-74.

Hout, M., & Fischer, C. (2002). Why more Americans have no religious preference: Politics and generations. *American Sociological Review, 67*, 165-190.

Johnstone, B., & Yoon, D. P. (2009). Relationships between the Brief Multidimensional Measure of Religiousness/Spirituality and health outcomes for a heterogeneous rehabilitation population. *Rehabilitation Psychology, 54*(4), 422-431.

Kapuscinski, A. N., & Masters, K. S. (2010). The current status of measures of spirituality: A critical review of scale development. *Psychology of Religion and Spirituality, 2*(4), 191-205.

Koenig, H. (2010). Spirituality and mental health. *International Journal of Applied Psychoanalytic Studies, 7*(2), 116-122.

Krippner, S., & Sulla, J. (2000). Identifying spiritual content in reports from ayahuasca sessions. *International Journal of Transpersonal Studies, 19*, 59-76.

Lajoie, D. H., & Shapiro, S. I. (1992). Definitions of transpersonal psychology: The first twenty-three years. *Journal of Transpersonal Psychology, 24*(1), 79-98.

Lukoff, D., & Lu, F. (2005). A transpersonal-integrative approach to spiritually-oriented psychotherapy. In L. Sperry & E. P. Shafranske (Eds.), *Spiritually oriented psychotherapy* (pp. 177-206). Washington, DC: American Psychological Association.

MacDonald, D. A. (2000). Spirituality: Description, measurement and relation to the Five Factor Model of personality. *Journal of Personality, 68*(1), 153-197.

MacDonald, D. A. (this volume). Philosophical underpinnings of transpersonal psychology as a science (Chapter 19).

MacDonald, D. A., & Friedman, H. L. (2001). The scientific study of spirituality: Philosophical and methodological considerations. *Biofeedback, 29*(3), 19-21.

MacDonald, D. A., Walsh, R., & Shapiro, S. (this volume). Meditation: Empirical research and future directions (Chapter 24).

Mansager, E. (2002). Religious and spiritual problem V-Code: An Adlerian assessment. *The Journal of Individual Psychology, 58*(4), 374-387.

Maslow, A. (1969a). The farther reaches of human nature. *Journal of Transpersonal Psychology, 1*(1), 1-9.

Maslow, A. (1969b). New introduction: Religions, values, and peak-experiences (new edition). *Journal of Transpersonal Psychology, 1*(1), 83-90.

Migdal, L., & MacDonald, D. A. (in press). Clarifying the relation between spirituality and well-being. *Journal of Nervous and Mental Disease.*

Miller, W. R., & Thoresen, C. E. (2003). Spirituality, religion, and health: An emerging research field. *American Psychologist, 58*(1), 24-35.

Miovic, M. (2004). An introduction to spiritual psychology: A review of the literature, East and West. *Harvard Review of Psychiatry, March/April,* 105-115.

Moberg, D. (2002). Assessing and measuring spirituality: Confronting dilemmas of universal and particular evaluative criteria. *Journal of Adult Development, 9*(1), 47-60.

Narramore, B. (n.d.). Christian graduate programs in psychology. Narramore Christian Foundation (n.p.). Retrieved from http://www.ncfliving.org/counselor_training.php

National Institute for Healthcare Research. (1998). *Scientific research on spirituality and health: A consensus report.* (A report based on the scientific progress in spirituality conferences). Rockville, MD: John Templeton Foundation.

Pappas, J. (2003). A construct validity study of the Self-Expansiveness Level Form: A multitrait-multimethod matrix and criterion approach. *Dissertation Abstracts International, 64*(01), 1545B (UMI No. 3085713).

Pappas, J., & Friedman, H. (2007). The construct of self-expansiveness and the validity of the Transpersonal Scale of the Self-Expansiveness Level Form. *The Humanistic Psychologist, 35*(4), 323-347.

Pargament, K. (1997). *The psychology of religion and coping: Theory, research, practice.* New York, NY: Guilford Press.

Pargament, K. (1999). The psychology of religion and spirituality? Yes and no. *International Journal for the Psychology of Religion, 9*(1), 3-16.

Pargament, K., & Sweeney, P. J. (2011). Building spiritual fitness in the Army: An innovative approach to a vital aspect of human development. *American Psychologist, 66*(1), 58-64.

Pargament, K. I., & Saunders, S. M. (Eds.). (2007). Special issue on spirituality and psychotherapy. *Journal of Clinical Psychology, 63*(10).

Pedersen, P., Lonner, W. J., Draguns, J. G., & Trimble, J. E. (Eds.). (2007). *Counseling across cultures* (6th ed.). Thousand Oaks, CA: Sage Publications.

Plante, T. G. (2009). *Spiritual practices in psychotherapy: Thirteen tools for enhancing psychological health.* Washington, DC: American Psychological Association.

Richards, S., & Bergin, A. (2000). Toward religious and spiritual competency for mental health professionals. In S. Richards & A. Bergin (Eds.), *Handbook of psychotherapy and religious diversity* (pp. 3-26). Washington, DC: American Psychological Association.

Saucier, G., & Skrzypinska, K. (2006). Spiritual but not religious? Evidence of two independent dispositions. *Journal of Personality, 75,* 1258-1292.

Smith, H. (2001). *Why religion matters: The fate of the human spirit in an age of disbelief.* New York, NY: HarperSanFrancisco.

Spaeth, D. (2000). Spirituality in history taking. *Journal of the American Osteopathic Association, 100,* 641-644.

Sperry, L., & Mansager, E. (2007). The relationship between psychology and spirituality: An initial taxonomy for spiritually-oriented counseling and psychotherapy. *The Journal of Individual Psychology, 63*(4), 359-370.

Sperry, L., & Shafranske, E. P. (2005). (Eds.), *Spiritually oriented psychotherapy*. Washington, DC: American Psychological Association.

Spiro, M. (1966). Religion: Problems of definition and explanation. In M. Banton (Ed.), *Anthropological approaches to the study of religion* (pp. 85-126). London, UK: Tavistock.

Steinfeld, G. J. (2000). Spiritual psychology and psychotherapy: Is there theoretical and empirical support? *Journal of Contemporary Psychotherapy, 30*(4), 353-380.

Stifoss-Hanssen, H. (1999). Religion *and* spirituality: What a European ear hears. *The International Journal for the Psychology of Religion, 9*(1), 25-33.

Turner, R. P., Lukoff, D., Barnhouse, R. T., & Lu, F. G. (1995). Religious or spiritual problem: A culturally sensitive diagnostic category in the DSM-IV. *Journal of Nervous and Mental Disease, 183*, 435-444.

Walker, D., Gorsuch, R., Tan, S., & Otis, K. (2008). Use of religious and spiritual interventions by trainees in APA-accredited Christian clinical psychology programs. *Mental Health, Religion & Culture, 11*(6), 623-633.

Walsh, R. (1993). The transpersonal movement: A history and state of the art. *Journal of Transpersonal Psychology, 25*(2), 123-139.

Walsh, R., & Vaughan, F. (1993). On transpersonal definitions. *Journal of Transpersonal Psychology, 25*(2), 199-207.

Wilber, K. (2000). *Integral psychology: Consciousness, spirit, psychology, therapy*. Boston, MA: Shambhala.

Wink, P., Dillon, M., & Fay, K. (2005). Spiritual seeking, narcissism, and psychotherapy: How are they related? *Journal for the Scientific Study of Religion, 44*, 143-158.

Wulff, D. (2003). The psychology of religion: An overview. In E. Shafranske (Ed.), *Religion and the clinical practice of psychology* (pp. 43-70). Washington, DC: American Psychological Association.

Zinnbauer, B. J., Pargament, K. I., Cole, B., Rye, M. S., Butter, E. M., Belavich, T. G., . . . Kadar, J. L. (1997). Religion and spirituality: Unfuzzying the fuzzy. *Journal for the Scientific Study of Religion, 36*(4), 549-564.

Zinnbauer, B., Pargament, D., & Scott, A. (1999). The emerging meanings of religiousness and spirituality: Problems and prospects. *Journal of Personality, 67*, 889-919.

4

Criticisms of Transpersonal Psychology and Beyond—The Future of Transpersonal Psychology

A Science and Culture of Consciousness

Harald Walach

After nearly half a decade of transpersonal psychology, to be precise 43 years after the foundation of the *Journal of Transpersonal Psychology* that gave the nascent movement an academic and scholarly appearance, it seems about time to pause and ask: What has the movement of transpersonal psychology really achieved? What is the impact, if any, it has made on the academic purveyance of psychology, its teaching and research, its application in clinical work, counseling, and education? What are the structural changes or improvements, if any? One can easily see that many of these questions seem to be rhetorical and have to be answered rather disappointingly in the negative. Although transpersonal psychology has tried to install itself as a new force with the remit to reform academic psychology, so far it has not really succeeded. Apart from three or so dedicated private graduate schools and training centers in the USA and two now discontinued postgraduate courses in the UK, to my knowledge there is no structural impact that can be perceived. Traditional psychology has proceeded on its trajectory, and chairs for transpersonal psychology funded by public funds of large schools or endowed chairs that radiate out are largely missing. Although new disciplines such as educational or organizational psychology have now succeeded in establishing themselves through new chairs and departments, the same is not true for transpersonal psychology. Why is that so? Curricula of psychology courses have changed over the past decades. New courses have been added, new topics and subjects have been taken in, honoring their importance. Transpersonal psychology, as a rule, and exceptions confirm this rule, is not one of them. New scientific disciplines within psychology have succeeded in making themselves visible, through scholarly outlets, conferences, and meetings, establishing their intellectual footprint. Transpersonal

The Wiley Blackwell Handbook of Transpersonal Psychology, First Edition.
Edited by Harris L. Friedman and Glenn Hartelius.
© 2013 John Wiley & Sons, Ltd. Published 2015 by John Wiley & Sons, Ltd.

psychology has not been nearly as successful as other disciplines within psychology. Although transpersonal psychology conferences exist, you will rarely find reports and headlines about findings presented there. What is wrong here?

Although transpersonal psychology and—to frame it in a broader context—spiritual approaches and techniques within the clinical counseling fields are popular among practitioners and seem to receive a warm welcome from many, this has not been at all reflected in academic representation. Let us take two examples, both from Germany. Thirteen years ago the German language journal, *Transpersonal Psychology and Psychotherapy* (now the *Journal for Consciousness Science*) was founded and has had a comparatively good circulation of roughly 1500 subscriptions—more than a lot of the professional journals in, say, psychosomatics or clinical psychology. This testifies to the interest of clinicians. But the university courses representing at least some aspect of transpersonal psychology are extremely rare. Currently in Germany there are only three university teachers with the necessary credentials to supervise PhD theses, who have some track record in publishing in this field, and enough interest to take on new students.

We recently did a representative survey among 909 German psychotherapists who are working under the statutory reimbursement system (Hofmann & Walach, 2011). Of their patients, 22% mentioned some sort of spiritual problem or topic and 66% of the therapists said that university or postgraduate training should give more attention to these issues. Two thirds of our respondents said that they have had a spiritual experience themselves, at least once, and 36% said they have had such experiences very often or repeatedly. This clearly shows that there is interest in spiritual issues on the practical level, because the topics are germane for patients and therapists alike, but this reality of life has not found its way into academic structures of teaching and research. Has transpersonal psychology succeeded in becoming an scholarly voice for all these practitioners?

Seen from a distance and with sober eyes, one has to admit that the success of transpersonal psychology as a discipline is indeed meager, to put it benevolently. A critic of the field would surely say: "Transpersonal psychology has failed as an academic-scientific discipline. It has not proven its worth and hence should just vanish." If some future for the academic study of transpersonal and spiritual phenomena is to be established, opening an inroad for spirituality into academic circles and allowing for the broadening of psychology as a field, it is necessary to assess critically the history of the transpersonal enterprise, its shortcomings and failures, listen to criticisms leveled against it, and understand the largely unspoken critique of mainstream science in order to determine the potential chance for transpersonal psychology.

In this chapter I wish to critique transpersonal psychology constructively. I will go briefly through the history of psychology as a discipline and through the history and sources of transpersonal psychology as a subdomain in order to understand the frictions and possible points of departure. I will then point out some criticisms and unsolved problems and develop a future perspective. My recommendation will be to reinvent the transpersonal enterprise along the lines originally intended by the founding fathers of psychology, William James and Franz Brentano: a psychology, a science—and culture—of consciousness, in order to get rid of some of the problems besetting transpersonal psychology. I do this from the vantage point of an academic teacher and researcher with a clinical training and experience in a transpersonal discipline, psychosynthesis, a long-standing spiritual practice in Zen meditation, the experience of being one of the founding members of the German Association of Transpersonal Psychology and Psychotherapy, and a former professor and course leader in one of the universities in the UK that was offering a postgraduate degree in transpersonal psychology and consciousness studies. I do this also with a firm commitment to the scientific enterprise, because I passionately believe that it is the only true international forum and joint venture of humankind that is comparatively successful and peaceful. At the same time I also believe that if science is to remain successful and helpful in the resolution of the problems on our agenda today then it will have to broaden its scope and paradigmatic stance by taking seriously some of the issues that led to the rise of transpersonal psychology.

A Historical Approach

In order to understand a current situation, historical analysis is normally useful. So it is appropriate to revisit briefly the history of psychology in general and that of transpersonal psychology in particular. At variance with most textbooks of psychology, I date the beginning of psychology as a scientific discipline to 1866. This is the year when the young professor of philosophy, the theologian and priest Franz Brentano (1838-1917), defended his position at the University of Würzburg in Germany. One of the famous theses was worded: "The true method of philosophy can only be the method of natural science" (Wehrle, 1989, p. 45). By that Brentano meant that philosophy had to become empirical and experimental. In 1871 he was to take up the philosophy chair at the University of Vienna. He made it clear that his interpretation of an empirical philosophy would be the new science and study of psychology. He also proposed that this method would have to proceed through thorough and careful introspection so as to understand the laws of the psyche. At the same time the vagaries of his private life were difficult. He was the priest responsible for drafting in 1869 the paper of the German bishops' council against Papal Infallibility, which was proclaimed in 1870. The German bishops' opposition against this move remained unheard. This led to Brentano's leaving the church. On top of this, he fell in love with a Jewish heiress of a big banking business in Vienna and he wanted to marry her. An apostatic priest marrying a Jewess in Catholic Vienna was a terrible scandal. Bretano was forced to resign, emigrate to Saxonia, marry there, come back and attempt to reclaim his chair. He was unable to do so, because the Austrian emperor refused to countersign the university's appointment documents. So Brentano was unable to resume his academic position, and his work remained undone. He was never able to write his important work, and what remained of his influence was indirect. Freud heard his lectures and put Brentano's teachings into the practice of inner hermeneutics so as to understand psychological content and derive laws from it (Merlan, 1945, 1949). Edmund Husserl was inspired by Brentano to develop his phenomenology (Husserl, 1919). Similarly, Carl Stumpf (1919) developed Gestalt psychology (Stumpf, 1919), and even Rudolf Steiner (1921), the founder of anthroposophy, studied with him (Steiner, 1921). Brentano himself was a deeply spiritual person, dedicated to daily contemplation, as he called it in the Catholic tradition, and was always looking for a way to reconcile the spiritual and the academic world, without a tangible success that he might have been able to pass on (Stumpf, 1919; Tiefensee, 1998).

The date often quoted as the year psychology was born is 1879 (Lück, 2002). This is the year when Wilhelm Wundt (1832-1920) opened his psychology laboratory at the University of Leipzig. It soon became the strange attractor for psychologists from around the world: William James and Stanley Hall were only some of those who visited (Brent, 1993). What is not well known is a very important episode in Wundt's life that has an important bearing on the topic (Kohls & Benedikter, 2010). Roughly at that time, in 1877, the professor of physics in Leipzig, Johann Karl Zöllner, became interested in studying mediumistic performances because he thought they would prove his theory of a fourth, spiritual dimension that could be incorporated into physics. The American medium Henry Slade was traveling through Europe and performing interesting feats: tables flew around, chairs hovered in the air, impossible-to-know information was given, and so forth. Hermann Ulrici, a professor of logic in Halle, wrote about those sessions, concluding that spiritism was of utmost scientific importance. To bolster his claim, he mentioned various renowned professors, among them Wilhelm Wundt. Wundt became furious (Wundt, 1879). He quickly came to understand that associating the nascent discipline of psychology with potentially fraudulent, but surely scientifically questionable performances of mediums was very dangerous, because it might threaten the new discipline's ability to be established within the academic system. In the attempt to join the established sciences, contact with and proximity to unscientific parapsychological phenomena had to be avoided at all costs. So Wundt included a clear warning about and prohibition against such studies in his book on hypnosis and in the foreword of the second edition of his psychology textbook and all further works (Kohls & Benedikter, 2010).

Sigmund Freud (1856-1939) is often misquoted as someone who had no interest in the occult and transpersonal phenomena (Simmonds, 2006). Although this is surely true on the outside, he was in fact quite interested in precognitive dreams, even in the immediate perception of his clients' states of mind in a phenomenon he called transference, which he recognized as having some similarity to clairvoyance (Freud, 1922, 1925). Freud's description of an open, receptive attentive state without content is very much akin to the phenomenological consciousness that Husserl would later advocate. Both Husserl and Freud were stimulated by Brentano's teaching. But Freud was also fighting for scientific recognition, and he knew that being associated with quackery and esotericism would be the death of psychoanalysis. So he made a scientific vow: no dealings with spiritual issues, please, in order to not endanger the still fragile flower of psychoanalysis. And psychoanalysis, true to its master's heritage, steered clear from the muddy waters of religion and transpersonal experiences.

Carl Gustav Jung (1875-1961) cannot be understood without his own spiritual experiences (Shamdasani, 1994, 1995, 1998a, 1998b, 2003, 2005). Already in 1913 he had his famous visions of floods of blood over Europe which inspired him to develop the process of active imagination in which he entered these visions, explored them, and came out again and described them. The results of these explorations were described and painted by him in *The Red Book*, which was edited only recently (Jung, 2009). Only later would Jung come to understand that his visions had been very powerful precognitive intuitions of what would happen a few years later during the Great War (1914-1919). He actually stated that he was happy when the war broke out, because this proved his visions correct and helped him to believe that he was not psychotic, but clairvoyant (Jung, 1967). All his later developments—the concept of a collective unconscious, of dynamic archetypes that structure individual psychic life, and the striving of developmental lines towards an emerging whole—can be seen as an unfolding of his original visions. It would be difficult to find any component in Jung's psychology that is not spiritual. But apart from creating an influential school of psychotherapy, what has Jungian psychology achieved? The academic mainstream has largely ignored it.

William James (1842-1910) is renowned as the founder of American psychology (James, 1981, 1984, 1985). His stance of radical empiricism is akin to Brentano's "scientific method" which he prescribed for psychology. His pragmatic, undogmatic approach, which was not predicated on any one of the prominent philosophical systems of his time, was flexible enough to accommodate fields as different as the study of religious experiences, clinical phenomena, and the stream of consciousness. In fact, one of the best and, in my view, still valid definitions of psychology stems from William James (1984) quoting George Trumbull Ladd, professor of philosophy at Yale: "The definition of Psychology may be best given in the words of Professor Ladd, as the description and explanation of states of consciousness as such" (p. 9).

Brentano, Wundt, James, Freud, and Jung—the five most important founding figures of psychology—were all open to transpersonal experiences, at least initially. Wundt and Freud later turned away and proclaimed a ban on the study of such phenomena. Jung was openly supportive of spiritual topics. Brentano was implicitly supportive, but failed for personal reasons to make his impact. William James was soon to be superseded by the behaviorist movement.

In Vienna the work that had been begun by Brentano was continued in philosophy by Ernst Mach, who succeeded Brentano in the philosophy chair, and Mach's colleagues Neurath, Schlick, and Carnap, who later formed the Vienna Circle, delineating the neopositivist movement that became so influential (Smith, 1994). Apart from some quite innovative ideas—to stick to sentences that were clear, logically analyzable and empirically supportable, to make science useful to humankind, to drop anything that was not really open to scrutiny and consensus—the neopositivists spoke out a clear-cut ban against what they saw as "metaphysics." By that term they meant a type of philosophy that was indulging in speculations, based on presuppositions that were outside empirical evidence. They banned religion and spiritual topics as unscientific and associated with an old type of thinking.

Positivists thought that old school philosophy was part of the past, and all studies of spirituality and religion with it. Such topics simply did not belong in the realm of science. Raimund Popper, although also trained and educated in Vienna, broke with the neopositivists and inaugurated his own model, critical rationalism, advocating empirical disproving of hypotheses. But in one thing he is in accord with his philosophical rivals; metaphysics was a no-go area, simply because there are no sentences derivable from metaphysics or religion that can be empirically invalidated—actually, to be a bit more accurate: metaphysics might be a good source of ideas that can later be tested empirically, Popper thought, but metaphysics itself is unscientific, because it is not testable.

In England, Bertrand Russell had formulated a philosophy that had some parallels with the neopositivist movement. At roughly the same time in the USA the behaviorist movement started to flourish. The common thread running through all these movements is the reliance on what can be directly observed, simple analysis of complex phenomena, denial of any "underlying" or "deep" structure to reality, and a refusal to take anything beyond, "higher," or "transcendent" into the purview of the scientific enterprise.

I ask forgiveness of specialists of the history of ideas for this rough-hewn picture of what is a very complex history reduced to a few pages. I do this to make the historical macrotrend against which transpersonal psychology emerged and which it has to confront understandable. This macrotrend can be reduced to the following tenets:

1   Embracing the scientific-experimental method as the best way to knowledge.
2   Using the analysis of outer relations to understand complex inner phenomena, i.e., analysis of forces as material interactions.
3   Sticking to an observation from the outside, a third-person-singular view, as the best and only perspective that can generate intersubjectively consensual knowledge.
4   Avoiding reference to entities that cannot be seen, analyzed, or otherwise empirically assessed.
5   Avoiding reference to occult, esoteric, and religious concepts and teachings, as they are perceived to be contrary to and irreconcilable with science.

If one looks at this historical sketch it is possible to formulate one grand criticism of transpersonal psychology, and if I am not mistaken there is not one writer in the field to which this would not apply.

No one has really taken this historical heritage and legacy seriously. Transpersonal psychology has not really understood the deep, deep cleavage that has to be bridged between scientific approaches in psychology—itself still a very young discipline in the making—and traditional or modern concepts of spirituality, spiritual experience, let alone a viable concept of the transcendent. Instead of historically understanding the nascent field of psychology, transpersonalists chided psychology for being too positivistic, scientific, and reductionist and not taking into consideration important human experiences. Although this is surely true, any criticism can and will only be heard after the person who wishes to criticize has arrived at a thorough understanding of what it is he or she is actually evaluating. No one seems to have really tried to achieve such a historical understanding (my emphasis here is on *historical*; for without a historical understanding, any systematic understanding is only half-baked).

This is my first prediction: Unless the field is able to live up to this legacy and offer ways by which spiritual and transpersonal experiences and topics can be integrated and researched, and at the same time stay true to the historical heritage of psychology as a discipline, it will not find a listening ear.

I believe the first truly deep and paradigmatic problem is the following: By choosing the trajectory it has, psychology has formed a certain type of world model for itself. Pepper (1942) called such implicit, tacit presuppositions world hypotheses. Collingwood (1940/1998) called them absolute presuppositions. They are *presuppositions,* because the system of science does not work without them. They are *absolute* because they are pervasive and are basic for all branches. More importantly, they are implicit and without open and rational debate or discourse. They form a coherent system and inform scientific disciplines, but the reflection upon those presuppositions is not part of the discipline itself. More importantly, such presuppositions, Collingwood stated, are actually not rationally debated and adopted. Rather, they stem from the cultural backdrop of a particular time. In the case of psychology, they stem from the movements and cultural preconditions I have tried to sketch. That is also the difficulty: It makes these presuppositions comparatively immune against attacks and criticisms, unless those attacks and criticisms also supply a better framework for the implicit or absolute presuppositions. Thomas Kuhn, in the wake of Collingwood and using his ideas, coined the term "paradigm" for such a set of preconditions, rules, and assumptions that form a discipline (Kuhn, 1955).

If a dispute arises *within* a paradigm about some issues, then there is a set methodology that is provided by the paradigm to resolve the conflict. This recipe does not work for disputes that are inter-paradigmatic, in which two sets of implicit presuppositions fight for priority. Transpersonal psychology belongs in both camps. A large part of the field, and I read some of the founding fathers' assertion as such, has wanted to simply be part of the huge game of science, just adding the odd rule, as it were, leaving the game as it is. But there is also a strong group of people who seem to be "anti-scientific," or against "reductionism," or against the way science is done, and would like some other approach. Implicitly what they do is challenge the paradigmatic assumptions of mainstream science and psychology, but without being really clear about what they are doing, it seems. This is surely always the case when someone says that transpersonal experiences of a transcendent reality have something to do with reality as such, to give an example. This is not simply a matter of "Is it true or not?" because the methods supplied by the current paradigm to make such decisions about truth or falsehood, the experimental method for instance, do not apply to cases like this.

Hence, at least part of the transpersonal enterprise is in fact an implicit or explicit *challenge to the entire history and set of methodologies by which science and scientific psychology* is done. The point is: you do not challenge a 800-pound gorilla with a thin stick. He either laughs at you or simply breaks your stick. If you want to challenge the whole history, tradition, and academic self-understanding of modern day psychology, you had better beef up your arsenal and know what you are doing. Rarely do transpersonal psychologists seem to understand what they are doing. In order to challenge the mainstream view what needs to happen is a thorough understanding of the presuppositions that the mainstream operates on, a profound critiquing of these presuppositions, and the provision of very, very good data indeed that could actually give adherents to the mainstream view enough reason to think twice about what *they* are doing.

None of this has happened. The critique of the mainstream from transpersonal quarters has been mild and not very profound. The data that have been offered as a reason to embrace a transpersonal rather than a materialistic-reductionist paradigm have been anecdotal at best, and the alternative philosophical framework accompanying transpersonal approaches has often been muddled. Thus, the critical impact of transpersonal psychology on the paradigmatic foundations of mainstream science has been "interesting" at best—in a British sense—which means, nothing to be bothered by.

What about the empirical base transpersonal psychologists have contributed using the methods of mainstream psychology to impact the discourse within the discipline, without challenging its foundations? Can you think of a set of experimental, empirical data, preferentially replicable, published in one of the major outlets of the field that has impacted the way psychologists think and work? If one is honest, there is not much to be gleaned from more than 40 years of activity. To be sure, parapsychologists have produced a wealth of anomalistic data, testifying that sometimes precognition can occur, sometimes telekinesis, sometimes remote viewing (Walach & Schmidt, 2005). But there is no theoretical consensus about how this could happen, let alone a really replicable set of data that can also convince critics (Alcock, 2003). The only coherent field is the field of meditation research, which has recently seen an upsurge (Ott, Hölzel, & Vaitl, 2011). The clinical implications of the manualized system of Mindfulness Based Stress Reduction have produced a host of publications that has led to these methods being widely offered (Grossman, Schmidt, Niemann, & Walach, 2004). Mindfulness Based Cognitive Therapy for depression relapse prevention (Williams, Teasdale, Segal, & Kabat-Zinn, 2007) has even made it into the British National Health Service. But this is hardly an achievement of transpersonalists. However, it is the only really perceptible impact that at least some spiritually inspired activity and research has made. Grofian Holotropic Breathwork has been around for about the same length of time (Grof, 1988, 2008). Although widely advocated with a colorful portfolio of benefits and transformative power, with many people going through trainings, one can observe a cruel law coming into play: unless you follow the rules of the game of science, use its methods to prove your worth, you will not become visible. The scientific studies of Holotropic Breathwork can be counted on one hand, at least those published in the peer-reviewed literature (Holmes, Morris, Clance, & Putney, 1996; Spivak, Kropotov, Spival, & Sevostyanov, 1994). None of these is a serious trial showing that Holotropic Breathwork is clinically superior to not doing anything, listening to loud music only, or lying together with friends for days on end and telling stories. One may be of the opinion that the experiences that can be had during such work are not amenable to scientific investigation, and perhaps this is true. But the clinical effects, if there are any, would be. Demonstrating those would be quite beneficial for the acceptability of the concept as a whole. It is this unwillingness to play the game of science—even when it would be easy to play without giving up anything of substance—that is one of the greatest obstacles for integration and change.

Thus, so far, transpersonal psychology has failed in a double sense: it has failed to really challenge the implicit foundations, the absolute presuppositions or paradigmatic assumptions of mainstream science and thus has not really proven its point; and it has also failed to provide solid empirical evidence that transpersonal experiences, transpersonal approaches, or transpersonal methods are in any way more worthwhile than traditional ones. The emphasis here is on "solid." There are surely a lot of data and studies around. But these are mostly pilot studies, are small, solitary, and not published in widely read journals. They surely do not disturb the sleep of the righteous.

In order to understand why the newly inaugurated transpersonal psychology has not convinced others that its approach is truly innovative and is helping to transform people to access their higher potential, it is important to now turn to what has been termed the spiritual positivism of transpersonal psychology, and also to the epistemological questions involved.

Spiritual Positivism of Transpersonal Psychology and the Problem of Epistemology

Some earlier concepts of transpersonal psychology assumed that there is a spiritual realm, transcendent but accessible through inner experience and spiritual practice or meditative discipline (Fontana, 2003; Soudková, 2002; Walsh, 1999; Welwood, 2002). Implicitly most seem to have been modeled along the lines of Buddhist injunctions: you go and sit down on your meditation cushion, recite the proper sutras, do your devotion, stick to the practice, and you will see for yourself. So it seemed clear. Similar to science, there is this prescription for what to do and out will come an experience or an insight about the nature of reality. Some earlier texts of Wilber (1997, 1998) and Walsh (1999) and others have suggested such a view. This has been dubbed spiritual positivism by Ferrer (1998, 2000, 2002). Thereby he means a fallacy that is similar to the fallacy of classical positivism: it is the assumption that there is a reality "out there," which is completely independent of the observer and indifferent to the instruments that are used to observe it. It was a painful process for science to understand that reality can only be accessed from certain perspectives, that reality gives itself up only from certain perspectives, and that a consensus about what this reality truly is, is quite difficult to reach. This is even more so for any transcendent and spiritual reality. To state that transcendent and spiritual realities are the same for, and accessible to, everybody is at best extremely naïve and probably simply wrong. Why is this so?

The Problem of Objectivism

Within the meta-reflection of scientific theory, it is meanwhile pretty clear that the innocent objective reality concept that can simply be observed is a dangerous simplification. How this reality appears to observers is dependent on the instruments used, the theoretical perspective employed, and the purpose under which observation is made. To someone looking at the night sky there are myriads of stars, but only if he or she is not observing from an area where light pollution is fogging visibility. To someone using a strong telescope this night sky looks quite different. To someone using radio or X-ray telescopes it looks different again. Someone without a theory will not even be able to use these instruments to any benefit at all and more than likely will not see much. The same is true for nearly all "realities." Bacteria, it is thought, cause some diseases and hence at least some of them seem clearly to be pathogens. Yet as humans, our skin, our gut, our orifices are home to myriads of them. In one cubic centimeter of our feces we have billions of bacteria. From the point of view of bacteria we are a rich soil to germ upon just as the 'real' soil is, for us, a substrate on which to grow crops. Only if some of our finely tuned immune processes become deranged will we suffer from the bacteria that we normally host. Why is something that is not even noticeable to us under normal circumstances suddenly a pathogen? It surely is the same "thing," is it not? Well, yes, and no. It carries all the same descriptors one can use to characterize it from the outside—genetic coding, surface receptors and antigenetic potential. But *in the context* of one reality, for instance a healthy organism, it is something else than *in another context* of say, an immune-compromised organism. Here it suddenly *becomes* something that it is not under other circumstances. So whether something is or is not, and what it is, depends on the context. It is not only the Buddhist philosophical tradition that has pointed to the doctrine of codependent arising or becoming. This is also something that has been prevalent in the West every now and then, one of the most prominent voices on the topic being the philosopher Leibniz.

Over the past 50 years, a complex debate has led to a refutation of the simple positivism that accepts a static reality out there that "only" has to be observed, described, and mapped. Philosophers of science have come to accept that every observation is "theory laden," to use Hanson's term (Suppe, 1977). Popper's criticism of positivism came exactly through the insight that one cannot observe even the simplest thing without a background theory. If one had no theory, one would have no clue what to look for, how to organize all the perceptions in the perceptual field into meaningful wholes, or how to interpret their relationships. Meaning is distilled out of what is perceived, because it is first imbued with meaning. As humans, we construct the reality we think is out there to a large degree. Modern neuroscience has brought up an interesting new term, the brain's dark energy (Raichle, 2006). By that is meant the fact that about 95% of the activities of the brain seem to concern traffic between neurons, and only 2% to 5% is traffic from the periphery—that is, sense organs—to the brain. To put it simply, input is the smallest amount of activity the brain is dealing with. Its main task seems to be to generate a representational image of what to expect from the world. Sensory input seems to be used to scan this representation for necessary corrections. That is to say, we do not perceive the world as it is, instead we construct the world as we expect it to behave and then we correct this expectation to a stronger or lesser degree depending on how we deal with incoming information.

What is true for individuals is also true for science as a joint human enterprise. A coherent picture of the world is constructed according to the scientific theories available. Empirical information is either used to elaborate this picture, or, if the information is too much at odds with our expectation, correct it. If too much information has amassed that cannot be reconciled with the current world view, some start to construct a new image of the world. If they are successful it will be possible to use the new model. This would then amount to a paradigm shift.

Now, if this is true for our everyday reconstruction of the world, and if this is true for scientific construction of the material world, what does this mean for a spiritual science?

Inner Experience and the Problem of Epistemology

Surely, any transpersonal "knowledge" would have to refer to some inner state or perception as its source and to something that cannot be directly perceived as a referent, "the Transcendent," "the Whole," "the Spiritual," "the Tao," "the

Dharma," whatever the names are that are then used. If one can analyze what happens here then it is indeed possible to construct a process analogous to perception. That was exactly how Brentano and James had seen it: inner perception of conscious experience. But what is it that is perceived? Can one simply apply the positivist formula that "whatever is perceived is there?" How does one go about the fact that some, in their transpersonal musings, perceive "spirits," "fairies," or "demons," some say they perceive "God," some say it is some divine intuitions, some call it emptiness, others say it is not really emptiness but something else, and so on? You can see the problem here. It is analogous to perception of the outside world, only even more complicated. In the outside world humans share a comparatively stable consensual domain where, most of the time, it is possible to agree upon such simple facts as, "the door is closed, you need to open it, if you want to go through it." In more complicated instances there is a scientific method to use to achieve consensus, a method that has had more than 500 years to mature and to develop.

However, in the inner realm of psychological inner experience there is no comparable thing. The referent of this experience is invisible by definition, only "experientially" accessible, if at all, and the access to this reality is surely not a simple one that normally does not occur outside some cultural consensus. So, when Buddhists meditate, they are likely to experience "dharma" or "emptiness," or if they are from a certain Zen lineage, "true self." When Carmelite nuns meditate and have inner experiences they normally experience Christ, or Mary, or some other religiously framed reality out of their own tradition. It may be possible to parallel such experiences, which, for instance, Saint Theresa of Avila, a Carmelite, described in her *Inner Castle*, with those described in the *Abidhamma*. But does that mean that Theresa has actually had experiences of the *Abidhamma*, or does that mean that all the Buddhas and monks having had those experiences have in fact experienced what Theresa called the Inner Christ? There is no criterion to say which one is better, or truer, than the other. It has been observed frequently that transpersonal psychology has had some Eastern bias (Friedman, 2002, 2005, 2009, 2010). It is quite obvious that there is no criterion that could identify what the referent of the experience actually is, and how it is to be described and named and talked about, if at all.

Put differently, inner experience is no innocent and simple access route to an unambiguous reality. On the contrary, inner experience is highly ambiguous, opaque, and dependent on assumptions. One can, of course, claim that there is such a thing as pre-conceptual experience where concepts do not enter. Some have called this, following Gebser's philosophy, "a-categorial" types of knowing (Atmanspacher & Fach, 2005; Hinterberger, 2011). While this is certainly true, it is also true that in order to enter into a discourse about this reality and its nature it is necessary to use categories and language, and these are dependent on culture, history, and language. So the spiritual experience of a religious seeker of the time around 20 CE in Palestine was likely influenced by the Jewish background of the culture, the expectations, the political situation, and so forth (Douglas-Klotz, 1999, 2002; Katz, 1983) and cannot easily be compared with the Indian Brahmanic culture of around 700 BCE, when the historical Gautama Buddha likely had his experience in Northern India. Also, the spiritual experience of the historical Jesus, a Jewish Rabbi, was likely different from the experience of Theresa of Avila, who was a Christian nun living within a nunnery in a thoroughly Christian culture in the Spain of the 16th century. A dissatisfied Christian going to a Zen Buddhist retreat but with all his or her Western roots and culture implanted not only in the mind but likely also in genes, will have a still different experience, if any.

That is not to say that there is no referent to such experiences. There may be such a thing as an a-categoreal core spiritual experience, which, however, needs reference to a cultural framework to be understood and expressed (Forman, 1998, 1999). But even if there is, there is no simple and easy access, and, most importantly, it is utterly naïve to think that just to "describe" the experience will be a description without reference to the "reality" that has been experienced.

The scientific injunction "take x, and do y, and you will find z" is complicated even for skilled scientists. A host of failed replications and debates are testimony to this, and only through huge struggles and debates does science succeed in creating a consensual understanding of the shared material world (Schmidt, 2009). The spiritual injunction "sit down, do y, and you will experience z" is even more complicated. This is so because the spiritual reality is more complicated to access, it seems, and because the discourse about the "true" nature of this reality is historically, culturally, and geographically much more fragmented than the scientific one. More importantly, it lacks the critical methodology that science has had 500 years to establish. There is only one proposition that is fairly sure here: that a naïve spiritual positivism is likely the worst theoretical background one can have. Yet this is exactly the background transpersonal psychology has brought to the topic for the first four decades of its existence. It seems that only a minority of people in the field have understood, let alone come to grips with the challenge here.

But there is another, even deeper challenge that needs to be looked in the eye here. This is the ontological challenge of what consciousness actually is, vis-à-vis, a mainstream science that is thoroughly materialistic. The problem is the following: if the ultimate reality in the world is "only" matter, and consciousness is derived from the intricate ordering of matter, then consciousness is a secondary phenomenon. How could it then have any direct access to reality? How can an inner experience then be anything else than just an idling game of a system on standby? What conceptual, philosophical, and epistemological reasons can there be to assume that a spiritual experience is really an experience of reality and not of some whimsical, ephemeral mental farting? Transpersonal psychology has simply assumed that inner experiences have some epistemological validity, without any understanding of the extremely difficult ontological ground upon which it is marching. I am not suggesting that the mainstream of science is right. But I am suggesting that it is unprofessional not to take into account the good arguments that a majority of scientists have, and produce a thorough refutation of this mainstream stance first, before indulging in one's own ontology and epistemology. In other words, one cannot talk about epistemology and how it is possible to glean knowledge from inner experience, without discussing ontology and the question of under which circumstances can this be possible in the first place. As far as I can see only a few people have tackled this issue, and very few with the requisite understanding of the problems.

Let me therefore sketch the problem of ontology a bit more clearly, then provide some arguments and potential solutions, and then discuss how transpersonal psychology has not met, but perhaps could meet, these challenges in the future.

The Problem of Ontology

The scientific worldview, shorthand for the set of assumptions underlying the way natural science operates and has been operating since Newton, is predicated on the assumption that matter is the more important, perhaps the only "real," stuff in the universe.

The French philosopher René Descartes (1596-1650) has prepared the field for it, unwittingly one has to say. In his book *Traité de l'homme* (*Treatise of Man*) (Descartes, 1664/2003), he proposed two revolutionary ideas. One idea was to separate the material from the mental realm describing matter as extended, solid, but also devoid of any vital principle of its own, and to assert that the mind has no extension, but is active as the principle of life. Thereby he only systematically described what Aristotle already had mentioned. What was new was the fact that Descartes conceived, unlike Aristotle, of two separable realms. This laid the groundwork for the later separation of the humanities and natural sciences, the latter being mainly dedicated to solving the puzzles around matter. The second revolutionary thought of Descartes was that he described *all* living beings, animals and human bodies alike, as mechanical automatons. Using the metaphors of the mechanical clockworks and toys of his time, he turned the idea around; if human craft could create clockworks of machinery that moved so elegantly as to imitate physiological movements, why not conceive of physiological bodies as machinery? This thought was extremely alien to a mind of the 17th century, but gradually gripped the imagination of scientists and laid the foundation for a mechanistic treatment of the physiological body. This move of Descartes also had an important consequence, which is only now seeing its fulfillment: Once the idea of the mechanization of nature had been consequently thought through and put into paradigmatic framings, there was no way of stopping this movement. On the contrary, it was only logical to extend it to the mind itself as well. Although Descartes carved out the mind from this mechanistic treatment of physiology, his successors extended the mechanistic metaphor to the mind.

What has been witnessed over the past decades is the consequence of the extension of the Cartesian program to the philosophy of consciousness and of mind. The mind is also seen as mechanical machinery. Modern brain science operates on the assumption that what can be seen in the brain *is* in fact operation of the mind. Some say the mind can emerge and become a separate kind of entity that has some causal influence on the material substrate, the brain. Some equate the operations of the mind with the operations of the brain. Some study mainly the functional relationships between neuronal entities assuming that the material substrate is irrelevant and only the function that is implemented by neurons is relevant. In fact what is relevant is that mainstream science is following this paradigmatic pull, conceptualizing the mind as machinery that is, ultimately, somehow identical with or causally dependent on its physiological substrate, the neuronal system in general and the brain in particular.

Such a view makes consciousness a secondary entity. If such a view is true, then consciousness is always late—and this is exactly the argument that is being used in modern discussions about the causal relevance of consciousness. A consciously experienced impulse to act is only experienced as such after all the neuronal antecedents have long before decided on the action (Burns, 1999; Libet, 1999; Wegner & Wheatley, 1999). Ultimately, the conscious self is a fiction created by extremely intricate neuronal machinery whose whole purpose is to secure survival of the system. For this survival it is useful to have a representation of the environment, as well as a representation of the system as an agent within this environment. But ultimately, the self is vacuous and appears as such, because the representational character is itself "opaque" to the system that is represented. Were it not opaque, an infinite regress would ensue that would again hamper the effectiveness of the representation (Metzinger, 2003).

Surely, in this view there is no such thing as "inner experience," except in a secondary and epistemologically irrelevant sense. This "inner experience" can only refer to states of the neuronal machinery and such states will have no relevance for knowledge of the world at large. What spiritual traditions claim—that inner experience arising from spiritual practice can tell us something about the world, only from another, namely inner perspective—is nonsensical from a modern, scientific point of view. Such a modern view will always counter that, whatever is experienced, when someone has a nice inner experience—a near-death experience, an experience of heavenly bliss, an experience of a transcendent reality, you name it—that will always be a reflection of the state of the neuronal system, nothing else. If the neuronal system is under strain, as in a situation close to death, then it will create some soothing experience to make the demise of the system palatable to itself (Marsh, 2010). If the neuronal system is under some deprivation, as in most spiritual practices, or in another way in exceptional circumstances, as in a continually hyperventilated and excited state that Holotropic Breathwork® induces, then it will create strange representations. To relate these strange representations to any reality is a scientific fallacy. Such experiences might be adaptive; they may help the system to restructure itself after some psychological stress, say after a crisis of meaning and purpose, or after a life-threatening or psychologically threatening situation. But to assume that these experiences have something to do with reality is silly at best and scientifically outrageous at worst.

To put it bluntly, unless transpersonal psychologists can also provide a solid theory of how consciousness as such can have its own epistemological relationship with reality, they will always be seen as those guys who have missed out on the problem and hence provide solutions that no one will cherish. In order to provide such a theory, some serious thinking about ontology needs to happen. This is nothing short of an enterprise of providing the scientific basis with a new paradigmatic option that can serve as a new platform apart from the mechanistic one that has followed from the Cartesian view. Make no mistake here, simple reference to some anomalistic and outlandish data—from Shamanic journeying, near-death studies, Holotropic Breathwork, parapsychological experiments—will not do. It will not do, because a paradigm and a theory is always stronger than data. As pointed out above, humans are predictive, theoretical animals. We form a theory about the world and replicate it until we are forced to change track. The same is true for science. A bunch of anomalistic data here and there will not bother anyone, except for those who wish to write the odd paper about how this bunch of data can also be interpreted without reference to any strange model of consciousness.

The Transpersonal Answer to the Challenge So Far

To me it seems as if no one has really understood the problem in its gravity. Transpersonalists have simply continued asserting that consciousness has some privileged status, without saying how this privileged status could be unified with the mainstream scientific effort. Some have simply tried to turn the wheel, or have not understood that a turning of the wheel would have to be involved if anyone were to take the proposal seriously, and tried to revert the discussion back to where it stood in about 1850, when the writings of Fichte, Schelling, and Hegel were still much debated and the idea of a mental activity as a prime source of everything, and hence "consciousness" in modern parlance, was a scientific option. One may dislike a historical point of view, but one thing about history is quite clear, it is next to impossible to turn the wheel back. The principle of "Wirkungsgeschichte"—the history of effects that ideas have created—introduced by the German philosopher and founder of philosophical hermeneutics Hans Georg Gadamer (1975) is important here; there is always some sense in what has happened. Put otherwise, there was a reason why the idealistic stance of "consciousness is primary, matter secondary" was given up by natural scientists in the middle of the 19th century. My personal interpretation is that this reason can be found in the fact that an idealistic philosophy in the sense of Schelling, Hegel, Fichte, and Plotinos for that matter, including probably most Vedanta styles of philosophy, does not allow for a fruitful notion of matter. One can of course lament and deplore this situation, but that does not undo it. The point to start from is the acceptance that the scientific community—scientists among whom are the most respected, most intelligent, and most powerful individuals—has at some point decided that it is more important and more fruitful to follow a paradigmatic model that allows for a solid analysis of matter and put the question of consciousness on hold.

This hold has now transformed into a busy kind of research along the very same line. Academic psychology has taken up that challenge and is moving along using the same paradigmatic assumptions as science does. This is where transpersonal psychology could come in. But it surely cannot come in stating that transpersonal psychology is possibly better for humankind, for psychology, and for integrating human experience by using implicitly—without open discussion and without really good arguments—a completely different set of assumptions than mainstream science. This is exactly what has happened, however, at least with a major part of the transpersonal movement. It was assumed that a psychology starting from an idealist assumption—that is, consciousness is primary, matter is secondary—is possible the same way as a psychology starting from a materialist assumption of matter as primary is possible, as most behaviorist, cognitivist, and neuroscientific approaches assume. Possible it is, to be sure, but ineffective, and this is what has been seen: ineffectiveness on a grand scale, despite a flood of publications, despite a host of assertions to the contrary.

The reason for this ineffectiveness, I argue, is that no one has really tackled the issue of ontology and argued a concise case, why in the first place and how in particular, could a different view be produced. Simple dualistic assertion will not do. That Cartesian conundrum as to how a separate substance, the mind—or consciousness—should affect a completely different one, namely matter, has never been solved. Science has just set aside the problem by cutting the Gordian knot with Ockham's razor, in effect stating "Forget the mind, it is only matter anyway or some sort of consequence of matter's organization."

A Brief Sketch of a Viable Alternative

I can only briefly sketch how a viable alternative would work and have to point the interested reader to our primary articles (Atmanspacher, Römer, & Walach, 2002; Römer & Walach, 2011; Walach, 2005; Walach & Römer, 2000, 2011). I think a minimal meeting ground between any spiritual claim—thus also of transpersonal psychology—mainstream science would be what I call the complementarist model of body-mind interaction. It starts from the assumption that complementarity, as originally introduced by Nils Bohr, one of the founding fathers of quantum mechanics, is a basic principle of nature, ontology, and epistemology alike (Bohr, 1937). Complementarity refers to the fact that an entity, a situation, or even a complex reality, can only be described by applying two seemingly contradictory statements at the same time (Atmanspacher & Primas, 2006). This is what the early theorists of quantum mechanics have discovered about the nature of the quantum. You can, for instance, describe its momentum and measure it exactly. But then you lose the knowledge of its position. You can measure its position, but then you lose all information about its momentum. Yet both, position and momentum, are necessary to characterize a particle. Although in classical, Newtonian physics, it is possible to measure position *and* momentum *independent* of each other at the same entity, say of a bullet shot from a gun, and thus predict trajectory and impact, this is no longer possible in quantum mechanics. Position and momentum of a quantum particle, say a photon, are both necessary to characterize the particle. Yet in quantum mechanics they are complementary, because they require measurement set-ups that are mutually exclusive. Technically speaking, so called canonical or complementary variables—position and momentum, time and energy, to name the best known ones—and complementarity are at the foundational basis of quantum mechanics (Kim & Mahler, 2000). They are irreducible, at least in the common conceptual framework that is currently most widely held. They are the source of the Heisenberg uncertainty relationship and they characterize the strange behavior of quantum systems. Two of them are worth mentioning here:

1   In quantum mechanics measurements impact the measured entity. Once position is measured, it is also changed. Only Newtonian physics knows a measurement without any impact on the measured, or rather, the impact of the measurement can be ignored.
2   In quantum mechanics complementary variables also define entanglement (Nadeau & Kafatos, 1999). Or put differently, entanglement is a special case of complementarity, namely the complementarity between the global variable, that is, the

description of a whole system, and the local variables, or descriptors of elements within the system. For instance, in a two photon system, where through down-conversion in a beam-splitting crystal two correlated photons have been produced from one single photon, the two photons form two elements of one system. The joint polarization of the system—the plane in which a wave is propagating—is the global variable. Individual photon polarizations are local variables. They are complementary to the global one—that is, their description is mutually exclusive. In mathematical terms: the polarizations are orthogonal. The system has to be described both by the global variable—spin 0—and the local variables—orthogonal polarizations—and both, the local and the global descriptions, are clearly incompatible or mutually exclusive within a classical logical framework. In quantum mechanics this is the reason why the two photons belonging to the one system described by one equation are "entangled," non-locally correlated. If you measure one particle and find as a result spin up, you know instantaneously that the other particle will be measured as down. This is true even if you could separate the two photons so far and measure at exactly the same time so that no messenger particle could travel between the two and convey the result of one of the measurements to the other particle. This is why this correlation is often called non-local, a technical term derived from the special theory of relativity, in which light is the maximum speed in the universe and hence all parts of the universe that are connected by light beams are called locally connected. The particles in such a quantum entanglement experiment are not locally connected, because light particles could not travel the distance between the measurement apparatuses, and hence the correlation is called non-local (Cushing, 1989; Mermin, 1989; Wessels, 1989).

   This theoretically predicted behavior of quantum systems has been empirically tested repeatedly and such entanglement has been observed, even at distances and with set-ups that make sure the correlation is really non-local (Salart, Baas, Branciard, Gisin, & Zbinden, 2008).
   Now, it is well known, and also very important for a proper understanding, that some quantum properties only pertain to quantum systems as such (Tegmark, 2000). Entanglement, as a quantum property, disappears very quickly with the interaction of particles and the environment (Yu & Eberly, 2009). This also defines why human observers see a world that behaves in a largely classical way (Römer, 2011).
   Nevertheless, it might still make sense to use the conceptual structures and framework of quantum mechanics. This is what we have done in forming a more general theory, Generalized Quantum Theory, which we stipulate is applicable to all sorts of systems and to systems of all make-ups (Atmanspacher, Filk, & Römer, 2006; Atmanspacher et al., 2002; Römer & Walach, 2011). Whether it is true and viable remains open to debate at this point, and I am claiming no more than general rational plausibility and some a priori reason. This a priori reason is the structural similarity and analogy between the make-up of systems (Baianu & Poli, 2011; Gernert, 1989; Zeleny, 1981). Ultimately this is an idea that is very old, but was again brought into the discussion by systems theory, claiming that some abstract principles of how systems are formed can be seen at all systemic levels, from atoms to molecules to organisms to

the Milky Way. In the same sense, our generalization of quantum theory claims that some principles of systemic similarity may perhaps be observed on every systemic level.

Complementarity was already suspected by Nils Bohr to play a role in epistemology and in other areas, when he, for instance, thought that ultimately the whole world might be governed by the principle of complementarity (Bohr, 1997; Rosenfeld, 1963). We have taken up this idea, which in its essence dates back to Heraclitus, but surely to Spinoza in the 17th century and, in another form, was taken up by Leibniz, his contemporaneous fellow philosopher who gave the idea another, more physical twist. And we have claimed that it is fruitful to conceptualize mind and matter, consciousness and brain, as two complementary descriptions of one entity, the human being (Walach & Römer, 2011). They are complementary in that they cannot be reduced to one another. Both are needed for a full description. And they are ultimate—that is, there is no other known entity that can serve as an explanation of both, except in a very speculative sense. We could, for instance, claim that there is still an underlying reality, the unified whole, Jung called it *unus mundus*—one world—that generates both mental and material ways of being (Atmanspacher, 2003; Atmanspacher & Primas, 2006). But that would be quite speculative and is not necessary at this level of conceptualization. What is necessary is the acknowledgement that both are ultimately of equal ontological dignity, that neither is "primary" or "superior" to the other. Rather they seem to co-arise and seem to be necessary to understand the human being.

Recently, some rather strong logical elements have been raised that are still not heard well enough (Hoche, 2008). They clearly show that to transition from mental concepts to material concepts or back is trespassing on categories and making severe category mistakes. Thus, I claim, a complementarist solution of the mind-body or consciousness-brain problem seems to be a rational proposal, plausible on the ground that it uses well-known principles of physics and extrapolates them, and it is non-reductionist. It allows consciousness its own status and thus also potentially its own epistemological role. If consciousness is co-primary with matter, one might not only have a route through the senses to understand the world, outer experience, but also the route through consciousness, inner experience. In other words, inner and outer experience are then also two complementary modes of relating to the world.

We have also generalized entanglement in our model. This follows naturally from the general description used above. We have produced a host of arguments and specifications elsewhere (Römer & Walach, 2011; Walach & Römer, 2011), hence I will keep it brief here. The mind actually fulfils some requirements known from quantum mechanics as being typical for quantum systems. For instance, if one "measures" a psychological state, say by introspection, that state is at the same time changed. This is a clear hint that we have some entity at hand that fulfils some requirements of a quantum description. We can conceive of mental and physical states as complementary to each other, but also as instances of descriptions that are complementary to a global systemic description, namely that of the whole person. In other words, we would assume that there holds also a generalized type of entanglement between appropriate mental and physical states. Thus, generalized entanglement would provide the "mechanism," albeit of a non-local kind, with no signaling happening, that co-ordinates the mental and the physical system. It then also becomes clear why mental states can be causal for physical states. It may also be rationally conceivable how human units, single persons, can form systems that again are non-locally coordinated into a kind of synergism that works without classical signals. A good example can be the extremely fine tuned coordination of artistic groups like ballet dancers, orchestras or choirs in exceptionally harmonious performances.

This, then, could foster the field of transpersonal psychology with a basis to stand on, and a minimal consensus with the mainstream: Consciousness as complementary to matter allows for epistemological access of consciousness to reality in its own right. Although the step to generalized entanglement is by no means dependent on, or consequent of that stipulation, it is a naturally occurring one, once one has accepted that the principles—I repeat, the principles, not the physics—of quantum mechanics may have relevance for the world at large. But I would like to leave it here, as we are clearly entering a highly contentious area. I have sketched this to demonstrate one thing: It is possible to use the theoretical structures offered by mainstream science and extend them to incorporate phenomena dealt with in the spiritual domain or in transpersonal psychology (Walach, 2011).

Four Roads into the Future

From here, there are several options to move forward, and all have been tried with more or less success:

1   Oppose the development of the mainstream, claiming that transpersonal psychology has so much more to offer, and that one should just abandon the Titanic that is sinking anyway and move about in little rafts. Only the Titanic is not sinking and the rafts have not gotten anywhere.
2   Try to offer a completely different ontology, for instance one of the older idealistic systems, or one of the Eastern ones, claiming that they are better suited to accommodate spiritual experiences. Only few people believe that there is anything worthwhile of which to take note.
3   Try to leave the paradigmatic foundations of science unchallenged accepting the course and route it has taken and say, "Well folks, like it or not, unless you go scientific, you will not be able to produce an impact and you will not be taken seriously."
4   Try to offer new paradigmatic foundations to science, accepting the route it has taken so far, but extending its scope by using the armament, the conceptual foundations, and the theoretical instruments science has in store. This is what I have tried to sketch above, and it goes without saying this is what I believe is the most fruitful and potentially the most powerful and also unifying approach.

The first route is what many Transpersonalists have done. They have created their little universes and their own rafts, some of them quite comfortable. In that category I would place a lot of the work done around altered states of consciousness, through Holotropic Breathwork or drugs (Griffiths, Richards, Johnson, McCann, & Jesse, 2008; Krippner & Sulla, 2000; Shanon, 2002). Some of this work is seeking relationship with the mainstream by using scientific methodology. This may be a first important step, but it may not be sufficient, because it is still happening in a context that is a bit like an isolated island or raft.

The second route is what some grand approaches to transpersonal psychology have tried. I would class Wilber's attempt here. If the conceptual foundations were more historically conscious of the problems in the history of science one could avoid the pitfalls. But as I see it at the moment, this attempt is not really working, because it neglects both the historical preconditions and the actual and current types of theorizing. The parallels between spiritual disciplines and science are too naïvely accepted at face value and the understanding of what science is and how it operates is coming too much from an outdated understanding of scientific background theory. Ultimately, it will be publication of ideas in peer-reviewed, mainstream journals, tapping into mainstream debates that will be the only means of influencing the discussion.

The first two approaches are also often associated with the founding of subcultures and special universes of discourse that are unconnected with the rest of the world and derive their own definitions and understanding from the fact that they are supposedly so much better than what the rest of the crowd is doing. This is a narcissistic motive and, in my view, a big problem of the whole field (Walach, 2008). In it, founders and leaders can feel important, collecting followers who support this interpretation, ultimately keeping both restricted in a narcissistic collusion that neither helps solve problems, nor moves our insight forward. A clear sign that this is happening, in my view, is whenever special circles of in-groups separate themselves from the "others," who are seen as not understanding as deeply. The history and presence of transpersonal psychology is full of this.

The third route comes in two flavors. One flavor relies on the mainstream scientific ground of the natural sciences and categorizes psychology as a natural science. Within such an approach, one can surely use the methods of science to study such transpersonal aspects, specific interventions, say, or construct questionnaires to capture transpersonal constructs as expansion or transpersonal trust (Friedman, 1983, 2002, 2009; Friedman & MacDonald, 2002; Kohls & Walach, 2008; MacDonald, LeClair, Holland, Alter, & Friedman, 2002). The other flavor uses a humanities approach and relies more on the discussion that has been produced within the cultural studies area. This has been dubbed Transpersonal Studies (Friedman, 2002). This is surely a viable route and some of the authors working within academic institutions use it (Lancaster, 2000, 2004, 2011).

The fourth route is what we have started and which I would naturally advocate as the best. It is, admittedly, likely also a bit more strenuous and difficult, but is the only one that I see as a viable, forward route that has a chance of creating impact.

So how could it work? I think the key would be the Science and the Culture of Consciousness.

Towards a Science and a Culture of Consciousness

The natural partners for transpersonal psychology are all those people who are trying to build a science of consciousness. Here, at present, a mainstream view that starts from materialist assumptions dominates. But this is so, because most other people have moved out. I think this mainstream view needs challenging. So far the challenging has happened so far from behind the hedge. It needs to happen in the open. That means writing and publishing in and for mainstream outlets, thus discussing the pertinent issues. For, after all, there are common topics: how to understand consciousness, what concepts are helpful, and where the common ground is.

From a practical point of view the common ground is the culture of consciousness (Metzinger, 2006). In a modern world with an exponential growth of information technology, cognitive capacities are taxed to the limit. Soon there will be an epidemic growth of incapacitated individuals who can no longer handle the amount of incoming information and whose cognitive capacities are crippled by information overload. Only some way of cultivating consciousness through practices that have naturally been the domain of transpersonal psychology and spiritual traditions—meditation, techniques to relax and collect the mind—will likely be reliable measures of relief here. This is where theory will meet practice and the notion of transformative practice will come into effect (Hartelius, Caplan, & Rardin, 2007). Thus there is common practical ground.

These issues will also let the areas of dissonance—the conceptual and philosophical issues—move towards the background in order for some practical solutions to come into focus. This may give a wholly different twist to the discussion. What transpersonal psychology does might even be defined as the study and culture of consciousness. Interestingly enough, the researchers studying the neuroscientific basis of consciousness and the neurocognitive models of consciousness, even though coming from a strictly materialist point of view, have realized one thing: The brain, substrate to the elusive phenomenon of consciousness, is itself being remodeled and changed by consciousness in action. Just learning how to juggle will have changed the thickness of the respective brain areas within a week (Driemeyer, Boyke, Gaser, Büchel, & May, 2008). In the same sense, all activities will have an effect feeding back on the brain, the substrate of our consciousness itself. In other words: consciousness and how it is directed will change the material basis of its own subsistence. This has also been shown for meditation: meditators have different brain structures than people who do not meditate (Ott et al., 2011).

If it is possible to show, empirically and with accepted methodology, that following a spiritual discipline will have an impact on people's lives, on their experience of difficulties and suffering, of illness and disease, then transpersonal psychology will have made a difference. If one replaces the terminology of "spirituality," "spiritual," "religion," and "religiosity," all of which have a denominational ring to them, by the term "culture of consciousness" then the enterprise is aligned with the thrust of science. By harnessing the insights and the power of science, it becomes possible to move away from a separatist position. That will still allow people to hold on to their own private creeds and belief systems. It will not abolish religion and it will not negate spirituality. But it will move them out of the domain of science and will move those elements that can be aligned with science closer to it. Once this has happened, the vision of the founding fathers and mothers of transpersonal psychology will have become true. Psychology will then have become more inclusive and will have introduced the idea of growth beyond what can be perceived at the moment.

References

Alcock, J. E. (2003). Give the null hypothesis a chance: Reasons to remain doubtful about the existence of PSI. *Journal of Consciousness Studies, 10*(6-7), 29-50.

Atmanspacher, H. (2003). Mind and matter as asymptotically disjoint, inequivalent representations with broken time-reversal symmetry. *Biosystems, 68,* 19-30.

Atmanspacher, H., & Fach, W. (2005). Akategorialität als mentale Instabilität. In W. Belschner, H. Piron & H. Walach (Eds.), *Bewusstseinstransformation als individuelles und gesellschaftliches Ziel* (pp. 74-115). Münster, Germany: Lit-Verlag.

Atmanspacher, H., Filk, T., & Römer, H. (2006). Weak quantum theory: Formal framework and selected applications. In A. Khrennikov (Ed.), *Quantum theory: Reconsiderations of foundations—American Institute of Physics, conference proceedings* (pp. 34-46). New York, NY: Melville.

Atmanspacher, H., & Primas, H. (2006). Pauli's ideas on mind and matter in the context of contemporary science. *Journal of Consciousness Studies, 13*(3), 5-50.

Atmanspacher, H., Römer, H., & Walach, H. (2002). Weak quantum theory: Complementarity and entanglement in physics and beyond. *Foundations of Physics, 32,* 379-406.

Baianu, I. C., & Poli, R. (2011). From simple to highly-complex systems: A paradigm shift towards non-Abelian emergent system dynamics and meta-levels. In B. Iantovics (Ed.), *Conference proceedings: Understanding intelligent and complex system* (pp. in print). Alba Iulia, Romania: Acta Universitatis Apulensis.

Bohr, N. (1937). Causality and complementarity. *Philosophy of Science, 4,* 289-298.

Bohr, N. (1997). *Collected works. Foundations of quantum physics I 1926-1932* (Vol. 6). Amsterdam, The Netherlands: North Holland.

Brent, J. (1993). *Charles Sanders Peirce. A life.* Bloomington, IN: Indiana University Press.

Burns, J. E. (1999). Volition and physical laws. *Journal of Consciousness Studies, 6*(10), 27-47.

Collingwood, R. G. (1998). *An essay on metaphysics* (Rev. ed.). Oxford, UK: Clarendon Press. (Original work published 1940)

Cushing, J. T. (1989). A background essay. In J. T. Cushing & E. Mcmullin (Eds.), *Philosophical consequences of quantum theory: Reflections on Bell's theorem* (pp. 1-24). Notre Dame, IN: University of Notre Dame Press.

Descartes, R. (2003). *Treatise of man (Traité de l'homme)* (Thomas S. Hall, Trans.). Amherst, NY: Prometheus Books. (Original work published 1664)

Douglas-Klotz, N. (1999). *The hidden gospel. Decoding the spiritual message of the Aramaic Jesus.* Wheaton, IL: Quest Books.

Douglas-Klotz, N. (2002). Beginning time: A new look at the early Jewish/Christian ritual time. *Cosmos: Journal of the Traditional Cosmological Society, 18,* 1-7.

Driemeyer, J., Boyke, J., Gaser, C., Büchel, C., & May, A. (2008). Changes in gray matter induced by learning—revisited. *PLoS One, 3*(7), e2669.

Ferrer, J. N. (1998). Speak now or forever hold your peace: A review essay of Ken Wilber's *The marriage of sense and soul: Integrating science and religion. Journal of Transpersonal Psychology, 30,* 53-67.

Ferrer, J. N. (2000). The perennial philosophy revisited. *Journal of Transpersonal Psychology, 32,* 7-30.

Ferrer, J. N. (2002). *Revisioning transpersonal theory: A participatory vision of human spirituality.* Albany, NY: State University of New York Press.

Fontana, D. (2003). *Psychology, religion, and spirituality.* Malden, MA: BPS Blackwell.

Forman, R. K. C. (Ed.). (1998). *The innate capacity: Mysticism, psychology, and philosophy* Oxford, UK: Oxford University Press.

Forman, R. K. C. (1999). *Mysticism, mind, consciousness.* Albany, NY: State University of New York Press.

Freud, S. (1922). Dreams and telepathy. In J. Strachey & A. Freud (Eds.), *The standard edition of the complete psychological works of Sigmund Freud* (Vol. 18, *Beyond the pleasure principle, group psychology and other works,* pp. 192-220). London, UK: Hogarth Press.

Freud, S. (1925). Some additional notes on dream interpretation as a whole. In J. Strachey & A. Freud (Eds.), *The standard edition of the complete psychological works of Sigmund Freud* (Vol. 19, *The ego and the id and other works,* pp. 123-138). London, UK: Hogarth Press.

Friedman, H. L. (1983). The Self-Expansiveness Level Form: A conceptualization and measurement of a transpersonal construct. *Journal of Transpersonal Psychology, 15,* 37-50.

Friedman, H. (2002). Transpersonal psychology as a scientific field. *International Journal of Transpersonal Studies, 21,* 175-187.

Friedman, H. (2005). Problems of romanticism in transpersonal psychology: A case study of Aikido. *The Humanistic Psychologist, 33,* 3-24.

Friedman, H. (2009). Xenophilia as a cultural trap: Bridging the gap between transpersonal psychology and religious/spiritual traditions. *International Journal of Transpersonal Studies, 28,* 107-111.

Friedman, H. (2010). Is Buddhism a psychology? Commentary on romanticism in "Mindfulness in Psychology." *The Humanistic Psychologist, 38,* 184-189.

Friedman, H. L., & MacDonald, D. A. (2002). Toward a working definition of transpersonal assessment. In H. L. Friedman & D. A. MacDonald (Eds.), *Approaches to transpersonal measurement and assessment* (pp. 123-140). San Francisco, CA: Transpersonal Institute.

Gadamer, H. G. (1975). *Wahrheit und Methode. Grundzüge einer philosophischen Hermeneutik.* Tübingen, Germany: Mohr (4. Aufl.).

Gernert, D. (1989). The formation of hierarchical structures as a key to self-organization. In G. J. Dalenoort (Ed.), *The paradigm of self-organization* (pp. 60-72). London, UK: Gordon & Breach.

Griffiths, R. R., Richards, W. A., Johnson, M. W., McCann, U. D., & Jesse, R. (2008). Mystical-type experiences occasioned by psilocybin mediate the attribution of personal meaning and spiritual significance 14 months later. *Journal of Psychopharmacology, 22*(6), 621-632.

Grof, S. (1988). *The adventure of self-discovery.* Albany, NY: State University of New York Press.

Grof, S. (2008). Brief history of transpersonal psychology. *International Journal of Transpersonal Studies, 27,* 46-54.

Grossman, P., Schmidt, S., Niemann, L., & Walach, H. (2004). Mindfulness based stress reduction and health: A meta-analysis. *Journal of Psychosomatic Research, 37,* 35-43.

Hartelius, G., Caplan, M., & Rardin, M. A. (2007). Transpersonal psychology: Defining the past, divining the future. *The Humanistic Psychologist, 35,* 1-26.

Hinterberger, T. (2011). Bewusstseinswissenschaften—Grundlagen, Modelle und Visionen. *Bewusstseinswissenschaften—Transpersonale Psychologie und Psychotherapie, 17*(2), 11-30.

Hoche, H.-U. (2008). *Anthropological complementarism. Linguistic, logical, and phenomenological studies in support of a third way beyond dualism and monism.* Paderborn, Germany: Mentis Verlag.

Hofmann, L., & Walach, H. (2011). Spirituality and religiosity in psychotherapy—A representative survey among German psychotherapists. *Psychotherapy Research, 21,* 179-192.

Holmes, S. W., Morris, R., Clance, P. R., & Putney, R. T. (1996). Holotropc breathwork: An experiential approach to psychotherapy. *Psychotherapy: Theory, Research, Practice, Training, 33,* 114-120.

Husserl, E. (1919). Erinnerungen an Franz Brentano. In O. Kraus (Ed.), *Franz Brentano: Zur Kenntnis seines Lebens uns seiner Lehre* (pp. 151-167). München, Germany: Beck.

James, W. (1981). *The works of William James: The principles of psychology.* Cambridge, MA: Harvard University Press.

James, W. (1984). *The works of William James: Psychology: Briefer course.* Cambridge, MA: Harvard University Press.

James, W. (1985). *The works of William James. The varieties of religious experience.* Cambridge, MA: Harvard University Press.

Jung, C. G. (1967). *Memories, dreams, reflections* (A. Jaffé, Ed.). London, UK: Collins.

Jung, C. G. (2009). *The red book: Liber novus.* (S. Shamdasani, Ed.). New York, NY: Horton.

Katz, S. T. (Ed.). (1983). *Mysticism and religious traditions.* New York, NY: Oxford University Press.

Kim, I., & Mahler, G. (2000). Uncertainty rescued: Bohr's complementarity for composite systems. *Physics Letters A, 269,* 287-292.

Kohls, N., & Benedikter, R. (2010). Origins of the modern concept of "Neuroscience." Wilhelm Wundt between empiricism and idealism: Implications for contemporary neuroethics. In J. Giordano & B. Gordijn (Eds.), *Scientific and philosophical perspectives in neuroethics* (pp. 37-65). Cambridge, UK: Cambridge University Press.

Kohls, N., & Walach, H. (2008). Validating four standard scales in spiritually practicing and non-practicing samples using propensity score matching. *European Journal of Assessment, 24,* 165-173.

Krippner, S., & Sulla, J. (2000). Identifying spiritual content in reports from Ayahuasca sessions. *International Journal of Transpersonal Studies, 19,* 59-76.

Kuhn, T. (1955). *The structure of scientific revolutions.* Chicago, IL: University of Chicago Press.

Lancaster, B. L. (2000). On the relationship between cognitive models and spiritual maps: Evidence from Hebrew language mysticism. *Journal of Consciousness Studies, 7*(11-12), 231-250.

Lancaster, B. L. (2004). *Approaches to consciousness: The marriage of science and mysticism.* Basingstoke, UK: Palgrave Macmillan.

Lancaster, B. L. (2011). The hard problem revisited: From cognitive neuroscience to Kabbalah and back again. In H. Walach, S. Schmidt, & W. B. Jonas (Eds.), *Neuroscience, consciousness and sprituality* (pp. 229-251). Dordrecht, The Netherlands: Springer.

Libet, B. (1999). Do we have free will? *Journal of Consciousness Studies, 6,* 47-57.

Lück, H. E. (2002). *Geschichte der Psychologie. Strömungen, Schulen, Entwicklungen* (3. überarb. Aufl. ed.). Stuttgart, Germany: Kohlhammer.

MacDonald, D. A., LeClair, L., Holland, C. J., Alter, A., & Friedman, H. L. (2002). A survey of measures of transpersonal constructs. In H. L. Friedman & D. A. MacDonald (Eds.), *Approaches to transpersonal measurement and assessment* (pp. 15-79). San Francisco, CA: Transpersonal Institute.

Marsh, M. N. (2010). *Out-of-body and near-death experiences: Brain-state phenomena or glimpses of immortality?* Oxford, UK: Oxford University Press.

Merlan, P. (1945). Brentano und Freud. *Journal of the History of Ideas, 6,* 375-377.

Merlan, P. (1949). Brentano and Freud—a sequel. *Journal of the History of Ideas, 10,* 451-452.

Mermin, N. D. (1989). Can you help your team tonight by watching on TV? More experimental metaphysics from Einstein, Podolsky, and Rosen. In J. T. Cushing & E. Mcmullin (Eds.), *Philosophical consequences of quantum theory: Reflections on Bell's theorem* (pp. 38-59). Notre Dame, IN: University of Notre Dame Press.

Metzinger, T. (2003). *Being no one: The self-model theory of subjectivity.* Cambridge, MA: MIT Press.

Metzinger, T. (2006, January). Der Begriff einer "Bewusstseinskultur." *e-Journal Philosophie der Psychologie*, n.p.

Nadeau, R., & Kafatos, M. (1999). *The non-local universe: The new physics and matters of the mind.* Oxford, UK: Oxford University Press.

Ott, U., Hölzel, B. K., & Vaitl, D. (2011). Brain structure and meditation: How spiritual practice shapes the brain. In H. Walach, S. Schmidt, & W. B. Jonas (Eds.), *Neuroscience, consciousness and spritiuality* (pp. 119-128). Dordrecht, The Netherlands: Springer.

Pepper, S. C. (1942). *World hypotheses: A study in evidence.* Cambridge, UK: Cambridge University Press.

Raichle, M. E. (2006). The brain's dark energy. *Science, 314*, 1249-1250.

Römer, H. (2011). Why do we see a classical world? In *Contributions to the Symposion in Honour of Basil Hiley, Helsinki, Finland, November 2010.*

Römer, H., & Walach, H. (2011). Complementarity of phenomenal and physiological observables: A primer on generalised quantum theory and its scope for neuroscience and consciousness studies. In H. Walach, S. Schmidt, & W. B. Jonas (Eds.), *Neuroscience, consciousness and spirituality* (pp. 97-107). Dordrecht, The Netherlands: Springer.

Rosenfeld, L. (1963). Niels Bohr's contribution to epistemology. *Physics Today, 16*(October), 47-54.

Salart, D., Baas, A., Branciard, C., Gisin, N., & Zbinden, H. (2008). Testing spooky actions at a distance. *Nature, 454*, 861-864

Schmidt, S. (2009). Shall we really do it again? The powerful concept of replication is neglected in the social sciences. *Review of General Psychology, 13*, 90-100.

Shamdasani, S. (1994). Introduction: Encountering Hélène. Théodore Flournoy and the genesis of subliminal psychology. In S. Shamdasani (Ed.), *From India to the planet Mars: A case of multiple personality with imaginary languages* (pp. xi-xliv). Princeton, NJ: Princeton University Press.

Shamdasani, S. (1995). Memories, dreams, omissions. *Spring, 57*, 115-137.

Shamdasani, S. (1998a). From Geneva to Zürich: Jung and French Switzerland. *Journal of Analytical Psychology, 43*, 115-126.

Shamdasani, S. (1998b). Introduction: Jung's journey to the East. In S. Shamdasani (Ed.), *The psychology of kundalini yoga. Notes of the seminar given in 1932.* London, UK: Routledge.

Shamdasani, S. (2003). *Jung and the making of modern psychology: The dream of a science.* Cambridge, UK: Cambridge University Press.

Shamdasani, S. (2005). *Jung stripped bare—by his biographers, even.* London, UK: Karnac.

Shanon, B. (2002). Ayahuasca visualizations: A structured typology. *Journal of Consciousness Studies, 9*(2), 3-30.

Simmonds, J. G. (2006). The oceanic feeling and a sea change: Historical challenges to reductionist attitudes to religion and spirit from within psychoanalysis. *Psychoanalytic Psychology, 23*, 128-142.

Smith, B. (1994). *Austrian philosophy. The legacy of Franz Brentano.* Chicago, IL: Open Court.

Soudková, M. A. (2002). The origins and development of transpersonal psychology: An American perspective. *Studia Psychologica, 44*, 175-200.

Spivak, L. I., Kropotov, Y. D., Spival, D. L., & Sevostyanov, A. V. (1994). Evoked potentials in holotropic breathing. *Human Physiology, 20*, 17-19.

Steiner, R. (1921). Franz Brentano: Ein Nachruf. In R. Steiner (Ed.), *Von Seelenrätseln.* Berlin, Germany: Philosophisch-anthroposophischer Verlag.

Stumpf, C. (1919). Erinnerungen an Franz Brentano. In O. Kraus (Ed.), *Franz Brentano: Zur Kenntnis seines Lebens uns seiner Lehre* (pp. 85-149). München, Germany: Beck.

Suppe, F. (Ed.). (1977). *The structure of scientific theories.* Urbana, IL: University of Illinois Press.

Tegmark, M. (2000). Importance of quantum decoherence in brain processes. *Physics Review, E 61,* 4194-4206.

Tiefensee, E. (1998). *Philosophie und Religion bei Franz Brentano (1838-1917)* (Vol. 14). Tübingen, Germany: Franckegg.

Walach, H. (2005). The complementarity model of brain-body relationship. *Medical Hypotheses, 65,* 380-388.

Walach, H. (2008). Narcicissm: The shadow of transpersonal psychology. *Transpersonal Psychology Review, 12*(2), 47-59.

Walach, H. (2011). Neuroscience, consciousness, spirituality—questions, problems and potential solutions: An introductory essay. In H. Walach, S. Schmidt, & W. B. Jonas (Eds.), *Neuroscience, consciousness and spirituality* (pp. 1-21). Dordrecht, The Netherlands: Springer.

Walach, H., & Römer, H. (2000). Complementarity is a useful concept for consciousness studies: A reminder. *Neuroendocrinology Letters, 21,* 221-232.

Walach, H., & Römer, H. (2011). Generalized entanglement: A nonreductive option for a phenomenologically dualist and ontologically monist view of consciousness. In H. Walach, S. Schmidt, & W. B. Jonas (Eds.), *Neuroscience, consciousness and spirituality* (pp. 81-95). Dordrecht, The Netherlands: Springer.

Walach, H., & Schmidt, S. (2005). Repairing Plato's life boat with Ockham's razor: The important function of research in anomalies for mainstream science. *Journal of Consciousness Studies, 12*(2), 52-70.

Walsh, R. (1999). *Essential spirituality. The 7 central practices to awaken heart and mind.* New York, NY: John Wiley & Sons.

Wegner, D. M., & Wheatley, T. (1999). Apparent mental causation. Sources of the experience of will. *American Psychologist, 54,* 480-492.

Wehrle, J. M. (1989). *Franz Brentano und die Zukunft der Philosophie. Studien zur Wissenschaftsgeschichte und Wissenschaftssystematik im 19. Jahrhundert* (Vol. 15). Amsterdam, The Netherlands: Rodopi.

Welwood, J. (2002). *Toward a psychology of awakening: Buddhism, psychotherapy, and the path of personal and spiritual transformation.* Boston, MA: Shambala.

Wessels, L. (1989). The way the world isn't: What the Bell theorems force us to give up. In J. T. Cushing & E. Mcmullin (Eds.), *Philosophical consequences of quantum theory: Reflections on Bell's theorem* (pp. 80-96). Notre Dame, IN: University of Notre Dame Press.

Wilber, K. (1997). *The eye of spirit: An integral vision for a world gone slightly mad.* Boston, MA: Shambala.

Wilber, K. (1998). *The marriage of sense and soul: Integrating science and religion.* New York, NY: Random House.

Williams, M., Teasdale, J., Segal, Z., & Kabat-Zinn, J. (2007). *The mindful way through depression: Freeing yourself from chronic unhappiness.* New York, NY: Guilford Press.

Wundt, W. (1879). *Der Spiritismus. Eine sogenannte wissenschaftliche Frage. Offener Brief an Herrn Prof. Dr. Hermann Ulrici in Halle.* Leipzip, Germany: Verlag Wilhelm Engelmann.

Yu, T., & Eberly, J. H. (2009). Sudden death of entanglement. *Science, 323,* 598-601.

Zeleny, M. (Ed.). (1981). *Autopoiesis. A theory of living organization.* New York, NY: Elsevier.

Part II
Transpersonal Theory

5

Revision and Re-Enchantment of Psychology

Legacy from Half a Century of Consciousness Research

Stanislav Grof

In 1962, Thomas Kuhn, one of the most influential philosophers of the 20th century, published his groundbreaking book *The Structure of Scientific Revolutions*. On the basis of 15 years of intensive study of the history of science, he was able to demonstrate that the development of knowledge about the universe in various scientific disciplines is not a process of gradual accumulation of data and formulation of ever more accurate theories, as usually assumed. Instead, it shows a clearly cyclical nature with specific stages and characteristic dynamics, which can be understood and even predicted.

The central concept of Kuhn's theory, which makes this possible, is that of a *paradigm*. A paradigm can be defined as a constellation of beliefs, values, and techniques shared by the members of the community at a particular historical period. It governs the thinking and research activities of scientists until some of its basic assumptions are seriously challenged by new observations. This leads to a crisis and emergence of suggestions for radically new ways of viewing and interpreting the phenomena that the old paradigm is unable to explain. Eventually, one of these alternatives satisfies the necessary requirements to become the new paradigm that then dominates the thinking in the next period of the history of science.

The most famous historical examples of paradigm shifts have been the replacement of the Ptolemaic geocentric system by the heliocentric system of Copernicus, Kepler, and Galileo; the overthrow of Becher's phlogiston theory in chemistry by Lavoisier and Dalton; and the conceptual cataclysms in physics in the first three decades of the 20th century that undermined the hegemony of Newtonian physics and gave birth to theories of relativity and quantum physics. Paradigm shifts tend to come as a major surprise to the mainstream academic community, because its members tend to mistake the leading paradigms for an accurate and definitive description of reality. Thus in 1900, shortly before the advent of quantum-relativistic physics, Lord Kelvin declared more than a 100 years ago, "There is nothing new to be discovered in physics now. All that remains is more and more precise measurements" (Jahn, 2001, p. 22).

The Wiley Blackwell Handbook of Transpersonal Psychology, First Edition.
Edited by Harris L. Friedman and Glenn Hartelius.

In the past five decades, various avenues of modern consciousness research have revealed a rich array of "anomalous" phenomena—experiences and observations that have undermined some of the generally accepted assertions of modern psychiatry, psychology, and psychotherapy concerning the nature and dimensions of the human psyche, the origins of emotional and psychosomatic disorders, and effective therapeutic mechanisms. Many of these observations are so radical that they question the basic metaphysical assumptions of materialistic science concerning the nature of reality and of human beings and the relationship between consciousness and matter.

In this chapter, I will summarize my observations and experiences from more than half a century of research into an important subgroup of non-ordinary states of consciousness for which I coined the name *holotropic*; these findings seriously challenge the existing scientific paradigms. Before I address this topic, I would like to explain the term *holotropic* that I will be using throughout this article. All these years, my primary interest has been to explore the healing, transformative, and evolutionary potential of non-ordinary states of consciousness and their great value as a source of new revolutionary data about consciousness, the human psyche, and the nature of reality.

From this perspective, the term "altered states of consciousness" (Tart, 1969) commonly used by mainstream clinicians and theoreticians is not appropriate, because of its one-sided emphasis on the distortion or impairment of the "correct way" of experiencing oneself and the world. (In colloquial English and in veterinary jargon, the term "alter" is used to signify castration of family dogs and cats.) Even the somewhat better term "non-ordinary states of consciousness" is too general, because it includes a wide range of conditions that are not relevant for the subject of this paper. Here belong trivial deliria caused by infectious diseases, tumors, abuse of alcohol, or circulatory and degenerative diseases of the brain. These alterations of consciousness are associated with disorientation, impairment of intellectual functions, and subsequent amnesia. They are clinically important, but lack therapeutic and heuristic potential.

The term "holotropic" refers to a large subgroup of non-ordinary states of consciousness that are of great theoretical and practical importance. These are the states that novice shamans experience during their initiatory crises and in later life induce in their clients for therapeutic purposes. Ancient and native cultures have used these states in rites of passage and in their healing ceremonies for millenia. They were described by mystics of all ages and initiates in the ancient mysteries of death and rebirth. Procedures inducing these states were also developed and used in the context of the great religions of the world—Hinduism, Buddhism, Jainism, Taoism, Islam, Judaism, Zoroastrianism, and Christianity.

The importance of holotropic states for ancient and aboriginal cultures is reflected in the amount of time and energy that the members of these human groups dedicated to developing *technologies of the sacred,* various procedures capable of inducing such states for ritual and spiritual purposes. These methods combine in various ways drumming and other forms of percussion, music, chanting, rhythmic dancing, changes in breathing, and cultivating special forms of awareness. Extended social and sensory isolation in a cave or desert, on arctic ice or high mountains is also an important means of inducing this category of non-ordinary states. Extreme physiological interventions used for this purpose include fasting, sleep deprivation, dehydration, use of powerful laxatives and purgatives, and even infliction of severe pain, body mutilation, and massive bloodletting. The ritual use of psychedelic plants has been by far the most effective tool for inducing healing and transformative non-ordinary states.

When I recognized the unique nature of these states of consciousness, I found it difficult to believe that contemporary psychiatry does not have a specific category and term for such theoretically and practically important experiences. Because I felt strongly that they deserve to be distinguished from "altered states of consciousness" and not be seen as manifestations of serious mental diseases, I started referring to them as *holotropic*. This composite word literally means "oriented toward wholeness" or "moving toward wholeness" (from the Greek *holos* = whole and *trepo/trepein* = moving toward or in the direction of something). The word holotropic is a neologism, but it is related to a commonly used term *heliotropism*—the property of plants to always move in the direction of the sun.

The name holotropic suggests something that might come as a surprise to an average Westerner: in our everyday state of consciousness we identify with only a small fraction of who we really are and do not experience the full extent of our being. Holotropic states of consciousness have the potential to help us recognize that we are not *"skin-encapsulated egos,"* as British philosopher and writer Alan Watts (1961/1974, p. 24, emphasis added) called it, but that, in the last analysis, we are commensurate with the cosmic creative principle itself. Or, to use the statement attributed to Pierre Teilhard de Chardin, French paleontologist and philosopher, "we are not human beings having spiritual experiences, we are spiritual beings having human experiences" (e.g., Covey, 2000, p. 47).

This astonishing idea is not new. In the ancient Indian Upanishads, the answer to the question: "Who am I?" is "Tat tvam asi." This succinct Sanskrit sentence means literally: "Thou art That," where "That" refers to the Godhead. It suggests that we are not *"namarupa"*—name and form (body/ego), but that our deepest identity is with a divine spark in our innermost being (*Atman*) which is ultimately identical with the supreme universal principle that creates the universe (*Brahman*). This revelation— the identity of the individual with the divine—is the ultimate secret that lies at the mystical core of all great spiritual traditions. The name for this principle could thus be the Tao, Buddha, Shiva (of Kashmir Shaivism), Cosmic Christ, Pleroma, Allah, and many others. Holotropic experiences have the potential to help us discover our true identity and our cosmic status (Grof, 1998). Sometimes this happens in small increments, other times in the form of major breakthroughs.

Psychedelic research and the development of intensive experiential techniques of psychotherapy in the second half of the 20th century moved holotropic states from the world of healers of ancient and preliterate cultures into modern psychiatry and psychotherapy. Therapists who were open to these techniques and used them in their practice were able to confirm the extraordinary healing potential of holotropic states and discovered their value as goldmines of revolutionary new information about consciousness, the human psyche, and the nature of reality. I became aware of the remarkable properties of holotropic states in 1956 when I volunteered as a beginning psychiatrist for an experiment with LSD-25. During this experiment, in which the pharmacological effect of LSD was combined with exposure to powerful strobo-scopic light (referred to as "driving" or "entraining" of the brainwaves), I had an overwhelming experience of cosmic consciousness (Grof, 2006).

This experience inspired in me a lifelong interest in holotropic states and research in this area has become my passion, profession, and vocation. Since that time, most of my clinical and research activities have consisted of systematic exploration of the therapeutic, transformative, heuristic, and evolutionary potential of these states. The half-century that I have dedicated to consciousness research has been for me an extraordinary adventure of discovery and self-discovery. I spent the first few decades conducting psychotherapy with psychedelic substances, initially at the Psychiatric Research Institute in Prague, Czechoslovakia, and then at the Maryland Psychiatric Research Center in Baltimore, MD, where I participated in the last surviving U.S. psychedelic research program. Since 1975, my wife Christina and I have worked with Holotropic Breathwork, a powerful method of therapy and self-exploration that we jointly developed at the Esalen Institute in Big Sur, California. Over the years, we have also supported many people undergoing spontaneous episodes of non-ordinary states of consciousness—psychospiritual crises or "spiritual emergencies," as Christina and I call them (Grof, & Grof, 1989; Grof, & Grof, 1991).

In psychedelic therapy, holotropic states are brought about by administering mind-altering substances, such as LSD, psilocybin, mescaline, and tryptamine or amphetamine derivatives. In Holotropic Breathwork, consciousness is changed by a combination of faster breathing, evocative music, and energy-releasing bodywork. In spiritual emergencies, holotropic states occur spontaneously, in the middle of everyday life, and their cause is usually unknown. If they are correctly understood and supported, these episodes have an extraordinary healing, transformative, and even evolutionary potential.

I have also been tangentially involved in many disciplines that are, more or less directly, related to holotropic states of consciousness. I have spent much time exchanging information with anthropologists and have participated in sacred ceremonies of native cultures in different parts of the world with and without the ingestion of psychedelic plants, such as peyote, ayahuasca, and Psilocybe mushrooms. This has involved contact with various North American, Mexican, South American, and African shamans and healers. I have also had extensive contact with representatives of various spiritual disciplines, including Vipassana, Zen, and Vajrayana Buddhism, Siddha Yoga, Tantra, and the Christian Benedictine order.

I have also closely followed the development of thanatology, the young discipline studying near-death experiences and the psychological and spiritual aspects of death and dying. In the late 1960s and early 1970s I participated in a large research project studying the effects of psychedelic therapy for individuals dying of cancer. I also have been privileged to know personally and experience some of the great psychics and parapsychologists of our era, pioneers of laboratory consciousness research, and therapists who had developed and practiced powerful forms of experiential therapy that induce holotropic states of consciousness.

My initial encounter with holotropic states was very difficult and challenging, both intellectually and emotionally. In the early years of my laboratory and clinical psychedelic research, I was bombarded daily with experiences and observations, that my medical and psychiatric training had not prepared me for. As a matter of fact, I was experiencing and observing things that were considered impossible in the context of the scientific worldview I had obtained during my medical training. Yet, those supposedly impossible things were happening all the time. I have described these "anomalous phenomena" in my articles and books (Grof, 2000, 2006).

In the late 1990s, I received a phone call from Jane Bunker, my editor at State University New York (SUNY) Press that had published many of my books. She asked me if I would consider writing a book that would summarize the observations from my research in one volume and would serve as an introduction to my already published books. She also asked if I could specifically focus on all the experiences and observations from my research that current scientific theories could not explain and suggest the revisions in our thinking that would be necessary to account for these revolutionary findings. This was a tall order, but also a great opportunity. My 70th birthday was rapidly approaching and a new generation of facilitators was conducting our Holotropic Breathwork training all over the world. A manual was needed covering the material taught in those training modules. Here was an opportunity to provide it.

The result of this exchange was a book with a deliberately provocative title: *Psychology of the Future*. The radical revisions in understandings of consciousness and the human psyche in health and disease that I suggested in this work fall into the following categories:

1   The Nature of Consciousness and Its Relationship to Matter
2   Cartography of the Human Psyche
3   Architecture of Emotional and Psychosomatic Disorders
4   Effective Therapeutic Mechanisms
5   Strategy of Psychotherapy and Self-Exploration
6   The Role of Spirituality in Human Life
7   The Importance of Archetypal Astrology for Psychology.

Unless thinking is changed in all these areas, the understanding of psychogenic emotional and psychosomatic disorders and their therapy will remain superficial, unsatisfactory, and incomplete. Psychiatry and psychology will be unable to genuinely comprehend the nature and origin of spirituality and appreciate the important role that it plays in the human psyche and in the universal scheme of things. These revisions are therefore essential for understanding the ritual, spiritual, and religious history of humanity—shamanism, rites of passage, the ancient mysteries of death and rebirth, and the great religions of the world. Without these radical changes in thinking, potentially healing and heuristically invaluable experiences ("spiritual emergencies") will be misdiagnosed as psychotic and treated by suppressive medication. A large array of the experiences and observations from the research of holotropic states will remain mystifying "anomalous phenomena," events that should not occur according to the current scientific paradigms. Mental health professionals will also have difficulty accepting the therapeutic power of psychedelic substances, mediated by profound experiences that are currently seen as psychotic—as demonstrated by the terms that mainstream clinicians and academicians use to describe them: experimental psychoses, psychotomimetics, or hallucinogens. This view reflects the inability to recognize the true nature of holotropic experiences as germane expressions of the deep dynamics of the psyche.

In view of my own initial resistance to the bewildering experiences and observations from researching holotropic states, as well as phenomena associated with them (such as astonishing synchronicities), I will not be surprised if the the proposed changes encounter strong resistance in the academic community. This is understandable, considering the scope and radical nature of the necessary conceptual revisions. Professionals in conventional academic and clinical circles tend to confuse "map and territory" and see current theories concerning consciousness and the human psyche in health and disease to be a definitive and accurate description of reality (Bateson, 1972). At issue here is not minor patchwork, known as *ad hoc hypotheses,* but a major fundamental overhaul. The resulting conceptual cataclysm would be comparable in its nature and scope to the revolution that physicists had to face in the first three decades of the twentieth century when they were forced to move from Newtonian to quantum-relativistic physics. In fact, the conceptual changes I am proposing would represent a logical completion of the radical changes in an understanding of the material world that have already occurred in physics.

The history of science abounds with examples of individuals who challenged the dominant paradigm; typically, their ideas were initially dismissed as products of ignorance, poor judgment, bad science, fraud, or even insanity. I am now in the ninth decade of my life, a time when researchers often try to review their professional career and outline the conclusions they have reached. More than half a century of research of holotropic states—my own, as well as that of many of my transpersonally oriented colleagues—has amassed so much supportive evidence for a radically new understanding of consciousness and of the human psyche that I have decided to describe this new vision in its entirety, fully aware of its controversial nature. The fact that the new findings challenge the most fundamental metaphysical assumptions of materialistic science should not be a sufficient reason for rejecting them. Whether this new vision will ultimately be refuted or accepted should be determined by unbiased future research of holotropic states.

1 The Nature of Consciousness and Its Relationship to Matter

According to the current scientific worldview, consciousness is an epiphenomenon of material processes; it allegedly emerges out of the complexity of the neurophysiological processes in the brain. This thesis is presented with great authority as an obvious fact that has been proven beyond any reasonable doubt. But on closer inspection, one discovers that it is a basic metaphysical assumption that is not supported by facts and actually contradicts the findings of modern consciousness research.

There is ample clinical and experimental evidence showing deep correlations between the anatomy, physiology, and biochemistry of the brain, on the one hand, and states of consciousness, on the other. However, none of these findings proves unequivocally that consciousness is actually generated by the brain. Even sophisticated theories based on advanced research of the brain—such as Stuart Hameroff's suggestion that the solution of the problem of consciousness might lie in understanding the quantum process in the microtubules of brain cells on the molecular and supramolec-ular level (Hameroff, 1987)—falls painfully short of bridging the formidable gap between matter and consciousness and illuminating how material processes could generate consciousness.

The origin of consciousness from matter is simply taken for granted as an obvious and self-evident fact, based on the metaphysical assumption of the primacy of matter in the universe. In fact, in the entire history of science, nobody has ever offered a plausible explanation for how consciousness could be generated by material processes, or even suggested a viable approach to the problem. Consider, for example, the book by Francis Crick (1995), *The Astonishing Hypothesis: The Scientific Search for the Soul*; the book's jacket carried a very exciting promise: "Nobel Prize-winning Scientist Explains Consciousness."

Crick's (1995) "astonishing hypothesis" was succinctly stated at the beginning of his book: "You, your joys and your sorrows, your memories and your ambitions, your sense of personal identity and free will, are in fact no more than the behavior of a vast assembly of nerve cells and their associated molecules. Who you are is nothing but a pack of neurons" (p. 3). At the beginning of the book, to simplify the problem of consciousness, Crick narrowed it to the problem of optical perception. He presented impressive experimental evidence showing that visual perception is associated with distinct physiological, biochemical, and electrical processes in the optical system from the retina through the optical tract to the suboccipital cortex. There the discussion ended as if the problem of consciousness had been satisfactorily solved.

In reality, this is where the problem begins. What exactly is capable of transforming biochemical and electric processes in the brain into a conscious experience of a rea-sonable facsimile of the object we as humans are observing, in full color, and projected into three-dimensional space? The formidable problem of the relationship between *phenomena*—things as one perceives them—and *noumena*—things as they truly are in themselves (*Dinge an sich*) was clearly articulated by Immanuel Kant (1999). Scien-tists focus their efforts on the aspect of the problem where they can find answers: the material processes in the brain. The much more mysterious problem—how physical processes in the brain generate consciousness—does not receive any attention, because it is incomprehensible and cannot be solved.

The attitude that Western science has adopted in regard to this issue resembles the famous Sufi story. On a dark night, Nasruddin, a satirical Sufi figure, is crawling on his knees under a candelabra. His neighbor sees him and asks: "What are you doing? Are you looking for something?" Nasruddin answers that he is searching for a lost key and the neighbor offers to help. After some time of unsuccessful joint effort, the neighbor has become confused and feels the need for clarification. He asks: "I don't see anything! Are you sure you lost it here?" Nasruddin shakes his head and points his finger to a dark area outside of the circle illuminated by the lamp and replies: "Not here, over there!" The neighbor is puzzled and inquires further: "So why are we looking for it here and not over there?" Nasruddin explains: "Because it is light here and we can see. Over there it's dark and we would not have a chance!"

Similarly, materialistic scientists have systematically avoided the problem of the origin of consciousness, because this riddle cannot be solved within the context of their conceptual framework. The idea that consciousness is a product of the brain naturally is not completely arbitrary. Its proponents usually refer to a vast body of very specific clinical observations from neurology, neurosurgery, and psychiatry, to support their position. The evidence for close correlations between the anatomy, neurophysiology, and biochemistry of the brain and consciousness is unquestionable and overwhelming. What is problematic is not the nature of the presented evidence but the conclusions that are drawn from these observations. In formal logic, this type of fallacy is called *non sequitur*—an argument wherein its conclusion does not follow from its premises. Although the experimental data clearly show that consciousness is closely connected with the neurophysiological and biochemical processes in the brain, they have very little bearing on the nature and origin of consciousness.

A simple analogy is the relationship between the TV set and the television program. The situation here is much clearer, because it involves a system that is human-made and its operation is well known. The final reception of the television program—the quality of the picture and of the sound—depends in a very critical way on the proper functioning of the TV set and on the integrity of its components. Malfunctioning of its various parts cause very distinct and specific changes in the quality of the program. Some of them lead to distortions of form, color, or sound, others to interference between the channels, and so on. Like the neurologist who uses changes in consciousness as a diagnostic tool, a television mechanic can infer from the nature of these anomalies which parts of the set and which specific components are malfunctioning. When the problem is identified, repairing or replacing these elements will correct the distortions.

Because the basic principles of the television technology are known, it is clear that the set simply mediates the program and that it does not generate it. It would be laughable to try examine and scrutinize all the transistors, relays, and circuits of the TV set and analyze all its wires in an attempt to figure out how it creates the programs. Even if this misguided effort were carried to the molecular, atomic, or subatomic level, there will be absolutely no clue as to why, at a particular time, a Mickey Mouse cartoon, a Star Trek sequence, or a Hollywood classic movie appear on the screen. The fact that there is such a close correlation between the functioning of the TV set and the quality of the program does not necessarily mean that the entire secret of the program is in the set itself. Yet this is exactly the kind of conclusion that traditional materialistic science draws from comparable data about the brain and its relation to consciousness.

Ample evidence suggests exactly the opposite, namely that under certain circumstances consciousness can operate independently of its material substrate and can perform functions that reach far beyond the capacities of the brain. This is most clearly illustrated by the existence of out-of-body experiences that can occur spontaneously, or in various facilitating situations—shamanic trances, psychedelic sessions, spiritual practice, hypnosis, experiential psychotherapy, and particularly near-death experiences. In all these situations consciousness can separate from the body and maintain its sensory capacity, while moving freely to various close and remote locations. Veridical out-of-body experiences are particularly interesting, because independent verification can in some cases confirm that the perception of the environment is accurate. In near-death situations, veridical out-of-body experiences can occur even in people who are congenitally blind for organic reasons (Ring & Cooper, 1999; Ring & Valarino, 1998). Many other types of transpersonal phenomena can also mediate accurate information about various aspects of the universe that had not been previously received and recorded in the brain (Grof, 2000).

Materialistic scientists have not been able to produce any convincing evidence that consciousness is a product of the neurophysiological processes in the brain. They have been able to maintain this conviction only by ignoring, misinterpreting, and even ridiculing a vast body of observations indicating that consciousness can exist and function independently of the body and of the physical senses. This evidence comes from parapsychology, anthropology, LSD research, experiential psychotherapy, thanatology, and the study of spontaneously occurring holotropic states of consciousness (spiritual emergencies; Grof, & Grof, 1989). All these disciplines have amassed impressive data demonstrating clearly that human consciousness is capable of functioning in many ways that the brain (as understood by mainstream science) cannot possibly function and that consciousness is a primary and further irreducible aspect of existence—an equal partner of matter or possibly superordinated to it.

2 Cartography of the Human Psyche

Traditional academic psychiatry and psychology use a model of the human psyche that is limited to postnatal biography and to the individual unconscious as described by Sigmund Freud. According to Freud, human psychological history begins after we are born; the newborn is a *tabula rasa,* a clean slate. Our psychological functioning is determined by an interplay between biological instincts and influences that have shaped our life since we came into this world—the quality of nursing, the nature of toilet training, various psychosexual traumas, development of the superego, our reaction to the Oedipal triangle, and conflicts and traumatic events in later life. According to this point of view, who we become and how we psychologically function is determined by our postnatal personal and interpersonal history.

The Freudian individual unconscious is also essentially a derivative of our postnatal history—a repository of what we have forgotten, rejected as unacceptable, and repressed. This underworld of the psyche (the *id* as Freud called it), is a realm dominated by primitive instinctual forces. To describe the relationship between the conscious psyche and the unconscious Freud used his famous image of the submerged iceberg, in which what had been assumed to be the totality of the psyche was just a small part of it, like the section of the iceberg showing above the surface of the water. Psychoanalysis discovered that a much larger part of the psyche, comparable to the submerged part of the iceberg, is unconscious and, unbeknownst to us, governs our thought processes and behavior.

Later contributions to dynamic psychotherapy added to etiological factors problems in the development of object relationships and interpersonal dynamics in the nuclear family (Bateson, Jackson, Haley, & Weakland, 1956; Blanck & Blanck, 1974, 1979; Satir, 1983; Sullivan, 1953), but shared with Freudian psychoanalysis the exclusive emphasis on postnatal life. Who we become and how we psychologically function is determined by what happened to us after we were born. In the work with holotropic states of consciousness induced by psychedelics and various non-drug means, as well as those occurring spontaneously, this model proves to be painfully inadequate. To account for all the phenomena occurring in these states, we must drastically revise our understanding of the dimensions of the human psyche. Besides *the postnatal biographical level* that it shares with traditional psychology, the new expanded cartography includes two additional large domains.

The first of these domains can be referred to as *perinatal,* because of its close connection with the trauma of biological birth. This region of the unconscious contains the memories of what the fetus experienced in the consecutive stages of the birth process, including all the emotions and physical sensations involved. These memories form four distinct experiential clusters, each of which is related to one of the stages of childbirth. I have coined for them the term *Basic Perinatal Matrices (BPM I-IV).*

BPM I consists of memories of the advanced prenatal state just before the onset of the delivery. BPM II is related to the first stage of the birth process when the uterus contracts, but the cervix is not yet open. BPM III reflects the struggle to be born after the uterine cervix dilates. And finally, BPM IV holds the memory of emerging into the world, the birth itself. The content of these matrices is not limited to fetal memories; each of them also represents a selective opening into the domains of the historical and archetypal collective unconscious, which contain motifs of similar experiential quality. Detailed description of the phenomenology and dynamics of perinatal matrices can be found in my various publications (e.g., Grof, 1975, 2000).

The official position of academic psychiatry is that biological birth is not recorded in memory and does not constitute a psychotrauma. The usual reason for denying the possibility of birth memory is that the cerebral cortex of the newborn is not mature enough to mediate experiencing and recording of this event. More specifically, the cortical neurons are not yet *myelinized*—completely covered with protective sheaths of a fatty substance called myelin. Surprisingly, this same argument is not used to deny the existence and importance of memories from the time of nursing, a period that immediately follows birth. The psychological significance of the experiences in the oral period and even "bonding"—the exchange of looks and physical contact between the mother and child immediately after birth—is generally recognized and acknowledged by mainstream obstetricians, pediatricians, and child psychiatrists (Kennel & Klaus, 1998; Klaus, Kennell, & Klaus, 1995).

The myelinization argument makes no sense and is in conflict with scientific evidence of various kinds. For instance, it has been established that memory exists in organisms that do not have a cerebral cortex at all. In 2001, an American neuroscientist of Austrian origin, Erik Kandel (2001), received a Nobel Prize in physiology for his research of memory mechanisms of the sea slug *Aplysia,* an organism incomparably more primitive than the newborn child. The assertion that the newborn is not aware of being born and is not capable of forming memory of this event also strongly conflicts with extensive fetal research showing that the fetus is extremely sensitive already in the prenatal stage (Tomatis, 1991; Whitwell, 1999). Given this evidence, the most likely explanation of the position of mainstream professionals is to attribute it to psychological repression and resistance due to the terrifying memory of biological birth.

The second transbiographical domain of the new cartography is best called *transpersonal,* because it includes a rich array of experiences in which consciousness transcends the boundaries of the body/ego and the usual limitations of linear time and three-dimensional space. This transcendence leads to experiential identification with other people, groups of people, other life forms, and even elements of the inorganic world. Transcendence of time provides experiential access to ancestral, racial, collective, phylogenetic, and karmic memories. Yet another category of transpersonal experiences can take one into the realm of the collective unconscious that the Swiss psychiatrist C. G. Jung (1968) called archetypal. This region harbors mythological figures, themes, and realms of all the cultures and ages, even those of which we have no intellectual knowledge.

In its farthest reaches, individual consciousness can identify with the Universal Mind or Cosmic Consciousness, the creative principle of the universe. Probably the most profound experience available in holotropic states is identification with the Supracosmic and Metacosmic Void, Primordial Emptiness, and Nothingness that is conscious of itself. The Void has a paradoxical nature; it is a *vacuum,* in the sense that it is devoid of any concrete forms, but it is also a *plenum,* because it seems to contain all of creation in a potential form.

In my books, I have classified transpersonal experiences in a strictly phenomenological and not hierarchical manner. The Hindu and Buddhist literature and Ken Wilber in his writings based on these Indian sources have taken the hierarchical approach of specifying the levels of consciousness on which various transpersonal experiences occur. To construct his map of psychospiritual development, Wilber used material from ancient spiritual literature, primarily from Vedanta Hinduism and both Theravada and Mahayana Buddhism. My own data are drawn from clinical observations in contemporary populations in a number of European countries, North and South America, and Australia, complemented by some limited experience with Japanese and East Indian experiential groups. However, despite the difference in the sources of data, it is not difficult to arrange transpersonal experiences in my classification in such a way that they closely parallel Wilber's description of the levels of spiritual evolution (e.g., Wilber, 1980).

My research has provided empirical evidence for the existence of most of the experiences included in Wilber's developmental scheme. It has also shown that the descriptions in ancient spiritual sources that Wilber draws on are still highly relevant for modern humanity. However, because the examples that Wilber used for various levels of psychospiritual development are rather scanty and incomplete, incorporating the observations from my research of holotropic states into his scheme requires some important additions and adjustments.

Wilber's (1980) scheme of the post-centauric spiritual domain includes the lower and higher subtle level, lower and higher causal level, and the level of the Ultimate or Absolute. According to him, the *low subtle,* or *astral-psychic, level of consciousness* is characterized by a degree of differentiation of consciousness from the mind and body which exceeds that achieved on the centaur level. The astral level, in Wilber's (1980) own words, "includes, basically, out-of-body experiences, certain occult knowledge, the auras, true magic, 'astral travel,' and so on" (p. 67). Wilber's description of the psychic level included various psi phenomena: ESP, precognition, clairvoyance, psychokinesis, and others. He also referred here to Patanjali's Sutras that include on the subtle level all the paranormal powers, mind-over-matter phenomena, or *siddhis* (Patanjali, 1990). In the *higher subtle realm,* consciousness differentiates itself completely from the ordinary mind and becomes what can be called the "overself" or "overmind" (Wilber, 1980, p. 68) In this domain, Wilber placed high religious intuition and inspiration, visions of divine light, audible illuminations, and higher presences—spiritual guides, angelic beings, ishtadevas, Dhyani-Buddhas, and God archetypes, which he saw as high archetypal forms of the human being.

Like the subtle level, the causal level can be subdivided into lower and higher. Wilber pointed out that the *lower causal realm* is manifested in a state of consciousness known as *savikalpa samadhi,* the experience of final God, the ground, essence, and source of all the archetypal and lesser-god manifestations encountered in the subtle realms. The *higher causal realm* then involves a "total and utter transcendence and release into Formless Consciousness, Boundless Radiance" (Wilber, 1980, p. 72) In this context Wilber referred to *nirvikalpa samadhi* of Hinduism, *nirodh* of Hinayana Buddhism, and to the eighth of the ten ox-herding pictures of Zen Buddhism.

On Wilber's last level, that of the *Absolute,* Consciousness awakens as its Original Condition and Suchness (*tathagata*), which is, at the same time, all that is, gross, subtle, or causal. The distinction between the witness and the witnessed disappears and the entire World Process then arises, moment to moment as one's own Being, outside of which and prior to which nothing exists.

In a hierarchical classification based on my own data, I would include in the low subtle or astral-psychic level experiences that involve elements of the material world, but provide information in a way that is radically different from everyday perception. Here belong, above all, experiences that are traditionally studied by parapsychologists (and some also by thanatologists and therapists), such as out-of-body experiences, astral travel, extrasensory perception phenomena, precognition, and clairvoyance. I would also add experiences of phenomena that are closely connected to material reality, but reveal aspects or dimensions that are not accessible to ordinary consciousness—the subtle or energy body, its conduits (*nadis* or *meridians*), fields (*auras*), and centers (*chakras*). Particularly relevant in this context is the concept of *crosspoints,* bridges between the visible and invisible reality, found in Tantric literature (Mookerjee & Khanna, 1977).

I would also include on the low subtle level some important transpersonal experiences that occur in my cartography but are not mentioned by Wilber. Here belong experiential identification with various aspects of space-time—other people, animals, plants, and inorganic materials and processes, as well as ancestral, racial, collective, phylogenetic, and karmic experiences. I have shown in my previous publications that all these experiences mediated by extrasensory channels provide access to accurate new information about the phenomena involved (Grof, 1975, 1985, 1987, 2000).

I would also add from my own classification a category of experiences that I call *psychoid,* using the term coined by Hans Driesch and adopted by C. G. Jung (Addison, 2009). This group includes situations in which intrapsychic experiences are associated with corresponding changes in the external world (or better in consensus reality). Psychoid experiences cover a wide range from Jung's (1972a) synchronicities and ceremonial magic to psychokinesis and other mind-over-matter phenomena, or *siddhis* (Grof, 1987) that Patanjali assigned to the subtle level of consciousness.

The categories of my map of transpersonal experiences that could be assigned to the high subtle level include visions of divine light and epiphany, encounters with various blissful and wrathful archetypal figures, communication with spirit guides and superhuman entities, contact with shamanic power animals, direct apprehension of universal symbols, and episodes of religious and creative inspiration (the "Promethean epiphany"; Grof, 2000, p. 67). The visions of archetypal beings or experiential identification with them can portray them in their universal form (e.g., the Great Mother Goddess) or in the form of their specific cultural manifestations (e.g. Virgin Mary, Isis, Cybele, Parvati, etc.).

Over the years, I have been privileged to be present in psychedelic and Holotropic Breathwork sessions of people having experiences from the lower and higher causal realms and possibly even those of the Absolute. I have also had personal experiences that I believe qualify for these categories. In my classification these episodes are described under such titles as experiences of the Demiurg, Cosmic Consciousness, Absolute Consciousness, or Supracosmic and Metacosmic Void.

The existence and nature of transpersonal experiences violate some of the most basic assumptions of materialistic science. They imply such seemingly absurd notions as relativity and the arbitrary nature of all physical boundaries, nonlocal connections in the universe, communication through unknown means and channels, memory without a material substrate, the nonlinearity of time, or consciousness associated with all living organisms, and even inorganic matter. Many transpersonal experiences involve events from both the microcosm and the macrocosm, realms that cannot normally be reached by unaided human senses, or from historical periods that precede the origin of the solar system, formation of planet earth, appearance of living organisms, development of the nervous system, and emergence of *Homo sapiens*.

Mainstream academicians and physicians adhering to the monistic materialistic worldview have no other choice but to deny the existence and authenticity of transpersonal experiences or relegate them to the category of anomalous phenomena. However, serious attempts have been made to provide for them a scientific conceptual framework and integrate them into a revolutionary new worldview. In an intellectual *tour de force* and a series of books, the world's foremost system theorist, interdisciplinary scientist, and philosopher, Ervin Laszlo (1993, 1999, 2003, 2004a, 2004b), has explored a wide range of disciplines, including astrophysics, quantum-relativistic physics, biology, and transpersonal psychology. He pointed out a wide range of phenomena, paradoxical observations, and paradigmatic challenges, for which these disciplines have no explanations. Drawing on revolutionary advances of 20th century's science, he offered a brilliant solution to the anomalies and paradoxes that currently plague many of its fields. Laszlo achieved this by formulating his *connectivity hypothesis,* which has as its main cornerstone the existence of what he called the *psi-field* and, more recently, renamed to the *Akashic field* (Laszlo, 2003, 2004b).

Laszlo has described it as a subquantum field that is the source of all creation and holds a holographic record of all the events that have happened in the phenomenal world. He equated this field with the concept of *quantum vacuum* (or better *quantum plenum*) that has emerged from modern physics (Laszlo, 2003, 2004b). Laszlo's connectivity hypothesis provides a scientific explanation for otherwise mysterious transpersonal experiences, such as experiential identification with other people and with representatives of other species, group consciousness, possibility of experiencing episodes from other historical periods and countries including past life experiences, telepathy, remote viewing, and other psychic abilities, out-of-body experiences, astral projection, the experience of the Supracosmic and Metacosmic Void, and others.

An alternative conceptual framework that can account for many of the baffling properties of transpersonal experiences is the process philosophy of the English mathematician, logician, and philosopher, Alfred North Whitehead (e.g., 1978). Whitehead's metaphysical system is of particular interest because it does not grant fundamental metaphysical status to matter but places central focus on experience or mind. According to process philosophy, the basic element of which the universe is made is not an enduring substance, but a moment of experience, called in his terminology *actual occasion*. The universe is composed of countless discontinuous bursts of experiential activity on all the levels of reality, from subatomic particles to human souls. The relevance of Whitehead's philosophy for transpersonal psychology and consciousness research has been explored in the writings of John Buchanan (1979, 2001, 2002, 2005), David Ray Griffin (1989, 1996), John Quiring (1996), Leonard Gibson (1998, 2006, 2010), and Grant Maxwell (2011).

Having spent more than half a century studying holotropic states of consciousness, I have no doubt that there exist transpersonal experiences which are ontologically real and are not products of metaphysical speculation, human imagination, or pathological processes in the brain. By the term ontologically real, I refer to a category of experiences that not only possess the subjective sense of reality, but whose contents also seem to reveal something of the nature or essential qualities of being or existence. It would be erroneous to dismiss all transpersonal experiences as products of fantasy, primitive superstition, or manifestations of mental disease, as has so frequently been done.

Anybody attempting to do that would have to offer a plausible explanation why these experiences have in the past been described so consistently by people of various races, cultures, and historical periods. He or she would also have to account for the fact that these experiences continue to emerge in modern populations under such diverse circumstances as sessions with various psychedelic substances, during experiential psychotherapy, in meditation of people involved in systematic spiritual practice, in near-death experiences, and in the course of spontaneous episodes of psychospiritual crisis. Detailed discussion of the transpersonal domain, including descriptions and examples of various types of transpersonal experiences can be found in my various publications (e.g., Grof, 1975, 1987, 2000).

In view of this vastly expanded model of the psyche, one could now paraphrase Freud's simile of the psyche as an iceberg by saying that everything Freudian analysis has discovered about the psyche represents just the tip of the iceberg showing above the water. Research of holotropic states has made it possible to discover and explore the vast submerged portion of the iceberg, which has escaped the attention of Freud and his followers, with the exception of the remarkable renegades Otto Rank and C. G. Jung. Mythologist Joseph Campbell, known for his incisive Irish humor, used a different metaphor: "Freud was fishing while sitting on a whale" (Tarnas, 1991, p. 423).

3 The Nature, Function, and Architecture of Emotional and Psychosomatic Disorders

To explain various emotional and psychosomatic disorders that do not have an organic basis (psychogenic psychopathology), traditional psychiatrists use a superficial model of the psyche limited to postnatal biography and the individual unconscious. This model suggests that these conditions originate in infancy and childhood as a result of various emotional traumas and interpersonal dynamics in the family of origin.

There seems to be general agreement among schools of dynamic psychotherapy that the depth and seriousness of these disorders depend on the timing of the original traumatization.

Thus, according to classical psychoanalysis, the origin of alcoholism, narcotic drug addiction, and manic-depressive disorders can be found in the oral period of libidinal development; obsessive-compulsive neurosis has its roots in the anal stage; phobias and conversion hysteria result from traumas incurred in the phallic phase and at the time of the Oedipus and Electra complex; and so on (Fenichel, 1945). Later developments in psychoanalysis linked some very deep disorders—autistic and symbiotic infantile psychoses, narcissistic personality, and borderline personality disorders—to disturbances in the early development of object relations (Blanck & Blanck, 1974, 1979). As I mentioned earlier, this does not apply to Rankian and Jungian therapists who understand that the roots of emotional disorders reach deeper into the psyche.

The above conclusions have been drawn from observations of therapists who use primarily verbal means. The understanding of psychogenic disorders changes radically if one employs methods that involve holotropic states of consciousness that engage levels of the unconscious generally inaccessible to verbal therapy. Initial stages of this work typically uncover relevant traumatic material from early infancy and childhood that is meaningfully related to emotional and psychosomatic problems and appears to be their source. However, when the process of uncovering continues, deeper layers of the unconscious unfold and additional roots of the same problems are found on the perinatal level and on the transpersonal level of the psyche.

Various ways of working with holotropic states—such as psychedelic therapy, Holotropic Breathwork, rebirthing, and primal therapy, or psychotherapy with people experiencing spontaneous psychospiritual crises—have shown that emotional and psychosomatic problems cannot be adequately explained as originating exclusively in postnatal psychotraumatic events. In my experience, the unconscious material associated with them typically forms multilevel dynamic constellations for which I have coined the term *systems of condensed experience* or *COEX systems* (Grof, 1975, 2000).

A typical COEX system consists of many layers of unconscious material that share similar emotions or physical sensations; the contributions to a COEX system come from different levels of the psyche. The more superficial and accessible layers contain memories of emotional or physical traumas from infancy, childhood, and later life. On a deeper level, each COEX system is typically connected to a certain aspect of the memory of birth—a specific BPM; the choice of this matrix depends on the nature of the emotional and physical feelings involved. For example, if the theme of the COEX system is victimization, this would be BPM II; if it is fight against a powerful adversary or sexual abuse, the connection would be to BPM III. For a positive COEX comprising memories of deeply satisfying and fulfilling situations it would be BPM I or BPM IV, and so on.

The deepest roots of COEX systems underlying emotional and psychosomatic disorders reach into the transpersonal domain of the psyche. They have the form of ancestral, racial, collective, and phylogenetic memories, experiences that seem to be coming from other lifetimes (*"past life memories"*; Grof, 2000, p. 238), and various archetypal motifs. Thus, for example, therapeutic work on anger and disposition to violence can, at a certain point, take the form of experiential identification with a tiger or a black panther. Or the deepest root of serious antisocial behavior can be a demonic archetype, while the final resolution of a phobia can come in the form of reliving and integrating of a past life experience, and so on.

The overall architecture of the COEX systems can best be shown with a clinical example. A person suffering from psychogenic asthma might discover in serial breath-work sessions a powerful COEX system underlying this disorder. The biographical part of this constellation might consist of a memory of near drowning at the age of seven, memories of being repeatedly strangled by an older brother between the ages of three and four, and a memory of severe choking during whooping cough or diphtheria at the age of two. The perinatal contribution to this COEX might be, for example, suffocation experienced during birth because of strangulation by the umbilical cord twisted around the neck. A typical transpersonal root of this breathing disorder might be an experience of being hanged or strangled in what seems to be a previous lifetime. Detailed discussion of COEX systems and their role in various forms of psychopathology, including additional examples, are available in several earlier of my publications (Grof, 1975, 1987, 2000).

4 Effective Therapeutic Mechanisms

Traditional psychotherapy recognizes only therapeutic mechanisms that operate on the level of the biographical material, such as weakening of the psychological defense mechanisms, remembering forgotten or repressed traumatic events, reconstructing the past from dreams or neurotic symptoms, attaining intellectual and emotional insights, analyzing of transference, and obtaining corrective experience in interpersonal relations. Psychotherapy involving holotropic states of consciousness offers many additional highly effective mechanisms of healing and personality transformation that become available when experiential regression reaches the perinatal and transpersonal levels. Such mechanisms include actual reliving of traumatic memories from infancy, childhood, biological birth, and prenatal life; past life memories; emergence of archetypal material; experiences of cosmic unity; and others.

I will illustrate this therapeutic dynamics by the story of a participant in one of the workshops facilitated by my wife and I at Esalen Institute in Big Sur, California, whom I will call Norbert. At the beginning of the workshop, Norbert complained about severe chronic pain in his left shoulder and pectoral muscle that had caused him great suffering and made his life miserable. Repeated medical examinations, including X-rays, had not detected any organic basis for his problem and all therapeutic attempts had remained unsuccessful. Serial Procaine injections had brought only brief transient relief for the duration of the pharmacological effect of the drug.

Norbert's breathwork session was long and very dramatic. In the sharing group following it, he described that there were three different layers in his experience, all of them related to the pain in his shoulder and associated with choking. On the most superficial level, he relived a frightening situation from his childhood in which he almost lost his life. When he was about seven years old, he and his friends were digging a tunnel on a sandy ocean beach. When the tunnel was finished, Norbert crawled inside to explore it. As the other children jumped around, the tunnel collapsed and buried him alive. He almost choked to death before he was rescued by the adults who arrived responding to the children's alarming screams.

When the breathwork experience deepened, Norbert relived a violent and terrifying episode that took him back to the memory of his biological birth. His delivery was very difficult, because his shoulder was stuck for an extended period of time behind the pubic bone of his mother. This episode shared with the previous one the combination of choking and severe pain in the left shoulder.

In the last part of the session, the experience changed dramatically. Norbert started seeing military uniforms and horses and recognized that he was involved in a fierce battle. He was even able to identify it as one of the battles in Cromwell's England. At one point, he felt a sharp pain in his left shoulder and realized that it had been pierced by a lance. He fell off the horse and experienced himself as being trampled by the other horses running over his body and crushing his chest. His broken rib cage caused him agonizing pain, and he was choking on blood, which was filling his lungs.

After a period of extreme suffering, Norbert's consciousness separated from his dying body, soared high above the battlefield, and observed the scene from a bird's eye view. Following the death of the severely wounded soldier, whom he recognized as himself in a previous incarnation, Norbert's consciousness returned to the present time and reconnected with his body, which was now pain-free for the first time after many years of agony. The relief from pain brought about by these experiences turned out to be permanent.

5 Strategy of Psychotherapy and Self-Exploration

The most astonishing aspect of modern psychotherapy is the number of competing schools with vast differences of opinion and lack of agreement concerning the most fundamental issues. What are the dimensions of the human psyche and what are its most important motivating forces? Why do symptoms develop and what do they mean? Which issues that the client brings into therapy are central and which are less relevant? What techniques and strategies should be used to correct or improve the emotional, psychosomatic, and interpersonal functioning of the clients? There are as many answers to these questions as there are schools.

The goal of traditional dynamic psychotherapies is to reach intellectual understanding of the human psyche, in general, and that of a specific client, in particular, and then use this knowledge to develop an effective therapeutic technique and strategy. An important tool in many modern psychotherapies is "interpretation," by which the therapist reveals to the client the "true" or "real" meaning of his or her thoughts, emotions, and behavior. This method is widely used in analyzing dreams, neurotic symptoms, behavior, and even seemingly trivial everyday actions, such as slips of the tongue or other small errors, Freud's (1914/1960) "Fehlleistungen." Another area in which interpretations are commonly applied is interpersonal dynamics, including transference of various unconscious feelings and attitudes on the therapist.

Therapists spend much effort trying to determine what is the most fitting interpretation in a given situation and what is the appropriate timing of this interpretation. Even an interpretation that is "correct" in terms of its content can allegedly be useless or harmful for the patient if it is offered prematurely, before the client is ready for it. A serious flaw of this approach to psychotherapy is that individual therapists, especially those who belong to diverse schools, attribute very different value to the same psychological content or behavior and offer for it diverse and even contradictory interpretations. I will illustrated this by a humorous example from my own psychoanalytic training.

As a beginning psychiatrist, I was in training analysis that involved three sessions a week for a period of over seven years; my analyst was the Nestor of Czechoslovakian psychoananalysis and president of the Czechoslovakian Psychoanalytic Association, Dr. Theodor Dosužkov. At the time of my analysis, Dr. Dosužkov was in his late 60s and it was known among his analysands—all young psychiatrists—that he had a tendency to doze-off occasionally during analytic hours. Dr.Dosužkov's habit was a favorite target of his students' jokes.

In addition to individual psychoanalytic training sessions, Dr. Dosužkov also conducted seminars in which his students shared reviews of books and articles, discussed case histories, and could ask questions about the theory and practice of psychoanalysis. In one of these seminars, a participant asked a "purely theoretical" question: "What happens if during analysis the psychoanalyst falls asleep? If the client continues free-associating, does therapy continue? Is the process interrupted? Should the client get refunded for that time, because money is such an important vehicle in Freudian analysis?"

Dr. Dosužkov could not deny that such a situation could occur in psychoanalytic sessions. He was aware that the analysands knew about his foible and he had to come up with an answer. "This can happen," he said. "Sometimes, you are tired and sleepy—you did not sleep well the night before, you are recovering from a flu, or are physically exhausted. But if you have been in this business a long time, you develop a kind of "sixth sense"; you fall asleep only when the stuff that is coming up is irrelevant. When the client says something really important, you wake up and you are right there!"

Dr. Dosužkov was also a great admirer of I. P. Pavlov, a Russian Nobel Prize-winning physiologist who derived his knowledge of the brain from his experiments with dogs. Pavlov wrote much about the inhibition of the cerebral cortex that occurs during sleep or hypnosis; he noted that occasionally there could be a "waking point" in the inhibited brain cortex. His favorite example was a mother who can sleep through heavy noises, but awakens immediately when her own child is moaning. "It is just like the situation of the mother Pavlov wrote about," explained Dr. Dosužkov, "with enough experience, you will be able to maintain connection with your client even when you fall asleep."

But Dr. Dosužkov's explanation was clearly flawed. What a therapist considers relevant in the client's narrative reflects his or her training and personal bias. If I had been working with an Adlerian, Rankian, or Jungian therapist instead of a Freudian one, they would have awakened at different times of the session—each at the moment when my narrative would bring something that, according to their training and judgment, was "relevant."

Because of the great conceptual differences between the schools of depth psychology, the question naturally arises as to which ones offer a more correct understanding of the human psyche in health and disease. If it were true that correct and properly timed interpretations are a significant factor in psychotherapy, one would expect to find great differences in the therapeutic success achieved by various schools. Their therapeutic results could be mapped on a Gaussian curve; therapists of the school with the most accurate understanding of the psyche and, therefore, most fitting interpretations would have the best results, while those belonging to orientations with less accurate conceptual frameworks would be distributed on the descending parts of the curve.

I do not know of any scientific studies that show clear superiority of some schools of psychotherapy over others, as measured by outcomes (Frank & Frank, 1991). If anything, the differences are found within the schools rather than between them—and such differences result from variations in the skills of the therapists within any given school. In each school there are better therapists and worse therapists. Also, very likely, the therapeutic results have very little to do with what the therapists think they are doing, such as the accuracy and good timing of interpretations, correct analysis of transference, tactical use of silence, and other specific interventions. Successful therapy probably depends on factors that are unrelated to intellectual brilliance and are difficult to describe in scientific language—the "quality of the human encounter" between therapists and clients, the feeling of the clients that they are unconditionally accepted by another human being, frequently for the first time in their life, or the hope that the client feels during the therapeutic process.

Given this disconcerting lack of agreement on the theory and practice of psychotherapy, a client with an emotional or psychosomatic disorder might just as well choose a psychotherapeutic school by flipping a coin. With each school comes a different explanation of the problem he or she brought into therapy and a different technique is offered as the method of choice to overcome it. Similarly, when a beginning therapist seeking training chooses a particular therapeutic school, that choice says more about the personality of the applicant than the value of the school.

The problem with many of the psychotherapeutic schools is that they correctly describe the dynamics on a certain level of the psyche but lack the understanding of the phenomena from other levels and try to interpret them in terms of their own limited conceptual framework. For example, Freud's system was limited to postnatal biography and the individual unconscious. He was not aware of the paramount importance of birth, except for a short period when he thought birth anxiety might be the template for all future anxieties (Freud, 1959). Freud also did not accept the existence of the collective unconscious and tried to interpret archetypal/mythological and parapsychological phenomena in terms of his narrow biological/biographical model. Otto Rank, who discovered the psychological importance of the trauma of birth, offered explanations of mythological and spiritual/religious motifs that described them as derivatives of perinatal dynamics. C. G. Jung, who discovered and described the vast domains of the historical and archetypal collective unconscious, was unable to see the psychological importance of the birth trauma. In an interview with Dr. Richard I. Evans, he laughingly dismissed Otto Rank's theory: "Oh, birth is not a trauma, it is a fact; everybody is born" (Segaller, 1957).

An effective psychotherapeutic system has to recognize and respect all levels of the psyche. The content that is explored and processed, as it unfolds from session to session, is determined by the client's own psychological process and unconscious dynamics. The therapist must have a broad enough conceptual framework to be able to accompany clients to any level of their unconscious psyche—biographical, perinatal, and/or transpersonal and support their respective experiences (Vaughan, 1993).

Therapy using the healing potential of holotropic states of consciousness can help to avoid the problem that plagues verbal techniques of psychotherapy: to determinine what in the client's narrative is relevant and choose the "correct" interpretation. The alternative that this approach offers actually confirms some ideas about the therapeutic process first outlined by C. G. Jung. According to Jung (1966), it is impossible to derive an effective psychotherapeutic technique from a purely intellectual understand-ing of the psyche. Jung realized in his later years that the psyche is not a product of the brain and is not contained in the skull. He started seeing it as the creative and generative principle of the cosmos (*anima mundi*) that permeates all of existence; the individual psyche of each individual is teased out of this unfathomable cosmic matrix. The boundaries between the anima mundi and the individual psyche are not absolute; they are permeable and can be transcended in holotropic states. The intellect is a partial function of the psyche that can help a person orient themselves in everyday situations; however, in and of itself, it is incapable to fathom the deepest mysteris of existence and comprehend and manipulate the psyche.

Victor Hugo (1863) said it beautifully in Les Misérables: "*There is one spectacle grander than the sea, that is the sky; there is one spectacle grander than the heavens; that is the interior of the soul*" (p. 127, emphasis added). Jung was aware of the fact that the psyche is a profound mystery and approached it with great respect. It was clear to him that the psyche is infinitely creative and cannot be described by a set of formulas that can then be used to correct the psychological processes of the clients. He suggested an alternative strategy for therapy that was significantly different from using intellectual constructs and external interventions.

What a psychotherapist can do, according to Jung, is to create a supportive envi-ronment, in which psychospiritual transformation can occur. This container can be compared to the hermetic vessel that makes alchemical processes possible. The next step then is to offer a method that mediates contact between the conscious ego and a higher aspect of the client, the Self. One of Jung's tools for this purpose was *active imagination,* involving continuation of a dream on the analyst's couch and its anal-ysis *in statu nascendi* (in the state of being born; cf. von Franz, 1997), rather than retrospective analysis of the dream from memory. This was different from Freud's interpretation of dreams from memories, sometimes months or even years old. The communication between the ego and the Self occurs primarily by means of symbolic language. In Jung's own words, active imagination is a process of consciously dialogu-ing with the unconscious *"for the production of those contents of the unconscious which lie, as it were, immediately below the threshold of consciousness and, when intensified, are the most likely to irrupt spontaneously into the conscious mind"* (Jung, 1972b, p. 68, emphasis supplied). In this kind of work, healing is not the result of brilliant insights and interpretations of the therapist; rather, the therapeutic process is guided from within the client's psyche.

In Jung's understanding, the Self is the central archetype in the collective uncon-scious and its function is to lead the individual toward order, organization, and whole-ness. Jung referred to this movement toward highest unity as the *individuation process.* The use of holotropic states for therapy and self-exploration essentially confirms Jung's perspective and follows the same strategy. The facilitators create a protective and sup-portive environment and help the clients enter a holotropic state. Once that occurs, the healing process is guided from within by the clients' own inner healing intelligence and the task of the facilitators is to support what is happening. This process automati-cally activates unconscious material with strong emotional charge that is close enough to consciousness to be available for processing on the day of the session.

In holotropic states, the psyche and the body manifest their capacity to function together as an integral self-organizing and self-healing system. The therapists and facilitators are thus spared the hopeless task of trying to determine what in the client's process is "relevant" and what is merely tangential. They simply support whatever is spontaneously emergting from moment to moment, trusting that the process is guided from within the client by an intelligence surpassing the intellectual under-standing which can be obtained by professional training in any of the schools of psychotherapy. Clients and participants in workshops and training might be using terms like COEX systems, BPMs, archetypes, and so on, but this will reflect their direct experiential engagement with whatever has spontaneously arisen and not be offered as interpretation by facilitators.

6 The Role of Spirituality in Human Life

The leading philosophy of Western science has been monistic materialism. Various scientific disciplines have described the history of the universe as the history of devel-oping matter and they accept as real only what can be measured and weighed. Life, consciousness, and intelligence are then seen as more or less accidental side-products of material processes. Physicists, biologists, and chemists recognize the existence of dimensions of reality that are not accessible to the senses—but only those that are physical in nature and can be revealed and explored by using various extensions of our senses, such as microscopes, telescopes, and specially designed recording devices, or laboratory experiments.

This kind of universe has no place for spirituality of any kind. The existence of God, the concept of invisible dimensions of reality inhabited by nonmaterial beings, the possibility of survival of consciousness after death, and the concept of reincarnation and karma are relegated to fairy tale books and handbooks of psychopathology. From a psychiatric perspective taking such phenomena seriously implies ignorance, unfamil-iarity with the discoveries of materialistic science, superstition, and primitive magical thinking. If intelligent persons believe in God or Goddess, they simply have not freed themselves from the infantile images of their parents as omnipotent beings and project them into Heaven or the Beyond. Direct experiences of spiritual realities, including encounters with mythological beings and visits to archetypal realms, are considered manifestations of serious mental diseases—psychoses.

Study of holotropic states has thrown new light on the problem of spirituality and religion. Key to this new understanding is the discovery that in these states it is pos-sible to encounter a rich array of experiences very similar to those that inspired the great religions of the world—visions of God and various divine and demonic beings, encounters with discarnate entities, episodes of psychospiritual death and rebirth, visits to Heaven and Hell, past life experiences, and many others. Modern research has shown beyond any doubt that these experiences are not products of fantasy or pathological processes afflicting the brain, but manifestations of archetypal material from the collective unconscious, and thus germane and essential constituents of the human psyche. Although these mythic elements are accessed intrapsychically in a process of experiential self-exploration and introspection, they are ontologically real, have objective existence. To distinguish transpersonal experiences from imaginary products of individual human fantasy or psychopathology, Jungians refer to this domain as *imaginal*.

French scholar, philosopher, and mystic, Henri Corbin (2000), who first used the term *mundus imaginalis*, was inspired to adopt this concept by his study of Islamic mystical literature. Islamic theosophers call the imaginal world—where everything existing in the sensory world has its analogue—*'alam a mithal*,' or the "eighth climate," to distinguish it from the "seven climates," or regions of traditional Islamic geography. The imaginal world possesses extension and dimensions, forms and colors, but these are not perceptible to the senses as they would be if they were properties of physical objects. But this realm is in every respect as fully ontologically real as the material world perceived by sensory organs and experiences of it can be verified by consensual validation by other people. The ontological reality of transpersonal experiences and events is also supported by theories that recognize and emphasize their participatory nature (Ferrer, 2002; Tarnas, 1991, 2006).

In view of these observations, the fierce battle that religion and science have fought over the last several centuries now appears ludicrous and completely unnecessary. Genuine science and authentic religion do not compete for the same territory; they represent two approaches to existence which are complementary, not competitive. Science studies phenomena in the material world, the realm of the measurable and weighable, whereas genuine spirituality and true religion draw their inspiration from experiential knowledge of the imaginal world as it manifests in holotropic states of consciousness. The conflict that seems to exist between religion and science reflects fundamental misunderstanding of both. As Ken Wilber has pointed out, there cannot possibly be a conflict between science and religion, if both of these fields are properly understood and practiced. If conflict seems to occur, one is likely dealing with "bogus science" and "bogus religion" (Wilber, 1999, p. 170). The apparent incompatibility is due to the fact that either side seriously misunderstands the other's position and very likely represents also a dubious version of its own discipline.

The only scientific endeavor capable of making any relevant and valid judgments about spiritual matters is consciousness research studying holotropic states, because truly informed opinion in this regard requires intimate knowledge of the imaginal realm. In his ground-breaking essay, *Heaven and Hell*, Aldous Huxley (1959) suggested that such concepts as Hell and Heaven represent intrapsychic realities experienced in a very convincing way during non-ordinary states of consciousness induced by psychedelic substances, such as LSD and mescaline, or various powerful non-drug techniques. The seeming conflict between science and religion is based on the erroneous belief that these abodes of the Beyond are located in the physical universe— Heaven in the interstellar space, Paradise somewhere in a hidden area on the surface of our planet, and Hell in the interior of the earth.

Astronomers have created and used extremely sophisticated devices, such as the Hubble Space Telescope, to explore carefully and map the entire vault of heaven. Results of these efforts, which have of course failed to find God and heaven replete with harp-playing angels and saints, have been taken as proof that such spiritual realities do not exist. Similarly, in cataloguing and mapping every acre of the planetary surface, explorers and geographers have found many areas of extraordinary natural beauty, but none of them matched the descriptions of Paradise found in the spiritual scriptures of various religions. Geologists have discovered that the core of the planet consists of layers of solid and molten nickel and iron and that its temperature exceeds that of the sun's surface—hardly a very plausible location for the caves of Satan.

Meanwhile, modern studies of holotropic states have brought strong supportive evidence for Huxley's insights. They have shown that Heaven, Paradise, and Hell are ontologically real and represent distinct and important states of consciousness that all human beings can under certain circumstances experience. Celestial, paradisean, and infernal visions are inherent aspects of the experiential spectrum of psychedelic inner journeys, near-death states, mystical experiences, as well as shamanic initiatory crises and other types of spiritual emergencies. Patients often tell their psychiatrists about experiences of God, Heaven, Hell, archetypal divine and demonic beings, and about psychospiritual death and rebirth. However, because of their inadequate super-ficial model of the psyche, psychiatrists dismiss these experiences as manifestations of mental disease caused by pathological processes of unknown etiology. They do not realize that matrices for these experiences exist in deep recesses of the collective unconscious psyche.

An astonishing aspect of transpersonal experiences occurring in holotropic states of various kinds is that their content can be drawn from the mythologies of any culture of the world, including those of which the individual has no intellectual knowledge. C. G. Jung (1967, 1968) discovered this extraordinary fact when he studied the mythological motifs occurring in the dreams and psychotic experiences of his patients. On the basis of his observations, he realized that the human psyche has access not only to the Freudian individual unconscious, but also to the collective unconscious, which is a repository of the entire cultural heritage of humanity. Knowledge of comparative mythology is thus more than a matter of personal interest or an academic exercise. It is a very important and useful guide for individuals involved in experiential therapy and self-exploration and an indispensable tool for those who support and accompany them on their journeys (Grof, 2006).

The experiences originating on deeper levels of the psyche, in the collective uncon-scious, have a certain quality that Jung referred to as *numinosity*. The word *numinous*—first used by Rudolf Otto—is relatively new and neutral and thus preferable to other similar expressions, such as religious, mystical, magical, holy, or sacred, which have often been used in problematic contexts and are easily misleading. The term numinosity applied to transpersonal experiences describes direct perception of their extraordinary nature which Otto (1917/1957) described with the terms "*mysterium tremendum*" (e.g., p. 12), "*fascinans*" (e.g., p. 52), and "*wholly other*" (e.g., p. 25)—something that cannot usually be experienced in everyday states of consciousness. They convey a very convincing sense that they belong to a higher order of reality, to a realm which is sacred.

In view of the ontological reality of the imaginal realm, spirituality is a very important and natural dimension of the human psyche and spiritual quest is a legitimate and fully justified human endeavor. It must be emphasized that this applies to genuine spirituality based on personal experience and does not provide support for ideologies and dogmas of organized religions. To prevent the misunderstanding and confusion that have compromised many similar discussions in the past, a clear distinction must be made between spirituality and religion.

Spirituality involves a special kind of relationship between the individual and the cosmos and is essentially a personal affair. By comparison, organized religion is institutionalized group activity that takes place in a designated location, a temple or a church, and involves a system of appointed officials who may or may not have had personal experiences of spiritual realities themselves. Once a religion becomes organized, it often loses the connection with its spiritual source and devolves into a secular institution that exploits human spiritual needs without satisfying them.

Organized religions tend to create hierarchical systems focusing on the pursuit of power, control, politics, money, possessions, and other worldly concerns. Under these circumstances, religious hierarchy tends to dislike and discourage direct spiritual experiences in its members, because they foster independence and cannot be effectively controlled. In such cases, genuine spiritual life continues only in the mystical branches, monastic orders, and ecstatic sects of the religions involved. People who have experiences of the immanent or transcendent divine open up to the spirituality found in the mystical branches of the great religions of the world or in their monastic orders, not necessarily in their mainstream organizations. A profound mystical experience tends to dissolve the boundaries between religions and reveals deep connections between them, while the dogmatism of organized religions tends to emphasize differences between various creeds and engender antagonism and hostility.

There is no doubt that the dogmas of organized religions—when interpreted literally—are generally in fundamental conflict with science, whether this science uses the mechanistic-materialistic model or is anchored in the emerging paradigm. However, the situation changes considerably when one examines authentic mysticism based on genuine spiritual experiences. The great mystical traditions have amassed extensive knowledge about human consciousness and about the spiritual realms in a manner that is similar to the critical approach used by scientists in acquiring knowledge about the material world. This includes methodologies for inducing transpersonal experiences, systematic collection of data, and intersubjective validation.

Like any other aspect of reality, spiritual experiences can be subjected to careful open-minded scientific research. Only such unbiased and rigorous study of transpersonal phenomena and of the challenges they present to materialistic understanding of the world can answer the critical question about the ontological status of mystical experiences: Can they reveal deep truth about some basic aspects of existence, as maintained by various systems of perennial philosophy and transpersonal psychology, or are they products of superstition, fantasy, or mental disease, as Western materialistic science sees them?

Mainstream psychiatry does not distinguish between a mystical experience and a psychotic experience and sees both as manifestations of mental disease. In its sweeping rejection of religion, psychiatry also does not differentiate primitive folk beliefs and the fundamentalist literal interpretations of religious scriptures from sophisticated mystical traditions or the great Eastern spiritual philosophies based on centuries of systematic introspective exploration of the psyche. Modern consciousness research has brought convincing evidence for the objective existence of the imaginal realm and has thus validated the main metaphysical assumptions of the mystical world view, the Eastern spiritual philosophies, and even certain beliefs of indigenous cultures.

7 The Importance of Archetypal Psychology and Transit Astrology

The greatest surprise I experienced during more than 50 years of consciousness research has been to discover the extraordinary predictive power of archetypal astrology. Because of my extensive scientific training, I was initially extremely skeptical about astrology. The idea that planets and stars could have anything to do with states of consciousness, let alone events in the world, seemed too absurd and preposterous to even consider. It took years and thousands of convincing observations for me to accept this possibility—a shift that required nothing less than a radical revision of my basic metaphysical assumptions about the nature of reality. Given the controversy that surrounds this issue, I would not have even discussed astrology in this presentation, had Richard Tarnas not published three remarkable books based on his meticulous ground-breaking research: *The Passion of the Western Mind* (Tarnas, 1991), *Prometheus the Awakener* (Tarnas, 1995), and *Cosmos and Psyche* (Tarnas, 2006).

Over the last 30 years, Rick and I have jointly explored astrological correlations of holotropic states. My main task has been to collect interesting clinical observations from psychedelic sessions, Holotropic Breathwork workshops and training, mystical experiences, spiritual emergencies, and psychotic breaks. Rick's main focus has been on astrological aspects of holotropic states of consciousness. This cooperation has yielded convincing evidence for systematic correlations between the nature, timing, and content of holotropic states of consciousness and planetary transits of the individuals involved.

The first indication that there might exist some extraordinary connections between astrology and my research of holotropic states was Rick's realization that my description of the phenomenology of the four basic perinatal matrices (BPMs), experiential patterns associated with the stages of biological birth, showed astonishing similarity to the four archetypes that astrologers link to the four outer planets of the solar system: BPM I to Neptune, BPM II to Saturn, BPM III to Pluto, and BPM IV to Uranus. It is important to emphasize that my description of the phenomenology of the BPMs was based on clinical observations made quite independently many years before I knew anything about astrology.

Even more astonishing was the discovery that in holotropic states the experiential confrontation with these matrices regularly occurs at the time when the individuals involved have important transits of the corresponding planets. Over the years, Rick and

I have been able to confirm this fact by thousands of specific observations and discover further astrological correlations for many other aspects of holotropic states. Because of these surprisingly precise correlations, astrology—particularly transit astrology—has turned out to be an invaluable instrument for consciousness research.

This is a vast and extremely important topic and I cannot do it justice in the context of this article. Interested readers will find more information in my two articles on holotropic states and archetypal astrology (Grof, 2009, in press), but adequate discussion of these remarkable findings will require a separate volume to be written by a professional astrologer. But I have seen enough evidence in the past 30 years to say at this point a few words concerning my present understanding of the relationship between the timing and nature of holotropic states, spontaneous or induced, and transit astrology.

It has been repeatedly seen that the experiences of the individuals who enter holotropic states of consciousness, seem to be attuned to and informed by the archetypal fields of the planets forming at the time of significant transits to their natal charts. This selectively activates the COEX system whose content has the corresponding archetypal qualities; this COEX then governs the inner experiences, as well as the perception of the external environment. The emerging unconscious material consists of biographical, perinatal, and transpersonal elements carrying these archetypal characteristics, often combined in very creative ways. The depth and intensity of this process depends on the power of the archetypal energies involved and on the number of previous experiences with holotropic states.

Although I understand that this brief summary will not have much impact on readers with no previous knowledge of astrology, I hope that it might inspire experienced astrologers to conduct their own research to verify or disprove these observations. There is currently an extraordinary renaissance of psychedelic research, with several major U.S. universities conducting new studies. Holotropic Breathwork workshops are available in many countries of the world, and spontaneous episodes of holotropic states abound. Those readers interested in verifying or disproving the conclusions made in this paper would thus have ample research material to work with.

In my opinion, archetypal astrology is the long-sought Rosetta stone of consciousness research. It provides a key for understanding the nature and content of present, past, and future holotropic states, both spontaneous and induced. However, it is important to emphasize that the astrological predictions, while extraordinarily accurate, are archetypically predictive and not concretely predictive. One of the striking properties of the archetypes exemplified by Richard Tarnas' pioneering research is their complex *multivalence*. Each archetype and archetypal combination has a rich spectrum of meanings, at the same time remaining true to its own specific nature. For example, although Saturn and Neptune each have a wide array of meanings, an experienced astrologer would never confuse any essential elements associated with one of these archetypes with those of the other.

The conceptual revisions outlined in this paper—based on my conclusions from more than 50 years of research—bring theoretical clarity to the world of depth psychology and help integrate the diverse positions of its competing schools. They also offer a radically different alternative to the confusing multiplicity of psychotherapeutic techniques employed by these schools, namely the self-healing and self-organizing intelligence of the client's psyche. When the paradigm shift currently occurring in Western science is successfully completed, responsible work with holotropic states incorporating archetypal astrology as a guide might emerge as one of the most promising trends in psychiatry, psychology, and psychotherapy.

When academic circles finally accept the basic tenets of transpersonal psychology, there will be no need for transpersonal psychology as a separate discipline. Because extrasensory access to new information can happen in connection with any category of transpersonal experiences, there will also be no need for parapsychology—a special discipline focusing on a small selection of phenomena in which ESP occurs, such as telepathy, clairvoyance, precognition, psychometry, or remote viewing. The psychology of the future would study the human psyche in its totality and with all its dimensions, infinitely larger than previously assumed and with more extraordinary capacities.

References

Addison, A. (2009). Jung, vitalism and "the psychoid": An historical reconstruction. *Journal of Analytical Psychology, 1*, 123-142.

Bateson, G. (1972). Form, substance and difference. In G. Bateson (Ed.), *Steps to an ecology of mind* (pp. 423-440). San Francisco, CA: Chandler.

Bateson, G., Jackson, D., Haley, J., & Weakland, J. (1956). Towards a theory of schizophrenia. *Behavioral Science, 1*, 251-264.

Blanck, G., & Blanck, R. (1974). *Ego psychology I: Theory and practice.* New York, NY: Columbia University Press.

Blanck, G., & Blanck, R. (1979). *Ego psychology II: Psychoanalytic developmental psychology.* New York, NY: Columbia University Press.

Buchanan, J. H. (1994). Universal feeling: Whitehead and psychology. *Dissertation Abstracts International, 55*(04), 0665b (UMI #9424802)

Buchanan, J. H. (2001). *Cosmic consciousness in a process cosmology.* Paper presented at the 86th Annual Congress of the International New Thought Alliance, Las Vegas, NV.

Buchanan, J. H. (2002). *Grof and Whitehead: Visions of a postmodern cosmology.* Atlanta, GA: Helios Foundation.

Buchanan, J. H. (2005, October). *Openness: Spirituality in a process psychology.* Paper presented at the Conference on Science and Spirituality, Wuhan, China.

Corbin, H. (2000). Mundus imaginalis, or the imaginary and the imaginal. In B. Sells (Ed.), *Working with images* (pp. 71-89). Woodstock, CT: Spring.

Covey, S. R. (2000). *Living the 7 habits: The courage to change.* New York, NY: Free Press.

Crick, F. (1995). *The astonishing hypothesis: The scientific search for the soul.* New York, NY: Scribner.

Fenichel, O. (1945). *The psychoanalytic theory of neurosis.* New York, NY: Norton.

Ferrer, J. (2002). *Revisioning transpersonal theory: A participatory vision of human spirituality.* Albany, NY: State University of New York Press.

Frank, J. D., & Frank, J. B. (1991). *Persuasion and healing: A comparative study of psychotherapy.* Baltimore, MD: Johns Hopkins University Press.

Freud, S. (1959). *Inhibitions, symptoms, and anxiety.* J. Strachey (Ed., & Trans.), *The standard edition of the complete psychological works of Sigmund Freud* (Vol. 20, pp. 75-175). London, UK: Hogart Press. (Original work published 1926)

Freud, S. (1960). *The psychopathology of everyday life*. Harmondsworth, UK: Penguin. (Original
    work published 1914)

Gibson, L. (1998, August). *Whitehead, LSD, and holotropic experience*. Paper presented at The
    Center for Process Studies, Claremont, California.

Gibson, L. (2006, July). *Holotropic breathwork as process psychotherapy*. Paper presented at the
    International Whitehead Conference, University of Salzburg, Austria.

Gibson, L. (2010). Whitehead and Grof: Resolving the ontological ambiguity of Jung's
    archetypes metaphysically and practically. *Tattva, Journal of Philosophy, 2*(1), 91-97.

Griffin, D. R. (1989). *Archetypal process: Self and divine in Whitehead, Jung, and Hillman*.
    Evanston, IL: Northwestern University Press.

Griffin, D. R. (1996, March). *Whitehead as a Transpersonal Philosopher*. Paper presented at the
    Transpersonal and Process Thought Conference, Esalen Institute, Big Sur, California.

Grof, C., & Grof, S. (1991). *The stormy search for the self: A guide to personal growth through
    transformational crises*. Los Angeles, CA: Jeremy P. Tarcher.

Grof, S. (1975). *Realms of the human unconscious: Observations from LSD research*. New York,
    NY: Viking Press. (Republished as *LSD: Doorway to the numinous*. Rochester, VT: Inner
    Traditions, 2009)

Grof, S. (1985). *Beyond the brain: Birth, death, and transcendence in psychotherapy*. Albany, NY:
    State University of New York Press.

Grof, S. (1987). *The adventure of self-discovery*. Albany, NY: State University of New York Press.

Grof, S. (1998). *The cosmic game: Explorations of the frontiers of human consciousness*. Albany,
    NY: State University of New York Press.

Grof, S. (2000). *Psychology of the future*. Albany, NY: State University of New York Press.

Grof, S. (2006). *When the impossible happens: Adventures in non-ordinary realities*. Louisville,
    CO: Sounds True.

Grof, S. (2009). Holotropic research and archetypal astrology. *Archai: The Journal of Archetypal
    Cosmology, 1*(1), 50-66.

Grof, S. (in press). An archetypal astrological analysis of holotropic states in psychedelic sessions
    and spiritual emergencies: Two case studies. *Archai: The Journal of Archetypal Cosmology*.

Grof, S., & Grof, C. (1989). *Spiritual emergency: When personal transformation becomes a crisis*.
    Los Angeles, CA: Jeremy P. Tarcher.

Hameroff, S. (1987). *Ultimate computing*. Amsterdam, The Netherlands: Elsevier.

Hugo, V. (1863). *Les misérables*. New York, NY: Carleton.

Huxley, A. (1959). *The doors of perception and heaven and hell*. Harmondsworth, UK: Penguin
    Books.

Jahn, R. G. (2001). 20th and 21st century science: Reflections and projections. *Journal of
    Scientific Exploration, 15*(1), 21-31.

Jung, C. G. (1966). *The practice of psychotherapy*. In *The collected works of C. G. Jung* (Vol. 16,
    2nd ed.). Princeton, NJ: Princeton University Press.

Jung, C. G. (1967). *Symbols of transformation*. In *The collected works of C. G. Jung* (Vol. 5; 2nd
    ed.). Princeton, NJ: Princeton University Press.

Jung, C. G. (1968). *The archetypes and the collective unconscious*. In *The collected works of C. G.
    Jung* (Vol. 9, Part 1; 2nd ed.). Princeton, NJ: Princeton University Press.

Jung, C. G. (1972a). Synchronicity: An acausal connecting principle. In *The structure and
    dynamics of the psyche* (pp. 417-420), *The collected works of C. G. Jung* (Vol. 8; 2nd ed.).
    Princeton, NJ: Princeton University Press.

Jung, C. G. (1972b). The transcendent function. In *The structure and dynamics of the psyche*
    (pp. 67-91), *The collected works of C. G. Jung* (Vol. 8; 2nd ed.). Princeton, NJ: Princeton
    University Press.

Kandel, E. R. (2001). The molecular biology of memory storage: A dialogue between genes and synapses. *Science, 294,* 1030-1038.

Kant, I. (1999). *Critique of pure reason.* Cambridge, MA: Cambridge University Press.

Kennell, J. H., & Klaus, M. (1998). Parental bonding: Recent observations that alter perinatal care. *Pediatrics in Review, 19*(4-12).

Klaus, M., Kennell, J. H., & Klaus, P. H. (1995). *Bonding: Building the foundations of secure attachment and independence.* Reading, MA: Addison Wesley.

Kuhn, T. (1962). *The structure of scientific revolutions.* Chicago, IL: University of Chicago Press.

Laszlo, E. (1993). *The creative cosmos.* Edinburgh, UK: Floris Books.

Laszlo, E. (1999). *The interconnected universe: Conceptual foundations of transdisciplinary unified theory.* Singapore, Republic of Singapore: World Scientific.

Laszlo, E. (2003). *The connectivity hypothesis: Foundations of an integral science of quantum, cosmos, life, and consciousness.* Albany, NY: State University of New York Press.

Laszlo, E. (2004a). Cosmic connectivity: Toward a scientific foundation for transpersonal consciousness. *International Journal of Transpersonal Studies, 23,* 21-31.

Laszlo, E. (2004b). *Science and the Akashic Field: An integral theory of everything.* Rochester, VT: Inner Traditions.

Maxwell, G. (2011). Archetype and eternal object: Jung, Whitehead, and the return of formal causation. *Archai: The Journal of Archetypal Cosmology, 3,* 51-71.

Mookerjee, A., & Khanna, M. (1977). *The tantric way.* London, UK: Thames & Hudson.

Otto, R. (1957). *The idea of the holy: An inquiry into the non-rational factor in the idea of the divine and its relation to the rational.* London, UK: Oxford University Press. (Original work published 1917)

Patanjali. (1990). *The yoga sutras of Patanjali* (C. Chapple & Yogi Ananda Viraj, Trans.). Delhi, India: Sri Satguru .

Quiring, J. (1996). Transpersonal psychology and process thought. *Process Perspectives, 20*(1), 6-7.

Ring, K., & Cooper, S. (1999). *Mindsight: Near-death and out-of-body experiences in the Blind.* Palo Alto, CA: William James Center for Consciousness Studies.

Ring, K., & Valarino, E. (1998). *Lessons from the light: What we can learn from the near-death experience.* New York, NY: Plenum Press.

Satir, V. (1983). *Conjoint family therapy.* Palo Alto, CA: Science & Behavior Books.

Segaller, S. (Director). (1957). *Jung on film* (An interview with Dr. Richard I. Evans, August 5-8, Zurich, Switzerland). Segaller Films.

Sullivan, H. S. (1953). *The interpersonal theory of psychiatry.* New York, NY: W. W. Norton.

Tarnas, R. (1991). *The passion of the Western mind: Understanding the ideas that have shaped our world view.* New York, NY: Ballantine.

Tarnas, R. (1995). *Prometheus the awakener: An essay on the archetypal meaning of the planet Uranus.* Woodstock, CT: Spring.

Tarnas, R. (2006). *Cosmos and psyche: Intimations of a new worldview.* New York, NY: Viking Press.

Tart, C. T. (1969). *Altered states of consciousness: A book of readings.* New York, NY: John Wiley & Sons.

Tomatis, A. A. (1991). *The conscious ear: My life of transformation through listening.* Barrytown, NY: Station Hill Press.

Vaughan, F. (1993). Healing and wholeness: Transpersonal psychotherapy. In R. Walsh & F. Vaughan (Eds.), *Paths beyond ego: The transpersonal vision* (pp. 160-165). Los Angeles, CA: Jeremy P. Tarcher.

von Franz, M.-L. (1997). *Alchemical active imagination*. New York, NY: C. G. Jung Foundation Books.

Watts, A. W. (1974). *Psychotherapy: East and West*. New York, NY: Ballantine Books. (Original work published 1961)

Whitehead, A. N. (1978). *Process and reality: An essay in cosmology* (Gifford Lectures delivered in the University of Edinburgh during the session 1927-1928, Corrected ed.). D. R.Griffin & D. W. Sherburne (Eds.). New York, NY: Free Press.

Whitwell, G. E. (1999). The importance of prenatal sound and music. *Journal of Prenatal and Perinatal Psychology and Health, 13*(3-4), 255-262.

Wilber, K. (1980). *The atman project*. Wheaton, IL: Theosophical.

Wilber, K. (1999). *The marriage of sense and soul: Integrating science and religion*. New York, NY: Broadway Books.

6

Altered States of Consciousness and Transpersonal Psychology

Albert P. Garcia-Romeu and Charles T. Tart

Given Western culture's wholesale rejection of altered states for so long, contemporary researchers of altered states of consciousness may feel like pioneers in an uncharted territory. However, for generations our human ancestors have journeyed to these realms even as scholars attempt to decipher and understand them today. Various aspects of altered states of consciousness have been studied in numerous fields including history, archaeology, cultural anthropology, religious studies, philosophy, psychology, and neuroscience, to name some of the most prominent. This chapter provides a survey of key highlights in altered states research to date, as the area is much too rich to examine in detail in the limited space allowed.

The review begins with a basic definition of major terms and concepts. Next, the historical roles of altered states of consciousness are presented, reaching back to ancient rites seemingly designed to induce altered states for the benefit of participants, such as the Eleusinian Mysteries in ancient Greece and various shamanic practices across cultures. Afterwards, the contributions of several 20th century thinkers are outlined. Trailblazing psychologists such as William James helped to build an initial framework for examining altered states of consciousness as early as 1902. Nevertheless, it was not until the 1960s that modern psychology began to consider the issue of consciousness and states of consciousness in earnest. Following along these lines, researchers such as Charles Tart and Stanislav Grof worked to create a place for the study of altered states and even advocate for the initiation of state-specific sciences and clinical interventions within modern-day psychological paradigms. Among the major contributions of these approaches was the inclusion of subjective first-person experience as admissible data for scientific inquiry.

Because those early days of altered states research, the use of modern computer technology and neuroimaging methods have allowed researchers to delve more deeply into the neural correlates of consciousness and altered states. These shifts have occasioned a renaissance of consciousness research, during which the study of altered states

The Wiley Blackwell Handbook of Transpersonal Psychology, First Edition.
Edited by Harris L. Friedman and Glenn Hartelius.

has branched out to include a wide variety of experiences ranging from hypnosis, trance, dreaming, and meditation, to mystical and transcendent experiences, intoxication through psychedelics or other substances, as well as out-of-body, near-death and other anomalous experiences. What might such diverse states have in common? Their main distinguishing feature is that they represent classes of experience in which subjects feel a marked *qualitative* distinction or alteration from their normal waking consciousness. This chapter will present the major multidisciplinary theories and findings regarding altered states of consciousness to date, and suggest possible directions for future research.

As a reminder of the intensity and power of altered states, before they are further analyzed, consider this account by Canadian physician Richard Maurice Bucke (1901/1969) occurring in 1872 and written in the third person to help maintain a sense of objectivity:

> It was in the early spring at the beginning of his thirty-sixth year. He and two friends had spent the evening reading Wordsworth, Shelley, Keats, Browning, and especially Whitman. They parted at midnight, and he had a long drive in a hansom (it was in an English city). His mind deeply under the influences of the ideas, images and emotions called up by the reading and talk of the evening, was calm and peaceful. He was in a state of quiet, almost passive enjoyment. All at once, without warning of any kind, he found himself wrapped around as it were by a flame colored cloud. For an instant he thought of fire, some sudden conflagration in the great city, the next he knew that the light was within himself. Directly afterwards came upon him a sense of exultation, of immense joyousness, accompanied or immediately followed by an intellectual illumination quite impossible to describe. Into his brain streamed one momentary lightning-flash of the Brahmic Splendor which has ever since lightened his life; upon his heart fell one drop of Brahmic Bliss, leaving thenceforward for always an after taste of heaven. Among other things he did not come to believe, he saw and knew that the Cosmos is not dead matter but a living Presence, that the soul of man is immortal, that the universe is so built and ordered that without any peradventure all things work together for the good of each and all, that the foundation principle of the world is what we call love and that the happiness of every one is in the long run absolutely certain. He claims that he learned more within the few seconds during which the illumination lasted than in previous months or even years of study, and that he learned much that no study could ever have taught . . . The illumination itself continued not more than a few moments, but its effects proved ineffaceable; it was impossible for him ever to forget what he at that time saw and knew, neither did he, or could he, ever doubt the truth of what was then presented to his mind. (pp. 9-10)

Experiences such as these are, in the eyes of many, the heart of transpersonal psychology, and it is therefore vital to understand, learn to produce, and control such transpersonal experiences, insofar as is possible.

Defining Key Terms

Consciousness

What is consciousness? The question has captivated philosophers, scientists, and countless other thinkers for thousands of years. Contemporary philosopher of mind David

Chalmers (1995) wrote, "Consciousness poses the most baffling problems in the science of the mind. There is nothing that we know more intimately than conscious experience, but there is nothing that is harder to explain" (p. 200). Taking this statement as a frame of reference, it is necessary to delineate carefully some of the main concepts underlying this chapter, namely consciousness, states of consciousness, and altered states of consciousness, before proceeding to examine some of the major multidisciplinary findings with respect to these topics.

Consciousness is itself a controversial term, so any definition would be tentative at best. Indeed, the act of defining is itself one small aspect of the totality of consciousness, so how can one ever expect the part to satisfactorily define the whole? However, for the purposes of this discussion, consciousness refers to the subjective awareness and experience of both internal and external phenomena. These phenomena may include but are not limited to: internal sensations, perceptions, thoughts, emotions, and the sense of self, as well as perception of all classes of external objects, events, and other stimuli. Part of the major problem in understanding and defining consciousness has been precisely how such a seemingly "external" object as a brain could possibly produce or experience subjective internal states. Such considerations lie outside the purview of this discussion. However, a number of authors have attempted to tackle the issue for interested readers (e.g., Baars, 1997; Blackmore, 2004; Chalmers, 1996; Combs, 2009; Dennett, 1991; Searle, 2004).

States of Consciousness and ASC

Moving forward, if consciousness refers to the subjective awareness and experience of internal and external phenomena, states of consciousness refer to the spectrum of ways in which experience may be organized. Tart (1975) defined a discrete state of consciousness as, "a unique, dynamic pattern or configuration of psychological structures" (p. 5). Classic examples of discrete states of consciousness include waking, dreaming, deep sleep, intoxication, hypnosis, and successfully induced meditative states, to name just a few. Working from this foundation, Tart suggested defining an "altered state" with respect to a "baseline state of consciousness" (p. 5), that being our ordinary waking state from which one conducts the majority of day-to-day affairs. This ordinary waking state is qualitatively distinct from dreaming, for instance, or from being under the influence of a significant amount of alcohol. Therefore, these alternate patterns or configurations of experience, which differ qualitatively from a typical baseline state, have been dubbed altered states of consciousness (ASC; Tart, 1969/1990). In light of postmodern critiques of normative baselines, these could also be called alternate states, so that no particular baseline is privileged (Rock & Krippner, 2007).

Altered states of consciousness have been exploited and explored in a variety of ways since the dawn of civilization (Ustinova, 2011). However, in the West ASCs have only begun to be seriously studied from the psychological perspective since the beginning of the 20th century. The following sections will present findings pertaining to the role of altered states in history, discuss the foundational work in 20th century psychology in defining the study of ASCs (Grof, 1975; James, 1902/1929; Tart, 1969/1990), and lead up to the present day conceptualization and research of altered states in fields such as psychobiology and neuroscience (Cahn & Polich, 2006; Vaitl et al., 2005).

Altered States throughout History

Prehistory

From the historical perspective, archaeological and anthropological findings have contributed to the contemporary understanding of altered states throughout time and across cultures. While prehistoric peoples by definition left no written records of their daily existence, such artifacts as cave paintings offer fascinating insight into the lives and minds of Paleolithic and Neolithic humans. Drawing on the neuropsychology of visual imagery in altered states, and anthropological data from contemporary communities that practice cave painting, the work of David Lewis-Williams (2002) suggested that early cave paintings (ca. 15,000 years ago) were heavily influenced by imagery related to altered states. Particular geometric motifs such as zigzags and spirals appear at multiple ancient sites, and are also characteristic of entoptic visions elicited during the onset of certain ASCs, such as fatigue or trance, thereby potentially linking altered states to some of the human species' earliest creative endeavors. Similarly, Yulia Ustinova (2011) cited the discovery of ancient musical instruments such as bird-bone pipes from as far back as 30,000 years ago, remarking that, "it is very probable that music and dancing were used for manipulation of consciousness as early as prehistory" (p. 49).

Indeed, some theorists have gone so far as to speculate that altered states of consciousness, specifically those evoked by such mind-altering plants as hallucinogenic mushrooms, may have played a major role in the evolution of human language and symbol use in prehistoric times (McKenna, 1992). The use of psychoactive plants can presumably be traced back to the period from 4200 to 6000 BCE, as evidenced by the appearance of opium poppy and hemp seeds at various Neolithic sites around Europe, as well as the cultivation of alcoholic beverages such as beer and wine in Mesopotamia and the Mediterranean dating back to 4000 BCE (Ustinova, 2011).

Ancient Greece

The religious and cultural life of ancient Greece offers further insight into the historical importance of ASCs. One major figure of the ancient Greek pantheon was Dionysus, son of Zeus, who was worshipped as the god of wine and intoxication as far back as 1500 BCE (Kerényi, 1976). Worship of Dionysus often involved ritual madness elicited by wine or mead, as well as dancing and music. These techniques served as a means of lowering participants' inhibitions, thereby producing an ecstatic state through which the spirit of the god could take possession of their bodies (Kerényi, 1976). In his scholarly exploration of the myth and cult of Dionysus, Walter Friedrich Otto (1965/1981) explained the phenomenon in this way, "Wine carries within it the wonders and secrets, the boundless wild nature of the god. The moment the belief in Dionysus became alive, the devout could learn from wine and could get an even deeper awareness of who he really was" (pp. 147-148).

The Eleusinian Mysteries, associated with the fertility goddess Demeter, represent another significant facet of ancient Greek life with potential links to ASCs. This rite was considered among the most important religious gatherings of the era, and was continuously practiced for nearly 2,000 years (Bowden, 2010). The Greater Eleusinian Mystery in particular was celebrated as far back as 1700 BCE at the town of Eleusis, near Athens, as a harvest festival with seemingly life-altering effects. Regarding this ritual, Terence McKenna (1992) wrote:

> There is little doubt that at Eleusis something was drunk by each initiate and each saw something during the initiation that was utterly unexpected, transformative, and capable of remaining with each participant as a powerful memory for the rest of their life. (p. 133)

True to its name, the precise nature of the Greater Mystery at Eleusis has remained difficult to ascertain, although several prominent thinkers have suggested the possibility that a hallucinogenic brew was imbibed there (Wasson, Hofmann, & Ruck, 1978).

Shamanism

Ancient Greece was not the only historical precedent for the use of altered states. In fact, rituals or practices employing some form of ASC are prevalent in a wide array of ancient cultures. Evidence abounds for the pre-Colombian use of mind-altering plants or plant-derivatives in numerous shamanic practices such as the ingestion of peyote in Mexico and ayahuasca in South America (Schultes & Hofmann, 1992). Shamanism is a cross-cultural phenomenon with early roots in Siberia, although evidence of such practices exists in various forms across Asia, Africa, Europe, and North and South America, some dating as far back as the Paleolithic Era (Price, 2001).

Shamanism has been defined in many ways, although Roger Walsh (2007) has offered this useful synthesis: "a family of traditions whose practitioners [shamans] focus on voluntarily entering altered states of consciousness in which they experience themselves or their spirit(s) interacting with other entities, often by traveling to other realms, in order to serve their community" (pp. 15-16). Shamanic rituals vary widely, although music, dancing, and the ingestion of mind-altering plants are often implicated (Winkelman, 2011). Struck by the prevalence of cross-cultural uses of plant medicines, ethnomycologist R. Gordon Wasson (1959) asked, "May not the sacred mushroom, or some other natural hallucinogen, have been the original element in all the Holy Suppers in the world?" (p. 333). Wasson (1968) was also among the first to suggest that an intoxicating plant-derivative called Soma, revered in the Vedic Indian religious tradition (ca. 1400 BCE) may have had hallucinogenic properties (McKenna, 1992; Wasson, 1968).

Yoga and Meditation

In addition to the use of mind-altering plants in ancient cultures, the development of yoga and meditative practices within Hinduism and early Buddhism dates back to at least 400 BCE (Shear, 2011). These disciplines were employed primarily as a means of purifying practitioners and aiding in their union with higher spiritual states (Feuerstein, 1998). Jonathan Shear (2011) stated that these Eastern traditions, "can enable the activity of the mind to settle down and disappear entirely so that its fundamental inner nature, independent of all the contents of ordinary awareness, can be experienced with clarity" (p. 140). Hence, meditation and yogic practices appear in the historical record as yet another ancient technology purposefully designed to induce altered consciousness.

Spirit and Diabolical Possession

A further explanatory framework for ASCs that gained popularity during the Middle Ages in the West (ca. 5th to 15th centuries CE) was that of spirit and diabolical possession, beliefs that are still embraced in some cultures even today (Sluhovsky, 2011). Not surprisingly, interpretations of Biblical texts have employed a similar framework for understanding the visions of Old Testament prophets such as Ezekiel (Ustinova, 2011). Although an in-depth discussion of the history of ASCs falls outside the scope of this chapter, interested readers may refer to Etzel Cardeña and Michael Winkelman's (2011a) comprehensive edited volume on the subject. It is worth noting, however, that at least until Late Antiquity (ca. 2nd to 8th centuries CE) the most prevalent contexts known to surround ASCs were largely creative, religious, or spiritual in nature, and in some cases these states were specifically invoked for the purposes of healing or transformation.

Altered States of Consciousness in 20th Century Psychology

William James

From the Enlightenment forward, investigations of ASCs were generally confined to the realms of hypnosis, mediumship, and intoxication (Cardeña & Alvarado, 2011), although this changed with the advent of psychological investigation into the nature of consciousness (James, 1902/1929). Specifically, James' radical empiricism, and study of first-person experience, both his own and that of others, provided a fertile ground for exploring ASCs, including mystical experiences and drug-induced states (James, 1902/1929). In many ways this work planted the seeds for a currently unfolding scientific revolution in the study of mind and consciousness away from stringent materialism, and towards the reintegration of first-person subjective experience within the scientific worldview (Beischel, Rock, & Krippner, 2011; Kuhn, 1962/1970; Tart, 1972, 2009).

In his seminal lectures on the varieties of religious experience delivered at Edinburgh in 1901 and 1902, James discussed a personal experience of nitrous oxide intoxication in his explanation of mysticism. Concerning the impressions this experience imparted, James (1902/1929) made this remark, perhaps the most oft-quoted and poignant statement regarding altered states of consciousness in the annals of Western psychology:

> Our normal waking consciousness, rational consciousness as we call it, is but one special type of consciousness, whilst all about it, parted from it by the filmiest of screens, there lie potential forms of consciousness entirely different. We may go through life without

suspecting their existence; but apply the requisite stimulus, and at a touch they are there in all their completeness, definite types of mentality which probably somewhere have their field of application and adaptation. No account of the universe in its totality can be final which leaves these other forms of consciousness quite disregarded. (pp. 378-379)

The lasting importance of this observation lays in part in James' assertion of the possible value of such states, in direct opposition to mainstream views of ASCs at the time, which generally considered ASCs as merely intoxication, anomaly, or pathology.

The Doors of Perception

Despite this early groundbreaking work, psychology as a field was largely dismissive of consciousness and ASCs until the latter half of the 20th century. This was for the most part due to the popularity of the behaviorist paradigm in psychology, which sought to remove such phenomena as mind and consciousness from the discourse of the day because they could not be directly observed by scientists (Watson, 1924/1958). Nevertheless, curious intellectuals continued to explore the landscapes afforded by altered states. In particular, the publication of Aldous Huxley's (1954) *The Doors of Perception* marked the beginnings of a turning point in popular opinion about the potentials of ASCs.

Huxley was a writer and social critic with widely varied interests, and in 1954 he published the results of his self-experimentation with mescaline, a synthetically produced derivative of the natural plant hallucinogen peyote. Therein, Huxley (1954) detailed the experience, describing it as an encounter with, "a world where everything shone with the Inner Light, and was infinite in its significance" (p. 20). His vivid portrayal of the strange mindscapes and unusual alterations of consciousness occasioned by mescaline generated enthusiastic interest in some circles. Along with Dr. Albert Hoffman's discovery of LSD in 1943, these writings and others like them foreshadowed a much wider cultural shift in the perception of ASC that was to come in the 1960s.

The 1960s

The sociocultural milieu of the 1960s was one of turbulence and widespread change. The ongoing conflict in Vietnam, the civil rights and women's liberation movements, and the birth of the hippie counter-culture were just a few of the currents emerging specifically in the USA during that time (Chinen, 1996a). A growing interest in non-Western spiritual traditions and the increasing popularity of marijuana and psychedelic drugs further fueled the exploration of ASCs among many members of the general public. Alongside these broader social transformations, the academic establishment was also slowly shifting.

Philosophical post-modernism questioned the idea that humans could discover a single objective truth through use of the scientific method (Chinen, 1996b; Smith, 1982). Doctrines such as relativism and constructivism from philosophy (Smith, 1982; Wilber, 1995), as well as developments in quantum physics (Battista, 1996), and computer science spawned talk of scientific revolution (Kuhn, 1962/1970). In the social sciences, the advent of existential, humanistic, and later transpersonal schools of psychology were also leading away from a behaviorist model, and toward the further exploration of consciousness in general, and ASCs in particular (Chinen, 1996a). At that time, such psychologists as Abraham Maslow (1962/1968), Tart (1969/1990, 1972, 1975), and Grof (1975) began making unprecedented strides in defining, researching, understanding, and working with altered states from within the Western paradigm.

Abraham Maslow

Frustrated with what he saw as the limitations of a pathology-based model in the psychology of the day, Maslow shifted the focus of his work toward high-functioning individuals. Maslow was a major figure in the development of humanistic and transpersonal psychology, which recognized the importance of individual human experience, the validity of mystical and spiritual experience, the interconnectedness of self with others and the world, and the potential for self-transformation (Hartelius, Caplan, & Rardin, 2007). His work explored the values and motivations of highly developed or "self-actualizing people," which he defined as, "those who have come to a high level of maturation, health, and self-fulfillment" (Maslow, 1962/1968, p. 71). Maslow's (1962, 1962/1968) research suggested a key role for peak experiences in spurring some people along towards these advanced stages of development (i.e., self-actualization). For Maslow, peak experiences were "moments of highest happiness and fulfillment" (1962/1968, p. 73), and included phenomena such as aesthetic, mystical, creative, and insightful experiences, among others. With this shift in orientation toward studying subjective experience and superlative functioning, psychology began to reconsider the role of consciousness in human development, and the potential value of ASCs.

Charles Tart

Another key thinker whose work helped to establish the validity of altered states in psychology was Tart (1969/1990, 1972, 1975). In the early 1960s, altered consciousness was still a nebulous concept, with fragmented research interests and no widely accepted or unified paradigm for conceptualization. Topics such as meditation, dreaming, hypnosis, and intoxication with various pharmacological agents were being studied; however, the common understanding of these phenomena as different classes of ASCs was still in its nascent stages (Tart, 1969/1990). In 1967, Tart began compiling research literature and theoretical writings from these and related areas, with the aim of providing a comprehensive edited volume entitled *Altered States of Consciousness: A Book of Readings*. The author's purpose as stated therein was to show, "that one could scientifically approach altered states of consciousness, . . . to make this a respectable field of investigation, to stimulate research, and to spread this information to the educated public" (Tart, 1969/1990, p. 8).

With the publication of this volume, the term "altered state of consciousness" was widely disseminated into the academic lexicon, and began thereafter to be used to define an entire class of experience and field of study. One of the still-classic works cited in the opening of the book defined ASCs in this way:

> any mental state(s), induced by various physiological, psychological, or pharmacological maneuvers or agents, which can be recognized subjectively by the individual himself (or by an objective observer of the individual) as representing a sufficient deviation in subjective experience of psychological functioning from certain general norms for that individual during alert, waking consciousness. (Ludwig, 1966, p. 225)

Continuing along these lines, Tart (1975) introduced a systems model of states of consciousness, that helped to lay the foundation for the study of ASCs by defining such key concepts as discrete and baseline states of consciousness, mentioned earlier, as well as examining the process of inducing ASCs. Furthermore, in proposing the development of *state specific sciences,* Tart (1972, 1973) proposed a foundational broadening of the scientific method, suggesting that science could and should be undertaken by trained observers from *within* various ASCs in order to fully explore the fundamental nature of consciousness.

Early Psychedelic Research

Other major work in defining the field of ASC came from early research with psychedelics. Scientists such as Grof and Walter Pahnke conducted groundbreaking investigations into the nature of the hallucinogenic experience with such substances as LSD and psilocybin (Grof, 1975; Pahnke, 1963; Pahnke, Kurland, Unger, Savage, & Grof, 1970). This work showed that in keeping with premodern uses of ASC, the carefully controlled administration of psychedelic substances could facilitate beneficial as well as religious and mystical experiences with profound and long-lasting effects (Doblin, 1991; Grof, 1975; Pahnke, 1963).

In a classic study conducted at Harvard University, known as the Good Friday Experiment, Pahnke (1963) orchestrated a double-blind, randomized controlled trial on the effects of psilocybin in eliciting mystical experiences. The research team administered either psilocybin or an active placebo (i.e., nicotinic acid, which produced somatic effects such as flushing), to 20 seminary students attending a Good Friday church service, and used questionnaires and interviews to assess the nature of their experiences. Pahnke found that participants who had received psilocybin were significantly more likely to report mystical experiences than those in the control group. Furthermore, in his 25-year follow up on Pahnke's (1963) study, Rick Doblin (1991) found that, "experimental subjects unanimously described their Good Friday psilocybin experience as having had elements of a genuinely mystical nature and characterized it as one of the high points of their spiritual life" (p. 13).

Other retrospective analyses of early psychedelic research further corroborate their potential value, for instance in the treatment of addiction, or in their ability to promote creativity (Krebs & Johansen, 2012; Krippner, 1985; Strassman, 1995). Grof (1975) wrote of psychedelics that, "It does not seem inappropriate and exaggerated to compare their potential significance for psychiatry and psychology to that of the microscope for medicine or the telescope for astronomy" (pp. 32-33). However, much of this work with hallucinogens was banned for decades due to legal and political issues surrounding the uses and abuses of such compounds, making psychedelic research with human subjects illegal and otherwise generally untenable until only recently. Fortunately, after several decades legitimate investigation into the benefits and underlying mechanisms of these and related substances is again underway (Addy, 2012; Fadiman, 2011; Griffiths & Grob, 2010; Griffiths, Richards, McCann, & Jesse, 2006; Grob et al., 2011; Parrott, 2007).

Altered States Come of Age

Since the pioneering work of figures such as James (1902/1929), Tart (1969/1990, 1972), and Grof (1975) in defining the field, many researchers and theorists have contributed to a growing body of ASC investigation. In their review of the psychobiology of altered states, Dieter Vaitl et al. (2005) noted that, "so far the evidence [for ASCs] is largely empirical in nature, and there is no overarching model for ASC" (p. 99). Dialogues and controversy regarding the nature of consciousness and the defining characteristics of ASCs are still ongoing in the literature (Revonsuo, Kallio, & Sikka, 2009; Rock & Krippner, 2007). However, a large corpus of research findings has been forthcoming over the past several decades.

Scientific advances and rigorous research have helped establish the study of ASCs produced by illness and injury (Avner, 2006), sleep and dreaming (Kokoszka & Wallace, 2011; LaBerge & Gackenbach, 2000), hypnosis (Kallio & Revonsuo, 2003), meditation (Cahn & Polich, 2005; Walsh, 1996), mystical and transcendent experiences (Beauregard, 2011; Griffiths et al., 2006), near-death experiences (NDEs; Greyson, 2000), and out-of-body experiences (OBEs; Blackmore, 2004; Blanke & Arze, 2005), among others. Over 15 years ago Walsh (1996, p. 167) noted more than 1,500 published studies on the effects of meditation alone, providing some frame of reference for the sheer volume of information that has been amassed in the various domains of ASC research. The following sections will provide a brief overview of major findings in key areas to date. Although, for a more detailed treatment of these and related topics see Cardeña and Winkelman (2011b), as well as Vaitl et al. (2005).

Sleep and Dreaming

Sleep and dreaming have become the traditional starting point in discussing ASCs, as they are the most commonly experienced and thus most familiar ASCs, occurring on a regular basis for most people. Sleep is a naturally occurring biological phenomenon regulated by circadian rhythms, hormones, and neurotransmitters in the brain, and is generally accompanied by a loss of consciousness of one's surroundings, and a well-documented pattern of physiological changes, including slowed heart rate and respiration (Kokoszka & Wallace, 2011). Through the study of electrophysiological activity in the brain during sleep and dreaming, researchers have identified several major phases in the sleep cycle. These have been labeled the hypnagogic period (transitioning from wake to sleep), sleep stages 1 through 4 (non-REM sleep), rapid eye movement sleep (REM; Aserinsky & Kleitman, 1953), and the hypnopompic period (emerging from sleep to waking). During normal sleep the person tends to cycle between non-REM and REM sleep in a regular pattern about four to six times each night, with the majority of remembered dreams occurring during REM sleep (Baruš, 2003).

Dreaming represents another classic form of an ASC. In dreams one may experience strange, complex, and sometimes convincing landscapes, events, and entire narratives seemingly generated without conscious effort (Vaitl et al., 2005). Various viewpoints have been proposed regarding the neural basis for dreams, as well as their inherent meaningfulness or lack thereof, although as yet little consensus has been reached as to the how and why of dreaming (Baruš, 2003; Freud, 1900/1950; Hobson, 1988; Taylor, 1998). Nevertheless, dreaming remains an active area of exploration with significant ramifications for the field of ASCs. One particular class of dreams, known as lucid dreams, offers a particularly intriguing glimpse into the nature of dreaming and consciousness. During lucid dreams, "we are explicitly aware that we are dreaming" (LaBerge & Gackenbach, 2000, p. 152), and one *simultaneously* feels as if consciousness is clear and lucid, very much like ordinary waking consciousness (Tart, 1983, 1984). The occurrence of lucidity affords the dreamer greater than normal insight and ability to control the contents of the dream. However, merely having the thought within an ordinary dream, "This is a dream," does not necessarily trigger the change to lucidity in consciousness that creates a lucid dream. Numerous volumes have been devoted to the theory and research of sleep and dreaming, but much is still not understood. For a useful review of the scientific literature see Stevan Harnad (2000).

Hypnosis

Dating back in its earliest forms to the 18th century, hypnosis has remained a relevant, though complex topic in the ASC literature. Hypnosis is defined from the behaviorist perspective as the ritualistic induction of a subject by a hypnotist (or self-induction by the subject, known as autohypnosis), with an emphasis on sleep-like states and automatic acceptance of suggestions. Other researchers see hypnosis as an ASC characterized by increased suggestibility (Beischel et al., 2011). In reality both approaches may be true, depending on the responses of individual subjects (Tart, 1970a). After induction, the hypnotist may then make suggestions that can alter the subject's beliefs, perceptions, and/or behaviors (Beischel et al., 2011), sometimes to radical degrees, such as inducing greatly decreased sensitivity to painful stimuli (Barber, 1998).

Hypnosis has been variously studied and employed as a treatment for pain relief and adjunct to psychotherapeutic interventions, demonstrating significant clinical usefulness (Barber, 1998; Lynn, Kirsch, Barabasz, Cardeña, & Patterson, 2000). However, the phenomenology and outcomes of hypnosis have manifested as notoriously idiosyncratic and difficult to replicate consistently (Farthing, 1992; Pekala & Kumar, 2000). Furthermore, the underlying mechanisms of hypnosis and its status as an ASC are as yet controversial (Baruš, 2003; Blackmore, 2004; Kallio & Revonsuo, 2003). Due to their potential value as a clinical and research tool, hypnotic phenomena plainly warrant further investigation at this time, and furthermore show marked potential for inducing transpersonal experiences (Tart, 1970b).

Meditation

There is considerable confusion in the discussion of meditation in the literature due to lack of discrimination between a wide variety of distinctive meditative procedures, which may or may not result in inducting a particular meditative ASC at a given time, so what is stated here must remain quite general. As with hypnosis, meditation is an intentionally induced state (Shear, 2011). Meditative techniques are largely rooted in ancient spiritual traditions, as previously mentioned, although current research looks at the effects of various meditative practices almost exclusively from a therapeutic perspective, for instance as a stress reliever, for which the various techniques are fairly effective (Barnes, Bloom, & Nahin, 2008).

From the modern-day perspective, Kevin Barrows and Bradly Jacobs (2002) defined meditation as, "the self-regulation of attention" (p. 12), noting the distinction between concentrative and mindfulness types of meditation. Concentrative meditation protocols call for focused attention on a single stimulus, such as the sensation of the breath, the flame of a candle, or a mantra, a special sound that is repeated by the meditator (Vaitl et al., 2005). Mindfulness meditation techniques involve, "a sustained nonreactive attention to one's ongoing mental contents and processes" (Samuelson, Carmody, Kabat-Zinn, & Bratt, 2007, p. 255), including thoughts, perceptions, and emotions. Both concentrative and mindfulness meditation techniques, when carried out successfully, have demonstrated clear physiological and phenomenological changes from ordinary waking consciousness (Cahn & Polich, 2006), and have been increasingly applied in recent years as useful adjuncts to traditional medical and psychological treatment (Barnes, et al., 2008).

In addition to apparent health-related benefits, a change in the sense of self is among the main features of meditation as a practice (which may or may not induce an ASC in a given session). Rael Cahn and John Polich (2006) described the reported outcomes of one kind of regular meditative practice as, "eliciting shifts toward expanded experience of self not centered on the individual's body schema and mental contents" (p. 181), in line with the aims of Eastern spiritual traditions which espouse meditation as a means of cultivating higher states of consciousness (Shear, 2011). Furthermore, a growing body of evidence suggests enhanced cognitive, affective, and visuospatial functioning in long-term meditators, providing added impetus to continue studying methods and effects of meditation (Hodgins & Adair, 2010; Kozhevnikov, Louchakova, Josipovic, & Motes, 2009; Sahdra et al., 2011).

Mystical and Transcendent Experiences

Following in the footsteps of James' (1902/1929) foundational work in the study of religious and mystical experience, contemporary researchers have continued to analyze and investigate these phenomena, along with similar experiences of a transcendent nature (Beauregard, 2011; Garcia-Romeu, 2010; Levin & Steele, 2005; MacLean, Johnson, & Griffiths, 2011; Waldron, 1998). Jeff Levin and Lea Steele (2005) wrote that transcendent experience, "typically evokes a perception that human reality extends beyond the physical body and its psychosocial boundaries," along with, "the perception of merging or identification with the source of being" (p. 89). These experiences occur across cultures, and may result from a number of triggering stimuli including prayer, fasting, being outdoors in nature, through ingestion of psychedelic substances, in times of personal crisis, as well as occurring spontaneously (Beauregard, 2011). Mystical and transcendent experiences have been found to occasion profound transformation in some individuals, including measurable positive changes in personality (MacLean et al., 2011; Waldron, 1998). These findings, along with others linking self-transcendence to increased well-being and ecological awareness (Garcia-Romeu, 2010; Levin & Steele, 2005) suggest a potentially vital role for mystical and transcendent experience in future ASC research.

OBEs and NDEs

This discussion of ASCs has been far from exhaustive, but in the interest of space only the most notable areas have been reviewed here. These and a wide variety of other ASCs, such as flow (Csikszentmihalyi, 1990) and dissociation (Tinnin, 1990), continue to be actively researched. For additional information interested readers may refer to Cardeña, Lynn, and Krippner's (2000), and Cardeña and Winkelman's (2011a, 2011b) thoroughgoing volumes.

This overview of ASC will conclude with a brief presentation of out-of-body experiences (OBEs) and near-death experiences (NDEs). Out-of-body experiences have been characterized by a sensation of being outside of one's physical body, "often floating or traveling away from the body" (Beischel et al., 2011, p. 115) and, more comprehensively, an OBE is defined by a perception that one is elsewhere than one's physical body *and* that one obviously possesses, from self-examination, a clear, non-dreamlike state of consciousness, comparable to waking consciousness (Tart, 1968). It has been estimated that some 10-15% of the general population have experienced an OBE, although research in diverse populations has found prevalence rates as high as 88% for instance in individuals who are highly prone to fantasy (Alvarado, 2000). Individuals who have undergone an OBE generally report positive aftereffects, including decreased fear of death (Alvarado, 2000). Similar to mystical and transcendent experiences, OBEs can occur under the influence of psychedelics, as well as spontaneously, and in conjunction with NDEs (Blackmore, 2004).

Greyson (2000) defined NDEs as, "profound psychological events with transcendental and mystical elements, typically occurring to individuals close to death or in situations of intense physical or emotional danger" (pp. 315-316). The NDE is typically characterized by the feeling of having survived one's own death, as well as particular overarching features derived from the work of pioneering NDE researcher Raymond Moody (1975), including "feelings of peace," "body separation," and "entering the light" (Blackmore, 2004, p. 360). As with OBEs, the aftereffects of NDEs have been reported as highly transformative, including increased spirituality and concern for others, and decreased fear of death (Greyson, 2000). NDEs may start as an OBE, with clear consciousness comparable to the ordinary waking state, but typically turn into ASCs, with experiencers insisting that words cannot adequately describe the experience because perception and cognition become so different. Both NDEs and OBEs have occurred across history and cultures (Blackmore, 2004), and continue to be investigated at this time as highly relevant areas in the conceptualization of ASCs.

Conclusion

In their review of the literature, Vaitl et al. (2005, p. 100) listed over 19 separate classes of ASCs, including such widely varied phenomena as orgasm, starvation, and psychosis. (Note the confounding here, too typical in the literature, between events or processes, which might induce an ASC, versus actual experiences of ASCs). Nevertheless, this does not seem to exhaust the spectrum of altered consciousness. Experiences such as having a cup of coffee or entering an intense emotional state may elicit moderate forms of ASCs. Citing the work of Roy Baumeister (1991), Elliot Aronson (2008) noted,

> Passionate love is, in many respects an altered state of consciousness, like that produced by marijuana or alcohol. Although this state is certainly exciting, it does not qualify as the best state to be in when one is making decisions with long-range, far-reaching consequences. (p. 390)

Likewise, dancing or listening to music may also induce various ASCs (Fachner, 2011). Hence, this review has only touched on the more prominent areas of inquiry into the nature of ASCs.

With these various branches of ASC research in mind, some thinkers have attempted the broader classification of ASCs within a unified framework. For instance, Roland Fischer (1971) referred to ergotropic (i.e., aroused) ASCs such as shamanic ecstasy, versus trophotropic (i.e., calm) states such as meditation. Similarly, Adolph Dittrich (1998) has drawn on international ASC research to derive three major dimensions of altered consciousness: oceanic boundlessness, dread of ego dissolution, and visionary restructuralization. Vaitl et al. (2005) proposed a four-dimensional descriptive system of ASCs encompassing activation, awareness span, self-awareness, and sensory dynamics. Ken Wilber (2000, 2006) has furthermore posited a multi-leveled system of ASCs consisting of gross, psychic, subtle, causal, and nondual states, as well as taking into account each individual's unique psychological development as part of the interpretive apparatus for experiencing ASC in particular ways. Although all of these can be helpful, it may be that the reality of ASCs is still far more varied and complex than any existing theoretical structure can contain.

In addition to such theories, other researchers have suggested the adoption of novel methodologies to investigate more effectively both subjective and objective phenomena related to ASC, such as psychophenomenology, neurophenomenology, and somatic phenomenology (Hartelius, 2007; Pekala, 1985, 1991; Varela, 1996). These approaches and others of this sort attempt to reconcile the difficulties posed by Chalmers' (1996) aptly named hard problem of consciousness, by incorporating both internal first-person states, with external objective measures such as psychological assessments or neuroimaging technologies. Despite these efforts, the field of ASC remains an area of lively debate and discourse, with few widely accepted explanations beyond the empirical findings. Nevertheless, the exploration and dialogue of scholars across disciplines are providing an ever-greater understanding of the complexities and dynamics of ASCs. Through this ongoing work the field of altered states research will continue to progress toward a more integrated understanding of these critical phenomena.

Future research will benefit from technological and theoretical advancements. Because ASCs have demonstrated the ability to connect humanity with "holistic perceptions and intuition, special forms of pre-self identification, nonverbal knowledge, and manifestations of intense emotional engagement and detachment" (Winkelman, 2011, p. 39), determining their potential values remains at the forefront of current research. Moving forward in establishing the state-specific sciences proposed by Tart (1972) and training ASC researchers not only to understand but also to employ these states for the betterment of humanity, remains an integral task. Furthermore, educating individuals in the existence, uses, and possible benefits of ASCs must be undertaken if there is hope of the transformation of contemporary Western culture from a monophasic (i.e., valuing only normal waking consciousness), to a polyphasic orientation, in which the spectrum of ASC is embraced as a toolkit for the ultimate advancement of society (Laughlin, McManus, & d'Aquili, 1990; Whitehead, 2011). In working toward such ends, it is important to look ahead to the future and create an infrastructure and cultural context wherein people may safely and constructively experience ASCs, while honoring our shared human heritage as a species that has explored ASCs since our earliest days.

References

Addy, P. H. (2012). Acute and post-acute behavioral and psychological effects of salvinorin A in humans. *Psychopharmacology, 220*(1), 195-204. doi:10.1007/s00213-011-2470-6

Alvarado, C. S. (2000). Out-of-body experiences. In E. Cardeña, S. J. Lynn, & S. Krippner (Eds.), *Varieties of anomalous experience: Examining the scientific evidence* (pp. 183-218). Washington, DC: American Psychological Association.

Aronson, E. (2008). *The social animal* (10th ed.). New York, NY: Worth Publishers.

Aserinsky, E., & Kleitman, N. (1953). Regularly occurring periods of eye motility and concomitant phenomena during sleep. *Science, 118*, 273-274.

Avner, J. R. (2006). Altered states of consciousness. *Pediatrics in Review, 27*(9), 331-338.

Baars, B. J. (1997). *In the theater of consciousness: The workspace of the mind.* New York, NY: Oxford University Press.

Barber, J. (1998). The mysterious persistence of hypnotic analgesia. *International Journal of Clinical and Experimental Hypnosis, 46*(1), 28-43.

Barnes, P. M., Bloom, B., & Nahin, R. L. (2008). Complementary and alternative medicine use among adults and children: United States, 2007. *National Health Statistics Reports, 12*(12), 1-23.

Barrows, K. A., & Jacobs, B. P. (2002). Mind-body medicine: An introduction and review of the literature. *The Medical Clinics of North America, 86*(1), 11-31.

Baruss, I. (2003). *Alterations of consciousness: An empirical analysis for social scientists.* Washington, DC: American Psychological Association.

Battista, J. R. (1996). Contemporary physics and transpersonal psychiatry. In B. W. Scotton, A. B. Chinen, & J. R. Battista (Eds.), *Textbook of transpersonal psychiatry and psychology* (pp. 195-206). New York, NY: Basic Books.

Baumeister, R. (1991). *Meanings of life.* New York, NY: Guilford Press.

Beauregard, M. (2011). Transcendent experiences and brain mechanisms. In E. Cardeña & M. Winkelman (Eds.), *Altering consciousness: Multidisciplinary perspectives* (Vol. 2, *Biological and psychological perspectives*, pp. 63-84). Santa Barbara, CA: Praeger.

Beischel, J., Rock, A. J., & Krippner, S. (2011). Reconceptualizing the field of altered consciousness: A 50-year retrospective. In E. Cardeña & M. Winkelman (Eds.), *Altering consciousness: Multidisciplinary perspectives* (Vol. 1, *History, culture, and the humanities,* pp. 112-135). Santa Barbara, CA: Praeger.

Blackmore, S. (2004). *Consciousness: An introduction.* New York, NY: Oxford University Press.

Blanke, O. & Arze, S. (2005). The out-of-body experience: Disturbed self-processing at the temporo-parietal junction. *The Neuroscientist, 11*(1), 16-24.

Bowden, H. (2010). *Mystery cults of the ancient world.* Princeton, NJ: Princeton University Press.

Bucke, R. M. (1969). *Cosmic consciousness: A study in the evolution of the human mind.* New Hyde Park, NY: University Books. (Original work published 1901)

Cahn, B. R., & Polich, J. (2006). Meditation states and traits: EEG, ERP, and neuroimaging studies. *Psychological Bulletin, 132*(2), 180-211. doi:10.1037/0033-2909.132.2.180

Cardeña, E., & Alvarado, C. S. (2011). Altered consciousness from the Age of Enlightenment through mid-20th century. In E. Cardeña & M. Winkelman (Eds.), *Altering consciousness: Multidisciplinary perspectives* (Vol. 1, *History, culture, and the humanities,* pp. 45-72). Santa Barbara, CA: Praeger.

Cardeña, E., Lynn, S. J., & Krippner, S. (Eds.). (2000). *Varieties of anomalous experience: Examining the scientific evidence.* Washington, DC: American Psychological Association.

Cardeña, E., & Winkelman, M. (Eds.). (2011a). *Altering consciousness: Multidisciplinary perspectives* (Vol. 1, *History, culture, and the humanities*). Santa Barbara, CA: Praeger.

Cardeña, E., & Winkelman, M. (Eds.). (2011b). *Altering consciousness: Multidisciplinary perspectives* (Vol. 2, *Biological and psychological perspectives*). Santa Barbara, CA: Praeger.

Chalmers, D. J. (1995). Facing up to the problem of consciousness. *Journal of Consciousness Studies, 3*(1), 200-219.

Chalmers, D. J. (1996). *The conscious mind.* New York, NY: Oxford University Press.

Chinen, A. B. (1996a). The emergence of transpersonal psychiatry. In B. W. Scotton, A. B. Chinen, & J. R. Battista (Eds.), *Textbook of transpersonal psychiatry and psychology* (pp. 9-18). New York, NY: Basic Books.

Chinen, A. B. (1996b). Western analytical philosophy and transpersonal epistemology. In B. W. Scotton, A. B. Chinen, & J. R. Battista (Eds.), *Textbook of transpersonal psychiatry and psychology* (pp. 217-227). New York, NY: Basic Books.

Combs, A. (2009). *Consciousness explained better: Towards an integral understanding of the multifaceted nature of consciousness.* St. Paul, MN: Paragon House.

Csikszentmihalyi, M. (1990). *Flow: The psychology of optimal experience.* New York, NY: Harper & Row.

Dennett, D. C. (1991). *Consciousness explained.* Boston, MA: Little, Brown.

Dittrich, A. (1998). The standardized psychometric assessment of altered states of consciousness (ASCs) in humans. *Pharmacopsychiatry, 31*(Suppl 2), 80-84.

Doblin, R. (1991). Pahnke's "Good Friday experiment": A long-term follow-up and methodological critique. *Journal of Transpersonal Psychology, 23,* 1-28.

Fachner, J. C. (2011). Time is the key: Music and altered states of consciousness. In E. Cardeña & M. Winkelman (Eds.), *Altering consciousness: Multidisciplinary perspectives* (Vol. 1, *History, culture, and the humanities,* pp. 355-376). Santa Barbara, CA: Praeger.

Fadiman, J. (2011). *The psychedelic explorer's guide: Safe, therapeutic, and sacred journeys.* Rochester, VT: Park Street Press.

Farthing, G. W. (1992). *The psychology of consciousness.* Engelwood Cliffs, NJ: Prentice-Hall.

Feuerstein, G. (1998). *The Yoga tradition: Its history, literature, philosophy and practice.* Prescott, AZ: Hohm Press.

Fischer, R. (1971). A cartography of ecstatic and meditative states. *Science, 174,* 897-904.

Freud, S. (1950). *The interpretation of dreams* (A. A. Brill, Trans.). New York, NY: Random House. (Original work published 1900)

Garcia-Romeu, A. P. (2010). Self-transcendence as a measurable transpersonal construct. *Journal of Transpersonal Psychology, 42*(1), 26-47.

Greyson, B. (2000). Near-death experiences. In E. Cardeña, S. J. Lynn, & S. Krippner (Eds.), *Varieties of anomalous experience: Examining the scientific evidence* (pp. 315-352). Washington, DC: American Psychological Association.

Griffiths, R. R., & Grob, C. S. (2010). Hallucinogens as medicine. *Scientific American,* December, 77-79.

Griffiths, R. R., Richards, W. A., McCann, U., & Jesse, R. (2006). Psilocybin can occasion mystical-type experiences having substantial and sustained personal meaning and spiritual significance. *Psychopharmacology, 187,* 268-283.

Grob, C. S., Danforth, A. L., Chopra, G. S., Halberstadt, A. R., McKay, C. M., Greer, G., & Hagerty, M., (2010). Pilot study of psilocybin treatment for anxiety in patients with advanced-stage cancer. *Archives of General Psychiatry, 68*(1),71-78. doi:10.1001/archgenpsychiatry.2010.116

Grof, S. (1975). *Realms of the human unconscious: Observations from LSD research.* New York, NY: Viking Press.

Harnad, S. (Ed.). (2000). Sleep and dreaming [Special issue]. *Behavioral and Brain Sciences, 23*(6).

Hartelius, G. (2007). Quantitative somatic phenomenology: Toward an epistemology of subjective experience. *Journal of Consciousness Studies, 14*(12), 24-56.

Hartelius, G., Caplan, M., & Rardin, M. A. (2007). Transpersonal psychology: Defining the past, divining the future. *The Humanistic Psychologist, 35*(2), 135-160.

Hobson, J. A. (1988). *The dreaming brain.* New York, NY: Basic.

Hodgins, H. S., & Adair, K. C. (2010). Attentional processes and meditation. *Consciousness and Cognition, 19,* 872-878.

Huxley, A. (1954). *The doors of perception.* New York, NY: Harper.

James, W. (1929). *The varieties of religious experience.* New York, NY: Random House. (Original work published 1902).

Kallio, S., & Revonsuo, A. (2003). Hypnotic phenomena and altered states of consciousness: A multilevel framework of description and explanation. *Contemporary Hypnosis, 20*(3), 111-164.

Kerényi, C. (1976). *Dionysos: Archetypal image of indestructible life.* (R. Manheim, Trans.) Princeton, NJ: Princeton University Press.

Kokoszka, A., & Wallace, B. (2011). Sleep, dreams, and other biological cycles as altered states of consciousness. In E. Cardeña & M. Winkelman (Eds.), *Altering consciousness: Multidisciplinary perspectives* (Vol. 2, *Biological and psychological perspectives,* pp. 3-20). Santa Barbara, CA: Praeger.

Kozhevnikov, M., Louchakova, O., Josipovic, Z. & Motes. M. (2009). The enhancement of visual-spatial efficiency through Buddhist deity meditation. *Psychological Science, 20*(5), 645-653.

Krebs, T. S., & Johansen, P. O. (2012). Lysergic acid diethylamide (LSD) for alcoholism: Meta-analysis of randomized controlled trials. *Journal of Psychopharmacology, 26*(7), 994-1002. doi:10.1177/0269881112439253

Krippner, S. (1985). Psychedelic drugs and creativity. *Journal of Psychoactive Drugs, 17,* 235-245.

Kuhn, T. S. (1970). *The structure of scientific revolutions* (2nd ed.). Chicago, IL: University of Chicago Press. (Original work published in 1962)

LaBerge, S., & Gackenbach, J. (2000). Lucid dreaming. In E. Cardeña, S. J. Lynn, & S. Krippner (Eds.), *Varieties of anomalous experience: Examining the scientific evidence* (pp. 151-182). Washington, DC: American Psychological Association.

Laughlin, C. D., McManus, J., & E.G. d'Aquili, E. G. (1990). Brain, symbol and experience: Toward a neurophenomenology of human consciousness. Boston, MA: Shambhala.

Levin, J., & Steele, L. (2005). The transcendent experience: Conceptual, theoretical, and epidemiological perspectives. *Explore, 1*(2), 89-101.

Lewis-Williams, D. (2002). *The mind in the cave*. London, UK: Thames & Hudson.

Ludwig, A. M. (1966). Altered states of consciousness. *Archives of General Psychiatry, 15,* 225-234.

Lynn, S. J., Kirsch, I., Barabasz, A., Cardeña, E., & Patterson, D. (2000). Hypnosis as an empirically supported clinical intervention: The state of the evidence and a look to the future. *International Journal of Clinical and Experimental Hypnosis, 48*(2), 239-259.

MacLean, K., Johnson, M., & Griffiths, R. (2011). Mystical experiences occasioned by the hallucinogen psilocybin lead to increases in the personality domain of openness. *Journal of Psychopharmacology, 25*(11), 1453-1461.

Maslow, A. H. (1962). Lessons from the peak experiences. *Journal of Humanistic Psychology, 2,* 9-18.

Maslow, A. H. (1968). *Toward a psychology of being* (2nd ed.). New York, NY: D. Van Nostrand. (Original work published 1962)

McKenna, T. (1992). *Food of the gods: The search for the original tree of knowledge, a radical history of plants, drugs, and human evolution*. New York, NY: Bantam Books.

Moody, R. A. (1975). *Life after life*. Covington, GA: Mockingbird Books.

Otto, W. F. (1981). *Dionysus: Myth and cult.* (R. B. Palmer, Trans.). Dallas, TX: Spring. (Original work published 1965)

Pahnke, W. N. (1963). Drugs and mysticism: An analysis of the relationship between psychedelic drugs and the mystical consciousness (Unpublished doctoral dissertation). Harvard University, Cambridge, MA.

Pahnke, W. N., Kurland, A. A., Unger, S., Savage, C., & Grof, S. (1970). The experimental use of psychedelic (LSD) psychotherapy. *JAMA, The Journal of the American Medical Association, 212*(11), 1856-1863.

Parrott, A. C. (2007). The psychotherapeutic potential of MDMA (3, 4 methylenedioxymethamphetamine): An evidence-based review. *Psychopharmacology, 191*(2),181-193.

Pekala, R. J. (1985). A psychophenomenological approach to mapping and diagramming states of consciousness. *Journal of Religion and Psychical Research,* 199-214.

Pekala, R. J. (1991). *Quantifying consciousness: An empirical approach*. New York, NY: Plenum Press.

Pekala, R. J., & Kumar, V. K. (2000). Operationalizing "trance" I: Rationale and research using a psychophenomenological approach. *American Journal of Clinical Hypnosis, 43*(2), 107-135.

Price, N. (Ed.). (2001). *The archaeology of shamanism*. London, UK: Routledge.

Revonsuo, A., Kallio, S., & Sikka, P. (2009). What is an altered state of consciousness? *Philosophical Psychology, 22*(2), 187-204.

Rock, A. J., & Krippner, S. (2007). Does the concept of "altered states of consciousness" rest on a mistake? *International Journal of Transpersonal Studies, 26,* 33-40.

Sahdra, B. K., MacLean, K. A., Ferrer, E., Shaver, P. R., Rosenberg, E. L., Jacobs, T. L., and Saron, C. D. (2011). Enhanced response inhibition during intensive meditation training predicts improvements in self-reported adaptive socioemotional functioning. *Emotion*, *11*(2), 299-312. doi:10.1037/a0022764

Samuelson, M., Carmody, J., Kabat-Zinn, J., & Bratt, M. A. (2007). Facilities mindfulness-based stress reduction in Massachusetts correctional facilities. *The Prison Journal*, *87*(2), 254-268.

Schultes, R. E., & Hofmann, A. (1992). *Plants of the Gods: Their sacred, healing and hallucinogenic powers*. Rochester, VT: Healing Arts Press.

Searle, J. R. (2004). *Mind: A brief introduction*. New York, NY: Oxford University Press.

Shear, J. (2011). Eastern approaches to altered states of consciousness. In E. Cardeña & M. Winkelman (Eds.), *Altering consciousness: Multidisciplinary perspectives* (Vol. 1, *History, culture, and the humanities*, pp. 139-158). Santa Barbara, CA: Praeger.

Sluhovsky, M. (2011). Spirit possession and other alterations of consciousness in the Christian Western tradition. In E. Cardeña & M. Winkelman (Eds.), *Altering consciousness: Multidisciplinary perspectives* (Vol. 1, *History, culture, and the humanities*, pp. 73-88). Santa Barbara, CA: Praeger.

Smith, H. (1982). *Beyond the post-modern mind*. New York, NY: Crossroads.

Strassman, R. J. (1995). Hallucinogenic drugs in psychiatric research and treatment. *Journal of Nervous and Mental Disorders*, *183*, 127-138.

Tart, C. T. (1968). A psychophysiological study of out-of-the-body experiences in a selected subject. *Journal of the American Society for Psychical Research*, *62*, 3-27.

Tart, C. T. (1970a). Self-report scales of hypnotic depth. *International Journal of Clinical and Experimental Hypnosis*, *18*, 105-125.

Tart, C. T. (1970b). Transpersonal potentialities of deep hypnosis. *Journal of Transpersonal Psychology*, *2*, 27-40.

Tart, C. T. (1972). States of consciousness and state-specific sciences. *Science*, *176*, 1203-1210.

Tart, C. T. (1973). State-specific sciences. *Science*, *180*, 1006-1008.

Tart, C. T. (1975). *States of consciousness*. New York, NY: E. P. Dutton.

Tart, C. T. (1983). Lucid dreaming. *Dictionary of Psychology*. Oxford, UK: Basil Blackwell.

Tart, C. T. (1984). Terminology in lucid dream research. *Lucidity Letter*, *3*(1), 4-6.

Tart, C. T. (Ed.). (1990). *Altered states of consciousness: A book of readings* (3rd ed.). New York, NY: John Wiley & Sons, Ltd. (Original work published 1969)

Tart, C. T. (2009). *The end of materialism: How evidence of the paranormal is bringing science and spirit together*. Oakland, CA: New Harbinger.

Taylor, J. (1998). *The living labyrinth: Exploring universal themes in myths, dreams, and the symbolism of waking life*. Mahwah, NJ: Paulist Press.

Tinnin, L. (1990). Mental unity, altered states of consciousness and dissociation. *Dissociation*, *111*(3), 154-159.

Ustinova, Y. (2011). Consciousness alteration practices in the West from prehistory to late antiquity. In E. Cardeña & M. Winkelman (Eds.), *Altering consciousness: Multidisciplinary perspectives* (Vol. 1, *History, culture, and the humanities*, pp. 45-72). Santa Barbara, CA: Praeger.

Vaitl, D., Birbaumer, N., Gruzelier, J., Jamieson, G., Kotchoubey, B., Kübler, A., and Weiss, T. (2005). Psychobiology of altered states of consciousness, *Psychological Bulletin*, *131*(1), 98-127. doi:10.1037/0033-2909.131.1.98

Varela, F. J. (1996). Neurophenomenology: A methodological remedy for the hard problem. *Journal of Consciousness Studies*, *3*(4), 330-349.

Waldron, J. L. (1998). The life impact of transcendent experience with a pronounced quality of noesis. *Journal of Transpersonal Psychology, 30*(2), 103-134.

Walsh, R. (1996). Meditation research: The state of the art. In B. W. Scotton, A. B. Chinen, & J. R. Battista (Eds.), *Textbook of transpersonal psychiatry and psychology* (pp. 167-175). New York, NY: Basic Books.

Walsh, R. (2007). *The world of shamanism: New views of an ancient tradition.* Woodbury, MN: Llewellyn.

Wasson, R. G. (1959). Division of Mycology: The hallucinogenic mushrooms of Mexico: An adventure in ethnomycological exploration. *Transactions of the New York Academy of Sciences, 21*(4) Ser. II, 325-339. doi:10.1111/j.2164-0947.1959.tb00681.x

Wasson, R. G. (1968). *Soma: Divine mushroom of immortality.* New York, NY: Harcourt Brace Jovanovich.

Wasson, R. G., Hofmann, A., & Ruck, C. (1978). *The road to Eleusis: Unveiling the secrets of the mysteries.* New York, NY: Harcourt Brace Jovanovich.

Watson, J. B. (1958). *Behaviorism.* Chicago, IL: University of Chicago Press. (Original work published 1924)

Whitehead, C. (2011). Altered consciousness in society. In E. Cardeña & M. Winkelman (Eds.), *Altering consciousness: Multidisciplinary perspectives* (Vol. 1, *History, culture, and the humanities,* pp. 181-202). Santa Barbara, CA: Praeger.

Wilber, K. (1995). *Sex, ecology, spirituality: The spirit of evolution.* Boston, MA: Shambhala.

Wilber, K. (2000). *Integral psychology: Consciousness, spirit, psychology, therapy.* Boston, MA: Shambhala.

Wilber, K. (2006). *Integral spirituality: A startling new role for religion in the modern and postmodern world.* Boston, MA: Integral Books.

Winkelman, M. (2011). Shamanism and the alteration of consciousness. In E. Cardeña & M. Winkelman (Eds.), *Altering consciousness: Multidisciplinary perspectives* (Vol. 1, *History, culture, and the humanities,* pp. 159-180). Santa Barbara, CA: Praeger.

7

Jung, Analytical Psychology, and Transpersonal Psychology

Alan G. Vaughan

Jung may have been the first to use the term *transpersonal* in his writings, although he wrote principally in German. In English translations of his work, however, his translators and editors often included the term. One work making specific reference to the term transpersonal, "The Personal and the Collective (or Transpersonal) Unconscious," can be found in his *Two Essays on Analytical Psychology* (Jung, 1966a, pp. 64-79). Jung also spoke about the mythological figures of the magician and demon as expressions of the unknown in human feeling that swept over a patient in treatment in which he made direct reference to the transpersonal, stating, "These attributes always indicate that contents of the transpersonal or collective unconscious are being projected" (Jung, 1966a, § 150). Whether or not he deliberately used that specific term, or whether his translators and editors chose to employ that term, it is clear that Jung thought of his approach to psychology, such as the collective unconscious and archetypes, in a way compatible with modern transpersonal psychology.

Jung (1966b) referred to his unique approach to psychology, which he called analytical psychology, as embracing both Freud's psychoanalysis and Adler's individual psychology (Jung, 1966b). Both Jung and Adler were early members of Freud's inner circle, and both eventually broke away from Freud to form their own schools. Jung's analytical psychology can be seen as a meta-psychology of individuation, the path by which each human being, through an inward journey of conscious engagement with the collective unconscious, becomes who she or he is meant to be. Jung used the term individuation "to denote the process by which a person becomes psychologically individual, that is a separate, indivisible unity or whole" (Jung, 1968a, § 490). This involves discovery of the self, namely the conscious and the larger collective unconscious, by engaging in conscious dialogue between the limited ego sphere of consciousness and the unconscious, which structurally is comprised of the personal unconscious and the collective unconscious.

The Wiley Blackwell Handbook of Transpersonal Psychology, First Edition.
Edited by Harris L. Friedman and Glenn Hartelius.
© 2013 John Wiley & Sons, Ltd. Published 2015 by John Wiley & Sons, Ltd.

In this journey toward individuation, the unconscious speaks to the ego in primordial language of symbols, images, affects, sensations and mythic narratives, all presented in dreams, waking fantasies, visions, and active imagination. The task of the ego is to learn the language of the unconscious, to enlarge its limited sphere of consciousness and to avail itself of the self-regulating aspects of the totality of psyche. The collective unconscious contains archetypes or psychoid pre-formations of the potential for all lived human experience, more commonly recognized as instincts that evolved from antiquity through perpetuity. Archetypes may be thought of as typical modes of apprehension, (Jung, 1968a, p. 4). Knowing the self and the journey toward individuation, in relation to the collective of humanity, are fostered in analytical depth psychotherapy, a process that involves historiographic amplification of the spiritual and creative dimensions of psyche or self, and many trans-cultural forms of creative expression.

Jung's Transpersonal Roots

Jung was interested in the transpersonal from childhood. He was the fourth child born to Paul Achilles Jung, a modest country parson in the Swiss Reformed Church whose wife, Emilie Preiswerk, was reported to have been a medium, engaged with the paranormal. His uncles on both sides of the family also were clergymen, so religion played a large role in his experience. As a child he was introspective and engaged with active imagination, visioning, the spiritual and imaginal realms, which were interests that continued through his medical education and later life. His investigation of the transpersonal occult phenomena, with his cousin Helene Preiswerk, became the subject of his medical school dissertation, a requirement for a medical degree from the University of Basel. He was interested in her experiences with visions, trance states, séances, fantasies, and mediums. This work was later published, in *The Collected Works*, as an essay, "On the Investigation of the Pathology and Psychology of So Called Occult Phenomena," in 1902 (Jung, 1975, pp. 3-88).

From childhood, Jung questioned his father's belief in Christian dogma, the meaning of religion, and god. The inner world of the spiritual, symbols, and symbolism were of primary interest to him as institutional religion receded in the shadow of prosperous mercantilism and industrialism. Recollections of his childhood interests in mysticism and mystical experience have been published in his famous autobiography, *Memories, Dreams, Reflections* (Jung, 1961), *The Seven Sermons to the Dead* (Jung, 1961, appendix), and more recently in his *The Red Book* (Shamdasani, 2009).

Jung was influenced by the work of Breuer, Janet, and especially Freud from the beginning of his career in psychiatry; however, recent scholarship shows that Jung's ideas about the unconscious were more influenced by Carl Gustav Carus, a physician who identified the unconscious as the essential ground of the soul, than by Freud (Shamdasani, 2003). The psychology of the unconscious as Jung conceptualized it may have originated with Carus, but Jung was also influenced by the philosophies of Leibniz, Kant, Schelling, Schopenhauer, and von Hartmann. Indirectly, the work of Nietzsche and Burckhardt also influenced Jung. It was Schelling's insight that the unconscious constituted the absolute foundation for consciousness, and that the unconscious as "the primeval foundation is not differentiated, but universal" (Shamdasani, 2003, pp. 164-165).

Jung (1961) read Freud's (1900/1913) book, *Interpretation of Dreams*, in 1900 and by 1903 from his own clinical practice, research and reading, developed a sense of the relationship between consciousness, the deeper and broader unconscious ground, including dreams and the concept of repression as a defense mechanism. Jung became Freud's colleague in 1907 and agreed with Freud that in some cases sexual trauma could account for presence of repression, but he also believed that there were cases involving neuroses in which the prominent causes did not include the question of sexuality. In sharing clinical cases with Freud during the six years of their colleague-ship, until 1913, Freud could not acknowledge any other cause for neuroses than sexuality, which became a major problem for Jung, who believed that Freud valued his own authority encoded in dogma over truth. Jung had little tolerance for dogma and his own negative father-son complex was stirring into consciousness, resulting in a break from Freud. A major part of this break involved Freud's stance on spirituality, as Jung disliked the fact that Freud reduced spirituality to mere repressed sexuality. Jung could not accept the view that culture was an artifact and consequence exclusively of repressed sexuality, and he thought that health, well-being, creativity, happiness, spirituality, aesthetics, social relations, purpose, and meaning were essential to a well-lived life as archetypal potentials from birth. Jung thought that psyche was the source of the libidinal energy that propelled humans toward individuation or optimal development. Psyche from his perspective encompassed sexual energy, but went beyond to creative expression, as well as to the destructive nature of the human species. Jung began to understand that personality is to the individual what culture is to the group, and he began to become more engaged with the ideas and experiences of the collective unconscious, comparative mythology, and symbolism, as experienced within himself, in his clinical practice, as well as in his research and writing. In September 1913, Jung and Freud met for the last time, and shortly thereafter Freud published a paper underscoring the incompatibility of his views with those of Jung and Adler (Alexander & Selesnick, 1966).

After his break with Freud, Jung withdrew from public life into what some call a period of creative illness (Ellenberger, 1981). During this time of extreme introversion, Jung began to journal in a series of personal notebooks, which appear in edited form as the recently published *The Red Book* (Shamdasani, 2009). The notebooks contained an autobiographical study of this transformative period, framing the architecture and laying the foundation for his theory, and guiding the remainder of his life's work. Using active imagination, painting, drawing, and writing, to explore his fantasies, visions, and dreams in context of his dialogue with the unconscious, he began to use metaphor and trans-cultural symbolism to amplify, interrogate, and confirm ideas that would evolve into his theories. He emerged from this period of eight years in 1921, concurrent with the publication of his book, *Psychological Types* (Jung, 1921/1923). This book was inspired by Jung's efforts to resolve destructive antagonisms and to accommodate views of personality theory held by Freud and Adler that differed from his own (Douglas, 2000). The system of typology he created both permitted and explained the different ways each of them experienced libido or psychic energy and reacted to the world. Jung went on to study alchemy and comparative mythology

(Campbell, 1971). Comparative mythology underscored the nature and character of his archetypal theory, while alchemy spoke to the nature of transformation that could be experienced in psychoanalysis, and the nature and language of the unconscious.

Analytical Psychology: Jung's Theory of Personality

Although Jung's theory of personality is complex, it is grounded in an architecture and engineered through the relational dynamics of several core constructs and related concepts. From the advent of the psychoanalytic movement born within the field of medicine in 1888, at the fringe of the new subspecialty psychiatry, psychoanalysis adopted a metaphysical language to help explain the human personality and mental states in relation to neurology and human biology. Some constructs were borrowed from religion and philosophy, and others from social sciences, such as cultural anthropology. Emerging from his encounter with the unconscious, Jung became clearer in his thinking and writing about the relational aspects of inner and outer psychological experience, as well as the self-regulating dynamics of psyche and the ego-self dialogue, the nature of archetypes and complex theory, the impact of Western culture on psyche, and the role of culture in relation to personality development of individuals and groups. His principal interests focused on the, psychology of religion spiritualism, the paranormal, mysticism, and occult phenomena.

Freud used the term metapsychology to cover his theories about the structure and function of the psyche, metaphorically referring to these as mental anatomy and physiology. It consists of theoretical abstractions, not directly observable entities. As an invented vocabulary that permits discussion of the psyche as if it possessed a reified structure, it was seen as a way to create a working model as an aid to understanding how the psyche operates. The symbolic or imaginary model was not seen as representing concrete measureable aspects of reality, but as inferential and heuristic. Jung continued this style of Freudian development in his theory of analytical psychology. His theory enlarged, extended, and offered novel and innovative thinking about human functions and the existential purpose and meaning of life. It was grounded in the common matrices of both species-specific human biology and cultural environmental historiography. In order to contextualize the main thrusts of Jung's complex theory, it is necessary to focus on the definition of some key terms.

Psyche. Jung preferred to use the terms psyche and psychic rather than mind or mental, because psyche refers to the entire mental apparatus, unconscious as well as conscious, whereas mind is generally used to designate those aspects of mental functioning that are completely conscious and the province of the ego domain.

Consciousness. In some of his thoughts about consciousness Jung wrote:

> When one reflects upon what consciousness really is, one is profoundly impressed by
> the extreme wonder of the fact that an event which takes place outside in the cosmos

simultaneously produces an internal image, that it takes place, so to speak, inside as well, which is to say: becomes conscious. (1961, p. 382)

For indeed our consciousness does not create itself—it wells up from unknown depths. In childhood it awakens gradually, and all through life it wakes each morning out of the depths of sleep from an unconscious condition. It is like a child that is born daily out of the primordial womb of the unconscious. (Jung, 1968a, § 935)

Consciousness from a Jungian vantage is divided into the personal unconscious and the collective unconscious. The personal unconscious is the product of interaction between the collective unconscious along with the physical and cultural environment, in which the individual develops. It contains everything that has passed or will pass through ego consciousness. Memories of past events are stored in the personal unconscious, generally accessible to consciousness upon will or external stimulus.

Complex and Personal Unconscious

Complexes are feeling-toned responses to ideas and experiences. They are functional units of the personal unconscious. This is as true for healthy people as it is for neurotic or psychotic individuals. Jung saw complexes as essential parts of the healthy mind. Complexes are autonomous and able to operate independent of consciousness or unconsciously, for example, in phenomena such as auditory or visual hallucinations, in visions or spirits that control mediums in trance states, or in multiple personalities. They can easily disturb or dislocate consciousness.

Collective Unconscious

The instincts and archetypes together form the collective unconscious. Jung called it collective because, unlike the personal unconscious, this level of the unconscious is not made up of individual and more or less unique contents, but of those that are universal and of regular occurrence (Jung, 1972a). Jacobi (1973) described this, as follows:

Whereas the so called personal unconscious comprises forgotten, suppressed, repressed, subliminally perceived contents originating in the life of the individual, the collective unconscious is made up of contents which regardless of historic era or social or ethnic group are the deposits of mankind's typical reactions since primordial times to universal human situations, such as fear, danger, the struggle against superior power, relations between children and parents, hate and love, birth and death, the power of the light and dark principles. (p. 10)

Jung spoke of the unconscious expressly and implicitly distinguishing between the personal and collective unconscious in the following language, in several of his principal works. Of the unconscious, for example, he stated:

Theoretically, no limits can be set to the field of consciousness, since it is capable of indefinite extension. Empirically, however, it always finds its limit when it comes up against the unknown. This consists of everything we do not know, which, therefore, is not related to the ego as the centre of the field of consciousness. The unknown falls into two groups of objects: those which are outside and can be experienced by the senses, and those which are inside and are experienced immediately. The first group comprises the unknown in the outer world; the second, the unknown in the inner world. We call this latter the territory of the unconscious. (Jung, 1968b, § 1)

Archetypes

Archetypes reside within the collective unconscious. Archetypes structure consciousness and hold potential for human experience mediated in interactions with the environment across cultures and the ages. Jung wrote about the archetypes in different places at different times in the *Collected Works*. The following quotation provides ground for understanding:

> The archetype in itself is empty and purely formal, nothing but a *facultas praeformandi*, a possibility of representation which is given *a priori*. The representations themselves are not inherited, only the forms, and in that respect they correspond in every way to the instincts, which are also determined in form only. The existence of the instincts can no more be proved than the existence of the archetypes, so long as they do not manifest themselves concretely. (Jung, 1968a, § 155)

The post Jungian scholar-analyst John Haule (2011a) has provided a contemporary definition of archetype, based on Jung's original work and grounded in the example of the particular archetype of language, as follows:

> The investigation of the language archetype allows us to list at least nine factors that describe what an archetype is:
>
> 1 An archetype is a species'-universal pattern
> 2 Of meaningful recognition, imagination and behavior
> 3 That resembles behaviors in closely related species,
> 4 Allowing us to trace a hypothetical line of inheritance back to a (possibly extinct) ancestor species,
> 5 And entails identifiable physiological alterations (brain-tracts, hormones, etc.).
> 6 As a result of hormones and autonomic nervous system involvement, archetypes are usually experienced as powerfully emotional, even numinous.
> 7 The archetype itself is an "empty program" that needs life-experience to 'fill' it,
> 8 And this filling process 'wires' the brain according to local and cultural styles of living,
> 9 With the result that "archetypal," in the sense of "mythic" images and expectations always take culture-specific forms. (p. 27)

In the architecture of Jung's theory, there is a functional relationship between the archetype as potential for species' specific experiences and the lived experience, which is the content of complexes.

Complex Theory and Archetypes

Thus, complexes are the means through which archetypes manifest themselves in personal psyche, the collective group psyche, and cultural environments. A complex is a group of associated ideas bound together by a shared emotional charge or a feeling toned response. It exerts a dynamic effect on conscious experience and on behavior (Stevens, 1991). Complexes have a bipolarity, positive and negative, which is conditioned by the quality of human experience of the archetype (e.g., good or bad mother complex). At the heart or center of each complex is a nuclear core of the collective unconscious, primordial images or archetypes. A close functional relationship exists between archetypes and complexes, in that complexes are personifications of archetypes. Complexes are the means through which archetypes manifest themselves and are experienced in the personal psyche and, in recent post Jungian thought (e.g., Singer & Kimbles, 2004), within the ethnic group psyche of the cultural complex.

Jung referred to the phenomenology and clinical aspects of complex theory, underlying neurosis and trauma in this manner:

> Complexes are psychic fragments which have split off owing to traumatic influences or certain incompatible tendencies. As the association experiments prove, complexes interfere with the intentions of the will and disturb the conscious performance; they produce disturbances of memory and blockages in the flow of associations; they appear and disappear according to their own laws; they can temporarily obsess consciousness, or influence speech and action in an unconscious way. In a word, complexes behave like independent beings, a fact especially evident in abnormal states of mind. In the voices heard by the insane they even take on a personal ego-character like that of the spirits who manifest themselves through automatic writing and similar techniques. (1972b, § 253)

Ego and Persona

In analytical theory, the ego is the focal point of consciousness manifest in cognitive-sensory functions. The ego mediates between subjective and objective realms of experience with a focus on decoding cultural symbols and adapting to acceptable norms of behavior. The persona is the packaging of the ego: the ego's public relations firm. For Jung, it is the role a person plays and is responsible for advertising to people how one wants to be seen and received. Social success depends on the quality of the persona. The best kind of persona to possess is one that adapts flexibly to different social situations, while at the same time being a good reflection of the ego qualities that stand behind it. Personas, developmentally, grow out of the need to adapt to expectations of parents, teachers, coaches, managers and society in the course of human development.

Shadow

The shadow possesses qualities opposite to those manifested in the persona. These two aspects of personality complement and counterbalance each other. The shadow compensates the pretension of the persona and the persona compensates for the antisocial propensities of the shadow. Although unconscious, the shadow does not cease to exist, but remains dynamically active. It carries the rejected aspects of the ego; and for the ego to own its content is painful, if not terrifying. Unconscious shadow is the basis for negative projection on to "other" at the individual and collective levels (e.g., racism, sexism, ageism, and all of the other "isms").

Self

The self can be viewed as the main archetype among the various archetypes. It is responsible for implementing the blueprint of life through each stage of the life cycle and bringing about the best adjustment that individual circumstances will allow. The self has teleological and ontological functions in that it has the innate characteristic of seeking its own fulfillment in life. The goal of the self is wholeness or individuation (becoming your unique self as complement to and distinct from the collective). Although the self is rooted in biology, it also carries one into spirit and mysteries of the soul. The ego is privy purely to conscious preoccupations, but the self has access to a much wider realm of existential experience. Jung (1966a) spoke of this, as follows:

> The self as a quantity that is super-ordinate to the conscious ego. It embraces not only the conscious but also the unconscious psyche, and is therefore, so to speak, a personality which we also are. . . . There is little hope of our ever being able to reach even approximate consciousness of the self, since however much we may make conscious there will always exist an indeterminate and indeterminable amount of unconscious material which belongs to the totality of the self. (§ 274)

Ego-Self Axis

Ego-Self Axis is the dialogue between the self and the ego. It presumes the differentiated capacity and ability of the ego to make meaning of communications emanating from the personal and collective unconscious, in the form of dreams (both personal and/or archetypal), fantasies, creative thought and productions, and more. As a general rule, the axis is cultivated through an in depth psychotherapy or analysis, but from other sources as well, such as spiritual practice and transcultural wisdom traditions.

Individuation

Jung saw the whole life cycle as a continuing process or metamorphosis that is commissioned and homostatically regulated by the self. He reasoned that the stages through which each human life proceeds are evolutionary extensions of those stages observable in non-human species (which he saw as our animal and plant brothers and sisters). Individuation is an expression of that biological process by which every living thing becomes what it was destined to become from the very beginning. Jung spoke of individuation in the following manner: "I use the term 'individuation' to denote the process by which a person becomes a psychological 'individual,' that is, a separate, indivisible unity or 'whole'" (Jung, 1968a, p. 275).

Theory of Opposites and the Transcendent Position

Based in the phenomenology of dialectics, opposites combined make a whole; for whatever is conscious, its opposite exists in the unconscious. The whole is the conscious and unconscious. The transcendent position is achieved with an expanded consciousness of dialecticism, able to hold and reconcile the perceptions and tensions of opposites in consciousness, which then yields new position or attitude: a third view, which then creates its own opposite to renew the cycle.

Jung and Transpersonal Psychology

Freud developed psychoanalytic theory using clinical case study methods within the frame of biological psychology. Adler along with Jung sought to expand this theoretical field and framework. Adler saw the importance of the family, will to power in the individual, and power dynamics within family structures. Jung, in contrast, offered the transcultural, historiographic, and transpersonal perspectives of the collective family of human species in his theory of archetypes and the collective unconscious. With the publication of *Symbols of Transformation,* Jung (1967) advanced the ideas that humans were in fact spiritual beings, with layers of consciousness that included our inherited evolutionary animal and tribal natures and ancestry. He asserted that transformations of libido or creative life energy included not only biological and social drives but transpersonal, ontological, and teleological agendas as well.

In his volume, *The Archetypes and the Collective Unconscious,* a collection of essays written over an extended period, Jung (1968a) argued for the triune levels of the psyche, the deepest being the fundamental psychic ordering, processing, and meaning-making of symbolic expressions of the collective unconscious, namely the transpersonal realm. Moreover, Jung explored these various dimensions in virtually all of his works, directly or indirectly. For example, in *Psychology and Religion: West and East,* Jung (1969) explored the transpersonal at great length as it manifests in world religions, wisdom traditions, spiritual practices, and other cultural patterns. In *Civilization in Transition* (Jung, 1978), he explored the transpersonal as it manifests in changing social forms. He also explored the transpersonal in *The Spirit in Man, Art, and Literature* (Jung, 1971) and, in his many essays on dream work, he indicated the importance of moving beyond the merely personal or reactive features of a dream to take note of their transpersonal features.

Jung's psychological theories of personality and analysis are not ego-driven fantasies, as many psychologies may be portrayed, but are a summons of ego consciousness toward honest and humble dialogue with the transpersonal features of the psyche. This includes dream work, mystical experience, active imagination, body work, and more (J. Hollis, personal communication 2012). The deeper relevance for understanding Jung's engagement with the transpersonal leads to two major points made by J. Hollis (personal communication, 2012):

1   We as individuals are present to a transpersonal history of humankind at all times, a reality, known or unbeknownst to us, and we are being influenced, moved and shaped by these historic and contemporaneous dynamic forces.

2   In a time of general spiritual impoverishment, decline of orthodoxy, failure of the
     systems of material capitalism and secular surrogates, the capacity of the individual
     to experience the numinous more directly not only offers a path out of the chaotic
     morass of modernism, but a path to a personal spirituality as well as a psychology.

Jung's principal interests in spiritualism, paranormal and occult phenomena, symbolism, and the psychology of religion, along with his research, clinical practice,
writing—and the training of Jungian analysts, underscore the importance of his work
to psychodynamic psychology in general and specifically to transpersonal psychology.
Undeniably, Jung was one of the major precursors, if not the actual founder, of a
transpersonal psychology.

Washburn's Approach to Transpersonal Psychology

Washburn (1988) is one noted transpersonal theorist who can broadly be seen as working in the Jungian depth tradition. He suggested that ego exists in relation to a superior
Dynamic Ground, which Jung referred to as the unconscious. Washburn indicated that
he does not think of transpersonal psychology as a sub-discipline of psychology, but
rather as a multidisciplinary inquiry aimed at a comprehensive understanding of human
nature, including relational psychodynamics, individual developmental and cognitive
psychology, the inner world of object relations theory, cultural-environmental religion,
and philosophy. As such, he suggested that transpersonal theory extends ideas about
the transpersonal field beyond the discipline of psychology. Transpersonal theory is
seen by him as integrative in character and borrows constructs from these and other
multiple sources. The architecture of Jung' theory is instrumental to the foundation
of Washburn's theoretical approach, particularly Jung's theory of the unconscious,
archetypes, complexes, ego-self axis, and the transcultural comparative study of mysticism, alchemy, spiritual and wisdom traditions, historiography, mythology, religion,
philosophy, art, symbols and symbolism, and cultural anthropology. These all figure
prominently in the architecture of analytical theory and support, as a foundation,
Washburn's multidisciplinary approach to transpersonal theory.
     Washburn's (2003) dynamic-dialectic paradigm has focused on deep sources of life
that have been submerged, but can be restored and integrated at a higher transpersonal
level. Washburn (1988) offered a triphasic stage model (pre-egoic, egoic, and trans-
egoic), which includes sensory, dynamic-relational and dialetical perspectives. The
primary influential sources of his thinking are Freud and Jung, although he values
contributions from psychoanalytic ego psychology, object relations theory, and the
post classical psychoanalytic work of Erick Erikson, Heinz Hartmann, and Margaret
Mahler, (Washburn, 1988, pp. 2-7). It is important for transpersonal psychology to
recognize the challenge suggested by Washburn in his approach to the theory and
its applications. He stated, "I have borrowed extensively from Jung, as I have as well
from Freud and from other representatives of psychodynamic thought. However, in
drawing heavily on thinkers such as these, I have not adhered closely to any of them,
but rather have gone my own way." (p. 7).

Although Washburn's (1988, 2003) approach to the pre-egoic and egoic stages of his theory integrates developmental psychodynamic theory, his third stage, the trans-egoic, integrates spiritual development and engagement with the collective unconscious or Dynamic Ground as a clear contribution to transpersonal theory. Washburn (1988) posited a bipolar constitution of the psyche, comprised of the non-egoic or physico-dynamic pole and the egoic or mental-egoic pole. There is a dialectical relationship between the two poles across the life span. The non-egoic is comprised of the Dynamic Ground thought to be energy, libido or spirit, sensuous bodily life, instincts, spontaneous feelings, imaginal autosymbolic cognitions, and nontemporal experience. Dynamics of the egoic or mental-egoic pole include ego and individuated selfhood, inner reflective mental life, cultivated personality, self-control and deliberate will, abstract operational cognition and temporal durational experience. His model of triphasic development, includes the neonatal state in the pre-egoic stage, egoic, and trans-egoic stage.

In the pre-egoic stage, or infant state, the egoic pole is not yet differentiated from the non-egoic pole. Ego exists preactively as a psychic potential within an undifferentiated dynamic matrix in the Dynamic Ground, or what Jung would have called the collective unconscious. In the pre-egoic stage, the egoic pole begins differentiation from the non-egoic pole, but remains weak and undeveloped. The emergent ego conscious is dominated by physico-dynamic or phylogentic potentials.

In the egoic stage, the ego establishes independence from the non-egoic pole, but only through dissociating itself from the non-egoic pole by means of original repression. The non-egoic pole is arrested and submerged, becoming the dynamic unconscious, while the ego assumes airs of a Cartesian self: an immaterial thinking thing. In the unfolding of selfhood, the non-egoic pole is alienated from consciousness and demoted to not-self: the id, or the non-egoic pole in arrested, pre-form. In the unfolding of selfhood, body ego differentiates from the Dynamic Ground and the egoic pole is identified with a bodily self or body-ego, which is not a well-defined or complete self. In identification with the one side of the Dynamic Ground, it participates in selfhood as the underlying primordial self.

During the trans-egoic stage, there is a higher level integration of the egoic pole, rerooted in the non-egoic pole in the Dynamic Ground. The power of the Dynamic Ground, as spirit, is sovereign and the ego is subject to its power. This Dynamic Ground is the aboriginal source existing prior to the activation of the eogic pole and from which selfhood emerges. In this stage of the unfolding of the self, the ego is rooted in and aligned with the Ground and the loyal subject of the spirit, which is sovereign.

Each of these developmental stages involves the ego's return or regression to the Dynamic Ground in service of transcendence. In this regression, the original repression (deemed necessary for developmental progression and differentiation of the self) gives way and the ego is reconnected with the non-egoic pole to which it regresses. The ego experiences resurging non-egoic potentials in their arrested pre-form. Regeneration in spirit can then occur. Here the ego, having given up resistance to the non-egoic potentials, is enhanced by re-engagement with these potentials, and thus is regenerated by the power of the Dynamic Ground or spirit. Integration of the two polar dimensions of psyche can then be experienced. In the reunion, their resources are fused into higher forms, integrated as a true bipolar system. Washburn conceived of a true two-in-one or *coincidentia oppositorium* in which the power of the Dynamic Ground, as spirit, is sovereign and the ego is subject.

Conclusion

Jungian scholarship continues, such as in the transpersonal theory of Washburn and the extended analytical theory of Sonu Shamdasani (2003). In particular, there has been a resurgence of interest generated by the recent publication of Jung's (2009) *Red Book,* and more original but previously unpublished work from Jung is expected to be published in the near future by the Philemon Foundation. In its breadth and depth, Jung's theory continues to generate interest in diverse disciplines, including neuroscience, attachment theory, and clinical practice (Haule, 2011a, 2011b; Knox, 2003; Stevens, 2003; Wilkerson, 2006); synchronicity and science (Haule, 2011a, 2011b), the cultural complex in theory and practice (Singer & Kimbles, 2004); comparative mythology and archetypal theory (Bolen, 1984, 1989; Bynum, 1999; Campbell, 1971; Edinger, 1972; Vaughan, 1980, 2010, 2013); political psyche (Samuels, 1993); and worldview, including transpersonal psychology. Washburn's work (2003) in particular has advanced the dialogue between structural hierarchal paradigm in transpersonal psychology (Wilber, 1996, 1998) and his own spiral dynamic perspective by seeking a reconciliation of differences in these two theories (Washburn, 2003). Jung's work represents pioneering contributions to transpersonal psychology, which not only continue to be influential on the field but, on its own, has a vibrant following.

References

Alexander, F., & Selesnick, S. (1966). *The history of psychiatry.* New York, NY: Harper & Row.

Bolen, J. (1984). *Goddesses in every woman: A new psychology for women.* New York. NY: Harper & Row.

Bolen, J. (1989). *Gods in everyman: A new psychology of men's lives and loves.* New York, NY: Harper & Row.

Bynum, E. B. (1999), *The African unconscious roots of ancient mysticism and modern psychology.* New York, NY: Teacher's College Press.

Campbell, J. (Ed.). (1971). *The portable Jung.* New York, NY: Viking Press.

Douglas, C. (2000). Analytical psychology. In R. Corsini & D. Wedding (Eds.), *Current psychotherapies* (6th ed.; pp. 113-147). Belmont CA: Brooks/Cole.

Edinger, E. (1972). *Ego and archetype.* Boston, MA: Shambhala.

Ellenberger, H. (1981). *The discovery of the unconscious.* New York, NY: Basic Books.

Freud, S. (1913). *The interpretation of dreams* (A. A. Brill, Trans). New York, NY: Macmillan. (Original work published 1900 [German])

Haule, J. (2011a). *Evolution and archetype.* In *Jung in the 21st century* (Vol. 1). New York, NY: Taylor & Francis.

Haule, J. (2011b). *Synchronicity and science.* In *Jung in the 21st century* (Vol. 2). New York, NY: Taylor & Francis.

Jacobi, J. (1973) *The psychology of C.G. Jung* (8th ed.). New Haven, CT: Yale University Press.

Jung, C. G. (1923). *Psychological types* (H. G. Baynes, Trans.). New York, NY: Harcourt, Brace. (Original work published 1921)

Jung, C. G. (1961). *Memories, dreams, reflections*. New York, NY: Pantheon Books.

Jung, C. G. (1966a). *Two essays on analytical psychology* (R. F. C. Hull, Trans.). In *The collected works of C. G. Jung* (Vol. 7, 2nd ed.). Princeton, NJ: Princeton University Press.

Jung, C. G. (1966b). *The practice of psychotherapy* (R. F. C. Hull, Trans.). In *The collected works of C. G. Jung* (Vol. 16, 2nd ed.). Princeton, NJ: Princeton University Press.

Jung, C. G. (1967). *Symbols of transformation* (R. F. C. Hull, Trans.). In *The collected works of C. G. Jung* (Vol. 5, 2nd ed.). Princeton, NJ: Princeton University Press.

Jung, C. G. (1968a). *The archetypes of the collective unconscious* (R. F. C. Hull, Trans.). In *The collected works of C. G. Jung* (Vol. 9, Part 1, 2nd ed.). Princeton, NJ: Princeton University Press.

Jung, C. G. (1968b). *Aion: Researches into the phenomenology of the self* (R. F. C. Hull, Trans.). In *The collected works of C. G. Jung* (Vol. 9, Part 2, 2nd ed.). Princeton, NJ: Princeton University Press.

Jung, C. G. (1969). *Psychology and religion: West and East* (R. F. C. Hull, Trans.). In *The collected works of C. G. Jung* (Vol. 11, pp. 558-575, 2nd ed.). Princeton, NJ: Princeton University Press.

Jung, C. G. (1971). *The spirit in man, art, and literature* (R. F. C. Hull, Trans.). In *The collected works of C. G. Jung* (Vol. 15, 2nd ed.). Princeton, NJ: Princeton University Press.

Jung, C. G. (1972a). On the nature of the psyche. 5. Conscious and unconscious. (R. F. C. Hull, Trans.). In *The structure and dynamics of the psyche* (pp. 184-190), *The collected works of C. G. Jung* (Vol. 8, 2nd ed.). Princeton, NJ: Princeton University Press.

Jung, C. G. (1972b). *The structure and dynamics of the psyche* (R. F. C. Hull, Trans.). In *The collected works of C. G. Jung* (Vol. 8). Princeton, NJ: Princeton University Press.

Jung, C. G. (1975). *Psychiatric studies* (R. F. C. Hull, Trans.). In *The collected works of C. G. Jung* (Vol. 1). Princeton, NJ: Princeton University Press.

Jung, C. G. (1978). *Civilization in transition* (R. F. C. Hull, Trans.). In *The collected works of C. G. Jung* (Vol. 10, 2nd ed.). Princeton, NJ: Princeton University Press.

Knox, J. (2003). *Archetype, attachment, analysis: Jungian psychology and the emergent mind*. New York: Routledge.

Samuels, A. (1993). *The political psyche*. New York, NY: Routledge.

Shamdasani, S. (2003). *Jung and the making of modern psychology: The dream of a science*. Cambridge, UK: Cambridge University Press.

Shamdasani, S. (Ed.). (2009). *The red book*. New York, NY: W. W. Norton.

Singer, T., & Kimbles, S. (2004). *The cultural complex: Contemporary Jungian perspectives on psyche and society*. New York, NY: Brunner-Routledge.

Stevens, A. (1991). *On Jung*. London, UK: Penguin Books.

Stevens, A. (2003). *Archetype revisited*. Toronto, Canada: Inner City Books.

Vaughan, A. (1980). A study of the transition of African American and African males from youth into young adulthood. In A. Kiev, W. J. Muya, & N. Sartorius (Eds.), *Future of Mental Health Services: Proceedings of a conference on the future of mental health services, Nairobi, Kenya, August 14-18, 1979* (pp. 146-159). Amsterdam, The Netherlands: Elsevier/North Holland.

Vaughan, A. (2010). *One world: Reflections on concepts of the emergent self, global citizenship and global culture*. Seattle, WA: Linkage.

Vaughan, A. (2013). Yoruba Orisha in archetypal transference and counter transference phenomena. Unpublished manuscript.

Washburn, M. (1988). *The ego and the dynamic ground.* Albany, NY: State University of New York Press.

Washburn, M. (2003). Transpersonal dialogue: A new direction. *Journal of Transpersonal Psychology, 35*(1), 1-19.

Wilber, K. (1996). *A brief history of everything.* Boston, MA: Shambhala.

Wilber, K. (1998). *The essential Ken Wilber.* Boston, MA: Shambhala.

Wilkerson, M. (2006). *Coming into mind: The mind-brain relationship: A Jungian perspective.* New York, NY: Taylor & Francis.

8

Integral Psychology

Brant Cortright

Integral Psychology is a phrase coined by the Indian psychologist Indra Sen in the 1930s to describe the psychology that comes out of Sri Aurobindo's integral yoga and integral philosophy (Sen, 1986). Sri Aurobindo was a Western-educated Indian sage who integrated the many disparate streams of Vedanta into a cohesive whole, as well as synthesized Tantra into a spiritual vision of the evolution of consciousness. He also provided rich, extensive phenomenological descriptions of inner, psychological, and spiritual dimensions of consciousness that have extensive implications for psychology. This chapter will provide an overview of Sri Aurobindo's psychological and spiritual thought and show how it provides an organizing framework for Western psychology (Aurobindo, 2007, 2012).

Sri Aurobindo was born in India in 1872, was educated in England from age 7 until he was 21 when he graduated from Cambridge University, and then returned to India where he lived until his death in 1950 (Heehs, 2008). Originally drawn to politics and the Indian independence movement, he soon shifted to yoga and spirituality. His rapid spiritual development following his enlightenment in 1908 allowed him to realize Nirvana and the impersonal Self or Atman and then flowered in the realization of the Personal Divine and the individual soul. He thus combined in himself the key realizations of the two major streams of spirituality in India and the world, namely that of the Personal Divine (mainstream Christianity, Judaism, Islam, and Indian Bhakti traditions) and the Impersonal Divine (Buddhism, Advaita Vedanta, Taoism.) As he would later write, most spiritual traditions stop at one realization or the other, which has perpetuated a kind of competition among the various religions of the world for which aspect of the Divine is most "ultimate." With Sri Aurobindo one finds a yogi who fused these two dimensions of spiritual realization within himself and who did not privilege either side of the Divine. Integral yoga sees the Divine as equally Personal and Impersonal, just as one's own spiritual identity has both personal and impersonal dimensions.

The Wiley Blackwell Handbook of Transpersonal Psychology, First Edition.
Edited by Harris L. Friedman and Glenn Hartelius.
© 2013 John Wiley & Sons, Ltd. Published 2015 by John Wiley & Sons, Ltd.

Sri Aurobindo's Western education gave him a great appreciation for the discoveries of the West, especially the exploration of the material world and science. He was the first to combine the Western theory of evolution with Indian spiritual traditions. For Sri Aurobindo, Darwin's discovery of evolution was momentous, but it was only the tip of the iceberg. The real story of evolution, he maintained, was not the development of species and bodies and forms, but the evolution of consciousness. Consciousness evolution is an inward process not visible on the surface. As consciousness evolves, it needs new bodies, new species, new forms to express the growing consciousness within.

Sri Aurobindo's integral philosophy uses the traditional Indian term of Brahman to describe the Divine, although in later life he increasingly used English rather than Sanskrit terms. The central idea is that Brahman created this universe by throwing itself into form (involution) to create matter via the "big bang." Brahman, which is best described by the terms existence (*sat*), consciousness (*chit*), and bliss (*ananda*), first creates matter, which is the most dense form of consciousness. Although the physical world appears to be "dead matter", devoid of consciousness, for Sri Aurobindo matter is secretly conscious but in a kind of sleep or torpor, it is unconscious although containing an evolutionary impulse. Matter slowly organizes and the next step of consciousness emerges, Life or the vital principle. Out of unicellular organisms first comes plants, and then as life becomes more complex there is the next step of evolution: the emergence of Mind. Animals have a rudimentary mind, according to integral philosophy, but one that is that is imprisoned by their senses. Only in human beings does mind emerge in its own fullness through language and the capacity for self-reflective thought.

With these three developments in consciousness—body, heart, and mind—Sri Aurobindo believed that the world is now ready for the next development of consciousness, the emergence of Spirit. As spirit emerges it uses the instrumentation of body, heart, mind to express itself in the world. Through this the soul's bliss, love, and peace radiate into the world as consciousness develops more expressive power in its ongoing development. The unfurling of consciousness is accompanied by development of increasing abilities and powers to engage with the world as the soul aligns with the Divine's evolutionary impulse. In the Indian tradition, the Divine creates this world for play, for *lila*. Shiva brings this world into manifestation through his dance, and Shiva dances for the sheer joy of dancing, out of the fullness of self-expression. As spirit emerges, the world becomes the soul's playground, an opportunity for further development and to bring the Divine light, love, joy, peace into the earth plane.

In the process spirit changes the instruments. Just as the Vital principle changed matter (living tissue is very different from inert matter), and just as the principle of Mind changed both matter (animal tissue is different from plant tissue) and the Vital principle (transforming it into emotions or feelings), so the principle of Spirit will change what came before, transforming the human body, heart, and mind to a higher vibration and more perfect instrument of spirit. This transformation was called by Sri Aurobindo *supramentalization,* and he believed that it would bring about a greater order to our life on earth, a life governed by spiritual oneness, universal love, wisdom, and freedom from the separative, aggressive, divisive ego that now characterizes the current level of evolution.

One important feature of the evolution of consciousness is the necessity for some kind of continuity of the developing consciousness. Because consciousness does not simply leap from a bacteria to an enlightened sage, but rather goes through a slow, graded, orderly development, this requires two things: the necessity for reincarnation, and a soul who undergoes this evolutionary growth. A growing consciousness needs many different bodies, forms, and expressions through which it can progress. For Sri Aurobindo reincarnation was both a theoretical necessity as well as a spiritual fact that was confirmable through a specific kind of introspection and consciousness development. Similarly, the evolving soul was a phenomenological reality that could be discovered by all persons who have a sincere aspiration and the meditative and spiritual discipline to do so. The soul is the evolutionary element within us and its emergence for each person is a turning point in the evolution of consciousness.

At the beginning of the human levels of evolution and for a long period following, the soul is concerned with building up the outer instruments of body, heart, and mind. The senses draw the person outward, and it is clear that many people are lost in outwardness and the surface of existence. But as consciousness evolves, it begins to turn the person within, revealing the riches of the inner world—peace, presence, love, wisdom, bliss.

Evolution begins slowly and unconsciously, meandering and with many false steps. As evolution proceeds it becomes more conscious. As it becomes more conscious it speeds up. The acceleration of consciousness evolution is what spiritual practice (yoga) is about, hence Sri Aurobindo's (2007) famous phrase, "All life is yoga," which was the subtitle to his masterwork of integration, *The Synthesis of Yoga*. That is, all life is a gradual self-finding and development, although it begins as an unconscious yoga. The true spiritual life begins when evolution becomes conscious and one can align with the evolutionary impulse within. The soul turning the person toward the inner spiritual life signals that the soul's growth has reached the point where it can be a significant influence in the person's life. Discovering the intrinsic joy, compassion, deep peace, and inner unity within changes the person's relationship to the outer world as the inner world opens.

Sri Aurobindo's integral philosophy is a contemporary statement of the perennial philosophy. Although some transpersonal theorists have criticized the perennial philosophy (Ferrer, 2000, 2002; Rothberg, 1986), there nevertheless has been nothing comparable to replace it as a comprehensive framework for situating spiritual experience. Huston Smith's (1976) scholarly statements of it enumerate four dimensions of outer reality: the physical plane, the intermediate plane, the celestial plane (Personal Divine) and the infinite plane (Impersonal Divine), which is broadly inclusive of the many diverse forms of spirituality. Although some commentators continue the competition for "most ultimate reality" by favoring one side or the other (Wilber, 1995), Sri Aurobindo's integral philosophy sees the Divine as Personal and Impersonal equally.

Although many Indian commentators have praised Sri Aurobindo as the "greatest Vedantic philosopher of all time," his decades exploring the inner world of Being have produced an extraordinarily detailed map of the psyche as well. The map of consciousness that emerges from integral yoga goes beyond the ego and the unconscious that has been the focus of Western psychology. What Sri Aurobindo stressed, much in line with other Eastern thinkers, was the importance of verifying these discoveries through one's own personal experience. It is not enough to simply read about higher or inner states of consciousness; one can, through a process of inner practice, verify these universal elements of human consciousness for oneself.

Integral yoga sees four levels of human consciousness. First is the outer consciousness consisting of a surface body, heart, and mind, which is that to which Western psychology has confined its research. Second is an inner, or subtle body, heart, and mind. Third is what is termed the true body, heart, and mind. Fourth is the central being, consisting of two aspects: the individual soul, and the atman or Buddha-nature.

The outer body, heart, and mind has further subdivisions that will be explored shortly. What is significant is that until recently, Western psychology—which begins from the outside and looks within—has primarily stopped here. Until the advent of transpersonal psychology, Western psychology has been fixated almost exclusively upon the surface manifestation of consciousness. Eastern and spiritual psychologies, on the other hand, begin from the inside and look without. These approaches to psychology have unambiguously affirmed that the true foundation of consciousness is spiritual, something to which Western psychology, until very recently, has been blind.

The second level of consciousness, according to Sri Aurobindo, consists of an inner or subtle body, an inner heart, and an inner mind. This inner level of consciousness is a much-expanded domain of awareness. The inner or subtle body consists of the energy body and auric field, the *chakras* (seven energy centers that organize the surface organism), subtle senses, and the ability to travel outside the physical body (out-of-body experiences.) The physical body results from the integrity of the subtle physical body. For example, Sri Aurobindo maintained that disease first begins by entering tears or holes in the auric envelope. Over time these energy disruptions eventually manifest as disease states in the outer body, a theory of disease with which some contemporary clairvoyants concur (Brennan, 1993; Myss, 1988). The inner emotional being or heart opens to a subtle world where cosmic waves of feelings are swirling and moving. Some enter into the individual, who then identifies these feelings as their own. Others pass by or are only a small influence. This intermediate plane also has beings and forces that seek to influence the person, for good or for ill. Openness to this world makes the psyche more of a public space than a separate, enclosed environment, although this influence is occult and too subtle for most people to experience without practice and intention. The inner mind opens to a much larger mind space that is not shut up in the tiny brain most people normally identify with. This much-expanded inner mind is open to the cosmic mind and to cosmic mind waves and thoughts. Fully half of what an individual experiences, according to Sri Aurobindo, comes from outside, but of the origins of thoughts, feelings, impulses, inspirations, and so forth, the person is typically not aware.

The world that the inner being opens to is closer to the Divine, but it forms an intermediate plane between the outer, physical world and Spirit. This intermediate plane is a mixture of light and dark, angelic and demonic, good and bad. While it is closer to the Divine, it is also closer to darker forces as well, forces that are hostile to the evolution and are therefore called hostile forces in integral yoga. But for a closer step to one's real nature it is necessary to go inward another level. The true mind, true heart, and true body are a third level of consciousness that is intimately connected to one's Divine nature. This level represents the atman on each plane of body, heart, and mind. It is the inner witness or observer consciousness and represents an essential dimension of each plane as it relates to the Impersonal Divine.

The inmost being is spiritual, and it consists of two aspects, personal and impersonal. On an inner plane behind the heart *chakra* lays the evolving soul, a portion of Personal Divine Being. This is one's spiritual individuality, one's unique soul, which develops over numerous lifetimes. The soul's nature is one of intrinsic bliss and joy, a deep peace, light and vision, and an inherent love. This love feels an inner unity with all people and creatures and creation and is not dependent upon outer circumstances. This psychic center enters the evolution and develops through life experience. After each lifetime the soul gathers the spiritual essence of the past life and makes a soul growth out of it, then prepares to reincarnate so that its evolution can continue. The soul, because it comes from the Divine whose nature is Truth, has an unerring guidance. It is the true evolutionary guide in life, the one infallible source of wisdom one can trust entirely. To awaken one's soul, to experience its joy and love and peace and light in daily life and make use of its inner guidance, is a central goal of integral yoga and integral psychology.

The other part of the individual's spiritual nature is the atman or Self (called in Buddhism Buddha-nature). This is the impersonal spiritual side that is one with Brahman. Its nature is therefore the same as that of Brahmah: *sat, chit, ananda* (existence, consciousness, bliss.) The atman stands above the evolution. It does not evolve or enter into the evolutionary play but stays forever in its wide, infinite peace supporting all parts of the life equally.

Whereas most religions stop with one realization or the other, integral yoga aims for the realization of both aspects of spiritual nature, and for uniting with both aspects of the Divine. However, because this is an evolutionary view of life, there is special importance given to the evolving soul, for this is the evolutionary element within us and the means of the transformation of consciousness in the world.

Each of these levels of identity is a world in itself. Most people, whose minds are drawn outward by their senses, identify exclusively with their outer body, heart, mind, or organism. But through an introspective or meditative process, inner perception can be trained and refined so that the veil that usually separates outer, surface identity from the inner planes can be pierced to reveal a much wider, deeper, vaster realm of consciousness. Spirituality, in this view, is not a matter of mere belief, but rather an experiential reality that appears when the proper conditions are met; when the surface mind is purified to the extent that the turbulence and noise of thought and emotion is quieted so there is some degree of peace and silence, one becomes capable of entering into the deeper realms of being. As the inner world opens up it becomes possible to find the spiritual reality of one's identity and the Divine that many religions have proclaimed for thousands of year.

Indra Sen was the first psychologist to realize the importance of integral yoga for psychology. In a series of writings and professional presentations from the 1930s through the 1970s, he laid out the central importance of the evolving soul (also called the "psychic being" or "psychic center" by Sri Aurobindo, 1997-2012) for psychology. Sen first tried to show how Freud's early writings were helpful but insufficient for understanding the psyche. He then turned to Jungian psychology and proposed that Jung's central archetype of the Self corresponds to the psychic being, although he argued that Jung's understanding was theoretical whereas integral psychology originated from the actual experience and realization of the soul. Given what has emerged about Jung's (2009) own deep engagements with the psyche, this critique might need to be softened—but the crucial distinction between theoretical knowledge and experience remains.

The first Western psychologist to write about integral psychology was Arya Mahoney, who published a series of articles outlining the experimental use of techniques he derived from integral yoga with psychotherapy clients, culminating in his book *Alchemy of the Soul* (Mahoney, 2007). Other Western writers to bring insights from integral yoga and philosophy into Western psychology include A. S. Dalal (2001), who published numerous collections of Sri Aurobindo's writings as well as amplified expositions of his yoga psychology. Matthijs Cornelissen (Cornelissen, Misra, & Varma, 2011) also advanced the field with a series of papers on integral psychology and a two-volume book on Indian psychology in which integral psychology figured prominently.

As another key writer in the field of integral psychology, Cortright has published a series of papers and the book *Integral Psychology* (2000, 2002, 2004, 2005a, 2005b, 2007, 2011), which further elucidated the integration of Western psychology with integral yoga. In this approach, Sri Aurobindo's map of consciousness becomes an integrating framework for all of Western psychology. Such a whole-person integrating framework has been notably missing in Western psychological scholarship since its inception.

Integral psychology begins with Sri Aurobindo's insight into the fourfold division of consciousness: the outer being (body, heart, mind), the inner being (inner or subtle physical, inner heart, inner mind), the true being (true body, heart, mind), and central being (evolving soul and atman or Buddha-nature). The province of Western psychology has historically been the outer being, but even with this most superficial part of the person, Western psychology has produced a wide array of theories and schools that put forth competing views in their attempts to understand the psyche. Sri Aurobindo's further subdivisions of the outer being provide an elegant way to understand the insights of Western psychology into body-heart-mind organism.

The level of mind is subdivided in integral psychology into physical mind, emotional mind, and mind proper. This tripartite division corresponds with the triune brain discovered by modern neuroscience: the ancient reptilian brain that runs the body and physiological systems, the mammalian emotional brain or limbic system responsible for feeling responses, and the neocortex, human's more recent evolutionary addition, which is the seat of abstract thinking, language, and the capacity for self-reflection. Most of current academic psychology research, together with cognitive-behavioral psychology, focuses on the level of mind. This first step inward reveals how thoughts ("self-talk") influence emotional life and how cognitions can be challenged, altered, and revised to assist people in reducing symptoms and coping more successfully with conditions ranging from certain kinds of depression to phobia to personality disorders. There is a great deal of research evidence that confirms its efficacy, and this level of intervention has had an important influence in the development of Western psychology.

However, many people seeking psychotherapy find this approach quite limited in their search for more thorough-going transformation. For more profound approaches to change and to understanding the psyche, it is necessary to turn to the depth psychologies. Depth psychology, which originated with Freud's seminal ideas, refers to a belief in the unconscious and the understanding that some forces of the psyche are beyond one's current conscious, rational control. The depth psychologies view emotion as central to understanding the psyche. Here again multiple schools have generated a bewildering array of theories that, based on the insights of integral yoga, can be synthesized into a coherent whole. Sri Aurobindo demarcated three levels of the emotional being: the lower emotional (consisting of the instinctual nature and animal inheritance), the central emotional level (where most people in today's world are centered, and consisting of concerns about self-esteem and relationships), and the higher emotional level (which partakes of a mentalized quality of images, creativity, and imagination). Note that the three levels of the emotional being do not have a value attached to them but simply refer to the frequency of the vibration of each level. The lower emotional has a slower, denser frequency as compared with the higher emotional or mental levels that vibrate at a higher frequency. This threefold division of the emotional being provides a way to understand and integrate the three major developments in psychoanalysis.

The lower emotional level corresponds to Freud's classical psychoanalysis. This first developmental step in Freud's thinking focused upon those aspects of the unconscious that are *instinctual*—that is, driven by instincts and impulses. Freud found two major instincts in the psyche: sex and aggression. This part of the psyche views the world through such a lens, and every person or event is colored by these instinctual concerns. Is each new person a potential partner or a competitor, does one feel safe or threatened? Animal desires are part of human heritage, and although Freud may have originally misunderstood how central sexual desires and aggressive instincts are, their role in psychological life can hardly be doubted.

The central emotional level corresponds to contemporary psychoanalysis. This is the relational model of the psyche that has by now subsumed Freud's earlier instinctual model. The self is primarily *relational* (not instinctual as Freud first thought, rather instincts help shape and orient what is the human being's more fundamental relational nature). The self emerges in a relational matrix, and the attachment patterns, the amount of self-esteem, the degree of self-cohesion versus vulnerability to fragmentation, place the self and its relational world at the center of psychological study. Do I feel related to others who are nourishing and who see me for who I am, or do I need to present an inauthentic, false self (as was necessary in the family of origin) that keeps me from being seen and from getting the emotional satisfactions I need? Do I feel good about myself, able to engage the world in a meaningful, gratifying way, or am I estranged from my skills and talents, unsure of my worth? This is the realm that self psychology, object relations, attachment-oriented schools, interpersonal schools, and family systems focus on. This also appears to be the level where most people spend most of their time.

The higher emotional level is *imaginal,* and corresponds to Jung's analytical psychology and includes the realm of fantasy and imagination. Symbol and image predominate here. This is the level that is closest to source of creativity (which is one's inner being, according to integral yoga), and the exploration of dreams, imagery, and creativity are the gateways to this level.

Although all schools of depth psychology point to the importance of emotion and emotion regulation for the psyche, psychoanalysis focuses on this directly. However, according to integral yoga this misses the central role of the body, for emotion emerges from bodily experiencing. The close relationship between somatic experiencing and emotion is one of the most profound discoveries of humanistic-existential psychology. The schools of humanistic-existential psychology include gestalt therapy and other existential schools (May, Angel, & Ellenberger, 1958; Perls, Hefferline, & Goodman, 1951), focusing (Gendlin, 1981), bioenergetics (Lowen, 1975), all the somatic therapies inspired by Wilhelm Reich's body focus—even Carl Rogers' client-centered therapy is grounded in this approach (Rogers, 2004). These schools have discovered that psychological wounding causes not only defenses to form and deficits in self-structure, but a dissociative move into the mind and out of the present sensory reality. All these schools value the importance of coming back into the here and now and one's organismic, physical reality as healing unfolds.

Thus, this structure of body, heart, and mind offers an integrating framework for the key elements of Western psychology. But integral psychology goes further. There is also the inner being (inner body, heart, and mind), the true being (true body, heart, and mind), and inmost of all the central being (soul and atman).

The inmost center of consciousness is the human being's spiritual ground, the true foundation of consciousness. As mentioned earlier this consists of the atman (or Buddha-nature), which is one's non-evolving identity with Brahman. The path to the realization of atman tends to be mindfulness practices. Sri Aurobindo stressed the difference between *experience, realization,* and *transformation.* Experience is temporary, although it opens new horizons of spiritual possibility. Realization is permanent, it allows continual access to a new dimension of consciousness, and according to Sri Aurobindo (2012) it is where most religions stop. The problem with realization is that it does not radically affect the outer nature. It is an inner freedom that is attained while the outer body, heart, mind are touched but not fundamentally changed. Transformation, on the other hand, brings inner realization out into the mind, heart, and the very cells of the body. For transformation to occur, the realization of the soul, not just the atman, is necessary, for the atman loses its hold on form but the soul is connected to the body, heart, and mind.

The evolving soul is the true self of the human being, what makes each one of us uniquely ourselves. It is eternal potential that develops into a unique expression of the Divine through time. Its voice is often drowned out in the noise and clamor of the body's demands, the heart's impulses and desires, the mind's constant thinking and imaging. Yet it struggles to express itself as best it can through these impediments, slowly refining one's outer nature over the course of many lifetimes, until it reaches the stage where it can be first an active influence and then an actual realization that radiates from the center of the heart. When the soul's immense love for all beings and creation begins to dawn, when its bliss and joy and deep contentment stir, when the soul's light and peace and aspiration to serve the Divine begin to be experienced, one's life changes dramatically. It becomes clear that what one is seeking cannot be satisfied by any amount of outer gratification. It is an inner union with the Divine to which the person aspires, and outer circumstances and relationship support the journey towards this Divine fulfillment.

Trusting inner guidance is a hallmark of integral psychology. The soul's unerring guidance, however, is easily overshadowed by the ego's desires and fears. For the soul communicates not so much by thought as by an essential feeling, according to Sri Aurobindo, warning by means of a sense of unease when one is straying from the soul's path and confirming with a feeling of ease, warmth, love, and "rightness" when the steps are true. However, learning to discern the soul's aspirations from the ego's desires is a lifetime's work (at least). Psychotherapy can be helpful in facilitating this process.

An integral approach to psychotherapy has two aims: first to heal the emotional wounding and suffering that every human beings experiences when incarnating, and second to awaken a person's deeper guidance and awareness of their true center (evolving soul). Healing emotional wounding brings up another important concept in integral psychology: *svabhava,* which means one's essential nature or authentic being. In Western psychology this corresponds to the idea of the authentic self. Different schools of depth psychology refer to this inborn potential in different ways. Gestalt therapy refers to organismic wisdom, Jung refers to the Self, psychoanalytic and existential writers refer variously to the real self, the authentic self, the true self, and these are contrasted with the false self or the defensively constructed self that most everyone needed to erect in childhood to cope with a mal-attuned early family system. In the view of Aurobindonian psychology one gets a confirming notion in *svabhava,* the essential or core self. The *Bhagavad Gita* goes so far to say the following one's essential nature leads to the highest spiritual realization, whereas following a path that is not truly one's own is harmful to spiritual development (Sargeant, 1984; see III, 35). In integral psychology, a central goal is working through and eroding the defensive structures of the self and allowing the authentic self to emerge more fully in its place.

Just as in traditional therapy, this goal means bringing coherence and integration to the ego, working through the unconscious defenses and earlier wounds and traumas, allowing the authentic self to emerge along with an increased capacity for intimacy, self-esteem, empowerment, and embodiment. While traditional therapies usually stop at a single goal—for example, greater capacity for emotion regulation or secure attachments or greater embodiment—integral psychology sees every therapy's goals as limited and seeks to unite them all in a vision of higher functioning on every level: body, heart, and mind. In bringing forth the authentic self with its abilities for meaningful and creative work, deep intimacy, and embodied self-knowledge, integral psychology looks beyond this to the refinement of one's surface nature by the evolving soul. The psychic center or evolving soul may not become an experiential reality for even the majority of clients, but a sense of trusting one's inner guidance generally does. As the soul's influence grows, some clients do experience and realize their deeper soul nature, while others sense it in glimpses.

Coherence of the surface self and a spiritual or soul refinement of the surface being are integral psychology's two goals. As the soul refinement proceeds, it transforms the vibration of the outer being so it becomes more responsive to the inner soul's light and love. A more spiritual view of life leads to valuing soul connections and soul relationships more deeply. Relationships, especially intimate relationships, are alive and vibrant to the extent that there is resonance on all four planes of our being: physical, emotional, mental, soul or spirit. At their current level of evolution most relationships have energetic vibrancy on only one or two levels, and before the transpersonal domain opens, most people are relatively content with people who only share some amount of physical, emotional, and mental congeniality. But as evolution proceeds, people are often less satisfied with a merely outer relationship. The inner soul longs for a spiritual communion with fellow seekers who share an inner light and soul spark. Intimate relationship, when one finds such a bond, opens to a new level of soul connection, a depth of sharing and resonance that goes far beyond what is possible with just the outer instruments.

Work, relationships, self-care, diet, exercise, and play are all brought under the soul's influence as outer life increasingly aligns with the inner. The instrumental human nature of body, heart, and mind are soul-infused, ennobled, brought to their highest possibilities as the integral transformation predicted by Sri Aurobindo manifests in the world and expresses more and more of its Divine possibilities.

References

Aurobindo, Sri. (1997-2012). *The complete works of Sri Aurobindo* (37 Vols.). Pondicherry, India: Sri Aurobindo Ashram Trust.

Aurobindo, Sri. (2007). *The synthesis of yoga*. Pondicherry, India: Aurobindo Ashram.

Aurobindo, Sri. (2012). *Letters on Yoga—I*. In *The complete works of Sri Aurobindo*. Pondicherry, India: Sri Aurobindo Ashram Trust.

Brennan, B. (1993). *Light emerging*. New York, NY: Bantam Books.

Cornelissen, M., Misra, G., & Varma, S. (Eds.). (2011). *Foundations of Indian psychology: Theories and concepts* (2 Vols.). New Delhi, India: Pearson Education.

Cortright, B. (2000). An integral approach to spiritual emergency. *Journal of Counseling and Guidance, 15,* 12-17.

Cortright, B. (2002). Integral psychotherapy as existential Vedanta. In M. Cornelissen (Ed.), *Consciousness and its transformation* (pp. 65-79). Pondicherry, India: All India Press.

Cortright, B. (2004). The meeting of East and West. In K. Joshi, M. Cornelissen, & A. Gupta (Eds.), *Consciousness, Indian psychology and yoga*. New Delhi, India: Indian Council of Philosophical Research.

Cortright, B. (2005a). Psychotherapy as the practice of discriminative awareness or Raja Yoga. In G. Shankar (Ed.), *Psychotherapy, yoga and spirituality*. New Delhi, India: Jahdamba.

Cortright, B. (2005b). Yoga and psychotherapy. In G. Shankar (Ed.), *Psychotherapy, yoga and spirituality*. New Delhi, India: Jahdamba.

Cortright, B. (2007). *Integral psychology*. Albany, NY: State University of New York Press.

Cortright, B. (2011). An integral approach to our psychic centre. In M. Cornelissen, G. Misra, & S. Varma (Eds.), *Foundations of Indian psychology: Theories and concepts* (pp. 198-210). Delhi, India: Pearson Education.

Dalal, A. S. (Ed.). (2001). *A greater psychology*. Los Angeles, CA: Tarcher.

Ferrer, J. N. (2000). The perennial philosophy revisited. *Journal of Transpersonal Psychology, 32*(1), 7-30.

Ferrer, J. N. (2002). *Revisioning transpersonal theory: A participatory vision of human spirituality*. Albany, NY: State University of New York Press.

Gendlin, E. (1981). *Focusing*. New York, NY: Bantam.

Heehs, P. (2008) *The lives of Sri Aurobindo*. New York, NY: Columbia University Press.

Jung, C. G. (2009). *The red book: Liber novus* (S. Shamdasani, M. Kyburz, & J. Peck, Eds. & Trans.). New York, NY: W. W. Norton.

Lowen, A. (1975). *Bioenergetics*. New York, NY: Penguin Books.

Mahoney, A. (2007) *Alchemy of the soul*. Nevada City, CA: Blue Dolphin Press.

May, R., Angel, E., & Ellenberger, H. (Eds.). (1958). *Existence*. New York, NY: Basic Books.

Myss, C. (1988) *The creation of health*. New York, NY: Three Rivers Press.

Perls, F., Hefferline, R., & Goodman, P. (1951). *Gestalt therapy*. New York, NY: Julian Press.

Rogers, C. (2004). *On becoming a person*. London, UK: Constable.

Rothberg, D. (1986). Philosophical foundations of transpersonal psychology. *Journal of Transpersonal Psychology, 18*, 1-34.

Sargeant, W. (Trans.). (1984). *Bhagavad gita*. Albany, NY: State University of New York Press.

Sen, I. (1986). *Integral psychology*. Pondicherry, India: Sri Aurobindo Ashram Press.

Smith, H. (1976). *Forgotten truth*. New York, NY: HarperCollins.

Wilber, K. (1995). *Sex, ecology, spirituality The spirit of evolution*. Boston, MA: Shambhala.

9

Transcend and Include

Ken Wilber's Contribution to Transpersonal Psychology

Allan Combs

As is true for many great thinkers, to understand Ken Wilber it is important to appreciate the growth of his ideas over time. Wilber himself helps in this task by dividing the history of his work into five more-or-less discrete phases that he has identified as Wilber-1, Wilber-2, and so on (2006b, June 6). Nevertheless, his own often-quoted mandate, "transcend and include," describes the overall trajectory of his thought surprisingly well (Wilber, 2000a, p. 9). Within this context he has always been interested in psychological and spiritual development carried upward to transpersonal levels. This theme especially dominated his writings through Wilber-3. Starting with Wilber-4 and continuing through Wilber-5, as well as at the time of this writing, he has concentrated his efforts more toward the formulation of a comprehensive philosophical worldview that extends beyond the scope of this chapter.

For clarity the topics on the following pages are laid out sequentially in terms of Wilber's five phases, always with an eye to the overall progression of his approach to transpersonal psychology.

Wilber-1: The Romantic Period (1975-1979)[1]

Major books:

The Spectrum of Consciousness (1977);
No Boundary (1979).

Nowadays it may be difficult to appreciate the force with which *The Spectrum of Consciousness* (Wilber, 1977) and the highly readable *No Boundary* (Wilber, 1979) arrived in the intellectual bazaar of the late 1970s, and in particular the community of psychologists. It was a time of paradigm changes. Thomas Kuhn's *The Structure of*

The Wiley Blackwell Handbook of Transpersonal Psychology, First Edition.
Edited by Harris L. Friedman and Glenn Hartelius.

Scientific Revolutions had been in print since 1962, but was getting more attention than ever. Popular books such as Gary Zukav's (1979) *Dancing Wu Li Masters*, Joseph Chilton Pearce's (1973) *Crack in the Cosmic Egg*, and Fritjof Capra's (1975) *Tao of Physics* took their places on bookstore shelves alongside Wilber's first two books. Excitement was in the air and things were changing. In spite of all this the number of psychologists who knew anything about transpersonal psychology outside of California was still very small. For example, I was living in Missouri in the late 1970s and was the only member of the *Association for Transpersonal Psychology* in the entire state.

In those days psychology was not only figuratively but also literally divided into three major camps. These were the so-called First Force, or behaviorism, dominating the academic world and associated at the time with B. F. Skinner (cf. Hastings, 1999). The Second Force included the psychodynamic psychologies of Sigmund Freud, Carl Jung, Erik Erikson, and others. These tended to exist at independent institutes outside of academia, and in private practice. Many were MDs. The Third Force of humanistic psychology was spearheaded by Abraham Maslow, Carl Rogers, Rollo May, and a few others. The animosity between these factions was real. The behaviorists were especially discourteous if not downright rude. Maslow was given little respect in his own department at Brandeis University and his students were often the brunt of contempt from other faculty members.

Wilber's first publications in the late 1970s were important because they organized the entire field of psychology into a single theoretical framework or "spectrum." In doing so they transformed transpersonal psychology from its beginnings in humanistic psychology, the West Coast human potentials movement, and explorations of the wisdom of the East, into nothing less than a container large enough to embrace virtually all of psychology's major schools of thought and practice. It is true that most highbrow academics turned their noses up at Wilber, an outsider with no credentials, but he was widely read by an intelligent general public that included many psychologists and academics as well. My own experience at the time, teaching at an undergraduate liberal arts university, was typical. After years of trying to help students make sense out of all the conflicting directions in which psychology was headed, I finally had a map that fanned them all out like cards on the table, creating a spectrum where each type of psychology took its rightful place beside the others.

Since that time it has never been possible to see psychology as quite the fragmented discipline it had previously been. This tendency to conceptualize across broad areas of knowledge has characterized Wilber's work ever since. Starting with Wilber-3, around the mid-1990s (see below), it began to stretch across all realms of human understanding, transitioning Wilber to the category of philosopher.

In the late 1970s, however, the theoretical underpinnings of Wilber's (1977) spectrum theory seemed much less important than the fact that someone was finally making sense out of the many disparate vectors that comprised psychology. As if this were not enough, he was including ideas about altered states of consciousness from Eastern psychologies. This did nothing to endear him to a stodgy academic audience, but along with his informal and lucid writing style his work was immediately recognized by a huge following of people seeking answers to just the kinds of questions he was addressing. The situation has not changed greatly since that time and

Wilber is still more admired by a wide intellectual readership than by the professional academic world. But, as Michael Murphy, co-founder of the Esalen Institute, has often noted, progress is made one funeral at time (personal communication, June 4, 2010), and Wilber's work is now tolerated, if not justly honored, by an increasing academic following.

The Spectrum

The basic idea of the spectrum of consciousness as presented in his first two books was simple enough, although grounded in an essentially Eastern notion of human nature most easily seen in the traditional levels of being, or "sheaths," of Vedanta philosophy (Wilber, 1977, 1979). Wilber did an excellent job of aligning these with Buddhist ideas and notions from Western mysticism as well. The result was a cascade of psychological structures by which the original ground of being, or formless nondual consciousness, is reduced by a series of splits, first into the total organism[2] against the environment, then the ego against the body, followed by the persona against the shadow. Each step reduces the inner life of the individual another step, and increases its alienation, first from the outer world and then from the shadow aspects of itself. This simple sequence of reductions also marks a series of contractions of a person's identity, ultimately arriving at a cleaving of the inner person into the persona, or conscious personality, and the shadow, Carl Jung's (1939) term for the entire inner menagerie of psychic life evicted from the conscious light of day.

An important aspect of this original spectrum was that it spanned not only a wide variety of psychologies, but also modes of psychological treatment (Wilber, 1977, 1979). Even at the time of the present writing this is an unusual feature of transpersonal theories, and is one reason for the considerable interest that Wilber garnered from the beginning. A close look at Figure 9.1, drawn from *No Boundary* (Wilber, 1979), also discloses examples of types of psychotherapy at each level.

These therapies range from simple counseling to deal with issues of the shadow and persona, to psychoanalysis and other treatments at the level of ego psychology, and on to various forms of existential and humanistic treatment at the organismic (or existential) level.

Wilber's spectrum included a variety of Western esoteric traditions as well as Eastern philosophies that, taken together, construct a series of transpersonal levels leading up to unity consciousness. Placing these on the same general continuum as well-known Western psychologies was a radical move, and one of the most important pieces of Wilber's model. It was a move of considerable importance to the young field of transpersonal psychology because it placed previously exotic ideas about Eastern notions of consciousness, and mystical states in general, into a common framework of discussion with familiar Western models of personality, the mind, and consciousness.

Wilber discussed these ideas at length, and especially in *No Boundary* (1979) considered them in terms of *The Perennial Philosophy,* an ancient idea indicating a basic unity of esoteric philosophies. In 1945, Aldous Huxley had practically reinvented

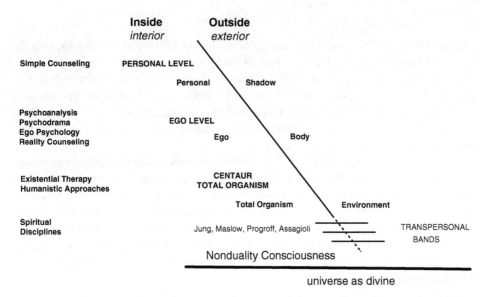

Figure 9.1 Spectrum of consciousness with suggested therapies from *No Boundary* (Wilber, 1979).

the ancient phrase (*philosophia perennis*) to refer to a set of basic themes he had discovered at the root of all religions. Most important among these was the notion of a divine reality as the origin of all being, and the fundamental ground of human consciousness. Giving actual descriptions of the mystical sense of cosmic unity, Wilber (1979) observed:

> So widespread is this experience of supreme identity that it has, along with the doctrines that purport to explain it, earned the name "The Perennial Philosophy." There is much evidence that this type of experience or knowledge is central to every major religion—Hinduism, Buddhism, Taoism, Christianity, Islam, and Judaism—so that we can justifiably speak of the "transcendent unity of religions" and the unanimity of primordial truth." (p. 3)

Here one sees the beginnings of a notion that would expand and grow in sophistication throughout Wilber's career, namely that the inner truth of human nature has a hierarchical structure. Later he would conceptualize the entire cosmos in this framework, but at this point he was struggling with how to organize the various structures of human experience. In the future he would also refer to this organization as the *Great Chain of Being,* referencing the Christian and more ancient notion of a cosmos vertically organized into a hierarchy of earthly and celestial beings (Lovejoy, 1960), and would draw from Sri Aurobindo's writings on the hierarchical organization of the inner structures of the human being as well (Aurobindo, 1971; Sobel & Sobel, 1984).

The Loss of Unity

Wilber (1977, 1979) spoke infrequently of evolution in his first two books, but the seeds were already present for later discussions of it as a central aspect of his thinking. The progressive cleaving of an original unified consciousness into smaller and smaller fragments resulting in many kinds of pain and suffering, each calling for its own form of therapy, gives the clear appearance of a kind of evolutionary path leading away from an infantile unity of being. Here there is also a calling to return to the state of that original unity.

Now, every great theory of psychology has a basic notion of motivation. For classical Freudian theory it was the release of libidinal energy, ultimately toward a state of final quiescence in death. For Abraham Maslow it was the urge to move toward a more adequate, fulfilling, and ultimately self-actualizing life. Late in his life, Maslow (1971) also added a calling to transcendence. Wilber (1980a) recognized this urge but reframed it in his book, *The Atman Project,* as a calling to return to one's original unity. He would soon reframe it again into an evolutionary model of growth and transformation.

Wilber-2: Lifespan Evolution, the Pre-Trans Fallacy, and the Historical Evolution of Consciousness (1980-1982)

Major books:

The Atman Project: A Transpersonal View of Human Development (1980a);
Up from Eden: A Transpersonal View of Human Evolution (1981).

The term *evolution* does not appear in the original indexes of either of Wilber's fist two books, *The Spectrum of Consciousness* (1977) and *No Boundary* (1979). During the Wilber-2 years, however, the idea of evolution became a central concept for Wilber, both as a metaphor for psychological growth and development, and for mapping transformations of consciousness across human history. These ideas would continue as a mainstay in his theoretical program from that time onward.

Exactly what did Wilber mean by *evolution?* He understands traditional science very well, and through his entire corpus he is inclined to take scientific findings and well-established scientific theories at their face value. For example, unlike many "new paradigm writers," with whom he has sometimes been wrongly bundled, he does not make fantastic claims about consciousness and quantum physics, the influence of mind over the material world, and the like. In fact, he has been quite critical of most such claims (e.g., Wilber, 2006a). Nevertheless, in different communities of discourse the term *evolution* has a variety of legitimate meanings. These range from ideas about the transformation of social and personal values over time, to the historical progress of scientific thought, and on to the evolution of biological species, including Darwinism and Neo-Darwinism. It is important to understand that Wilber has not set himself against any of these, although he has argued that certain of them, such as Neo-Darwinism, have been overstretched and do not explain everything they claim to explain (Wilber, 1995).

When he is not referring to established ideas about evolution from traditional disciplines, however, Wilber has his own slant on the concept. In the following passage from the 1996 edition of *The Atman Project* he wrote:

> The course of human development—*and evolution at large*—is from subconscious to self-conscious to superconscious; from prepersonal to personal to transpersonal; from under-mental to mental to over-mental; from pre-temporal to temporal to trans-temporal, by any other name: eternal. (p. 8)

In the above sense, psychological growth is all about evolution, whether it be about the individual or the history of human culture. Note, however, that this conception of evolution is more of an unfolding, or progressive movement toward fulfillment in unity consciousness, than like standard biological ideas on the topic.

As Wilber would point out many times in his later work, this notion fits hand-in-glove with ideas about spiritual evolution articulated in the writings of the great 20th century Indian yoga-sage Sri Aurobindo (e.g., Wilber, 2006a). It also fits comfortably with the history of human consciousness described by the 20th century German cultural historian Jean Gebser (e.g., 1972, 1949/1986). The latter, as with Sri Aurobindo, will continue from this time on to be among Wilber's most highly regarded influences. Sri Aurobindo's thought is described in greater detail in Chapter 7 of this book, so it will be treated here only in passing. Gebser's thinking, however, is addressed in more detail below.

With the above in mind, one can see that, despite the new emphasis on evolution, Wilber-2 is not dramatically different than Wilber-1; a point Wilber himself has emphasized (Wilber, 1997, see pp. 153-154). It also helps explain why he spoke at length about *involution* in his first two books (Wilber, 1977, 1979), even before he began speaking of *evolution,* and has continued to speak about it ever since.

Involution

Involution, as Wilber has used the term, is an ancient idea that refers to the indwelling or movement of the spirit. It is found, for example, in the works of Sri Aurobindo (e.g., 1990) and described by the Indian philosopher and historian Ananda Coomaraswamy (e.g., 1947), both familiar to Wilber. The idea is that spirit projects or steps itself downward, permeating and finally losing itself in the various levels of being. Then for Wilber (1980a, 1981), as for Sri Aurobindo, evolution is a reversal of this course, one in which spirit progressively manifests and discovers itself again. This is the deep basis of the growth and transformation of consciousness in the individual and in history. In the historical context it is an idea reminiscent of Hegel and the German Romantics. Indeed, speaking of Hegel, Wilber (1981) stated in *Up From Eden* that "his shadow falls on every page" (p. 314). More recently he has said,

> The notion of a prior involutionary force does much to help with the otherwise impenetrable puzzles of Darwinian evolution, which has tried, ever-so-unsuccessfully, to explain why dirt would get right up and eventually start writing poetry. (Wilber, 1999, p. 12)

Sri Aurobindo (1980) had proposed similar ideas based on traditional levels of being as found in Hindu thought, especially in Vedanta.

Multiple Levels of Individual Evolution

During this period Wilber (1980a) expanded and articulated his original spectrum into no less than 17 levels (Table 9.1), and in the Appendix to *The Atman Project* compared them, level by level, to a wide variety of contemporary psychologies, as well as concepts from the Kabbalah and Sri Aurobindo's writings, and several traditional Buddhist and Hindu systems of thought. This propensity to take basic ideas and articulate them into multiple categories, then comparing and aligning them with other systems of thought, would become a hallmark of Wilber's work through much of his career.

Not surprisingly, observers wondered how he manages to organize such diverse bodies of information, and how he succeeds in synthesizing them. This is a question that would continue to intrigue his readers, and his critics. The answer would seem to be that he is an amazingly prodigious reader with an equally prodigious memory. Beyond that, he has always had a gift for synthesis. According to his friend Jack Crittenden (2001), his style is to approach any field of knowledge by searching for the most general ideas that will be accepted by virtually all representatives of that field. Crittenden offered the example of religion: What can all religions agree about? That Jesus Christ is the savior of humankind? Certainly not. That God as a divine being is the supreme creator and ruler of the cosmos? Not that either. That there exists some ultimate divine or creative principle? Perhaps this latter one. Wilber then takes

Table 9.1   Levels of Development, from *The Atman Project* (Wilber, 1980a)

Pleromatic
Uroboric
Axial-body

Pranic-body
Image-body

Membership-cognition
Early egoic/personic
Middle egoic/personic
Later egoic/personic

Mature Ego

Biosocial
Centaur

Low subtle

High subtle

Low causal

Hi causal

Ultimate

such overarching ideas as true and seeks even higher principles that will pass muster across a variety of different fields, always in search of general principles that have broad application and wide potential acceptance.

The Pre-Trans Fallacy

The clearest distinction between Wilber-1 and Wilber-2 comes in the form of the pre-trans fallacy (Wilber, 1980b). A simple but powerful idea, it refers to the mistake of conflating infantile or pre-egoic experiences with advanced or trans-egoic ones. Figure 9.2 illustrates this concept.

Here is a lifecycle pattern, drawn from *The Atman Project* (Wilber, 1980a), familiar from Wilber-1, but shown as a circle. Beginning in infancy, at the bottom, life moves upward and outward on the left, transitioning from an infantile state of "blooming buzzing confusion" (James, 1890/1981, p. 462) through childhood and adolescence, and on toward fully adult ego development. If growth continues, the individual moves on around and down to the right through a series of trans-egoic states toward a return to unity with the spirit.

The pre/trans fallacy comes into play when pre-egoic experience or behavior is mistakenly labeled as trans-egoic (Wilber, 1980b). For instance, infancy and childhood experiences have often been romantically taken to be spiritual, when in fact they are simply pre-egoic and pre-personal. In other words having no ego is not equivalent to being trans-egoic. When Wilber first proposed this idea many critics were incensed by his rejection of the authenticity of childhood spirituality. He stuck to his guns

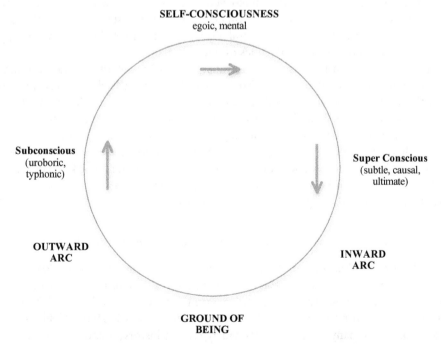

Figure 9.2 General life cycle, suggested from *The Atman Project* (Wilber, 1980a).

however, and did not revisit the issue in detail again until the publication of *Integral Spirituality* in 2006, as will be seen.

Once recognized, many instances of the pre/trans fallacy can be found in the American culture. Wilber (2006a) has been especially critical of the New Age culture that seemed to identify everything from ecstatic dancing, to swimming with dolphins and weekend "shamanism," as spiritual. In a similar vein Wilber (1983b, 1995) identified certain psychologists as indulging the pre/trans fallacy. These included Carl Jung, for mistaking certain nonrational and undifferentiated states as spiritual or post-egoic experiences, while Freud did the opposite, mistaking genuine mystical experiences as infantile and pre-egoic. Wilber noted that this reductionist attitude toward post-egoic experiences has dominated much of psychology and psychiatry ever since.

Interestingly, although the pre/trans fallacy played a significant role in Wilber's thinking throughout the Wilber-2 period, the term did not actually occur in either *The Atman Project* (1980a) or *Up From Eden* (1981). It appeared for the first time in print in a *ReVision Journal* article during 1980, simply titled "The Pre/Trans Fallacy" (1980b).

Transformation vs. Translation

In *The Atman Project* (1980a), Wilber first proposed the important distinction between *transformations* and *translations*. On reflection, this is a common sense idea. It simply states that personal transformations shift one "upward" toward growth when the deep or formative structures of consciousness or the self change appropriately; this needs to be distinguished from how one can shift laterally through different forms of expression while staying at the same level. The former indicates structural growth while in the latter the form of expression changes while the structure stays the same. Wilber wrote about these in fairly general terms, but later, in Wilber-3 he would apply the same ideas in terms of specific lines of development.

As an example, consider Lawrence Kohlberg's (1981) well-known stages of moral development. Suppose that a man whose moral thinking is based on external sources of authority belongs to a church that denounces gay marriage. It is likely that he will adopt this moral view as well. However, if for other reasons he later finds himself to be a member of a church that actually approves of such marriage then his own views are also likely to change. This would not be because he has undergone a fundamental transformation to a higher and more accepting structure of moral thinking, but simply that his source of authority has changed position, producing the translation in his moral reasoning to the approval of such marriages.

Jean Gebser: The History of Consciousness and Culture

With the 1981 publication of *Up from Eden: A Transpersonal View of Human Evolution* Wilber entered new territory by fashioning a theory of the history of human consciousness. In doing so he relied heavily on the scholarship of the mid-20th century German cultural historian and poet Jean Gebser (1972, 1949/1986). Gebser was at ease with many languages, was widely read in history, literature, and the arts, and was a personal acquaintance of many of the great minds of the mid-20th century (Feuerstein, 1987; Thompson, 1998). His most important discovery came when he realized that the turn of the 20th century had brought with it a new form of consciousness surfacing in the arts as well as science, mathematics, jurisprudence, and other fields (Gebser, 1949/1986). The key to this new consciousness was an escape from the rigid boundaries—what he termed "perspectival consciousness" (p. 19)—that had dominated much of human experience since the Renaissance. Put most simply, he found a new fluidity in, for example, the art of Picasso, the poetry of Rilke, the physics of Heisenberg, and so on, all pointing to a new *structure of consciousness* in which time and space, and even the sense of self, had become fluid and holistic. Gebser termed this new form of experience *integral consciousness.*

Having discovered the emergence of this new integral consciousness, Gebser began to consider the long span of human history, and doing so discovered what he believed to be several other structures of consciousness that had dominated different periods, each representing a different way of experiencing and interpreting reality (e.g., Feuerstein, 1987). He proposed five such structures that had unfolded in sequence. These overlapped greatly, but during each period one particular structure rose to dominate much of human experience. Briefly, the five structures are as sketched here.

The archaic structure of consciousness. This is Gebser's (1949/1986) term for the transitional structure of consciousness that existed before the first fully human experience arose. He claimed quite honestly to know little about it because of the enormous time between then and now, and the absence of detailed artifacts representing that period. But he believed that there must have been a transition time when the first humans began to emerge from their prehominid ancestors.

Interestingly, this period of emergence has been researched intensively since Gebser in the mid-20th century, and even since Wilber wrote *Up from Eden* in 1981, so a much richer story can be told today about archaic consciousness, and indeed scholars are doing exactly that (e.g., Donald, 1991; Mithen, 1996).

The magical structure of consciousness. The magical structure of consciousness interprets the world in terms of magical forces (Gebser, 1949/1986). Georg Feuerstein (1987) characterized its principle features as egolessness, identity with a group or tribe; point-centered perception in which any location can be substituted for any other (as in "sympathetic magic"); space and time are experienced as fluid (telepathy and synchronicity are commonplace); human life is interwoven with the experience of nature; and power is exercised and experienced through magic.

Now, consistent with Wilber's theme of "transcend and include," each structure of consciousness remains with humanity even as history moves forward and newer structures come into ascendance. For instance, music and rhythm are intimately associated with the magical structure and even today have the power to arouse people emotionally and to transport them to imaginal landscapes beyond mundane reality. On the pathological side, magical thinking is still a common element in states of grief and anxiety, and on the opposite side sometimes vaunted by New Age writers and filmmakers as the path to love and riches. Interestingly, Anna Freud's (1936/1987) classic defense mechanisms rely heavily on magical operations such as repression, projection, reaction formation, and the like.

The mythical structure of consciousness. Structures of consciousness are characterized by the kinds of answers they provide to basic questions such as "What is the purpose of life?" "What happens to us when we die?" and "How was the world created?" (Combs, 2002). Magical cultures even today tell creation stories about tricksters and magic. Mythic stories of creation, however, come from grand narratives of gods and goddesses that, unlike the local spirits of magical cultures, rule over the entire cosmos. The agricultural revolution that took place more or less 12,000 years ago brought with it the first widespread worship of fertility goddesses associated with the night, the moon, and the earth (e.g., Cunliffe, 2011; Thompson, 1981). During early historical times male gods who were associated with the sky and the sun would replace these (e.g., Thompson, 1981). These male gods arose, for example, in the grand mythical pantheons of Egypt, Mesopotamia, Greece, and in the Germanic mythologies. Similar systems of mythology were developing in India and China as well (Duiker & Spielvogel, 2010).

The mythic structure of consciousness is associated with narratives and poetry, and along with these a richness of the imagination. Most of the great religions are about such narratives, and afford meaning to those who live according to the aspirations they provide. Even nonreligious persons often have some personal story, or myth, that gives purpose to their lives (Feinstein & Krippner, 1988).

The mental structure of consciousness. Gebser (1949/1986) did not think of these historical structures as sequentially improving, each superior to the one before. Indeed, he felt that the modern mental structure, which dominates the current moment of history, was in some ways the most restrictive one of all. Although mental consciousness began with the Greek and later Roman philosophers, modern mental consciousness, as Gebser saw it, began in the Renaissance when artists, architects, and writers first acquired perspectival consciousness. The latter places the individual viewer at a fixed location in the visual landscape, and solidifies the ego at a fixed subjective position in the head, contrary to mythic consciousness, which seems to have found its center in the heart.

There is no need for a detailed description of the mental structure here because it is today's dominant mode of understanding reality. It relies on the faculties of reason and logic. Today, for example, one may visit shamans or religious healers, but if a medical condition is sufficiently serious, most people usually end up placing themselves in the hands of scientifically informed physicians. This is an example of how contemporary society places its trust in the mental structure.

Gebser (1949/1986) believed that each structure of consciousness had its own strengths and weaknesses. The scientific and other intellectual achievements of the mental structure are unquestionable, but beginning with the Age of Enlightenment there has been a tendency toward wrangling over details, which Gebser referred to as *ratio*, in part because it represents a division of the whole into smaller and smaller parts that are niggled over in nonproductive nitpicking. Thus, he felt that the mental structure carries the seeds of its own trivializing. He believed this tendency toward hair-splitting wrangling lies at the root of many of the modern world's problems.

The integral structure of consciousness. The integral structure began to emerge, according to Gebser (1949/1986), around the turn of the 20th century, but may take centuries to become widely dominant. In the meantime he predicted strife on a wide scale, just as is now seen in the early 21st century political arena. As the German philosopher and a leader of the German Green Party, Rudolf Bahro (1994) has pointed out, the major political divisions in the world today run directly along the lines that separate different structures of consciousness.

Gebser first recognized the integral structure of consciousness in the paintings of Pablo Picasso and Paul Klee, where multiple viewpoints appear simultaneously as integral wholes (Feuerstein, 1987); and in the poetry of Rainer Maria Rilke, where time seems a fluid quality of experience. Full blown integral consciousness experiences the world in a kind of subtle or "diaphanous" light, while at the same time paradoxically it is more real and solid than in previous structures of experience. Although he usually avoided comparisons with Eastern philosophies, Gebser noted a fundamental similarity between integral consciousness and Zen satori.

Gebser and Wilber. We could say much more about Gebser's ideas (e.g., Combs, 2002, 2003, 2009), but the important thing here is to understand his influence on Wilber, first seen in *Up From Eden* (1981), and continuing along with Sri Aurobindo's influence to the present day. Even in the above brief sketch of Gebser's structures of consciousness, it is apparent how easily they align with Wilber's ideas of lifespan evolution. This alignment becomes more apparent in Wilber-3, which moves more explicitly into the language of developmental psychology. In short, Gebser's outline of the history of human consciousness seems nothing less than a mirror of the developmental history of the individual. The single point of disagreement concerns the nature of integral consciousness.

As has been seen, Wilber's (2000a) model of conscious evolution in the individual includes several transpersonal stages beyond the development of an adult ego. Gebser (1949/1986), on the other hand, brings history to a kind of fulfillment and conclusion with the emergence of the integral structure. My own view is that there are two explanations for this disparity, neither of which excludes the other (Combs, 2009). The first is that Gebser was essentially a cultural historian, although psychologically sophisticated, and he was simply reporting what he was seeing. The other is that Wilber was viewing several stages of higher personal development where Gebser was simply seeing a single structure. Gebser (1949/1986), for instance, suggested that certain historical figures such as Meister Eckhart in the 14th century and Nicholas of Cusa in the 15th century had already achieved integral consciousness, but an informal reading of their writings also suggests that they had experiences at very high levels of consciousness. On the other hand it is doubtful that Picasso or Klee, for example, experienced such rarified states of experience, though all are included in Gebser's examples of integral consciousness. Although they experienced integral consciousness in Gebser's sense, they did not, at least on an ongoing basis, experience the higher structures of consciousness that Wilber described.

Before moving on to Wilber-3 let me note that while it is not in the purview of this chapter to review criticisms that have been directed at Wilber's work, his overview of the evolution of consciousness, combined with the notion of the pre-trans fallacy, has easily engendered more *ad hominem* criticism than anything else he has done. It is difficult to pinpoint exactly what the problem is here, in part because most of this criticism appears frankly uninformed and vehemently argued by those who have not carefully read his work. It seems, however, there is a popular notion that Wilber has nothing but distain for primary cultures, and shamans in particular. Because Wilber has shown no interest in primary cultures, except in Paleolithic times, nor in modern shamans, such accusations seem curiously without support. This is a complex issue, however, especially considering that many contemporary tribal peoples as well as modern shamans are not the same at all as our Paleolithic ancestors (Combs & Krippner, 2003). In any case, it is not an issue that Wilber has addressed.

Wilber-3: Lines of Development, the Spectrum of Pathology, and the Beginnings of a New Paradigm (1983-1993)

Major books:

Eye to Eye: The Quest for the New Paradigm (1983a);
A Sociable God: A Brief Introduction to a Transcendental Sociology (1983b);
Quantum Questions: Mystical Writings of the World's Great Physicists (Ed., 1984c);
Transformations of Consciousness: Conventional and Contemplative Perspectives on Development (1986; Ed. with J. Engler & D. Brown);
Grace and Grit (1991).

Wilber-3 is often characterized by the introduction of *developmental lines*, first discussed in *A Sociable God* (Wilber, 1983b). This is the concept that individual development proceeds along several different paths at different rates. For example, a person might grow at an average rate in terms of moral development, rapidly in mathematical or musical skills, slowly in artistic judgement, and so on. The result is the everyday fact that different people have different distributions of abilities, or if one prefers, types of intelligence. These lines of development, as well as the overall growth of the personality, are navigated by a core self-system that is the individual's locus of identity and organization.

Now, the concept of lines was already well known in developmental psychology. For example, Piaget (1952; Flavell, 1963) had used the term *décalage* to refer to different rates of growth across diverse areas of intelligence. Nevertheless, for Wilber this represents an important shift because it comes directly from research in developmental and cognitive psychology. Despite the wide range of material in his previous scholarship, he had tended to rely on psychiatric theories such as those of Freud and Jung, as well as neo-analytic ego theory, rather than mainstream developmental research in the field of psychology. Beginning with the introduction of lines of development he began to pay close attention to such developmental research. Along with this came the recognition of other dimensions of individual differences, especially personality types. Although he did not explore lines or types deeply, he would come to speak of levels, lines, and types as important identifying features for each individual.

Psychopathology and Types of Treatment

This was a highly productive period for Wilber, during which he continued to cultivate his earlier thinking about levels of development and forms of psychopathology. In a two-part journal article published in 1984 (Wilber, 1984a, 1984b), and in the 1986 book, *Transformations of Consciousness* (Wilber, Engler, & Brown, 1986) he presented detailed discussions of this topic, suggesting for each stage of development a major form of pathology as well as a modality of treatment. These can be seen in Table 9.2. This was scholarly work, relying on the literatures of ego development and psychopathology, as well as offering considered reflections on disorders that can occur at the highest levels of development and their treatments.

Each major stage is marked by a "fulcrum," or milestone in the transformation of consciousness or the self to the next level of growth. It is beyond the scope of this chapter to go into detail about the individual levels and their transitions, but it is my own view that this work represents Wilber's finest contribution to transpersonal psychology, and indeed to the field of psychology in general. In it one sees his major developmental stages organized in a systematic fashion, the ways each can miscarry into pathology, and suggested treatment modalities for each. This is not to say that the model is entirely correct, but it does an excellent job of organizing a broad range of psychological phenomena and is rich material for discussion and exploration in greater detail. It is not possible to know the extent to which these ideas have actually influenced the thinking of psychologists since that time, but judging from the author's personal experience it is safe to say that its effect has not been trivial.

Table 9.2 Levels of Development shown beside Fulcrums with Characteristic Pathologies and Treatment Modalities, suggested from *Transformations of Consciousness* (Wilber et al., 1986)

Fulcrums of self-development	*Characteristic psychopathology*	*Treatment modalities*
Ultimate (F-10)		
Causal (F-9)	Causal Pathology	Path of Sages
Subtle (F-8)	Subtle Pathology	Path of Saints
Psychic (F-7)	Psychic Disorders	Path of Yogis
Existential (F-6)	Existential Pathology	Existential Therapy
Formal-Reflexive (F-5)	Identity Neurosis	Introspection
Rule/Role (F-4)	Script Pathology	Script Analysis
Rep-Mind (F-3)	Psychoneurosis	Uncovering Techniques
Phantasmic-Emotional (F-2)	Narcissistic-Borderline	Structure-Building Techniques
Sensory physical		
Undifferentiated Matrix (F-1)	Psychoses	Physiological/Pacification

New Paradigms

During this period from 1983 to 1993 Wilber was beginning to seriously explore diverse epistemologies for understanding and acquire knowledge in general. In *Eye to Eye* (Wilber, 1983a, pp. 2-3), for example, he wrote of Saint Bonaventure's "three eyes of knowing." These are:

1   Eye of flesh (monologic/sensibilia/physical senses);
2   Eye of mind (dialogic/intelligibilia/rational senses);
3   Eye of spirit (translogic/transcendelia/inner senses).

Each represents a different epistemology and a different domain of knowledge acquisition.

At this point one can begin to see that the proper understanding of these three eyes of knowing, including their strengths and weaknesses, foreshadowed Wilber's later ideas about *epistemological pluralism* and *integral methodological pluralism*.

Wilber-4, -5, and Beyond: All Quadrants, All Levels (1995—the present)

Major books:

Sex, Ecology, Spirituality (1995);
The Eye of Spirit (1997);
The Marriage of Sense and Soul (1998);
Integral Psychology (2000a);
A Theory of Everything (2000b);
Integral Spirituality (2006a; also Volume 2 of *The Kosmos Trilogy* and
The Many Faces of Terrorism at various locations on the Worldwide Web).

The 1995 publication of *Sex, Ecology, Spirituality* (often referred to as SES) marked a major turning point in Wilber's work. Although apparent in his earlier publications, especially *Eye to Eye* (1983a), at this point there was no question that he had become a philosopher. He claims he had actually quit referring to himself as a transpersonal psychologist as far back as the early 1980s (Wilber, 2012), but in SES the thrust of his thinking moved towards the creation of a broad philosophical system.

SES (Wilber, 1995) reconceived the entire cosmos, both in its objective and its subjective dimensions, as *holons*. According to Wilber a holon is a whole process or structure that is part of a larger process or structure, which in turn is part of a still larger one, and so forth, while in the downward direction it is composed of smaller processes or structures made of still smaller ones all the way down. The idea, familiar nowadays in systems science, was suggested in part by Arthur Koestler in *Janus: A Summing Up* (1979), his last complete book. The title refers to the two-faced god, Janus, one face pointing toward larger more inclusive structures and the other toward smaller included ones. Wilber (1983a) had already introduced these ideas in a preliminary way in *Eye to Eye*. In SES and his following publications he was to raise this concept to an inclusive régime comparable to Gottfried Wilhelm Leibniz's Monadology (Leibniz, 1714/2012). Indeed, in SES Wilber made numerous references to Leibniz and the nature of his monads.

To explore the system of thought that grew out of the ideas developed in SES (Wilber, 1995) would take our discussion well beyond the limits of this chapter. One important idea, however, was the notion that every holon has four dimensions, or four aspects, often represented by the well-known four quadrant diagram shown in Figure 9.3. That is, each holon has a subjective inner reality, represented by the left two quadrants, and an objective outer reality represented by the right two quadrants. The two upper quadrants represent singular or individual aspects of the holon, and the bottom two represent plural or social aspects. For example, seen as a holon a person has an experiential interior (upper left), while at the same time is part of some larger experiential community or communities (lower left). In similar fashion this person possesses a physical body (upper right) that is part of some community or communities of other bodies (lower right). In terms of fields of inquiry the upper left represents phenomenology and much of psychology, the lower left language and hermeneutics, the upper right behaviorism and objective science, and the lower right systems science. However, these examples only scratch the surface of an enormously complex and comprehensive theoretical framework, one that Wilber (2006) further expanded in *Integral Spirituality* to include interiors and exteriors for each of the four quadrants. For instance, the "interior of the interior" of the upper left quadrant represents "raw" experience. An example is the tangible feel of a toothache or the taste of an orange. At the same time the exterior of the interior of the upper left

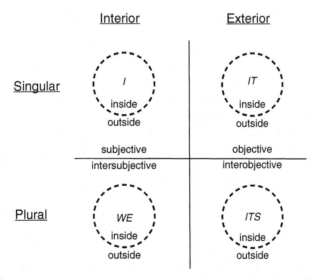

Figure 9.3 The four quadrants shown with interiors and exteriors for each quadrant, suggested from *Integral Spirituality* (Wilber, 2006a).

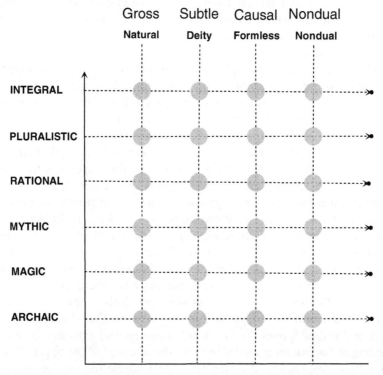

Figure 9.4 A Wilber-Combs lattice, suggested from *Integral Spirituality* (Wilber, 2006a).

quadrant represents the view of an inner observer, or in Wilber's terms, "the look of the feel."

This complete system allowed Wilber to place the individual within a rich framework of quadrants as well as levels of development, collectively termed the AQAL or "All-Quadrants All-Levels" model (e.g., Wilber, 2000b). Adding developmental lines and personality types, as well as the fact that a person can be in any of a number of states of consciousness, creates what Wilber informally has called the "kosmic address."

During this period Wilber also paid considerable attention to methodological issues, leading to a set of considerations referred to together as *Integral Methodological Pluralism* (Wilber, 2006a). Its implications are beyond the scope here, but in essence suggest a comprehensive range of types of inquiry based on the multiple perspectives presented in the AQAL format.

Following his own edict to transcend and include, in *Integral Psychology* Wilber (2000a) continued to examine questions of personal growth and transformation, reframing many of his previous ideas in terms of the newer AQAL model. In *Integral Spirituality* (Wilber, 2006a) he discussed at length the implications of the AQAL model as a set of *perspectives* leading to a complete "post-metaphysical" worldview. The latter is an idea suggested by contemporary European philosophers, especially Jürgen Habermas (e.g., 1985).

In the meantime Wilber continued to improve on earlier ideas about development. In *Integral Spirituality* (Wilber, 2006a) he introduced the Wilber-Combs Lattice, a concept that solved a problem that had troubled many of his readers since Wilber-2 and the pre-trans fallacy. This was the implication that the experience of a child must always be pre-egoic, thus any claims of childhood spirituality had to be considered as instances of the pre-trans fallacy.

The Wilber-Combs Lattice

The issue of childhood spirituality was related to the puzzling fact that many people who have not reached advanced levels of personal development report temporary but powerful experiences of subtle or "higher" states of consciousness, in other words spiritual experiences (see Figure 9.4). But according to Wilber's earlier models such states of consciousness are identified with advanced developmental levels of the self. In this way of thinking it was not possible for children, or young people in general, retarded people, and so on, to have authentic spiritual experiences. The solution to this enigma occurred to both Wilber and Combs (this author) independently, and is presented in detail by Wilber (2006a) in *Integral Spirituality*, and in my own book, *Consciousness Explained Better* (Combs, 2009). Ideas leading up the Wilber-Combs Lattice had actually been explored in a preliminary way by Wilber in SES (1995), and by this author in *The Radiance of Being* (Combs, 2002).

It now seems an obvious solution, but like so many "obvious" ideas, it was only apparent after the fact. Put simply, people have spontaneous experiences of higher or mystical states of consciousness, *peak experiences* in Maslow's (1962, 1971) terms, but when they return to everyday consciousness they interpret them to others and themselves through their own structure of development. A child may be deeply moved by such an experience, but will interpret it in the language of a child. Add this to the fact that people at all levels of personal growth occasionally have transient mystical or peak experiences and one has the basis for the wide range of reports given for such experiences.

Summing Up: Wilber's Legacy to Transpersonal Psychology

One of the most important functions of a good scientific theory is to summarize the important observations of a field of inquiry, while providing a roadmap of the territory—that is, putting some degree of organization onto the collection of disparate facts and observations that constitute that field. Wilber's early publications, whether correct or incorrect in detail, did this effectively for transpersonal psychology, as well as for the field of psychology in general, and as such made a contribution of significant proportions. Through most of the 1980s Stanislav Grof's (1975, 1985, 1988) holographic model of the psyche was the only other major transpersonal theory of consciousness, and it did not attempt to detail stages of growth or types of therapy, nor integrate broad fields of knowledge. By the late 1980s Michael Washburn's (1988) view of how transpersonal experiences arise became another contender, but as with Grof's holographic model, did not address the wider range of issues that characterized

Wilber's work. Contemporary theorist Jorge Ferrer (e.g., 2002) offers a postmodern view of transpersonal experiences that relies strongly on social and historical context, but again does not address the range of purely psychological issues that Wilber has spoken to in the history of his writings.

Wilber's early publications had created broad interest in the previously almost unheard-of field of transpersonal psychology in large part by placing it in the same theoretical context as traditional psychological theory, while including Eastern ideas as well. In these ways he has provided an important service to the field of psychology.

Notes

1. All such dates are approximate.
2. *Organism* was actually a term used in experimental psychology at the time to refer to an animal that was the subject in an experiment, but it had recently been popularized by the humanistic psychologist, Carl Rogers, to refer to the entire human being, body and mind, conscious and unconscious.

References

Aurobindo, S. (1971). *Letters on yoga* (Vols. 1-3). Pondicherry, India: All India Press.

Aurobindo, S. (1980). *The synthesis of yoga*. Pondicherry, India: Sri Aurobindo Ashram Press.

Aurobindo, S. (1990). *The life divine*. Wilmot, WI: Lotus Light.

Bahro, R. (1994). *Avoiding social and ecological disaster: The politics of world transformation*. Bath, UK: Gateway Books.

Capra, F. (1975). *Tao of physics: An exploration of the parallels between modern physics and eastern mysticism*. Berkeley, CA: Shambhala.

Combs, A. (2002). *The Radiance of being: Understanding the grand integral vision; Living the integral life*. St. Paul, MN: Paragon House.

Combs, A. (2003). Inner and outer realities: Jean Gebser in a cultural/historical perspective. *Integrative Explorations: Journal of Culture and Consciousness, 7-8*, 22-34. [Also available at http://www.cejournal.org/GRD/Realities.htm]

Combs, A. (2009). *Consciousness explained better: Towards an integral understanding of the multifaceted nature of consciousness*. St. Paul, MN: Paragon House.

Combs, A., & Krippner, S. (2003). Process, structure and form: An evolutionary transpersonal psychology of consciousness. *International Journal of Transpersonal Studies, 22*, 47-60.

Coomaraswamy, A. K. (1947). *Time and eternity*. Ascona, Switzerland: Artibus Asial.

Crittenden, J. (2001). Foreword in K. Wilber, *The eye of the spirit: An integral vision of a world gone slightly mad* (pp. vii-xii). Boston, MA: Shambhala.

Cunliffe, B. (2011). *Europe between the oceans: 9000 BC-AD 1000*. New Haven, CT: Yale University Press.

Donald, M. (1991). *Origins of the modern mind: Three stages in the evolution of culture and cognition*. Cambridge, MA: Harvard University Press.

Duiker, J. D., & Spielvogel, J. J. (2010). *The essential world history. To 1800* (6th ed.). (Vol. 1). Stamford, CT: Wadsworth.

Feinstein, D., & Krippner, S. (1988). *Personal mythology: The psychology of your evolving self*. Los Angeles, CA: Jeremy P. Tarcher.

Ferrer, J. N. (2002). *Revisioning transpersonal psychology*. Albany, NY: State University of New York Press.

Feuerstein, G. (1987). *Structures of consciousness: The genius of Jean Gebser*. Lower Lake, CA: Integral.

Flavell, J. H. (1963). *The developmental psychology of Jean Piaget*. New York, NY: Van Nostrand.

Freud, A. (1987). *The writings of Anna Freud* (Vol. 2, Ego and the mechanisms of defense). Madison, CT: International Universities Press. (Original work published 1936)

Gebser, J. (1972). Foundations of the aperspectival world. *Main Currents, 29*, 2.

Gebser, J. (1986). *The ever-present origin.* (N. Barstad and A. Mickunas, Trans.). Athens, OH: Ohio University Press. (Original work published 1949)

Grof, S. (1975). *Realms of the human unconscious: Observations from LSD research*. New York, NY: Viking Press.

Grof, S. (1985). *Beyond the brain: Birth, death, and transcendence in psychotherapy*. Albany, NY: State University of New York Press.

Grof, S. (1988). *The adventure of self-discovery: Dimensions of consciousness and new perspectives in psychotherapy and inner exploration*. Albany, New York, NY: State University of New York Press.

Habermas, J. (1985). *The theory of communicative action*. Boston: Beacon Press.

Hastings, A. (1999). Transpersonal psychology: The fourth force. In D. Moss (Ed.), *Humanistic and transpersonal psychology: A historical and biographical sourcebook* (pp. 192-208). Westport, CN: Greenwood Press.

Huxley, A. (1945). *The perennial philosophy*. New York, NY: Harper & Row.

James, W. (1981). *The principles of psychology*. Cambridge, MA: Harvard University Press. (Original work published 1890)

Jung, C. G. (1939). Conscious, unconscious, and individuation (R.F.C. Hull, Trans). In *Collected works of C. G. Jung* (Vol. 9, Part 1, pp. 275-289). Princeton, NJ: Princeton University Press.

Koestler, A. (1979). *Janus: A summing up*. New York, NY: Vintage.

Kohlberg, L. (1981). *Essays on moral development* (Vol. 1). San Francisco, CA: Harper & Row.

Kuhn, T. (1962). *The structure of scientific revolutions*. Chicago, IL: University of Chicago Press.

Leibniz, G. (1714/2012). *The monadology*. Seattle, WA: Createspace.

Lovejoy, A.O. (1960). *The great chain of being: A study of the history of an idea*. New York, NY: Harper.

Maslow, A. (1962). *Toward a psychology of being*. Princeton, NJ: Van Nostrand.

Maslow, A. (1971). *The further reaches of human nature*. New York, NY: Viking.

Mithen, S. (1996). *The prehistory of the mind*. London, UK: Thames & Hudson.

Pearce, J. C. (1973). *Crack in the cosmic egg: Challenging constructs of mind and reality*. London, UK: Lyrdbird Press.

Piaget, J. (1952). *The origins of intelligence in children*. New York, NY: Basic Books.

Sobel, J. & Sobel, P. (1984). *The hierarchy of minds: The mind levels*. New York, NY: Vantage Press.

Thompson, W. I. (1981). *The time falling bodies take to light: Mythology, sexuality, and the origins of culture*. New York, NY: St. Martin's Press.

Thompson, W. I. (1998). *Coming into being: Artifacts and texts in the evolution of consciousness*. Basingstoke, UK: Palgrave Macmillan.

Washburn, M. (1988). *The ego and the dynamic ground*. Albany, NY: State University of New York Press.

Wilber, K. (1977). *The spectrum of consciousness*. Wheaton, IL: Theosophical Publications.

Wilber, K. (1979). *No boundary: Eastern and Western approaches to personal growth.* Los Angeles, CA: Center Publications.

Wilber, K. (1980a). *The atman project: A transpersonal view of human development.* Wheaton, IL: Quest. (2nd ed. published by Quest, 1996)

Wilber, K. (1980b). The pre/trans fallacy. *ReVision Journal, 3*(2), 51-73.

Wilber, K. (1981). *Up from Eden: A transpersonal view of human evolution.* Garden City, NY: Anchor-Doubleday.

Wilber, K. (1983a). *Eye to eye: The quest for the new paradigm.* New York, NY: Anchor-Doubleday.

Wilber, K. (1983b). *A sociable God: A brief introduction to a transcendental sociology.* New York, NY: New Press.

Wilber, K. (1984a). The developmental spectrum and psychopathology, Part I: Stages and types of pathology. *Journal of Transpersonal Psychology, 16*(1), 75-117.

Wilber, K. (1984b). The developmental spectrum and psychopathology, Part II: Treatment modalities. *Journal of Transpersonal Psychology, 16*(2), 137-166.

Wilber, K. (Ed.). (1984c). *Quantum questions: Mystical writings of the world's great physicists.* Boston, MA: Shambhala.

Wilber, K. (1991). *Grace and grit: Spirituality and healing in the life and death of Treya Killam Wilber.* Boston, MA: Shambhala.

Wilber, K. (1995). *Sex, ecology, spirituality: The spirit of evolution.* Boston, MA: Shambhala.

Wilber, K. (1996). *The atman project.* Boston, MA: Shambhala.

Wilber, K. (1997). *The eye of the spirit: An integral vision of a world gone slightly mad.* Boston, MA: Shambhala.

Wilber, K. (1998). *The marriage of sense and soul: Integrating science and religion.* New York, NY: Random House.

Wilber, K. (1999). *The collected works* (Vol. 2, *The atman project; Up from Eden*). Boston, MA: Shambhala.

Wilber, K. (2000a). *Integral psychology: Consciousness, spirit, psychology, therapy.* Boston, MA: Shambhala.

Wilber, K. (2000b). *A theory of everything: An integral vision for business, politics, science, and spirituality.* Boston, MA: Shambhala.

Wilber, K. (2006a). *Integral spirituality: A startling new role for religion in the modern and post-modern world.* Boston, MA: Shambhala.

Wilber, K. (2006b, June 6). *What we are, that we see.* Retrieved August 11, 2012, from http://www.kenwilber.com/blog/show/46

Wilber, K. (2012). *On critics, Integral Institute, my recent writing, and other matters of little consequence: A Shambhala interview with Ken Wilber* [Part 1: The demise of transpersonal psychology]. Retrieved August 11, 2012, from http://wilber.shambhala.com/index.cfm//#interview

Wilber, K., Engler, J., & Brown, D. (1986). *Transformations of consciousness: Conventional and contemplative perspectives on development.* Boston, MA: Shambhala.

Zukav, G. (1979). *Dancing Wu Li masters: An overview of the new physics.* New York, NY: William Morrow.

10

Transpersonal Philosophy

The Participatory Turn

Glenn Hartelius and Jorge N. Ferrer

There have arguably been just two major philosophical paradigms in transpersonal psychology since its founding: perennialist and participatory. Although there are a variety of other theoretical orientations, few of these have articulated their philosophical situation in any detail. In the absence of an explicit alternate philosophy the context of transpersonal inquiry defaults back to a modern philosophy, one that considers reality as limited to a relationship between objective world and rational mind. Within such a frame, the spiritual and non-ordinary experiences that are central to the development of the transpersonal approach are little more than distortions of normal consciousness, induced perhaps by biological or chemical imbalances. The "insights" of the world's great mystics and spiritual teachers are then ascribed to pathological conditions (Leuder & Thomas, 2000); transpersonal theories that take into account the wisdom of spiritual traditions are little more than wishful imaginings built on delusion (Ellis & Yeager, 1989). Having one or more effective philosophical frames is therefore critical to the success of a transpersonal approach.

It will first be necessary to distinguish between theoretical orientations and philosophical frameworks. After that perennial philosophy will be introduced, along with the critiques that have moderated its influence within transpersonal psychology. Due to participatory philosophy's rather public dispute with perennialist approaches, the relationship between these two is addressed in abbreviated form. With this background, participatory philosophy will be examined as a suitable container for the transpersonal project.

The Wiley Blackwell Handbook of Transpersonal Psychology, First Edition.
Edited by Harris L. Friedman and Glenn Hartelius.
© 2013 John Wiley & Sons, Ltd. Published 2015 by John Wiley & Sons, Ltd.

Philosophies and Theoretical Orientations

In order to clarify the distinction between philosophies and theoretical orientations, it may be of use to briefly review the work of transpersonal scholars who have developed the latter. These include Abraham Maslow, Stanislav Grof, and Charles Tart, whose theories have been prominent within transpersonal psychology.

Maslow, the one who among the founders of the field held the greatest stature within psychology at large, died in 1970 (Hoffman, 2008), just two years after the announcement of transpersonal psychology's founding (Sutich, 1968). Much of Maslow's scientific work had been on primate and human behavior and motivation, conducted with standard scientific methodologies (e.g., Maslow, 1943, 1954; Maslow & Harlow, 1932). By the time he participated in the founding of transpersonal psychology, he recognized that a philosophical shift was underway (Maslow, 1969), and articulated both a critique of scientific objectivity as applied in psychology (Maslow, 1966) and the rudiments of an alternative psychological paradigm (Maslow, 1962/1999). He expressed concern that the impersonal stance, assuming a subject-object dichotomy and emotional detachment from that which is studied, was fictitious and distorting; he felt this issue to be of particular import in the study of human beings (Maslow, 1961). Yet in his short tenure in the transpersonal field he contributed little specific substance to the construction of a philosophical alternative to the modernist frame.

Grof (e.g., 1975/1996, 1985, 2003) brought to the nascent field what was perhaps the most important empirical data of its early years: his research on the potential psychotherapeutic effects of the psychedelic LSD. Based on his review of over 2,600 session reports, Grof (1973) formulated a multilayered model of the unconscious, broadly situated within psychodynamic theory and closest, perhaps, to the work of Otto Rank (1929) on birth trauma. Although its initial theories were constructed largely on interpretations of qualitative data, psychodynamic psychology generally considers itself as an evidence-based scientific psychology (e.g., Borden & Clark, 2012; Shedler, 2010); in this regard Grof's early work had no need of an alternate philosophy. Later, when situating the findings from psychedelic research within a broader spiritual and cultural context, Grof (e.g., 1983, 1998) adopted the perennialist philosophy prevalent within transpersonalism (cf. Lahood, 2007a).

Hypnosis and parapsychology were the domains of Tart's (e.g., 1964, 1966) early research, conducted within the sphere of a modernist science. By the time he formulated his concept of altered states of consciousness, Tart (1971) had rejected the notion that the scientific method can be applied only to objective data. While stepping back from the philosophical task, he aptly noted the need for a philosophy of knowing that would allow for using experiential knowledge in a scientific way. He further refined this into a call for state-specific sciences, suggesting that the methods of science can be applied within an altered state of consciousness just as it is within a rational state of consciousness in traditional science (Tart, 1972, 2000). This important insight informs Varela's (1996) neurophenomenology and Hartelius' (2007, 2009) somatic phenomenology as an approach to a phenomenological-empirical science. While he developed concepts that have profound philosophical implications, Tart stopped short of offering a philosophical container that would situate a state-specific science of the sort that he proposed.

Perennial Philosophy

The first transpersonal theorist to attempt a philosophy was Ken Wilber (e.g., 1975), who fused perennial philosophy with psychology. Perennialist thought takes many forms, but its essence is that spiritual traditions use culturally diverse language and symbols to represent what is essentially the journey to a single spiritual ultimate (Ferrer, 2000a, 2002). It suggests that a single truth underlies all traditions and is the goal of all paths. Early forms of this line of reasoning can be found in "the Neoplatonism of Philo of Alexandria or the Platonic-Christian synthesis of St. Augustine" (Ferrer, 2000a, p. 8); it was first named perennial philosophy by 16th century Catholic scholar Agostino Steuco, who drew on similar concepts from earlier writers such as Marsilio Ficino, Pico della Mirandola, and Nicolas de Cusa (Schmitt, 1966). In recent times this approach has been further developed by such traditionalist scholars as René Guenon (2001) and Frithjof Schuon (e.g., 1953/1984), and popularized by others such as Madame Helena Blavatsky (1888/1978), Swami Vivekananda (1947), and most famously, Aldous Huxley (1945).

Ferrer (2000a) has identified five different types of perennialist thought. His simplest, or *basic* form, holds that "there is only one path and one goal for spiritual development" (p. 10). The *esotericist* form admits there are many religious paths but only a single spiritual or mystical goal. The *perspectivist* form allows for still more complexity, believing that while there are many paths and many goals in differing spiritual traditions, these all represent "different perspectives, dimensions, or manifestations of the same Ground of Being or Ultimate Reality" (Ferrer, 2000a, p. 10). The closely related *typological* form tends to hold that there are a "limited number of types of mysticism that run across the different traditions...and affirms that [these are] diverse expressions or manifestations of a single kind of spiritual experience or ultimate reality" (Ferrer, 2000a, p. 11). Finally, the *structuralist* form accepts that there are many different mystical paths and goals, but considers these as diverse surface structures reflecting a deep structure that is universal.

Wilber (e.g., 1981) developed for transpersonal psychology a structuralist version of perennial philosophy that combined developmental psychology with spiritual evolution. In this view, human beings evolve spiritually through a pre-given series of *structures of consciousness,* each of which *transcends and includes* prior levels. This approach is an intuitively attractive way to resolve tensions between differing traditions of thought in a tolerant and inclusive manner, and Wilber (e.g., 1987, 1993, 2003, 2006) has constructed increasingly sophisticated iterations of his model. From around 1975 until recent years, perennial philosophy appears to have been the dominant philosophical paradigm within the transpersonal approach (Ferrer, 2000a; Rothberg, 1986).

However, perennial philosophy requires assumptions and leads to conclusions that, on careful examination, are problematic; Ferrer (2000a, 2002) has identified five such issues. A primary example is *objectivism*: in order for diverse spiritual traditions to be reflections of a single spiritual order, the divine must necessarily be real in an objective sense. Although human representations of this way may be manifold, the truth itself must not be affected by the cultural or psychological location of the spiritual practitioner. Regardless of the language used, a Hindu or Buddhist or Christian will follow what is at some deep level the same journey of personal transformation toward the divine—a formulation that a priori obliterates any meaningful spiritual plurality (or diversity) and forces the convergence of all traditions to submit to a single spiritual ultimate conveniently resembling that favored by one or another variant of perennialist thought.

At the same time, while the divine order must be objectively real in order for this consistency to hold true, that order cannot be objectively perceived or located or measured. Its existence is intuited through spiritual apprehension and comparison of accounts from different spiritual and especially mystical traditions. This brings forward three additional interrelated assumptions: *essentialism,* which holds that what is common among spiritual traditions is both more foundational and has the greatest explanatory power, and an *a priori philosophical stance* that embraces a *nondual monistic metaphysic* (i.e., the belief that there is a single, timeless and formless reality hidden beneath the appearances of the world that is paradoxically the same as the latter; Ferrer, 2000a). In other words, perennialism begins with the assumption that there is a single truth underlying various traditions, then collects evidence of their similarities to show that this is true. Because this evidence, on close examination, tends not to support a one-truth model, it is often filtered and sorted in different ways so it can be seen to fit the desired end. This can lead to *intolerant and dogmatic* conclusions: spiritual traditions that do not assume a nondual divine ultimate, for example, must therefore be inferior, inauthentic, or partial in their grasp of truth; and others who challenge the particular perennialist formula for interpreting the data from different traditions are wrongheaded, lacking in insight, or just unimportant.

In addition to these five shortcomings, Ferrer (2002) has articulated three specific critiques of perennialism. First and perhaps most obvious is the fact that the more closely accounts from different mystical traditions are compared, the more they can be seen to differ (Ferrer, 2011a), making it difficult to hold that the same spiritual truths underlie all the world's spiritual traditions (Ferrer, 2002). Second, it is rationally dubious to propose an objective domain of reality that is nevertheless unseen, immeasurable, and inaccessible to public observation; it is even more awkward to suggest that encountering this reality through deep inner experience constitutes objective empirical inquiry. This position requires a definition of objectivity that is indefensible within critical thought. Third, a perennialist model necessarily retains an experiential division between subject and object: it is through individual subjective experience that the transcendently objective divine is perceived. Ferrer (2002) has identified these as critiques of *perennialism, inner empiricism,* and *experientialism,* respectively.

Philosophically, the larger issue in perennialism is its retention of a Cartesian worldview in which subject and object are separate; this is what Ferrer (2002) has called *subtle Cartesianism.* In fact, something akin to Cartesian dualism seems necessary for a perennialist view: If the divine order is not objective and separate from the differently-conditioned subjectivities of spiritual seekers, then it cannot remain invariable, it cannot be the object of inner empirical inquiry, and the whole notion of a single ultimate spiritual truth becomes logically untenable. It may be noteworthy that the substantive articulation of perennialist views followed soon after the rise of divisions between rational philosophy and spiritual authority in medieval Christian culture, for dualistic assumptions appear to be essential to a perennial view—however complex or sophisticated.

Integral Philosophy: A Viable Alternative?

Although Wilber's (e.g., 1975, 1981, 1993) early philosophical offerings to transpersonal psychology were clearly perennialist, it is fair to ask whether this term can also be applied to his later work. The relevance here is whether Wilber's development into integral philosophy is sufficiently different to present a viable alternative framework for transpersonal concepts. Wilber (e.g., 1997, 1998, 1999, 2000a) has himself critiqued certain forms of perennial philosophy. He has regularly claimed that critics—whom he has assigned to a lower evolutionary rung of thought and spiritual development—direct their attacks at misunderstandings of his ideas (e.g., Wilber, 2000b), and has implied that he has not identified himself with the perennial philosophy since the mid-1980s (Wilber, 2012). Yet critics and defenders alike have continued to characterize his work as a version of perennialism (e.g., Ferrer, 2011a; Rowan, Daniels, Fontana, & Walley, 2009), and he himself has praised aspects of a perennial approach long after he reportedly ceased to identify with it (e.g., Wilber, 2000b). His alternative to perennialist thought is what he has called integral post-metaphysics (e.g., Wilber, 2006); the question is whether this latter approach effectively overcomes the liabilities of perennialism without losing its benefits.

For Wilber (2006), post-metaphysical thinking replaces the pre-given ontological structures of consciousness (through which evolution progresses) with levels of being and knowing that are collectively constructed by humans through the process of evolution back toward the divine, so that these levels of evolution are themselves dynamic and evolving. If the levels of evolution are relatively stable it is because they are "Kosmic habits" (p. 240), not because they are ahistorical, pre-given, Platonic archetypes. With this re-definition of the evolutionary structures of consciousness, Wilber claimed to have overcome the philosophical shortcomings of perennialism.

Yet as Wilber has shifted the ontological status of these Kosmic habits to his upper left-hand quadrant (interior-individual), Wilber (2006) has apparently *reduced* spiritual realities by assigning them to the inner realm of the individual, whether or not that is his intention (see Ferrer, 2011a). This maneuver seems strikingly similar to Schleiermacher's (1799/1996) attempt to protect spiritual truths from modern and postmodern critiques by relegating them to the realm of inner individual experience. Wilber (2006) has explicitly expressed both this motivation and this strategy:

> The Great Chain of Being . . . which represents the essence of those premodern traditions, is actually dealing with realities and phenomena that are almost *entirely* in the Upper-Left quadrant. (p. 44, emphasis in original)

Apparently aware that this might be seen as a demotion, Wilber (2006) continued:

> This is not a negative put-down, but a positive address: these folks were consummate phenomenologists that would explore and master those realms [i.e., inner individual subjectivity] with genius and intensity often yet to be matched. But the Great Traditions did not . . . really know about the . . . other quadrants. (p. 44)

Wilber was arguably unpacking what he believed are the merits of the demotion in the context of his motivation, and he explicitly stated that religious practitioners were phenomenologists exploring the depths of their own individual subjectivity.

It is, however, possible to construct a more generous reading of Wilber's intent in the context of his overall thought. By subjectivity Wilber (e.g., 1977) has consistently referred to the subjective aspect of a singular reality that is neither subjective nor objective, but that "*can be approached either subjectively or objectively*" (p. 47, emphasis in original). Later, in his all-quadrant all level model (AQAL), Wilber (e.g., 2000a) also determined that phenomena could be approached either individually or collectively, yielding four quadrants: "the interior and the exterior of the individual and the social" (Wilber, 1995, p. 120). The Upper-Left quadrant refers to the interior-individual (interior referring to subjective), Upper-Right is exterior-individual (exterior referring to objective), Lower-Left is interior-collective, and Lower-Right is exterior-collective (see Wilber, 2000a, Fig. 5 on p. 62). These quadrants are also the *four strands* that make up each *holon,* holons being the structures that make up the world (Wilber, 1995). The four aspects (strands, quadrants) of appearance reflect the deeper, unitary, formless, nondual reality that lies behind them; as the deeper reality emerges through these quadrants, it is necessarily distorted because each is only a partial reflection of its wholeness. At the same time, each strand remains "intimately related and indeed dependent upon all the others, but none...can be reduced to the others" (Wilber, 1995, p. 120). The interdependence of these strands or quadrants reflects his position that within the nondual awareness that underlies them, the substance of all four quadrants is an inseparable, integral whole. If one takes this as context, then the quadrants are in some sense entangled with each other through the underlying nondual substrate so that *assigning* spiritual truths to a particular quadrant does not, within Wilber's model, necessarily *reduce* them to that quadrant—for the quadrant itself is not a reduction of the underlying, irreducible nondual awareness but rather a lens or portal into it.

One problem with this more liberal interpretation is that since Wilber has not explicitly offered it, it is arguably forced to apply such a reading to these passages. More serious yet is the fact that if one were to apply this logic to Wilber's work broadly, then it is hard to understand how any reductionism at all would be possible. Wilber has consistently critiqued modernist science for approaching reality only through the objective lenses of the right-hand quadrants (this is Wilber's, e.g., 1995, 2000b, *flatland,* a world of exteriors with no interiors), yet if Wilber's assignment of spiritual truths almost exclusively to the Upper Left Quadrant is not largely reductionist, then neither is an objectivist approach to the world.

The central issue, however, is not whether one adopts a strict or generous interpretation of Wilber's statements regarding the relationship of spiritual realities to the domain of individual subjectivity; nor is the problem confined to the fact that his structures of consciousness were pre-given in earlier iterations of his thought, for Wilber (2006) has rejected the pre-givenness of his structures of consciousness and concluded that he has thereby become post-metaphysical. The issue is that for Wilber, his four quadrants are the appearances of a single nondual reality that lies behind them, a reality that is not apparent except through them (e.g., Wilber, 2000a). This one reality is by definition a metaphysical construct: a dimension that is behind the realm of appearances while also one with them (cf. Ferrer, 2011a; van Inwagen, 1998).

As Wilber (2006) himself has noted, metaphysics cannot survive in the context of critical thought. Philosophical appeal to a hidden dimension is akin to inserting a step into a series of mathematical computations that reads, "then a miracle occurs" (Harris, 1994, p. 1); it is the equivalent of secret evidence in judicial proceedings. Wilber (2006) has defined metaphysics in specific, limited terms: as the pre-Kantian belief that humans experience the world as it is, rather than as structures constructed within the mind on the basis of sensory data. He has then moved beyond metaphysics as defined in that narrow way. Kant's critique was also of just such a narrow metaphysical stance. Instead, he posited that there is a world of objective things-in-themselves (or noumena) directly behind the world of appearances (or phenomena) that are presented to the mind. Although Wilber's work overcomes pre-Kantian metaphysics, it operates within a Kantian metaphysical dualism.

Wilber's (2006) integral post-metaphysics remains deeply, centrally, metaphysical. His model works the way it is intended only so long as his four quadrants of reality (interior-individual, interior-collective, exterior-individual, and exterior-collective) function as integral aspects of a deeper, nondual reality. Yet it is precisely this timeless and formless reality that is a metaphysical construct—metaphysical in the sense that it is a deeper reality lying behind the appearances of the world (Ferrer, 2011a; van Inwagen, 1998). This reality is seemingly available only through the private subjective experience of individuals who are sufficiently evolved to apprehend it, and who interpret their experience in a manner consistent with Wilber's thought. This nondual metaphysical concept, and the associated elevation of a nondual realization as the zenith of universal spiritual development and evolution, has been central to his work since his first book (Wilber, 1977), continues to be central in his most recent book (Wilber, 2006), and signals that his work remains perennialist in nature (cf. Ferrer, 2002, 2011a).

Without this metaphysical claim, there are four quadrants but they are no longer the manifest aspects of a hidden nondual whole—they are just four separate fragments of reality. His individual-collective categories are not philosophically controversial, which means one is left with a world divided into subject and object; there is no other reality lying behind them to which one can appeal in order to solve the difficult philosophical problems of reconciling inner and outer dimensions. If this is the situation, when Wilber (2006) relegated "the invaluable and profound truths of the premodern [spiritual] traditions" (p. 46) to his Upper-Left quadrant, he was effectively acceding to modernist critiques of spirituality that dismiss it as something concocted subjectively.

Displaced from its metaphysical context, this move seems to relinquish a central element of Wilber's project to modernism: Spirituality is then a kind of subjective experience that is entirely made up by humans. Yet rather than merely being imposed at the societal level by such institutions as, say, the medieval Christian church, these constructs are now made inescapable by collective coercion from within. Ferrer (2002), following Popper's (1994) thought, has critiqued this as the "myth of the framework": the notion that "mystics and religious practitioners are prisoners of their cultures and conceptual frameworks, and that spiritual knowledge must always be shaped by or screened through such frameworks" (Ferrer, 2011a, p. 9).

So, either Wilber's system remains metaphysical and perennialist, in which case it does not withstand the scrutiny of critical thought, or else it renounces the metaphysical claim that is at its heart, in which case it has not addressed the Cartesian issues that lie at the root of modernism and postmodernism. Either way, he does not appear to defend successfully the significance of human spirituality in a critical contemporary context. Wilber's challenge, no different from that of contemporary society, is of being caught on the horns of the Cartesian dilemma, unable to unite subjective and objective domains of reality and therefore subject to the limitations of both. It is in response to this difficulty that participatory thought has emerged as a fully post-Cartesian alternative.

Participatory Philosophy

The alternative that has emerged in transpersonal thought, and that has quickly met with considerable success, is a participatory philosophy as articulated by Jorge N. Ferrer (e.g., 2000b, 2001, 2002, 2008a, 2010, 2011b; Ferrer & Sherman, 2008a) and others (e.g., Heron, 1992, 2006; Kelly, 2008; Kremer, 1994; Tarnas, 1991). This approach offers what may be a more effective context for spirituality because it presents a substantive challenge to Cartesian dualism. As noted, a critique of the subject-object divide was raised by Maslow at the beginning of the transpersonal project.

The roots of the philosophy currently underlying science come from René Descartes (1596-1650), who proposed that matter had extension in space but had no consciousness, whereas mind (or soul) had consciousness but no extension in space (Hatfield, 2008). From this came the Western assumption that mind and matter exist as wholly separate domains of reality: matter came to be understood as being devoid of mind, and mind came to be seen as wholly separate from the material world. This way of thinking is called Cartesian dualism, after Descartes.

Participatory thought, by contrast, understands the world to be a dynamic and open-ended living system that is continually involved in cocreating itself (Ferrer, 2011b). This conclusion is the result of a transformational leap in Western thought, based directly on insights gained from a transpersonal perspective. Early Western philosophy understood knowledge to be a relationship between rational mind and objective world. Reason allowed the mind to be a neutral agent in gathering objective information—a view that fueled an exuberant, naïve objectivism in the Age of Enlightenment. What this view offered was, after all, the tantalizing prospect of absolutely certain knowledge.

Kant's critique of this perspective began the long development toward postmodernism. He grasped that what the mind perceives is mental phenomena based on the interaction of sensory data and the mind's innate categories; it puts together an image that seems to be a real world, but can only ever largely be a construction within the mind. The objective world remains essentially beyond the reach of perception. Nietzche (1967) famously described this as a world in which the same situation can be interpreted in completely opposite ways: it is one in which "there are no facts" (p. 47). Rather than witness to an objective world, the mind is locked within subjectivity.

In both of these alternatives, the human mind is something quite separate from the material world: either it observes objective reality from a wholly different dimension, or else it is sequestered from objective reality. Building on the insights of the Western philosophical tradition of romanticism (cf. Sherman, 2008; Tarnas, 1991), participatory thought offers a third alternative, thereby offering a possible step beyond postmodernism: that mind and nature are necessarily woven of the same fabric (cf. Bateson, 1979). If this is so, then the human mind is not an isolated capsule of subjectivity adrift in a lifeless world. Rather, the mind is made of the same stuff as the world: consciousness in some form goes all the way down to the basic materials of physicality (Chalmers, 1995; De Quincey, 1994; Heron, 1992). The mind can know the world because through the mind, the world knows itself (Tarnas, 1991; Velmans, 2008).

Modern human beings were displaced from their centrality in the physical universe by Copernicus, from their ability to know that world directly by Kant, and from their biological uniqueness within it by Darwin (Tarnas, 1991). As the world closed in, the human person, confined within suffocating biological and deterministic forces, seemed little more than a helpless pawn with the misfortune of consciously witnessing its own fate. Population pressures built, scientific advances eradicated the role of divine forces that might intercede, and the world descended into two wars exemplifying raw struggle for evolutionary dominance. Civilization seemed capable of annihilating itself through nuclear war. Yet at this very moment depth psychology began to open the psyche, as it were, from the bottom, giving birth to a revitalized place for humanity within the cosmos (cf. Tarnas, 2006).

Freud's model of the psyche is often visualized as an iceberg in which the ego is but a small part that emerges from the waters of the unconscious; in Jung's view the ego might instead be pictured as an island that, if followed deeply enough into the unconscious, becomes the whole world. The individual mind is itself an intimate part of the cosmos, but feels alienated on the island of the individual self because it has forgotten how to swim in the waters that connect it with the community of life. As this formerly unconscious realm of mind is recovered, the relationship to world is transformed: no longer wandering alone through a world of inanimate objects, humanity is welcomed home into a community of subjects (Berry, 1996).

In Western society the process of recovering for humankind something beyond ego consciousness has been the work of transpersonal psychology, humanistic psychology, and depth psychology, and has on a popular level given rise to transcendentalists, the Beat generation, hippies, and the New Age movement. Through self-exploration, transformational practices such as meditation or communion with nature, and psychedelics, recent generations have struggled to open the door that modernism closed, and that postmodernism dismissed as illusory: the door to communion with the creative, inspiring presence of life itself.

It is transpersonal research, specifically the work of Stanislav Grof, which offers a substantive empirical bridge between deep psyche and world. Grof's (e.g., 1983) work used reports from several thousand LSD sessions to map the process of individuals as they opened progressively deeper aspects of their unconscious minds, moving first through levels represented by Freudian theory, re-experiencing the archetype-rich titanic traumas associated with biological birth, then expanding into experiences resonant with collective realms described by Jung (Grof, 1983, 1985, 1998; Tarnas, 1991). Through substance-induced biological disinhibition of the mind-body (cf. Cahart-Harris et al., 2012), the person recovered an unconscious history at once biologically rooted and archetypally patterned, suggesting "that nature itself, including the human body, was the repository and vessel of the archetypal, *that nature's processes were archetypal processes*" (Tarnas, 1991, pp. 427-428, emphasis supplied). The depths of the mind appeared to converge with the biological origins of the body in archetypal process.

These archetypes are neither fixed, pre-given structures, nor constructed by collective humanity (as Wilber [2006] has suggested), nor even templates for evolutionary progress toward some foreordained ultimate (cf. Ferrer, 2002, 2008a), but are themselves products of the irrepressible mystery that urges itself into manifestation through a thousand forms: not as products, but themselves as participants in ever-unfolding emancipatory process. As the mystery unfolds it may in retrospect be seen as evolutionary progression, but to project this past trajectory onto the future is to miss the open, prolific, creative dynamism inherent in the ongoing invention of the world.

Transpersonal psychology in particular has recognized that this journey into the depths of the psyche has much in common with mystical paths that inform the great spiritual traditions of the world. From a participatory perspective these are not all facets of the same path, and do not all lead to the same goal (cf. Ferrer, 2002, 2008a). Spirituality may be broadly defined as the urge within individuals and communities to find relationship with the whole of their world or some larger part of it, with the larger presences—nature-based or theistic, personal or impersonal. Yet as the ego is woven back into the fabric of life, it loses its imagined power to see all the world—or all the world's spirituality—from a privileged and neutral position. It is no longer the observer who can take in the whole painting from afar; it is part of the canvas, and it is *located* on that canvas. Although it can broaden its location (cf. Friedman, 1983) through experience and empathic conversation, it cannot escape its *locatedness* (cf. Haraway, 1988); this locatedness is the substance of its belonging, at once its vitality and its limitation.

Every person's experience is unique, in part, because their locatedness is unique; I may be standing next to my wife and sharing an event, but if she is on my right, then I am on her left—and this will be among the least of the differences in our respective experiences. Biology, gender, belief, community, culture, and geography can all be understood as aspects of locatedness, and a person's locatedness is imbued into every relationship. This is also true of spiritual relationships with the whole of one's world, or with some larger aspect of it. If someone wishes to describe how all spiritual traditions fit together *from their unique and limited perspective,* imbued with the qualities of their particular locatedness, that is quite different from claiming to see, *from a privileged perspective* (as is typically the case with perennialism), how all spiritual traditions are in reality related to a single ultimate dimension. This applies no less to participatory views, which is why participatory thinkers advance their claims as necessarily situated rather than universal, and offered in the spirit of creative emancipatory contributions to the global conversation rather than as objective representations of the truth (e.g., Ferrer, 2002; Ferrer & Sherman, 2008a).

Ferrer (2002, 2008a; Ferrer & Sherman, 2008a) has used a participatory frame to suggest a context for understanding spiritual experience and transpersonal phenomena. In modern and postmodern contexts, spiritual and mystical processes are thought to occur entirely within the subjectivity of the individual—they are inherently private rather than relational, and therefore have no ontological reality. The experience may make you feel better, but it cannot be real in the way that rocks and geraniums in the garden are real. From a participatory stance, by contrast, spiritual and mystical experiences are *participatory events,* cocreated encounters with spiritual powers and presences that are ontologically real. They are not made up inside a private mind, but are something that happens in the shared world. Nor are these experiences something happening *to* the individual, but actions that world and self bring forth together— a process Ferrer (2008a) has called *participatory enaction.* Self and world, part and whole, shape each other reciprocally in an ongoing process of mutually transforming participation.

With this understanding, spiritual and mystical experiences are ontologically real, and they are unique. Each tradition that arises around these encounters bears its own distinctive character, yet in the broadest sense it is possible to recognize spirituality as a category of human aspiration, experience, and expression. It is a richly variegated category—no less blooming with creative diversity than the language and arts of love—and accordingly resists reduction to any but the subtlest of commonalities. To describe spiritual traditions as "rivers leading to the same ocean" (Ferrer, 2002, p. 144) may not do justice to the sheer fecundity of the spiritual impulse; perhaps it is more aptly envisioned as "an ocean with many shores" (p. 133). The ocean in this metaphor should not suggest a common pre-given spiritual reality, but rather a shared human capacity for cocreating ontological possibilities that overcome egocentricism, dissociation, and eco-social injustice.

As the currents of different traditions mingle, a participatory stance invokes mutual respect for the ways in which each individual and each community brings their particular insights and contributions (Ferrer, 2010, 2011b). In place of ranking various spiritual traditions by how well they reflect some constructed ideal or pre-given reality, Ferrer has suggested they might be evaluated on three criteria: how well they free their members from narcissism and self-centeredness (egocentrism test), how well they foster the development of the whole person (dissociation test), and how effectively they "foster ecological balance, social and economic justice, religious and political freedom, class and gender equality, and other fundamental human rights" (eco-social-political test; Ferrer, 2011b, p. 7; cf. Heron, 2006). This evaluation of emancipatory qualities, however, has been proposed within a "relaxed spiritual universalism" (Ferrer, 2008a, p. 156) that rescues the ultimate unity of the mystery and allows for cross-cultural qualitative distinctions without making these the tools of some new ontological hierarchy. The mystery to which they point, relentlessly teeming with potential, cannot serve as basis for any static hierarchy because it creatively advances in multiple ontological directions.

Conclusion

Wilber's model served transpersonal psychology at a time when Maslow, its most prominent founder, had died, and a philosophical container was needed in which to cultivate the fledgling field. It should be noted that the vulnerability of his system at the level of philosophy should not obscure the fact that Wilber has contributed numerous useful and articulate concepts to the transpersonal approach, nor the fact that as an author with a broad popular following he continues to inspire many. Wilber's model is certainly among the most sophisticated perennialist systems ever constructed by a single person, and his work deserves respect as a significant accomplishment.

That said, the participatory turn offers a new way forward for transpersonal psychology, as well as for other approaches that require a post-Cartesian philosophical
context. Since its formal introduction in 2002 it has been embraced by a number of
transpersonal and religious scholars (see Ferrer, 2011b; Ferrer & Sherman, 2008b;
Lahood, 2007b), explicated as an approach to spiritual practice (Ferrer, 2003, 2008b),
applied to graduate and integral education (e.g., Ferrer, 2011c; Ferrer, Romero, &
Albareda, 2005; Nakagawa & Matsuda, 2010), sketched into a cosmology (Adams,
2010), and used as starting point for a re-definition of empiricism (Hartelius, 2009).
It finds scholarly touch points in Gendlin's (1997) process model for a philosophy of
the implicit, in the phenomenological concept of lifeworld (e.g., Luft, 2011), and in
the humanist-existentialist concept of presence (e.g., Schneider, 2010), among others.
As a non-hierarchical, emancipatory approach to understanding spiritual experience
and spiritual knowing, it is itself an invitation to dialogue: to shared participation in
the unfolding of life and the cosmos.

References

Adams, W. W. (2010). Nature's participatory psyche: A study of consciousness in the
    shared earth community. *The Humanistic Psychologist, 38*(1), 15-39. doi:10.1080/
    08873261003635708

Bateson, G. (1979). *Mind and nature: A necessary unity* (Advances in systems theory, complex-
    ity, and the human sciences). New York, NY: Hampton Press.

Berry, T. (1996, April 9). Ethics and ecology. Paper presented to the Harvard Seminar on
    Environmental Values.

Blavatsky, H. P. (1978). *The secret doctrine* (3 vols.; B. de Zirkoff, Ed.). Wheaton, IL: Theo-
    sophical. (Original work published 1888)

Borden, W., & Clark, J. J. (2012). Contemporary psychodynamic theory, research, and practice:
    Implications for evidence-based intervention. In T. L. Rzepnicki, S. G. McCracken, & H.
    E. Briggs (Eds.), *From task-centered social work to evidence-based and integrative practice:
    Reflections on history and implementation* (pp. 65-87). Chicago, IL: Lyceum Books.

Carhart-Harris, R., Erritze, D., Williams, T., Stone, J., Reed, L., Colasanti, A., & Nutt, D.
    (2012). Neural correlates of the psychedelic state as determined by fMRI studies with
    psilocybin. *Proceedings of the National Academy of Science (PNAS), 109*(6), 2138-2143.
    doi:10.1073/pnas.1119598109

Chalmers, D. J. (1995). Facing up to the problem of consciousness. *Journal of Consciousness
    Studies, 2*(3), 200-219.

De Quincey, C. (1994). Consciousness all the way down? An analysis of McGinn's critique of
    panexperientialism. *Journal of Consciousness Studies, 1*(2), 217-229.

Ellis, A., & Yeager, R. J. (1989). *Why some therapies don't work: The dangers of transpersonal
    psychology*. Buffalo, NY: Prometheus Books.

Ferrer, J. N. (2000a). The perennial philosophy revisited. *Journal of Transpersonal Psychology,
    32*(1), 7-30.

Ferrer, J. N. (2000b). Transpersonal knowledge: A participatory approach to transpersonal
    phenomena. In T. Hart, P. Nelson, & K. Puhakka (Eds.), *Transpersonal knowing: Exploring
    the farther reaches of consciousness* (pp. 213-252). Albany, NY: State University of New York
    Press.

Ferrer, J. N. (2001). Towards a participatory vision of human spirituality. *ReVision: A Journal of Consciousness and Transformation 24*(2), 15-26.

Ferrer, J. N. (2002). *Revisioning transpersonal theory: A participatory vision of human spirituality*. Albany, NY: State University of New York Press.

Ferrer, J. N. (2003). Integral transformative practice: A participatory perspective. *The Journal of Transpersonal Psychology, 35*(1), 21-42.

Ferrer, J. N. (2008a). Spiritual knowing as participatory enaction: An answer to the question of religious pluralism. In J. N. Ferrer & J. H. Sherman (Eds.), *The participatory turn: Spirituality, mysticism, religious studies* (pp. 135-169). Albany, NY: State University of New York Press.

Ferrer, J. N. (2008b). What does it mean to live a fully embodied spiritual life? *International Journal of Transpersonal Studies 27*, 1-11.

Ferrer, J. N. (2010). The plurality of religions and the spirit of pluralism: A participatory vision of the future of religion. *International Journal of Transpersonal Studies, 28*, 139-151.

Ferrer, J. N. (2011a). Participation, metaphysics, and enlightenment: Reflections on Ken Wilber's recent work. *Transpersonal Psychology Review, 14*(2), 3-24.

Ferrer, J. N. (2011b). Participatory spirituality and transpersonal theory: A ten-year retrospective. *Journal of Transpersonal Psychology, 43*(1), 1-34.

Ferrer, J. N. (2011c). Teaching the Graduate Seminar in Comparative Mysticism: A Participatory Integral Approach. In W. Parsons (Ed.), *Teaching Mysticism* (pp. 173-192; American Academy of Religion Series). Oxford, NY: Oxford University Press.

Ferrer, J. N., Romero, M. T. & Albareda, R. V. (2005). Integral transformative education: A participatory proposal. *The Journal of Transformative Education 3*(4), 306-330.

Ferrer, J. N., & Sherman, J. H. (2008a). Introduction: The participatory turn in spirituality, mysticism, and religious studies. In J. N. Ferrer & J. H. Sherman (Eds.), *The participatory turn: Spirituality, mysticism, religious studies* (pp. 1-78). Albany, NY: State University of New York Press.

Ferrer, J. N., & Sherman, J. H. (Eds.). (2008b). *The participatory turn: Spirituality, mysticism, religious studies*. Albany, NY: State University of New York Press.

Friedman, H. (1983). The Self-Expansiveness Level Form: A conceptualization and measurement of a transpersonal construct. *Journal of Transpersonal Psychology, 15*(1), 37-50.

Gendlin, E. T. (1997). *A process model*. New York, NY: Focusing Institute. Retrieved from http://www.focusing.org/gendlin/docs/gol_2202.html

Grof, S. (1973). Theoretical and empirical basis of transpersonal psychology and psychotherapy: Observations from LSD research. *Journal of Transpersonal Psychology, 5*(1), 15-53.

Grof, S. (1983). East and West: Ancient wisdom and modern science. *Journal of Transpersonal Psychology, 15*(1), 13-36.

Grof, S. (1985). *Beyond the brain: Birth, death and transcendence in psychotherapy*. Albany, NY: State University of New York Press.

Grof, S. (1996). *Realms of the human unconscious: Observations from LSD research*. London, UK: Souvenir Press. (Original work published 1975)

Grof, S. (1998). Human nature and the nature of reality: Conceptual challenges from consciousness research. *Journal of Psychoactive Drugs, 30*(4), 343-357. doi:10.1080/02791072.1998.10399710

Grof, S. (2003). Implications of modern consciousness research for psychology: Holotropic experiences and their healing and heuristic potential. *The Humanistic Psychologist, 31*(2-3), 50-85.

Guenon, R. (2001). *The collected works of Rene Guenon* (J. R. Wetmore, Ed.; 23 vols.). Hillsdale, NY: Sophia Perennis.

Haraway, D. (1988). Situated knowledges: The science question in feminism and the privilege of partial perspective. *Feminist Studies, 14*(3), 575-599. doi:10.2307/3178066

Harris, S. (1994). *Chalk up another one: The best of Sidney Harris.* New Brunswick, NJ: Rutgers University Press.

Hartelius, G. (2007). Quantitative somatic phenomenology. *Journal of Consciousness Studies, 14*(12), 24-56.

Hartelius, G. (2009). *Participatory empiricism: Toward a phenomenological-empirical science for human psychology. Dissertation Abstracts International,* 70(07) 0392B (UMI #3367157).

Hatfield, G. (2008). René Descartes (E. N. Zalta, Ed.). *The Stanford encyclopedia of philosophy.* Stanford, CA: Metaphysical Research Lab/Center for the Study of Language and Information.

Heron, J. (1992). *Feeling and personhood: Psychology in another key.* London, UK: Sage.

Heron, J. (2006). *Participatory spirituality: A farewell to authoritarian religion.* Morrisville, NC: Lulu Press.

Hoffman, E. (2008). Abraham Maslow: A biographer's reflections. *Journal of Humanistic Psychology, 48,* 439-443. doi:10.1177/0022167808320534

Huxley, A. (1945). *The perennial philosophy.* New York, NY: Harper & Row.

Kelly, S. (2008). Participation, complexity, and the study of religion. In J. N. Ferrer & J. H. Sherman (Eds.), *The participatory turn: Spirituality, mysticism, religious studies* (pp. 113-133). Albany, NY: State University of New York Press.

Kremer, J. (1994). *Looking for Dame Yggdrasil.* Red Bluff, CA: Falkenflug Press.

Lahood, G. (2007a). The participatory turn and the transpersonal movement: A brief introduction. *ReVision: A Journal of Consciousness and Transformation, 29*(3), 2-6. doi:10.3200/REVN.29.3.2-6

Lahood, G. (Ed). (2007b). The participatory turn, Part 1 and 2 [Monograph]. *ReVision: A Journal of Consciousness and Transformation,* 29(3-4).

Leuder, I., & Thomas, P. (2000). *Voices of reason, voices of insanity.* Philadelphia, PA: Routledge.

Luft, S. (2011). *Subjectivity and lifeworld in transcendental phenomenology.* Evanston, IL: Northwestern University Press.

Maslow, A. H. (1943). A theory of human motivation. *Psychological Review, 50*(4), 370-396. doi:10.1037/h0054346

Maslow, A. H. (1954). The instinctoid nature of basic needs. *Journal of Personality, 22,* 326-347. doi:10.1111/j.1467-6494.1954.tb01136.x

Maslow, A. H. (1961). Are our publications and conventions suitable for the personal sciences? (Comment). *American Psychologist, 16*(6), 318-319. doi:10.1037/h0039674

Maslow, A. H. (1966). *The psychology of science: A reconnaissance.* New York, NY: Harper & Row.

Maslow, A. H. (1969). The farther reaches of human nature. *Journal of Transpersonal Psychology, 1*(1), 1-9.

Maslow, A. H. (1999). *Toward a psychology of being* (3nd ed.). New York, NY: John Wiley & Sons. (Original work published 1962)

Maslow, A. H., & Harlow, H. F. (1932). Comparative behavior of primates: II. Delayed reaction tests on primates at Bronx Park Zoo. *Comparative Psychology, 14*(1), 97-107. doi:10.1037/h0072093

Nakagawa, Y. & Y. Matsuda (Eds.). (2010). *Integral approach: Integral Transformative Inquiry.* Kyoto, Japan: Institute of Human Sciences, Ritsumekian University.

Nietzche, F. (1967). *The will to power* (W. Kaufmann, Ed.). New York, NY: Random House.

Popper, K. (1994). The myth of the framework. In M. A. Nottumo (Ed.), *The myth of the framework: In defense of science and rationality* (pp. 33-64). New York, NY: Routledge.

Rank, O. (1929). *The trauma of birth*. New York, NY: Dover. (Original work published 1924 [German])

Rothberg, D. (1986). Philosophical foundations of transpersonal psychology. *Journal of Transpersonal Psychology, 18*(1), 1-34.

Rowan, J., Daniels, M., Fontana, D., & Walley, M. (2009). A dialogue on Ken Wilber's contribution to transpersonal psychology. *Transpersonal Psychology Review, 13*(2), 5-41.

Schleiermacher, F. (1996). *On religion: Speeches to its cultured despisers* (R. Crouter, Trans.). Cambridge, UK: Cambridge University Press. (Original work published 1799)

Schmitt, C. (1966). Perennial philosophy: Steuco to Leibniz. *Journal of the History of Ideas, 27,* 505-532. doi:10.2307/2708338

Schneider, K. J. (2010). An existential-integrative approach to experiential liberation. *The Humanistic Psychologist, 38*(1), 1-14. doi:10.1080/08873261003635815

Schuon, F. (1984). *The transcendent unity of religions*. Wheaton, IL: Theosophical. (Original work published 1953)

Shedler, J. (2010). The efficacy of psychodynamic psychotherapy. *The American Psychologist, 65*(2), 98-109. doi:10.1037/a0018378

Sherman, J. H. (2008). A genealogy of participation. In J. N. Ferrer & J. H. Sherman (Eds.), *The participatory turn: Spirituality, mysticism, religious studies* (pp. 81-112). Albany, NY: State University of New York Press.

Sutich, A. (1968). Transpersonal psychology: An emerging force. *Journal of Humanistic Psychology, 8,* 77-78. doi:10.1177/002216786800800108

Swami Vivekananda (1947). *The complete works of Swami Vivekananda* (8 vols.). Hollywood, CA: Vedanta Press.

Tarnas, R. (1991). *The passion of the Western mind: Understanding the ideas that have shaped our world view*. New York, NY: Ballantine Books.

Tarnas, R. (2006). *Cosmos and psyche: Intimations of a new world view*. New York, NY: Viking.

Tart, C. T. (1964). A comparison of suggested dreams occurring in hypnosis and sleep. *International Journal of Clinical and Experimental Hypnosis, 12*(4), 263-289. doi:10.1080/00207146408409114

Tart, C. T. (1966). ESPATESTER: An automatic testing device for parapsychological research. *Journal of the American Society of Psychical Research, 26,* 256-269.

Tart, C. T. (1971). Scientific foundations for the study of altered states of consciousness. *Journal of Transpersonal Psychology, 3*(2), 93-133.

Tart, C. T. (1972). States of consciousness and state-specific sciences. *Science, 176,* 1203-1210. doi:10.1126/science.176.4040.1203

Tart, C. T. (2000). Investigating altered states on their own terms: State-specific sciences. In M. Velmas (Ed.), *Investigating phenomenal consciousness: New methodologies and maps.* (pp. 255-278). Amsterdam, The Netherlands: John Benjamins.

van Inwagen, P. (1998). The nature of metaphysics. In S. Laurence & C. Macdonald (Eds.), *Contemporary readings in the foundations of metaphysics* (pp. 11-21). Malden, MA: Blackwell.

Varela, F. (1996). Neurophenomenology. *Journal of Consciousness Studies, 3*(4), 330-349.

Velmans, M. (2008). Reflexive monism. *Journal of Consciousness Studies, 15*(2), 5-50.

Wilber, K. (1975). *Psychologia perennis:* The spectrum of consciousness. *Journal of Transpersonal Psychology, 7*(2), 1-21.

Wilber, K. (1977). *The spectrum of consciousness*. Wheaton, IL: Theosophical.

Wilber, K. (1981). *Up from Eden: A transpersonal view of human evolution*. New York, NY: Doubleday/Anchor.

Wilber, K. (1987). The spectrum model. In D. Anthony & K. Wilber (Eds.), *Spiritual choices: The problems of recognizing authentic paths to inner transformation* (pp. 327-348). St. Paul, MN: Paragon House.

Wilber, K. (1993). The great chain of being. *Journal of Humanistic Psychology, 33*(3), 52-65. doi:10.1177/00221678930333006

Wilber, K. (1995). *Sex, ecology, spirituality: The spirit of evolution.* Boston, MA: Shambhala.

Wilber, K. (1997). *The eye of spirit: An integral vision for a world gone slightly mad.* Boston, MA: Shambhala.

Wilber, K. (1998). *The marriage of sense and soul: Integrating science and religion.* Boston, MA: Shambhala.

Wilber, K. (1999). *One taste: The journals of Ken Wilber.* Boston, MA: Shambhala.

Wilber, K. (2000a). *Integral psychology.* Boston, MA: Shambhala.

Wilber, K. (2000b). *A theory of everything: An integral vision for business, politics, science and spirituality.* Boston, MA: Shambhala.

Wilber, K. (2003). Waves, streams, states, and self: An outline of integral psychology. *The Humanistic Psychologist, 31*(2-3), 22-49. doi:10.1080/08873267.2003.9986925

Wilber, K. (2006). *Integral spirituality: A startling new role for religion in the modern and postmodern world.* Boston, MA: Shambhala.

Wilber, K. (2012). On the nature of post-metaphysical spirituality: Response to Habermas and Weis. Retrieved from http://wilber.shambhala.com/html/misc/habermas/index.cfm (Original work published 2001 as Vom Wesen einder postmetaphysische Spiritualität, *Transpersonale Psychologie und Psychotherapie, 7*(2), 33-49)

11

Transpersonal Self-Expansiveness as a Scientific Construct

Harris L. Friedman

I have previously argued that there is a need to build meaningful Mid-Range Transpersonal Psychology Theory (M-R TPT) in a way that avoids the traps of grand theory and mini-theory (Friedman, 2002, this volume). Self-expansiveness (Friedman, 1981, 1983) is one among many possible transpersonal concepts and constructs that can be useful for that purpose. In this chapter, I discuss the construct of self-expansiveness in some detail, including how it can be operationalized, some empirical findings supporting both its validity and utility, and some of its future implications. In addition, to place this one construct within a broader context, I discuss the need for systematically developing and researching other transpersonal concepts and constructs to further transpersonal psychology as both a science and a praxis.

Self-Expansiveness as a Scientific Construct

The construct of self-expansiveness originated from my own experiences, which I used as personal (but non-scientific) data to formulate it. I considered myself a *psychonaut* at the time I created this construct, as I had been engaging regularly for several years in deep inner explorations using my own varieties of meditation, augmented by ample doses of helpful psychedelics. I developed the construct of self-expansiveness because it helped me make sense of some of my own transpersonal experiences, and I chose to research it because I thought it might have utility for others, as well as be expedient for developing M-R TPT, which I saw as a way to build a sorely needed science of transpersonal psychology. I also wanted to test the external validity of my own inner musings gained as a psychonaut against the challenges of bringing one of these notions into the larger consensual world of outer experiences, namely into the competitive arena of science. Last, I was committed to doing a transpersonal,

The Wiley Blackwell Handbook of Transpersonal Psychology, First Edition.
Edited by Harris L. Friedman and Glenn Hartelius.
© 2013 John Wiley & Sons, Ltd. Published 2015 by John Wiley & Sons, Ltd.

yet empirical, dissertation to win my doctorate, and using a self-report approach to measure this construct seemed, naïvely in retrospect, relatively easy to accomplish.

I started by framing the construct of self-expansiveness as a way to conceptualize and operationalize a transpersonal approach devoid of metaphysical speculation, especially "theocentric" assumptions that plague this area of research (i.e., most measures of spiritual and transpersonal concepts are based on religious assumptions, especially those involving notions of a divinity; see MacDonald & Friedman, 2002). In this way, self-expansiveness is not based on anything supernatural but, nevertheless, self-expansiveness as a construct may be tapping into notions similar to how some view spirituality, and measures of self-expansiveness overlap in important ways with some measures of spirituality (e.g., Pappas & Friedman, 2007, 2012).

Self-expansiveness rests on the view that the self-concept can be relatively narrowly construed, limited to the isolated individual bound in the here-and-now of the present, or can expand to include others, nature, and even a transpersonally constituted identity where the sense of self can extend to allow for boundless identity with all of existence. I designated the process of self-expansion to occur across three arbitrarily delineated levels (personal, middle, transpersonal) within two dimensions (spatial and temporal). The spatial dimension includes contracted and expanded properties, while the temporal dimension consists of past and future properties. These are expressed graphically in a cartography (see Figure 11.1), as well as verbally in various descriptions of the construct. In this regard, the possibility of transcendence beyond space and time is outside of the map, but may be implied by the areas beyond where the map ends.

Transpersonal self-expansiveness focuses on the notion of the self, but it only focuses on one aspect of the self, namely self-concept. Thus it does not focus on the "I" or self as it is directly experienced, but rather on the "me" that is viewed as an object, albeit

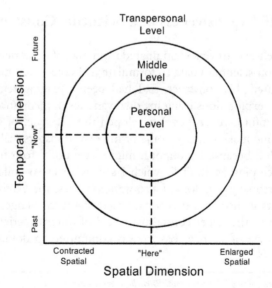

Figure 11.1 The original cartography of self-expansiveness. Adapted from Friedman (1981, 1983).

an object delineated as special to the person as compared with all other objects viewed as not-me (James, 1890). The self has played a major role in psychology throughout its history, as it is the primary organizing basis for many psychological topics (Leary & Tangney, 2003), as well as for integrating one's own experiences, including through structuring levels of self-identity (Pederson, 1994). The notion of self as experienced can be equated to consciousness itself, and is a metaphysical notion every bit as obscure as transcendence, which defies scientific efforts to pin it down (Frager & Fadiman, 2005). However, self-concept, the running symbolic register of one's experiences, which is coded in narrative and other forms of memory, is a delimited construct as compared to the lived self. I saw it as theoretically and empirically amenable to scientific efforts and capable of being woven into theories that are as potentially falsifiable as any in psychology (Friedman, 1981, 1983), simply being a cluster of attitudes and beliefs about one's self in answer to the question, "who am I?"

It is no surprise that contemporary psychology has tended to emphasize the self-concept rather than attempting to examine directly the experiencing self. As an aside, phenomenological methods continue to attempt to tackle the self as directly lived. However, I note that such phenomenological methods inevitably bring whatever direct experience that might be captured through introspection back into some symbolically mediated way that essentially is just another form of self-concept. This is not meant to denigrate phenomenology as a method, as I see it as very valuable, but to clarify that the subjective (or first-person perspective) products of phenomenological inquiry always have to be translated into some objective (or third-person perspective) product to become part of the scientific process.

Even with reducing my focus to the self-concept, and bracketing the more difficult topic of lived self (along with other metaphysical concepts, such as transcendence), there were still many obstacles to developing self-expansiveness as a construct. For example, there is a proliferation of confusing terms used to describe self-concept, resulting in a huge and fragmented literature (Byrne, 2002). These include terms combining the prefix "self" with a plethora of suffixes, such as -construal (e.g., Marx, Stapel, & Muller, 2005), -definition (e.g., Robbins, Pis, & Pender, 2004), -esteem (e.g., Esposito, Kobak, & Little, 2005), -knowledge (e.g., Lieberman, Jarcho, & Satpute, 2004), -identity (e.g., Webb, 2004), -perception (e.g., Weiss & Amorose, 2005), and -representation (e.g., Reinert, 2005), just to mention a few. No consensual way to approach self-concept as a whole has yet been recognized within mainstream psychology (Chen, Chen, & Shaw, 2004), although I suggest the construct of self-expansiveness may provide opportunity for such an integration.

In addition, there are many vantages from which to look at self-concept. For example, the divide between individualistic and relational approaches is often invoked (e.g., Markus & Kitayama, 1994). I see these as inseparable sides of a coin (i.e., human individuals rarely if ever are apart from a social context, while human social systems exist only through their individual inhabitants), so that either, without taking its complement into consideration, is lacking in wholeness. Additional vantages to self-concept include biological emphasizing anatomical and physiological aspects of self-concept (e.g., Lieberman, et al., 2004), ecological emphasizing relatedness of self-concept to the non-human environment (e.g., Bragg, 1996), and temporal emphasizing relatedness of self-concept to past and possible future aspects of a person (e.g., Newby-Clark

& Ross 2003). There are also many specific aspects of self-concept that have gained attention, such as the moral (Lewis, 2003) and artistic (Vispoel, 1995) components of self-concept. One often overlooked aspect of the self-concept in Western psychology that is germane to transpersonal psychology is spirituality (Poll & Smith, 2003), as many cultural traditions consider spirituality central to understanding self-concept (e.g., Asian Indian; Friedman, MacDonald, & Kumar, 2004). I note that including spirituality as part of the self-concept does not necessarily reify spirituality, but may simply deal with the importance of people's spiritual beliefs and attitudes about spirituality when defining themselves, and this approach can still bracket the ontological status of the object of their beliefs and attitudes. For example, in his pioneering work, MacDonald (2000) organized the nomothetic network composed of various measures of spirituality, but he was explicit that his resulting 5-factor approach did not measure spirituality itself but, rather, only its expressions (i.e., MacDonald sidestepped the difficult ontological problems in claiming to conceptualize and measure spirituality per se, just as I am focusing only on self-concept rather than the more elusive self).

To these numerous perspectives on self-concept, only a few of which have been mentioned, I have added transpersonal self-expansiveness (Friedman, 1981, 1983) as something new. Transpersonal self-expansiveness is based on the fact that one's sense of self can expand beyond ("trans") the individual self seen as an isolated monad (i.e., the self-concept is inherently malleable, governed only by the extent with which one can identify aspects of the world as being part of who one sees oneself to be). The boundaries between self and world are fluid, even as understood through the filter of self-concept as a more stable trait (the "me") than the ever-shifting state of consciousness (the "I"). As a trait, this can vary across individuals who vary in their identification or sense of interconnection with different aspects of the world, including on possible transpersonal dimensions. Following James' (1890) insights about the self, Maslow (1968) discussed how the self can expand beyond its usual biographic, personal, and egoic sense toward the transpersonal. Walsh and Vaughan (1993) similarly described transpersonal experiences "in which the sense of identity or self extends beyond (trans) the individual or personal to encompass wider aspects of humankind, life, psyche or cosmos" (p. 203). Many others have emphasized such an approach (e.g., Daniels, 2005), but no one else has systematically grounded their views in a comprehensive way, nor has anyone else provided a corresponding way to make such a view empirically accessible. Just as the individual and collective notions of the self-concept are complementary, I think all domains of the self-concept are likewise complementary and even necessary for wholeness, and these various notions can be subsumed under the construct of self-expansiveness.

What I have added of especial value in creating the construct of self-expansiveness is a way to understand all these many aspects of self-concept, including a transpersonal aspect, through a cartography defined by space and time coordinates, which shows how the boundary between me and not-me can be delineated. Hunt (1999) and many others have pointed out that space and time are conceptual givens, perhaps the most basic orienting categories for adaptively tracking one's sense of self. More specifically, the self-expansiveness cartography positions space and time dimensions orthogonally, providing a map through which self-concept can be depicted. This allows a graphical way to express spatially enlarged and contracted aspects of self-concept, as well as aspects temporally extended into past and future . These then can be used to delineate boundaries of self-concept in terms of self-expansiveness, including transpersonal self-expansiveness. Where the spatial and temporal dimensions intersect is labeled the present (or "here-and-now"). Moving out from this intersection in four directions defined by the bifurcation of two lines, there are defined self-concept quadrants (i.e., temporal future, temporal past, spatial contracted, spatial enlarged), each of which encompasses the possibility of an expansive self-concept, such that one can identify with content in each of these quadrants in ways that are beyond the individual (i.e., seen existing as an isolated organism in the present).

The construct of self-expansiveness, and its cartography, provides a way to integrate many conventional, and seemingly disparate, approaches to self-concept, each of which can be placed on the map as an aspect of a larger whole, while all of which taken together define the larger whole. Its periphery, distant from the center, is seen as transpersonal. It reconciles the individualistic and relational dichotomy, as well as integrates the biological, environmental, and temporal aspects of self-concept, as these are all placed in relationship through its cartography. For example, an enlarged spatial self-concept includes both environmental and relational aspects of self-concept, whereas a contracted spatial self-concept may include only biological aspects of self-concept (i.e., for those who see themselves only in biologically reductive ways). Similarly, past and future temporal expansiveness includes aspects of self-concept related to time. Transpersonal self-expansiveness, and its cartography, unifies all of these perspectives within a singular holisitic framework.

The construct of transpersonal self-expansiveness rests on the radical assumption that no absolute limits can be placed on what is included or excluded in one's self-concept. This implies that the individual (a term whose root "divid" relates to being divided or separate) self can identify with all aspects of existence, including all that exists in space and time as encompassed by a transpersonally expansive self-concept, and become whole rather than divided from the cosmos. This radical view stems from James' (1890) profound insight that all boundaries placed around individuals' self-concepts are just arbitrary limitations placed on the potentially largest Self (i.e., using the capital "S" to express the most expansive sense of an all encompassing self). Individuals might include the entirety of existence within their self-concept, which then becomes a Self-concept rather than a lesser self-concept. Note, this does not address possible ultimate concerns that go beyond any predication of existence, as in the possibility of supernatural or metaphysical issues (e.g., transcendence). The further reaches of this less bounded self-concept, although still limited to the natural (i.e., that which exists in space and time), is literally transpersonal in terms of being *trans* or beyond the limiting *personal* sense of being an isolated monad, as in the prevailing Western notions of an individual self separated from the cosmos. I specified the transpersonal level of self-concept as emerging when it extends "sufficiently beyond the here-and-now, such that there is a dissolution of the individual's perception of self as an isolated biosystem existing only in the present" (Friedman, 1983, p. 39). Through this, the self-concept can be seen as potentially expanding beyond separateness, as an isolated presence in space and time, to encompass all conventional notions of the self (such as being biological, ecological, social, and temporal), while scientifically integrating these many conventional views and also including a transpersonal perspective that is well defined by being grounded within a naturalistic frame of reference.

Transpersonal self-expansiveness is therefore unlike other transpersonal constructs that rely on metaphysical and supernatural assumptions, as it limits its depiction of self-concept to time and space. This also differs from the numerous religious and spiritual approaches that appeal to supernatural and metaphysical notions, such as to a soul or nonduality, as the construct of transpersonal self-expansiveness brackets these untestable speculations. It should be again noted that, although the cartography of self-expansiveness is limited to the material world of space and time, its circular boundary does allow for what might go beyond its circumference to be displayed on its map, but this territory is undefined. In this sense, the possibility of the transcendent may be implied, but is not reified.

There are several conventional approaches in psychology to self-concept that resemble the construct of transpersonal self-expansiveness. For example, Aron and Aron (1986, 1996) used the term self-expansiveness in their model that views self-concept as capable of incorporating others by constituting a larger identity in which selves overlap, but their approach limits self-expansiveness only to the social realm. Likewise, Mayer and Frantz's (2004) connectedness to nature construct is quite similar to self-expansiveness, but limits expansion of the self-concept only to the realm of nature. Burris and Rempel's (2010) amoebic self theory also addresses the bodily and social domains of the self in a similar way as self-expansiveness. There are also a few emerging views encompassing multiple aspects of self-concept, such as a recent approach and associated measure of connectedness with three aspects of self: oneself, others and nature, and the transcendent (Meezenbroek et al., 2012). However, self-expansiveness as a construct predates, and is much more comprehensive than, all of these other approaches, and it uniquely offers a way to conceptualize the transpersonal, while it also subsumes all these domains of self-concept.

There are a number of arguments that can be made for the worth of self-expansiveness as a construct. One is that it is often referenced in scholarly writings, including within mainstream psychology (e.g., Cahn & Polich, 2006), as well as within the transpersonal literature (e.g., Haimerl & Valentine, 2001). It is important to also note that its cartography is flexible, such that its orientation can be transposed while keeping its fundamental form. Specifically, the transpersonal level can be flipped into becoming the new intersection of the space-time lines (where the personal level previously was at the here-and-now), while the personal level can become the new periphery (see Friedman & Pappas, 2006). This transposability feature is common in other recognized cartographies, such as when different projections can all be used to map the same territory (e.g., the less-known Gall-Peters projection as an alternative to the more common Mercator projection in mapping the earth), which evidences the underlying stability of the territory being mapped. In other words, that this transposition can occur without significant loss of meaning adds to the credence of the construct. In addition, because it can be discussed verbally (as in this chapter's written description), as well as mapped in pictorial form, it gains additional credence. However, the strongest evidence for the worth of self-expansiveness as a construct is based on growing empirical research, which is discussed later in this chapter.

The cartography can also be expanded in a variety of novel ways. For example, I created it as a horizontal or flat two-dimensional approach to depicting self-expansiveness. However, additional dimensions can be added, such as by supplementing the space-time coordinates with various third, or even higher order, dimensions. One additional orthogonal dimension that I explored, but on which I have never published, was to add a vertical dimension of cognitive complexity, as an attempt to map some of the developmental stages that Wilber (2001) used in his grand theory. Another approach that I explored was to find a more nuanced way to conceptualize the extent of identification with each level mapped by the cartography, which I used by shading the areas mapped in the cartography to display the extent of integration of one's identification at each level (Friedman, 1984). Thus far, however, I have mostly stayed with the basic approach I have outlined simply because it is more manageable, but I hope it is evident that there are many heuristic avenues to extend the construct of self-expansiveness, and build better scientific approaches that can accompany its further development.

The Self-Expansiveness Level Form

The construct of self-expansiveness would merely be another interesting notion if it were not empirically testable. In order to conduct a quantitative empirical dissertation within transpersonal psychology, I elected to use self-report approaches. However, I needed an appropriate psychometric instrument, as there were no explicitly transpersonal measures at the time. This has changed since my dissertation was started in 1975, and now many measures relevant to transpersonal research have emerged (see MacDonald, Friedman, & Kuentzel, 1999; MacDonald, Kuentzel, & Friedman, 1999; MacDonald, LeClair, Holland, Alter, & Friedman, 1995), but none have all of the advantages related to the construct of self-expansiveness. MacDonald and I have discussed a number of important methodological issues related to transpersonal scientific research relying on such instruments and, despite the importance of measurement for conducting quantitative transpersonal scientific studies, we have emphasized that all measures have limitations, as follows: "Although we are of the opinion that such approaches are fruitful avenues to gain reliable and useful knowledge, we do not believe that measurement can ever capture the inherent complexity or 'suchness' of many important transpersonal constructs that may, by their very nature, defy language, conceptualization, and exact measurement" (Friedman & MacDonald, 2002a, p. ix). To this, I add that many of the constructs used in transpersonal psychology should perhaps be relegated to the area of transpersonal studies, as they are outside of the purview of science.

When planning my dissertation, as there were no explicitly transpersonal measures, I created a self-report instrument, the Self-Expansiveness Level Form (SELF; Friedman, 1981, 1983), as one operationalization of my construct. It consists of 18 items accompanied with a Likert-type rating scale, and is published, including scoring instructions, in both of these early works. The SELF serves as a measure of the level of expansiveness of self-concept from the personal present into various aspects of spatial and temporal identity. I tried to avoid metaphysical and supernatural references, even though almost all other spiritual and transpersonal measures ask about issues filled with these (e.g., such as asking about prayer, which unavoidably implies a transcendent entity toward whom prayer is being addressed, or meditation, which often implies grounding within a religious system of belief, such as Buddhism with its inherent metaphysical assumptions). Rather, the SELF solely uses items congruent with the naturalistic cartography that frames self-expansiveness as a scientific construct.

The SELF measures the three different levels of possible self-expansiveness. The first is the personal level, which refers to the extent to which individuals identify with their selves in the present, for example with their behaviors, feelings, physical body, and thoughts. This level is seen as operationalizing the prevailing Western approach to self-concept, which focuses on the person as an isolated organism existing in the here-and-now of space-time. The next is the middle level, which refers to an intermediate expansiveness of the self-concept. In that level individuals identify with relationships extending beyond the individual who is seen as an isolated monad, with their physical and social contexts as well as with their personal past and future. These align with the diverse understandings of self-concept, such as the social-relational, ecological, biological, and temporal. Middle-level items include willingness to identify with childhood experiences (past) and imagined possible self projected into time (future), current family members (enlarged spatial) and parts of one's body, such as one's heart (contracted spatial). The middle level of self-expansiveness has not yet been adequately developed conceptually or empirically, which is reflected in current limitations of the SELF Middle Scale. It is possible that it will someday be further developed into a number of differing subscales rather than remaining a univariate scale (although this rests on empirical questions requiring research, which has not been done yet).

Last and most importantly, the SELF allows for measuring transpersonal aspects of self-concept, which are defined as being sufficiently distinct from the individual seen as an isolated monad, yet is still connected in some distant ways to the individual. Transpersonal items on the SELF include willingness to identify with the atoms within the body (extremely contracted spatial), all life (extremely enlarged spatial), distant ancestors (extreme past), and future descendents (extreme future) who may not have human form. These are seen as transpersonal insofar as they go considerably beyond identifying with obvious connections to the individual, but they still are in some ways connected. For example, my thoughts are clearly connected to me as an individual, as is my personal past and family, resulting in these being personal-level items. But my atoms and your atoms are indistinguishable (other than being located within my or your body) and my distant ancestors who may not have had human form are also indistinguishable from those of yours (even though both your and my genetic heritages connecting each of us to these ancestors are within our respective bodies). The construct of transpersonal self-concept is thus presented as a radical extension of other more conventional approaches to the self-concept in psychology, but still within the realm of science.

In my dissertation (Friedman, 1981), I constructed this measure through a multiyear process of iterations, involving over one thousand students as coresearchers using qualitative, quantitative, and graphical strategies to forge finally a meaningful set of items that hung together coherently (i.e., converged) and were distinct (i.e., diverged) from unrelated constructs, all as a scientific process driven by the meaning of the construct I wanted to operationalize. The scope of this effort is what led me to state previously in this chapter that any preconception I held that this task would be easy was clearly naïve. This work involved both empirical and theory-driven considerations. I also demonstrated that the two most well-developed scales of the SELF (i.e., Personal and Transpersonal Scales) have acceptable reliability, as well as construct validity (e.g., the Transpersonal Scale correlated positively with a measure of mystical experience and other measures of theoretically related constructs, as well as diverged from measures of some theoretically unrelated constructs such as intelligence and social desirability). Finally the SELF Transpersonal Scale demonstrated that it could differentiate between known transpersonal and student groups in its initial samples.

MacDonald, Tsagarakis, and Holland (1994) first replicated some of my original research on the SELF, and extended my findings by conducting further comparisons with another related measure. Upton (1998) conducted a similar replication and extension. Together with colleagues, I continued this line of research with additional validation and extension studies, such as one that showed the SELF Transpersonal Scale is empirically distinct from the five-factor model in trait psychology (MacDonald, Gagnier, & Friedman, 2000) and can be at least partially replicated in an Asian Indian sample (Friedman, et al., 2004). More recent validations studies have looked further at bolstering the evidence for the validity of the SELF Transpersonal Scale, as well as for comparing it with an alternately worded version (Pappas & Friedman, 2007), other validation studies have used qualitative (Feuer, 2009) and graphical strategies (Pappas & Friedman, 2012). With some of these latter approaches employing variants of the original SELF, either alternately worded or presented in graphical formats, it is evident that the SELF is merely one operationalization of the construct of self-expansiveness. In that regard, it is important to emphasize that, if a construct can withstand numerous operationalizations, and retain fidelity to its intended meaning, this lends additional support to it being seen as worthwhile, as opposed to just being an artifact of a method or some other capricious factors. This logic is similar to the argument that the cartography can be transposed without losing its meaning (as in Friedman & Pappas, 2006), supporting the robustness of the construct of self-expansiveness. That is, when a construct can be approached in different ways and still retain its meaning, it is more likely to be something meaningful. Likewise, validating a measure also validates the underlying construct that the measure supposedly operationalizes.

In addition to these validation studies, a number of other studies have used the SELF in exploring transpersonal issues, including with organizational leaders (Bursten, 1989), spiritual practices (Majeski, 1998), transformative education (Gaynor, 1999), creative arts teaching (Lindsey-North, 1999), body work (Wang, 2000), creativity in musicians (Guzman, 2003), worldviews of scientists (Kuhar, 2005), energy work (Marlowe, 2010), pro-environmental behavior (Hoot & Friedman, 2011), and para-psychology (Rock, Storm, Harris, & Friedman, 2013), to name a few. These studies employed self-expansiveness as a variable in studies in which various hypotheses were tested, furthering M-R TPT.

Currently, the SELF is also being used in a variety of ongoing studies. For example, it is being used to evaluate the outcome of several psychedelic research studies being conducted at Harvard University (see Friedman, 2006). These ongoing studies are approaching psychedelics mainly as biochemical agents (e.g., exploring how LSD might influence serotonin levels), but the SELF was also added to the battery of measures to explore whether transpersonal aspects of psychedelic experiences might also be important, perhaps even crucial, for understanding possible salutary effects of these substances. Currently a team of international colleagues and I are also using the SELF in a large cross-cultural study in which data were gathered from over a dozen nations, using both English and translated versions of the SELF. I am also beginning to look more closely at the Personal Scale in two other ongoing research projects. In addition, the SELF is currently being used in approximately a dozen exploratory studies about which I know at this time, and there are several additional ones being contemplated about which I know. That self-expansiveness and its related measure, the SELF, have been able to generate this considerable research activity is important to the scientific process, whereas grand and mini-theoretical approaches (see Friedman, this volume) have not been very successful in generating research, despite the fact that they might more broadly capture the imagination of those searching for personally satisfying, if not empirically supported, so-called answers to the most perplexing life questions. All of this suggests that a burgeoning research tradition within transpersonal psychology is being facilitated by the construct of self-expansiveness and the SELF, while grand theory and mini-theory have been relatively sterile.

As I see the greatest strength of self-expansiveness to be in its applicability for building M-R TPT, it should be re-emphasized that the SELF is only one operationalization of this construct. Alternatively, self-expansiveness can be operationalized using many other procedures, including quantitatively (e.g., through various alternate measurement strategies that are numerically expressed; Friedman, 1981), qualitatively (e.g., through various categorization or other strategies that are expressed in natural language; Feuer, 2009), graphically (e.g., through various strategies that are expressed pictorially; Pappas & Friedman, 2012), and in potentially many other empirical ways (e.g., psychophysiologically). The SELF has also led to the development of a number of such similar measures as of ecological self-expansiveness (St. John, 2004) and the Self-Expansiveness Circles Test (Pappas & Friedman, 2012). There are also many emerging measures that seem to be grasping toward parts of what the SELF more comprehensively captures. The SELF has also been translated into many languages in addition to English for studies in various cultures (e.g., Kustner, 2002), as well as used in different cultural contexts in its English version (e.g., Friedman, et al., 2004). These variants and many usages illustrate the generativity of this approach.

Concerns with Identification in the Construct and Measure of Self-Expansiveness

However, all is not without problems with self-expansiveness, as the process of identification is fundamental to self-expansiveness and needs to be seen in a nuanced way, and not as an absolute either/or. There are gradations in the ability by which the individual can identify with different aspects of the world as they are measured by the SELF through using a Likert-type scale. However, identification processes are ambiguous, so those taking the SELF may answer with different underlying assumptions steering their responses. For example, identification is not necessarily the same as positing exact equivalence, which is a possible interpretation of its meaning. If I were to identify with a character in a novel, I would be observing salient similarities in some vital aspects of my life with that of the character; however, I would not be saying that I am necessarily that character *in toto*. Others might see this differently, and answer accordingly. One specifically perplexing concern is that I based this construct of self-expansiveness on the assumption that one's full potential includes the capacity to expand one's self-concept to identify with all within the expanse of space and time, as well as possibly even beyond in scientifically inexpressible ways, yet the process of identification undergirding this is not specified in my approach.

This also leads to some concerns about my assumption that there are advantages to encouraging greater self-expansiveness through identification with a larger range of that with which it is possible for one to identify. It can also be argued conversely, in my perspective, that perhaps "disidentification" would be a better strategy to pursue for transpersonal healing and growth. The self-concept can be deconstructed in the process of disidentification until there is nothing left that can be construed as constituting the self. This alternate strategy to self-expansiveness is used in some psychotherapies (e.g., Assagioli, 1965) and in some traditional meditation practices (e.g., Maharshi, 2008). However, I believe that taken to the extremes, an identification with the All, or a complementary disidentification leading to the Void, might merge together in the same destination. One analogy to clarify this can be drawn from the geometric circle, which consists of a line closing back unto itself. Regardless of at what point on a circle one might enter, following the circle to its conclusion will eventually lead to the same destination, as it curves back on itself to include all of its points. Similarly, perhaps following the different paths of identification and disidentification can, like following a circular path, both come together, eventually leading to the equivalence of the All and the Void (as in the wordplay of the equivalence of the *now-here* with the *nowhere*). This discussion involves philosophical speculation about the relationship between possible universal consciousness and the possible lack of all consciousness (as in superconscious nothingness), which is a speculative topic that science cannot address cogently. However, this topic requires comment because some transpersonal thinkers have been critical of the construct of self-expansiveness on this ground, as in expressing concern that it might promote a form of narcissism (e.g., Louchakova & Lucas, 2007). In addition, adherents to a number of traditions promoting disidentification see the self only as an illusion, perhaps even the most fundamental and destructive of illusions, and consequently reject the worth of self-expansiveness on the basis that it might exacerbate, rather than remedy, that illusion. For example, some research with the SELF has found such a pattern of disidentification within certain populations (e.g., Majeski, 1998, in studying Westerners engaged in Tibetan Buddhist meditation), which makes the SELF invalid as a measure for that group. In this regard, I was very careful to give interpretive instructions on scoring the SELF to encourage users to look for patterns of disidentifiers, and not to automatically exclude them from being considered possibly high in transpersonal ways other than self-expansiveness (see Friedman, 1983).

This problem with identification is just one of the many paradoxes that limit scientific inquiry in the transpersonal. Despite these wrinkles in this fundamental assumption underlying the construct of self-expansiveness, I think following a path involving greater self-expansiveness has advantages, as well as possible disadvantages, over exclusively following a path involving disidentification, at least within the contemporary Western context, similarly to how Wilber's (2001) acknowledgement of the crucial role of identification as the self develops from a lower to higher identities, which he saw as the basic process that enables the self to progress up his view of the vertical consciousness hierarchy. That is, I think it is crucial to examine empirically how the self might progress from constricted to expansive identification. All of this must be considered in building M-R TPT, and especially when applying it for human betterment.

Transpersonal Praxis: Implications for Assessment and Therapy

Another way to evaluate the usefulness of a construct is to consider whether it has any practical value, which is a pragmatic issue. The SELF provides a potentially useful tool for assessment, although it is in need of further development for such a purpose, such as by standardizing norms on different populations. Such standardization is a prerequisite before the SELF could be responsibly used in any but exploratory clinical applications due to the high stakes inherent in such applications. However, the scale provides a potential assessment avenue for beginning clinical work conceptualized as transpersonal. I have written previously on possible uses of the SELF for assessment within clinical settings (Friedman & MacDonald, 1997, 2002b), including using it for differential diagnosis of transpersonal from psychotic states, which often present similarly (Johnson & Friedman, 2008). In brief, having a reliable and valid measure of transpersonal self-concept adds a dimension not currently available in the clinical armamentarium, and this can also be used to build evidence-based transpersonal clinical interventions. The SELF also holds broad possibilities for assessment outside of the clinical areas, such as in organizational settings (e.g., for recruiting transformational leaders). Information on the construct of self-expansiveness can also be gathered in more individualistic and less structured ways than using the SELF or similar measures, such as through using interviews or other testing approaches (e.g., projective tests and psychophysiological procedures) based on the construct. As self-expansiveness is just one among many potential constructs that can be used in developing M-R TPT, the SELF is just one measure operationalizing self-expansiveness that could be used for transpersonal assessment.

I have also preliminarily designed a model for a transpersonal psychotherapy based on the construct of self-expansiveness, which I call *Self-Expansiveness Therapy* (SET). It operates under the assumption that the optimum development of human potential relates to having a holistic vision of oneself, defined as being able to identify with all aspects of one's potential identity, namely to be greatly self-expansive. SET provides an integrative approach to therapy that addresses the entire cartography that frames the construct of self-expansiveness. Note, I use the broader term therapy, as opposed to psychotherapy, because to be holistic in a transpersonal way implies treating not just from a psychological approach (as in *psycho*-therapy), but using many therapeutic approaches, such as including social systems and somatic interventions (which are not psychotherapies per se), as well as transpersonal approaches.

In brief, each aspect of the cartography of self-expansiveness can be linked with a therapeutic approach. Starting with the present, there are many psychotherapies focused on bringing the person to the here-and-now, such as Gestalt therapy and bioenergetics that emphasize the experienced body. Behavioral therapy and cognitive therapy also deal in the present, focusing on present behavior and thoughts respectively, while experiential therapies focus on affect. Incidentally, these are the four domains (i.e., behavior, body, cognition, and emotion) addressed in items of the Personal Scale of the SELF, which measures identification with the self in the present. And, of course, there is the burgeoning area of mindfulness therapies.

However, it is important to note that, just as the self-concept of an individual is not limited to the present, neither should a holistic therapy be limited that way. In fact, one view as to what makes humans unique among other creatures known to us is the ability to be conscious of an expansive sense of self. In terms of the temporal dimension and using a visual analogy, to be able to look ahead by using "foresight" to predict possible future occurrences in order to plan accordingly and to be able to look backwards by using "hindsight" to garner lessons from the past are both important human abilities. Continuing this visual analogy in terms of the spatial dimension, to have "farsight" into distant aspects of the world or to have "insight" into internal aspects within oneself are also important human abilities. From this, the construct of self-expansiveness implies that, to be fully whole as a human, one needs to identify expansively, not just in the present. There is no evidence that other life forms can extrapolate beyond themselves into time and space anywhere near as well as is possible with our human abilities to be self-expansive. Consequently, our ability to conceptualize ourselves beyond the limitation of the present using insight, farsight, foresight, and hindsight, even to the point where we might identify with transpersonal phenomena, constitutes what I think is our essential humanness. Those who proffer platitudes, such as *live only in the present, as that is all that is,* may miss that the present is also capable of being expansive, and it should not be reduced to only the narrow here-and-now. In contrast, as important as the present is, it can also be seen as but one possible point in space and time, whereas optimally developed humans can embrace all points in space and time as part of an expansive transpersonal identity.

Consequently, SET uses the self-expansiveness cartography as a grid for understanding how various therapies can address the complete range of human potential in relationship to the self-concept. As a comprehensive and integrative therapeutic model, it subsumes other therapies that only deal with parts of the whole. For examples of extant therapies that expand their focus away from the present temporally, there is the psychodynamic emphasis on understanding one's developmental narrative though focus on the personal past. Reminiscence therapies with the elderly can also be seen this way, as can regressive hypnosis and inner child work. In contrast, reality therapy, with its focuses on future consequences, can be seen as focused on the personal future, as can vocational counseling and broader life planning approaches. These future-oriented approaches also veer from the present temporally. For examples of extant therapies that expand their focus away from the present spatially, biofeedback can be viewed as addressing issues involving contracted space, a going inward on the spatial dimension by working with specific subsystems of the human body (e.g., the heart). Similarly, relationship therapies can be seen as addressing issues involving expanded space, as can any therapies applied within important reference groups with which the person might strongly identify. This can also include ecological therapies that relate individuals to their physical, rather than social, environment.

Going further into the middle level beyond the personal, but not yet the transpersonal, are political (e.g., Marxist) and feminist therapies, which can allow individuals to deal with their psychological issues in a greatly expanded temporal context, such as through historical analysis of human predicaments. Likewise, dealing with distant future scenario planning involves a greatly expanded temporal approach, such as the story of the seventh generation planning used by the traditional Cherokee people, in which decisions were historically made within tribal councils based on their implications for the next seven generations. Likewise, whole-earth environmental therapies can be seen as operating in a greatly expanded spatial level. At the greatly contracted spatial level would be therapies that intervene at the cellular and molecular level, such as using principles of psychoneuroimmunology and traditional aruvedic medicine. These are clearly not just personal, yet not quite transpersonal either, which is why I place them still in a middle level.

Then there is the non-transcendent transpersonal level. At the contracted spatial level would be energy healing, such as possibly acupuncture. At the level of expanded spatial, there is no extant whole-earth healing method, but perhaps focused on cultivating a sense of awe by pondering the vastness of the universe may be an important approach to develop for this purpose. Likewise, at the past and future temporal levels, there are no extant therapies focusing on the origins of man (or life) or the future of all living beings as we evolve (or possibly will fail to adapt and sink back into nothingness). Perhaps these areas, where there are gaps in terms of extant therapies, would be best addressed by some meditative practices, and even by the study of science, which enables us to extrapolate ourselves in these extreme ways. If humans could properly position themselves in time and space in a transpersonal way, one can only speculate about the many implications, such as caring more about our earth and its multispecies inhabitants.

Then there is the possible ultimate level of the transcendent transpersonal, about which I think nothing per se can be meaningfully stated. This can be seen, however, as related to many transpersonal therapies, such as deep meditative or prayer traditions that do not rely on words but, rather on direct unmediated experience, but I will not discuss these approaches in any depth, as their goals are what I consider to be ineffable and they are outside of the realm of science.

As a clinical psychologist, I am keenly interested in clinical implications of self-expansiveness. Responsible clinical practitioners could practice from a transpersonal scientific framework, conducting outcome studies and honing clinical interventions to ensure they are worthwhile by using this construct as one guide among many possible scientific guides. By using the cartography of self-expansiveness, a broader view of what can be accomplish though transpersonal assessments and therapies is also achievable. The approach to assessment offered by the SELF and to therapy offered by SET provides a transpersonal alternative, complementing extant conceptual frameworks, and can make various therapies more holistic by uniting them under this overarching construct that recognizes the personal and the transpersonal, and all levels in between, without forsaking any. As a therapist, I believe it is necessary to be holistic, which involves working with the entire range of human existence. If clinicians focus on fixing people in little ways, then perhaps those being treated might just become better suited for destruction. Would anyone, for example, want to help a despot (e.g., Hitler) deal with possible guilt and anxiety so that he or she would be unencumbered and free to wreak greater havoc? In a recent paper (Friedman & Robbins, 2012), I have described the goal of resiliency training in the US Army as suffering from this potential problem. By being holistic in the ways outlined through the self-expansiveness cartography, therapy can be made more responsible to the largest whole. It can even provide a unifying ground for potentially resolving larger cultural dilemmas, such as ethnic conflicts, which is an area where I have begun to apply the construct of self-expansiveness (see Friedman, 2004; Machinga & Friedman, in press). Thus, transpersonal clinicians do not need to adhere to a romantic view of the world (see Friedman, 2005). Likewise they also do not just need to be used as pawns subjugating others to increasingly repressive and inhumane social policy. The construct of self-expansiveness enables conceptualization in which these stark alternatives can be placed into a much broader perspective, which provides a way to heal (i.e., make whole) and grow both individuals and larger systems in a transpersonal way.

Concluding Thoughts

Self-expansiveness has been presented as a potentially useful construct for building and testing M-R TPT, as well as furthering transpersonal applications for human betterment. Self-expansiveness is not a theory per se but, as a construct, it can be used in building various theories. It could also be seen as a model, as it is a complicated construct that has several components. Its worth is in the clarity of its conceptualization, grounded in space and time, and the way in which it is empirically accessible, such as through measurement by the SELF. To summarize briefly the construct of self-expansiveness, it provides an understanding of the self-concept through position in space and time, the most basic categories to which humans are oriented. It focuses on the self-concept as a narrative that individuals create to understand cognitively their lives. Consistent with many transpersonal, as well as conventional psychological, understandings, the concept of self is given centrality, but in this case is limited to its aspect known as self-concept, which is empirically accessible. Self-expansiveness is portrayed both verbally and through a cartography based on the dimensions of space and time, depicting how people can position their sense of self in a horizontal, rather than vertical and hierarchical, way. This map hinges on the process of identification through which one can expand the self-concept onto different contents of the map. The limits of the self-concept are undefined, extending to whatever occurs through identification in the map-making process. In this regard, the Self, representing a transpersonal view of a maximally expanded self, may approach toward the transcendent, even though the transcendent and similar notions are beyond definition and outside of any mapping or other symbolic process. However, the residual non-transcendent or material manifestation in the space-time cartography allows for a tentative pointing to possible non-transcendent aspects of the transpersonal.

It is interesting to imagine the widespread acceptance of a model of holistic health that would include the transpersonal in a comprehensive way, and applications that include, but are not restricted to, clinical praxis. For example, programs dealing with criminal offenders could focus on the development of expanded self-concept that might potentially lead to empathy for victims and responsible acceptance of useful social roles. Corporate leaders could be encouraged to develop an expanded sense of self, focusing on environmental sensitivity and social justice. Politicians could be expected to have an expanded self-concept encompassing deep empathy toward all of their constituents, even with an ultimate focus toward world peace and prosperity. I believe that developing M-R TPT can uniquely be used to address some of the most important challenges facing humankind, and the construct of self-expansiveness may play an important role in this. Being able to discuss pressing concerns that threaten human existence cogently from a transpersonal perspective that avoids metaphysical and supernatural language is more likely to be received positively within contemporary culture than a discussion using metaphors based on antiquated and parochial worldviews, especially those that might be divisive.

I also advocate for further development of M-R TPT by pursuing cumulative research on other transpersonal concepts and constructs, including but not privileging self-expansiveness, as this one construct is not necessarily uniquely important, even though the larger notion of the transpersonal is. Concepts used in natural language, such as the expressions of spirituality (MacDonald, 2000) and awe (Bonner & Friedman, 2011), may provide similar opportunities to build and test theories, and I am currently involved in research with both of these approaches. There is also ample room to develop new constructs that could be valuable. Perhaps some of the grand theories, which I have criticized for being empirically inaccessible (Friedman, 2002, this volume), can be mined for their parts that could be useful in building M-R TPT in ways that are amenable for empirical exploration. The major point is that there is a need for systematically developing and empirically researching concepts and constructs to further transpersonal psychology as both a science, including for use in both theory and research, and as a praxis. It is my hope that this work will also lead to an expansion of psychology as a discipline. The construct of self-expansiveness coherently links a transpersonal perspective to conventional understandings of a self-concept, provides a basis for assessment and a way to integrate many therapies, and offers many other possible benefits. As such, self-expansiveness can be shown to be much more than just an anomalous add-on to mainstream approaches, but a way to significantly advance them. Along with other empirically accessible transpersonal concepts and constructs, self-expansiveness can become an increasingly important part of a growing scientific and applied transpersonal contribution to humanity.

References

Aron, A., & Aron, E. (1986). *Love as the expansion of self: Understanding attraction and satisfaction*. New York, NY: Hemisphere.

Aron, A., & Aron, E. (1996). Love and expansion of the self: The state of the model. *Personal Relationships, 3*, 45-58.

Assagioli, R. (1965). *Psychosynthesis: A collection of basic writings.* New York, NY: Penguin.

Bonner, E., & Friedman, H. (2011). A conceptual clarification of the experience of awe: An interpretative phenomenological analysis. *The Humanistic Psychologist, 39*, 222-235.

Bragg, E. (1996). Towards ecological self: Deep ecology meets constructionist self-theory. *Journal of Environmental Psychology, 16* (2), 1996.

Burris, C. T., & Rempel, J. K. (2010). If I only had a membrane: A review of amoebic self theory. *Social and Personality Psychology Compass, 4*, 756-766.

Bursten, L. (1989). Constructed realities and transformation of consciousness: A holonomic approach. *Dissertation Abstracts International, 50*(05), 0565B (UMI #8917275).

Byrne, B. (2002). Validating the measurement and structure of self-concept: Snapshots of past, present, and future research. *American Psychologist, 57*(11), 897-909.

Cahn, B., & Polich, J. (2006). Meditation states and traits: EEG, ERP, and neuroimaging studies. *Psychological Bulletin, 132*(2), 180-211.

Chen, S., Chen, K., & Shaw, L. (2004). Self-verification motives at the collective level of self-definition. *Journal of Personality and Social Psychology, 86*(1), 77-94.

Daniels, M. (2005). *Shadow, self, spirit: Essays in transpersonal psychology.* Exeter, UK: Imprint Academic.

Esposito, A., Kobak, R., & Little, M. (2005). Aggression and self-esteem: A diary study of children's reactivity to negative interpersonal events. *Journal of Personality, 73*(4), 887-905.

Feuer, C. (2009). Exploring the ecological validity of the construct of self-expansiveness and an instrument designed to measure it. *Dissertation Abstracts International, 70*(08), 0795B (UMI #3368981).

Frager, R., & Fadiman, J. (2005). *Personality and personal growth* (6th ed.). Upper Saddle River, NJ: Prentice Hall.

Friedman, H. (1981). The construction and validation of a transpersonal measure of self-concept: The Self-Expansiveness Level Form. *Dissertation Abstracts International, 42*(02), 0079B (UMI #8117150).

Friedman, H. (1983). The Self-Expansiveness Level Form: A conceptualization and measurement of a transpersonal construct. *Journal of Transpersonal Psychology, 15*, 37-50.

Friedman, H. (1984, August). *A humanistic-transpersonal theory of personality.* Paper presented at the American Psychological Association Annual Conference, Toronto, Canada.

Friedman, H. (2002). Transpersonal psychology as a scientific field. *International Journal of Transpersonal Studies, 21*, 175-187.

Friedman, H. (2004). Frameworks for peace: Reframing the conflict in Fiji. *International Journal of Transpersonal Studies, 23*, 118-124.

Friedman, H. (2005). Problems of romanticism in transpersonal psychology: A case study of Aikido. *The Humanistic Psychologist, 33*, 3-24.

Friedman, H. (2006). The renewal of psychedelic research: Implications for humanistic and transpersonal psychology. *The Humanistic Psychologist, 34*(1), 39-58.

Friedman, H. (this volume). The role of science in transpersonal psychology: The advantage of middle-range theory (Chapter 17).

Friedman, H., & MacDonald, D. (1997). Towards a working definition of transpersonal assessment. *Journal of Transpersonal Psychology, 29*, 105-122.

Friedman, H., & MacDonald, D. (Eds.). (2002a). *Transpersonal measurement and assessment.* San Francisco, CA: Transpersonal Institute.

Friedman, H., & MacDonald, D. (2002b). Using transpersonal tests in humanistic psychological assessment. *The Humanistic Psychologist, 30*, 223-236.

Friedman, H., MacDonald, D., & Kumar, K. (2004). Cross-cultural validation of the Self Expansiveness Level Form with an Indian sample. *Journal of Indian Psychology, March*, 44-56.

Friedman, H., & Pappas, J. (2006). The expansion of the personal self and the contraction of the transcendent self: Complementary processes of transcendence and immanence. *Journal of Transpersonal Psychology, 38*(1), 41-54.

Friedman, H., & Robbins, B. (2012). The negative shadow cast by positive psychology: Contrasting views and implications of humanistic and positive psychology on resiliency. *The Humanistic Psychologist, 40*, 87-102.

Gall-Peters projection (n.d.) In *Wikipedia*. Retrieved from http://en.wikipedia.org/wiki/Gall%E2%80%93Peters_projection

Gaynor, D. R. (1999). Changes in cognitive structure associated with experiences of spiritual transformation. *Dissertation Abstracts International, 60*(05), 0669B (UMI #9932120).

Guzman, C. V. (2003). Creativity, spirituality and self-expansiveness in the process of writing popular music. *Dissertation Abstracts International, 64*(11), 0795b (UMI #311353).

Haimerl, C., & Valentine, E. (2001). The effect of contemplative practices on intrapersonal, interpersonal, and transpersonal dimensions of the self-concept. *Journal of Transpersonal Psychology, 33*, 37-52.

Hoot, R., & Friedman, H. (2011). Sense of interconnectedness and pro-environmental behavior. *International Journal of Transpersonal Studies, 30*(1-2), 89-100.

Hunt, H. (1999). Transpersonal and cognitive psychologies of consciousness: A necessary and reciprocal dialogue. In S. Hameroff, A. Kaszniak, & D. Chalmers (Eds.). *Toward a Science of Consciousness III: The third Tucson discussions and debates* (pp. 449-458). Cambridge, MA: MIT Press.

James, W. (1890). *The principles of psychology.* New York, NY: Henry Holt.

Johnson, C., & Friedman, H. (2008). Enlightened or delusional? Differentiating religious, spiritual, and transpersonal experience from psychopathology. *Journal of Humanistic Psychology, 48*(4), 505-527.

Kuhar, R. M. (2005). An exploration of the impact of education and engagement in science on scientists' metaphysical beliefs and spirituality. *Dissertation Abstracts International, 66*(09), 0669B (UMI #3182443).

Kustner, U. (2002). Effectiveness of a meditative method of therapy based on Buddhist psychology and practice: A pilot study. *Journal for Meditation and Meditation Research, 2*, 31-47.

Leary, M., & Tangney, J. (2003). The self as an organizing construct in the behavioral sciences. In M. Leary & J. Tangney (Eds.), *Handbook of self and identity* (pp. 3-14). New York, NY: Guilford.

Lewis, Y. (2003). The self as a moral concept. *British Journal of Social Psychology, 42*, 225-237.

Lieberman, M., Jarcho, J., & Satpute, A. (2004). Evidence-based and intuition-based self-knowledge: An fMRI study. *Journal of Personality and Social Psychology, 87*(4), 421-435.

Lindsey-North, J. L. (1999). Fanning the flame: Transforming teachers by fostering transpersonal understandings through the arts. *Dissertation Abstracts International, 60*(03), 0327A (UMI #9923134).

Louchakova, O., & Lucas, M. (2007). Self as the clinical category: Reflections on culture, gender and phenomenology. *Journal of Transpersonal Psychology, 39*, 111-136.

MacDonald, D. A. (2000). Spirituality: Description, measurement and relation to the Five Factor Model of personality. *Journal of Personality, 68*(1), 153-197.

MacDonald, D., & Friedman, H. (2002). Assessment of humanistic, transpersonal and spiritual constructs: State of the science. *Journal of Humanistic Psychology, 42*, 102-125.

MacDonald, D., Friedman, H., & Kuentzel, J. (1999). A survey of measures of spiritual and transpersonal constructs: Part one—research update. *Journal of Transpersonal Psychology, 31*, 137-154.

MacDonald, D., Gagnier, J., & Friedman, H. (2000). The Self-Expansiveness Level Form: Examination of its validity and relation to the NEO Personality Inventory Revised. *Psychological Reports, 86*, 707-726.

MacDonald, D., Kuentzel, J., & Friedman, H. (1999). A survey of measures of spiritual and transpersonal constructs: Part two—additional instruments. *Journal of Transpersonal Psychology, 31*, 155-177.

MacDonald, D., LeClair, L., Holland, C., Alter, A., & Friedman, H. (1995). A survey of measures of transpersonal constructs. *Journal of Transpersonal Psychology, 27*, 1-66.

MacDonald, D., Tsagarakis, C., & Holland, C. (1994). Validation of a measure of transpersonal self-concept and its relationship to Jungian and five factor model conceptions of personality. *Journal of Transpersonal Psychology, 26*, 175-201.

Machinga, M., & Friedman, H. (in press). Developing transpersonal resiliency: An approach to healing and reconciliation in Zimbabwe. *International Journal of Transpersonal Studies, 32*(1).

Maharshi. R. (2008). *Who am I?: The teachings of Bhagavan Sri Ramana Maharshi* (24th ed.). Tamil, India: Sri Ramanasramam (downloaded from http://www.sriramanamaharshi .org/bookstall/downloadbooks.html)

Majeski, R. A. (1998). The relationship of transpersonal self-transcendence, extraversion, openness to experience, and psychological well-being in mature adult female meditators and non-meditators. *Dissertation Abstracts International, 59*(10), 0117B (UMI #9908987).

Markus, H., & Kitayama, S. (1994). A collective fear of the collective: Implications for selves and theories of selves. *Personality and Social Psychology Bulletin, 20*, 568-579.

Marlowe, J. (2010). Quantum mechanics and mysticism: An investigation of transformative experiences in Matrix Energetics seminars. *Dissertation Abstracts International, 71*(09), 0669B (UMI #3418276).

Marx, D., Stapel, D., & Muller, D. (2005). We can do it: The interplay of construal organization and social comparisons under threat. *Journal of Personality & Social Psychology, 88*(3), 432-446.

Maslow, A. H. (1968). *Toward a psychology of being.* New York, NY: Van Nostrand.

Mayer, F. & Frantz, C. (2004). The Connectedness to Nature Scale: A measure of individuals' feeling in community with nature. *Journal of Environmental Psychology, 24*, 503-515.

Meezenbroek, E., Garssen, B., van den Berg, M., Tuytel, G., van Dierendonck, D., Visser, A., & Schaufeli, W. (2012). Measuring spirituality as a universal human experience: Development of the Spiritual Attitude and Involvement List (SAIL). *Journal of Psychosocial Oncology, 30*(2), 141-167.

Newby-Clark, I., & Ross, M. (2003). Conceiving the past and future. *Personality and Social Psychology Bulletin, 29*(7), 807-818.

Pappas, J., & Friedman, H. (2007). The construct of self-expansiveness and the validity of the Transpersonal Scale of the Self-Expansiveness Level Form. *The Humanistic Psychologist, 35*(4), 323-347.

Pappas, J., & Friedman, H. (2012). The importance of replication: Comparing the Self-Expansiveness Level Form Transpersonal Scale with an alternate graphical measure. *The Humanistic Psychologist, 40*, 364-379.

Pederson, D. M. (1994). Identification of levels of self-identity. *Perceptual and Motor Skills, 78*, 1155-1167.

Poll, J., & Smith, T. (2003). The spiritual self: Toward a conceptualization of spiritual identity development. *Journal of Psychology and Theology, 31,* 129-142.

Reinert, D. (2005). Spirituality, self-representations, and attachment to parents: A longitudinal study of Roman Catholic college seminarians. *Counseling and Values, 49* (3), 226-238.

Robbins, L., Pis, M., & Pender, N. (2004). Physical activity self-definition among adolescents. *Research & Theory for Nursing Practice: An International Journal, 18*(4), 317-330.

Rock, A. J., Storm, L., Harris, K., & Friedman, H. (2013). Shamanic-like journeying and psi-signal detection: I. In search of the psi-conducive components of a novel experimental protocol. *Journal of Parapsychology, 76*(2), 321-347.

St. John, D. (2004). *An ecopsychological self: Model and measure.* Ann Arbor, MI: Dissertation Abstracts International.

Upton, J. M. (1998). Measures of personality and transpersonality: Correlations between the "big five" factors of the "NEO PI-R" and five transpersonal inventories. *Dissertation Abstracts International, 59*(05), 0669B (UMI #9833358).

Vispoel, W. P. (1995). Self-concept in artistic domains: An extension of the Shavelson, Hubner, and Stanton (1976) model. *Journal of Educational Psychology, 87,* 134-153.

Walsh, R. & Vaughan, F. (Eds.). (1993.). *Paths beyond ego: The transpersonal vision.* New York, NY: Jeremy P. Tarcher/Putnam.

Wang, L. S.-C. (2000). Using zero-balancing to reveal the connection between physical and psycho/spiritual qualities. *Dissertation Abstracts International, 61*(04), 0669B (UMI #9969182).

Webb, J. (2004). Organizations, self-identities, and the new economy. *Sociology, 38*(4), 719-738.

Weiss, M., & Amorose, A. (2005). Children's self-perceptions in the physical domain. *Journal of Sport & Exercise Psychology, 27*(2), 226-244.

Wilber, K. (2001). *A theory of everything: An integral vision for business, politics, science, and spirituality.* Boston, MA: Shambhala.

12

Neuroscience and the Transpersonal

B. Les Lancaster

Fundamentals: On Explanatory and Methodological Pluralism

This chapter concerns the role that neuroscience has played, and may be expected to play in the future, in the understanding of experiences and systems of thought associated with the transpersonal. Fundamental to this agenda is the question of where neuroscience fits into the range of approaches associated with transpersonal psychology. Simply glancing at the titles of recent scholarly works in this field brings the central issue clearly into focus: Alexander Fingelkurts and Andrew Fingelkurts (2009) asked, "Is our brain hardwired to produce God, or is our brain hardwired to perceive God?"; *Sacred or Neural?* is the direct question in the title of Anne Runehov's (2007) book. The central premise would seem to be that if the brain "produces God" then there is effectively nothing "sacred" about such experiences; whereas were the brain in some way tuning in to—"perceiving"—God, the role of the sacred is secured. In this chapter, I hope to demonstrate that such a dichotomy is somewhat misleading, and that a transpersonal perspective can give a richer vision of the ways in which neuroscience contributes to an understanding of spirituality and mysticism.

Table 12.1 goes some way to contextualizing the role of neuroscience, placing it at one end of a spectrum that moves up through the level of cognitive and neuropsychological, to that of the psychodynamic, and finally to the level of spiritual/mystical. The table collates different approaches to consciousness and the mind (Lancaster, 2004) in terms of their position on three critical issues:

- What are the explanatory structures on which the approach relies in advancing knowledge?
- What methods does it employ?
- What value is ascribed to the notion that deep change, or transformation, is amongst the goals of studying consciousness?

The Wiley Blackwell Handbook of Transpersonal Psychology, First Edition.
Edited by Harris L. Friedman and Glenn Hartelius.
© 2013 John Wiley & Sons, Ltd. Published 2015 by John Wiley & Sons, Ltd.

Table 12.1 Critical Parameters which Differentiate Across a Range of Approaches Relevant to Transpersonal Psychology

Approach	Explanatory structures	Ascribed value re. transformation	Methods
Level 4: Spiritual/mystical	Transcendent systems • Spirit/soul • Godhead	ultimate	Contemplative/concentrative
Level 3: Psychodynamic	Systems of the psyche • Self/ego • Other conscious and unconscious complexes	individuation therapeutic	
Level 2: Cognitive & neuropsychological	Cognitive systems/informational systems • Representations • Constructed thought patterns	therapeutic developmental	Hermeneutic
Level 1: neuroscientific	Neurochemical systems • Patterns of neural activity; brain regions • Intra-neural structures	To be 'normal' only	Scientific

The first two issues are central to the status of the approach. Where there is general agreement on these, the approach may be considered an *academic discipline*. Any discipline has an agreed area of inquiry, agreed methods, and agreed explanatory structures. In this case the topic of inquiry is the mind, and each of the approaches listed makes use of different levels of explanatory structures as given in Table 12.1. Methodology is not so straightforward inasmuch as the boundaries between the levels are permeable (hence the arrows in Table 12.1): whilst scientific methodology is a defining hallmark of neuroscience, for example, insights deriving from hermeneutic and/or contemplative methods may be critical for interpreting scientifically-derived data. It is fallacious to think that the highly sophisticated images of brain function that characterise neuroscience today determine neuroscientific theories; the theories are driven by intuitive ideas of the how the mind works, which are shaped only partly by the data and images. Similarly, as shall be seen, spiritual traditions themselves can gain from the fruits of scientific methodologies, which may operate in interaction with contemplative or hermeneutic methods.

The third issue concerns the human potential for radical transformation to enriched ways of being. Spiritual and mystical traditions are essentially directed towards this goal, using terms such as enlightenment, salvation, and higher union to convey it. Therapeutic psychology similarly holds promises of individual transformation in terms of overcoming neurosis and so forth. Understanding the factors involved in achieving these kinds of transformation is at the heart of transpersonal psychology, and may be seen as perhaps the most important unitive factor amongst transpersonalists—whilst there may be disagreements over the merits of different authors' models of the mind, and the relative value of various kinds of practices designed to promote deep change, all within the transpersonal movement agree that there is something essentially *real* about these soteriological aspirations. The point for the present purposes is that this becomes an issue that fundamentally divides researchers sharing an overarching interest in the mind. Again, details may be discerned from Table 12.1, but in brief, neuroscience is at odds with the transpersonal orientation inasmuch as its terms of reference do not include the potential value in spiritually-oriented transformation. Studying the brain of an epileptic patient, for example, may be viewed as valuable for the hope that some form of cure may be produced, enabling the patient to achieve a greater degree of normality. It is only when one begins to bridge the levels of Table 12.1 that questions of more interest from a transpersonal perspective begin to open up, as in the study of the seemingly spiritual experiences observed in rare cases of temporal lobe epilepsy, for example.

A range of disciplines bridge the levels of Table 12.1. Cognitive neuroscience, for example, integrates the lower two levels; neuropsychoanalysis (Solms, 2000; Solms & Turnbull, 2002) covers the lower three levels. In my view, the defining feature of transpersonal psychology is that it integrates across *all the levels* in its approach to understanding the mind and processes of transformation (Lancaster, 2004). It is this fact that enables a description of the ways in which neuroscience contributes to transpersonal psychology. In broad terms, its contribution takes one of three potential forms (Lancaster, 2010): identification of the neural *correlates* of specific spiritual practices; clarification of *models* of the mind as transmitted in spiritual and mystical traditions; and exploration of the *correspondences* posited in mystical systems of thought as pertaining between higher and lower realms in a given cosmological hierarchy (i.e. equivalence in structure and function between macrocosm and microcosm).

The first of these three has dominated discussions in this area. Thus, the questions referred to above ("sacred or neural?" etc.) have been asked within the context of the research identifying neural correlates of spiritual experience. Do the observations that there are identifiable neural correlates imply that the spiritual experience is generated by the brain, or might they point to the reality of the supposed external source of such experience, namely *God* or *Absolute Being*? This whole area of research is addressed in the following section, but the more general point of concern at the outset is recognition that neuroscience impacts on the transpersonal in the two further, distinctive ways identified above (to be explicated in the succeeding two sections). The stark dichotomy of neural versus sacred may be modulated somewhat in the light of these other approaches.

Neural and Cognitive Correlates of Spiritual Practice

Simply identifying the brain regions that are active whilst a person is involved in a spiritual practice is of little value unless one can further specify the kinds of mental processes to which those regions contribute. For this reason, cognitive as well as neural correlates must be considered, because many spiritual teachings specify the goals to which their practices are directed in terms that can be understood by psychologists as cognitive. An example is the Buddhist *vipassana* practice, which is traditionally described as developing a form of *meta-awareness* (Lutz, Dunne, & Davidson, 2007), meaning that practitioners might be expected to develop increased ability to avoid their attention being grabbed by distracting stimuli.

A study by Heleen Slagter et al. (2007) put this claim to the test by examining the *attentional blink* in participants before and after a three-month vipassana retreat, during which the participants meditated 10-12 hours per day. As the term implies, the attentional blink is a cognitive equivalent to the blink of the eyelid; when two visual stimuli are presented in quick succession amongst a stream of such stimuli, awareness of the second is often obscured by processing of the first. This obscuring effect is operative with inter-stimulus intervals between about 200 and 500ms. Results from the study showed greater improvements in the ability to detect the second stimulus when presented within this inter-stimulus time frame amongst the retreat participants than amongst controls (novice meditators). In addition to this behavioral measure, the study examined electrophysiological responses to the visual stimuli. Amongst those attending the retreat, there was a relative decrease in the amplitude of the evoked P3b wave to the first visual stimuli. This positive wave in the evoked potential is thought to relate to attentional resource allocation, and the authors suggested that the increased ability to detect the second stimulus came about on account of a lowering in the level of cognitive resources being devoted to the first stimulus. This lowering of resources being devoted to the first stimulus is clearly in accord with the goal of cultivating "bare attention" as promoted traditionally in the teachings about vipassana. In other words, in cognitive and neurophysiological terms, vipassana meditation seemed to be achieving exactly what the teachings state that it should achieve—at least in this one dimension.

Connected to control of attention is the ability to detach from habitual modes of cognitive processing. Such *cognitive flexibility* requires assertion of control to overcome the way that features of the world automatically grab attention. Only by attenuating the automaticity (Deikman, 1966) is it possible to re-frame the approach one adopts in a given situation. A classic example of such a habitual mode leading to inappropriate processing is the *Stroop effect*. John Ridley Stroop (1935) demonstrated that the ability to read a color word (e.g. "red") was compromised when the word was written in ink of a color that conflicted with the word (e.g., "red" written in blue ink). The Stroop effect demonstrates that the color which is before the eyes captures one's attention, even when instructed to ignore it.

An obvious question therefore arises in relation to the claimed effects of meditation on attention: Does meditation lead to increased cognitive flexibility as evidenced through decreased interference on a Stroop task? Studies by Heidi Wenk-Sormaz (2005) and Adam Moore and Peter Malinowski (2009) answer this question affirmatively. Moore and Malinowski's study showed that participants' scores on a scale of mindfulness correlated with their accuracy on the Stroop task, and that meditators achieved higher mindfulness scores than non-meditators. Using an fMRI technique, Elisa Kozasa et al. (2012) observed lower levels of activation in the brain regions associated with attention amongst meditators, by comparison with nonmeditators, when responding to a Stroop task. The authors suggested that the meditation training had led to more efficient control of attention.

A further example of automatic processing is found in the phenomenon of *binocu-lar rivalry*. When two different images are presented to the two eyes simultaneously, the viewer generally sees one or the other, not some kind of superimposition of one on the other. Typically, the image seen alternates randomly. Olivia Carter et al. (2005) studied this phenomenon in a group of Tibetan Buddhist monks. In an interesting methodological strategy, the researchers had the monks act as their own controls by engaging in two different meditative practices, each predicted to have different consequences for the rivalry task. One was a practice the authors translated as "one-point," which entailed maintaining attention on a single object and reducing distraction by other internal or external events. The other practice entailed developing compassion and emanating loving-kindness. For obvious reasons in terms of the goals of the practices, the one-point meditation was hypothesized as likely to give greater stability on the binocular rivalry test. This was indeed the outcome: The compassion practice resulted in no changes from the baseline level of perceptual stability, whereas 50% of monks had highly increased stability both during, and following, the one-point practice.

In addition to these various cognitive effects, meditation has been reported to have positive consequences for emotional life, with periods of practice resulting in "positive mood, emotional stability and resilience to stress and negative life events" (Rubia, 2009, p. 2). Many studies have demonstrated these effects using behavioral and social measures, and conclusions are reinforced by research using brain imaging techniques which have shown that emotionally-oriented meditation activates areas of the brain known to have important roles in emotion-related processing. When researchers studied the areas of the brain activated by emotional stimuli whilst expert meditators engaged in loving-kindness-compassion meditation, they found that meditators had increased levels of activity in areas of the limbic system (insular and cingulate cortices) known to play central roles in emotion (Lutz, Brefczynski-Lewis, Johnstone, & Davidson, 2008). Moreover, these neural changes were correlated with changes in heart rate, suggesting that compassion meditation induces a recalibration of the neural systems that co-ordinate peripheral indices of emotion (Lutz, Greischar, Perlman, & Davidson, 2009).

An earlier study (Lutz, Greischar, Rawlings, Ricard, & Davidson, 2004) showed that those with long-term experience of Tibetan compassion meditation had developed greater integration across widespread regions of the brain. The researchers studied the power in the gamma band of the EEG, a measure of synchrony in neural patterns of firing. Compared to controls, the long-term practitioners displayed higher levels of synchrony not only during their meditation but also at baseline prior to meditating. This latter observation is striking because it suggests the influence of meditation on the individuals' general state. After all, the purpose of a regular practice is not simply to engender a given state at the time of the practice but to transform the practitioner in the longer term. Because the goal of the meditation in this study is to bring about a global state of compassion, the global coupling amongst widespread brain regions is especially suggestive. As the authors suggested, it seems that the meditators' brains had indeed been transformed to a more unified state.

A primary objective of many forms of meditation is a state of equanimity, in which one becomes detached from emotional disturbance. Neurophysiological support for the effectiveness in this regard of a form of Yoga meditation (*Sahaja Yoga*), intended to generate thoughtless awareness, comes from an EEG-based study in which participants were shown distressing movie clips (Aftanas & Golosheykin, 2005). Controls showed increases in EEG gamma synchrony over anterior cortical regions in response to the clips, suggesting that these regions associated with affect were activated by the clips. The EEG patterns of long-term meditators, by comparison, displayed none of these changes, implying that some degree of equanimity on this measure had been achieved. There is now extensive research showing the effects of mindfulness practices on emotional control, suggesting that there are potential gains for psychological and physical health by achieving the sort of control over emotional reactivity that meditation can bring (Chambers, Gullone, & Allen, 2009).

In addition to the various functional effects of meditation, it has been reported that meditation produces substantive and lasting structural changes in the brain. Sara Lazar et al. (2005) reported that brain regions associated with attention were thicker in meditators than in nonmeditators; Luders, Toga, Lepore, and Gaser (2009) showed greater volume of grey matter in regions related to emotional control; and Peter Vestergaard-Poulsen et al. (2009) found higher grey matter density in lower brain stem regions associated with breath control (for review see Hinterberger, Kohls, Kamei, Feilding & Walach, 2011). Other changes in brain activity associated with meditation have been reviewed by B. Rael Cahn and John Polich (2006) and Lutz, et al. (2008). As a generalization, meditation directed at control of attention results in activation of frontal areas known to be involved in higher-order executive functions; and open monitoring meditation, in which there is no specific focus for the attention, with the meditator monitoring internal and/or external events more generally, activates brain regions concerned with vigilance and monitoring of signals arriving through the sensory systems. As stated above in relation to the study of cognitive functions behaviorally, the data from study of the brain indicates that the practices are doing precisely what they are traditionally said to be doing.

But what of the more numinous aspects of spiritual practice? Is it possible to point to neural concomitants of an experience of the divine, for example? And, if this is possible, are these patterns of brain activity all there is to such mystical experience? Mario Beauregard and Vincent Paquette (2006, 2008) approached these questions through studies of Carmelite nuns who had experienced mystical states of union with God. Clearly, it is not possible to turn on such encounters at will, simply to fit in with the researchers' monitoring of the brain. The closest the authors could come to studying these mystical states was to ask the nuns to remember and attempt to relive the most intense mystical experience they had encountered. As it turned out, recalling the experience did lead to significant reliving, inasmuch as self-reports following the study gave high scores on measures designed to evaluate mystical experience.

Beauregard and Paquette assessed brain activity through fMRI (the 2006 study) and EEG analysis (2008). The studies made comparisons across a baseline condition of rest, a control condition in which the nuns were asked to recall and relive their most intense encounter with a *human,* and the above condition in which the nuns viewed the encounter as having been with *God.* The fMRI study showed patterns of activity in both the control and mystical conditions consistent with a lowered sense of self, as might be expected if one were merging with another (increases in activity of left and right superior parietal lobes); higher emotion, which related to the nuns' subjective reports of peace and unconditional love (left caudate nucleus, left cingulate); and imagery (regions of visual cortex). The particular observations of interest concern the comparison between the control and mystical conditions. Amongst a range of differences between these two conditions, activity in the right middle temporal cortex was higher in the mystical condition, leading Beauregard and Paquette to suggest such activation reflected the subjective sense of having contacted a spiritual, rather than a human, entity.

This conclusion regarding the role of the right temporal cortex was reinforced by the EEG study, which showed greater gamma power over this region in the mystical vs. control conditions. Other findings included increased theta power over frontal areas, interpreted by the authors as relating to feelings of peace, joy, and unconditional love; and long-distance alpha synchrony over regions of the right hemisphere, considered to reflect an inhibition of sensory processing during the mystical condition.

Studies such as this leave many questions unanswered. From a neuropsychological perspective, the proposed functions of particular areas involve much supposition; it is one thing to note commonalities in activations associated with emotion in general, for example, but quite another to propose that a particular aspect of the activation relates to unconditional love. There is a questionable level of circularity involved in the way in which categories obtained through subjective reports are imposed on the brain imaging data. The most defensible conclusion from this research is the one that the authors make to the effect that the substitution of a divine for a spiritual *other* does generate a distinctive pattern of activity in the brain. The scientific data alone cannot, however, indicate whether the spiritual experience points beyond its subjectivity. In the face of this, however, Beauregard and Denise O'Leary (2007) asserted that, "the evidence supports the view that individuals who have RSMEs [religious, spiritual, and/or mystical experiences] do in fact contact an objectively real 'force' that exists outside themselves" (p. 290).

It is for reasons such as this over-confident assertion that Coles (2008, p. 1954) referred to the attempt to make theological pronouncements on the basis of neuroscientific research as "an embarrassment," inasmuch as "over-interpreted accounts of poor experiments are recycled to construct grand schemes to explain religious experience" (p. 1954; re: neurotheology see also Ashbrook, 1984; d'Aquili & Newberg, 1999). This may be an overly harsh critique of the quality of the experiments, but he is right about over-interpretation. Moreover, as Brandt, Clément, and Re Manning (2010) observed, the complexities of religious discourse make it inadvisable to try to fit the rich variety of religious activities under the umbrella of a perennialist notion of experiencing the Absolute. In summary, neuroscience has clearly demonstrated that spiritual practices can generate changes in line with the emotional and cognitive consequences to be expected from the relevant spiritual teachings. Nevertheless, as Fingelkurts and Fingelkurts (2009, p. 312) put it, "neuroscientific arguments tell us nothing about the true nature of religious experience or God."

Models of Mind in Neuroscience and Mysticism:
Potential for Integration

It would be a mistake to think that the various spiritual and mystical traditions are concerned only with ultimate experiences. The nature of the mind is a central topic for these traditions, and there is therefore scope to address the extent to which these models accord with neuroscientific data, and the potential for generating models of mind that integrate scientific and mystical data. Different traditions emphasize different psychological functions in their understanding of the mind. Thus Buddhism has much to say about the minutiae of perception; Kabbalah explores the nature of thought beneath the limen of consciousness; Sufism is rich in its discussions of imagination; and the Advaita Vedanta school of Hinduism details the propensity of mind to split reality into subjects and objects. In all cases, the goal is not simply to specify the function of these mental processes for its own sake, but to advance the quest for transformation. It is through coming to know the inner processes that one is able to harness them in quest of the aspiration to a higher state of being.

I have previously examined in detail the insights into the nature of perception in the Wisdom literature (*Abhidhamma*) of Therevadan Buddhism, and their relation to perceptual processes as understood in cognitive neuroscience (Lancaster, 1997a, 1997b, 2004). The consonance between these diverse approaches is epitomized by their respective understanding of "moments" of consciousness. In line with the overarching Buddhist teaching that all is impermanent and in constant flux, Abhidhamma teaches that perception may be deconstructed into a series of successive moments of consciousness. Consciousness is not a continuous stream but consists of successive moments, each of which arises as a conditioned response to previous events, endures briefly, and then decays, having conditioned the next moment in the sequence. The sense that consciousness is a continuous stream is, on this view, illusory. According to Abhidhamma, a normal act of perception comprises 17 moments of consciousness, which are grouped into a number of stages. Using the example of vision, Aung (1910/1972, p. 126) named these stages as follows:

> [First] consciousness of the kind that apprehends sensations . . . rises and ceases. Immediately after this there rise and cease in order—visual consciousness, seeing just that visible object; recipient consciousness receiving it; investigating consciousness investigating it; determining consciousness determining it.

These moments of consciousness are understood as being incredibly brief; according to the Buddhist texts, millions of such moments may occur in the duration of one lightning flash! Such a time-scale (allowing for hyperbole in the texts) places them in the same time-scale as the brain processes occurring en route to perception. At least one neuroscientific formulation of the brain's role in perception bears a striking parallel to the Buddhist scheme because it posits that successive stages in the brain's processing of sensory data give rise to "micro-consciousnesses" (Zeki, 2003; Zeki & Bartels, 1999). Semir Zeki (2003) argued that the processing that occurs in distinct visual regions of the brain—processing of color information, of movement information, and so forth—eventuates in distinct micro-consciousness; as he succinctly put it, "a processing site is also a perceptual site" (p. 214). The central point he made is that, despite an introspective sense to the contrary, consciousness *is not unified,* that there are many consciousness*es* distributed in time and space, a formulation that clearly accords with Buddhist ideas.

Further parallels between the cognitive neuroscience of perception and specific stages identified in the Abhidhamma may be discerned (Lancaster, 1997a, 1997b, 2004):

1 The Abhidhamma stage of *visual consciousness* corresponds to the neural activities in the various regions of the visual cortex through which specific properties of the visual stimulus (color, movement, etc.) become encoded as patterns of firing amongst specialized neural groups.

2 *Recipient consciousness* corresponds to the oscillations in neural responses which signal involvement of (preconscious)[1] memory systems. The neural systems in lower processing areas (stage 1) connect with those in higher areas where connections with objects previously experienced are established. These lower-higher connections are crucial for intelligible perceptions to arise. Putting it simply, one does not merely see colors, shapes, movements, and so forth, one sees meaningful objects, and their meaningfulness can only arise through memory connections.

3 *Investigating consciousness* corresponds to activation of memory structures (engrams) that have elements in common with the current visual stimulus (as mediated through the visual processing areas in stage 1).

4 *Determining consciousness* corresponds to the matching between sensory neural activity (stage 1) and the output from memory (stage 3). The engram that most closely matches the sensory pattern becomes dominant with other, competing engrams being inhibited. In this sense, the meaning of the object is *determined.*

These four stages in the neural account follow each other automatically. The pattern in the sensory array results in a specific pattern of activation in the higher, memory-related neural areas, and competing patterns are inhibited as a dominant pattern arises. It is significant to note that the Buddhist schema makes the same point: that these four stages come as an all-or-none package.

There are two further perceptual stages identified in Abhidhamma, not mentioned in the earlier quote from Aung: *running consciousness* and *registering consciousness.* To complete the account:

5 *Running consciousness* corresponds to the incorporation of whatever has been determined through stage 4 into the on-going "I-narrative," which eventuates in the normal, everyday state of consciousness. The neurocognitive account may be aligned with the Buddhist view of no-self (the absence of any separate, stable entity that is the self) by recognizing that the sense of I arises through a constructive process; there is no on-going, substantive I, just a narrative that generates the sense of self as a putative center of the mind. This center *seems* to be the receiver of impressions, the director of thinking, and instigator of free-willed actions. Much research in neuroscience attests to the fact, consistent with Buddhist theory, that it is none of these things.

6 *Registering consciousness* is the final stage identified by Abhidhamma texts, and
   corresponds to the way in which the experience arising through stage 5 becomes
   stored in memory.

Considerably more detail of these stages as they are described in the Abhidhamma,
together with the evidence for relating them to stages in neural processing may be
found in Lancaster 1997a, 1997b, 2004. Not only is the evidence for the correspondences given here strong, but incorporation of the Buddhist ideas into an understanding of the nature of perception clarifies aspects that are unclear from the neuroscientific
data themselves. This material thus exemplifies a dialogue between cognitive neuroscience and Buddhism that may lead to significant refinements of ideas in both camps.

This approach, through which insights promulgated within a spiritual tradition
might be integrated with neuroscientific data, is further exemplified by Lancaster's
(2000, 2004) work on kabbalistic language mysticism and Stephen Kaplan's (2009)
analysis of the mental process of *grasping* as developed in the Advaita Vedanta school
of Hinduism. Kaplan noted significant parallels between the Advaitans' analysis of the
role of mental grasping in establishing the sense of subject and object, and the view
from cognitive neuroscience of the way in which the brain's parietal lobe is involved in
establishing a sense of self. Research into the role of the parietal lobe in this regard can
be summarized by stating that it generates the sense of being an embodied subject in
a world where objects constitute an external space; the parietal lobe is crucial for being
able to situate oneself in relation to this sort of objective world. The point of interest
concerns how this crucial cognitive skill develops. There is much neuropsychological
evidence to support the view that the parietal lobe is central for the ability to grasp
for objects. In cases where it is damaged, for example, the patient may lose this ability
to reach for an object in its correct spatial location. Eugene d'Aquili and Andrew
Newberg (1999) argued that the ability to grasp accurately is the primitive forerunner
of the spatial awareness that is taken for granted, through which self is localized in
relation to the apparently objective world it inhabits.

As Kaplan (2009) noted, this neuropsychological formulation seems to be anticipated by the etymology of the Sanskrit term *grah*, meaning "to grasp," because the
term relates to the act of perception and the division between perceiver and perceived,
subject and object. This etymology becomes an explicit teaching about the manner
in which a sense of self is established by mental grasping. From a soteriological perspective such grasping is restrictive, because the resulting sense of separation between
subject and object is an illusion that holds the person back on the path of transformation. Kaplan drew attention to the precise correspondence between Advaitan
philosophy and the neuroscientific understanding of the role of the parietal lobe in its
spatial functions: Physical grasping is viewed by both approaches as the primary deter-
minant of the full-blown mental state in which self is established as separate from the
outer world.

Kaplan (2009) summarized the major aspects of Advaitan philosophy in three points:
First, the fundamental human problem is the appearance of the duality of the grasper
and the grasped; second, this presentation of duality is associated with sense perception; and third, the ultimate aim of the religious life cannot be realized until the
illusory nature of the duality of *grāhaka-grāhya* [grasper-grasped] is realized. Kaplan

concluded, much as I have from my examination of the Abhidhamma's view of perception, that there is "a fascinating confluence of ideas" (p. 262) between these two traditions, of Advaita and cognitive neuroscience. Both traditions have come to the conclusion that this fundamental distinction between the embodied self and objects existing spatially beyond the self comes about as a construction of the mind, and that the grasping function lies at the root of the distinction.

This "confluence of ideas" is not merely fascinating, but has the potential to lead to new understandings and generative hypotheses. By interrelating the two vantage points on the mind—the one neuroscientific and the other spiritual—one can achieve a form of *triangulation*. The use of two perspectives may enable a more accurate view to be built up than would be achieved by either alone.

Neuroscience and Esotericism

In the earlier section on neuroscientific studies of spiritual practices, it was shown that the evidence supports the value of the practices in terms of general psychological goals—the control of attention or emotion, for example. The primary goals of most religions, however, entail notions of higher, even heavenly, realms and transcendent levels of being. This final section will explore the putative role of neuroscience in relation to these metaphysical notions as they impinge on transpersonal psychology.

In occult and mystical traditions, study of the human mind is understood as yielding insights into so-called higher realms. "From the 'I' of flesh and blood you may learn about the 'I' of the Holy One, blessed be He," runs a rabbinic text (*Genesis Rabbah* 90:1; *Leviticus Rabbah* 24:9). The lower intimates the higher on account of the principle of correspondence, upon which a large proportion of esoteric teachings are based. As Corbin (1958/1969) expressed it in his study of Sufism, "to everything that is apparent, literal external, exoteric . . . there corresponds something hidden, spiritual, internal, esoteric" (p. 78). As he remarked, this concept is the "central postulate of esotericism and esoteric hermeneutics." In the words of the *Zohar*, the major text of Kabbalah, "The Holy One, blessed be He . . . made this world corresponding to the world above, and everything which is above has its counterpart here below," and He "made man corresponding to the pattern above, for all is according to wisdom and there is not a single part of man which is not based on the supernal wisdom" (*Zohar* 2:20a; 1:186b). The "pattern above" alludes to the face of divinity turned towards this world. In other words, God and man are *isomorphic* in that they "share the same structure and are logically equivalent" (Shokek, 2001, p. 6). In Elliot Wolfson's (2005) poetic phrase, "God, world, and human are intertwined in a reciprocal mirroring" (p. 32).

Neuroscientific studies exploring the effects of spiritual practices—reviewed earlier—fit into the established physicalist paradigm which holds the brain to be the agent of psychological functions. In terms of Table 12.1, Level 1 explores the medium through which activity associated with Level 4 is expressed—the brain as vehicle of changes brought about by spiritual practice. The esoteric doctrine of isomorphism suggests a different paradigm: the brain as mirror of cosmic principles. Clearly, the assumptions here are of a different order than those associated with the physicalist paradigm. Supposed higher realms and macrocosmic principles are not the stuff of science. Yet the most important challenge for transpersonal psychology may be to find a paradigm that interconnects notions of consciousness beyond the brain or higher spiritual realities with an extended vision of science. In such a context the question as to whether or not neuroscience might support the esoteric teachings of isomorphic hierarchical levels of being becomes of considerable interest.

A similar "fascinating confluence of ideas" as discerned in the previous section is evident here. Core kabbalistic teachings about the macrocosm reveal an uncanny consonance with key principles of brain operation, in particular as these principles relate to consciousness (for detail, see Lancaster, 2004, 2011a, 2011b). In brief, there are two key principles of the brain's functioning that have been correlated with consciousness: *binding,* meaning the generation of coherence amongst assemblies of neurones, and *recurrent processing,* which refers to the impact of descending neural pathways on activity in ascending pathways. The kabbalistic teachings to which these seem to relate are those of *unification* and *reflexivity* respectively.

As far as the consonance between binding and unification is concerned, both involve harnessing diverse elements together by means of establishing coherence. In the brain it is the coherence in oscillatory firing patterns between diverse groups of neurones that signals their integration. As eloquently argued by Christoph von der Malsburg (1997), the level of consciousness correlating with brain activity depends critically on such coherence:

> We experience mind states of different degrees of consciousness, and ... the difference is made by the difference in the degree of coherence, or order ... between different parts of the brain. Let us, then, describe a state of highest consciousness as one characterized by global order among all the different active processes. ... A globally coupled state could be one in which all the different [parts] are phase-locked to each other. (pp. 196-197)

The analogy with kabbalistic teaching is that coherence across different levels in the created hierarchy is viewed as bringing about the highest mystical states:

> "One"—to unify everything from there upwards as one; to raise the will to bind everything in a single bond; to raise the will in fear and love higher and higher as far as *En-Sof* [the limitless essence of God]. And not to let the will stray from all the levels and limbs but let it ascend with them all to make them adhere to each other, so that all shall be one bond with *En-Sof. (Zohar* 2:216b)

Moving on to the fit between recurrent processing and reflexivity, both depend on activity at a lower level triggering activity in a higher level, which in turn acts back on the lower level bringing about the intended effect. In neuroscience this system has been identified in relation to the brain's sensory processing systems, with the lower level comprising brain structures concerned with immediate properties of the sensory stimulus and the higher structures being those dealing with memory. The *meaning* of the sensory stimulus is determined when the activity from the higher centers impacts on the lower regions through recurrent processing, and eventuates in conscious recognition. Indeed, Victor Lamme (2006, p. 499) argued that such recurrent processing "is the key neural ingredient of consciousness" (p. 499). As he asserted, "We could even define consciousness as recurrent processing" (p. 499).

The analogous teachings in Kabbalah need some unpacking from their context in order that the parallel with these findings in neuroscience might become evident. The *Zohar* enunciates the core teaching in its poetic language:

> Come and see. Through the impulse from below is awakened an impulse above, and through the impulse from above there is awakened a yet higher impulse, until the impulse reaches the place where the lamp is to be lit and it is lit...and all the worlds receive blessing from it. (*Zohar* 1: 244a)

The central imagery of the Kabbalah presents a picture of the realms existing between that of humanity and the Ultimate. The "impulse from below" arises through human spiritual work and brings about resonances throughout the successive intermediary realms reaching to the Ultimate. The "lamp" symbolically refers to an aspect of the Godhead which is capable of bestowing the divine influx, or "blessings," back into the human sphere.

We see here the fundamental operational pattern of the macrocosm as understood in Kabbalah. It is but a small stretch of the imagination to see this pattern in the brain systems for consciousness mentioned above in terms of recurrent processing. A sensory stimulus triggers activity in lower centres, which "awakens" activity in higher centres, through which the "lamp" that brings the "blessing" of consciousness is kindled.

Just as was discovered in the previous section more directly, there is in these indirect allusions from spiritual traditions evidence that their accumulated wisdom stands the test of being measured against research findings in neuroscience. Perhaps it should be put the other way round: research is catching up, as it were, with the spiritual and mystical wisdom which, through diverse teachings around the globe, has built up a highly sophisticated view of the mind and its organ, the brain. It might be better still to express the point as a recognition that these findings reach towards a unified stance through which the fruits of insight and revelation coming from spiritual traditions blend with the scientific research effort into consciousness. The spiritual traditions bring not only knowledge of the mind but also the ways of transformation; science brings the power to subject claims that are measurable in neuroscientific and psychological terms to rigorous investigation. That blending of disciplines has advanced considerably over recent years.

Note

1. Confusion arises on account of problems with terminology. Most neuroscientists would refer to the very rapid early stages of perceptual processing as being *preconscious*. Thus, the memory activity mentioned here is not the normal conscious function of recall, which comes later. Rather, this stage is one in which the initial perception is being built up through relating the incoming stimuli with stored images to which they relate. It is occurring within a few hundred milliseconds of the stimulus falling on the retina, before normal conscious perception comes about. Zeki (2003), with his arguments about micro-consciousnesses—which very much fit

with the Buddhist view—is, in fact, out of step with most neuroscientists in this regard. Here is not the place to go further into this issue (see Lancaster, 2004), involving, as it does, the differing reasons why Buddhists and neuroscientists would be interested in processes of the mind such as perception.

References

Aftanas, L. I., & Golosheykin, S. A. (2005). Impact of regular meditation practice on EEG activity at rest and during evoked negative emotions. *International Journal of Neuroscience*, *115*, 893-909.

Ashbrook, J. (1984). Neurotheology: The working brain and the work of theology. *Zygon*, *19*, 331-350.

Aung, S. Z. (1972). *Compendium of philosophy* (R. Davids, Rev. & Ed.). London, UK: Pali Text Society. (Original work published 1910)

Beauregard, M., & O'Leary, D. (2007). *The spiritual brain: A neuroscientist's case for the existence of the soul.* New York, NY: HarperCollins.

Beauregard, M., & Paquette, V. (2006). Neural correlates of a mystical experience in Carmelite nuns. *Neuroscience Letters*, *405*, 186-190.

Beauregard, M., & Paquette, V. (2008). EEG activity in Carmelite nuns during a mystical experience. *Neuroscience Letters*, *444*, 1-4.

Brandt, P. Y., Clément, F., & Re Manning, R. (2010). Neurotheology: Challenges and opportunities. *Schweizer Archiv für Neurologie und Psychiatrie*, *161*, 305-359.

Cahn, R., & Polich, J. (2006). Meditation states and traits: EEG, ERP, and neuroimaging studies. *Psychological Bulletin*, *132*, 180-211.

Carter, O. L., Presti, D., Callistemon, C., Liu, G. B., Ungerer, Y., & Pettigrew, J. D. (2005). Meditation alters perceptual rivalry in Tibetan Buddhist monks. *Current Biology*, *15*, R412-R413.

Chambers, R., Gullone, E., & Allen, N. B. (2009). Mindful emotion regulation: An integrative review. *Clinical Psychology Review*, *29*, 560-572.

Coles, A. (2008). God, theologian and humble neurologist. *Brain*, *131*, 1953-1959.

Corbin, H. (1969). *Creative imagination in the Sufism of Ibn Arabi* (R. Manheim, Trans.). Princeton, NJ: Princeton University Press. (Original work published 1958)

D'Aquili, E. G., & Newberg, A. B. (1999). *The mystical mind: Probing the biology of religious experience.* Minneapolis, MN: Fortress Press.

Deikman, A. J. (1966). Deautomatization and the mystic experience. *Psychiatry*, *29*, 324-338.

Fingelkurts, A. A., & Fingelkurts, A. A. (2009). Is our brain hardwired to produce God, or is our brain hardwired to perceive God? A systematic review on the role of the brain in mediating religious experience. *Cognitive Processing*, *10*, 293-326.

Hinterberger, T., Kohls, N., Kamei, T., Feilding, A., & Walach, H. (2011). Neurophysiological correlates to psychological trait variable in experienced meditators. In H. Walach, S. Schmidt, & W. B. Jonas (Eds.), *Neuroscience, consciousness, and spirituality* (pp. 129-155). New York, NY: Springer.

Kaplan, S. (2009). Grasping at ontological straws: Overcoming reductionism in the Advaita Vedanta—neuroscience dialogue. *Journal of the American Academy of Religion*, *77*, 238-274.

Kozasa, E. H., Sato, J. R., Lacerda, S. S., Barreiros, M. A. M., Radvany, J., Russell, T. A., and Amaro, E., Jr. (2012). Meditation training increases brain efficiency in an attention task. *NeuroImage*, *59*, 745-749.

Lamme, V.A.F. (2006). Towards a true neural stance on consciousness. *Trends in Cognitive Sciences, 10,* 494-501.

Lancaster, B. L. (1997a). The mythology of *anatta:* Bridging the East-West divide. In J. Pickering (Ed.), *The authority of experience: Readings on Buddhism and psychology* (pp. 170-202). Richmond, Surrey, UK: Curzon Press.

Lancaster, B. L. (1997b). On the stages of perception: Towards a synthesis of cognitive neuroscience and the Buddhist *Abhidhamma* tradition. *Journal of Consciousness Studies, 4,* 122-142.

Lancaster, B. L. (2000). On the relationship between cognitive models and spiritual maps: Evidence from Hebrew language mysticism. *Journal of Consciousness Studies, 7,* 231-250.

Lancaster, B. L. (2004). *Approaches to consciousness: The marriage of science and mysticism.* Basingstoke, UK: Palgrave Macmillan.

Lancaster, B. L. (2010). Cognitive neuroscience, spirituality and mysticism: Recent developments. In I. Clarke (Ed.), *Psychosis and spirituality: Exploring the new frontier* (2nd ed.). New York, NY: John Wiley & Sons.

Lancaster, B. L. (2011a). The cognitive neuroscience of consciousness, mysticism and psi. *International Journal of Transpersonal Studies, 30,* 11-22.

Lancaster, B. L. (2011b). The hard problem revisited: From cognitive neuroscience to Kabbalah and back again. In H. Walach, S. Schmidt, & W. B. Jonas (Eds.), *Neuroscience, consciousness, and spirituality* (pp. 229-251). New York, NY: Springer.

Lazar, S. W., Kerr, C. E., Wasserman, R. H., Gray, J. R., Greve, D. N., Treadway, M. T., and Fischl, B. (2005). Meditation experience is associated with increased cortical thickness. *Neuroreport, 16,* 1893-1897.

Luders, E., Toga, A. W., Lepore, N. & Gaser, C. (2009). The underlying anatomical correlates of long-term meditation: Larger hippocampal and frontal volumes of gray matter. *NeuroImage, 45,* 672-678.

Lutz, A., Brefczynski-Lewis, J., Johnstone, T., & Davidson, R. J. (2008). Regulation of the neural circuitry of emotion by compassion meditation: Effects of meditative expertise. *PLoS ONE 3,* e1897. doi:10.1371/journal.pone.0001897

Lutz, A., Dunne, J. D., & Davidson, R. J. (2007) Meditation and the neuroscience of consciousness: An introduction. In P. D. Zelazo, M. Moscovitch, & E. Thompson (Eds.), *The Cambridge handbook of consciousness* (pp. 499-551). Cambridge, UK: Cambridge University Press.

Lutz, A., Greischar, L. L., Perlman, D. M., & Davidson, R. J. (2009). BOLD signal in insula is differentially related to cardiac function during compassion meditation in experts vs. novices. *NeuroImage, 47,* 1038-1046.

Lutz, A., Greischar, L. L., Rawlings, N. B., Ricard, M., & Davidson, R. J. (2004). Long-term meditators self-induce high-amplitude gamma synchrony during mental practice. *Proceedings of the National Academy of Sciences of the United States of America, 101,* 16369-16373.

Moore, A., & Malinowski, P. (2009). Meditation, mindfulness and cognitive flexibility. *Consciousness and Cognition, 18,* 176-186.

Rubia, K. (2009). The neurobiology of meditation and its clinical effectiveness in psychiatric disorders. *Biological Psychology, 82,* 1-11.

Runehov, A. L. C. (2007). *Sacred or neural? The potential of neuroscience to explain religious experience.* Göttingen, Germany: Vandenhoeck & Ruprecht.

Shokek, S. (2001). *Kabbalah and the art of being.* London, UK: Routledge.

Slagter, H. A., Lutz, A., Greischar, L. L., Francis, A. D., Nieuwenhuis, S., Davis, J. M., & Davidson, R. J. (2007). Mental training affects distribution of limited brain resources. *PLoS Biology, 5*(6), e138. Retrieved from http://www.ncbi.nlm.nih.gov/pubmed/17488185

Solms, M. (2000). A psychoanalytic contribution to contemporary neuroscience. In M. Velmans (Ed.), *Investigating phenomenal consciousness: New methodologies and maps*. Amsterdam, The Netherlands: John Benjamins.

Solms, M., & Turnbull, O. (2002). *The brain and the inner world: An introduction to the neuroscience of subjective experience*. New York, NY: Other Press.

Stroop, J. R. (1935). Studies of interference in serial verbal reactions. *Journal of Experimental Psychology, 18*, 643-661.

Vestergaard-Poulsen, P., van Beek, M., Skewes, J., Bjarkam, C. R., Stubberup, M., Bertelsen, J., & Roepstorff, A. (2009). Long-term meditation is associated with increased gray matter density in the brain stem. *Wolters Kluwer Health, 20*, 170-174.

von der Malsburg, C. (1997). The coherence definition of consciousness. In M. Ito, Y. Miyashita, & E. T. Rolls (Eds.), *Cognition, computation, and consciousness* (pp. 193-204). Oxford, UK: Oxford University Press.

Wenk-Sormaz, H. (2005). Meditation can reduce habitual responding. *Alternative Therapies in Health and Medicine 11*, 42-58.

Wolfson, E. (2005). *Language, eros, being: Kabbalistic hermeneutics and poetic imagination*. New York, NY: Fordham University Press.

Zeki, S. (2003). The disunity of consciousness. *Trends in Cognitive Sciences, 7*, 214-218.

Zeki, S. & Bartels, A. (1999). Toward a theory of visual consciousness. *Consciousness and Cognition. 8*, 225-259.

Part III
Transpersonal Methodologies

13

Transpersonal Research and Future Directions

Rosemarie Anderson[1] and William Braud

As a scientific endeavor, transpersonal psychology had an auspicious beginning with the inaugural issues of the *Journal of Transpersonal Psychology* (Sutich, 1969). From 1969 through 1980, the first 11 years of *Journal of Transpersonal Psychology* contained articles by distinguished psychologists, including Roberto Assagioli, Daniel Goleman, Stanislof Grof, Lawrence Leshan, Abraham H. Maslow, and June Singer; physicists Fritjof Capra and David Bohm; lineage teachers in worldwide spiritual traditions, including, Chogyam Tungpa Rinpoche, Sheikh Robert Frager, Roshi Jiyu Kennett, Ram Dass (Richard Alpert), Swami Radha, Tharthang Tulku Rinpoche, and Brother David Steindl-Rast; and philosophers Ken Wilber and Alan Watts. Although the majority of of these articles are theoretical in nature, the authors typically reflect on what they had learned about the transcendent or ultimate dimensions of human experience through their research and spiritual practice. Therefore, from the beginning, transpersonal psychology has been an integrative scientific disciple, understanding "science" as all knowledge and spiritual practice that contributes to our collective understanding of the human condition, especially as related to what Abraham Maslow (1969) aptly termed the "farther reaches of human nature."

Overview of Research Methods Used in Transpersonal Research

Over the past 40-plus years, the articles in both the *Journal of Transpersonal Psychology* and *International Journal of Transpersonal Studies* have been a mix of theoretical and empirical articles. Empirical articles, both qualitative and quantitative, increased from 4% in the 1970s to 12% in the 1980s, 15% in the 1990s, and 17% in the 2000s, with 57% of the empirical articles qualitative, 31% quantitative, and 11% mixed-methods in nature (Hartelius, Rothe, & Roy, 2013). Although most fields of scientific endeavor tend to

The Wiley Blackwell Handbook of Transpersonal Psychology, First Edition.
Edited by Harris L. Friedman and Glenn Hartelius.

proceed from theoretical to empirical over time, usually over several decades, defining transpersonal concepts in operational terms has been challenging and slow going. This is not surprising. Because the authors of this chapter were trained as experimental psychologists in the 1970s, we understand that "translating" metaphysical and spiritual terms and experiences into concepts and especially measurable phenomena needs to proceed carefully and slowly while being mindful that some transpersonal phenomena may not be strictly measurable at all, given their inherent complexity. Therefore, the field of transpersonal psychology may always require mature meta-theorizing in order to integrate the mind-body-spirit nexus without diminishing any of the phenomena, interconnections, or the possibility that transpersonal and spiritual experiences are inherently changing as history moves forward.

What follows in this chapter is an articulation of the various research methods—both mainstream and explicitly transpersonal—as applied to the study of transpersonal phenomena. We conclude with our own recommendations about future directions for transpersonal research.

Quantitative Approaches to Transpersonal Research

The study of *transpersonal experiences* and the relationship of these experiences to human development has been, and remains, a dominant topic in transpersonal research. Braud (1998a, 2011a) suggested a useful framework for organizing the types of questions that can be asked about such experiences. One can explore any experience in terms of (a) the *nature* of the experience itself; (b) how might the experience be *conceptualized* and how might conceptualizations change through time; (c) how does the experience unfold and develop, what features might accompany it, and which conditions might facilitate or impede it; and (d) what are the *outcomes* or "fruits" of the experience? The types of questions in this four-fold framework are aligned with the four major respective aims of well-established scientific research: to describe, explain, predict, and control the topic under investigation. Researchers have developed specific methods that are optimally suited for addressing these respective questions and aims. Quantitative research methods are especially effective for investigating the *process* and *outcomes* of transpersonal experiences; these methods are particularly useful in exploring issues and questions (c) and (d) above. In this section we describe the dominant quantitative and psychometric approaches used in transpersonal research and indicate their respective strengths, limitations, and challenges.

For exploring the outcomes or fruits of transpersonal experiences, experimental, quasi-experimental, and single-participant designs are especially useful. Causal-comparative and correlational designs are especially effective for investigating process-related questions. All five of these quantitative approaches typically make use of well-established psychometric assessments; excellent reviews of the most transpersonally relevant assessments can be found in a series of articles by MacDonald and colleagues (MacDonald, Friedman, & Kuentzel, 1999; MacDonald, Kuentzel, & Friedman, 1999; MacDonald, LeClair, Holland, Alter, & Friedman, 1995).

From a transpersonal perspective, correlational designs (including bi-variate and multi-variate correlations; multiple regression, discriminant function, canonical, and factor analyses) can determine which factors might covary with or set the stage for transpersonal experiences, and which types of persons or types of preparations tend to foster or interfere with certain experiences. Causal-comparative approaches (group statistical methods for searching for other, "causal," differences among groups already known to differ in some characteristic of interest) also are useful in this regard. The weaknesses of these designs are ambiguity of concluding causality in the case of correlations, ambiguity of causal "direction" in causal-comparative designs, and an inability to identify and assess possible extraneous and confounding variables.

Experimental and quasi-experimental designs are excellent for confidently determining effects of specifically defined and manipulated variables and for confidently concluding the existence of specific types of outcomes of transpersonal experiences. A major weakness of experimental designs is that in order to allow measurement, studied events usually must be simplified in order to bring them into the laboratory, and this may remove them from their more complex, natural contexts and result in artificial and even trivial findings especially as related to the multi-leveled nature of transpersonal and spiritual experiences. An additional limitation of quasi-experimental designs is that the absence of true random assignment of participants to conditions opens them to undetermined influences of possible unidentified extraneous variables. So-called single-subject designs, of the type used in Skinnerian and behavior modification studies, rarely are used in transpersonal research. However, because of their careful experimental rather than statistical control of variables, such designs could be very useful for determining and tracing the accompaniments and "fruits" of ongoing transpersonal experiences such as meditation or various spiritual practices. A weakness of such designs is that which is found for one participant or for a small number of participants might not generalize well to other individuals.

The approaches treated above may be supplemented by surveys and by action research methods (in which one carefully studies one's practical application work), the results of which can be quantified. Meta-analysis (which is the statistical analysis of the findings of a large body of similar quantitative studies) can be particularly useful in synthesizing research findings on similar topics. In addition, specialized quantitative approaches, such as physiological and biomedical assessments and designs (specialized methods and instrumentation for measuring somatic variables) and parapsychological assessments and designs (for exploring exceptional human experiences and abilities such as telepathy, clairvoyance, precognition, psychokinesis, and direct healing) could be used.

Quantitative methods emphasize "objective" third-person accounts to the disadvantage of "subjective" first-person accounts; some methods (e.g., experiments) tend to be used in artificial contexts that may not be relevant to the real life contexts in which experiences and events naturally occur. Such methods can overly simplify and trivialize experiences by reducing what is studied to what is readily measurable, losing much of the richness and personal meaning of experiences.

Qualitative Approaches to Transpersonal Research

In transpersonal psychology, qualitative research approaches are well-suited for investigating questions (a) and (b) noted above—the *nature* of transpersonal experiences and how the experiences are *conceptualized, interpreted, and understood,* especially by those who experience them. Question (a) can be explored by means of various descriptive qualitative approaches (phenomenological, experiential, heuristic, narrative, life stories, case studies, feminist, and ethnographic methods), and question (b) can be addressed by various theoretical and interpretive approaches (meta-theorizing, grounded theory, hermeneutic analyses, textual and discourse analyses, and historical and archival methods).

The descriptive qualitative approaches mentioned in (a) above address transpersonal experiences as they naturally and spontaneously occur in the lived world of participants and through a first-person perspective, as well as the meanings and personal impacts of the experiences, especially as these are self-perceived and constructed by the participants themselves. The approaches mentioned in (b) above can help identify patterns among varied research findings and hence can support analysis, synthesis, integration, interpretation, and theorizing regarding findings, as these are performed and construed by the research investigators.

In addition to the methods already mentioned, a number of new approaches have been proposed, including the experiential research method, cooperative inquiry, interpretive phenomenological analysis, participatory research, and cultural approaches. These strongly emphasize the direct experiences, voices, and full participation of the individuals being studied, in all stages of the research project.

Qualitative methods are excellent for eliciting and documenting "subjective," first-person accounts, especially of very noteworthy experiences. However, they deemphasize "objective," third-person aspects and the *degrees* to which certain factors are present or absent (although this may be possible by quantifying the density of various emerging themes), usually do not allow *causal* conclusions to be drawn (although it rarely is recognized that qualitative methods might indicate or at least suggest causality if used creatively and carefully), and often simply yield confirmations or deepenings of what already is known about the phenomena being researched. Properly conducted, qualitative designs can alter initial "lenses" or understandings and suggest new ones. Some qualitative methods may foster the development of conceptualizations, interpretations, and theories, although many play down this aspect, preferring to focus upon rich *descriptions* of experiences.

Useful additional information about all of the quantitative and qualitative research methods may be found in Anderson and Braud (2011), Braud and Anderson (1998), and Wertz, Charmaz, McMullen, Josselson, Anderson, and McSpadden (2011).

Mixed Methods and Modern Modeling Methods Research

Because research praxis privileges using methods and procedures that optimize the study of a particular phenomenon and the long-range purposes of a study, various types of quantitative and qualitative procedures have been employed and combined in psychology and the human sciences for decades. However, in the past 20 years, there has been an upsurge of interest in and the use of mixed methods. This expansion has largely been spurred by the development of sophisticated qualitative methods in the past 30 or 40 years. With the many well-developed qualitative methods and procedures now in place, combining the strengths of quantitative and qualitative methods provides a wide variety of research approaches with which to address complex problems. In combining quantitative and qualitative approaches the strengths of each are added one to another and to some extent attenuate the limitations of the other. Some mixed-methods researchers now refer to mixed-methods research as a "third movement" in the development of research methodology, following quantitative and qualitative methods (Tashakkori & Teddlie, 2003). Although individual researchers often use mixed-methods studies, increasingly mixed-method studies are led by multidisciplinary teams of researchers who provide a wide-range of research expertise and perspectives on a research topic (Creswell & Plano Clark, 2011; National Institutes of Health, 2010).

Mixed-methods research no longer refers to the mere combination of quantitative and qualitative methods in one study. Rather, the field of mixed methods provides specific mixed-methods designs, value-based discussions about combining methods and analyzing data, and philosophic rationales for using these methods, merging and analyzing quantitative and qualitative databases, and interpreting findings gathered from difference sources. Various philosophic differences are held among mixed-methods researchers, including social constructivist worldviews, transformative perspectives that encourage social change (Greene, 2007; Hesse-Biber, 2010; Mertens, 2009) and pragmatic perspectives, which privilege the research problem over methodological "purity."

While allowing that more complex designs are commonplace, Creswell and Plano Clark (2011) provided four basic types of mixed-methods designs:

1   Convergent designs: The combination of qualitative and quantitative data within one study and an analysis and comparison of the merged data and results.
2   Sequential designs: A qualitative study is followed by a quantitative study to understand more fully a topic or vice versa.
3   Embedded designs: Some quantitative data is collected within a qualitative study or vice versa.
4   Multiphase designs: Multiple studies, which may include quantitative, qualitative, and mixed-methods designs, conducted over extended periods time and linked by a common purpose.

Modern modeling methods (or what is sometimes known as the "new statistics") may be considered a mixed-methods approach to research. These new statistical approaches and their corresponding software programs can analyze all data—quantitative or qualitative—that can be coded. Specific procedures within modern modeling methods include structural equation modeling, multi-level modeling, longitudinal modeling, growth curve models, and Bayesian statistical modeling (Hoyle, 2012; McGrath, 2011). The software programs now available analyze large databases, which include data from many sources, and predict the likelihood of anticipated outcomes. For example, based on successes of characteristics of past movies and characteristics of movie plots and actors, modern modeling models are now being used to predict which movies are likely to become blockbuster hits (Gladwell, 2006). These same procedures can analyze multidisciplinary databases relevant to healthcare, complex social problems, patterns of surveillance related to security issues, longitudinal analysis of developmental processes, global and environmental trends.

The advance of modern modeling methods' analytic procedures and software programs have already attracted some of the most eminent statisticians in universities and companies in North America and Europe, in part because the public, governments, and industry have much to gain from their outcome predictions. Modern modeling methods conferences, weekend seminars, and summer school training sessions are growing in number. While modern modeling methods are essentially advanced statistical procedures, the capacity of these procedures to integrate and analyze large amounts of data quickly may put modern modeling methods at the forefront of the evolution of research methodology in psychology and the human sciences in the years to come. While many may critique these modern modeling methods as overly simplifying data—especially qualitative data—to numerical or textual codes and separating data from their interpretative contexts, the power of these procedures to predict the likelihood of outcomes for complex phenomena, including transpersonal phenomena, cannot be overstated.

Transpersonal Approaches to Research

In the mid 1990s, three approaches to research were developed at the Institute of Transpersonal Psychology, now Sofia University. Intuitive inquiry was developed by Rosemarie Anderson and integral inquiry by William Braud. Organic inquiry was developed by Jennifer Clements with early assistance from Dorothy Ettling, Lisa Shields, Nora Taylor, and Dianne Jenett. All three approaches were introduced in Braud and Anderson (1998). After a decade of use and refinement of procedures, the three approaches were described in detail in Anderson and Braud (2011) in individual chapters by Anderson, Braud, and Clements. What follows are brief overviews of the transpersonal approaches to research.

Intuitive Inquiry

Intuitive inquiry affirms intuition, compassion, and service as central to research and to understanding anything important about life at all. Acknowledging a world in flux and challenging world views that separate the knower, the lover, from what is known, intuitive inquirers tend toward insights that "break set" with established theory and scholarship, transforming not only their understanding of the research topic but often their personal lives. In research reports, the "tale" of an intuitive inquiry is reported fully and projected toward the future as an impetus for individual, ethical, and collective change.

Intuitive inquiry has been influenced by many philosophical and methodological approaches. Among the prominent influences are the embodied phenomenology of Maurice Merleau-Ponty (1945/1962, 1964/1968), the biblical hermeneutics of Friedrich Schleiermacher (1977), the philosophic hermeneutics of Hans-Georg Gadamer (1976, 1998), feminist research approaches (Fine, 1992; Nielsen, 1990; Reinharz; 1992), heuristic research (Moustakas, 1990), Eugene Gendlin's (1991, 1992) "thinking beyond patterns," and many scholars describing intuitive and embodied practices among indigenous peoples (Abram, 1996; Luna & Amaringo, 1991; Sheridan & Pineault, 1997).

Five Cycles of Hermeneutic Interpretation

Intuitive inquiry involves an interpretative process between the parts and the whole of the texts known as the hermeneutic circle. The method invites the transformation of the researcher's understanding of the topic, procedurally contained by five successive cycles of interpretation. Each cycle allows the researcher's psyche to roam freely within its procedural boundaries, which contain specific activities unique to that cycle. Overall, the five cycles pivot around the researcher's intuition, integrating intellectual understanding as the course of an inquiry unfolds.

Cycle 1: Clarifying the research topic through imaginal dialogue. Traditionally in research praxis, a researcher typically chooses a research topic based on research in an area of interest and identifies a relevant next study. However, in intuitive inquiry, a topic of study arises from the researcher's interests and passions. To clarify a topic, intuitive inquirers select a text, broadly defined, that attracts their attention repeatedly and relates in a general way to the researcher's interests. Texts for Cycle 1 have included photographs, paintings, mandalas, collages, sketches, symbols, sculptures, song lyrics, movies, poems, sacred texts, scripture, interview transcripts, recorded dreams, and journal accounts of a meaningful transformative experience. Although no intuitive inquirer has yet used quantitative "texts" in Cycle 1, statistical findings, graphs, and figures based on empirical findings could be used.

Once the text is identified, intuitive inquirers begin a process of imaginal dialogue with the text, spending time each day reading, listening to, or viewing the identified text. Thoughts, ideas, daydreams, conversations, impressions, visions, and intuitions are recorded in a noninvasive manner. This process of engagement with the text completes when the creative tension with the text resolves and a compelling, manageable, clear, focused, concrete, researchable, and promising emerges.

Cycle 2: Reflecting on extant topical texts and developing the preliminary interpretive lenses. After completing a review of the theoretical and empirical literature on the topic, the researcher identifies a set of texts from this literature for Cycle 2. The texts selected express compelling and varying understandings of the topic to help the intuitive inquirer grasp the range and depth of understanding already existing in the literature. Thereafter, again via imaginal dialogue, the researcher engages with these texts to discern and distill the researcher's understanding of the research topic *prior* to data gathering. Generating these preliminary interpretive lenses is usually quick and easy, feeling more like creative imagination or brainstorming than a formal process. Ten to 12 are usually sufficient to capture the intuitive inquirer's pre-understanding of the topic.

Cycle 3: Collecting data and preparing a descriptive analysis of data. Cycle 3 has two phases. First, the researcher collects original or archival data. Second, the researcher presents a descriptive analysis of data that invites readers to come to their own conclusions about them before they read the researcher's interpretations in Cycles 4 and 5.

To date, most researchers using intuitive inquiry have collected original empirical data in the form of interviews or stories from research participants who meet specific criteria as informants relevant to the topic of study (Coleman, 2000; Dufre-chou, 2004; Esbjörn-Hargens, 2004; Manos, 2007; Phelon, 2004; Rickards, 2006; Shepperd, 2006; Unthank, 2007). However, in a study of true joy among Christian mystics, Carlock (2003) chose a set of writings from historical mystics related for Cycle 3 because of the spiritual depth of the historical mystical sources and Rickards (2006) made extensive use of historical narratives and journal accounts provided by female World War II espionage agents. Several researchers have collected embodied writing (Anderson, 2001, 2002a, 2002b) accounts from participants (Dufrechou, 2004; Netzer, 2008; Shepperd, 2006) or examples of participants' artistic expression (Hill, 2003; Hoffman, 2004; Manos, 2007; Rickards, 2006).

A wide variety of analytic procedures can be used in Cycle 3 of intuitive inquiry. To date, descriptive analyses of data have included edited interview transcripts (Esbjörn, 2003, Esbjörn-Hargens, 2004), portraits of participants (Coleman, 2000; Rickards, 2006), historical portraits (Carlock, 2003), portraits accompanied by illustrative exam-ples of participants' art (Manos, 2007), aspects of discourse analysis plus interviewee stories (Unthank, 2007), portraits plus common themes in interviews (Brandt, 2007), common themes in interviews plus artistic expression (Perry, 2009), a series of par-ticipants' embodied writings (Dufrechou, 2004; Netzer, 2008; Shepperd, 2006), and common themes plus integral mandala artwork (Cervelli, 2009). The analytic pro-cedures of action and participatory research, case study, focus group, ethnographic, grounded theory, heuristic, narrative, and empirical phenomenological research could be adapted to Cycle 3 of intuitive inquiry as well. These summary accounts of the data are as descriptive as possible, allowing the readers to read the descriptive analyses and come to their own conclusions prior to the researcher's interpretation in Cycle 4.

Cycle 4: Transforming and refining interpretive lenses. Cycle 4 has two phases. First, the researcher presents a set of Cycle 4 interpretive lenses, refining and transforming Cycle 2 lenses in the light of researcher's personal engagement with the data gathered in Cycle 3. Cycle 2 lenses are modified, removed, rewritten, expanded, etc., reflecting the researchers more developed and nuanced understanding of the topic at the conclusion of the study. Second, the researcher provides a lens-by-lens comparison of Cycle 2 and Cycle 4 lenses, which articulates the changes made.

Cycle 5: Integration of findings and literature review. As is conventional at the end of a research study, in Cycle 5, the intuitive inquirer returns to the theoretical and empirical literature on the topic and reevaluates it in light of the findings of the study. Epistemologically speaking, the researcher stands back from the research process and considers all aspects of it anew, as though drawing a larger hermeneutic circle around the entire study.

Unique to intuitive inquiry as a research method, the intuitive inquirer attempts to express trajectories that emerge from the findings that suggest new or more refined ways of being human in the world. Researchers are called to explore topics that require attention by the culture at large and in the hope that they will generate breakthrough insights along the way. Implicitly, intuitive inquiries consider, "What does the future ask of us?" In so doing, intuitive inquiry hopes to both continue and break set with established scientific discourse on a topic.

Additional information about intuitive inquiry may be found in the following articles and book chapters: (Anderson, 1998, 2000, 2004a, 2004b, 2011a, 2011b).

Integral Inquiry

Ultimate truth, if there be such a thing, demands the concert of many voices.
Carl Jung (1993, p. xiv)

Integral inquiry is an inclusive and integrated research approach as a way of honoring and addressing topics of transpersonal and spiritual import. The approach includes and integrates aspects of the research enterprise that conventional research approaches deliberately keep separate. Inclusion and integration take place in three major areas. First, a research session may simultaneously provide opportunities for knowledge gain for the discipline; clinical, educational, and other benefits for the research participants; and psychospiritual growth and the possibility of transformative change for the researcher, the research participants and the eventual readers of the research report. Second, a greater understanding of the topic of inquiry is made possible through attention to the nature of experiences, their history and conceptualization, their dynamic unfolding and the processes that facilitate or inhibit them, and their outcomes or "fruits." Third, in the course of the investigation, the integral inquirer practices many complementary forms of knowing, being, and doing, including conventional, tacit, intuitive, body-based, feelings-based, and "direct" forms of knowing; ordinary and nonordinary states of consciousness; analytical/linear and nonanalytical/nonlinear ways of working with data; and alternative ways of expressing findings (themes, narratives, metaphors, similes, symbols, and nonverbal creative expressions). Integral inquiry integrates both quantitative and qualitative data collection and analysis and, therefore, is a mixed-methods approach to research.

When this approach was being developed in the 1990s, the term *integral* already was being used—in the Integral Yoga and Integral Yoga Psychology of Sri Aurobindo (1948/2000), and in the integral structure of consciousness described by Jean Gebser (1949/1986)—and later would be used for the Integral Psychology of Ken Wilber (2000). The naming of *Integral Inquiry* was not inspired by any of these three uses; however, the approach does have considerable overlaps with these other views.

The essential features of this inclusive, pluralistic, pragmatic, radically empirical, flexible, and open research approach can be described, most succinctly, in a "by the numbers" format.

1 *Goal:* The overall goal of the approach is to acquire and increment both knowledge and wisdom.
2 *Desired Outcomes:* Integral inquirers seek two outcomes for any research project: information regarding the studied topic (an academic and nomothetic aim) and transformation of all involved participants.
3 *Phases and Modes of Inquiry:* Like all other research approaches, integral inquiry addresses three major phases of inquiry: study design and data collection, data analysis, and interpretation, and the communication of findings to others.

4   *Types of Research Questions:* A distinctive feature of integral inquiry is its emphases
    on four major types of research questions that can apply to any research topic: (a)
    what is the nature of the experience (or of the process, condition, trait, or state
    being studied); (b) how has the experience (or other aspect of the topic) been
    conceptualized and what has been learned about it, historically; (c) how has the
    experience unfolded or developed, what set the stage for it, what helps and what
    hinders it, and what accompanies it; and (d) what are the outcomes or fruits of
    the experience ? A variety of specific methods are used to explore these respective
    question types.

5   *Utility of the Inquiry:* The integral inquirer chooses research projects whose
    conduct and findings promise to be useful to five types of "recipients" of the
    project: the research participants, the researcher, the reader/consumer of the
    final research report, the investigator's discipline and field of study, and society
    as a whole.

6   *Whole Person Involvement:* Throughout all phases of a research project, both the
    researcher and the research participants (and even the audience of the reported
    findings) are invited to involve six aspects of their being in the process of
    the inquiry: their body, emotions, intellect, spirit, relationships, and creative
    expression (six major facets around which the curricula and holistic pedagogy
    of the Institute of Transpersonal Psychology, now Sofia University, have been
    developed.)

7   *Foci of Intention:* During the course of an inquiry, the researcher is invited to
    focus attention and intention upon seven aspects of the project: right inquiry,
    right participants, right expression (on the part of the research participants),
    right reception (of the participants' offerings, by the researcher), right expres-
    sion (by the researcher to the project's audience), right reception (of the study
    and its findings by the "consumer"), and right uses and practice of what has
    been learned.

8   *Modes of Knowing:* Throughout a research project, both researcher and research
    participants (as well as the audience of the study's findings) are invited to use
    eight modes of knowing in order to increase their knowledge, appreciation,
    and understanding of what is to be learned in the project: sensory impressions,
    words and thoughts, images, feelings, intuitions, realizations in altered conditions
    of consciousness, sensory and motor automatisms (automatic, "unconscious"
    reactions), and paranormal and direct means of knowing (knowing through being
    or becoming the object of knowing).

9   *Sources of Inspiration:* Rather than focusing only on what has been found and
    thought about one's topic in a narrow recent literature review time frame and in
    one's own narrow discipline or area of study, the integral inquirer is invited to
    have his or her research project informed by nine additional sources: the natural
    sciences; psychology; sociology; anthropology; philosophy; literature; the arts;
    the various spiritual, wisdom, and folk traditions; and personal and anecdotal
    evidence.

10 *Communication of Findings:* The researcher is encouraged to use a variety of
    means of expressing findings and communicating these to one's intended audi-
    ences. These include the following ten means: statistical summaries; figures
    and graphs; tabulated results; themes and distillates; participant narratives; the

researcher's own descriptive narration; images and expressive art (including electronic formats); poetry, metaphor, and symbols; fiction; and presentations and performances for professionals and the general public.

Just as integral inquiry recognizes the value of including a wide range of methods, practices, and principles, transpersonal psychology and established psychology itself might be similarly broadened to include a wider range of emphases. Such a broadened form of psychology—an *inclusive and integrated psychology*—would allow itself to be informed by the methods, findings, theories, implications, and applications of all disciples within mainstream psychology and also would welcome inputs from related areas of study such as parapsychology and psychical research, spiritual and wisdom traditions, the humanities, and the arts. Such inclusiveness and integration, as exemplified in integral inquiry, also could serve as a model for similarly expanding the substantive content and approaches of scholarly disciplines other than psychology.

Additional and detailed information about integral inquiry may be found in a number of articles and book chapters (Braud, 1994, 1998a, 1998b, 1998c, 2002, 2006, 2011b, 2011c).

Organic Inquiry

Organic inquiry is an emerging approach to qualitative research that attracts people and topics related to psychospiritual growth and development. The psyche of the researcher becomes the subjective instrument of the research, working in partnership with liminal and spiritual influences. A three-step process of preparation, inspiration, and integration guides both the data collection and the analysis.

This approach (initially called organic research) was originated in the mid-1990s by Jennifer Clements, with early assistance from Dorothy Ettling, Lisa Shields, Nora Taylor, and Dianne Jenett, as they were searching for avenues of research that could include the sacred. At the time, Clements, Ettling, Shields, Taylor, and Jenett were either faculty or doctoral students at the Institute of Transpersonal Psychology, now Sofia University. They wanted a way of working in which the positive values of cooperation and interdependency were appreciated, in which diversity would foster equality rather than separation, and where spiritual experience would not be forced into the shadow of rational thought (Clements, Ettling, Jenett, & Shields, 1998, 1999).

Called *organic inquiry* because it is a living and therefore mutable process, the approach invites transformative change, which includes not only information, but also a transformation that provides changes to both mind and heart. The approach offers a process for cultivating these changes in the researcher, participants, and readers of the research through the telling of stories. Stories present findings using both feeling and thinking styles in order to offer the reader an opportunity to interpret the stories' transformative implications for themselves. Stories are offered to the reader by way of the individual stories of the participants, composite participant story, and the story of how the researcher has changed as a result of the study. Throughout the course of the study and the reading of research findings by others, the researcher, participants, and final readers are asked to be alert to possible transformative changes that are indicated by greater movements toward self, Spirit, and service to others.

Perhaps the most important aspect of organic inquiry is its emphasis on transformation. The approach incorporates the idea that research can include spirit, body, and feeling as well as mind. Guided by transpersonal psychology's many models of human development and the psychological types identified by Carl Jung (1921/1971), organic inquiry uses the context of a particular topic to offer *transformative change,* defined as a resulting restructuring of worldview that provides some degree of movement along a lifetime path toward transpersonal development.

The organic orientation includes the assumption of the mystical traditions that divine/human interaction is available to one who is open. The terms *liminal* and *liminal realm* describe a state beyond ego that may be visited by the individual psyche to gather useful experience, a state in which the ego is barely perceptible. We may learn to cross the threshold (*limen*) beyond ego, gather experience, and to return "so that the deeper ground of the archetypal field can be seen, experienced, and allowed to flower" (Hopcke, 1991, p. 118). Crossing the threshold takes the psyche to a less structured and less familiar state, where experience may be witnessed, but not created or controlled by ego. The term *liminal* is used to indicate a more neutral influence beyond ego.

In using this approach, the researcher works with her or his own story and with those of the research participants—stories of the particular experience being studied. Analysis, which involves the cognitive integration of liminal encounters with the data, may result in transformative changes (especially in terms of greater movements toward self, Spirit, and service) in the researcher's understanding and experience of the topic, as evidenced by important ways in which the researcher's story changes as a result of having encountered those of the research participants. Stories, as evocative vehicles of feeling as well as thinking, present a diverse and intimate view of the topic in order to engage the individual reader in a parallel process of transformative interpretation—transformations of head and of heart.

In organic inquiry, validity is assessed by asking the question, "Is this useful to me?" The project has *transformative validity* when it succeeds in affecting the individual reader through identification with, and change of, her or his prevailing story, as witnessed in the arenas of self, Spirit, and service. The responses of early readers can give some indication of a study's potential transformative validity.

An organic image. The characteristics and growth of an organic study are suggested by the image of the growth of a tree. The five major characteristics of organic inquiry—*sacred, personal, chthonic, related,* and *transformative*—are cumulative rather than successive. They happen simultaneously rather than in any given order.

Sacred: preparing the soil. Before a seed is planted, the earth is prepared. Similarly, participation in the organic approach calls for spading up old habits and expectations to cultivate a sacred perspective.

Personal: planting the seed. Planting the seed represents the initial experience of the topic by the researcher. The best topic will have passionate meaning because it has been the occasion for the researcher's own psychospiritual growth.

Chthonic: the roots emerge. Just as the developing roots of a tree are invisible and beyond intention, an organic inquiry has an underground life of its own because of its subjective and spiritual sources. As with a living tree, the process is allowed to evolve and change.

Related: growing the tree. Participants' stories are the branches that join and inform the trunk story of the research.

Transformative: harvesting the fruit. The fruits of organic inquiry are the transformative changes it offers, changes of mind and heart, particularly for its readers.

Additional information about organic inquiry approach may be found in the following sources: Clements (2002, 2004, 2011) and Clements, Ettling, Jenett, & Shields (1998, 1999).

Researcher Preparedness and Transpersonal Skills

In all forms of research—quantitative, qualitative, and transpersonal—the researcher herself or himself is actually the most important "tool" in the investigation. This is because the many qualities and skills of the researcher help determine all aspects of the research project—from choosing what to study and in which manner to how the collected data are analyzed, interpreted, and presented. A useful way to consider the many researcher qualities is to speak of the *preparedness* or *adequateness* of the researcher. The established research literature has addressed only a narrow range of these researcher characteristics and skills and how these might be identified, enhanced, and optimally used in research projects.

Skills typically treated in research methods textbooks, as well as at research sites themselves, generally are limited to the cognitive, intellectual skills of practicing keen observation, engaging in critical thinking, efficient problem-solving, finding and evaluating relevant information, effectively analyzing data, clearly communicating one's findings to one's professional peers, and maintaining an "objective," uninvolved stance throughout the investigation. These skills are essential in the preparation of the transpersonal researcher, but they are not enough. In order to investigate topics of transpersonal relevance in sufficient depth and thoroughness, it is necessary to supplement these conventionally treated skills with a set of additional skills that rarely are addressed in research training.

These skills can be called *integral research skills* because when used together they can help provide a complete and integrated (integral) appreciation of the topic being studied. They can be called *transpersonal research skills* for two reasons. First, many of these have provided the basis for practices that are of importance in spiritual and wisdom traditions that have transpersonal relevance. Second, a practice may be considered transpersonally relevant if it is carried out with a transpersonal intention, such as increased self-awareness, an expanded sense of identity, or expanded ways of knowing, doing, and being in the world, beyond the usual egoic modes of functioning. Once identified, these skills can be enhanced through training and used in all phases of any research project.

In this brief section, we can provide only a quick overview of 10 of these integral or transpersonal skills, along with brief descriptions of how each skill can be practiced and used in the various phases of research.

- *Working with intention*: Awareness of, and deliberate framing of, intentions (attention directed toward a specific goal) for all phases of a research project; facilitates the realization of study aims
- *Quieting and slowing*: Sets the stage for use of other skills, relaxes and quiets, reduces distractions and "noise" at many levels, reduces structures and constraints, allows change, allows fuller observations and appreciation of more subtle aspects of what is studied
- *Working with attention*: Practice in deploying, focusing, and shifting attention; deautomatizing attention; attending to different forms and channels of information; changing focal plane or magnification of attention; developing witnessing consciousness; so-called *meditation* is really a special way of deploying attention
- *Auditory skills*: Practice in devoting more complete attention to external and internal sounds and to sound memories and sound imagination
- *Visual skills, imagery, visualization, imagination*: Practice in devoting more complete attention to outer and inner sights and images; use of memory images, visualization, spontaneous and guided imagery; active imagination; empowered imagination
- *Kinesthetic skills*: Practice in knowing, remembering, and expressing knowing and being through gross and subtle movements
- *Proprioceptive skills*: Practice in identifying and attending to subtle visceral and muscular sensations; working with felt senses, feelings, affective knowing
- *Direct knowing, intuition, empathic identification*: Identifying with the object of knowing; knowing through presence, empathy, sympathy, compassion, love, being, becoming, participation; parapsychological processes
- *Accessing unconscious processes and materials*: Reducing egoic control; tacit knowing; liminal and transitional conditions; incubation; attention to vehicles that carry previously unconscious information; identifying unconscious tendencies
- *Play and the creative arts*: Fostering curiosity, creativity, and insight; encouraging beginner's mind; provides novelty, new combinations; encourages excitement, enthusiasm, exploration

Detailed treatments of each of these 10 skills, along with specific experiential exercises for their systematic training and use in the three major research phases of any transpersonal study—planning a study and collecting data, analyzing and interpreting data, and communicating one's findings to one's reading or listening audience—may be found in Anderson and Braud (2011).

Finally, we call to your attention still another set of skills and tools that can be of great use in transpersonal research. These are the 13 thinking tools described by R. and M. Root-Bernstein (1999). The Root-Bernsteins have convincingly demonstrated the power of these tools as they commonly are used by creative individuals in many different areas of science, mathematics, the humanities, and the arts, and they present ways to identify and learn to better use these tools. The 13 tools they present are processes of *observing, imaging, abstracting, recognizing patterns, forming patterns, analogizing, body thinking, empathizing, dimensional thinking, modeling, playing, transforming,* and *synthesizing.*

Future Directions for Transpersonal Research

Transpersonal scholarship and research is likely to become increasingly empirical, inclusive of quantitative, qualitative, and mixed-method approaches to research. In concluding this review of transpersonal research, we have three concluding recommendations:

1   If transpersonal psychology and transpersonal studies wish to influence mainstream scientific dialogue in the human sciences and humanities, transpersonal researchers need to stay current with the waves of methodological innovations now occurring in psychology and throughout the human sciences. Currently, because descriptive data seem to better portray the subtlety and depth of transpersonal and spiritual experiences, most transpersonal researchers are trained and gravitate toward using qualitative approaches to research. However, in order to stay current with current developments in the psychology and the human sciences, transpersonal researchers will need to train themselves quantitative and mixed-method approaches or at least participate in research teams that include quantitative researchers trained in the various new statistics now available.

2   Allow for research methods, procedures, and expressions that do not fit into current methodological parameters and let the fruits of research outcomes direct future use of the methods and procedures employed. All research praxes are informed by the historical periods and people they serve. The methods we use now will change to serve new times and circumstances. It is impossible to know what one does not know or what methods will be required in the future, especially with regard to the study of experiences among minority groups and indigenous and non-Western cultures.

3   Retaining the tradition already established in the field, many transpersonal researchers remain aware that transpersonal and spiritual phenomena themselves may morph, transcending and including what has gone before. In transpersonal and spiritual research, one is studying at least in part the ineffable and the changing. The numinous may always eclipse human understanding. Therefore, may a spirit of generosity and humility abound in transpersonal research efforts. Allow that human and global consciousness may be changing in ways that cannot be known. Of course, there is a desire and need to be precise and rigorous and to use the best of research methods available. However, as rigorously as one can use the methods of our times, the users are only researchers and scholars in pursuit of understanding—understandings that may change under the gaze of inquiry, as new methods of research are developed, and as history unfolds. Both within psychology and throughout the human sciences, research methods continue to be developed and paradigms of knowledge are shifting. Just staying in touch and trained in the new research methods and procedures both qualitative and

qualitative is challenging enough given how many there are each year. However, more challenging is always to aver and commit oneself to the study of transpersonal phenomena that ever changes and is always in part outside of one's grasp.

Note

1. William Braud died on May 13, 2012. We have been friends and intellectual partners for 20 years. With gratitude, I wish to acknowledge his many contributions to transpersonal scholarship and my life.

References

Abram, D. (1996). *The spell of the sensuous: Perception and language in a more-than-human world.* New York, NY: Pantheon Books.

Anderson, R. (1998). Intuitive inquiry: A transpersonal approach. In W. Braud & R. Anderson, *Transpersonal research methods for the social sciences: Honoring human experience* (pp. 69-94). Thousand Oaks, CA: Sage.

Anderson, R. (2000). Intuitive inquiry: Interpreting objective and subjective data. *ReVision: Journal of Consciousness and Transformation, 22*(4), 31-39.

Anderson, R. (2001). Embodied writing and reflections on embodiment. *Journal of Transpersonal Psychology, 33*(2), 83-96.

Anderson, R. (2002a). Embodied writing: Presencing the body in somatic research, Part I, What is embodied writing? *Somatics: Magazine/Journal of the Mind/Body Arts and Sciences, 13*(4), 40-44.

Anderson, R. (2002b). Embodied writing: Presencing the body in somatic research, Part II, Research Applications. *Somatics: Magazine/Journal of the Mind/Body Arts and Sciences, 14*(1), 40-44.

Anderson, R. (2004a). Guest editor, intuitive inquiry. *The Humanistic Psychologist, 32*(4).

Anderson, R. (2004b). Intuitive inquiry: An epistemology of the heart for scientific inquiry. *The Humanistic Psychologist, 32*(4), 307-341.

Anderson, R. (2011a). Intuitive inquiry: Exploring the mirroring discourse of disease. In F. Wertz, K. Charmaz, L. McMullen, R. Josselson, & R. Anderson (Eds.), *Five ways of doing qualitative analysis: Phenomenological psychology, grounded theory, discourse analysis, narrative research, and intuitive inquiry* (pp. 243-278). New York, NY: Guilford.

Anderson, R. (2011b). Intuitive inquiry: The ways of the heart in human science research. In R. Anderson and & W. Braud (Eds.), *Transforming self and others through research: Transpersonal research methods and skills for the human sciences and humanities* (pp. 15-70). Albany, NY: State University of New York Press.

Anderson, R., & Braud, W. (2011). *Transforming self and others through research: Transpersonal research methods and skills for the human sciences and humanities.* Albany, NY: State University of New York Press.

Aurobindo, Sri. (2000). *The synthesis of yoga.* Pondicherry, India: Sri Aurobindo Ashram Press. (Original work published serially 1914-192, and in book form 1948)

Brandt, P. L. (2007). Nonmedical support of women during childbirth: The spiritual meaning of birth for doulas. *Dissertation Abstracts International, 68*(07) 0669B (UMI #3274206).

Braud, W. (1994). *Toward an integral methodology for transpersonal studies.* Working Paper Number 1994-1 of the William James Center for Consciousness Studies, Institute of Transpersonal Psychology, Palo Alto, CA. Retrieved from http://www.inclusive psychology.com/archives.html

Braud, W. (1998a). An expanded view of validity. In W. Braud & R. Anderson (Eds.), *Transpersonal research methods for the social sciences: Honoring human experience* (pp. 213-237). Thousand Oaks, CA: Sage.

Braud, W. (1998b). Can research be transpersonal? *Transpersonal Psychology Review, 2*(3), 9-17.

Braud, W. (1998c). Integral inquiry: Complementary ways of knowing, being, and expression. In W. Braud & R. Anderson (Eds.), *Transpersonal research methods for the social sciences: Honoring human experience* (pp. 35-68). Thousand Oaks, CA: Sage.

Braud, W. (2002). The ley and the labyrinth: Universalistic and particularistic approaches to knowing. *Transpersonal Psychology Review, 6*(2), 47-62.

Braud, W. (2006). Educating the "more" in holistic transpersonal higher education: A 30+ year perspective on the approach of the Institute of Transpersonal Psychology. *Journal of Transpersonal Psychology, 38*(2), 133-158.

Braud, W. (2011a). *An expanded form of research and disciplined inquiry.* Retrieved fromhttp://inclusivepsychology.com/essays.html

Braud, W. (2011b). Integral inquiry: The principles and practices of an inclusive and integrated research approach. In R. Anderson & W. Braud (Eds.), *Transforming self and others through research: Transpersonal research methods and skills for the human sciences and humanities* (pp. 71-130). Albany, NY: State University of New York Press.

Braud, W. (2011c). Integrating Yoga epistemology and ontology into an expanded integral approach to research. In M. Cornelissen, G. Misra, & S. Varma (Eds.), *Foundations of Indian psychology,* (Vol. 1, pp. 288-311). New Delhi, India: Pearson.

Braud, W., & Anderson, R. (1998). *Transpersonal research methods for the social sciences: Honoring human experience.* Thousand Oaks, CA: Sage.

Carlock, S. E. (2003). The quest for true joy in union with God in mystical Christianity: An intuitive inquiry study. *Dissertation Abstracts International, 65*(04) 0669B (UMI #3129583).

Cervelli, R. L. (2009). An intuitive inquiry into experiences arising out of the Holotropic Breathwork® technique and its integral mandala artwork: The potential for self-actualization. *Dissertation Abstracts International, 70*(12) 0669B (UMI #3380360).

Clements, J. (2002). *Organic inquiry: Research in partnership with spirit.* Unpublished manuscript, Institute of Transpersonal Psychology, Palo Alto, CA.

Clements, J. (2004). Organic Inquiry: Toward research in partnership with spirit. *Journal of Transpersonal Psychology, 36,* 26-49.

Clements, J. (2011). Organic inquiry: Research in partnership with spirit. In R. Anderson & W. Braud (Eds.), *Transforming self and others through research: Transpersonal research methods and skills for the human sciences and humanities* (pp. 131-159). Albany, NY: State University of New York Press.

Clements, J., Ettling, D., Jenett, D., & Shields, L. (1998). Organic research: Feminine spirituality meets transpersonal research. In W. Braud & R. Anderson (Eds.), *Transpersonal research methods for the social sciences: Honoring human experience* (pp. 114-127). Thousand Oaks, CA: Sage.

Clements, J., Ettling, D., Jenett, D., & Shields, L. (1999). *If research were sacred: An organic methodology* (Rev. ed.). Retrieved from http://www.serpentina.com/research-x.html

Coleman, B. (2000). Women, weight, and embodiment: An intuitive inquiry into women's psycho-spiritual process of healing obesity. *Dissertation Abstracts International, 61*(04) 0669B (UMI #9969177).

Creswell, J. W., & Plano Clark, V. L. (2011). *Designing and conducting mixed methods research.* (2nd ed.). Thousand Oaks, CA: Sage.

Dufrechou, J. (2004). We are one: Grief, weeping, and other deep emotions in response to nature as a path toward wholeness. *The Humanistic Psychologist, 32*(4), 357-378.

Esbjörn, V. C. (2003). Spirited flesh: An intuitive inquiry exploring the body in contemporary female mystics. *Dissertation Abstracts International, 64*(06) 0669B (UMI #3094309).

Esbjörn-Hargens, V. (2004). The union of flesh and spirit in women mystics. *The Humanistic Psychologist, 32*(4), 401-425.

Fine, M. (1992). *Disruptive voices: The possibilities of feminist research.* Ann Arbor, MI: University of Michigan Press.

Gadamer, H. (1976). On the problem of self-understanding. In D. E. Linge (Ed. & Trans.), *Philosophical hermeneutics* (pp. 44-58). Berkeley, CA: University of California Press. (Original work published 1962)

Gadamer, H. (1998). *Truth and method* (2nd rev. ed. J. Wiensheimer & D. Marshall Trans.). New York, NY: Continuum. (Original work published 1960)

Gebser, J. (1986). *The ever-present origin* (N. Barstad & A. Mickunas, Trans.). Athens, OH: Ohio University Press. (Original work published 1949 [German])

Gendlin, E. T. (1991). Thinking beyond patterns: Body, language, and situations. In B. den Ouden & M. Moen (Eds.), *The presence of feeling in thought* (pp. 25-151). New York, NY: Peter Lang.

Gendlin, E. T. (1992). The primacy of the body, not the primacy of perception. *Man and World, 25*(3-4), 341-353.

Gladwell, M. (2006). So predictable [Video file]. Retrived from http://www.newyorker.com/online/video/2006/10/09/predictable

Greene, J. C. (2007). *Mixed methods in social inquiry.* San Francisco: John Wiley & Sons.

Hartelius, G., Rothe, G., & Roy, P. (2013). A brand from the burning: Defining transpersonal psychology. In Friedman, H., & Hartelius, G. (Eds.), *The Wiley-Blackwell handbook of transpersonal psychology* (pp. 1-22). Malden, MA. Wiley-Blackwell.

Hesse-Biber, S. N. (2010). *Mixed methods research: Merging theory with practice.* New York, NY: Guilford.

Hill, R. F. (2003). Mountains and mysticism: Climbing in thin air and transformation. *Dissertation Abstracts International, 64*(10) 0669B (UMI #3110309).

Hoffman, S. L. (2004). Living stories: Modern storytelling as a call for connection. *The Humanistic Psychologist, 32*(4), 379-400.

Hopcke, R. H. (1991). On the threshold of change: Synchronistic events and their liminal context in analysis. In N. Schwartz-Salant & M. Stein (Eds.), *Liminality and transitional phenomena* (pp. 115-132). Wilmette, IL: Chiron.

Hoyle, R. H. (2012). *Handbook of structural equation modeling.* New York, NY: Guilford.

Jung, C. G. (1971). *Psychological types* (R. F. C. Hull, Trans.). In *The collected works of C. G. Jung* (Vol. 6, 2nd ed.). Princeton, NJ: Princeton University Press. (Original work published 1921)

Jung, C. G. (1993). Foreword. In E. Neumann, *The origins and history of consciousness* (pp. xiii-iv). Princeton, NJ: Princeton University Press.

Luna, L. E., & Amaringo, P. (1991). *Ayahuasca visions: The religious iconography of a Peruvian shaman.* Berkeley, CA: North Atlantic Books.

MacDonald, D. A., Friedman, H. L., & Kuentzel, J. G. (1999). A survey of measures of spiritual and transpersonal constructs: Part one—research update. *Journal of Transpersonal Psychology, 31*(2), 137-154.

MacDonald, D. A., Kuentzel, J. G., & Friedman, H. L. (1999). A survey of measures of spiritual and transpersonal constructs: Part two—additional instruments. *Journal of Transpersonal Psychology, 31*(2), 155-177.

MacDonald, D. A., LeClair, L., Holland, C. J., Alter, A., & Friedman, H. L. (1995). A survey of measures of transpersonal constructs. *Journal of Transpersonal Psychology*, *27*(2), 171-235.

Manos, C. (2007). Female artists and nature: An intuitive inquiry into transpersonal aspects of creativity in the natural environment. *Dissertation Abstracts International*, *68*(07) 0669A (UMI #3270987).

Maslow, A. H. (1969). The farther reaches of human nature. *Journal of Transpersonal Psychology*, *1*(1), 1-19.

McGrath, R. E. (2011) *Quantitative models in psychology*. Washington, DC: American Psychological Association.

Merleau-Ponty, M. (1962). *Phenomenology of perception* (C. Smith, Trans.). London, UK: Routledge & Keegan Paul. (Original work published 1945 [French])

Merleau-Ponty, M. (1968). *The visible and the invisible* (A. Lingis, Trans.). Evanston, IL: Northwestern University Press. (Original work published 1964 [French])

Mertens, D. M. (2009). *Transformative research and evaluation*. New York, NY: Guilford.

Moustakas, C. (1990). *Heuristic research: Design, methodology, and applications*. Newbury Park, CA: Sage.

National Institutes of Health, Office of Behavioral and Social Sciences Research. (2010). *Best practices for mixed methods research in the human sciences*. Washington, D.C: Author. Retrieved from http://obssr.od.nih.gov/scientific_areas/methodology/mixed_methods_research/introduction.aspx

Netzer, D. (2008). Mystical poetry and imagination: Inspiring transpersonal awareness of spiritual freedom. *Dissertation Abstracts International*, *69*(08) 0669B (UMI #3316128).

Nielsen, J. M. (Ed.). (1990). *Feminist research methods: Exemplary readings in the social sciences*. Boulder, CO: Westview Press.

Perry, A. (2009). Does a unitive mystical experience affect authenticity? An intuitive inquiry of ordinary Protestants. *Dissertation Abstracts International*, *70*(02) 0669B (UMI #3344550).

Phelon, C. R. (2004). Healing presence in the psychotherapist: An intuitive inquiry. *The Humanistic Psychologist*, *32*(4), 342-356.

Reinharz, S. (1992). *Feminist methods in social sciences*. New York, NY: Oxford University Press.

Rickards, D. E. (2006). Illuminating feminine cultural shadow with women espionage agents and the dark goddess. *Dissertation Abstracts International*, *68*(10) 0669B (UMI #3286605).

Root-Bernstein, R., & Root-Bernstein, M. (1999). *Sparks of genius: The thirteen thinking tools of the world's most creative people*. Boston, MA: Houghton Mifflin.

Schleiermacher, F. (1977). *Hermeneutics: The handwritten manuscripts*. In H. Kimmerle (Ed.; D. Luke & J. Forstman, Trans.). Missoula, MT: Scholars Press. (Original work published 1819)

Shepperd, A. E. (2006). The experience of being deeply moved: An intuitive inquiry. *Dissertation Abstracts International*, *67*(05), 0669B (UMI #3221764).

Sheridan, J., & Pineault, A. (1997). Sacred land—sacred stories. In R. Davis-Floyd & P. S. Arvidson (Eds.), *Intuition: The inside story* (pp. 57-80). New York, NY: Routledge.

Sutich, A. (1969). Some considerations regarding transpersonal psychology. *Journal of Transpersonal Psychology*, *1*(1), 11-20.

Tashakkori, A., & Teddlie, C. (2003). *Mixed methodology: Combining qualitative and quantitative approaches*. Thousand Oaks, CA: Sage.

Unthank, K. W. (2007). "Shame on you": Exploring the deep structure of posttrauma survival. *Dissertation Abstracts International*, *68*(07) 0669B (UMI #3270986).

Wertz, F. J., Charmaz, K., McMullen, L. M., Josselson, R., Anderson, R., & McSpadden, E. (2011). *Five ways of doing qualitative analysis: Phenomenological psychology, grounded theory, discourse analysis, narrative research, and intuitive inquiry.* New York, NY: Guilford Press.

Wilber, K. (2000). *Integral psychology: Consciousness, spirit, psychology, therapy.* Boston, MA: Shambhala.

14

Neurophenomenology
Enhancing the Experimental and Cross-Cultural Study of Brain and Experience
Charles D. Laughlin and Adam J. Rock

As far as we can discern, the sole purpose of human existence is to kindle a light in the darkness of mere being.

C. G. Jung, *Memories, Dreams, Reflections*

At this point in the history of social and behavioral science a discussion of methods that is not grounded upon both a neuroepistemology and a neurophenomenology soon will not be worth considering. Why? Because it is now known that consciousness is a function of the internal organization of the brain (Changeux, 1985; Damasio, 2010; Koch, 2004; LeDoux, 2003; Nunez, 2010; Purves, 2010). Every thought, image, feeling, intuition, awareness and sensory experience is mediated by the organ of experience—the brain. Thus questions having to do with how we know, what we can and cannot know, gender-related styles of knowing, the symbolic nature of knowing, how consciousness constructs its world of experience, and how it interacts with the unconscious psyche are really questions about how the brain is organized and develops, and what limiting factors are imposed upon knowing by the organization of the brain and by the physical and sociocultural environments of the developing brain (Mesquita, Barrett, & Smith, 2010). Before we discuss the origin and meaning of the concept of neurophenomenology it would be prudent to explicate the concepts of consciousness and phenomenology.

Consciousness and Phenomenology

Numerous philosophers (e.g., Block, 1995, 2002; Forman, 1996) have suggested that much of the ambiguity associated with the term "consciousness" is due to the fact that a variety of meanings have been attributed to the term. While a "universally accepted definition" is yet to be formulated, consciousness studies are, however, "generally

The Wiley Blackwell Handbook of Transpersonal Psychology, First Edition.
Edited by Harris L. Friedman and Glenn Hartelius.
© 2013 John Wiley & Sons, Ltd. Published 2015 by John Wiley & Sons, Ltd.

definable by a set of phenomena" (Wallace & Fisher, 1987, p. 12). It is salient that, in some cases, the components of the concept of consciousness range from awareness coupled with unconscious functioning (Krippner, 1972), to attention, awareness and memory (Farthing, 1992). In the context of the present chapter, we are concerned with consciousness in the sense of one being consciously aware of something. Thus, we will only consider the conscious awareness aspect of the concept of consciousness.

Almost a century ago, Edmund Husserl (1913/1970), borrowing from Franz Brentano (1838-1917; see Brentano 1874/1973) characterized the structure of human consciousness as being intentional. That is, from Husserl's perspective, "All consciousness...is consciousness of something" (Sartre, 1958, p. li). In this sense, consciousness is characterized by "aboutness" (Moran, 2000); for example, one may be consciously aware of craving. Similarly, in *Being and Nothingness,* Jean-Paul Sartre (1958) constructed the term "positional self-consciousness" to denote the observation that one's consciousness is always directed toward a "transcendent object:" "All that there is of intention in my actual consciousness is directed toward the outside, toward the table; all my judgments or practical activities, all my present inclinations transcend themselves; they aim at the table and are absorbed in it" (p. lii).

Subsequently, Thomas Natsoulas' (1978) seminal theoretical study of consciousness reiterated the assertions of Husserl and Sartre: "One's being conscious, whatever more it might mean, must include one's being aware of something" (p. 910). Adam Rock and Stanley Krippner (2007a, 2007b) have contended that a review of the cognitive psychology literature provides support for Husserl's intentionality thesis. That is to say, numerous cognitive psychologists (e.g., Benjafield, 1992; Matlin, 1998; Nairne, 1997; Solso, 2001) have defined consciousness as one's awareness of "objects" in physical (i.e., "external") and phenomenal (i.e., "inner") space. Consider, for example, a research participant who is exposed to the sound of monotonous drumming during a shamanic journeying experiment. The participant will be consciously aware of, for example, the physical stimulus and his or her subjective experience pertaining to the stimulus (e.g., alterations in time perception, fluctuations in positive affect, enhanced vividness of visual mental imagery).

The previously stated term "phenomenal space" may be further explicated by considering Ned Block's (2002) notion of *phenomenal consciousness* (or *p-consciousness*), which refers to one's conscious awareness of phenomenology. Block equates p-consciousness to experience; thus, p-consciousness properties constitute experiential properties, specifically, the "experiential properties of sensations, feelings and perceptions...thoughts, wants and emotions" (p. 206). For Block, the "totality of the experiential properties of a state are 'what is it like' to have it" (p. 206). For example, one may be p-conscious of the experiential properties of drinking a chocolate milkshake; that is, the "what is it like" to drink the milkshake.

In a manner consistent with Block (2002), David Chalmers (1996) used the term "phenomenal concept of mind" to denote conscious experience. Put simply, this concept of mind is characterized by its qualitative feel or qualia: the "way things seems to us" (Dennett, 2002, p. 226). Consider, for example, a standard cue-reactivity experiment of alcohol craving in which an alcohol cue is presented to a heavy drinker. Extrapolating from Daniel Dennett, the way the alcohol cue looks to the heavy drinker (i.e., the subjective visual quality of the glass of alcohol) is his or her visual experience or quale, how the alcoholic beverage tastes to the heavy drinker is his or her gustatory quale, and so on.

Similarly, Dennett (1993) observed that psychologists and philosophers employ the term "phenomenology" in a rather all-inclusive sense to denote all constituents of conscious experience (e.g., pains, imaginings, mental imagery). Dennett has divided phenomenology—what he has termed "phenom"—into three distinct kinds: (1) external world experiences (e.g., visual, auditory, and tactile sensations linked to physical stimuli); (2) internal world experiences (e.g., daydreams, inner-monologues, intuitions, epiphanies); and (3) experiences of affect (e.g., joy, fear, pain, "sensations" of thirst and hunger). One might argue that this tripartite division is evident in the phenomenology of craving. For example, in the previously outlined cue-reactivity experiment the heavy drinker would encounter external world experiences in the form of visual, olfactory, gustatory, and tactile sensations of the alcohol stimulus. Furthermore, internal world experiences such as recollections of previous drinking acts, anticipation (i.e., cognitively rehearsing the future act of drinking the presented alcoholic beverage), and inner-monologues (e.g., "I'd love a drink"), may occur. Finally, affect experiences (e.g., "sensations" of thirst and craving) may also be present. It should also be evident that Dennett's tripartite division co-maps with Block's (2002) notion of p-conscious properties (i.e., the "experiential properties of sensations, feelings and perceptions . . . thoughts, wants and emotions"; p. 206). For instance, Dennett's external world, internal world, and affect experiences broadly equate with Block's sensations, perceptions, and emotions, respectively.

Ronald Pekala and Etzel Cardeña (2000) suggested that phenomenology "is a term that refers to a philosophy, a research approach, and, in a more general way, the study of experience" (p. 59). It is the "study of experience" that is the focus of this chapter. In the next section we will examine the natural biological basis of lived experience.

Neurophenomenology: Origin and Meaning of the Concept

In 1986, Professor Kiyohiko Ikeda of Yamanashi University, Japan, invited Charles Laughlin to an international meeting to discuss the role of structuralism in biology. Biologists from around the world had begun applying structuralist theory to the origin of species and to other problems that they felt were not amply explained by Darwinian theory alone. Professor Ikeda had read Laughlin's earlier work, *Biogenetic Structuralism* (Laughlin & d'Aquili, 1974), that had been translated into Japanese, and thought he might have something to contribute. The workshop on structuralism in biology occurred at the Biological Laboratory, Kansai Medical University, Osaka, Japan, during December 7-11, 1986. Approximately 50 scholars attended the meeting, among whom were biologists Brian Goodwin, David M. Lambert, Atuhiro Sibatani, and David Elder (Sibatani, 1987).

Francisco Varela also attended and showed considerable interest in Laughlin's paper, which was entitled "The prefrontosensorial polarity principle: Toward a neurophenomenology of intentionality" (Laughlin, 1988). Varela was very taken with the idea of neurophenomenology, and later in 1989 wrote to ask Laughlin to do a book exploring the idea for the Shambhala Publications *New Science Library* series, which Varela edited. The book Laughlin wrote with his late colleagues John McManus and Eugene d'Aquili, entitled *Brain, Symbol and Experience: Toward a Neurophenomenology of Human Consciousness* (1990), came out in that series (later republished by Columbia University Press). Among other things, the book explored the phenomenology of the great philosopher, Edmund Husserl and argued that the essential structures discovered during the course of phenomenological investigation must be mediated by universal properties and structures of the nervous system.

Varela appropriated the concept of neurophenomenology from that work and made it his own (Varela, 1996, 1999)—for example, "In brief, I approach temporality by following a general research direction *I have called neurophenomenology,* in which lived experience and its natural biological basis are linked by mutual constraints provided by their respective descriptions" (Varela, 1999, p. 267, emphasis added). So far as we know, Varela did not credit Laughlin's group for having developed either the concept or the approach. But what is far more important here is that he effectively caused a schism in the neurophenomenology literature into two streams of thought, one that for simplicity's sake we will label the *cognitive neurophenomenologists* and the other the *cultural neurophenomenologists.*[1] They are fairly distinct strains and are usually characterized by not referencing the works done by the other—in our opinion a very silly and deplorable situation, which we hope to remedy here.

Neurophenomenology: The Cognitive Neurophenomenologists

The cognitive neurophenomenologists are primarily philosophers and neuroscientists influenced by Varela (1996, 1999; see Rudrauf, Lutz, Cosmelli, LaChaux, & Le Van Quyen, 2003, for a summary of Varela's work), who have defined the approach in a way that requires the naturalization of phenomenology (Varela, 1997). Varela (1996) went on to elaborate:

> On the one hand, we are concerned with a process of external emergence with well-defined neurobiological attributes, on the other, with a phenomenological description that stays close to our lived experience. The nature of the sought-after circulation one seeks is no less than that of mutual constraints of both accounts, including both the potential bridges and contradictions between them. What is the specific nature of the passages between these two accounts in the case at hand? (p. 305)

Following Varela's lead, cognitive neurophenomenologists tend to define the approach within the contexts of philosophy of mind and cognitive neuroscience. Psychologists who do apply neurophenomenology tend to do so to experimental work, while philosophers use the approach as a kind of "naturalized epistemology" (Kornblith, 1985). Cognitive neurophenomenologists have worked on a variety of problems, including the embodiment of consciousness (Thompson, Lutz, & Cosmelli, 2005; Thompson & Varela, 2001), self-consciousness (Lutz, 2007), the so-called "hard problem" of consciousness (Bayne, 2004), hypnosis (Cardeña, Lehmann, Jönsson, & Terhune, 2007), Whiteheadian metaphysics (Marstaller, 2009), the "spontaneity" of consciousness (Hanna & Thompson, 1999), the problem of relating first person reports to third-person biobehavioral research (Lutz & Thompson, 2003;

Thompson, 2006), and the problem of the neural correlates of consciousness (Noë & Thompson, 2004).

Neurophenomenology: The Cultural Neurophenomenologists

The cultural neurophenomenologists are mainly anthropologists working in the areas of dreaming, the senses, medical anthropology, symbolism, and of course *transpersonal anthropology* (Laughlin, 1989, 1994). Research is almost always naturalistic and non-experimental. If there is one characteristic that distinguished this branch it is that, unlike most academic philosophers and psychologists, there is a primary focus on culture.[2] Indeed, the lack of serious concern for culture and cross-cultural comparison has been an ethnocentric bias that has typified psychology for decades. "On the one hand, it is generally agreed that the need and ability to live in the human medium of culture is one of the central characteristics of human beings. On the other hand, it is difficult for many academic psychologists to assign culture more than a secondary, often superficial role in the constitution of our mental life" (Cole, 1996, p. 1; see also Berry, Poortinga, Breugelmans, Chasiotis, & Sam, 2011).

In keeping with the field of anthropology, the value of neurophenomenology is naturalistic and introspective, and application is directed toward diverse subjects encountered in cross-cultural comparison, and ethnographic and applied fieldwork; for example, consciousness (Laughlin, 1988), religion and spiritual practices (Dornan, 2004; Krippner & Combs, 2002; Laughlin, 1992, 2011; Peters, 2004; Rodd, 2003; Vásquez, 2011; Winkelman, 1996a, 1996b, 2010), theory (Laughlin & Throop, 2006; Laughlin et al., 1990; Peters, 2000; Throop, 2003b;), the anthropology of experience (Desjarlais & Throop, 2011), time consciousness and culture (Laughlin, 1992; Laughlin & Throop, 2008), dreaming and dream cultures (Kirmayer, 2009; Laughlin, 2011), the structure of the ancient mind (Dornan, 2004; Laughlin & Loubser, 2010), the nature of the "ethnographic epoché" (Throop, 2012) and healing (Groisman & Sell, 1996).

Neurophenomenologies

The most direct method for ascertaining the relations between consciousness and the nervous system is by way of combining the methods of phenomenology and neuroscience into a kind of neurophenomenology. Neurophenomenology is a powerful method that relies upon a dialogue between descriptions of the essential properties of consciousness as ascertained through trained contemplation on the one hand, and the structures and processes of the brain discovered in neuroscience on the other hand. When Laughlin originally defined the method of neurophenomenology, he paired research in the neurophysiology of experience with the methods used in Husserlian transcendental phenomenology. There was a reason for specifying Husserlian phenomenology, for the concept is a very fuzzy one in philosophy—there are as many phenomenologies as there are phenomenologists (Kockelmans, 1967). For many phenomenologists (like Heidegger and his notion of *Dasein*), the term simply means what we as humans learn from reflecting upon our own experience. But for the authors, that

definition amounts to what might be called "naïve" phenomenology—philosophical
reflections on the order of: "As I reflect upon the green of the leaves on the tree outside my study window." In our opinion, the value of neurophenomenological research
depends both on the advances in neuropsychology and in the disciplined application
of what Laughlin and his colleagues have called *mature contemplation* (Laughlin et al.,
1990, Chapter 11; d'Aquili, Laughlin, & McManus, 1993). Varela did pick up on this
element of Laughlin's earlier program, for he was, as d'Aquili, McManus and Laughlin
were, a practicing meditator. He clearly had more than naïve phenomenology in mind
(cf. Rudrauf et al., 2003), as evidenced by his discussion of Husserl, Merleau-Ponty,
and Heidegger (Varela, 1999), and by his attitude reflected in:

> However, a simple undisciplined introspective approach is not the solution; the "just-take-
> a-look" or "seeing inside" attitude must be overcome. Neurophenomenology implies
> "gathering a research community armed with new pragmatic tools for the development
> of a science of consciousness." This involves a "call for transforming the style and values
> of the research community itself," in other words, that researchers themselves, as they
> are specialists in neurosciences for instance, become specialists in the phenomenology of
> conscious experience: "My proposal implies that every good student of cognitive science
> who is also interested in issues at the level of mental experience, *must inescapably attain a
> level of mastery in phenomenological examination in order to work seriously with first-person
> accounts.*" (Varela & Shear, 1999, p. 2, emphasis in original)

Although Laughlin is a practicing Buddhist,[3] his work in phenomenology focused
upon the method of Husserlian *transcendental phenomenology*—that is, introspection
carried out by a trained meditator who has succeeded in "bracketing" or "reducing"[4]
all received assumptions (what Husserl called the *natural attitude*) about his/her
consciousness, and has realized the real (illusory) nature of the ego. Only then can a
phenomenologist accurately discover the essential properties of his/her consciousness
and then seek to account for such elements by way of neuroscience. This bracketing
or "setting aside" of one's natural attitude leads to a state of consciousness[5,6] which
Husserl (1931/1977) called the *phenomenological* or *transcendental epoché*.

The pursuit and maturation of the *phenomenological attitude* (Husserl, 1931/1977;
Koestenbaum, 1967; Miller 1984; Schmitt, 1967) produces a state of mind marked
by astonishment and wonder, and by a cognition relatively free of the constraints of
received, culturally conditioned frames of reference (see Fink, 1981; for an Eastern
view of this state of mind, see Suzuki, 1970). This freedom allows the inner-directed
study of the factors of consciousness as objects of awareness, rather than conditioned
attention to phenomena naively presumed from the natural attitude to be "out there"
somewhere and requiring response (see Funke, 1981). The contemplative comes to
realize that each and every state of mind is componental and unitary. In addition, the
mature contemplative can slow the process of entrainment down to the very simple so
as to discern the atomic levels of experience: pixels, temporal epochs, impermanence
of objects, purity, parallel processes, componental nature of the empirical ego, or
"me" (and cognized ego, or "I"), causation, and invisible causation.

This is a very crucial point, for even if one has access to the very finest neuroscience
available, but the phenomenological data remain naïve (pre-epoché, pre-reduction),

then very likely the neurophenomenology will be naïve as well, and very likely erroneous. For example, it is apparent to most mature contemplatives known by the authors that they, as we ourselves, at some point in their meditative careers came to realize that sensory data are pixelated, particulated, or granular to perception (Laughlin, 1992; Laughlin et al., 1990). In other words, there comes a time when many contemplatives reach a specific epoché within which they are able to perceive that their entire sensorium (conscious sensory field) is made up of points (dots, granules, particles, *bindus, yods,* and so forth). After the epoché, the sensorium is experienced as a field of pixels that is perceptually and cognitively distinguishable into sensory modes, and within sensory modes into forms and events. The fundamental act of perception is the abstraction and reinforcement of invariant features within the order of an unfolding and dissolving field of dots (see Gibson, 1979). In our experience, apprehending the pixelated nature of the senses is easiest to realize visually, but eventually sounds, tastes, touches are all seen to be made up of sensory particles. Once one realizes this epoché, one may easily apprehend the texture of the sensorium at will. Furthermore, when concentration upon sensory molecular pixels reaches a sufficient intensity, awareness of gross sensory objects is lost.

Whether or not a theorist has attained this "pixelation" epoché is evident by how they experience and think about their own consciousness, and what understanding of consciousness they project upon others. For instance, Chalmers (1996), the Australian philosopher of mind, has famously defined what he called "the hard problem" of consciousness. By that he meant, after all the mental functions are explained by reference to their underlying neurophysiology, the fact of experience remains a puzzle. "Why is it that when our cognitive systems engage in visual and auditory information-processing, we have visual or auditory experience: the quality of deep blue, the sensation of middle C? . . . It is widely agreed that experience arises from a physical basis, but we have no good explanation of why and how it so arises. Why should physical processing give rise to a rich inner life at all?" (Chalmers, 1995, p. 201). Nowhere in his presentation of the "hard problem" did he evince the epoché noted above. He did not seem to realize that his patch of "deep blue" is (1) pixelated, and (2) a cognitive operation of his own brain. A patch of blue is the brain's symbolic representation of electromagnetic energies striking the retinae. In other words, blue pixels are the brain's way of representing a specific range of electromagnetic frequencies to itself. When one realizes that *all sensory experience is a cognitive act on the part of the brain,* then the so-called "hard problem" vanishes, or is at least rendered easier.

Necessity of Mature Contemplation

Some scholars accept the importance of disciplined phenomenology and some do not. Following Varela's lead closely, neuroscientist Antoine Lutz (2002) noted that

neurophenomenological investigation requires a specific, rigorous technique. What is needed here is to overcome the "just-take-a-look" attitude with regard to experience that is pervasive in cognitive protocols or the dominant philosophy of mind. Western and Eastern phenomenological traditions have been favored, as we will see later, as appropriate

pragmatic tools, but other first-person approaches are being explored. The phenomenological methodology relies on the cultivation of a gesture of reflexive awareness, called
phenomenological reduction. . . . The goal of this methodological reduction is to attain
intuitions of the descriptive structural invariants of an experience. (p. 133)

In a subsequent study, Lutz (2007) applied the method to correlate self-awareness
of seizure onset with the underlying neurobiology of awareness—an ingenious project
that involved training epileptics to recognize the "prodromes," or onset signals that
arise before seizure.

By contrast, philosopher Lars Marstaller (2009) has applied the perspective to the
process philosophy of Alfred North Whitehead. He argued that Whitehead's "phenomenology" can be used to "extend" the range of neurophenomenological exploration. Although Laughlin has long considered Whitehead to be a remarkably astute
contemplative (Laughlin, 1973; Laughlin & d'Aquili, 1974), by no stretch of the
imagination is his approach a phenomenology in the disciplined Husserlian sense,
or even of the Buddhist *vippasana* variety. Whatever value Marstaller's essay has for
metaphysics, it represents how rapidly the application of neurophenomenology can
be watered down in the phenomenology department. This slippage into naïve phenomenology can be apparent even in work by authors who are themselves meditators,
as seems to be the case in Laurence Kirmayer's (2009) study in which he used the
term neurophenomenology as a kind of shorthand for emphasizing the relationship
between the experience and the neurobiology of nightmares. Indeed, some writers
have gone so far as to question the need for phenomenological training at all in
carrying off a neurophenomenology. Philosopher Tim Bayne (2004) wrote:

At the heart of neurophenomenology is the claim that Husserlian phenomenology has
a unique and privileged method of describing the first-person nature of consciousness.
Phenomenology is unique in that it is importantly different from the standard first-person
methodologies employed in consciousness studies; and it is privileged in that it is more
rigorous than such methodologies. I have my doubts about both claims. I say this with
some tentativeness, for my knowledge of the phenomenological tradition is limited. But
let me explain why I am inclined to think that the phenomenological method is neither
unique nor privileged. (p. 351)

Bayne went on to exhibit a very typical ignorance of phenomenological methods. This
kind of criticism has been leveled at phenomenology for decades, both in philosophy
and in psychology, almost always by scholars who have not trained themselves in
the method, and who have not experienced the distinct states of consciousness the
method evokes.

Neurophenomenology of Time Consciousness

A factor that is often missed by philosophers debating phenomenology is that mature
contemplation leads through a series of transpersonal[7] experiences, resulting in
irreversible changes in self-awareness and ego-identification. These changes allow
"seeing" in new ways, ways that pre-epoché commentators cannot know from direct

experience—the kind of difference in seeing alluded to in such Zen aphorisms as "before awakening chop wood, after awakening chop wood."

There are numerous realizations pertaining to the essential structures of consciousness that are available to mature, disciplined phenomenology that are also amenable to a neurophenomenological treatment. One of the problems that attracted both Varela (1999) and Laughlin (1992)—presumably independently[8]—was the structure of time-consciousness. This was a very natural problem for phenomenologists, and Husserl wrote one of his finest studies on the subject—*The Phenomenology of Internal Time-Consciousness* (Husserl, 1905/1964; see also Kortooms, 2002). Both Varela and Laughlin grounded their analyses upon the Husserlian reduction that Laughlin discussed at length, but which Varela did not treat. In any event, Husserl (1905/1964; see also Landgrebe, 1981; Miller, 1984) saw the "primal impressional datum" of perception as being a synthesis of recently past acts of perception ("retention"), of the streaming present ("now points") and of the anticipated future ("protention"). As Husserl (1905/1964) noted:

> the continuity of running-off [unfolding] of an enduring Object is a continuum whose phases are the continua of the modes of running-off of the different temporal points of the duration of the Object.... Since a new now is always presenting itself, each now is changed into a past, and thus the entire continuity of the running-off of the pasts of the preceding points moves uniformly "downward" into the depths of the past.... Every primordially constitutive process is animated by protentions which voidly constitute and intercept what is coming, as such, in order to bring it to fulfillment. (pp. 49-50, 76)

These three phases of temporal unfolding constitute a "perceptual epoch" (not to be confused with *the* epoché)—retention, the "now" point, and protention combining to form the naïve "present." The relations among memories of patterns abstracted from recently past epochs are, as Husserl (1905/1964) noted, "primordial"—that is, fundamental to how consciousness works, fundamental to the neural organization mediating perceptual acts. These are cognitions that entrain with what is happening in the sensorium "right now" to produce the perception of enduring objects and the sense of continuity of events.

The phases of the perceptual epoch are not theoretical distinctions, they are phenomenologically apparent. As a contemplative's concentration upon the flow of sensory experience increases and the mind slows down its processes, the sensory flow is revealed to present in a continuous, but pulsing, iterative flow (Dainton, 2006; Damasio, 1999). It is by studying the discernible *fine structure*[9] of perceptual epochs, the relations between epochs, and the temporal binding of epochs that one is able to discover the essential and universal nature of time-consciousness—what Maurice Bloch (1977) called "universal time"; the experience of time that underlies the very structure of subjective life regardless of one's particular cultural heritage. After completing the requisite reductions, the mature contemplative is prepared to watch this process unfold in their own experience. Not only is the sensorium comprised of pixels, it flickers, and this flickering is quite distinctive. But it is a harder characteristic of perception to realize than merely apprehending sensorial points.

For one thing, the so-called "now-point"[10] is not a "durationless interface between past and future" (Dainton, 2006, p. 120). Perceptual epochs are not instantaneous. Contemplatives know this because the reduction to the pure "now" involves the falling away of retention and protention until all one is aware of is the intermittent streaming of sensory data, as well as patterns and topographical relations among patterns (color, tonal, textural relations, spatial, and geometric relations, etc.) as they arise and pass away in the sensorium. In this reduction to the actual now, all gross cognitive and behavioral acts such as recognition, anticipation, reaction, rememoration, and so forth, have dropped away. The stream of data (e.g., in the case of speech, the sounds transmitted through the air by the speaker's vocalizations) arise simultaneously within epochs and then pass away. There is clearly some very short duration involved in this process, but it would be impossible to measure it using phenomenological methods alone. Perceptual epochs are thus not really snapshot-like. They are neither static, nor instantaneous. They are themselves what Husserl called "temporal objects"; they are objects of experience that have a durational expanse, however minute. The data that arise and pass away in epochs "take time" to present. But any and all data or patterns arising within any one epoch are experienced as simultaneous (see Pastor, Day, Macaluso, Friston, & Frackowiak, 2004).

The temporal organization of experience is thus a very complex matter, and involves areas of the brain in addition to those mediating perceptual epochs. It would not be unfair to say that the whole brain is involved in temporal processing. The role of the brain's prefrontal cortex (PFC) in selecting, exciting, and ordering sensorial activity into a temporally meaningful plan has been discussed elsewhere (Laughlin, 1988; Laughlin et al., 1990; see also Pribram, 1971). Laughlin has suggested that phenomenal experience is constituted within the dialogue between PFC imposed order ("intentional meaning") and sensorial order ("perceptual meaning"). Part of the dialogue between prefrontal and sensorial structures seems to involve septo-hippocampal centers in the midbrain. Orbitofrontal projections from prefrontal cortex richly innervate the hippocampus and dorsolateral prefrontal projections enter the lateral septal area (see Gray, 1982). These areas are also connected to secondary sensory areas and seem to receive sensory information that is already abstracted from the initial processing in the primary sensory cortex. All of this processing is designed to extract, make meaningful, and act upon the world as portrayed in perceptual epochs. Temporal-causal associations, durational motion in space, the general sense of the "streaming" of consciousness are all grounded upon the primordial structure of the perceptual epoch.

Cultural Neurophenomenology

Other applications could be examined from a cognitive neurophenomenological point of view. However, the discussion will now turn to the difference a cultural aspect makes in the analysis. Psychologists until recently have tended to ignore the impact of culture upon the functioning of the mind. In their attempt to approximate the rigors of scientific methods practiced in the so-called "hard" sciences, psychology often produces a naïve scientism in theory-building and empirical research. In striving to focus on the transcultural structures of perception, cognition, memory, and so on, psychology can often be faulted for presenting an overly a-cultural, and therefore ethnocentric, understanding of human mentation. Moreover, in relying heavily on laboratory experimentation, psychologists have all too often ignored the ways in which consciousness is concretely manifest in everyday life, especially in the lives of non-Western peoples. This failing in psychology is nowhere more evident than in accounts of transpersonal experiences.

In order to introduce the role of culture in experience, Laughlin and his colleague, C. Jason Throop, have developed what they call a *cultural neurophenomenology* (Laughlin & Throop, 2006, 2008, 2009). This is an approach that integrates the results of neurophenomenological analysis into a cross-cultural perspective—an approach that requires a confluence of at least three skill sets: (1) a working knowledge of neuroscience, especially neurophysiology, (2) post-epoché, mature contemplation, and (3) a working knowledge of comparative ethnology (Eggan, 1954). One of the things we are able to show using this method is how cultural conditioning (i.e., enculturation, socialization) can produce variations in the everyday presentation of essential neurocognitive and perceptual structures among different peoples. The result is a perspective that in true Jamesian fashion[11] is rooted in experience and is capable of incorporating both the neurobiological and cultural influences upon individual experience. Such a new language consists of a set of terms that allows for a currency of exchange between the domains of individual experience, culture, and extramental reality without shifting back and forth between incommensurable languages of mentality and physicality.

Although Husserl's work is rarely viewed in this way, it is thoroughly cognizant of the role played by culture in conditioning consciousness. It is, after all, culture that (in part) conditions a person's natural attitude toward phenomena, and that must be bracketed before mature phenomenology may be accomplished. Furthermore, there are really two directions of study implied in Husserl's approach, one inward to the discovery of the structures of one's own subjectivity, and one outward to explore the historical and cultural influences on that subjectivity. One is incomplete without the other, and what we are terming a cultural neurophenomenology is predicated on the integration of both movements. Indeed, this is precisely the point that Husserl (1913/1970) was making in his classic book, *The Crisis in the European Sciences and Transcendental Phenomenology,* when he argued:

> [for] an autonomous philosopher with the will to liberate himself from all prejudices, he must have the insight that all the things he takes for granted are prejudices, that all prejudices are obscurities arising out of a sedimentation of tradition—not merely judgments whose truth is as yet undecided—and that this is true even of the great task and idea, which is called 'philosophy.' All judgments which count as philosophical are related back to this task, this idea. A historical, backward reflection of the sort under discussion is thus actually the deepest kind of self-reflection aimed at self-understanding in terms of what we are truly seeking as the historical beings we are. (p. 72)

Cultural Neurophenomenology of Time-Consciousness

A return to the neurophenomenology of time consciousness will show how the addition of the cultural ingredient allows for a cross-cultural application of the method. It has been seen that all brains process the temporal dimension of perception in the same way. The brain retains and binds a working memory of recently past now moments (retention) to the real now point and anticipated future now points (protention). The now point is the sensorium refreshing its presentation every fraction of a second, and to the mature contemplative may appear as a flickering of the sensory field. If data present in the same now point, then they are perceived as simultaneous. If they are presented in different now points, they will be perceived as occurring in time. This is a rudimentary cognitive act, and is the primordial structure of lineal time.

In the past, much was made in anthropology about how the time maps of traditional peoples differ from those of Western society. Traditional (sometimes called "primitive") peoples, according to this view, have a fundamentally different mentality than so-called civilized folk, and thus live more in the present, and cognize time as a system of recurrent cycles, while Westerners live with their minds riveted on the future and cognize time in a lineal series of episodes (see e.g., Evans-Pritchard, 1939; Levy-Bruhl, 1923/1966;). The latter time-map was assumed to be the product of the industrial revolution and facilitated by the invention of clocks. Such dualistic accounts of cultures and their time-maps have more recently come into disrepute as being both over-simplistic and empirically inaccurate (Adam, 1990; Gell, 1992; Ten-Houten, 2005). A moment's reflection about the Western time-map shows that life is lived out in a welter of recognized, recurring cycles—day and night, a weekly round of days ("TGIF"), annual seasons, such recurring holidays as Christmas, Easter, Veterans Day, birthdays, annual vacations, a daily cycle of more or less ritualized meals (breakfast, lunch, high tea, dinner, night time snack), annual round of sports seasons, and on-and-on. By the same token, as Alfred Gell (1992) has pointed out, if traditional peoples are only aware of cycles of recurring events, how is it possible that they can distinguish last year's event from other different events of the same kind in previous years—an ability they obviously have, or they could have no sense of history.

Culture thus influences the way one orients themself to duration—usually durations over minutes, hours, and years. As with other aspects of experience, one becomes conditioned to integrate everyday life within a worldview that emphasizes a particular standpoint with respect to time, causation, and history. All humans may experience sensory time-consciousness in the same way, but just which objects and events receive one's awareness will vary from person to person and from group to group. How the sense of temporal continuity and cyclicity is integrated will be informed from personal history and a particular society's worldview. The most dramatic and forceful of influences will be the cosmology of the group to which one belongs, including its stock of lore and mythic stories, its cycle of ritual enactments and the teachings of its purveyors (shamans, healers, parents, instructors, teachers, leaders, and so forth).

Cultural Neurophenomenology of Lucid Dreaming

Another example of the application of the cultural neurophenomenological approach is in relating lucid dream experiences to neurophysiological processes. One of the most common sources of transpersonal experience is in dreaming, especially when dreams are lucid. A dream is considered lucid by psychologists if one becomes aware within the dream that one is in fact dreaming and not awake (LaBerge, 1980, 1985). Usually something causes the individual to wake up in a dream, almost always during the rapid eye movement (REM) state (Ogilvie, Hunt, Sawicki, & McGowan, 1978). Those who participate in sleep lab research are taught to maintain lucidity, exercise control, and communicate with researchers using predefined signals (LaBerge, Nagel, Dement, & Zarcone, 1981). All the indications are that lucidity in dreaming is mediated by increased involvement of prefrontal cortical areas of the forebrain.

Anthropologically speaking, the normal psychological take on lucidity from a cross-cultural point of view tends to be quite ethnocentric. Lucidity is uncommon among Western dreamers because they are raised in a materialist, technocratic society that pays scant attention to dreaming and other alternative states. Normal dreaming for Westerners tends to involve minimal awareness and recall, as well as bizarre ideation. This is undoubtedly caused by the lack of prefrontal cortical mediation of higher cognitive functioning during dreaming. However, many societies on the planet do value their dreaming and consider dreams to be as real as waking states. Hence lucidity is quite common in non-Western cultures (Laughlin, 2011). What is usually ignored by non-Western lucid dreamers is the awareness of waking up in the dream, hyper-awareness of the dream ego, and emphasis upon the exercise of control so important in sleep lab research. Again, the cultural dimension impacts the variety of dream phenomenology, and in most cases of non-Western dream cultures, people take lucidity for granted. Such cultures routinely seek interaction with the otherwise invisible spiritual dimension, information from ancestors and other entities, and divinatory insight into the future, all of which are typically alien to Western ways of knowing.

Conclusion

Neurophenomenology is a powerful explanatory and research tool that goes a long ways toward controlling for the consciousness "gap" between the worlds of experience and extramental reality (Laughlin & Throop, 2009; Roy, Petitot, Pachoud, & Varela, 1999). It is especially powerful when the phenomenology is that of mature contemplation, and not merely first person descriptions of experience (Gallagher & Sørensen, 2006). Unfortunately, there is and will continue to be a temptation on the part of researchers to water down the need for skilled phenomenology. In some cases there will be no alternative, as when the researcher is depending upon first person reports of subjects and patients who may or may not have been trained as phenomenologists. But learning to become a mature contemplative—a pre-requisite for anything like a Husserlian transcendental phenomenology—is a transpersonal project. One cannot become a mature contemplative without transforming one's self, one's ego. Hence, there may be a resistance on the part of many to undertake the rigors of this kind of training.

This discussion only begins to explore the range of problems that might profitably come within the purview of a neurophenomenological analysis. For cognitive neurophenomenology, the implications are radical, in that the approach requires considerable alteration in the design of laboratory or clinical research protocols. For cultural neurophenomenologists, the challenge is to acquire the requisite training in neuroscience (or add a neuroscientist to the team) as well as learn to use transpersonal field methods to access the experiences had by one's non-Western hosts while in alternative states of consciousness.

Notes

1. The latter term was coined by anthropologist C. Jason Throop.
2. With the notable exception of the field of cross-cultural psychology (Berry et al., 2011; van de Vijver, Chasiotis, & Breugelmans, 2011).
3. Laughlin was a Tibetan Buddhist monk for seven years and studied under a number of Tantric masters, including Namgyal Rinpoche, Kalu Rinpoche, and especially the great Sakya lama, Chogye Trichen Rinpoche, his preceptor. Varela was also a Buddhist, studying under Trungpa Rinpoche.
4. "Reduction" is given its root meaning by Husserl—"return," "go back"—and refers to his dictum "return to the things themselves," or how things present themselves to consciousness while ignoring all received knowledge about those things.
5. Rock and Krippner (2007a, 2007b, 2011, 2012) have argued that "states of consciousness" may be more accurately referred to as "states of phenomenology."
6. A state of consciousness is typically defined as "[the set] of mental episodes (e.g., perceptions, feelings, thoughts) of which one is or can readily become directly aware. Typically a stream of such states [of consciousness] occurs while one is conscious" (Natsoulas, 1978, p. 912). It may be observed that the notion of a "state of consciousness" retains the characteristic of intentionality exemplified by the conscious awareness component of the concept of consciousness. In the context of the definitional boundaries of the term "state of consciousness," it is evident that conscious awareness' transcendent object is a set of mental episodes and, extrapolating from Block (2002), the experiential properties of this set constitute phenomenology.

    However, Tart (1975) has argued that terms such as "states of consciousness" and "altered states of consciousness" have "come to be used too loosely, to mean whatever is on one's mind at the moment" (p. 5). Consequently, Tart (1975) developed the term "discrete states of consciousness" (d-SoC) in an attempt to rectify this terminological problem. A d-SoC may be defined as "a unique configuration or system of psychological structures or subsystems... that maintains its integrity or identity as a recognizable system in spite of variations in input from the environment and in spite of various (small) changes in the subsystems" (p. 62).

    Pekala (1985) asserted that, from Tart's (1975) perspective, it is the pattern or configuration of these different structures or subsystems (i.e., phenomenological elements) that constitutes a d-SoC. In contrast, Singer (1977) argued that it is the intensity of these different elements, rather than the pattern, that defines a d-SoC. Pekala and Wenger (1983) synthesize the essential aspects of Tart's (1975) and Singer's (1977) conceptions to define a SoC as the "particular intensity and pattern of associated phenomenological parameters that characterize one' s subjective experience during a given time" (p. 252-253).
7. Hartelius, Caplan, and Rardin (2007) conducted a thematic analysis of 160 definitions of transpersonal psychology from 1968 through 2002, collected from the published literature and from colleagues within the field. Three themes emerged from their analysis, which broadly capture the fundamental constituents of definitions of transpersonal psychology: (i) beyond-ego, (ii) integrative/holistic, and (iii) transformative. With regards to (i), the term "ego" is not being used in the Freudian sense of the mediator between the id and superego. Instead, ego refers to one's individual sense of self with a precise space-time

location. Thus, (i) suggests that transpersonal psychology is concerned with experiences whereby one's self-sense transcends the ordinary spatial and temporal limitations (cf. Friedman, 1983). In terms of (ii), the terms "integrative/holistic" suggest that transpersonal psychology is concerned with the whole person within the context of his/her life-world. Therefore, transpersonal psychologists do not engage in forms of reductionism (e.g., biological), nor do they consider individuals in isolation from their natural world, social group, and so forth. As for (iii), the term "transformative" suggests that transpersonal psychologists focus on practices (e.g., meditation) that allow the individual to attain conscious states (e.g., *samadhi*) and stages (altruism, compassion, enlightenment) that are ultimately more positive and meaningful relative to ordinary waking states or conventional human development. Extrapolating from the results of Hartelius et al. (2007), a transpersonal experience is an, ultimately, positive transformative experience characterized by the transcendence of ego.

8. Varela does not cite Laughlin's earlier study, so it is assumed he was unaware of it.
9. John Stroud's (1967) useful term "fine structure" is used here to refer to distinct, elemental and universal patterns discernable within experience by mature, trained introspection.
10. This was originally William James' (1890/1981) term.
11. See Laughlin and McManus (1995) on the relevance of William James to an anthropology of consciousness, and Throop (2003a) on the significance of James' writings about the temporal structure of consciousness.

References

Adam, B. (1990). *Time and social theory*. Philadelphia, PA: Temple University Press.

Bayne, T. (2004). Closing the gap? Some questions for neurophenomenology. *Phenomenology and the Cognitive Sciences 3*, 349-364.

Benjafield, J. G. (1992). *Cognition*. Englewood Cliffs, NJ: Prentice-Hall International.

Berry, J. M., Poortinga, Y. H., Breugelmans, S. M., Chasiotis, A., & Sam, D. L. (2011). *Cross-cultural psychology: Research and applications* (3rd ed.). Cambridge, UK: Cambridge University Press.

Bloch, M. (1977). The past and the present in the present. *Man, 12*(2), 278-292.

Block, N. (1995). On a confusion about a function of consciousness. *Behavioral and Brain Sciences, 18*, 227-247.

Block, N. (2002). Concepts of consciousness. In D. Chalmers (Ed.), *Philosophy of mind: Classical and contemporary readings* (pp. 206-218). New York, NY: Oxford University Press.

Brentano, F. (1973). *Psychology from an empirical standpoint (Psychologie vom empirischen Standpunkte* (A. Rancurello et al., Trans.). New York, NY: Humanities Press. (Original work published 1874)

Cardeña, E., Lehmann, D., Jönsson, P., & Terhune, D. (2007). The neurophenomenology of hypnosis. *Proceedings of the 50th Annual Conventions of the Parapsychological Association*, 17-30.

Chalmers, D. (1995). Facing up to the problem of consciousness. *Journal of Consciousness Studies, 2*(3), 200-219.

Chalmers, D. (1996). *The conscious mind: In search of a fundamental theory*. Oxford, UK: Oxford University Press.

Changeux, J.-P. (1985). *Neuronal man: The biology of mind*. Oxford, UK: Oxford University Press.

Cole, M. (1996). *Cultural psychology*. Cambridge, UK: Harvard University Press.

Dainton, B. (2006). *Stream of consciousness: Unity and continuity in conscious experience* (rev. paperback ed.). London, UK: Routledge.

Damasio, A. 1999). *The feeling of what happens: Body and emotion in the making of consciousness.* New York, NY: Harcourt.

Damasio, A. (2010). *Self comes to mind: Constructing the conscious brain.* New York, NY: Pantheon.

D'Aquili, E. G., Laughlin, C. D., & McManus, J. (1993). Mature contemplation. *Zygon, 28*(2), 133-176.

Dennett, D. C. (1993). *Consciousness explained.* London, UK: Penguin.

Dennett, D. C. (2002). Quining qualia. In D. Chalmers (Ed.), *Philosophy of mind: Classical and contemporary readings* (pp. 226-246). New York, NY: Oxford University Press.

Desjarlais, R., & Throop, C. J T. (2011). Phenomenological approaches in anthropology. *Annual Review of Anthropology, 40*, 87-102.

Dornan, J. (2004). Beyond belief: Religious experience, ritual, and cultural neurophenomenology in the interpretation of past religious systems. *Cambridge Archaeological Journal, 14*(1), 25-36.

Eggan, F. (1954). Social anthropology and the method of controlled comparison. *American Anthropologist, 56*, 743-763.

Evans-Pritchard, E. E. (1939). Nuer time reckoning. *Africa, 12*(2), 189-216.

Farthing, G. W. (1992). *The psychology of consciousness.* Englewood Cliffs, NJ: Prentice-Hall.

Fink, E. (1981). The problem of the phenomenology of Edmund Husserl. In W. McKenna, R. M. Harlan, & L. E. Winters (Eds.), *Apriori and world* (pp. 21-55). The Hague, The Netherlands: Martinus Nijhoff.

Forman, R. K. C. (1996). *What does mysticism have to teach us about consciousness?* Revised version of a paper delivered to "Towards a Science of Consciousness 1996" (Tuscon II), April.

Friedman, H. (1983). The Self-Expansiveness Level Form: A conceptualization and measurement of a transpersonal construct. *Journal of Transpersonal Psychology, 15*(1), 37-50.

Funke, G. (1981). A transcendental-phenomenological investigation concerning universal idealism, intentional analysis and the genesis of habitus. In W. McKenna, R. M. Harlan and L. E. Winters (Eds.), *Apriori and world* (pp. 71-113). The Hague, The Netherlands: Martinus Nijhoff.

Gallagher, S. & Sørensen, J. B. (2006). Experimenting with phenomenology. *Consciousness and Cognition, 15*, 119-134.

Gell, A. (1992). *The anthropology of time.* Oxford, UK: Berg.

Gibson, J. (1979). *The ecological approach to visual perception.* Boston, MA: Houghton Mifflin.

Gray, J. A. (1982). *The neuropsychology of anxiety.* Oxford, UK: Oxford University Press.

Groisman, A. & Sell, A. B. (1996). Healing power: Neurophenomenology, culture, and therapy of Santo Daime. In M. Winkelman & W. Andritzky (Eds.), *Yearbook of cross-cultural medicine and psychotherapy* (Vol. 4, pp. 279-287). Berlin, Germany: Verlag fur Wissenschaft und Bildung.

Hanna, R., & Thompson, E. (1999). Neurophenomenology and the spontaneity of consciousness. *Canadian Journal of Philosophy, 29*, 133-162.

Hartelius, G., Caplan, M., & Rardin, M. A. (2007). Transpersonal psychology: Defining the past, divining the future. *The Humanistic Psychologist, 35*(2), 1-26.

Husserl, E. (1970). *Logical investigations* (Vol. 2). London, UK: Routledge & Kegan Paul. (Original work published 1913)

Husserl, E. (1964). *The phenomenology of internal time-consciousness.* Bloomington, IN: Indiana University Press. (Original work published 1905)

Husserl, E. (1977). *Cartesian meditations: An introduction to phenomenology*. The Hague: Martinus Nijhoff. (Original work published 1931)

James, W. (1981). *The principles of psychology*. Cambridge, MA: Harvard University Press. (Original work published 1890)

Kirmayer, L. J. (2009). Nightmares, neurophenomenology and the cultural logic of trauma. *Culture, Medicine and Psychiatry, 33*, 323-331.

Koch, C. (2004). *The quest for consciousness: A neurobiological approach*. Englewood, CO: Roberts.

Kockelmans, J. J. (1967). *Phenomenology: The philosophy of Edmund Husserl*. Garden City, NY: Doubleday.

Koestenbaum, P. (1967). Introduction. In E. Husserl (Ed.), *The Paris lectures* (pp. ix-xxvii). The Hague, The Netherlands: Martinus Nijhoff.

Kornblith, H. (Ed.). (1985). *Naturalizing epistemology*. Cambridge, MA: Bradford.

Kortooms, T. (2002). *Phenomenology of time: Edmund Husserl's analysis of time-consciousness*. Dortrecht, The Netherlands: Kluwer.

Krippner, S. (1972). Altered states of consciousness. In J. White (Ed.), *The highest state of consciousness* (pp. 1-5). Garden City, NY: Doubleday.

Krippner, S. & Combs, A. (2002). The neurophenomenology of shamanism: An essay review. *Journal of Consciousness Studies, 9*(3), 77-82.

LaBerge, S. (1980). Lucid dreaming as a learnable skill: A case study. *Perception and Motor Skills, 51*, 1039-1042.

LaBerge, S. (1985). *Lucid dreaming*. Los Angeles, CA: Tarcher.

LaBerge, S, Nagel, L., Dement, W., & Zarcone, V. (1981). Lucid dreaming verified by volitional communication during REM sleep. *Perceptual and Motor Skills, 52*, 727-732.

Landgrebe, L. (1981). *The philosophy of Edmund Husserl*. Ithaca, NY; Cornell University Press.

Laughlin, C. D. (1973). The influence of Whitehead's organism on Murray's personology. *Journal of the History of the Behavioural Sciences, 9*(3), 251-257.

Laughlin, C. D. (1988). The prefrontosensorial polarity principle: Toward a neurophenomenology of intentionality. *Biology Forum, 81*(2), 243-260. (Also published in K. Ikeda (Ed.), *Foundation of structuralist biology*. Tokyo, Japan: Kaimeisha [Japanese])

Laughlin, C. D. (1989). Transpersonal anthropology: Some methodological issues. *Western Canadian Anthropologist, 5*, 29-60.

Laughlin, C. D. (1992). Time, intentionality, and a neurophenomenology of the dot. *The Anthropology of Consciousness, 3*(3-4), 14-27.

Laughlin, C. D. (1994). Transpersonal anthropology, then and now. *Transpersonal Review, 1*(1), 7-10.

Laughlin, C. D. (2011). Communing with the gods: The dreaming brain in cross-cultural perspective. *Time & Mind, 4*(2), 155-188.

Laughlin, C. D., & d'Aquili, E. G. (1974). *Biogenetic structuralism*. New York, NY: Columbia University Press.

Laughlin, C. D., & Loubser, J.H.N. (2010). Neurognosis, the development of neural models, and the study of the ancient mind. *Time & Mind, 3*(2), 135-158.

Laughlin, C. D., & McManus, J. (1995). The relevance of the radical empiricism of William James to the anthropology of consciousness. *Anthropology of Consciousness, 6*(3), 34-46.

Laughlin, C. D., McManus, J., & d'Aquili, E. G. (1990). *Brain, symbol and experience: Toward a neurophenomenology of human consciousness*. New York, NY: Columbia University Press.

Laughlin, C. D., & Throop, C. J. (2006). Cultural neurophenomenology: Integrating experience, culture and reality through Fisher information. *Journal Culture & Psychology, 12*(3), 305-337.

Laughlin, C. D., & Throop, C. J. (2008). Continuity, causation and cyclicity: A cultural neurophenomenology of time-consciousness. *Time & Mind*, *1*(2), 159-186.

Laughlin, C. D., & Throop, C. J. (2009). Husserlian meditations and anthropological reflections: Toward a cultural neurophenomenology of experience and reality. *Anthropology of Consciousness*, *20*(2), 130-170.

LeDoux, J. (2003). *Synaptic self: How our brains become who we are*. New York, NY: Penguin.

Levy-Bruhl, L. (1966). *Primitive mentality*. Boston, MA: Beacon Press. (Original work published 1923)

Lutz, A. (2002). Toward a neurophenomenology as an account of generative passages: A first empirical case study. *Phenomenology and the Cognitive Sciences*, *1*(2), 133-167.

Lutz, A. (2007). Neurophenomenology and the study of self-consciousness. *Consciousness and Cognition*, *16*, 765-767.

Lutz, A., & Thompson, E. (2003). Neurophenomenology: Integrating subjective experience and brain dynamics in the neuroscience of consciousness. *Journal of Consciousness Studies*, *10*(9-10), 31-52.

Marstaller, L. (2009). Towards a Whiteheadian neurophenomenology. *Concrescence: The Australasian Journal of Process Thought*, *10*, 57-66.

Matlin, M. W. (1998). *Cognition* (4th ed.). Fortworth, TX: Harcourt Brace.

Mesquita, B., Barrett, L. F., & Smith, E. R. (Eds.). (2010). *The mind in context*. New York, NY: Guilford.

Miller, I. (1984). *Husserl, perception, and temporal awareness*. Cambridge, MA: MIT Press.

Moran, D. (2000). *Introduction to phenomenology*. New York, NY: Routledge.

Nairne, J. S. (1997). *Psychology: The adaptive mind*. Pacific Grove, CA: Brooks/Cole.

Natsoulas, T. (1978). Consciousness. *American Psychologist*, *33*, 906-914.

Noë, A., & Thompson, E. (2004). Are there neural correlates of consciousness? *Journal of Consciousness Studies*, *11*(1), 3-28.

Nunez, P. L. (2010). *Brain, mind, and the structure of reality*. Oxford, UK: Oxford University Press.

Ogilvie, R. D., Hunt, H. T., Sawicki, C., & McGowan, K. (1978). Searching for lucid dreams. *Sleep Research*, *7*, 165.

Pastor, M., Day, B. L., Macaluso, E., Friston, K. J., & Frackowiak, R. S. J. (2004). The functional neuroanatomy of temporal discrimination. *Journal of Neuroscience*, *24*(10), 2585-2591.

Pekala, R. J. (1985). A psychophenomenological approach to mapping and diagramming states of consciousness. *Journal of Religion and Psychical Research*, *8*, 199-214.

Pekala, R. J., & Cardeña, E. (2000). Methodological issues in the study of altered states of consciousness and anomalous experiences. In E. Cardeña, S. J. Lynn, & S. Krippner (Eds.), *Varieties of anomalous experience: Examining the scientific evidence* (pp. 47-82). Washington, D.C.: American Psychological Association.

Pekala, R. J., & Wenger, C. F. (1983). Retrospective phenomenological assessment: Mapping consciousness in reference to specific stimulus conditions. *Journal of Mind and Behavior*, *4*, 247-274.

Peters, F. H. (2000). Neurophenomenology. *Method & Theory in the Study of Religion*, *12*(1-4), 379-415.

Peters, F. H. (2004). Neurophenomenology of the supernatural sense in religion. *Method & Theory in the Study of Religion*, *16*(2), 122-148.

Pribram, K. H. (1971). *Languages of the brain*. Englewood Cliffs, NJ: Prentice-Hall.

Purves, D. (2010). *Brains: How they seem to work*. Upper Saddle River, NJ: Pearson Education.

Rock, A. J., & Krippner, S. (2012). States of consciousness or states of phenomenology? In A E. Cavanna & A. Nani (Eds.), *Consciousness: States, mechanisms and disorders* (pp. 55-65). Hauppauge, NY: Nova Science.

Rock, A. J., & Krippner, S. (2007a). Does the concept of "altered states of consciousness" rest on a mistake? *International Journal of Transpersonal Studies, 26,* 33-40.

Rock, A. J., & Krippner, S. (2007b). Shamanism and the confusion of consciousness with phenomenological content. *North American Journal of Psychology, 9*(3), 485-500.

Rock, A. J., & Krippner, S. (2011). States of consciousness redefined as patterns of phenomenal properties: An experimental application. In D. Cvetkovic & I. Cosic (Eds.), *States of consciousness: Experimental insights into meditation, waking, sleep and dreams. The Frontiers collection* (pp. 257-278). Paris, France: Springer-Verlag.

Rodd, R. (2003). *Maripa:* To know everything: The experience of power as knowledge derived from the integrative mode of consciousness. *Anthropology of Consciousness, 14*(2), 60-88.

Roy, J.-M., Petitot, J., Pachoud, B., & Varela, F. J. (1999). Beyond the gap: An introduction to naturalizing phenomenology. In J. Petitot, F. J. Varela, B. Pachoud, & J. M. Roy (Eds.), *Naturalizing phenomenology* (pp. 1-80). Stanford, CA: Stanford University Press.

Rudrauf, D., Lutz, A., Cosmelli, D., LaChaux, J.-P., & Le Van Quyen, M. (2003). From autopoiesis to neurophenomenology: Francisco Varela's exploration of the biophysics of being. *Biological Research, 36,* 21-59.

Sartre, J. P. (1958). *Being and nothingness: An essay on phenomenological ontology.* New York, NY: Philosophical Library.

Schmitt, R. (1967) Husserl's transcendental-phenomenological reduction. In J. J. Kockelmans (Ed.), *Phenomenology: The philosophy of Edmund Husserl and its interpretation* (pp. 58-68). Garden City, NY: Doubleday.

Sibatani, A. (1987). On structuralist biology. *Biological Forum, 80,* 558-564.

Singer, J. L. (1977). Ongoing thought: The normative baseline for alternate states of consciousness. In N. E. Zinberg (Ed.), *Alternate states of consciousness* (pp. 89-120). New York, NY: Free Press.

Solso, R. L. (2001). *Cognitive psychology* (5th ed.). Boston, MA: Allyn & Bacon.

Stroud, J. M. (1967). The fine structure of psychological time. *Annals of the New York Academy of Sciences, 138,* 623-631.

Suzuki, S. (1970). *Zen mind, beginner's mind.* New York, NY: Weatherhill.

Tart, C. T. (1975). *States of consciousness.* New York, NY: Dutton.

TenHouten, W. D. (2005). *Time and society.* Albany, NY: State University of New York Press.

Thompson, E. (2006). Neurophenomenology and contemplative experience. In P. Clayton (Ed.), *The Oxford handbook of science and religion* (pp. 226-235). Oxford, UK: Oxford University Press.

Thompson, E., Lutz, A., & Cosmelli, D. (2005). Neurophenomenology: An introduction for neurophilosophers. In A. Brook & K. Akins (Eds.), *Cognition and the brain: The philosophy and neuroscience movement* (pp. 40-97). Cambridge, UK: Cambridge University Press.

Thompson, E., & Varela, F. J. (2001). Radical embodiment: Neural dynamics and consciousness. *Trends in Cognitive Sciences, 5*(10), 418.

Throop, C. J. (2003a). Articulating experience. *Anthropological Theory, 3*(2), 219-241.

Throop, C. J. (2003b). Minding experience: An exploration of the concept of experience in the French anthropology of Durkheim, Lévy-Bruhl, and Lévi-Strauss. *Journal of the History of the Behavioral Sciences, 39*(4), 365-382.

Throop, C. J. (2012). On inaccessibility and vulnerability: Some horizons of compatibility between phenomenology and psychoanalysis. *Ethos, 40*(1), 75-96.

van de Vijver, F. J. R., Chasiotis, A., & Breugelmans, S. M. (Eds.). (2011). *Fundamental questions in cross-cultural psychology.* Cambridge, UK: Cambridge University Press.

Varela, F. J. (1996). Neurophenomenology: A methodological remedy for the hard problem. *Journal of Consciousness Studies, 3*(4), 330-349.

Varela, F. J. (1997). The naturalization of phenomenology as the transcendence of nature: Searching for generative mutual constraints. *Revue de Phénoménologie, 5,* 355-385.

Varela, F. J. (1999). The specious present: A neurophenomenology of time consciousness. In P. Jean, F. J. Varela, B. Pachoud & J. M. Roy (Eds.), *Naturalizing phenomenology: Issues in contemporary phenomenology and cognitive science* (pp. 266-329). Stanford, CA: Stanford University Press.

Varela, F. J., & Shear, J. (Eds.). (1999). The view from within: First-person methodologies in the study of consciousness (Special Issue). *Journal of Consciousness Studies, 6* (2-3).

Vásquez, M. A. (2011). *More than belief: A materialist theory of religion.* Oxford, UK: Oxford University Press.

Wallace, B., & Fischer, L. E. (1987). *Consciousness and behavior* (2nd ed.). Boston, MA: Allyn & Bacon.

Winkelman, M. J. (1996a). Neurophenomenology and genetic epistemology as a basis for the study of consciousness. *Journal of Social and Evolutionary Systems, 19*(3), 217-236.

Winkelman, M. J. (1996b). Shamanism and consciousness: Metaphorical, political and neurophenomenological perspectives. *Transcultural Psychiatric Research Review, 33,* 69-80.

Winkelman, M. J. (2010). *Shamanism: A biopsychosocial paradigm of consciousness and healing* (2nd ed.). Santa Barbara, CA: Praeger.

15

Quantitative Assessment of Transpersonal and Spiritual Constructs[1]

Douglas A. MacDonald and Harris L. Friedman

Over the past three decades, interest in spirituality and associated constructs/ phenomena has been increasing among scientists, practitioners, and laypersons. As a function of this interest, there has been an impressive rise in the number of studies appearing in the literature that attempt to examine these subjects with varying degrees of rigor and, by association, there is now a staggering number of standardized assessment tools designed specifically to assess spirituality as well as a gamut of other constructs relevant to transpersonal psychology (e.g., see MacDonald, Kuenztel, & Friedman, 1999; MacDonald, LeClair, Holland, Alter, & Friedman, 1995).

However, although we are strongly supportive of research on topics that contribute to the transpersonal area, a cursory inspection of the available literature reveals two notable negative trends. First, we have observed a virtual absence of shared measures and/or methodologies across investigations—that is, many studies involve the development of new assessment technologies, most often without efforts being made to address or incorporate extant measures. Consequently, the literature presents a highly confusing picture as to the status of quantitative instrumentation and the actual state of scientific knowledge involving spirituality and humanistic/transpersonal psychology.

Second, the vast majority of research and test development efforts are being put forth not by transpersonal psychologists but instead by investigators from a number of conventional areas of psychology including clinical psychology, social psychology, health psychology, and the psychology of religion. Medicine and nursing have also been quite active in the generation of new tests and measurement tools. By extension, it appears that humanistic and transpersonal psychologies are contributing considerably less to the growing scientific interest and evolving research, a fact of which has been noted by advocates of the emerging positive psychology movement and used by it as a basis on which to marginalize and exclude humanistic/transpersonal psychology from the realm of scientific psychology (e.g., see Seligman & Csikszentmihalyi, 2000, p. 7).

The Wiley Blackwell Handbook of Transpersonal Psychology, First Edition.
Edited by Harris L. Friedman and Glenn Hartelius.
© 2013 John Wiley & Sons, Ltd. Published 2015 by John Wiley & Sons, Ltd.

The purpose of this chapter is to present information regarding the status of quantitative assessment as it applies to the definition and measurement of constructs arising from, or related to, spirituality and transpersonal psychology. Our express aim in providing this information is to assist transpersonal psychologists in becoming aware of available technologies and to compel researchers to more seriously consider the incorporation of such technologies in ongoing research. For the sake of clarity, the chapter is structured around four general questions: (a) What arguments support the use of quantitative assessment in transpersonal research? (b) What types of measures are currently available in the literature? (c) What does the available empirical literature that uses these measures report about the relation of spiritual and humanistic/transpersonal concepts to human functioning? (d) What are the recommendations for investigators interested in doing transpersonal research?

Arguments Supporting the Quantitative Assessment of Spiritual and Transpersonal Concepts

In general, transpersonal psychology has eschewed the use of objective tests, formalized assessment, and conventional empirical research methodologies on the grounds that they are reductionistic and unable to do justice to the inherent richness, complexity, and often ineffability, of subjective human experience. In the place of such data gathering strategies, qualitative research methods, such as the phenomenological method (e.g., Giorgi, 1997; Patrik, 1994; Walsh, 1995), have been advanced as providing greater accessibility to the lived world of experience in a manner which has come to be seen by many as being more consistent with the underlying worldview and values promoted by third and fourth force psychologies.

To be sure, the limitations of operationalization (i.e., the definition of a construct according to how it is measured) are great and we concur with the basic criticism of reductionism. However, we also contend that all conceptual modalities of knowing are inherently reductionistic to some degree; although we subscribe to the position that the best way of understanding or knowing an experience or state of consciousness is to experience it directly oneself, any attempt either to communicate that to another or, indeed, to process internally that experience with conceptual thought is bound to be at least somewhat reductionistic. Further, we are of the view that qualitative methodologies provide perspectives on data that are simply not available through more conventional (e.g., psychometric) means and, as such, have an important place in the armamentarium of available research methods. Of course, they too suffer from their own unavoidable reductionistic implications. Therefore, we believe that quantitative methods, and most centrally psychometric testing, provide an important avenue of information and should not be dismissed as an illegitimate research tool. Briefly, here are some points for consideration. For the interested reader, these issues are discussed at greater length in a number of our existing publications (e.g., Friedman, 1983; Friedman & MacDonald, 1997; MacDonald, 2011; MacDonald et al., 1995; MacDonald & Friedman, 2001; MacDonald, Friedman, & Kuentzel, 1999; MacDonald, Kuentzel, & Friedman, 1999; MacDonald, Tsagarakis, & Holland, 1994).

First, the problems with operationalization and reductionism associated with psychometric testing are not unique to humanistic and transpersonal concepts, theory, and experience. These problems exist in all areas of psychological and social science research. However, despite these limitations, the development and application of tests has flourished in all psychological sciences. Why? Because they provide information which, notwithstanding its shortcomings, is open to verification and replication through a standardized methodology that enables the comparison of findings and the evolution of a body of cumulative knowledge. Following from this, it appears reasonable to us to argue that there may be benefits of testing for humanistic and transpersonal psychologies also.

Second, much of the literature concentrates on transcendent states of consciousness and, as such, creates the impression that spiritual and transpersonal experience represents the totality of the area. It must be pointed out, however, that transpersonal psychology is not exclusively concerned with experience. Rather, it is a much broader enterprise. Perhaps nowhere better is this communicated than by Walsh and Vaughan (1993, p. 203), who defined transpersonal psychology as "the area of psychology that focuses on the study of transpersonal experiences and related phenomena. These phenomena include the causes, effects, and correlates of transpersonal experiences and development, as well as the [theories], disciplines and practices inspired by them." If one takes this definition at face value, it may readily be contended that the study of relevant theory and behavior, both of which are much more amenable to conventional scientific inquiry than experience, is as central to defining a scientific transpersonal psychology as is the exploration of non-ordinary experience.

Third and most generally, in response to the sweeping changes in service provision arising from economic (e.g., increased involvement of third party payers such as insurance companies) and legal (e.g., increased likelihood of malpractice litigation) factors, psychometric testing and formalized psychological assessment are finding use as one of the primary modalities through which psychological service providers justify and validate clinical diagnoses and interventions. However, Friedman and MacDonald (1997) noted that,

> in showing reluctance to embrace assessment...transpersonal practitioners appear to be putting themselves at unnecessary risk...Without significant energy being directed at demonstrating the validity and usefulness of [relevant] theory and associated practices, transpersonal psychological practice can be seen as being in an increasingly defenseless position relative to the larger psychological and scientific community, since...practitioners are not making satisfactory attempts at being accountable for the quality and effectiveness of their work to their clients, their profession, and their science. (p. 106)

Stated differently, due to social and political factors, both the science as well as the practice of transpersonal psychology may be in jeopardy because of the gross underutilization of recognized technologies in verifying theory and professional judgment. In this vein, psychometric tests appear to hold the potential of adding credibility to transpersonal theory and practices due to their wide acceptance within scientific and social institutions.

Taken together, these points should make apparent the need for, and the possibility of, psychometric testing in the humanistic and transpersonal areas. As a matter of clarity and summarization, psychometric testing may be seen as providing six concrete benefits for transpersonal research. As stated by MacDonald et al. (1995), these may be described as follows:

> 1) once adequate training in psychometrics and test construction is obtained, tests are relatively easy to construct, use, score, and interpret; 2) tests can be completed in a relatively short period of time and can be administered both individually or to groups; 3) tests allow for standardized measurement of a construct thereby making it easier to compare findings from different studies and easier to replicate existing findings; 4) tests allow for fast accumulation of empirical literature on a wide variety of theories and phenomena; 5) tests can be used to verify transpersonal theory...and 6) tests allow for easier comparison between transpersonal conceptions and mainstream psychological concepts. (p. 175)

Available Instrumentation

Literature reviews (MacDonald et al., 1995; MacDonald, Kuentzel, & Friedman, 1999) have revealed more than 100 extant instruments of spirituality and transpersonal constructs. In order to give the reader some idea of their breadth and flavor, Table 15.1 presents a partial listing of some of the tests that we felt were representative of the range of available tools and which appear to hold some promise for research.

Table 15.1   Listing of Selected Extant Measures of Spirituality and Related Constructs

Spirituality
Expressions of Spirituality Inventory (MacDonald, 2000)
Psychomatrix Spirituality Inventory (Wolman, 1997)
Spiritual Orientation Inventory (Elkins, Hedstrom, Hughes, Leaf, & Saunders, 1988)

Well-being
Integration Inventory (Ruffing-Rahal, 1991)
Mental, Physical, and Spiritual Well-Being Scale (Vella-Brodrick & Allen, 1995)
Spiritual Well-Being Scale (Paloutzian & Ellison, 1982; Ellison, 1983)

Experience and Consciousness
Assessment Schedule for Altered States of Consciousness (Van Quekelberghe et al., 1991)
Ego Permissiveness Inventory (Taft, 1969, 1970)
Mystical Experiences Scale (Hood, 1975)
Phenomenology of Consciousness Inventory (Pekala, 1982; Pekala, Steinberg, & Kumar, 1986)

Beliefs, Orientation, and Identity
Ego Grasping Orientation (Knoblauch & Falconer, 1986)
Feelings, Reactions, Beliefs Survey (Cartwright & Mori, 1988)
Self-Expansiveness Level Form (Friedman, 1983)
Transpersonal Orientation To Learning (Shapiro & Fitzgerald, 1989

As can be seen in the table, we present 14 measures grouped into four general categories; (a) Spirituality, (b) Well-Being, (c) Experience and Consciousness, and (d) Beliefs, Orientation, and Identity. Please note that these categories are being used for illustrative purposes and not because they are an accurate and reliable taxonomic classification system. Nonetheless, all instruments included here are standardized paper-and-pencil measures.

Spirituality category. All measures listed in the spirituality category define and assess spirituality as a multidimensional construct. Given our knowledge of the existing instrumentation, the conceptualization of spirituality as involving more than one component appears to be the rule rather than the exception (i.e., most instruments define spirituality as consisting of two or more dimensions). In many cases, religion and/or religiousness finds representation either through the formal inclusion of items or scales or through the (usually) inadvertent confounding of religion and spirituality.

A   *Spiritual Orientation Inventory* (Elkins, Hedstrom, Hughes, Leaf, & Saunders, 1988). This measure is comprised of 85 items that are unequally divided into nine subscales. The subscales, in turn, embody the major features of spirituality identified by the test authors through their content analysis of available relevant literature. The subscales consist of the following: (i) Transcendent Dimension, (ii) Meaning and Purpose in Life, (iii) Mission in Life, (iv) Sacredness in Life, (v) Material Values, (vi) Altruism, (vii) Idealism, (viii) Awareness of the Tragic, and (ix) Fruits of Spirituality. This instrument is rare in that it is only one of a few that assess a model of spirituality that has good support of its content validity (i.e., the nine components of spiritual orientation have been seen by a range of experts as representing key elements of the construct). Further, this test embodies one of the first, and, to date, one of the most effective, efforts at devising a measure of spirituality which minimizes the confound with conventional religion and religiousness.

B   *Psychomatrix Spirituality Inventory* (Wolman, 1997). Designed to tap what spirituality means to Americans, the PSI is a 105-item test that encapsulates "seven clearly differentiated categories" (Wolman, 1997, p. 80) of spirituality. The items themselves were developed through the extensive surveying of persons ranging from lay people to experts in the areas of religion and spirituality and the dimensions derived from analyses of scores obtained from a sample of about 700 participants. The categories are as follows: (i) Awareness of a Higher Power; (ii) Spiritual Activities or Practices, (iii) Use of Healing Practices, (iv) Experience of Physical and Emotional Trauma, (v) Body Awareness, (vi) Religious History, and (vii) Current Religious Practices. The method of development of the PSI (i.e., social survey research) is noteworthy since the dimensions appear to represent aspects of spirituality that are of significant interest to investigators in a range of fields (e.g., conventional and alternative medicine; nursing; clinical, health and rehabilitation psychology; psychology of religion).

C   *Expressions of Spirituality Inventory* (MacDonald, 2000). Named as such so as to avoid the reification of spirituality in measurement, the Expressions of Spirituality

Inventory (ESI) is a 98-item test developed to assess a five dimensional measurement model of spirituality. The model itself was constructed through the factor analyses of several representative measures of spirituality and related constructs. In essence, the five dimensions may be best understood as capturing (at least some of) the major facets of spirituality as represented in existing paper-and-pencil tests. The dimensions consist of the following: (i) Cognitive Orientation Towards Spirituality (i.e., spiritual beliefs and perceptions), (ii) Experiential/Phenomenological Dimension (i.e., spiritual experience), (iii) Existential Well-Being, (iv) Paranormal Beliefs, and (v) Religiousness.

Well-being category. Measures in this category all concern themselves with the assessment of positive states of functioning and/or factors contributing to quality of life.

A *Integration Inventory* (Ruffing-Rahal, 1991). This 37-item instrument was developed to serve as a measure of well-being integration in older persons. The test author equates the notion of well-being integration with the Jungian concept of individuation (i.e., the conscious differentiation and integration of aspects of the psyche into itself) and sees the questionnaire as tapping the meaningfulness of daily life. Although not utilized in much research to date, this test is unique in attempting to assess objectively a concept akin to the theorizing of Jung.

B *Mental, Physical, and Spiritual Well-Being Scale* (Vella-Brodrick & Allen, 1995). Based on the earlier Holistic Living Inventory (Stoudenmire, Batman, Pavlov & Temple, 1985), this 30-item scale was constructed to serve as an easy to use measure of holistic health and well-being. As its name indicates, it consists of three subscales that assess mental, physical, and spiritual aspects of well-being. Initial psychometric work suggests that this test produces scores with decent reliability and validity.

C *Spiritual Well-Being Scale* (Paloutzian & Ellison, 1982; Ellison, 1983). The SWBS is perhaps the single most commonly used instrument in the literature. It consists of 20 items divided into two subscales; Religious Well-Being and Existential Well-Being. This two component model of spiritual well-being was derived from the work of Moberg (1971; Moberg & Brusek, 1978) who described the construct as consisting of vertical (i.e., well-being in relation to a Higher Power) and horizontal (i.e., well-being independent of anything religious) dimensions. Although some difficulties with factor structure and score distributions with certain populations have been shown to exist, the available research using this test suggests that it holds very good potential for exploring the relation of spirituality to psychological functioning.

Experience and consciousness category. In this category, we include measures designed explicitly to assess experience and states of consciousness. Akin to the spirituality measures, all of these measures are multidimensional.

A *Assessment Schedule for Altered States of Consciousness* (Van Quekelberghe, Altstotter-Gleich, & Hertweck, 1991). This measure is composed of 325 items that are divided across 14 subscales. The subscales, in turn, embody major categories of altered states experience. The ASASC was developed in order to serve as a comprehensive measure of non-ordinary states of consciousness. The subscales are: (i) Personal Data (e.g., demographic/descriptive information as well as items on history of substance use and involvement in consciousness altering practices); (ii) Extraordinary Mental Processes (e.g., unusual trains of thought); (iii) Parapsychology, Own Experiences; (iv) Parapsychology, Own View; (v) Esoterics (e.g., astrology, spiritual healing); (vi) Positive Mystic Experiences; (vii) Negative Mystic Experiences; (viii) Imagination; (ix) Dreams; (x) Dissociation; (xi) Hallucinations; (xii) Hypersensitiveness; (xiii) Changed Feeling of Time and Space; and (xiv) Change (i.e., long term effects of non-ordinary experiences on functioning). The inclusiveness and comprehensiveness of this test is impressive and its design facilitates the use of selected subscales for any given research purpose, thereby minimizing the administration of undesirable or redundant questions.

B   *Ego Permissiveness Inventory* (Taft, 1969, 1970). This 72-item test taps a nine-factor conception of ego permissiveness (i.e., the ego's ability to relinquish "some of its power in order to allow the actualization of the [positive] potentialities of the pre-conscious and unconscious aspects of the personality"; Taft, 1969, p. 36). The nine factors are (i) Peak Experiences, (ii) Dissociated Experiences; (iii) Acceptance of Fantasy, (iv) Belief in the Supernatural, (v) Automatic Thought, (vi) Confidence in Cognitive Control, (vii) Cognitive Adaptability, (viii) Playfulness versus Endogenous Arousal, and (ix) Emotional Arousal from Social Sources. Subsequent to his initial efforts (i.e., Taft 1969), Taft (1970), re-factored the items and revised the measure to consist of eight 10-item subscales labeled (i) Peak Experiences, (ii) Dissociated Experiences, (iii) Openness to Inner Experiences, (iv) Belief in the Supernatural, (v) Emotional Extraversion, (vi) Intrinsic Arousal, (vii) Controlled Adaptability, and (viii) Intellectual Control. Although he found an additional factor in his second analyses (called Cognitive Regression), he did not include it in his revised instrument.

C   *Mystical Experiences Scale* (Hood, 1975). The M-Scale is a 32-item instrument designed to assess eight of the nine dimensions of mystical experience identified by Stace (1960) in his phenomenological analysis of reports of such experience (i.e., all of Stace's dimensions except paradoxicality). The dimensions are (i) Ego Quality, (ii) Unifying Quality, (iii) Inner Subjective Quality, (iv) Temporal/Spatial Quality, (v) Noetic Quality, (vi) Ineffability, (vii) Positive Affect, and (viii) Religious Quality. Next to the Spiritual Well-Being Scale, the M-Scale has been among the most commonly used measures in research.

D   *Phenomenology of Consciousness Inventory* (Pekala, 1982; Pekala, Steinberg, & Kumar, 1986). The PCI is a 53-item paper-and-pencil measure which is designed to tap 12 major dimensions of phenomenological experience including (i) Positive Affect, (ii) Negative Affect, (iii) Altered Experience, (iv) Visual Imagery, (v) Attention, (vi) Self-Awareness, (vii) Altered Awareness, (viii) Internal Dialogue, (ix) Rationality, (x) Volitional Control, (xi) Memory, and (xii) Arousal. Due to its relative comprehensiveness, the PCI may be seen as a reasonably good tool for use in place of, or, more ideally, as augmentation to, qualitative research methods.

Beliefs, orientation, and identity category. In our final category, we include instruments that assess a more eclectic variety of constructs.

A   *Ego Grasping Orientation* (Knoblauch & Falconer, 1986). The EGO is a 20-item true/false measure of Taoist orientation designed to measure ego grasping, a concept defined as "a dualistic stance that is marked by the person's attempts to make things more positive while striving to eliminate the negative aspects of human experience" (Knoblauch, 1985, p. 55). The concept itself was developed based upon a therapeutic adaptation of the Taoist concepts of yin-yang, wu-wei, and te.

B   *Feelings, Reactions, Beliefs Survey* (Cartwright & Mori, 1988). This 130-item instrument taps nine main aspects of personality functioning as delineated by Carl Rogers. These are labeled (i) Focusing Conscious Attention, (ii) Openness to Feelings in Relationships, (iii) Trust in Self as an Organism, (iv) Fully Functioning Person, (v) Feeling Uncomfortable with People, (vi) Struggling with Feelings of Inferiority, (vii) Feeling Ambivalent in Relationships, (viii) Openness to Transcendent Experiences, and (ix) Religio-Spiritual Beliefs. This measure is distinctive in its attempt to formalize and operationalize central personality functions as seen by Rogers.

C   *Self-Expansiveness Level Form* (Friedman, 1983). This is an 18-item test designed to measure a model of self-concept delineated according to three levels of self-expansiveness. Self-expansiveness is defined as "the amount of True Self which is contained within the boundary demarcating self from not-self through the process of self-conception" (Friedman, 1983, p. 38). The three levels of self-expansiveness were derived through the use of a spatial-temporal cartography of self-concept (i.e., identity defined as existing in time and space). Each level of self-concept corresponds to a subscale on the measure. The personal subscale is concerned with the here-and-now level of identity. The transpersonal subscale, conversely, taps aspects of self-concept in which identity extends sufficiently beyond the present time and place to involve the dissolution of self as a separate egoic entity. The Middle subscale occupies the area between the Personal and Transpersonal and, although not developed conceptually by Friedman, appears to relate to self-concept as involving an expanded sense of identity beyond the personal level that does not qualify as sufficiently expanded as to be considered transpersonal (e.g., identification with social behavior and the environment). This instrument is one of the only existing tests designed to explicitly incorporate transpersonal theories of identity.

D   *Transpersonal Orientation to Learning* (Shapiro & Fitzgerald, 1989). This 40-item measure was constructed to tap the extent to which a person's attitudes and beliefs about learning and education are transpersonal in nature. The test authors comment that a transpersonal orientation to learning advocates the use of educational environments as contexts for facilitating spiritual development. As such, transpersonally-minded individuals give considerable weighting to intuitive and receptive modes of consciousness in education as opposed to the usual rational/ logical modes. The 40 items of the instrument are equally divided into four subscales that the test authors developed from the results of an item-level factor analysis. The subscales are (i) Fantasy Techiques Applied in Schools, (ii) Mysticism Preferred to Science as an Epistemology, (iii) Mystical/Occult/Paranormal Techniques Applied to Schools, and (iv) Transcendent Consciousness. This assessment tool was devised by educational researchers to use in exploring the role of transpersonal value systems in education. As such, it is the only measure of its kind.

Scientific Knowledge Derived Through Spiritual and Transpersonal Measures

What does the available empirical literature that uses standardized measures report about the relation of spiritual and transpersonal concepts to human functioning? Does it provide strong evidence of a positive link between spirituality and health? Two general comments can be made about the literature. First, it is in such disarray that the discovery of cogent trends is challenging. The task is made significantly more difficult by the fact that there is not a formally developed nomological net of transpersonal constructs. That is, as we have already commented, there is little agreement between measures on what constitutes any given construct and, by association, little basis on which to assume any equivalence of measurement. Ostensibly, if one cannot assume that tests claiming to measure the same construct are, in fact, measuring the same construct, then one cannot assume that the findings obtained with one test are applicable or generalizable to findings involving other tests.

Second, in virtually all studies that report a significant relationship between some aspect or element of spirituality and functioning, the effect size is poor to marginal at best. For example, the religiousness-addictions research has been one of the more salient areas that demonstrates a robust inverse relationship, an association which has held up across different demographic groups and substances. However, when these findings are examined, it has been observed that the upper limit of effect size falls at a correlation of about .25 (Connors, Tonigan, & Miller, 1996). Such a correlation is equivalent to explaining just over 6% of the variance between these variables. Clearly, whether or not a finding is significant, when it only accounts for 6% of the score variance on average, it is difficult to substantiate its clinical and pragmatic import.

Notwithstanding effect size considerations, the burgeoning studies examining the relation of spirituality and associated transpersonal constructs to psychological and physical functioning may yield a more intelligible picture if there were an empirically based organizational model through which the findings could be structured and interpreted. The emphasis on empirically based is important because such an organizational model could only have scientific value if it empirically demonstrates how different operationalizations of transpersonal constructs relate to, and influence, one another. In other words, if the organizational model does not lend to the development of a nomological net of constructs and to the identification of central structural elements within that net, then, from a scientific standpoint, it remains practically impossible to determine which, if any, existing theoretical model offers the most valid and useful perspective for understanding the available findings. With this empirical requirement in mind, the five dimensional model of spirituality devised by MacDonald (1997, 2000) may be seen as a viable candidate for bringing order to the literature.

As stated earlier in the context of describing the ESI, MacDonald (2000) developed a five factor model of spirituality based upon the factor analyses of several representative measures of spirituality and associated constructs. Spirituality is approached by MacDonald as a broad order construct domain that subsumes most constructs falling in the realm of transpersonal psychology (i.e., he essentially adopts the position that the study of spirituality is synonymous with transpersonal psychology) as well as many related subdisciplines (e.g., parapsychology, psychology of religion, existential psychology). Each of the five factors are presented by MacDonald as embodying robust common dimensions that account for a wide range of constructs.

In order to give an idea of its potential as an organizing framework, Table 15.2 shows the classification of 17 tests (or subscales from these tests) across the dimensions as per MacDonald's correlational and factor analytic findings. If the table is closely inspected, it will be noted that the test or subtest classifications appear theoretically consistent for the most part. That is, measures that were designed to tap certain constructs seem to contribute to factors that are conceptually similar. For example, measures of spiritual experience seem to belong to the factor identified as such; measures of religiousness, paranormal beliefs, and existential well-being appear to do so also. There are, however, a few tests that do not follow the same trend. In particular, the Spirituality Assessment Scale and the Spirituality Self-Assessment Scale, two measures intended to tap general spirituality, as well as the Index of Core Spiritual Experience, a test designed to assess spiritual experience, are all categorized on dimensions which do not appear immediately consistent with their theoretical underpinnings. MacDonald's (1997, 2000) examination of the content of these measures provides an answer for this. The former two measures of general spirituality mostly contain items which concern themselves with self-perceived functioning and quality of life without any reference to anything overtly spiritual or religious (e.g., I am happy; I feel strong; My life is rewarding), thus explaining why they were found to significantly contribute to the Existential-Well-Being dimension and were categorized as measures of such. In a similar vein, the Index of Core Spiritual Experience, though designed to serve as a non-theistic measure of spiritual experience, consists of items that are heavily laden with theistic terminology and concepts. Consequently, it seems reasonable that the scale would load on a religiousness factor in analytic work and it appears appropriate to categorize the instrument in the Religiousness dimension.

With the illustration of how the five dimensions can organize existing measures of spirituality and related constructs completed, one can now turn to the application of these dimensions to assist in understanding of how spirituality relates to conventional psychological variables. We will adopt two approaches to accomplishing this task. First, we briefly summarize some of the empirical trends that emerge for each dimension separately as they relate to the available literature. Second, based upon some of the empirical work with using the ESI (e.g., MacDonald, 2000; MacDonald & Holland, 2002a, 2002b, 2002c, 2003), we provide summary information on some of the empirical correlates of the each of the five dimensions in MacDonald's (2000) model.

Table 15.2   Categorization of Spirituality Instruments Based Upon Factor Analytic and Correlational Results

---

Cognitive Orientation Towards Spirituality
Spirituality Assessment Scale-Innerness
Spiritual Orientation Inventory-All subscales save Transcendent Dimension
Death Transcendence Scale-Religious Mode
Intrinsic-Extrinsic Religious Orientation Scale-Intrinsic Religiousness
Spiritual Well-Being Questionnaire-Subjective Spiritual Well-Being

Experiential/Phenomenological Dimension
Mystical Experiences Scale-All eight subscales
Peak Experiences Scale
Spirituality Assessment Scale-Transcendence
Spiritual Orientation Inventory-Transcendent Dimension and Sacredness in Life
Assessment Schedule for Altered States of Cons.-Positive Mystical Experiences
Death Transcendence Scale-Mystical Experience
Ego Permissiveness Inventory (Taft, 1969)-Peak Experience and Dissociated Experience

Existential Well-Being
Ego Grasping Orientation
Spirituality Assessment Scale-Innerness, Transcendence, Unifying Consciousness, Purpose and
    Meaning in Life
Spirituality Self-Assessment Scale
Spiritual Well-Being Questionnaire-Self-Satisfaction
Spiritual Well-Being Scale-Existential Well-Being

Paranormal Beliefs
Paranormal Beliefs Scale-Extraordinary Life Forms, Precognition, Psi Beliefs, Spiritualism,
    Superstitiousness, Witchcraft
Transpersonal Orientation to Learning-Mystical/Occult/Paranormal Techniques to Learning
Assessment Schedule for Altered States of Consciousness-Parapsychology, Own Beliefs and
    Esoterics
Ego Permissiveness Inventory-Belief in the Supernatural

Religiousness
East-West Questionnaire-Man and the Spiritual, Eastern and Man and the Spiritual, Western
Index of Core Spiritual Experience
Intrinsic Religious Motivation Scale
Mystical Experiences Scale- Religious Quality
Paranormal Beliefs Scale-Traditional Religious Beliefs
Death Transcendence Scale- Religious mode
Intrinsic-Extrinsic Religious Orientation Scale- Intrinsic religiousness
Spiritual Well-Being Questionnaire-Christian Faith, Personal Piety, Religious Cynicism
Spiritual Well-Being Scale-Religious Well-Being

Note. Table adapted from MacDonald (1997).

Research Trends in the Literature

Cognitive Orientation Towards Spirituality. This dimension refers to spirituality as expressed through non-religious means. In particular, it embodies beliefs, attitudes, and perceptions about the relevance of spirituality to one's daily functioning. When the literature is examined from the perspective of this dimension, surprising little research is found. In fact, there is a real paucity of studies exploring how non-theistically based conceptions of spirituality relate to psychological functioning. This appears to be largely the result of the limited number of existing spirituality measures that partition out religiousness. However, there are some indications that persons who are high on this dimension may tend to demonstrate higher levels of self-actualization and ego resiliency and lower levels of depression (e.g., Ellason, 1992; Tloczynski, Knoll, & Fitch, 1997; Zainuddin, 1993).

Experiential/phenomenological dimension. As its name implies, this dimension involves spiritual and mystical experience. Unfortunately, the research using measures that fall under this dimension provides a mixed picture of how spiritual experience relates to psychological functioning. For example, there are a number of studies that find positive associations with self-actualization and personality variables suggestive that spiritual experiences are connected with a healthy orientation towards self. However, for every study that supports such an association, there seems to be another that either fails to replicate it or finds the opposite pattern of results. One finding that seems fairly robust, incidentally, is a positive correlation between spiritual experience and temporal lobe signs (see Lukoff & Lu, 1988; MacDonald et al., 1995; MacDonald, Friedman & Kuentzel, 1999).

Existential well-being. This dimension involves aspects of spirituality relating to existential aspects of human functioning. More specifically, it appears to involve three general components: purpose and meaning in life (derived from any source), a sense of inner strength and perception of self as able to cope with the basic issues of life, and a relaxed orientation towards self and day-to-day matters. Research involving this dimension of spirituality appears to be the most consistent in its support of a positive relation with health and well-being and a negative association with pathology and general dysfunction. As examples, existential well-being seems to be robustly and negatively associated to depression, anxiety, and adjustment problems (MacDonald, 2000).

Paranormal beliefs. In contrast to the research with Existential Well-Being, research involving paranormal beliefs has generally shown a positive relation with indices of pathology and with psychological variables typically thought of as reflecting negative aspects of functioning. For example, paranormal beliefs have been found to be related to unusual thought and behavioral patterns including psychotic disorders (e.g., schizophrenia, schizotypy), external locus of control, suggestibility, and temporal lobe signs (MacDonald et al., 1995; MacDonald, Friedman, & Kuentzel, 1999).

Religiousness. In MacDonald's model, religiousness refers to what is more conventionally known as intrinsic religious orientation or engaging in religious practice for its own sake. Extrinsic religious orientation (i.e., using religion as a means to accomplish another end, such as acquiring social status in one's community) and formal aspects of institutional religion are explicitly excluded. Both nondenominational beliefs about the existence of a higher power and religious practice (including prayer, meditation, and attendance at religious services) comprise the two key components of this dimension. In his survey of the religious commitment- mental health literature, Gartner (1996) noted that the manner in which religiousness relates to psychological and physical functioning varies as a function of mode of measurement. In particular, hard variables (e.g., behavioral observations, physiological indices) have been observed to produce more consistent positive associations between religiousness and health as compared to soft variables (e.g., psychometric tests) that themselves generate more neutral to negative relations. He attributes this difference in findings to the fact that hard variables tend to be more objective and accurate indicators of religiousness and functioning while standardized tests often operationalize health in terms which pathologize religion (e.g., MMPI and Personal Orientation Inventory both have religion items which are used as indicators of dysfunction). Nonetheless, in his review of existing studies, Gartner reports that religiousness appears to demonstrate different patterns of relationship with different variables. Evidence supportive of an association with mental health is found in studies on physical health and mortality, treatment outcome, marital satisfaction and divorce, general well-being, antisocial behavior, and depression. Evidence consistent with a religiousness-pathology connection is noted with authoritarianism, dogmatism, tolerance of ambiguity, suggestibility and dependence, self-actualization, and temporal lobe epileptic signs. Inconsistent evidence has been observed with anxiety, psychosis, self-esteem, sexual disorders, prejudice, and intelligence/education.

Empirical Findings Using the Expressions of Spirituality Inventory It should be apparent from this brief literature overview that even with an organizing model, there exist considerable points of ambiguity and murkiness. Why does such ambiguity exist? Is it because the available research is poorly done across the board? Is it because the various aspects of spirituality actually do produce different configurations of relationships with different variables and/or different populations?

Table 15.3 presents a summary of empirical findings obtained by MacDonald (1997, 2000) and MacDonald and Holland (2002a, 2002b, 2002c, 2003) involving the ESI Dimensions and a number of psychological variables. Included in the table are correlational results between the ESI and two comprehensive measures of personality (i.e., the NEO Personality Inventory-Revised [NEO-PI-R] and the Temperament and Character Inventory [TCI]), two measures of pathology (i.e., the Minnesota Multiphasic Personality Inventory [MMPI-2] and the Complex Partial Epileptic Signs), and two additional constructs of general interest (i.e., boredom proneness and social desirability). In all cases, data were obtained from university student samples.

As can be seen in Table 15.3, although there are some points of overlap, basically, each of the five dimensions produce a differential pattern of findings across all measures. For three of the dimensions, the findings appear generally consistent with our

Table 15.3 Significant Empirical Correlations for the Five Dimensions of the Expressions of Spirituality: Inventory with Selected Conventional Psychological Constructs

ESI Dimensions	Variable Domains		
	Personality	*Pathology*	*Other*
Cognitive Orientation Towards Spirituality	NEO-PI-R: **E, O, A, C** TCI: **C**, NS (−), **P, RD, SD, ST**	MMPI-2: None CPES: (+)	BPS: (−) Social Desire: (+)
Experiential/ Phenomenological Dimension	NEO-PI-R: **E, O** TCI: HA (−), **P, ST**	MMPI-2: Si (−) CPES: (+)	BPS: No relation Social Desire: No
Existential Well-Being	NEO-PI-R: N (−), **E, A, C** TCI: **C**, HA (−), **P, SD**	MMPI-2: Hs (−), D (−), Hy, Pd (−), Pa (−), Pt (−), Sc (−), Si (−) CPES: (−)	BPS: (−) Social Desire: (+)
Paranormal Beliefs	NEO-PI-R: **O** TCI: **NS, ST**	MMPI-2: Pa CPES: (+)	BPS: No relation Social Desire: No
Religiousness	NEO-PI-R: **A, C** TCI: **C**, NS (−), **RD, SD, ST**	MMPI-2: Pd (−) CPES: No relation	BPS: No relation Social Desire: (+)

Note. NEO-PI-R = NEO Personality Inventory-Revised, N = Neuroticism, E = Extraversion, O = Openness, A = Agreeableness, C = Conscientiousness; TCI = Temperament and Character Inventory, RD = Reward Dependence, NS = Novelty Seeking, HA = Harm Avoidance, P = Persistence, C = Co-operativeness, SD = Self-Directedness, ST = Self-Transcendence; MMPI-2 Hs = Hypochondriasis, D = Depression, Hy = Hysteria, Pd = Psychopathic Deviate, Pa = Paranoia, Pt = Psychasthenia, Sc = Schizophrenia, Si = Social Introversion; CPES = Complex-Partial Epileptic Signs; BPS = Boredom Proneness Scale. Boldface items generated correlations of .30 or greater. (+) and (−) denote positive and negative correlation, respectively. Findings for NEO-PI-R and social desirability taken from MacDonald (2000). Findings for the TCI taken from MacDonald and Holland (2002a). Findings for the MMPI-2 taken from MacDonald and Holland (2003). Findings for CPES taken from MacDonald and Holland (2002b). Findings for boredom proneness taken from MacDonald and Holland (2002c).

literature overview. That is, Existential Well-Being seems to most clearly demonstrate an inverse relation with measures of pathology and neuroticism; Paranormal Beliefs seems to produce a pattern of association with measures of unusual thought processes and non-ordinary temporal lobe activity, and the Experiential/Phenomenological Dimension shows a bidirectional constellation of relationships indicating the presence of links to both positive and negative aspects of functioning.

The results for the remaining two ESI dimensions, on the other hand, are less copacetic with the research. In the case of Religiousness, although the obtained significant results appear congruent with existing studies, nonsignificant relations with indices of depression, antisocial behavior, addictions (not included in the table), and temporal lobe signs do not replicate available findings. Cognitive Orientation Toward Spirituality, while producing a set of coefficients with the TCI and NEO-PI-R suggestive of healthy personality correlates, did not obtain any significant correlations with

MMPI-2 scales and a positive correlation was observed with a measure of complex-partial epileptic signs.

When the trends in the research are taken into consideration, what can be said about spirituality and human functioning? Assuming that the ESI and its underlying factor model are robust, only one conclusion seems defensible: spirituality and associated transpersonal constructs are not related to psychological and physical functioning in a simple unidirectional manner. Rather, it appears that the association is best charac-terized as complex, multidirectional, and at least partly the product of how constructs are operationalized.

Recommendations for Future Research

In light of all that we have discussed, we have a number of recommendations for anyone interested in using psychometric tests to scientifically explore the domains of spirituality and humanistic/transpersonal psychology. As we are sure the reader will note, many of these recommendations are relevant to virtually all psychological research. Despite the universal applicability of some of these suggestions, however, we believe it prudent to make explicit all elements of the research process which require augmentation or revision in order for investigations in the transpersonal domains to reach a level of rigor which is at least on par with the quality of science done in mainstream psychology.

1   When employing psychometric tests as the quantitative method, studies should incorporate multidimensional measures of constructs of interest and/or multiple measures. This should be done in response to the fact that most concepts and phenomena of interest to humanistic and transpersonal researchers are complex and unlikely to be adequately represented by a simple one-dimensional test.
2   Consistent application of same method and tests across studies is essential. Research traditions and subdisciplines are built and maintained through the ongoing use of a theory and/or methodology in exploring a phenomena/behavior.
3   Pay attention to issues around statistical power. Because effect sizes tend to be weak, efforts need to be made to best augment the power of variables used in an investigation. This can be done through sample size (larger samples have greater power), by selecting measures that are known to demonstrate sensitivity to the vari-able of interest (e.g., including some hard behavioral measures), and by choosing appropriate statistics.
4   Give regard to possible confounding variables and co-variates and make efforts to address them. Variables such as age, sex, ethnicity/culture, and intelligence, as well as a variety of social (e.g., socioecomonic status) and socialization factors (e.g., education, early exposure to religion/spirituality) need to be controlled so their effects can be explained and/or eliminated.
5   Efforts should be made within studies to provide some evidence of the replicability of findings. That is, whenever possible, studies should focus on producing reliable empirical findings through the replication of results with a different sample or methodology.

6   Exercise caution in the interpretation of information coming from tests. Do not
    reify tests or scientific concepts. Interpret and report findings appropriately with
    sensitivity given to their limitations (especially in terms of generalizability). One
    specific area of difficulty that has become the focus of some criticism concerns
    the confound of spirituality with well-being (e.g., Koenig, 2008). In particular,
    it has been noted that many tests of spirituality define and measure the construct
    in a way that causes cross-contamination of spirituality with psychological well-
    being outcomes (i.e., many tests include items related to wellness and positive
    affectivity as parts of spirituality). By extension, research that finds a significant
    association between spirituality and well-being needs to be interpreted with cau-
    tion since, at minimum, the strength of the relationship will likely be artificially
    inflated.

Conclusion

As stated in the introduction, interest in topics central to humanistic and transpersonal psychologies is blooming in all segments of society, including within the scientific establishment. However, in this age of acceptance and exploration of ideas
once taboo in empirical traditions, a time when one would assume that humanistic/
transpersonal psychology should be serving a leading role, what, in fact, is happening is that these psychologies are becoming marginalized and even excluded from
scientific developments due to their lack of commitment to recognized psychological
research methods. It is our sincere hope that investigators take heed of the arguments
and information presented here and make strong efforts to have humanistic and
transpersonal psychology placed back in the forefront of spirituality and consciousness
studies.

Note

1. This chapter is an adaptation of a paper by MacDonald and Friedman (2002), which in turn
   was based upon a paper presented at the 108th Annual Convention of the American Psychological Association at Washington, DC, August 2000. A version of this paper has also published in a journal of SAGE/SOCIETY as: MacDonald, D. A., & Friedman, H. L. (2002).
   Assessment of humanistic, transpersonal, and spiritual constructs: State of the Science. *Journal of Humanistic Psychology*, 42(4), 102-125. Available at http://online.sagepub.com

References

Cartwright, D., & Mori, C. (1988). Scales for assessing aspects of the person. *Person Centered
    Review, 3*, 176-194.

Connors, G. J., Tonigan, J. S., & Miller, W. R. (1996). A measure of religious background and behavior for use in behavior change research. *Psychology of Addictive Behaviors, 10*(2), 90-96.

Elkins, D. N., Hedstrom, L. J., Hughes, L. L., Leaf, J. A., & Saunders, C. (1988). Toward phenomenological spirituality: Definition, description, and measurement. *Journal of Humanistic Psychology, 28*(4), 5-18.

Ellason, J. W. (1992). *Cognitive coping styles associated with multiple personality disorder.* Master's Thesis, Texas Women's University.

Ellison, C. W. (1983). Spiritual well-being: Conceptualization and measurement. *Journal of Psychology and Theology, 11*(4), 330-340.

Friedman, H. L. (1983). The Self-Expansiveness Level Form: A conceptualization and measurement of a transpersonal construct. *Journal of Transpersonal Psychology, 15*(1), 37-50.

Friedman, H. L., & MacDonald, D. A. (1997). Toward a working definition of transpersonal assessment. *Journal of Transpersonal Psychology, 29*(2), 105-122.

Gartner, J. (1996). Religious commitment, mental health, and prosocial behavior: A review of the empirical literature. In E. P. Shafranske (Ed.). *Religion and the clinical practice of psychology* (pp. 187-214). Washington, DC: American Psychological Association.

Giorgi, A. (1997). The theory, practice, and evaluation of the phenomenological method as a qualitative research procedure. *Journal of Phenomenological Psychology, 28*(2), 235-260.

Hood, R. W. (1975). The construction and preliminary validation of a measure of reported mystical experience. *Journal for the Scientific Study of Religion, 14,* 29-41.

Knoblauch, D. L. (1985). Applying Taoist thought to counseling and psychotherapy. *American Mental Health Counselors Association Journal, 7,* 52-63.

Knoblauch, D. L., & Falconer, J. A. (1986). The relationship of a measured Taoist orientation to Western personality dimensions. *Journal of Transpersonal Psychology, 18*(1), 73-83.

Koenig, H. G. (2008). Concerns about measuring spirituality in research. *Journal of Nervous and Mental Disease, 196*(5), 349-355.

Lukoff, D., & Lu, F. G. (1988). Transpersonal psychology research review topic: Mystical experience. *Journal of Transpersonal Psychology, 20*(2), 161-184.

MacDonald, D. A. (1997). The development of a comprehensive factor analytically derived measure of spirituality and its relationship to psychological functioning. *Dissertation Abstracts International, 61*(09) 0115B (UMI #NQ52412).

MacDonald. D. A. (2000). Spirituality: Description, measurement and relation to the five factor model of personality. *Journal of Personality, 68*(1), 153-197.

MacDonald, D. A. (2011). Studying spirituality scientifically: Reflections, considerations, and recommendations. *Journal of Management, Spirituality and Religion, 8*(3) 195-210.

MacDonald, D. A., & Friedman, H. L. (2001). The scientific study of spirituality: Philosophical and methodological considerations. *Biofeedback Newsmagazine, 29*(3), 19-21.

MacDonald, D. A., & Friedman, H. L. (2002). Assessment of humanistic, transpersonal, and spiritual constructs: State of the science, *Journal of Humanistic Psychology, 42*(4), 102-125

MacDonald, D. A., Friedman, H. L., & Kuentzel, J. G. (1999). A survey of measures of spiritual and transpersonal constructs: Part one—Research update. *Journal of Transpersonal Psychology, 31*(2), 137-154.

MacDonald, D. A., & Holland, D. (2002a). Examination of the psychometric properties of the Temperament and Character Inventory Self-Transcendence dimension. *Personality and Individual Differences, 32,* 1013-1027.

MacDonald, D. A., & Holland, D. (2002b). Spirituality and self-reported complex-partial epileptic-like signs. *Psychological Reports, 91,* 785-792.

MacDonald, D. A., & Holland, D. (2002c). Spirituality and boredom proneness. *Personality and Individual Differences, 32,* 1113-1119.

MacDonald, D. A., & Holland, D. (2003). Spirituality and the MMPI-2. *Journal of Clinical Psychology, 59*(4), 399-410.

MacDonald, D. A., Kuentzel, J. G., & Friedman, H. L. (1999). A survey of measures of spiritual and transpersonal constructs: Part two—Additional instruments. *Journal of Transpersonal Psychology, 31*(2), 155-177.

MacDonald, D. A., LeClair, L., Holland, C. J., Alter, A., & Friedman, H. L. (1995). A survey of measures of transpersonal constructs. *Journal of Transpersonal Psychology, 27*(2), 171-235.

MacDonald, D. A., Tsagarakis, C. I., & Holland, C. J. (1994). Validation of a measure of transpersonal self-concept and its relationship to Jungian and Five Factor Model conceptions of personality. *Journal of Transpersonal Psychology, 26*(2), 175-201.

Moberg, D. O. (1971). Spiritual well-being: Background and issues. Washington, DC: White House Conference on Aging.

Moberg, D. O., & Brusek, P. M. (1978). Spiritual well-being: A neglected subject in quality of life research. *Social Indicators Research, 5,* 303-323.

Paloutzian, R. F., & Ellison, C. W. (1982). Loneliness, spiritual well-being and the quality of life. In Peplau & Perlman (Eds.). *Loneliness: A sourcebook of current theory, research, and therapy* (pp. 224-237). New York: John Wiley.

Patrik, L. E. (1994). Phenomenological method and meditation. *Journal of Transpersonal Psychology, 26*(1), 37-54.

Pekala, R. J. (1982). *The phenomenological of consciousness inventory (PCI).* Thorndale, PA: Psychophenomenological Concepts.

Pekala, R. J., Steinberg, J., & Kumar, C. K. (1986). Measurement of phenomenological experience: Phenomenology of Consciousness Inventory. *Perceptual and Motor Skills, 63,* 983-989.

Ruffing-Rahal, M. A. (1991). Initial psychometric evaluation of a qualitative well-being meaure: The Integration Inventory. *Health Values, Health Behavior, Education, and Promotion. 15*(2), 10-20.

Seligman, M. E. P., & Csikszentmihalyi, M. (2000). Positive psychology: An introduction. *American Psychologist, 55*(1), 5-14.

Shapiro, S. B., & Fitzgerald, L. F. (1989). The development of an objective scale to measure a transpersonal orientation to learning. *Educational and Psychological Measurement, 49,* 375-384.

Stace, W. T. (1960). *Mysticism and philosophy.* Philadelphia, PA: Lippincott.

Stoudenmire, J., Batman, D., Pavlov, M., & Temple, A. (1985). Validation of a holistic living inventory. *Psychological Reports, 57,* 303-311.

Taft, R. (1969). Peak experiences and ego permissiveness: An exploratory factor study of their dimensions in normal persons. *Acta Psychologica, 29,* 35-64.

Taft, R. (1970). The measurement of the dimensions of ego permissiveness. *Personality: An International Journal, 1*(2), 163-184.

Tloczynski, J., Knoll, C., & Fitch, A. (1997). The relationship among spirituality, religious ideology, and personality. *Journal of Psychology and Theology, 25*(2), 208-213.

Van Quekelberghe, R., Altstotter-Gleich, C., & Hertweck, E. (1991). Assessment Schedule for Altered States of Consciousness: A brief report. *Journal of Parapsychology, 55,* 377-390.

Vella-Brodrick, D. A., & Allen, F.C.L. (1995). Development and psychometric validation of the Mental, Physical, and Spiritual Well-Being Scale. *Psychological Reports, 77,* 659-674.

Walsh, R. (1995). Phenomenological mapping: A method for describing and comparing states of consciousness. *Journal of Transpersonal Psychology, 27*(1), 25-56.

Walsh, R. N., & Vaughan, F. E. (1993). On transpersonal definitions. *Journal of Transpersonal Psychology, 25*(2), 199-207.

Wolman, R. (1997). Spirituality: What does it mean to you? *New Age Journal, September/October*, 78-81.

Zainuddin, R. (1993). Needs as determinants of orientation towards spirituality. *Journal of the Indian Academy of Applied Psychology, 19*(1-2), 31-38.

16

The Role of Science in Transpersonal Psychology

The Advantages of Middle-Range Theory

Harris L. Friedman

For transpersonal psychology to thrive, both as science and praxis, it must rely on empirical evidence, not simply faith or dogma, to support its claims (Friedman, 2002). Whether starting inductively from empirical observations, deductively from extant beliefs, or more intuitively through some process of abduction, transpersonal concepts must be amenable to empirical approaches to be part of the scientific process. In this regard, empirical refers to being accessible to experience via the senses, both outer (e.g., vision) and inner (e.g., proprioception), congruent with how contemporary cognitive psychologists (e.g., Solso, 2001) include consciousness as awareness of "objects" in both physical and phenomenal space.

It could perhaps also apply to other ways of experiencing (e.g., using active imagination; Jung, 1997), if these could be brought into a consensual framework for others to corroborate, as some agreed upon referent is always needed for the data gleaned from scientific observations. This requires that truth claims can be disputed (and neither embraced as part of an untestable faith, nor foisted upon others as authoritarian dogma). In essence, science requires that any appropriately trained observer be able to replicate scientific claims, rather than having to blindly accept them. Scientific theories integrate empirically accessible concepts into a type of structure, which can be seen as an explanatory mechanism (see Bunge, 1997) based on some organizing principles (e.g., logic, mathematics, graphical depictions) that provide for what can be called explanation, and also the ability to make predictions (hypotheses) that are testable using empirical data (see Jaccard & Jacoby, 2010). For a scientific theory to grow, it needs to build upon the iterative interplay of both empirical data and theory. Scientific theories cannot be isolated from empirical observations or they would only be philosophical speculations, while traditional worldviews (e.g., astrological systems) and even contemporary religious faiths (e.g., Buddhism) are not part of science per se, insofar as they do not rely on empirical evidence for their claims. In previous writings, I have criticized portraying both astrology (Friedman, 2002) and Buddhism (Friedman,

The Wiley Blackwell Handbook of Transpersonal Psychology, First Edition.
Edited by Harris L. Friedman and Glenn Hartelius.

2009, 2010) as sciences. Although both are not sciences in my view, they can be used to further science in many ways (e.g., as in generating scientific theories reframing their beliefs and practices). One starting place for building scientific transpersonal theory is to operationally define (i.e., in a way that is empirically accessible through a specified procedure) concepts that serve as the fundamental components of theory. For this purpose, I developed a construct (i.e., a type of concept that is created specifically to be used in science), which I called "self-expansiveness" (Friedman, 1981, 1983). It refers to how the boundary drawn around one's sense of self (i.e., self-concept) can vary from being narrowly constrictive to broadly expansive. Although I maintain that self-expansiveness can provide a fruitful way to create and develop a variety of transpersonal psychology theories, it is just one among many other possible concepts that offers heuristic potential for empirically developing and testing such theories through programs of cumulative research, as well as for furthering evidence-based transpersonal psychology praxis.

Theory and Science

Transpersonal psychology can be seen as an attempt to replace traditional spiritual and folk psychological worldviews with perspectives congruent with those of modern science, that can develop scientifically through empirical research. Specifically this means making these perspectives amenable for empirical exploration. In this way, transpersonal psychology straddles conventional science and other disciplines focusing on spirituality and related concerns, attempting to meld them together in a way that benefits from the openness of empiricism, while still considering some of the most profound questions typically relegated to non-scientific pursuits by the mainstream. Transpersonal psychology as a science also is focused on applications, namely empirically informed practice.

Scope of Theory

One way to view theories is to look at their scope, or the range of phenomena they attempt to explain (Jaccard & Jacoby, 2010). The leading transpersonal theories have been in the tradition of "grand theory" (as delineated from mini- and middle-range theory; Merton, 1968), which means they often attempt to explain too much and by doing so they end usually up explaining little of scientific worth. Two examples of such over-reaching transpersonal work are Wilber's (2001) *A Theory of Everything* and Laszlo's (2004) *Science and the Akashic Field: An Integral Theory of Everything*, both of which unabashedly profess to explain everything. Essentially what such grandiose works provide are mythic accounts about reality. These may provide comforting illusions of sense-making to the largest questions of meaning and purpose, but they also may operate outside of a framework of science. Such works are more similar to the explanatory stories told around campfires since the advent of humankind (and to the many current religious ideologies that invoke supernatural and metaphysical causation). Although these accounts could provide not only comfort, but also socio-cultural adaptation (i.e., by unifying disparate groups under common beliefs), they also often led to strife—as people are all too willing to kill over their differing untestable beliefs about such matters. As closed systems, grand theories cannot be questioned empirically and are therefore unavoidably authoritarian, whether based on inner faith or enforced by external power. The Freudian tradition is an example of a grand theory, as it can be used post hoc to explain virtually everything, from art history to zoological evolution, without being able to provide definitive tests of its assertions. In contrast, more useful scientific theories require openness and the capacity for growth, while grand theories offer little opportunity for generating improvements through empirical efforts. Although there are thriving traditions of psychoanalysis that continue to evolve, these are more influential within the humanities and other non-scientific disciplines than in psychology. Grand theories result in scientific stagnation, making them more akin to folk psychology and religion, in which open questioning is discouraged, if not banned. Many of the approaches that have dominated transpersonal psychology since its inception suffer the problem of being grand theories and, thereby, outside of the scientific realm.

Perhaps Wilber's (e.g., 2001) extensive work is the best example of this. It spins complex conjectures employing esoteric language that is mostly without empirical referents. This is not to deny that some empirical work has been conducted on its notions (e.g., Sehrbrock, 2007). However, the sheer mass of Wilber's work is overwhelming, which is exacerbated by the fact that it is constantly being revised (MacDonald, 2007), while his scholarly eruditeness can lull readers into passively accepting its many empirically unfounded conclusions. Problems with Wilber's approach are clearly pointed out by Ferrer (2002), among other critics. My main concern is that, like the legendary King Procrustes, Wilber attempts to place everything into universal categories, providing a so-called perennial vision that embraces everything, whether or not it fits well into his system (and, when something does not fit so well, Wilber does not hesitate to make post hoc adjustments to ensure it fits). Wilber's approach also suffers from employing many supernatural and metaphysical concepts, such as the notion of non-duality, which elude empirical examination. In my view, his grand theory veers closely toward becoming a new religion, while at best it is a philosophical, but not scientific, effort. Although no science, including psychology, is totally free of underpinning philosophical assumptions, the history of psychology has been one of evolving from philosophy, which engages in speculations that do not require subsequent empirical evidence. This is not to denigrate philosophy, which in itself is a valuable enterprise, but simply to delineate it from science, including transpersonal psychology. The first step in developing a scientific transpersonal psychology is to escape from the shadow of such grand theory by creating theories that are empirically accessible and able to generate testable hypotheses that can challenge their claims and foster their evolution.

One avenue of such escape would be to seek refuge in what can be called mini-theories (Merton, 1968), which attempt to avoid overly large generalizations by making sense of specific phenomena within delimited contexts. For example, in attempting to explain the diversity of various transpersonal systems across cultures by imposing a singular universal structure upon them, which could be seen as oppressively colonialistic, mini-theories can explain how they differentially operate within their local contexts as indigenous psychologies (Allwood & Berry, 2006). These allow for ways to understand diverse spiritual traditions from an emic (or cultural insider) perspective, which could be adaptive in cross-cultural encounters (e.g., in under-standing a specific spiritual path from the perspective of those who are immersed in it). Just as there was fear that anthropologists would "go native" when involved in cross-cultural research by abandoning their etic (or cultural outsider) discipline, there is a similar occupational hazard for transpersonal psychologists, who also frequently go native by embracing exotic traditions and thereby abandoning scientific efforts (see Wallis, 2003). This relates to the frequent confound in transpersonal psychol-ogy in which traditional worldviews and spiritual approaches are often taken whole as being themselves psychologies, when in fact they are typically not scientific, but based on metaphysical and supernatural assumptions (Friedman, 2002, 2005, 2009, 2010). This makes cultivating an emic perspective potentially hazardous for those who desire to maintain their so-called scientific objectivity through keeping an etic perspective. However, having an emic perspective can be useful, if the etic perspec-tive can also be kept intact. For example, while challenging beliefs held by many practitioners within the martial art of Aikido, I brought an outsider's scientific per-spective onto transpersonal a practice in which I long had been involved as an insider (Friedman, 2005).

Ferrer's (2002) participatory approach appears to be arguing for mini-theories when it champions the diversity of all spiritual traditions as seen on their own terms. He apparently minimizes their commonalities in an effort to avoid promoting the hege-mony he critiqued in Wilber's (e.g., 2001) grand theory. Such mini-theories allow for acknowledging and respecting cultural differences, but essentially they build silos that separate, abnegating the possibility of finding useful connections. This can lead to con-sidering all transpersonal systems as incommensurate, rather than part of potentially meaningful patterns (i.e., scientific laws) that can further development of scientific theory. Unfortunately, Ferrer's participatory approach, like the grand theory he aptly critiqued, does not offer any specific strategies that would position it well as a scien-tific approach. Rather, it appears to promote only a vague research agenda, which I think could be subsumed under the long tradition of inter-subjectivity studies (see Fuchs & Jaegher, 2009). Organic inquiry (e.g., Clements, 2004) is an example of an approach to building mini-theories within transpersonal psychology congruent with Ferrer's participatory vision, as it explicitly does not seek to generalize results from its data and advocates full (including from transpersonal perspectives) participation of the researcher with little regard for any so-called objectivity in its data-near descriptive research. I see the products of this type of research as being similar to journalism, and at the borderline of the scientific tradition by virtue of being more descriptive than interpretive (however note, journalism is a worthwhile endeavor in and of itself, and is not clearly distinguishable from social sciences; Weaver & McCombs, 1980).

In between the two extremes, namely grand theories that attempt to explain every-thing and mini-theories that avoid explaining much of anything, are "middle-range" theories (Boudon, 1991; Friedman, 2002; Merton, 1968). Rather than trying to explain everything, these theories carve out a limited, but not so limited as to be just local, context in which to explain how things might operate, and they attempt mod-est generalizations across local situations in search of regularities without becoming fixated on either grandiosely explaining everything or humbly denying the possi-bility of any useful explanations. Middle-range approaches focus on balancing the interplay between theory and data without privileging either, while recognizing the equal importance of both, providing a solid foundation upon which to further develop scientific theory. In contrast, grand theories can be seen as overly focused on building one-size-fits-all theory to the exclusion of attending to the specifics of data, while mini-theory can be seen as overly focused on gathering specific data to the exclusion of building generalizable theory. As must be evident, I am a strong proponent of middle-range transpersonal psychology theory (M-R TPT), which I position within a post-positivistic epistemology (Popper, 2001/1937) congruent with methodological pluralism (Dawson, Fischer, & Stein, 2006; Robbins & Friedman, 2009). My approach neither claims that M-R TPT needs to be veridical to any ontological truth, nor does it privilege any singular empirical method as inherently better or worse, but it is pragmatic for building a science of transpersonal psychology, as well as supporting transpersonal praxis.

Concepts and Constructs

To build M-R TPT, transpersonal psychology needs scientific concepts that are amenable to clear operationalization for testing hypotheses that derive from theories, as theories again are simply linkages between and among concepts. This in turn can lead to further theory building and then further empirical research in an open and iterative cycle that characterizes the scientific process, and differentiates it from closed approaches. Scientific strategy facilitates progress, rather than stagnation, and differentiates transpersonal psychology as a science from traditional worldviews and religions, as well as philosophy (note, my intent is not to denigrate traditional worldviews, religions, or philosophy, but to separate them as different, but neither better nor worse, from science). However, it is especially important that transpersonal psychology not attempt to be a New Age religion by advocating for stances that are supernatural and metaphysical, while hypocritically posing as a science.

Consequently, building M-R TPT first involves developing clearly defined concepts that are empirically accessible. Concepts can be gleaned from natural language, but to build a theory of scientific worth using terms employed in natural language can be quite problematic. For example, one natural language concept that is relevant to transpersonal psychology is "awe," but it is a quite ambiguous term, so I and a colleague recently used qualitative methods to clarify it (see Bonner & Friedman, 2011). This type of clarification is especially important within transpersonal psychology, where natural language terms often employ contradictory traditional usages, which can be especially difficult to define when imbued with supernatural and metaphysical baggage. Additionally difficult is when the meaning of words radically change over time—as in the case of awe, which has shifted from originally describing an overwhelming sense of fear (e.g., as reflected in the recent U.S. military campaign titled "shock and awe") to now describing a predominantly positive emotion (e.g., the ubiquitously overused slang of "awesome" as a positive exclamation). In our recent research, Bonner and I focused on clarifying this term to make it more useful for building M-R TPT, and our intent was to operationalize it through later creating an empirical measure useful for testing M-R TPT involving awe. A natural language term that is clarified this way takes on less ambiguous meaning by being specified in ways delineating what it does and does not mean, preparing it for operationalization and making it more useful for theory building.

Constructs are a special type of concept that are acknowledged as being artificially created (i.e., not used in natural language) and have scientifically designated meanings, even if they may refer only to imaginary entities without clear veridical connection with any reality. To avoid the problems with imprecisely specified natural language terms, it may be simpler to coin a new, more precise, term not found in ordinary usages. In that sense, scientific constructs, although expressed in natural language terms, are created for theoretical purposes. As such, they do not need to be real in any veridical sense when used to build theory, and often it is important to refrain from prematurely reifying them, as they can simply be temporary place markers for what may or may not later justify the ontological status of being deemed "real." However, to be part of science, there has to be some potential at least for them to earn such a status by being amenable to empirical observation. One current example of a construct is the Higg's boson or so-called "god particle." It has long been a sought prize in modern physics as a needed complement for extant theories in physics, despite that its actual existence was until recently only speculative—and whether or not its existence has recently been empirically verified is subject to much debate (Ellwanger, 2012). The point is, prior to being supposedly found, the Higg's boson was constructed as something needed to have scientific theory make sense, so it was only a place marker for what was not yet known, yet was seen as a useful fiction for building and testing theory. What made the Higg's boson within the realm of science, and not within the realm of the supernatural and metaphysics, is that as a construct it was potentially amenable to empirical scrutiny, even if that had to wait until a huge super-collider was built to test for its existence. Many transpersonal notions used in grand theory, such as non-duality (Wilber, 2001), are unavoidably metaphysical and supernatural. In contrast, science as an empirical endeavor is limited to the study of the physical and natural, namely that which is phenomenal (i.e., can be experienced empirically). Terms without empirical referents, such as nonduality, pose insurmountable scientific challenges when employed as building blocks for developing M-R TPT. At a minimum, to begin specifying the diverse meaning of these terms into narrower categories would surely offend some in spiritual traditions who might use the terms in their own parochial ways, while finding empirical referents for them would be impossible.

When an adequate natural language concept does not exist, but a new concept is created to be useful for theory building and testing, it is called a construct (i.e., something constructed, rather than given). Consequently, I coined the neologism "self-expansiveness" (Friedman, 1981, 1983), which I defined as referring to the flex-ibility in the boundaries everyone draws around their sense of self (i.e., self-concept), and I emphasized that this boundary, which can range from quite narrow to quite expansive, includes the possibility of transpersonal self-expansiveness. Note that, after the advent of search engines, I recently found that some others had used this same term in different contexts and with different meanings than I ascribed to it, but my usage was constructed for a specific purpose, namely to be used to build and test M-R TPT. Self-expansiveness is presented as not being necessarily the best concept (or construct) for building M-R TPT, rather it is just one among many potential contenders, such as awe, that holds heuristic potential for developing M-R TPT by being operationalizable for empirically testing.

Why Transpersonal Psychology Should Be Scientific

I have long advocated that transpersonal psychology should be a science (e.g., Friedman, 1981, 1983). In an earlier "manifesto" (Friedman, 2002), I made a number of arguments for this conclusion, which I briefly summarize in this section. I start with the fact that transpersonal psychology is positioned as a subfield of the discipline of psychology by virtue of its name. As such, transpersonal psychology is widely recognized, and benefits by being seen, as a science. Juxtaposing the terms transpersonal and psychology clearly implies that whatever transpersonal psychology might be, it relates to psychology, which makes it part of a recognized scientific endeavor. Regarding the academic aspects of transpersonal psychology, this understanding places it within psychology departments, while in terms of praxis, it opens the door for legitimacy in the eyes of those seeking and paying for professional services. In the clinical arena, potential clients seeking traditional healing (e.g., from someone invoking a supernatural intervention within a religious tradition) or New Age healing (e.g., from someone employing a pseudoscientific energy device) would clearly not expect the same protections or expertise based on science as they would if going to a licensed psychologist. Anyone claiming to be an applied psychologist would be seen as having at least some scientific background and training when claiming that title, even if not possessing actual expertise. Likewise, when a scholar produces a work as a psychologist, there are expectations related to the scientific basis of such a product. Even if the term transpersonal is used as a qualifier, specifying the type of psychology being practiced or produced, it does not act as a disqualifier that allows one to operate outside of the scientific tradition. Those who use the term transpersonal psychology but eschew science, yet garner benefits from their practices and work products through being associated with the science of psychology, are perpetuating a potential ethical, and possible legal, breach.

Beyond this encumbrance lies a more basic issue, namely is it even possible for transpersonal psychology to actually be a science? Braud (1998), among others, raised this question, and many reject the possibility of a scientific transpersonal psychology, despite that I advocate for this on many grounds (see Friedman, 2002). After all, central aspects of the transpersonal are often defined as being ineffable, dealing with realities beyond the ordinary senses and transcending all conceptualizations. However, science is founded on empiricism, and the scientific process operating in transpersonal psychology can be described as an effort toward reducing that which was formerly seen as ineffable into that which literally makes sense (as in being in accord with the world as one can empirically find it through the senses). But what about aspects of the transpersonal that are clearly outside the bounds of science, such as non-duality and other empirically inaccessible concepts (e.g., soul) that seem to transcend ordinary reality? People usually experience the world, including themselves, through an implicit Cartesian divide, which perceptually splits their sense of subjectivity from objectivity, separating the sense of self as lived from a world that is perceived as being other than the self, including dividing their own sense of self into the subjective "I" and objective "me" (James, 1890). So how can such a radical divide be handled by scientific approaches, as transcendent states (e.g., nonduality, unitive consciousness, etc.) would abnegate all conventional bases of knowledge involving separation between knower and known? These questions pose a conundrum that lead me to the conclusion that transpersonal psychology cannot be scientific unless it is constrained into abandoning its focus on transcendence. Although disallowing speculations about transcendence, by labeling that as non-scientific, reduces the scope of its study, I see it as unavoidably necessary if transpersonal psychology is to be scientific. Some might see this stance as destroying the heart of transpersonal psychology, and leaving only trivial concerns for it to study. However, this is the trap that I believe underlies the continuing fascination of transpersonal psychology with grand theory, including the many problems stemming from such a fascination.

To escape this trap, I believe it has to be forthrightly acknowledged and accepted that there are areas within the transpersonal that truly elude scientific efforts. The solution I proposed (Friedman, 2002) involves delimiting transpersonal psychology using one simple maneuver, namely dividing that which is transpersonal into two components: its transcendent and non-transcendent aspects. In this regard, a scientific transpersonal psychology can bracket all concern about the transcendent, as that is not amenable to empirical approaches or even conceptualization itself. In fact, whatever transcendence might be and/or not be (as the most basic state of being itself cannot necessarily be predicated or denied to it) is undefined, but I loosely take it to be anything that is supernatural and metaphysical (e.g., that might be outside of space and time). Again, science can only deal with the natural and physical.

Conceptualization, which is one of the foundations of science, seems logically to require a Cartesian split between knower and known, and any direct, non-mediated knowing would not be conceptual but of another ilk that is outside of the parameters of science. By bracketing sticky metaphysical and supernatural issues, and focusing instead only on the non-transcendent aspects of the transpersonal, a scientific transpersonal psychology can be developed. This does not mean, however, that the transcendent cannot be studied, only that it cannot be studied under the guise of psychology, which is a scientific endeavor. To study the transcendent directly would involve way more than science could ever capture, as approaching the transcendent would seem to require going beyond both limited concepts and data into other possible non-scientific frameworks and ways of knowing. This bracketing, which I have championed, requires acknowledgement that transcendence eludes efforts to reduce it into a scientific paradigm, as it is avowedly supernatural and metaphysical.

However, such bracketing does not prohibit a scientific transpersonal psychology from dealing with many other important, even crucial, transpersonal concerns through M-R TPT. But it does undermine the metaphysical and supernatural notions prevalent within transpersonal grand theories, while it also avoids the cacophony of focusing only on local understandings as in mini-theories. Despite possible protestations that might allude to potential ways to directly research the transcendent (and that somehow would surmount the Cartesian divide), frankly I have never seen a successful example, nor do I think this is possible while maintaining a scientific vantage (and I eagerly await being proven wrong in this regard). Instead, I accept that science is unavoidably caught in this divide and has to operate within limited parameters that allow it to study only empirical phenomena. Grand theory may attempt to bypass this divide by offering fancy construals that are inclusive of everything, but these are empirically unfounded, while mini-theory does not even approach the divide by instead staying close to the particulars.

For those who want to study the transcendent, there are non-scientific approaches that remain available, such as through religion, poetry, and other artistic expressions, seeking direct attainment via meditation, contemplation, and many other avenues, which all can be called aspects of transpersonal studies and can involve a plethora of non-scientific transpersonal practices (Friedman, 2002). These endeavors are neither intrinsically more or less valuable than science, but they are not science. Likewise, there are many other sciences besides psychology that can study the transpersonal from nonpsychological perspectives, such as transpersonal anthropology and sociology. Collectively, all disciplines that study the transpersonal can be subsumed under transpersonal studies, whereas a subset of these can be seen as scientific, one of which is transpersonal psychology. My solution does not foreclose on the legitimate right to study or practice the transpersonal in any way, but it does require clarity that non-scientific approaches to transpersonal studies are not part of psychology. Simply put, not all ways to know are scientific, and both scientific and nonscientific ways have their relative advantages and disadvantages. This delineation also makes it clear what transpersonal psychology can and cannot entertain as a science, namely again that the transcendent is outside of the boundary that science can successfully consider.

What Is Left for Transpersonal Psychology to Study?

Some might think that this leaves transpersonal psychology to only consider trivial issues, while it abandons its major concern on transcendence. However, science can be quite broadly construed, even if it cannot deal with transcendence, and can deal with many exciting and important issues that are not transcendent. That which is transpersonal does not have to only be supernatural and metaphysical, as there is a realm of the non-transcendent transpersonal that is amenable to science, which I am trying to carve out for M-R TPT. For example, to feel a merger of one's identity with another during the experience of love-making can be transpersonally self-expansive, yet this may be a transpersonal experience that is non-transcendent, namely an experience that only overcomes the sense of being an isolated individual but that does not necessarily lead to any supernatural or metaphysical experience. A sense of dyadic oneness, in which two are merged in identity but still exist as separate from others within the larger cosmos, is not the same as a non-dual experience of unity with the entirety of the cosmos and beyond—and that obliterates any possibilities of conceptualization. Although both can be seen as transpersonal, the former would be non-transcendent and amenable to scientific study, whereas the latter would be transcendent and outside of the purview of science.

Regarding the methods of science, James (1890) proposed a radical empiricism, which is congruent with my vision of transpersonal psychology as a science. For example, people ordinarily perceive from an inside versus outside perspective toward the world, delineated by using their skin as the boundary. Conventional science tends to only look outward, but what occurs both within and outside of the skin is within the purview of science, such that science can focus on inner data, even if they seem subjective and resistant to objectification, as well as more conventionally can focus on outer data, such as things and other persons. Inner data can be obtained through phenomenological methods and, with the advent of new technologies, through scientific apparatuses, such as electroencephalographs, which are simply sensory extenders (see Krippner & Friedman, 2009). Scientific data can also be collected from various states of consciousness, including alternate (i.e., to ordinary waking consciousness in Western culture; see Tart, 1975) states. To be seen as empirical data, all that is required is that information be amenable (or potentially amenable) to the senses, although it needs to be recognized that the senses can operate under many different consciousness states (e.g., under the influence of psychedelic substances; Friedman, 2006). As long as phenomenological data from an alternate state can be accessed with some degree of reliability (again, a prerequisite for being a scientifically valid observation), either by the same researcher across time or by others, it can be studied scientifically. Thus a community of meditators who share common practices that alter their ordinary consciousness in reliable ways can be seen as producing empirical data that are accessible to science. Insofar as some in such a community might have what could be described as transcendent experiences, these would be outside the realm of science to directly study (i.e., I would see these direct experiences as noumenal, not phenomenal). But these could be brought into scientific study as remembrances that are translated into concepts, despite that transcendent experiences themselves would not be amenable to science. So the stories such allegedly transcendence-experiencing meditators might tell should be seen as different from their direct experiences, and their stories could yield good data for science as stories. Last on this point, I must admit that I am not even comfortable calling so-called transcendent experiences an "experience," as that places the term back into limiting Cartesian concepts, so even that term should itself only be seen as a loose metaphor for an ineffability.

From such a broad perspective on science, why would studying the transcendent directly be out of scientific bounds? Perceiving phenomena is at the heart of empiricism and is based on a differentiation, such as in signal detection theory where a sensory input, at its simplest, is either deemed present or absent. From a transcendent frame, such basic delineation falls meaningless, similar to how the so-called laws of physics appear to break down under the conditions in a black hole. Any attempt to impose categorization onto transcendence is simply off the mark, as it reduces it to a symbol, such as language or mathematics or perhaps a graphical relationship, but such symbols are not "it," only faint shadows of whatever it might be and not be simultaneously. Even if one were to have a transcendent experience in any meaningful sense, it cannot be attributed to that one as an individual, as at the point of such experience individuality would seem to dissolve. Likewise, to try to conceptualize about it later would necessarily portray it in reduced terms, and even to attempt to remember it would seem to be only a translated blur reconstructed within dualistic memory. One could extemporaneously dance or sing as an attempted depiction of a transcendent experience, but even such a free expression would only be at best a loose translation of the ineffable. To attempt to capture anything that could be meaningfully called transcendent within a scientific frame with its demands for logical consistency and empirical accessibility is more than challenging as, in my opinion, it is simply not possible.

Conclusion

This chapter outlines a guide to building M-R TPT as an alternative to both grand theory and mini-theory. In order to build M-R TPT, emphasis is placed on developing concepts, including constructs, that are empirically accessible and relevant to transpersonal psychology. This requires bracketing concepts that are metaphysical and supernatural, as they are outside of the purview of science. A viable transpersonal psychology based on such development can lead to useful theories, cumulative programs of research, and applied practices that are empirically supported. One construct that could be useful for this purpose is self-expansiveness, which is discussed in greater depth in another chapter (Friedman, this volume). It is introduced to provide a concrete example of how M-R TPT can be pursued. However, other concepts, such as awe, are also potentially useful for such a purpose.

References

Allwood, C., & Berry, J. (2006). Origins and development of indigenous psychologies: An international analysis. *International Journal of Psychology, 41*(4), 243-268.

Bonner, E., & Friedman, H. (2011). A conceptual clarification of the experience of awe: An interpretative phenomenological analysis. *The Humanistic Psychologist, 39*, 222-235.

Boudon, R. (1991). What middle-range theories are. *Contemporary Sociology, 20*(4), 519-522.

Braud, W. (1998). Can research be transpersonal? *Transpersonal Psychology Review, 2*(3), 9-17.

Bunge, M. A. (1997). Mechanism and explanation. *Philosophy of the social sciences, 27*, 410-465.

Clements, J. (2004). Organic inquiry: Toward research in partnership with Spirit. *Journal of Transpersonal Psychology, 36*(1), 26-49.

Dawson, T., Fischer, K., & Stein, Z. (2006). Reconsidering qualitative and quantitative research approaches: A cognitive developmental perspective. *New Ideas in Psychology, 24*, 229-239.

Ellwanger, U. (2012). A Higgs boson near 125 GeV with enhanced di-photon signal in the NMSSM. *Journal of High Energy Physics, 44*(3), 1-9.

Ferrer, J. (2002). *Revisioning transpersonal theory: A participatory vision of human spirituality.* Albany: State University of New York Press.

Friedman, H. (1981). The construction and validation of a transpersonal measure of self-concept: The Self-Expansiveness Level Form. *Dissertation Abstract International, 42*(02), 0079B (UMI #8117150).

Friedman, H. (1983). The Self-Expansiveness Level Form: A conceptualization and measurement of a transpersonal construct. *Journal of Transpersonal Psychology, 15*, 37-50.

Friedman, H. (2002). Transpersonal psychology as a scientific field. *International Journal of Transpersonal Studies, 21*, 175-187.

Friedman, H. (2005). Problems of romanticism in transpersonal psychology: A case study of Aikido. *The Humanistic Psychologist, 33*, 3-24.

Friedman, H. (2006). The renewal of psychedelic research: Implications for humanistic and transpersonal psychology. *The Humanistic Psychologist, 34*(1), 39-58.

Friedman, H. (2009). Xenophilia as a cultural trap: Bridging the gap between transpersonal psychology and religious/spiritual traditions. *International Journal of Transpersonal Studies*, *28*, 107-111.

Friedman, H. (2010). Is Buddhism a psychology? Commentary on romanticism in "Mindfulness in Psychology." *The Humanistic Psychologist*, *38*, 184-189.

Friedman, H. (this volume). Transpersonal self-expansiveness as a scientific construct (Chapter 11).

Fuchs, T., & Jaegher, H. (2009). Enactive intersubjectivity: Participatory sense-making and mutual incorporation. *Phenomenological Cognitive Science*, *8*, 465-486. Retrieved from https://www.klinikum.uni-heidelberg.de/fileadmin/zpm/psychatrie/fuchs/Enactive_Intersubjectivity.pdf

Jaccard, J., & Jacoby, J. (2010). *Theory construction and model-building skills: A practical guide for social scientists*. New York, NY: Guilford.

James, W. (1890). *The principles of psychology*. New York, NY: Henry Holt.

Jung, C. (1997). *Jung on active imagination*. Princeton, NJ: Princeton University Press.

Krippner, S., & Friedman, H. (Eds.). (2009). *Mysterious minds: The neurobiology of psychics, mediums, and other extraordinary people*. Santa Barbara, CA: Praeger.

Laszlo, E. (2004). *Science and the Akashic field: An integral theory of everything*. Rochester, VT: Inner Traditions.

MacDonald, D. A., (2007, March 28). Where's that wascally Wilber? The challenges of hitting a moving target [A review of the book Where's Wilber At?]. *PsycCRITIQUES - Contemporary Psychology: APA Review of Books*, *52*(13), Article 5.

Merton, R. (1968). *Social theory and social structure*. New York, NY: Free Press.

Popper, K. (2001). *The logic of scientific discovery*. New York, NY: Routledge. (Originally published in 1937)

Robbins, B., & Friedman, H. (Eds.) (2009). Special issue on methodological pluralism [entire]. *The Humanistic Psychologist*, *37*(1).

Sehrbrock, J. (2007). Preliminary evidence for the effectiveness of integrally informed psychotherapy. *Journal of Integral Theory and Practice*, *2*(1), 40-59.

Solso, R. L. (2001). *Cognitive psychology* (5th ed.). Boston, MA: Allyn and Bacon.

Tart, C. T. (1975). *States of consciousness*. New York, NY: Dutton.

Wallis, R. (2003). *Shamans/Neo-Shamans: Ecstasy, alternative archaeologies and contemporary Pagans*. New York, NY: Routledge

Weaver, D., & McCombs, M. (1980). Journalism and social science: A new relationship? *Public Opinion Quarterly*, *44*(4), 477-494.

Wilber, K. (2001). *A theory of everything: An integral vision for business, politics, science, and spirituality*. Boston, MA: Shambhala.

17

Philosophical Underpinnings of Transpersonal Psychology as a Science

Douglas A. MacDonald

As to any truth-declaring system, truth is undeclarable; so 'an enunciation of truth' is just the name given to it.

The Buddha

The preceding quote attributed to Gotama Buddha and taken from the Diamond Sūtra (translation by A. F. Price & Wong Mou-lam, 1990, p. 42) succinctly captures the inherent nature and workings of science as I understand them, while also communicating a fundamental dilemma with which science is confronted but, when acknowledged with humility, honesty, and integrity, forms a solid basis from which science operates. That dilemma can be posed as an innocent question—how do I know that what I think I know is, in actually, what there is to know? The question can be applied to anything we think we know or want to know—objects, people, experiences, ideas, emotions, systems, and even the act and processes of knowing itself. Stated a different way, how do I know that my experiences, my symbols, my words, my ideas, my speculations, my theories, and so forth convey/embody truth? This question is especially pertinent to transpersonal psychology, which attempts to address some of the most difficult questions possible.

Within the context of these questions, science can be seen as a way of both determining truth and, at the same time, a way of examining claims to truth. Its primary aim and goal is to serve as a vehicle through which humans can know the cosmos and themselves, as well as everything above, below, between, within, and beyond these things. Yet as a necessary and dynamic component of this, it is also a way of reflecting upon the nature of truth and knowing in a manner that is self-critical and open to revision. Science is not a static entity, but a fluid process in which mechanisms for

The Wiley Blackwell Handbook of Transpersonal Psychology, First Edition.
Edited by Harris L. Friedman and Glenn Hartelius.
© 2013 John Wiley & Sons, Ltd. Published 2015 by John Wiley & Sons, Ltd.

generating, examining, testing, and revising truth claims are rendered transparent—and made openly available to anyone who takes the time to learn and participate in the process.

A Brief Overview of Conventional Science

The origins of science may be traced back to the Greek thinker Thales of Miletus (640-546 BCE), who is credited with starting the critical tradition in Western philosophy (Leahey, 1987). Many systems of thought claim access to truth but do not have any means through which to verify and, if deemed erroneous, revise such claims. These are closed systems, as found in religion and schools of thought in which knowledge by authority is assumed to a sufficient basis for determinations of verdicality. In contrast, the critical tradition led to both rational and experiential grounds as a method of openly testing and improving upon ideas as representations and explanations of reality.

In the time following the birth of the critical tradition, epistemology emerged as a formal branch of philosophy expressly concerned with knowledge. This inspired the possibility of acquiring "true" knowledge by devising sophisticated systems of thought which, in turn, fostered the creation of methods that have contributed to the growth of science. In essence, when looked at within the history of philosophy, science can be thought of as an integration of two seemingly disparate approaches to knowledge—rationalism (i.e., the use of reasoning as a means of determining truth) and empiricism (i.e., the school of thought which maintains that knowledge can only be obtained through experience). Although the discoveries of Copernicus, Kepler, and Galileo were momentous and demonstrated the explanatory power of linking rationality to observation, the best argumentation for the synthesis of these two traditions can seen in the work of Immanuel Kant. In his *Critique of Pure Reason,* Kant (1771/1996) discussed the inherent limitations of each approach and proffered a philosophy that permitted theory and reason to be used as the basis of attributing meaning to experience. In essence, he offered experience as the testing grounds to ascertain the extent to which theory conforms to and illuminates our apprehension of ourselves and the cosmos. In Kant's thinking, both theory and experience mutually inform each other and, concomitantly, compel each other to flourish. When left in isolation, however, theory without experience becomes mere metaphysics and experience without theory loses all substantive meaning.

With that stated, from the time of the ancient Greeks up to the present, there has been tacit recognition that the world of appearances and reality (i.e., the world as-it-really-is) may not be the same. Said in a different way, our perception and the true nature and qualities of whatever it is we perceive may not actually have any objective correspondence. Plato, for instance, maintained that objects and things cannot be known as they really are, but only as approximations, and imperfect ones at that, of what he viewed as eternal Forms or Ideas. Other approaches, including linguistics, phenomenology and postmodern philosophies (e.g., social constructionism, deconstructionism), have also presented argumentation that the signs and symbols used to codify experience are ultimately imperfect representations of experience. Within the auspices of psychology, a number of well-known theorists (e.g., George Kelly, 1955;

Carl Rogers, 1974; the early Gestalt psychologists like Wertheimer, 1944, and Köhler, 1969) put forth similar arguments that knowledge of reality independent of our own subjective perception is likely not possible. For instance, Rogers maintained that what is knowable is defined entirely by our subjective field of experience. Kelly advanced the notion of constructive alternativism, which is based on the premise that it is impossible to know something separate from our constructs (i.e., structuring ideas and thoughts). And the Gestaltists advanced the idea of psychological isomorphism—that our experience parallels but is different from the objects within our experience. Ostensibly, such views about the relation of perception to knowledge raise some very basic questions about the nature and qualities of knowledge itself. Is knowledge something that is absolute and objective, which is discovered, or is it a construction derived from some intra- and/or inter-subjective process, as is maintained by many postmodern schools of thought?

Science, curiously enough, has acknowledged the problem of indeterminacy of perception and with what we call the challenge of establishing the goodness-of-fit of ideas, concepts, and theories to experience, and vice versa. Its response to this problem is that concepts and theories are representations of things in experience that may or may not be real, but which, nevertheless, have value in their capacity to account for and explain events occurring in experience. Extending from this, scientific knowledge, especially in the context of any psychological science, can be understood as the product of the interaction of theory with experience. The extent to which they both conform to each other—most generally and commonly manifested in terms of the ability of theory to allow science to accurately and meaningfully predict and control events occurring within experience—reflects the unique power of science. Implicit in this notion is the recognition that we can never with absolute certainty prove that our theories and models are the same as our experience. Similarly, we can never prove that our experience is a pristine, flawless and complete embodiment of whatever it is that we are experiencing. A map is not the territory that it represents, but merely an approximate model. The utility of the map, in providing us with a way of orienting ourselves within the terrain as we experience it, is the basis on which the validity of the map is ascertained. To confuse the map and the terrain that it represents, specifically to assume that the map is something that is equivalent to the terrain itself, is a fallacy known as reification (also known as hypostatization). Science tries to guard itself against the reification of concepts and ideas, and only advances the view of equivalency of the two when the evidence suggesting the goodness-of-fit between the concept and the experience is invariant across time, place, and researcher.

Nested within this discussion thus far is another important set of considerations, namely, the problems of bias and distortion as they manifest in scientific inquiry and resultant knowledge claims. Especially in the past few decades, science has come to recognize that the basis on which we assert to have valid knowledge may be influenced by a variety of factors including situational, contextual, personal, socio-cultural, and political factors. Science is a human creation, after all, and the limitations introduced by our humanness contribute to a range of difficulties, ranging from imprecision and inexactness to misinterpretation and overgeneralization all the way to frank dissimulation and fraud. Because of this, science has tried to build within itself self-monitoring and self-corrective mechanisms to identify false claims in order to either modify them, or, if needed, purge them from the corpus of scientific knowledge. Among these mechanisms are an impressive armamentarium of strategies aiming toward the following: (a) reducing the likelihood that personal motivations and errors in thinking of a researcher result in biases in how scientific research is designed and executed, and its resulting data interpreted (e.g., disclosure of potential conflicts of interest and adherence to the rules of rationality in linking theory to data prior to acquiring the data, taking care to identify cultural influences on theory and/or data and their interpretation); (b) ensuring that researchers adopt rigorous designs including standardized approaches to gathering data so as to minimize the chances that situationally specific influences, including researcher/experimental biases and effects, and sampling biases do not lead to erroneous/misrepresentative data and conclusions (i.e., that experiences of the phenomenon of interest are comparable and as similar as possible, while controlling for potential nuisance and confounding influences on a phenomenon that may undermine defendable and theory-driven interpretations of findings); (c) introducing rigor in how theory is tied to experience and data so as to permit for precision in identifying the fit between the two (e.g., developing logical and testable hypotheses as extensions of the theory and ruling out competing hypotheses as providing better fit to the data); and (d) making the scientific process and outcomes transparent to others so that the ideas, method, and data can be replicated and extended by independent researchers (e.g., peer review and scrutiny of findings by members of the scientific community). Thus all sciences may be viewed as attempting to produce and test knowledge claims which are minimally biased, grounded on a logical and empirically demonstrable link between theory and experience, and are rendered open to criticism and revision.

Science is a Philosophy and More

Science as an epistemological endeavor remains very much a branch of philosophy in its reliance on untestable assumptions, albeit it is also an empirically informed branch that has added value in some contexts. As such, science is not the only way to obtain knowledge, and the assumptions and conclusions of science regarding the nature of knowledge and the processes by which knowledge claims can be understood and evaluated are not the only valid or useful ones. There are multiple ways of conceptualizing what knowledge is and how to acquire it, including from transpersonal perspectives (e.g., see Tart, 1975; Walsh & Vaughan, 1980; Wilber, 1990, 1995, 2001). However undeniably, when one considers the developments made over the past few hundred years in many fields of inquiry, science has accomplished things that no other area of inquiry has been able to do and, by association, earns a privileged status among epistemologies. Ostensibly, argumentation about the validity of science based upon its pragmatic products has resulted in science gaining increased status and import with business, government, and the general public, as manifested by the resources and mechanisms put into place to support it (e.g., incorporation in educational curricula, public and private funding of scientific research, etc.).

By its very nature, science is a social enterprise. As noted by Kuhn (1970) in his Weltanschauung (i.e., World View) analysis, science, including theory development and methodology, flows from, and is grounded upon, necessary a priori assumptions that themselves are not verified or even verifiable with the theories and methods, but which require agreement among a community of people in order for science to operate and progress. It is important to emphasize this—the assumptions are themselves not "provable" by the conventional rules of science. They are taken as givens. Science is based upon a community of people subscribing to the same assumptions about what is knowable, what is knowledge, and what you need to do to acquire and validate the veridicality of knowledge claims. In this way, it could be argued that science and religious systems, if not all organized human social systems, share in common the utilization of certain axioms that themselves are not questioned, but serve the functional purpose of allowing for organized communication and social behavior. Kuhn referred to the collection of assumptions as the disciplinary matrix which, when combined with shared exemplars (i.e., models of what constitutes appropriate methodology), constitutes the paradigm of a science. As he aptly pointed out, if one wants to be part of science and do things that are recognized as contributing to science, then one needs to agree with the assumptions and utilize methods congruent with the shared exemplars.

Bunge (2006), a philosopher of science who has authored more than 50 books on the scientific paradigm, has well-defined views on what assumptions are needed to make an epistemological system a science. Following his lead, science is characterized as having the following features: (a) the rules of logic and rationality are followed to direct deductive reasoning regarding the interpretation of data and experience (when doing confirmatory or theory-testing research), as well as to guide inductive inference-making (in the case of exploratory science), but, in the case of the latter, does not claim onto itself to validate the inferences, as validation is dependent upon experimentation and empiricism; (b) language and semiotic systems are assumed to meaningfully represent phenomena and putative facts, so that scientific propositions match the facts to which they refer; (c) ontological materialism or naturalism serves as the basis of all that is knowable and real, as "all real things are material (possess energy)...and ideas in themselves, however true or useful, are fictions" (p. 34); (d) epistemological realism is assumed, namely that it is possible to know reality, albeit imperfectly, and that scientific theories can and do represent aspects of the real world; (e) secular ethics, which balance the quest for knowledge with consideration for the impact of science on the well-being of others and the world, are important, and; (f) epistemic socialism is followed, which does not rely on the dictates of some unassailable authority but, rather, is informed and influenced by a community of experts who themselves must be accountable to the scientific community. Housed within point "c" are four additional philosophical features that Bunge cited as requisite components of science: moderate skepticism (i.e., the belief that scientific knowledge is fallible and can be improved upon); moderate empiricism (i.e., all hypotheses must be empirically testable and verifiable); moderate rationalism (i.e., scientific knowledge develops though the interaction of induction and deduction along with experience); and scientism (i.e., the belief that "whatever is knowable and worth knowing is best known scientifically" [p. 34]). It is noteworthy that Bunge has applied his view of the philosophy of science to existing disciplines and the extent to which they demonstrate adherence to these assumptions, concluded that the "hard" sciences (i.e., physics, chemistry, biology) implicitly meet his principles, while the "soft" sciences (i.e., social sciences including psychology) only satisfy some of them. In this regard, transpersonal psychology remains one of the softest of sciences.

Measurement, Quantification, and Science

Thus far, I have discussed the nature of science as an epistemological system and have tried to illustrate that, at least in its intended form, it can be viewed as a multifaceted endeavor that is simply concerned with truth and knowledge. I have also attempted to communicate that contrary to many caricatures of it, science does not subscribe to the view that its products (i.e., theories, models, explanations, and knowledge) are in any way absolute. They are approximations and representations, which can be criticized and revised and nothing more. However, one thing that needs to be made explicit is the place of measurement and quantification in science.

Despite the fact that there are a variety of methods used in science that place very little weight on measurement, quantification of phenomena is often equated with science. It should be noted that nothing stated thus far makes quantification a requirement for science. Ethology, for example, is a branch of biology that relies extensively on naturalistic observation and description as the basis for its empirical research. It is quite clear that qualitative and observational methods devoid of measurement are used in many scientific fields, including in some areas of psychology, such that quantification is not the only approach to meaningful and systematic inquiry and knowledge acquisition.

However, quantitative methods are prominent in many sciences in that, first, measurement often provides strong support for the approximation to reality of a phenomenon and, second, the demonstrated success of mathematics as a logic system for organizing data. In regard to the first, if something is measurable, then that provides information as to its ontological status and empirical accessibility (i.e., it means that it is part of the natural world and is available to experience). In addition, it better ensures reliability of empirical data because, when a system of measurement is used to quantify a variable, it helps standardize it so that it can be compared across studies. Second, since the emergence of formal mathematics (and geometries), the elegance and rigorous logic of these systems have demonstrated with tremendous success their capacity to account for and help explain/predict natural phenomena. In essence it can be said that quantitative methods serve to bolster two of the basic assumptions of the scientific paradigm, namely those of naturalism and the potency of rationality and logic to elucidate truth.

Physics is perhaps the most putative example of a scientific discipline that has benefited from quantification, relying upon the measurement of material processes with increasing power and lucidity to articulate the fundamental properties of matter and energy. However, psychology has also made some significant advances as a function of measurement. For example, psychophysics, arguably the first real expression of psychology as a scientific discipline, was able to quantitatively investigate the covariation of physical phenomena with psychological experience to such a level of effectiveness that it produced its first "laws" (i.e., Fechner's law, Weber's law, and Steven's law; D'Amato, 1970). Thereafter, thanks to the work of Galton and Cattell, the latter of whom developed the first formal "mental" test in 1890, psychometrics was created as an approach to defining and meaningfully measuring aspects of consciousness, cognition, and human psychology, which permitted study of phenomena previously considered to be outside the purview of scientific inquiry (Leahey, 1987).

Science and Transpersonal Psychology

Since its inception as a discrete area of inquiry in the late 1960s, transpersonal psychology has struggled with its identity and its relationship to science. This struggle can be seen both in the numerous publications dedicated to its definition, vision, and goals (e.g., Hartelius, Caplan, & Rardin, 2007; Lajoie & Shapiro, 1992, 1996; Valle, 1989; Vaughan, 1985; Walsh & Vaughan, 1993), and in the variety of criticisms raised regarding the applicability of conventional science to transpersonal psychology, including several proposals for new methods and even new paradigms that would better permit the meaningful study of the transpersonal than what appears capable with mainstream approaches (e.g., Davis, 2009; Shear, 2007; Tart, 1975; Taylor, 2009; Wilber, 1990, 1995).

Consequently, some in transpersonal psychology have adopted a variety of positions that put it at odds with established scientific assumptions, and that have created the appearance that scientific methods do a disservice to the inherent integrity of the subfield (see Friedman, 2002). For example, it is relatively common for transpersonal psychologists to allege reductionism as a fundamental problem of science (e.g., Wilber, 2001). Because of the subscription of science to naturalism/materialism, rationality, and linguistic/semiotic representationalism, it tends to take transpersonal phenomena, such as spiritual experiences, and reduce them to mechanisms (e.g., biological) and/or logical propositions, which simply do not conform or do justice to the real nature, quality, and significance of such phenomena. This criticism has merits, at least insofar as one might view transpersonal phenomena as ontologically real and of a source and quality that is not reducible to material processes in the first place. However, to view transpersonal phenomena in this way is to advance an assumption that there is more to reality than nature. From the perspective of a critic of transpersonal psychology, such an assumption could be viewed as no more substantiated or verifiable than that of naturalism itself. In addition, such an assumption results in the equally intractable problem of transcendental reductionism (i.e., everything including nature itself is reduced to transcendent causes, mechanisms, and processes). Consequently, the criticism of reductionism can be viewed as holding little value in advancing transpersonal science.

Another criticism more specific to the use of quantitative methodologies relates to the reductionism of the quality of an experience to a quantity. It is perhaps stated most succinctly by Wilber (1990, p. 26), "once you have translated the world into empiric measurement and numbers, you have a world without quality, guaranteed." This criticism too appears to have some legitimacy, as quantification of any phenomenon or aspect of functioning does tend to move it away from a more holistic experience. However, implicit to Wilber's stance is the assumption that qualitative methods are somehow more appropriate than quantitative ones for the study of transpersonal phenomena, a position that has been used by some to devise an ever broadening array of qualitative modes of inquiry (e.g., see Anderson & Braud, this volume). Regardless of the promise and pitfalls of qualitative methods, I do think it important to point out that when any experience, transpersonal or otherwise, is codified in any way (e.g., linguistically, symbolically, imaginally), it involves reductionism, because it takes an experience as it is experienced and forces it into a representational system in a way that simply cannot be inclusive of its apprehensive wholeness.

This also ties in with the problem of reification in transpersonal psychology. The confusion of ideas, concepts, and theories with the reality that they are supposed to illuminate is very common, and can cause many problems. To cite one main-stream example, many people including scientists, politicians, and educators, mis-takenly believe that IQ tests measure intelligence in some absolute way—and use a person's performance on such tests to make high stakes decisions that affect the way people live. This fails to realize that such tests only measure equivocal indicators of intelligence, which are typically based upon only one theory of intelligence that itself is only supported by limited empirical research. Intelligence tests are thus only opera-tionalizations of a theory and, at best, are only an approximation of what intelligence really is (whatever that might be). In many instances, transpersonal psychologists also engage in similar reification of their concepts. Ambiguous notions, such as optimal well-being, self-transcendence, and the like are discussed in the literature as if they are as ontologically real, often without serious consideration given to the possibility that they, like all concepts, may be only approximations of what is truly real and knowable. To naively assume that such concepts have a consensual meaning is problematic, and such a closed stance is antithetical to the growth and development of a science.

It should be noted that these critiques do not apply to all transpersonal theo-ries, such as those of Tart (1969) and Ferrer (2002). The former, for example, avoided many of these assumptions in building a way to conceptualize states of con-sciousness, while the latter pointed out many ways in which such assumptions are flawed and need careful deconstruction. Nevertheless, for the further development of transpersonal psychology as a science, these sorts of problems need to be carefully addressed.

One area where I think it may be especially important to focus is on the relation-ship of the scientific worldview, which has thus far been explicated, to what might be called mystical worldviews, which are composed of many diverse traditions that should not be assumed to be necessarily the same. Contemplative and spiritual tradi-tions have been a major inspiration for the subdiscipline's creation and have served as the major focus of its theory development. Like science, mystical traditions provide assumptions and methods (e.g., prayer, meditation) aimed, at least in part, at realiz-ing an epistemological goal. However, they seldom subscribe to a view of knowledge as something that can be represented in any way, as practically all such traditions acknowledge the ineffability and non-reducibility of mystical experience and insight, despite proclaiming that such experience is available to anyone and everyone who humbly and authentically tries to attain it. These mystical worldviews place empha-sis not on knowledge and its acquisition, as does science, but rather on knowing as an immediate apprehension of things-as-they-are. They tend to foster an experiential awareness, which is not mediated by symbols, abstractions, ideas or even by person-hood. Here is where transpersonal psychology has the potential to bring something unique, if not essential, to the realm of science—it provides a way of thinking about how theories and methods geared toward the generation of knowledge may be reconciled with the mystical aspiration of knowing things-as-they-are. It can provide a template and framework for moving science in the direction of perfecting its theory and methods from being mere representations of reality to being vehicles of experiential access to knowing itself. In so doing, it does not need to limit itself to challenging and/or refuting existing assumptions and methods of science. Rather, it simply needs to foster a way of understanding and facilitating an improved goodness-of-fit between knowledge and experience.

In some ways, transpersonal psychology is already demonstrating success in cultivating greater openness to mystical worldviews by science. One excellent example involves meditation, which has become an intensely studied topic over the past four decades (e.g., see MacDonald, Walsh, & Shapiro, this volume). Another example is spirituality. Like meditation, spirituality has generated an incredible amount of scientific research in the past several years, particularly in psychology, nursing, and medicine, and it is now seen as an important component of health and well-being. Both of these areas of inquiry have flourished because of transpersonal psychology and its advocacy for them.

Considerations for Furthering Transpersonal Science

Scientific advances in the studies of meditation and spirituality evidence that transpersonal science is possible, but these have mostly been conducted from conventional scientific frames of reference and have not really tackled the difficult challenges in scientific transpersonal psychology. This requires carefully thinking through a variety of issues at both the paradigmatic and methodological levels. There are three such intertwined relevant areas—the assumption of naturalism, the challenges of representationalism as manifested in goodness-of-fit, and the viability and variety of quantitative methods with particular attention given to psychometric tests.

Is Ontological Materialism a Requirement for Science?

Naturalism, at least as depicted by Bunge (2006) is something that presents some fundamental problems to transpersonal psychology. By limiting the purview of what is knowable only to those things that are part of material and energetic processes, it would seem that anything and everything that is at the heart of the subdiscipline is essentially taken off the table for legitimate scientific inquiry. Indeed, if the stance of transpersonal psychology is that there is a transcendent dimension to reality that exists independently of the natural world and of human experience, then this is difficult to address in any scientific way. However, I think there are other possible points of entry into exploring a way of reframing this situation so that a positive resolution is possible. Conceptions of the transcendent as a separate dimension of reality are inherently metaphysical and idealist in nature, and comprise essential parts of most established religious and theological systems. As I have argued (MacDonald, 2011a; MacDonald & Friedman, 2001), as well as others (e.g., Friedman, 2002; Helminiak, 2008; Slife,

Hope, & Nebeker, 1999), such a metaphysical stance presents irresolvable issues, because its concepts and tenets do not and cannot conform to empiricism (whether sensory or otherwise) as a means of verification. Alternatively, if the transcendent were viewed in purely experiential terms, something that is suggested by most, if not all, extant schools of mysticism, then it could be positioned that the transcendent and transpersonal are just extensions of the continuum of all human experience, and can comfortably be treated in terms that are not dystonic with naturalism. Within this context, it might be said that the assumption of naturalism may be better reconceived as that of experientialism—anything that is available to human experience is a legitimate focus of scientific study.

With that in mind, if naturalism were to be replaced with experientialism, then it would be incumbent upon researchers to exercise considerable discernment in the theories and explanations ascribed to experience. Given the recognized levels of reality (e.g., physical, biological, psychological, social, spiritual), and their mutual interplay and influence on each other, transpersonal researchers (and indeed all researchers) would need to make sure that competing explanations for a given experience or phenomenon associated with one or more of the levels are incorporated into study designs, and are tested. In fact, this is something that is already a part of psychological science. In particular, it has been recognized for some time that a variety of conceptual models may demonstrate reasonably good fit to experience. In order to show that one model is better than another, both need to be tested empirically to examine whether one model reflects greater explanatory power in accounting for variation in the variables comprising the model.

In this vein, if transpersonal researchers want to demonstrate that transcendent experience reflects a transcendent reality, and that such a reality has correlative or causal influences on other levels of reality, then it would be necessary for the researchers to show that their model of transcendent reality accounts for experience (which can be indicated by data based on experience). In fact, all data are ultimately experiential, as humans can only know the world through experience. It is also incumbent that any such model would show improvement over conventional models based upon other levels (e.g., physical, biological, psychological, and social). This is likely to prove to be a tricky task, because conventional explanations based upon material and/or psychosocial factors have available to them a variety of recognized processes and synergisms that are embedded in the assumption of naturalism. For instance, in his articulation of naturalism, Bunge (2006) made mention of three principles that are used to structure how science views the organization and operation of material phenomena and which can be used to account for how elements of the material reality may function and influence one another. These are dynamism (i.e., the recognition that all material processes are in a state of constant change), systemism (i.e., all things are either a system or a part of a system), and emergentism (i.e., all systems have emergent properties that cannot be explained as a function of the components alone). Transpersonal researchers would need to develop and test explanations based upon claims of a transcendent reality that accommodate these features of naturalism in order to make any assertions about the ontology and empirical relevance of a transcendent dimension to existence.

The Problem of Goodness-of-Fit

One way to understand science is to view it as trying to establish a good fit between its representations (whether they be concepts, theories, or models) and experience. Data from a study are the concrete experiences that are used as the ground on which the representation (i.e., map) is juxtaposed. Depending upon the kind of phenomenon being studied, as well as the skills in constructing maps, the ability to produce evidence of goodness-of-fit that will be recognized, replicated, and agreed upon will vary. Sensory experience, for example, permits for relatively discrete assignment of representative symbols/signs (e.g., words, pictures) to relatively discrete objects (e.g., trees, atoms). In the case of this class of experiences, which are energetic and materialistic by their very nature, we often can assume that the assignment of the representative symbol is exclusive (i.e., the sign/symbol only applies to one object in experience and not others). Because of this exclusivity, we can then apply rules of reasoning/logic to our symbols to inductively specify relations between objects (e.g., no relation, either of covariation or causation) and then generate specific hypotheses that can be tested by gathering data (experiencing) the objects. Conventional science has tended to give primacy to sense experience as the preferred mode to acquire knowledge of the world, mostly because of its easy replicabilty—as it is the form of experience that can most readily be reproduced over time and across experients. In addition, there can be a fairly high level of agreement in the reliability of the experience and the objects of experience as associated to representational signs/symbols. Based on this, the ability of research grounded on sensory experience to establish a strong goodness-of-fit with theory is the most straightforward.

Mental experiences (i.e., experiences of mental phenomena), on the other hand, are not as reliable as sensory experience because they are not readily available across experients or within the same experient over time in a way that allows for near consensual agreement among researchers regarding the correspondence of the experience to the symbols/signs used to represent it. Stated differently, because the researcher cannot firmly establish the discrete relation between a representational symbol/sign and a discrete content of experience in a way that other researchers can easily agree upon, the confidence in the sign/symbol-experience relation is weakened. By association, the capacity for researchers to find evidence of a strong goodness-of-fit between theory and data is also weaker as compared to researchers using sensory data. As faced by psychological science, the problem of establishing a clear relation between sign and signified has contributed to difficulties in producing precise concepts which, in turn, has contributed to a proliferation of theories in every area of study (e.g., intelligence, personality, emotion). This phenomenon is not seen to anywhere near the same extent in the hard sciences, which limit their empiricism and theory development to sense experience (e.g., physics, chemistry, and biology).

With transpersonal, and especially in regard to possible transcendent experiences, researchers are placed in an even more difficult position regarding the generation of an agreeable link between representational symbol/sign and the experience, because of the very fact that such experiences are essentially viewed as being beyond linguistic codification and representation. In this class of experiences, the ability to establish goodness-of-fit between word, theory, and experience is reduced to the point at which it may be seen as futile in even trying to engage in any form of scientific inquiry. This fact, namely the indeterminancy of sign-signifed relations with transpersonal phenomena, may be understood as a major contributing factor to the difficulties transpersonal psychology has had making progress as a science in the deeper aspects of its exploration. It is relatively simple to look at whether meditators or people who see themselves as spiritual might be healthier in some conventional ways, but really looking deeply at transpersonal issues, such as how meditation might lead to a transcendent state, is impeded by the fact that there is limited consensus as to even what it is that is being studied.

Notwithstanding the increased difficulties facing mental and especially transpersonal experience and phenomena, it is still possible to engage in meaningful scientific research. In particular, it can be argued that, if a language or representational system contains words/symbols that are defined in a manner that differentiates the meaning of the word/symbol from other words/symbols, those words/symbols can be used to represent something discrete in experience that is not reducible to what is represented by the other words. In the case of both psychological and transpersonal experiences, there are extensive lexicons of words and terms in almost all languages that are designed to discretely represent the varying qualities of those experiences. Importantly, some research has been done to not only help substantiate this view (e.g., Oxman, Rosenberg, Schnurr, Tucker, & Gala, 1988), but to also demonstrate that it is possible to reliably scale and quantify experiential states to permit for standardized measurement (e.g., Back & Bourque, 1970; Bourque & Back, 1968, 1971; MacDonald, 2000a; MacDonald, LeClair, Holland, Alter, & Friedman, 1995).

Quantitative Methods in Transpersonal Research

Extending from the last point, quantitative transpersonal research becomes a possibility when we can identify discrete components of experience that we can then define in terms of one or more dimensions relevant to our interests and that can be enumerated. Examples of this include: frequency of occurrence (e.g., how often a type of experience happens within a specified period of time; how often does a person engage in a specific behavior); strength of agreement or belief (e.g., how strongly does a person believe in, or agree with, statements describing an element of their experience as being characteristic of him/her); intensity (e.g., how potent is a stimulus dimension within experience such as brightness, loudness, emotionality, and so forth); speed/response latency (e.g., the amount of time needed to complete a task); and accuracy (e.g., the ability to solve a problem), to name just a few. The challenge here is to be sure that one is (a) careful in making sure that the component of experience in which there is interest can be made conceptually discrete from other components of experience; and (b) rigorous in ensuring that the concept representing the component of experience is reliably associated with an actual component of experience. Stated differently, researchers need to be sure that the operationalization of their concepts are linked in a rational way to the concept itself and the experience that the concept is intended to elucidate. In addition, any operationalization must show reliability (i.e., consistency across time and experience) and validity (i.e., empirical evidence that it is assessing what it is conceptually supposed to be assessing). These are things that have presented difficulties for the development of measurement tools of transpersonally relevant concepts. For example, there is now a breathtaking array of paper-and-pencil self-report tools claiming to assess spirituality. However, many of them suffer from problems with the inadequate differentiation of spirituality from religion and from well-being (Koenig, 2008, MacDonald, 2000b; Meezenbroek, Garssen, van den Berg, van Dierendonck, Visser, & Schaufeli, 2010; Migdal & MacDonald, 2013), as well as other problems. This has proven to be a problem in meditation research (e.g., see MacDonald, Walsh & Shapiro, this volume), as well as in other areas of transpersonal psychology.

In a variety of publications, I have argued in support of the development, validation, and utilization of psychometric tests in humanistic and transpersonal research, and have presented information on a wide number of available tests (Friedman & MacDonald, 1997, 2002, 2006; MacDonald, 2000b; MacDonald & Friedman, 2002, 2009; MacDonald, Friedman & Kuentzel, 1999; MacDonald, Kuentzel, & Friedman, 1999; MacDonald et al., 1995). Although there are many benefits for the use of such quantitative assessment tools (see MacDonald & Friedman, this volume), there are also other ways to gather meaningful transpersonal data (e.g., using phenomenological and psychophysiological approaches).

An Example of Transpersonal Science as Applied to Measurement

In order to give the reader a more detailed sense of how my approach to science within a transpersonal psychological framework looks in action, I briefly share a program of research on which I have been working for the past 20 years. It is important to state that I do not cite myself because I think that my own research is the only example; there are others in the transpersonal community who have also done scientific work that is quite reputable and serve as good exemplars (e.g., Friedman, this volume-a, -b).

Throughout much of my life, I have had an intense fascination with transpersonal/transcendent states and modes of consciousness and, as I pursued my studies in psychology, I became more and more interested in exploring ways of making them legitimate topics of scientific investigation. However, as I delved into the literature across a wide range of disciplines, I kept encountering criticisms of such topics, which seemed to conclude that transpersonal consciousness is something that is simply not appropriate for scientific study. Thematically, many of these criticisms appeared to revolve around the observation that there is no consensus on what these phenomena really are and on how they can be defined in a way that would permit meaningful study. This prompted me to learn more about measurement, statistics, and scientific method. What emerged from this learning process was both a vision of how to utilize conventional methods to study an inherently transpersonal concept (i.e., spirituality) and a specific desire to try to find a way of devising a definition and measurement tool that would be seen as meeting the standards of rigor espoused by the scientific community.

My efforts began with three assumptions, namely: (a) anything available to experience is available for scientific inquiry (i.e., the assumption of experientialism); (b) although words have been argued in the spiritual and transpersonal literature to be insufficient in describing and explaining spirituality, words may be used to provide an approximate representation of spirituality and spiritual experience based upon the normative use of language when discussing spirituality as an exclusive topic of study (i.e., assumptions about representationalism); and (c) spirituality is not just an experiential state but also embodies the full range of associated cognitive, affective, and behavioral correlates associated with the occurrence of spiritual experience. As an additional consideration, included within my assumptive base in order to be sure to best delineate what is and is not spirituality, I gave extensive thought about the relation of spirituality to religion and parapsychological phenomena, and elected to take up the stance that intrinsic religiousness and paranormal phenomena should be included under the rubric of spirituality.

With these assumptions settled upon, I then completed a two-part study that comprised my doctoral dissertation (MacDonald, 1997), which was aimed at devising a descriptive model of spirituality and a tool to quantitatively measure it. In the first part, I reviewed available quantitative instruments designed to assess spirituality and related constructs and selected a representative sample of measures using a variety of inclusionary criteria (e.g., measures had to be unique in how they conceptualized spirituality, and have evidence of reliability and validity). Thereafter, I analyzed the responses on these measurement tools from a reasonably large sample ($n = 534$) and found evidence of a small number of latent constructs (i.e., factors) that seemed to represent the common descriptive features of spirituality as reflected in existing tests.

Wanting to be sure that my findings were not an artifact of my analyses on a single sample nor the product of the specific tests I used, the second stage of my study primarily involved constructing original test items that appeared to reflect what each of the factors embodied and utilizing those items as the basis of a new test. This test, along with several others not used in stage one of the project, were then given to a large sample ($n = 938$). The analyses of the new test items produced a five-factor solution that appeared very similar to those found in stage one. Based on this, I used a statistical approach to item selection and either reassigned or eliminated items that did not seem to contribute to the reliable and valid measurement of one of the factors. This process resulted in the creation of the Expressions of Spirituality Inventory (ESI; MacDonald, 1997, 2000a). As a necessary part of test development, the second stage of the study also included an examination of scale reliability via an analysis of inter-item response consistency and scale validity as manifested in convergent and discriminant correlations with other measures as well as the tests ability to significantly differentiate between groups of people known to differ in their spirituality. The evidence in both cases provide strong support for the psychometric properties of the test.

While doing my research (past and present), and in my publications (e.g., see MacDonald, 2000a), I have always tried to be explicit with my assumptions and with the limitations of my methodology. In my unpublished test manual (MacDonald, 2000b), which I provide to all researchers who request a copy of the instrument, I

326

Douglas A. MacDonald

am clear that the ESI does not measure spirituality but rather its expressions, which onto themselves are just approximations of what spirituality may be. I have always maintained that spirituality itself is not directly measurable. Nevertheless, based upon my initial work, I have used the ESI as a tool to examine the relation of spiritual constructs to a variety of variables and aspects of functioning, including psychopathology (MacDonald & Holland, 2003), boredom proneness (MacDonald & Holland 2002a), complex-partial epileptic signs (MacDonald & Holland, 2002b), empathy and altruism (Huber & MacDonald, 2012), well-being (Migdal & MacDonald, 2013), and even work and organizational variables (Affeldt & MacDonald, 2010). And importantly, the ESI has been used to help validate other measures of spiritual and transpersonal constructs, including the Self-Expansiveness Level Form (MacDonald, Gagnier, & Friedman, 2000), the Self-Transcendence dimension of the Temperament and Character Inventory (MacDonald & Holland, 2002c), and the Spiritual Fitness Assessment (Kassab & MacDonald, 2011). In addition, it has helped with theory development (e.g., see MacDonald, 2009 and 2011b for a model of spiritual identity based upon the ESI dimensions). Finally, I have not ceased being critical of the measure and its underlying factor model, and I am currently collaborating with a number of researchers on determining if the ESI holds up across cultures and languages (MacDonald et al., 2013) as well as exploring its correlates to brain states measured via qEEG (Ikanga et al., 2012). The creation of the ESI as a quantitative measure of a transpersonal construct has proven fruitful for facilitating considerable empirical research while, at the same time, not violating the tenets of a scientific transpersonal psychology.

Conclusion

Gotama Buddha in the quote cited at the beginning of this chapter had anticipated (probably quite unintentionally) the basis for the scientific worldview—there is truth, but it cannot be articulated and still remain truth. Consequently, anything that is an authentic vehicle or expression of truth will simply be called a vehicle or expression of truth—and will not be confused with truth itself. This is how I, as a psychological researcher have chosen to reconcile the conventional scientific worldview toward applications in transpersonal psychology. I approach transpersonal psychology as a subdiscipline of psychology, which I define as the scientific study of consciousness, particularly non-ordinary states, modes, processes, and structures of consciousness with the intent of: (a) elucidating its nature, characteristics, expressions, functions, correlates, causes, and products; and (b) facilitating greater exploration of the relation of representations of experience to experience itself with the express purpose of illuminating and making available the direct knowing of reality as-it-really-is. For me, quantitative science is a vehicle that can be used to venture on a journey of exploring truth. However, it is not the only vehicle, and its assumptions, activities, and outcomes are not the final authority on reality or experience. For example, in some settings, quantitative approaches might be more useful while, in other settings, qualitative approaches might be more useful. But, as a mode of inquiry, science broadly construed has much to offer transpersonal psychology by being participatory, systematic, rigorous, critical, self-correcting, and open to revision.

References

Affeldt, D. L., & MacDonald, D. A. (2010). The relationship of spirituality to work and organizational attitudes and behaviors in a sample of employees from a health care system. *Journal of Transpersonal Psychology, 42*(2), 192-208.

Anderson, R., & Braud, W. (this volume). Transpersonal research and future directions (Chapter 13).

Back, K. W., & Bourque, L. B. (1970). Can feelings be enumerated? *Behavioral Science, 15*(6), 487-496.

Bourque, L. B., & Back, K. W. (1968). Values and transcendental experiences. *Social Forces, 47*(1), 34-38.

Bourque, L. B., & Back, K. W. (1971). Language, society, and subjective experience. *Sociometry, 34*, 1-21.

Bunge, M. (2006). The philosophy behind pseudoscience. *Skeptical Inquirer, 30*(4), 29-37.

D'Amato, M. R. (1970). *Experimental psychology: Methodology, psychophysics, and learning.* New York: McGraw-Hill.

Davis, J. (2009). Complementary research methods in humanistic and transpersonal psychology: A case for methodological pluralism. *Humanistic Psychologist, 37*(1), 4-23.

Ferrer, J. (2002). *Revisioning transpersonal theory: A participatory vision of human spirituality.* Albany: State University of New York Press.

Friedman, H. L. (2002). Transpersonal psychology as a scientific field. *International Journal of Transpersonal Studies, 21*, 175-187.

Friedman, H. L. (this volume-a). The role of science in transpersonal psychology: The advantages of middle-range theory (Chapter 16).

Friedman, H. L. (this volume-b). Transpersonal self-expansiveness as a scientific construct (Chapter 11).

Friedman, H. L., & MacDonald, D. A. (1997). Toward a working definition of transpersonal assessment. *Journal of Transpersonal Psychology, 29*(2), 105-122.

Friedman, H. L., & MacDonald, D. A. (2002). Using transpersonal tests in humanistic psychological assessment. *The Humanistic Psychologist, 30*, 223-236.

Friedman, H. L., & MacDonald, D. A. (2006). Humanistic testing and assessment. *Journal of Humanistic Psychology, 46*(4), 510-529.

Hartelius, G., Caplan, M., & Rardin, M. A. (2007). Transpersonal psychology: Defining the past, divining the future. *Humanistic Psychologist, 35*(2), 135-160.

Helminiak, D. A. (2008). Confounding the divine and the spiritual: Challenges to a psychology of spirituality. *Pastoral Psychology, 57*(3-4), 161-182.

Huber, J. T., & MacDonald, D. A. (2012). An investigation of the relation between altruism, empathy, and spirituality. *Journal of Humanistic Psychology, 52*(2), 206-221.

Ikanga, J., MacDonald, D. A., McMahon, A., Lilley, S. C., Gedge, E. R., Barbat, S., Switzer, K. A., & Deering, D. E. (2012, February). *Spirituality and resting brain activity in a sample of university students.* Poster presented at the 40th annual meeting of the International Neuropsychological Society, Montreal, Quebec, Canada.

Kant, I. (1996). *Critique of Pure Reason* (W. Pluhar, Trans.). Indianapolis, IN: Hackett. (Originally published in 1771)

Kassab, V., & MacDonald, D. A. (2011). Examination of the psychometric properties of the Spiritual Fitness Assessment. *Journal of Religion and Health, 50*(4), 975-985.

Kelly, G. (1955). *The psychology of personal constructs.* New York, NY: Norton.

Koenig, H. G. (2008). Concerns about measuring "spirituality" in research. *Journal of Nervous and Mental Disease, 196*(5), 349-355.

Köhler, W. (1969) *The task of Gestalt psychology.* Princeton, NY. Princeton University Press.

Kuhn, T. S. (1970). *The structure of scientific revolutions* (Enlarged edition). Chicago, IL: University of Chicago Press.

Lajoie, D. H., & Shapiro, S. I. (1992). Definitions of transpersonal psychology: The first twenty-three years. *Journal of Transpersonal Psychology, 24*(1), 79-98.

Lajoie, D. H., & Shapiro, S. I. (1996). Definitions of transpersonal psychology: The first 23 years. In G. H. Jennings (Ed.), *Passages beyond the gate: A Jungian approach to understanding the nature of American psychology at the dawn of the new millennium* (pp. 279-294). Needham Heights, MA: Simon & Schuster Custom Publishing.

Leahey, T. H. (1987). *A history of psychology* (2nd ed.). Englewood Cliffs, NJ: Prentice-Hall.

MacDonald, D. A. (1997). The development of a comprehensive factor analytically derived measure of spirituality and its relationship to psychological functioning. *Dissertation Abstracts International, 61*(09) 0115B (UMI #NQ52412).

MacDonald, D. A. (2000a). Spirituality: Description, measurement and relation to the Five Factor Model of personality. *Journal of Personality, 68*(1), 153-197.

MacDonald, D. A. (2000b). *The expressions of spirituality inventory: Test development, validation, and scoring information.* Unpublished test manual.

MacDonald, D. A. (2009). Identity and spirituality: Conventional and transpersonal perspectives. *International Journal of Transpersonal Studies, 28,* 86-106.

MacDonald, D. A. (2011a). Studying spirituality scientifically: Reflections, considerations, and recommendations. *Journal of Management, Spirituality and Religion, 8*(3) 195-210.

MacDonald, D. A. (2011b). Spiritual identity: Individual approaches. In S. J. Schwartz, K. Luyckx, & V. L. Vignoles, (Eds). *Handbook of identity theory and research: Domains and categories* (Vol. 2, pp. 531-544). New York, NY: Springer.

MacDonald, D. A., & Friedman, H. L. (2001). The scientific study of spirituality: Philosophical and methodological considerations. *Biofeedback Newsmagazine, 29*(3), 19-21.

MacDonald, D. A., & Friedman, H. L. (2002). Assessment of humanistic, transpersonal, and spiritual constructs: State of the Science. *Journal of Humanistic Psychology, 42*(4), 102-125.

MacDonald, D. A., & Friedman, H. L. (2009). Measures of spiritual and transpersonal constructs for use in yoga research. *International Journal of Yoga, 2*(1), 2-12.

MacDonald, D. A., & Friedman, H. L. (this volume). Quantitative assessment of transpersonal and spiritual constructs (Chapter 15).

MacDonald, D. A., Friedman, H. L., Brewczynski, J., Holland, D., Gubrij, Z., Kumar, S. K. K., & Ikeda, Y. (2013). Spirituality across cultures and languages. Manuscript in preparation.

MacDonald, D. A., Friedman, H. L., & Kuentzel, J. G. (1999). A survey of measures of spiritual and transpersonal constructs: Part one- Research update. *Journal of Transpersonal Psychology, 31*(2), 137-154.

MacDonald, D. A., Gagnier, J. J., & Friedman, H. L. (2000). The Self-Expansiveness Level Form: Examination of its validity and relation to the NEO Personality Inventory—Revised. *Psychological Reports, 86,* 707-726.

MacDonald, D. A., & Holland, D. (2002a). Spirituality and boredom proneness. *Personality and Individual Differences, 32,* 1113-1119.

MacDonald, D. A., & Holland, D. (2002b). Spirituality and self-reported complex-partial epileptic-like signs. *Psychological Reports, 91,* 785-792.

MacDonald, D. A., & Holland, D. (2002c). Examination of the psychometric properties of the temperament and character inventory self-transcendence dimension. *Personality and Individual Differences, 32*, 1013-1027.

MacDonald, D. A., & Holland, D. (2003). Spirituality and the MMPI-2. *Journal of Clinical Psychology, 59*(4), 399-410.

MacDonald, D. A., Kuentzel, J. G., & Friedman, H. L. (1999). A survey of measures of spiritual and transpersonal constructs: Part two—Additional instruments. *Journal of Transpersonal Psychology, 31*(2), 155-177.

MacDonald, D. A., LeClair, L., Holland, C. J., Alter, A. & Friedman, H. L. (1995). A survey of measures of transpersonal constructs. *Journal of Transpersonal Psychology, 27*(2), 171-235.

MacDonald, D. A., Walsh, R., & Shapiro, S. (this volume). Meditation: Empirical research and future directions (Chapter 24).

Meezenbroek, E., Garssen, B., van den Berg, M., van Dierendonck, D., Visser, A., & Schaufeli, W. B. (2010). Measuring spirituality as a university human experience: A review of questionnaires. *Journal of Religion and Health.* doi:10.1007/s10943010-9376-1

Migdal, L., & MacDonald, D. A. (2013). Clarifying the relation between spirituality and well-being. *Journal of Nervous and Mental Disease, 201*(4), 274-280.

Oxman, T. E., Rosenberg, S. D., Schnurr, P. P., Tucker, G. J., & Gala, G. (1988). The language of altered states. *Journal of Nervous and Mental Disease, 176*(7), 401-408.

Price, A. F., & Wong, M. (1990). *The diamond sutra and the sutra of Hui-Neng.* Boston, MA: Shambhala.

Rogers, C. (1974). *Toward a science of the person.* New York, NY: Norton.

Shear, J. (2007). Eastern methods for investigating mind and consciousness. In M. Velmans & S. Schneider (Eds.). *The Blackwell companion to consciousness* (pp. 697-710). Malden, MA: Wiley-Blackwell.

Slife, B. D., Hope, C., & Nebeker, R. S. (1999). Examining the relationship between religious spirituality and psychological science. *Journal of Humanistic Psychology, 39*(2), 51-85.

Tart, C. (1969). *States of consciousness.* New York, NY: E.P. Dutton.

Tart, C. T. (Ed). (1975). *Transpersonal psychologies.* New York: Harper.

Taylor, E., (2009). The Zen doctrine of "no-method". *Humanistic Psychologist, 37*(4), 295-306.

Valle, R. S. (1989). The emergence of transpersonal psychology. In R. S. Valle & S. Halling (Eds). *Existential-phenomenological perspectives in psychology: Exploring the breadth of human experience* (pp. 257-268). New York, NY: Plenum Press.

Vaughan, F. (1985). Transpersonal vision. *ReVision, 8*(1), 11-15.

Walsh, R. N., & Vaughan, F. (1980). *Beyond ego: Transpersonal dimensions in psychology.* Los Angeles, CA: Jeremy P. Tarcher.

Walsh, R., & Vaughan, F. (1993). On transpersonal definitions. *Journal of Transpersonal Psychology, 25*(2), 199-207.

Wertheimer, M. (1944). Gestalt theory. *Social Research, 11*, 78-99.

Wilber, K. (1990). *Eye to eye: The quest for the new paradigm* (expanded edition). Boston, MA: Shambhala.

Wilber, K. (1995). *Sex, ecology, spirituality: The spirit of evolution.* Boston, MA: Shambhala.

Wilber, K. (2001). *A theory of everything: An integral vision for business, politics, science, and spirituality.* Boston, MA: Shambhala.

Part IV
Transpersonal Experiences

18

Exploring the Nature of Exceptional Human Experiences

Recognizing, Understanding, and Appreciating EHEs

Genie Palmer and Arthur Hastings

A variety of experiences fill up our lives as human beings living on this planet. This continuum of human experiences includes ordinary, everyday experiences on one end and extraordinary, exceptional experiences on the other end. On the extraordinary side is a set of experiences that are often considered unusual, rare, and out-of-the-ordinary. The field of parapsychology calls them *anomalous* experiences (Cardeña, Lynn, & Krippner, 2000) and typically views them as neither normal nor natural human experiences. Within the field of transpersonal psychology, these experiences are called *exceptional human experiences* (EHEs) and are studied particularly for their meanings and their transformational potentials in the lives of the experiencers. EHEs consist of mystical experiences, psychic experiences, encounter experiences, unusual death-related experiences, exceptional human performances, healing experiences, desolation/nadir experiences, and dissociation experiences. The aim of this chapter is to explore the nature of EHEs and discover beneficial aspects and important life impacts of experiences that are often ignored, devalued, and forgotten, and to uncover and discover the multifaceted nature of these gems of human experiences. These are considered in the context of theoretical and research areas that may contribute to a broader understanding of these experiences.

Background

Throughout history, written reports have appeared regularly describing exceptional human experiences. As understanding of the nature of these experiences changed over time, so have the names applied to them evolved. In the early 20th century, American psychologist and philosopher, William James (1902/1958) wrote in depth about *religious experiences*. During the human potential movement of the 1960s, psychologist Abraham Maslow (1964) wrote extensively about *peak experiences* and

The Wiley Blackwell Handbook of Transpersonal Psychology, First Edition.
Edited by Harris L. Friedman and Glenn Hartelius.
© 2013 John Wiley & Sons, Ltd. Published 2015 by John Wiley & Sons, Ltd.

how such experiences might lead to living a more self-actualized life. Later, Stanislav Grof (1973) identified a range of experiences he called *transpersonal experiences* and defined them as "involving an expansion or extension of consciousness beyond the usual ego boundaries and the limitations of time and space" (pp. 48-49). Sociologist James McClenon (1994) described such experiences as wondrous events due to their apparent magical and blissful qualities. In the early 1990s, theorist and parapsychology researcher Rhea White (1993) began studying and gathering a full range of unusual human experiences from peak or mystical (highest point) experiences to nadir or despair (lowest point) experiences and coined the term, *exceptional human experiences* (EHEs). Following in White's footsteps, parapsychologist and transpersonal researcher William Braud (2003, 2012) has written extensively on EHEs and their meanings and life impacts and has described such experiences as *nonordinary and transcendent experiences.* A more complete list of names can be found in Palmer and Braud (2002) and Braud (2003).

Although viewed as rare and unusual, EHEs are reported widely in the general population and may be considered more common than expected. Numerous surveys (Farha & Steward, 2006; Haraldsson & Houtkooper, 1991; Harris Interactive, 2008; Moore, 2005; Newport & Strausberg, 2001; Palmer, 1979; Pew Research Center, 2009; Rice, 2003) in the USA and internationally have consistently indicated belief in a variety of these experiences. Yet, EHEs remain an out-of-the-ordinary experience– often misunderstood, not discussed or shared, and even discouraged and feared.

What are EHEs?

In her original work, White (1993) documented approximately 100 types of EHEs and organized the experiences into five major categories: mystical and unitive experiences, psychic experiences, encounter experiences, unusual death-related experiences, and exceptional normal experiences. Later, White and Brown (2000) reorganized and expanded the list to include over 200 types of experiences in nine categories. The list is much too long to reproduce here, and will be reflected only as experiences are discussed as examples; Braud (2012) summarized and distilled the work of White (1997); White and Brown (1998, 2000); and Palmer (1999). (See Palmer, 1999, for an early EHE Glossary with definitions of categories and subcategories; see also White, 2000, for a list of potential EE/EHEs.)

EHEs Narratives

The personal accounts presented here come from people in all walks of life, demonstrating the variety of people who have reported having an extraordinary experience of this type. The following examples, supplemented with brief descriptions, offer a sense of the nature of these remarkable experiences.

Nature-Related Experience

Samantha Dowdall's (1998) mixed-method study focused on people who reported nature-related EHEs. One hundred and twenty-six participants from 30 states within the USA and seven countries reported one or more of these experiences. Results indicated that many of the participants' personal stories of healing influenced their decisions to protect the earth. One participant found healing in her garden following the death of both parents and the ending of her marriage. Dowdall noted that this and many other extraordinary experiences reported in her study happened under rather ordinary circumstances. One participant reported the following account:

> I was in my mid 50s, had recently lost both parents and a long term marriage had ended in a protracted and ugly divorce. There was an overgrown clump of sword fern in the yard that I wanted to take up and divide. It had a huge network of fine but tough roots that were intertwined and reluctant to yield. As I followed them and worked with them, I found my life—my family, my teachers, my children, all my relationships changing. I saw my Creator, my higher power entertwined [sic] in all the mess. Though I didn't understand the pattern, I knew it all was as it should be.
>
> Now my hands working in my garden have become my spiritual director. As I plant, prune, uproot, in the company of birds, butterflies, neighbors, cats, all of us living and breathing together, the Universe is here in my small plot of land. (Dowdall, 1998, pp. 318-319).

Dowdall's study pointed to decades-long questions around how to motivate more people to take action given the current world environmental crises. She queried if fear and guilt have not worked, what will? Perhaps personal association with the natural world and the recognition and sharing of our nature-related experiences may be the best triggers and teachers of all (Dowdall, 1998).

Channeling

One of the forms of EHEs is channeling. This means that the person is receiving and transmitting messages that come spontaneously to the individual through mental or physical channels of information—including words, automatic writing, and speaking from trances. In EHEs, it is understood to mean that the message comes from some source outside the self of the person (Hastings, 1991). The case of Jane Roberts is instructive.

Roberts was a writer of poetry, short stories (including science fiction), and novels. She was interested in psychic and extrasensory perception and so began experimenting with an Ouija Board. To her surprise, the board spelled out messages within five sessions. Four sessions later she began saying the words aloud, speaking the words as they came into her mind. Becoming more experienced later, she would voluntarily go into a full trance and speak messages that were said to come from "Seth," who said he was a non-physical being speaking through her body. Seth described himself as an "energy essence personality," a being who had had other incarnations and realities. He never claimed that he was a separate being. Robert, Jane's husband, kept records of these discourses. Seth began to dictate books through Jane (Hastings, 1991; Roberts, 1970, 1974).

Through Seth's messages and her own ideas, Jane developed a model she called Aspect Psychology. The idea was that as individuals we are an aspect of a larger consciousness. This is a larger entity outside of time and space (what some would call the soul). Usually humans are not aware of this wider entity, and are in the conventional reality for mental training, knowledge, feedback, and learning. The larger self is engaged in living several physical lives in other times or realities, experienced simultaneously.

Roberts, an experienced and serious writer herself, wrote several books in addition to the channeled Seth books, suggesting how an individual might incorporate the levels of consciousness discussed by Seth. Roberts also wrote a volume expressing how the philosopher and psychologist William James might view the world now, from his vantage point on the other side (Roberts, 2001). Another concept that marks the Seth teachings is a detailed discussion of how beliefs and assumptions shape the realities that individuals live within. The channeling of Roberts gives evidence that one can use exceptional experiences as doorways to a wider understanding and consciousness.

Out-of-Body Experiences, Past Life Recall, and Other EHEs

The case of psychic Anne Armstrong provides an example of sensitivity with exceptional human experiences (Armstrong & Armstrong, 2010). In her 20s Anne began having what would be considered spontaneous EHEs. She would experience being outside of her body, observing her body from another part of the room, in the altered state called out-of-body experience. This was frightening for her. She wondered if she were going to die. Her husband said that

> She constantly felt as if she and her body were not securely connected. There was the sense that her feet were not touching the ground; she would turn or move and the body didn't; she was frequently aware of the existence of another reality, and of beings that were not part of our physical world (Armstrong & Armstrong, 2010, p. 40).

Anne was hypersensitive to the environment, including people's emotions and levels of consciousness. She described colors around the head (called an aura) that reflected the person's state of mind. Initially she complained of migraine and other headaches that seemed to have no cause. Medical treatment was not helpful. She finally found a therapist who used hypnotism to bring psychological and psychic experiences to the surface. Anne and her husband learned hypnosis and practiced hypnotizing each other. Anne began to "remember" what seemed to be a traumatic past life in ancient Rome. She felt herself in a large male body that was being tortured and killed. Releasing these apparent memories seemed to reduce the traumatic reactions.

Anne could sense the emotions of others, including material from the unconscious as well as conscious minds. The release of the painful experiences perhaps opened a way to be aware of other people's feelings, reactions, and sensations. Anne was overrun by this information. The material would flow through her while she was cooking, trying to sleep, carrying on a conversation, and other daily activities. Researchers (Brown & White, 1997; Palmer, 1979; Palmer & Braud, 2002) in EHEs and parapsychology have suggested that one kind of exceptional experience often leads to further experiences.

Finally she turned the tables on the situation. Speaking aloud, she said something like this: "I don't know who you are that is doing this, or why you are doing it, but I want it to stop. I don't want to have this always running through my head. I will do the work, but I want it to be only when I am willing for it to come. If you do not agree, I will do everything I can to stop you" (A. Hastings, personal communication, 1984). Anne got agreement on this. She was able to direct her attention to a person or situation, turn on the psychic awareness, and communicate what she perceived. Then she could turn it off when she was finished.

During one period in her life after she had resolved the memories of the hypnosis sessions, she and Jim traveled to Europe, visiting Rome and Italy. Her sensitivity to the environment presented her with images of ancient times. When they visited Hadrian's Villa, Anne said "You will never believe what I am seeing. I am seeing this Villa as it was nearly 2000 years ago. I see the lavish parties, just as they were then" (Armstrong & Armstrong, 2010, p. 63). Later, as they approached another building Anne felt her body begin to move, her hips turn, and a discomfort in the lower part of her body. A sign told them that this was the red light district of the city. By the time they reached their hotel she was exhausted, feeling, she said, like she had been making love all day. Was this her energy? Was it the pent up energy of the location? They did not know.

Anne did not make claims of glory. She felt that everyone could access their psychic abilities with practice and training. She taught groups on how to utilize intuition, how to work with kundalini, and practiced as a psychic reader for people who wished to get her perception of a relationship, conflict, or decision. She was a modest person. Each psychic person had some skills and not others. She once said, "I can't find lost children" (A. Hastings, personal communication, 1984).

Encounter/Apparition Experience

Dianne Arcangel (2004, 2005) conducted an international study that included participants from the USA, Canada, and 17 other countries, designed to collect data pertaining to the effect that encounter experiences have on recipients. Over a five-year period, she surveyed almost 600 participants for the study, with 98% reporting some degree of comfort from the experience. Arcangel noted that encounter experiences serve a primary purpose as catalysts for growth. Here is one description of a visual encounter.

A sixteen-year-old girl named Katie was involved in a serious car accident in which her friend was killed. As the driver, the friend lost control of the car, careening it into a backward spin down an embankment and into the woods (Arcangel, 2005). The car was destroyed to the degree that the highway patrol could not identify the make or model and the investigating officer wanted to know how the survivor was able to escape from it, alive and unharmed. Katie reported that when the car stopped, she had the feeling of someone lifting her out of the car. Confused after the accident, she did not know what to do or where to go, when suddenly she saw her beloved grandfather who had recently died, pointing in one direction. Because she recognized her grandfather's image and trusted he was there to help her, she followed his gesture, came to the road, and was able to get help from a passing motorist. After seeing the wreckage, the family members were shocked that Katie survived without any injury.

Katie had previously commented to her family that she is sure her grandfather is there for any major events in her life.

Peak Experience

Long before he became the sixth person to walk on the moon in 1971, Apollo 14 astronaut Edgar Mitchell had a keen interest in psychic phenomena and research. Whereas his planned telepathy experiments from the lunar spaceship did not turn out as planned, Mitchell (1974) was rewarded with an extraordinary event that most of us will never experience in the same way:

> The first thing that came to mind as I looked at Earth was its incredible beauty. Even the spectacular photographs do not do it justice. It was a majestic sight–a splendid blue and white jewel suspended against a velvet black sky. How peacefully, how harmoniously, how marvelously it seemed to fit into the evolutionary pattern by which the universe is maintained. In a peak experience, the presence of divinity became almost palpable and I *knew* that life in the universe was not just an accident based on random processes. This knowledge came to me directly–noetically. (p. 29)

He further described his experience:

> For me, seeing our planet from space was an event with some of the qualities traditionally ascribed to religious experience. It triggered a deep insight into the nature of existence– the sort of insight that radically changes the inner person. My thinking–indeed, my consciousness–was altered profoundly. I came to feel a moral responsibility to pass on the transformative experience of seeing earth from the larger perspective. But further, the rational man in me had to recognize the validity of the nonrational cognitive process. (p. 34)

Spontaneous Healing Experience

Alternative medicine researcher Larry Dossey (2011) pointed to a major failing within the medical profession regarding healing experiences. "There is an aspect of NDEs that should evoke the greatest interest in medicine, but which has gone almost unnoticed: In some cases, the disease that nearly caused the individual to die has vanished on awakening, or does so soon thereafter" (p. 59). As an example, Dossey retold the story of Mellen-Thomas Benedict, a stained-glass artist who experienced near-death in 1982:

> Benedict was dying from an inoperable brain tumor. He was offered chemotherapy but declined, wanting to maintain as high a quality of life as possible in the time he had left. Having no health insurance he entered hospice care, which lasted about 18 months. He woke up one morning around 4:30 AM and knew this was the day he would die. He told his hospice nurse, and they agreed that she would leave his dead body undisturbed for at least six hours, because he had read that "all kinds of interesting things happen when you die." Suddenly he experienced being outside his body. He had a sense of panoramic vision and saw a magnificent shining light, the most beautiful thing he had

ever seen. It seemed a conduit to the Source or the Higher Self. . . . Then the light turned into an exquisitely gorgeous mandala of human souls. He felt all his negative judgments and cynical attitudes about his fellow human beings giving way toward a view that was equally hopeful and positive. He conversed with the Great Light. He rode a stream of consciousness through the galaxy and glimpsed the entire universe. He felt he was in pre-creation before the Big Bang. His consciousness expanded to infinity. It was revealed to him that there is no death, only immortality. With this assurance, the entire process then reversed itself and he returned to his body. His hospice nurse found Benedict without vital signs. For an hour and a half she could not detect any pulse, blood pressure, or heart sounds, even with an amplified stethoscope. She honored their agreement and left his body alone. Then Benedict suddenly awakened. On seeing the light outside, he tried to get up and go to it, falling out of bed. The nurse heard a clunk and found him on the floor. Within three days he was feeling normal, yet happier than he had ever felt in his life. He was discharged from hospice. Three months later a friend suggested that he return to his physician to be tested again. Benedict resisted; he was afraid of getting bad news. He eventually complied and a follow-up brain scan was done. As his physician looked at the before-and-after scans, he said, "Well, there is nothing here now." Benedict responded cheerfully, "Really, it must be a miracle?" "No," the unimpressed doctor said, "these things happen. They are called spontaneous remission[s]." (Dossey, 2011, pp. 59-60)

Desolation/Nadir Experiences

Stories abound regarding heroic yet traumatic efforts of the Holocaust survivors; Victor Frankl's dramatic account of turning tragedy into transformation is a well-known story. However, everyday accounts of Desolation/Nadir experiences are hard to come by, possibly because few researchers explore such experiences in depth or individuals are not willing to share such personally challenging stories. Rominger (2010) provided an account from one participant in his article examining the similarities and differences between a pleasant NDE and a distressing one and the creative use of artwork for possible growth and transformation. One middle-aged Caucasian male participant, who assumed the name of Charles for the study purpose, reported his childhood NDE. Around the age of seven, Charles hit the back end of a car as he rode his bicycle, causing part of the car to penetrate his eye socket through to his skull. He recalled hearing family members scream as he hovered near a streetlight and watched his family place him into their car and take him to the hospital.

Thirty years later, Charles still vividly recalled the dreadful feelings of foreboding darkness all around him, of hovering over his body and attempting to re-enter only to slip out again, and of fear that he was going to be in serious trouble with his parents (Rominger, 2010). Charles reported that after the experience, he was sure he would go to hell when he died, that he became ambivalent towards life, and experienced a troubled adolescence that continued into his early adulthood. He also described emotional distancing with family relationships and his church. As part of the study requirements, Charles had drawn a series of four art pieces, with drawings of an all-consuming darkness in the early pictures, then a gradual lightening of colors in later pictures, depicting more balance between dark and light which he described as love. The final drawing showed Charles, "now looking toward an emerging sun after seeing the debris that a violent storm had deposited on the shores next to a deep ocean" (Rominger, 2010, p. 22). Charles's artwork, according to Rominger, served as a metaphor of his transforming inner experience. Because of his study participation, Charles shared his distressing experience with his wife, the first time he had told any family members.

This experience may have remained a Desolation/Nadir experience for so long because Charles did not have enough family support following his experience as a young person and therefore was unable to share and work through the event appropriately. The study dialogue and artwork provided him a healthy and more positive outcome. An essential aspect of these experiences and what qualifies them as EHEs is that whereas the experiencer may have feelings of desolation and despair for years following the event, the experience often serves as a trigger for eventual growth and development.

This next section focuses on theoretical underpinnings and empirical research associated with EHEs, much of which has previously been described in various articles by Braud (2003, 2012) and several studies by Genie Palmer (1999), Palmer and Braud (2002, 2010), and Braud and Associates (2007).

Theoretical Issues

Theories allow speculation about the nature of EHEs. Braud (2012) distinguished the first three models or theories presented here and highlighted their association with the accompaniments, impacts, outcomes or aftereffects of EHEs. The two additional models provide further understanding of the impacts of these experiences.

The "EHE Process"

As a stage model, the EHE process as created White (1997, 1998a) and Brown (1998) includes recognition of and working with an experience to nurture and grow it from an anomalous experience (AE) into an exceptional experience (EE) and eventually into a meaningful EHE. When a spontaneous AE occurs in one's life, initially and in most instances, the experience occurs outside one's ordinary consciousness or self-concept and goes no further. At this stage, the experience may be ignored, dismissed, dissociated, or considered a legitimate anomaly simply for intellectual curiosity. However, if the experiencer becomes aware of the AE and chooses to work with it and discover its possible meaning, the experience has the potential to become an EE. Delving deeper into the experience may lead to uncovering more meaning and greater significance of the EE in one's life and to discover other related experiences. As the process deepens further, the EE becomes an exceptional *human* experience and has the potential to change one's identity, from a separate ego-self to what White (1997) called a more inclusive "All-Self" (p. 89) with a new view of self, lifeview, and worldview, and can lead to actualizing one's true potential as a human being.

Human lives are made up of a story or narrative that each person tells about themselves, their lives, and world. Whether these are positive, life potentiating stories or negative, depotentiating ones, such narratives provide ways of making meaning out of one's life. Most narratives are heavily influenced by the culture a person lives in and its current paradigm. The role of narrative is essential to the EHE process for as soon as people have such an experience, their current life story provides either agreement or disagreement as to whether the EHE becomes part of their new life story or is thrown out and ignored (White, 1997).

A useful way of working with one's EHEs is through writing, particularly the art of EHE autobiography as proposed by White (1998a). Instead of reviewing one's life in terms of outer major events with their ups and downs as is typical in most autobiographical writings, one discloses those subjective experiences that may have profoundly influenced one's life and have been kept as secret, even to oneself. In essence, one writes the story of their life through the lens of human experiences that have touched them deeply and, both figuratively and literally, moved them out of their ordinary reality into something more—a place they may not have been before. Many of these experiences prompt positive actions in life that might not otherwise have been taken. Writing about experiences helps the integration of these experiences into a new identity and lifeview (White, 1998a).

The Role of Disclosure

Disclosing life experiences, especially the more unusual events of one's life, is the foundation for psychotherapy and counseling practices, and provides practical evidence for the psychological and physical benefits of such disclosure. Several viewpoints lend further understanding of disclosure and point to its value for working with one's EHEs.

Following years of research in the areas of physiological and psychological associations of confession, disclosure and confiding of important life experiences and events, Pennebaker (1995, 1997) has found that disclosure of traumatic experiences, either verbally or written, especially those previously not shared with others, are associated with improvements in health and well-being as measured by various assessments. Pennebaker (1995) pointed out an essential feature of the act of disclosure in therapy is its allowance for an experience to be translated into words, and that this disclosure process could provide more valuable feedback than what is received from the therapist. This act of putting an experience into words creates a structure or organization for it, leading to assimilation of the experience. Stiles (1995) acknowledged for assimilation to take place, particularly with upsetting events, repeated disclosure over time is necessary. Stiles declared "Only after the problem has been identified and owned—that is, as it is in the process of becoming intellectually and emotionally assimilated—is it recognized and expressed as being associated with the self" (p. 85). Some EHEs may initially come as upsetting or distressing events that require one to take time, to disclose gradually, safely, and frequently in order to fully "own" it and assimilate it into a new identify and worldview.

Driver (1991), a theologian, used the expression "confessional performance" to describe a type of self-disclosure that is not used in the sense of confessing one's sins or crimes, but more as a profession of one's beliefs, an act of revealing one's self. Self-revelation involves mystery and a sense of awe. In confessional performance, beliefs are translated into actions; one is in a sense "coming out" of the closet of inhibition and taking a stand, going public. This act of profession is a kind of speaking that brings light to something hidden in the dark; it is speaking the truth about it to oneself and to others. Driver's ideas offer relevance to an understanding of EHEs in that through a process of confessing or professing these experiences and revealing more of oneself, it may be possible to come to know one's true identity more fully and appreciate the reality of such experiences.

The "Broaden and Build" Theory of Positive Emotion

Fredrickson's (2002) "broaden-and-build theory of positive emotion" has been actively researched for the past two decades and is highly regarded in the field of positive psychology. Prior to that, positive emotions had essentially been ignored while traditional empirical studies focused on negative emotions, which were deemed necessary for our ancestors' survival–fight or flight (Fredrickson, 2002).

Positive emotion or "positivity" refers to a broadened state of mind that builds enduring personal resources and may also have benefited our ancestors by leaving them with extra physical and psychological resources, such as knowledge of the environment and an ability to cope with stress (Fredrickson, 2002, 2009).

Fredrickson and Losada (2005) confirmed multiple benefits of positive emotions. They concluded that positive emotions bring about alterations in one's state of mind and bodily systems; lead to increases in intuition and creativity, recovery rates, immune functions, happiness, psychological growth, and resilience to adversity; and positively affect longevity. The authors discovered a positivity ratio (2.9:1) of higher positivity to negativity which has the potential to lead to long-term human flourishing–optimal functioning that includes goodness, generativity, growth, and resilience.

Fredrickson (2009) asserted the work on positivity has allowed her to find an answer to the riddle of "*What good are positive emotions?*" (p. 19). Work with EHEs suggests a similar question, what good are exceptional human experiences? Recognizing and working with one's EHEs has the potential to allow experiencers to open up to or "broaden" their experiences and to "build" on their coping skills to better deal with life stresses (Braud and Associates, 2007).

Need-Related Theory of EHEs

Noted parapsychologist, Rex Stanford (1974), concluded that spontaneous psi (psychic phenomenon) events might be need-related and suggested the term as a model, psi-mediated instrumental response (PMIR). According to Stanford's need-related model, these spontaneously-occurring experiences happen without conscious awareness on the part of a person having the experience of the need or even of the realization that an extraordinary event has fulfilled that need. Ring (1991) offered an intriguing perspective on a need-related view of EHEs. He examined four case histories of NDErs whose lives prior to the experience were filled with deep pain and torment and reported that their NDEs served as a "compensatory gift" or "amazing grace" for the receiver.

After years of study and research on psi and after examining his personal psi experiences, Braud (1994) concluded that psi tends to occur in need-related circumstances and that such experiences serve a purpose or function. Need-related aspects of EHEs may be essential in discovering important meanings and interpretations of these experiences (Palmer & Braud, 2002). In a technologically-complex and materialistic society, problems of alienation and identity abound, leaving many people with unmet needs and feelings of disconnection. Honoring and welcoming EHEs can serve to connect and re-connect individuals to themselves, others, and the world around them, bringing much-needed meaning into their lives.

Transpersonal Theory of Participatory Events

Ferrer (2002) has suggested a shift is needed from viewing transpersonal and spiritual experiences as experiential as opposed to a participatory event. Ferrer has called this *the participatory turn* to better understand spiritual or transpersonal experiences. He proposed that such experiences be viewed not only as individual experiences but as participatory events that also occur in a relationship, a community, a collective identity, or a place. Ferrer used the analogy of a party or celebration to explain a participatory event–an experiential event that requires certain conditions be fulfilled. By not reducing spiritual and transpersonal phenomena to only human inner experiences, such experiences can be better understood as transcending human boundaries and realities, and as *cocreated events* (Ferrer, 2011). Viewing EHEs from this position suggests another possible stage in their development–from an *exceptional experience* to an *exceptional human experience* to a *participatory event* in which the event can be more fully integrated in one's spiritual growth and development, and worldview.

Relevant Research Findings

Delving into empirical research on the topic of EHEs produces some pertinent studies to further understanding about the nature of these experiences. Given this relatively young field, few studies are available; however, what stands out is how important, meaningful, and transformative these life experiences can be, as indicated in the studies that follow.

Spirituality and Well-being

In their questionnaire study, Kennedy and Kanthamani (1995) surveyed a convenience sample of 120 people who expressed an interest in parapsychology and who also reported having at least one paranormal or transcendent experience. Overall results showed an increase in interest and belief in spiritual matters and an increased sense of well-being. Specifically, findings indicated that a large percentage of the respondents believed their life is guided or watched over by a higher force or being, are certain of life after death, became significantly more spiritual or religious, and better understood and accepted death. Participants also indicated decreases in fear of death, depression or anxiety, isolation and loneliness, and worry and fears about the future. Most of the participants indicated that positive effects resulted from a combination of more than one psychical and/or transcendent experience. The amount of changes noted in the study was positively associated with the number of reported experiences. While

45% of the respondents indicated their experience caused temporary fear mixed with positive feelings, only 9% indicated that their experiences had been frightening with no positive effects.

Social Relevance

Zangari and Machado (1996) studied the incidence and social relevance of psychic experiences occurring in the daily lives of 181 Brazilian university students with 89.5% reporting at least one experience. The types of experiences reported included ESP, poltergeist, out-of-body experiences, apparitions, haunting, and past-life memories. The study highlighted how cultural aspects can influence people's beliefs in these types of experiences. Brazil is a country where general acceptance of psychic events is the norm and where people are highly encouraged to have such experiences; therefore, reporting on these experiences is considered natural. In the study, 80% of the participants reported psychic experiences that had highly influenced or changed their lives in important ways. Participants reported these experiences saved them or another person from illness, severe emotional crisis, accidents, or death; changed their attitudes about self, humanity, society, spiritual beliefs, meaning of life, and death; and influenced their decisions about lifestyle, school, friends, job, marriage, and health.

Triggers, Concomitants, and Aftereffects

Brown and White (1997) explored a variety of EHEs in search of triggers, concomitants, and aftereffects through the narrative accounts obtained from 50 participants. Overall findings revealed all 50 essayists reported at least one long-term aftereffect, with 31 indicating their experiences were exceptional and life changing. Through a process of qualitative thematic content analysis, numerous themes and patterns emerged. The top triggers for EHEs included meditation and prayer, along with various crisis situations, such as depression, spiritual emergencies, and death of another. It is interesting to note that the range of concomitants or accompaniments of the experiences included physical, physiological, psychological, and spiritual aspects. For physical, top themes were body luminosity, lights, colors, and being touched; for physiological, top themes included energy influx, weeping, weightlessness, and hyperacuity; for psychological, top themes were cognitive shift, boundaries dropping away, amazement, and connectedness; and for spiritual aspects, top themes to emerge were ego surrender and overwhelming wonder, awe, and joy. With respect to the aftereffects of these experiences, themes emerged of altered outlook, changed attitudes, personal growth, increased interest in spirituality, and increased well-being, suggesting the transformative nature of these experiences.

Disclosure and Well-being

The nature, accompaniments, and life impacts of five categories of EHEs, including mystical, psychic, unusual death-related, encounter, and exceptional normal experiences were studied by Palmer and Braud (2002) using correlational and qualitative thematic analysis along with an experimental design and standardized assessments. A sample of 70 US participants who reported having these experiences were selected to participate in either individual or psychoeducational groups to explore possible beneficial outcomes of working with and disclosing EHEs. The 70 study participants self-disclosed a total of 1,715 experiences that ranged from a low of 2 experiences to a high of 101 experiences. Psychic experiences were most often reported, with death-related experiences the least often. Mystical/unitive experiences were reported by a majority of the participants as having the most profound impact on their lives and being the most beneficial. Frequent and/or profound EHEs were positively and significantly correlated to high levels of meaning and purpose in life, high levels of spirituality, "thin" or permeable boundaries, and a tendency toward transformative life changes. Disclosure was positively and significantly associated with meaning and purpose in life, positive attitudes and well-being, and reduced stress symptoms.

The study's disclosure intervention provided participants with an opportunity to share their experiences in new ways by helping them move from superficially talking about their experiences to a deeper and more expanded level of awareness of disclosure of EHEs (Palmer & Braud, 2002). The deeper awareness and disclosure allowed for working through any fears surrounding the experiences to discovering their more positive meanings and life impacts. Emergent themes from the qualitative data confirmed important accompaniments of EHEs. Well-being aspects emerged from the qualitative data and provided further evidence for a cluster of qualities or *a well-being cluster* or *wellness syndrome*. Included in this cluster were aspect of increased meaning, openness, and need-related aspects, increased and beneficial aspects of disclosure, increased positive physiological and psychological attitudes, and various aspects of spirituality. Additional themes of transformative change also emerged.

"Broaden and Build" with EHEs

Braud and Associates (2007) conducted two studies involving aspects of Fredrickson's (2009) broaden-and-build model of positive emotions in a new context—that of EHEs. In the first, Braud and his student researchers designed and carried out a mixed methods study in which they explored whether or not 144 research participants' responses might be "broadened"—that is, become more numerous, expansive, and open—immediately following the imaginal reliving of a selected EHE as compared with a control/contrast of imagined typical experiences.

Study findings suggested two types of "broadening" within the imaginal reliving group who reported incidence of EHEs in everyday life. Correlational results pointed to one type, a greater broadening, expansiveness, and openness of responsiveness, as seen with positive emotions. Self-schema assessment suggested a second type, that of "'broadening'–a more extensive and inclusive appreciation of self identity" (p. 4). Qualitative results for the imaginal reliving group revealed responses suggestive of opening up to more transpersonal and spiritual qualities, which is consistent with the "broadening" hypothesis as proposed by Fredrickson (2002) for positive emotions.

A follow-up qualitative study explored the "building" aspect of the broaden-and-build model in the context of spiritually relevant EHEs. Fifty new participants who reported the occurrence of spontaneous EHEs in everyday life answered questions about the nature, triggers, accompaniments, meanings, and aftereffects of their more important, dramatic, or profound EHEs. Questions related to the "building" aspect included various influences of the experiences on coping and well-being accompaniments or aftereffects of that EHE. Two sets of themes emerged from the data. Nine major themes revealed how EHEs had helped the participants cope more effectively with stress, adversity, and problem solving. Eight themes or areas reported by the 48 participants revealed that EHEs had helped improve their well-being, with spiritual well-being reported as the most influenced by EHEs (Braud and Associates, 2007).

Life and Work Impacts

In a qualitative study, Palmer and Braud (2010) explored possible life and work impacts, including transpersonal-related impacts, of reported psychical experiences from a sample of 65 volunteer participants from the Institute of Transpersonal Psychology (now Sofia University)—faculty, students, administration, staff, and alumni. Participants reported a maximum of 3 psychical experiences, chosen from a Glossary that defined 22 of the most well-known psychical experiences, and were asked to submit written accounts of their most important, dramatic and meaningful experiences and any associated life and work impacts. A total of 150 psychical experiences were reported that included 20 types of the listed experiences. Fourteen types of self-reported life and work impacts emerged from data using qualitative thematic content analysis. Results for impacts included that 83% reported increased well-being (increased overall, physical, psychological, and spiritual well-being); 71% reported life impacts (changed life, had profound life impact, provided guidance, helped one apply lessons in life, and influenced a later life interest); 66% reported increased understandings, prompted realizations, and new self-perceptions; and 43% reported enhanced growth, spiritual growth, and psychospiritual growth. Other impacts included increased understanding and confirmation of psychical experiences; increased awareness and consciousness; impacts on work; increased sense of connectedness; fostering of inquiry and questioning; increased validation or confirmation; calls to action; and increased love, gratitude, and disclosure. This study expanded thinking about the role of EHEs in relation to Fredrickson's (2002) "broaden and build" model of positive emotions.

Meaning Making

In 1982, Twemlow, Gabbard, and Jones did a large-scale study of 339 out-of-body (OBE) experiencers. Reporting on the findings, Gabbard and Twemlow (1984) emphasized that for the experiencer, OBEs are almost never considered trivial, but are experiences described as having a sense of purpose and meaning, that effects are long lasting, and that they often produced dramatic impacts on their lives. More than half of the participants in the study claimed their lives had been changed. Participants generally reported a sense of calm, peace, and quiet during the experience and positive meanings and impact from the experiences, including feelings of joy, a desire to disclose the experience with others, greater awareness of reality, and change of beliefs in life after death. Gabbard and Twemlow (1984) pointed out that what was most obvious from the study is the participants' description of their OBEs as suggestive of peak and mystical experiences.

Kennedy, Kanthamani, and Palmer (1994) surveyed 500 randomly selected Duke University students, asking them about transcendent or spiritual experiences (overwhelming feelings of peace and unity with the entire creation or profound inner sense of Divine presence) and psychical experiences (ESP, precognition, telepathy, mind-over-matter, and OBEs). Of the 105 responses, 59% reported having had these experiences, with 41% reporting psychical experiences and 42% reporting transcendent experiences; 91% of those reporting transcendent experiences and 46% reporting psychical experiences considered them valuable. The study revealed that two factors, in particular, contributed to a person's sense of purpose and meaning—expressing artistic creativity and observing spiritual or religious beliefs—which correlated positively with reports of anomalous experiences. Findings concluded that the students who reported having psychic and spiritual experiences had a greater sense of meaning in life, and. specifically, participants who observed religious or spiritual beliefs tended to report a healthy lifestyle.

With a focus on reaching a deeper understanding and uncovering the meanings and impacts of anomalous experiences, Wilde and Murray (2010) studied out-of-body-experiences (OBEs) and near-death-experiences (NDEs), using interpretative phenomenological analysis (IPA) as their qualitative approach. Fifteen participants who had either of these experiences were recruited and interviewed. Three major themes emerged from the data: the art and practice of disclosing an anomalous experience, integrating an anomalous experience, and the transformational effects or impacts on the self and embodied nature of anomalous experiences.

Although a strong wish to disclose their spontaneous OBEs existed for some participants, such disclosure was viewed as challenging, especially in the work place and with family; the participants did not know what information to share and with whom (Wilde & Murray, 2010). For a few of the participants, the study became their first opportunity to disclose their OBEs. Important issues were raised by the study as to how society, in general, views anomalous experiences. The interpretations that participants assigned to their experiences were an important aspect in the study. For example, one participant viewed these experiences as highly valued and considered them experiences to be "treasured and protected" and not "justified or explained" (Wilde & Murray, 2010, p. 64).

The authors noted that these experiences impacted the experiencers' evolving sense of self and may have served as an adaptive form of behavior and creative solutions to problem solving (Wilde & Murray, 2010). In creating more meaning out of these unforeseen experiences, participants moved from a place of initial confusion to one of interpreting them as positive, life-affirming events. With their new interpretations, participants took positive actions in searching for more information, support, and further understanding of their experiences and in bringing more meaning to their lived experience. Finally, the authors pointed to a larger area of meanings and impacts of working with and researching anomalous experiences, in that research of this kind can be useful to health care professionals and psychologists in dealing with clients' experiences.

Practical nature of EHEs

The practical and useful nature of EHEs make these experiences to welcome, treasure, honor, and appreciate. Some EHEs can have a dramatic, life changing impact; less dramatic EHEs can play an equally important role in everyday life situations; still other EHEs may have a negative side or bear negative aftereffects, especially the more profound and intense events. These experiences can be frightening, causing fear and resistance around disclosure, fears of being seen as crazy or weird, ambivalence about having such experiences, or difficulty in finding a place for such experiences to fit into their current identity and worldview. Subsequently, such experiences may be outlawed and possibly rejected and/or kept secret. Confronting the fear and resistance by working with and through such experiences holds the potential for self transformation and for changing one's view of self, life, and the world.

Several approaches are available to guide individuals in working with their EHEs to uncover positive and useful meanings, to find helpful interpretations, and to realize their full worth. For example, Hastings (1983) has offered a counseling approach for working through fears or anxieties that might arise with some EHEs, along with practical wisdom for dealing with these potentially valuable and useful experiences. Genie Palmer (1999) suggested a process of spiritual guidance and psychoeducational group work as a way to encourage disclosure of EHEs and foster their potential meanings and spiritual aspects. The EHE autobiography process as described by White (1998b) presents a way to write about one's lifelong experiences. Pennebaker's (2004) unique writing process offers a way to write about the more challenging EHEs. By utilizing an art-based process, Rominger (2010) pointed to useful and creative way to work with EHEs, especially with NDEs.

History suggests that accounts of experiences like EHEs have existed as long as humans have had the words to write about them. Such experiences have an obvious hold on today's culture as evidenced by their strong attraction in media such as television programs and cinema. Yet, it is rare to hear people in the everyday walk of life reveal these experiences. If EHEs are spoken about, it is often to explain away the experiences or judge them or the experiencers. White (1997) reminded us that these experiences are behind some of the most important events in history and some of the most significant inventions, theories, and discoveries. EHEs have changed lives, saved some, and transformed others; they have been reported to be some of the most important experiences we can have as human beings. It is important, then, to recognize and understand EHEs and when appropriate, to appreciate and cherish them as healthy and positive human experiences.

References

Arcangel, D. (2004). The afterlife encounter survey: Phase 1. *Journal of the American Society for Psychical Research, 98*(3-4), 121-145.

Arcangel, D. (2005). *Afterlife encounters: Ordinary people, extraordinary experiences.* Charlottesville, VA: Hampton Roads.

Armstrong, J., & Armstrong, A. (2010). *Awakening the divine within: Kundalini the gateway to freedom*. New York, NY: iUniverse.

Braud, W. (1994). Honoring our natural experiences. *Journal of the American Society for Psychical Research, 88*(4), 293-308.

Braud, W. (2003). Nonordinary and transcendent experiences: Transpersonal aspects of consciousness. *Journal of the American Society for Psychical Research, 97*(1-2), 1-26.

Braud, W. (2012). Health and well-being benefits of exceptional human experiences. In C. Murray (Ed.), *Mental health and anomalous experience* (pp. 107-124). New York, NY: Nova Science.

Braud, W., & Associates. (2007, August). *Extending positive psychology's "broaden-and-build" theory to a spiritual context*. Paper presented at the 115th Annual Convention of the American Psychological Association, San Francisco, CA.

Brown, S. V. (1998). The EHE process: The objective standpoint. In R. A. White (Ed.), *Exceptional human experience: Special issue, background papers II. The EHE Network, 1995-1998: Progress and possibilities* (pp. 51-52). New Bern, NC: Exceptional Human Experience Network.

Brown, S. V., & White, R. A. (1997). Triggers, concomitants, and aftereffects of EHEs: An exploratory study. *Exceptional Human Experience, 15*(1), 150-156.

Cardeña, E., Lynn, S. J., & Krippner, S. (2000). Introduction: Anomalous experiences in perspective. In E. Cardeña, S. J. Lynn, & S. Krippner (Eds.), *Varieties of anomalous experience: Examining the scientific evidence* (pp. 3-24). Washington, DC: American Psychological Association.

Dossey, L. (2011). Dying to heal: A neglected aspect of NDEs. *Explore, 7*(2), 59-62.

Dowdall, S. A. (1998). Roots of the spirit: Interrelationships among ecological actions and attitudes, nature-related exceptional human experiences, spirituality, and well-being. *Dissertation Abstracts International, 59*(05) 0669B (UMI #9833350).

Driver, T. F. (1991). *The magic of ritual: Our need for liberating rites that transform our lives and our communities*. San Francisco, CA: HarperSanFrancisco.

Farha, B., & Steward, G. (2006). Paranormal beliefs: An analysis of college students. *Skeptical Inquirer, 30*(1), 37-40.

Ferrer, J. N. (2002). *Revisioning transpersonal theory: A participatory vision of human spirituality*. Albany, NY: State University of New York Press.

Ferrer, J. N. (2011). Participatory spirituality and transpersonal theory: A ten-year retrospective. *Journal of Transpersonal Psychology, 43*(1), pp. 1-34.

Fredrickson, B. (2002). Positive emotions. In C. R. Snyder & S. J. Lopez (Eds.), *Handbook of positive psychology* (pp. 120-134). New York, NY: Oxford University Press.

Fredrickson, B. L. (2009). *Positivity: Top notched research reveals the 3 to 1 ratio that will change your life*. New York, NY: Random House.

Fredrickson, B. L., & Losada, M. F. (2005). Positive affect and the complex dynamics of human flourishing. *American Psychologist, 60*(7), 678-686.

Gabbard, G. O., & Twemlow, S. W. (1984). *With the eyes of the mind: An empirical analysis of out-of-body states*. New York, NY: Praeger.

Grof, S. (1973). Varieties of transpersonal experiences: Observations from LSD psychotherapy. *Journal of Transpersonal Psychology, 4*, 45-80.

Haraldsson, E., & Houtkooper, J. M. (1991). Psychic experiences in the multinational human values study: Who reports them? *Journal of the American Society for Psychical Research, 85*(2), 145-165.

Harris Interactive. (2008). More Americans believe in the devil, hell and angels than in Darwin's theory of evolution: Nearly 25% of Americans believe they were once another person. Retrieved from http://www.harrisinteractive.com/harris_poll/index.asp?PID=982

Hastings, A. (1983). A counseling approach to parapsychological experience. *Journal of Transpersonal Psychology, 15*(2), 143-167.

Hastings, A. (1991). *With the tongues of men and angels: A study of channeling.* Fort Worth, TX: Holt, Rinehart and Winston.

James, W. (1958). *The varieties of religious experience.* New York, NY: Penguin Classics. (Original work published 1902)

Kennedy, J. E., & Kanthamani, H. (1995). An exploratory study of the effects of paranormal and spiritual experiences on people's lives and well-being. *Journal of the American Society for Psychical Research 89,* 249-264.

Kennedy, J. E., Kanthamani, H., & Palmer, J. (1994). Psychic and spiritual experiences, health, well-being, and meaning in life. *Journal of Parapsychology, 58,* 353-383.

Maslow, A. H. (1964). *Religion, values, and peak-experiences.* Columbus, OH: Ohio State University Press.

McClenon, J. (1994). *Wondrous Events.* Philadelphia, PA: University of Pennsylvania Press.

Mitchell, E. D. (1974). *Introduction: From outer space to inner space.* New York, NY: G. P. Putnam's Sons.

Moore, D. W. (2005). Three in four Americans believe in paranormal: Little change from similar results in 2001. *Gallup Poll News Service.* June 16. Retrieved from http://www.gallup.com/poll/16915/Three-Four-Americans-Believe-Paranormal.aspx

Newport, F., & Strausberg, M. (2001). *Americans' belief in psychic and paranormal phenomena is up over last decade.* Retrieved April 30, 2010, from http://www.gallup.com/poll/4483/americans-belief-psychic-paranormal-phenomena-over-last-decade.aspx

Palmer, G. T. (1999). Disclosure and assimilation of exceptional human experiences: Meaningful, transformative, and spiritual aspects. *Dissertation Abstracts International, 60*(05) 0669B (UMI #9932122).

Palmer, G., & Braud, W. (2002). Exceptional human experiences, disclosure, and a more inclusive view of physical, psychological, and spiritual well-being. *Journal of Transpersonal Psychology, 34,* 29-61.

Palmer, G., & Braud, W. (2010). *Psychical experiences and their life and work impacts for members of a professional academic transpersonal community.* Unpublished manuscript.

Palmer, J. (1979). A community mail survey of psychic experiences. *Journal of the American Society for Psychical Research, 3*(3), 221-251.

Pennebaker, J. W. (1995). *Emotion, disclosure, & health.* Washington, DC: American Psychological Association.

Pennebaker, J. W. (1997). *Opening up: The healing power of expressing emotions.* New York, NY: Guilford Press.

Pennebaker, J. W. (2004). *Writing to heal: A guided journal for recovery from trauma and emotional upheaval.* Oakland, CA: New Harbinger Press.

Pew Research Center. (2009, December). *Eastern, new age beliefs widespread: Many Americans mix multiple faiths.* Retrieved December 23, 2009, from http://pewforum.org/newassets/images/reports/multiplefaiths/multiplefaiths.pdf

Rice, T. W. (2003). Believe it or not: Religious and other paranormal beliefs in the United States. *Journal for Scientific Study of Religion, 42*(1), 95-106.

Ring, K. (1991). Amazing grace: The near-death experience as a compensatory gift. *Journal of Near-Death Studies, 10*(1), 11-39.

Roberts, J. (1970). *The Seth material.* Englewod Cliffs, NJ: Prentice-Hall.

Roberts, J. (1974). *The nature of personal reality.* Englewood Cliffs, NJ: Prentice-Hall.

Roberts, J. (2001). *The afterdeath journal of an American philosopher: The world view of William James.* Manhasset, NY: New Awareness Network.

Rominger, R. (2010). Postcards from heaven and hell: Understanding the near-death experience through art. *Art Therapy: Journal of the American Art Therapy Association, 27*(1), 18-25.

Stanford, R. G. (1974). An experimentally testable model for spontaneous psi events. *Journal of the American Society for Psychical Research, 68*(1), 34-57.

Stiles, W. B. (1995). Disclosure as a speech act: Is it psychotherapeutic to disclose? In J. W. Pennebaker (Ed.), *Emotion, disclosure & health* (pp. 71-91). Washington, DC: American Psychological Association.

Twemlow, S. W., Gabbard, G. O., & Jones, F. C. (1982). The out-of-body experience: A phenomenological topology based on questionnaire response. *American Journal of Psychiatry, 139*(4), 450-455.

White, R. A. (1993). Working classification of EHEs. *Exceptional Human Experience: Background Papers, 11*(2), 149-150.

White, R. A. (1997). Dissociation, narrative, and exceptional human experience. In S. Krippner & S. Powers (Eds.), *Broken images, broken selves: Dissociative narratives in clinical practice* (pp. 88-121). Washington, DC: Brunner-Mazel.

White, R. A. (1998a). The EHE process: The subjective standpoint. In R. A. White (Ed.), *Exceptional human experience: Special issue, background papers II. The EHE Network, 1995-1998: Progress and possibilities* (pp. 49-50). New Bern, NC: Exceptional Human Experience Network.

White, R. A. (1998b). How to write an EHE autobiography. In R. A. White (Ed.), *Exceptional human experiance: Special issue, background papers II. The EHE Network, 1995-1998: Progress and possibilities* (pp. 81-83). New Bern, NC: Exceptional Human Experience Network.

White, R. A. (2000). *List of potential EE/EHEs* (3rd ed.). Retrieved July 1, 2012, from http://www.ehe.org/display/ehe-pagedc08.html?ID=3

White, R. A., & Brown, S. V. (1998). Classes of EE/EHEs. In R. A. White (Ed.), *Exceptional human experience: Special issue, background papers II. The EHE Network, 1995-1998: Progress and possibilities* (pp. 43-45). New Bern, NC: Exceptional Human Experience Network.

White, R. A., & Brown, S. V. (2000). *Dictionary of EHE-related terms: An experiencer's guide.* Retrieved July 29, 2012, from http://www.ahhh-thelight.com/rw_ehe_terms.htm

Wilde, D. J., & Murray, C. D. (2010). Interpreting the anomalous: Finding meaning in out-of-body and near-death experiences. *Qualitative Research in Psychology, 7*(1), 57-72.

Zangari, W., & Machado, E. R. (1996). Survey: Incidence and social relevance of Brazilian university students' psychic experiences. *European Journal of Parapsychology, 12,* 75-87.

19

Psychedelic-Induced Experiences
James Fadiman and Andrew Kornfeld

This chapter considers how psychedelic substances affect consciousness, using the lens of a transpersonal approach to psychology. Transpersonal psychology's point of view is especially suitable to grapple with this question due not only to its continuing interest in altered states of consciousness (Hartelius, Caplan, & Rardin, 2007; Tart, 1975), but also to its long-standing relationship with psychedelic research. Several early founders of both the *Journal of Transpersonal Psychology* and Association of Transpersonal Psychology were involved in psychedelic research prior to the founding of the discipline, and discovered that the emerging field resonated with their own worldviews (Roberts & Winkelman, this volume).

By contrast, mainstream psychology has historically distanced itself from this area of study, perhaps in part because so many reports of psychedelic-induced effects include data historically shunned, denied, or pathologized by science in general. These effects include out-of-body experiences, spiritual or transcendent states of consciousness, disidentification with one's personality, and seemingly spontaneous healing. Indigenous uses include divination, communication with the spirit world, the plant kingdoms and the full scope of paranormal phenomenon. Despite a recent thaw in mainstream psychology's stance toward psychedelic research (Friedman, 2006), there is still considerable skittishness about taking the data and its implications seriously.

Dimension of Psychedelic Experience

There are at least three loosely associated groups of psychedelics. The most researched group includes lysergic acid diethylamide or LSD-25 (hereafter called LSD), psilocybin, mescaline, and the plants and fungi that contain them: certain morning glory seeds, Hawaiian wood rose[1], mushrooms, Peyote, San Pedro, and others. Important

The Wiley Blackwell Handbook of Transpersonal Psychology, First Edition.
Edited by Harris L. Friedman and Glenn Hartelius.
© 2013 John Wiley & Sons, Ltd. Published 2015 by John Wiley & Sons, Ltd.

members of the second group include substances used mainly in ritual settings: dimethyltryptamine (DMT), ayahuasca, and ibogaine. The third group contains "alphabetamines," so-named because they share an amine group, and because they represent a constantly expanding list of created compounds with a wide and under-researched range of psychological effects (Erowid.org, 2012).

Psychedelics can also be described in terms of the chemical classes to which they belong. Many are either tryptamines such as LSD, DMT, and Psilocybin, or phenethy-lamines such as mescaline, MDMA (3,4-methylenedioxy-*N*-methylamphetamine), and 2C-B (4-bromo-2,5-dimethoxyphenethylamine). Although certain experts consider MDMA non-psychedelic, it exhibits several properties similar to those of psychedelics in its lasting spiritual and healing effects. Some researchers distinguish between those psychedelics that are naturally occurring and those that are synthesized, others discriminate in terms of levels of toxicity, and so forth. This chapter will focus more on the first group, and especially on the research about LSD.

Psychedelic Effects

LSD-25 is the 25th variation of lysergic acid synthesized by Dr. Albert Hofmann (1979/2005). Several other congeners of lysergic acid became pharmaceutical products sold by the Sandoz Pharmaceutical Company for applications such as the treatment of migraine headaches. As the initial animal tests of LSD-25 revealed nothing of interest, it was put away and almost forgotten. In 1943, Hofmann felt an urge to retest it, and got a tiny amount into his system by mistake. The rest is history. LSD was, for a while, the most researched psychiatric drug in the world. From this work it has been learned that ingesting LSD or one of the other substances from the first group can lead to any of the following outcomes.

Psychosis modeling. These substances can evoke a psychotic experience (Grof, 2008). It has been suggested by Stanislav Grof that this property could be employed to give mental health workers an opportunity to experience the full terror that psychotic patients undergo.

Mental health improvements. Use of psychedelics has caused reductions in long-established neurotic patterns and in the range of difficulties and diagnoses that might be found in patients at an adult mental health clinic (Fadiman, 2011; Grof, 2008; MacLean, Johnson, & Griffiths, 2011; Savage, Fadiman, Savage, & Harman, 1964).

Reduction or elimination of chronic allergies. Andrew Weil (2004) was cured of a life-long cat dander allergy while on a recreational dose of LSD. The first author has collected other reports of the permanent reduction or elimination of chronic allergies. For example, Joshua (personal communication, 2011), inspired by Weil's story, reported that "during my first and only experience taking LSD, I deliberately exposed myself to pollens that had caused me to have allergic reactions for as long as I can remember. I took LSD in a field and sniffed the flowers and grasses telling myself that I did not need to have allergic reactions to them. I did not have allergic reactions. And since that day, I have rarely reacted to allergens." Also inspired by Weil,

Tim (personal correspondence, 2012) reported, "I had a wonderful experience on psychedelic mushrooms. The amount taken was relatively small (about 1.75 grams). While meditating, I essentially 'wished' my allergies away, concentrating very hard on 'defeating' the allergies so my body was in balance.... The next day...I noticed that I was feeling amazing, which I attributed to the amazing experience the past night...in the coming days that I continued feeling this way, and stopped taking my allergy medicine. Today (about 9 months later), I have not needed any medicine and have no allergies.... After having allergies and taking medication daily for ten full years, about half my life, this is amazing."

Cluster headache prevention. There are no conventional medical treatments that have proven effective in preventing cluster headaches, often considered the most painful of all forms of headache. However, it has been reported that 92% of individuals using either psilocybin or LSD between cluster headaches seemingly prevented an expected headache (Sewell & Halpern, 2007; www.Clusterbusters.com).

Alcoholism reduction. Abram Hoffer (1970), reporting on studies done in the 1960s, noted that, "The one striking conclusion that every scientist using psychedelic therapy (high dose) with alcoholics found the same percentage of recoveries...about 50 percent were able to remain sober or to drink much less" (p. 361). Most of these studies gave LSD to treatment-resistant older alcoholics, who had essentially zero abstinence or controlled drinking after many prior treatment failures. Before the legal use of LSD was curtailed, the Public Health Department of the Canadian province of Saskatchewan had declared that a single high dose LSD treatment of alcoholism was to be considered, "no longer experimental" and "to be used where indicated" (Unger 1962, p. 5).

Scientific breakthroughs. One research group reported that psychedelics were useful in making creative insights into complex problems including the development of a linear accelerator beam-steering device, in a new model of the photon, a vibratory microtone, and even in commercial building design (Harman, McKim, Mogar, Fadiman, & Stolaroff, 1966). Two Nobel Prize winners, Francis Crick and Kary Mullis, have attributed their discoveries in part to their LSD use (Brown, 2013); Crick co-discovered the double helical structure of DNA, and Mullis invented the most widely used technique in molecular biology called Polymerase Chain Reaction (PCR).

Anxiety relief. In use with terminally ill patients, psychedelic therapy has been shown effective in easing anxiety (Grob et al., 2011, Grob & Danforth, 2013; Kast, 1970; Kolp, Young, Friedman, Krupitsky, Jansen, & O'Connor, 2007).

Mystical experience. Psychedelic substances frequently produce profound transcendent or mystical experiences; some people consider these among the most important experiences in their lives (Doblin, 1991; Griffiths, Richards, McCann, & Jesse, 2006, 2008; Huxley 1954, 1956; MacLean, et al., 2011; Pahnke, 1967).

Enhanced quality of life. Individuals taking microdoses (10-20 μg LSD, which is one fifth to one tenth of a recreational dose) have reported to the first author improvements in daily activities and self-awareness, without sensory or visual enhancements or distortions. Charles (Fadiman, 2011; pseudonyms used unless otherwise specified) observed, "What seems to happen is that the 'flow' space described by Mihaly Csikszentmihalyi . . . is a lot easier to access and stay in. . . . You are doing what you do professionally, you are doing it well, time passes quickly, and you are pleased with your output" (p. 201).

Madeline reported that "sub-doses . . . allow me to increase my focus, open my heart, and achieve breakthrough results all remaining integrated within my routine" (Fadiman, 2011, p. 203).

According to Stephen Gray, "One of the results of this sharpness was that my guitar playing became more focused and agile. . . . On those nights my playing was definitely more on the mark. Also noticed my ability to recollect lyrics was noticeably superior to my norm" (Fadiman 2011, p. 208; real name used with permission).

Jeanette (age 19) recorded this in her diary: "4/25: micro day. Calmly worked through different emotional blocks throughout the school day, and felt a lot of unconscious material being processed" (Unpublished report).

Given this range of experiences, it is evident these substances do not fit the standard biochemical, pharmaceutical profile. Psychedelic researchers first need to take into account the strength and the nature of internal and external variables that influence the effects. The most important of these are the emotional and intellectual expectations ("set"), the physical and psychological atmosphere surrounding the ingestion ("setting"), and the dose taken.

Theories of Psychedelic Action

It is almost axiomatic that humans are not primarily rational beings. Offered a choice between something that appears difficult and something that appears easier, people typically go for the easier option (Kahneman, 2011). Given the complexity of explaining effects of such substances as LSD, it is not surprising that initial theories were simply carted over from existing scientific disciplines. For example, if LSD were just another pharmaceutical, it could be assumed to have a major mode of action that could be observed from physical changes and subject reports. As aspirin lowers fevers, emetics induce vomiting, and statins lower cholesterol irrespective of the time, place, or attitude of the person taking these drugs, so might LSD's action be clearly measurable and unrelated to the patient's mood or setting. This was the frame within which early research on LSD was conducted.

Often, experimental pharmaceutical drugs are administered in laboratories or in hospitals. After the dose has been given, one waits for its effects to take place, then dispassionately observes the subject's reactions, measures vital signs, takes blood, asks for urine samples, and may request the performance of specific tasks. Having recorded all this over a number of subjects, researchers can assume that they have completed a realistic, objective, scientific analysis of the new substance.

The results from this kind of early testing led to a theory that LSD was a psychoto-mimetic—a substance that, in normal subjects, created reality distortions such as those of patients during psychotic episodes. Studies conducted in laboratory and hospital settings commonly produced data that suggested generally upsetting, sometimes ter-rifying, imagery-filled, sensory-distorted experience for 6-12 hours, as well as height-ened sensitivity to emotional distance. The effects of just an infinitesimal dose of a few hundred micrograms of LSD appeared to match much of the territory spanned by psychotic symptoms.

In retrospect, it is possible to suggest that subjects, in an unfamiliar state of height-ened sensitivity, may have become frightened or paranoid in the care of a hospital staff that worked with appropriate professional clinical detachment taking temperatures and blood pressure, and extracting fluids, and quite likely ignoring what seemed to them incoherent statements from the person on LSD. However, even in these settings, some subjects reported that the world was transformed into astonishing beauty and that they were overwhelmed by feelings of bliss and love—and described moments of great personal insight. The statements, while noted, were not considered central to the effects of the drug. Calling it a drug had already framed a set of expectations, which we can see in hindsight, may have predisposed the researchers and even the subjects towards the observed outcomes.

Even Hoffman's (1979/2005) first intentional LSD experience had many psychotic-like features. He reported:

> A demon had invaded me, had taken possession of my body, mind, and soul. I jumped up and screamed, trying to rid my body of him, but sank down again helpless...everything in my field of vision wavered and distorted as if in a curved mirror.... There was absolutely no feeling of time...
>
> I asked my assistant to call for a doctor....
>
> I was afraid that I gone insane and..., at the climax, I had the feeling I was out of my body. I had the feeling that I was going to die...Through that very diffi-cult experience—horribly difficult—after 4 or 5 hours the feelings began to change. (pp. 49-51)

Not long thereafter, a young Czech psychiatrist, Grof, was given a dose of LSD while seated in one corner of a room in a psychiatric clinic. At one point the experimenter was curious if a strobe light would modify Grof's experience. Staring at it, Grof (1993) lost awareness of his surroundings:

> I was hit by a radiance that seemed comparable to the light at the epicenter of a nuclear explosion, or perhaps the light of supernatural brilliance said in Oriental scriptures to appear to us at the moment of death.
>
> This thunderbolt catapulted me out of my body. First, I lost my awareness of my imme-diate surroundings, then the psychiatric clinic, then Prague and finally the planet.... My consciousness seemed to explode into cosmic dimensions....
>
> The Divine manifested itself and took me over in a modern scientific laboratory in the middle of a scientific experiment conducted in a Communist country with a substance produced in the test tube of a twentieth-century chemist. (pp. 15-16)

Because of experiences such as those of Grof and others, a different evaluation of these substances gradually emerged. Unlike other classes of pharmaceuticals, effects of psychedelics such as LSD are enormously influenced by the subjects' mental state and attitude as well as their environment. The "environment" is not only the physical setting but includes the behavior and attitudes of the people present. The generally accepted theory now is that skillful use of a positive set and setting generally leads to positive experiences.

By the time Aldous Huxley was first given a psychedelic, it was in the comfort of his own home. He had a guide, a psychedelic researcher experienced in establishing a positive set and setting, who, while playing music, encouraged Huxley to relax into the new feelings and sensations. Huxley did, assured that he was being taken care of and in no danger.

> We played the Bach B-minor suite and the "*Musical Offering*" and the experience was overpowering. Bach was a revelation. The tempo of the pieces did not change; nevertheless they went on for centuries and they were a manifestation, in the plane of art, of perpetual creation...An expression of the essential all-rightness of the universe. (Horowitz & Palmer, 1999, p. 86)

On another occasion, Huxley asked his sister,

> Did you get what I have got so strongly?...An overpowering sense of gratitude, the desire to give thanks to the Order of Things for the privilege of this particular experience....And then there is the intense feeling of compassion...One can never be the same again. (Horowitz & Palmer, 1999, p. 115)

Huxley's report reflects elements of the standard set and setting that has been developed on the basis of the personal experiences of a number of psychotherapists and scientist—one that maximizes the likelihood of an experience of great pleasure, beauty, and enhanced sensory awareness. In this "best practices" situation many subjects have had, as Grof related, an entheogenic experience of personal transcendence (Harman & Fadiman, 2011). Dependent on dose and intention, the experience can involve anything from increases in mathematical understanding to actively overcoming trauma to exhibition of life-transforming unitive and mystical qualities.

Similarly, it is now known that it is possible to turn around a disturbing, terrifying, and even debilitating drug-induced exposures including those that sometimes occur at festivals such as Boom in Portugal or Burning Man in Nevada. These festivals have well-trained psychedelic guides available who regularly turn disturbing experiences into positive ones, just as Hoffman's (1979/2005) experience introduced earlier:

> When I came back from this strange world, our normal world...was a wonderful world...very enjoyable...I closed my eyes and had beautiful colored visions.
> In the morning I was completely fresh. The sensation of well-being and renewed life flowed through me. When I later walked in the garden...Everything glistened and sparkled in a fresh light. (p. 48)

In psychedelic research, attention to set and setting is of critical importance individually, culturally, and cross-culturally. All current American and European therapeutic studies use slight variations of the physical setting and mental set developed by Al Hubbard and others in the sixties (Sherwood, Stolaroff, & Harman, 1962). In South America, the best-known psychedelic therapeutic centers, such as *Takiwasi* in Peru (Tindall, 2008), operate with a cross-cultural component, as they are staffed by both indigenous healers and Westerners (a large number of indigenous groups still maintain traditional methods; Davis, 1997).

Explanatory Mechanisms

Because psychedelic research was effectively prohibited for more than forty years, scientists are only now only starting to uncover the delicate mechanisms occurring in the brain during and after psychedelic induced experiences. Psychedelics work by binding to receptors on the surface of neurons (brain cells). LSD, which works almost exclusively on the serotonin system, mimics the neurotransmitter by binding to its different receptor types and eliciting excitatory and inhibitory responses. The variety of serotonin receptors, the way in which LSD binds to them, and the excitatory/inhibitory responses may explain the complex and profound states of consciousness experienced by someone on LSD (Nichols, 2004).

Researchers in England measured changes in cerebral blood flow during the peak of a psilocybin-induced psychedelic experience using a functional magnetic resonance imagining (fMRI). They discovered, counter to expectations, diminished blood flow to the medial prefrontal cortex (mPFC) and the posterior cingulate cortex (PCC). The prefrontal cortex, a relatively new evolutionary brain region, is more developed in humans and deals with complex thinking—filtering the world around us. It may be that by shutting off this brain region, participants were able to experience vivid sensory stimuli that they would have otherwise written off as something non-important in the background. Even more interestingly, the PCC is the part of the brain associated with self-identity (Carhart-Harris et al., 2012), which may explain the reported transpersonal phenomena of ego death while experiencing the effects of psychedelics.

These findings, however, relate to possible processes responsible for the transient experiences while under the influence of a psychedelic substance. A more significant phenomenon that also requires explanation is how a *single* psychedelic-induced experience can create lasting cognitive and emotional transformation such as major shifts in personality or in chronic mental health. Examples of this are the soldier who no longer exhibited symptoms of treatment-resistant post-traumatic stress disorder after MDMA psychotherapy (Mithoefer, Wagner, Mithoefer, Jerome, & Doblin, 2010), the teacher whose depression lifted after a single dose of ketamine[2] (ketamine has psychedelic properties at certain doses; Hamilton, 2012), the terminally ill cancer patient who has come to terms with death after an experience with psilocybin (Grob et al., 2011), or the perfectly healthy woman who experienced one of the most spiritually significant moments in her life with psilocybin (Griffiths et al., 2011).

Such results are entirely different from the effects of psychoactive prescription medication such as anti-depressants, benzodiazepines, amphetamines, and so forth, which must be taken frequently to maintain a desired shift in intellectual/emotional mood or attitude. When individuals stop the medication, the changed traits often revert to the state they were in before the medication was given. A possible explanation is that such an experience activates the brain process known as neuroplasticity—the brain's ability to change itself. Associating neuroplasticity with psychedelics is a new theoretical turn, and the conceptualization presented in this chapter appears to be novel.

Neuroscience commonly focuses on how the brain initiates physical human action. For example, when a person reaches for an object, an array of motor command neurons fire action potentials (the way neurons turn on and off), which cause the proper muscle movements and the intended actions in the world. This process relates to how the brain shapes its environment. In recent years, neuroscience has given more attention to how *environment and experiences shapes the brain* (Doidge, 2007). Neuroplasticity is at the foundation of what makes human and sentient beings. It is activated by interactions with the environment—the people, events, and situations we encounter every day of our lives. It is the reason why we can solve complex problems, create artistic masterpieces, and ponder the origins of the universe. As you read this chapter, your approximately 100 billion neurons are strengthening, weakening, creating new connections and destroying old among the some 10,000 synapses per neuron. This process allows each person to remember and recast information previously acquired and to evaluate future alternatives. Multiple neurons connecting with one another form what is called a brain map (Doidge, 2007).

Each neuron (or brain cell) within the human brain is shaped similar to a tree, with the branches representing small protrusions called dendrites and the roots representing terminal buttons. Dendrites function to receive information, while terminal buttons send information to other neurons in the form of neurotransmitters. It is important to remember that neurons do not touch, but communicate via synapses.

Interestingly, 2,5-dimethoxy-4-iodoamphetamine or DOI is an uncommon psychedelic phenethelamine compound that shares a mechanism similar to LSD and other psychedelics. Jones et al. (2009) observed rapid increases in dentritic size after a single dose of DOI, indicating that these neurons have more potential form synaptic connections.

Further, certain types of protein neurotransmitter receptors are thought to be involved with the long term strengthening and weakening of synapses. Numerous studies have demonstrated that these receptors become activated upon the administration of various psychedelic tryptamines, such as LSD, psilocybin, and DMT (Aghajanian & Marek, 1997, 1999; Puig, Celada, az-Mataix, & Artigas, 2003; Beique, Imad, Mladenovic, Gingrich, & Andrade, 2007). This may indicate that psychedelic compounds activate synaptic change above and beyond what these synapses would do normally.

If a single psychedelic experience is able to create durable changes in personality and mental and emotional health, as has been reported, then it seems that these substances may be able to uniquely catalyze the formation of new brain maps. To the degree that such a suggestion can be experimentally supported, this suggests that *psychedelics are neuroplasticity activators*—significantly enhancing one of the most important adaptive processes in the brain.

Research by Ronald Duman and Nick Li (2012) offered preliminary evidence to support this characterization of the impact of psychedelics. Their work demonstrated that ketamine can accelerate the formation of new synapses between neurons through a process known as *synaptogenesis*. Duman reported physical data demonstrating that, just hours after the administration of ketamine in rats, increased synaptogenesis was taking place. Neuroplastic activation appears to be a useful explanatory mechanism consistent with the data about major, rapid, and durable mental and emotional changes after therapeutic psychedelic experiences. It is highly possible that, by switching off the mPFC and PCC brain regions, unique neuroplastic events are enabled to occur in greater number.

Summary and Conclusions

Research into psychedelics has opened new areas of inquiry: Early LSD work led to intensified study of serotonin—now a major area of research—and continues to lead to advances in neuropsychology. It is generative research not only because it may demonstrate the potential therapeutic effects of psychedelics, but because at times it produces novel and implication-rich results that may lead to more effective study of mind and brain. Several major observations can be offered:

1. Psychedelic substances do not cause experiences, but do facilitate novel experiences of considerable duration, mostly beneficial but some harmful. Beneficial results include profound spiritual and mystical experiences, improvement in a variety of mental health conditions including anxiety and alcoholism, enhancement in quality of life, and the cultivation of practical, creative insights into complex problems, physical health benefits such as reduction or elimination of chronic allergies and prevention of cluster headaches, and possible source of insights into the nature of psychosis.

2. Research on consciousness needs to be more context-based with multiple variables observed simultaneously. Enough is known about the effect of psychedelics to give up the notion that one can isolate the effects of a substance merely because one can isolate the substance. Yet a remarkable amount of early research assumed that LSD's impact, as with other pharmaceuticals, was negligibly affected by factors such as set and setting. The emergence of these latter as important variables suggests that LSD and similar substances affect systems that are much closer to the center of sentience itself, and may therefore be variable in ways that are more dynamic, more individualized, and less mechanically predictable.

By way of analogy, it would be of little use to control for whether respondents sat with ankles crossed while answering questions on standard self-report measures: the variable is not properly calibrated to the research. For a similar reason, taking a psychedelic at a concert or during a ritual in a rainforest may be no more or less meaningfully controlled than taking it in a laboratory, therapy room, or a hospital— and standardizing doses or the accompanying music for a psychedelic session is not necessarily useful. The lability of response to psychedelics is such that a multivariate approach is not only more useful, but inescapable, because the salient variables present in even the simplest of designs are already multiple.

A six variable model, originally developed to improve the therapeutic benefit of high-dose LSD therapy in the 60s, may be a useful tool for psychedelic studies, in order to support prediction and evaluation of short- and long-term psychedelic effects. The variables are:

> Set (intellectual and emotional expectations)
> Setting (physical and psychological atmosphere)
> Substance and amount (drug and dose)
> Sitter (others in attendance)
> Session (what occurs during the drug active phase.)
> Situation (subject's psychosocial context)
> (summarized from Fadiman, 2011, pp. 14-38, 258, 265)

One test of the robustness of a multivariate model is to determine whether a change in any one variable affects the nature, scope, duration, strength, and residual effects of the intervention.

3. Psychedelic substances, used correctly, are valuable tools to study facets of consciousness including self-healing, visionary experience, spiritual transformations, religious conversion, and altered states of consciousness. After a 40-year research hiatus, there is now a beginning understanding of how these substances affect physical, mental and spiritual functioning. Perhaps it is fortunate that, because psychedelic research has never been funded nor seen as potentially profitable by any pharmaceutical company, the full range of effects have been reported. Psychedelics, as with most other powerful compounds, have anticipated desirable and undesirable effects, less prominent effects, and rare effects. Because almost all psychedelics are not yet legal, but widely used and easily available, the non-profit group Erowid has created a web-based data repository to collect and make available as complete a library of reports about these substances as possible. In June 2012, a visitor to Erowid.org can access some 22,500 "trip reports" on 517 substances, compounds, and mixtures. This informal, unsystematic collection of anecdotal qualitative reports, while often messy, is now available to researchers as preliminary data that may help to inform and shape more formal research.

In reviewing the literature on substances and human experiences, it is necessary to remain alert to the potential for distortions or suppression of data. Resistance to psychedelic research is an example of this issue, but not an isolated case. Perhaps because of the overwhelming financial and political power of pharmaceutical companies, some published medical research may pass over mental distress caused by using profitable drugs. An example can be seen with the case of the antimalarial agent Larium. Although the United States is a major research center for pharmaceutical products, reports of nightmares, suicides, and even murders attributed to the use of Larium by researchers outside the USA are discounted if not denied by the company producing the drug (Koen, 2009; Nevin, Poetrusiak, & Caci, 2008; www.lariaminfo.org).

4. Neuroplasticity and the suppression of certain brain regions appear to be a valuable conceptual tool in reframing hitherto inexplicable research findings. Research on psychedelics is still in preliminary stages. The present early effort to explain their effects in creating beneficial long-term psycho-emotional change must necessarily piece together evidence drawn from the testing of various substances that produce similar experiences. On this basis, it is possible to suggest that psychedelics in the class that includes LSD, psilocybin, and ketamine at certain doses function as neuroplasticity activators, perhaps promoting the development of new brain maps by significantly enhancing synaptogenesis and inhibiting the function of brain areas associated with complex conscious thought such as the mPFC and PCC. Much more work needs to be done to test this preliminary sketch of how psychedelics might impact brain and mind, but hypotheses that fit with observed data are crucial for directing future research.

Future Directions for Psychedelic Research

What can transpersonal psychology offer observational and experimental psychedelic science? First, transpersonal psychology's interest in non-ordinary states, and in bringing to bear on psychology the insights from spiritual and indigenous traditions of many cultures, informs a broad context within which psychedelic research can be seen as indispensable. The Western assumption that only one state of mind reflects reality is typical of a *monophasic* culture; by contrast, it is likely that the majority of the world's cultures are *polyphasic,* recognizing that different states of consciousness contribute to the perception of reality (Bourguignon & Evascu, 1977; Laughlin, McManus, & d'Aquili, 1990). For example, of 274 cultures, Richard Blum (1969) found only four that did not use psychoactive substances, suggesting that these and the states they facilitate are quite typical of human culture.

With the exception of early psychologists such as William James, transpersonal psychology was the first aspect of the field to seriously engage with these phenomena. As a pioneering contributor, transpersonal psychology is an obvious participant in the further development of psychedelic research. Yet it is uniquely suited for this task because it is not just interested in the scientific study of various states of consciousness, but in a *polyphasic science* that does not demand psychedelic phenomena be interpreted only through the monophasic lens of standard science (cf. Tart, 1972).

Transpersonal psychology is able to contribute to rigorous scientific research into the various impacts of psychedelic experience, but it is also able to design and interpret research from a perspective that considers these experiences as something more than delusional. This is perspective is essential for useful study; just as the deciphering of ancient Egyptian hieroglyphs would have been difficult without the assumption that they represented intelligible writing, so the study of psychedelic experiences is hampered if it does not accept that these states have some inherent value.

There are, of course, many specific areas of research that need further development—from more sophisticated research designs, to more effective design and utilization of set and setting, expanded research on the reported mental, emotional, and physiological benefits of psychedelic experience, and research on a wide variety of plants and laboratory-produced substances not yet under study. Other aspects deserving inquiry are the effects of long-term recreational use of psychedelics, long-term use within recognized psychedelic churches, and use in such churches by young children (e.g., Doering-Silveira et al., 2005).

Farther out, after psychedelic experiences are themselves better understood, it may be that these states might be utilized in systematically exploring other non-ordinary phenomena such as near-death experiences, clairvoyance, telepathy, and distant healing (Tart, 2009), plants as teachers (Buhner, 2002; Harpignies, 2007), non-primate problem-solving and its implications (e.g., if unicellular slime mold can solve a maze, this raises questions regarding the nature of intelligence; Nakagaki, 2001; Narby 2006), and non-human intelligent entities with or without physical form (Tindall, 2008). Such explorations might come full circle and connect scientific society with humanity's indigenous roots:

> Ayahuasca and iboga, too, it seems to me, precipitate you, even if you are a materialist, rationalist, atheist academic, into a sphere that is the spitting image of the one described by shamans the world over, filled with discarnate entities, dead people, people were not yet born, talking animals, and all sorts of things." (Narby, Koumen, & Ravalec, 2010, p. 84)

Notes

1. Morning glory seeds and Hawaiian wood rose seeds contain lysergic acid amide (LSA), a close relative of lysergic acid diethylamide (LSD).
2. All other anti-depressants do not seem to have any effect for 2-6 weeks.

References

Aghajanian, G. K., & Marek, G. J. (1997). Serotonin induces excitatory postsynaptic potentials in apical dendrites of neocortical pyramidal cells. *Neuropsychopharmacology, 36,* 589-599.

Aghajanian, G. K., & Marek, G. J. (1999). Serotonin, via 5-HT2A receptors, increases EPSCs in layer V pyramidal cells of prefrontal cortex by anasynchronous mode of glutamate release. *Brain Research, 825,* 161-171.

Beique, J. C., Imad, M., Mladenovic, L., Gingrich, J. A., & Andrade, R. (2007). Mechanism of the 5-hydroxytryptamine 2A receptor-mediated facilitation of synaptic activity in prefrontal cortex. *Proceedings of the National Academy of Science USA, 104,* 9870-9875.

Blum, R. (1969). *Society and drugs: Social and cultural observations.* San Francisco, CA: Jossey-Bass.

Bourguignon, E., & Evascu, T. L. (1977). Altered states of consciousness within a general evolutionary perspective: A holocultural analysis. *Behavior Science Research, 12,* 197-216.

Brown, D. J. (2013) *The new science of psychedelics: At the nexus of culture, consciousness, and spirituality.* Rochester, VT: Park Street Press.

Buhner, S. (2002) *The lost language of plants: The ecological importance of plant medicines to life on earth.* White River Junction, VT: Chelsea Green.

Carhart-Harris, R., Erritze, D., Williams, T., Stone, J., Reed, L., Colasanti, A., & Nutt, D. (2012). Neural correlates of the psychedelic state as determined by fMRI studies with psilocybin. *Proceedings of the National Academy of Science (PNAS), 109*(6), 2138-2143.

Davis, W. (1997) *One river: Explorations and discoveries in the Amazon rain forest.* New York, NY: Simon & Schuster.

Doblin, R. (1991). Pahnke's "Good Friday experiment": A long-term follow-up and methodological critique. *Journal of Transpersonal Psychology, 23*(1), 1-28.

Doering-Silveira, E., Grob, C., Dobkin de Rios, M., Lopez, M., Alonso, E., Tacla, L., & Da Silveira, D. (2005) Ayahuasca in adolescence: A preliminary psychiatric assessment. *Journal of Psychoactive Drugs, 37,*129-133.

Doidge, N. (2007) *The brain that changes itself: Stories of personal triumph from the frontiers of brain science.* New York, NY: Viking.

Duman, R., & Li, N. (2012). A neurotrophic hypothesis of depression: Role of synaptogenesis in the actions of NMDA receptor antagonists. *Philosophical Transactions of the Royal Society Biological Sciences, 367,* 2475-2484.

Erowid.org. (2012). *Erowid [website].* San Francisco, CA: Author.

Fadiman, J. (2011) *The psychedelic explorer's guide: Safe, therapeutic, and sacred journeys.* Rochester, VT: Park Street Press.

Friedman, H. (2006). The renewal of psychedelic research: Implications for humanistic and transpersonal psychology. *The Humanistic Psychologist, 34*(1), 39-58.

Griffiths, R. R., Johnson, M. W., Richards, W. A., Richards, B. D., McCann, U., & Jesse, R. (2011) Psilocybin occasioned mystical-type experiences: Immediate and persisting dose-related effects. *Journal of Psychopharmacology, 218,* 649-665.

Griffiths, R., Richards, W., McCann, U., & Jesse, R. (2006). Psilocybin can occasion mystical-type experiences having substantial and sustained personal meaning and spiritual significance. *Psychopharmacology, 187*(3), 268-283.

Griffiths, R., Richards, W., McCann, U., & Jesse, R. (2008) Mystical-type experiences occasioned by psilocybin mediate the attribution of personal meaning and spiritual significance 14 months later. *Journal of Psychopharmacology, 6,* 621-632.

Grob, C., & Danforth, A. (2013) Psychedelic psychotherapy near the end of life. In T. Roberts (Ed.), *The psychedelic future of the mind: How entheogens are enhancing cognition, boosting intelligence, and raising values* (pp. 102-117). Rochester, VT: Park Street Press.

Grob, C., Danforth, A., Chopra, G., Hagerty, M., McKay, C., Halberstadt, A., & Greer, G. (2011). Pilot study of psilocybin treatment for anxiety in patients with advanced-stage cancer. *Archives of General Psychiatry, 68*(1), 71-78.

Grof, S. (1993). *The holotropic mind: The three levels of human consciousness and how they shape our lives.* New York, NY: HarperOne.

Grof, S. (2008). *LSD psychotherapy.* Santa Cruz, CA: Multidisciplinary Association for Psychedelic Studies.

Hamilton, J. (2012). "I wanted to Live": New depression drugs offer hope for toughest cases. National Public Radio.

Harman, W., & Fadiman, J. (2011). A questionnaire study of psychedelic experiences. In J. Fadiman (Ed.), *The psychedelic explorer's guide: Safe, therapeutic, and sacred journeys* (pp. 296-302). Rochester, VT: Park Street Press.

Harman, W., McKim, R., Mogar, R., Fadiman, J., & Stolaroff, M. (1966). Psychedelic agents in creative problem-solving: A pilot study. *Psychological Reports, 19,* 211-227.

Harpignies, J. (2007). *Visionary plant consciousness: The shamanistic teachings of the plant world.* Rochester, VT: Park Street Press.

Hartelius, G., Caplan, M., & Rardin, M.-A. (2007). Transpersonal psychology: Defining the past, divining the future. *The Humanistic Psychologist, 35*(2), 135-160.

Hoffer, A. (1970). Treatment of alcoholism with psychedelic therapy. In B. Aaronson & H. Osmond (Eds.), *Psychedelics: The uses and implications of hallucinogenic drugs* (pp. 357-366). New York, NY: Doubleday.

Hofmann, A. (2005). *LSD: My problem child.* Santa Cruz, CA: Multidisciplinary Association for Psychedelic Studies (MAPS). (Original work published 1979 [German])

Horowitz, M., & Palmer, C. (1999). *Moksha: Aldous Huxley's writings on psychedelics and the visionary experience.* Rochester, VT: Park Street Press.

Huxley, A. (1954). *The doors of perception.* New York, NY: Harper.

Huxley, A. (1956). *Heaven and hell.* London, UK: Chatto & Windus.

Jones, K. A., Srivastava, D. P., Allen, J. A., Strachan, R. T., Roth, B. L., & Penzes, P. (2009). Rapid modulation of spine morphology by the 5-HT2A serotonin receptor through kalirin-7 signaling. *Proceedings of the National Academy of Science USA, 106,* 19575-19580.

Kahneman, D. (2011). *Thinking fast and slow.* Farrar, NY: Strauss & Giroux.

Kast, E. (1970). A concept of death. In B. Aaronson & H. Osmond (Eds.), *Psychedelics: The uses and implications of hallucinogenic drugs* (pp 366-381). New York, NY: Doubleday, New York.

Koen, D. (2009, February 11). The dark side of Larium. *CBSnews.com.* Retrieved from http://www.cbsnews.com/2100-500164_162-538144.html

Kolp, E., Young, M. S., Friedman, H., Krupitsky, E., Jansen, K., & O'Connor, L.-A. (2007). Ketamine-enhanced psychotherapy: Preliminary clinical observations on its effects in treating death anxiety. *International Journal of Transpersonal Studies, 26,* 1-17.

Laughlin, C. D., McManus, J., & d'Aquili, E. G. (1990). *Brain, symbol and experience: Toward a neurophenomenology of human consciousness.* Boston, MA: Shambhala.

MacLean, K., Johnson, M., & Griffiths, R. (2011). Mystical experiences occasioned by the hallucinogen psilocybin lead to increases in the personality domain of openness. *Journal of Psychopharmacology, 29* doi:10.1177/0269881111420188.

Mithoefer, M., Wagner, M., Mithoefer, A., Jerome, L., & Doblin, R. (2010). The safety and efficacy of +/− 3,4-methylenedioxymethamphetamine-assisted psychotherapy in subjects with chronic, treatment-resistant posttraumatic stress disorder: The first randomized controlled pilot study. *Journal of Psychopharmacology, 25*(4), 439-452.

Nakagaki, T. (2001). Smart behavior of true slime mold in a labyrinth. *Research in Microbiology, 152,* 767-770.

Narby, J. (2006) *Intelligence in nature.* New York, NY: Tarcher/Penguin.

Narby, J., Koumen, J., & Ravalec, V. (2010) *The psychotropic mind: The world according to ayahuasca, iboga, and shamanism.* Rochester, VT: Park Street Press.

Nevin, R., Pietrusiak, P., & Caci, J. (2008). Prevalence of contraindications to mefloquine use among USA military personnel deployed to Afghanistan. *Malaria Journal, 7*:30. doi:10.1186/1475-2875-7-30.

Nichols, D. (2004). Hallucinogens. *Pharmacology & Therapeutics, 101*(2), 131-181.

Pahnke, W. N. (1967). LSD and religious experience. In R. Debold & R. Leaf (Eds.) *LSD, man, and society* (pp. 60-85). Middletown, CT: Wesleyan University Press.

Puig, M. V., Celada, P., az-Mataix, L., & Artigas, F. (2003). In vivo modulation of the activity of pyramidal neurons in the rat medial prefrontal cortex by 5-HT2A receptors: relationship to thalamocortical afferents. *Cerebral Cortex, 13,* 870-882.

Roberts, T., & Winkelman, M. (this volume). Psychedelic induced transpersonal experiences, therapies, and their implications for transpersonal psychology (Chapter 25).

Savage, C., Fadiman, J., Savage, E., & Harman, W. (1964). LSD. Therapeutic effects of the psychedelic experience. *Psychological Reports, 14,* 111-120.

Sewell. A., & Halpern, J. (2007). Response of cluster headache to psilocybin and LSD. In M. Winkelman & T. Roberts (Eds.), *Psychedelic medicine: New evidence for hallucinogenic substances as treatments* (Vol. 1, pp. 98-103). Westport, CT: Praeger.

Sherwood, N., Stolaroff, M., & Harman, W. (1962) The psychedelic experience: A new concept in psychotherapy. *The Journal of Neuropsychiatry, 3,* 370-375.

Tart, C. T. (1972). States of consciousness and state-specific sciences. *Science, 176,* 1203-1210.

Tart, C. T. (1975). *States of consciousness.* New York, NY: E. P. Dutton.

Tart, C. T. (2009). *The end of materialism: How evidence of the paranormal is bringing science and spirit together.* Oakland, CA: New Harbinger.

Tindall, R. (2008) *The jaguar that roams the mind: An Amazonian plant spirit odyssey.* Rochester, VT: Park Street Press.

Unger, S. (1962). Apparent results of referrals of alcoholics for LSD therapy. *Report of the Bureau, Saskatchewan Department of Public Health.* p. 5.

Weil, A. (2004). *The natural mind* (Rev. ed.). New York, NY. Mariner Books.

20

Near-Death Experiences and Transpersonal Psychology

Focus on Helping Near-Death Experiencers

Cheryl Fracasso, Bruce Greyson, and
Harris L. Friedman

The transpersonal nature of the near-death experience (NDE) challenges the limitations of mainstream psychology and supports the need for transpersonal psychology. Raymond Moody (1975) is credited with coining the term NDE, while noting several predominant characteristics that challenge what Westerners are socialized into believing is "reality." Some of these include seeing a bright light, floating through a tunnel, having an out-of-body experience with vivid sensory awareness, telepathic communications with spiritual beings and deceased relatives, family, and friends, having a life review (i.e., recalling the highlights of one's life)—and all of these can occur when a person is deemed clinically, as well as nearly, dead. In addition, occurring after these unusual experiences are many profound aftereffects that can dramatically and permanently change the lives of NDE experiencers (NDErs). NDEs may result in post-integration issues, such as psychospiritual crises that may require therapeutic intervention to resolve.

Whether or not the aftereffects cause significant adjustment problems, the transpersonal realms experienced starkly contrast with ordinary consensual reality, and therefore can potentially disrupt NDErs' worldviews as they try to make sense out of the profound state they have experienced. The ineffability of the experience only adds to the confusion, because many struggle with the inadequacy of words when trying to communicate their experience to others. To compound the issue, the past 37 years of research have indicated that a large percentage may initially question their own sanity due to having experienced a different state of awareness that does not conform to three-dimensional space-time rules—which only reinforces ambivalence to share their experience with others (Duffy & Olsen, 2007; Greyson, 1997, 2005, 2010; James, 2004; Simpson, 2001). However it is not just NDErs who are often left confused, but scientists who study this phenomenon with open minds are also left wondering, as it contradicts so much of the prevailing materialistic perspective.

The Wiley Blackwell Handbook of Transpersonal Psychology, First Edition.
Edited by Harris L. Friedman and Glenn Hartelius.
© 2013 John Wiley & Sons, Ltd. Published 2015 by John Wiley & Sons, Ltd.

Whether these experiences are real or some confabulation of the brain is not the issue at hand for transpersonal psychologists to decide. Rather, it is important to keep in mind that it *is real* in the mind of the experiencer. The fact that millions of people have reported NDEs with consistent characteristics in all ages, genders, and cultures is simply not something that can be easily ignored. Although many theories have been proposed over the past few decades to try to explain NDEs, or perhaps better yet "explain them away," each has fallen short of being able to account adequately for all characteristics reported, let alone *why* these consistent characteristics have prevailed for centuries, regardless of religion or prior personal or spiritual beliefs. (For an overview of these theories and their limitations, see Greyson, Kelly, & Kelly, 2009; Greyson, 2010.) This makes the NDE a unique phenomenon in a class of its own that is different from other transpersonal experiences, and therefore, deserves to be recognized as such. The aim of this chapter is to present information on what is known about NDEs, as well as common aftereffects, to better inform transpersonal psychologists and those interested in transpersonal phenomena, about the NDE and its implications for working with NDErs.

Incidence: How Common are NDEs?

Over the past 37 years, it has been estimated that as many as 10-40% of those who survive a clinical crisis are reporting NDEs and that, due to improved techniques of resuscitation, these numbers are expected to increase (Parnia, Spearpoint, & Fenwick, 2007; van Lommel, van Wees, Meyers, & Elfferich, 2001). In a recent analysis, Nancy Zingrone and Carlos Alvarado (2009) found that the incidence rate in "retrospective studies combined is 35 percent, whereas that of prospective studies combined is 17 percent" (p. 34). However, Suzanne Simpson (2001) and many others (e.g., Duffy & Olsen, 2007; James, 2004) highlighted that the actual occurrence of NDEs may be significantly higher, because many NDErs may be reluctant to talk about their experience post-NDE due to fears of being labeled as "crazy."

Noting these limitations in obtaining accurate incidence rates of NDEs, earlier studies showed slightly higher occurrences prior to when Bruce Greyson's (1983) NDE Scale was developed to screen for the validity of NDEs using clear criteria. For example, a prospective study by Kenneth Ring (1980) found that 40% out of 102 individuals who came close to death and/or were resuscitated reported a NDE, while a Gallup Poll conducted in 1982 (Gallup & Proctor, 1982) revealed that nearly 8 million people reported a NDE (which equates to nearly 35% reported by those who presumably came close to death). In another prospective study, Greyson (1986) assessed 61 patients who were admitted to the hospital for a suicide attempt and found that 16 reported a NDE. It seems likely that these numbers will continue to rise as medical advances enable the resuscitation of more and more people from the brink of death.

More recently, Pim van Lommel and colleagues (2001) conducted an 8-year prospective study on 344 survivors of cardiac arrest in 10 Dutch hospitals and found that 18% reported an NDE and, out of these, 12% reported a core experience with several features originally noted by Moody (1975). Although these rates are considerably lower than those reported in earlier findings, van Lommel and colleagues found that the occurrence of NDEs was not associated with fear of death prior to the cardiac arrest, medication, duration of unconsciousness, or length of cardiac arrest. Another prospective study conducted by Parnia, Waller, Yeates, and Fenwick (2001) examined 63 consecutive survivors of cardiac arrest in a British cardiac care unit and found that 11% reported a NDE. Likewise, Schwaninger, Eisenberg, Schechtman, and Weiss (2002) assessed 174 consecutive survivors of cardiac arrest over a four-year period and found that 23% reported a NDE. Similarly, Greyson (2003) conducted a prospective study in which he examined 1,595 patients consecutively admitted to a tertiary cardiac care inpatient unit over a period of thirty months. Greyson found that 10% of the patients who survived cardiac arrest reported a NDE.

Demographics

NDEs have been reported in a broad array of populations and circumstances. There has been no differential prevalence found for religion (McClenon, 2006a), race (Greyson, 2003; McClenon, 2005), age (Britton & Bootzin, 2004; van Lommel et al., 2001), gender (Audain, 1999; Greyson, 1997, 2001, 2003; Parnia et al., 2007), or education and socioeconomic status (Greyson, 1997). Furthermore, NDErs have been shown to be psychologically healthy using various measures (Greyson, 2007; Greyson et al., 2009; Parnia et al., 2007; Wren-Lewis, 2004), and do not meet clinical criteria for post-traumatic stress disorder (PTSD) or dissociative disorders as outlined in the *DSM-IV-TR* (American Psychiatric Association (APA), 2000; Christian, 2005; Greyson, 2001, 2007; Morris & Knafl, 2003; Wren-Lewis, 2004).

Likewise, NDEs are reported in a wide variety of medical crises, such as surgery, cardiac arrest, accidents/injuries, childbirth, allergic reactions, acute and/or terminal illness, drowning, military combat, and extreme emotional stress, to name a few (Britton & Bootzin, 2004; Greyson, 1997, 2001, 2003; Greyson et al., 2009;; Moody, 1975; Parnia et al., 2001, 2007; Ring, 1980; van Lommel et al., 2001). Morse, Conner, and Tyler (1985) found gender differences between the types of clinical crises that provoked a NDE, as well as differences in children, but overall, reports by children and adults generally consisted of the same key characteristics.

Cross-Cultural Research

Rich data have been gleaned from cross-cultural research, which strongly suggest that many characteristics of NDEs appear to be a universal phenomenon. Although research has shown that cultures may interpret the meaning of the NDE differently (i.e., attributing the light or spiritual beings to their specific religious/spiritual ideology), Greyson et al. (2009) pointed out that the essential characteristics appear to remain the same (i.e., seeing a light, out-of-body experience [OBE], life review, seeing deceased spirits/relatives/loved ones, enhanced telepathic/psychic abilities, etc.).

For example, a recent study conducted in Iran found that Muslim NDErs reported similar criteria to Western accounts (Fracasso, Aleyasin, Friedman, & Young, 2010). Out of 19 participants, 62% reported encountering a light, 53% reported coming to a border or boundary and said they were "sent back," 42% reported hearing an unidentifiable voice, 41% reported a life review, 37% reported seeing scenes from the future, 32% reported OBEs, 26% reported seeing deceased relatives or religious (holy) spirits, and 21% reported sensing the presence of deceased relatives and/or religious (holy) spirits. Likewise, 53% reported they were able to communicate and receive information telepathically in this state of consciousness, and 74% reported enhanced psychic abilities post-NDE.

Other researchers have found similar results. Allan Kellehear (2008) conducted a cross-cultural comparison of data through 2005 and found that non-Western NDEs had many similarities to Western accounts, with only a few minor differences. Cultures examined were China, India, New Zealand, Hawaii, Western New Britain, Native America, Tibet, Guam, and Africa. Kellehear found that all non-Western NDEs included reports of meeting/seeing deceased relatives or supernatural beings and experiencing other realms of pure, unlimited knowledge, as commonly reported in Western NDEs. In contrast, Kellehear found that reports of the tunnel experience were not described in most non-Western accounts, although reports of floating through darkness were common, which appears to resemble the tunnel experience. Belanti, Perera, and Jagadheesan (2008) suggested these differences may be due to socio-cultural influences surrounding how one interprets the meaning of the experience, language barriers, and/or religious beliefs.

Interestingly, James McClenon (2005) analyzed 28 African-American narratives from 1,832 anomalous experiences collected in North Carolina to compare elements of the NDE with ritual healing ceremonies. McClenon reported that a majority of the NDE narratives revealed more negative emotions than the rituals. Following this, McClenon (2006b) analyzed eight Kongo NDEs from Central Africa and found that they all reported out-of-body experiences, "other realms" of pure knowledge, and communication with supernatural beings, which lends further support to the universality of this experience. In Satwant Pasricha's (2008) survey of 60 villages in India (36,100 people), she found that four individuals out of every 10,000 reported a NDE. As in Western NDEs, Pasricha found the most commonly reported elements were seeing a bright light, a sensation of a "cave" (commonly referred to as a tunnel in Western accounts), extrasensory experience as well as extreme feelings of peace. Australian reports of NDEs have also suggested that approximately 8% of the population reported NDEs, with a 36% prevalence rate reported among those who had a close brush with death (Perera, Padmasekara, & Belanti, 2005).

NDE Aftereffects

It is also well documented that there are several profound aftereffects commonly associated with NDEs, including both positive as well as negative post-integration issues that appear to occur over a period of 15 years or more (Bush, 1991; Christian, 2005; Groth-Marnat & Summers, 1998; Insinger, 1981; Noyes, Fenwick, Holden, & Christian, 2009; Sutherland, 1992). Research has shown that in a substantial number of cases, clinical intervention may be needed to help NDErs integrate their NDE into their daily lives—although many researchers view even these difficult aftereffects as positive post-integration growth opportunities in which shallow parts of the old self are left behind as NDErs seek to integrate deeper values (Holden, 2009). Many researchers have found high rates of divorce due to radical changes in lifestyle values (Christian, 2005), some became suicidal during certain phases (longing to return to the peaceful realm experienced during their NDE), while others struggled with depression, perhaps due to not having the experience validated by friends, family, and/ or practitioners (Bush, 1991; Groth-Marnat & Summers, 1998; Noyes et al., 2009).

Positive Long-Term Aftereffects

Positive long-term effects of NDEs commonly cited in the literature include an increased sense of purpose and meaning in life (Britton & Bootzin, 2004; Greyson, 1996, 1997, 2009; Moody, 1975; Noyes et al., 2009; Ring, 1980; van Lommel et al., 2001; Zingrone & Alvarado, 2009), feelings of unity, love, and compassion towards all of life (Greyson, 2001; Holden, Long, & MacLurg, 2006; James, 2004; Parnia et al., 2001), a decreased interest in obtaining material wealth (Stout, Jacquin, & Atwater, 2006), a desire to eat healthier (many reported eating more vegetables and desiring less red meat), a decreased fear of death, and an increased desire to be of service to others (Brumm, 2006; Christian, 2005; Kinnier, Tribbensee, Rose, & Vaughan, 2001; Moody, 1975; Morris & Knafl, 2003; Ring, 1980; Sabom, 1982; Wren-Lewis, 2004). Many NDErs also reported a decreased desire to consume certain chemicals found in some foods and/or addictive type of substances, such as caffeine, alcohol, and nicotine (James, 2004; Ring, 1992).

Long-Term Post-Integration Issues

Some of the commonly cited long-term, post-integration issues include frustration with finding one's purpose in life, confusion about the true meaning of life, high rates of depression, anxiety, anger, as well as problems integrating the experience into his or her daily life (Christian, 2005; Duffy & Olsen, 2007; Greyson, 2001, 2007; James, 2004; Morris & Knafl, 2003; Olsen & Dulaney, 1993; Simpson, 2001; Wren-Lewis, 2004). Furthermore, NDErs commonly report a growing sense of isolation from others due to feeling different, and/or being reluctant to talk about the experience out of fears of being rejected or ridiculed (Greyson et al., 2009). Mori Insinger (1981) suggested this sense of isolation may lead to higher rates of depression, and these findings are consistent with subsequent studies (Christian, 2005; Greyson, 2007; Greyson & Harris, 1987; Morris & Knafl, 2003; Wren-Lewis, 2004). However, it should be noted that depression and anxiety are normal responses to a NDE and the profound aftereffects often take years to integrate; therefore, pathological conditions need to be differentiated from the normal course and outcome of the NDE. Again, research has shown that NDErs have a significantly high rate of divorce post-NDE, perhaps due to drastic changes in lifestyle values, which may place strain on interpersonal relationships (Christian, 2005; Greyson et al., 2009; Morris & Knafl, 2003; Wren-Lewis, 2004). Whether this is a sign of pathology or one of moving toward healthier and more fulfilling relationships has not been determined. Likewise, John Wren-Lewis (2004) found that positive life changes also co-existed with higher rates of personal distress, making this picture confusing.

In a study conducted by Stout, et al. (2006), participants were asked what their main struggles and challenges were post-NDE. Stout and colleagues found six key themes consistently reported: (1) difficulty processing a radical shift in reality, (2) difficulty accepting their return back to this life, (3) difficulties sharing their experience with others and/or lack of validation or understanding from family and/or friends, (4) a growing sense of isolation due to the inability to talk about the experience with others, (5) challenges adjusting to heightened chemical sensitivities and intuitive gifts, and (6) difficulty finding/living their life purpose and integrating new spiritual values into daily life.

Other integration issues include a lack of boundaries post-NDE. Greyson (2007) suggested this may be due to the state of unconditional love and "Oneness" that was experienced during the NDE, and that many struggle with integrating back into a society that predominantly lives by the belief that individuals are separate from each other. In fact, Greyson noted many are not able go back to that prior way of living and thinking, which may present several adjustment issues, especially because family or friends may not understand their new values. Moreover, it is important to note that this sense of unity and oneness is not just an intellectual *belief* for many, but rather, becomes a central part of their new reality.

Other issues surround responses from family and/or friends. In addition to lack of validation and sometimes being disbelieved, Greyson (1997, 2007) suggested some may put the NDEr up on a pedestal expecting superhuman powers from them. The extreme of either of these responses can put immense pressure on NDErs, leading them to not feel understood, while reinforcing a desire to suppress the experience.

Mental Health Studies

Over the past few decades, several studies have been conducted to assess NDErs' mental health. Although many may experience higher rates of depression and anxiety, it is important to note that this may be a normal reaction to an extraordinary event, and that the profound changes that often accompany a NDE that may take several years to successfully integrate. Therefore, we highly encourage practitioners to take this into consideration, and discourage the use of diagnostic labels that may not be appropriate and applicable to many in the NDE population. The APA's (2000) *Diagnostic and Statistical Manual of Mental Disorders* (4th ed., text rev.; *DSM-TR-IV*) has created a specific diagnostic label under V Code 62.89 for "Spiritual or Religious Problem" for issues that do not qualify as a pathological disorder, which may more succinctly represent the NDE and its normal aftereffects than other psychodiagnostic labels (see Lukoff, Lu, & Turner, 1998).

Dissociative and Post-Traumatic Stress Disorders

Researchers have found some NDErs report recurring auditory hallucinations that they describe as "internal voices" (Bentall, 2000). However, Richard Bentall found that 97% who reported recurrent hallucinations found these experiences to be positive, and that NDErs did not meet clinical criteria for dissociation, schizophrenia, or post-traumatic stress disorder as outlined in the *DSM-IV-TR* (APA, 2000). Subsequent studies conducted by Greyson and Mitchell Liester (2004) found the same results, indicating that NDErs highly valued these experiences and functioned better psychologically as a result.

Other studies have focused on post-traumatic stress disorder (PTSD) and dissociative symptoms following a NDE. Out of 194 NDErs, Greyson (2001) did find higher rates of intrusive PTSD symptoms compared to non-experiencers, but not more avoidance symptoms. Greyson suggested that avoidant-type behavior may be more related to feelings of being different than others and not gaining validation, versus related to trauma caused by the NDE. These findings are consistent with earlier findings from Glen Gabbard and Stuart Twemlow (1984), who found that NDErs were psychologically healthy and did not differ from normal controls. More recently, Parnia et al. (2007) confirmed these findings and also reported that NDErs did not score significantly higher than normal controls for PTSD or dissociative disorders.

However, more research is needed on those who report distressing NDEs. Richard Bonenfant (2001) reported one case of a six-year-old boy who suffered PTSD following a distressing NDE during a car accident. Bonenfant stated, "The boy's parents reported that their son suffered from restlessness, anxiety, and nightmares for months following his NDE" (p. 93). Although in this case it is difficult to determine whether the symptoms were the result of the car accident or the NDE, distressing NDEs need to be explored further to determine if the aftereffects present psychological challenges that differ from pleasurable NDE accounts.

Schizotypal Personality Disorder and Psychotic Disorders

As for schizotypal personality disorder and brief psychotic disorders, studies have shown that NDErs differ in a number of ways. Schizotypal personality disorder consists of perceptual and cognitive deficits that include pervasive interpersonal deficits that are not seen in NDErs (Gabbard & Twemlow, 1984; Irwin, 1993; Locke & Shontz, 1983). David Lukoff, Lu, and Turner (1995) suggested that NDEs can be differentiated from brief psychotic disorders by their acute onset following a stressful event, in addition to their good premorbid functioning and positive attitude post-NDE.

To our knowledge, there are no studies in the academic databases presently that have shown NDErs to meet criteria for any of the psychotic disorders. This is not to say that this diagnostic category might not be applicable to some (perhaps pertaining to those who had a mental health disorder prior to their NDE); however, as of this date, those who had prior mental health disorders (especially of a psychotic nature) have not been adequately studied to compare psychological functioning pre- and post-NDE. Moreover, previous psychological diagnoses of any such psychotic disorders would need to be differentiated from the NDE itself, as it is not common for NDEs to present with psychotic aftereffects.

Childhood Antecedents & Personality Characteristics

Gabbard and Twemlow (1984) proposed NDEs are more likely to occur in individuals who have personality characteristics prone to dissociation, absorption, or fantasy-proneness. According to Gabbard and Twemlow, traits such as absorption allow an individual to screen out the external world and focus on internal characteristics, which make it more likely to experience a NDE under states of stress or trauma. Furthermore, this theory proposed that individuals who report NDEs may be more prone to fantasizing or daydreaming, and that the NDE is simply a psychological defense that may occur under a high state of stress or trauma. However, several studies show contradictory results and do not reveal significant relationships between NDEs and fantasy-proneness personality traits (Britton & Bootzin, 2004; Brumm, 2006; Greyson, 2003; Wren-Lewis, 2004).

In addition, Ring (1992) compared 74 NDErs and 54 controls and found several childhood antecedents in NDErs that he called *the encounter-prone personality* (p. 145). While Ring found no statistical differences between the groups on fantasy-proneness, a higher percentage of NDErs reported a sensitivity to *alternate realities* (p. 127), and reported more psychic experiences as a child. Examples included awakening in the night and seeing nonphysical beings, telepathic communication, premonitions, and other psi-related activity. Ring also found a higher percentage of NDErs reported childhood abuse or trauma, and/or reported a stressful childhood due to severe illness. Ring suggested that experiencing prior trauma or a stressful childhood may foster the development of dissociative type of symptoms, leading to a sense of depersonalization and absorption proneness, thus making some more susceptible to having a NDE. To our knowledge, findings of this have not been researched further, so remain an area that needs to be explored to assess whether these childhood antecedents are consistent in larger samples.

Therapeutic Challenges

Research has indicated that there are both interpersonal and intrapersonal NDE aftereffects that may occur in various stages, and about which mental health practitioners could benefit from being aware. Some of the main issues involve disclosure barriers and various integration issues that range from grief work, depression, divorce, career changes, addressing any anomalous aftereffects (electrical sensitivity and/or ongoing psi-related phenomena), and addressing distressing NDEs (Foster, James, & Holden, 2009).

Disclosure Barriers

Some initial barriers to working with a NDE client may surround reluctance to talk about the experience due to fears of being labeled as mentally ill, as well as many questioning their own sanity (Duffy & Olsen, 2007; Greyson, 1997; James, 2004; Simpson, 2001). Cassandra Musgrave (1997) explored 51 NDErs' attitudes post-NDE and, among many positive aftereffects, found that 76% reported a reluctance to disclose their experience due to fears of being ridiculed or rejected. Moreover, Regina Hoffman (1995a, 1995b) explored disclosure tendencies and needs in 50 NDErs and found these tended to occur in stages. The first stage entailed a sense of shock and surprise in trying to make sense out of the NDE. Once the initial shock was handled, a need to have the experience validated tended to occur. Following this, the impact the NDE had on their lives started to become apparent, accompanied by the need to actively explore spiritual and psychological implications of their experience. The final stage entailed how to integrate this experience into their lives which, as Cherie Sutherland (1992) and many other researchers have noted (e.g., Greyson, 2007; Greyson & Harris, 1987), can take years.

Other researchers have suggested the initial reaction to a NDE plays a critical role in the course and outcome of its aftereffects, which may require a team-oriented approach to client care from the moment the NDE occurs (James, 2004). Because NDEs are commonly happening in medical care facilities, there have been widespread training efforts in this last decade focused on educating medical practitioners about NDEs, and how to help a client who may have experienced one (Duffy & Olsen, 2007; James, 2004; Simpson, 2001). Mental health practitioners can benefit from learning about some of the guidelines medical practitioners have implemented in an effort to increase communication among professionals, and to deliver proper treatment and referrals to the NDE population.

In order to break through client reluctance to discuss their NDE and any aftereffects, mental health practitioners can begin the dialogue by asking clients who have survived a medical crisis if they remember anything during their period of unconsciousness, and then assess client openness from there. Additionally, it is recommended that clients be assured that many others have reported similar experiences (while not discounting the uniqueness of their experience), and to educate them about the nature of this phenomenon in order to reduce fears they may have about discussing their experience.

Psychotherapeutic Strategies

Several treatment approaches have been recommended by practitioners who have worked with the NDE population, which are predominantly focused on helping clients integrate this experience into their daily lives. Although empirical research needs to be done to test the efficacy of these methods, the below strategies were put together by a panel of NDE researchers who have spent years working with the NDE population (Greyson & Harris, 1985). The following is a recent list of strategies outlined by Greyson (1996, 1997, 2007).

Therapeutic Approaches Immediately Following a NDE

Appreciate unexpectedness. Because clients have not had time to prepare (due to not expecting a traumatic experience to happen), a key to working with NDErs is an appreciation of the unexpectedness of the experience.

Reorientation. Immediately following the NDE, clients may be extremely confused and disoriented. Researchers suggest that grounding techniques geared towards stimulating tactile senses may help them become more aware of body consciousness.

Clarify and reflect. Avoid interpreting the meaning or reason the NDE occurred, and instead listen attentively and help the client clarify and reflect on the experience.

Diagnostic labels. Immediately following a NDE, if clients do have another psychological disorder make sure they understand the NDE is a distinct phenomenon not related to their other diagnoses.

Education. Provide NDErs and their family and friends literature on NDEs to ensure them many others have reported this experience, and that the experience is not abnormal. However, ensure that "normalizing" the experience does not discount the uniqueness of their experience.

Avoid victimization. Avoid a sense of victimization by encouraging the client to grieve for the loss of the ego (or shallower parts of the old self that they may choose to leave behind).

Expression of ineffable. Help clients try to express the ineffability of the experience through non-verbal therapies, such as hypnosis, guided imagery, or art therapy.

Here and now approach to therapy. Using a here-and-now approach to therapy may help clients integrate the experience into their daily lives. Helping them realize what the experience means, and how this impacts daily living can help them make sense out of the experience and facilitate growth.

Couples or family counseling. Because of the high divorce rate among the NDE population, it is important to offer couples or family counseling early on to help family members understand the dramatic lifestyle changes that NDErs may undergo. This can help the client gain validation and support from family and/or friends, and may reduce the later onset of feelings of alienation and isolation, which can result in changes such as divorce.

Support groups. Refer the NDEr to support groups such as the International Association for Near-Death Studies (IANDS: www.iands.org) so that they can explore problems and solutions with other NDErs. Researchers suggest this may help reduce the sense of bizarreness about the experience.

Spiritual crisis. For those who present with psychospiritual crisis, grounding techniques such as mindfulness meditation or yoga have been found to be effective in helping clients get reoriented to the here-and-now. Additionally, meditation may help clients relive the experience and gain new insights into how to integrate the experience into daily living.

Long-Term Therapeutic Approaches

Before entering into a therapeutic relationship with a client who has undergone a NDE, Greyson (1996, 1997, 2007) pointed out it is important for mental health practitioners to realize that the NDE and its aftereffects may impact the therapist's own psychospiritual growth. Therefore, Greyson suggested it is important for the therapist and client to both discuss what their expectations are in therapeutic relationship, as well as desired outcomes. Below are some useful techniques (Greyson, 2007).

Limits on therapeutic relationship. Researchers found it is important to clarify at the onset of therapy that the NDE is distinct from other problems and to clarify specific issues resulting from the NDE. If a client presents with various issues, it may be helpful to refer to the client to another therapist to help with non-NDE related problems to avoid a conflict of interest when helping clients integrate the NDE.

Trust. It may take clients a little longer to trust even the most sensitive and compassionate mental health practitioners due to the contrasting difference between experiences encountered during the NDE and consensual reality. Likewise, therapists may struggle with believing things shared by the client and so it is imperative for mental health practitioners to be aware of their own thoughts, feelings, and biases.

Flexibility in frequency and length of sessions. In order to establish rapport with NDErs, rigid adherence to traditional therapeutic approaches that encourage an objective, analytical stance should be avoided. Researchers have found this only serves to distance the client and may interfere with fostering client's psychospiritual growth. Likewise, length and frequency of sessions should be more flexible to allow clients to explore ineffable concepts and overwhelming emotions that may result.

Encourage grief work. Due to the dramatic impact NDEs commonly have on lifestyle values, beliefs, and attitudes, it is recommended that mental health practitioners should help clients grieve parts of their ego that may been radically transformed, or "died" as a result of the NDE.

Free association of anomalous details. Researchers suggest therapists should encourage clients to explore anomalous details of the experience on numerous levels such as through dream analysis, guided imagery, art therapy, and/or meditation. Encouraging clients to engage both right and left brain hemispheres may help clients describe ineffable experiences and may provide insights into specific problems of integration.

Explore life purpose. Because many clients struggle with being sent back, and question their life purpose, exploring new values can help reveal underlying problems the client may be struggling to integrate. For example, many report they "chose to come back to life," and it may be helpful to explore why they chose to come back. Additionally, feelings of guilt and remorse may be related to their return, so these are important areas to explore with the client.

Explore fears of unwanted aftereffects. It is important to help clients distinguish the NDE versus the aftereffects of the NDE. This can help clients reject or resist negative aftereffects without having to devalue the NDE itself.

Explore family dynamics. Drastic changes in lifestyle, values, and beliefs can often dramatically alter relationships with family and/or friends, and leave clients feeling alienated and isolated. Therefore, some researchers have found it helpful to make home visits and/or encourage family therapy.

Support groups. Although it is important for clients to gain validation from other NDErs, because of the transpersonal nature of the NDE one downside to group therapy with other NDErs is that it can sometimes encourage clients to devalue worldly matters, which can lead to further problems. Therefore, therapists can help clients reaffirm the importance of the here-and-now, as well as what can be learned from the NDE.

Encourage constructive action. Once clients have integrated the aftereffects of a NDE and internalized new beliefs, values, and sense of life purpose, it is important to encourage them to help others. Experts who have worked with NDErs suggest the therapeutic work is done when clients have found a way to actualize a sense of unconditional love experienced during the NDE and share it with others. In summary, once NDErs are able to adapt the various stages of integration into their daily lives and reach out and help others, Greyson (1996, 1997, 2007) suggested the therapeutic relationship should potentially come to a close.

Conclusion

NDErs frequently are permanently and powerfully altered by their experience, which can lead to good or challenging short-term outcomes—and even the challenging short-term outcomes are seen by some as part of the post-NDE integration process that can lead to good long-term outcomes. There are no extant scientific theories that sufficiently explain NDEs to discount their veridicality, leaving this one of the most interesting phenomena that calls for the openness inherent in transpersonal, rather than conventional materialistic, perspectives. Regardless of whether NDEs are ontologically real or not, NDErs are affected deeply by their NDEs. For clinicians working with NDErs, we present some guidelines for assessing and treating this population. Likewise, scientists who study NDEs and NDErs are often deeply affected by many aspects of the phenomena, such as their commonality across cultures that provides indirect evidence that NDEs are not just a product of culturally learned expectations. We think studying NDEs provides perhaps the most interesting window to explore the limits of the most basic assumptions of Western materialism, and to build transpersonal understandings that might go beyond these limits.

References

American Psychiatric Association (2000). *Diagnostic and statistical manual of mental disorders* (4th ed., text rev.). Washington, DC: Author.

Audain, L. (1999). Gender and trauma in the near-death experience: An epidemiological and theoretical analysis. *Journal of Near-Death Studies, 18*, 35-49.

Belanti, J., Perera, M., & Jagadheesan, K. (2008). Phenomenology of near-death experiences: A cross-cultural perspective. *Transcultural Psychiatry, 45*(1), 121-133.

Bentall, R. P. (2000). Hallucinatory experiences. In E. Cardeña, S. J. Lynn, & S. Krippner (Eds.), *Varieties of anomalous experience: Examining the scientific evidence* (pp. 85-120). Washington, DC: American Psychological Association.

Bonenfant, R. J. (2001). A child's encounter with the devil: An unusual near-death experience with both blissful and frightening elements. *Journal of Near-Death Studies, 20,* 87-100.

Britton, W. B., & Bootzin, R. R. (2004). Near-death experiences and the temporal lobe. *Psychological Science, 15,* 254-258.

Brumm, K. (2006). A study of near-death experiences and coping with stress. *Journal of Near-Death Studies, 24,* 153-173.

Bush, N. E. (1991). Is ten years a life review? *Journal of Near-Death Studies, 10,* 5-9.

Christian, S. R. (2005). Marital satisfaction and stability following a near-death experience of one of the marital partners. *Dissertation Abstracts International, 66*(11) 0158A (UMI #3196139).

Duffy, N., & Olsen, M. (2007). Supporting a patient after a near-death experience: Recovering from cardiac arrest, your patient reports an out-of-body experience. Do you know how to respond? *Nursing, 4,* 46-48.

Foster, R., James, D., & Holden, J. (2009). Practical applications of research on near-death experiences. In J. Holden, B. Greyson, & D. James (Eds.), *The handbook of near-death experiences: Thirty years of investigation* (pp. 235-258). Santa Barbara, CA: ABC-CLIO.

Fracasso, C. L., Aleyasin, S. A., Friedman, H. L., & Young, M. S. (2010). Near-death experiences in a small sample of Iranian Muslims. *Journal of Near-Death Studies, 29,* 265-272.

Gabbard, G. O., & Twemlow, S. W. (1984). *With the eyes of the mind: An empirical analysis of out-of-body states.* New York, NY: Praeger.

Gallup, G., & Proctor, W. (1982). *Adventures in immortality: A look beyond the threshold of death.* New York, NY: McGraw Hill.

Greyson, B. (1983). The Near-Death Experience Scale: Construction, reliability, and validity. *Journal of Nervous and Mental Disorders, 171,* 369-375.

Greyson, B. (1986). Incidence of near-death experiences following attempted suicide. *Suicide and Life-Threatening Behavior, 16,* 40-45.

Greyson, B. (1996). The near-death experience as a transpersonal crisis. In B. Scotton, A. Chinen, & J. Battista (Eds.), *Textbook of transpersonal psychiatry and psychology* (pp. 302-326). New York, NY: Basic Books.

Greyson, B. (1997). The near-death experience as a focus of clinical attention. *Journal of Nervous and Mental Disease, 185*(5), 327-334.

Greyson, B. (2001). Posttraumatic stress symptoms following near-death experiences. *American Journal of Orthopsychiatry, 71,* 368-373.

Greyson, B. (2003). Incidence and correlates of near-death experiences in a cardiac care unit. *General Hospital Psychiatry, 25,* 269-276.

Greyson, B. (2005). "False positive" claims of near-death experiences and "false negative" denials of near-death experiences. *Death Studies, 29,* 145-155.

Greyson, B. (2007). Review: Near-death experiences: Clinical implications. *Revista Psiquitatria Clinica, 34,* 49-57.

Greyson, B., Kelly, E. W., & Kelly, E. F. (2009). Explanatory models for near-death experiences. In J. M. Holden, B. Greyson, & D. James (Eds.), *The handbook of near-death experiences: Thirty years of investigation* (pp. 213-234). Santa Barbara, CA: Praeger/ABC-CLIO.

Greyson, B. (2010). Implications of near-death experiences for postmaterialist psychology. *Psychology of Religion and Spirituality, 2,* 37-45.

Greyson, B., & Harris, B. (1987). Clinical approaches to the near-death experiencer. *Journal of Near-Death Studies, 6,* 41-52.

Greyson, B., & Liester, M. B. (2004). Auditory hallucinations following near-death experiences. *Journal of Humanistic Psychology, 44,* 320-336.

Groth-Marnat, G., & Summers, R. (1998). Altered beliefs, attitudes, and behaviors following near-death experiences. *Journal of Humanistic Psychology, 38,* 110-125.

Hoffman, R. M. (1995a). Disclosure habits after near-death experiences: Influences, obstacles, and listener selection. *Journal of Near-Death Studies, 14,* 29-48.

Hoffman, R. M. (1995b). Disclosure needs and motives after a near-death experience. *Journal of Near-Death Studies, 13,* 237-266.

Holden, J. M. (2009). Veridical perception in near-death experiences. In J. M. Holden, B. Greyson, & D. James (Eds.), *The handbook of near-death experiences: Thirty years of investigation* (pp. 185-211). Santa Barbara, CA: Praeger/ABC-CLIO.

Holden, J. M., Long, J., & MacLurg, J. (2006). Out-of-body experiences: All in the brain? *Journal of Near-Death Studies, 25,* 99-107.

Insinger, R. M. (1981). The impact of near-death experiences on family relationships. *Journal of Near-Death Studies, 9,* 141-181.

Irwin, H. J. (1993). The near-death experience as a dissociative phenomena: An empirical assessment. *Journal of Near-Death Studies, 12,* 95-103.

James, D. (2004). What emergency department staff need to know about near-death experiences. *Topics in Emergency Medicine, 26,* 29-34.

Kellehear, A. (2008). Census of non-western near-death experiences to 2005: Overview of the current data. *Journal of Near-Death Studies, 4,* 249-265.

Kinnier, R. T., Tribbensee, N. E., Rose, C. A., & Vaughan, S. M. (2001). In the final analysis: More wisdom from people who have faced death. *Journal of Counseling & Development, 79,* 171-177.

Locke, T. P., & Shontz, F. C. (1983). Personality correlates of the near-death experience: A preliminary study. *Journal of American Soc Psychical Research, 77,* 311-318.

Lukoff, D., Lu, F., & Turner, R. (1995). Cultural considerations in the assessment and treatment of religious and spiritual problems. *The Psychiatric Clinics of North America, 18*(3), 467-485.

Lukoff, D., Lu, F., & Turner, R. (1998). From spiritual emergency to spiritual problem: The transpersonal roots of the new DSM-IV Category. *Journal of Humanistic Psychology, 38*(2), 21-50.

McClenon, J. (2005). Content analysis of a predominantly African-American near-death experience collection: Evaluating the ritual healing theory. *Journal of Near-Death Studies, 23,* 159-181.

McClenon, J. (2006a). Origins of belief in life after death: The ritual healing theory of near-death experiences. In L. Storm & M. Thalbourne (Eds.), *The survival of human consciousness: Essays on the possibility of life after death.* Jefferson, NC: McFarland.

McClenon, J. (2006b). Kongo near-death experiences: Cross-cultural patterns. *Journal of Near-Death Studies, 25,* 21-34.

Moody, R. A. (1975). *Life after life.* Covington, GA: Mockingbird Books.

Morris, L. L., & Knafl, K. (2003). The nature and meaning of the near-death experience for patients and critical care nurses. *Journal of Near-Death Studies, 21,* 139-167.

Morse, M. L., Conner, D., & Tyler, D. (1985). Near-death experiences in a pediatric population. *American Journal of Disabled Children, 139,* 595-600.

Musgrave, C. (1997). The near-death experience: A study of spiritual transformation. *Journal of Near-Death Studies, 15,* 187-201.

Noyes, R., Jr., Fenwick, P., Holden, J. M., & Christian, R. (2009). Aftereffects of pleasurable Western adults near-death experiences. In J. M. Holden, B. Greyson, & D. James (Eds.), *The handbook of near-death experiences: Thirty years of investigation* (pp. 41-62). Santa Barbara, CA: Praeger/ABC-CLIO.

Olsen, M., & Dulaney, P. (1993). Life satisfaction, life review, and near-death experiences in the elderly. *Journal of Holistic Nursing, 11,* 368-382.

Parnia, S., Spearpoint, K., & Fenwick, P. B. (2007). Near-death experiences, cognitive function, and psychological outcomes of surviving cardiac arrest. *Resuscitation, 74,* 215-221.

Parnia, S., Waller, D. G., Yeates, R., & Fenwick, P. (2001). A qualitative and quantitative study on the incidence, features, and aetiology of near-death experiences. *Resuscitation, 48,* 149-156.

Pasricha, S. K. (2008). Near-death experiences in India: Prevalence and new features. *Journal of Near-Death Studies, 26,* 267-282.

Perera, M., Padmasekara, G., & Belanti, J. (2005). Prevalence of near-death experiences in Australia. *Journal of Near-Death Studies, 24*(2), 109-115.

Ring, K. (1980). *Life at death.* New York, NY: Quill.

Ring, K. (1992). *The omega project. Near-death experiences, UFO encounters, and mind at large.* New York, NY: William Morrow.

Sabom, M. B. (1982). *Recollections of death: A medical investigation.* New York, NY: Harper & Row.

Schwaninger, J., Eisenberg, P. R., Schechtman, K. B., & Weiss, A. N. (2002). A prospective analysis of near-death experiences in cardiac arrest patients. *Journal of Near-Death Studies, 20,* 215-232.

Simpson, S. M. (2001). Near-death experience: A concept analysis as applied to nursing. *Journal of Advanced Nursing, 36,* 520-526.

Stout, Y. M., Jacquin, L. A., & Atwater, P. M. H. (2006). Six major challenges faced by near-death experiencers. *Journal of Near-Death Studies, 25,* 49-62.

Sutherland, C. (1992). *Transformed by the light: Life after near-death experiences.* Sydney, Australia: Bantam.

van Lommel, P., van Wees, R., Meyers, V., & Elfferich, I. (2001). Near-death experience in survivors of cardiac arrest: A prospective study in the Netherlands. *Lancet, 358,* 2039-2045.

Wren-Lewis, J. (2004). The implications of near-death experiences for understanding posttraumatic growth. *Psychological Inquiry, 15,* 90-92.

Zingrone, N. L., & Alvarado, C. S. (2009). Pleasurable Western adult near-death experiences: Features, circumstances, and incidence. In J. M. Holden, B. Greyson, & D. James (Eds.), *The handbook of near-death experiences: Thirty years of investigation* (pp. 17-40). Santa Barbara, CA: Praeger/ABC-CLIO.

21

Transpersonal Sexual Experiences
Jenny Wade

The relationship between sex and spirituality is one of the most controversial and least understood in contemporary society as well as in transpersonal studies. For centuries, the major world religions have promoted the renunciation of sensual pleasure—especially celibacy—as the path of spiritual aspiration. At the mild end of the continuum, sex is considered a distraction from the spiritual path, and at the severe, a defilement that can separate an individual permanently from the Absolute. Why all the charge about sex? Perhaps because it is actually a doorway to the transpersonal, one that anybody can access without the need for clergy, teachers, drugs, ritual, sacrifice, or donations. What would happen if humanity reclaimed its inherent capacity for direct access to transpersonal wisdom, ecstasy, and Spirit?

The connection between sex and spirituality has been known since ancient times. Its transformative power appears in one of the world's oldest documents, the *Epic of Gilgamesh,* recorded about 4,000 years ago from an oral tradition about a historical king of Uruk who lived about 2700 BCE. In it Enkidu, a furry creature more animal than human, grazes alongside the other animals and drinks with them at their watering hole. One day, a goddess commanded a priestess of sacred sex named Shamhat to leave the temple and go make love to Enkidu in the wilderness. Through their week-long sex bout, Enkidu attained a higher state of being:

> Shamhat unclutched her bosom, exposed her sex, and he took in her voluptuousness.
> She was not restrained, but took his energy.
> She spread out her robe and he lay upon her....
> His lust groaned over her;
> for six days and seven nights, Enkidu stayed aroused,
> and had intercourse with the [sacred] harlot
> until he was sated with her charms.
> But when he turned his attention to his animals,

The Wiley Blackwell Handbook of Transpersonal Psychology, First Edition.
Edited by Harris L. Friedman and Glenn Hartelius.

the gazelles saw Enkidu and darted off,
the wild animals distanced themselves from his body....
But then he drew himself up, for his understanding had broadened....
The [sacred] harlot said to Enkidu:
"You are beautiful, Enkidu, you are become like a god." (Kovacs, 1989, p. 9)

Enkidu walked upright like a human being, increased in intelligence, and became partly divine—thanks to transpersonal sex. The ancient Near East retained its traditions of transpersonal sex with the rise of civilization and centralized religious establishment, unlike many other cultures. Priestesses engaged in ritual sex with worshippers and enacted the holy union of Goddess and God (*heiros gamos*) in a variety of cultures in rites poorly understood by outsiders then, much less now (cf., Avagianou, 2008; Budin, 2006; Keesling, 2006; Lapinkivi, 2008; Nissinen, 2008; Nyberg, 2008; Pongratz-Leisten, 2008; Rikala, 2008; Roth, 2006; Smith, 2008; Teppo, 2008; Zimmerman, 2008). Exactly what sacred sex felt like or meant in fertility cults and sexual mystery schools such as those of Isis, Pan, Ishtar, Cybele, and Dionysus has been lost.

This has not stopped unwarranted speculation, with the result that today much of what is claimed about "sacred sex," "Goddess worship," and "sacred prostitutes" bears little resemblance to historical practice within the context of the originating spiritual systems and cultures. Although such revisionist practices may address strong needs in today's seekers, they cloud what can be known with certainty about the potential of sex for spiritual opening. Furthermore, they can be misleading, as spiritual-sexual experiences require no special knowledge. Sexually-based spiritual experiences are irrepressible human dynamics that continue to crop up in the face of ignorance, denial, and religious oppression. Because it is not talked about today, when people have transpersonal sexual experiences, they are often at a loss to understand them. Like other transpersonal experiences, sexual ones have the potential for immense healing, life enhancement, personal transformation, and spiritual realization (e.g., Elfers, 2009; Little, 2009; MacKnee, 2002; Wade, 1998, 2000, 2004). However, they are so powerful that, if misunderstood or mishandled, the results can sometimes be harmful: psychological damage, sexual exploitation, dysfunctional relationships, even suicide (Bragdon, 1988, 1990; Wade, 2004). Only by understanding transpersonal sexual experiences can they be facilitated, managed, and worked through to realize their optimal positive potential.

Untangling the Myths and History of Spirituality and Sex

According to popular myth, the so-called Venus figurines—some 60-odd Paleolithic female statuettes with exaggerated breasts, bellies, and buttocks found from France to Siberia—represent "the Goddess" of a fertility cult (e.g., Eisler, 1987, 1995; Gimbutas, 1982, 1989, 1991). Not only is it impossible to know anything for certain about such prehistoric artifacts, critics of these Goddess theories point out the undesirability of human (versus animal) fecundity prior to the rise of agriculture (e.g., Tannahill, 1980), which undermines the notion of matriarchal hunter-gatherer societies central to many of these Goddess theories, and how flawed such theories are generally (e.g., Eller, 2000; Fleming, 1969; Goodison & Morris, 1998; Hutton, 1991). A felt need for the feminine in Western religions has resulted in a popular resurgence of purportedly ancient "Goddess" traditions, including the "triple goddess" archetype of maiden-mother-crone and many Pagan, Wiccan, and Western esoteric (magick) rituals, including a version of the *heiros gamos* called the Great Rite (e.g., Wagar, 2009). Credible evidence of such ancient religions is ambiguous at best (e.g., Avagianou, 2008; Budin, 2006; Keesling, 2006; Lapinkivi, 2008; Nissinen, 2008; Nyberg, 2008; Pongratz-Leisten, 2008; Rikala, 2008; Roth, 2006; Smith, 2008; Teppo, 2008; Zimmerman, 2008)—if not entirely nonexistent. (For instance, poet and novelist Robert Graves invented the "triple goddess" for one of his books, *The White Goddess,* and made it clear that he did not believe his vision had ever existed in reality [Hutton, 1991, p.145]).

Similarly, little is known about indigenous peoples' connections between sexuality and spirituality, although the separation of sex and spirit into distinct categories is likely a late, colonial importation (e.g., Hoppál, 1987; Kehoe, 2000; Vitebsky, 1996). Not only does the diversity of indigenous cultures make it impossible to generalize, but also information about extinct, non-literate cultures is inferential as well as woefully incomplete. The vast majority of surviving indigenous cultures have been so disrupted by colonialism that direct transmission from the knowledge lineage has been lost, even assuming that such individuals would share esoteric matters with outsiders in the first place (e.g., Sigal, 2000, 2011). The popular desire for a more embodied religion has led to an extensive spread of neo-shamanism (e.g., Hoppál, 1987; Kehoe, 2000; Vitebsky, 1996; Walsh, 2007; York, 2003), including a sexual branch called Chuluaqui Quodoushka, falsely alleged to derive from Native American traditions (e.g., Giago, 1993; Hagan, 1992).

Other misunderstandings cloud the picture, such as that the major Eastern religions are commonly held to be more sexually oriented than the Western ones. Although sectarian exceptions exist in any religion, generally speaking the Eastern and Western world religions all retain significant sexual symbolism, but incarnate sexuality, especially with regard to women, was repressed (e.g., Anderson & Zinsser, 1988; Spretnak, 1991). Even traditions that ideologically venerate females, such as Jewish mysticism, certain Gnostic sects, Tantra, and Taoism, came to exclude women from full initiation and to relegate them to an instrumental role in the self-transformation of male seekers (e.g., McDaniel, 1989).

Hinduism, like the ancient Near-Eastern religions, prominently features divine couples, such as the god Shiva and goddess Shakti whose mating in thousands of forms produced all the species of creation; however, carnal desire is to be avoided because it ties humanity to the world of illusion (e.g., Courtright, 2006). Nyaya, Yoga, and Vedanta Hinduism, as well as most classic Sanskrit texts, hold that the elimination of desire is essential to realization. The *Kama Sutra* is not some mystical sex treatise, but rather a practical lovemaking guide for householders (as opposed to seekers) who are expected by middle age to be mostly free of sexual urges and ready to devote their later years to spiritual pursuits (Kakar, 1994). Hindu Tantra is a yogic practice that began relatively late as "reverse spirituality," part of a political rebellion against religious convention that advocated engaging in taboo acts, specifically consuming forbidden food and drink and engaging in unclean or proscribed activities, including sex (e.g., Courtright, 2006; Parrinder, 1996; Tannahill, 1980; D. G. White, 2003). These acts became ritualized into a path of realization based on the "crazy wisdom" that the Absolute can be found everywhere, even in what is vile. Nevertheless, in traditional Tantra, actual sex with a partner is given up as quickly as possible so that the (male) practitioner can activate his own sexual energy without the need for coitus with a woman to reach full realization.

Classic Buddhist texts, such as the *Visuddhimagga,* likewise enjoin practitioners to eschew attachment to sensual pleasure. Serious practitioners were expected to be celibate, if not ascetic, and indeed the cessation of sexual desire distinguishes the successful seeker (Cole, 2006; Faure, 1998; Tannahill, 1980; van Gulik, 1974). Theravada and Mahayana Buddhism incorporate the same kinds of austerities that distinguish Hinduism and Jainism (Pagels, 1979). Vajrayana Buddhism (a Tantric form deriving from indigenous Tibetan and Indian sources) demands high levels of contemplative attainment before seekers can participate in ritualized sexual practices that have more to do with meditation than with lovemaking (Faure, 1998; van Gulik, 1974).

Taoist sex, based on the male and female principles of yang and yin, advocates lengthy lovemaking sessions in which the goal is to protract the number and duration of the woman's orgasm while the man assiduously withholds ejaculation. The point is not enjoyment so much as the promotion of the man's health and "immortality," considered to be fed by the woman's orgasmic energy and lubrication and by his retention of semen, thought to be irreplaceable life essence (e.g., Eskildsen, 1998; Kohn, 1992; Parrinder, 1996; Saso, 1997). Taoist sexual methods can involve austerities, up to and including celibacy (Komjathy, 2007).

In summary, the neo-Tantric and neo-Taoist forms that have sprung up in the West, similar to the neo-indigenous and Goddess forms discussed above—bear slight resemblance to the original practice (e.g., Komjathy, 2007; Urban, 2000, 2003; D. G. White, 2003), though they may have beneficial effects.

Of the major Western religions, sex played a much greater role in Judaism than in Christianity or Islam. To this day Judaism retains a more institutionalized place for the feminine, as well. Jews were supposed to marry and have children, especially the men who aspired to become spiritual leaders (e.g., Berger, 2006). In fact, sex within marriage was considered a religious duty, although sects varied in terms of how often it was appropriate to engage in sex and how much to enjoy it (Pagels, 1979; Tannahill, 1980). During the Middle Ages Kabbalism, a mystical form of Judaism, emerged, which put forward coitus as a powerful spiritual act that enabled humans to participate in the masculine and feminine aspects of God sustaining the cosmos. Shekinah, the feminine personification of God, is variously viewed as God's daughter given to the world as its wife and as the Divine Mother and protector of the world (Ariel, 1988; Berger, 2006; Hoffman, 1992; Waite, 1960).

Christianity began diverging into a tradition that revered celibacy and asceticism early on. Jesus differed from the mainstream Judaism of his time in condoning practices that would limit procreation, such as forbidding divorce for a wife's infertility (Matthew 19:4-6), as well as connecting celibacy with eternal life (Luke 20:34-36). The apostle Paul went further, recommending celibacy as the path to salvation, even in marriage (1 Corinthians 7:1-35). Indeed Christian orthodoxy from the first century to the present interprets sex as an integral part of the "original sin" that separated humanity from God—if not the sin itself (e.g., Johnson & Jordan, 2006; Ware, 1997; Weisner-Hanks, 2000). Celibacy and asceticism have a long history in Christianity. Gnostic and other Christian mystical traditions, which have always incorporated sexual imagery, including the feminine aspects of God, such as Sophia, were largely persecuted out of existence. Their sacred texts (including the Gnostic Gospels, Jewish Pseudepigrapha, Christian Apocrypha, and Dead Sea scrolls) were denied canonical validity or suppressed.

In contrast, sexuality is consecrated in the Qu'ran (e.g., 2:25, 3:15, 4:57), and Mohammed's supernatural acts of sexual prowess and virility demonstrate his exalted status. Islam technically considers sexuality a natural, healthy drive in men and women alike. In fact, the Qu'ran condemns taking vows of celibacy for spiritual purposes (57:27). Later Moslem scholars downplayed Mohammed's sexuality (Parrinder, 1996), and mainstream Islam became sexually conservative, as reflected by the laws in contemporary Moslem cultures. Even some famous contemplatives, such as Ibn 'Arabi, whose influence remains strong in Sufism, recommended celibacy (Schimmel, 1997). However, generally speaking, mystical forms of Islam are rife with a feminine principle and a sacralization of intercourse (Al-Hibri & Habti, 2006). For example, Baul contemplatives liken the spiritual relationship between Allah and Mohammed, between Allah and the seeker, and between the seeker and spiritual teacher to the love between a man and a woman "whose body is the temple of Allah and within whom is the unwritten Qu'ran" (McDaniel, 1989, p. 164).

To summarize, regardless of how far religions have attempted to separate sexuality from spirituality in practice, they still retain sexual symbolism even in mainstream forms. The female and male principles of yin and yang are essential to Taoist thought as the spiritual forces that interpenetrate all of manifest creation. The Indian *yoni* (vagina) and *lingam* (penis) symbolize many levels of spirituality in Hinduism and Buddhism both, including the arrival of the individual soul in the World Soul (Atman) or nirvana (popularly "enlightenment") as well as the presence of nirvana in the material world. The mantram central to Hinduism and Buddhism, *om mani padme hum,* the jewel in the lotus, is actually a sexual metaphor for spiritual realization. The Bible's Song of Solomon is an ecstatic, frankly erotic declaration of sexual love sacred to Jews, Christians, and Moslems. The Church as the Bride of Christ is an obviously sexual metaphor. The mystical branches of all of these religions are frankly sexual, but how literally can any of these symbols or contemplative practices be understood to involve actual sex?

Even when the obscure euphemisms of classic sex manuals, such as the Taoist *Fang-nei-chi* and *I-shin-po,* render techniques more or less clear, the states of attainment they produce are barely conveyed. About all that can be said is that the spiritual underpinnings for Tantric and Taoist texts maintain that the Absolute resides in the physical universe, including the human body, not separate from it. Consequently the body is a valid medium for spiritual realization. Classic Tantra and Vajrayana Buddhism strive for a meditative process that will transcend the duality of masculine and feminine (loosely, sex), as it does other dualities, thereby identifying the practitioner with the Nondual Whole. Such traditions, along with other cosmologies that are reliant on dualities representing sexual opposites, regard a kind of mystical hermaphrodite as the closest human likeness to the Absolute (e.g., Henriques, 1963; Tannahill, 1980; van Gulik, 1974).

With the greater acceptance of same-sex liaisons in many cultures today, the seemingly heteronormative male-female, masculine-feminine dualities central to such venerable traditions have been viewed as problematic by some (e.g., Hutchins, 2002; Sell, 2001). However, the notion of a mystical hermaphrodite is embodied in the institutionalized sacred roles of sexually ambiguous, third-gender humans recognized in a number of cultures (Henriques, 1963). Such people, as revered representatives of an important aspect of spiritual reality, are held to have sacred powers, for instance, the *hijras* and *jogappas* of India (e.g., Bradford, 1983; Nanda, 1993; Piedmont, 1996); the *berdaches* or Two-Spirit people of Native America (e.g., Jacobs, Thomas, & Lang, 1997; Roscoe, 1998; Tafoya, 1992; Zuber-Chall, 2012); and the *nat kadaws, meinmasha, acault* or *achauk* of Myanmar (Coleman, Colgan, & Gooren, 1992; Ho, 2009). Depending on the culture, these people may cross gender lines and may or may not have sex ("true" *hijras,* for example, are expected to be castrated or celibate, although many do engage in sex, including prostitution).

Given that the mainstream versions of most of the world religions restrict sexual expression of various kinds or view it as antithetic to spirituality, most people are enculturated to feel shameful about sex and to be misinformed about its positive connection with spirituality.

Sacred Sex Today

If little is known about spiritual sexual traditions historically, and modern recreations of these traditions owe much more to contemporary Western sensibilities than to the original practices, what claims can legitimately be made for transpersonal sex? First, transpersonal sex does exist. And second, it just happens—in the absence of instruction, religious belief, or special techniques. Sex studies have inadvertently uncovered transpersonal experiences that occur spontaneously during lovemaking to unsuspecting people (e.g., Maurer, 1994; Ogden, 2006), as these examples show:

> When we make love, it's like I disappear. Athletes talk about being in the zone—this is like being in the zone for hours. It's not like I'm doing anything or making anything happen. In some religions they say, It's the dance, not the dancer. This is like I'm being danced. . . .
>
> So what have we got here, angels or what?. . I say to myself. .: There are these two people, and they're an expression of God's love. That's such a new thought to me that I don't even know what I mean by it. So where is this coming from? . . . It's coming from God, or grace, or somewhere. I can't even believe I'm saying this. I used to be a Marxist!—Alex (Maurer, 1994, pp. 456-459)

> There is a unitive energy where the two truly become one. And once in a while, you transcend even that, and you become one with the universe. At times I have experienced that. It's like a great light, but that doesn't exactly describe it, either. . . . That is just the doorway you pass through into something beyond, something transcendent.—Roseanne (Bonheim, 1997, pp. 40-41)

> When we made love, I would experience my body dissolving, and there would just be flowers, thousands of flowers. Sometimes we seemed to be under the ocean, swimming

like fishes. Everything would drop away except this consciousness of unfolding and melting and dissolving and flowing.—Hannah (Bonheim, 1997, p. 81)

Similarly studies of transpersonal experiences have uncovered their source to be sex (e.g., Greeley, 1974; Grof, 1975, 1985, 1988, 1998; Hardy, 1979; Kreutzer, 1978; Laski, 1961; Maslow, 1987). For instance, Laski's research (1961) on "transcendent ecstasy" revealed that for 43% of her participants it occurred when they were making love. Maslow (1987) found that sex produced what he called peak experiences:

There were the same feelings of limitless horizons opening up to the vision.... great ecstasy and wonder and awe, the loss of placing in time and space with, finally, the conviction that something extremely important and valuable had happened, so that the subject is to some extent transformed. (p. 164)

As can be seen from the quotes above, sex can trigger altered states with transpersonal qualities similar to those associated with mysticism, even among the uninitiated. Neo-tantric practices can produce similar effects:

The only sense of form...came from the movement...I felt myself to be radiance, tangible radiance and bliss. It was the two of us, and so my sense of what I was was completely inclusive of him.—Sara (Sokol, 1989, p. 125)

There was no me...I remember looking over at the door to my apartment and thinking, "there is no difference between door jambs and smog." There is no difference between anything whatsoever...There is only apparent difference...I felt as if I had just been born in that moment, or that I had been asleep all my life and had just awakened...I was simply being what I AM, and what everyone else IS, in truth.—Trisha (Feuerstein, 1992, pp. 35-36)

However, any deliberate method to create a transpersonal experience can influence, and perhaps limit, the kinds of states that practitioners access (Tart, 1972, 1975). To date, no systematic research of different sexual-spiritual practices has been done, although independent anecdotal accounts and small studies suggest profound states may be realized using these methods with positive results for the individuals and couples involved. Besides the informal reports of Jalaha Bonheim (1997), Georg Feuerstein (1992), and Dell Sokol (1986, 1989), Cheryl Kruse (2002) and Lisbeth Holbrook (2008) have both conducted small qualitative studies of Western neo-tantric practitioners. Kruse's sample (2002) comprised ten couples, mostly college educated, aged 40-73, who had practiced neo-Tantra from one to ten years (other demographic information is not available). Holbrook's (2008) sample of 13 included 11 from the same neo-Tantric yoga community. Of the thirteen, 9 were female, and 10 were Caucasian. This mostly college-educated sample was aged 24-59 with no predominant trend in spiritual background (only 3 listed the Ipsalu Tantra Kriya Yoga tradition of the neo-Tantric community from which they were recruited as their spiritual affiliation).

More studies have been done on the transpersonal experiences that arise spontaneously and involuntarily when people are making love without training. These adventitious events therefore represent the range of humanity's innate potential, unconditioned by special practices or ideologies. Because they can happen to anyone without warning, unsuspecting people may not understand what is occurring, may attach an unwarranted significance to the events, and may be profoundly affected by them, positively or negatively, as the research shows. Studies include: Emma Bragdon's (1988, 1990) analysis of sex triggering transpersonal openings, including crises within the larger context of spiritual emergencies; Chuck MacKnee's (2002) study of the "profound sexual and spiritual encounters" of five male and five female "practicing Christians"; Jenny Wade's (1998, 2000, 2001, 2004) publication of qualitative research culminating in a sample of 91 men and women who reported "nonordinary, mystical, or transcendent or altered-state sex"; Anne Little's (2009) replication of Wade's mixed-population study with an all-lesbian sample of 69 women; and John Elfers' (2009) study of four men and four women who had utilized their transpersonal sexual experiences as the foundation for continued self-transformation practices. Of these, Wade's (2004) is the largest, heterogenous study comprising 77 heterosexual, 18 homosexual, and 7 bisexual men and women aged 26-70, 80 of them Caucasian, with 86 college graduates or above. (Scantling & Browder's 1993 study of 536 women focused on the nonordinary experiences of 68 high scorers on the Telegen Absorption Scale, which the authors dubbed "supersex" but avoided discussing in transpersonal terms, despite some matches with transpersonal phenomena.)

An overview of the findings of these studies presents what is currently known about people's inherent capacity for transpersonal sex, but it should be noted that where demographic information is available, these samples tend to represent the experiences of Westerners, primarily American Caucasians who, for the most part—though certainly not exclusively—have grown up acculturated to a Judeo-Christian society, if they were not actually reared in those traditions. The reflection of two relatively large all-female studies (Little, 2009; Scantling & Browder, 1993) may give a slight sex bias to the results, but to date all of the mixed-sex findings suggest that men as well as women have the same experiences. These general findings may be summed up as follows:

1 Transpersonal sexual experiences have no obvious connection to sexual mechanics or technique (Wade, 2004). They can begin prior to touching, happen when "just" holding hands or kissing, or occur after sex when the couple is resting. They include heterosexual, gay, and lesbian lovemaking (Elfers, 2009; Little, 2009; Wade, 2001, 2004) as well as mainstream and less conventional techniques, such as bondage-domination-sado-masochism (BDSM), cross-dressing, and so on. They can also occur during masturbation (Bonheim, 1997; Wade, 2004).

2 Transpersonal sexual experiences seem unrelated to physiological differences associated with male and female arousal (Elfers, 2009; Holbrook, 2008; Little, 2009; MacKnee, 2002; Wade 2001, 2004). In other words, men and women have the same types of experiences.

3 Orgasm, which is a discrete altered state, is not the same as the transpersonal experiences people describe, is not confused with them, and does not have a causal relationship with transpersonal states (e.g., Wade, 2004). In Wade's sample,

orgasm occurred before, during, and/or after the transpersonal experience, and was frequently considered irrelevant, or even a nuisance that detracted from the more compelling bliss of the transpersonal state.

4   A history of sexual abuse, although connected with dissociative altered states, did not cause transpersonal experiences (Wade, 2004). People with histories of sexual abuse described their transpersonal experiences as quite different and as helping heal their sexual problems, including the tendency to dissociate (Elfers, 2009; Little, 2009; Wade, 2004).

5   The nature of the couples' relationship is unrelated to transpersonal experience (Wade, 2004). Transpersonal sex is not restricted to "true love," nor does it sacralize relationships as "meant to be," nor mean that a partner is "the one." In fact, such interpretations can be extremely harmful. Transpersonal sexual experiences can occur under any circumstances: during one-night stands, in long-term relationships, with despised partners, and when people feel they are doing something morally wrong (such as an adulterous affair, or a forbidden act).

6   Sexual transpersonal states have no discernable relationship to the participants' spiritual beliefs, length or type of practice, or levels attained during spiritual practices (e.g., Maurer, 1994; Wade, 2004). Strong contradictions between the person's belief systems and the transpersonal experience can result in profound disruptions (the person fears going crazy, for example), which may be repressed or have negative outcomes (such as broken relationships), or conversely, which may produce life-enhancing outcomes (such as spiritual awakening). When the transpersonal events are congruent with, or interpreted through, the person's existing belief system, they tend to strengthen it (Holbrook, 2008; MacKnee, 2002; Wagar, 2009).

7   The range of transpersonal experience produced spontaneously during sex includes ones very like, if not phenomenologically indistinguishable from, those associated with other triggers, such as drugs, trance, meditation, and the like (e.g., Bragdon, 1988, 1990; Little, 2009; Wade, 2001, 2004) and well mapped by other researchers of altered states (e.g., Grof, 1988; R. A. White, 1994, 2001). They include, but are not limited to:

- Various paranormal phenomena, such as out-of-body experiences, clairsentience, and telepathy
- Kundalini (unusual energy and physical experiences, including speaking in tongues and other phenomena associated with Hindu yogic practices)
- Past lives
- Visions, including seeing angelic and demonic beings
- Channeling and possession
- Otherworldly travel and shapeshifting, including connections with power animals or animal guides, as in shamanism
- Supernatural and transpersonal connections with Nature
- The Void (nonduality or "enlightenment" in the Eastern traditions)
- Unio mystica (nonduality in the Western traditions)

Many of these transpersonal experiences feature the phenomenological hallmarks of spiritual attainment recognized in well-established traditions. Although it is impossible to provide examples of all of these here, this last point can be illustrated by a brief comparison with aspects of the nondual states of Samadhi or nirvana in Buddhism. In Table 21.1 texts from experts on Buddhism and nonduality on the left are juxtaposed with excerpts on the right from lovers (who are not Buddhists nor meditators) describing what happened during sex. For reasons of space, these comparisons involve just the experience of illumination, transcendence of spatial categories, and collapsing the flow of time into the Eternal Now.

As with other transpersonal events, not all transpersonal sexual experiences are blissful (Bragdon, 1988, 1990; Wade, 2004). Frightening percepts and imagery can emerge with powerful intensity. Strong energetic disruptions, such as those associated with kundalini awakening, can be disturbing as well as disabling. Although classic and neo-Tantric methods are designed to activate latent energetic potentials in the human body—potentials that can be cultivated by other practices, such as martial arts, or adventitiously evoked—awakening these energies can create a host of persistent unwanted percepts, making people feel physically or mentally ill. The collapsing of ego boundaries or uncontrollable eruption of threatening imagery that may occur during sex can cause psychological regression and psychotic symptoms. As with other transpersonal experiences, the imagery that arises can represent unconscious material that has not yet been integrated by the personality (Elfers, 2009; Little, 2009; Wade, 2004). Wade has suggested (2004) that, for this reason, some partners, are more likely to evoke transpersonal experiences in their lovers because the relationship animates primal erotic relationships, such as those with caretakers. It may be that frightening transpersonal sexual experiences have been under-reported.

Exactly what causes transpersonal sexual experiences is unknown—is it some kind of divine grace or participation in the Great Mysterious, or is it a matter of cultivating certain techniques? Certainly traditional and neo-Tantric and neo-Taoist practices, according to all anecdotal evidence, are effective in bringing about transpersonal states during sex. It seems likely that such practices have refined a number of natural elements of lovemaking, somewhat like the way the basic positions of ballet refine aspects of natural human movement. Just as anyone, including children or the untaught, can dance—and dance traditions have sprung up worldwide—anyone can have a transpersonal sexual experience. Those spontaneous, naturally arising experiences may be formalized by practice into certain conventions that enhance, refine, or constrain them into the patterns valued by each culture, including the ones that produce the most predictable results.

For example, the repetitive movements and vocalizations that frequently accompany (untaught) lovemaking resemble the repetitive movements of trance-dancing and the practice of chanting. Repeated stimulation of one sensory channel, such as stroking a particular place on the partner's body, can overload and overwhelm that channel until it extinguishes, as many repetitive activities cultivated in spiritual practices do. Furthermore, lovemaking often involves a combination of physical and mental relaxation with high levels of alertness and single-pointed concentration without discursive thought, such as when attention is absorbed in a lover's touch or gazing into the lover's eyes. These conditions are the same as those cultivated for meditation in many traditions, only the object of concentration is different. Scantling and Browder (1993) determined that the women most able to become absorbed in their experience were the ones most likely to have "supersex," noted above. Is it surprising, then, that

Table 21.1   Comparisons of Illumination, Transcendence of Spatial Categories, and Collapsing the Flow of Time into the Eternal Now

	Illumination
Experts' text	*Lovers' text*
All at once the roshi [Zen teacher], the room, every single thing disappeared in a dazzling stream of illumination and I felt myself bathed in a delicious, unspeakable delight.... For a fleeting moment I was alone—I alone was...Then the roshi swam into view. Our eyes met and we burst out laughing."I have it! I know! There is nothing, absolutely nothing. I am everything and everything is nothing!" (Kapleau, 1989, p. 239)	Everything in the room was suddenly lost in a bright, white light. Then suddenly everything appeared again as though the floodwaters of the light were receding only with form.... But there was really no separation between the things: the bed, the dresser, the window, my lover, me. I was not separate from everything, though objects had the usual edges.... There was only being. It was all part of me, and I was all of it, just the is-ness. (Wade, 2004, p. 171)
Spatial Nonduality	
Form does not differ from Voidness, and Voidness does not differ from Form...Voidness and existence are complementary to each other...not in opposition. [An] enlightened being sees both aspects at the same time... *Voidness is simply a term denoting the nonsubstantial and nonself nature of beings*...(Chang, 1959, p. 45. Original emphasis.)	I'm there, and my partner's there,...and everything in the room is connected. There's no space between us, and yet I can actually see from one standpoint the outline of her body as a separate thing. But that's just an outline within the fullness of being...On the one hand, everything is being. On the other hand, being is not full of a whole bunch of forms, but the appearance of a whole bunch of forms. It's very real from one standpoint, but at the same time you can see straight through it. (Wade, 2004, p. 172)
Temporal Nonduality (Eternal Now)	
Eternity is not an awareness of *everlasting time*, but an awareness which is itself *totally without time*. The eternal moment is a timeless moment. (Wilber, 1979, p. 62)	Experience drops away into nothingness, without the flow of time, without even desire because in that moment everything is there.
For time to fly away there would have to be a separation [between it and things]. Because you imagine that time only passes, you do not learn the truth of being-time (Dogen, cited in Kapleau, 1989, p. 311)	There can be no desire because that suggests something to desire, something separate, and everything is there; there is nothing that isn't there in that moment. Desire suggests a future, wanting something *out there* in time. But there's no time, so there's no *out there* there. Time just doesn't exist somehow. (Wade, 2004, p. 174)

meditation and sex may produce similar effects? Absorption, the foundational practice of most contemplative paths, is a quality anybody can cultivate.

A common factor in neo-Tantric and neo-Taoist techniques—and one anecdotally and only incidentally reported (Little, 2009; Wade, 2004)—is considerable time spent in lovemaking. The longer couples engage, the more likely, it seems, that a transpersonal experience may result. People who are seriously interested in having such experiences might do well to take lessons in neo-Tantric or neo-Taoist techniques to increase their likelihood, irrespective of the ideology attached to any one path. It is not the beliefs, but the innate capacity that seems to make these experiences possible, and that can be amplified by refinement.

Practice developing any of these inherent qualities can help, but it should never be assumed that this alone causes the experience. All the practice in the world may only open the door to the Great Mysterious on the other side—or make visible and tangible something that has always been there, as the venerable spiritual-sexual traditions teach.

The Effects of Transpersonal Sexual Experiences

Transpersonal sexual experiences, like other transpersonal experiences, have enormous beneficial potential. Aside from the ancient traditions, such as Tantra and Vajrayana Buddhism that claim to be the path to spiritual realization, and Taoism that utilizes such practices for health and longevity, their modern revisionist paths are popular because they: help people overcome sexual shame and oppression; improve technique and orgasmic ability, generally; produce experiences of deeper connectedness with partners and greater relationship satisfaction; enhance a sense of spirituality; present the relationship as an avenue for personal and couple growth; and enhance connectedness with the human community at large (Kruse, 2002).

The research on people who are not engaging in practices to bring about transpersonal sexual states presents a much broader range of effects. Because these individuals were surprised by what happened and were not ideologically predisposed to connect transpersonal phenomena with sex, they were both unprepared and unsupported. If, as sometimes happened, transpersonal phenomena countered their beliefs, especially a materialistic worldview, some denied or repressed such experiences and sought to stop them or feared they were "going crazy" (Wade, 2004). Some denied any connection with Spirit or supernatural phenomena, even if they could not explain it. Others, as noted above, may be negatively affected. Wade (2004) found participants whose egoic structures had collapsed, requiring considerable psychotherapy or other methods to enable them to function as well as before—and not everyone was able to achieve this prior level of functioning. Her records, as well as Little's (2009), include people who became addicted to the "high" and intense connection possible with transpersonal sex, to their own detriment or to that of others. They also include people who clung to partners with whom transpersonal sex occurred even when the relationships were dysfunctional, convinced that the partner must be somehow "the one" and the relationship "hallowed" or unique. Furthermore, sex, like other transpersonal experiences, may involve bringing unconscious material into awareness through metaphorical imagery or dramatic dynamics. People unaccustomed to working with such material or unable to recognize and contextualize it when it does occur may find it threatening and difficult to process.

But the vast majority reported extraordinary benefits in excess of those identified in the admittedly few and small studies of neo-Tantric practitioners:

- Personal healing, including the resolution of internal conflict, especially: self-acceptance and loss of shame around sexuality, sexual identity, and gender issues (Elfers, 2009; Little, 2009; MacKnee, 2002; Wade, 2004); resolution of sexual dysfunction, especially association with having been sexually abused (Elfers, 2009; Little, 2009; MacKnee, 2002; Wade, 2004); and the resolution of personal loss (MacKnee, 2002).
- Empowerment and purpose, including feeling revitalized and motivated to help themselves and others realize more completeness in sexuality and spirituality (Elfers, 2009; Little, 2009; MacKnee, 2002; Wade, 2004).
- Enhanced relationships, especially greater connection with the partner, decreased defensiveness, and increased compassion, all of which are further extended to other relationships, including non-human relationships with nature and the environment as a whole (Elfers, 2009; Little, 2009; MacKnee, 2002; Wade, 2004). Additionally Elfers (2009) found that some participants generalized their sexual interests to become polyamorous after their transpersonal sexual experiences.
- Conviction that Spirit is real and present, variously expressed (Little, 2009; MacKnee, 2002; Wade, 2004). In MacKnee's practicing Christian sample (2002), this took the form of affirming beliefs in God, deeper knowledge of God, trust in God, and deep gratitude for having been graced with such experiences. In Wade's (2004) mixed sample, people's experience frequently countered their consciously held beliefs, resulting in spiritual awakening. Some former atheists and agnostics became spiritual seekers as a result of their sexual experiences, and others, whose transpersonal experiences countered the religions they espoused, converted to traditions better aligned with what they perceived during sex.
- Personal growth, including discarding limiting beliefs, ceasing dysfunctional behavior and relationships, and discovering new paranormal abilities (Elfers, 2009; Little, 2009; Wade, 2004).

Even when the experiences and their results were interpreted to be positive, they were often so profound that they challenged the person's most basic assumptions and values, with results that could be disruptive. Some found that their present lovers, family, or friends were not supportive of what, for the experiencers, was a compelling revelation. That caused relationship breaks, job changes, or the abandonment of secular pursuits for spiritual seeking. These changes were mirrored by those lovers who had frightful or challenging experiences. Sometimes they were so disturbed, they shed relationships and partners in an effort to avoid a repeat of a threatening experience. Even when they subsequently invested personal or professional effort to integrate them, usually with the same kinds of positive results listed above, their lives had often taken a new direction with some former circumstances left behind. Whatever the sacrifices, virtually everyone thought the gifts of transpersonal sex were worth the life changes they produced. As one self-described hard-core materialist and atheist, who dismissed anything he could not prove scientifically, said of his life after transpersonal sex:

> I knew there would be no scientific explanations. [Since that sexual experience] I've studied accounts of peak and near-death experiences, glimpses and openings, awakenings and other forms of mystical expression. I understand what happened to me by now but have felt a need, as I grow older, to transmit some of this to others who suffer so much with their needless fears and doubts.... I have a bad case of what Alan Watts labeled the "divine madness" and I never want to be cured.... In some mysterious way, I was touched by God.... I'm embarrassed, but mostly I consider myself the luckiest man alive... (Wade, 2004, pp. 73-4)

Conclusion

Sex, despite the teachings of centuries of mainstream religions, is an avenue of great spiritual potential, as was better appreciated in ancient times and indigenous cultures. Research indicates that it is a natural capacity all humans possess, probably to a greater or lesser extent like any talent, such as musical or athletic ability. Some people may be born with perfect pitch or the ability to play by ear whereas others can become professional performers with lessons and constant practice and even those who may seem relatively tone deaf can learn to discriminate sounds with teaching.

Transpersonal sexual experiences, if they occur spontaneously to unsuspecting people, may be frightening or destabilizing, especially when people have no idea such phenomena exist. But when unconditioned by expectations, ideological indoctrination, or technique, such experiences also may produce a much broader range of positive, transformative effects than even those produced by the deliberate practices of Tantra, Taoism, and the like. Cultivating practices that are conducive to transpersonal sexual experiences resembles cultivating the practices of many other spiritual disciplines, except that the focus on the body specifically involves sexuality and that the practices most frequently involve partnering of some kind. Because human relationships are so often complicated, the results of spiritual sexual practices tend to enhance connection and compassion, although in other ways they produce the same kinds of transformation, higher values, and life enhancement as recognized, formal spiritual practices, such as the mystical paths of the "world religions."

Their most distinguishing feature, perhaps, is their potential for reconciling the material world—especially the exigencies of embodiment—with the spiritual realm, so often viewed in opposition to bodily needs. This ability to transcend what many people view as irreconcilable polarities, including the body as a source of great shame or spiritual defilement, is perhaps best summarized by the words of experiencers. According to "Colleen," a woman who had been sexually abused starting when she was only two years old, transpersonal sex transfigured her life and her sense of Spirit:

> It made me feel like sex is really big and really vast and there's a lot more there than I was taught, not just in what happened to me, but these visions the media and religion teach us, too.

Sex is absolutely sacred, absolutely holy. There's nothing dirty or bad about it. It's something to be awestruck about.

It reminds me that this is what the universe is *really* all about: feeling that life is so joyous and so blessed. Sex, me, God, all of it, is absolutely beautiful, absolutely spiritual and overflowing, just overflowing with love.

References

Al-Hibri, A., & Habti, R. M. (2006). Islam. In D. S. Browning, M. C. Green, & J. Witte (Eds.), *Sex, marriage, and the family in the world religions* (pp. 150-225). New York, NY: Columbia University Press.

Anderson, B. S., & Zinsser, J. P. (1988). *A history of their own: Women in Europe from prehistory to the present* (Vol. 1). New York, NY: Harper & Row.

Ariel, D. S. (1988). *The mystic quest: An introduction to Jewish mysticism.* New York, NY: Schocken.

Avagianou, A. A. (2008). *Heiros gamos* in ancient Greek religion: The human aspect of a sacralized ritual. In M. Nissinen & R. Uro, (Eds.), (*Sacred marriages: The divine-human sexual metaphor from Sumer to early Christianity* (pp. 145-172). Winona Lake, IN: Eisenbrauns.

Berger, M. S. (2006). Judaism. In D. S. Browning, M. C. Green, & J. Witte (Eds.), *Sex, marriage, and the family in the world religions* (pp. 1-76). New York, NY: Columbia University Press.

Bonheim, J. (1997). *Aphrodite's daughters: Women's sexual stories and the journey of the soul.* New York, NY: Simon & Schuster.

Bradford, N. (1983). Transgenderism and the cult of Yellama: Heat, sex and sickness in South Indian ritual. *Journal of Anthropological Research 39*(3), 307-322.

Bragdon, E. (1988). *A sourcebook for helping people in spiritual emergency.* Los Altos, CA: Lightening Up.

Bragdon, E. (1990). *The call of spiritual emergency.* San Francisco, CA: Harper & Row.

Budin, S. L. (2006). Sacred prostitution in the first person. In C. A. Faraone & L. K. McClure (Eds.), *Prostitutes & courtesans in the ancient world* (pp. 77-92). Madison, WI: University of Wisconsin Press.

Chang, G. C. C. (1959). *The practice of Zen.* New York, NY: Harper & Row.

Cole, A. (2006). Buddhism. In D. S. Browning, M. C. Green, & J. Witte (Eds.), *Sex, marriage, and the family in the world religions* (pp. 299-365). New York, NY: Columbia University Press.

Coleman, E., Colgan, P., & Gooren, L. (1992). Male cross-gender behavior in Myanmar (Burma): A description of the acault. *Archives of Sexual Behavior, 21*(3), 313-321.

Courtright, P. B. (2006). Hinduism. In D. S. Browning, M. C. Green, & J. Witte (Eds.), *Sex, marriage, and the family in the world religions* (pp. 226-290). New York, NY: Columbia University Press.

Eisler, R. T. (1987). *The chalice and the blade: Our history, our future.* San Francisco, CA: Harper & Row.

Eisler, R. T. (1995). *Sacred pleasure: Sex, myth and the politics of the body.* San Francisco, CA: Harper San Francisco.

Elfers, J. (2009). When eros is a god: Cultivating the ecstatic potentials of sexuality as transpersonal development. *Dissertation Abstracts International, 70*(02) 0669B (UMI #3344935).

Eller, C. (2000). *The myth of matriarchal prehistory: Why an invented past won't give women a future*. Boston, MA: Beacon.

Eskildsen, S. (1998). *Asceticism in early Taoist religion*. Albany, NY: State University of New York Press.

Faure, B. (1998). *The red thread: Buddhist approaches to sexuality*. Princeton, NJ: Princeton University Press.

Feuerstein, G. (1992). *Sacred sexuality: Living the vision of the erotic spirit*. Los Angeles, CA: Jeremy P. Tarcher.

Feuerstein, G. (1998). *Tantra the path of ecstasy*. Boston, MA: Shambhala.

Fleming, A. (1969). The myth of the mother-goddess. *World Archaeology, 1*(2), 247-261.

Giago, T. (1993, January 27). Phony Indians. *The Baltimore Sun*. Retrieved from: http://articles.baltimoresun.com/1993-01-27/news/1993027046_1_cherokee-nation-indian-tribe

Gimbutas, M. (1982). *The goddesses and gods of old Europe*. Berkeley, CA: University of California Press.

Gimbutas, M. (1989). *The language of the goddess*. San Francisco, CA: Harper & Row.

Gimbutas, M. (1991). *The civilization of the goddess*. San Francisco, CA: HarperSanFrancisco.

Goodison, L., & Morris, C. (Eds.). (1998). *Ancient goddesses: The myths and the evidence*. Madison, NJ: University of Wisconsin Press.

Greeley, A. M. (1974). *Ecstasy: A way of knowing*. Englewood Cliffs, NJ: Prentice Hall.

Grof, S. (1975). *Realms of the human unconscious*. New York, NY: Viking Press.

Grof, S. (1985). *Beyond the brain: Birth, death and transcendence in psychotherapy*. Albany, NY: State University of New York Press.

Grof, S. (1988). *The adventure of self-discovery: Dimensions of consciousness and new perspectives in psychotherapy and inner exploration*. Albany, NY: State University of New York Press.

Grof, S. (1998). *The cosmic game: Explorations of the frontiers of human consciousness*. Albany, NY: State University of New York Press.

Hagan, H. E. (1992, September). The plastic medicine people circle. *Sonoma County Free Press*. Retrieved from: http://www.sonomacountyfreepress.com/features/spirg-hagan.html

Hardy, A. (1979). *The spiritual nature of man: A study of contemporary religious experience*. Oxford, UK: Clarendon Press.

Henriques, F. (1963). *Prostitution and society: Primitive, classical & oriental*. New York, NY: Citadel.

Ho, T. (2009). Transgender, transgression, and translation: A cartography of nat kadaws: Notes on gender and sexuality within the spirit cult of Burma. *Discourse, 31*(3), 273-317, 396.

Hoffman, E. (1992). *The way of splendor: Jewish mysticism and modern psychology*. Northvale, NJ: Aronson.

Holbrook, L. J. (2008). Psychological characteristics of altered states of consciousness experienced during transcendent sex. *Dissertation Abstracts International, 69*(05) 0669B (UMI #3307969).

Hoppál, M. (1987). Shamanism: An archaic and/or recent system of beliefs. In S. Nicholson (Ed.), *Shamanism* (pp. 76-100). Wheaton, IL: Quest.

Hutchins, L. (2002). Bisexual women as emblematic sexual healers and the problematics of the embodied sacred whore. *Journal of Bisexuality 2*(2/3), 205-226.

Hutton, R. (1991). *The pagan religions of the ancient British Isles: Their nature and legacy*. Oxford, UK: Blackwell.

Jacobs, S. E., Thomas, W., & Lang, S. (1997). *Two-spirit people: Native American gender identity, sexuality, and spirituality*. Urbana, IL: University of Illinois.

Johnson, L. T., & Jordan, M. D. (2006). Christianity. In D. S. Browning, M. C. Green, & J. Witte (Eds.), *Sex, marriage, and the family in the world religions* (pp. 77-147). New York, NY: Columbia University Press.

Kakar, S. (1994). Ramakrishna and the mystical experience. *Annual of Psychoanalysis, 20,* 215-234.

Kapleau, P. (Ed.). (1989). *The three pillars of Zen* (Rev. ed.). Boston, MA: Beacon.

Keesling, C. (2006). Heavenly bodies: Monuments to prostitutes in Greek sanctuaries. In C. A. Faraone & L. K. McClure (Eds.), *Prostitutes and courtesans in the ancient world* (pp. 59-76). Madison, WI: University of Wisconsin Press.

Kehoe, A. (2000). *Shamans and religion: An anthropological exploration in critical thinking.* London, UK: Waveland.

Kohn, L. (1992). *Early Chinese mysticism: Philosophy and soteriology in the Taoist tradition.* Princeton, NJ: Princeton University Press.

Komjathy, L. (2007). *Cultivating perfection: Mysticism and self-transformation in early Quanzhen Daoism.* Sinica Leidensia (Vol. 75). Boston, MA: Brill.

Kovacs, M. G., (Trans.). 1989. *The epic of Gilgamesh.* Stanford, CA: Stanford University Press.

Kreutzer, C. S. (1978). Whatever turns you on: Triggers to transcendent experiences. *Journal of Humanistic Psychology, 18*(3), 77-80.

Kruse, C. L. (2002). Couples' experiences of sacred sex/Tantra practices. *Dissertation Abstract International, 63*(02) 0392B (UMI #3042885).

Lapinkivi, P. (2008). The Sumerian sacred marriage and its aftermath in later sources. In M. Nissinen & R. Uro (Eds.), *Sacred marriages: The divine-human sexual metaphor from Sumer to early Christianity* (pp. 7-42). Winona Lake, IN: Eisenbrauns.

Laski, M. (1961). *Ecstasy in secular and religious experiences.* Los Angeles, CA: Jeremy P. Tarcher.

Little, A. (2009). Beyond the closet and through the doors of perception: The transcendent sexual experiences of 69 women. *Dissertation Abstracts International, 70*(07), 0669B (UMI #3360373).

MacKnee, C. M. (2002). Profound sexual and spiritual encounters among practicing Christians: A phenomenological analysis. *Journal of Psychology and Theology, 30*(3), 234-244.

Maslow, A. H. (1987). *Motivation and personality* (Rev. ed.). New York, NY: Harper & Row.

Maurer, H. (1994). *Sex: An oral history.* New York, NY: Viking.

McDaniel, J. (1989). *The madness of the saints: Ecstatic religion in Bengal.* Chicago, IL: University of Chicago Press.

Nanda, S. (1993). Hijras: An alternative sex and gender role in India. In G. Herdt (Ed.), *Third sex, third gender: Beyond sexual dimorphism in culture and history* (pp. 373-417). New York, NY: Zone.

Nissinen, M. (2008). Song of Songs and sacred marriage. In M. Nissinen & R. Uro (Eds.), *Sacred marriages: The divine-human sexual metaphor from Sumer to early Christianity* (pp. 173-218). Winona Lake, IN: Eisenbrauns.

Nyberg, K. (2008). Sacred prostitution in the Biblical world? In M. Nissinen & R. Uro (Eds.), *Sacred marriages: The divine-human sexual metaphor from Sumer to early Christianity* (pp. 305-320). Winona Lake, IN: Eisenbrauns.

Ogden, G. (2006). *The heart and soul of sex: Making the ISIS connection.* Boston, MA: Trumpeter Books.

Pagels, E. (1979). *The Gnostic gospels.* New York, NY: Vantage.

Pagels, E. (1988). *Adam, Eve, and the serpent.* New York, NY: Random House.

Parrinder, G. (1996). *Sexual morality in the world's religions.* Oxford, UK: Oneworld.

Piedmont, O. (1996). The veils of Arjuna: Androgyny in gay spirituality, East and West. *Dissertation Abstracts International, 57*(06) 0392B (UMI #9633907).

Pongratz-Leisten, B. (2008). Sacred marriage and the transfer of divine knowledge: Alliances between the gods and the king in ancient Mesopotamia. In M. Nissinen & R. Uro (Eds.), *Sacred marriages: The divine-human sexual metaphor from Sumer to early Christianity* (pp. 43-74). Winona Lake, IN: Eisenbrauns.

Rikala, M. (2008). Sacred marriage in the New Kingdom of Ancient Egypt: Circumstantial evidence for a ritual interpretation. In M. Nissinen & R. Uro (Eds.), *Sacred marriages: The divine-human sexual metaphor from Sumer to early Christianity* (pp. 115-144). Winona Lake, IN: Eisenbrauns.

Roscoe, W. (1998). *Changing ones: Third and fourth genders in Native North America.* New York, NY: St. Martins.

Roth, M. T. (2006). Marriage, divorce, and the prostitute in ancient Mesopotamia. In C. A. Faraone & L. K. McClure (Eds.), *Prostitutes and courtesans in the ancient world* (pp. 21-39). Madison, WI: University of Wisconsin Press.

Saso, M. (1997). The Taoist body and cosmic prayer. In S. Cloakley (Ed.), *Religion and the body* (pp. 231-247). Cambridge, UK: Cambridge University Press.

Scantling, S., & Browder, S. (1993). *Ordinary women, extraordinary sex: Every woman's guide to pleasure and beyond.* New York, NY: Dutton.

Schimmel, A. (1997). "I take off the dress of the body": Eros in Sufi literature. In S. Cloakley (Ed.), *Religion and the body* (pp. 262-288). Cambridge, UK: Cambridge University Press.

Sell, I. M. (2001). Third gender: A qualitative study of the experience of individuals who identify as being neither man nor woman. *Dissertation Abstracts International, 62*(04) 0669B (UMI #3011299).

Sigal, P. H. (2000). *From moon goddesses to virgins: The colonization of Yucatecan Maya sexual desire.* Austin, TX: University of Texas Press.

Sigal, P. H. (2011). *The flower and the scorpion: Sexuality and ritual in early Nahua culture.* Durham, NC: Duke University Press.

Smith, M. S. (2008). Sacred marriage in the Ugaritic texts? The case of KTU/CAT 1.23 (Rituals and myths of the goodly gods). In M. Nissinen & R. Uro (Eds.), *Sacred marriages: The divine-human sexual metaphor from Sumer to early Christianity* (pp. 83-114). Winona Lake, IN: Eisenbrauns.

Sokol, D. (1986). Spirituality and sexuality: A phenomenological exploration of transcendental states in sexuality (Tantra, matriarchal, patriarchal, kundalini, yoga). *Dissertation Abstracts International, 47*(07) 0392A (UMI #8625587).

Sokol, D. (1989). Spiritual breakthroughs in sex. In G. Feuerstein (Ed.), *Enlightened sexuality: Essays on body-positive spirituality* (pp. 112-140). Freedom, CA: Crossing.

Spretnak, C. (1991). *States of grace: The recovery of meaning in the postmodern age.* San Francisco, CA: Harper.

Tafoya, T. (1992). Native gay and lesbian issues: The two-spirited. In B. Berson (Ed.), *Positively gay* (pp. 253-259). Berkeley, CA: Celestial Arts.

Tannahill, R. (1980). *Sex in history.* New York, NY: Stein & Day.

Tart, C. (1972). States of consciousness and state-specific sciences. *Science, 176,* 1203-1210.

Tart, C. (1975). *States of consciousness.* New York, NY: E. P. Dutton.

Teppo, S. (2008). Sacred marriage and the devotees of Ishtar. In M. Nissinen & R. Uro (Eds.), *Sacred marriages: The divine-human sexual metaphor from Sumer to early Christianity* (pp. 75-92). Winona Lake, IN: Eisenbrauns.

Urban, H. B. (2000). The cult of ecstasy: Tantrism, the New Age, and the spiritual logic of late capitalism. *History of Religions, 39*(3), 268-304.

Urban, H. B. (2003). *Tantra: Sex, secrecy, politics, and power in the study of religion.* Berkeley, CA: University of California Press.

van Gulik, R. H. (1974). *Sexual life in ancient China: A preliminary survey of Chinese sex and society from ca. 1500 B.C. till 1644 A.D.* Leiden, The Netherlands: Brill.

Vitebsky, P. (1996). *The shaman: Voyages of the soul—Trance, ecstasy and healing from Siberia to the Amazon.* New York, NY: Macmillan/Duncan Baird.

Wade, J. (1998). Meeting God in the flesh: Spirituality in sexual intimacy. *ReVision, 21*(2), 35-41.

Wade, J. (2000). The love that dares not speak its name. In T. Hart, P. Nelson, & K. Puhakka (Eds.), *Transpersonal knowing: Exploring the horizon of consciousness* (pp. 271-318). Albany, NY: State University of New York Press.

Wade, J. (2001). Mapping the courses of heavenly bodies: The varieties of transcendent sexual experience. *Journal of Transpersonal Psychology, 32*(2), 103-122.

Wade, J. (2004). *Transcendent sex: When lovemaking opens the veil.* New York, NY: Paraview Pocket Books.

Wagar, S. (2009). The Wiccan "Great Rite"—*Hieros Gamos* in the modern West. *Journal of Religion and Popular Culture, 21*(2), 1-38.

Waite, A. E. (1960). *The holy Kabbalah: A study of the secret tradition in Israel as unfolded by sons of the doctrine for the benefit of the elect dispersed through the lands and ages of the greater exile.* New Hyde Park, NY: University Books.

Walsh, R. (2007). *The world of shamanism: New views of an ancient tradition.* Woodbury, MN: Llewellyn.

Ware, K. (1997). "My helper and my enemy;" The body in Greek Christianity. In S. Cloakley (Ed.), *Religion and the body* (pp. 90-110). Cambridge, UK: Cambridge University Press.

Weisner-Hanks, M. E. (2000). *Christianity and sexuality in the early modern world: Regulating desire, reforming practice.* London, UK: Routledge.

White, D. G. (2003). *The kiss of the Yogini: "Tantric sex" in its South Asian context.* Chicago, IL: University of Chicago Press.

White, R. A. (1994). Exceptional human experience and the more we are: Exceptional human experience and identity. Retrieved from: http://ehe.org/display/ehe-pagea229.html?ID=70

White, R. A. (2001). What are exceptional human experiences? New Bern, NC: EHE Network. Retrieved from: http://ehe.org/display/ehe-page3439.html?ID=6

Wilber, K. (1979). *No boundary: Eastern and Western approaches to personal growth.* Boston, MA: Shambhala.

York, M. (2003). *Pagan theology: Paganism as a world religion.* New York, NY: New York University Press.

Zimmerman, R. (2008). The love triangle of Lady Wisdom: Sacred marriage in Jewish wisdom literature? In M. Nissinen & R. Uro (Eds.), *Sacred marriages: The divine-human sexual metaphor from Sumer to early Christianity* (pp. 243-258). Winona Lake, IN: Eisenbrauns.

Zuber-Chall, S. (2012). Gender and sexuality in indigenous North America, 1400-1850. *Choice, 49*(5), 957-958. Retrieved from: http://search.proquest.com/docview/921022903?accountid=25304

22

Parapsychology

Adam J. Rock, Lance Storm, Harvey J. Irwin, and Julie Beischel

Parapsychology, a term coined by Max Dessoir (1889), refers to the study of a range of unexplained phenomena that are considered paranormal or ostensibly paranormal. These phenomena include *extra-sensory perception, psychokinesis,* and *life after death* (also known as *survival of consciousness*—these three phenomena are each defined in subsequent sections below). In the 1930s, J. B. Rhine adopted the term parapsychology, and it has been used ever since. The term parapsychology has come to supersede the term *psychical research,* although some parapsychologists often think of psychical research as specifically referring to afterlife research, which is also a parapsychological topic.

A phenomenon is classified as paranormal if it cannot be understood in the context of conventional scientific standards, on the assumption that no scientific rule, or law, or sufficiently proven theory, exists to explain the nature of the phenomenon. According to Thalbourne (2003), conventional scientists even see paranormal processes as "physically impossible and outside the realm of human or animal capabilities" (p. 83). Many scientists prefer to explain paranormal phenomena as nothing more than fraud, or artifacts of some kind of careless or unwitting laboratory practice (Hansel, 1980). Others believe that reports of significant effects (i.e., effects not expected by chance) are merely the result of a range of statistically creative (i.e., exploratory) processes that reveal nothing of real interest to science (e.g., see Hyman, 2010), but such assumptions are constantly challenged (e.g., see Storm, Tressoldi, & Di Risio, 2010a).

Parapsychology differs from the similar field of anomalistic psychology, a term coined by Zusne and Jones (1982), in that the latter covers a broader range of phenomena than pure parapsychology, which may still be of a paranormal nature, but also are popularly attributed to supernatural, magical, or occult processes. Anomalistic phenomena thereby may include UFOs, astrology, and crypto-zoological creatures such as the Loch Ness Monster. In addition, anomalistic psychology tends to have a more explicitly sceptical orientation than parapsychology.

The Wiley Blackwell Handbook of Transpersonal Psychology, First Edition.
Edited by Harris L. Friedman and Glenn Hartelius.
© 2013 John Wiley & Sons, Ltd. Published 2015 by John Wiley & Sons, Ltd.

Of some concern to advocates and critics alike are the practical advantages, if any, of parapsychology. To address this issue, Neppe (2005) proposed that parapsychology is one of the most important of all the areas of scientific endeavour for five major reasons:

1 Its implications broaden our worldview, and are so profound in its more radical framework;
2 It allows the development of cosmological theories and new scientific endeavours may develop as a consequence;
3 Its methodology serves as a model for both the physical and humanistic sciences to adopt;
4 It extends the methodology issue because the subjective approach in parapsychology extends its usefulness even further in the social and medical sciences; and,
5 Partly as a synthesis of the above, it should be accepted as a major legitimate scientific endeavour as the implications of the findings are so fundamental, ubiquitous, and versatile for almost all our sciences. (p. 56)

Neppe's last point is particularly pertinent in that the impact of the parapsychological findings on the sciences and the humanities could be far-reaching and of some consequence. It is perhaps this key point that encourages such reserved attitudes in the more conservative circles of academia and the population at large. Nevertheless, parapsychology has been applied in public institutions (e.g., U.S. Department of Defense; see McMoneagle, 1997, 2000), positive outcomes have been attained in crime solving (see Schouten, 1993, 1994), and edifying and/or profitable results have been achieved in archaeology and anthropology (see Schwartz, 1983, 2000, 2005). Further possible applications inherent in the parapsychological findings will become clearer throughout this chapter.

The purpose of this chapter is to provide an introduction to parapsychology for transpersonal scientists, practitioners, and students. However, the interested reader may wish to seek out more comprehensive surveys (e.g., Irwin & Watt, 2007).

Categories of Psi

Over the years, parapsychologists have created a taxonomy (classification system) of psi experiences. Irrespective of whether or not the nominated types of psi entail distinct underlying processes, the terms are useful in describing psi experiences and experimental procedures. In the subsequent subsections this traditional taxonomy and its nomenclature will be outlined.

Extra-Sensory Perception

The term extrasensory perception (ESP) was coined by J. B. Rhine (1934) to cover any form of communication between minds or brains that is not explicable in conventional scientific terms. Rhine also used the shorthand term *psi* (a Greek letter pronounced

Table 22.1 The Traditional 3 × 2 Taxonomy of ESP according to Temporal Location and Nature of the Presumed Target-Event

Nature of presumed target-event	Temporal location of presumed target-event		
	Past	*Present*	*Future*
Mental	Retrocognitive Telepathy	Contemporaneous Telepathy	Precognitive Telepathy
Physical	Retrocognitive Clairvoyance	Contemporaneous Clairvoyance	Precognitive Clairvoyance

"sigh") to denote "paranormal causation" or "paranormal process" (Thalbourne, 2003, p. 92; psi also includes psychokinesis, described in the next section).[1] Since normal scientific explanations are inadequate in describing the nature and mechanism underlying the purportedly extrasensory process, ESP is often considered a paranormal phenomenon. On this basis, ESP is also referred to as *paranormal (or anomalous) cognition.*

The term ESP embraces three classes of paranormal communication: telepathy, clairvoyance, and precognition. Telepathy refers to the "paranormal acquisition of information concerning the thoughts, feelings or activity of another conscious being" (Thalbourne, 2003, p. 125). Clairvoyance is defined as "paranormal acquisition of information concerning an object or contemporary physical event; in contrast to telepathy, the information is assumed to derive directly from an external physical source" (Thalbourne, 2003, p. 18). Precognition is defined as "a form of extrasensory perception in which the target is some future event that cannot be deduced from normally known data in the present" (Thalbourne, 2003, p. 90).

Table 22.1 shows that ESP target-events are traditionally classified as either mental or physical in nature. From Table 22.1 it can be seen that, temporally speaking, target-events may be in the past (i.e., retrocognitive), the present (i.e., contemporaneous), or the future (i.e., precognitive).

Although meta-analytic studies (summaries of sets of studies) have often demonstrated weak ESP effects, parapsychologists agree that ESP is consistent and relatively demonstrable under laboratory conditions, as is indicated in studies by (i) Storm, Tressoldi, and Di Risio (2010b) for the Ganzfeld (described below); (ii) Milton (1998) for remote viewing (RV); and (iii) Steinkamp, Milton, and Morris (1998) for clairvoyance and precognition.

Perhaps of even greater interest to transpersonal psychologists is the phenomenological study of ESP (Irwin, 1994). Largely pioneered by Louisa Rhine, wife of J. B. Rhine, some parapsychologists have compiled collections of case reports of spontaneous ESP experiences with a view to identifying the descriptive characteristics of these experiences and the place they have in the life of the experient (the person who has the experience). This type of research is termed *process-oriented* because it focuses on phenomenology (the way things are experienced by the experient), rather than attempting to demonstrate that psi exists.

Table 22.2   The Traditional Taxonomy of PK According to Temporal Location

Nature of presumed target-event	Temporal location of presumed target-event		
	Past	*Present*	*Future*
Physical	Retroactive Psychokinesis	Contemporaneous Psychokinesis	Preactive Psychokinesis

Psychokinesis

The term psychokinesis (PK) was coined by J. B. Rhine (1934) to cover any form of mind-matter interaction that is not explicable in conventional scientific terms. Since normal scientific explanations are inadequate in describing the nature and mechanism underlying the *psychokinetic* process (mental impact on matter), PK is often considered a paranormal phenomenon. On this basis, PK is also referred to as *paranormal (or anomalous) action.*

Table 22.2 shows how PK target-events are restricted to physical events. From Table 2, it can be seen that PK effects can cross the temporal barrier, so that effects may be elicited in the past, the present, or the future.

PK can be classified also as either micro-PK or macro-PK. Micro-PK refers to psychokinetic effects that are not directly observable by the unaided human eye (i.e., they occur at the quantum-mechanical level), as is indicated, for example, in the unobservable sub-atomic process of psychokinetically perturbed random nuclear decay underlying the binary outputs characteristic of random event generation (REG) or random number generation (RNG; see Radin & Nelson, 1989, 2003). Macro-PK generally refers to the directly observable effects of paranormal action on biological organisms (e.g., species' behaviors), the fall of dice, psychokinetic metal-bending (PKMB), and related phenomena.

Most meta-analytic studies show that PK effects are generally even weaker than ESP effects, but parapsychologists agree that like ESP, PK is consistent and, therefore, relatively demonstrable under laboratory conditions, as is indicated by the following studies: (i) Braud and Schlitz (1991) on direct mental interactions with living systems (DMILS); (ii) Radin and Ferrari (1991) on dice throwing experiments, and (iii) Radin and Nelson (2003) on RNG experiments.

Survival of Consciousness

There are many parapsychological experiences that seem to imply post-mortem survival such as apparitional experiences, near-death experiences (NDEs), out-of-body experiences (OBEs), and reincarnation experiences. Some of these experiences are covered in other chapters in this volume. Consequently, this section will focus on apparent spirit communication, which is commonly referred to as mediumship.

Over a century of mediumship research concludes that certain skilled mediums are able to report accurate and specific information about the deceased loved ones (termed *discarnates*) of living people (termed *sitters*) during anomalous information reception (AIR); that is, without any prior knowledge about the discarnates or sitters, in the absence of sensory feedback, and without using deceptive means (e.g., Beischel, Biuso, Boccuzzi, & Rock, 2011). However, mediumship findings (reviewed by Braude, 2003; Fontana, 2005; Gauld, 1983) *en bloc* do not directly address which parapsychological mechanisms are involved in AIR by mediums. That is, the data, in and of themselves, support multiple hypotheses including: (a) the survival of consciousness (i.e., life after death; the continued existence, separate from the body, of at least portions of an individual's consciousness or personality after physical death), (b) the psychic reservoir hypothesis (i.e., that all information since the beginning of time is stored somehow and somewhere in the universe and mediums are accessing that cosmic store rather than communicating with the deceased; reviewed in Fontana, 2005), and (c) super-psi (also called super-ESP; discussed in detail in Braude, 2003, and reviewed in Fontana, 2005). Super-psi, the retrieval of information through telepathy with the living, clairvoyance, and/or precognition, is deemed super by its ostensible requirement of "more refined and extensive psychic functioning than we discover in controlled laboratory studies" (Braude, 2003, p. 11). In the super-psi explanation, a medium may receive information through multiple psi processes:

> telepathically from the mind of the sitter (even though the latter may not be consciously thinking about the information at the time), telepathically from the minds of people elsewhere, clairvoyantly from the environment, or even precognitively from the future moment when the sitter checks on the facts given in the communications and finds them to be correct. (Fontana, 2005, p. 104)

However, it is important to note that the survival hypothesis also requires some form of psi in order for information to be transferred from the discarnate to the medium. Indeed, either "the medium acquires her knowledge of discarnate minds by telepathically scanning their minds or ... the discarnate person is telepathically sending information to a medium's mind. In either case, living agent telepathy is operative" (Sudduth, 2009, p. 177). Sudduth (2009) termed this "survival psi" and described it as "a highly refined and efficacious sort of psi functioning ... indistinguishable from the degree or kind of psi required by the super-psi hypothesis" (p. 184).

Psi-conducive Stimulus Conditions

Parapsychologists have devoted much of their research to the identification of circumstances and experimental procedures that may effectively elicit psi. Efforts to identify what elicits psi are termed *process-oriented*; they are aimed at understanding *how* psi works. In contrast, *proof-oriented* research simply aims to show that extra-chance performance can be obtained under controlled conditions.

The Ganzfeld

Bem and Honorton (1994) have asserted that, "Historically, psi has often been associated with meditation, hypnosis, dreaming, and other naturally occurring or deliberately induced altered states of consciousness" (p. 5).[2] Perhaps the most widely used technique in this context is the Ganzfeld ("total field"), which may be defined, in broad terms, as a "homogeneous perceptual environment" (Bem, 1993, p. 102). Specifically, the Ganzfeld consists of an undifferentiated visual field created by viewing a red light through halved opaque ping-pong balls taped over a percipient's eyes. Additionally, an analogous auditory field is produced by the percipient listening to stereophonic white or pink noise (i.e., a monotonous hissing sound; Bem, 1993). Therefore, as a procedure whereby a sender (agent) is required to "psychically communicate" (Milton & Wiseman, 1999, p. 387) a picture target or movie-film target to an isolated receiver (percipient) who is in the Ganzfeld condition of *homogeneous sensory stimulation*, the Ganzfeld evidently induces an altered state of consciousness (ASC), which is considered psi-conducive. If the percipient correctly selects the target rather than one of the decoys, this is termed a *hit*. The five major independent Ganzfeld meta-analyses (Bem & Honorton, 1994; Bem, Palmer, & Broughton, 2001; Honorton, 1985; Storm & Ertel, 2001; Storm, Tressoldi, & Di Risio, 2010b) report hit rates ranging from between 31.6% and 36.7% (in which 25% is a chance occurrence).

Dreaming

Researchers have also investigated what is now referred to as *dream-psi,* that is, the occurrence of psi during a dream. This domain had its greatest impact through work done at the Maimonides Dream Laboratory (Ullman, Krippner, & Vaughan, 1974). The field originated with the idea that many people report telepathic and premonitory dreams, and indeed a vast collection of unexplained anecdotal accounts collected by J. B. Rhine's wife, Louisa Rhine, attests to the prevalence of these experiences (L. E. Rhine, 1962). Participants at the Maimonides laboratory were asked to dream about a target picture and the experimenters compared resulting dream motifs to the target material. In some sense, the psi process could be encapsulated in the dream process, and the psi target seemed embedded in imaginal form as dream content.

Results from the Maimonides dream studies were mixed and complex, collected by a small team of researchers with diverse methodologies, different statistical testing procedures, and different goals. As Storm (2006) conservatively stated: "These findings do indicate that the 'average' dream-psi study is not likely to elicit evidence of psi, but when the collection is looked at over a 40-year period, there is an extremely strong indication of a correspondence between dream motifs and target material under laboratory conditions" (p. 146).

Meditation

A handful of studies were conducted that directly investigated the alleged psi-conduciveness of meditation (e.g., Honorton, 1997; Palmer, Khamashta, & Israelson,

1979; Rao, Dukhan, & Rao, 2001; Rao & Puri, 1978; Rao & Rao, 1982; Roney-Dougal & Solfvin, 2006), but the results were inconsistent.

Furthermore, as Steinkamp (2005) indicated in her meta-analysis of forced-choice studies (i.e., experiments in which an individual is forced to choose from various options), enhanced psi abilities after meditation might partly be the result of psychological factors. For example, participants may have greater confidence after meditating, and their beliefs might, in turn, couple with the experimenter's belief that meditation will help. In other words, it is unclear whether the enhancement of psi is due to the state of consciousness as such, to some concomitant factor like belief, or to some combination of both (on belief as a psi-conducive variable, see Lawrence, 1993).

Hypnosis

For a time, the main focus of researchers (e.g., Honorton & Krippner, 1969; Kumar & Pekala, 2001; Pekala & Cardeña, 2000) came to be the extrasensory experient's state of mind; it was thought that ESP was somehow related to *distinctive states of consciousness,* such as dissociation brought about by such factors as somnambulism, absorbing preoccupation, and mental fatigue. Progress proved slow, but it was inevitable that parapsychologists would more seriously investigate hypnosis since it was seen as a potential experimental procedure for bringing about a passive, dissociative state thought to be conducive to psi. However, in a review by Stanford and Stein (1994), results were mixed, depending on the personality and style of the experimenter. They also noted that participant selection played a part.

Relaxation

Anecdotal and experimental reports of alleged psychic phenomena in meditative or relaxed states suggested an avenue of research for parapsychologists (e.g., Braud & Braud, 1973, 1974). Honorton (1977) cursorily reviewed the relaxation literature and, having found some indication that relaxation could "enhance psi receptivity" (p. 457), advocated relaxation as a psi-conducive condition.

Storm and Thalbourne (2001) collected 21 ESP studies from 1946 to 1992 that featured relaxation as a treatment condition. They found that 52% of studies with a relaxation condition ($n = 11$) produced significantly stronger effects compared to the non-relaxation studies ($n = 10$); this success rate is about ten times higher than would be expected by chance.

Summary

The Ganzfeld, dreaming, meditation, hypnosis, and relaxation are all ostensibly psi-favorable test conditions. However, in recent years parapsychologists (e.g., Alvarado, 1998; Braud, 2005) have questioned whether these procedures really facilitate psi. Perhaps other factors such as sampling or experimenter effects are psi-conducive and the test conditions themselves have no inherently psi-enhancing properties (Braud, 2005).

Models of Psi

On the basis of experimental investigations of the circumstances under which psi may occur, parapsychologists began to devise descriptions of the psi process. Models or theories of psi include electromagnetic theories (e.g., Persinger, 1975), energy field theories (e.g., Wasserman, 1956), observational theories (e.g., Schmidt, 1975), memory models of ESP (e.g., Irwin, 1979), and many others. The most influential of these models is perhaps the noise-reduction model, which is arguably the dominant paradigm in contemporary parapsychology. This section will briefly consider the noise-reduction model, the psi-meditated instrumental response model, decision augmentation theory, the theory of psychopraxia, and the imagery cultivation model (for a comprehensive review of parapsychological models see Irwin & Watt, 2007.)

The Noise-Reduction Model

Honorton (1977, 1993) conceptualized psi as a weak cognitive signal usually masked by internal cognitive and external noise, or unwanted stimulation. On that basis, he proposed the noise-reduction model of psi (Honorton, 1974, 1993).

Braud (2002) also endorsed a model of mental quietude and he, too, described the Ganzfeld as an ASC similar to that obtained in meditation (i.e., stillness of mind or cognitive quietude). In Alvarado's (1998) words, Braud (1978) "articulated" the possible sources of noise including "sensory and perceptual noise, bodily and autonomic activity, mental activities . . . [and] excessive striving to obtain ESP information" (p. 44).

Theoretically, by modifying the "signal-to-noise ratio" (i.e., reducing the noise), using any of the above-described treatments (i.e., hypnosis, dreaming, meditation, and relaxation), the presumed psi information could be better detected. Parker (2005) clarified this model:

> The common feature, as Honorton described it, is the elimination of "noise" or unwanted sources of stimulation. By "noise" was meant not just external stimulation and sources of distraction but also inner chatter. The objective is to still the mind in order for internal imagery to spontaneously manifest; or, expressed in another way, the brain requires a minimal level of stimulation and in the absence of an external source, it will turn internally for this (p. 73).

The Psi-Mediated Instrumental Response Model

The psi-meditated instrumental response (PMIR) model (Stanford, 1974a,b) suggests that psi experiences arise because they fulfil a goal-orientated or adaptive need for the individual in his or her environment. Thus, according to the PMIR model the individual has a need or disposition for the psi experience to occur. However, Stanford asserted that the individuals may not be consciously aware of the factors (e.g., feelings, behaviors, desires, images) that constitute a psi-mediated response.

Decision Augmentation Theory

Decision Augmentation Theory (DAT) contends that individuals integrate information obtained via anomalous cognition (AC) or psi into the decision-making process along with the usual inputs (e.g., information from the environment; May, Utts, & Spottiswoode, 1995). This process culminates with a human decision that predisposes a desired outcome. May and his colleagues asserted that, "In statistical parlance, DAT says that a slight, systematic bias is introduced into the decision process by AC" (p. 199). Consider the following question, "When should we schedule our next parapsychological experiment and who should be the experimenter?" According to DAT, AC biases decisions in order to produce the desired outcome.

The Theory of Psychopraxia

The term *psychopraxia* is derived from two Greek words: *psyche,* which means soul, mind, or self, and *praxia,* from which derives the word, practice (derived from *prattein,* meaning to accomplish or bring about). Psychopraxia theory (Thalbourne, 2004) attempts to unify both normal and paranormal psychology, and motor action and cognition, so that the conceptual distinction between (i) ESP and PK, and (ii) normal information-acquisition and normal motor control might be eliminated, because, for example, both sides of the dichotomy are instances of action (Storm & Thalbourne, 2000).

The Imagery Cultivation Model

According to Storm and Rock's (2009a, 2011) imagery cultivation (IC) model, the active cognitive process of mental imagery cultivation allows the experient to access the unconscious domain of the human psyche, which is a wellspring of psi images. The IC model contends that during an altered state (e.g., shamanic journeying[3]), the psi signal is somehow embedded in the cultivated imagery. Here, one is reminded of the Maimonides dream-psi experiments in which the experimenters investigated whether the dream motifs corresponded to the target material. Thus, the IC model challenges the noise-reduction model's emphasis on mental quietude. The IC model has received recent empirical support (Storm & Rock, 2009b).

The Psychology of Belief in Psi

Another topic of interest both to parapsychologists and to their critics is the nature of belief in paranormal phenomena. Many parapsychologists may argue that their own belief in the reality of psi is founded on their scrutiny of the relevant experimental literature. Again, some critics, having examined the same literature with a more jaundiced eye, may declare their *disbelief* in psi is based on the same source. Irrespective of the veridicality of these self-observations, the fact remains that the paranormal beliefs of members of the general population typically have a far different origin.

Why do people embrace paranormal beliefs? A superficial answer might be that believers have had parapsychological experiences themselves and base their conviction on this evidence (e.g., Coll & Taylor, 2004). Contrary to this view, however, many psi phenomena endorsed by people have not been personally experienced and, further, many disbelievers have had similar experiences, which they have chosen to interpret in non-paranormal terms (Irwin, 1985). Thus, belief may influence (the interpretation of) parapsychological experiences as much as or even more than the reverse.

Another factor to consider is the contribution of sociocultural influences. It seems clear that the *form* of paranormal beliefs held by a person is strongly governed by cultural factors such as socialization within the family, peer group processes, dissemination of paranormal concepts in the media, and (both explicit and implicit) instruction in the context of other social institutions such as schools, the church, and cults (Vyse, 1997). The issue remains, however, as to why a person should be susceptible to these influences, that is, what factors psychologically predispose a person to develop belief in the paranormal. Broadly speaking, there have been two productive approaches to this issue. Each of these will be briefly described and assessed in turn (for a more comprehensive analysis see Irwin, 2009).

The first approach may be dubbed the *cognitive deficits hypothesis* in that it holds the paranormal believer to be illogical, irrational, credulous, and even downright foolish (e.g., Alcock, 1981) or, in less polemical terms, to be characterized by common inherent flaws in their everyday thought processes. Research into paranormal believers' intelligence and reasoning abilities has yet to yield unequivocal support for the cognitive deficits hypothesis, although—rather than reasoning skills—the factor of reasoning *style* is emerging as a key correlate of paranormal belief. Thus, believers often tend to use an experiential-intuitive reasoning style in preference to an analytical-rational one (e.g., Aarnio & Lindeman, 2005) and to reach interpretations of events with insufficient reality testing (Irwin, 2003).

At the same time, it is virtually a psychological axiom that personal beliefs are held because they serve significant psychodynamic needs of the individual. In seeking to understand paranormal belief, some researchers therefore have focused their attention on the psychological functions served by these beliefs. This perspective is known as the *psychodynamic functions hypothesis*. In this context, research suggests a pivotal role is played by a need to feel life events can be within one's capacity to control (Blackmore & Troscianko, 1985), a need that perhaps may be exacerbated by a failure in childhood to establish an adequate sense of autonomous control over life (Watt, Watson, & Wilson, 2007). A person's underlying paranormal beliefs may then be activated by stress evoked by a situation in which the need for control becomes acute (Dudley, 1999; see also Irwin, 2009, for a detailed model of the development of paranormal belief in terms of reasoning style and the need for control).

Parapsychology and Transpersonal Psychology

It is noteworthy that numerous parapsychologists (e.g., Charles Tart, Stanley Krippner, Michael Daniels) are also distinguished transpersonal psychologists. Hartelius, Caplan, and Rardin (2007) conducted a thematic analysis of 160 definitions of transpersonal psychology from 1968 through 2002 collected from the published literature and from colleagues within the field. Three themes emerged from their analysis that broadly capture the fundamental constituents of definitions of transpersonal psychology: (1) beyond-ego, (2) integrative/holistic, and (3) transformative. With regard to (1), the term ego is not being used in the Freudian sense of the mediator between the id and superego. Instead, ego refers to one's individual sense of self with a precise space-time location. Thus, (1) suggests that transpersonal psychology is concerned with experiences whereby one's self-sense transcends the ordinary spatial and temporal limitations (Friedman, 1983). From there, (2) the term integrative/holistic suggests that transpersonal psychology is concerned with the whole person within the context of his/her life-world. Therefore, transpersonal psychologists do not engage in forms of reductionism (e.g., biological), nor do they consider individuals in isolation from their natural world, social group, and so on. As for (3), the term transformative suggests that transpersonal psychologists focus on practices (e.g., meditation) that allow the individual to attain conscious states (e.g., *samadhi*) that are ultimately more positive and meaningful relative to ordinary waking states; it also refers to developmental stages such as self-actualization. Extrapolating from the results of Hartelius et al. (2007), a transpersonal experience is, ultimately, a positive transformative experience characterized by the transcendence of ego.

One particularly useful transpersonal map is Grof's (1975, 1988, 1993) cartography of the transpersonal dimensions of the human psyche. Grof's model includes three transpersonal categories: First, phenomena that take place within consensual space-time reality (i.e., the shared physical universe) but transcend its normal boundaries (i.e., spatial and temporal expansion and contraction). Precognition and retro-cognition involve the transcendence of normal temporal boundaries by allowing one to perceive future events and past events, respectively. Clairvoyance involves the transcendence of normal spatial boundaries by allowing one to perceive a contemporaneous physical event outside the range of one's normal vision. Grof's second category refers to phenomena that take place beyond consensual space-time reality (i.e., in a dimension beyond the physical universe, e.g., the afterlife). Psi experiences that fall into this category include mediumship and NDEs. The final category denotes phenomena of a psychoid nature, whereby the distinction between mind and matter is transcended. Grof (1975, 1988, 1993) has classified micro-PK and macro-PK as psychoid effects. Thus, from Grof's perspective, many transpersonal experiences are psi experiences. However, in Daniels' (2005) view, a psi experience is only transpersonal "if the effect of this experience is in some way to transform the person's sense of self to encompass a wider or deeper reality" (pp. 49-50).

Given the slippery, elusive phenomena investigated by parapsychologists, it is of paramount importance that experimentation is characterized by stringent methodological controls. Consequently, broadly speaking, parapsychologists tend to be extremely good methodologists. In light of Neppe's (2005) contention that parapsychological methodology might serve as a model for other sciences to adopt, coupled with the aforementioned relationship between transpersonal experiences and psi experiences, transpersonal psychology might benefit from a dialogue with parapsychology.

Conclusion

The existence of psi phenomena remains contentious, even among transpersonal psychologists (Krippner & Friedman, 2010). Yet parapsychology has the potential to be one of the most important of all the areas of scientific endeavors (cf. Neppe, 2005). Indeed, an understanding of the nature of psi could have radical philosophical and scientific implications for our current physicalistic worldview. Furthermore, if numerous transpersonal experiences are, in fact, also psi experiences, then parapsychological research has the potential to elucidate the nature of the transpersonal. It is the authors' view that parapsychologists and transpersonal psychologists would benefit from engaging in cross-fertilization of their respective sub-disciplines.

Notes

1. Psi (from the Greek letter Ψ = 'psi') comes from Thouless and Wiesner (1947), who proposed a unitary process underlying ESP and PK (psychokinesis). Paradoxically, they went on to use the Greek symbols Ψ_γ (psi-gamma) and Ψ_κ (psi-kappa) as labels for ESP and PK, respectively, in order to indicate that ESP and PK were "different aspects of one process" (Thouless & Wiesner, 1947, p. 179).
2. Rock and Krippner (2007a, 2007b, 2011a, 2012) argue that "altered states of consciousness" are more accurately referred to as "altered states of phenomenology."
3. Rock and Krippner (2011b) explain that, "shamanism can be described as a body of techniques and activities that supposedly enable its practitioners to access information that is not ordinarily attainable by members of the social group that gave them privileged status. These practitioners use this information in attempts to meet the needs of this group and its members" (p. 7).

References

Aarnio, K., & Lindeman, M. (2005). Paranormal beliefs, education, and thinking styles. *Personality and Individual Differences, 39,* 1227-1236.

Alcock, J. E. (1981). *Parapsychology: Science or magic? A psychological perspective.* Elmsford, NY: Pergamon Press.

Alvarado, C. S. (1998). ESP and altered states of consciousness: An overview of conceptual and research trends. *Journal of Parapsychology, 62,* 27-63.

Beischel, J., Biuso, M., Boccuzzi, M., & Rock, A. (2011, June). *Anomalous information reception by research mediums under quintuple-blind conditions: Can the mind exist without the body?* 30th Annual Meeting of the Society for Scientific Exploration, Boulder, Colorado.

Bem, D. J. (1993). The ganzfeld experiment. *Journal of Parapsychology, 57,* 101-110.

Bem, D. J., & Honorton, C. (1994). Does psi exist? Replicable evidence for an anomalous process of information transfer. *Psychological Bulletin, 115,* 4-18.

Bem, D. J., Palmer, J., & Broughton, R. S. (2001). Updating the ganzfeld database: A victim of its own success? *Journal of Parapsychology, 65,* 207-218.

Blackmore, S., & Troscianko, T. (1985). Belief in the paranormal: Probability judgements, illusory control, and the "chance baseline shift." *British Journal of Psychology, 76,* 459-468.

Braud, W. G. (1978). Psi-conducive conditions: Explorations and interpretations. In B. Shapin & L. Coly (Eds.), *Psi and states of awareness* (pp. 1-34). New York, NY: Parapsychology Foundation.

Braud, W. G. (2002). Psi-favorable conditions. In V. W. Rammohan (Ed.), *New frontiers of human science* (pp. 95-118). Jefferson, NC: McFarland.

Braud, W. (2005). The farther reaches of psi research: Future choices and possibilities. In L. Storm & M. A. Thalbourne (Eds.). (2005). *Parapsychology in the 21st century: Essays on the future of psychical research* (pp. 38-62). Jefferson, NC: McFarland.

Braud, W. G., & Braud, L. W. (1973). Preliminary explorations of psi- conducive states: Progressive muscular relaxation. *Journal of the American Society for Psychical Research, 67,* 27-46.

Braud, W. G., & Braud, L. W. (1974). Further studies of relaxation as a psi-conducive state. *Journal of the American Society for Psychical Research, 68,* 229-245.

Braud, W. G., & Schlitz, M. A. (1991). Consciousness interactions with remote biological systems: Anomalous intentionality effects. *Subtle Energies, 2,* 1-46.

Braude, S. E. (2003). *Immortal remains: The evidence for life after death.* Lanham, MD: Rowman & Littlefield.

Coll, R. K., & Taylor, N. (2004). Probing scientists' beliefs: How open-minded are modern scientists? *International Journal of Science Education, 26,* 757-778.

Daniels, M. (2005). *Shadow, self, spirit: Essays in transpersonal psychology.* Exeter, UK: Imprint Academic.

Dessoir, M. (1889). Die Parapsychologie. *Sphinx, 7,* 341-344.

Dudley, R. T. (1999). The effect of superstitious belief on performance following an unsolvable problem. *Personality and Individual Differences, 26,* 1057-1064.

Fontana, D. (2005). *Is there an afterlife? A comprehensive overview of the evidence.* Blue Ridge Summit, PA: NBN.

Friedman, H. (1983). The Self-Expansiveness Level Form: A conceptualization and measurement of a transpersonal construct. *Journal of Transpersonal Psychology, 15*(1), 37-50.

Gauld, A. (1983). *Mediumship and survival: A century of investigations.* Chicago, IL: Academy Chicago.

Grof, S. (1975). *Realms of the human unconscious: Observations from LSD research.* New York, NY: Viking Penguin.

Grof, S. (1988). *The adventure of self-discovery.* Albany, NY: State University of New York Press.

Grof, S. (1993). *The holotropic mind: The three levels of human consciousness and how they shape our lives.* New York, NY: Harper Collins.

Hansel, C. E. M. (1980). *ESP and parapsychology: A scientific reevaluation.* Buffalo, NY: Prometheus.

Hartelius, G., Caplan, M., & Rardin, M. A. (2007). Transpersonal psychology: Defining the past, divining the future. *The Humanistic Psychologist, 35*(2), 1-26.

Honorton, C. (1974). State of awareness factors in psi activation. *Journal of the American Society for Psychical Research, 68,* 246-256.

Honorton, C. (1977). Psi and internal attention states. In B. B. Wolman (Ed.), *Handbook of parapsychology* (435-472). New York, NY: Van Nostrand Reinhold.

Honorton, C. (1985). Meta-analysis of psi ganzfeld research: A response to Hyman. *Journal of Parapsychology, 49,* 51-91.

Honorton, C. (1993). Rhetoric over substance: The impoverished state of skepticism. *Journal of Parapsychology, 57,* 191-214.

Honorton, C. (1997). The ganzfeld novice: Four predictors of initial ESP performance. *Journal of Parapsychology, 61,* 143-158.

Honorton, C., & Krippner, S. (1969). Hypnosis and ESP performance: A review of the exper-
    imental literature. *Journal of the American Society for Psychical Research, 63,* 214-252.
Hyman, R. (2010). Meta-analysis that conceals more than it reveals: Comment on Storm et al.
    (2010). *Psychological Bulletin, 136,* 486-490. doi:10.1037/a0019676
Irwin, H. (1979). *Psi and the mind: An information processing approach.* Metuchen, NJ: Scare-
    crow Press.
Irwin, H. J. (1985). A study of the measurement and the correlates of paranormal belief. *Journal
    of the American Society for Psychical Research, 79,* 301-326.
Irwin, H. J. (1994). The phenomenology of parapsychological experiences. In S. Krippner,
    S. Hart, E. Schneck, M. Ullman, & R. O. Becker (Eds.), *Advances in parapsychological
    research.* (Vol. 7, pp. 10-76). Jefferson, NC: McFarland.
Irwin, H. J. (2003). Reality testing and the formation of paranormal beliefs. *European Journal
    of Parapsychology, 18,* 15-27.
Irwin, H. J. (2009). *The psychology of paranormal belief: A researcher's handbook.* Hatfield, UK:
    University of Hertfordshire Press.
Irwin, H. J., & Watt, C. A. (2007). *An introduction to parapsychology* (5th ed.). Jefferson, NC:
    McFarland.
Krippner, S., & Friedman, H. L. (Eds). (2010). *Debating psychic experience: Human potential
    or human illusion?* Santa Barbara, CA: Praeger.
Kumar, V. K., & Pekala, R. (2001). Relation of hypnosis-specific attitudes and behaviors to
    paranormal beliefs and experiences. In J. Houran & R. Lange (Eds.), *Hauntings and
    poltergeists: Multidisciplinary perspectives* (pp. 260-279). Jefferson, NC: McFarland.
Lawrence, T. R. (1993). Gathering in the sheep and goats: A meta-analysis of forced-choice
    sheep-goat ESP studies, 1947-1993. *Proceedings of the 36th Annual Convention of the
    Parapsychological Association,* pp. 75-86.
May, E. C., Utts, J. M., & Spottiswoode, J. P. (1995). Decision augmentation theory: Toward
    a model of anomalous mental phenomena. *Journal of Parapsychology, 59,* 195-220.
McMoneagle, J. (1997). *Mind trek: Exploring consciousness, time, and space through remote
    viewing.* Charlottesville, VA: Hampton Roads.
McMoneagle, J. (2000). *Remote viewing secrets: A handbook.* Charlottesville, VA: Hampton
    Roads.
Milton, J. (1998). A meta-analysis of waking state of consciousness, free-response ESP stud-
    ies. In N. L. Zingrone, M. J. Schlitz, C. S. Alvarado, & J. Milton (Eds.), *Research in
    parapsychology 1993* (pp. 31-34). Lanham, MD: Scarecrow Press.
Milton, J., & Wiseman, R. (1999). Does psi exist? Lack of replication of an anomalous pro-
    cess of information transfer. *Psychological Bulletin, 125*(4), 387-391. doi:10.1037/0033-
    2909.125.4.387
Neppe, V. M. (2005). Why parapsychology is amongst the most important of the sciences.
    Australian Journal of Parapsychology, 5(1), 4-22.
Palmer, J., Khamashta, K., & Israelson, K. (1979). An ESP ganzfeld experiment with tran-
    scendental meditators. *Journal of the American Society for Psychical Research, 73*(4), 333-
    348.
Parker, A. (2005). Psi and altered states of consciousness. In L. Storm & M. A. Thalbourne
    (Eds.), *Parapsychology in the 21st century: Essays on the future of psychical research* (pp.
    65-89). Jefferson, NC: McFarland.
Pekala, R. J., & Cardeña, E. (2000). Methodological issues in the study of altered states
    and anomalous experiences. In E. Cardeña, J. Lynn, & S. Krippner (Eds.), *Varieties of
    anomalous experience* (pp. 47-82). Washington DC: American Psychological Association.
Persinger, M. A. (1975). ELF waves and ESP. *New Horizons, 1*(5), 232-235.

Radin, D. I., & Ferrari, D. C. (1991). Effects of consciousness on the fall of dice: A meta-analysis. *Journal of Scientific Exploration, 5,* 61-83.

Radin, D. I., & Nelson, R. D. (1989). Evidence for consciousness-related anomalies in random physical systems. *Foundations of Physics, 19*(2), 1499-1514.

Radin, D. I., & Nelson, R. D. (2003). Research on mind-matter interaction (MMI): Individual intention. In W. B. Jones & C. C. Crawford (Eds.), *Healing, intention, and energy medicine: Research and clinical implications* (pp. 39-48). Edinburgh, UK: Churchill Livingstone.

Rao, K. R., Dukhan, H., & Rao, P. V. K. (2001). Yogic meditation and psi scoring in forced-choice and free-response tests. In K. Ramakrishna (Ed.), *Basic research in parapsychology* (2nd ed.; pp. 287-306). Jefferson, NC: McFarland.

Rao, K. R., & Puri, I. (1978). Subsensory perception (SSP), extrasensory perception (ESP) and transcendental meditation (TM). *Journal of Indian Psychology, 1,* 69-78.

Rao, P. V. K., & Rao, K. R. (1982). Two studies of ESP and subliminal perception. *Journal of Parapsychology, 46,* 185-208.

Rhine, J. B. (1934). *Extra-sensory perception.* Boston, MA: Bruce Humphries.

Rhine, L. E. (1962). Psychological processes in ESP experiences: Part II. Dreams. *Journal of Parapsychology, 26,* 172-199.

Rock, A. J., & Krippner, S. (2007a). Does the concept of "altered states of consciousness" rest on a mistake? *International Journal of Transpersonal Studies, 26,* 33-40.

Rock, A. J., & Krippner, S. (2007b). Shamanism and the confusion of consciousness with phenomenological content. *North American Journal of Psychology, 9*(3), 485-500.

Rock, A. J., & Krippner, S. (2011a). States of consciousness redefined as patterns of phenomenal properties: An experimental application. In D. Cvetkovic & I. Cosic (Eds.), *States of consciousness: Experimental insights into meditation, waking, sleep and dreams. The Frontiers collection* (pp. 257-278). Paris, France: Springer-Verlag.

Rock, A. J., & Krippner, S. (2011b). *Demystifying shamans and their world: A multi-disciplinary study.* Exeter, UK: Imprint Academic.

Rock, A. J., & Krippner, S. (2012). States of consciousness or states of phenomenology? In A. E. Cavanna & A. Nani (Eds.), Consciousness: States, mechanisms and disorders (pp. 55-65). Hauppauge, NY: Nova Science.

Roney-Dougal, S. M., & Solfvin, J. (2006). Yogic attainment in relation to awareness of precognitive targets. *Journal of Parapsychology, 70*(1), 91-120.

Schmidt, H. (1975). Toward a mathematical theory of psi. *Journal of the American Society for Psychical Research, 69,* 301-319.

Schouten, S. A. (1993). Applied parapsychology studies of psychics and healers. *Journal of Scientific Exploration, 7*(4), 375-401.

Schouten, S. A. (1994). An overview of quantitatively evaluated studies with mediums and psychics. *Journal of the American Society for Psychical Research, 88,* 221-254.

Schwartz, S. (1983). Preliminary report on a prototype applied parapsychological methodology for utilization in archaeology, with a case report. In W. G. Roll, R. L Morris, & R. White (Eds.). *Research in parapsychology 1981* (pp. 25-27). Metuchen, NJ: Scarecrow.

Schwartz, S. (2000). *The Alexandria project.* New York, NY: The Author's Guild.

Schwartz, S. (2005). *The secret vaults of time.* Charlottesville, VA: Hampton Roads.

Stanford, R. G. (1974a). An experimentally testable model for spontaneous psi events. I. Extrasensory events. *Journal of the American Society for Psychical Research, 68,* 34-57.

Stanford, R. G. (1974b). An experimentally testable model for spontaneous psi events. II. Psychokinetic events. *Journal of the American Society for Psychical Research, 68,* 321-356.

Stanford, R. G., & Stein, A. G. (1994). A meta-analysis of ESP studies contrasting hypnosis and a comparison condition. *Journal of Parapsychology, 58,* 235-269.

Steinkamp, F. (2005). Forced-choice ESP experiments: Their past and their future. In L. Storm & M. A. Thalbourne (Eds.). *Parapsychology in the 21st century: Essays on the future of psychical research* (pp. 124-163). Jefferson, NC: McFarland.

Steinkamp, F., Milton, J., & Morris, R. L. (1998). A meta-analysis of forced-choice experiments comparing clairvoyance and precognition. *Journal of Parapsychology, 62,* 193-218.

Storm, L. (2006). Meta-analysis in parapsychology: II. Psi domains other than ganzfeld. *Australian Journal of Parapsychology, 6,* 135-155.

Storm, L., & Ertel, S. (2001). Does psi exist? Comments on Milton and Wiseman's (1999) meta-analysis of ganzfeld research. *Psychological Bulletin, 127,* 424-433.

Storm, L., & Rock, A. J. (2009a). Imagery cultivation vs. noise reduction: Shamanic-like journeying as a psi-conducive alternative to the ganzfeld protocol. *Australian Journal of Parapsychology, 9*(1), 5-31.

Storm, L., & Rock, A. J. (2009b). Shamanic-like journeying and psi: I. Imagery cultivation, paranormal belief, and the picture-identification task. *Australian Journal of Parapsychology, 9*(2), 165-191.

Storm, L., & Rock, A. J. (2011). *Shamanism and psi: Imagery cultivation as an alternative to the ganzfeld protocol.* Adelaide, Australia: Hyde Park Press.

Storm, L., & Thalbourne, M. A. (2000). A paradigm shift away from the ESP-PK dichotomy: The theory of psychopraxia. *Journal of Parapsychology, 64,* 279-300.

Storm, L., & Thalbourne, M. A. (2001). Paranormal effects using sighted and vision-impaired participants in a quasi-ganzfeld task. *Australian Journal of Parapsychology, 1,* 133-170.

Storm, L., Tressoldi, P. E., & Di Risio, L. (2010a). A meta-analysis with nothing to hide: Reply to Hyman (2010). *Psychological Bulletin, 136*(4), 491-494. doi:10.1037/a0019840.

Storm, L., Tressoldi, P. E., & Di Risio, L. (2010b). Meta-analyses of free-response studies 1992-2008: Assessing the noise reduction model in parapsychology. *Psychological Bulletin, 136*(4), 471-485. doi:10.1037/a0019457.

Sudduth, M. (2009). Super-psi and the survivalist interpretation of mediumship. *Journal of Scientific Exploration, 23,* 167-193.

Thalbourne, M. A. (2003). *A glossary of terms used in parapsychology.* Charlottesville, VA: Puente Publications.

Thalbourne, M. A. (2004). *The common thread between ESP and PK.* New York, NY: Parapsychology Foundation.

Thouless, R. H., & Wiesner, B. P. (1947). The psi process in normal and "paranormal" psychology. *Proceedings of the Society for Psychical Research, 48,* 177-196. (Abridged version published in *Journal of Parapsychology,* 1948, *12,* 192-212)

Ullman, M., Krippner, S., & Vaughan, A. (1974). *Dream telepathy.* Baltimore, MD: Penguin Books.

Vyse, S. A. (1997). *Believing in magic: The psychology of superstition.* New York, NY: Oxford University Press.

Wasserman, G. D. (1956). An outline of a field theory of organismic form and behavior. In G. E. Wolstenholme & E.C.P. Millar (Eds.), *Ciba Foundation symposium on extrasensory perception* (pp. 53-72). Boston, MA: Little, Brown.

Watt, C., Watson, S., & Wilson, L. (2007). Cognitive and psychological mediators of anxiety: Evidence from a study of paranormal belief and perceived childhood control. *Personality & Individual Differences, 43,* 335-343.

Zusne, L., & Jones, W. H. (1982). *Anomalistic psychology: A study of extraordinary phenomena of behaviour and experience.* Hillsdale, NJ: Erlbaum Associates.

Part V

Transpersonal Approaches to Transformation, Healing and Wellness

23

Transpersonal Perspectives on Mental Health and Mental Illness

Jacob Kaminker and David Lukoff

A distinctive feature of transpersonal psychology is its attention to and acceptance of non-ordinary states of consciousness, including spiritual crises. A medical model of mental health often pathologizes such states without discernment, potentially stigmatizing unique but potentially meaningful experiences that fall outside of consensus reality. While the importance of spirituality to mental health is gaining recognition, as evidenced by the wide acceptance of the recovery model (Surgeon General, 1999), there is a still much progress to be made.

Transpersonal psychology recognizes the significant evidence that many of these states of consciousness are not only quite common in the population at large (Gallup, 2002), but often lead to greater realization of human potential (Lukoff, 2007). Knowledge of such experiences, as well as of religious and spiritual diversity issues, can be considered a necessity for clinicians in order to for them to offer appropriate guidance to clients, and also to raise awareness of their own biases and thereby limit the impact that these biases might otherwise have (O'Connor & Vandenberg, 2005).

This chapter offers a transpersonal perspective on non-ordinary states of consciousness as they relate to mental health. This entails a discussion of the commonalities and differences among transpersonal theorists on the nature of extraordinary human states, as well as on how a transpersonal view relates to mainstream psychology. The discussion is framed within a clinical perspective that allows for the diversity of human experience.

Pathologizing Spirituality

The mental health professions have a long history of ignoring and pathologizing religion and spirituality in all forms (Lukoff, Lu, & Turner, 1992). For instance, Sigmund Freud described religion as an obsessional neurosis (Freud, 1927/1989), and

The Wiley Blackwell Handbook of Transpersonal Psychology, First Edition.
Edited by Harris L. Friedman and Glenn Hartelius.
© 2013 John Wiley & Sons, Ltd. Published 2015 by John Wiley & Sons, Ltd.

Albert Ellis (1980) asserted that "the less religious [patients] are, the more emotionally healthy they will tend to be" (p. 637). These statements exemplify what has been a general dismissiveness towards religiosity throughout the history of psychology. There has also been a strong tendency to pathologize extraordinary human experiences. Although the intention of diagnosis is to provide structure and comfort, the result is often to the contrary. According to James Nelson (2009),

> While a view of mental disorder as illness was designed to remove guilt and restore the dignity of people with problems, in fact it dehumanizes them, picturing individuals as pathological or underdeveloped and in need of outside manipulation from an expert. (p. 349)

This trend is slowly transforming. Beginning in the 1990s and with increasing vigor, mainstream psychology has begun to recognize the relationship between spirituality and mental health (Nolan, Dew, & Koenig, 2011). However, the focus of research has largely been on the connection between spirituality and the "less debilitating mental illnesses such as depression and anxiety," while "severe mental conditions such as chronic psychosis are rarely examined" (p. 384). One result of this omission is a lack of attention to the potential risks and benefits of non-ordinary states, including both those fostered through spiritual practice and spontaneous states. According to a review of the literature,

> reasons for this deficit may include: the belief that religion or spirituality are part of the pathology of mental illness...; lack of interest in or education about religion and spirituality among mental health professionals...; and possible competition for clients, as both clergy and mental health professionals are experts on human suffering. (Nolan et al., 2011, p. 386)

These gaps in the literature are unfortunate in light of the commonness of such experiences. Surveys have consistently found that over one-third of the people in the United States report intense religious experiences that in some sense lifted them outside of themselves (cf. Greeley, 1974; Hay & Morisy, 1978). Another study by David Yamane and Megan Polzer (1994) found that about one half of Americans surveyed had experienced religiously-related ecstasy, with significant differences in percentage based on denomination, region, and race. These differences can likely be accounted for by the diversity of goals in spiritual practices and of the language for describing the experiences. In any case, the overwhelming evidence points to the commonality of perceiving something that was understood to be outside of oneself.

In addition, much of the scripture throughout world religions contains descriptions of prophets whose experiences of ecstasy and religious experiences contained visions and imagery, which some mental health professionals may erringly diagnose as pathological. Auditory and visual hallucinations have played an essential role in religion for thousands of years. Accounts range from Biblical prophets and saints to shamans, as well as the famous Daemon voice guide of Socrates. Modern psychiatrists have retroactively diagnosed all of them as having had mental disorders (Leuder & Thomas, 2000).

The *DSM-IV-TR* (American Psychiatric Association, 2000) specifically notes that clinicians assessing for schizophrenia in socioeconomic or cultural situations different from their own must take cultural differences into account: "In some cultures, visual or auditory hallucinations with a religious content may be a normal part of religious experience (e.g., seeing the Virgin Mary or hearing God's voice)" (American Psychiatric Association, 2000, p. 306). For example, in a study of visual hallucinations among Hispanic clinic patients, Juan Lata (2005) found that phenomena typically deemed as psychotic may occur in connection with spiritual experiences. Common examples include visions of loved ones, saints, angels, Jesus, and Mary.

Transcending Egoic Boundaries

This potential for pathologizing non-ordinary experiences, despite content and outcome, derives from the commonalities between transpersonal phenomena and psychosis as well as some dissociative diagnoses. One reason for these commonalities is the shared characteristic of transcending of the usual boundaries of the self. Creative pursuits and spiritual practices represent attempts to willingly deconstruct or transcend the normal boundaries of the self for the purpose of psychospiritual growth or new creative possibilities (Akkach, 1997; Peters, 1989; Swan, 2008).

Throughout recorded history, there have been accounts of the muse in the creative process (Nachmanovitch, 1991) and spiritual traditions have described the transcending of ego boundaries in the forms of spontaneous visions or revelations (Kornfield, 1993), psychic experiences (Caplan, 1999), and spiritual awakenings such as kundalini experiences (Sovatsky, 1999). Popular culture, spiritual communities, and many notable figures from the artistic and literary worlds have acknowledged both the frequency and the potential benefits of transcending egoic boundaries. Transpersonal psychology attempts to reconcile the differences between the long history of spiritual wisdom and modern science. Newberg, d'Aquili, and Rause (2001) have even gone so far as to suggest that the need to transcend the self is a basic neurobiological need. This can be experienced as euphoric and transcendent, or it can be terrifying when it is experienced as a sort of death of the acquired sense of self.

Research has shown that spirituality helps to foster coping skills, which, in turn, improves prognosis for people with schizophrenia (Shah et al., 2011). One explanation for this phenomenon is that spirituality provides a roadmap for the unknown territory beyond the individual human experience. In other words, it helps to make sense of the realms glimpsed through psychosis and may provide a structure for reintegration. In this regard, it is particularly helpful to understand spirituality in its diversity, since traditions that are unfamiliar may be more readily pathologized.

Diversity Issues

While diversity issues have become a mainstay in clinical theory, the recognition of spiritual diversity issues by the psychological community has lagged behind. Chad Johnson and Harris Friedman (2008) have pointed out that the values of the clinician weigh heavily on differential diagnosis of these issues. Issues that are likely to impact diagnosis of mystical experiences include clinician theoretical orientation and openness to spirituality (Allman, De La Roche, Elkins, & Weathers, 1992). According to David Greenberg and Eliezer Witztum (1991), therapists can only responsibly diagnose clients after becoming familiar with their religious tradition.

A study by Shawn O'Connor and Brian Vandenberg (2005) presented clinical vignettes to 110 mental health professionals from a variety of settings. Each vignette represented a client from a different religious denomination, namely Catholic, Mormon, and Nation of Islam. Participants were randomly assigned to one of four conditions, each with slightly different vignette packets. In each, "the religious beliefs of the individuals in the vignettes were identified as either being integral to a religious tradition or not and also as either resulting in a threat to harm another or not" (O'Connor & Vandenberg, 2005, p. 610). They found that "nonreligious clinicians may be more likely to impute pathology to religious ideation than religious clinicians" (p. 613). In addition, pathology rating were significantly higher for the Nation of Islam vignette than the Mormon and higher for the Mormon that the Catholic. What the researchers termed "beliefs not explicitly identified as belonging to an established religion" were considered significantly more pathological (p. 613). Finally, and more clinically appropriately, when the vignettes included harmful consequences, ratings of pathology were higher. The results of this study demonstrate the effect on clinician bias with regard towards more culturally marginal religious traditions as well as towards unfamiliar presentations of spirituality.

Transpersonal Perspectives on Mental Health

Some transpersonally-oriented treatment centers have focused on the ability of the client to make meaning of the experience. Victor Frankl (1959/1984), one of the intellectual forefathers of transpersonal psychology, believed that meaning-making is a distinctly human characteristic that allows us to triumph in the face of suffering. His own discoveries on this subject developed during his internment in a Nazi concentration camp. One of Abraham Maslow's (1969) major contributions to the field is the concept of self-transcendence, which he understood in his later years as being at the top of the developmental hierarchy of needs. Some of the states experienced in spiritual practice, including those with psychotic features, can help to foster this stage of self-transcendence. These two contributions from Frankl (1959/1984) and Maslow (1969) can be understood as creating the foundation for transpersonal psychology's perspective on non-ordinary states.

Freud (1930/1961) influenced modern psychology's explanation of mystical states by reducing them to an "oceanic experience" marked by "infantile helplessness" and a "regression to primary narcissism" (p. 21). In contrast to Freud, other theorists have opened the door to viewing mystical experiences as a sign of health and a powerful agent of transformation, including Carl Jung (1952a) and Evelyn Underhill (1955). Additionally, studies have found that people reporting mystical experiences scored lower on psychopathology scales and higher on measures of psychological well-being than controls (Hood, 1974; Hood, Hill, & Spilka, 2009). Within transpersonal psychology, there are various understandings of the nature of non-ordinary states of consciousness. Each understanding has different implications for the understanding of mental health and mental illness, especially when it comes to the nature of regressive states, the linear nature of spiritual growth, and how to relate to the mainstream forces of the medical model of mental health.

Of the theorists who can be identified as transpersonal, some descend from the Jungian tradition and believe that something essential is being discovered through regressive states (Jung, 1952b). Roberto Assagioli (1965/1989), Jung's contemporary, also noticed the link between transpersonal experiences and the healing of trauma through regressive states. Stanislav Grof and Christina Grof (2010) joined them in recognizing the healing power of regression. They developed *holotropic breathwork* practices designed to invoke these states in the interest of transformation. Michael Washburn (1994), who has identified with the psychodynamic tradition, has called this type of pursuit "regression in the service of transcendence" (p. 242). From this perspective, it is important to explore regressive states with awareness in order to heal trauma and to grow spiritually.

Ken Wilber (1980) has argued that this prizing of regressive states reflects a *pre/trans fallacy*, one that erroneously understands regressive, or pre-personal states as offering spiritual wisdom in the same way as transpersonal states. Although Wilber validly points to the need for discrimination in the valuing of non-ordinary states, a number of scholars have argued against the notion that lines can be drawn so simply (Grof, 1998; Schavrien, 2008; Taylor, 2009; Washburn, 1998). More practical distinctions may emerge as the study of non-ordinary states matures.

R. Elliot Ingersol (2002) has suggested an integral approach to diagnosis that avoids the "disease model" in the *DSM* (p. 115) and instead looks at consciousness through Wilber's (1995) All Quadrants All Levels (AQAL) model. This model views consciousness through four quadrants, with each being focused either internally or externally and either individual or collective. The interior-individual (I) quadrant contains subjective experience, interior-collective (we) represents paradigms and cultures, exterior individual (it) describes the brain and physical body, and exterior-collective (its) includes government, social systems, and the physical environment (Wilber, 2007). Within each are developmental levels that describe the evolution of the human, societal, or cosmic dimensions of each quadrant. This model comes from Wilber's understanding of the commonalities between spiritual traditions and models of consciousness. Washburn (2003) has described this view as *structural-hierarchal* in that it "stresses a hierarchy of achieved structural abilities and capacities" (p. 1).

Phenomenological approaches, such as those of William James (1902/1958), Edmund Husserl (1913/1931), and Ron Valle (1998) focus on the structure of experience in transpersonal phenomena. Attention is directed towards the lived experience, as free as possible from interpretation or metaphysical assumptions. Rather than seeking objectivity, this approach denies that unmediated experience of an external material world is possible, because subjectivity shapes every perception (Polkinghorne, 1989). The empirical focus of inquiry then shifts from observing the material world to observing experience itself as it were, focusing on subjectivity rather than objectivity. Within transpersonal psychology, this has expressed itself as an ongoing interest in examining and describing inner subjective experience in the way that attempts to parallel how traditional science describes outer objects and events (e.g., Tart, 2004; Welwood, 1979; cf. Ruzek, 2007). This stance developed in response to the fact that much of mainstream psychology has dismissed consciousness and experience as valid objects of study (cf. Tart, 2004), especially in earlier decades. The interest in subjective experience, shared by humanistic psychology, has represented a significant contribution to the larger field.

Yet examining human experience within the subjective category it was assigned by science created its own set of problems that early transpersonal scholarship at times overlooked: Accepting the subject-object divide of modernist thought placed transpersonal research in a scientifically indefensible position. In response to this dilemma, Jorge Ferrer (2000, 2002) proposed that the transpersonal field rely instead on participatory thought (Skolimowski, 1994; Tarnas, 1991), which challenges the notion of dividing reality into categories of subject and object. In Ferrer's (2000; Ferrer & Sherman, 2008) participatory view, transpersonal states and spiritual experiences are transforming encounters with the world, not private delusions. Because these events are not intrapsychic or confined to an individual, but rather transcend subject-object dualism, this approach allows such events as the auditory hallucinations of schizophrenia to be reframed as potentially meaningful encounters—either with repressed or dissociated parts of the psyche, or, in a Jungian sense, with aspects of the collective unconscious (Suri, 2011).

David Lukoff (2011) has advocated integrating acceptance of spirituality into the mainstream by depathologizing extraordinary human experiences whenever possible. This does not mean that spiritual and religious problems do not require clinical attention, but rather that it is important to diagnose the problem correctly, so as to encourage potential psychospiritual growth and to avoid attaching undue stigma or unnecessary psychopharmacological intervention.

In recent history, one of the most significant shifts on this issue in the mental health field has been marked by the addition to the *DSM-IV* of the V-code for Religious and Spiritual Problems. The acceptance of this new category by the American Psychiatric Association Task Force on *DSM-IV* was based on a proposal documenting the extensive literature on the frequent occurrence of religious and spiritual issues in clinical practice, the lack of training provided to mental health professionals, and the need for a diagnostic category to support training and research in this area of clinical practice (Lukoff et al., 1992). Lukoff, Francis Lu, and C. Paul Yang (2010) have proposed the following categories based on a review of the literature:

- Religious problems
  - Loss or questioning of faith
  - Changes in membership, practices, and beliefs (including conversion)
  - New Religious Movements and cults
  - Life-threatening and terminal illness
- Spiritual problems
  - Anomalous experiences (i.e., mystical experiences, near-death experiences, psychic experiences and alien abduction experiences)
  - Meditation and spiritual practice-related experiences
  - Possession experiences

Regardless of the belief of the mental health professional in the validity of these anomalous phenomena, studies have shown that experients show physiological reactions when describing the phenomena that demonstrate the subjective truth of the experience (Cardeña, Lynn, & Krippner, 2002; McNally et al., 2004). Therefore, the appropriate therapeutic stance is to respect this subjective experience and treat the resultant trauma and help the experient to integrate the insights. Among the most commonly described phenomena in transpersonal psychology that requires this therapeutic stance is the spiritual emergency.

Spiritual Emergency

Spiritual emergency must be differentiated from *spiritual emergence* in that the latter involves a slower integration of a spiritual experience into the worldview, whereas the former comes in the form of a crisis, a sudden explosion of consciousness that often resembles psychosis (Grof & Grof, 1992). A vivid demonstration of spiritual emergency comes in the form of Lukoff's (1991) self-case study. At 23 years of age, Lukoff experienced a spiritual emergency that met the *DSM-II* criteria in effect at the time for an Acute Schizophrenic Episode and meets the *DSM-IV* criteria for a Hallucinogen-induced Delusional Disorder.

For two months, Lukoff (1991) was convinced that he had uncovered the secrets of the cosmos, and that he was both Buddha and Christ in a new reincarnation. This was triggered by taking LSD for the first time. He described how the experience began:

> I awoke just after midnight. Although I had slept for only two hours, I felt rested—in fact, I was full of energy and eager to get back to writing in my journal. But first a quick trip to the bathroom. While there, I stopped in front of the mirror and gazed at my reflection. Suddenly I noticed that my right hand was glowing, giving off a white light. My thumb was touching my forefinger in the ancient mudra position of the meditating Buddha. Immediately the meaning of this sign was clear to me: I had been Buddha in a previous life. Then another thought came: Buddha had been reincarnated as Jesus Christ. Therefore, I had also been Jesus Christ. Now, in this moment, the luminous image in the mirror was awakening me to my true purpose: to once again bring the human race out of its decline. My journal writing was actually the creation a "new Bible," a Holy Book which would unite all people around the common tenants of a single belief system. Instead of unifyng just one social group, as Buddha and Christ had, my mission was to write a book that would create a new worldwide society free of conflict and full of loving relationships. (p. 25)

During the most acute stage, which lasted a week, he slept little and held conversations with the "spirits" of eminent thinkers in the social sciences and humanities. He had discussions with contemporary persons including R. D. Laing, Margaret Mead, and Bob Dylan, as well as individuals no longer living, such as Jean-Jacques Rousseau, Freud, Jung, and—of course—the Buddha and Christ. Based on these conversations, he produced a 47-page "Holy Book" that he expected would unite all the peoples of the world in the project of designing a new society. He sent xeroxed copies to friends and family so that they too could be enlightened.

As the grandiosity began to fade over the next two months, Lukoff began to read Jung and Joseph Campbell to find some perspectives on his experience. Then he spent four and a half years in Jungian analysis and also worked with Wallace Black Elk, a Lakota Medicine Man, to integrate the experience and incorporate it into his personal mythology. He finished his graduate studies in clinical psychology and now understands this experience as a form of a shamanic initiatory crisis. Today, he is a leading voice in the movement to bring awareness to the spiritual benefits of these states and to reform the pathologization of spirituality in mental health. If he had been directed to a medical model mental health practitioner at the time, it is likely that his life would have taken a very different turn, possibly involving medication and hospitalization.

Differential Diagnosis

Paul Jerry (2003) has pointed out that "diagnosis is a dynamic and on-going process with revisions and changes occurring throughout the therapeutic process," but that differential diagnosis is essential before prescribing treatment. According to him, "one would likely intervene with medication and hospitalization for the psychotic, a course of treatment that could be disastrous for the transcending client" (p. 45). However, researchers such as John Perry (1974), Loren Mosher and Alma Menn (1979), and John Bola and Mosher (2003), have demonstrated the effective treatment of psychosis with limited psychopharmacological intervention, through helping clients to make meaning of their experiences.

It is also necessary to rule out any substance-related causes including intoxication and withdrawal. Differential diagnosis between a substance-induced experience and a psychotic break is also important, as there are both similarities and differences (Nelson & Sass, 2008). Although differential diagnosis with substances is important, clinical trials of psilocybin, the active ingredient in hallucinogenic mushrooms, have shown lasting positive effects similar to that of a mystical experience (Griffiths, Johnson, Richards, McCann, & Jesse, 2011). In light of this data, the value of a substance-induced experience should not be disregarded though abuse or dependency on the given substance should be assessed.

Pathological and spiritual experiences cannot be always distinguished from each other in form or content, but need to be assessed in the light of the values and beliefs of the individual, as well as the social context. Similarities exist between transpersonal experiences and pathological experiences, but there are diagnostic features that necessitate different case conceptualizations and clinical interventions. However, Johnson and Friedman (2008) have pointed out that psychopathology generally has higher levels of decompensation and terror than mystical experience.

Lukoff (2005) has presented criteria for differential diagnosis between what he has called visionary spiritual experience (VSE) and psychotic disorders. Unlike psychotic disorders, VSEs have "good pre-episode functioning, acute onset of symptoms during a period of three months or less, [a] stressful precipitant to the psychotic episode, [and] a positive, exploratory attitude toward the experience" (Lukoff, 2005, p. 242). Further, a VSE must be without "significant risk for homicidal or suicidal behavior," and typically includes "ecstatic mood, a sense of newly gained knowledge, and delusions with spiritual themes (which most psychotic disorders do not include)" (Phillips, Lukoff, & Stone, 2009, p. 8).

Aside from diagnosing experiences, another dimension of differential diagnosis is religious pathology. Some theorists have formalized their observations into diagnostic models (Spero, 1985; Lovinger, 1996). The primary themes of these models can be simplified into highlighting how much the client's spirituality brings them hope over despair and helps them connect, rather than distance themselves from others and from life.

Treatment

In treatment, Jerry (2003) has observed that it is first important to ask whether the transpersonal material is being pursued for the therapist's interest or whether it is central to the client's goals in therapy. If it is important to the therapy, there are two questions in treatment planning: (1) "how do the clients' psychological/characterological structures of personality affect their interpretation of the experience?" (Jerry, 2003, p. 50), and (2):

> given the constellation of symptoms, interpretations and orientation to the experience, which of these psychological distortions will become the grist for the therapeutic mill? In other words, having a sense of the nature of the reaction to the experience (say, paranoia), will this become the focus of therapy because it is the most likely to transform itself (say from paranoia to security)? (p. 51)

Some residential treatment approaches have addressed the spiritual dimensions of psychosis. Perry (1974), who founded Diabysis, a Jungian-oriented group treatment home for people experiencing a first psychotic episode, found themes including the destruction of the world, a cosmic fight between good and evil, the appearance of a messiah that the client identifies with, and a sense of a rebirth of the world into a more loving place. Perry encouraged clients to express and explore the symbolic aspects of their psychotic experiences. Therapy, conducted thrice weekly, consisted of listening to clients and helping them to interpret the powerful and spiritual symbols within their hallucinations and delusions. Medications were rarely used. Perry reported that severely psychotic clients became coherent within two to six days without medication. The outcomes appeared better for those who had had fewer than three previous psychotic episodes. Diabysis closed down in 1980 due to budget cutbacks in the mental health system.

A similar program, Soteria House, located in San Jose, California, provided more empirical support for this model (Mosher & Menn, 1978). Soteria House ran from 1971 to 1983, roomed six clients, with three to four staff on the premises at one time. The staff was trained to view psychotic experiences as a developmental stage that can lead to growth, and that often contain a spiritual component of mystical experiences and beliefs. Medication was typically not prescribed unless a client showed no improvement after six weeks (only 10% of clients used medication at Soteria), because it was believed to stunt the possible growth-enhancing process of the psychotic episode (Mosher & Menn, 1979).

Outcomes from Soteria were compared to a traditional program: a community mental health center inpatient service consisting of daily pharmacotherapy, psychotherapy, occupational therapy, and group therapy (Mosher, Menn, & Mathews, 1975). Clients' length of stay was longer at Soteria than in the comparison program (mean of 166 days versus 28 days), but most patients recovered in six to eight weeks without medication (Mosher, Hendrix, & Fort, 2004). A recent meta-analysis of data from two carefully controlled studies of Soteria programs found better two-year outcomes for Soteria patients in the domains of psychopathology, work, and social functioning compared with similar clients treated in a psychiatric hospital (Bola & Mosher, 2003).

Lukoff led the development of a holistic program for patients with diagnoses of schizophrenia that addressed the spiritual side of their lives (Lukoff, Wallace, Liberman, & Burke, 1986). He contrasted the effectiveness of a 12-week holistic health program with a social skills training group, randomly assigning inpatients at a state mental hospital to either treatment. The holistic program consisted of 20 minutes each of daily yoga and meditation. Clients also attended a weekly "Growth and Schizophrenia" session examining the positive, and especially the spiritual dimensions of their hallucinations and delusions. Overall, the study provided some support to the idea that spiritual interventions can be used in persons with schizophrenia without causing harm, and with possible benefits.

Conclusion

With its focus on describing symptoms and making diagnoses, the medical model of psychology leads anomalous or non-ordinary human experiences to become pathologized. Many of these states of consciousness can be better understood as the transcending of egoic boundaries, bringing both risks and benefits. With a therapeutic focus on helping the client to make meaning of the experience, clients can show improvement in many areas, even when compared to their pre-episodic functioning.

Diagnosis is a crucial first step in treatment planning. Differential diagnosis should discern substance-induced, psychotic, and dissociative states from spiritual problems. These need to be diagnosed with attention to the clients' values, beliefs, and social context. Treatment of psychosis without medication is often possible in a highly controlled environment, but the support does not currently exist for these types of facilities. Greater public awareness of the efficacy of this approach should foster both the perceived need for and funding of this type of treatment center.

Knowledge of religious and spiritual beliefs and practices is an important diversity issue in clinical practice. It is crucial for clinicians to familiarize themselves with their clients' religious and spiritual problems, religious traditions, and spiritual practices in order to avoid bias and to help them utilize their experience in service of psychospiritual growth. As the mental health community is beginning to accept the importance of these issues to clients, clinical training programs should incorporate more education on these topics.

Given their potential for enhancing well-being and their known pitfalls, spiritual practices should be more central to the field of psychology for understanding of the mind, psychospiritual development, and mental health. Future research can focus on the risks and benefits of specific practices in the context of traditional spiritual wisdom.

The *DSM-IV* V-code for Spiritual and Religious Problems has expanded public consciousness of spiritual diversity issues in clinical practice and has guided clinicians on how to approach these common human experiences. Further popular acceptance would allow for these issues to be acknowledged as primary, rather than secondary reasons for seeking treatment.

References

Akkach, S. (1997). The world of imagination in Ibn Arabi's ontology. *British Journal of Middle Eastern Studies, 24*(1), 97-113.

Allman, L. S., De La Roche, O., Elkins, D. N., & Weathers, R. S. (1992). Psychotherapists' attitudes towards clients reporting mystical experiences. *Psychotherapy, 29*, 564-569.

American Psychiatric Association. (2000). *Diagnostic and statistical manual* (4th ed., text rev.). Washington, DC: Author.

Assagioli, R. (1989). Self-realization and psychological disturbances. In S. Grof & C. Grof (Eds.), *Spiritual emergency: When personal transformation becomes a crisis* (pp. 27-48). Los Angeles, CA: Tarcher. (Original work published 1965)

Bola, J. R., & Mosher, L. R. (2003). Treatment of acute psychosis without neuroleptics: Two-year outcomes from the Soteria project. *Journal of Nervous and Mental Disease, 6*, 219-229.

Caplan, M. (1999). *Halfway up the mountain: The error of premature claims to enlightenment.* Prescott, AZ: Hohm Press.

Cardeña, E., Lynn, S., & Krippner, S. (Eds.). (2002). *Varieties of anomalous experience: Examining the scientific evidence.* Washington, DC: American Psychological Association.

Ellis, A. (1980). Psychotherapy and atheistic values: A response to A. E. Bergin's psychotherapy and religious issues. *Journal of Consulting and Clinical Psychology, 6*, 635-639.

Ferrer, J. N. (2000) Transpersonal knowledge: A participatory approach to transpersonal phenomena. In T. Hart, P. Nelson, & K. Puhakka (Eds.), *Transpersonal knowing: Exploring the horizon of consciousness* (pp. 213-252). Albany, NY: State University of New York Press.

Ferrer, J. N. (2002). *Revisioning transpersonal theory: A participatory vision of human spirituality.* Albany, NY: State University of New York Press.

Ferrer, J. N., & Sherman, J. H. (2008). *The participatory turn: Spirituality, mysticism, religious studies.* Albany, NY: State University of New York Press.

Frankl, V. E. (1984). *Man's search for meaning.* New York, NY: Washington Square Press (Original work published 1959).

Freud, S. (1961). *Civilization and its discontents.* New York, NY: W. W. Norton. (Original work published 1930)

Freud, S. (1989). *The future of an illusion.* New York, NY: W. W. Norton. (Original work published 1927)

Gallup, G. (2002). *The 2001 Gallup poll: Public opinion.* Lanham, MD: Rowman & Littlefield.

Greeley, A. (1974). *Ecstasy: A way of knowing.* Englewood Cliffs, NJ: Prentice Hall.

Greenberg, D., & Witztum, E. (1991). Problems in the treatment of religious patients. *American Journal of Psychotherapy, 45*, 554-565.

Griffiths, R. R., Johnson, M. W., Richards, B. D., McCann, U., & Jesse, R. (2011). Psilocybin occasioned mystical-type experiences: Immediate and persisting dose-related effects. *Psychopharmacology, 218*(4), 649-665.

Grof, S. (1998). Ken Wilber's spectrum psychology: Observations from clinical consciousness research. In D. Rothberg & S. Kelly (Eds.), *Ken Wilber in dialogue: Conversations with leading transpersonal thinkers* (pp. 85-116). Wheaton, IL: Theosophical.

Grof, S., & Grof, C. (1992). *The stormy search for self: A guide to personal growth through transformational crisis.* New York: Tarcher.

Grof, S., & Grof, C. (2010). *Holotropic breathwork: A new approach to self exploration and therapy.* Albany, NY: State University of New York Press.

Hay, D., & Morisy, A. (1978). Reports of ecstatic, paranormal, or religious experience in Great Britain and the United States: A comparison of trends. *Journal for the Scientific Study of Religion, 17*(3), 255-268.

Hood, R. (1974). Psychological strength and the report of intense religious experience. *Journal for the Scientific Study of Religion, 13*(1), 65-71.

Hood, R. W., Hill, P. C., & Spilka, B. (2009). *The psychology of religion: An empirical approach* (4th ed.). New York, NY: Guilford.

Husserl, E. (1931). *Ideas towards a pure phenomenology and phenomenological philosophy.* New York, NY: Humanities. (Original work published 1913)

Ingersoll, R. E. (2002). An integral approach for teaching and practicing diagnosis. *Journal of Transpersonal Psychology, 34*(2), 115-116.

James, W. (1958). *The varieties of religious experience.* New York, NY: New American Library of World Literature. (Original work published 1902)

Jerry, P. (2003) Challenges in transpersonal diagnosis. *Journal of Transpersonal Psychology, 35*(1), 43-59.

Johnson, C. V., & Friedman, H. L. (2008). Enlightened or delusional? Differentiating religious, spiritual, and transpersonal experiences from psychopathology. *Journal of Humanistic Psychology, 48*(4), 505-527.

Jung, C. G. (1952a). *Psychology and religion* (R. F. C. Hull, Trans.). In *The collected works of C. G. Jung* (Vol. 1). Princeton, NJ: Princeton University Press.

Jung, C. G. (1952b). *Symbols of transformation* (R. F. C. Hull, Trans.). In *The collected works of C. G. Jung* (Vol. 5). Princeton, NJ: Princeton University Press.

Kornfield, J. (1993). *A path with heart: A guide through the perils and promises of spiritual life.* New York, NY: Bantam.

Lata, J. (2005). *Visual hallucinations in Hispanic clinic patients: A need to assess for cultural beliefs.* San Juan, Puerto Rico: Carlos Albizu University.

Leuder, I., & Thomas, P. (2000). *Voices of reason, voices of insanity.* Philadelphia, PA: Routledge.

Lovinger, R. J. (1996). Considering the religious dimension in assessment and treatment. In E. P. Shafranske (Ed.), *Religion and the clinical practice of psychology* (pp. 327-364). Washington, DC: American Psychological Association.

Lukoff, D. (1991). Divine madness: Shamanistic initiatory crisis and psychosis. *Shaman's Drum, 22,* 24-29.

Lukoff, D. (2005). Spiritual and transpersonal approaches to psychotic disorders. In S. G. Mijares & G. S. Khalsa (Eds.), *The psychospiritual clinician's handbook: Alternative methods for understanding and treating mental disorders* (pp. 233-257). New York, NY: Haworth Reference Press.

Lukoff, D. (2007). Visionary spiritual experiences and mental disorders. *Southern Medical Journal, 100*(6), 635-641.

Lukoff, D. (2011). Visionary spirituality and mental disorders. In E. Cardeña & M. Winkelman (Eds.), *Altering consciousness: Multidisciplinary perspectives* (Vol. 1, pp. 301-325). Santa Barbara, CA: Praeger.

Lukoff, D., Lu, F., & Turner, R. (1992) Toward a more culturally sensitive DSM-IV: psychoreligious and psychospiritual problems. *Journal of Nervous and Mental Disease, 180,* 673-682.

Lukoff, D., Lu, F., & Yang, P. (2010). DSM-IV Religious and Spiritual Problems. In J. Peteet & F. Lu (Eds.), *Religious and spiritual considerations in psychiatric diagnosis: A research agenda for DSM-V* (pp. 187-214). Washington, DC: American Psychiatric Association Press.

Lukoff, D., Wallace, C. J., Liberman, R. P., & Burke, K. (1986) A holistic health program for chronic schizophrenic patients. *Schizophrenia Bulletin, 6,* 274-282.

Maslow, A. (1969). The farther reaches of human nature. *Journal of Transpersonal Psychology, 1*(2), 1-9.

McNally, R. J., Lasko, N. B., Clancy, S. A., Macklin, M. L., Pitman, R. K., & Orr, S. P. (2004). Psychophysiological responding during script-driven imagery in people reporting abduction by space aliens. *Psychological Science, 15*(7), 493-497.

Mosher, L., Hendrix, V., & Fort, D. (2004) *Soteria: Through madness to deliverance.* Philadelphia, PA: Xlibris Corporation.

Mosher, L., & Menn, A. (1978). Community residential treatment for schizophrenia: Two-year follow-up. *Hospital and Community Psychiatry, 6,* 715-723.

Mosher, L., & Menn, A. (1979). Soteria: An altenative to hospitalization. In H. R. Lamb (Ed.), *Alternatives to acute hospitalization* (pp. 73-84). San Francisco, CA: Jossey-Bass.

Mosher, L., Menn, A., & Mathews, S. (1975) Soteria: Evaluation of a home-based treatment for schizophrenia. *American Journal of Orthopsychiatry, 6,* 455-467.

Nachmanovitch, S. (1991). *Free play: The power of improvisation in life and the arts.* New York, NY: G. P. Putnam's Sons.

Nelson, J. M. (2009). *Psychology, religion, and spirituality.* New York, NY: Springer.

Nelson, B., & Sass, L. A. (2008). The phenomenology of the psychotic break and Huxley's trip: Substance use and the onset of psychosis. *Psychopathology, 41*(6), 346-355.

Newberg, A., d'Aquili, E., & Rause, R. (2001). *Why God won't go away: Brain science and the biology of belief.* New York, NY: Ballantine Books.

Nolan, J., Dew, R., & Koenig, H. G. (2011). The relationship between religiousness/spirituality and schizophrenia: Implications for treatment and community support. In M. Ritsner (Ed.), *Handbook of schizophrenia spectrum disorders* (Vol. 3, *Therapeutic approaches, comorbidity, and outcomes,* pp. 383-420). New York, NY: Springer.

O'Connor, S., & Vandenberg, B. (2005). Psychosis or faith? Clinicians' assessment of religious beliefs. *Journal of Consulting and Clinical Psychology, 73*(4), 610-616.

Perry, J. (1974). *The far side of madness.* Englewood Cliffs, NJ: Prentice Hall.

Peters, L. G. (1989). Shamanism: Phenomenology of a spiritual discipline. *Journal of Transpersonal Psychology, 21*(2), 115-137.

Phillips, R., Lukoff, D., & Stone, M. (2009). Integrating the spirit within psychosis: Alternative conceptualizations of psychotic disorders. *Journal of Transpersonal Psychology, 41*(2), 61-79.

Polkinghorne, D. E. (1989). Phenomenological research methods. In R. S. Valle & S. Halling (Eds.), *Existential-phenomenological perspectives in psychology: Exploring the breadth of human experience* (pp. 41-60). New York, NY: Plenum Press.

Ruzek, N. (2007). Transpersonal psychology in context: Perspectives from its founders and historians of American psychology. *Journal of Transpersonal Psychology, 39*(2), 153-174.

Schavrien, J. (2008). Shakespeare's late style and renewal through the feminine: A full spectrum, all-quadrant approach. *Journal of Transpersonal Psychology, 40*(2), 199-223.

Shah, R., Kulhara, P., Grover, S., Kumar, S., Malhotra, R., & Tyagi, S. (2011). Relationship between spirituality/religiousness and coping in patients with residual schizophrenia. *Quality of Life Research, 20*(7), 1053-1060.

Skolimowski, H. (1994). *The participatory mind*. London, UK: Arkana.

Sovatsky, S. (1999). *Eros, consciousness and kundalini: Deepening sensuality through Tantric celibacy and spiritual intimacy*. Rochester, VT: Inner Traditions International.

Spero, M. H. (Ed.). (1985). *Psychotherapy of the religious patient*. Springfield, IL: Charles C Thomas.

Surgeon General (1999). *Mental health: A report of the Surgeon General*. Bethesda, MD: Author.

Suri, R. (2011). Making sense of voices: An exploration of meaningfulness in auditory hallucinations in schizophrenia. *Journal of Humanistic Psychology, 51*(2), 152-171.

Swan, W. (2008). C. G. Jung's psychotherapeutic technique of active imagination in historical context. *Psychoanalysis and History, 10*(2), 185-204.

Tarnas, R. (1991). *The passion of the Western mind*. New York, NY: Harmony Books.

Tart, C. T. (2004). On the foundations of transpersonal psychology: Contributions from parapsychology. *Journal of Transpersonal Psychology, 36*(1), 66-90.

Taylor, S. (2009). Beyond the pre-trans fallacy: The validity of pre-egoic spiritual experience. *Journal of Transpersonal Psychology, 41*(1), 22-43.

Underhill, E. (1955). *Mysticism: A study in the nature and development of man's spiritual consciousness*. New York, NY: Meridian.

Valle, R. S. (Ed.), (1998), *Phenomenological inquiry in psychology: Existential and transpersonal dimensions*. New York, NY: Plenum Press.

Washburn, M. (1994). *Transpersonal psychology in psychoanalytic perspective*. Albany, NY: State University of New York Press.

Washburn, M. (1998). The pre-trans fallacy reconsidered. In D. Rothberg & S. Kelly (Eds.), *Ken Wilber in dialogue: Conversations with leading transpersonal thinkers* (pp. 62-83). Wheaton, IL: Theosophical.

Washburn, M. (2003). Transpersonal dialogue: a new direction. *Journal of Transpersonal Psychology, 35*(1), 23-40.

Welwood, J. (1979). Self-knowledge as the basis for an integrative psychology. *Journal of Transpersonal Psychology, 11*(1), 23-40.

Wilber, K. (1980).The pre/trans fallacy. *Re-Vision, 3*, 51-72.

Wilber, K. (1995). *Sex, ecology, spirituality: The spirit of evolution*. Boston: Shambhala.

Wilber, K. (2007). *The integral vision*. Boston: Shambhala.

Yamane, D., & Polzer, M. (1994). Ways of seeing ecstasy in modern society: Experiential-expressive and cultural-linguistic views. *Sociology of Religion, 55*, 1-25.

24

Meditation

Empirical Research and Future Directions

Douglas A. MacDonald, Roger Walsh, and
Shauna L. Shapiro

Since its inception as a unique subdiscipline in the late 1960s, transpersonal psychology has been actively involved in the exploration of technologies and practices (both ancient and modern) that are thought to facilitate the expression of higher modes, states, and traits of consciousness. Of particular interest has been the variety of methods of transformation collectively referred to as meditation that are integral parts of many established spiritual, religious, and mystical traditions. In fact, at a time when mainstream scientists and clinicians tended to view such practices in highly suspect terms (e.g., Alexander & Selesnick, 1966), articles on meditation aimed at both fostering empirical research as well as a greater understanding of its philosophy, practice, and significance were appearing in the then recently founded *Journal of Transpersonal Psychology* (e.g., Goleman, 1971, 1972; Osis, Bokert, & Carlson, 1973; Tart, 1971; Timmons & Kamiya, 1970; Trungpa, 1973; Van Nuys, 1971). Currently, meditation has become not only a topic of intense study, but is something that has been increasingly incorporated into psychotherapeutic systems and practice (e.g., Brazier, 1995; Corsini, 2001; Hayes, Follette, & Linehan, 2004; Kabat-Zinn, 2003; Linehan, 2007; Segal, William, & Teasdale, 2002; Walsh & Vaughan, 1993; Wilber, 2000). In light of these exciting developments, transpersonal psychology may be viewed as having played a pivotal and pioneering role in making meditation accessible to Western psychology. In this chapter, we would like to provide an overview of some of the research that has been done on meditation with primary attention directed toward investigations identifying its physical and neurological manifestations and correlates, as well as to studies examining its impact on psychological and social functioning.

Meditation Defined

Before launching into a discussion of the available research, it is important to first provide a working definition of what meditation is. While it may seem to be a

The Wiley Blackwell Handbook of Transpersonal Psychology, First Edition.
Edited by Harris L. Friedman and Glenn Hartelius.
© 2013 John Wiley & Sons, Ltd. Published 2015 by John Wiley & Sons, Ltd.

relatively straightforward task, arriving at an acceptable definition is deceptively challenging due to the fact that there are multiple meditative practices that employ different techniques for similar, although not necessarily identical, purposes. As well, meditation as it has been traditionally practiced is virtually never a stand-alone activity but rather is an embedded part of a larger system of beliefs and lifestyle associated with authentic and culturally grounded spiritualities including but not limited to Hinduism, Buddhism, Taoism, Confucianism, Judaism, Christianity, and Islam. Within the confines of Western science and psychology, meditation practices have tended to be decontextualized from their original culturally framed meaning systems and treated as a psychological technology that can be studied and/or utilized separate from these meaning systems (i.e., they are generally used in a secularized manner without explicit regard given to their contributions to spiritual development). However, even when treated as a mere technique, there have been calls for more formal operationalizations of, and demarcation criteria for, meditation so as to permit better standardization of research and comparison of the findings across studies because existing definitions have not been sufficient in both precision and scope in addressing differences across the various meditative systems (e.g., Bond et al., 2009; Cardoso, de Souza, Camano, & Leite, 2004). In order to give a sense of how meditation has been conceptualized in the psychological and transpersonal literature, Table 24.1 presents a variety of definitions provided over the past five decades. In all cases, these definitions were proffered by their respective authors as ways of thinking about meditation in general and without allegiance or advantage given to any specific technique or system.

As we are sure the reader will note, the definitions in the table show a fair degree of similarity but also some conspicuous differences. More recent definitions tend to emphasize the mechanisms involved in the practice of meditation, namely, the intentional manipulation of attentional processes. As well, many definitions make reference to goals or intended outcomes of meditation practice. However, most of these are construed in terms of well-accepted aspects of psychological health without any overt mention of ostensible spiritual outcomes. For the sake of this chapter, we will be adopting the definition devised by Walsh and Shapiro (2006) which characterizes meditation as "a family of self-regulation practices that focus on training attention and awareness in order to bring mental processes under greater voluntary control and thereby foster general mental well-being and development and/or specific capacities such as calm, clarity, and concentration" (pp. 228-229). One of the main benefits of this definition is that it permits for an efficient differentiation between meditation as a pure practice in attentional training from related activities that may include features or aspects of such training but either incorporate other elements, such as breath manipulation or body postures and movement (e.g., yoga, Tai Chi, Qi Gong), and/or are more centrally concerned with the contents of awareness and effecting change in such contents as is the case with visualization, hypnosis, and psychotherapy.

With a working definition settled upon, an emergent detail that requires some discussion concerns the varieties of meditative techniques. Efforts have been made to categorize meditation systems based upon known non-ordinary states of consciousness thought to be associated with such systems (e.g., Fischer, 1971; Goleman, 1972, 1988; Naranjo & Ornstein, 1971). Nevertheless, there has been little substantive advancement in how meditative systems are organized and typed, particularly in terms of the specific goals of practice (Walsh & Shapiro, 2006). Scientists and clinicians have

Table 24.1 Sample Definitions of Meditation in the Psychological and Transpersonal Literature

Source	*Definition*
Naranjo & Ornstein (1971)	"Meditation is concerned with the development of a *presence,* a modality of being, which may be expressed or developed in whatever situation the individual may be involved" (p. 8)
White (1974)	"... meditation is primarily a means to an end: enlightenment. It is a tool for learning spiritual psychology, a technique for expanding consciousness." (p. xix).
Wise (1974)	"Meditation is a mental discipline in which relationships are revealed. It is a process of pattern-recognition in which the mind is raised above the particulars to receive universals which give coherence to the particulars" (p. 69)
Epstein & Lieff (1986)	"Meditation may be conceptualized as a process of attentional restructuring wherein the mind can be trained ... to pay attention undistractedly to a series of changing objects. This perceptual retraining allows a finely honed investigation of the rapidly changing self-concepts that perpetuate the sense of self" (p. 58)
Washburn (1988)	"the practice of pure steadfast attention" (p. 143)
Ramaswami & Sheikh (1989)	"... a set of techniques designed to alter our normal mode of consciousness and bring about a harmonious reintegration of the human personality" (p. 434)
Goleman (1991)	Meditation is "the self-regulation and retraining of attentional habits" (p. 192)
Jevning, Wallace, & Beidebach (1992)	"a stylized mental technique ... repetitively practiced for the purpose of attaining a subjective experience that is frequently described as very restful, silent, and of heightened alertness, often characterized as blissful" (p. 415)
Shapiro & Walsh (2003)	"Meditation can be defined as a family of practices that train attention and awareness, usually with the aim of fostering psychological and spiritual well-being and maturity" (p. 88)
Cardoso et al. (2004)	"Meditation ... utilizes a (1) specific technique (clearly defined), involving (2) muscle relaxation somewhere during the process and (3) 'logic relaxation': a necessarily (4) self-induced state, using a (5) self-focus skill" (p. 59)
Cahn & Polich (2006)	"... practices that self-regulate the body and mind, thereby affecting mental events by engaging a specific attentional set" (p. 180)
Bond et al. (2009)	The essence of meditation ... "is its use of (a) a defined technique, (b) logic relaxation, and (c) a self-induced state" (p. 129)
Kristeller (2011)	"Meditation ... is a cognitive process that involves the cultivation of a certain type of attention and moment-to-moment, nonjudgmental awareness of one's immediate experience, whether narrowly or more broadly focused" (p. 201)

generally adopted the stance of categorizing meditation techniques along the lines of how attention is directed with the main distinction being made between concentrative (i.e., attention focused on an object, sense, image, or idea) versus mindfulness (i.e., attention but non-attachment to the field of experience) approaches (Cahn & Polich, 2006; Shapiro & Walsh, 2003). A parallel distinction has been made more recently between focused attention and open-monitoring techniques (Lutz, Slagter, Dunne, & Davidson, 2008). With that stated, in the past few years, some meditation researchers have tried to create a third category. Travis and Shear (2010) have proposed automatic self-transcending (i.e., techniques aimed at transcending their own activity) as a new type, and have provided some experimental data showing that in contrast to focused attention (claimed to be linked to beta and gamma brain wave activity) and open monitoring (tied to increased theta activity), self-transcending methods are associated with elevated alpha1 activity. Alternatively, others (e.g., Kristeller, 2011) have advocated for guided or directed meditation to be treated as a third category. With these techniques, specific contents (e.g., symbols, images, passages, and even movements) that are viewed as meaningful and illuminative of particular aspects of self and consciousness are used as the focus of meditation practice. Whether or not these new categories garner recognition and support by experts, practitioners, and researchers has yet to be seen.

What Does the Research Tell Us about the Effects of Meditation?

As noted by Walsh and Shapiro (2006), the two most commonly studied forms of meditation are mindfulness as typically (although not exclusively) understood within the context of the Buddhist vipassana tradition, and Transcendental Meditation (TM), a system of meditation developed by Marharishi Mahesh Yogi based upon Hindu meditative traditions that is often viewed as being primarily concentrative, but which includes an observing/witnessing component in more advance stages of practice. However, with that in mind, perusal of the available research reveals that a fairly broad array of techniques described as meditation have been the focus of at least some studies. This includes such practices as Sahaja yoga, Kundalini yoga, Kriya yoga, Raja yoga, Vihangam yoga, Qigong meditation, Ananda Marga meditation, Zen meditation, Deity meditation, Loving Kindness meditation, Compassion meditation, Acem meditation, guided meditation, and mantram meditation, just to name a few of the more notable ones. Ostensibly, and as mentioned earlier, direct comparison and integration of empirical findings based upon the various systems is difficult to do, since it has not been established empirically that different meditative systems result in the same effects (Neumann & Frasch, 2006; Shapiro & Walsh, 2003).

Additionally, even within more researched approaches such as TM or mindfulness, there is significant divergence in terms of type of participants studied (e.g., novice versus experienced meditators), whether the study was focused on experiential states attained during active practice versus trait changes in biopsychosocial functioning arising from practice, and the quality of study design, including the measurement of variables relevant to meditation. In fact, scholars who have sampled the extant investigations have identified a number of problems with the research that are important to state up front, because they will mitigate the confidence one can have in the robustness of the available findings (Baer, 2003; Cahn & Polich, 2006; Canter & Ernst, 2003; Chiesa & Serretti, 2010; Neumann & Frasch, 2006; Ospina et al., 2008; Walsh & Shapiro, 2006). These difficulties include, but are not necessarily limited to, the following: (a) small sample sizes that diminish statistical power and generalizability of results to populations, (b) use of self-selected participants that introduce issues with selection bias and expectancy effects, (c) inadequate control/comparison groups that make it difficult to determine the extent to which state and trait changes can be attributed to meditation practice, (d) poor use of randomized trials that could result in potential problems with undetected and systematic sources of error influencing meditation outcomes, (e) insufficient descriptions of actual meditative techniques employed to allow for exact replication in future studies and that raise concerns around treatment integrity, (f) inconsistent use of technology, especially with electroencephalography (EEG; e.g., different studies use a varying number of sensors and placement of sensors is not standardized across studies) and inadequate resolution of translational images, (g) over-utilization of self-report assessment and measurement tools creating potential problems with response biases and social desirability, (h) difficulties accessing state-specific subjective experiences traditionally ascribed to meditative practice (e.g., Samadhi, transcendental awareness) without disturbing and distorting ongoing meditative processes in order to study their concomitant psychological and physiological expressions, (i) indeterminacies in the reliable use of language to capture subjective meditative experiences to allow for meaningful comparisons across experients and (j) insufficient measures of phenomenological states and constructs germane to meditative philosophy and technique. An additional issue deserving special mention relates to general problems that have been identified with data analysis in the translational imaging research (e.g., fMRI) that raise concerns about the meaning and reliability of findings in such studies (e.g., Bennett, Baird, Miller, & Wolford, 2012; Vul, Harris, Winkleman, & Pashler, 2009). Clearly, the reader should be able to appreciate that there is a need to exercise careful and critical judgement when examining the available findings and reaching any strong conclusions about what science concludes regarding the effects of meditation.

Notwithstanding the deluge of criticisms, the burgeoning research does afford the opportunity to get some sense of how meditation may impact functioning. Due to space limitations, we cannot exhaustively review all of these studies here. Fortunately, there are a wide variety of published sources that attempt to review and bring order to the empirical research, which the reader may want explore (e.g., for general reviews, see Andresen, 2000; Murphy & Donovan, 1997; Shapiro & Walsh, 1984, 2003; Walsh & Shapiro, 2006; for TM research see Alexander, Rainforth, & Gelderloos, 1991; Alexander, Robinson, Orme-Johnson, Schneider, & Walton, 1994; Alexander, Walton, Orme-Johnson, Goodman, & Pallone, 2003; Canter & Ernst, 2003; for mindfulness meditation see Baer, 2003; Chiesa, Calati, & Serretti, 2011; Germer, Siegel, & Fulton, 2005; Grossman, Niemann, Schmidt, & Walach, 2004; Kabat-Zinn, 2003; for EEG and brain imaging studies see Cahn & Polich, 2006; for psychological effects see Sedlmeier et al., 2012). In this chapter, we would like to touch upon general trends and salient findings to help illustrate the potency of meditation across most recognized domains of human functioning.

Physiological Findings

For several decades, efforts have been made to identify the somatic and neuro-physiological effects of meditation on practitioners. While initially viewed within conventional scientific circles as something that simply facilitates a relaxation response (Benson, 1984), research now compellingly suggests that meditation has much farther reaching correlates to physiological changes, both in terms of state (i.e., changes occurring while actively meditating) and trait (i.e., lasting effects on body functions arising from practice). For instance, meditation is associated with indicators of heightened physiological rest, states of calmness, and improved stress responsiveness and well-being, including reduced heart rate and rate of respiration, lower plasma lactate and cortisol levels, increased heart rate variability, increased skin resistance, and more stable phasic skin resistance (Burg, Wolf, & Michalak, 2012; Mohan, Sharma, & Bijlani, 2011; Shapiro & Walsh, 2003; Zeidan, Johnson, Gordon, & Goolkasian, 2010). At the same time, meditation appears to simultaneously foster elevated aware-ness as reflected in a variety of neurophysiological indices including increased cerebral blood flow, markedly increased levels of plasma arginine vasopressin, and faster H-reflex recovery (Shapiro & Walsh, 2003). More recent studies suggest that medi-tation reduces stress-induced immune responses (decreased plasma interlukin-6; Pace et al., 2009) and is associated with improved immunoreactivity (Tang et al., 2007).

Considering the neurological findings more specifically, Cahn and Polich (2006) provided an excellent overview and analysis of the EEG and translational imaging research up to that time, including evoked potential (EP), and event-related potential (ERP) studies. Overall, although they identify numerous inconsistencies of results across investigations, their work also helps highlight areas where relatively congruent findings have been observed. Some of these include the following: (a) increases in alpha and theta brainwave power and reductions of overall frequency during active meditation; (b) increased alpha power in experienced meditators when at rest; (c) increased theta activity in the frontal midline area associated with lower anxiety; (d) increased alpha-theta coherence both within and between cerebral hemispheres during meditation practice and in seasoned meditators when at rest; (e) potential lateralized (left-right) brain state and trait changes involved in emotional experience; (f) although associated with sleeplike states of consciousness, meditative states are not the same and advanced meditators have been shown to produce and maintain higher alpha and theta power during all stages of sleep, including dreaming and deep sleep; (g) high-frequency gamma band activity increases in meditators, especially for practices involving affect regulation; (h) EP and ERP research suggests that meditation may change cortical auditory processing (associated with shorter response latencies to audi-tory information); (i) neuroimaging (i.e., positron emission tomography [PET], sin-gle photon emission computed tomography [SPECT], functional magnetic resonance imaging [fMRI]) studies have identified several potentially significant brain structures which appear to be implicated in meditation, including the cingulate, prefrontal, and orbitofrontal cortices and the superior parietal lobe.

Since the publication of Cahn and Polich (2006), a considerable number of EEG, ERP, and neuroimaging studies have appeared in the literature that have replicated and/or broadened the findings of previous research. Although still plagued with many of the methodological problems identified above, some of the more interesting and corroborative findings reported in the literature regarding meditation practice include the following: (a) increased inter-hemispheric coherence in the frontal lobes (Travis & Arenander, 2006); (b) improved functional connectivity between multiple brain regions, most notably between auditory and medial visual networks (Kilpatrick et al., 2011), several structures in the default-mode network (e.g., medial prefrontal and cingulate cortices; Brewer et al., 2011) and attentional networks (Hasenkamp & Barsalou, 2012), and greater structural connectivity of major projection, commissural, and association pathways (Luders, Clark, Narr, & Toga, 2011); (c) differential activation of brain regions involved with attention and emotion (Brefczynski-Lewis, Lutz, Schaefer, Levinson, & Davidson, 2007), including enhanced involvement of the prefrontal cortex (Cheng, Borrett, Cheng, Kwan, & Cheng, 2010; Davanger, Ellingsen, Holen, & Hugdahl, 2010) hippocampal structures (Engström, Pihlsgard, Lundberg, & Soderfeldt, 2010), and structures implicated in improved responses to pain (Zeidan et al., 2011); (d) increased frontal theta activity and concurrent decreased activity in parietal and occipital areas (Baijal & Srinivasan, 2010) and elevated occipital gamma power in experienced practitioners (Cahn, Delorme, & Polich, 2010); (e) enhanced alpha wave modulation in the primary somatosensory neocortex (Kerr et al., 2011); (f) larger auditory mismatch negativity amplitudes suggesting improved pre-attentive perception (Srinivasan & Baijal, 2007); (g) increased cortical (i.e., gray matter) volume and density in a variety of structures, including the cingulate gyrus, putamen, insula, temporal gyrus and the temporal-parietal junction, hippocampus, orbitofrontal cortex, thalamus, cerebellum, corpus callosum, and lower brain stem (Grant, Courtemanche, Duerden, Duncan, & Rainville, 2010; Hölzel et al., 2008, 2011; Lazar et al., 2005; Luders, Toga, Lepore, & Gaser, 2009; Luders, Phillips et al., 2012; Pagnoni & Cekic, 2007; Vestergaard-Poulsen et al., 2009); (h) reduced P3a amplitude linked with lower automatic reactivity to auditory stimuli (Cahn & Polich, 2009); (i) increased cerebral blood flow in long-term meditators in a variety of structures including the prefrontal cortex, parietal cortex, thalamus, putamen, caudate, and the midbrain, as well as greater thalamic asymmetry as compared to non-meditators (Newberg et al., 2010); (j) significantly reduced late positive potential ERP in frontal regions when presented with negative emotional visual stimuli (Sobolewski, Holt, Kublik, & Wrobel, 2011); (k) significant differences in plasma catecholamine levels compared to non-mediators (Jung et al., 2012); and (l) significantly greater gyrification (i.e., cortical folding) in the precentral gyrus, fusiform gyrus, cuneus, and anterior dorsal insula (Luders, Kurth et al., 2012).

In summary, when considered in its totality, the physiological research provides very strong indications that meditation contributes to changes in brain and body functions. In terms of somatic correlates and outcomes, studies suggest that meditation effects manifest in terms of improved stress responses, and greater state and trait expressions of calmness and relaxedness as seen in a variety of body systems (e.g., respiration, hormones, blood and circulatory systems). Neurologically, investigations done to date seem to point to improved integration and harmonization of brain structure activation, greater control over cognitive resources, especially those associated to brain structures implicated in executive functions and automatic processing (such as the default network), strengthened affect regulation, and enhanced perceptual processes. Neuroanatomically, a number of recent studies indicate that the brain structures may actually change in terms of size, neuronal density, morphological distribution and organization, and efficiency of operations.

We now turn to the research focusing more on behavioral, cognitive, attitudinal, emotional, and social correlates and effects linked to meditative practice.

Psychological and Social Findings

As discussed by Walsh and Shapiro (2006), although problems with expectancy and design factors have been argued to account for some of the trends in results, most notably as they relate to alleged cognitive benefits (e.g., see Canter & Ernst, 2003; also see Chiesa et al., 2011 for a more general review of cognitive abilities research), studies done up to that time have identified a variety of associations between meditation practice and psychological and social functioning. Included among the research findings are correlates between meditation and increased perceptual sensitivity, learning capabilities, memory, processing speed, concentration, reaction time, motor skills, perceived self-control, academic performance, self-esteem, empathy, and creativity (e.g., Andresen, 2000; Cranson et al., 1991; Dillbeck, Assimakis, & Raimondi, 1986; Murphy & Donovan, 1997; Shapiro, Schwartz, & Bonner, 1998; So & Orme-Johnson, 2001). Also reported in the research prior to 2006 are findings linking meditation to greater levels of interpersonal functioning, coping skills, marital satisfaction, and maturation (e.g., higher levels of ego and moral development), as well as to positive changes in personality (e.g., reduced trait anxiety/neuroticism), self-actualization, spirituality, and the expression of more advanced states and stages of consciousness (e.g., Alexander & Langer, 1990; Alexander et al., 1991; Emavardhana & Tori, 1997; Nidich, Ryncarz, Abrams, Orme-Johnson, & Wallace, 1983; Shapiro & Walsh, 2003; Tloczynski & Tantriells, 1998; Travis, Arenander, & DuBois, 2004; Walsh & Shapiro, 2006).

Since 2006, and akin to the physiological research, a large number of investigations have been done aiming at identifying the impact meditation has on a variety of psychological and social variables. In the name of brevity, only a synopsis of some of the more notable trends in findings are reported here. Meditation is associated with: (a) improved self-regulatory control as manifested in response inhibition during training and enhanced self-reported socioemotional functioning (Sahdra et al., 2011); (b) strengthened processing efficiency of emotional information (Ortner, Kilner, & Zelazo, 2007; Roberts-Wolfe, Sacchet, Hastings, Roth, & Britton, 2012); (c) improved attention (Prakash et al., 2010; Semple, 2010; Van den Hurk, Giommi, Gielen, Spekens, & Barendregt, 2010) including visual attentional processing (Hodgins & Adair, 2010), executive functioning (Zeidan, Johnson, Diamond, David, & Goolkasian, 2010), cognitive flexibility (Moore & Malinowski, 2009) and bottom-up processing (Van den Hurk, Janssen, Giommi, Barendregt, & Gielen, 2010); (d) reduced negative affect, fatigue, and mental confusion (Zeidan, Johnson, Gordon, et al., 2010), diminished need for sleep (Kaul, Passafiume, Sargent, & O'Hara, 2010), lower perceived stress and improved emotional intelligence (Chu, 2010), and lower somatization and anxiety (Yunesian, Asiani, Vash, & Yazdi, 2008); (e) higher and more stable self-esteem (Burg & Michalak, 2012), more congruent implicit and explicit self-esteem (Koole, Govorun, Cheng, & Gallucci, 2009), and enhanced psychological well-being (Falkenström, 2010; Josefsson, Larsman, Broberg, & Lundh, 2011; Keune & Forintos, 2010); (f) lower pain sensitivity (Zeidan, Gordon, Merchant, & Goolkasian, 2010) and; (g) an increase in values relating to universalism, benevolence, transcendence, and collectivism (Justo & Luque, 2009).

As a valuable and much needed contribution to the literature that is worth outlining here, Sedlmeier et al. (2012) completed a quantitative meta-analysis of the empirical studies focused on examining the effects of meditation in non-clinical samples of adult practitioners on a variety of psychological variables, including positive and negative emotions, emotion regulation, empathy, state and trait anxiety, neuroticism, perception, cognition, learning, attention, memory, intelligence, mindfulness, behavior, stress, self-concept, self-realization, personality, perception, and well-being. After eliminating approximately 75% of the 595 investigations they uncovered due primarily to methodological problems and noting that most research lacks a theoretical basis, they determined that the average global effect size across the remaining 163 studies they analyzed reflected a medium effect (e.g., for all studies, the typical magnitude of effect falls at $r = .28$ or $d = .58$). Sedlmeier and colleagues indicated that this finding is generally comparable to the effect sizes seen in meta-analytic studies of psychotherapy effectiveness (e.g., Lipsey & Wilson, 1993; Wampold, 2001). They also asserted that the effects of meditation do not appear to be explainable in terms of simple relaxation or cognitive restructuring, and that effect sizes seem to be consistently higher for variables involving negative affect as compared to cognitive variables.

Clinical Findings and Interventions

Thus far, our overview of the available research on meditation has been mostly focused on studies that look at meditation as a discrete practice using non-clinical (i.e., healthy) research participants. As mentioned at the beginning of this chapter, meditation has been increasingly integrated into clinical interventions and at present there is a fairly extensive body of literature looking at the effects of meditation and/or meditative techniques incorporated into conventional therapies (e.g., mindfulness-based cognitive behavioral therapies) on both physical and psychological health and pathology with clinical samples.

Considering first investigations on the effects of meditation on physical and psychosomatic disorders, research indicates that meditation practice may contribute to the amelioration of a variety of conditions, particularly those in which stress plays a role. This includes cardiovascular disorders, such as coronary heart disease, hypertension and hypercholesterolemia (Olivo, Dodson-Lavelle, Wren, Fang, & Oz, 2009; Schneider et al., 2005), asthma, stuttering, type II diabetes, primary dysmenorrhea, and premenstrual dysphoric disorder (Murphy & Donovan, 1997). Meditation also seems to facilitate positively immune function in cancer patients, and attenuate distress symptoms in fibromyalgia, rheumatoid arthritis, and cancer patients, as well as in people suffering from HIV and a variety of chronic pain syndromes including migraines

(Bormann & Carrico, 2009; Carlson, Speca, Patel, & Goodey, 2003; Davidson et al., 2003; Foley, Baillie, Huxter, Price, & Sinclair, 2010; Kabat-Zinn, 2003; Kvillemo & Bränström, 2011; Labelle, Campbell, & Carlson, 2010; Morone, Greco, & Weiner, 2008; Shigaki, Glass, & Schopp, 2006; Wachholtz & Pargament, 2008; Weissbecker et al., 2002; Williams, Kolar, Reger, & Pearson, 2001; Zautra et al., 2008). In addition, there are indications that meditation may augment and improve treatments for such conditions as psoriasis, prostate cancer, atherosclerosis, and epilepsy (Kabat-Zinn, 2003; Lansky & St. Louis, 2006; Zamarra, Schneider, Besseghini, Robinson, & Salerno, 1996).

Turning to psychotherapeutic effects, individuals from differing populations manifesting a range of psychopathologies appear to benefit. Included are such disorders as ADHD, anxiety, depression and suicidality, bipolar disorder, eating disorders, insomnia, panic and phobic disorders, and trauma disorders (Barnhofer et al., 2007, 2009; Bormann, Thorp, Wetherell, Golshan, & Lang, 2012; Boteva, 2008; Evans et al., 2008; Farb, Anderson, & Segal, 2012; Kozasa et al., 2008; Kristeller & Wolever, 2011; Lee et al., 2007; Manzaneque et al., 2011; Miklowitz et al., 2009; Miller, Fletcher, & Kabat-Zinn, 1995; Ong, Shapiro, & Manber, 2008; Rosenthal, Grosswald, Ross, & Rosenthal, 2011; Shapiro et al., 1998; Walsh & Shapiro, 2006; Weber et al., 2010; Zylowska et al., 2008). Further, meditation practice has been shown to alleviate anxiety, aggression, and recidivism in prisoners and criminal offenders, to reduce use of both legal and illegal drugs in incarcerated persons, and to improve relapse prevention in recovered alcoholics and substance users (Alexander et al., 2003; Bowen et al., 2006; Gelderloos, Walton, Orme-Johnson, & Alexander, 1991; Himelstein, 2011; Singh et al., 2008; Zgierska et al., 2008). Research also suggests that meditation-based interventions may prove helpful for children and individuals with intellectual and developmental disabilities (e.g., Black, Milam, & Sussman, 2009; Burke, 2010; Singh et al., 2007, 2011) and for caregivers of mentally ill patients (e.g., Oken et al., 2010).

Although the cited literature may create the impression that meditation and meditation-therapy combinations are ubiquitously effective with a variety of health conditions, it is important to keep in mind that some therapeutic effects may dissipate if practice is discontinued, and adherence and compliance may present significant challenges (e.g., de Lisle, Dowling, & Allen, 2011). While earlier studies have suggested that treatment completion rates and post-intervention continuation of meditation are significantly high (e.g., Baer [2003] reported a completion rate of 85%; Kabat-Zinn, Massion, Herbert, & Rosenbaum, 1997, and Miller et al., 1995, found 75% of participants continued to meditate 6-48 months post-intervention and 56% after three years), there are indications that clinical researchers and practitioners have not been diligent in monitoring treatment adherence and between-session meditation practice and that, by extension, claims regarding the application and effectiveness of meditation in treatment may not be what they appear to be (Toneatto & Nguyen, 2007; Vettese, Toneatto, Stea, Nguyen, & Wang, 2009).

There is also another factor to consider with regard to the utilization of meditative practices—the potential for negative effects. An axiom in medicine states that any treatment that is powerful enough to provide therapeutic benefit is also powerful enough to harm. Meditation is no exception and some literature suggests that practice can contribute to problems in functioning, particularly in those with serious pre-existing pathologies (Elmer, MacDonald, & Friedman, 2003; Germer et al., 2005; Grof & Grof, 1989; Kuijpers, van der Heijden, Tuinier, & Verhoeven, 2007; Walsh, 2000; Walsh & Vaughan, 1993; Wilber, Engler, & Brown, 1986). As a prudent and recent development, efforts are now starting to be made to identify client characteristics that would contraindicate the utilization of meditation (Dobkin, Irving, & Amar, 2012).

Reorienting our discussion from health conditions to the interventions themselves, as noted earlier in the chapter, there are numerous therapeutic systems now available that attempt to integrate conventional psychotherapeutic modalities and meditative practices. As articulated by Walsh and Shapiro (2006), as well as others (Arkowitz & Mannon, 2002), these systems may be divided into three kinds: theoretical integration, technical eclecticism, and the search for underlying common factors. Examples of theoretical integration can be found in the fields of Diamond/Ridhwan, psychosynthesis, transpersonal, and integral psychologies (Walsh & Vaughan, 1993; Wilber, 2000), as well as in the recently developed mindfulness-integrated cognitive-behavioral therapy (Cayoun, 2011). Common therapeutic factors have been explored and proffered by Baer (2003), Kabat-Zinn (2003), and Walsh (1999, 2000). However, of the three kinds, approaches embodying technical eclecticism have seen the greatest growth, with the majority of them involving a combination of mindfulness with established psychotherapeutic techniques. Specific examples include Kabat-Zinn's (2003) mindfulness-based stress reduction (MBSR), mindfulness-based cognitive therapy, dialectical behavior therapy, mindfulness-based art therapy, acceptance and commitment therapy, and control therapy (Dimidjian & Linehan, 2003; Segal et al., 2002; Shapiro & Astin, 1998). Outside of Western psychology, eclecticism has found expression in Japanese Morita and Naikan therapies (Corsini, 2001). Many of these approaches have initial research support and some, such as MBSR, already meet the criteria for "probably efficacious" treatments (Baer, 2003; Fjorback, Arendt, Ømbøl, Fink, & Walach, 2011; Grossman et al., 2004; Piet & Hougaard, 2011; Sipe & Eisendrath, 2012).

An aside. A variety of questions are raised from the developments in both practice and research. For instance, are there other ways of combining and integrating meditation and therapy that could result in empirically demonstrable improvement in health and well-being? Because both therapy and meditation have been shown to facilitate enhanced awareness (Walsh & Shapiro, 2006) would *all* therapies benefit from the inclusion of meditation in whole or in part? Does meditation either as an adjunct or as an integrated part of therapy lead to more cost-effective treatment and/or healthcare utilization? Last, is there potential in using meditation as a practice to prevent and/or protect from conditions for which it has been shown to have benefit?

For the last two questions, some literature has appeared to provide answers. In terms of cost-effectiveness, there is evidence that the incorporation of meditation into medical practice may substantively reduce health care utilization and costs (Herron, 2011). With regard to the use of meditation as a prophylactic, some have pondered and even advocated for the introduction of meditative practice on a large scale (e.g., in educational systems and employment settings) and/or in the training of clinicians with the available research suggesting that doing so holds promise (Bruce, Manber, Shapiro,

& Constantino, 2010; Campion & Rocco, 2009; Davis & Hayes, 2011; Deurr, 2004; Shapiro, Astin, Bishop, & Cordova, 2005; Shapiro, Brown, & Astin, 2011; Shapiro, Brown, & Biegel, 2007; Walach et al., 2007; Wisner, Jones, & Gwin, 2010).

Exceptional Findings

In addition to the effects of and correlates to meditation described thus far, there is research indicating that advanced meditation practitioners demonstrate remarkable capacities traditionally thought in Western science and psychology to be outside the realm of possibility. These include development of willful and deliberate control of the autonomic nervous system, and of lucid dream and lucid non-dream sleep states of consciousness (Mason et al., 1997), heightened integrative cognitive capacities accompanied with a virtual elimination of ego-drive conflicts (Jonte-Pace, 1998; Wilber et al., 1986), control of binocular rivalry and motion-induced blindness (Carter et al., 2005), development and cultivation of synesthesia (Walsh, 2005), ability to inhibit totally the startle response and to respond with equanimity, relaxation, and compassion to any visual stimuli, including those that ordinarily elicit a response of intense disgust, and ability to accurately perceive facial microexpressions that are generally very difficult to discern (Goleman, 2003). Lastly, consistent with Hindu philosophy which indicates that spiritual development fostered by advanced meditation practice may be accompanied by the emergence of siddhis, or psychic abilities, a recent parapsychological meta-analysis has found that meditators, as well as people who believe in the paranormal, have a performance advantage in free response ganzfeld studies compared to other research participants (Storm, Tressoldi, & Di Risio, 2010).

Are All Meditative Systems the Same in Their Effect on Functioning?

An important issue that has existed in the meditation literature for a long time concerns whether or not different systems of meditation produce the same or different effects on practitioners. This question can actually take two forms—do secularized meditative techniques work the same as spiritually focused ones? Also, do the discrete systems of meditation (e.g., TM and mindfulness) have the same effects?

In regard to the first query, the vast majority of published research, especially the clinical studies, has tended to employ secularized versions of meditation. With that in mind, we were able to uncover two recent investigations that give explicit consideration to the effects of spiritually-focused meditation (SpM) as compared to secularized meditation (SeM). In one study (Cole et al., 2012), it was found that SpM produced better treatment outcomes as compared to SeM and a control group in terms of greater reduction in depression and increased positive emotions in patients with metastatic melanoma. The researchers reported that, along with the enhanced outcomes, patients expressed a preference for meditation programs that explicitly included spiritually based material. In the second study, Wachholtz and Pargament (2008) compared SpM to internally focused SeM, externally focused SeM, and muscle relaxation in the treatment of migraine headaches. They found the SpM outperformed all other treatment conditions as reflected in significantly greater reductions in headaches, anxiety, and negative affect, as well as more substantively improved pain tolerance, self-efficacy, and existential well-being. Although it is clear that additional research is needed, these initial findings suggest that meditation has better effects if practiced within a spiritual context.

Turning to the second question, there are a growing number of studies that directly compare different techniques (e.g., Lehmann et al., 2012; Levenson, Ekman, & Ricard, 2012; Perlman, Salomons, Davidson, & Lutz, 2010). However, an impressive meta-analysis of research exploring the psychological effects of meditation in healthy individuals done by Sedlmeier and colleagues (2012) provides a very good sense of what the extant research has determined regarding the different systems of meditation. In particular, they partitioned their analyses in such a manner in which they not only looked at global combined effects of meditation, but also at the effects of TM as compared to mindfulness as compared to other approaches both generally and specifically as they relate to a variety of psychological variables. What they found was that, while there were no meaningful global effect size differences across the three sets of meditative systems, there is evidence showing differential effect sizes in terms of their impact on specific aspects of psychological functioning. In particular, and only for analyses in which they could reliably compare TM and mindfulness, they found that TM had the strongest effect sizes in terms of its impact on negative emotions, state and trait anxiety, neuroticism, self-realization, and learning and memory while mindfulness meditation had the strongest effects on self-concept and in the reduction of negative features of personality. Given these results, as well as the preponderance of available studies, it appears reasonably safe to say that although meditation regardless of system has an impact on psychological functions, different forms of meditation seem more effective in facilitating change in very specific areas of functioning. Consequently, it appears that there may be a need on the part of meditation advocates to be a bit more discerning in terms of which types of meditation they recommend for use by people in both general and clinical populations. Obviously, further research is needed to verify the findings of Sedlmeier et al. (2012).

How and Why? Theories of Meditation

With a burgeoning body of empirical literature indicating that meditation has fairly clear, and measureable effects on mind, body, and experience, an important question emerges—how does meditation result in these changes? The lack of a coherent and integrative theory that permits for the generation of specific testable hypotheses has plagued meditation research and, unfortunately, most published studies lack a clear theoretical basis (Sedlmeier et al., 2012). However, this is not due to a lack of trying for there are, in fact, many explanations in the literature as to how meditation may work. As stated by Walsh and Shapiro (2006), three kinds of explanations have been given which they called metaphoric, mechanistic, and process.

Metaphoric explanations are typically given in the philosophical systems from which the meditation systems are derived. Classic metaphors common to these explains include purification of the mind of toxicity, freeing the mind and self of illusions and conditioning, awakening the mind from its trance state, calming disturbances, rebalancing the mind and self, unfolding innate potentials, enlightenment, and uncovering one's true identity (Walsh, 1999). Mechanistic explanations, alternatively, are what are typically advanced by contemporary scientists. Although arguably metaphoric in their own right, because the mind and brain are seen as analogous to a machine, a variety of psychological (e.g., relaxation, exposure, desensitization, dyhypnosis, deautomatization, catharsis, counterconditioning, insight, self-monitoring, self-control, self-acceptance, and self-understanding) and physiological mechanisms (e.g., reduced arousal, modified autonomic activity, stress immunization, and hemispheric synchronization and laterality shifts) have been put forth in the literature (Baer, 2003; Cahn & Polich, 2006; Davidson et al., 2003; Murphy & Donovan, 1997; Sedlmeier et al., 2012). Last, process explanations place emphasis on the features of experience and consciousness in a manner that is not reductionistic (as mechanistic explanations are criticized by some for doing—see Rosch, 1999; Wilber, 2000), but which can accommodate the interplay and interaction of mechanisms at one or more levels of a system without itself being reduceable to those mechanisms. Walsh and Shapiro (2006) pointed out two potentially important processes that may be central to understanding meditation—the refinement of awareness and disidentification. In terms of the former, they make reference to the fact that heightened awareness is something that is not only common to virtually all meditative practices (Walsh, 1999; Wong, 1997), but is also seen as highly germane to psychotherapy (Perls, 1969; Raskin & Rogers, 1995; Whitmont, 1969). Disidentification on the other hand, is a process in which awareness observes but does not identify with the contents of experience (including thoughts, feelings, and images). Although referred to by different names in various theories (e.g., decentration, decentering, detachment, observing self, metacognitive awareness, de-embedding; Martin, 1997; Wilber, 2000), disidentification has been advanced as a requisite process for personal growth and transformation.

Conclusions and Directions for Future Research

Clearly, there is a need for an approach to conceptualizing and studying meditation that gives due regard and respect for its history, complexity, and sheer potency in effecting change in human consciousness and functioning. While current theoretical and empirical efforts can be characterized as a good start, it should be apparent to the reader that there is still a considerable amount of work that needs to be done in order to facilitate the growth of a meaningful and illuminative understanding of meditation. With everything we have discussed in mind, we end this chapter with a set of recommendations for future research.

1   Considerable attention should be given to devising synergistic and complex models of meditation that aim to integrate the disparate theories and explanations currently offered by scientist, clinician, and meditative practitioner alike, so as to permit for a more holistic understanding of the nature, processes, and effects of meditation. A promising candidate that may function well in this capacity is the

integral model of Wilber (2000). At the same time, such models need to be meticulously specified and articulated so as to allow for the generation of meaningful and precise hypotheses that can be rigorously studied.

2   Methodologically, there is a need for much greater care in the design of studies. This includes such elements as better using theory to guide the development of research expectations, selecting participants in a way that ensures sufficient power and generalizability of findings and/or allows for detailed examination of theoretically relevant mechanisms, processes, and outcomes (as would be the case in studying advanced meditators), utilizing study designs that permit the examination of changes and effects both cross-sectionally and longitudinally, inclusion of appropriate comparison groups when trying to establish effects of practice, resisting the tendency of over-relying on a single methodology (e.g., self-report measures, translational imaging technologies) out of recognition that doing so may introduce systematic biases in knowledge claims, and better ensuring adherence and integrity of meditation practice by study participants. Also, it is important to articulate whether a pure attentional form of meditation is being used or if it is being augmented with additional technique, such as breath manipulation or body movements because it is difficult to determine what components would be responsible for any changes seen.

3   Deserving mention in its own right, significant efforts should be given to developing and validating measures of constructs relevant to theories of meditation so as to permit standardized assessment of variables that can be replicated across investigation (see MacDonald, LeClair, Holland, Alter, & Friedman, 1995 for measures that have been developed for meditative, phenomenological, and transpersonal research).

4   Greater thought should be given to possible mediating, moderating, and contextual factors and how they impact meditation (e.g., age, gender, ethnicity, religious affiliation and commitment, length of meditation practice, expectancies). Especially important here is consideration of the value/belief context (e.g., spirituality) in which meditation is practiced, as well as the role of lifestyle (Walsh, 2011) in how meditation works.

5   Research is needed that looks at potential negative effects of meditation, as well as the differential effects of specific forms of meditation so that informed decisions about how, when, and with whom meditation is used can be made responsibly.

6   Expand the focus of meditation research to look at the role and influences of personality, development, and maturation. In the same vein, along with continued studies of the potential value of meditation in the treatment of illness and pathology, extend investigations into the realm of examining the exceptional effects of meditation to determine how it can facilitate higher states of personal and social functioning and well-being.

References

Alexander, C. & Langer, E. (Eds.). (1990). *Higher stages of human development*. New York, NY: Oxford University Press.

Alexander, C. N., Rainforth, M. V., & Gelderloos, P. (1991). Transcendental meditation, self-actualization, and psychological health. *Journal of Social Behavior and Personality*, *6*(5), 189-247.

Alexander, C. N., Robinson, P., Orem-Johnson, D. W., Schneider, R. H., & Walton, K. G. (1994). The effects of transcendental meditation compared to other methods of relaxation and meditation in reducing risk factors, morbidity, and mortality. *Homeostasis*, *35*(4-5), 243-263.

Alexander, C., Walton, K., Orem-Johnson, D., Goodman, R., & Pallone, N. (Eds.). (2003). *Transcendental meditation in criminal rehabilitation and crime prevention*. New York, NY: Haworth Press.

Alexander, F., & Selesnick, S. (1966). *The history of psychiatry*. New York, NY: Harper & Row.

Andresen, J. (2000). Meditation meets behavioral medicine. *Journal of Consciousness Studies*, *7*(11-12), 17-74.

Arkowitz, H., & Mannon, B. (2002). A cognitive-behavioral assimilative integration. In F. Kaslow & J. Lebow (Eds.), *Comprehensive handbook of psychotherapy* (Vol. 4, pp. 317-337). New York, NY: John Wiley & Sons.

Baer, R. (2003). Mindfulness training as a clinical intervention: A conceptual and empirical review. *Clinical Psychology: Science and Practice*, *10*(2), 125-143.

Baijal, S., & Srinivasan, N. (2010). Theta activity and meditative states: Spectral changes during concentrative meditation. *Cognitive Processing*, *11*(1), 31-38.

Barnhofer, T., Duggan, D., Crane, C., Hepburn, S., Fennell, M. J. V., & Williams, J. M. G. (2007). Effects of meditation on frontal-alpha asymmetry in previously suicidal individuals. *NeuroReport: For Rapid Communication of Neuroscience Research*, *18*(7), 709-712.

Barnhofer, T., Crane, C., Hargus, E., Amarasinghe, M., Winder, R., & Williams, J. M. G. (2009). Mindfulness-based cognitive therapy as a treatment for chronic depression: A preliminary study. *Behaviour Research and Therapy*, *47*(5), 366-373.

Bennett, C. M., Baird, A. A., Miller, M. B., & Wolford, G. L. (2012). Neural correlates of interspecies perspective taking in the post-mortem Atlantic salmon: An argument for proper multiple comparisons correction. *Journal of Serendipitous and Unexpected Results*, *1*(1), 1-5.

Benson, H. (1984). *The relaxation response*. New York, NY: Avon.

Black, D. S., Milam, J., & Sussman, S. (2009). Sitting-meditation interventions among youth: A review of treatment efficacy. *Pediatrics*, *124*(3), e532-e542.

Bond, K., Ospina, M. B., Hooton, N., Bialy, L., Dryden, D. M., Buscemi, N., ... Carlson, L. E. (2009). Defining a complex intervention: The development of demarcation criteria for "meditation." *Psychology of Religion and Spirituality*, *1*(2), 129-137.

Bormann, J. E., & Carrico, A. W. (2009). Increase in positive reappraisal coping during a group- based mantram intervention mediate sustained reductions in anger in HIV-positive persons. *International Journal of Behavioral Medicine*, *16*(1), 74-80.

Bormann, J. E., Thorp, S. R., Wetherell, J. L., Golshan, S., & Lang, A. J. (2012). Meditation-based mantram intervention with veterans with posttraumatic stress disorder: A randomized trial. *Psychological Trauma: Theory, Research, Practice, and Policy*. Advance online publication. doi:10.1037/a0027522

Boteva, K. (2008). Mindfulness meditation in patients with mood disorders. Feasibility, safety, and efficacy. *International Journal of Child Health and Human Development*, *1*(2), 135-154.

Bowen, S., Witkiewitz, K., Dillworth, T. M., Chawla, N., Simpson, T. L., Ostafin, B. D., ... Marlatt, G. A. (2006). Mindfulness meditation and substance use in an incarcerated population. *Psychology of Addictive Behaviors*, *20*(3), 343-347.

Brazier, D. (1995). *Zen therapy: Transcending the sorrows of the human mind.* New York, NY: John Wiley & Sons.

Brefczynski-Lewis, J. A., Lutz, A., Schaefer, H. S., Levinson, D. B., & Davidson, R. J. (2007). Neural correlates of attentional expertise in long-term meditation practitioners. *PNAS Proceedings of the National Academy of Sciences of the United States of America, 104*(27), 11483-11488.

Brewer, J. A., Worhunsky, P. D., Gray, J. R., Tang, Y., Weber, J., & Kober, H. (2011). Meditation experience is associated with differences in default mode network activity and connectivity. *PNAS Proceedings of the National Academy of Sciences of the United States of America, 108*(50), 20254-20259.

Bruce, N. G., Manber, R., Shapiro, S. L., & Constantino, M. J. (2010). Psychotherapist mindfulness and the psychotherapy process. *Psychotherapy Theory, Research, Practice, and Training, 47*(1), 83-97.

Burg, J. M., & Michalak, J. (2012). Achtsamkeit selbstwert und selbstwertstablität/ Mindfulness, self-esteem, and self-esteem stability. *Zeitschrift für Klinische Psychologie und Psychotherapie: Forschung und Praxis, 41*(1), 1-8.

Burg, J. M., Wolf, O. T., & Michalak, J. (2012). Mindfulness as self-regulated attention: Associations with heart rate variability. *Swiss Journal of Psychology, 71*(3), 135-139.

Burke, C. A. (2010). Mindfulness-based approaches with children and adolescents: A preliminary review of current research in an emergent field. *Journal of Child and Family Studies, 19*(2), 133-144.

Cahn, B. R., Delorme, A., & Polich, J. (2010). Occipital gamma activation during Vipassana meditation. *Cognitive Processing, 11*(1), 39-56.

Cahn, R., & Polich, J. (2006). Meditation states and traits: EEG, ERP, and neuroimaging studies. *Psychological Bulletin, 132*(2), 180-211.

Cahn, B. R., & Polich, J. (2009). Meditation (vipassana) and the P3a event-related brain potential. *International Journal of Psychophysiology, 72*(1), 51-60.

Campion, J., & Rocco, S. (2009). Minding the mind: The effects and potential of a school-based meditation programme for mental health promotion. *Advances in School Mental Health Promotion, 2*(1), 47-55.

Canter, P. & Ernst, E. (2003). The cumulative effects of Transcendental Meditation on cognitive function: A systematic review of randomized controlled trials. *Wiener klinische Wochenschrift Gesellschaft der Ärzte in Wien, 115*(21-22), 758-766.

Cardoso, R., de Souza, E., Camano, L., & Leite, J. R. (2004). Meditation in health: An operational definition. *Brain Research Protocols, 14*, 58-60.

Carlson, L. E., Speca, M., Patel, K. D., and Goodey, E. (2003). Mindfulness-based stress reduction in relation to quality of life, mood, symptoms of stress and immune parameters in breast and prostate cancer outpatients. *Psychosomatic Medicine, 65*, 572-581.

Carter, O., Presti, D., Callistemon, C., Liu, G. B., Ungerer, Y., & Pettigrew, J. D. (2005). Meditation alters perceptual rivalry in Tibetan Buddhist monks. *Current Biology, 15*(11), R412-R413.

Cayoun, B. A. (2011). *Mindfulness-integrated CBT: Principles and practice.* New York, NY: Wiley-Blackwell.

Cheng, R. W. F., Borrett, D. S., Cheng, W., Kwan, H. C., & Cheng, R. S. S. (2010). Human prefrontal cortical response to the meditative state: A spectroscopy study. *International Journal of Neuroscience, 120*(7), 483-488.

Chiesa, A., Calati, R., & Serretti, A. (2011). Does mindfulness training improve cognitive abilities? A systematic review of neuropsychological findings. *Clinical Psychology Review, 31*(3), 449-464.

Chiesa, A., & Serretti, A. (2010). A systematic review of neurobiological and clinical features of mindfulness meditations. *Psychological Medicine, 40*(8), 1239-1252.

Chu, L. (2010). The benefits of meditation vis-à-vis emotional intelligence, perceived stress and negative mental health. *Stress and Health: Journal of the International Society for the Investigation of Stress, 26*(2), 169-180.

Cole, B. S., Hopkins, C. M., Spiegel, J., Tisak, J., Agarwala, S., & Kirkwood, J. M. (2012). A randomized clinical trial of the effects of spiritually focused meditation for people with metastatic melanoma. *Mental Health, Religion, & Culture, 15*(2), 161-174.

Corsini, R. (Ed.). (2001). *Innovative psychotherapies* (2nd ed.). New York, NY: John Wiley.

Cranson, R. W., Orme-Johnson, D. W., Gackenbach, J., Dillbeck, M. C., Jones, C. H., & Alexander, C. N. (1991). Transcendental meditation and improved performance on intelligence-related measures: A longitudinal study. *Personality and Individual Differences 12*(10), 1105-1116.

Davanger, S., Ellingsen, Ø., Holen, A., & Hugdahl, K. (2010). Meditation-specific prefrontal cortical activation during Acem meditation: An fMRI study. *Perceptual and Motor Skills, 111*(1), 291-306.

Davidson, R. J., Kabat-Zinn, J., Schumacher, J., Rosenkranz, M., Muller, D., Santorelli, S. F., … Sheridan, J. F. (2003). Alterations in brain and immune function produced by mindfulness meditation. *Psychosomatic Medicine, 65*, 564-570.

Davis, D. M., & Hayes, J. A. (2011). What are the benefits of mindfulness? A practice review of psychotherapy-related research. *Psychotherapy, 48*(2), 198-208.

De Lisle, S. M., Dowling, N. A., & Allen, J. S. (2011). Mindfulness-based cognitive therapy for problem gambling. *Clinical Case Studies, 10*(3), 210-228.

Deurr, M. (2004). *A powerful silence: The role of meditation and other contemplative practices in American life and work.* Northampton, MA: Centre for Contemplative Mind in Society.

Dillbeck, M. C., Assimakis, P. D., & Raimondi, D. (1986). Longitudinal effects of the transcendental meditation and TM-Sidhi program on cognitive ability and cognitive style. *Perceptual Motor Skills, 62*(3), 731-738.

Dimidjian, S., & Linehan, M. (2003). Defining an agenda for future research on the clinical applications of mindfulness practice. *Clinical Psychology: Science and Practice 10*, 125-143.

Dobkin, P. L., Irving, J. A., & Amar, S. (2012). For whom may participation in a mindfulness-based stress reduction program be contraindicated? *Mindfulness, 3*(1), 44-50.

Elmer, L. D., MacDonald, D. A., & Friedman, H. L. (2003). Transpersonal psychology, physical health and mental health: Theory, research, and practice. *Humanistic Psychologist, 31*(2-3), 160-181.

Emavardhana, T., & Tori, C. D. (1997). Changes in self-concept, ego defense mechanisms, and religiosity following seven-day Vipassana meditation retreats. *Journal for the Scientific Study of Religion, 36*(2), 194-206.

Engström, M., Pihlsgård, J., Lundberg, P., & Söderfeldt, B. (2010). Functional magnetic resonance imaging of hippocampal activation during silent mantra meditation. *Journal of Alternative and Complementary Medicine, 16*(12), 1253-1258.

Epstein, M. D., & Lieff, J. D. (1986). Psychiatric complications of meditation practice. In K. Wilber, J. Engler, & D. P. Brown, *Transformations of consciousness: Conventional and comtemplative perspectives on development* (pp. 53-63). Boston, MA: Shambhala.

Evans, S., Ferrando, S., Findler, M., Stowell, C., Smart, C., & Haglin, D. (2008). Mindfulness-based cognitive therapy for generalized anxiety disorder. *Journal of Anxiety Disorders, 22*(4), 716-721.

Falkenström, F. (2010). Studying mindfulness in experienced meditators: A quasi-experimental approach. *Personality and Individual Differences, 48*(3), 305-310.

Farb, N. A. S., Anderson, A. K., & Segal, Z. V. (2012). The mindful brain and emotion regulation in mood disorders. *Canadian Journal of Psychiatry, 57*(2), 70-77.

Fischer, R. A. (1971). A cartography of the ecstatic and meditative states. *Science, 174,* 897-904.

Fjorback, L. O., Arendt, M., Ømbøl, E., Fink, P., & Walach, H. (2011). Mindfulness-based stress reduction and mindfulness-based cognitive therapy: A systematic review of randomized controlled trials. *Acta Psychiatrica Scandinavica, 124*(2), 102-119.

Foley, E., Baillie, A., Huxter, M., Price, M., & Sinclair, E. (2010). Mindfulness-based cognitive therapy for individuals whose lives have been affected by cancer: A randomized controlled trial. *Journal of Consulting and Clinical Psychology, 78*(1), 72-79.

Gelderloos, P., Walton, K., Orme-Johnson, D., & Alexander, C. (1991). Effectiveness of the transcendental meditation program in preventing and treating substance misuse: A review. *International Journal of the Addictions, 26*(3), 293-325.

Germer, C., Siegel, R., & Fulton, P. (2005). *Mindfulness and psychotherapy.* New York, NY: Guilford.

Goleman, D. (1971). Meditation as meta-therapy: Hypotheses toward a proposed fifth state of consciousness. *Journal of Transpersonal Psychology, 3*(1), 1-25.

Goleman, D. (1972). The Buddha on meditation and states of consciousness: II. A typology of meditation techniques. *Journal of Transpersonal Psychology, 4*(2), 151-210.

Goleman, D. (1988). *The meditative mind: The varieties of meditative experience.* New York, NY: Putnam.

Goleman, D. (1991). Meditation and consciousness: An Asian approach to mental health. In S. Boorstein (Ed.). *Transpersonal psychotherapy* (pp. 188-199). Stanford, CA: JTP Books.

Goleman, D. (Ed.). (2003). *Destructive emotions.* New York, NY: Bantam.

Grant, J. A., Courtemanche, J., Duerden, E. G., Duncan, G. H., & Rainville, P. (2010). Cortical thickness and pain sensitivity in Zen meditators. *Emotion, 10*(1), 43-53.

Grof, S., & Grof, C. E. (1989). *Spiritual emergency.* Los Angeles, CA: Jeremy P. Tarcher.

Grossman, P., Niemann, L., Schmidt, S., & Walach, H. (2004). Mindfulness-based stress reduction and health benefits: A meta-analysis. *Journal of Psychosomatic Research, 57,* 35-43.

Hasenkamp, W., & Barsalou, L. W. (2012). Effects of meditation experience on functional connectivity of distributed brain networks. *Frontiers in Human Neuroscience, 6*(1), Article 38.

Hayes, S. C., Follette, V. M., & Linehan, M. (Eds.). (2004). *Mindfulness and acceptance: Expanding the cognitive-behavioral tradition.* New York, NY: Guilford Press.

Herron, R. E. (2011). Changes in physician costs among high-cost transcendental mediation practitioners compared with high-cost nonpractitioners over five years. *American Journal of Health Promotion, 26*(1), 56-60.

Himelstein, S. (2011). Meditation research: The state of the art in correctional settings. *International Journal of Offender Therapy and Comparative Criminology, 55*(4), 646-661.

Hodgins, H. S., & Adair, K. C. (2010). Attentional processes and meditation. *Consciousness and Cognition: An International Journal, 19*(4), 872-878.

Hölzel, B. K., Carmody, J., Vangel, M., Congleton, C., Yerramsetti, S. M., Gard, T., & Lazar, S. M. (2011). Mindfulness practice leads to increases in regional brain gray matter density. *Psychiatry Research: Neuroimaging, 191*(1), 36-43.

Hölzel, B. K., Ott, U., Gard, T., Hempel, H., Weygandt, M., Morgan, K., & Vaitl, D. (2008). Investigation of mindfulness meditation practitioners with voxel-based morphometry. *Social Cognitive and Affective Neuroscience, 3*(1), 55-61.

Jevning, R., Wallace, R. K., & Beidebach, M. (1992). The physiology of meditation: A review: A wakeful hypometabolic integrated response. *Neuroscience & Biobehavioral Reviews, 16*(3), 415-424.

Jonte-Pace, D. (1998). The Swami and the Rorschach. In R. Forman (Ed.), *The innate capacity: Mysticism, psychology, and philosophy* (pp. 137-169). New York, NY: Oxford University Press.

Josefsson, T., Larsman, P., Broberg, A. G., & Lundh, L. (2011). Self-reported mindfulness mediates the relation between meditation experience and psychological well-being. *Mindfulness, 2*(1), 49-58.

Jung, Y., Kang, D., Byun, M., Shim, G., Kwon, S., Jang, G., ... Kwon, J. (2012). Influence of brain-derived neurotrophic factor and catechol O-methyl transferase polymorphisms on effects of meditation on plasma catecholamines and stress. *Stress: The International Journal on the Biology of Stress, 15*(1), 97-104.

Justo, C. F., & Luque, M. N. (2009). Efectos de una programa meditación en los valores de una muestra de estudiantes universitarios/Effects of a meditation program on values in a sample of university students. *Electronic Journal of Research in Educational Psychology, 7*(3), 1157-1174.

Kabat-Zinn, J. (2003). Mindfulness-based interventions in context: Past, present, and future. *Clinical Psychology: Science and Practice, 10*(2), 144-156.

Kabat-Zinn, J., Massion, A., Hebert, J. R., & Rosenbaum, E. (1997). Meditation. In J. Holland (Ed.), *Textbook of psycho-oncology.* Oxford, UK: Oxford University Press.

Kaul, P., Passafiume, J., Sargent, C. R., & O'Hara, B. F. (2010). Meditation acutely improves psychomotor vigilance and may decrease sleep need. *Behavioral and Brain Functions, 6,* Article 47.

Kerr, C. E., Jones, S. R., Wan, Q., Pritchett, D. L., Wasserman, R. H., Wexler, A., ... Moore, C. I. (2011). Effects of mindfulness mediation training on anticipatory alpha modulation in primary somatosensory cortex. *Brain Research Bulletin, 85*(3-4), 96-103.

Keune, P. M., & Forintos, D. P. (2010). Mindfulness meditation: A preliminary study on meditation practice during everyday life activities and its association with well-being. *Psihologijske Teme, 19*(2), 373-386.

Kilpatrick, L. A., Suyenobu, B. Y., Smith, S. R., Bueller, J. A., Goodman, T., Creswell, J. D., ... Naliboff, B. D. (2011). Impact of mindfulness-based stress reduction training on intrinsic brain connectivity. *NeuroImage, 56*(1), 290-298.

Koole, S. L., Govorun, O., Cheng, C. M., & Gallucci, M. (2009). Pulling yourself together: Meditation promotes congruence between implicit and explicit self-esteem. *Journal of Experimental Social Psychology, 45*(6), 1220-1226.

Kozasa, E. H., Santos, R. F., Rueda, A. D., Benedito-Silva, A. A., DeMoraes, O., Felipe, L., Leite, J. R. (2008). Evaluation of Siddha Samadhi yoga for anxiety and depression symptoms: A preliminary study. *Psychological Reports, 103*(1), 271-274.

Kristeller, J. (2011). Spirituality and meditation. In J. D. Aten, M. R. McMinn, & E. L. Worthington, Jr. (Eds). *Spiritually oriented interventions for counseling and psychotherapy* (pp. 197-227). Washington, DC: American Psychological Association.

Kristeller, J. L., & Wolever, R. Q. (2011). Mindfulness-based eating awareness training for treating binge eating disorder: The conceptual foundation. *Eating Disorders: The Journal of Treatment and Prevention, 19*(1), 49-61.

Kuijpers, H. J. H., van der Heijden, F. M. M. A., Tuinier, S., & Verhoeven, W. M. A. (2007). Meditation induced psychosis. *Psychopathology, 40*(6), 461-464.

Kvillemo, P., & Bränström, R. (2011). Experiences of a mindfulness-based stress-reduction intervention among patients with cancer. *Cancer Nursing, 34*(1), 24-31.

Labelle, L. E., Campbell, T. S., & Carlson, L. E. (2010). Mindfulness-based stress reduction in oncology: Evaluating mindfulness and rumination as mediators of change in depressive symptoms. *Mindfulness, 1*(1), 28-40.

Lansky, E. P., & St. Louis, E. K. (2006). Transcendental meditation: A double-edged sword in epilepsy? *Epilepsy and Behavior, 9*(3), 394-400.

Lazar, S. W., Kerr, C. E., Wasserman, R. H., Gray, J. R., Greve, D. N., Treatway, M. T., ... Fischl, B. (2005). Meditation experience is associated with increased cortical thickness. *NeuroReport: For Rapid Communication of Neuroscience Research, 16*(17), 1893-1897.

Lee, S. H., Ahn, S. C., Lee, Y., Choi, T., Yook, K., & Suh, S. (2007). Effectiveness of a meditation-based stress management program as an adjunct to pharmacotherapy in patients with anxiety disorder. *Journal of Psychosomatic Research, 62*(2), 189-195.

Lehmann, D., Faber, P. L., Tei, S., Pascual-Marqui, R. D., Milz, P., & Kochi, K. (2012). Reduced functional connectivity between cortical sources in five meditation traditions detected with lagged coherence using EEG tomography. *NeuroImage, 60*(2), 1574-1586.

Levenson, R. W., Ekman, P., & Ricard, M. (2012). Meditation and the startle response: A case study. *Emotion, 12*(3), 650-658.

Linehan, M. (2007). *Dialectical behavior therapy in clinical practice: Applications across disorders and settings.* New York, NY: Guilford Press.

Lipsey, M. W., & Wilson, D. B. (1993). The efficacy of psychological, educational, and behavioral treatment: Confirmation from meta-analysis. *American Psychologist, 48,* 1181-1209.

Luders, E., Clark, K., Narr, K. L., & Toga, A. W. (2011). Enhanced brain connectivity in long-term meditation practitioners. *NeuroImage, 57*(4), 1308-1316.

Luders, E., Kurth, F., Mayer, E. A., Toga, A. W., Narr, K. L., & Gaser, C. (2012). The unique brain anatomy of meditation practitioners: Alterations in cortical gyrification. *Frontiers in Human Neuroscience, 6,* Article 34.

Luders, E., Phillips, O. R., Clark, K., Kurth, F., Toga, A. W., & Narr, K. L. (2012). Bridging the hemispheres in meditation: Thicker callosal regions and enhanced fractional anisotropy (FA) in long-term practitioners. *NeuroImage, 61*(1), 181-187.

Luders, E., Toga, A. W., Lepore, N., & Gaser, C. (2009). The underlying anatomical correlates of long-term meditation: Larger hippocampal and frontal volumes of gray matter. *NeuroImage, 45*(3), 672-678.

Lutz, A., Slagter, H. A., Dunne, J. D., & Davidson, R. J. (2008). Attention regulation and monitoring in meditation. *Trends in Cognitive Sciences, 12*(4), 163-169.

MacDonald, D. A., LeClair, L., Holland, C. J., Alter, A., & Friedman, H. L. (1995). A survey of measures of transpersonal constructs. *Journal of Transpersonal Psychology, 27*(2), 171-235.

Manzaneque, J. M., Vera, R. M., Ramos, N. S., Godoy, Y. A., Rodriguez, F. M., Blanca, M. J., ... Enguix, A. (2011). Psychobiological modulation in anxious and depressed patients after a mindfulness meditation programme: A pilot study. *Stress and Health: Journal of the International Society for the Investigation of Stress, 27*(3), 216-222.

Martin, J. (1997). Mindfulness: A proposed common factor. *Journal of Psychotherapy Integration, 7,* 291-312.

Mason, L., Alexander, C., Travis, F., Marsh, G., Orme-Johnson, D., & Gackenbach, J. (1997). Electrophysiological correlates of higher states of consciousness during sleep in long term practitioners of the Transcendental Meditation program. *Sleep, 20a,* 201-110.

Miklowitz, D. J., Alatiq, Y., Goodwin, G. M., Geddes, J. R., Fennell, M. J. V., Dimidjian, S., ... Williams, J. M. G. (2009). A pilot study of mindfulness based cognitive therapy for bipolar disorder. *International Journal of Cognitive Therapy, 2*(4), 373-382.

Miller, J., Fletcher, K. & Kabat-Zinn, J. (1995). Three-year follow-up and clinical implications of a mindfulness-based intervention in the treatment of anxiety disorders. *General Hospital Psychiatry, 17,* 192-200.

Mohan, A., Sharma, R., & Bijlani, R. L. (2011). Effect of meditation on stress-induced changes in cognitive functions. *Journal of Alternative and Complementary Medicine, 17*(3), 207-212.

454   *Douglas A. MacDonald, Roger Walsh, and Shauna L. Shapiro*

Moore, A., & Malinowski, P. (2009). Meditation, mindfulness and cognitive flexibility. *Consciousness and Cognition: An International Journal, 18*(1), 176-186.

Morone, N. E., Greco, C. M., & Weiner, D. K. (2008). Mindfulness meditation for the treatment of chronic low back pain in older adults: A randomized controlled pilot study. *Pain, 134*(3), 310-319.

Murphy, M. & Donovan, S. (1997). *The physical and psychological effects of meditation* (2nd ed.). Petaluma, CA: Institute of Noetic Sciences.

Naranjo, C., & Ornstein, R. E. (1971). *On the psychology of meditation.* New York, NY: Viking Press.

Neumann, N., & Frasch, K. (2006). Meditation aus neurobiologischer Sicht-Untersuchungsergebnisse bildgebender Verfahren [The neurological dimension of meditation: Results from neuroimaging studies]. *Psychotherapie Psychosomatik Medizinische Psychologie, 56*(12), 488-492.

Newberg, A. B., Wintering, N., Waldman, M. R., Amen, D., Khalsa, D. S., & Alavi, A. (2010). Cerebral blood flow differences between long-term meditators and non-meditators. *Consciousness and Cognition: An International Journal, 19*(4), 899-905.

Nidich, S. I., Ryncarz, R. A., Abrams, A., Orme-Johnson, D. W. & Wallace, R. K. (1983). Kohlbergian cosmic perspective responses, EEG coherence and the TM and TM-Sidhi program. *Journal of Moral Education, 12*(3), 166-173.

Oken, B. S., Fonareva, I., Haas, M., Wahbeh, H., Lane, J. B., Zajdel, D., & Amen, A. (2010). Pilot controlled trial of mindfulness mediation and education for dementia caregivers. *Journal of Alternative and Complementary Medicine, 16*(10), 1031-1038.

Olivo, E. L., Dodson-Lavelle, B., Wren. A., Fang, Y., & Oz, M. C. (2009). Feasibility and effectiveness of a brief meditation-based stress management intervention for patients diagnosed with or at risk for coronary heart disease: A pilot study. *Psychology, Health & Medicine, 14*(5), 513-523.

Ong, J. C., Shapiro, S. L., Manber, R. (2008). Combining mindfulness meditation with cognitive-behavior therapy for insomnia: A treatment-development study. *Behavior Therapy, 39*(2), 171-182.

Ortner, C. N. M., Kilner, S. J., & Zelazo, P. D. (2007). Mindfulness meditation and reduced emotional interference on a cognitive task. *Motivation and Emotion, 31*(4), 271-283.

Osis, K., Bokert, E., & Carlson, M. (1973). Dimensions of meditative experience. *Journal of Transpersonal Psychology, 5*(2), 109-135.

Ospina, M. B., Bond, K., Karkhaneh, M., Buscemi, N., Dryden, D. M., Barnes, V., ... Shannahoff-Khalsa, D. (2008). Clinical trials of meditation practices in health care: Characteristics and quality. *Journal of Alternative and Complementary Medicine, 14*(10), 1199-1213.

Pace, T. W. W., Negi, L. T., Adame, D. D., Cole, S. P., Sivilli, T. I., Brown, T. D., ... Raison, C. I. (2009). Effect of compassion meditation on neuroendocrine, innate immune, and behavioral responses to psychosocial stress. *Psychoneuroendocrinology, 34*(1), 87-98.

Pagnoni, G., & Cekic, M. (2007). Age effects on gray matter volume and attentional performance in Zen meditation. *Neurobiology of Aging, 28*(10), 1623-1527.

Perlman, D. M., Salomons, T. V., Davidson, R. J., & Lutz, A. (2010). Differential effects of pain intensity and unpleasantness of two meditation practices. *Emotion, 10*(1), 65-71.

Perls, F. (1969). *Gestalt therapy verbatim.* Lafayette, CA: Real People Press.

Piet, J., & Hougaard, E. (2011). The effect of mindfulness-based cognitive therapy for prevention of relapse in recurrent major depressive disorder: A systematic review and meta-analysis. *Clinical Psychology Review, 31*(6), 1032-1040.

Prakash, R., Dubey, I., Abhishek, P., Gupta, S. K., Rastogi, P., & Siddiqui, S. V. (2010). Long-term Vihangam yoga meditation and scores on tests of attention. *Perceptual and Motor Skills, 110*(3, Pt 2), 1139-1148.

Ramaswami, S., & Sheikh, A. A. (1989). Meditation East and West. In A. A. Sheikh & K. S. Sheikh (Eds). *Healing East and West: Ancient wisdom and modern psychology* (pp. 427-469). New York, NY: John Wiley & Sons.

Raskin, N., & Rogers. C. (1995). Person-centered therapy. In R. Corsini & D. Wedding (Eds.), *Current psychotherapies*, (5th ed.; pp. 128-161). Itasca, IL: F. E. Peacock.

Roberts-Wolfe, D., Sacchet, M., Hastings, E., Roth, H., & Britton, W. (2012), Mindfulness training alters emotional memory recall compared to active controls: Support for an emotional information processing model of mindfulness. *Frontiers in Human Neuroscience, 6*, Article 15.

Rosch, E. (1999). Is wisdom in the brain? *Psychological Science, 10*, 222-224.

Rosenthal, J. Z., Grosswald, S., Ross, R., & Rosenthal, N. (2011). Effects of transcendental meditation in veterans of Operation Enduring Freedom and Operation Iraqi Freedom with posttraumatic stress disorder: A pilot study. *Military Medicine, 176*(6), 626-630.

Sahdra, B. K., MacLean, K. A., Ferrer, E., Shaver, P. R., Rosenberg, E. L., Jacobs, T. L.,...Saron, C. D. (2011). Enhanced response inhibition during intensive meditation training predicts improvements in self-reported adaptive socioemotional functioning. *Emotion, 11*(2), 299-312.

Schneider, R. H., Alexander, C. N., Staggers, F., Orme-Johnson, D. W., Rainforth, M., Salerno, W.,...Nidich, S. (2005). A randomized controlled trial of stress reduction in African Americans treated for hypertension for over one year. *American Journal of Hypertension, 18*, 88-98.

Sedlmeier, P., Eberth, J., Schwarz, M., Zimmerman, D., Haarig, F., Jaeger, S., & Kunze, S. (2012). The psychological effects of meditation: A meta-analysis. *Psychological Bulletin, 138*(6), 1139-1171. doi:10.1037/a0028168.

Segal, Z., William, J. M., & Teasdale, J. (2002). *Mindfulness-based cognitive therapy for depression*. New York, NY: Guilford Press.

Semple, R. J. (2010). Does mindfulness meditation enhance attention? A randomized controlled trial. *Mindfulness, 1*(2), 121-130.

Shapiro, D., & Astin, J. (1998). *Control therapy*. New York, NY: John Wiley & Sons.

Shapiro, S., Astin, J., Bishop, S., & Cordova, M. (2005). Mindfulness-based stress reduction and health care professionals. *International Journal of Stress Management, 12*(2), 164-176.

Shapiro, S. L., Brown, K. W., & Astin, J. (2011). Toward the integration of meditation into higher education: A review of research evidence. *Teachers College Record, 113*(3), 493-528.

Shapiro, S. L., Brown, K. W., & Biegel, G. M. (2007). Teaching self-care to caregivers: Effects of mindfulness-based stress reduction on the mental health of therapists in training. *Training and Education in Professional Psychology, 1*(2), 105-115.

Shapiro, S., Schwartz, G., & Bonner, G. (1998). Effects of mindfulness-based stress reduction on medical and premedical students. *Journal of Behavioral Medicine, 21*, 581-599.

Shapiro, D. H., & Walsh, R. (Eds.). (1984). *Meditation*. New York, NY: Aldine.

Shapiro, S., & Walsh, R. (2003). An analysis of recent meditation research and suggestions for future directions. *The Humanistic Psychologist, 31*, 86-114.

Shigaki, C. L., Glass, B., & Schopp, L. H. (2006). Mindfulness-based stress reduction in medical settings. *Journal of Clinical Psychology in Medical Settings, 13*(3), 209-216.

Singh, N. N., Lancioni, G. E., Manikam, R., Winton, A. S. W., Ashvind, N. A., Singh, J., & Singh, A. D. A. (2011). A mindfulness-based strategy for self-management of aggressive behavior in adolescents with autism. *Research in Autism Spectrum Disorders, 5*(3), 1153-1158.

Singh, N. N., Lancioni, G. E., Winton, A. S. W., Adkins, A. D., Singh, J., & Singh, A. N. (2007). Mindfulness training assists individuals with moderate mental retardation to maintain their community placements. *Behavior Modification, 31*(6), 800-814.

Singh, N. N., Lancioni, G. E., Winton, A. S. W., Singh, A. N., Adkins, A. D., & Singh, J. (2008). Clinical and benefit-cost outcomes of teaching a mindfulness-based procedure to adult offenders with intellectual disabilities. *Behavior Modification, 32*(5), 622-637.

Sipe, W.E.B., & Eisendrath, S. J. (2012). Mindfulness-based cognitive therapy: Theory and practice. *Canadian Journal of Psychiatry, 57*(2), 63-69.

So, K., & Orme-Johnson, D. (2001). Three randomized experiments on the longitudinal effects of the Transcendental Meditation technique on cognition. *Intelligence, 29*(5), 419-440.

Sobolewski, A., Holt, E., Kublik, E., & Wróbel, A. (2011). Impact of meditation on emotional processing: A visual ERP study. *Neuroscience Research, 71*(1), 44-48.

Srinivasan, N., & Baijal, S. (2007). Concentrative meditation enhances preattentive processing: A mismatch negativity study. *NeuroReport: For Rapid Communication of Neuroscience Research, 18*(16), 1709-1712.

Storm, L., Tressoldi, P. E., & Di Risio, L. (2010). Meta-analysis of free response studies, 1992- 2008: Assessing the noise reduction model in parapsychology. *Psychological Bulletin, 136*(4), 471-485.

Tang, Y., Ma, Y., Wang, J., Fan, Y., Feng, S., Lu, Q., . . . Posner, M. I. (2007). Short-term meditation training improves attention and self-regulation. *PNAS Proceedings of the National Academy of Sciences of the United States of America, 104*(43), 17152-17156.

Tart. C. (1971). A psychologist's experience with transcendental meditation. *Journal of Transpersonal Psychology, 3*(1), 135-140.

Timmons, B., & Kamiya, J. (1970). The psychology and physiology of meditation and related phenomena: A bibliography. *Journal of Transpersonal Psychology, 2*(1), 41-59.

Tloczynski, J., & Tantriells, M. (1998). A comparison of the effects of Zen breath meditation or relaxation on college adjustment. *Psychologia, 41*, 32-43.

Toneatto, T., & Nguyen, L. (2007). Does mindfulness meditation improve anxiety and mood symptoms? A review of the controlled research. *Canadian Journal of Psychiatry, 52*(4), 260-266.

Travis, F., & Arenander, A. (2006). Cross-sectional and longitudinal study of effects of transcendental meditation practice on interhemispheric frontal asymmetry and frontal coherence. *International Journal of Neuroscience, 116*(12), 1519-1538.

Travis, F., Arenander, A., & DuBois, D. (2004). Psychological and physiological characteristics of a proposed object-referral/self-referral continuum of self-awareness. *Consciousness and Cognition, 13*, 401-420.

Travis, F., & Shear, J. (2010). Focused attention, open monitoring and automatic self- transcending: Categories to organize meditations from Vedic, Buddhist, and Chinese traditions. *Consciousness and Cognition: An International Journal, 19*(4), 1110-1118.

Trungpa, C. (1973). An approach to meditation. *Journal of Transpersonal Psychology, 5*(1), 62-74.

Van den Hurk, P. A. M., Giommi, F., Gielen, S. C., Spekens, A. E. M., & Barendregt, H. P. (2010). Greater efficiency in attentional processing related to mindfulness meditation. *Quarterly Journal of Experimental Psychology, 63*(6), 1168-1180.

Van den Hurk, P. A. M., Janssen, B. H., Giommi, F., Barendregt, H. P., & Gielen, S. C. (2010). Mindfulness meditation associated with alterations in bottom-up processing: Psychophysiological evidence for reduced reactivity. *International Journal of Psychophysiology, 78*(2), 151-157.

Van Nuys, D. (1971). A novel technique for studying attention during meditation. *Journal of Transpersonal Psychology, 3*(2), 125-133.

Vestergaard-Poulsen, P., VanBeek, M., Skewes, J., Bjarkam, C. R., Stubberup, M., Bertelsen, J., & Roepstorff, A. (2009). Long-term meditation is associated with increased gray matter density in the brain stem. *NeuroReport: For Rapid Communication of Neuroscience Research, 20*(2), 170-174.

Vettese, L. C., Toneatto, T., Stea, J. N., Nguyen, L., & Wang, J. J. (2009). Do mindfulness meditation participants do their homework? And does it make a difference? A review of the empirical literature. *Journal of Cognitive Psychotherapy, 23*(3), 198-225.

Vul, E., Harris, C., Winkleman, P., & Pashler, H. (2009). Puzzlingly high correlations in fMRI studies of emotion, personality, and social cognition. *Perspectives on Psychological Science, 4*(3), 274-290.

Wachholtz, A. B., & Pargament, K. I. (2008). Migraines and meditation: Does spirituality matter? *Journal of Behavioral Medicine, 31*(4), 351-366.

Walach, H., Nord, E., Zier, C., Dietz-Waschkowski, B., Kersig, S., & Schüpbach, H. (2007). Mindfulness-based stress reduction as a method for personnel development: A pilot evaluation. *International Journal of Stress Management, 14*(2), 188-198.

Walsh, R. (1999). *Essential spirituality: The seven central practices.* New York, NY: John Wiley & Sons.

Walsh, R. (2000). Asian psychotherapies. In R. Corsini & D. Wedding (Eds.), *Current Psychotherapies* (6th ed., pp. 407-444). Itasca, IL: F. E. Peacock.

Walsh, R. (2005). Can synesthesia be cultivated? *Journal of Consciousness Studies, 12*(4-5), 5-17.

Walsh, R. (2011). Lifestyle and mental health. *American Psychologist, 66*(7), 579-592.

Walsh, R., & Shapiro, S. L. (2006). The meeting of meditative disciplines and Western psychology: A mutually enriching dialogue. *American Psychologist, 61*(3), 227-239.

Walsh, R., & Vaughan, F. (Eds.). (1993). *Paths beyond ego.* Los Angeles, CA: J. Tarcher.

Wampold, B. E. (2001). *The great psychotherapy debate: Model, methods, and findings.* Mahweh, NJ: Erlbaum.

Washburn, M. (1988). *The ego and the dynamic ground: A transpersonal theory of human development.* Albany, NY: State University of New York Press.

Weber, B., Jermann, F., Gex-Fabry, M., Nallt, A., Bondolfi, G., & Aubry, J. M. (2010). Mindfulness-based cognitive therapy for bipolar disorder: A feasibility trial. *European Psychiatry, 25*(6), 334-337.

Weissbecker, I., Salmon, P., Studts, J. L., Floyd, A. R., Dedert, E. A., & Sephton, E. (2002). Mindfulness-based stress reduction and sense of coherence among women with fibromyalgia. *Journal of Clinical Psychology in Medical Settings, 9*(4), 297-307.

White, J. (Ed). (1974). *What is meditation?* Garden City, NY: Anchor Books.

Whitmont, E. (1969). *The symbolic quest.* Princeton, NJ: Princeton University Press.

Wilber, K. (2000). *The eye of spirit.* In *The collected works of Ken Wilber* (Vol. 7.). Boston, MA: Shambhala.

Wilber, K., Engler, J., & Brown, D. (Eds.). (1986). *Transformations of consciousness: Conventional and contemplative perspectives on development.* Boston, MA: New Science Library/Shambhala.

Williams, A., Kolar, M. M., Reger, B. E., & Pearson, J. C. (2001). Evaluation of a wellness-based mindfulness stress reduction intervention: A controlled trial. *American Journal of Health Promotion, 15*, 422-432.

Wise, C. C. (1974). A meditation on meditation. In J. White (Ed.), *What is meditation?* (pp. 61-84). Garden City, NY: Anchor Books.

Wisner, B. L., Jones, B., & Gwin, D. (2010). School-based meditation practices for adolescents: A resource for strengthening self-regulation, emotional coping, and self-esteem. *Children & Schools, 32*(3), 150-159.

Wong, E. (1997). *The Shambhala guide to Taoism.* Boston, MA: Shambhala.

Yunesian, M., Asiani, A., Vash, J. H., & Yazdi, A. B. (2008). Effects of transcendental meditation on mental health: A before-after study. *Clinical Practice and Epidemiology in Mental Health, 4,* Article 25.

Zamarra, J. W., Schneider, R. H., Besseghini, I., Robinson, D. K., & Salerno, J. W. (1996). Usefulness of the transcendental meditation program in the treatment of patients with coronary artery disease. *American Journal of Cardiology, 78,* 77-80.

Zautra, A. J., Davis, M. C., Reich, J. W., Nicassario, P., Tennen, H., Finan, P., ... Irwin, M. R. (2008). Comparison of cognitive behavioral and mindfulness meditation interventions on adaptation to rheumatoid arthritis for patients with and without history of recurrent depression. *Journal of Consulting and Clinical Psychology, 76*(3), 408-421.

Zeidan, F., Johnson, S. K., Diamond, B. J., David, Z., & Goolkasian, P. (2010). Mindfulness meditation improves cognition: Evidence of brief mental training. *Consciousness and Cognition: An International Journal, 19*(2), 597-605.

Zeidan, F., Johnson, S. K., Gordon, N. S., & Goolkasian, P. (2010). Effects of brief and sham mindfulness on mood and cardiovascular variables. *Journal of Alternative and Complementary Medicine, 16*(8), 867-873.

Zeidan, F., Martucci, K. T., Kraft, R. A., Gordon, N. S., McHaffie, J. G., & Coghill, R. C. (2011). Brain mechanisms supporting the modulation of pain by mindfulness meditation. *Journal of Neuroscience, 31*(14), 5540-5548.

Zgierska, A., Rabago, D., Zuelsdorff, M., Coe, C. M., Miller, M., & Fleming, M. (2008). Mindfulness meditation for alcohol relapse prevention: A feasibility pilot study. *Journal of Addiction Medicine, 2*(3), 165-173.

Zylowska, L., Ackerman, D. L., Yang, M. H., Futrell, J. L., Horton, N. L., Hale, T. S., ... Smalley, S. L. (2008). Mindfulness meditation training in adults and adolescents with ADHD: A feasibility study. *Journal of Attention Disorders, 11*(6), 737-746.

25

Psychedelic Induced Transpersonal Experiences, Therapies, and Their Implications for Transpersonal Psychology

Thomas B. Roberts and Michael J. Winkelman

Psychedelics and other natural and synthetic substances have an ability to induce a range of transpersonal experiences. The predominance of spiritually-related experiences from these substances has led to the development of the concept of entheogen—reflecting their potential to produce an internal experience of communing with god. The similarity of the drug-induced transpersonal experiences and those induced spontaneously or through behavioral and mental practices attests to their common biological bases in human nature. These biological bases involve the similarity of these exogenous substances to neurotransmitters, particularly the neuromodulator serotonin, and therefore their ability to serve as neurotransmitters. These neurocognitive effects of psychedelics demand a neurophenomenological model that addresses the relationship of both endogenous and exogenous neurotransmitter substances to the nature of perceived reality. These biological foundations also make them important tools for understanding the nature of brain functions, their relationships to mental processes, and the consequential relationship of brain and mind to personal experience, particularly the emotions, health, and spirituality. This chapter presents a neurophenomenological model of psychedelic-induced transpersonal experiences, therapeutic processes that they induce, and their implications for transpersonal theory. The pharmacological effects of psychedelics also enables them to address a range of psychological and emotional maladies. The chapter concludes with a brief overview of the multidisciplinary implications of psychedelics for the sciences and society.

Introduction

Transpersonal pioneer and renowned investigator of LSD Stan Grof (2009) characterized transpersonal experiences as "the feeling of the individual that his consciousness expanded beyond the usual ego boundaries and the limitations of time and space"

The Wiley Blackwell Handbook of Transpersonal Psychology, First Edition.
Edited by Harris L. Friedman and Glenn Hartelius.
© 2013 John Wiley & Sons, Ltd. Published 2015 by John Wiley & Sons, Ltd.

(p. 157). Friedman (1983) elaborated on this characterization of transpersonal experiences by reference to the degree or level of self-expansiveness, "which is defined as the amount of the self which is contained within the boundary demarcating self from non-self through the process of *self-conception*" (p. 38). For Friedman, the transpersonal dimension is reflected in "the degree to which individuals manifest expanded self-concepts [that] reflects the extent to which they accept or deny their unity with their true unbounded selves" (p. 39), and "the degree of identification with aspects of reality beyond that which is ordinarily conceived as being an aspect of the individual" (p. 41). These psychedelic-induced transpersonal experiences are eminently of a spiritual nature, although the political reactions they engendered have often dominated the public view of the substances that induce them.

Psychedelic, Entheogenic, and Transpersonal Experiences

The spiritual aspect of psychedelic experiences led a group of psychedelic scholars to invent the term *entheogen* as a synonym that emphasizes this quality (Ruck, Bigwood, Staples, Ott, & Wasson, 1979); it was also an attempt to reduce hostile public connotations that the term psychedelic has had due to its countercultural associations. The reframing of psychedelics as entheogens—with its etymological reference to producing the experience of god within (*theos* being Greek for god)—exemplifies and personalizes this conceptualization of identification with the universe beyond the personal self. This extrapersonal dimension is emphasized in the Greek etymological roots of entheogen referring to "the god within" or "animated with deity"; and *gen/genesis*, "action of becoming." Mark Hoffman and Carl Ruck (2004) defined *entheogen* as "any substance that, when ingested, catalyzes or generates an altered state of consciousness deemed to have spiritual significance" (pp. 111-112). Thus, *entheogen*, rather than psychedelic, is more exactly limited to instances when people feel a sense of sacredness, when spiritual experiences occur, and/or when these events are given a spiritual interpretation. This distinction also reflects empirical findings about mystical experiences; Hood's (1995) Mystical Experience Scale distinguishes a group that does experience a sense of sacredness from a group that does not; however, the experiences of both groups qualify as mystical.

Not all psychedelic experiences qualify as transpersonal; only those that have clear shifts in ego identity or location in time and/or space are relevant. Walls breathing and music seeming to arise in one's head do not count; they are personal experiences. But psychedelic experiences do encompass a broad range of transpersonal experiences, perhaps all. Grof (2001) has listed over two dozen transpersonal experiences such as archetypes, ancestral memories, and racial memories, and the *Journal of Transpersonal Psychology* (*JTP*) has included additional examples such as mystical experiences with their sense of ego-transcendence resulting in a sense of unity, existing outside of time, and a sense of becoming one with something else or even the whole cosmos (Lajoie, Shapiro, & Roberts, 1991).

It is this broader sense of surpassing personal identity that provided the original concept of transpersonal. In the 1970s as now, the term "transpersonal" was often understood as another word denoting a group of people acting together or interacting, almost a synonym of *social, collective, group,* and *interpersonal.* These words all make the assumption that individuals are separate beings who interact with each other. Transpersonal psychologists do not deny this, but emphasize that the perception of separateness depends on one's mind-body state, and more importantly, that the transpersonal states or experiences weaken or even erase conventional personal boundaries. That is, doing away with one's personal boundaries—*transpersonal*—is a psychologically different process from maintaining those boundaries while interacting with other separate, also bounded individuals, who all maintain their individual identity—interpersonal, collective, or group. This distinction has weakened over the years; in a survey of common usage of *transpersonal,* Hartelius, Caplan, and Rardin (2007) reported the growth of broader meanings: "the major subject areas of the field can be summed up in three themes: beyond-ego psychology, integrative/holistic psychology, and psychology of transformation" (p. 135).

Ego transcendence is a the key feature of psychedelics' entheogenic effects, which are known for evoking a characteristic engagement with some personalized transpersonal domains. Anthropologists and ethnobotanists (e.g., Dobkin de Rios, 1984; Furst, 1972; Harner, 1973; Rätsch, 2005; Schultes & Hofmann, 1979) have provided evidence of the similar psychological and cognitive dynamics associated with entheogen traditions worldwide. These pre-modern entheogenic uses share some commonalities in engaging a dramatic encounter with a spiritual world or the supernatural, bringing the mythical world to life; inducing an experience of the separation of one's soul or spirit from the body and its travel to the supernatural world; activating latent powers or abilities within and outside of the person; establishing personal relationships, even identity with animals and the experience of transformation into an animal; provoking experiences of death, transformation and rebirth; providing information through visions; and producing healing (Winkelman & Hoffman, in press).

When the cross-cultural literature on psychedelic-induced transpersonal experiences is considered as a whole, what is primarily reported is entheogenic, an experience that is most often intrinsically experienced as spiritual (Winkelman & Hoffman, in press; also see Arthur, 1999; Dobkin de Rios, 1984; Furst, 1976; Harner, 1973; Heinrich, 1995; Labate & MacRae, 2010; Rätsch, 2005; Ruck, Hoffman, & Celdrán, 2011; Ruck, Staples, & Heinrich, 2011; Rush, 2011; Schultes, Hofmann, & Rätsch, 1998; Wasson, 1968, 1980; Wasson, Kramrisch, Ott &, Ruck, 1986). This is the fundamental interpretation provided in hundreds of documented cultures around the world and across time. Beings experienced as both physical and spiritual entities have provided the foundations for human life and culture and the fundamental concepts of self and the purpose they have in the universe.

Not only are psychedelics central to many religious and spiritual traditions worldwide, they have also been central to the foundations of transpersonal psychology; many founders of transpersonal psychology include scholars whose lifetime professional writings include psychedelic topics. It is difficult to overestimate the influence of psychedelics on transpersonal studies. From their twin births during the hopeful period of the 1960s, through the dark decades of anti-psychedelic propaganda, and now in the twenty-first century's renaissance of psychedelic studies, transpersonal psychology and psychedelics have matured together and supported each other in a positive intellectual co-dependence.

The Partnership of Transpersonal Psychology and Psychedelics

Although there are historical antecedents to the word *transpersonal* (Vich, 1988), the parents in its current uses in psychology blend positive psychology (Compton & Hoffman, 2012), Abraham Maslow's (1968) "transcenders," and the psychedelic psychology of Stanislav Grof (2012). Toward the end of his life as he studied self-actualizers, Maslow realized they formed two separate groups. Beyond the self-actualizers were the self-transcenders, leading Maslow to update his needs hierarchy to put self-transcendence at the top above self-actualization (Maslow, 1967, 1968, 1969; Roberts, 1978). In the Preface to the second edition of *Toward a Psychology of Being* (1968, pages iii-iv) Maslow reported this new top to his needs hierarchy:

> I should say also that I consider Humanistic, Third Force Psychology, to be transitional, a preparation for a still "higher" Fourth Psychology, transhuman, centered in the cosmos rather than in human needs and interest, going *beyond* humanness, identify, *self-actualization* and the like. (pp. iii-iv, emphases added)

He further distinguished between self-actualizers and people who had peak experiences as the title of his chapter "Self-actualization and Beyond" shows in James Bugental's (1967) anthology *Challenges of Humanistic Psychology*. Maslow (1969) distinguished self-actualizers from transcenders on the basis of 20 characteristics:

> The other type (transcenders?) may be said to be much more aware of the realm of Being ... to have unitive consciousness and "plateau experiences" more or less often, and to have or to have had peak experiences (mystic, sacral, ecstatic) with illuminations or insights or cognitions which changed their view of the world and of themselves, perhaps occasionally, perhaps as a usual thing.
>
> It may be said of the "merely healthy" self-actualizers that, in an overall way, they fulfill the expectations of McGregor's Theory Y. But of the individuals who have transcended self-actualization we must say that they have not only fulfilled but transcended or surpassed Theory Y. They live at a level which I shall here call Theory Z for convenience and because it is on the same continuum as Theories X and Y and with them form a hierarchy. (p. 32; interior citations omitted)

Naturally enough, ways of triggering self-transcendence, mystical experiences, sacral and ecstatic states attracted his attention, and the psychedelic work of Stanislav Grof provided one piece of evidence. In *Religions, Values, and Peak-Experiences*. Maslow (1970) mentioned Grof's psycholytic work as important in providing nadir-experiences, the opposite of peak experiences (p. xiv) and later noted that, "these deductions from the nature of intense peak-experiences are given some support by general experience of LSD and psilocybin" (p. 76). Because many humanistic psychologists rejected any idea of spirituality, cosmic awareness, mystical experience, and related ideas, in 1967, Maslow, Grof, and others decided to found a new post-humanistic psychology. Together they coined the term transpersonal (Grof, 2012).

The editorial board of the early *JTP* was well-populated with psychedelic psychologists, scholars whose writings then and later included many of the primary publications about psychedelics: James Fadiman, Stanislav Grof, Walter Pahnke, Huston Smith, and Alan Watts. Over the years the board has also included Stanley Krippner, Charles Tart, and Frances Vaughan, who have all had professional interests in psychedelics. Ram Dass' *The Only Dance There Is* (1974) was first published as a series of *JTP* articles in 1970, 1971, and 1973, as were early drafts of chapters from Grof's (1975) key book *Realms of the Human Unconscious,* most notably his 1972 article entitled, "Varieties of Transpersonal Experiences: Observations from LSD Psychotherapy."

During its first decades, the *Journal of Transpersonal Psychology* dared to be one of the rare professional publications to report on psychedelic research. To the editors' and authors' honor, these were published during an era of intense governmental and media antipsychedelic propaganda when other journals were intimidated not to publish anything positive about psychedelics. Roger Walsh (1983) reported this fear when he submitted an article, "The journal editor was willing to accept the paper provided I remove any reference to positive effects of psychedelics" (p. 115). From these beginnings under difficult birth conditions and shunned childhood, psychedelics are spreading transpersonal ideas throughout the world of ideas and into other disciplines.

The Psychobiology of Psychedelics

The ubiquitous relationship of psychedelics and spiritual and other transpersonal experiences spans human history and prehistory. From ancient mushroom-shaped shamanic dancers engraved in the rocks of Africa to contemporary religions such as The Peyote Religion/Native American Church, Santo Daime, and Uniao do Vegetal, the use of a class of substances called psychedelics and hallucinogens appear almost intrinsically and inevitably linked to spiritual experiences (Arthur, 1999; Dobkin de Rios, 1984; Furst, 1972; Harner, 1973; Heinrich, 1995; Labate & MacRae, 2010; Rätsch, 2005; Roberts, 2001; Ruck et al., 2011; Ruck et al., 2001; Rush, 2011; Schultes et al., 1998; Wasson, 1968, 1980; Wasson et al., 1986). That this entheogenic effect is intrinsic rather than merely an effect of expectations is established in the double-blind clinical studies of Griffiths, Richards, McCann, & Jesse (2006, 2008). The similarity in cross-cultural use of entheogenic substances and the associated beliefs and experiences regarding their nature reflects effects on a common underlying human biological substratum which provides psychophysiological and psychopharmacological mechanisms for explaining both their ability to induce experiences of the sacred, as well as psychedelics' therapeutic properties (e.g., Winkelman & Roberts, 2007).

The biological basis of psychedelic-inspired mystical experiences, independent of expectation, is illustrated in the study by Griffiths et al. (2006) at the Medical Institute of Johns Hopkins University that provided objective evidence that psilocybin can directly induce mystical experiences and produce persistent effects on participants' attitudes, moods, and behaviors. The comparison with controls showed that psilocybin produced higher ratings on scales assessing the mystical oceanic boundlessness, visionary experiences; introvertive and extrovertive mysticism; a sense of unity with all of the universe; intuitive knowledge and transcendence of time and space; noetic experience characterized by a sense of sacredness; and significantly higher levels of peace, harmony, joy, and intense happiness. This careful clinical study illustrates that psychedelic-induced transpersonal experiences involve both the intrinsic biological properties of these substances and the structure of the human brain.

The Power of Transpersonal Variables

From a transpersonal perspective, the Johns Hopkins psilocybin studies open a broad avenue of experimental transpersonal research. Instead of considering such topics as meaningfulness, sacredness, altruism, and open-mindedness through the armchair theorizing of personal anecdotes, theology, vague observations, and historical examples, psychedelics bring experimental exactness to these topics. In a 14-month follow-up to the Griffiths et al. (2006) study, Griffiths et al. (2008) found that 11% of their volunteer subjects reported that their mystical experience was the single most significant experience of their lives, and an additional 67% rated it as one of their five most significant experiences. MacLean, Johnson, and Griffiths (2011) found, "in participants who met criteria for having had a complete mystical experience during their psilocybin session, Openness remained significantly higher than baseline more than 1 year after the session" (p. 1453). To assure that reported open-mindedness was not self-delusions, friends and family were interviewed before and after the sessions to confirm the self-reports. Mystical experience was the transpersonal variable that made the difference.

Psychoactives as Human Enhancers

E. O. Smith (1999) reviewed evidence that fitness benefits accrued to our human ancestors as a consequence of their ability to respond to these psychoactive substances. Many adaptive mechanisms could have been involved in human physiological and cultural use of consciousness-altering chemicals that provide relaxation, strength, anxiety reduction, pain endurance, enhanced bonding, nutrients, and many other effects. Sullivan and Hagen (2002; also see Sullivan, Hagen, & Hammerstein, 2008) reviewed evidence of a long-term evolutionary relationship between psychotropic plant substances and humans' cognitive capacities that indicate there were selective benefits of substance use. They characterized these benefits in terms of the ability of plants to provide neurotransmitter analogues that served as substitutes for endogenous transmitters that are rare or otherwise limited by dietary constraints. These are primarily in the monoamine neurotransmitters such as serotonin, as well as acetylcholine, norepinephrine, and dopamine that are crucial for normal brain function and require dietary precursors.

Psychedelics as Psychointegrators

Although entheogenic substances are found in a wide variety of families and genera, their effects primarily derive from similar chemicals compounds known as indoleamines, which have direct and indirect effects on the brain's neurotransmitter systems. The major classes of indoleamines—tryptamines (e.g., DMT, LSD, psilocin,

and psilocybin) and phenylethylamines (e.g., mescaline, MDMA [ecstacy], 2C-B)—
exert similar influences on serotonergic neurons (Nichols, 2004; Nichols & Chemel,
2006; also see Fantegrossi, Mernane, & Reissig, 2008) and produce similar experiential effects (for review see Hintzen & Passie, 2010; Passie, Halpern, Stichtenoth,
Emrish, & Hintzen, 2008).

A general macro-effect of entheogens involves high-voltage slow-wave synchronous
brain wave activity that increases the connectivity between the behavioral brain and
emotional brain, and between these lower brain areas and the frontal cortex (for discussion see Winkelman, 2010). These systematic changes in the overall dynamics of
brain processes are reflected in high-voltage brain wave discharges of a slow wave
frequency (typically theta, 3-6 cycles per second). These biochemically based physiological dynamics are primarily based in serotonin disinhibition and the consequent loss
of its inhibitory effects on dopamine and the mesolimbic structures, enhancing the
activity of lower brain structures, particularly the thalamic area that gates information
ascending from the peripheral nervous system.

Vollenweider's (1998) research on the mechanisms of action of psychedelics illustrates these macro level effects on the major cortical loops, particularly the frontal-
subcortical circuits that provide one of the principal organizational networks of the
brain. These involve neuronal linkages that constitute feedback loops of the cortical
areas of the frontal brain with the thalamus of the brain stem region and other lower
brain regions such as basal ganglia, substantia nigra, and the thalamus. Vollenweider attributed the consciousness-altering properties of psychedelics to their selective
effects on the brain's cortico-striato-thalamo-cortical feedback loops wherein the thalamus limits the ascending information to the frontal cortex from the environment
and body; psychedelics disable this disinhibition process, increasing access to the flow
of information that is ordinarily inhibited. This information overwhelms the frontal
cortex, leading to an alteration of experience of self, other, environment, and the
internal world of psychological structures and projections.

This model of psychedelic effects on the brain is shared by other models of alterations of consciousness. Dietrich (2003) proposed that a variety of altered states of
consciousness (ASCs; endurance running, dreaming, hypnosis, drug-induced states,
and meditation) involve a temporary deregulation of the prefrontal cortex (PFC) and
associated higher order functions. The common effects of this disruption are manifested in the loss of the roles of the frontal lobes, a subtraction of certain faculties
or experiences, reducing awareness to a lower condition within the hierarchy of conscious states. The different agents and activities that lead to this deregulation do so
in distinct ways that produce unique phenomenological characteristics of religious
experiences. Dietrich proposed that these different forms of hypofrontality involve
a general principle of a hierarchical and progressive disengagement with the more
sophisticated cognitive skills and levels of consciousness involving self-awareness and
planning (e.g., self-reflection, sense of time, planning) being compromised first, followed by lower-level systems. The deregulation of the PFC allows a number of unusual
self-experiences related to more ancient brain functions.

These effects of psychedelics, as well as other shamanistic ASCs, provoke a consciousness of these evolutionarily earlier structures of the brain (see Winkelman,
2010). Entheogens' effects on neurotransmission underlie a widespread premodern

466 Thomas B. Roberts and Michael J. Winkelman

use in shamanistic healing practices. Therapeutic effects are produced by the pharmacological and ritual activation of emotional processes of the limbic system and paleomammalian brain that underlie self-formation, attachment, and social bonding. Winkelman (2007a) has reviewed how these manipulations provoke the integration of lower level brain processes in ways that produce therapeutic effects, for example through the integration of traumatic memories into consciousness. These effects epitomize psychointegration, in which biological stimulation by entheogens expands awareness of repressed aspects of the self and the personal unconscious. Winkelman proposed that this reflects an enhanced awareness of processes in the lower structures and may involve what psychiatrist Stanislav Grof (1992) discussed as the transbiological realms of perinatal and transpersonal domains, including archetypal and mystical dimensions. It is this activation of lower brain structures that likely underlies the many different healing effects of entheogens.

"A Vaster Panoply of Human Experience": Transpersonal Psychology and Psychedelics

In addition to coining the term "transpersonal", helping to found the Transpersonal Institute, serving on its Editorial Board, and publishing in *JTP*, Grof's psychedelic clinical therapy and research formed a basis for transpersonal psychology's scientific credibility. While doing low-dose or *psycholytic* LSD clinical research in Prague, he discovered to his own surprise that some of his patients remembered their own births and even had transpersonal experiences. Later at the Maryland Psychiatric Research Institute, he and his research team developed high-dose psychedelic psychotherapy and honed the treatment protocol to include music, blindfolds, a relaxed setting, and similar precursors of today's laboratory and clinical techniques. From a transpersonal perspective, this work was proof-of-concept research that showed it is possible to elicit transpersonal experiences experimentally. These findings advanced transpersonal topics such as meaningfulness, spirituality, sacredness, mystical experiences, identity, ego-loss, archetypes, ancestral memories, and noetic knowing from armchair speculation to experimentation.

Grof's pioneering psychedelic findings have implications beyond psychotherapy in understanding the human mind. Psychedelics amplify or magnify human psychological experiences. Using LSD as a sort of microscope to examine the mind, psychiatrist Grof conducted over 4000 sessions and later reviewed records of several thousand additional sessions. Thus, Grof's sampling of the human mind is immense. In *Higher Wisdom*, psychiatrists Roger Walsh and Charles Grob (2005) evaluated Grof's knowledge of the human mind with perhaps only a little hyperbole: "He has therefore perhaps seen a vaster panoply of human experience than anyone else in history" (p. 119). Just as the microscope benefited biology and medicine by allowing scientists to assemble hundreds of individual magnified close-ups into detailed pictures of the human body—for example, a microscopic atlas of the liver—Grof has pieced together a psychedelics-based atlas of the human mind. Using the Freudian trope of

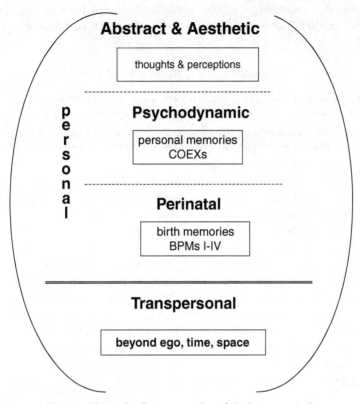

Figure 25.1 Grof's cartography of the human mind.

the mind having depth, Grof arranged his data into layers (see Figure 25.1). This map moves understanding of the human mind forward by integrating aspects of perceptual, Freudian-psychodynamic, Rankian-birth, and the Jungian collective unconscious psychologies into one overall model.

Abstract and Aesthetic Level

This is the shallowest level and what most people think of as psychedelic—sensory amplification and distortion of sight and sound and/or intensity of thoughts and emotions. Art, design, music, and popular culture portray these, but they have little to do with psychotherapy. In fact, in order not to have their clients distracted by perceptual changes, psychotherapists encourage clients to use blindfolds and earphones. Unlike recreational sessions whose intent may be to powerfully experience music, in therapeutic sessions the music is part of the psychotherapeutic process, selected to intensify inner awareness. Although experiences of chemical stimulation at the abstract and aesthetic level may be useful in exploring sensory and perceptual process, Grof (2009) wrote, they "represent the most superficial level of LSD experiences. They do not reveal the unconscious of the subject and do not have any psychodynamic significance" (p. 40). The next three levels are packed with significance.

Personal History, Biographical Level

In order to present a well-structured theory, Grof has presented his map layer-by-layer, but during sessions, a feeling, thought, or memory at one level may connect with others at different levels, so the client may ricochet around from level to level. In fact, these transitions help depict the client's mind by tracking the connections among levels in his or her emotional structure.

Coming from a strong psychodynamic tradition, Grof (2001) has named this the personal history level, or Freudian level, and concurs with some psychoanalytical thought, "Psychosexual dynamics and the basic conflicts described by Freud are manifested with unusual clarity and vividness even in the sessions of naïve subjects" (p. 66). But he has added to the Freudian perspective. Rather than the Freudian structures such as the Oedipal complex and penis envy, Grof discovered that emotions, thoughts, fantasies, and experiences collect together in a large number of clumps, which he has called *systems of condensed experience,* or *COEX systems.* "A COEX system can be defined as a specific constellation of memories (and associated fantasies) from different life periods of the individual" (Grof, 2001, p. 68). Each COEX has an emotional theme such as fear or loss, or a positive theme such as love and safety, and they largely determine the personality structure at this level of the mind. COEX systems are personally useful in understanding why, say, someone may overreact to a small annoyance as if it were a major threat; the annoyance activates a larger COEX. COEXs link to birth experiences that have similar emotional and physical feelings, and any particular experience on the personal history level will also activate its corresponding part on the perinatal level.

Perinatal, or Birth Level

There are four stages in the perinatal level. Grof (1992) has called these clusters Basic Perinatal Matrices (BPMs). They give pre-birth structure to the post-birth personal history level, to which subsequent life experiences attach their feelings—both emotional and physical. It is handy to think of the BPMs as four computer folders. At birth each BPM's size and power comes from pre- and perinatal life. In addition to the files that come from birth-related experiences, as a person lives their life new experiences are filed in their respective folders—that is, in the ones with which they have most resonance. To extend the folder metaphor, just as memories are stored in COEX folders on the personal history level, they are stored in BPM folders on the perinatal level.

Good womb and bad. BPM I is associated with life in the womb, usually the "good womb," and typically gives feelings of relaxation and all needs being taken care of; however, some fetuses experience a "bad womb," and many fetuses may experience bad episodes.

Contractions, trapped. BPM II, the "no-exit hell," starts with contractions but when the cervix is not open enough; typical feelings are those of being trapped with no hope of escape. The entrapment may be physical or emotional as when one is trapped in a bad relationship or job.

Birth canal, titanic struggle. Grof has named BPM III "titanic struggle." It occurs as the fetus struggles down the birth canal; movies and TV shows often spend most of their time expressing this action-based BPM and invoking the feelings of BPM III. They often go back and forth between BPM III and II as heroes and heroines fight, are successful, are trapped again, and so on.

Emergence, success. Finally, BPM IV happens when the baby emerges, and is accompanied by feelings of success, glory, celebration, and triumph. Grof's BPM series provides an exceedingly fertile collection of observations and ideas for the social sciences and the arts as well as psychiatry.

Perinatal ideas provide a rich set of ideas not only for understanding ourselves as humans, but also for interpreting movies such as *Snow White* and *Fight Club,* aspects of philosophy and history, and the imagery political leaders use to work people up into a war-like mood (Roberts, 2013). This is not to say they use a perinatal chain of imagery intentionally, but these images emerge because they unconsciously feel right. Grof's (1977) "The Perinatal Roots of Wars, Totalitarianism, and Revolutions," described this pro-war rhetoric. For example, when preparing citizens for war, leaders often provoke the feelings of entrapment, being squeezed, and and having no escape, thus activating the unconscious memory of the fetuses' experience of being trapped in the womb before the cervix is open—a need for room to live—*lebensraum,* as Hitler phrased it. This is followed by the "cosmic struggle" and war imagery, struggle, and the battle of moving down the birth canal. Finally leaders' imagery visualizes victory, success, and glory paralleling actual emergence and birth—"The glorious thousand-year Reich" as Hitler symbolized it. If people became aware of how the interplay of their own birth experiences and this imagery can be activated intentionally or unintentionally, they might become less violence prone. If nations realize this, they might become less bellicose.

Transpersonal Level

After inventing the psychedelic method of producing transpersonal experiences experimentally, Grof (2009) started to categorize them guided by his definition of transpersonal: "The common denominator of this otherwise rich and ramified group of phenomena is the feeling of the individual that his consciousness expanded (1) beyond the usual ego boundaries and limitations of (2) time and (3) space" (p. 157; numbers added). He listed 26 kinds of transpersonal experiences; six fall within the usual area of objective reality and 20 outside of it. For most scientists, their assumptions about what our minds can know are limited by what is known about what is in mainstream Western culture in an ordinary mind-body state. Transpersonal experiences support the assumption that what can be known varies from one state to another (Roberts, 2013); this epistemological perspective was the basis of Tart's (1972) notion of "state specific sciences." Thus, the single-state assumptions of Western culture and science are disputed by the findings of transpersonal psychology and its multistate view of reality and evidence of state-specific knowledge and abilities.

Psychedelic Psychotherapies

These transpersonal theories of the mind imply that these parts of the mind contain both specific sources of psychopathologies and their respective resources for treating them. Historically and in current clinical research on psychedelics, the research volunteers and clinical patients take their doses during an all-day session and are accompanied by session guides, usually a man and a woman. With these cautions, this procedure is akin to taking anesthetics. A patient is administered an anesthetic by a qualified anesthesiologist who attends the patient constantly; similarly, a qualified psychedelic psychotherapist attends a patient undergoing psychedelic psychotherapy. There is one exception: the pharmacological use of psychedelics, which will be discussed below. State-of-the art guidelines are provided by Passie (2007) and Mithoefer, Wagner, Mithoefer, Jerome, and Doblin (2011). Fadiman's (2011) *The Psychedelic Explorer's Guide* and Goldsmith's (2011) *Psychedelic Healing* have described these procedures in more detail.

A treatment session itself is typically the third step of a four-step process. Before that, patients and research volunteers are screened for physical and mental health. Second, before their session days, clinical patients and research volunteers develop rapport and learn to trust their guides. In order not to have surprise experiences that may frighten them, volunteers and patients learn what kinds of experiences they may have. After the session, both the same day and on a following day, they meet with their guides who help them make sense of their experiences and integrate them into their lives.

In addition to indigenous and shamanic approaches (see Winkelman 2007b), there are four main types of psychedelic sessions: psycholytic and psychedelic—which developed from Grof's work—entactogenic, and pharmacological.

Psycholytic

The purpose of psycholytic use—the dissolving or releasing of repression of memories—is to allow repressed material from a patient's unconscious to become conscious. Doses are low enough for the patient and psychiatrist to discuss memories when they emerge. This discussion-type treatment may last several drug-free sessions, and new doses are used only if required to dislodge more memories. In psycholytic use, psychedelics are very much just an adjunct to talking therapy. Although there is no set order of autobiographical memories emerging before perinatal ones, generally perinatal memories appear as related post-birth memories are exposed and dealt with. From a transpersonal perspective the perinatal level is significant. Grof (2009) reported, that becoming exposed to one's perinatal level opens up "deep repositories of spiritual and religious experiences that appear to form an intrinsic part of the human psyche and are independent of the individual's cultural and religious background and programming"

(p. 97). Although everyone has a birth experience as part of his or her individual life—as a personal level event—perinatal experiences form a highway from the three personal levels of the mind—abstract and aesthetic, biographical, perinatal—to the transpersonal level.

Psychedelic

There are two purposes for psychedelic, high dose therapy. The first is to produce a powerful, mystical experience in the client, and as mystical experiences include senses of ego-loss, self-transcendence, and time distortion, this method of psychotherapy is at the heart of transpersonal psychology. Treatment may be a few times, or even only once. The mystical, peak experience is itself psychotherapeutic. Because the psychedelic is used to produce the mystical experience, this portrays a different mechanism of action from the usual pharmacological mechanisms of common psychotherapeutic drugs. Current research—sometimes clinical and sometimes preclinical—focuses on such topics as treatment of depression (Carhart-Harris et al., 2012), post-traumatic stress disorder (Mithoefer et al., 2011), obsessive-compulsive disorders (Moreno, Delgado, & Galenberg, 2012), death anxiety (Grob et al., 2011), addictions and alcoholism (Kolp, Krupitsky, Friedman, & Young, 2009; www.ibogaine.org), neuroses and psychoses (Grof, 2001). Substances being researched to elicit therapeutic mystical experiences include not only the peyote employed by the Native American church, but also LSD, psilocybin, ibogaine, ketamine, ayahuasca, and several extracts and chemical congeners. These investigative therapeutic treatments rely not only on pharmacological and psychotherapeutic actions, but also on the power of set and setting (Johnson, Richards, & Griffiths, 2008). Reviews of research on these and related diagnostic categories are in the two-volume work, *Psychedelic Medicine: New Evidence for Hallucinogenic Substances as Treatments,* co-edited by Winkelman and Roberts (2007). *The Pharmacology of LSD: A Critical Review* exemplifies the kinds of thorough reviews needed for other substances (Hintzen & Passie, 2010). Psychedelic research from the 1960s on the use of psychedelics to treat autism and what would now be called Asperger's syndrome (Mogar & Aldrich, 1969) is being re-examined and may be resumed soon with adults.

Twenty-first century research has used the psychedelic model, but now with psilocybin favored over LSD. Grob et al.'s (2011) pilot study of reducing death anxiety typifies this use. In addition, the psilocybin team at Johns Hopkins has produced a series of psilocybin studies that looks at mystical experiences, meaningfulness, spirituality, openness, and altruism (Griffiths et al., 2006, 2008; MacLean et al., 2011).

The second type of psychedelic psychotherapeutic experience pushes the boundaries of transpersonal psychology even further. From Grof's (2006) perspective, the manifestation of an apparently pathological symptom may actually be the emergence of a therapeutic process, but because it does not seem part of this culture's usual beliefs about objective reality, it is often misclassified it as a symptom. This is not to deny that some neuroses and psychoses have organic and traumatic roots, but at times apparent symptoms are actually emerging therapeutic actions. Grof has suggested that humans have a sort of "inner radar" that locates both a problem and its solution, no matter how peculiar. Although the solutions may seem strange, idiosyncratic, even bizarre, for some reason when patients let their unconscious guide them, go forward with the process, and let their symptoms fully unfold, their symptoms and the underlying causes are often seemingly relieved (Grof, 2006). It may be instructive to think of this as a psychological parallel to throwing up tainted food; both are natural self-purging processes and should not be stopped.

Among the transpersonal events of non-objective reality that Grof (2006) has witnessed during psychedelic sessions are a woman who relived being accused as a witch in colonial Salem, several other apparent past-life recalls, another who felt transformed into a tree, and past life recalls that provide a sense of forgiveness that was later verified with the forgiven person miles away, and casting out of a satanic possession. Originally, Grof reported these cases as phenomenological descriptions of his patients' experiences without commenting on whether they were "real" or not (as in the reporting of dreams), but these and other transpersonal experiences seem to be becoming more credible to him, as the title of his 2006 book hints, *When the Impossible Happens*.

Entactogenic

This word is specifically applied to MDMA, more commonly called "Ecstasy". Exactly what to call this substance when it is used as a therapeutic agent is still unresolved; it has been referred to as an *empathogen,* and an *anxiolytic* (anxiety dissolving) or *antianxiety agent*. Although MDMA is not a proper psychedelic, it is commonly associated with these substances, so it will be considered here. The purpose of MDMA psychotherapy is to allow the client to reduce or even wholly disconnect the fear or other stressful feeling associated from the memory of a traumatic event, so its use for post traumatic stress disorder is paramount. MDMA was originally used primarily for couples and relationship therapy but without a record of clinical research studies (Holland, 2001). Michael Mithoefer, a psychiatrist in South Carolina, is now in the midst of government approved pilot clinical research studies. Originally involved with civilian therapy, he is now treating military, war-related cases (Mithoefer et al., 2011). The ability to separate from one's fears may be a beneficial use of ego-transcendence directed at a particular memory, or the feeling of being secure and in "safe hands" may be a therapeutic trait of mystical experiences. In spite of anecdotal reports, transpersonal research instruments have yet to track down any possible transpersonal elements of MDMA psychotherapeutic sessions.

Pharmacological

Unlike the other kinds of psychedelic psychotherapy, this type of therapy is pharmacological, not just psychological or transpersonal; in this sense it is an exception to the typical therapeutic uses of psychedelics. Serendipitously, a sufferer from cluster headaches discovered that psychedelics ended his suffering by preventing the periodic recurrence of these "suicide headaches" A group has been formed to examine this lead further (www.clusterbusters.com).

Wider Intellectual Prospects

Psychedelics form an experimental base for transpersonal psychology, one that is growing firmer as additional studies appear. In addition, psychedelic research embeds transpersonal psychology in larger intellectual frameworks. What might the transpersonal-psychedelic combination contribute to future large-scale intellectual projects? Experimental evidence, a wider evidential base, enriched conceptual base, and extended humanities, a view of the human mind that includes many mind-body states are several of the benefits (Roberts, 2013).

Consilience

Eminent biologist Edward O. Wilson (1998) proposed building a scaffold of knowledge that integrates the range of evidence and ideas from the subatomic, through the physical, chemical, biological, and so on to abstractions. One step toward linking these various levels might be to have an input (independent variable) at one level and its effects (dependent variable) measured at another, thus linking the levels. Psychedelics may be especially apt at this. As the recent work at Johns Hopkins Medical Institute shows (Griffiths et al., 2006, 2008) psilocybin not only effects biological processes but links all the way up to abstractions such as meaningfulness, spirituality, mystical experiences, openness of personality (MacLean et al., 2010), and other altered states phenomena (Roberts, 2013). As described in this volume, other transpersonal psychotechnologies such as meditation offer similar cross-level connections. Naranjo (1996) has provided an interpretation of psychedelic experiences in reference to the principles of the psychology of meditation.

Experimental Studies

Studies of mystical experiences, senses of sacredness, blessedness, resting in "caring, loving hands," awe, similar spiritual and religious concepts, and intense religious experiences have largely relied on historical records and ages-old texts. Now, these aspects of transpersonal spirituality are open to experiment. Their significance for religious studies was heralded by famed scholar of religions Huston Smith decades ago (see Smith, 2000; also Roberts, 2012, 2013).

Multistate Theory

One assumption behind transpersonal psychology is that individuals can produce and use many mind-body states—states of consciousness—in addition to an ordinary, default state (Tart, 1975). Over the years, one way or another, this central theme has likely been expressed in every volume of the *Journal of Transpersonal Psychology*. In addition to psychedelics, the journal features transpersonal psychotechnologies such as various kinds of meditation, biofeedback, body work, breathing exercises, the martial arts, dreams, hypnosis, and so on. Building on Tart's (1969) admonition to include all states in a full psychology, psychedelic and transpersonal ideas fit within multistate theory's four main concepts: (1) including all states, (2) mind-body state as variable, (3) psychotechnologies—methods—for producing states, and (4) residence. Residence recognizes that all human abilities are expressions of their home states, and they vary in strength and kinds from state to state. Furthermore, rare and unusual abilities may reside in states other than a default ordinary state. Thus, multistate theory provides an intellectual backing for transpersonal observations and theory (Roberts, 2013).

Transpersonal Contributions

As with religious studies, psychedelics are carrying transpersonal ideas into other disciplines; although, at this time their influences in the arts and humanities are not so as strong as those in anthropology, pharmacology, psychology, and psychotherapy. The psychedelics have been central to the expanding considerations of altered consciousness, which have applications across the disciplines of the humanities, social and physical sciences (Cardeña & Winkelman 2011). Current academic concerns in transpersonal theory also have implications that range from the arts to zoology (Hintzen & Passie, 2010; Roberts 2011, 2013). In practical fields, education and business may begin to catch up. There is hardly a field that is not beginning to be enriched by transpersonal perspectives, and psychedelics commonly carry those ideas.

Conclusions

While it is safe to say that transpersonal psychology could exist without psychedelics, it may be just as safe to say that transpersonal psychology would not exist without psychedelics. The intrinsic power of psychedelics to induce transpersonal experiences explains their primordial association with mystical traditions worldwide and underscores the need to explicate their physiological and cognitive properties as keys to a deeper understanding of the nature of transpersonal experiences and the human mind.

Internet and General Periodical Resources

With additional research being published frequently, the following resources are among the best ways to keep up with recent reports and future ones as they appear:

- Death anxiety. Grob and Danforth (2013). "Links to Videos and Web Sites." In "Psychedelic Psychotherapy Near the End of Life,"
- Johns Hopkins Psilocybin Research. (2012). Meaningfulness, spirituality, openness, and altruism. Griffiths et al. www.csp.org/psilocybin.
- Psychedelic Research around the World. (2012). Multidisciplinary Association for Psychedelic Studies. www.csp.org/research
- Our Research. (2012). Heffter Research Institute. http://www.heffter.org/research-hucla.htm

- Beckley Foundation Research. (2012). www.beckleyfoundation.org/research/
- U. S. National Institute of Health. (2012). www.clinicaltrials.gov (Hint: search "hallucinogen" rather than "psychedelic.)

Via articles on psychedelics in respected professional publications and general periodicals, transpersonal ideas are making their way into wider society. Here are several examples:

- 2006. *The Chronicle of Higher Education.* Researchers Explore New Visions for Hallucinogens. (Brown)
- 2008. *The Lancet.* Research on Psychedelics Moves into the Mainstream. (Morris)
- 2010. *American Psychological Association Monitor.* Research on Psychedelics Makes a Comeback. (Novotney)
- 2010. *Scientific American.* Hallucinogens as Medicine. (Griffiths & Grob)
- 2011. *The Economist.* Acid Tests. Research into Hallucinogenic Drugs Begins to Shake Off Decades of Taboo.
- 2012. Is the World ready for Medical Hallucinogens? *The New York Times Magazine* (Slater)

References

Arthur, J. (1999) *Mushrooms and mankind.* San Diego, CA: Book Tree.

Brown, S. (2006). Researchers explore new visions for hallucinogens. *The Chronicle of Higher Education,* Dec. 8. Retrieved from http://chronicle.com/weekly/v53/i16/16a01201.htm

Bugental, J. (Ed.). (1967). *Challenges of humanistic psychology.* New York, NY: McGraw-Hill.

Cardeña, E., & Winkelman, M. (Eds.). (2011). *Altering consciousness: Multidisciplinary perspectives* (2 Vols.). Santa Barbara, CA: Praeger.

Carhart-Harris, R. L., Leech, R., Williams, T. M., Erritzoe, D., Abbasi, N., Bargiotas, T., & Nutt, D. J. (2012). Implications for psychedelic-assisted psychotherapy: A functional magnetic resonance imaging study with psilocybin. *British Journal of Psychiatry.* Retrieved from http://bjp.rcpsych.org/content/early/2012/01/18/bjp.bp.111.103309. doi:10.1192/bjp.bp.111.103309

Compton, W., & Hoffman, E. (2012) *Positive psychology: The science of happiness and flourishing.* Belmont, CA. Wadsworth. Cengage Learning.

Dietrich, A. (2003). Functional neuroanatomy of altered states of consciousness: The transient hypofrontality hypothesis. *Consciousness and Cognition, 12,* 231-256.

Dobkin de Rios, M. (1984). *Hallucinogens: Cross-cultural perspectives.* Albuquerque, NM: University of New Mexico Press.

The Economist. (2011, June 23). Acid tests. Research into hallucinogenic drugs begins to shake off decades of taboo. Author.

Fadiman, J. (2011). *The psychedelic explorer's guide: Safe, therapeutic, and sacred journeys.* Rochester, VT: Park Street Press.

Fantegrossi, W., Mernane, K., & Reissig, C. (2008). The behavioral pharmacology of hallucinogens. *Behavioral Pharmacology, 75,* 17-33.

Friedman, H. L. (1983). The self-expansiveness level form: A conceptualization and measurement of a transpersonal construct. *Journal of Transpersonal Psychology, 15*(1), 37-50.

Friedman, H. (2006). The renewal of psychedelic research: Implications for humanistic and transpersonal psychology. *The Humanistic Psychologist, 34*(1), 39-58.

Furst, P. (1976). *Hallucinogens and culture*. San Francisco, CA: Chandler & Sharp.

Goldsmith, N. M. (2011). *Psychedelic healing: The promise of entheogens for psychotherapy and spiritual development*. Rochester, VT: Healing Arts Press.

Griffiths, R. R., Richards, W., McCann, U., & Jesse, R. (2006). Psilocybin can occasion mystical-type experiences having substantial and sustained personal meaning and spiritual significance. *Psychopharmacology, 187*(3), 268-283.

Griffiths, R. R., Richards, W., McCann, U., & Jesse, R. (2008). Mystical-type experiences occasioned by psilocybin mediate the attribution of personal meaning and spiritual significance 14 months later. *Journal of Psychopharmacology, 6*, 621-632.

Griffiths, R. & Grob, C. (2010). Hallucinogens as medicine. *Scientific American, 303*(6), 76-79.

Grob, C. S. & Danforth, A. (2013). Psychedelic psychotherapy near the end of life. In T. Roberts, *The psychedelic future of the mind* (Chapter 7). Rochester, VT: Inner Traditions/ Bear.

Grob, C. S., Danforth, A. L., Chopra, G. S., Hagerty, M., McKay, C. R., Halberstadt, A. L., & Greer, G. R. (2011). Pilot study of psilocybin treatment for anxiety in patients with advanced-stage cancer. *Archives of General Psychiatry, 68*(1), 71-78.

Grof, S. (1972). Varieties of transpersonal experience: Observations from LSD psychotherapy. *Journal of Transpersonal Psychology, 4*(1), 45-80.

Grof. S. (1975). *Realms of the human unconscious: Observations from LSD research*. New York, NY: Viking Press. (Republished in 2009 as *LSD: Doorway to the numinous*, by Park Street Press, Rochester, VT)

Grof, S. (1977). The perinatal roots of wars, totalitarianism, and revolutions: Observations from LSD research. *The Journal of Psychohistory, 4*(3), 269-308.

Grof, S. (1992). *The holotropic mind*. San Francisco, CA: Harper Collins.

Grof, S. (2001). *LSD psychotherapy*. Sarasota, FL: Multidisciplinary Association for Psychedelic Studies.

Grof, S. (2006). *When the impossible happens*. Boulder, CO: Sounds True.

Grof, S. (2009). *LSD: Doorway to the numinous*. Rochester, VT: Inner Traditions.

Grof, S. (2012). Maslow's fourth force: A brief history of transpersonal psychology. In *Healing our wounds: The holotropic paradigm shift*. Newcastle, WA: Stream of Experience.

Harner, M. (Ed.). (1973). *Hallucinogens and shamanism*. New York, NY: Oxford University Press.

Hartelius, G., Caplan, M. & Rardin, M. A. (2007). Transpersonal psychology: Defining the past, divining the future. *The Humanistic Psychologist. 35*(2), 1-26.

Heinrich, C. (1995). *Strange fruit: Alchemy and religion, the hidden truth*. London, UK: Bloomsbury.

Hintzen, A. & Passie, T. (2010). *The pharmacology of LSD: A critical review*. New York, NY: Oxford University Press.

Hoffman, M. & Ruck, C. A. P. (2004). Entheogens (psychedelic drugs) and shamanism. In M. N. Walter & E. J. N. Fridman (Eds.), *Shamanism: An encyclopedia of world beliefs, practices and cultures* (Vol. 1, pp. 111-117). Santa Barbara, CA: ABC-Clio.

Holland, J. (2001). *Ecstasy: The complete guide*. Rochester, VT: Park Street Press.

Hood, R. W., Jr. (1995). *Handbook of religious experience*. Birmingham, AL: Religious Education Press.

Johnson, M., Richards, W., & Griffiths, R. (2008). Human hallucinogen research: Guidelines for safety. *Journal of Psychopharmacology, 22*(6), 603-620.

Kolp, E., Krupitsky, E., Friedman, H., & Young, S. (2009). Entheogen-enhanced transpersonal psychotherapy of addictions: Focus on clinical applications of ketamine for treating alcoholism. In A. Browne-Miller (Ed.), *The Praeger international collection on addictions* (Vol. 3, pp. 403-417). Westport, CT: Praeger.

Labate, B., & MacRae, E. (Eds). (2010). *Ayahuasca, ritual and religion in Brazil.* London, UK: Equinox.

Lajoie, D., Shapiro, S., & Roberts, T. (1991). A historical analysis of the statement of purpose in *The Journal of Transpersonal Psychology. The Journal of Transpersonal Psychology, 23*(2), 175-182.

MacLean, K. A., Johnson, M. W., & Griffiths, R. R. (2011). Mystical experiences occasioned by the hallucinogen psilocybin lead to increases in the personality domain of openness. *Journal of Psychopharmacology, 25*(11), 1453-1462. doi: 10.1177/0269881111420188

Maslow, A. (1967). Self-actualization and beyond. In J. Bugental (Ed.), *Challenges of humanistic psychology* (pp. 279-286). New York, NY: McGraw-Hill.

Maslow, A. (1968). Preface to the Second Edition. *Toward a psychology of being.* Princeton, NJ: Van Nostrand.

Maslow, A. (1969). Theory Z. *Journal of Transpersonal Psychology, 1*(2), 31-47.

Maslow, A. (1970). *Religions, values, and peak-experiences.* New York, NY: Penguin, New York.

Mithoefer, M. C., Wagner, M. Y., Mithoefer, A. T., Jerome, L., & Doblin, R. (2011). The safety and efficacy of {+/−}3,4-methylenedioxymethamphetamine-assisted psychotherapy in subjects with chronic, treatment-resistant posttraumatic stress disorder: The first randomized controlled pilot study. *Journal of Psychopharmacology, 25*(4), 439-452.

Mogar, R. E., & Aldrich, R. W. (1969). The use of psychedelic agents with autistic schizophrenic children. *Behavioral Neuropsychiatry, 1*(8), 44-50. Retrieved at http://www.neurodiversity.com/library_mogar_1969.html

Moreno, F., Delgado, P., & Gelenberg, A. (2012). Effects of psilocybin in obsessive-compulsive disorder [study protocol]. Retrieved from http://www.maps.org/research/psilo/azproto.html

Morris, K. (2008). Research on psychedelics moves into the mainstream. *The Lancet, 371,* 1491-1492.

Naranjo, C. (1996). The interpretation of psychedelic experiences in light of the psychology of meditation. In M. Winkelman & W. Andritzky (Eds.), *Yearbook of cross-cultural medicine and psychotherapy 1995: Sacred Plants, Consciousness and healing* (pp. 75-90). Berlin, Germany: Verland & Vetrieb.

Nichols, D. (2004). Hallucinogens. *Pharmacology and Therapeutics, 101,* 131-181.

Nichols, D., & Chemel, B. (2006). The neuropharmacology of religious experience: Hallucinogens and the experience of the divine. In P. McNamara (Ed.), *Where God and science meet: The psychology of religious experience* (pp. 1-34). Westport, CT: Greenwood.

Novotney, A. (2010). Research on psychedelics makes a comeback. *American Psychological Association Monitor, 41*(10), 10.

Passie, T. (2007). Contemporary psychedelic therapy: An overview. In M. Winkelman & T. Roberts (Eds.), *Psychedelic medicine* (Vol. 1, pp. 45-68). Westport, CT: Praeger/Greenwood.

Passie, T., Halpern, J., Stichtenoth, D., Emrish, H., & Hintzen, A. (2008). The pharmacology of lysergic acid diethylamide: A review. *CNS Neuroscience & Therapeutics, 14,* 295-314.

Ram Dass. (1974). *The only dance there is.* Garden City, NY: Anchor/Doubleday.

Rätsch, C. (2005). *The encyclopedia of psychoactive plants: Ethnopharmacology and its applications* (J. Baker, Trans.). Rochester, VT: Park Street Press. (Original work published 1998 as *Enzyklopädie der psychoaktiven Pflanzen*, Aarau, Switzerland: AT Verlag)

Roberts, T. B. (1978). Beyond self-actualization. *ReVision, 1*(1), 42-46.

Roberts, T. B. (2011, December 8). *Psychedelic additions to the house of intellect.* Lecture delivered at MAPS 25th Anniversary Celebration, Oakland, CA. Retrieved from http://niu.academia.edu/ThomasRoberts/Talks/63819/Psychedelic_Additions_to_the_House_of_Intellect_PowerPoint

Roberts, T. B. (2012). *Spiritual growth with entheogens.* Rochester, VT: Inner Traditions.

Roberts, T. B. (2013). *The psychedelic future of the mind: How entheogens are enhancing cognition, boosting intelligence, and raising values.* Rochester, VT: Inner Traditions.

Ruck, C. A. P., Bigwood, J., Staples, D., Ott, J., & Wasson, R. G. (1979). Entheogens. *Journal of Psychoactive Drugs, 11*(1-2), 145-146.

Ruck, C., Hoffman, M., & Celdrán, J. (2011). *Mushrooms, myth and mithras: The drug cult that civilized Europe.* San Francisco, CA: City Lights Books.

Ruck, C., Staples, B., & Heinrich, C. (2001). *The apples of Apollo: Pagan and Christian mysteries of the Eucharist.* Durham, NC: Carolina Academic Press.

Rush, J. (2011). *The mushroom in Christian art: The identity of Jesus in the development of Christianity.* Berkeley CA: North Atlantic Books.

Schultes, R., & Hofmann, A. (1979). *Plants of the gods.* New York, NY: McGraw-Hill.

Schultes, R., Hofmann, A. & Rätsch, C. (1998). *Plants of the gods: Their sacred, healing and hallucinogenic powers* (2nd ed.). Rochester, VT: Healing Arts Press.

Slater, L. (2012). Is the world ready for medical hallucinogens? A kaleidoscope at the end of the tunnel. *The New York Times Magazine, April 22*, 56-60, 66.

Smith, E. O. (1999). Evolution, substance abuse, and addiction. In E. S. Trevathan & J. McKenna (Eds.), *Evolutionary medicine* (pp. 375-405). New York, NY: Oxford University Press.

Smith, H. (2000). *Cleansing the doors of perception: The religious significance of entheogenic plants and chemicals.* Los Angeles, CA: Jeremy P. Tarcher.

Sullivan, R., & Hagen, E. (2002). Psychotrophic substance-seeking: Evolutionary pathology or adaptation? *Addiction, 97*, 389-400.

Sullivan, R., Hagen, E., & Hammerstein, P. (2008). Revealing the paradox of drug reward in human evolution. *Proceedings of the Royal Society, B, 275*, 1231-1241.

Tart, C. (Ed.). (1969). *Altered states of consciousness* (3rd ed.). San Francisco, CA: HarperSanFrancisco.

Tart, C. (1972). States of consciousness and state-specific sciences. *Science, 176*, 1203-1210.

Tart, C. (1975). *States of consciousness.* New York, NY: E.P. Dutton.

Vich, M. (1988). Some historical sources of the term "transpersonal." *Journal of Transpersonal Psychology, 20*(2), 107-110.

Vollenweider, F. (1998). Recent advances and concepts in the search for biological correlates of hallucinogen-induced altered states of consciousness. *Heffter Review of Psychedelic Research, 1*, 21-32.

Walsh, R. (1983). Psychedelics and self-actualization. In L. Grinspoon & J. B. Bakalar (Eds.), *Psychedelic reflections* (pp. 115-120). New York, NY: Human Sciences Press.

Walsh, R., & Grob, C. (Eds.). (2005). *Higher wisdom: Eminent elders explore the continuing impact of psychedelics.* Albany, NY: State University of New York Press.

Wasson, G. (1968). *Soma: Divine mushroom of immortality.* New York, NY: Harcourt Brace Jovanovich.

Wasson, G. (1980). *The wondrous mushroom: Mycolatry in Mesoamerica.* New York, NY: McGraw-Hill.

Wasson, G., Kramrisch, S., Ott, J. & Ruck, C. (1986). *Persephone's quest: Entheogens and the origins of religion.* New Haven, CT: Yale University Press.

Wilson, E. O. (1998). *Consilience: The unity of knowledge.* New York, NY: Knopf.

Winkelman, M. (2007a). Therapeutic bases of psychedelic medicines: Psychointegrative effects. In M. Winkelman & T. Roberts (Eds.), *Psychedelic medicine: New evidence for hallucinogenic substances as treatments* (Vol. 1, pp. 1-19). Westport, CT: Praeger.

Winkelman, M. (2007b). Shamanic guidelines for psychedelic medicines. In M. Winkelman & T. Roberts (Eds.), *Psychedelic medicine: New evidence for hallucinogenic substances as treatments* (Vol. 2, pp. 143-168). Westport, CT: Praeger.

Winkelman, M. (2010). *Shamanism: A biopsychosocial paradigm of consciousness and healing.* Santa Barbara, CA: ABC-CLIO.

Winkelman, M., & Hoffman, M. (in press). Entheogens. In Kocku von Stuckrad and Robert Segal, (Eds.), Vocabulary for the study of religion. Leiden, The Netherlands: Brill.

Winkelman, M., & Roberts, T. (Eds.). (2007). *Psychedelic medicine: New evidence for hallucinogenic substances as treatments* (2 Vols.). Westport, CT: Praeger/Greenwood.

26

Transpersonal Dimensions of Somatic Therapies

Don Hanlon Johnson

In speaking of the fixation of the body, we are not referring to purely physical attachment—lust, let's say—as a purely physical matter. We are talking about the mind-body situation, the body aspect of our mind, the solidity aspect of it which needs constant feeding, reinforcement. It needs continual reassurance that it is solid. The basic Hinayana practice of simplifying every activity of the mind into just breathing or body movement reduces the intensity of the Rudra of body.

Chogyan Trungpa & Herbert V. Guenther, 1975, p. 9

Transpersonal psychology emerged in the middle of the last century primarily under the impact of widespread experiences that called into question dominant notions of the personal self in Western psychology. The experiences that first shaped the field came out of early contacts with older wisdom traditions—Hinduism, Buddhism, and Taoism. Access and attraction to these teachings were accelerated by the use of psychoactive substances. More slowly but steadily the earth-centered spiritualities of indigenous peoples have come to play a part in shaping the development of a different notion of the self. Still somewhat on the margins of the field, a wide range of somatic practices developed during the late 19th and early 20th centuries also radically change the mainstream notions of the physical matrix that supports various notions of the self in ways that join with those other movements. After an introductory account of the general territory of body-based transcendence, what follows is an account of how various body-centered practices lead to transpersonal experiences, with implications for a more expansive practice of psychotherapy.

The Wiley Blackwell Handbook of Transpersonal Psychology, First Edition.
Edited by Harris L. Friedman and Glenn Hartelius.
© 2013 John Wiley & Sons, Ltd. Published 2015 by John Wiley & Sons, Ltd.

The Territory

The movement in Life Against Death *was certainly moving down into the body and finding the reality to be bodily. But after I had gotten there, another movement set going which might be expressed this way: "but the body when you find it, is not just a body."*

(Norman O. Brown, 1970, p. 4)

Norman O. Brown uttered that statement in 1970 in an interview in a Santa Cruz underground newspaper. It was a crystalline expression of what I had been finding in the few years earlier. I had been a member of the Roman Catholic religious order of Jesuits for some ten years, during which we meditated one hour each morning, and for some short periods during the day; each year, we engaged in an 8-day silent retreat; and once I completed a 30-day silent retreat. Of the many different practices we were taught, several involved bodily awareness: breathing, posture, sensory attentions. Despite intense devotion to these practices over a decade, I lived a dissociated life, my consciousness largely living within abstract theological and biblical worlds, with little feeling for my breathing, kneeling, and sitting body nor for the palpable bodies of others.

In 1967 Gia-Fu Feng, a Chinese refugee and Taoist practitioner, invited me and a handful of Jesuit friends to join him in his pre-dawn meditation at his center on the summit of the Santa Cruz mountains just above our theological school. We entered his meditation room looking out over the fog-laced redwoods, and were instructed simply to sit and pay attention to our breath. There was something about the environment and the teaching vocabulary that prompted my sudden direct attunement to my actual breathing. In that hour, all the contents of the previous ten years of meditation—sacred images and phrases, mystical teachings, intellectual meanings—came crashing together. When I found my breathing, I found it was not just breathing.

That door opened to a journey with various methods of body cultivation that took something of this form:

- When I found touch in massage training and Rolfing, I found it was not just touch;
- When I found gestures and movements in working with such practices as Continuum and Body-Mind Centering, I found they were not just gestures and movements;
- When I found postures in Rolfing and Aston-Patterning, I found they were not just postures.

It was a door whose shapes I was able to discern because of my earlier philosophical studies in which I had read Plato, Descartes, Galileo, and Husserl. I could say very clearly what mind-body dualism was, how it came about, and what its implications were for our lives. But until now, I had not directly and consciously felt it in my being. I knew maps for the [territory] that I would have to traverse from then on.

I was not alone. For only one example, some 50 years earlier, the Tasmanian actor F. Matthias Alexander (1969) wrote a similar passage about his experiments that led to the creation of the Alexander Technique:

> I must admit that when I began my investigation, I, in common with most people, conceived of "body" and "mind" as separate parts of the same organism, and consequently believed that human ills, difficulties and shortcomings could be classified as either "mental" or "physical" and dealt with on specifically "mental" or specifically "physical" lines. My practical experiences, however, led me to abandon this point of view and readers of my books will be aware that the technique described in them is based on the opposite conception, namely, that it is impossible to separate "mental" and "physical" processes in any form of human activity. (p. 161)

But as I pursued this journey into the direct experience of the body, I came to realize that my experience was not universal, but radically Western, rooted in the consciousness-shaping forces of classical Greek philosophy, Christian theology, modern Western philosophy, and empirical science. I came to realize that these seemingly abstract ideas were engraved in my neuromuscular pathways by living within the structures of classrooms, exercise, dance, medical practices, and sports, which were peculiar to Western Europe and the United States. I eventually discovered that these practices, which shape the sensibilities of people growing up in this culture, are different from those in other cultures.

The late Japanese philosopher Yasuo Yuasa (1987) has written extensively about the different kind of sensibility that is evoked in the shaping practices of China, India, Korea, and Japan—martial arts, meditation, calligraphy, music, and so forth. The core of his work is the argument that sustained attention over a lifetime to the refinement of these practices and their experiential results are essential to the evolution of consciousness itself in the mature adult.

> One of the characteristics of Eastern Body-Mind theories is the priority given to the questions, "How does the relationship between the mind and the body come to be (through cultivation)?" or "What does it become?" The traditional issue in Western philosophy, on the other hand is "What is the relationship between the mind-body?' In other words, in the East one starts from the experiential assumption that the mind-body modality changes through the training of the mind and body by means of cultivation or training. Only after assuming this experiential ground does one ask what the mind-body relation is. That is, the mind-body issue is not simply a theoretical speculation but it is originally a practical, lived experience, involving the mustering of one's whole mind and body. The theoretical is only a reflection on this lived experience. (Yasuo, 1987, p. 18)

Encountering these very different cultural notions of sensibility helped me articulate the meaning and implications of my turn towards the body. What was lacking in both the meditation and academic teachings I received was this Asian notion of the intellectual and spiritual importance of cultivating one's sensibilities by long-term sustained practice of various bodily potentialities, and that theory depends on the cultivation of lived experience. Although in my Jesuit training we deliberately incorporated shifts of posture from sitting to standing to kneeling, we were not taught to pay intricate attention to what happened in each posture and in the shifts from one to another. When we practiced breathing meditation, our focus was on the words of the mantra (e.g., the Jesus prayer), not the actual experience of breathing itself.

What is given us at birth is the raw material for a human life, literally to be shaped both willy-nilly by parents, caregivers, and the media; sometimes more consciously by taking on practices designed to harmonize the links between body-shaping and the evolution of consciousness. This process of shaping the self and of consciousness itself is not well understood, not simply because of the pervasiveness of dualism, but also because it takes sustained use of specific body practices to make sense of it. It is as if a scholar would claim authority in studying Zen texts without practicing zazen. In the words of Husserl's phenomenological method, one must cultivate the particular attitude that constitutes a particular experiential territory. Within that newly found territory, the reality in question is now available to one who is ready to attend to it.[1] It was my prior studies of Husserl that helped me grasp more clearly what happened to me in Gia-Fu Feng's zendo: when I learned to shift my attention into the intricacies of sitting and breathing, adopting the Zen *Einstellung* or attitude, I found myself in a new experiential realm. And there, right before me, were the vast treasures of the transpersonal realm for which I had been searching for several years.

Marcel Mauss (1973) introduced the phrase "techniques of the body" to designate various body-shaping practices within a culture or particular community. These include the most obvious and deliberate forms of body-shaping present in methods of exercise, dance, sports, physical therapy, and body therapies. But more importantly, they also include everyday, non-thematized practices—infant-holding methods, the use of tools, walking, sitting. He called attention to the obvious but rarely noticed fact that simple activities, which one tends to think of as "natural"—sitting, diving, digging trenches—are highly evolved, culture- and gender-specific ways of shaping individuals according to the peculiar needs and aesthetic of that culture. These techniques accomplish two things. On the objective side, they give habitual shape to the protean bodies of our human birth. On the side of subjectivity, they help create our body-images, our felt sense of self, the body-schema. That body schema locates us within the perceived world; it forms the basis for our sense of our boundaries, where I stop and you begin; how responsive I am to outside information and how permeable to human intercourse. The shaping process is defined and transmitted in our social institutions: religion, the military, fashion and the media, sports, art, medicine. They reflect the tenacious forces of gender, ethnicity, and social class. Styles of shaping bodies parallel other expressions of a society's tastes in such forms as architecture, music, dance, and art.

In the development of a psychotherapist or a spiritual teacher, the shaping involves habituating oneself for listening, intuiting, dreaming, silence, and the range of sensibilities that are essential for these works.

Somatic Transpersonal Dimensions

To introduce a modicum of clarity into these complex issues, I am going to weave analyses of different kinds of transformative body practices into three strands of the transpersonal dimension, showing the relation of embodiment to each:

1   the dissolution of the fixity of the "I," the illusion that it is a thing;
2   affecting the neuromuscular barriers that keep one from a full and direct encounter with present reality;
3   the transcendence of ordinary awareness.

This is, needless to say, an artificial division, since the transcendence of the rigidly personal entails the whole package. But it helps as a way of articulating how various kinds of transformative body practices facilitate the crossover to the transpersonal and the therapeutic values inherent in that move.

Neuromuscular Fixities

Ida Rolf's (1977) work is often situated within the realm of physical therapy or alternative medicine even though she always rejected that interpretation. The goal of her intricate system of manipulations was to reduce the many ways in which an individual's body fights the field of gravity instead of harmonizing with it. In that fight, it builds up a network of hardened connective tissues (fascia, ligaments, tendons) that over time creates an illusory sense of being a hardened object, a machine with pulleys and levers, or a computer.

> Let me reiterate what I have often said before: I am not primarily interested in the relief of symptoms, either physical or mental. I personally am interested in the potential of humans, and human potential *per se* neither includes nor excludes the palliation of symptoms. The question remains: to what extent could Rolfers create a small population able to live within the gravity field without an on-going, everlasting war, without the constant expenditure of precious human energy merely to carry on life within the gravity field? If we could create such a population, what would be its characteristics? (Rolf, 1977, p. 3)

It was the cessation of that "ongoing, everlasting war" with the earth's field that originally drew so many, including myself, to this practice—the surprising feeling of gliding together through the world, suddenly uncluttered. Time and again over several decades, I have left Rolfing sessions with that intensely pleasurable feeling of just being here as I stand and move, with my attention freed of the pushes and pulls that so often occupy me; I am in a spacious and fresh world of consciousness.

Ida Rolf's (1977) work emerged out of the pre-medicalized field of osteopathy, an intricate system of connective tissue manipulation developed in the 19th century by Andrew Still and William Sutherland. Sutherland considered that this work of enhancing the link between one's body and the energy forces of the cosmos was carrying on older esoteric European traditions. The key to that link for him is the cerebrospinous fluid, whose pulses throughout the body reflect our relationship with the larger fields of the universe. A handful of practitioners managed to carry forward the original genius of the founders despite the colonization of the field by mainstream medicine—Eliott Blackman, Viola Frymann, John Upledger (Upledger & Vredevoog, 1983), Fritz Smith, Michael Shea (2007), Hugh Milne (1995), Harold I. Magoun (1983). They have managed to train large populations of young practitioners to do this remarkable work. It involves the cultivation of the circulation of the cerebrospinous fluid and its awareness, resulting in profound experiences of harmony with the ancient fields of bioenergies. It is an indescribably luscious experience to feel the utter peace and freedom from the daily hassles of embodiment when one of these practitioners guides one into what they often call a still point, an experience exactly like ones that emerge in sustained meditation.

Naked Awareness

In the 1930s, Charlotte Selver (1977) and Carola Speads brought to New York a radical method for cultivating the senses, which was originally developed by Elsa Gindler in Berlin. The work is deceptively simple: spending hours over years exploring the sensations of the simplest activities: sitting, standing up, reaching, touching, tasting. Alan Watts in California happened upon it and saw it as a Western version of Zen. He invited Selver to visit California where her work was enthusiastically embraced by Suzuki Roshi, founder of San Francisco Zen Center and Michael Murphy the founder of Esalen Institute. She had a quiet but enormous impact on the founders of humanistic psychology, most of whom studied her work. She wrote little and spoke with great care. In this passage, she addressed her spare version of the transpersonal theme:

> What people call "mystic"—the experiences one has, for instance in breathing, in balance, or whatever it is, on contact with another person—this can be very clearly experienced and yet experienced as a wonder, too. In other words, I feel it would be marvelous if one could work to pinpoint certain very clear revelations, which come out of experience and which in themselves are astonishing. The revelations can come from the very smallest experience. For instance, eating. (Selver, 1977, p. 17)

Another student of Gindler's, Lily Ehrenfried (1956), escaped to France where she taught until her death in her late 90s. She wrote a beautiful book on the spiritual dimensions of working over time to awakening the fullest ranges of our human sensory capacities. Its title summarizes the transpersonal relevance of this work: *From the Education of the Body to Spiritual Balance* (Ehrenfried, 1956).

Judith Aston created a method of working with the body using both movement instructions, guided touch, and manipulation of connective tissues with the goal of helping a person gain access to what she has sometimes called a neutral space, a configuration of the body in which the pulls and collapses due to many causes are largely put out of play.

> "Neutral" means your available optimal alignment for now. It's a position that creates the least stress and the most support for your body. Finding your Neutral is about honoring who you are at any given time.

Your Neutral will be unique to your body, mind and spirit. Your joints, history, surgeries, limitations, fears, successes, emotions and thoughts all make up one person, you, in this present moment. Your Neutral will take into account everything about you and it will change as you do. So if you are grieving the loss of a loved one, your Neutral will reflect that feeling at that particular time, as it would reflect joy at other times. (Aston, 2007, pp. 16-17)[2]

Using hands and carefully crafted words, the method helps one to arrive right here, neither tensed for action or contracting in fear, but just alive for the now. Her formulation is an embodied version of a widely recognized transpersonal notion of presence, where the inner conversations, with their floodings of memories and images, lose their power and a person is simply available for what is here now. Her formulation articulates the somatic dimension of this notion, expressing how the intricate matrices of muscle, bone, and connective tissues add to the mental detritus to pull one away from the currently real. Under the impact of her teaching, it is shocking to realize how much useless, self-defeating bodily actions one brings to the simplest events of life— sitting at a computer, in conversation with friends, driving a car. As one learns how to do just what one is doing and no more, there is a delicious feeling of emptiness, an absence of the dispersal of self that so typically clouds our perceptions of the real. In her recognition of this transpersonal aspect of her work, she introduced her book with this quote from Pema Chodron (2007): "Pleasant happens. Unpleasant happens. Neutral happens. What we gradually learn is to not move away from being fully present" (p. 78).

Beyond the Ordinary

Emilie Conrad Da'Oud's "Continuum" is a method of conscious body movement that helps one discover dimensions of embodied consciousness that are in the far-reaches of conventional thinking (Conrad, 2007). It involves long sustained periods of noticing, and sometimes initiating the most minute kinds of movement in the manner, she has said, of dropping a pebble in a pond and watching the ripples radiate. She came to her work out of an early history as a New York dancer and a four-year stay in Haiti where she studied African dance and spirituality.

As I let myself become increasingly anguished by the limits humans unknowingly agree to, I also began to see something else. I intuited that at an organismic level of pulsating life force, human beings were interacting among species and environments that our more conventional selves were unaware of.

I began to see human beings as biomorphic—we include all life forms. The movements of these forms went far beyond my dance classes, my nationality, gender, and species description. I had been searching for these "unqualified" movements all of my life.

What is it to join life in this way? What is it to magnify the subtle worlds of movement that silently flicker and pulsate inside of us? What is it to feel movement as a cosmic play in which form becomes mutable? These are the inquiries we make in Continuum. (Conrad, 1997, p. 62)

What originally struck me about entering this method was its almost luscious disruption of what I thought of as the basic framework of bodily movement. She likened that conventional framework to industrial age metaphors, pulley and levers, up-down-out. The movements triggered by her directions put me in a completely unfamiliar world of creatures—sea anenomes, slime molds, centipedes, seaweeds waving in the tides. Not grid-bound, not Cartesian coordinates. The consciousness that I found emerging from this work is indeed cosmic, although not in the more ethereal use of this term, but in a radically embodied sense of being within the ever-moving fluids, air, energetic pulsations of the earth, its beings, and the larger cosmic attractors.

Bonnie Bainbridge Cohen's *Body-Mind Centering* (2008) is similar to "Continuum" in its evoking unfamiliar states of body-embedded consciousness that link individuals to the vast worlds of living beings (Hartley, 1989). She has a genius at guiding people into a variety of unique kinds of consciousness that are different from one another depending on

- where they originate: from situating one's awareness in, for example, the bones, the lymph glands, the blood, the muscles; or
- what kind of sensibility is in play: touch, seeing, voicing; or
- what kind of overall body state is attended to: feeling, sensing, emoting, thinking.

It is almost a miraculous feeling to sense the precise discriminations of changes of consciousness as she evokes one sense of being in one's fluids, then one's bones, then one's muscles. With the familiar language of Western culture, it is very difficult to express such experiences.

> Generally, when anatomy is taught as I learned it, and as I see it taught elsewhere, you're given visual pictures of it. We have an image of it, but we don't have the kinesthesia of it within ourselves. Maybe we'll even say, "Oh, I have this bone or this muscle *in* me," but it's an intellectual concept, rather than the information coming through viscerally from the proprioceptors of that thing itself. The information is *always* coming in viscerally, but each person is selective in terms of what they choose to acknowledge. The studying that we're doing at the school [School for Body/Mind Centering] is highly selective in terms of receiving input; we go from one system to the other—now we're going into the senses, now we're going to *acknowledge the information* from the skeleton, now from the eye, now from the muscles, now from the organs, from the glands, the brain, the blood, etc. (Cohen, 2008, p. 64)

Authentic Movement is another widespread discipline that involves similar altered states. It is of special relevance to transpersonal psychology because its founders developed their work out of a psychological perspective that included not only perceptions and sensations, but feelings, emotions, dream awareness, and tracking of thoughts themselves. Its origins are in the work of Mary Whitehouse (1995; Frantz, 1999), one of the founders of Dance Therapy, and developed by a handful of others. The emphasis is on long and sustained practice of movement usually in groups or pairs. One person adopts the role of non-critical witness, eyes open, present to what is happening, creating an atmosphere of containment so that the mover is free to attend to what wants to happen—impulses, images, feelings. The presence of the witness helps create a feeling of safety that allows new and possibly fearful experiences to emerge in movement. The mover often moves with eyes closed. At the end of a period of movement, which may last from a few minutes to an hour or more, there is a disciplined period of discourse whose aim is to allow words to emerge in the same way that movements emerged, not talking about the experience, neither judging it nor interpreting, but allowing words and thoughts to come from out of the experience in the same way that the movements arose. This practiced discourse in a non-judgmental atmosphere of safety is makes Authentic Movement especially valuable in developing new theories of psychotherapy. The moving, speaking, writing, allow the mover to claim forgotten or rejected dimensions of the self as well as fractured links between thinking, moving, and direct experience.

Mary Whitehouse expressed how she came to develop this practice that she called "Movement in Depth:"

> What I began to understand during the beginning of my work in movement in depth was that in order to release a movement that is instinctive (i.e., not the "idea" of the person doing that movement nor my idea of what I want them to do), I found that I had to go back toward not moving. In that way I found out where movement actually started. It was when I learned to see what was authentic about movement, and what was not, and when people were cheating, and when I interfered, and when they were starting to move from within themselves, and when they were compelled to move because they had an image in their heads of what they wanted to do; it was then that I learned to say "Go ahead and do your image, never mind if you are thinking of it," and when to say "Oh, wait longer. Wait until you feel it from within. (Frantz, 1999, p. 23)

The practice involves teaching people how to wait for movement to arise and evolve as one gives oneself to it within an atmosphere of quiet attention. It is a sustained, tutored, disciplined waiting for movement—and words—to come from the self, instead of from habitual movements—or words—or moving and speaking as others would have us.

> A word about what this way of working with the body requires. There is necessary an attitude of inner openness, a kind of capacity for listening to one's self that I would call honesty. It is made possible only by concentration and patience. In allowing the body to move in its way, not in a way that would look nice, or that one thinks it should, in waiting patiently for the inner impulsive, in letting the reactions come up exactly as they occur on any given evening—new capacities appear, new modes of behavior are possible, and the awareness gained in the specialized situation goes over into a new sense of one's self. (Whitehouse, 1995, p. 250)

Janet Adler (2007) who has carried this work forward under the name *Authentic Movement,* deliberately developing its transpersonal dimensions, wrote of her early work with autistic children that inspired her eventual engagement with Authentic Movement:

> With the children and within the discipline of Authentic Movement, there is much learning about distinguishing between when we are here and when we are not here. In

times of grace there is a shared presence and in these moments...ritual occurs. When this happens, an immediate sense of inherent order becomes apparent within a felt sense of sacred space. (p. 25)

The Intertwinings: With Others and the World

There are two particularly important results of the marriage of certain kinds of somatic practices and transpersonal psychology. The first has to do with resolving an old tension between the transpersonal realm and the tangible worlds of body and earth. In the account above, you can see that the cultivation of various regions of our bodily reality leads to a consciousness in which the illusion of a bounded self undergoes a metamorphosis. One becomes ever more aware that humans are a network of interactions in the environment—air, food, bacteria, cells, the looks and touches of others—within which we find some bare core of agency, the "I can" of Edmund Husserl (Behnke, 2003). Husserl's student Maurice Merleau-Ponty formulated this interconnection as "intercorporeity" to replace the more abstract "intersubjectivity," to emphasize our congenital insertion into the web of relationships that makes up the Real (Merleau-Ponty, 1968). In that view, the pervasive troubles of alienation, isolation, and narcissism are secondary in the archaic processes of self-shaping, rooted not in nature but nurture. Individuation is an adult achievement; sociality is our body of birth. In this revisioning of our intercorporeal origins, Western thought joins with the Buddhist notion of interdependence, realized in the flesh. With this easing of the boundaries between flesh, cells, and higher states of consciousness, the therapeutic task of gaining some purchase over the sorrows of everyday life is rendered less problematic.[3]

A second, and intimately related result of the marriage is an enhanced capacity to deal with the great challenge of our time, the destruction of our ecosystem and the species that nurture it. It has been hard to mobilize the vast numbers of people necessary to change destructive public policies. Part of the difficulty results from a cultural alienation from our soulful connection with flesh, for it is our skin, lungs, and senses that interface our consciousness with air, water, sounds of crickets, sweep of great herons. Not enough people feel that our consciousness, our minds, souls, ideals are intertwined with the earth in which we are embedded. As we become more aware of this intertwining, perhaps there is some hope that we will succeed in turning away from destruction.

Notes

1. Husserlian Phenomenology has played a crucial role in my finding ways to articulate the layers of meaning in these many brilliant body practices. His intricate methods have been drastically oversimplified in the field of psychology. For an account of the method of constitutive phenomenology, cf. the article on that topic by Fred Kersten (1997). Elizabeth Behnke (e.g., 2003) has done a great service in her Study Project in The Phenomenology of the Body (sppb@openaccess.org) in which she has brought together little noticed Husserlian

texts with various body practices to demonstrate the radically transformative power in this classical tradition.

2. Her notion of neutral space is similar to Edmund Husserl's notion of the "null-body." Cf. Elizabeth Behnke's article on Husserl in The Encyclopedia of Philosophy, Table of Contents: Section 4: www.iep.utm.edu/husspemb/#H6<http://www.iep.utm.edu/husspemb/#H6>

3. There are increasing signs that the well-established bioenergetic approach to therapy initi- ated by Wilhelm Reich and carried forward by Stanley Keleman, Alexander Lowen, John Pierrakos, and others, will make increasingly significant contributions to transpersonal psy- chology by fostering the sense of self as a biological organism. Even though the founders were virulently secular in resistance to the toxic mystical and spiritual climate of pre-war Germany they managed to lay the foundations for a materialist sense of self that was not atomistic/mechanistic but embedded within the dense interdependent networks of biolog- ical evolution.

References

Adler, J. (2007). From autism to the discipline of Authentic Movement. In P. Pallaro (Ed.), *Authentic Movement. Moving the body, moving the self* (Vol. 2, pp. 24-31). Philadelphia, PA: Kingsley.

Alexander, F. M. (1969). *The resurrection of the body.* New York, NY: Dell.

Aston, J., Ross, K., & Bridgeman, K. R. (2007). *Moving beyond posture: In your body on the earth.* Incline Village, NV: Judith Aston.

Behnke, E. (n.d.). Null-body, protean body, potent body, neutral body, wild body. Author. Retrieved from http://www.donhanlonjohnson.com/syllabi/behnkenullbody.html (Available from author sppb@openaccess.org)

Behnke, E. (2003). Embodiment work for the victims of violation: In solidarity with the com- munity of the shaken. In C. -F. Cheung, I. Chvatik, I. Copoeru, L. Embree, J. Iribarne, & H. R. Sepp (Eds.), *Essays in celebration of the founding of the Organization of Phenomeno- logical Organizations.* Author. Retrieved from www.o-p-o.net

Brown, N. O. (1970, September). *Free spaghetti dinner interview.* Unpublished manuscript, Norman O. Brown Papers. University Library Special Collections and Archives, University of California, Santa Cruz, CA.

Chodron, P. (2007). *Practicing peace in times of war.* Boston, MA: Shambhala.

Cohen, B. B. (2008). *Sensing, feeling, and action: The experiential anatomy of Body-Mind Centering.* Northampton, MA: Contact Editions.

Conrad, E. (1997). Continuum. In D. H. Johnson (Ed.), *Groundworks: Narratives of embodi- ment.* Berkeley, CA: North Atlantic Press.

Conrad, E. (2007). *Life on land: The story of continuum.* Berkeley, CA: North Atlantic Books.

Ehrenfried, L. (1956). *De l'education du corps à l'équilibre de l'esprit.* Paris, France: Aubier Montaigne.

Frantz, G. (1999). An approach to the center: An interview with Mary Whitehouse. In P. Pallaro (Ed.), *Authentic Movement: Essays by Mary Starks Whitehouse, Janet Adler and Joan Chodorow* (pp. 17-38). Philadelphia, PA: Jessica Kingsley.

Hartley, L. (1989). *Wisdom of the body moving: An introduction to Body-Mind Centering.* Berkeley, CA: North Atlantic Books.

Kersten, F. (1997). Constitutive phenomenology. In L. Embree (Ed.), *The encyclopedia of phenomenology* (pp. 110-114). New York, NY: Springer.

Magoun, H. I. (Ed.). (1983). *Osteopathy in the cranial field.* Author.

Mauss, M. (1973). The techniques of the body (B. Brewer, Trans.). *Economy and Society*, *2*, 70-88.

Merleau-Ponty, M. (1968). The intertwining—the chiasm. In *The visible and the invisible* (A. Lingis, Trans.). Evanston, IL: Northwestern University Press.

Milne, H. (1995). *The heart of listening: A visionary approach to craniosacral work*. Berkeley, CA: North Atlantic Books.

Rolf, I. (1977, December). Dr. Rolf Says. *Rolf Lines* (no vol., n.p.).

Selver, C. (1977). Interview with Ilana Rubenfeld. *Somatics*, *1*(2), 13-17.

Shea, M. J. (2007). *Biodynamic sacral therapy*. Berkeley, CA: North Atlantic Books.

Trungpa, C., & Guenther, H. V. (1975). *The dawn of tantra*. Berkeley, CA: Shambala.

Upledger, J., & Vredevoog, J. (1983). *Craniosacral therapy*. Seattle, WA: Eastland Press.

Whitehouse, M. S. (1995). The Tao of the body. In D. H. Johnson (Ed.), *Bone, breath, and gesture* (pp. 241-252). Berkeley, CA: North Atlantic Books.

Yasuo, Y. (1987). *The body: Toward an Eastern mind-body theory*. Albany, NY: State University of New York Press.

27

Hypnosis and Transpersonal Psychology

Answering the Call Within

Ian E. Wickramasekera II

For well over two centuries the Western world has struggled to understand and utilize the phenomenon referred to today as hypnosis (Forrest, 1999) for what it can reveal about the nature of human existence and its ultimate potential. Hypnotic phenomena have been alternately viewed through a lens that lacks critical self-examination or that dismissed hypnosis as unworthy of attention. Yet hypnosis has called certain individuals to understand its mysteries despite the dangers that many researchers have encountered. The tradition of transpersonal psychology in particular owes a great debt to the pioneers of hypnosis, who frequently suffered ridicule and misfortune for providing a Western paradigm that has led to important developments in the fields of clinical psychology, consciousness studies, mind-body medicine, and parapsychology. Historically, the myriad phenomena of hypnosis have provided some of the best illustrations of the core ideas and concepts that one finds today in transpersonal psychology.

A brief historical examination of hypnosis will highlight its relationship to the fields of consciousness studies, mind-body medicine, parapsychology, and transpersonal psychology. The journey will begin with the early and largely forgotten days of Abbé Faria, then proceed through the eras of James Braid, Sigmund Freud, Milton Erickson, Ernest Hilgard, Ian Stevenson, and J. B. Rhine, all of whom answered the call to understand and utilize hypnotic phenomena in their own way. Next the focus will shift to an examination of the clinical effectiveness and utility of hypnotic phenomena—of which every transpersonal psychologist should have some awareness. Highlighted will be the four major traditions of clinical hypnosis employed in clinical psychology and mind-body medicine, which are routinely employed to help alleviate human suffering. Hypnosis can help integrate the body, mind, and spirit of human beings in an empirically verifiable manner that has come to satisfy even the most skeptical of former critics. The analysis will finish with a look to the present and possible future work of modern hypnosis researchers that is of particular relevance to transpersonal psychology. Research

The Wiley Blackwell Handbook of Transpersonal Psychology, First Edition.
Edited by Harris L. Friedman and Glenn Hartelius.
© 2013 John Wiley & Sons, Ltd. Published 2015 by John Wiley & Sons, Ltd.

in hypnosis continues to be on the leading edge of discoveries that challenge conventional understandings of human nature and human potential. Hypnosis may also be of critical assistance in future studies of the nature of mind using methods of neuroscience and neurophenomenology (Lutz & Thompson, 2003); from a transpersonal perspective it can be anticipated that such combined efforts might reach similar perspectives as the ancient wisdom teachings of many mystical traditions such as Dzogchen and Tibetan Buddhism (Varela, Thompson, & Rosch, 1991; Wangyal, 2011).

A Transpersonal History of Hypnosis

Transpersonal psychology has a highly diverse background (Tart, 1975; Walsh & Vaughan, 1993), but the tradition of hypnosis is probably one of the oldest and most colorful contributors from within the Western world. Research in hypnosis has been of paramount importance to the field of consciousness studies and in particular to the study of altered states of consciousness. Perhaps more than any other approach, it has provided evidence for polypsychic models of identity (Frederick, 2005; Hilgard, 1977) that cast doubt on the simple models of a continuous and unitary selfhood that transpersonal psychologies have critiqued (e.g., Tart, 1975; Walsh & Vaughan, 1993). Research in hypnosis led to the creation of psychodynamic terms such as the ego and the unconscious mind (Breuer & Freud, 1895/1999), which in turn have been essential to the translation of the ancient literature of Eastern mystical traditions that have been highly influential within transpersonal psychology. Any history of transpersonal psychology without reference to the development of hypnosis is therefore incomplete. The true origins of hypnosis began with the life of a man whose ideas have taken hundreds of years to fully appreciate (Carrer, 2006).

Over two centuries ago in Paris, France, there lived a man whose clinical work and ideas foresaw some of the most advanced understandings and current practices of clinical psychology, mind-body medicine, parapsychology, and transpersonal psychology. His name was José Custódio de Faria (1746-1819), although he is more widely known in the annals of the history of hypnosis as Abbé Faria (Carrer, 2006). Faria utilized an open-minded yet critical examination of the phenomenon of animal magnetism (Forrest, 1999) as a starting place for his original discoveries about hypnosis, which he named *lucid sleep* (Faria, 1819/2006). Most scholars and physicians of his day either accepted animal magnetism uncritically as a kind of energy-medicine or dismissively as some sort of dangerous charlatanism. Faria began his investigations of animal magnetism by attending séances where he witnessed specially trained magnetists apply their energies to patients who often went into epileptic convulsions after the supposed energy was applied. The most amazing effects of animal magnetism often occurred after the patient finished convulsing, when many subjects seemed to experience profound alterations of their consciousness, ignore painful stimuli, spontaneously recover from illnesses, receive telepathic communications, predict future events, and even diagnose and treat other people's medical illnesses. All that seemed necessary to make these amazing experiences happen was for the magnetist to apply the secrets of animal magnetism to the patient using esoteric-looking hand gestures, sometimes with an unusual device known as the baquet. Franz Anton Mesmer (1734-1815) had earlier developed a kind of secret society of magnetists around him called the Society of Harmony. Mesmer effectively served as the grand magus of the society and all its members paid him vast amounts of adoration, money, and prestige in order to learn the secrets of animal magnetism (Forrest, 1999).

The genius of Abbé Faria was to dare to challenge the Society of Harmony and medicine in general by originating a simpler and yet more elegant explanation for what was happening in the séances of animal magnetism. Faria boldly dared to hypothesize that the energies these people experienced did not come from the magnetist, but from within the patients' own mind, body, and spirit. He posited instead these people had a special gift to utilize their mind-body relationship in ways that had previously not been discovered in human beings. Faria praised the abilities of these patients to transcend the normal expectations of human potential using the phenomena of lucid sleep (hypnosis), and he dismissed the magnetists' belief that they wielded a miraculous energy. He referred to a person gifted at hypnosis as an *epopte,* meaning, those who see clearly (Forrest, 1999). He maintained that an epopte was a person who had a special gift to experience mind-body phenomena due to a combination of psychophysiological and spiritual factors (Carrer, 2006). Faria's ideas about the characteristics of an epopte are similar to Eastern ideas about the characteristics of an advanced meditator (Ray, 2000).

Although his work far pre-dated psychology, Abbé Faria's ideas about hypnosis were distinctively psychological and even transpersonal in their orientation as he mixed together his close observations of human behavior with ideas about body, mind, and spirit learned in obtaining his doctorate in theology while becoming a Catholic priest. Though he used different terms, his original writings stressed that common psychophysiological factors as well as special spiritual factors underlie what happens in hypnotic phenomena (Faria, 1819/2006). His theory rested on the basic assumption that commonplace notions about human nature are impoverished compared to our full potential—an assumption common in both humanistic and transpersonal psychology (e.g., Tart, 1975; Walsh & Vaughan, 1993).

Faria was also one of the first to investigate the polypsychic nature of identity (Frederick, 2005; Hilgard, 1977). Faria (1819/2006) described a number of individuals with whom he worked who seemed to be able to contact normally dormant or hidden aspects of their personality and sense of self through hypnosis (Faria, 1819/2006). Faria developed entirely new methods of hypnosis such as *age regression* in which he asked his subjects to revisit scenes from their past memories. Furthermore, he did not shy away from discussing his observations of parapsychological phenomena and developing a kind of psychophysiological and spiritual theory for how these phenomena occur (Carrer, 2006). Faria can be named as one of the first to realize a transpersonal explanation for altered states of consciousness, parapsychological phenomena, and the polypsychic nature of identity, in the way those terms are used in the West, while at the same time developing clinical methods that aided patients heal themselves using their own mind/body relationship. Abbé Faria could rightly be called one of the most important early pioneers in clinical psychology, consciousness studies, parapsychology, and transpersonal psychology.

Sadly, Abbé Faria was largely ridiculed in his own time, both by the tradition of animal magnetism and the medical establishment of his day. To make matters worse, a popular theatrical play was written about him in which he was thoroughly ridiculed, turning even the general public against him (Forrest, 1999). He left Paris shortly after the play's debut and died within a year with no known marker for his grave. He was largely forgotten in later years by other scholars of hypnosis due to the rarity of his only book (i.e., Faria, 1819/2006), and to the fact it was written in an obscure form of French (Carrer, 2006). However, as will be seen, a number of important scholars after his time have acknowledged his influence upon their ideas.

A number of influential people took up Faria's ideas and methods including James Braid (1843/1960), who was largely responsible for giving hypnosis its name in Western society. Braid followed Faria's notion that hypnosis represented a kind of mind/body ability that most human beings possess to some degree; Braid also dismissed earlier theories of animal magnetism even though they were still influential in his day (Forrest, 1999). Hippolyte Bernheim (1891/1980) later observed that a kind of trusting relationship with the hypnotist seemed essential in order for the hypnotized person to respond successfully to a hypnotic suggestion, whether in or out of the experience of trance. Bernheim successfully used methods of hypnosis to help patients with medical issues and psychophysiological disorders, and he credited Abbé Faria for sparking many of his ideas about hypnotic suggestibility.

Sigmund Freud can be said to have developed most of his key ideas in psychoanalysis through his early years of using Bernheim and Jean Martin Charcot's methods of hypnosis with patients who had psychosomatic illnesses. In *Studies on Hysteria* (Breuer & Freud, 1895/1999), the authors noted that some of their patients were able to recall memories during hypnosis that they otherwise could not remember during waking consciousness. This informed Freud as he developed his theories of repression, the unconscious, and a polypsychic theory of identity (Frederick, 2005; Hilgard, 1977). In Freud's polypsychic theory of identity, the ego is the only part of our mind that is generally well known to the person, and it frequently struggles with other unconscious parts of one's true nature.

It is noteworthy that some of the terms Freud developed such as ego, have been indispensable to translators of Eastern mystical texts and Western occultists alike (Crowley, 1929/1976), even though Freud's theorizing tended to denigrate mystical phenomena (Epstein, 1995). His ideas about ego clearly point to some of the forms of self-deception that Eastern mystical traditions have discussed under terms such as maya, illusion, and ignorance (Ray, 2000). However, unlike Eastern traditions that hold out the prospect of getting beyond the egoic veil of illusion and arrive at one's true nature (e.g., Wangyal, 2011), Freud was entirely pessimistic about this potential. Freud's point of view seemed to be that the best one can do as therapists is to move people who are suffering deeply to a more tolerable and common level of everyday unhappiness (Epstein, 1995).

It is perhaps telling that Freud eventually found the methods of hypnosis as distasteful as he did those of mysticism such as meditation. It has been suggested that he invented a number of psychoanalytic processes such as free association and dream interpretation in part to avoid the more profound cathartic experiences and alterations in consciousness that he observed with hypnosis (Fromm & Nash, 1997). What is certain is that when he abandoned hypnosis and eschewed mysticism, he closed a door that would not open again for nearly a hundred years (Epstein, 1995).

A small community of clinicians and scholars kept the hypnotic tradition alive and significantly expanded upon the scientific literature of hypnosis during the 20th century (Barabasz & Watkins, 2004) despite Freud's abandonment of the tradition that helped form his ideas. Foremost among these daring people are names such as Clark Hull, Milton Erickson, and Ernest Hilgard who were all determined to create a culture of scientific legitimacy around the uses of hypnosis in medicine, psychotherapy, and research.

Quietly, over many decades of research these scholars and their many colleagues created a body of scientific literature that has put hypnosis research in a much more respectable light than where Freud had left it. Much of this research has completely dismissed the traditional misconceptions that people have about hypnosis. There is now good evidence that hypnotic ability is a normal and highly stable trait that most people have to some degree, and which can be measured with highly reliable psycho-metric instruments (Hilgard, 1965, 1979). It is also known that hypnosis produces various phenomenological experiences such as altered states of consciousness in some individuals but not in everyone, not even in all of those who have good levels of hypnotic ability (Pekala & Kumar, 2000). Research has shown that hypnosis does not appear related to gullibility, waking suggestibility, or low intelligence (Nash, 2001); it appears to enhance the effectiveness of psychotherapy and medical procedures for anxiety, depression, pain, psychophysiological disorders, stress, trauma, and many related problems. For this reason hypnosis has, in the 20th century, been endorsed as a valid method for clinical and research purposes by respected groups such as the American Academy of Sciences, the American Medical Association, the American Psychological Association, and the British Medical Association (Barabasz & Watkins, 2005). This approval has been hard-won, and many hypnosis researchers have tended to shy away from controversial topics such as the investigation of anomalous phenomena during much of the past 100 years, perhaps in order to avoid appearing unscientific. However, there are a number of developments in hypnosis research with import for consciousness studies and parapsychology.

One of the most frequently debated topics in hypnosis research has centered on whether an altered state of consciousness is important for the production of hypnotic behaviors and experiences (Kirsch & Lynn, 1995). Early theorists such as Faria, Braid, and Charcot posited that an altered state of consciousness was a critical element in the production of hypnotic behaviors. However, this view has been called into question by other early theorists such as Libeault and Bernheim (Forrest, 1999), who expounded upon a view that suggestibility was more important than altered states of consciousness in explaining the nature of hypnosis. Paradoxical research has accumulated over time that is difficult to reconcile with either a purely altered state or non-state perspective (Kirsch & Lynn, 1995). For instance, many studies have now demonstrated that some individuals can experience profound hypnotic phenomena without a significantly altered state of consciousness (Barber, 2000; Kirsch & Lynn, 1995; Pekala & Kumar, 2005); ironically, it has also been shown that hypnotic ability does not correlate strongly with waking suggestibility or gullibility.

The community of hypnosis became sharply divided for a time between state theorists who discussed the importance of altered states of consciousness and non-state theorists who discussed the importance of a variety of social factors like role-taking and expectancy as the primary mediators of hypnotic phenomena (Kirsch & Lynn, 1995). Both state and non-state theorists have developed strong lines of evidence to support their views, which has made it nearly impossible to define hypnosis in a way that is acceptable to everyone in the field. However, more recently one of the world's most respected non-state theorists has published data from fMRI studies of the brain during hypnosis that appear to demonstrate the importance of altered states of consciousness (Kirsch, 2011). It would seem that from an empirical point of view a synthesis of both positions is necessary, because the evidence is strong on both sides no matter how paradoxical or illogical this viewpoint may seem. So far only a few unified theories of hypnosis have emerged that attempt to integrate both state and non-state aspects of hypnotic phenomena (Barber, 2000) although it certainly seems to be a direction that some researchers are taking (Pekala & Kumar, 2005; Wickramasekera II, 2007a).

Research and theorizing about possible correspondences between hypnotic and parapsychological phenomena was another very important development in the tradition of hypnosis during the 20th century. Many early researchers of parapsychology turned to hypnosis with the hope that it could enhance the reliability and magnitude of anomalous phenomena. However, a number of prominent parapsychologists have published data demonstrating that adding hypnosis to their experiments did not seem to reliably augment the production of paranormal phenomena such as clairvoyance and telepathy. J. B. Rhine conducted a number of parapsychological experiments with hypnosis throughout his career and later wrote that hypnosis was "not the kind of thing we need at this stage in ESP research" (Rhine, 1952, p. 367) due largely to the failure of any researcher to discover how hypnosis could actually enhance the production of paranormal phenomena.

Another early blow to hypnosis and parapsychological researchers occurred when it was shown that hypnosis was also not a reliable method to use when interviewing people about their memories of previous lives or other anomalous phenomena (Stevenson, 1994). Unfortunately, a good number of people in the general public, and even within the tradition of psychotherapy, falsely believe that the use of hypnotic regression techniques can reliably enhance people's memories of the past. A mountain of evidence has emerged within the past 50 years demonstrating conclusively that hypnosis does not reliably enhance people's memories of past events—though hypnosis does reliably inflate people's confidence in the veracity of their memories (Laurence & Perry, 1983). Worse yet, it has been found that some people can actually develop false memories (pseudo-memories) of events that never happened when they are asked even mildly suggestive questions during hypnosis (Laurence & Perry, 1983).

A classic experiment in this line of research was initiated by Laurence and Perry (1983) in which they age-regressed their experimental participants a few weeks back in time and asked them to report on slightly unusual phenomena that, the researchers suggested, had happened one night while the participants slept. Most of the highly hypnotizable subjects in their experiment then produced pseudo-memories of events that most likely never happened. However, even more ethically concerning was the fact that some of the participants' confidence in the reality of these pseudo-memories was not shaken when they were later told about the deception involved in the experiment. Hypnosis had seemed to boost the participants' confidence in the veracity of these pseudo-memories in a manner that has clearly caused many to wonder about the ethics of using hypnosis to enhance biographical recall (Barber, 1998). A number of prominent parapsychological researchers abandoned using hypnotic age regression techniques for these reasons (Stevenson, 1994). However, age regression techniques have nevertheless been helpful in resolving clinical issues, as will be discussed below.

Research involving hypnosis and other altered states of consciousnesses has more recently started to become helpful in the study of anomalous phenomena. A number of researchers have demonstrated evidence that people who tend to experience hypnotic phenomena also tend to report having more experiences with anomalous phenomena (Pekala, Kumar, & Marcano, 1995). This has led some to propose that measures of hypnotic ability could be used as a screening tool for finding particularly gifted people with paranormal abilities (Wickramasekera, 1986). Meanwhile a number of research paradigms seem to have come closer to demonstrating the proper methods of using altered states of consciousness to actually enhance the production of paranormal phenomena (Cardeña, 2010) such as the Ganzfeld studies of Charles Honorton and his colleagues (1990).

Looking back at the history of hypnosis, it is paradoxically true that both much and little has been accomplished regarding the explanation of its mysteries. The field has made good progress in establishing itself within science and medicine, despite the fact that this process has taken over two centuries. The hypnosis community has come much closer to making hypnosis a respectable subject of scientific inquiry and an accepted treatment method to which clinicians can routinely turn. The focus will now turn to a review of the dominant clinical paradigms employed in hypnosis today.

A Transpersonal Look at the Current Landscape of Clinical Hypnosis

The landscape of clinical hypnosis has evolved significantly over time. This section will briefly examine some of the major clinical traditions in existence today and look to their relevance from a transpersonal perspective. The four primary paradigms taught within the hypnosis community are the psychoanalytic, Ericksonian, socio-cognitive, and health/medical approaches. Each will be considered in terms of its ideas and methods, along with commentary from a transpersonal viewpoint.

The Psychoanalytic Tradition of Clinical Hypnosis

In a fascinating evolution of ideas and methods, the 20th century began with Freud abandoning the use of hypnosis, but ended with a healthy and influential contingent of psychoanalytic clinicians and researchers thriving within the hypnosis community (Fromm & Nash, 1997). Freud himself seems to have had trouble completely parting ways with hypnosis. He was quoted in 1935 as saying:

> There has to this day never been a better demonstration of the existence of the uncon-
> scious than the phenomenon of hypnosis. When philosophers talk about the impossibility
> of the unconscious, one can only advise them to witness an hypnosis; but people don't
> want to be shown that is the way human beings are. (Wortis, 1954, p. 160)

It should not be too surprising, then, that a number of influential psychoanalytic thinkers of the 20th century wished to return to the fertile ground of hypnosis and psychoanalysis that Freud had rejected.

Among these was Erika Fromm, one of the leading proponents of the ego psychology model in the 20th century (Fromm & Nash, 1997). She often credited Gill and Brenman's (1959) model of hypnosis as a "regression in service of the ego" as an important starting point of her approach to integrating psychoanalysis and hypnosis. Fromm taught her students that hypnosis was an altered state of consciousness that itself could enhance a patient's access to unconscious material while also enhancing their ego receptivity and experiential openness in psychotherapy (Fromm & Nash, 1997). Gill and Brenman (1959) observed that their methods of hypnoanalysis seemed to dramatically improve the efficacy and speed of psychoanalytic psychotherapy. The authors observed that this increase in efficacy of hypnoanalysis compared to normal psychoanalytic psychotherapy was due to the increased rate at which transference phenomena occur when hypnosis is utilized in psychotherapy. Nash and Spinler (1989) later demonstrated that normal people undergoing routine demonstrations of hypnosis do actually seem to engage in transference phenomena such as idealizing their hypnotist and seeing them as an especially wise person. Erika Fromm was an excellent teacher of this style of hypnotic treatment and she taught her students how to use methods such as age regression to resolve psychological trauma. These patients were often reported to be more amenable for treatment when hypnosis was used to enhance the patient's ego receptivity (Fromm & Nash, 1997). Some of Fromm's ideas about hypnosis having the effect of increasing ego receptivity were additionally supported by research suggesting that highly hypnotizable individuals seem more open experientially than other people (Tellegen & Atkinson, 1974) while also tending to score more highly on measures of empathy (Wickramaksekera II & Szlyk, 2003).

The ego psychology model bears much in common with the ego states model (Watkins & Watkins, 1997) in that it also incorporates many ideas about hypnosis as a regression in service of the ego and utilizes similar methods such as age regression in hypnoanalysis. However, a distinguishing feature of the ego states model is its detailed focus on the polypsychic aspects of human nature. This model can be said to be polypsychic in the sense that its proponents argue that every person has a continuum of ego states within rather than a singular sense of self (Watkins & Watkins, 1997). The term polypsychic is used in this tradition to indicate that the self is made up of many different self structures (e.g., parts) that take hold of us and through which we live and experience the world around us at times. A person normally transitions through their various parts in a rather integrated way that allows them to bring out their industrious parts at work, their playful parts at home, their compassionate parts in with other people's suffering, and so on. At other times some of these parts of our self may remain dormant and relatively un-integrated such as when a person cannot accept some aspect of themselves (Frederick, 2005).

The ego states model and its therapeutic methods are aimed at integrating the conflicting *parts* of a patient (the ego states) to work together more harmoniously and to share access to explicit memories across ego states. The model is highly regarded by clinicians who frequently treat patients with dissociative disorders since the methods of ego states therapy can be utilized to integrate these patients' fragmentary experiences of self along with their traumatic experiences. However, the methods are also aimed at working with much less pathological situations in psychotherapy such as when a person experiences suffering over their inability to accept some part of themselves fully. Situations of this sort commonly emerge when individuals are ashamed of their sexuality, gender, or past actions in life due to the myriad forms of judgment that people tend to hold against themselves—something that discourages them from being more authentic (Rogers, 1957).

The ego psychology and ego states treatment models can be said to be useful to transpersonal psychology due to their focus on enhancing the receptivity of the ego while confronting the ego's tendency towards self-deception. Psychoanalytic hypno-analysis and transpersonal psychotherapy both frequently try to help people achieve greater levels of awareness, openness, and insight while utilizing altered states of consciousness in some fashion (Fromm & Nash, 1997; Tart, 1994; Trungpa, 1973). The major difference comes about through the more optimistic view of transpersonal psychology that the ego can in some way be transcended through methods such as meditation (Trungpa, 1973). At the same time, some early ego psychologists experimented with using more transpersonal oriented methods such as LSD together with hypnoanalysis (Gill & Brenman, 1959); however, this is not typical of the current ego psychology approach.

The Ericksonian Tradition of Clinical Hypnosis

Milton Erickson is often cited as one of the greatest teachers of clinical hypnosis of the 20th century (Haley, 1993). Milton Erickson had tremendous impact on the hypnosis community through his work, co-founding the American Society of Clinical Hypnosis, editing the *American Journal of Clinical Hypnosis,* and spending countless hours training the next generation of clinicians. Many people think of hypnosis as a form of psychotherapy where one uses hypnosis to bypass the client's resistance. However, Erickson is credited with teaching the hypnosis community that "Hypnosis is not a process of taking control of people. It's a process of giving them control of themselves by providing feedback that they wouldn't ordinarily have" (Grinder & Bandler, 1981, p. 13). A close analysis of Erickson's methods and theories of clinical hypnosis demonstrates some surprising convergences between the Ericksonian tradition of clinical hypnosis and the humanistic/transpersonal traditions of psychology (Gunnison, 1985; Rogers, 1986). Some humanistic and transpersonal psychologists have held negative viewpoints of hypnosis. For example, Carl Rogers (1957), in his original writings on client-centered psychotherapy, described the clinical use of directive therapy techniques such as hypnosis as being unnecessary and potentially unhelpful. However, the similarity between Erickson and Rogers quickly emerges in light of the unusually intuitive style of empathy that Erickson utilized with hypnosis (Rogers, 1985, 1986).

Erickson's approach towards clinical hypnosis and psychotherapy appears to have been motivated by an empathic commitment to his patients. One of Erickson's most widely used methods, known as *utilization* (Erickson, Rossi, & Rossi, 1976) in the Ericksonian tradition, refers to the therapist's effort to use the client's own energy, skills, and potentials (Lankton, 2012a) in psychotherapy to help them accomplish their goals. Ericksonian therapists are required to learn how to become extraordinarily empathically attuned to their clients as a part of their training on how to utilize what their patient is doing in psychotherapy. For example, Erickson directed his students to observe even the minutest aspects of their patient's behavior such as their pupil diameter and breathing patterns (Erickson & Rossi, 1979), which Ericksonians sometimes refer to as *minimal cues*. Erickson encouraged his students to utilize their client's minimal cues by doing things such as pacing their vocal patterns to match with the client's respiration rate. Ericksonian hypnotists rarely follow standardized hypnotic scripts with their patients in favor of empathically utilizing what their clients bring to each moment in psychotherapy. Most Ericksonian therapists instead work to enter into a profound experience of being in the here-and-now with their clients while in trance, and the focus is on the present rather than the past (Lankton, 2010). My own research in this area has demonstrated that hypnosis actually seems to be a surprisingly empathy-laden experience (Wickramasekera II, 2007a; Wickramasekera II & Szlyk, 2003), consistent with the methods and ideas of the Ericksonian tradition.

Thus the essential elements of psychotherapy that Carl Rogers termed as empathy and unconditional positive regard can readily be found in Ericksonian therapy, as has been remarked upon by Carl Rogers himself (Gunnison, 1985; Rogers, 1985, 1986; Wickramasekera II, 2004b). Rogers (1985) suggested that the highly empathic context of client-centered psychotherapy may actually encourage therapists and their clients to enter into a trance together. Many therapists have probably found themselves entranced in some way by the intensity of a good empathic exchange with a patient. Rogers (1985) speculated that perhaps Erickson's gift for helping his patients may have come from the increased access to unconscious material that he might have had through utilizing hypnosis in therapy. He praised Milton Erickson for his ability to use this kind of hypnotic-empathy by saying:

> This concept helps me to explain how I can know and relate to the inner core of my client without any conscious knowledge of that core. It seems that Erickson had a very great gift for this kind of mysterious communication. (Rogers, 1985, p. 566)

The Ericksonian tradition tends to be more open than some to discussing anomalous experiences. Two well-known psychologists within the American Society of Clinical Hypnosis have recently created a workshop where they discuss the integration of anomalous experiences in psychotherapy (Accaria & Appel, 2005). Although these factors—empathy and consideration of anomalous experiences—might make the Ericksonian approach particularly attractive to transpersonal psychologists, in-depth knowledge of all four of the major hypnotic traditions is essential to a complete understanding of the potential of hypnotic phenomena.

The Socio-Cognitive Tradition of Hypnosis

The socio-cognitive tradition is perhaps the most frequently misunderstood school of hypnosis (Kirsch & Lynn, 1995). The tendency of altered states theorists has been to ignore the importance of the social psychological factors that this approach emphasizes

(Council, 1999); conversely, non-state theorists such as those of the socio-cognitive tradition have tended to ignore or to even deny the existence of the phenomenological experience of altered states of consciousness in hypnosis (Barber, 2000; Kirsch & Lynn, 1995). For this reason, transpersonally oriented psychologists or therapists might eschew the social cognitive tradition. However, as will be seen, much of what socio-cognitive theorists have uncovered about the nature of hypnosis is also useful to transpersonal theorists and practitioners.

Socio-cognitive theorists have a long tradition of producing some of the finest and most important scientific articles on the clinical effectiveness of hypnosis in dealing with issues such as anxiety and depression (Kirsch, Montgomery, & Saperstein, 1995; Schoenberger, Kirsch, Gearan, Montgomery, & Pastyrnak, 1997). Furthermore, these socio-cognitive authors have created relatively simple and elegant methods of integrating hypnosis with cognitive-behavioral therapy (CBT) that have been shown to significantly increase the latter's effectiveness. One meta-analysis in this area demonstrated that patients receiving hypnosis integrated with CBT received better treatment outcomes 70% of the time when compared with patients who received CBT without hypnosis (Kirsch, et al., 1995). Today this approach to integrating hypnosis with CBT is regarded as highly effective and helpful even by people who are critical of theoretical aspects of the model of CBT itself (Lankton, 2012b).

Many of the explanations of hypnosis that socio-cognitive theorists have put forth have considerable relevance for transpersonal psychology. Ted Sarbin is known as one of the most influential socio-cognitive theorists of the 20th century, and his work has often highlighted how the interpersonal and social context of hypnosis can cause people to adopt a *social role* that guides their behaviors and experiences during hypnosis (Sarbin, 1950). A surface level reading of this idea might seem to suggest that socio-cognitive theorists are saying that people fake hypnosis using the roles and expectations they believe are expected of them (Kirsch & Lynn, 1995). However, what socio-cognitive theorists are describing is a process by which individuals create an expectation or role for themselves and then come to *believe-in* this role with a *hallucinated-intensity* (Sarbin, 1998). The model also states that all experiences of the self/ego are "constructed, role-governed, and performed" (Lynn, Pintar, Stafford, Marmelstein, & Lock, 1998, p. 137) as a kind of *believed-in imagining*.

This view of the self as believed-in imagining is similar to views of self as illusory that are found in the Eastern mystical traditions that inform transpersonal psychology (Wickramasekera II, 2004a, 2007b). For instance, in the Dzogchen tradition the self is said to arise from ignorance of one's true nature. One creates a fictional sense of self in part to calm anxieties over ignorance of one's true nature, which is normally invisible due to the form of dualistic consciousness that is utilized in order to cling to a familiar sense of self (Wangyal, 2011). Consider the following quotation from the Bon Dzogchen teacher, Tenzin Wangyal Rinpoche, (Wangyal, 2011) on how one creates a fictional sense of self:

> Our cultural and family upbringing, our religious training, along with all our personal encounters and physical and emotional sensitivities, contribute to shaping our hopes, fears, perspectives, and sense of self. To achieve true self-realization, you must ultimately shed the conceptual, dualistic view that you have cultivated over a lifetime. (p. 25)

It can be said that one of the main points of utilizing altered states of consciousness in Dzogchen and Tibetan Bon-Buddhism is to help one learn to open to the reality of who we as humans are innately, through methods of meditation. This is but one example of how the socio-cognitive tradition has generated useful clinical methods, theories, and data that can be utilized from within a transpersonal framework, despite a difference of opinion regarding the value of altered states of consciousness.

The Medical/Health Tradition of Hypnosis

One of the most promising developments in the hypnosis community within the last 50 years has been its ability to reliably demonstrate the beneficial physiological effects of hypnosis on the body (Covino, Wexler, & Miller, 2010). It has been known for hundreds of years that hypnosis can relieve pain, but it is only within the past 20 years that good evidence has been developed for how it is accomplished within the brain. In the 1990s Pierre Rainville and his colleagues published a series of paradigm-shifting papers for the neuroscience community that demonstrated how hypnosis alleviated pain through affecting the emotional and sensory pain processing centers of the brain (Rainville, Carrier, Hofbauer, Bushnell, & Duncan, 1999). Furthermore, a number of excellent studies have appeared demonstrating that hypnosis works well for alleviating pain in clinical contexts (Montgomery, DuHamel, & Redd, 2000; Patterson & Jensen, 2003), and even tends to provide cost savings through reduced utilization of medical services and drugs (Lang & Rosen, 2002). This successful research on hypnotic analgesia has gone a long way towards convincing the medical community that it is time to embrace hypnosis in alleviating chronic pain and other related health problems. The use of hypnosis has also been established to some degree with asthma, eating disorders, irritable bowel syndrome, obesity, sleep disorders, smoking cessation, wound healing, and simply coping with the stress of being a medical patient (Covino et al., 2010; Ginandes, Brooks, Sando, Jones, & Aker, 2003; Palsson, 2006).

The effective research that has been done with hypnosis in medical settings has opened a great deal of territory for clinicians within the transpersonal tradition who are interested in mind/body medicine (Achterberg, 2002; Dossey, 1995). It has been my experience that the medical community generally welcomes any clinician who can reliably help their patients. I have frequently been asked by my medical colleagues if I could help a particular patient or disorder with hypnosis. However, I have never been asked about transpersonal psychology while at a hospital or medical clinic. Transpersonal psychology appears to enjoy quite a bit less stigma within medical settings than in academic or psychiatric contexts, where it has sometimes garnered negative attention (e.g., Ellis & Yeager, 1989).

A Transpersonal Look at the Future of Hypnosis

There are two interrelated trends within the hypnosis community of interest to transpersonal clinicians and scholars. The first trend concerns the astonishing pace at which concepts and methods from mystical traditions such as Dzogchen, Bon,

Tibetan Buddhism, and Taoism are becoming integrated with hypnosis. The second trend concerns the increasing utilization of methods of hypnosis to provide new insights into advanced questions about the nature of mind and identity within neuroscience and neurophenomenology. These two developments are likely to draw many people to take a fresh look at transpersonal psychology, since the tradition has been a haven for people who are not afraid to answer the call to understand and help others more fully utilize their body, mind, and spirit.

The Secret Wisdom of All Ages and Hypnosis

This look to the future begins by examining the current trend towards the integration of the methods and theories of ancient mystical traditions with hypnosis. For many years, Stanley Krippner and his colleagues have been conducting cross cultural and psychophysiological research on hypnosis and its relationship to the mystical and shamanistic practices of various cultures (Hageman, Krippner, & Wickramasekera II, 2008; Krippner, 2004). Krippner (2004) has documented numerous correspondences between the hypnotic-like practices in various shamanistic traditions and the Western traditions of hypnosis. The door to understanding hypnosis and its relationship to mysticism is now opening much wider than in former years.

Mindfulness meditation is probably the most popular of the ancient wisdom methods to have become integrated within psychotherapy and medical communities (Kabat-Zinn, 1990; Walsh & Shapiro, 2006). It seems as if almost every major tradition of psychotherapy recognizes and recommends the practice of mindfulness meditation, despite the fact that very little has been said about the ultimate nature of mind that is said to arise through practicing mindfulness (Trungpa, 1973; Wickramasekera II, 2004b). The big exception is of course the tradition of transpersonal psychology, which has celebrated and studied many different mystical traditions' viewpoints on the nature of mind (Tart, 1975; Walsh & Vaughn, 1993; Wickramasekera II, 2004a, 2004b, & 2007b). It seems likely that transpersonal writings on mystical practices such as Dzogchen, gTummo, kundalini yoga, mahamudra, and mindfulness meditation (Ray, 2000) will become more influential outside the transpersonal community as the rest of the psychological community awakens to the deeper potential of human nature that can be glimpsed during various meditation practices. This is already happening within the hypnosis community in which ideas about hypnosis and meditation practices have led to the development of promising initial clinical methods, research, and theory (Barabasz & Watkins, 2005; Hageman et al., 2008; Holroyd, 2003; Spiegel, White, & Waelde, 2010; Wickramasekera II, 2004a, 2007b; Yapko, 2011).

As an example of how some knowledge of hypnosis can help one understand the esoteric techniques of ancient wisdom cultures, consider the ancient practices of mantra meditation in which one meditates on sacred sounds or phrases that are repeated thousands of times (Wangyal, 2011). Many of these mantras contain subtle psychological and spiritual meanings embedded within them. The Bon-Buddhist mantra, OM MA TRI MU YE SA LE DU, for example, contains a complete roadmap for how to work with various aspects of suffering (Wangyal, 2005). Every small sound within the mantra addresses a kind of wisdom that helps alleviate the sufferings of life. A meditator can use the mantra as a practice to gain insight/awareness into the nature of suffering while meditating on the sacred sounds that transfer a blessing of sorts. Similarly, the mantra can be used to reestablish the insight/awareness during daily life just by repeating the mantra again outside of formal practice. This is much like the clinical practice of using post-hypnotic suggestions to help clients deal with various emotional conflicts in their lives. For instance, I commonly teach my patients to utilize the post-hypnotic suggestion, "calm, relaxed, and free," to activate a calm, relaxed, and quiescent state of mind. My patients can then later use the post-hypnotic suggestion whenever negative emotions might overwhelm them. Dzogchen practitioners use mantras in a hypnotic-like fashion (Krippner, 2004), and we can understand part of their potential as being related to post-hypnotic suggestions. However, mantras are quite different from post-hypnotic suggestions in that people usually do not conceive of post-hypnotic suggestions as being sacred sounds.

The similarity between post-hypnotic suggestions and mantras is but one small example of the shared territory between hypnosis and the ancient wisdom traditions (Holroyd, 2003). These traditions have produced many advanced theories about the nature of mind that are now capable of being examined utilizing advanced techniques in neuroscience such as functional magnetic resonance imaging (fMRI). So the integration of wisdom traditions into hypnosis will necessarily interact with another trend that involves the explosion of research in neuroscience and neurophenomenology, utilizing methods of hypnosis.

Neurophenomenology and Hypnosis

There has been a steadily increasing amount of research in neuroscience utilizing hypnosis as a method to investigate the physiological correlates of phenomenological experiences. The technology of neuroscience has become so precise that it is now possible to map the physiological correlates of even subtle phenomenological experiences such as altered states of consciousness (Lutz & Thompson, 2003). The paradigm of neurophenomenology attempts to build a bridge between subjective experiences of mind with the objective evidence of what happens simultaneously in the body (Lutz & Thompson, 2003). Neurophenomenology draws from the pioneering methods and ideas of Charles Laughlin (1988), a transpersonal anthropologist, and colleagues (Laughlin, McManus, & d'Aquili, 1990). This approach was adopted by Francesco Varela and colleagues (Varela et al., 1991), and developed in a more cognitive direction as an approach to understanding the workings of the brain and mind, drawing on the philosophy of *embodiment* (cf. Merleau-Ponty, 1962). Neurophenomenology essentially studies the ways in which subjective experiences of mind reciprocally interact, affect, and emerge with the objective physiological processing of experiences. It is thus a philosophy of how experience is grounded in a circular interaction between internal subjective experience and the objectively observable bodily processes associated with those experiences. Experiences of mind are said to arise as an emergent property of a mind that is fully embodied in its experience. This idea of an *embodied mind* is quite different from the previous paradigm in neuroscience, which simply studied the objective correlates of mind in a disembodied way. Aanstoos (1991) has nicely summarized the inherent limitation of a disembodied approach in neuroscience by saying that "we will never understand the first person experience of one's body by reducing it to a third person perspective" (p. 1).

Pierre Rainville's groundbreaking research into hypnosis and pain perception (Rainville et al., 1999) is an excellent example of how hypnosis can be useful to neuroscience, and potentially also to neurophenomenology. Rainville and his colleagues utilized hypnosis as a precise control that allowed them to examine the distinct phenomenological experiences of how pain feels to human beings in different conditions. In some experimental conditions they utilized hypnosis to reduce the sensory aspects of pain, while in others conditions they asked the participants to use hypnosis to block only the emotional aspects of their pain. The results suggested that hypnosis could reduce both the emotional and sensory aspects of pain. This experiment demonstrates how it is possible to train participants to experience and report on precise mental phenomena in a manner that parallels what early gestalt psychologists were attempting (Gardner, 1985). Rainville and his colleagues were among the first researchers to demonstrate that the anterior cingulate in the brain plays a critical role in mediating hypnotic phenomena as has also been found in meditation studies (Rainville et al., 1999; Spiegel et al., 2010). Thus there is a kind of emerging neurophenomenological argument that the experiences of hypnosis and meditation are embodied in similar ways. However, these studies only scratch the surface of the available phenomenological tools that could be used in the future research on the neurophenomenology of hypnosis and meditation.

The hypnosis community has invented two rigorous approaches to gathering phenomenological data from participants experiencing hypnotic phenomena. One of these approaches is based on using detailed phenomenological interviews with participants about their hypnotic experiences and is known as the experiential analysis technique (Sheehan, 1992). The other approach utilizes experience inventories that have been finely tuned over 20 years of research to provide empirical data on the major and minor types of phenomenological experiences that people report having during a variety of altered states of consciousness (Pekala & Kumar, 2000). This last approach has the benefit of deriving empirical data from the experience ratings that people register on a brief experience inventory called the Phenomenology of Consciousness Inventory (PCI). The PCI has been demonstrated to be reliable and valid measure of altered states of consciousness such as a person's ability to experience hypnosis (Pekala & Kumar, 2000).

The methods of neurophenomenology and hypnosis combined promise to give novel and groundbreaking transpersonal models of identity and parapsychological phenomena. It has been known for many years that some highly hypnotizable individuals without a dissociative disorder can utilize hypnosis to experience a temporary disruption of their experience of themselves as a solid, continuous, and unitary self (Hilgard, 1977). The field is now just a few steps away from using the methods of hypnosis and neurophenomenology to examine how the experience of self is embodied in human beings. Studies in this area could help understand the experiential embodiment of realized beings who have transcended the illusion of self as well as those who suffer from disorganized views of self seen in dissociative disorders. Perhaps studies in this area may even suggest methods of biofeedback that will help more people improve their sense of awareness, compassion, and presence just as ancient traditions have taught for thousands of years. This could actually happen if it is possible to discover how our highest human potential is embodied in the brain/mind, and then choose methods of biofeedback to reinforce that embodiment. Perhaps after more research in this area with Eastern methods that encourage identity transformation such as gTummo (Benson et al., 1982), an embodied understanding of the self will be gained, along with methods to achieve its transcendence. It should not be too surprising if evidence is uncovered related to the embodiment of anomalous phenomena using this type of approach, as has already been seen in a few early studies (Achterberg et al., 2005).

Conclusion: Answer the Calling

I do not know what I may appear to the world, but to myself I seem to have been only like a boy playing on the sea-shore, and diverting myself in now and then finding a smoother pebble, or a prettier shell than ordinary, whilst the great ocean of truth lay all undiscovered before me.

Isaac Newton (1855/2005)

Anyone with a transpersonal background is uniquely suited to answer the call to understand the mysteries of hypnosis and what they can reveal about the ultimate potential of human nature. Pioneers of the traditions of hypnosis and transpersonal psychology have already embraced all the underlying phenomena and methods necessary to take the next steps forward. I would like to make an impassioned plea to anyone who is interested in transpersonal psychology to learn more about the realms of hypnosis, neurophenomenology, and the ancient wisdom teachings reviewed in this chapter. Everyone could have a part to play in the effort to help the Western world awaken to the true nature of body, mind, and spirit whether they primarily think of themselves as a healer, practitioner, researcher, and/or a teacher. I make my plea at a time when the traditions of hypnosis and some ancient wisdom schools such as Dzogchen are waning (Wangyal, 2005, 2011; Wickramasekera II, 2010) due in part to a decline in the numbers of people who are committed enough to keep the traditions alive. However, this is rather ironic as the scientific understanding of these mysteries has grown to great heights, and this would be an excellent time to revive these traditions. The way is clear for everyone to play their unique part in this effort to understand and utilize the gifts of our human body, mind, and spirit. It may be that there will be danger and ridicule, just as Abbé Faria and countless others before encountered. However, the chance to swim in the oceans of wisdom is just too great to resist if you happen to get the calling to take up hypnosis and transpersonal psychology.

References

Aanstoos, C. (1991). Embodiment as ecstatic intertwining. In C. Aanstoos (Ed.), *Studies in humanistic psychology* (pp. 94-111). Carrollton, GA: West Georgia College.

Accaria, P., & Appel, A. (2005). *A gathering of healers*. Workshop presented at the Annual Meeting of the American Society of Clinical Hypnosis.

Achterberg, J. (2002). *Imagery in healing*. Boston, MA: Shambhala.

Achterberg, J., Cooke, K., Richards, T., Standish, L., Kozak, L., & Lake, J. (2005). Evidence for correlations between distant intentionality and brain function in recipients: A functional magnetic resonance imaging analysis. *The Journal of Alternative and Complementary Medicine, 11*(6), 965-971.

Barabasz, A., & Watkins, J. (2005). *Hypnotherapeutic techniques* (2nd ed.). New York, NY: Routledge.

Barber, J. (1998). Hypnosis and memory: A hazardous interplay. *Journal of Mental Health Counseling, 19*, 305-318.

Barber, T. X. (2000). A deeper understanding of hypnosis: Its secrets, its nature, its essence. *American Journal of Clinical Hypnosis, 42*, 208-272.

Benson, H., Lehmann, J. W., Malhotra, M. S., Goldman, R. F., Hopkins, J., & Epstein, M. D. (1982). Body temperature changes during the practice of gTummo yoga. *Nature, 295*, 234-236.

Bernheim, H. (1980). *New studies in hypnotism*. New York, NY: International University Press. (Original work published 1891)

Braid, J. (1960). *Braid on hypnotism: The beginnings of modern hypnosis*. New York, NY: Julian Press. (Original work published 1843)

Breuer, J., & Freud, S. (1999). *Studies on hysteria* (J. Strachey, Trans.). New York, NY: Basic Books. (Original work published 1895)

Cardeña, E. (2010). Anomalous experiences during deep hypnosis. In M. Smith (Ed.), *Anomalous experiences: Essays from parapsychological and psychological perspectives* (pp. 93-107). New York: Praeger.

Carrer, L. (2006). *José Custódio de Faria: Hypnotist, priest and revolutionary*. New York, NY: Trafford.

Council, J. R. (1999). Hypnosis and response expectancies. In I. Kirsch (Ed.), *Expectancy, experience, and behavior* (pp. 383-402). Washington, DC: American Psychological Association.

Covino, N., Wexler, J., & Miller, K. (2010). Hypnosis and medicine: In D. Barrett (Ed.), *Hypnosis and hypnotherapy* (Vol. 2, pp. 177-196). Santa Barbara, CA: Praeger.

Crowley, A. (1976) *Magick in theory and practice*. New York, NY: Dover. (Original work published 1929)

Dossey, L. (1995). *Healing words*. New York, NY: HarperCollins.

Ellis, A., & Yaeger, R. (1989). *Why some therapies don't work: The dangers of transpersonal psychology*. Buffalo, NY: Prometheus.

Epstein, M. (1995). *Thoughts without a thinker*. New York, NY: Basic Books.

Erickson, M. H., & Rossi, E. L. (1979). *Hypnotherapy: An exploratory casebook*. New York, NY: Irvington.

Erickson, M. H., Rossi, E. L., & Rossi, S. I. (1976). *Hypnotic realities*. New York, NY: Irvington.

Faria, J. C. (1819). *Causas do sono lúcido*. Paris, France. (Translation from Carrer, 2006).

Forrest, D. (1999). *Hypnotism: A history*. New York, NY: Penguin.

Frederick, C. (2005). Selected topics in ego state therapy. *International Journal of Clinical & Experimental Hypnosis, 53*(4), 339-429.

Fromm, E., & Nash, M. (1997). *Psychoanalysis and hypnosis*. New York, NY: International Universities Press.

Gardner, H. (1985). *The mind's new science*. New York, NY: Basic Books.

Gill, M. M., & Brenman, M. (1959). *Hypnosis and related states: Psychoanalytic studies in regression*. New York, NY: International Universities Press.

Ginandes, C., Brooks, P., Sando, W., Jones, C., & Aker, J. (2003). Can medical hypnosis accelerate post-surgical wound healing? Results of a clinical trial. *American Journal of Clinical Hypnosis, 45*(4), 333-351.

Grinder, J., & Bandler, R. (1981). *Trance-formations.* Moab, UT: Real People Press.

Gunnison, H. (1985). The uniqueness of similarities: Parallels of Milton Erickson and Carl Rogers. *Journal of Counseling and Development, 63,* 561-564.

Hageman, J., Krippner, S., & Wickramasekera, I. E., II. (2008). Sympathetic reactivity during meditation. *Subtle Energies and Energy Medicine, 19*(2), 23-48.

Haley, J. (1993). *Jay Haley on Milton Erickson.* New York, NY: Brunner/Mazel.

Hilgard, E. R. (1965). *Hypnotic susceptibility.* New York, NY: Harcourt, Brace, & World.

Hilgard, E. R. (1977). *Divided consciousness: Multiple controls in human thought and action.* New York, NY: John Wiley & Sons.

Hilgard, E. R. (1979). The Stanford hypnotic susceptibility scales as related to other measures of hypnotic responsiveness. *American Journal of Clinical Hypnosis, 21,* 68-83.

Holroyd, J. (2003). The science of meditation and the state of hypnosis. *American Journal of Clinical Hypnosis, 46*(2), 109-28.

Honorton, C., Berger, R. E., Varvoglis, M. P., Quant, M., Derr, P., Schechter, E. I., & Ferrari, D. C. (1990). Psi communication in the ganzfeld: Experiments with an automated testing system and a comparison with a meta-analysis of earlier studies. *Journal of Parapsychology, 54,* 99-139.

Kabat-Zinn, J. (1990). *Full catastrophe living.* New York, NY: Delta.

Kirsch, I. (2011). The altered state issue: Dead or alive? *International Journal of Clinical and Experimental Hypnosis, 59*(3), 350-362.

Kirsch, I., & Lynn, S. J. (1995). The altered state of hypnosis. *American Psychologist, 50*(10), 846-858.

Kirsch, I., Montgomery, G., & Sapirstein, G. (1995). Hypnosis as an adjunct to cognitive-behavioral psychotherapy: A meta-analysis. *Journal of Consulting & Clinical Psychology, 63,* 214-220.

Krippner, S. (2004). Trance and the trickster: Hypnosis as a liminal phenomenon. *International Journal of Clinical and Experimental Hypnosis, 53,* 97-118.

Lang, E. V., & Rosen, M. P. (2002). Cost analysis of adjunct hypnosis with sedation during outpatient interventional radiologic procedures. *Radiology, 222,* 375-382.

Lankton, S. (2010). Ericksonian approaches to hypnosis and therapy. In D. Barrett (Ed.), *Hypnosis and hypnotherapy: Applications in psychotherapy and medicine* (Vol. 2, pp. 1-48). Santa Barbara, CA: Praeger.

Lankton, S. (2012a). Ericksonian approaches to hypnosis and therapy. In D. Barrett (Ed.), *Hypnosis and hypnotherapy* (Vol. 2, pp. 1-48) Santa Barbara, CA: Praeger.

Lankton, S. (2012b). Editorial. *American Journal of Clinical Hypnosis, 54,* 245-246.

Laughlin, C. D. (1988). The prefrontosensorial polarity principle: Toward a neurophenomenology of intentionality. *Biology Forum, 81*(2), 243-260. (Also published in K. Ikeda (Ed.), *Foundation of structuralist biology.* Tokyo, Japan: Kaimeisha [Japanese])

Laughlin, C. D., McManus, J., & d'Aquili, E. G. (1990). *Brain, symbol and experience: Toward a neurophenomenology of human consciousness.* New York, NY: Columbia University Press.

Laurence, J. R, & Perry, C. (1983). Hypnotically created memory amongst high hypnotizable subjects. *Science, 222,* 523-524.

Lutz, A., & Thompson, E. (2003). Neurophenomenology: Integrating subjective experience and brain dynamics in the neuroscience of consciousness. *Journal of Consciousness Studies, 10,* 31-52.

Lynn, S. J., Pintar, J., Stafford, J., Marmelstein, L., & Lock, T. (1998). Rendering the implausible plausible: Narrative construction, suggestion, and memory. In J. de Rivera &

T. R. Sarbin (Eds.), *Believed-in imaginings: The narrative construction of reality* (pp. 23-144). Washington, DC: American Psychological Association.

Merleau-Ponty, M. (1962). *The phenomenology of perception*. New York, NY: Routledge.

Montgomery, G. H., DuHamel, K. N., & Redd, W. H. (2000). A meta-analysis of hypnotically induced analgesia: How effective is hypnosis? *International Journal of Clinical and Experimental Hypnosis, 48*, 138-153.

Nash, M. R. (2001). The truth and hype of hypnosis. *Scientific American, 285*, 46-55.

Nash, M. R., & Spinler, D. (1989). Hypnosis and transference: A measure of archaic involvement. *International Journal of Clinical and Experimental Hypnosis, 37*(2), 129-144.

Newton, I. (2005). *Memoirs of Newton* (D. Brewster, Ed.). Edinburgh, UK: Thomas Constable. (Original work published 1855)

Palsson, O. (2006) Standardized hypnosis treatment for irritable bowel syndrome: The North Carolina Protocol. *International Journal of Clinical and Experimental Hypnosis, 54*, 51-64.

Patterson, D. R., & Jensen, M. P. (2003). Hypnosis and clinical pain. *Psychological Bulletin, 129*, 495-521.

Pekala, R. J., & Kumar, V. K. (2000). Operationalizing "trance" I: Rationale and research using a psychophenomenological approach. *American Journal of Clinical Hypnosis, 43*(2), 107-135.

Pekala, R. J., & Kumar, V. K. (2005). States, traits, and provocative debates: The state/nonstate controversy with particular reference to operationalizing "hypnotism." *Psychological Hypnosis, 14*, 13-18.

Pekala, R. J., Kumar, V. K., & Marcano, G. (1995). Anomalous/paranormal experiences, hypnotic susceptibility, and dissociation. *Journal of the American Society for Psychical Research, 89*, 313-332.

Rainville, P., Carrier, B., Hofbauer, R. K., Bushnell, M. C., & Duncan, G. H. (1999). Dissociation of sensory and affective dimensions of pain using hypnotic modulation. *Pain, 82*, 159-171.

Ray, R. (2000). *Indestructible truth: The living spirituality of Tibetan Buddhism*. Boston, MA: Shambhala.

Rhine, J. B. (1952). Extrasensory perception and hypnosis. In L. LeCron (Ed.), *Experimental hypnosis* (pp. 359-368). New York, NY: Macmillan.

Rogers, C. R. (1957). The necessary and sufficient conditions of therapeutic personality change. *Journal of Consulting Psychology, 21*(2), 95-103.

Rogers, C. R. (1985). Reaction to Gunnison's article on the similarities between Erickson and Rogers. *Journal of Counseling and Development, 63*, 565-566.

Rogers, C. R. (1986). Rogers, Kohut, and Erickson: A personal perspective on some similarities and differences. *Person Centered Review, 1*, 125-140.

Sarbin, T. R. (1950). Contributions to role-taking theory: I. Hypnotic behavior. *Psychological Review, 57*, 225-270.

Sarbin, T. R. (1998). Believed-in imaginings: A narrative approach. In J. de Rivera & T. R. Sarbin (Eds.), *Believed-in imaginings: The narrative construction of reality* (pp. 15-30). Washington, DC: American Psychological Association.

Schoenberger, N. E., Kirsch, I., Gearan, P., Montgomery, G., & Pastyrnak, S. L. (1997). hypnotic enhancement of a cognitive behavioral treatment for public speaking anxiety. *Behavior Therapy, 28*(1), 127-140.

Sheehan, P. W. (1992). The phenomenology of hypnosis and the Experiential Analysis Technique. In E. Fromm & M. R. Nash (Eds.), *Contemporary hypnosis research* (pp. 364-389). New York, NY: Guilford Press.

Spiegel, D., White, M., & Waelde, L. (2010). Hypnosis, mindfulness meditation, and brain imaging. In D. Barrett (Ed.), *Hypnosis and hypnotherapy* (pp. 37-52). Santa Barbara, CA: Praeger.

Stevenson, I. (1994). A case of the psychotherapist's fallacy: Hypnotic regression to "previous lives." *American Journal of Clinical Hypnosis, 36,* 188-193.

Tart, C. (1975). *Transpersonal psychologies.* New York, NY: Harper & Collins.

Tart, C. (1994). *Living the mindful life.* Boston, MA: Shambhala.

Tellegen, A., & Atkinson, G. (1974). Openness to absorbing and self-altering experiences ("absorption"), a trait related to hypnotic susceptibility. *Journal of Abnormal Psychology, 83,* 268-277.

Trungpa, C. (1973). *Cutting through spiritual materialism.* Boston, MA: Shambhala.

Varela, F., Thompson, E., & Rosch, E. (1991). *The embodied mind.* Boston, MA: MIT Press.

Walsh, R., & Shapiro, S. (2006). The meeting of meditative disciplines and Western psychology: A mutually enriching dialogue. *American Psychologist, 61*(3), 227-239.

Walsh, R., & Vaughan, F. (1993). *Paths beyond ego: The transpersonal vision.* New York, NY: Tarcher.

Wangyal, T. (2005). *The six realms of the wheel of existence.* Unpublished transcript for a 3 week retreat conducted at the Ligmincha Institute in Charlottesville, VA, July.

Wangyal, T. (2011). *Tibetan yogas of body, speech, and mind.* Ithaca, NY: Snow Lion.

Watkins, J. G., & Watkins, H. H. (1997). *Ego states: Theory and therapy.* New York, NY: W. W. Norton.

Wickramasekera, I. E. (1986, November). *Parapsychological verbal reports, hypnotizability, and stress-related disorders.* Paper presented at Parapsychology and Human Nature: The 35th Annual Conference of the Parapsychology Foundation, Washington, DC.

Wickramasekera, I. E., II (2004a, March). *How research in hypnosis illuminates the Tibetan Buddhist philosophy of mind.* Paper presented at the Annual Meeting of American Society of Clinical Hypnosis in Anaheim, CA, USA.

Wickramasekera, I. E., II. (2004b). The kalyanamitra and the three necessary and sufficient conditions of client-centered psychotherapy. *Journal of Humanistic Psychology, 44*(4), 485-493.

Wickramasekera, I. E., II. (2007a). Empathic aspects of absorption and incongruence. *American Journal of Clinical Hypnosis, 50*(1), 59-69.

Wickramasekera, I. E., II. (2007b, August). *How research in hypnosis illuminates the Bön-Buddhist model of self.* Paper presented the 2007 Annual Convention of the American Psychological Association, San Francisco, CA, USA, August.

Wickramasekera, I. E., II. (2010). Pedagogical perspectives on teaching hypnosis. In D. Barrett (Ed.), *Hypnosis and hypnotherapy* (Vol. 1, pp. 145-160). Santa Barbara, CA: Praeger.

Wickramasekera, I. E., II, & Szlyk, J. (2003). Could empathy be a predictor of hypnotic ability? *International Journal of Clinical and Experimental Hypnosis, 51*(4), 390-399.

Wortis, J. (1954). *Fragments of an analysis with Freud.* New York, NY: Simon & Schuster.

Yapko, M. (2011). *Mindfulness and hypnosis: The power of suggestion to transform experience.* New York, NY: Norton.

28

Dreaming and Transpersonal Psychology

Daniel Deslauriers

As a universal expression of Being, dreaming addresses the entire spectrum of human experience. With boundless creative variations, dreams have the potential to bring to light the deepest yearnings and the existential struggles that frame the human spiritual quest. A dream is a quasiphysical, immersive virtual experience, unfolding in a narrative fashion but in an indeterminate time-bound manner. Its imagery and felt-sense are closely tied to the core emotional concerns of the dreamer (Bosnak, 2007; Cartwright, 2010; Kramer, 2007), lending the dream experience a sense of realness and believability.

Transpersonal psychology can complement the emerging view of dreaming proposed by science (Lancaster, 2011). This view generally asserts that neurophysiological changes associated with different stages of sleep are, in their diversity, essential for learning, and for the maintenance of physical health, immunity, as well as psychological wellbeing. Dreaming is described as a spontaneously arising and endogenously produced hallucinatory experience, known to occur when certain neurophysiological conditions are met, such as in REM (Rapid Eye Movement) sleep—a high-activation brain state, coupled with atonia (where antigravity muscles are temporarily paralyzed), that recurs at regular intervals 4-5 times or every 90-120 minutes, each night. Night dreams are thus distinct from waking mental imagery and daydreaming, although they may share similarities in the form of thought exhibited. Adults, absent brain trauma affecting dream production or recall (Solms, 1997), will normally experience REM sleep nightly, and are likely to report dreams if awaken during this stage. Although sleep clearly plays a restorative role, dreaming appears crucial for psychological integration. On that basis, we can extrapolate that dreaming can address core concerns that interface with spiritual experiences and psychospiritual development (Bogzaran & Deslauriers, 2012).

For those pondering the transpersonal nature of dream experiences (e.g., Lancaster, 2004), science's description of the underlying biological mechanisms is illuminating

The Wiley Blackwell Handbook of Transpersonal Psychology, First Edition.
Edited by Harris L. Friedman and Glenn Hartelius.

but falls short of capturing the richness of the phenomena associated with dreaming. A number of transpersonal experiences known to occur during dreams still challenge a neurophysiological view of the brain-mind. Other than pointing out some of its general features (Hobson, 2000), neuroscientists are still puzzled by the question of dream *content*. Why do certain dreams arise at a given time in a person's life, often presaging events to come? What enables dreaming to be more susceptible to psi experience (Krippner, Bogzaran, de Carvalho, 2002)? What is the psychophysiology of extraordinary dreams (Bulkeley, 2011), and what explains their healing potential?

Scientific experiments cannot easily summon on demand the kind of impactful and life-transforming experiences that dreamers report—especially the sort of transpersonal encounters such as numinous dreams, visitation dreams, or other more subtle non-dual experiences. As a result, dream reports collected in laboratory setting do not properly reflect the wider spectrum of dreams and their potentialities (Hunt, 1989a, 2000). Furthermore, little is known experimentally about the role of dreaming skills across the entire arc of life development, because the study of the impact of dreams does not cover long periods. Some highly impactful dreams may occur on rare occasions over one's lifetime, but their impact may be felt, and their understanding unfolded, over a number of years (Bogzaran, 2006; Knudson & Minier, 1999). With the exception of laboratory research on lucid dreams (Hearne, 1978; LaBerge, 2000; Voss, Holzmann, Tuin, & Hobson, 2009, Wehrle et al., 2007) and on dream and sleep witnessing (Mason, Alexander, Travis, Gackenbach, & Orme-Johnson, 1995), most research on transpersonal dreams has relied on retrospective reports (Bogzaran, 1989; Esser, 2012) including numerous autobiographical reports (Garfield, 1979; Gillespie, 1987; Hervey de Saint-Denis, 1867/1982; Jung, 1965; Kelzer, 1987; Sparrow, 1976; Wagonner, 2009; Womack, 2002).

A comprehensive theory of dreaming should address not only the fundamental level of dream production (e.g., the neurocorrelates of a particular state of consciousness) but it ought to have a broad scope: How satisfactorily does it explain the wide range of dream experience possible, not just normative or prevalent dreams? In order to understand the full spectrum of dreaming and its impact on the whole being, the neurosciences must strive to be phenomenologically accurate. Transpersonal psychology's contribution lies in part in the comprehensiveness of the phenomenological range of dream experiences that it considers.

The Paradox of Dreaming as a State of Consciousness

It is generally admitted that waking, dreaming, and sleep represent discrete states of consciousness. However, the boundary separating the states of dreaming from waking is not fixed. Paradoxically, most early REM dreams are forgotten before awakening, leaving no trace in memory. For this reason, dreaming status as a state of consciousness has been problematic (Hobson, 2009). At the other end of the spectrum, impactful dreams (such as nightmares) can take an indelible character. These dreams tend to spill over into waking, leaving strong impression and are thus more easily consigned to memory. For most dreams however, the process of recall may require voluntary attention, as one learns to navigate the waters where dreaming and waking join in the hypnopompic (sleep awakening) stage. Dream recall tends to increase when one begins to pay closer attention to one's dreams (beginning with fragments, or residual felt-sense). A fuller recall may take the form of re-playing the dream imagery in one's mind as a mean to anchor the dream in memory, before writing it down at a later time.

The boundary between dreams and self-reflective consciousness (normally associated with waking) can be also explored *inside* the dream itself. Once the skill of dream recall is stabilized, the dreamer can learn to increase reflective cognizance of the dream state, and perhaps achieve full dream lucidity, that is, being fully aware, during the dream, that one is dreaming.

Although REM is an innate biological program, dreaming and recall are subject to development, as part of a more encompassing ability to transact between states of consciousness. Dreaming, especially lucid dreaming, becomes more than an experience, but also an achievement, one that dreamers can elect to refine throughout their lifetime.

Self-Organization, Self-Reference, and Developmental Flourishing

Transpersonally oriented authors (e.g., Bogzaran, 1991; Cortright, 2007; Wilber, 2000) tend to see dreaming as a naturally arising altered state of consciousness that intersects with the ongoing psychospiritual developmental trajectory of the dreamer. To be able to articulate one's experience dialectically, as viewed and understood from each state (dreaming self as viewed from a waking perspective, and vice-versa) is a core element of spiritual intelligence (Deslauriers, 2000), characterizing a postconventional stage of human development (Van den Daele, 1992).

Dreams can become a readily available training ground for attention and awareness in the context of wider contemplative practice (Gordon, 2006). This draws on the fact that consciousness in dreams is both *self-organizing* and *self-referential*. Self-organizing natural systems are those that are structured by their own internal processes. Self-organization leads to the spontaneous emergence of order without the direct imposition of outside instructions or rules. For example, in the insect world, an ant colony is a complex self-organized system. For Lewis (2000), "human development is just one exemplar of the universal tendency towards higher-order coherence" (p. 36). Self-organization enables the emergence of novelty and helps explain how, without predetermination, these novel forms become increasingly complex with development. Self-organization in dreams is most clearly captured at the onset of dreams. Dreams occur on their own accord, when the "dreaming brain 'relaxes' into natural pattern of activity" (Combs & Krippner, 2009, p. 49). While there is no one "in charge," the highly activated REM dreaming brain form patterns of experience that are organized around residual moods and waking life concerns. The latter play the role of "attractors" in the process of self-organization. "Such fluidity... [serves to] enlarge the attractors through which brain activity flows, effectively allowing easier connections to be made between feelings, memories, and the productions of the imagination" (Combs & Krippner, 2009, p. 49-50). If dreaming is the expression of a self-organizing system, the question arises as to the extent to which psychospiritual concerns serve as a basin of attractors of their own, interacting within the framework of the other attractors named above. Just as insight in problem-solving dreams tends to occur following focused practice and incubation, one may ask if spiritual insight in dreams are breakthroughs that come on the heel of prolonged practice while awake.

Self-reference, for its part, inflects a particular direction of self-organization: self-states are mirrored in dream imagery (Rossi, 1985). Dreams not only build from experiences and memories, but a notable aspect of dreaming is the presence of a virtual self, a "dream ego" around which the dream narrative unfolds. The experience of dreaming is thus unlike "watching a movie" made by someone else. The proper metaphor may be an immersive virtual environment that is being created by the dreamers, as it goes along. This immersive nature lends the dreaming experience a noetic and self-validating quality, similar to that ascribed to mystical experiences by William James (1902).

If it is true that the dream is a mirror of the self, a more immediate rendering of that truth is enacted in lucid dreaming. For the self to cultivate the skills and ability to wake up to self-created images and interact with them brings about new choices and potential prospects. Self-inquiry and self-transformation seems to increase through the act of reflection within lucid dreams (Hunt, 2000). If the dreamer can rest safely in the knowledge that dream experience is ultimately evanescent, transient, and happening within the bounds of the dreaming mind, emotions such as fear and anxiety can be recognized, diffused, and even transformed (Wallace, 2012). Dreams can become the training ground for skills linked with self-flourishing: radical self-acceptance, healthy surrendering to the unknown, and the development of witnessing clarity and dispassionate engagement with the imaginal world. Alternatively, a lucid dreamer can experiment with the capacities, the limitations, and eventual the letting go of the "I-self."

To the extent that dreams display a broad range of transformative experiences, one could surmise that dreaming is a primordial candidate for the way by which transpersonal experience takes form and become *cognized or embodied* (albeit in virtual form). Due to its virtual immersive nature, dreaming can provide a clear sense of "what it is like" to live with an open heart, to have a taste of oneness, to touch the plenum of the void, or to be initiated to a sense of multidimensional being-ness or to surrender to light (Bogzaran & Deslauriers, 2012). These numinous experiences are the source of profound noetic insight and at the same time, they often bring a sense of deep healing (Corbett, 2007) and deeper understanding about one's life purpose.

A prospective function of dreams has also been linked to the exploration of "possible selves" (Kahan, 2011). If indeed one of the main purposes of dreaming is to explore potential scenarios within the safe place of the imagination, the experience of dream begs the question as to the teleological, or the final cause associated with the spontaneous display of what appears, on the face of it, as some form of illuminative wisdom. Jung (1974) has rightly pointed out that the contact with the numinosum (not only the content of the image) is, in itself, healing (see also Bogart, 2009; Corbett, 2007).

Social and cultural views on dreams can affect the development of self-reflective abilities related to dreams. Children develop a felt sense of what dreaming is, as they learn to differentiate dream experience from waking consciousness (Foulkes, 1999; Laurendeau & Pinard, 1962).

The increasing complexity in dreaming plots is also associated with developmental stages at the pre-formal and formal levels (Foulkes, 1999). Post-formal stages of adult development have not received the same attention, perhaps since there is no consensus on their nature nor about the characteristics of full maturity of the human potential. Van den Daele (1992) has offered a typographical model that takes into account the deepening of complexity within a person's thought-process whereas ego development and dream complexity closely follow each other. For van den Daele (1992), "dreams of greater complexity tend to address issues of greater generality for the inner world, for objective social interests, or for social significance" (p. 311).

Post-formal development, however, is not only characterized by more complex thinking; deeper understanding may come with non-intellectual intuition that accompanies other forms of human flourishing including the ineffable but paradoxical self-perceptual depth that arises with non-dual experience (in dreams or waking; Gackenbach, Cranson, & Alexander, 1986). Strong numinous experiences in dreams, and what Tibetan literature refers to as "dreams of clarity" (Wangyal, 1998, p. 93), can bring a subtle but profound re-organization of the sense of self (Wallace, 2012). Experience of non-duality in dream may sensitize one to an embraceful ground of being from which one is not separate and to the existential condition that requires or accompanies such illumination. For example, Tandan (2011) discussed a personal dream whose plot forces upon her the choice between a pill that would put her to sleep or be beheaded. She saw this forced choice as emblematic of the existential issues that accompany spiritual transformation when embracing the death of an egocentric part of self.

Dream Experience, Dream Consciousness

As one explores the role of dreaming in human flourishing and self-realization, it is important to look at how dreaming itself supports the transformative process. The following phenomenological categories lend an appreciative gaze on some prominent regularities and peculiarities of dreaming.

Social and relational aspects. A close look at dream content reveals that dreamers rarely find themselves alone in dreams; one finds the almost ubiquitous presence of others, who the dreamer either observes or interacts. The fact that dreams have a strong intersubjective or relational aspect may also give a clue as one of their role: To attune the individual with the complex and constantly changing emotional landscape that human living requires (Bogzaran & Deslauriers, 2012). This relational dimension of dreaming is also at the source of what might be called horizontal transpersonal experiences, in which the self-boundaries are expanded in contact with others in dreams, including numinous contact with the departed in visitation dreams; with spiritual teachers in guidance or teaching dreams; or in dreams where one is emulating an aspect of a teacher.

Relational connections are not limited to the human world. Many dreams may voice aspects of a larger ecological distress with dreams scenarios presenting apocalyptic disasters or animals pleading for help or imparting existential lessons (Jaenke, 2010). Dreams of healing often find the dream self in a natural setting, as if it were being seen fresh and anew; the natural surroundings suddenly become suffused with boundless life force. Some dreamers, especially in the presence of sleep paralysis (Cheyne, 2001; Hurd, 2011; McNally & Clancy, 2005), will encounter spiritual entities, often taking the form of "presences" whose identity may vary (based on the belief system of the dreamers): angelic presence, alien entities, or invisible beings making themselves known through the message they impart to the dreamer. The feeling tone of such dreams can be quite ominous (Cheyne, 2001), lending some of these experiences a dark numinous quality (Dennis, 2001; Hunt 1989b).

Time and space. Dreams are known to present strong variations of the spectrum of time-space-awareness when compared with the more linear display of consciousness in waking. In considering the dimensions of space and time and consciousness, it is noteworthy that dreams often take place in a time that is different than the present life of the waking person, sometimes mixing past, present, and future (e.g., a deceased loved one appears in a dream as youthful and healthy). The linearity of time in dreams is not as sharp as in waking. Dreamers are at pains to recount the actual order of events because it often seems as if everything was happening "all at once," or the order of events was somewhat unknown, and the dream could have happened in any order.

Alternatively, the idea of space in dreams is closely related to the habits of the senses overlaid on the imaginal landscape of the dream. The notion of distance (as in near and far) may lose its defining characteristics, especially in lucid dreaming in which the mere thought of visiting a distant place may elicit one's presence there, eliminating the distance that separates "here" and "there."

Some dreams also express capacities that supersede the waking limitations that are associated with embodied presence in space (dreams of flying, or breathing underwater are common examples), or the explorations of wider dimensions of space (hyperspace lucidity; Bogzaran, 1994, 2003). Such dreams tend to convey strong transpersonal tones: the dreamer may feel elated, but at the same time a sense of inner-calm pervades. These sensations often carry over in waking. Thematically, these dreams carry a sense of personal mastery as the dreamer naturally settles in a state of flow. To contrast them with other types of impactful dreams, Kuiken and Sikora (1993) called them *transcendent* dreams. The later have led dreamers to consider previously ignored spiritual possibilities (e.g., a feeling of self-renewal or an ineffable sense of peace, love, or awe). In some reports, the dreams' impact includes forms of ecstatic release, a deep sense of spaciousness or timelessness wherein life suffuses all things, and an attenuation of the separation between self and world.

Narrative form. Dream reports most frequently take on a story form, despite the numerous bizarre elements and time variations that occur in dreaming. The story schema also serves as shorthand for the particular perspective embedded within any given state of consciousness. From the privileged stand point of the dreamer, the dream is most likely experienced from the vantage point of an "I" that stands in for the narrator, or more precisely the narrator's dream ego, dream self, or dream body. In contrast to the single perspectival stance of waking, dreams can also present a view of the world from multiple perspectives at once—for example, where one can observe a scene simultaneously from one's own eyes and from a bird's eye view—or from layered vantage points such as a dream within a dream.

Perspective and self-awareness. While dreamers may not always be critically aware of their inherent state of consciousness (unless one becomes lucid in a dream), self-reflective awareness (or metacognition) is still present in dreams in multiple forms: self-talk, goal-orientation, emotional self-monitoring, evaluation of the effectiveness of dream behavior, and evaluation of other's action (Kahan, 2001). These self-reflective skills are the basis upon which one can build the further skill of dream lucidity, the full the recognition, within the dream, of the fact that one is dreaming.

The virtual but vanishing quality of dreaming takes on particular importance when looking at dream from an ontological perspective. That evanescent quality imparts the dream state its dream-like quality. This evanescent quality has been similarly applied to waking phenomena when referring to their dream-likeness, and the role of the mind as a reality-constructing apparatus.

Altered states within dreams. A multiplicity of states are displayed *within* our dreams: for example, vigilance, contemplative witnessing, self-reflection, mystical rapture, and even "high" dreams where one dreams of being under the influence of a substance (Tart, 1969).

Dream impact. Although the imaginal world of dreams vanishes upon awakening, it often leaves emotional and mnemonic impressions. This is especially true in the case of strongly impactful dreams. Following Jung's classic nomenclature of *big dreams,* religious historian and dream researcher Kelly Bulkeley (2011) has attempted a basic mapping of a highly impacful dream. As can be seen in his model, he identifies four categories of big dream experiences (called "prototypes") along two axes: a *relational* axis (horizontal), expressing the quality of feeling between the dreamer and other characters, and an *elemental* axis (vertical).

The relational axis shows dreams oscillating between aggressive prototypes at one extremity to sexual prototypes on the other. The most intense manifestations of the aggressive prototype are nightmares: negatively charged dreams, suffused with anxiety or fear, and themes of harm avoidance dreams. At times, negative dreams appear to have a strong transpersonal overtone connected to what has been called the experience of the dark numinous. For example, reflecting on his own impactful dreams as a child, Harry Hunt (1989a) wrote that these "negative numinosities...were infinite, they were vast and total, malevolent and evil, and they were very powerful. They were certainly the most powerful things I had ever known" (n. p.). The other extremity of the horizontal (relational) axis describes impactful dreams of a sexual nature.

The vertical line in Bulkeley's model represents an *elemental axis,* reflecting the degree to which a dream is characterized by either increasing complexity and structure (uppermost) or fragmentation and decay (lowermost). Dreams reflecting the latter are extremely memorable and almost always unpleasant *gravitational* dreams such as falling, being paralyzed, losing one's teeth or body parts, crashing, being swept away by a wave, watching things fall apart. Religious renditions of this reality are images of apocalypse and cataclysm. These dreams seem to express an awareness of the truth of entropy: life is a kind of existential defiance against decay but to which one surrenders at death.

Bulkeley (2011) has placed "mystical dreams" at the upper end of the axis, including dreams that express

> the capacity to envision transcendental freedom from the oppressive limitations of gravity, entropy and death . . . : flying dreams, visitation dreams, in which the living presence defies the finality of physical death; and healing dreams; . . . ecstatic dreams of brilliant light, lucid self-awareness and divine union, along with aesthetically creative dreams of astonishing beauty and cosmic harmony. (p.17)

Dream impact can also takes the form of *dream sanctification*. Perceiving dreams as sacred appears to increase the amount of meaning and strength gained from them (Pargament & Mahoney, 2002). Research also showed that those who sanctified their dreams (e.g., viewed them as a manifestation of God, of a higher power, or as having sacred qualities) exhibited more stress-related growth, spiritual growth, and positive emotion towards an identified waking stressor related to the dream (Phillips & Pargament, 2002). Their study suggested "that spirituality and religion should be considered in explorations of dreams as a form of coping" (p.150).

Purposes & Functions of Dreaming in the Light of Transpersonal Experiences

Dreaming has been ascribed multiple functions.[1] These are often couched in functional relationship to the waking mind. As a state characterized by fluid and hyperconnected cognition (Hartmann, 2000), dreaming is postulated to provide insights into real-life issues, artistic, scientific, or concrete problems. Sleep and dreaming processes also appear to be crucial to the formation of long-term memory and learning, in particular the transfer of experience from short-term memory (meditated by the hippocampus) to the cortex, which translates as situated learning. This function is understood within the rubric of neuroplasticity.

Many regard dreams' emotional content as a cue to their purpose: Dreaming may serve to metabolize waking emotional experience, orienting one within the ever-changing social field that humans inhabit as social beings (Cartwright, 2010; Kramer, 2007; Neilsen, Deslauriers, & Baylor, 1991). For Hartmann, (2000) dreaming cross-connects new experience with known schemas. Most dreams contain a central image that serves to elucidate metaphorically the emotional state of the dreamer. Thus dreams can be described as an embodied integrative mechanism (Bosnak, 2007).

Revonsuo (2000) has taken a bio-evolutionary view to describe the advantages of mentally rehearsing one's own reaction against imagined threats. His theory helps explain the prevalence of negative emotions in dreams, including nightmares. For him, dreaming is a prime expression of the threat rehearsal function. Those who can foresee, in dreams, the negative implications of their choices, or the potential consequences of exterior threats, are more likely to prepare for them in actuality. Although the threat rehearsal function may indeed provide an evolutionary advantage, the theory overstates the facts and excludes a wide number of dreams, including spiritually transformative dreams. I counter that the rehearsal function does not apply exclusively to negative emotions, or to the presence of a threat. The multiplicity of dream content provides evidence that the dreamer can explore and rehearse anything. The rehearsal capacity applies to flourishing capacities (Wangyal, 1998), or skill learning (de Koninck, Christ, Hebert, & Rinfret, 1990), just as well as it does to threats.

Phenomenological study of dreaming that draws directly from life experience suggests that dreaming is *not* a unitary phenomenon (Hunt, 1989a). Given the many types of dreams that exist, dreaming likely serves numerous functions, such as is true for waking thought. A helpful way to understand this complexity would be to consider the many dream functions as relating to different levels of organization of our being, such as cognitive, emotional, behavioral (Noreika, Windt, Lenggenhager, & Karmin, 2010).

A case in point may be the sizable numbers of extraordinary dreams, most of which associates with transpersonal experience. Krippner et al. (2002) have identified some of the following types:

- Spiritual and visitation dreams
- Healing dreams
- Precognitive dreams
- Telepathic dreams
- Clairvoyant dreams
- Mutual dreams
- Collective dreams
- Out of body dreams
- Dreams within dreams
- Past life dreams
- Initiation dreams
- Lucid dreams

This list points out that dreaming, seen from the perspective of an extended self, may serve a host of functions that link the individuals to larger processes. From a transpersonal lens, *dreaming may express the psychic precipitates of a transpersonal encounter*. One could use a biological metaphors to describe this process: Just as the membrane of a cell enables the permeable exchange giving form to its nested and purposeful existence, a dream may mediate the fluid boundaries between self and others, between parts of self, between self and world, and between self and no-self. Informational exchanges take the form of somatic felt sense, feelings, emotions, images (archetypal or otherwise) and stories, presented with exquisite details in the subtle medium of consciousness.

Belief systems, scientific or traditional, influence what dreaming is by ascribing particular functions to dreams, and by defining what kinds of dreams are possible or most

valued. The reliance on naturalistic explanation of dreams as the endogenous production of individual minds, however correct, tends to minimize the extent to which
individual minds are part of larger collective minds that manifest within relationships,
within groups or even at a more global level, within nested and interdependent complex systems. A transpersonal perspective on dreams may be a serious placeholder for
the possibility that one does not dream *exclusively* for oneself. While dreams arise in
the individual monad, their import may extend beyond the individual. Dreams may
arise for the benefit of a group or for other beings who share the biosphere with
humans, and whose fate may be at our mercy.

The phenomenological reports of extraordinary dreams also suggest an "evolutive"
aspect of the unconscious described by Taylor (2009). This aspect may help refine
the dialogue about the functions of dreaming, seen here as allowing for a wider
spectrum of creative expression of the mind while building upon the instrumental
functions. These include: prospective exploration, metaphorical problem-solving and
insight, emotional integration and self-perceptual depth (Kuiken, Lee, Eng, & Singh,
2006), but also relational or empathetic perception (other-centered perceptual depth).
None of these functions calls for capacities that stand apart of normal human functioning. But the intentional sphere of application pertains to the full flourishing of
the human capacities and how these may be imagined or virtually expressed by the
dreaming mind.

In some extraordinary dreams, not only a *configuring* function (Van den Deale,
1992) but also a *prefiguring* one may be at play as dreaming provides an embodied
noesis of transpersonal events. Embodied noesis can be briefly defined as the sense
of knowing that arises, through immediacy, from *having* a particular experience (in
this case, a dream). The next section illustrates important research that attempted to
capture this dimensions of dreaming, showing how dream may give rise to existential
and spiritual insight, and how dreams can play an important role in the process of
psychospiritual development.

Phenomenological Research: Transpersonal Dream Practice and Self-Inquiry

Among the few published dream studies directly engaging transpersonal themes,
Bogzaran (1989) attempted to resolve some of the major methodological challenges,
such as the difficulty to make contact with transpersonal phenomena within the time-
frame of the research. Using a quasi-experimental design, she asked proficient lucid
dreamers to engage with the Divine within their lucid dreams, over an experimental
period of two weeks. Prior to engaging in the process of formulating an incubation
phrase, dreamers were asked to reflect in writing about their own notions of the Divine.
Participants were then asked to formulate an intention (incubation phrase) with the
goal to remember it (and repeat it) in the dream once they achieved lucidity. Most
dreamers who succeeded to complete this complex task reported having impactful,
and for some, very transformative experiences. The findings showed that dreamers
either conceived of the Divine in a personalized or impersonalized manner. Incubation phrases also reflected a propensity toward either actively seeking the Divine,

or receptively open oneself to it. This mirrors Hunt (2007)'s Weberian analysis of contemporary spirituality, showing two distinct modes of transpersonal or spiritual orientation: otherworldly or innerworldly. Bogzaran demonstrated that, thematically, the participant's lucid encounter tended to correlate with their pre-dream notion of the Divine (either as a personalized or impersonal encounter), and that activities in the dreams tended to reflect the active or receptive nature of the incubation task. The study demonstrated not only the possibility of invoking transpersonal experiences in dreams and also how one's belief system can impact the experience, and the outcome of the dreams.

In his narrative study, Esser (2012) replicated the research protocol but modified the task by asking dreamers to invite *kundalini* in their awareness during their lucid dreams, and to meditate or witness the dream. As in Bogzaran's study, the narratives shared by dreamers include numerous transformative experiences showing the intense and prolonged impact that this kind of inquiry can produce on the dreamer, including shifts in identity, revision of the dreamer's perception of ultimate reality, and a greater sense of fulfillment. Dreamers also reported ways by which dream mediated somatic (and subtle body) experience such as energy surging in their dream self and their physical body, sensual or sexual feeling, spontaneous movements of the physical body, accompanied by strong emotional release, including for example a deep feeling of gratitude.

Although peak experiences are most often reported in waking experience, Esser (2012) and Bogzaran's (1989) studies show that dreams can be the source of powerful and life-transforming peaks. Such practices can be very effective in inviting mystical-like experiences.[2] Although it could be argued that experience in the dreaming state might have more subtle effects than waking experience, one should bear in mind that lucid dreaming, as with contemplative practices, tends to accentuate feeling of clarity and participation in the psychic realms. As a result these dreams are often felt as numinous, and potentially as more impactful than similar kinds of experiences in a waking state.

These two research studies demonstrate the impactful changes that dreamers may encounter when they put in practice a combination of a dream cultivation strategy and a dream awareness strategy. One could argue that the research protocol creates a situation that mimics the intensity of similar practices conducted in more traditional religious settings, but the research goals align with the ethos of an open-ended inquiry.

Dream Understanding and Dream Practices

A broad range of practices can be identified across cultures. These practices take account of the multifaceted nature of dreaming: as a special form of consciousness and as the source of creative material. Many dream practices further connect dreaming to other states of consciousness beyond waking including; contemplative awareness and witnessing such as found in meditation: shamanic states of consciousness such as found in journey work, or states associated with the dying process. Many dreamers have often turned to religious teachings or indigenous science, as these tend to include traditional developmental models (see for example, Mason & Orme-Johnson,

2010). For example, Tibetan Buddhism contains specific practices taught as a means of exploring the nature of mind (Wangyal, 1998). In indigenous traditions, dreaming has been used for diagnosis and healing (Tedlock, 2005), and dreams are highly regarded for their visionary potential (Irwin, 1996, 2001).

To make sense of the wide array of dream practices, I have proposed that most practices fall into one of four broad categories (Deslauriers, 2009): (1) dream cultivation practices, often referred to as dream incubation; (2) dream awareness practices connected with dream lucidity; (3) dream understanding practices by those who seek to derive meaning from dreams, one's own or that of others; and (4) performative dream practices that connect insight with actions in the world. Understood sequentially, these practices involve the use of intentionality before the dream occurs (pre-sleep incubation), during the dream itself (lucid dreaming), or once one remembers a dream as in dream interpretation or dream action or ritual.

An integral approach to dreaming articulates each set of practices in relation to the others and the skills developed in one can be put to use in another. This enables the dreamer to unfold the full arc of the dreaming experience. For example, a dreamer may decide to set an intention before going to sleep, which could include that of becoming lucid in one's dream. If the dreamer has previously mastered the skill of lucidity, s/he may decide to address a pre-set intention during the dream. Upon waking, the dreamer may elect to reflect on the dream using a particular modality. Finally s/he may decide to take a particular action inspired from the dream, or to express its content in creative form, as a means to externalize, embody the dream, or in order to share it with others. Actions can take the form of a personal ritual that may help the dreamer anchor the existential or spiritual meaning derived from the dream. These practices are sensitive to the transpersonal context of dreamwork especially when an effort is made to relate them to the developmental journey or the spiritual beliefs of the dreamer. Davis (2004) discussed how to incorporate spirituality with Hill's cognitive-experiential dream interpretation model (Hill and Rochlen, 2002).

A trend toward participatory and embodied approach to dream experience can be traced in the past decades. Shying away from intellectual dream interpretation offered by a professional using a particular psychological lens (e.g., self-psychology, Jungian, or archetypal), the dreamer is now seen at the center of the interpretive work most likely guided by open-ended query from a therapists or facilitator who can model this form of self-inquiry (Bogart, 2009; Kelzer, 1999).

A host of interpretive and noninterpretive approaches exists using modalities as varied as movement, voice and sound (Doehner, 2012), meditation (DeCicco & Murkar, 2012), dream re-enactment and creative expression. Bogzaran and Deslauriers (2012) proposed an *Integral Dream Practice* that fosters a phenomenological attitude toward dreams. This attitude emphasizes: *dreams as experience* (as opposed to a symbolic text to be interpreted); the cultivation of *somatic awareness* when approaching dreams noninterpretively; *phenomenological creativity* in which dream experiences are regarded as a spontaneous creation of deep inner structures. When engaging in Integral Dream Practice the dreamer is guided to unfold a co-creative relationship among many aspects of their self. It encourages the dreamer to "enter the imaginal realm, to express the 'psychic automatism' and only later to articulate the process by way of reflection. This allows for a natural arising of insights and for possible meaning to be integrated as part of evolving consciousness" (Bogzaran & Deslauriers, 2012, p. 219).

Non-interpretive embodied approaches invite the dreamer to go back to the dream by the means an imaginal re-entry into the dream. Jung (1965) opened the door to this form of self-inquiry with the practice of "active imagination." Diverse modalities can foster a sense of being re-immersed in the dream world, including following the somatic felt sense that is connected to various dream images. *Dream re-entry* has proven to be an effective method in bringing lucidity to the dream experience, meeting the dream image in a dream-like state. It can also facilitate the exploration of alternative endings of dreams that is, in which the dreamer continues the path of resolutions suggested in the dream but not necessarily completed.

Conclusion

Kahn & Gover (2010) summed up dreaming consciousness as a thinking form that is boundless in content and creativity. It is perhaps the most naturally widespread form of altered consciousness that humans have known. In exploring the dreaming (as content and process) from a transpersonal perspective, I have noted how a developmental perspective reveals the increasing complexity in dreams with maturity and how dreams and dreamwork foster psychospiritual skills development. Dreams can help reveal the broad outline of one's spiritual life and its finer contours. The epistemological and ontological gaze of transpersonal psychology helps disclose the wide-ranging phenomenology of human flourishing and the role played by dreaming in this evolutionary and maturational process, both in its self-referential aspect (understood metaphorically as a vertical connection between ego and Self), or relational aspect (horizontal connections) revealing one's situatedness within complex ecological, cultural, and relational matrices.

For Hunt (2007), a psychology focused on numinous experiences and their effect on the course of life must navigate between false reductionism and over-belief. In this chapter, I have tried to chart an argument that heeds this counsel. Although dreams are connected to complex mind-brain processes, I avoided positing the origins of dreams as simply biologically produced. Similarly, I tried to avert dualistic explanation ascribing the origin of dreams to a transcendent source. Perhaps spirituality is self-organized just like as dreams are. One's own personal history, teleological orientation, and sense of calling will influence the way one approaches spiritual realities and how they disclose themselves. Dreams are part of this complex dialogical process. They are partners in self-realization, showing limitations of one's understanding, and giving inklings of how a true-for-oneself spirituality might feel, as opposed to a true-for-everyone spirituality.

Notes

1. Given that most of REM dreams are not recalled, it appears that dreaming can fulfill its psychobiological functions without the dreamer becoming aware of its content. The question thus arises as to whether any function of dreams has something to do with its particular content (Blagrove, 2011). Does a particular outcome obtain (be it insight, learning, or

mood regulation) because one has simply dreamt or because one had *that* particular dream? The answer still remains a puzzle for scientists.

2. Bogzaran and others have, however, warned about the strong aftereffects that these unusual peak experiences in dreams may have especially if they occur without proper context or supervision (such as that provided within a spiritual or religious group). Such effects can include psychological disorientation, or a feeling of loneliness as dreamers may not know whom to turn to share their experience. It is not uncommon that a dreamer needs time to make sense and integrate the learning of such an occurrence. Whereas the contemplative goals of lucid dreams may be to cultivate a lucidity in waking awareness, from a clinical perspective, one should distinguish this healthy pursuit from a pathological sense of derealization.

References

Blagrove, M. (2011). Distinguishing continuity/discontinuity, function, and insight when investigating dream content. *International Journal of Dream Research, 4*(2), 45-47.

Bogart, G. (2009). *Dreams and self-healing: Unfolding the symbols of the unconscious.* London, UK: Karnac.

Bogzaran, F. (1989). Experiencing the divine in the lucid dream state. *Masters Abstracts International, 29*(01) 0392 (UMI #1340429).

Bogzaran, F. (1991). Experiencing the divine in the lucid dream state. *Lucidity Letter, 10* (1 & 2), 169-176.

Bogzaran, F. (1994). Images of the lucid mind: A phenomenological study of lucid dreaming and modern painting. *Dissertation Abstracts International, 57*(08) 0392A (UMI #9702150).

Bogzaran, F. (2003). Lucid art and hyperspace lucidity. *Dreaming, 13*(1), 29-42.

Bogzaran, F. (2006). The spiritual dimensions of lucid dreaming. *Elixir, 2,* 23-32.

Bogzaran, F. & Deslauriers, D. (2012). *Integral dreaming: A holistic approach to dreams.* Albany, NY: State University of New York Press.

Bosnak, R. (2007). *Embodiment. Creative imagination in medicine, art and travel.* New York, NY: Routledge.

Bulkeley, K. (2011). Big dreams: The science of highly memorable dreams. In S. Kakar, (Ed.), *On dreams and dreaming* (pp. 1-20). Delhi, India: Viking.

Cartwright, R. (2010). *The twenty-four hour mind. The role of sleep and dreams in our emotional life.* New York, NY: Oxford University Press.

Cheyne, J. A. (2001). The ominous numinous sensed presence and "other" hallucinations. *Journal of Consciousness Studies, 8*(5-7), 133-150.

Combs, A. L., & Krippner, S. (2009). Daylife, dreamlife and chaos theory. In S. Krippner and D. Joffe Ellis (Eds.), *Perchance to dream: The frontiers of dream psychology* (133-145). New York, NY: Nova Science.

Corbett, L. (2007). *Psyche and the sacred. Spirituality beyond religion.* New Orleans, LA: Spring Journal Books.

Cortright, B. (2007). *Integral psychology: Yoga, growth, and opening the heart.* Albany, NY: State University of New York Press.

Davis, T. L. (2004). Incorporating spirituality into dream work. In C. E. Hill (Ed.), *Dream work in therapy: Facilitating exploration, insight, and action* (pp. 149-168). Washington, DC: American Psychological Association.

DeCicco. T. L., & Murkar, A. (2012, June). *Meditative dream re-entry: A protocol for using meditation for dream interpretation.* Presentation at the International Conference for the Study of Dreams. Abstract available at http://asdreams.org/2012/abstracts.html#D

De Koninck, J., Christ, G., Hebert, G., & Rinfret, N. (1990). Language learning efficiency, dreams and REM sleep. *Psychiatric Journal of the University of Ottawa, 15*(2), 91-92.

Dennis, S. L. (2001). *Embrace of the daimon: Sensuality and the integration of forbidden imagery in depth psychology.* York Beach, ME: Nicolas-Hays.

Deslauriers, D. (2000). Dream in the light of emotional and spiritual intelligence. *Advanced Development Journal, 9,* 105-122.

Deslauriers, D. (2009). Transcultural strategies for working with dreams. In S. Krippner & D. Joffe Ellis (Eds.), *Perchance to dream: The frontiers of dream psychology* (43-57). New York, NY: Nova Science.

Doehner, S. (2012, June). *A sound imagination: When sound transforms images.* Paper presented at the International Conference for the Study of Dreams. Retrieved June 2012 from http://asdreams.org/2012/abstracts.html#D

Esser, T. (2012, June). *Lucid dreaming meditation: Invited experiences of kundalini, the divine, and nonduality.* Paper presented at the International Conference for the Study of Dreams. Retrieved June 2012 from http://asdreams.org/2012/abstracts.html#E

Foulkes, D. (1999). *Children's dreaming and the development of consciousness.* Cambridge, MA: Harvard University Press.

Gackenbach, J., Cranson, R., & Alexander, C. (1986). Lucid dreaming, witnessing dreaming, and the Transcendental Meditation technique: A developmental relationship. *Lucidity Letter, 5*(2), 34-41.

Garfield, P. (1979). *Pathway to ecstasy: The way of the dream mandala.* New York, NY: Holt, Rinehart & Winston.

Gillepsie, G. (1987). Dreamlight: Categories of visual experience during lucid dreaming. *Lucidity Letter, 6*(1), 164-168.

Gordon, D. (2006). *Mindful dreaming: A practical guide for emotional healing through transformative mythic journeys.* Berkeley, CA: New Page Books.

Hartmann, E. (2000). The psychology and physiology of dreaming: A new synthesis. In L. Gamwell (Ed.), *Dreams 1900-2000: Science, art and the unconscious mind* (pp. 61-76). Ithaca, NY: Cornell University Press.

Hearne, K. M. T. (1978). Lucid dreams: An electro-physiological and psychological study. *UMI Dissertations Publishing* 0722 (UMI #U426618).

Hervey de Saint-Denis, L. (1982). *Dreams and the means of directing them.* M. Schatzman (Ed.), N. Fry (Trans.). London, UK: Duckworth (original work poublished 1867 [*Les Rêves et Les Moyens de les Diriger,* Paris: Amyat (French)]).

Hill, C. E., & Rochlen, A. B. (2002). The Hill cognitive-experiential model of dream interpretation. *Journal of Cognitive Psychotherapy, 16*(1), 75-89.

Hobson, J. A. (2000). *Dreaming as delirium: How the brain goes out of its mind.* Cambridge, MA: MIT Press.

Hobson, J. A. (2009). REM sleep and dreaming: Towards a theory of protoconsciousness. *National Review of Neuroscience, 10*(11), 803-813.

Hunt, H. T. (1989a). *The multiplicity of dreams.* Harvard University Press.

Hunt, H. T. (1989b). Lucidity Association Chair, Interviewed by K. Belicki. *Lucidity Letter, 8*(1). Retrieved from http://spiritwatch.ca/lucidity_1989_june.html

Hunt, H. T. (2000). Experiences of radical personal transformation in mysticism, religious conversion, and psychosis: A review of the varieties, processes, and consequences of the numinous. *The Journal of Mind and Behavior, 21*(4), 353-398.

Hunt, H. T. (2007). *Lives in spirit. Precursors and dilemmas of a secular Western mysticism.* Albany, NY: State University of New York Press.

Hurd, R. (2011). *Sleep paralysis: A guide to hypnagogic visions & visitors of the night.* Los Altos, CA: Hyena Press.

Irwin, L. (1996). *The dream seekers: Native American visionary traditions of the Great Plains.* Norman: University of Oklahoma Press.

Irwin, L. (2001). Sending a voice, seeking a place: Visionary traditions among Native women of the Plains. In K. Bulkeley (Ed.), *Dreams: A reader on religious, cultural and psychological dimensions of dreaming* (93-119). New York, NY: Palgrave.

Jaenke, K. (2010). Earth dreaming. In C. Chalquist (Ed.), *Rebearths: Conversations with a world ensouled* (pp. 187-202). Walnut Creek, CA: World Soul Books.

James, W. (1902). *The varieties of religious experience. A study in human nature.* NY: Random House.

Jung, C. G. (1965). *Memories, dreams, reflections.* A. Jaffé (Ed.): New York, NY: Vintage Books.

Jung, C. G. (1974). *Dreams.* Princeton, NJ: Princeton University Press.

Kahan, T. L. (2001). Consciousness in dreaming: A metacognitive approach. In K. Bulkeley (Ed.), *Dreams: A reader on the religious, cultural, and psychological dimensions of dreaming* (333-360). New York, NY: Palgrave.

Kahan, T. L. (2011). Possible Selves: Dreaming and the liberation of consciousness. In S. Kakar, (Ed.), *On dreams and dreaming* (pp. 109-126). Delhi, India: Viking.

Kahn, D., & Gover, T. (2010). Consciousness in dreams. *International Review of Neurobiology, 92,* 181-195.

Kelzer, K. (1987). *The sun and the shadow: My experiment with lucid dreaming.* Virginia Beach, VA: A.R.E. Press.

Kelzer, K. (1999). *Deep journey: Experiential psychotherapy with dreams, personal archetypal tales and trance states.* Berkeley, CA: North Atlantic Books.

Knudson, R. M., & Minier, S. (1999) The on-going significance of significant dreams: The case of the bodiless head. *Dreaming, 9,* 235-245.

Kramer, M. (2007). *The dream experience. A systematic exploration.* New York, NY: Routledge.

Krippner, S., Bogzaran, F., & de Carvhalo (2002). *Extraordinary Dreams and how to use them.* Albany, NY: State University of New York Press.

Kuiken, D., Lee, M. N., Eng, T. C., & Singh, T. (2006). The influence of impactful dreams on self-perceptual depth and spiritual transformation. *Dreaming, 16,* 258-279.

Kuiken, D., & Sikora, S. (1993). The impact of dreams on waking thoughts and feelings. In A. Moffitt, M. Kramer, & R. Hoffman (Eds.), *The functions of dreams* (pp. 419-475). Albany, NY: State University of New York Press.

LaBerge, S. (2000). Lucid dreaming: Evidence and methodology. *Behavioral and Brain Sciences, 23*(6), 962-964.

Lancaster, B. L. (2004). *Approaches to consciousness: The marriage of science and mysticism.* New York, NY: Palgrave MacMillan.

Lancaster, B. L. (2011). The cognitive neuroscience of consciousness, mysticism and psi. *The International Journal of Transpersonal Studies, 30*(1-2), 11-22.

Laurendeau, M., & Pinard, A. (1962). *Causal thinking in the child, a genetic and experimental approach.* New York, NY: International University Presses.

Lewis, M. D. (2000). The promise of dynamic systems approaches for an integrated account of human development. *Child Development, 71*(1), 36-43.

Mason, L. I., Alexander, C. N., Travis, F., Gackenbach, J., & Orme-Johnson, D. (1995). EEG correlates of higher states of consciousness during sleep. *Sleep Research, 24,* 152.

Mason, L. I., & Orme-Johnson, D. W. (2010). Transcendental consciousness wakes up in dreaming and deep sleep. Commentary on "The neurobiology of consciousness: Lucid dreaming wakes up" by J. Allan Hobson. *International Journal of Dream Research, 3*(1), 28-32.

McNally, R. J., & Clancy, S. A. (2005). Sleep paralysis, sexual abuse, and space alien abduction. *Transcultural Psychiatry, 42*(1), 113-122.

Nielsen, T. A., Deslauriers, D., & Baylor, G. W. (1991). Emotions in dream and waking event reports. *Dreaming, 1*(4), 287-300.

Noreika, V., Windt, J. M., Lenggenhager, B., & Karim, A. A. (2010). New perspectives for the study of lucid dreaming: From brain stimulation to philosophical theories of self-consciousness. Commentary on "The neurobiology of consciousness: Lucid dreaming wakes up" by J. Allan Hobson. *International Journal of Dream Research, 3*(1), 36-45.

Pargament, K. I., & Mahoney, A. (2002). Spirituality: Discovering and conserving the sacred. In C. R. Snyder (Ed.), *Handbook of positive psychology* (pp. 646-659). New York, NY: Oxford University Press.

Phillips, R. E., & Pargament, K. I. (2002). The sanctification of dreams: Prevalence and sanctification. *Dreaming, 12*(3), 141-153.

Revonsuo, A. (2000). The reinterpretation of dreams: An evolutionary hypothesis of the function of dreaming. *Behavioral and Brain Science, 23,* 877-901.

Rossi, E. L. (1985). *Dreams and the growth of personality* (2nd ed.). New York, NY: Brunner/ Mazel.

Solms, M. (1997). *The neuropsychology of dreams: A clinico-anatomical study.* Mahwah, NJ: Erlbaum.

Sparrow, S. (1976). *Lucid dreaming: Dawning of the clear light.* Virginia Beach, VA: A.R.E. Press.

Tandan, M. (2011). The way leads through yourself to beyond yourself: Dreaming in a Himalayan Monastery. In S. Kakar, (Ed.), *On dreams and dreaming* (pp. 146-167). Delhi, India: Viking.

Tart, C. (1969). *Altered states of consciousness.* Garden City, NY: Doubleday Anchor.

Taylor, E. (2009). *The mystery of personality: A history of psychodynamic theories.* New York, NY: Springer.

Tedlock, B. (2005). *The woman in the shaman's body: Reclaiming the feminine in religion and medicine.* New York, NY: Bantam.

Van den Daele, L. (1992). Direct interpretation of dreams: Typology. *The American Journal of Psychoanalysis, 52*(4), 307-326.

Voss, U., Holzmann, R., Tuin, I., & Hobson, J. A. (2009). Lucid dreaming: A state of consciousness with features of both waking and non-lucid dreaming. *Sleep, 32,* 1191-1200.

Waggoner, R. (2009). *Lucid dreaming: Gateway to the inner self.* Needham, MA: Moment Point Press.

Wallace, B. A. (2012). *Dreaming yourself awake: Lucid dreaming and Tibetan dream yoga for insight and transformation.* B. Hodel (Ed.): Boston, MA: Shambhala.

Wangyal, T. (1998). *The Tibetan yogas of dreams and sleep.* Ithaca, NY: Snow Lion.

Wehrle, R., Kaufmann, C., Wetter, T. C., Holsboer, F., Auer, D. P., Pollmächer, T., & Czisch, M. (2007). Functional microstates within human REM sleep: first evidence from fMRI of a thalamocortical network specific for phasic REM periods. *European Journal of Neurosciences, 25,* 863-871.

Wilber, K. (2000). *One taste: Daily reflections on integral spirituality.* Boston, MA: Shambhala.

Womack, Y. (2002). *Guardians of the gate: An investigation of numinous presence, "visions of the Divine" in dreams.* Köln, Germany: Lambert Academic.

29

Expressive and Creative Arts Therapies

Kim A. Bella and Ilene A. Serlin

Creative and expressive arts have long been an experiential practice for exploring questions of a spiritual and transpersonal nature, as well as a support for actively probing various dimensions of experience (Allen, 1995; Coppin & Nelson, 2005; Finley, 2008; McNiff, 1998b). Expressive and creative arts therapy incorporate this perspective in a therapeutic approach that combines creative expression and imaginal processes, such as painting, drawing, music, psychodrama, drama, dance/movement, storytelling, and poetry with psychotherapeutic techniques that focus on personal growth and development, transformation and healing, self-awareness, and emotional and spiritual well-being. The arts therapies promote conscious and intentional use of art-based modalities and creative processes in an effort to foster healthy cognitive, emotional, physical, spiritual, and social functioning, and they are widely employed in a variety of settings ranging from clinical, therapeutic, educational, community, medical, and rehabilitative (International Expressive Arts Therapies Association [IEATA], 2012; National Coalition of Creative Arts Therapies Association [NCCATA], 2012). An essential ingredient in any therapeutic process is promoting the awareness of the client's undigested material, and the arts therapies aid in the facilitation of integrating physical, emotional, cognitive, spiritual, and creative elements so these aspects can be harmonized, communicated, and expressed for enhanced functioning.

Expressive and creative arts therapies offer an avenue for individuals to express themselves in ways that might be challenging in a more traditional therapeutic approach or setting. According to Malchiodi (2005), combining verbal and nonverbal forms of expression with a variety of techniques and styles can help improve and enrich client communication. Although not strictly nonverbal, as in the case of poetry, storytelling, and drama, the extra-verbal aspects of creative expression allow for the elucidation from the nonverbal to the verbal, thereby providing an opportunity for a richer, multidimensional, and expanded approach to health and healing. For example, in a recent study conducted on the experience of being psychologically, creatively, and spiritually

The Wiley Blackwell Handbook of Transpersonal Psychology, First Edition.
Edited by Harris L. Friedman and Glenn Hartelius.
© 2013 John Wiley & Sons, Ltd. Published 2015 by John Wiley & Sons, Ltd.

stuck (Bella, 2011), the expressive arts technique utilized as part of the methodology helped facilitate a direct communication with the participants' immediate experience that had not been revealed with the verbal approach. As one participant described his post-drawing experience:

> I notice a shift as I acknowledge that [stuckness]. It feels a little smoother, a little bit less stuck now. I can feel that there's more acceptance around it now. I can still feel that there's a part of me that doesn't want it to be there, but then there's another part that's just willing to let it take its course, too. (p. 71)

He found another layer of meaning for himself while engaged in the nonverbal aspect of the project. Another participant described her experience:

> I feel this thing like an arrow, and it's in my head, and it's fuzzy like clouds. Right now, in this moment, I don't feel stuck. I feel like I have a lot of energy that's been released, released and unleashed. I feel a clarity with it. It's not disorganized energy, and it's not frenetic energy, but it feels clear, like a pathway. (p. 110)

She moved fluidly, following her experience moment-by-moment in a direct and immediate way, acknowledging that the drawing helped her to engage and deepen her process as she drew it. For each of these individuals, more information became available to them as they tapped into a different mode of expression enabling them to communicate a visual representation of their internal state, which led to a shift in both their experience and its expression.

Expressive and Creative Arts Therapies Distinction

Expressive arts therapy and creative arts therapy have sometimes been used synonymously. However, while the primary focus for both approaches is utilizing the arts as the vehicle for healing (Serlin, 2007b), there is a distinction between the two modalities. Expressive arts therapy applies an integration of all creative processes using a wide range of media (i.e., visual arts, dance, music) while creative arts therapy employs a specific arts modality (i.e., art therapy). Both approaches attempt to foster wholeness and healing through psychological, physical, and spiritual wellness (IEATA, 2012; NCCATA, 2012; Serlin, 2007b).

A creative arts therapist is a professional schooled in a specific modality, such as art therapy (trained in art and therapy), from a program designed specifically for that field, which reflects that specific approach to healing. For example, an art therapist working with a traumatized client would employ art-making as the mode of communication when words might not be available. This process can then "give a voice" to painful and traumatic experiences and provide meaning through the use of metaphors and symbolic images. By comparison, an expressive arts therapist is trained in a variety of arts-based modalities and might explore a client's issue through a variety of modalities, such as writing, a painting process, a sound, and/or a movement, tailoring the session in each case to the client's needs. In general, expressive art therapists can be seen as having "breadth" and creative arts therapists as having "depth."

The Transpersonal Psychology Approach in Arts Therapies

The arts therapies include a range of psychological perspectives, such as psychoanalytic, psychodynamic, cognitive, behavioral, and neuroscientific. However, for purposes of this chapter, the focus is on the transpersonal orientation, which includes the spiritual as well as the psychological dimension of experience. Although traditional psychological approaches work with one or more of the psychological, emotive, cognitive, and even somatic and mythological dimensions of human experience, transpersonal psychology includes all these within a philosophical and psychological perspective that grounds all these modalities within a broader spiritual context. Transpersonal psychology is an integrative discipline that combines the psychological with the spiritual, and this approach seeks to include and embody the multidimensionality of the "whole person" experience that includes ordinary and non-ordinary states of consciousness, self-actualization, diverse worldviews and perspectives, direct experience, and analytical intellect, which provides an "integrative human psychology" (Hartelius, Caplan, & Rardin, 2007). Expressive arts therapies fit well within the framework of transpersonal psychology as the arts therapies fields also seek to be multi-dimensional, multi-modal, and integral. As Serlin (2007b) has pointed out, "art is crucial for the healing journey because it touches and also expresses the whole complex human person, including levels of mind, body, and spirit" (p. 107).

The theoretical underpinning of the arts therapies rests on the premise of *intermodality*, in which the capacities and potentiality of a client can be expressed and explored through a range of sensory modalities in a therapeutic setting (Knill, Levine, & Levine, 2005). Two key elements of the expressive arts therapies are the "capacity of the arts to respond to human suffering," and the role of imagination in the "creative source of meaning" (Levine & Levine, 1999, p. 11). Also integral to the arts therapies approach is play, aesthetics, experimentation, and creative expression, which are essential to psychological well-being (Knill et al., 2005; Levine & Levine, 1999). In this respect, the arts therapies provide a range of possibilities for suffering to be explored and healing to occur.

History of Expressive and Creative Arts Therapies

The arts therapies have been practiced down throughout the ages, ranging from the ancient Greeks' use of art to work through emotional blocks that helped cleanse the psyche (Serlin, 2007a), to dance rituals for healing (Backman, 1972), to the use of role-playing and psychodrama with World War I veterans (Moreno, 1946). For example, early humans understood and celebrated the mysteries of creation and the divine by movement of the body through dance, which offered the possibility for transformation and healing, connection to the sacred, and meaning in a complex world (Serlin, 1993). Considered by some as "humankind's first psychotherapists" (Walsh, 1990), shamans were healers who incorporated physical and psychological components to their work using a wide repertoire of practices—ritual, singing, drumming, drama, dance, use of symbols and imagery—to cure the presenting illness, similar to current practices in expressive arts therapies (Serlin, 1993).

At the core of expressive arts therapies is creative expression, and May (1975) suggested that "creativity is the most basic manifestation of a man or woman fulfilling his or her own being in the world" (p. 40). Barrow (1996) described creativity as a process millions of years in the making; Almaas (2004) contended that creativity is the fundamental nature of life to express itself; Provencal and Gabora (2007, p. 255) stated that "art is a universal language, and that people engage in art naturally;" and Bohm and Peat (1987) spoke of it as a fundamental force in the universe. Creativity and creative expression are a natural movements in a natural process, and the disruption of the natural flow of the creative process and its creative expression can create ripples on a variety of levels that can impact one's life with sometimes severe and unintended consequences. Von Franz (2001) contended that significant mental illness and spiritual emergencies can also be the outcome of a stymied or stunted creative process. The expressive arts therapies, therefore, can be a valuable tool in helping to keep the natural flow of the universe moving inside each of us.

Benefits of and Supportive Research on Expressive and Creative Arts Therapies

Research on the efficacy of art therapy and creative arts has provided substantial acknowledgement of the health benefits of the creative process and artistic expression (Allen, 1995; Baráth, 2003; Barone & Eisner, 2012; Feder & Feder, 1981; McNiff, 1992; Serlin, 2007a). These may include stress reduction, increased life expectancy, enhanced immune system functioning, and an increase in physical and physiological health (Kiecolt-Glaser, McGuire, Robles, & Glaser, 2002; Pennebaker, 1990; Serlin, 2007a). Expressive art therapies have been successful in a wide range of therapeutic settings in work with groups and individuals with mental health concerns ranging from the mild to the severe. For example, the International Society for Traumatic Stress Studies (ISTSS, 2011) cited evidence that expressive arts therapies can help reduce the major symptoms of post-traumatic stress disorder (PTSD) and improve overall functioning. Evidence also suggests that these therapies support increases in emotional control and enhanced body image and reductions in depression, sleep problems, and anxiety. Provencal and Gabora (2007) also cited evidence of the therapeutic benefits of art creation, whereby personal issues and challenges, either traumatic or mundane, can be dealt with by allowing painful memories to surface and be released.

Expressive arts therapies are often process-based approaches that allow for the full expression of the human experience. An advantage of expressive arts therapies is that they often provide a concrete artifact that can offer the opportunity for continued contemplation at a later time (Koff-Chapin, 1996), which may enrich an individual's experience. Koff-Chapin (1996) went on to explain that expressive arts therapies can help bypass the rational mind and allow for direct, immediate experience based on the present moment rather than on past causes, reasons, or beliefs. This in turn allows for an intuitive and innate holding of the therapeutic process and produces an artifact that can uncover and reveal further insights not readily available through other therapies and methodologies (Heron & Reason, 1997; Koff-Chapin, 2005; McNiff, 1998a; Rappaport, 2009). The importance of the artifact is based on the effectiveness it provides in contributing to the healing of the individual, not necessarily on the artifact itself.

When a structured belief system receives input that has been filtered through the lens of the mind, distortions on the cognitive level can occur, and an arts-based artifact may also help unravel a mental misrepresentation. When perceptions of reality are skewed, it is possible to look to the language of art to help translate and comprehend information received from the inner and outer environment. Sommers-Flanagan (2007) interviewed psychologist Natalie Rogers:

> With expressive art, we are concerned as much about the process as we are about the product. The intent—just as in client-centered therapy—is to peel away the layers of defense and find our true nature. Art allows us to go into our pain, rage, and grief. Using art sometimes is much more effective than words to deal with some of these very difficult emotions. (p. 123)

Rappaport (2009) concurred, stating that "art captures the totality of the experience in one moment" (p. 79) and allows for an activation of the "inner witness" that can provide distance and space for further exploration and integration of the experience. This process of nonverbal creative expression is a form of embodied inquiry that can be meditative, utilizing an expressive art to support expanding awareness and insight, as well as helping to make meaning during difficult and challenging times. Rudolf Arnheim (1992), a perceptual psychologist, said,

> Art serves as a helper in times of trouble, as a means of understanding the conditions of human existence and of facing the frightening aspects of those conditions, as the creation of a meaningful order—these most welcome aids are grasped by people in distress and used by the healers who come to their assistance. But the blessings experienced in therapy can reach further; they can remind artists everywhere what the function of art has been and will always be. (p. 170)

At the core of many creative therapeutic approaches is the role of the imagination and working with images. According to McNiff (1998a), images and the imagination possess energy. Levine (2000) stated, "we need to harness the energetic dimension of aesthetic experience and join it to the articulate expression of artistic form" (para. 10). Through images, one is called upon to come forth and engage fully and dynamically to the energy radiating from creative expression. Images call upon the person to face (and reflect) their human existence and discover deeper truths, as in Levine's (2000) discussion of Gadamer's (2004) *Truth and Method*:

> Truth is the uncovering of the meaning of being. Such an uncovering demands that we enter into a dialogic relationship with that which we seek to understand, a relationship

in which not only the being of the thing we study, but also our own being comes into question. The experience of a work of art is for Gadamer an archetype of the revelation of truth. To understand the work demands more than a detached objectivity; rather, we confront the work with our own existence in a passionate encounter in which it speaks to us in a way that shatters our preconceptions. (para. 12)

Levine (2000) went on to say that truth is revealed when feeling and form can be united together, the imagination can be trusted as the conduit for the unfolding of that truth, and that truth is revealed in the embodied forms through presence itself or a "coming into being of the world (para. 15)." The practical application of revealing the truth of one's innermost being in the world through the expressive arts therapy lens can be found in numerous settings, within a variety of populations (e.g., individual, family, community, global), and among a wide range of treatments. Major mental illness, abuse, addiction, trauma and stress, and life-threatening illnesses are only a few of the conditions where expressive arts therapies have been successfully applied. Serlin (2007a) described her work of using expressive arts therapies with patients suffering from cancer: "Expressive therapies help patients get in touch with that part of the cancer that is symbolic and understand what it means. The meaning of the illness is expressed through imagery and metaphor" (p. 88). An example of a collective thread she cited from a cancer patient study:

> One image that appeared with frequency was that of *speed*. Women in a support group . . . drew pictures of frenzied lines and talked of the overwhelming speed of modern life, of lacking time to rest, to digest, or to reflect. A cancer cell can be seen symbolically as a cell out of control, speeding and multiplying crazily. These pathologies of time, space, and composition, disorders of postmodernity, show up in the experience and symbolic representation of disconnection and speed in the body. (Serlin, 2007a, p. 88)

In understanding feelings through image and metaphor, patients were able to regain a sense of control in their lives and helped to boost their self-esteem (Serlin, 2007a). Other studies have shown that expressive arts therapy can help patients increase their vitality, improve their body image, reduce their risk for life-threatening illnesses such as heart disease, cancer, and HIV, increase breast cancer survival rates, regulate high blood pressure, manage pain, and decrease depression (Cohen & Walco, 1999; Serlin, 2007a; Serlin, Classen, Frances, & Angell, 2000; Spiegel, Bloom, Kraemer, & Gottheil, 1989). Serlin (2007a) discussed how symbolic language provides a vehicle for the not easily conceptualized and not easily expressed aspects of experience, thus allowing a full range of capacities and guidance to unfold. Nonverbal expression, experienced through metaphors, symbols, and images (to name a few), provide a portal through which balance of the mind, body, and spirit can be achieved for the individual, for the community, and for the greater whole (Serlin, 2007a).

Rossi (1986) proposed that there is an interrelatedness between the mind and the body, and that how one processes emotions can assist or inhibit their ability to heal when beset by physical illness effects (Pert, 1997). Pert (1997) explained that when processing emotions, neuropeptide receptors facilitate the regulation of immunocytes, thereby enhancing the immune system. Dance therapy has been shown to increase immune system functioning due to the positive expression of emotions (Pert, 1997). In her movement therapy work with cancer patients, Serlin (2007a) related one patient's experience as follows:

> Meaning like when I walk into the group sometimes I'm real constricted, my body is constricted. I'm stressed. I'm tensed, you know, and then all of a sudden we start with some of the conversation, the movement, the stories and I'm just a different human being. It gives spaciousness to my cells so it allows them to breathe and allows them to flow more freely and then it gives spaciousness to my spirit because all of a sudden I'm free, and joy or pain or whatever comes out. So that's where I find the healing in the work. (p. 87)

Serlin (2007a) suggested that the findings here imply that balance can be achieved in the neuropeptide receptor network when emotions are expressed, and that this contributes to health and healing. ISTSS (2011) also explained the importance of brain functioning, emotions, and the specific manner in which an individual processes a traumatic event. The practices of expressive arts therapies help to activate right-brain functioning, thus providing a pathway to the nonverbal. The ability to tap into the right brain and express oneself physically and emotionally through expressive arts therapy can help alleviate stress and provide a boost in self-confidence, self-esteem, and a healthy body image (Serlin, 2007a). Expressive arts therapies have also been used effectively in dealing with issues of trauma experienced by children and adults alike. Through the use of the creative arts process, individuals who have experienced a traumatic event can find a "way to access nonverbal material or content that is unavailable to words" (ISTSS, 2011, p. 603). This type of process-oriented creative expression may be a valuable tool to aid individuals in working through the effects of the trauma.

Epistemological Perspectives

Transpersonal psychology is exemplified by a multi-modal or a many-ways of knowing orientation (Braud & Anderson, 1998), and expressive arts therapies bases its approach on accessing information and healing on multiple levels from various ways of knowing. Some aspects include peak and mystical experiences, indigenous ways, intuitive insights, contemplative traditions, sacred plant medicines, rituals, guided imagery, and other practices that can cultivate consciousness and increase self-understanding. For example, Gardner's (1982) multiple intelligences model allows for an expanded awareness of experience and access to different levels of aptitude and capacities based on information from the visual-spatial, musical, interpersonal, intrapersonal, bodily-kinesthetic, linguistic, and logical-mathematical realms. A case in point is Ilene Serlin's work as a dance therapist, which emphasizes the cultivation and unfoldment of the bodily-kinesthetic intelligence, enabling access to inner wisdom and knowing from a somatic sensitivity perspective (Stern, 1998). Additionally, Vaughan's (2002) description of spiritual intelligence allows for a multi-perspective approach that aims to find integration between the spiritual inner world and the materialistic outer life to open the heart, illuminate the mind, and inspire the soul. Goleman's (1995) emotional intelligences pave the way for a way of knowing and being in the world that encompasses self-awareness, self-control, and the ability to build relationships and community. The arts therapies provide an opportunity to practice and reflect on unfolding and illuminating the wisdom within that can support the process of healing and self-actualization.

Heron (1992) described four different ways of knowing—experiential, presentational, propositional, and practical knowing. He proposed these definitions:

> Experiential knowing—imaging and feeling the presence of some energy, entity, person, place, process or thing—is the ground of presentational knowing. Presentation knowing—an intuitive grasp of the significance of patterns as expressed in graphic, plastic, moving, musical and verbal art-forms—is the ground of propositional knowing. And propositional knowing—expressed in statements that something is the case—is the ground of practical knowing—knowing how to exercise a skill. (p. 122)

All aspects of a multidimensional approach to knowing are integral to the expressive arts therapies. One explores and discovers something from direct experience (experiential knowing), then express it in a creative way to gain understanding (presentational knowing), articulate it in a way that concretizes it (propositional knowing), and put the insights into action (practical knowing; Heron & Reason, 1997). Expressive arts therapy applies all levels of this approach in its practices, with presentational knowing as the primary representational modality. According to McNiff (2008), presentational knowing can yield understanding and insights that can be more accessible than many other forms of expression, and some scholars assert that presentational knowing can also offer innovative and novel approaches to generate understanding and transformation that are difficult to access by other means (Barone, 1995; Cole & Knowles, 2008; Greene, 1995). Rather than relying solely on cognitive understanding alone, the artistic rendering of one's inner landscape can provide a treasure trove of information. As an example, Rappaport (2009) described the experience of one of her focusing-oriented art therapy clients where she had drawn an image of her internal space after a contemplative exercise:

> My heart is locked inside a box and the tears are buried inside. I feel all of this pain but I won't let myself really feel it. The blue around the heart is all of the sadness and the black is a depressed feeling. I feel so heavy. I wish I could cry. (p. 125)

In this case, the drawing provided a visual depiction of previously unknown material that was accessed through creative avenues. Inner experience can often be represented in a visual form as a way of making meaning of personal, subjective experience that can be difficult to express in language (Seeley & Reason, 2008) as shown in the experience referenced above.

Research by Osterhold, Rubiano, and Nicol (2007) suggested that experiential and presentational knowing are integral elements that help to facilitate the whole-person experience in a direct and immediate way. These particular ways of knowing can help get underneath one's ideas and beliefs, and can provide access to parts of oneself that cannot be expressed wholly in words. Heron and Reason (2008) stated that:

> presentational knowing is made manifest in images which articulate experiential knowing, shaping what is inchoate into a communicable form, and which are expressed nondiscursively through the visual arts, music, dance, and movement ... and is a ... fundamental part of the process of inquiry, and its expression is both a meaningful outcome in its own right, and a vital precursor to propositional outcomes. (para. 24)

Mullett's (2008) research on creative engagement utilizing art, poetry, and song created a bridge between what is experienced and the expression of that experience. She found that creative expression of experience was a major factor in facilitating transformational changes in people's lives, further validating different ways of knowing and expressive arts therapies as valid instruments of inquiry and tools of transformation. Seeley and Reason (2008) also found the value of exploring direct, immediate experience using multi-modal ways of knowing results in a vibrant and diverse discovery of novel ideas and creative expressions.

Robbins (1986) indicated that the primary goal of therapy is to find congruence between the inner and outer reality of individual's experience, and an important element in the expressive arts therapies is being able to shape the raw material of one's experience, often from an emotional level, into a symbol or image (or sound or movement) that facilitates healing (Serlin, 2007a). When a person creates, the very act itself opens up a space between them and their emotions, allowing an objectification of the emotions, and thus offering a development in the capacity to discriminate between them (Feinstein & Krippner, 2009; Jung, 1966; Serlin, 1999). Hence, expressive arts therapies can be a valuable tool in exploring the full range of the human experience and can provide a foundation for a broader and deeper acknowledgement of the transpersonal nature of the self.

Creative Arts Therapies

The following sections briefly outline some of the major creative arts therapies (practices and methods also utilized by expressive arts therapists) focusing specifically on art therapy, music therapy, dance/movement therapy, and drama/psychodrama therapy.

Art Therapy

According to the American Art Therapy Association (2012), art therapy can be defined as the:

> therapeutic use of art making, within a professional relationship, by people who experience illness, trauma or challenges in living, and by people who seek personal development. Through creating art and reflecting on the art products and processes, people can increase awareness of self and others, cope with symptoms, stress and traumatic experiences; enhance cognitive abilities; and enjoy the life-affirming pleasures of making art. (n.p.)

Art therapy has been successfully used in a multitude of settings with a wide variety of applications and positive outcomes using physical and/or psychological measures such as in the treatment of schizophrenia (Teglbjaerg, 2011), grief and loss (Cheng, Lo, Chan, & Woo, 2010), torture survivors (Gray, 2011), depression (Bar-Sela, Atid, Danos, Gabay, & Epelbaum, 2007), HIV/AIDS symptom relief (Rao, Nainis, Williams, Langner, Eisin, & Paice, 2009), diabetes (Stuckey, 2009), and cancer (Serlin, 2007a), to name a few.

Dance/Movement Therapy

The American Dance Therapy Association (ADTA, 2009) has defined dance/movement therapy as the "psychotherapeutic use of movement to further the emotional, cognitive, physical, and social integration of the individual base on the empirically supported premise that the body, mind, and spirit are interconnected (n.p.)." The ADTA (2009) detailed that:

> Dance/movement therapy focuses on movement behavior as it emerges in the therapeutic relationship. Expressive, communicative, and adaptive behaviors are all considered for group and individual treatment. Body movement, as the core component of dance, simultaneously provides the means of assessment and the mode of intervention for dance/movement therapy. (n.p.)

Serlin (2007a) explained that dance therapy draws on stretching, rhythm, emotive expression, and other movements, integrating them with imagery and expression and a strong therapeutic relationship and building on those benefits. For example, stroke patients in expressive therapy classes attain needed exercise and build their coordination skills, as well as getting a boost of self-esteem, and that the patient learns to transform illness or physical pain through the sheer joy of movement (Serlin, 2007a).

Drama Therapy

According to the National Association for Drama Therapy (NADT, 2012), drama therapy is described as an:

> active, experiential approach to facilitating change. Through storytelling, projective play, purposeful improvisation, and performance, participants are invited to rehearse desired behaviors, practice being in relationship, expand and find flexibility between life roles, and perform the change they wish to be and see in the world. (n.p.)

Drama therapy is a participatory and engaged approach that can "provide the context for participants to tell their stories, set goals and solve problems, express feelings, or achieve catharsis. Through drama, the depth and breadth of inner experience can be actively explored and interpersonal relationship skills can be enhanced. Participants can expand their repertoire of dramatic roles to find that their own life roles have been strengthened" (NADT, 2012, para. 1).

Drama therapy is a spontaneous, creative, and playful method, which allows for a greater amount of freedom, experimentation, and transformation to explore emotional states by the means of dramatic action (Kedem-Tahar & Kellermann, 1996). They explained that drama therapists "use a wide range of exercises built on music, movement, sound, mime, physical relaxation, narratives, guided daydreaming, imagery and play" (p. 29) using "various stage props, such as dolls, masks, costumes, make-up and inanimate objects" (p. 29) to enact stories and myths. Drama therapy is process-oriented rather than outcome-oriented, progressing through various stages and it may entail either a pre-constructed theme or an improvisation on the spot (Kedem-Tahar & Kellerman, 1996).

Psychodrama

The American Society of Group Psychotherapy & Psychodrama (ASGPP, 2012), describes psychodrama as the:

> guided dramatic action to examine problems or issues raised by an individual (psychodrama) or a group (sociodrama). Using experiential methods, sociometry, role theory, and group dynamics, psychodrama facilitates insight, personal growth, and integration on cognitive, affective, and behavioral levels. It clarifies issues, increases physical and emotional well being, enhances learning and develops new skills. (n.p.)

Psychodrama encourages patients/clients to act out scenes using role-plays and dramatizations to explore real-life situations, dreams, fantasies, past memories, and future events (Kedem-Tahar & Kellermann, 1996).

Kedem-Tahar and Kellerman (1996) described the difference between psychodrama and drama therapy, "in psychodrama, the 'soul' (psyche) is the aim and the 'action' (drama) is the means, the opposite is true for drama therapy in which drama itself (as pure art) is the aim and the psyche is the means (of expression)" (p. 30). Serlin (2007a) elaborated, drama therapy is more closely related to theater using fictional narratives and psychodrama encourages the use of role-playing with the patient/client as the protagonist of the story.

Music Therapy

According to the American Music Therapy Association (AMTA, 2011), music therapy is defined as an:

> established health profession in which music is used within a therapeutic relationship to address physical, emotional, cognitive, and social needs of individuals. After assessing the strengths and needs of each client, the qualified music therapist provides the indicated treatment including creating, singing, moving to, and/or listening to music. Through musical involvement in the therapeutic context, clients' abilities are strengthened and

transferred to other areas of their lives. Music therapy also provides avenues for communication that can be helpful to those who find it difficult to express themselves in words.
Research in music therapy supports its effectiveness in many areas such as: overall physical rehabilitation and facilitating movement, increasing people's motivation to become
engaged in their treatment, providing emotional support for clients and their families,
and providing an outlet for expression of feelings. (para. 2)

Some aspects of music therapy may include singing, improvisational techniques,
interactive musical play, and active music-making, singing, interactive music play, and
improvisational techniques (AMTA, 2011).

Summary

Transpersonal approaches to the expressive arts utilize the intellectual, emotive, affective, experiential, sensorial, and imaginal aspects of human experience as pathways to
wholeness, healing, and spiritual development. It is the multidimensionality of expressive arts that distinguishes it from other transpersonal psychological approaches and
thereby has the potential to contribute to a fuller understanding of human experience and making meaning of the world. The expressive arts-based therapy approaches
reposition therapy within the realm of local, personal, everyday places and events in
which individuals may "meaningfully (and aesthetically) express both our individual
and wider truths through that which we create" (Seeley & Reason, 2008, p. 17).
When individuals mindfully explore the boundaries and potentials of their immediate
experience, they are engaging in a rich, participatory, and truthful discovery process
that can yield productive, meaningful, and fulfilling results about both themselves and
the world itself (Sullivan, 2005). In this way, creative approaches reveal new knowledge both about the depth and potential of the human being as well as the nature of
the creative spiritual ground from which human experience arises. At its most potent,
creative expression becomes a lived-in-the-moment inquiry that reveals the variety,
depth, aliveness, and fullness of the spiritual dimension of existence expressing itself
as a creative human experience in the world. Within this larger context, expressive arts
and creative arts therapists can be seen as healers who combine art, ritual, diagnosis,
and treatment to restore wholeness, health, and well-being to individuals as well as
the world.

References

Allen, P. B. (1995). *Art is a way of knowing*. Boston, MA: Shambhala.
Almaas, A. H. (2004). *Inner journey home: Soul's realization of the unity of reality*. Boston, MA:
    Shambhala.
American Art Therapy Association. (2012). Retrieved from http://www.americanartthera
    pyassociation.org
American Dance Therapy Association. (2009). Retrieved from http://www.adta.org
American Music Therapy Association. (2011). Retrieved from http://musictherapy.org

American Society of Group Psychotherapy and Psychodrama. (2012). Retrieved from www. asgpp.org

Arnheim, R. (1992). *To the rescue of art.* Berkeley, CA: University of California Press.

Backman, L. (1972). *Religious dances.* London, UK: Allen & Unwin.

Baráth, Á. (2003). Cultural art therapy in the treatment of war trauma in children and youth: Projects in the former Yugoslavia. In S. Krippner & T. McIntyre (Eds.), *The psychological impact of war trauma on civilians: An international perspective* (pp. 155-170). Westport, CT: Praeger.

Barone, T. (1995). The purposes of arts-based education research. *International Journal of Education Research, 23*(2), 169-180.

Barone, T., & Eisner, E. (2012). *Arts based research.* Thousand Oaks, CA: Sage Publications.

Barrow, J. (1996). *The artful universe: The cosmic source of human creativity.* New York, NY: Oxford University Press.

Bar-Sela, G., Atid, L., Danos, S., Gabay, N., & Epelbaum, R. (2007). Art therapy improved depression and influenced fatigue levels in cancer patients on chemotherapy. *Psychooncology. 16*(11), 980-984.

Bella, K. (2011). The Tao of stuckness: A heuristic art-based inquiry into following the thread of stuck experience. *Dissertation Abstracts Internaitonal, 73*(04) 0392B (UMI #349011).

Bohm, D., & Peat, D. (1987). *Science, order, and creativity: A dramatic new look at the creative roots of science and life.* New York, NY: Bantam Books.

Braud, W., & Anderson, R. (1998). *Transpersonal research methods for the social sciences: Honoring human experience.* Thousand Oaks, CA: Sage Publications.

Cheng, J., Lo, R., Chan, F., & Woo, J. (2010). A pilot study on the effectiveness of anticipatory grief therapy for elderly facing the end of life. *Journal of Palliative Care. 26*(4), 261-269.

Cohen, S., & Walco, G. A. (1999). Dance/movement therapy for children and adolescents with cancer. *Cancer Practice, 7*(1), 34-42.

Cole, A. L., & Knowles, J. G. (2008). Arts-informed research. In J. G. Knowles & A. Cole (Eds.), *Handbook of the arts in qualitative research* (pp. 55-70). Thousand Oaks, CA: Sage Publications.

Coppin, J., & Nelson, E. (2005). *The art of inquiry: A depth psychological perspective* (2nd ed., Rev.). Putnam, CT: Spring.

Feder, E., & Feder, B. (1981). *The expressive arts therapies: Art, music and dance as psychotherapy.* Englewood Cliffs, NJ: Prentice-Hall.

Feinstein, D., & Krippner, S. (2009). *Personal mythology: Using ritual, dreams, and imagination to discover your inner story* (3rd ed.). Fulton, CA: Energy Psychology Press.

Finley, S. (2008). Arts-based research. In J. G. Knowles & A. Cole (Eds.), *Handbook of the arts in qualitative research* (pp. 71-82). Thousand Oaks, CA: Sage Publications.

Gadamer, H.-G. (2004). *Truth and method* (2nd rev. ed., J. Weinsheimer & D. G. Marshall Trans.) New York, NY: Crossroads.

Gardner, H. (1982). *Art, mind and brain.* New York, NY: Basic Books.

Goleman, D. (1995). *Emotional intelligence.* New York, NY: Bantam Books.

Gray, A. E. L. (2011) Expressive arts therapies: Working with survivors of torture. *Torture, 21*(1), 39-47.

Greene, M. (1995). *Releasing the imagination: Essays on education, the arts, and social change.* San Francisco, CA: Jossey-Bass.

Hartelius, G., Caplan, M., & Rardin, M.-A. (2007). Transpersonal psychology: Defining the past, divining the future. *The Humanistic Psychologist, 35*(2), 1-26.

Heron, J. (1992). *Feeling and personhood: Psychology in another key.* London, UK: Sage.

Heron, J., & Reason, P. (1997). Participative knowing and an extended epistemology. *Qualitative inquiry, 3*(3), 274-294.

542   *Kim A. Bella and Ilene A. Serlin*

Heron, J., & Reason, P. (2008). Extending epistemology within a co-operative inquiry. Retrieved September 18, 2008, from: http://www.human-inquiry.com/EECI.htm

International Expressive Arts Therapy Association (IEATA). (2012). Retrieved from http://www.ieata.org

International Society for Traumatic Stress Studies. (2011). *Guidelines 16 and 17.* Retrieved at http://www.istss.org/TreatmentGuidelines/3337.htm

Jung, C. (1966). On the relation of analytic psychology to poetry. In R. F. C. Hull (Trans.), *The collected works of C. G. Jung: Spirit in man, art, and literature* (Vol. 15, pp. 131-193). Princeton, NJ: Bollingen.

Kedem-Tahar, E., & Kellermann, P. F. (1996). Psychodrama and drama therapy. *The Arts in Psychotherapy, 23*(1), pp. 27-36.

Kiecolt-Glaser, J. K., McGuire, L., Robles, T., & Glaser, R. (2002). Psychoneuroimmunology and psychosomatic medicine: Back to the future. *Psychosomatic Medicine, 64,* 15-28.

Knill, P. J., Levine, E. G., & Levine, S. K. (2005). *Principles and practice of expressive arts therapy: Towards a therapeutic aesthetics.* Philadelphia, PA: Jessica Kingsley.

Koff-Chapin, D. (1996). *Drawing out your soul: The touch drawing experience* (2nd ed.). Langley, WA: Center for Touch Drawing.

Koff-Chapin, D. (2005). (Autobiographical article). In P. R. Jacobson (Ed.), *Eyes of the soul: Exploring inspiration in art.* Grafenau, Germany: Optimum Druck. Retrieved September 18, 2008 from: http://www.touchdrawing.com/4Deborah/DKCarticles.html

Levine, S. K. (2000). Researching imagination: Imagining research. *POIESIS: A Journal of the Arts and Communication, 2,* 88-93.

Levine, S., & Levine, E. (Eds). (1999). *Foundations of expressive arts therapy: Theoretical and clinical perspectives.* Philadelphia, PA: Jessica Kingsley.

Malchiodi, C. (2005). *Expressive therapies.* New York: Guildford Press.

May, R. (1975). *The courage to create.* New York, NY: W. W. Norton.

McNiff, S. (1992). *Art as medicine: Creating a therapy of the imagination.* Boston, MA: Shambhala.

McNiff, S. (1998a). *Art-based research.* Philadelphia, PA: Jessica Kinglsey.

McNiff, S. (1998b). *Trust the process: An artist's guide to letting go.* Boston, MA: Shambhala.

McNiff, S. (2008). Art-based research. In J. G. Knowles & A. Cole (Eds.), *Handbook of the arts in qualitative research* (pp. 29-40). Thousand Oaks, CA: Sage.

Moreno, J. L. (1946). *Psychodrama.* New York, NY: Beacon House.

Mullett, J. (2008). Presentational knowing: Bridging experience and expression with art, poetry and song. In T. Reason & H. Bradbury (Eds.). *The SAGE Handbook of Action Research.* doi:10.4135/9781848607934

National Association of Drama Therapy (NADT). (2012). Retrieved from http://www.nadt.org

National Coalition of Creative Arts Therapies Association (NCCATA). (2012). Retrieved from http://www.nccata.org

Osterhold, H., Rubiano, E., & Nicol, D. (2007). Rekindling the fire of transformative education: A participatory case study. *Journal of Transformative Education, 5*(3), 221-245.

Pennebaker, J. W. (1990). *Opening up: The healing power of expressing emotions.* New York, NY: Guilford Press.

Pert, C. (1997). *Molecules of emotion: Why you feel the way you feel.* New York, NY: Charles Scribner & Sons.

Provencal, A., & Gabora, L. (2007). A compelling overview of art therapy techniques and outcomes: A review of Art Therapy Has Many Faces. *Psychology of Aesthetics, Creativity, and the Arts, 1*(4), 255-256, doi:10.1037/1931-3896.1.4.255b

Rao, D., Nainis, N., Williams, L., Langner, D., Eisin, A., & Paice, J. (2009). Art therapy for relief of symptoms associated with HIV/AIDS. *AIDS Care, 21*(1), 64-69.

Rappaport, L. (2009). *Focusing-oriented art therapy: Accessing the body's wisdom and creative intelligence*. Philadelphia, PA: Jessica Kingsley.

Robbins, A. (1986). *Expressive therapy: A creative arts approach to depth-oriented treatment*. New York, NY: Human Sciences Press.

Rossi, E. L. (1986). *The psychobiology of mind-body healing*. New York, NY: W.W. Norton.

Seeley, C., & Reason, P. (2008). Expressions of energy: An epistemology of presentational knowing. In P. Liamputtong & J. Rumbold (Eds.), *Knowing differently: Arts-based & collaborative research* (pp. 25-46). New York, NY: Nova Science.

Serlin, I. A. (1993). Root images of healing in dance therapy. *American Dance Therapy Journal, 15*(2), 65-75.

Serlin, I. A. (1999). Imagery, movement and breast cancer. In C. Clark (Ed.), *The encyclopedia of complementary health practices* (pp. 408-410). New York, NY: Springer-Verlag.

Serlin, I. A. (2007a). Expressive therapies. In M. Micozzi (Ed). *Complementary and integrative medicine in cancer care prevention: Foundations & evidence-based interventions* (pp. 81-94). New York, NY: Springer.

Serlin, I. A. (2007b). Theory and practices of arts therapies: whole person integrative approaches to healthcare. In I. Serlin (Ed), *Whole person healthcare: The arts and health* (Vol. 3, pp. 107-120). Westport, CT: Praeger Publishers.

Serlin, I., Classen, C., Frances, B., & Angell, K. (2000). Support groups for women with breast cancer: Traditional and alternative expressive approaches. *The Arts in Psychotherapy, 27*(2), 123-138.

Sommers-Flanagan, J. (2007). The development and evolution of person-centered expressive art therapy: A conversation with Natalie Rogers. *Journal of Counseling and Development, 85*(1), 120-125.

Spiegel, D., Bloom, J., Kraemer, H., & Gottheil, E. (1989). Effect of psychosocial treatment on survival of patients with metastatic breast cancer. *Lancet, 2*, 888-891.

Stern, E. M. (1998) The dialogue of movement: An interview/conversation with Ilene Serlin and E. Mark Stern. *Psychotherapy Patient, 10*(3/4), 47-52.

Stuckey, H. (2009). Creative expression as a way of knowing in diabetes adult health education: An action research study. *Adult Education Quarterly, 60*(1), 46-64. doi:10.1177/0741713609334139

Sullivan, G. (2005). *Art practice as research: Inquiry in the visual arts*. Thousand Oaks, CA: Sage.

Teglbjaerg, H. S. (2011). Art therapy may reduce psychopathology in schizophrenia by strengthening the patients' sense of self: A qualitative extended case report. *Psychopathology, 44*, 314-318. doi:10.1159/000325025

Vaughan, F. (2002). What is spiritual intelligence? *Journal of Humanistic Psychology, 42*(2), 16-33.

Von Franz, M. L. (2001). *Creation myths* (Rev. ed.). New York, NY: Shambhala.

Walsh, R. (1990). *The spirit of shamanism*. Los Angeles, CA: Jeremy P. Tarcher.

30

Psychospiritual Integrative Practices

Kathleen Wall, Fabrice Nye, and Eric FitzMedrud

The ego person in us cannot transform itself by its own force or will or knowledge or by any virtue of its own into the nature of the Divine; all it can do is to fit itself for the transformation and make more and more its surrender to that which it seeks to become.

Sri Aurobindo, 1984/1921, p. 80

The purpose of the integrative practices discussed in this chapter is to transform consciousness and all aspects of life. People engage in these practices to bring out the best in themselves and society, and to create a life worth living. The focus of this chapter is on *practices,* with the assumption that they are continuously utilized, pervading life, and are not limited to brief encounters with a facilitator. This chapter reviews what makes a practice integrative, surveys integrative practices, gives a detailed description of one integrative practice to illustrate the state of the field, and provides future directions for integrative practices.

Before attempting to review psychospiritual integrative practices we faced many questions. Which practices count as psychospiritual? Which are integrative? What differentiates a practice from a therapy or a tradition? Cortright, Kahn, and Hess (2003) offered a description of integral that includes body, heart, mind, and spirit. Wilber's (2000) integral theory and the All-Quadrants, All-Levels (AQAL; Wilber, 2006, p. 26) framework expand the integral range further to include six domains: physical, emotional-sexual, psychological, meditative/contemplative, community, and nature (Ferrer, 2003). The word *integral* is used regularly in transpersonal psychology, while the word *integrative* is used broadly in social sciences and medicine. In writings about integral practices a common description is that the practice transforms the

The Wiley Blackwell Handbook of Transpersonal Psychology, First Edition.
Edited by Harris L. Friedman and Glenn Hartelius.

practitioner. The intended transformation pertains to the person's consciousness as is described by Luskin (2004):

> Transformative practices that arose out of the religious traditions of the world are specific tactics designed to bring about transformation through spiritual insight. Their goal is to lead a practitioner to an enhanced awareness of spirit and a corresponding diminishment of identification with the mental and physical aspects of life. Intentional transformative practices aim to change the mind, body, and spirit of an individual or group by altering their perception of the relationship among these three elements so that spirit becomes predominant. (p. S-15)

In another definition, transformation involves a "shift in worldview followed by a dramatic restructuring of core values" (Schlitz, Vieten, & Amorok, 2007, p. 25). Schlitz and her colleagues added that "a sense of the sacred is often intimately connected with transformative experiences" (p. 29). Wilber (1980) differentiated transformation from changes that affect only the surface structure of consciousness, which he called *translations*. With these theoretical categories in mind we began our search and review process.

Review of Psychospiritual Integrative Practices

Literature Search

In this review, psychospiritual is defined as:

> a wide range of therapeutic systems which embrace a spiritual dimension of the human being as fundamental to psychic health and full human development and which utilize both psychological and spiritual methods (such as meditation, yoga, dream-work, breathwork) in a holistic, integrated approach to healing and inner growth. (Gleig, 2010, p. 738)

In an attempt to identify psychospiritual integrative practices in research databases we searched first for *spirituality* in the subject to ensure the practice had a spiritual component. Second, we searched for one of the following somewhere in the article: meditation, contemplation or contemplative, integrative or integral, psychospiritual or psychospiritual, and transformative, transformation, or transformational. Third, we searched for one of the following terms in the abstract or title: practice, intervention, or therapy. This search in multiple databases yielded an initial 37 potential psychospiritual integrative practices.

The following criteria were then applied to ensure the practice was indeed a psychospiritual integrative practice: first, the practice must be an autotelic practice—it must have a purpose in itself and not be intended or designed only for the treatment of or recovery from some illness or deficiency in health. This criterion helped differentiate psychospiritual practices from treatments. It eliminated, among other practices, a variety of integrations of spiritual principles with cognitive behavioral therapy. The second criterion was that the practice includes spirituality in an explicit way. This criterion required some interpretation because, for example, though Mindfulness-Based Stress Reduction (MBSR; Kabat-Zinn, 1990) training does not explicitly identify its spiritual components, we took the meditation origins and practices to be inherently spiritual in the broadest sense of that term. In contrast, HeartMath literature (Childre, Martin, & Beech, 2000) mentions spirituality as valued by the HeartMath approach but makes no mention of spirituality within its approach. Based on this information we counted MBSR as passing our criterion but not HeartMath. Reasonable people may disagree with this assessment. The third criterion was that a practitioner must be able to engage in the practice in some independent way after learning it. This criterion eliminated several culturally embedded practices that are primarily mediated by healers or guides. This criterion reflects a bias in this review toward practitioner autonomy but is not an evaluation of such practices. The final criterion required that there be at least one peer-reviewed quantitative research publication that indicated possible psychological benefits of the practice. This helped confirm that the practice integrated psychological benefits with purported spiritual benefits.

Recognizing that while these criteria helped to identify a manageable subset of psychospiritual integrative practices, it might also have excluded some valid candidates, we also conducted a validity check on the search criteria. Prior to searching we identified 13 practices that we thought our search might locate. Of these, 5 were among the 37 potential practices identified by our search, and all 5 of those passed our criteria set. The remaining 8 validity check practices were each searched for each independently as planned and any literature found checked to determine whether the practice passed the qualifying criteria. Only one of these practices, the Hoffman Quadrinity Process (Laurence, 2004), passed all of the criteria. An analysis of the articles on the Hoffman Quadrinity Process and keywords associated with those articles, revealed that the descriptor "alternative," as in "alternative healing" or "alternative therapy," would have located that article. A search of multiple databases adding that term was conducted, but no additional practices were identified for consideration.

Of the promising 37 practices thus identified, 12 passed all four criteria. Those 12 practices were condensed into a list of 9 when the 3 yoga practices were consolidated into a single category, and when nonspecific "prayer" was included in the "centering prayer" review. These practices are reviewed in brief below.

Psychospiritual Integrative Practices

The eight point program of passage meditation (PM). Passage Meditation (PM) was first systematized and taught at University of California Berkeley, during the 1960s by Indian Fulbright scholar Eknath Easwaran. Instructions and trainings are available at www.easwaran.org (Blue Mountain Center of Meditation, 2012) and in Flinders, Oman, Flinders, and Dreher (2010).

PM includes: (a) Thirty minutes of meditation on a memorized inspirational spiritual text that embodies spiritual ideals; (b) repetition of a "mantram," a holy name or phrase repeated during daily activities calms the mind and interrupts time urgency and negative thoughts, this is a bridging tool between formal meditation and daily life;

(c) slowing down, to allow time for inner reflection and sensitivity to others; (d) one-pointed attention involves doing only one thing at a time with full attention to train the mind to be more emotionally stable and less reactive to interruptions and emotions; (e) training the senses directs practitioners to discriminate in lifestyle choices, to make healthier choices, avoiding excessive drinking, overeating and unhealthy media; (f) putting others first encourages movement from one's own private self-interest to the needs of others; (g) spiritual association with other practitioners to offer and receive support, work together for a selfless goal, meditate and associate with other spiritual seekers; and (h) daily inspirational reading from the wisdom traditions is recommended.

Flinders, Oman, and Flinders (2007) reviewed research on PM, including two randomized controlled studies on health professionals and college students. Positive changes were found in stress, well-being, spirituality, self-confidence, and increase in forgiveness. A shorter form of PM focusing on mantram repetition, slowing down, and "one-pointed" attention reduced post traumatic stress disorder symptom severity, psychological distress, and increased quality of life in U.S. war veterans. With healthy community-dwelling adults, in a randomized controlled study, placement in the mantram repetition group was associated with less stress and depression compared with participants in the placebo mantram and no treatment control groups (Bormann, 2010). This growing body of research on PM, including randomized controlled trials indicates it has promise for improving quality of life for a range of psychological distress and for people simply wishing to improve their lives (Bormann, 2010). (NB: in this section the term "mantram" is used, but the Transcendental Meditation section in this chapter refers to the "mantra"; the term is used within each section as it is used in the literature about that practice.)

Hoffman quadrinity process. As described by Laurence (2004), the Hoffman Quadrinity Process is an emotional education program based on the theory that negative patterns and emotions take root in childhood from unrealistic expectations from one's parents. The process focuses on forgiveness of one's parents. It concentrates on four aspects of self: physical, emotional, intellectual, and spiritual. It is delivered in an 8-day, intensive residential workshop using a variety of methods and develops a participant's relationship with a spiritual self.

Only one research study was found that evaluated the psychological benefits of the Hoffman Quadrinity Process. Levenson's (2003) review used a quasi-experimental design to assess differences between a control group of participants who expressed interest but no plans in attending the Hoffman Quadrinity Process training and an experimental group who planned to and then did attend a training in the practice. Their results found that the experimental group did report significant positive change compared to baseline but when comparing repeated measures of the control and experimental groups, the results were less clear. In that comparison, the experimental group did not show as significant a difference from the control group in depression scores but did show significant differences from the control group on positive psychological variables.

Although the results of this study were promising, the results may be an artifact caused by differences between the experimental and control groups in characteristics such as help-seeking behavior. Therefore, as with many of the other practices in this chapter, the evidence base of the Hoffman Quadrinity Process is extremely limited and no conclusion can yet be drawn about this training practice.

Integral transformative practice®. Integral Transformative Practice (ITP), a trademark of Integral Transformative Practice International, includes a series of physical exercises (yoga and aikido), relaxation, and meditation 5 times per week; taking responsibility for one's own practice; practice with a community of ITP practitioners (in person or electronically); 3 hours of aerobic exercise weekly; conscious eating; intellectual development; a long-term individual affirmation to reflect desired change in mental, physical, and spiritual well-being; and finding ways to offer help to those in need, to ameliorate unnecessary waste and suffering in the world, and advance the evolution of our species and society to a more balanced, peaceful, and joyful condition.

Recent uncontrolled research on ITP (Vieten, Estrada, Cohen, Radin, Schlitz, & DeLorme (manuscript in preparation). A version of this paper is available at http://www.itp-international.org/library/print/summary-ions-transformation-study) reported on 53 ITP practitioners from 7 ITP groups in the US with average age of 55 over the course of 1 year. That research found statistically significant improvements in self-reported general physical health, quality of life, and psychological well-being. It also found a reduction in participants' health symptoms. More involvement in the practices predicted greater psychological well-being, quality of life, and self-transcendence but not improved physical health. The degree of self-transcendence predicted physical health, which in turn mediated improvements in psychological well-being. In the study self-transcendence was described as (a) a desire to discover meaning in life, (b) growing spirituality involving both an expansion of self-boundaries and an increased appreciation for present moment experiences, or (c) growth in wisdom described in the contemplative traditions. Though this uncontrolled study has promising findings, the results are subject to confirmation bias, it lacks a control group, and does not have any additional research supporting the results. Researchers and practitioners should view these results with caution despite the promise they hold.

Mindfulness-based stress reduction®. Developed in a medical setting for patients with chronic pain MBSR, trademarked by Kabat-Zinn, is derived from ancient Buddhist and yoga practices. Mindfulness is defined as paying attention, nonjudgmentally, in the present moment, and on purpose (Kabat-Zinn, 1990).

The three key components are sitting mindfulness (Vipassana), body scan meditations, and hatha yoga. The standard format is 8 weekly, highly experiential, 3-hour sessions and an all-day intensive. The program includes home practice of meditation exercises. The sitting meditation training begins with focusing on the breath, repeatedly returning the attention to it when it wanders away. The mindfulness training then expands to nonjudgmental observation of thoughts, feelings, sensations and stimuli as they enter the meditator's consciousness.

MBSR and associated therapies have given rise to an increasingly richer body of outcome research (e.g., Cohen-Katz et al., 2005; Sephton et al., 2007; Shapiro, Schwartz, & Bonner, 1998). Other disciplines have emerged that incorporate mindfulness in alignment with cognitive-behavioral therapies, such as dialectical behavior therapy (DBT; Linehan, 1993a, 1993b), mindfulness-based cognitive therapy (MBCT; Segal,

Williams, & Teasdale, 2002), and acceptance and commitment therapy (ACT; Hayes, Strosahl, & Wilson, 1999; Hayes, Strosahl, & Houts, 2005).

Prayer. This review includes mention of several types of prayer including centering prayer because prayer comes in different types: supplication, devotion, intercession, gratefulness, and contemplative prayer (Stanley, 2009). Centering Prayer is one form of contemplative prayer. The research supporting the evidence base for prayer as a psychospiritual integrative practice includes both centering prayer and contemplative prayer. Centering Prayer was developed by Meninger, Pennington, and Keating in the 1970s as a distillation of the monastic contemplative experience as it was practiced by the Desert Fathers and Mothers in the third and fourth centuries (Keating, 2005). This Christian tradition was transmitted through several routes (Johnston, 1996; Pennington, 1982). The term "Centering Prayer" was coined by Thomas Merton (Bourgeault, 2004).

A description of the four guidelines for Centering Prayer is given elsewhere (Keating, 2005). For this discussion it is important to note that the sacred word used in Centering Prayer should not be confused with a mantram. The sacred word, unlike the mantram, is not repeated constantly. Instead, as Blanton (2011) wrote, "it is only used when practitioners observe that they are being attracted by a thought. The sacred word is gently used to return the person's attention back to God's presence" (p. 136).

Contemplative prayer has been observed to be correlated with improvements in heart rate variability (Stanley, 2009), existential well-being and religious satisfaction (Poloma & Pendleton, 1991), and to be effective in reducing both depression (Johnson et al., 2009) and anxiety (Finney & Malony, 1985). But each of these studies have serious methodological limitations including small N, correlational self-report method, uncontrolled pilot method, and quasi-experimental design. Further research is needed to examine the effects of Centering Prayer and other types of prayer for psychotherapeutic intervention before drawing any conclusions about the efficacy of this practice for spiritual or psychological well-being.

Psychospiritual integrative therapy. See the detailed review in the next section of this chapter.

Qigong, or chi gong. Qigong or chi gong, a set of practices of which tai chi is one, is an ancient Chinese spiritual practice with many different forms and schools. What the schools have in common is the utilization of postures or movements to mobilize essential life energy. For a more thorough review of the history, schools, and goals of many different types of qigong see Tsang, Cheung, and Lak (2002). Although much of the literature in English on qigong focuses on the beneficial physical (e.g., heart disease; Ng et al., 2012) or psychological (Chan, Lee, Suen, & Tam, 2010; Lavretsky et al., 2011; Tsang, Mok, Yeung, & Chan, 2003) effects of the practice for a geriatric population, the practice is neither solely for the elderly nor solely for the prevention or cure of ailments.

There is a great deal more evidence for the benefits of qigong practices on physical health than on mental health. The mental health literature suggests both positive psychological benefits (Tsang et al., 2003) and decreases in mental health symptoms

(Lavretsky et al., 2011). Of note about the mental health studies thus far cited, several are randomized controlled trials, including the studies by Lavretsky et al. (2011) and Chan et al. (2010). This is far from an exhaustive list of the available rigorous studies especially when expanding to studies of the physical health benefits. Therefore, qigong is one of the integrative practices with strong emerging evidence to suggest that it is health promoting in addition to being an ancient and revered spiritual practice.

Transcendental meditation®. Transcendental meditation is a technique that originates from the Indian Vedic tradition, and was taught by Maharishi Mahesh Yogi beginning in the 1950s. The term Transcendental Meditation was trademarked by Maharishi. The technique consists mainly of mentally repeating a simple mantra. The mantra is not used for its spiritual significance, but in order to prevent cognitive activity. Mantra meditation is practiced twice a day for 20 minutes (Maharishi Mahesh Yogi, 1963; Orme-Johnson, 1988; Roth, 1994). The mantra is given out by a TM teacher during a private interview, and chosen on the basis of the meditator's age and gender (Lowe, 2011). New meditators are asked not to reveal the mantra that their instructor had assigned to them. The mantras used in TM have evolved through the years, and are now available on the internet (Doughney, 2004).

TM has been shown to have a beneficial impact on psychosocial stress and anxiety, as well as smoking and alcohol abuse (Rainforth et al., 2007), and to significantly reduce blood pressure (Anderson, Liu, & Kryscio, 2008; Nidich et al., 2009). Although TM meta-analyses have "found a superiority of transcendental meditation (TM) compared to other methods of relaxation and meditation" (Sedlmeier et al., 2012, p. 2), most of the research on TM including these meta-analyses have been carried out by researchers directly involved in or linked to the Maharishi University of Management, which has a vested interest in TM's dissemination (Canter, 2003; Sedlmeier et al., 2012).

Yoga. Yoga is one of six branches of classical Indian philosophy. The word *yoga* is derived from the Sanskrit for "join" or "yoke" referring to the union of the individual self with the Universal self. Patanjali systematized the philosophies and practices in *The Yoga Sutras* (Satchidananda, 1999), which persist as the definition of modern practices of yoga. Patanjali identified eight practices of yoga: (a) yamas (restraints or ethical disciplines: harmlessness, truthfulness, nonstealing, right use of vital force, and nonattachment); (b) niyamas (individual observances of disciplines: purity, content-ment, self-discipline, self-inquiry, and surrender the sense of separateness from the Divine); (c) asana (postures); (d) pranayama (breath control); (e) pratyahara (with-drawal of senses from control by externals); (f) dharana (concentration); (g) dhyana (meditation); and (h) samadhi (absorption, self-realization, enlightenment).

Many styles of yoga are practiced including Iyengar, Ashtanga, Vini, Kundalini, Bikram, Art of Living, and Integral. A research review (Fields, 2011), including sev-eral randomized controlled trials, indicates yoga has been helpful in reducing job stress, anxiety, depression, improving the quality of sleep, and for improving a host of pain syndromes and physical health problems. That review theorizes on possible mechanisms of action including stimulating of pressure receptors leading to enhanced vagal activity and reduced cortisol, which may in turn lead to reduced depression and enhance immune function. There are many research studies conducted in India, where yoga philosophy and multiple yogic practices tied to a specific lineages are included in the intervention. For example, a randomized control trial of 180 perimenopausal women in fourteen centers of Swami Vivekananda Yoga Research Foundation in Bangalore, India (Chatta, Nagarathna, Padmalatha, & Nagendra, 2008). Yoga groups and physical exercise control groups practiced 1 hour daily for 5 days per week for 8 weeks. Yoga groups, but not control groups had statistically significant improvements in hot flushes, night sweats and cognitive functions of remote memory, mental balance, attention and concentration, delayed and immediate recall, verbal retention and recognition. There is a large body of research on yoga that point to salutatory effects on health and well-being. A major challenge is that several very different practices are labeled "yoga." Specification of practices would allow for comparisons of effectiveness.

Psychospiritual Integrative Therapy: An Integrative Transformative Practice

Psychospiritual Integrative Therapy (PSIT; Wall, 2010; Wall, Corwin, & Koopman, 2012) is illustrated here to provide a more detailed description of an emerging integrative practice. PSIT is a good practice to illustrate the state of the field because among the family of integrative practices, the state of PSIT's development is between those with more research evidence (e.g., MBSR, TM, and qigong) and those with little or none as evidenced by the fact that 7 of the 13 practices used in our search validity check did not turn up in the literature search or did not meet our criteria for inclusion. PSIT has one experimental research study that suggests its efficacy and a few other studies utilizing a variety of other qualitative and quantitative research methods. PSIT is integrative because it has both a transpersonal intention—to assist people in actualizing their highest aspiration or life purpose—and specific psychological and spiritual processes. The psychological and spiritual processes help the participants develop skill in transforming personal patterns so they may actualize an aspirational life purpose. The theoretical underpinnings, process, and research on PSIT will be discussed.

Theoretical Underpinnings of PSIT

PSIT is informed by the cosmology of the evolution of consciousness articulated in the Integral Yoga of Sri Aurobindo (1984) and his collaborator Mirra Alfassa. This cosmology posits that human consciousness evolves into a higher spiritualized and integral consciousness. Further, this evolution is seen as fulfilling the purpose of existence to transform the consciousness of all life into an integral consciousness. So, to further the transformation of the consciousness of all life, this cosmology requires action in the world to transform mental and material life forms, not just spiritual enlightenment for an individual. Few practices are prescribed by Sri Aurobindo for those in pursuit of integral consciousness other than aspiration and surrender.

PSIT was developed to provide more tools and practices to assist individuals to actualize their higher aspiration in life. PSIT is nonsectarian, relying on an individual sense of the sacred and spiritual experiences rather than religious beliefs; therefore it is suitable to people from most religions or those who have none. It encourages personal experience of spirituality, meaning, and purpose in life not just mental beliefs.

PSIT Practices

PSIT has a dual focus. At a trait level it aims to facilitate deep transformation as defined above. At the behavioral level it is a "tool kit" of practices to be utilized repeatedly in order to act in the world in ways that are in harmony with fulfilling one's higher life purpose. PSIT is a flexible intervention that can be used for groups or individuals. This section will describe the activities of PSIT, a brief vignette to illustrate a client's experience of those activities, and review the integrative qualities of the process.

There are seven main processes in PSIT. They are: (a) clarifying an aspiration in life, also referred to as a higher purpose, through reflection and creative expression; (b) discerning personal patterns that aid that aspiration (referred to as a personified *helper*) and personal patterns that frustrate expression of that aspiration (referred to as a personified *hinderer*); (c) developing of witness consciousness through mindfulness meditation and movement based on MBSR (Kabat-Zinn, 1990); (d) accepting the *helper* and the *hinderer* through imagined and enacted dialogue with those personifications while in witness consciousness; (e) cultivating a personal sense of the sacred through Passage Meditation (Flinders et al., 2010); (f) surrendering the motivations of the helper and hinderer to the divine as experienced by the participant as facilitated by movement, drawing, and writing in journals; (g) planning for how to enact the personal aspiration; and, (h) sharing the changes with others in the group, facilitators, and/or significant others to affirm the changes and externalize the internal process. For more information on PSIT facilitator's trainings and manuals contact the first author (see also Corwin, Wall, & Koopman, 2012; Wall, Corwin, & Koopman, 2012).

The PSIT steps will be presented below in the form of a vignette. First, as Hillary (pseudonym) begins a PSIT group she finds, through reflection, that she feels purposeful when she helps others. Grappling with some confusion about what her highest aspiration or life purpose could be, she decides that "to help others" is her highest aspiration. Contemplation of spiritual readings, writing (journaling) and creative expression in the form of drawing helped her clarify the aspiration.

Second, Hillary acknowledges personal patterns that help and hinder the actualization of her aspiration. She is guided to mindfully experience postures, bodily sensations, feelings, thoughts, images, motivations, and a sense of spirit that express the helper and hinderer. Hillary described her helper as energetic and kind and her hinderer as depressive and judgmental. She found herself rejecting her hinderer, with strong emotional reactions, as she was convinced that it had nothing good to add to her life.

Third, through exercises designed to develop witness consciousness, Hillary reduces identification with her temporary and ever changing aspects including her helper and hinderer. This witness consciousness produces a re-perceiving (Shapiro, Carlson, Astin, & Freedman, 2006) that helps Hillary create a more flexible and expanded view of the self which leads to behavioral flexibility (Hayes, 2004). The witness consciousness allowed her to be less emotionally reactive to her hinderer.

The fourth practice in PSIT invites Hillary to develop acceptance of the helper and hinderer and, through a guided dialogue, understand their motivations. Hillary uses her witness consciousness to develop a nonjudgmental acceptance that her helper is motivated by boundless energy to help others. Her hinderer wants to protect her from overextending herself and depleting her energy.

The fifth practice primes Hillary for connecting with a personal sense of the sacred by having her bring in a personally meaningful poem, prayer, or lyrics. Hillary shares the few lines from a favorite poem that reminds her of her personal feeling of the sacred.

With this sense evoked, the PSIT facilitator invites Hillary into the sixth step to surrender the motivations of the helper and hinderer to the sacred. In PSIT, surrender is an active process of aligning the participant's will with their perception of divine will rather than clinging to egoic notions of control (Aurobindo, 1993). This type of surrender paradoxically promotes active coping with adversity (Cole & Pargament, 1999; Pargament, 1997). Like some PSIT participants, Hillary had some difficulty wanting to surrender, especially the motivations of her helper. She also achieved a full sense of surrender to the sacred only after several sessions. Hillary, experiences a transformation of her helper as it gains energy by experiencing her spiritual connection, and devotes herself to compassionately caring for herself as well as others. Hillary's hinderer's depression lifts, although it is not banished, when she experiences a sense of spiritual support. Hillary also experiences a decrease in her sense of burden as she trusts the sacred more and releases a felt need to be personally responsible for events outside her control.

As the PSIT process comes to a close with the seventh step, the participant is encouraged to create a plan for actualizing their aspiration consistently in daily life. Hillary develops a plan for regular spiritual meditation for self-care and to help her discern the best balance for her energy between caring for others and self-care.

Finally, Hillary shares with the group how her aspiration changed during the process, the changes in her helper and hinderer, the sense of peace she felt in the meditations, and her plan for actualizing her aspiration.

Repeated practice of the PSIT process in group or individually is encouraged to reinforce the participant's ability to continually transform their multiple helpers and hinderers in order to consistently fulfill one's highest aspiration, creating a meaningful, purposeful life. Workbooks, recordings of guided meditations, and reflection on their journals provide material support when repeating the practices. Forming and joining alumni groups to support the practices in community is also recommended.

Research on Psychospiritual Integrative Therapy

PSIT research, like some integrative practices presented in this chapter (e.g., Integral Transformative Practice, Hoffman Process), is a practice with a small body of research suggesting its possibility for improving quality of life. Research on PSIT has been conducted on small groups of people with cancer. The validation of PSIT as a treatment intervention is, thus, in its infancy. This section will briefly review four PSIT studies for their findings and methodological limitations—potentials and challenges that are common among integrative practices.

Results of an uncontrolled feasibility study with 24 breast cancer survivors indicate that participants in a PSIT group experienced statistically significant increases in psychological, physical, and functional well-being, with moderate to large effect sizes, however social/family well-being did not increase significantly (Garlick, Wall, Corwin, & Koopman, 2011). The participants experienced a decrease in mood dysfunction, especially depression, anger, fatigue, and tension, while their sense of vigor increased. There was no significant decrease in confusion. A sense of spiritual well-being, especially a sense of meaning and peace grew in the participants. Their scores increased on measures of post traumatic growth, especially experiencing new possibilities and personal strength. Emotional well-being showed a small increase at the 4-week follow-up, while other scores decreased. This suggests that participants continued to integrate the emotional skills, but not others from the PSIT process after the intervention stopped leading to questions about the persistence of the practice.

McDonald, Wall, Corwin, Brooks and Koopman (2013) conducted a qualitative study of 12 PSIT participants and 12 community breast cancer support group participants. They found that PSIT participant narratives included more existential and spiritual development themes and that those participants had more desire to live life fully as compared to narratives of participants in community support groups. PSIT participants also reported gaining more specific skills for coping than community support group participants and improved relationships after developing the detached and nonjudgmental awareness characteristic of witness consciousness in PSIT and increased spirituality. However, both participant groups were helped in restoring a new sense of normalcy after their world view was shattered by the experience of cancer raising questions as to whether less integrative practice groups are equally facilitative of coping, in this case with cancer.

A study of the experience of surrender (Rosequist, Wall, Corwin, Achterberg, & Koopman, 2012) in 12 breast cancer PSIT group participants, found that with repetition, most, although not all, participants were able to experience a sense of completeness of surrender as facilitated by PSIT practices. This surrender increased a self-reported sense of peacefulness, purpose, optimism, higher quality of life (QL), and an active coping process as described by participants' self-report on an open-ended questionnaire. The components for PSIT were reported as promoting changes in spiritual well-being and QL in a multiple case studies comparison of four female breast cancer participants in PSIT who changed the most and least in measures of spirituality (Rettger, 2011). Rettger also found that people whose pre-post intervention scores had the highest percentage change on measures of spiritually also changed most on QL measures. Similarly, spiritual well-being and self-transcendence mediated QL in 31 cancer group participants (Johnson, 2011). Both of these PSIT studies were small and uncontrolled. However, they suggest a relationship between spirituality and QL reported in other research discussed below.

The limitations of the studies reviewed include no control group, lack of generalizability, small numbers, possible demand characteristics, and convenient samples. Yet, the qualitative studies provide a rich description of the range of experience, both difficult and facilitative for participants of PSIT. Despite their limitations, the studies reviewed above show the feasibility of PSIT to impact both the spiritual and psychological well-being of participants. As with the developers of other integrative practices, PSIT researchers would like to conduct more rigorous studies with diverse populations especially with a population of those who are not struggling with a major illness yet wish to improve the quality of life. PSIT has been conducted with a broader population though not researched with this group. However, obtaining resources for research on PSIT and other integrative practices has proven challenging.

Future Directions

The transpersonal vision of integrative practices, reviewed here, is a lofty transformation of consciousness and all aspects of life. Transpersonal psychology is better served to advance science and improve psychospiritual integrative practices, by researching whether and how integrative practices work. The investigation of the components responsible for profound change allows for refinement of components responsible for change and to de-emphasize components that are not active in the transformative process. Integrative practices are being developed with a variety of emphases, as the brief review above shows. Research studies on their effects are emerging but, except for a few modalities those studies are sparse and lack rigor. However, some research is emerging on the components of these practices. Some integrative practice components being studied are: compassion (such as that conducted by Stanford's Center for Compassion and Altruism Research and Education; Goetz, Keltner, & Simon-Thomas, 2010; Simon-Thomas et al., 2011), forgiveness (Harris et al., 2006), and meditation (Shapiro et al., 2006; Oman, Thoresen, & Hedberg, 2010). The findings of those research efforts indicate that integrative practices include components that have a capacity to change the consciousness of the participants in positive ways. Forgiveness and compassion and their associated emerging practices, although aligned with the transpersonal vision in their participatory approach (see Ferrer, 2011), were not reviewed in this chapter because their lack of explicit inclusion of spiritual components. If a practice is found to cultivate the goals of spiritual practice such as compassion, forgiveness, calm, and relational connection, future transpersonal research might also properly study that practice.

Research on components or possible mechanisms of psychospiritual integrative practices is emerging. For instance, Shapiro et al. (2006) posited that *reperceiving*, that is the shift in perspective resulting from distancing oneself from the drama of one's narrative, is a mechanism of action of mindfulness that fosters self-regulation, cognitive flexibility, values clarification, and exposure. Schlitz et al. (2007) suggested that the notion of surrender may paradoxically "open a door to an entirely new way of being" (p. 39). Other components that deserve to be studied are: gratitude, self-transcendence, and purpose in life. The relationship of spirituality and a greater sense of quality of life also deserve further research. This relationship was noted in studies of two practices reviewed here, ITP and PSIT. Furthermore there is a growing body of literature on the positive relationship between spirituality, and quality of life (Plante & Thoresen, 2007). For example in two large studies, spirituality was found to significantly predict quality of life in cancer patients at baseline and 6 months later (Yanez et al., 2009).

Neural correlates of well-being are being studied with integrative practices as well. Urry et al. (2004) documented a correlation between activation of a left posterior region of the superior frontal cortex and "both eudaimonic well-being, understood as purpose, mastery, strong relationships, and self-acceptance, and hedonic well-being, operationalized as the subjective sense that life is satisfying" (p. 370). Hanson and Mendius (2009) have pointed out that the brain's neuroplasticity allows incremental alterations in the neural structure and that the accumulating impact of positive material produced by integrative practices will over time change the brain. However, though research on integrative practices suggests positive changes in participant well-being (Luskin, Reitz, Newell, Quinn, & Haskell, 2002; Vieten, Estrada, Cohen, Radin, Schlitz, & DeLorme (manuscript in preparation). A version of this paper is available at http://www.itp-international.org/library/print/summary-ions-transformation-study) and neuropsychology research has shown that increases in well-being correlate with changes in neural activation, there is little research that documents changes in neural cactivation as a result of participation in an integrative practice. A study of the neural correlates and mechanisms of the benefits from integral practices and their components would be beneficial to the field.

Although many of the practices here are directly or indirectly informed by centuries old traditions, even new integrative practices draw upon ancient technologies. Yet, 21st century technologies may also have much to offer to the practitioner. Where practitioners once had to travel to find their community of the spirit and a teacher willing to work with them, teaching programs are now available on the internet (e.g., Hamilton, 2012), creating a virtual community. Multimedia links embedded in books guide practices (e.g., Goldstein, 2012). Virtual reality also allows people in search of healing to use gaming technology to get better (e.g., Kanani, 2011; National Institutes of Health, 2011). The confluence of time-tested practices with modern tools of dissemination and connection may prove to boost the reach of integrative practices.

Our search eliminated those practices without an explicit spiritual subject, yet we identified many practices that appear to value spirituality without making the spiritual content explicit. We propose that those practices too may be considered within the domain of transpersonal psychology and be reviewed subsequently. We also delimited our review to practices that may be engaged in independently, yet this distinction is arbitrary at best and discriminatory at worst. A later review should separately consider those practices such as 12-step spirituality, sweat lodges, and other culturally embedded and connected practices, which require facilitation, mediation, other interpersonal environments.

A research challenge for the field to overcome is the necessity for longitudinal studies to investigate the results of longer term effects of executing standardized integrative practices. Because of the nature of integrative practices, some practitioners and researchers might expect that longer term or more frequent practices may yield increasing improvements over time but it is also possible that greater effects are experienced early in practices when there is the greatest room for improvement and that thereafter, ongoing improvement rates taper off. It would also be interesting to investigate the dose (either the amount of time daily for a regular practice or the effects of concentrated practice as might happen on a retreat) required for integrative practices to yield significant and sustained improvements in well-being. This dose research is especially relevant given that research has found brain changes after an

8-week mindfulness meditation course (Davidson et al., 2003). Another challenge is the clearer description of the processes used in such practices as yoga and qigong. It is difficult to compare outcomes when different practices are used, yet all labeled yoga or qigong. Yet many practices utilize a variety of modalities that may be helpful for different people at different times in life.

Many questions remain about integrative practices such as: How much is enough? What are the effects of longer term practices? How do people continue practicing when they reach plateaus in their perceived progress? As in physical exercise, what is an optimal level? Are certain practices better at meeting certain participant needs? These questions and more will require research to investigate, yet the ground work to establish the evidence base for most of these practices is small, nonexistent, and/or has serious methodological limitations. Therefore, diverse as these methods are, a unifying research strategy for the field of integrative practices using successively more complex and rigorous research (e.g., from qualitative studies to quasi-experimental pilots to randomized control trial designs, progressively) would both winnow the field and might help the practices to more effectively bring transformation to progressively larger audiences. Research discerning the effective components and degree of efficacy of integrative practices may allow these practices to become more than proprietary marketing tools, ensure their longevity beyond the life span of their creators, and improve their ability to transform the consciousness of practitioners.

References

Anderson, J. W., Liu, C., & Kryscio, R. J. (2008). Blood pressure response to transcendental meditation: A meta-analysis. *American Journal of Hypertension, 21*(3), 310-316. doi: 10.1038/ajh.2008.268

Aurobindo, Sri (1984). *The synthesis of yoga.* Pondicherry, India: Sri Aurobindo Ashram Press. (Original work published 1921)

Aurobindo, Sri (1993). *The Integral Yoga: Sri Aurobindo's teachings and method of practice.* Pondicherry, India: Sri Aurobindo Ashram Press.

Blanton, P. G. (2011). The other mindfulness practice: Centering prayer & psychotherapy. *Pastoral Psychology, 60,* 133-147. doi:10.1007/s10089-010-0292-9

Blue Mountain Center of Meditation. (2012). In *Learning how to meditate.* Retrieved, September 11, 2012 from http://www.easwaran.org/learning-how-to-meditate.html

Bormann, J. E. (2010). Mantram repetition: A "portable contemplative practice" for modern times. In T. G. Plante (Ed.), *Contemplative practices in action: Spirituality, meditation, and health* (pp. 35-59). Santa Barbara, CA: Praeger.

Bourgeault, C. (2004). *Centering prayer and inner awakening.* Cambridge, MA: Cowley.

Canter, P. H. (2003). The therapeutic effects of meditation. *British Medical Journal, 326*(7398), 1049-50. doi:10.1136/bmj.326.7398.1049

Chan, A. W. K., Lee, A., Suen, L. K. P., & Tam, W. W. S. (2010). Effectiveness of a Tai chi Qigong program in promoting health-related quality of life and perceived social support in chronic obstructive pulmonary disease clients. *Quality of Life Research, 19,* 653-664. doi:10.1007/s11136-010-9632-6

Chatta, R., Nagarathna, R., Padmalatha, V., & Nagendra, H. R. (2008). Effect of yoga on cognitive functions in climacteric syndrome: A randomized controlled study. *BJOG: An International Journal of Obstetrics and Gynaecology, 115*(8), 991-1000. doi:10.111/j.1471-0528.2008.01749.x

Childre, D., Martin, H., & Beech, D. (2000). *The HeartMath solution*. New York, NY: Harper-One.

Cohen-Katz, J., Wiley, S., Capuano, T., Baker, D. M., Deitrick, L., & Shapiro, S. (2005). The effects of mindfulness-based stress reduction on nurse stress and burnout: A qualitative and quantitative study, part III. *Holistic Nursing Practice, 19*(2), 78-86. doi:10.1097/00004650-200503000-00009

Cole, B. S., & Pargament, K. I. (1999). Spiritual surrender: A paradoxical path to control. In W. R. Miller (Ed.), *Integrating spirituality into treatment: Resources for practitioners* (pp. 179-198). Washington, DC: American Psychological Association. doi:10.1037/10327-009

Cortright, B., Kahn, M., & Hess, J. (2003). Speaking from the heart: Integral T-groups as a tool for training transpersonal psychotherapists. *Journal of Transpersonal Psychology, 35*(2), 127-142.

Corwin, D., Wall, K., & Koopman, C. (2012). Psychospiritual Integrative Therapy: Psychological intervention for women with breast cancer. *The Journal for Specialists in Group Work, 37*(3), 252-273. doi:10.1080/01933922.2012.686961

Davidson, R. J., Kabat-Zinn, J., Schumacher, J., Rosenkranz, M., Muller, D., Santorelli, S. F., ... Sheridan, J. F. (2003). Alterations in brain and immune function produced by mindfulness meditation. *Psychosomatic Medicine, 65*(4), 564-570. doi:10.1097/01PSY.0000077505.67574.E3

Doughney, M. (2004). In *The TM and TM-Sidhi techniques*. Retrieved August 25, 2012, from http://minet.org/mantras.html

Ferrer, J. N. (2003). Integral transformative practice: A participatory perspective. *Journal of Transpersonal Psychology, 35*(1), 21-42.

Ferrer, J. N. (2011). Participatory spirituality and transpersonal theory: A ten-year retrospective. *The Journal of Transpersonal Psychology, 43*(1), 1-34.

Fields, T. (2011). Yoga clinical research review. *Complementary Therapies in Clinical Practice, 17*(1), 1-8. doi:10.1016/j.ctcp.2010.09.007

Finney, J., & Malony, H. (1985). An empirical study of contemplative prayer as an adjunct to psychotherapy. *Journal of Psychology and Theology, 13*, 284-290.

Flinders, T., Oman, D., & Flinders, C. L. (2007). The eight-point program of passage meditation: Health effects of a comprehensive program. In T. G. Plante & C. E. Thoresen (Eds.), *Spirit, science and health: How the spiritual mind fuels physical wellness* (pp. 72-93). Westport, CT: Praeger.

Flinders, T., Oman, D., Flinders, C., & Dreher, D. (2010). Translating spiritual ideals into daily life: The eight-point program of passage meditation. In T. G. Plante (Ed.), *Contemplative practices in action: Spirituality, meditation, and health* (pp. 35-59). Santa Barbara, CA: Praeger.

Garlick, M., Wall, K., Corwin, D., & Koopman, C. (2011). Psycho-Spiritual Integrative Therapy for women with primary breast cancer. *Journal of Clinical Psychology in Medical Settings, 18*(1), 78-90. doi:10.1007/s10880-011-9224-9

Gleig, A. (2010). *Psychospiritual*. In D. A. Leeming, K. Madden, & S. Marlan (Eds.), *Encyclopedia of Psychology and Religion*, (pp. 738-739). New York, NY: Springer.

Goetz, J. L., Keltner, D., & Simon-Thomas, E. (2010). Compassion: An evolutionary analysis and empirical review. *Psychological Bulletin, 136*(3), 351-374. doi:10.1037/a0018807

Goldstein, E. (2012). *The now effect: How this moment can change the rest of your life*. New York, NY: Atria.

Hamilton, C. (2012). *Integral enlightenment online course*. Retrieved April 24, 2012, from http://integralenlightenment.com/online-course/info/

Hanson, R., & Mendius, R. (2009). *Buddha's brain: The practical neuroscience of happiness, love and wisdom*. Oakland, CA: New Harbinger.

Harris, A. H. S., Luskin, F., Norman, S. B., Standard, S. S., Bruning, J. J., Evans, S. S., & Thoresen, C. E. (2006). Effects of a group forgiveness intervention on forgiveness, perceived stress, and trait-anger. *Journal of Clinical Psychology, 62*(6), 715-733. doi:10.1002/jclp.20264

Hayes, S. (2004). Acceptance and Commitment Therapy and the new behavior therapies. In S. Hayes, V. M. Follette, & M. M. Linehan (Eds.), *Mindfulness and acceptance: Expanding the Cognitive-Behavioral tradition* (pp. 1-29). New York, NY: Gilford Publishing.

Hayes, S. C., Strosahl, K. D., & Wilson, K. G. (1999). *Acceptance and commitment therapy: An experiential approach to behavior change.* New York, NY: Guilford.

Hayes, S. C., Strosahl, K. D., & Houts, A. (Eds.). (2005). *A practical guide to acceptance and commitment therapy.* New York, NY: Springer.

Johnson, A. V. (2011). An investigation of spiritual mediators of quality of life and mood among cancer survivors participating in psycho-spiritual integrative therapy. *Dissertation Abstracts International, 73*(06) 0669B (UMI #3495279).

Johnson, M., Dose, A., Pipe, T., Petersen, W., Huschka, M., Gallenberg, M., ... Frost, M. H. (2009). Centering prayer for women receiving chemotherapy for recurrent ovarian cancer: A pilot study. *Oncology Nursing Forum, 36*(4), 421-428. doi:10.1188/09.ONF.421-428

Johnston, W. (Ed.). (1996). *The cloud of unknowing.* New York, NY: Image Books.

Kabat-Zinn, J. (1990). *Full catastrophe living.* New York, NY: Delacorte.

Kanani, R. (2011, September 19). Gaming for social change: An in-depth interview with Jane McGonigal. *Forbes.* Retrieved from http://www.forbes.com

Keating, T. (2005). *Manifesting God.* New York, NY: Lantern Books.

Laurence, T. (2004). *The Hoffman process.* New York, NY: Bantam.

Lavrestsky, H., Alstein, L. L., Olmstead, R. E., Ercoli, L. M., Riparetti-Brown, M., St. Cyr, N., & Irwin, M. R. (2011). Complementary use of Tai chi chih augments escitalopram treatment of geriatric depression: A randomized controlled trial. *The American Journal of Geriatric Psychiatry, 19*(10), 839-850. doi:10.1097/JGP.oB013e318 20ee9ef

Levenson, M. R. (2003, August). *Symptom reduction and positive mental health: Evaluation of an alternative therapy.* Paper presented at the American Psychological Association annual conference, Toronto, Canada. Abstract retrieved from http://web.ebscohost.com

Linehan, M. M. (1993a). *Cognitive-behavioral treatment of borderline personality disorder.* New York, NY: Guilford.

Linehan, M. M. (1993b). *Skills training manual for treating borderline personality disorder.* New York, NY: Guilford.

Lowe, S. (2011). Transcendental meditation, Vedic science and science. *Nova Religio, 14*(4), 54-76. doi:10.1525/nr.2011.14.4.54

Luskin, F. (2004). Transformative practices for integrating mind–body–spirit. *The Journal of Alternative and Complementary Medicine, 10*(1), S-15-S-23. doi:10.1089/acm.2004.10.S-15

Luskin, F., Reitz, M., Newell, K., Quinn, T. G., & Haskell, W. (2002). A controlled pilot study of stress management training of elderly patients with congestive heart failure. *Preventive Cardiology, 5*(4), 168-172.

Maharishi Mahesh Yogi. (1963). *Science of being and art of living.* New York, NY: Signet.

McDonald, C., Wall, K., Corwin, D., Brooks, C., & Koopman, C. (2013). The effects of Psycho-Spiritual Integrative Therapy and community support groups on coping with breast cancer: A qualitative analysis. *European Journal of Person Centered Healthcare.*

National Institutes of Health. (2011). *Clinical trial of a rehabilitation game—SuperBetter.* Retrieved April 24, 2012, from http://clinicaltrials.gov/ct2/show/study/NCT0139 8566

Ng, S., Wang, C., Ho, R. T., Ziea, E. T., Wong, V. C. T., & Chan, C. L. (2012). Tai chi exercise for patients with heart disease: A systematic review of controlled clinical trials. *Alternative Therapies, 18*(3), 16-22.

Nidich, S. I., Fields, J. Z., Rainforth, M. V., Pomerantz, R., Cella, D., Kristeller, J., ... Schneider, R. H. (2009). A randomized controlled trial of the effects of transcendental meditation on quality of life in older breast cancer patients. *Integrative Cancer Therapies, 8*(3), 228-234.

Oman, D., Thoresen, C. E., & Hedberg, J. (2010). Does passage meditation foster compassionate love among health professionals? A randomized trial. *Mental Health, Religion, & Culture, 13*(2), 129-154. doi:10.1080/13674670903261954

Orme-Johnson, D. W. (1988). The cosmic psyche—An introduction to Maharishi's Vedic psychology: The fulfillment of modern psychology. *Modern Science and Vedic Science, 2*(2), 113-163.

Pargament, K. I. (1997). *The psychology of religion and coping: Theory, research, and practice.* New York, NY: Guilford Press.

Pennington, B. (1982). *Centering prayer.* New York, NY: Image Books.

Plante, T. G., & Thoresen, C. E. (Eds.). (2007). *Spirit, science, and health: How the spiritual mind fuels physical wellness.* Westport, CT: Praeger.

Poloma, M. M., & Pendleton, B. F. (1991). The effects of prayer and prayer experiences in measures of general well-being. *Journal of Psychology & Theology, 19*(1), 71-83.

Rainforth, M. V., Schneider, R. H., Nidich, S. I., Gaylord-King, C., Salerno, J. W., & Anderson, J. W. (2007). Stress reduction programs in patients with elevated blood pressure: A systematic review and meta-analysis. *Current Hypertension Reports, 9*(6), 520-528. doi:10.1007/s11906-007-0094-3

Rettger, J. P. (2011). A multiple case study exploration of women coping with primary breast cancer participating in a psycho-spiritual integrative therapy group. *Dissertation Abstracts International, 72*(07) 0669B (UMI #3450900).

Rosequist, L., Wall, K., Corwin, D., Achterberg, J., & Koopman, C. (2012). Surrender as a form of active acceptance among breast cancer survivors receiving Psycho-Spiritual Integrative Therapy. *Supportive Care in Cancer, 20*(11), 2821-2827.

Roth, R. (1994). *Maharishi Mahesh Yogi's transcendental meditation* (2nd ed.). New York, NY: Donald I. Fine.

Satchidananda, S. (1999). *The Yoga Sutras of Patanjali, Translation and Commentary.* Buckingham, VA: Integral Yoga Publications.

Schlitz, M., Vieten, C., & Amorok, T. (2007). *Living deeply: The art and science of transformation in everyday life.* Oakland, CA: New Harbinger.

Sedlmeier, P., Eberth, J., Schwarz, M., Zimmermann, D., Haarig, F., Jaeger, S., & Kunze, S. (2012). The psychological effects of meditation: A meta-analysis. *Psychological Bulletin, 138*(6), 1139. doi:10.1037/a0028168.

Segal, Z. V., Williams, J. M., & Teasdale, J. D. (2002). *Mindfulness-based cognitive therapy for depression: A new approach to preventing relapse.* New York, NY: Guilford.

Sephton, S. E., Salmon, P., Weissbecker, I., Ulmer, C., Floyd, A., Hoover, K., & Studts, J. L. (2007). Mindfulness meditation alleviates depressive symptoms in women with fibromyalgia: Results of a randomized clinical trial. *Arthritis Care & Research, 57*(1), 77-85. doi:10.1002/art.22478

Shapiro, S. L., Carlson, L. E., Astin, J. A., & Freedman, B. (2006). Mechanisms of mindfulness. *Journal of Clinical Psychology, 62*(3), 373-386. doi:10.1002/jclp.20237

Shapiro, S. L., Schwartz, G. E., & Bonner, G. (1998). Effects of mindfulness-based stress reduction on medical and premedical students. *Journal of Behavioral Medicine, 21*(6), 581-599. doi:10.1023/A.1018700829825

Simon-Thomas, E. R., Godzik, J., Castle, E., Antonenko, O., Ponz, A., Kogan, A., & Keltner, D. J. (2012). An fMRI study of caring vs. self-focus during induced compassion and pride. *Social Cognitive and Affective Neuroscience, 7*(6), 635-648.

Stanley, R. (2009). Types of prayer, heart rate variability, and innate healing. *Zygon, 44*(4), 825-846. doi:10.1111/j.1467-9744.2009.01036.x

Tsang, H. W. H., Cheung, L., & Lak, D. C. C. (2002). Qigong as a psychosocial intervention for depressed elderly with chronic physical illness. *International Journal of Geriatric Psychiatry, 17*(12), 1146-1154. doi:10.1002/gps.739

Tsang, H. W. H., Mok, C. K., Yeung, Y. T. A., & Chan, S. Y. C. (2003). The effect of Qigong on general and psychosocial health of elderly with chronic physical illness: A randomized clinical trial. *International Journal of Geriatric Psychiatry, 18*(15), 441-449. doi:10.1002/gps.861.

Urry, H. L., Nitschke, J. B., Dolski, I., Jackson, D. C., Dalton, K. M., Mueller, C. J., ... Davidson, R. J. (2004). Making a life worth living: Neural correlates of well-being. *Psychological Science, 15*(6), 367-372. doi:10.1111/j.0956-7976.2004.00686.x

Vieten, C., Estrada, M., Cohen, A. B., Radin, D., Schlitz, M. M., & DeLorme, A. (manuscript in preparation). A version of this paper is available at http://www.itp-international.org/library/print/summary-ions-transformation-study). Effects of engaging in a community-based integral practice program on health and well-being.

Wall, K. (2010). *Psycho-spiritual integrative therapy group facilitator's manual.* Palo Alto, CA: Institute of Transpersonal Psychology.

Wall, K., Corwin, C., & Koopman, C. (2012). Reaping fruits of spirituality through Psycho-Spiritual Integrative Therapy in cancer recovery. In T. G. Plante (Ed.), *Religion and positive psychology: Understanding the psychological fruits of faith* (pp. 233-246). Santa Barbara, CA: Praeger.

Wilber, K. (1980). *The atman project: A transpersonal view of human development.* Chicago, IL: Quest.

Wilber, K. (2000). *Integral psychology: Consciousness, spirit, psychology, therapy.* Boston, MA: Shambhala.

Wilber, K. (2006). *Integral spirituality.* Boston, MA: Shambhala.

Yanez, B., Edmondson, D., Stanton, A. L., Park, C. L., Kwan, L., Ganz, P. A., & Blank, T. O. (2009). Facets of spirituality as predictors of adjustment to cancer: Relative contributions of having faith and finding meaning. *Journal of Consulting and Clinical Psychology, 77*(4), 730-741. doi:10.1037/a0015820

31

The Diamond Approach

John V. Davis, Theodore Usatynski, and Zvi Ish-Shalom

The Diamond Approach is a contemporary spiritual teaching and path for exploring the nature of reality as it is experienced through human consciousness, an exploration that leads to inner freedom and maturity. It aims for a full, free, and personal embodiment of one's potential in one's experience and one's life. Providing a systematic and psychologically-sophisticated method for exploring the nature of consciousness and reality, the Diamond Approach enables students to investigate their inner experience, discover and integrate the inner truth of their being, work through the obstacles to realizing and expressing that truth, and develop as authentic, creative, and fulfilled human beings. Since its origins in the mid-1970s, it has gained respect from a number of transpersonal psychologists and spiritual teachers, and the body of students studying it, both formally and informally, has grown rapidly. Its map of consciousness, articulation of the processes of spiritual development, and methods will be of interest and value to many transpersonal psychologists.

Although the Diamond Approach is not a transpersonal psychology, per se, it responds to many of the questions central to transpersonal psychology: What is the nature of optimal human development and spiritual maturity? What is the nature and fate of the sense of individual identity and self-transcendence? How can we most effectively work with the barriers and difficulties on a spiritual path? Many of its responses to these questions will be familiar to transpersonal psychologists and spiritual seekers. However, it also offers new and insightful answers to these questions, offering more effective ways of understanding and engaging inner development. Understanding, as an integration of concepts, direct experience, and lived expression, is at the heart of its methods. Although its teachings offer richly detailed, broad-ranging, often subtle, and even profound psychological insights, it is primarily a spiritual path which entails living a life engaged with the world, not apart from it.

The Diamond Approach views reality as the eternal truth in a variety of manifest and unmanifest dimensions. Its view is multi-faceted, precise, and inclusive. As a

The Wiley Blackwell Handbook of Transpersonal Psychology, First Edition.
Edited by Harris L. Friedman and Glenn Hartelius.
© 2013 John Wiley & Sons, Ltd. Published 2015 by John Wiley & Sons, Ltd.

modern Western teaching, the Diamond Approach values and cultivates the specific ways in which reality manifests through the individual person. It is grounded in a view of reality that is seen both as a shared field in which differentiated particulars arise and as an absolute nonduality beyond concepts and perception. Its understanding is nonhierarchical in the sense that it does not privilege particulars or the universal, duality or nonduality, being or nonbeing, the rich beauty of the world or the boundless purity of transcendence. All are expressions of the endless possibilities of the totality of reality.

The Diamond Approach embraces both *recovery* of one's connection to true nature and *development* of one's capacity to live as true nature. The first aim arises from the view that one's inner truth or *essence* becomes unavailable to consciousness due to conditioning, habit, psychodynamic defenses, structuring of the inherent openness of individual consciousness, and other factors. With a gradual recovery of this connection, essence is increasingly experienced in differentiated qualities, among them joy, strength, compassion, passion, support, value, and a felt-sense of basic trust in the world, along with many others. Without access to these qualities, psychological and spiritual development is arrested or distorted, resulting in misidentifying oneself as a separate entity dissociated from the ground of being and its essential qualities. The resulting loss of contact with essence leads to suffering and compulsive attempts to regain essential qualities. Recovery of one's inherent connection to essence leads to fulfillment, self-realization, and the embodiment and authentic expression of these qualities. Its second aim recognizes that individual consciousness matures and transforms toward greater aliveness, openness, dynamism, sensitivity, clarity, and transparency to reality. Conscious access to essence enables one to re-engage the full potential of development. Aspects of this process, its stages, and vicissitudes have been described by developmental psychology, transpersonal psychology, and spiritual wisdom traditions. The recovery aspect of this work leads to a deeply satisfying sense of homecoming, while the developmental aspect is an adventure of personal evolution without end.

Over the past 40 years, A. H. Almaas has articulated an extensive body of written and oral teachings on the Diamond Approach. As with all wisdom traditions, it is difficult to reduce the subtlety, depth, and richness of this knowledge into a few pages. Furthermore, the Diamond Approach, being a modern Western teaching of human development, often borrows terms from other traditions. In some cases, these terms will have slightly different meanings from their traditional context. We have attempted to explicate these terms as clearly as possible according to the conceptual paradigms of the Diamond Approach.

History and Development

The Diamond Approach has been developed and articulated primarily by A. H. Almaas (the pen-name for Hameed Ali) through several series of books and through his spiritual work school, the Ridhwan School. It is its own logos, understanding, and method, arrived at through phenomenological inquiry and testing through its teachings. Although its insights arose on their own through Almaas and his collaborators, it draws on multiple sources of wisdom to articulate its findings, including both classical and modern psychodynamic theory and various spiritual wisdom traditions, including Sufism, Buddhism, Gurdjieffian Fourth Way work, Vedantism, and contemplative Christianity and Judaism. However, Almaas has described the Diamond Approach as arising first through his direct experience that then found expression in various conceptual frameworks.

Almaas, who was born in Kuwait in 1944, has described his early training in physics as an attempt to understand the nature of reality (Schwartz, 1996). However, in the early 1970s, he began exploring various forms of psychological and spiritual work. Claudio Naranjo's group, *Seekers After Truth,* seems to have been an important influence on the early development of the Diamond Approach. For many years, Almaas collaborated with Karen Johnson and Faisal Muqaddam. Although Muqaddam left the Diamond Approach to found his own school, Almaas and Johnson continue to work together. In 1974, Almaas began teaching what he called the Returning Process, drawing from the Fischer-Hoffman Process. A group of students asked him to begin an ongoing group in 1975. That group grew steadily in Colorado and California. A few years later, he began training a small group of students to teach the Diamond Approach, the Ridhwan Foundation was formed as a church, and in 1983, the first group of teachers other than Almaas, Johnson, and Muqaddam was ordained. In 1987, the basic teachings of the Diamond Approach were organized and offered as the Diamond Heart Training, and the work is sometimes referred to by this name. Experiencing steady growth and expansion, (as of 2012) the Ridhwan Foundation offers groups in North America, Europe, Australia, and New Zealand with approximately 4000 students, 120 ordained teachers, and active seminary training programs in the USA and Europe.

Almaas has been prolific in presenting the Diamond Approach through several series of books. His first books described the orientation of the Diamond Approach and one of its foundational concepts, essence (Almaas, 1984/1998). The *Diamond Heart* books 1 through 5 (Almaas, 1987/2000a, 1988/2000b, 1990/2000c, 1997/2000d, 2011) are primarily transcriptions of talks to students and present a deepening series of teachings. The *Diamond Mind* books (Almaas, 1986/2000i, 1988/2000a, 1996/2000h) present detailed technical explorations of the dynamics of spiritual development. *The Diamond Body* (Almaas, 2002, 2006, 2008) series outlines the methodology and practices of the Diamond Approach. Almaas has also presented a broad overview of the Diamond Approach path (2004), an autobiographical account (1995/2000f), and the use of the enneagram in spiritual realization (1998/2000e). A number of Almaas' books are also available in translation. Davis (1999) has written an introductory overview of the Diamond Approach, and several other Diamond Approach teachers have written books influenced by the Diamond Approach (Brown, 1999: Maitri, 2001, 2005). For more on the history of the Diamond Approach, A. H. Almaas, and his writings, see his website (http://ahalmaas.com).

Methods of the Diamond Approach

The Diamond Approach uses a wide range of contemplative practices and experiential techniques, including classic forms of concentration and mindfulness meditations, body-sensing practices, chanting, visualization, movement, psychodynamic methods, and somatic work. Although many of these practices are similar to those found in other contemplative and psychotherapeutic approaches, they are used in the context of the Diamond Approach in ways that are often unique to its logos and orientation. The books in Almaas' *Diamond Mind* series include case studies and examples of students working with him and give a flavor of the main methods of the Diamond Approach.

Inquiry

Inquiry is both the primary source for the Diamond Approach's map of inner experience and spiritual development and its primary method (Almaas, 2002). Described as the open and open-ended investigation into one's experience in the present moment, inquiry leads to greater awareness of present experience, a fuller understanding of that experience, and freedom for the unfolding, expansion, and evolution of consciousness. The practice of inquiry contains many subtleties and undergoes its own process of development as the student's soul matures. Initially, inquiry is taught and practiced as a specific method for exploring present experience with a teacher, with a fellow practitioner, or alone. With sufficient experience and understanding of the practice, inquiry becomes spontaneous, a way of being in the world. Although one still practices it as a specific method, it becomes recognizable as on ongoing process of exploring all experience in a deeper, freer, and more open way. Ultimately, the Diamond Approach sees inquiry and the understanding it leads to as a coemergence of individual experience and the dynamic unfolding of being.

At the beginning of the path, a student practicing inquiry is primarily exploring the surface layers of his or her experience: the thoughts, feelings, or sensations that arise in response to a particular question or topic. Insofar as one is identified with the ego-self, one's range of experience will be limited to those experiences that can be incorporated into its more-or-less predefined set of self-images. Inquiry systematically challenges this range. This practice calls for self-compassion, curiosity, resilience, steadfastness, sincerity, a love of truth for its own sake, and other qualities. At the same time, it reveals the limitations and impediments to these qualities, exposing the unconscious dynamics and imprints underlying and reinforcing them. This exposure allows understanding of these limitations and leads to the recovery and deeper integration of essential qualities. In this way, inquiry is a self-reinforcing practice.

With maturation, the practice of inquiry will naturally open up the student's consciousness to deeper states of being, more expanded capacities for experience, and more spiritually mature traits of consciousness. Two primary conditions allow inquiry to unfold in an optimal way. The first is the capacity for some degree of essential presence, and the second is a sincere interest in, and love for, the truth for its own sake. In addition, each essential aspect contributes unique capacities and support for inquiry, including, for example, the Will aspect (with its characteristics of resilience and steadfastness), the Compassion aspect (with an open-hearted tolerance toward all experience, including pain), the Curiosity aspect (bringing an interest and even joy in the process of inquiry), and the Strength aspect (with a robust, courageous, and impassioned engagement with one's immediate experience). The practice of inquiry calls on these qualities of Being while, at the same time, developing the student's capacity to recognize these qualities as part of their own being. Almaas' book, *Space-cruiser Inquiry* (2002), describes the stages of inquiry and the importance of these and other essential aspects for inquiry.

The Practice of Inquiry

Inquiry is always focused on present experience. The attitude of inquiry is open to whatever might arise in experience, regardless of whether or not it is familiar, comfortable, or expected and however an experience might arise somatically, emotionally, and cognitively. This openness reveals the inclusive stance of inquiry. It is open-ended in the sense that it has no particular goal. While inquiry may lead to experiences of unconditional love, will, clarity, or joy (as well as many other essential qualities), none of these are given primacy. Rather, inquiry continually leads to greater presence, aliveness, understanding, freedom, and other open-ended qualities of experience.

Any experience can be the starting point for inquiry, although in the context of a Diamond Approach group teaching, a specific focus for an inquiry is typically given. These focused inquiries are intended to support students' personal exploration of the teachings. Whether it begins with a specific topic or not, inquiry tends to proceed in an integrative way which includes perceptions, memories, insights, emotions, body sensations, intuition, and awareness of subtle energies. When memories arise, they are explored in one's present experience; for example, through the sensations or emotions that the memories trigger. Associations to past experiences can deepen understanding of patterns. As inquiry proceeds from one experience to another, awareness tends to open to deeper levels of experience and, eventually, direct and immediate experiences of true nature.

Among the barriers to realization inquiry exposes are psychodynamic imprints of early history, structural limitations such as identification with oneself as an ego-self or with primitive instinctual drives, or with so-called phenomenological issues rooted in misunderstandings of the perception and experience of true nature. As these issues are worked through and understood, the energy bound up in them is made available to consciousness, leading to a shift in experience. This shift may feel like an insight, a release of energy, a strong (or subtle) emotional state, or a spaciousness in one's awareness. However, these kinds of shifts are not its aim, and they are not final. Instead, they open one to a deeper experience of true nature or to a deeper issue or obstacle. Although inquiry follows a thread of experience, it is rarely linear and often surprising in what it reveals.

Developmental and Supportive Practices

The Diamond Approach also uses certain practices to develop specific capacities and to help illuminate distortions, obscurations, and opacities in one's consciousness. Since *presence* is the central doorway this path uses to access all aspects and dimensions of reality, there are two specific practices particularly emphasized to develop the capacity to sense presence directly: Sensing, Looking, and Listening (a body-sensing practice that is practiced continuously at every stage of the journey), and the *Kath* meditation (a concentration practice which serves many functions but whose central purpose at the beginning of the path is to develop grounded presence). Other methods are used strategically at various points of the teaching to invite specific essential aspects or dimensions of reality into one's awareness. These include various chants, visualizations, and concentration and awareness practices. These methods have the additional function of preparing one's consciousness to more fully engage the practice of inquiry. Body-centered practices are also important to the Diamond Approach as support for inquiry and unfoldment of experience. The use of somatic practices within the logos of the Diamond Approach is reflected in the name given to these practices, *Diasomatic Inquiry*, or, "inquiry through the body."

Formats

There are two main formats used by the Ridhwan School to disseminate the teachings of the Diamond Approach. It is taught primarily through personal contact in a private session with a teacher trained and ordained in the Diamond Approach. (Because the Ridhwan School is recognized in the USA as a church, teachers are considered ministers and, following a lengthy training and assessment process, are ordained to teach the Diamond Approach.) Focused on the student's immediate experience, these private sessions reflect the open and open-ended nature of inquiry most directly. Sessions may be, at various times and in attunement with the student's needs, supportive, confrontational, focused on the teacher-student relationship, or quietly contemplative. Diasomatic Inquiry is usually a central part of private sessions as well.

Generally, students are also part of an ongoing group within the Ridhwan School, and these groups include both large group teaching meetings and smaller open-ended groups facilitated by a Diamond Approach teacher. Teaching meetings are often scheduled over a 3-day period or in a week-long retreat format and may be residential or not. At a typical three-hour large group teaching meeting, the group will meditate together, the teacher will present a talk on the material, and students will engage in a focused inquiry exercise with others (usually in dyads or triads) to explore the topic first-hand.

Although these formats have served as the central organizing structures of this path, they continue to evolve along with the teaching itself. It should also be emphasized that students continue their practice of inquiry, meditation, and, from time to time, other specific practices, in their daily lives. At the heart of the Diamond Approach is the recognition that one's ordinary, day-to-day life is the optimal context to practice and live fully one's realization.

Central Concepts

Before presenting some of the most important concepts in the Diamond Approach, it is necessary to reiterate the challenge of presenting the subtlety, depth, and richness of these concepts in a few words. It usually takes many days of teaching to introduce them to students and many years to integrate them into one's life and spiritual work. Also reiterated is the sense of the Diamond Approach as an organic and dynamic revelation. These concepts are central in the Diamond Approach at the present time, and as a living tradition, they are subject to revision and expansion. Perhaps most importantly, all are encouraged to test them in their own experience.

Essence and Presence

Almaas' first published writing dealt with *presence* and *essence*, their various manifestations, and the ways they become obscured from consciousness, and these concepts continue to be of central importance in the Diamond Approach (Almaas, 1984/1998). Generally, Almaas has used the terms *essence* and *true nature* interchangeably, but sometimes he has used essence to refer to the manifestation of true nature within the individual, and true nature to refer to the ontological nature of all experience and the fundamental ground of being. True nature is pure, unconditioned, unconditional, timeless, and boundless. However, it differentiates into specific qualities and dimensions much as white light differentiates into the full spectrum of colors. *Presence* refers to the central experiential property of essence, the self-aware inner nature of experience, and the ground of being. Generally thinned or nonexistent in ordinary experience, presence is often experienced initially as fullness and richness of experience, a present-centered immediacy, and a unified medium of consciousness. It is also often experienced as spacious or flowing.

Among the differentiated qualities of essence are Strength, Compassion, Will, Joy, Power, Intelligence, Curiosity, Personhood, Identity, and many others. The Diamond Approach offers a detailed understanding with precise experiential qualities and functions for each of them. For example, the Strength essence is the foundation for experiences of vitality, dynamism, energy, initiative, separation, and autonomy as well as strength. Initially, it may appear to inner awareness as a red color. As this aspect of essence arises in a more open and developed consciousness, it is also the foundation for discriminating awareness and living according to true nature rather than the fixations, reifications, and contractions of the ego-self. Each essential aspect has similarly unique and multi-layered experiential qualities and functions, as well as emotional, cognitive, and somatic issues associated with it. The methods of the Diamond Approach help students recognize and work through the unconscious conflicts and issues that obscure the natural manifestation of the essential aspects and facilitate maturation so that essence can be experienced and expressed more completely and freely.

Soul

The Diamond Approach understands the *soul* to be the living organ of consciousness; a field of presence, awareness, perception, knowing, and functioning. This use of the term *soul* is based on its use in ancient Western thought as the self rather than its use in many contemporary psychological systems. Roughly equivalent to individual consciousness, the soul is the medium through which all individual experience takes place and the vital energy of sentient beings. Thus, the soul is an organ (or organism) of consciousness and the expression of being. The soul's intrinsic properties include sensitivity, impressionability, dynamism, and potentiality. When the soul is influenced by essence, she embodies and expresses the qualities of true nature—spaciousness,

freedom, and full aliveness, for example.[1] Furthermore, as a living organ of consciousness, the soul develops and matures. Her potential is to develop in accordance with
reality manifesting through essential aspects, but because of her impressionability and
potentiality, the soul can also be shaped by the structures of ego and the imprints of
conditioning. Thus, the soul expresses her intrinsic properties in various degrees of distortion or transparency in every human experience and at every stage of development,
whether one is living as the ego-self, essential presence, or transcendent nonduality.

Initially, the soul is patterned in distinct ways by early experiences, its manifestation
as a physical body, and its interactions with complex social and cultural environments.
In the perspective of the Diamond Approach, these experiences allow the soul to
develop the capacities necessary to become more explicitly aware of the faceted nature
of consciousness itself and to realize and embody more of the full range of essential
aspects and dimensions of being. Experiencing oneself as a bounded and contracted
ego-self, while limited, is still an experience that is arising in the field of the soul.
If the soul identifies herself as an ego-self, then the properties of the soul will not
have the freedom to express themselves fully. The soul's sensitivity becomes dulled,
impressionability becomes brittle, dynamism is deadened, and potential is unrealized.
As unconscious material is understood and digested through the practice of inquiry,
one becomes more transparent to his or her essential nature. Furthermore, as needs
for reflection, support, and nourishment on many levels are met, the soul evolves and
matures, becoming increasingly self-aware and self-reflective, more integrated, more
transparent to essence, more fully functional, and more free.

The Development of the Soul and the Theory of Holes

One of the most important contributions of the Diamond Approach is its comprehensive and systematic understanding of how early childhood experiences cause individuals
to lose touch with the essential qualities inherent to the human soul and the implications of these losses for optimal mental health and full realization. These childhood
experiences have a direct impact on spiritual development in adult life. No parent or
early environment can fully recognize the essential qualities innately present in infants
and children or provide the conditions for the child's soul to fully develop according to essence. When these various forms of essence are not supported—or actively
discouraged—the child loses access to essence and a compensating ego structure takes
it place. This view does not blame parents and caregivers; it simply recognizes the
resulting developmental arrests and "forgetting" that affect virtually everyone.

This loss of direct access to essence leaves a gap in consciousness, a dissociation
referred to as a *hole*, and this hole remains largely unconscious because it is covered
up by a compensating ego structure. The core of the ego structure is a *self-image*, a
set of thoughts, feelings, embodied energy patterns, and relational tendencies with
which the individual identifies. For example, a mother may discourage her infant's
natural attempts to separate. The infant perceives that his or her intensely strong
energy is upsetting to the mother and restrains himself/herself, leaving an experience
of weakness, frustration, and deficiency. In adult life, this can manifest as a feeling
of deficient emptiness, incapacity, and lack of deep fulfillment in many life situations

as the individual is unconsciously identified with the self-image of being small and weak. The adult compensates for this weakness, imitating or approximating the "lost" quality of essential strength and vitality with aggression, for example.

There are many such ways that direct contact with essence is lost or abandoned in early development and many attempts in the adult ego-personality to cope with this loss. However, all involve avoidance of the hole resulting from the loss of contact with essence. Therefore, the methods of the Diamond Approach encourage students to inquire into the self-image in order to experience the corresponding loss of essence that is always at the root of a hole. When the self-image and the hole are explicitly experienced from the perspective of present reality, the self-image and the experience of a hole dissolve. In this process, what felt like a deficient emptiness (the hole) is revealed as a contracted form of spacious consciousness, and the specific form of essence obscured by the ego structure is free to manifest. To continue our example of the Theory of Holes, exploring one's aggressive reactivity and reactive anger leads to an underlying feeling of frustration, weakness, and deficient emptiness, which if explored with sufficient sincerity and openness, reveals an experience of space and release. Rather than stopping the process of inquiry here, the Diamond Approach encourages students to continue exploring. Typically, an experience of genuine, unconditional strength and robust vitality arises in this space. Each aspect of essence has particular issues associated with it and a particular experience of the hole that is felt when that aspect of essence is lost to consciousness.

Personal Essence, the Pearl Beyond Price

The Diamond Approach is oriented to living and expressing one's realization in daily life. Students and teachers are expected to engage in all the activities of contemporary culture, including relationships, family, work, service, and community life. The various issues, difficulties, and accomplishments that naturally arise from these activities become material for the practice of inquiry and the soul's maturation. The Diamond Approach views the common issues of engaging with the world, such as responsibility, autonomy, intimacy, power, sexuality, and physicality, not as problems to be transcended but as doorways to further realization and development of the potentials of consciousness.

The Diamond Approach helps individuals systematically recognize, disidentify from, and metabolize a broad range of ego structures formed during childhood. At the same time, students discover that any of the ego structures, self-images, and conditioned expressions of the ego-self (anger, fear, contraction, for example) can lead to essence. This combination of disidentification and discovery is central in the processes of the Diamond Approach. Through these processes, an inner autonomy of being can be developed. True autonomy here means freedom from the restrictive influences of unconscious self-images, reactivity, and relational patterns. It is based on unconditional value for one's being and integrity in one's actions. Qualities of essence are integrated into one's personal being, and the qualities of essence enable harmonious and effective functioning. The soul naturally embodies and expresses respect, contactfulness, and personalness. Within the Diamond Approach, this result of embodying a mature, personal, integrated, functional, and consistent expression of essence in the world is referred to as the *Personal Essence* or the *Pearl Beyond Price* and is described in Almaas' (1988/2000g) book by the same name.

This essential aspect is often experienced as a soft, round, and full presence that feels luminescent and authentic. In contrast to other essential aspects that are whole and complete in themselves, the Pearl is the one quality of essence that develops. This means that the depth and breadth of the Pearl can expand throughout the spiritual journey by integrating more qualities and dimensions of essence in more areas of life. This allows the soul to experience multiple aspects of essence simultaneously. Through this development, the soul feels increasingly personal, dignified, and heartful. Furthermore, this personalness is not based on self-images or imprints of the past. As the soul opens to her boundless nature, the Personal Essence integrates more and more dimensions of being, bringing these riches into the world through personal and human expression. In this way, the Personal Essence resolves one of the great paradoxes of spiritual work: how to be personal and boundless at the same time.

Self-Realization and the Point of Existence

The Diamond Approach recognizes that self-recognition is an inherent potential of human consciousness. The soul can become directly aware of her inner nature in ways that are different from the conventional sense of identity constructed by the ego. This self-knowing can be direct, immediate, free from the influences of the past, and independent of the reflections of others. The formation of the ego-identity has been the central focus of self-psychologists, most notably Kohut (1971) and Kernberg (1975), and the Diamond Approach has drawn on this body of knowledge to explore the possibilities of self-recognition beyond the ego-identity. In *The Point of Existence: Transformations of Narcissism in Self-Realization*, Almaas (1996/2000h) described the process by which individuals realize *essential identity* or the *Point* and the phenomenology of this essential aspect.

The Point is experienced directly as the presence of the true inner nature of the self. As the ego-identity develops, one loses touch with the essential identity and one's sense of value, uniqueness, and significance come to be derived from self-images that require mirroring from others. Realization of the Point requires that one venture into an empty void, where the shell of the ego-identity no longer functions to cover up the insecurity and meaninglessness that lies at the core of the ego, the hole of identity. This is understandably a challenging part of the Work and requires confronting painful wounds as the narcissistic supports for identity fall away revealing the ego's inherent deficient emptiness. From this deep sense of deficiency and emptiness, first space and then the Point arise, infusing consciousness with an inherent sense of value and meaning. Almaas has called this aspect the Point since it often is experienced as a timeless, dimensionless point of light. The need for external confirmation of one's identity fades away, as well as the corresponding need for inner confirmation through self-representations. As the Point, one knows oneself to be essence, and as this realization of essential identity deepens, the sense of self-recognition can expand far beyond the familiar boundaries of the physical body and self-images based on the past into the deeper dimensions of being.

Diamond Vehicles

As one's realization deepens and as one identifies more with essence than the ego-self, deeper and more subtle types of wisdom are needed on the spiritual path. The Diamond Approach details how organized patterns of knowledge, known as *Diamond Vehicles,* can arise in the soul. Diamond Vehicles are often experienced as messengers or teachers, supporting the soul's development at particular junctures of the spiritual path. They disclose precise knowledge of the relationship of essence to the soul and what is needed for further realization. This knowledge presents itself in the form of a structure composed of all essential aspects, each related to specific concerns on the spiritual path. They gather essential aspects to support the soul's unfolding, providing an understanding of how each specific quality of essence contributes to the soul's development, while also revealing the obstacles to further realization.

The essential qualities are often experienced in these structures as illuminated gems of wisdom with a sense of aesthetic rapture, and each Diamond Vehicle has a specific shape and function. The diamond-like nature of these vehicles reflects a clarity and objectivity as the knowledge of these vehicles addresses fundamental issues common to all human beings, especially those on a spiritual path. Various Diamond Vehicles show how each essential aspect contributes to understanding, pleasure, love, knowledge, humanness, and the support for one's identity as true nature. Although these and other such wisdom vehicles have been identified and are part of the advanced teachings of the Diamond Approach, Almaas has indicated that that there are perhaps many other vehicles.

Boundless Dimensions

Being has both personal and boundless dimensions. The latter refers to the ways the soul experiences the infinite nature of reality beyond the structures (both egoic and essential) of a separate self-entity. Phenomenologically, the boundless dimensions are accessed by inquiring into the inner nature of all experience. Any experience is a differentiation of being into a rich, wondrous, and ultimately loving manifestation of reality. Further inquiry reveals the inner nature of this rich beauty as a pure presence without differentiation, and as this presence, reality comes to know itself by being itself. Inquiry into the pure presence of an experience reveals its inner nature to be pure awareness, free of all concepts. Co-emergent with these boundless dimensions is the constant upwelling, flow, and completely fresh expression of being in each moment. The source of all phenomena is an absolute emptiness and mystery beyond being and non-being. Almaas has named these co-emergent boundless dimensions, respectively, Divine Love, the Supreme, the Nonconceptual (or the Nameless), the Logos, and the Absolute.

The Absolute is the most fundamental and subtle dimension, and each subsequent dimension is considered increasingly differentiated and knowable, although all are fundamentally inseparable, much like the physical dimensions of height, width, and length. These dimensions form the ontological ground of all experience and phenomena. The Absolute provides the basis of spaciousness, openness, and unlimited potential in all inner and outer experience. The Logos is the source of unfolding and transformation. Pure awareness enables the capacity for perception. Pure presence gives rise to the capacity for discrimination and knowing. Divine Love is the source of differentiated essential qualities and eventually, affect. When the Personal Essence arises in the boundless dimensions, they are experienced in a personal, though non-egoic, way, and they are expressed in authentic functioning. When the Point arises on the boundless dimensions, one knows oneself as each dimension in a nondual way.

While articulating these dimensions of true nature, the Diamond Approach also describes the specific issues and obstacles involved in their realization and integration, increasing the potential for direct experience and realization of these subtle dimensions. As human beings, we lose touch with our boundless nature through misunderstandings about the nature of reality. These misunderstandings arise from several sources, including an instinctual orientation to the external, that is, the surface of phenomena without recognition of their inner nature, and a variety of psychodynamic issues related to the development of a sense of separate identity. Through direct exploration, we can come to recognize these boundless dimensions and work through the veils and obstacles to each. Thus, spiritual teachings that are profoundly deep and subtle become more accessible to a wider body of students.

Journeys of Ascent and Descent

The Diamond Approach is generally taught to students in a systematic fashion. The teachings of the more accessible essential aspects are followed by the teachings of the Pearl and the Point. This is generally followed by exploration of the Diamond Vehicles and the Boundless Dimensions. According to Almaas, this order reflects the unfolding of the Diamond Approach in his own experience. The teachings are also organized in this manner because accumulated experience has shown that the understanding of the more subtle teachings requires considerable learning, maturation, and integration of many diverse spiritual qualities and capacities. In the logos of the Diamond Approach, this arrangement of the teachings and the soul's realization is considered the *Journey of Ascent*. The more advanced teachings of the Diamond Approach also reflect the unfolding and expression of the Absolute as it becomes manifest in the world. These teachings of the *Journey of Descent* emphasize the integration of the various qualities of essence (especially the Diamond Vehicles) into one's daily life in the world (Almaas, 2004). This includes the understanding of freedom from within the transcendent and manifest perspectives of the five boundless dimensions.

View of Totality

Almaas has continuously acknowledged that no path can provide a full and final description of reality, and indeed, this view is expressed in the Diamond Approach's continuing evolution as a spiritual system. Ultimately, true nature is beyond any concepts and descriptions and beyond any system or teaching. In the broadest sense, the Diamond Approach does not take any of its descriptions of the spiritual path to be final. For example, from the perspective of the boundless dimensions, the nature of reality is clearly nondual. At the same time, human consciousness generally arises through dualistic structures. To be a "true individual," means knowing oneself as both boundless presence and a unique expression of that presence. The Diamond Approach recognizes that all experiences, perspectives, and dimensions are co-emergent and always existing, at least in potential. It does not privilege one above another. The perspective of a child is not less valid than that of a realized adult; in some ways, a child's consciousness is more open and fluid and in other ways less developed and capable. The most contracted and painful experiences express reality as do the most sublime; both are forms that reality can take. Similarly, absolute transcendent emptiness is not more fundamentally real or valuable than the manifest beauty of the world or the normal experience of taking a shower. Reality includes all the potentials of existence and nonexistence, an ineluctable mystery that can never be encompassed by any individual consciousness or spiritual path. Because it is so radically open, this view includes all other views, including views of individual realization, enlightenment, mystical union, and liberation. Almaas has called this all-inclusive perspective the *View of Totality,* and its implications for both daily life and the spiritual journey are limitless. The view of totality opens up the understanding of unconditional freedom independent from any spiritual or material condition.

Assessment

Contributions

Since the Diamond Approach is continuing to develop, often in ways that are new and surprising, both to its founders and its students, it is difficult to assess its contributions and challenges. Probably its most important contribution is simply that it provides a precisely articulated view along with a core practice, inquiry, which can be engaged by many students at varying levels of personal and spiritual development. Thus, it makes spiritual work more widely available. Within this broad contribution, several specific contributions can be identified.

Nonduality of psychological and spiritual work. The Diamond Approach has several particular contributions for those pursuing spiritual realization and maturity and for transpersonal psychologists. It is based on the seamlessness of psychological and spiritual work. Rather than seeing these domains as sequential or parallel, the Diamond Approach works with them as aspects of one whole. This perspective has several implications. It makes it easier to recognize the influence of essence on development, even in early life, and the influence of psychodynamics, even in the higher stages of transpersonal development. For example, the Strength essence mentioned in previous examples functions initially for the infant's survival. One may recognize this in the infant's loud and robust attempts to get fed or comforted and, somewhat later, as the infant comes to know herself or himself as an independent and autonomous person. This aspect of essence functions in a similar way throughout the lifespan, for example supporting life transitions and healthy relationships. In transpersonal stages of development, the Strength essence expresses itself in dynamic and courageous inquiry and other spiritual practices and in the discernment and discriminating wisdom characteristic of spiritual maturity (Walsh, 2000). On the other hand, early imprints regarding strength, boldness, courage, and anger (as well as other essential aspects) limit the soul's maturity even in very refined stages of spiritual realization. Although it is sometimes useful to discriminate psychological and spiritual elements of human development, in the view of the Diamond Approach, each reflects and supports the soul's needs at particular developmental stages; this development is one unified process.

The unity of the psychological and the spiritual is also evident in the Diamond Approach's understanding of the inner critic or superego (Brown, 1999). Some transpersonal and spiritual approaches have also recognized a *spiritual superego* inasmuch as evaluative and judgmental comparisons inhibit spiritual development and further reinforce the narcissistic tendencies of the ego-self. Both Washburn (1994) and Wilber (1997) have noted that the *repressive barrier* formed by self-judgment is a major obstacle to the transpersonal stages of human development.

While the superego and other mechanisms of self-judgment are well known in psychology, the emphasis in the Diamond Approach is freeing consciousness from its limitations and not simply removing a source of suffering. Early in the work with the Diamond Approach, students are taught to recognize and defend against the cognitive, emotional, and somatic inhibitions of the superego. This allows the open and immediate exploration of present experience necessary for spiritual development. Furthermore, the Diamond Approach brings its understanding of essence into the work with the superego. Brown (1999) has shown how various essential aspects such as Compassion, Strength, and Value are necessary for a more complete resolution of these obstacles. Although the superego and its impacts have been described by many psychological theorists and some spiritual teachers, it has been seen simply as a barrier. However, the Diamond Approach's orientation is that all phenomena are expressions of True Nature, regardless of how they may arise in our experience. From this orientation, the superego can be seen as a distortion or approximation of essential qualities of guidance, support, and protection. This view casts the superego, and indeed all egoic structures, in a profoundly different light. Rather than a structure to be rejected (further fueling the tendencies toward self-judgment), the superego reflects a distortion of essence. Through a combination of defending oneself and understanding the roots of the superego, the soul can reclaim more of its inherent depth.

These well-established methods for reducing the repressive influences of the superego are one example of the broader metapsychological insights of the Diamond Approach. One of the primary strengths of the Diamond Approach is the ways it draws on extensive knowledge of how the ego develops and functions. The ego and its age-appropriate structures are seen as necessary developmental achievements, providing capacities for effective functioning and spiritual discovery. It adds to this knowledge an understanding of how the ego also inhibits the soul's further development and how to help students systematically metabolize and release the ego in order to further purify and develop the soul. Taken together, these views and practices offer a major contribution to the practical methodology of transpersonal practice and exemplify the nonduality of the psychological and the spiritual.

Personalness and the personal essence. Many spiritual wisdom traditions hold the view (some explicitly, others implicitly) that the realized condition is at odds with living a rich personal life in the conventional world. The realm of personal experience is seen by many traditions as a limited expression of the ego-self that needs to be transcended in order to realize the ultimate impersonal truth. The Diamond Approach's understanding of the Personal Essence or the Pearl Beyond Price, and its emphasis on the realization and development of this essential aspect, clarifies the relationship between the human experience of personalness, authentic contact, and functioning in the world with the boundless experiences of nonduality. In order to be a complete human being, the personal must be experienced as nondual and the nondual must be experienced as personal (Almaas, 1988/2000g). The emphasis on the development of the Pearl is thus an important contribution of the Diamond Approach for practitioners of any tradition, since this approach to spiritual development offers an embodied perspective that is more aligned with the contemporary lifestyles of the Western world.

Boundless dimensions. As described above, Almaas has identified five fundamental dimensions of reality. Each of these has been described in other spiritual wisdom traditions, and often one or another is posited as the ultimate nature of reality. However, the Diamond Approach provides an inclusive view that recognizes each dimension without privileging one over another. These five dimensions are co-emergent and, in the view of the Diamond Approach, must be included in a full account of reality.

View of totality. From the perspective of the View of Totality as articulated in the Diamond Approach, there is no particular end state that is more real or ultimate than any other. While this view is consistent with some of the deepest teachings of various spiritual traditions, it contrasts with many popular views of spiritual development. The View of Totality has arisen within this context and can be seen as both a response to, and a further contribution towards, the evolutionary needs of spirituality. It posits a view that includes the insights and realizations of all traditions and paths from every walk of life; in fact, it is fundamentally an openness to all possible experiences, both known and unknown. This view provides an orientation to the spiritual journey that is more aligned with the contemporary reality in that it does not require faith in, allegiance to, or cultivation of any particular condition of realization. Moreover, since the View of Totality is nonhierarchical, it also recognizes the experience of the ego-self, for example, to be just as valuable an expression of reality as is the revelation of a sublime nondual realm. This perspective provides an all-inclusive orientation to the full range of experience—both dual and nondual—that many traditional systems do not embrace. In order to distinguish this View of Totality from a naïve relativism, in his more recent teachings, Almaas has emphasized that the View of Totality can only be realized after one has begun to integrate both the personal and the transcendent dimensions of essence.[2]

Challenges

Almaas' writings have contributed to the dialogue of transpersonal psychology (e.g., Cortright, 1997). Wilber has commented on the Diamond Approach, offering both sincere appreciation and pointed critiques (Wilber, 1997). Much of this debate has centered on the nature of spiritual experiences during childhood. Almaas has responded extensively to Wilber's critiques on this matter from theoretical and experiential perspectives (Almaas, 2004). According to Almaas, this dialogue has helped to clarify the specific understanding of the Diamond Approach and its relation to other transpersonal psychologies. It has also revealed how difficult it is to compare one system to another. In general, these discussions have helped the entire field recognize the need for an increasingly precise understanding of the dynamics of transpersonal development. This precision helps to highlight distinct differences as well as to underscore the many fundamental commonalities that exist among the various paradigms of transpersonal psychology.

One of the main criticisms of the Diamond Approach is that it is syncretistic and does not really possess a unique logos and understanding. Almaas has continually emphasized that the Diamond Approach is its own teaching with a precise logic, organization, and capacity to develop the human soul and that it has arisen from his direct experience (as well as the experiences of his collaborators and students). As a modern teaching, it exists in parallel with many other psychological and spiritual methodologies. Almaas has deliberately chosen to use concepts and terms from various academic, psychological, and spiritual traditions in his teachings because he feels these terms provide the most accurate conceptual and linguistic means of conveying the Diamond Approach's teachings. His use of specific terms and concepts from other systems opens his teachings to charges of appropriation. However, he has expressed that he is using these concepts to articulate the experiential wisdom of the Diamond Approach within its own logos and that his use of certain terms is not intended to fully match the way they are used in their original context.

In his published works as well as his trainings, Almaas has also compared and contrasted the Diamond Approach with concepts and paradigms from other spiritual traditions as he understands them. While such comparisons serve particular functions for teaching students on a path, they also naturally lend themselves to criticism, especially in scholarly circles. He may not be simply appropriating but misappropriating. In this regard as well, Almaas has expressed that his intention is not to interpret other traditions *per se,* but rather to use those concepts and practices as a means of more clearly elucidating the teachings of the Diamond Approach. This carries with it certain theoretical and practical problems that are not easily resolved by any modern transpersonal or spiritual system. Such use of concepts and practices from other traditions remains a question for the Diamond Approach.

Although still under the direction of Almaas, the Ridhwan School, the organization with responsibility for offering the Diamond Approach teachings, training teachers, and overseeing the activities of DA teachers and students, is growing and transitioning. Almaas is still active in teaching and writing but moving toward a less direct role in the organization itself. At the same time, the organization continues to grow at an increasing rate. As with many such organizations, it remains to be seen how the organization will respond to the next generation of leaders and teachers and how this will affect the Diamond Approach teachings. In conclusion, it appears that the Diamond Approach has reached a broad level of acceptance and influence and will continue to inform the field of transpersonal psychology as well as the development of humanity in general.

Notes

1. Almaas typically uses the feminine when referring to the soul. A thorough discussion of this choice can be found in his book *Inner Journey Home* (2004).
2. As of this writing, Almaas is preparing a manuscript on the View of Totality that will deal extensively with this material.

References

Almaas, A. H. (1998). *Essence: The Diamond Approach to inner realization/The elixir of enlightenment.* York Beach, ME: Samuel Weiser. (Original work published 1984)

Almaas, A. H. (2000a). *Diamond Heart book one: Elements of the real in man.* Boston, MA: Shambhala. (Original work published 1987)

Almaas, A. H. (2000b). *Diamond Heart book two: Freedom to be.* Boston, MA: Shambhala. (Original work published 1988)

Almaas, A. H. (2000c). *Diamond Heart book three: Being and the meaning of life.* Boston, MA: Shambhala. (Original work published 1990)

Almaas, A. H. (2000d). *Diamond Heart book four: Indestructible innocence.* Boston, MA: Shambhala. (Original work published 1997)

Almaas, A. H. (2000e). *Facets of unity: The enneagram of holy ideas.* Boston, MA: Shambhala. (Original work published 1998)

Almaas, A. H. (2000f). *Luminous night's journey: An autobiographical fragment.* Boston, MA: Shambhala. (Original work published 1995)

Almaas, A. H. (2000g). *The Pearl Beyond Price: The integration of personality into being: An object relations approach.* Boston, MA: Shambhala. (Original work published 1988)

Almaas, A. H. (2000h). *The Point of Existence: Transformations of narcissism in self-realization.* Boston, MA: Shambhala. (Original work published 1996)

Almaas, A. H. (2000i). *The Void: Inner spaciousness and ego structure.* Boston, MA: Shambhala. (Original work published 1986)

Almaas, A. H. (2002). *Spacecruiser inquiry: True guidance for the inner journey.* Boston, MA: Shambhala.

Almaas, A. H. (2004). *The inner journey home: Soul's realization of the unity of reality.* Boston, MA: Shambhala.

Almaas, A. H. (2006). *Brilliancy: The essence of intelligence.* Boston, MA: Shambhala.

Almaas, A. H. (2008). *The unfolding now: Realizing your true nature through the practice of presence.* Boston, MA: Shambhala.

Almaas, A. H. (2011). *Diamond Heart book five: Inexhaustible mystery.* Boston, MA: Shambhala.

Brown, B. (1999). *Soul without shame: A guide to liberating yourself from the judge within.* Boston, MA: Shambhala.

Cortright, B. (1997). *Psychotherapy and spirit: Theory and practice in transpersonal psychotherapy.* Albany, NY: State University of New York Press.

Davis, J. (1999). *The Diamond Approach: An introduction to the teachings of A. H. Almaas.* Boston, MA: Shambhala.

Kernberg, O. (1975). *Borderline conditions and pathological narcissism.* New York, NY: Jason Aronson.

Kohut, H. (1971). *The analysis of the self.* New York, NY: International Universities Press.

Maitri, S. (2001). *The spiritual dimension of the enneagram: Nine faces of the soul.* New York, NY: Tarcher.

Maitri, S. (2005). *The enneagram of passions and virtues: Finding the way home*. New York, NY: Tarcher.

Schwartz, T. (1996). *What really matters: Searching for wisdom in America*. New York, NY: Bantam.

Walsh, R. (2000). *Essential spirituality: The 7 central practices to awaken the heart and mind*. New York, NY: John Wiley & Sons.

Washburn, M. (1994). *Ego and the dynamic ground: A transpersonal theory of human development*. Albany, NY: State University of New York Press.

Wilber, K. (1997). *The eye of spirit: An integral vision for a world gone slightly mad*. Boston, MA: Shambhala.

32

Transpersonal Psychotherapies
Vitor Rodrigues and Harris L. Friedman

One application of transpersonal psychology is to alleviate mental health concerns and promote optimum growth through psychotherapies. Transpersonal psychotherapies share much in common with other psychotherapies, but also have important differences. In terms of common ground with other approaches, they are relational, implying a therapist and one or more individuals together aiming at some therapeutic effect. They also imply a view about human development, human disturbances, and the way both interact. In addition, they employ some specific methods or techniques. Within the therapeutic relationship, an assessment (which may or may not be formal or involve a diagnosis) is made, objectives are established, and a therapeutic process ensues. Transpersonal psychotherapists also undergo professional training, which typically includes experiencing personally the therapeutic process they are learning to later practicing with clients. However, in addition to these widely shared commonalities, there are some salient differences between transpersonal psychotherapies and most, but not all, other psychotherapies.

The Essential Role of Consciousness

Transpersonal psychotherapies tend to focus on the essential role of consciousness, while psychotherapeutic change is sought through changing consciousness states, including identity as reflected in accumulated states of consciousness. Consciousness can be defined as the ability to be aware of internal mental processes (e.g., emotions, images, thoughts, etc.) and external perceptual experiences (e.g., auditory, gustatory, olfactory, tactile, visual, etc.) in terms of relatedness to being a particular person (Presti, 2011). Transpersonal psychotherapies are based on the assumption that consciousness is at the core of what being human means. This defines the human broadly as being a physiological, emotional, intellectual, social and spiritual consciousness system in

The Wiley Blackwell Handbook of Transpersonal Psychology, First Edition.
Edited by Harris L. Friedman and Glenn Hartelius.
© 2013 John Wiley & Sons, Ltd. Published 2015 by John Wiley & Sons, Ltd.

its totality. LeShan (1984) made the point that the most perfect, high-processing, intelligent android would never qualify as human, although a very imperfect, ugly, crippled, ill-tempered, but self-aware being would.

Transpersonal psychotherapists tend to focus their clinical attention on clients' conscious experience of themselves, including cognition, emotion and behavior within their identity structure. In turn, identity can be considered to be the most concrete, observable, manifestation of consciousness, while being also the main experience organizer (Louchakova & Lucas, 2007). Identity has also been conceptualized as the active builder of both comprehension of and action upon reality (McCombs, 1989). In this way, transpersonal psychotherapies are integrative, as they acknowledge the fact that the core identification of each individual can vary to include emotions, the body, cognition, inner perception, and so on. Spirituality is also a core part of identity (Griffith & Griggs, 2001). Consequently, transpersonal psychotherapists tend to welcome, and many times make use of, the contributions from various psychotherapeutic models that specialize in each area of possible identity. One model of how various transpersonal psychotherapies can be integrated conceptually based on identity is provided by Self-Expansiveness Therapy (Friedman, this volume).

Since the beginning of the transpersonal movement, extraordinary experiences, which had previously been seen as outside of the purview of psychology, began to be increasingly viewed as important psychological processes, especially as they began happening to many people through use of psychedelic substances (Friedman, 2006). From their client's reports and from their own personal experiences, it became quite obvious to many psychologists that human beings could experience big changes in the intensity and quality of their consciousness, including its range and the content of experiences, without it being seen as being psychopathological. Exceptional human experiences even became seen as showing human beings at their best (see Cardeña, Lynn, & Krippner, 2000; Cardeña & Winkelman, 2011). As more people started to report very intense and expansive states of consciousness that often produced positive, not just psychopathological, after-effects, transpersonal psychotherapies began to be recognized, drawing from earlier pioneering psychotherapists in Europe, such as Assagioli's (1970) psychosynthesis and Jung's (1952) depth psychology.

A Special Role for Spirituality

Transpersonal psychotherapists also generally assume that what can broadly be called spirituality is an important part of consciousness and identity. Walach (2009) described spirituality as "having as a common definitional core, some experiential, notional, behavioral or intentional relationship with some transcendent reality, out of which arises meaning, solace or motivation for an individual" (p. 2). About five billion of the planet's population has some form of spiritual adherence or practice (Hitchcock & Esposito, 2004), and this should be acknowledged in delivering responsible psychotherapies. Recent research has also shown that spirituality can be very positive to physical and mental health (Comer, 2004; Koenig, McCullough, & Larson, 2001). It is a matter of regret that mainstream psychologists have mostly ignored and/or debunked spirituality for so long (and many still do), even though the vast majority of their clients are religious or have some spiritual practice as important components in their lives. Transpersonal psychotherapists tend to rectify this omission by allowing spiritual experiences and concepts to be explicitly incorporated into psychotherapy, such as helping clients deal with spiritual dilemmas and by integrating spirituality as a potentially helpful force within their lives.

A Framework Explaining the Process of Transpersonal Psychotherapy

Being a relational process, what typically happens during a transpersonal psychotherapy session can described by taking into account both therapists' and clients' perspectives, and the interactive nature of events between them. The following provides a framework explaining how transpersonal psychotherapy can work as a process. However, not all transpersonal psychotherapists necessarily follow this approach.

One fundamental aspect that requires mention is that transpersonal psychotherapy is not defined by just using some techniques that modify consciousness, but requires integration into a process that includes a psychotherapeutic relationship, starting with an evaluation, goal setting, unfolding of sessions for self-exploration and therapeutic gain, as well as ongoing and a final evaluation. All of this occurs within a co-operative process at which the therapist acts mostly as catalyst for the client's self-knowledge and healing. This relationship happens inside a safe environment, perhaps that can even be seen as a healing field, where at least during some of the time both therapist and patient may be in a modified state of consciousness and exchange information and energy at levels that can include lower unconsciousness, normal consciousness, and higher consciousness. This is one reason why we think transpersonal psychotherapists must undergo a demanding training, allowing them to monitor themselves and become available at several levels simultaneously, increasing their capacity to resonate with their clients.

The Psychotherapist's Side

Transpersonal psychotherapists can be experts in the management of consciousness states, including what Roberts (1989) called the ability to do tertiary thinking thinking. They can gain this expertise by engaging in various spiritual traditions or from using modern versions for modifying consciousness states. Transpersonal psychotherapists can operate within ordinary consciousness or in alternate states of consciousness, which might allow them to better resonate with their clients, especially if their clients are also in alternate states of consciousness or are dealing with the sequelae of such alternate states. Access to alternate states can put transpersonal psychotherapists in touch with their best capacities for creativity, wisdom, empathy, and love, and allow them to address their clients' suffering and disturbance with their own radiant health (Wegela, 2003). Rodrigues (2008) has also termed this unconditional love, and has argued that such love is both health protective and health promoting at the mental and physical levels. Transpersonal psychotherapists can act as catalyst for their clients' inner healer

(Grof, 2000), bringing forward their deepest wisdom and capabilities for insight and self-healing, which can be accessed through modified states of consciousness. Transpersonal psychotherapists can help their clients process experiences and insights through verbal dialogue, but transpersonal psychotherapies also often go beyond using just verbal techniques to include use of a full array of classic and contemporary transformative practices to help clients get both deeper and faster insights about themselves. These can be seen as restructuring their identity by dealing both with their personal *self* and their deeper *Self* (Rodrigues, 2010). A range of techniques often used in transpersonal psychotherapies have been called psychotechnologies (e.g., Grof, 2000) and include varying practices, such as meditation, hypnosis, drumming and chanting, trance dance, breathwork, active imagination, guided imagery, deep relaxation, biofeedback, binaural tones, and so on. Transpersonal psychotherapists tend to trust the inner potential and inner wisdom of their clients as coming from their higher Self and from the normal tendency of consciousness to grow, expand, and find healthy expressions.

At the same time, transpersonal psychotherapists need to be able to evaluate by making important distinctions between lower and higher levels of conscious processes happening to them and their clients (Assagioli, 1970), including using frameworks, such as the delineation among pre-personal, personal, and transpersonal states (Wilber, 2000). This can also include a variety of assessment approaches (Friedman & Mac-Donald, 2002; MacDonald & Friedman, 2002), which are especially important in distinguishing between higher states (such as enlightenment) and lower states (such as psychosis; Johnson & Friedman, 2008).

The Client's Side

Clients engaged in transpersonal psychotherapies may or may not get into modified states of consciousness through using various psychotechnologies. When employed, these alternate states of consciousness may help them find inspiration and intuition, as well as increase creativity and clarity of mind. They may also help clients in distancing from painful wounds from the past or, quite the opposite, help clients in exploring these wounds to get better understandings of what they are doing to the clients. This may allow clients to get a faster and deeper understanding of themselves, their symptoms and psychological processes, and ways for making needed changes.

These techniques can be used in a secure space provided by the therapist, which can facilitate the access to deeper levels of the psyche (unconscious, conscious, or possibly even superconscious), including accessing past memories, repressed material, and preverbal processes, as well as possible sources of higher wisdom. Clients can learn ways to focus on emotions and their corresponding body correlates (e.g., tensions, fatigue, etc.) to amplify and decrease them, understand their origin, and change their disturbed patterns, as well as gain many other benefits. One very positive aspect of the techniques inducing consciousness modification is that often they, by themselves, generate very pleasurable emotional experiences, including states of stillness and clarity of mind that allow clients to discover new possibilities for well-being.

Sometimes specific transpersonal concerns will bring clients to transpersonal psychotherapists, who would be more likely to have expertise about spiritual experiences, dilemmas, and crises than would conventional psychotherapists (Geels, 2011), as well as would likely be better in dealing with extraordinary experiences, which could be dismissed by conventional psychotherapists as merely psychopathological. One example of the contemporary recognition of the importance of spiritual crises is the creation of the category of religious and spiritual problems within the *Diagnostic and Statistical Manual of Mental Disorder IV-TR* (American Psychiatric Association, 1994). Transpersonal psychology bridges psychology and spirituality, and its practitioners sometimes work with clients having various questions and problems that arise from spiritual experiences, such as concerns resulting from participation in contemporary and indigenous practices (Rodrigues, 2010). These experiences can affect the client's mental health not only in positive, but sometimes in challenging, ways. For example, these experiences could lead to different forms of spiritual emergencies, including: (1) shamanic crisis, (2) the awakening of kundalini, (3) episodes of unitive consciousness (peak experiences), (4) psychological renewal through return to the center (our deepest and "true" nature), (5) the crisis of psychic opening, (6) past-life experiences, (7) communications with spirit guides and channeling, (8) near-death experiences, (9) experiences of close encounters with UFOs, and (10) possession states. There are a number of transpersonal approaches related to discerning the differences between clinical psychopathology and what can often be better diagnosed as spiritual emergency, an area pioneered by Grof and Grof (1990).

Concerning the objectives to be defined for each session, clients and therapists will have their own agendas, and these may or may not be in concert. However, generally speaking therapists' agenda may follow goals related to more conventional or humanistic approaches to psychotherapy, such as the promotion of human traits and qualities that favor optimal functioning and well-being, including happiness, optimism, hope, resilience, forgiveness, creativity, flow and peak experiences, emotional intelligence, hardiness, self-efficacy, and self-esteem, as well as pursuing less conventional transpersonal goals. In this regard, transpersonal psychotherapies can be closely in line with humanistic and positive psychology goals, while also addressing transpersonal goals not usually the focus in humanistic and positive psychology, such as increasing self-expansiveness (Friedman, this volume) and higher functioning (Wilber, 2000).

The Relationship

The relationship between clients and transpersonal psychotherapists often involves verbal exchanges, such as feedback from clients about their feelings and perceptions during self-exploration. This can include mutual feedback as sessions unfold, and also can acknowledge and manage very well-known relationship phenomena common to all psychotherapies, such as transference, counter-transference and resistance (Descamps, 2006). A key part of transpersonal psychotherapies would be for the therapist and client to both be paying close attention to their inner worlds (with its emotions, symbols, thoughts, sensations) as they interact with each other, as well as to the consciousness of the client and psychotherapist. This will often also involve going further than most psychotherapies toward paying attention to the cultural and social environment, particularly as they might pertain to spirituality and extraordinary experiences. Although different approaches to psychotherapy seem to have relatively similar impact by relying on common relational factors, the strong psychotherapeutic alliance often forged in transpersonal psychotherapies may be due to open acceptance of spiritual and anomalous phenomena, which might otherwise be denigrated (or simply disqualified as being unreal) by conventional psychotherapists. This, in fact, may be key to the effectiveness of treating clients experiencing such phenomena by using transpersonal approaches.

Some transpersonal psychotherapists claim also to have experiences with various subtle energies and might pay attention to possible information transfers between them and their clients, which could be seen as energy transference and countertransference. To some transpersonal psychotherapists, the setting for transpersonal psychotherapies may feel like sacred spaces, where they can meet their clients' deepest recesses, a psychic field experienced "through resonance, [which] can help awaken and open the inner being of the client … and can work toward the opening of the client's psychic center" (Cortright, 2007, pp. 156-157). Indeed some research seems to be showing that the emphasis from transpersonal psychotherapy in the intense preparation of the therapist to deal with subtle (possibly even psychic) phenomena, as well as being aware of energy events and learning to be deeply present with patients may also be of key importance. For instance, McCraty, Atkinson, and Tomasino (2001) mentioned that there is a heart electromagnetic field that extends several feet from the body and could possibly transfer emotional information between therapist and client, while Carpenter (2002) showed that anomalous communication might take place between therapist and clients during sessions.

Another interesting area in the transpersonal psychotherapeutic relationship often concerns experience of time, which may entail the possibility of slowing down or accelerating time at the subjective level shared by client and psychotherapist. This type of phenomena is commonly acknowledged among hypnotherapists, as hypnotic states can frequently bring about time distortions (see Nash & Barnier, 2008).

The Session

Transpersonal psychotherapy sessions may unfold through several possible stages that were identified by Saldanha (1997), as follows: clients *acknowledge* the symptom or trouble; characterize it through some amount of *identification* (e.g., assigning a color, a weight, a shape, a size, to the emotion) and *direct experience* of it; have some *catharsis* (such as expressing the deep buried emotions associated with a past trauma and bodily tension); start making some distance by *de-identifying* from the symptom, using inner wisdom (found through modification of consciousness) to *transmute* the contents or experiences that are troublesome, and finding insights, new meanings, or new postures in life; experience some personal *transformation* accompanied by a feeling of change; last, *elaborate* on the experience and its implications, and find ways to *integrate* it in their current life. During sessions, simple relaxation techniques can help clients reduce stress, as well as open to inner dimensions (e.g., bodily feelings) and lower defensiveness, while meditation techniques may bring increased benefits (Donovan, Murphy, & Taylor, 1997). Other psychotechnologies, such as Holotropic Breathwork (Grof & Grof, 2010), can help clients access deeply modified states of consciousness. In short, many classic and modern spiritual practices can be brought into transpersonal psychotherapy sessions.

Identity and Development

Transpersonal, yet nonpathological states of consciousness can generate deep changes at many levels of the human self-concept, as recent work is showing (e.g., Cardeña & Winkelman, 2011). Ellsworth, Scherer, and Goldsmith (2009) stressed the fact that emotions influence thought and result from the organism's appraisal of its circumstances as favorable or unfavorable, novel or familiar, pleasant or unpleasant, and compatible or incompatible. Actually, emotions seem to be crucial in all human evaluations about both the outside physical-social world and the inner world of sensation, feeling, cognition, and volition. An organism will differently react to any stimulus as it perceives pleasure-pain and threat-security (Everly & Lating, 2002). It follows that emotion is always connected with evaluation, and evaluation is only possible against some standard (e.g., the importance of something for the organism's survival).

In this regard, identity can be seen as constituting the most fundamental standard for what concerns human beings, because humans evaluate almost everything, inside and outside, against their self-concept. For example, the way people perceive and conceive of themselves as a moral, affective, cognitive, biologic, or spiritual beings is fundamental to everything else. So if people believe and feel that they are only their bodies, a knife being held to assault them would be more traumatizing than if they believe and feel that they are immortal souls. Similarly, if someone's core identity seems to be primarily about being a wife, the possibility of divorce would be a lot more painful than if that person's identity instead flows around being compassionate and loving, rather than this social role. The main observable unit that shows the unique way each one of us is consciously integrating body, emotion, and cognition is identity. Transpersonal psychotherapy approaches often assume that changes in states of consciousness are accompanied with momentary (at least) changes in identity, while the stronger the change in consciousness, the deeper the probable change in identity.

Identity can change through dramatic modifications in consciousness that arise naturally. As Maslow (1968) discussed early in the development of transpersonal psychology, peak experiences can change intensely and positively what people think they are. One area where such potential for consciousness change can be quite dramatically found involves near-death experiences (NDEs; Atwater, 2011). Near-death experiencers (NDErs) often change the ways they think about themselves, frequently towards a feeling that they are more than their physical bodies and that they will survive bodily death as conscious and thinking beings. Belschner (2005) discussed how transpersonal psychotherapy may deal with extraordinary experiences, such as NDEs, that seem to go against modern and normative views of reality, as NDErs often describe experiencing nonlinear time and space that transcend the ordinary three dimensions. NDErs and other with extraordinary experiences often describe other anomalous experiences, such as merging with objects, expanding to limitless space, and not necessarily being constrained by a need for stability or some environment dependency. In this regard, transpersonal psychotherapy is especially well-equipped to help clients dealing with issues of life and death (Hennezel & Leloup, 1997, Kubler-Ross, 1995; LeLoup, 2001; Simonton, 2002).

Intentionally modifying states of consciousness as part of transpersonal psychotherapy may provide deeper and faster access to opportunities for changing identity. Many models and techniques for transpersonal psychotherapy can be found to operate this way. As an example, Holotropic Breathwork (Grof & Grof, 2010) is one approach no one can afford to ignore in the transpersonal field. Although the Grofs' model does not represent a full psychotherapeutic approach (with the typical development of a psychotherapeutic relationship over time), it brings in instruments of high quality for promoting dramatic changes in states of consciousness and for deep inner experience. These ideas revolve around the importance of perinatal experiences, which have received some research confirmation (Chamberlain, 1998; Holmes, Morris, Clance, & Putney, 1996).

The Grofs' (2010) work can be seen as related to a group of regression therapy models, such as the ones developed by TenDam (1996), Netherton and Shiffrin (1979), and Woolger (2004). These allow clients to experience past memories (from any moment in their biographical life or possibly in previous ones). These can involve traumatic or pleasant memories, but they all supposedly can bring a better understanding of clients' personal characteristics. Techniques for eliciting these can vary (e.g., hypnosis, breathwork, body touch, exaggeration of body symptoms, visualization, verbalizing core feelings or assumptions, etc.), but they all share the fact that therapists stay in close proximity and interaction with clients during sessions. These allow clients to explore deep feelings, memories, and experiences from the past that seem to be playing some important role in the present. Then the contents and experiences are used to produce some sort of wisdom and reprogramming in the client with the therapist's assistance, all of this while the client is in a modified state of consciousness. The intense and close interaction happening there is a good model for what can be a seen as a typical transpersonal psychotherapy session, including consciousness modification, deep insight during sessions that can become highly emotional and include catharsis, intense interaction, an emphasis on reprogramming, finding new meanings for life, and making new decisions. Many times, regression therapists will try to help clients by making sure they are really getting in touch with their so-called inner healer and not just finding some easy escape from emotional troubles or just confirming their personal ego's structure of fears, desires, and other emotional contents.

One therapeutic effects of such consciousness modification concerns the ability to explore deep memories, which can possibly include past lives (Bowman, 1997; Stevenson, 1997; Woolger, 2004). Whereas conventional psychotherapies might dismiss such possibilities, transpersonal psychotherapies can remain open to these as possibilities. Transpersonal psychotherapies can also help clients investigate and change maladaptive patterns that may be based on perinatal experiences, such as described by Grof (2000) in his system of condensed experiences (COEX). These COEX are composed of dynamic memory constellations, which have similar themes (Blin & Chavas, 2011). In transpersonal psychotherapy, the psychotherapeutic relationship during modified states of consciousness can help clients bring these COEX patterns into present experience and decide if and when they want to change them. Transpersonal psychotherapists are uniquely positioned to provide appropriate techniques to help catalyse such changes, whether dealing with perinatal experiences or those of past lives. However, aside from ego-adjustment and symptom relief, heavy emphasis is placed on the patient's deep healing from their core Self into radiant health (Wegela, 2003), which may include inner expansion, wisdom, creativity, and joy.

One major contribution from Grof (2000), and also other authors dealing with regression therapy, has been the way to bring to clinical practice different views on human development that are typical of transpersonal psychology. Kasprow and Scotton (1999, p. 12) stated that transpersonal views are not only concerned "with the diagnosis and treatment of psychopathology associated with the usual stages of human development from infancy through adulthood, but also with difficulties associated with developmental stages beyond that of the adult ego." For example, Armstrong (2007), described 12 stages of human life (including from prebirth to death, dying, and beyond death), as the "spirit down" part of our journey into a baby's body and a "body up" journey of human development. In his view, during our experience we adapt to the world and its ways as persons and we recall our inner heritage as souls, such that our development takes place under two influences: biology and spirit. We add to this that indeed transpersonal views may also consider diagnosis and treatment of ailments rooted in times before the ego, such as perinatal or even possible past lives.

Wilber's (2000) model, although it is not coming from a clinician, does have a powerful influence on many transpersonal psychotherapies. He ascribes to his integral psychology the task of studying the functions of consciousness (perceiving, desiring, wanting, acting), the structures of consciousness (body, mind, soul, spirit), the states of consciousness (vigilance, sleep, dream, meditation), the modes of consciousness (aesthetic, moral, scientific), and the development of consciousness (from prepersonal to personal to transpersonal, and from subconscious to conscious to superconscious). This theory allows a perspective in which clinicians can place their own and their clients' experiences into various developmental levels: sensory-motor; emotional-phantasmal; the representative mind (the preoperational in Piagetian terms); the role/rule mind (the concrete operational in Piagetian terms); the formal/reflective mind (or formal operational in Piagetian terms); vision logic; psychic; subtle; causal; and finally nondual.

Relevant Research and Future Trends

The evidence for transpersonal psychotherapy is relatively lacking compared to the many more conventional psychotherapies. However, there are case studies (e.g., Clinton, 2006; Deatherage, 1975; Galegos, 1983; Miller, 2005; Segall, 2005; Urbanowski & Miller, 1996), as well as other research studies (e.g., Clinton, 2006; Deatherage, 1975; Grepmair et al., 2007; Holmes et al., 1996; Peres & Nasello, 2007; Peres, Newberg, et al., 2007; Peres, Simão, & Nasello, 2007). Grof's (2000) model, as one example, has received supporting evidence in a number of doctoral dissertations about its theoretical value, therapeutic efficacy, how it can help in self-discovery, reducing fear and increasing self-confidence, love and compassion, and bringing useful life-changes, and even its power to uncover archetypal depths of the human mind (Archambault, 2010; Binns, 1997; Brouillette, 1997; Cervelli, 2009; Hanratty, 2002; Pressman, 1993).

Meditation, one of transpersonal psychotherapy's most powerful tools, is used as an important way to change consciousness states and expand them, and as part of procedures to increase self-awareness in clients and to help them take distance from, and learn to identify and de-identify with, identity structures. For example, Grepmair et al. (2007) showed that mindfulness training can increase the efficiency of therapy, while coincidentally it produces an intense aware presence from therapists. Similarly, research also shows that metacognitive awareness can play a very important role in learning emotion regulation (Wells, 2000). Meditation may also contribute to the development of a trusting relationship between therapist and client. Growing evidence coming from neuroplasticity and also from cognitive-behavioral research is showing the efficacy of meditation for psychological and for psychosomatic disturbances (Begley, 2008; Davidson, 2004; Davidson et al., 2003; Hirai, 1989; Johanson, 2006; Mace, 2007; Segall, 2005; Travis, 2006).

In the future, research on transpersonal psychotherapy could benefit from more standardized studies with randomized comparison groups to be evaluated prior and post sessions, using both conventional and explicitly transpersonal psychometric instruments (MacDonald, Kuentzel & Friedman,1999a, 1999b). Along with these, qualitative studies exposing the phenomenology of therapeutic sessions in detail and possibly connecting them with ongoing phenomena at the psychological, neurobiological, and energetic levels would be useful. Mixed-method studies with the aid of qualitative and quantitative instruments for diagnosis, monitoring, and outcome evaluation would also help in understanding in greater detail processes that might be happening as clients are served, including what results are produced.

The burgeoning research in the general field of consciousness studies and neurobiology offers much promise for future understandings of transpersonal psychotherapies. New measuring devices for both consciousness states and possibly energy states may allow transpersonal psychotherapists to conduct better research. Transpersonal psychotherapy, and transpersonal research in general, is likely to become more driven by advancing technology through the use of biofeedback and related mind-brain machines (e.g., brainwave entrainment machines using sound, design music, flashes of light and so on; Huang & Charyton, 2008), energy scanning devices (see Korotkov, 2002), intense environment-changing devices such as flotation tanks (Kjellgren, Lyden, & Norlander, 2008), and sophisticated real-time measures of both brain and immunological parameters. Probably new consciousness-modifying drugs will be added to already existing ones as possible candidates for helping psychotherapeutic modification of consciousness, as more novel substances are being developed and used (Kolp, Krupitsky, Friedman, & Young, 2009; Mishor, McKenna & Callaway, 2011; Nichols & Chemel, 2011). All of this may also have an impact on society, as it possibly contributes to a deep change in the concept of humans as being more than just bunches of neurons processing information inside structures of bones and cells.

Similarly, transpersonal psychotherapy may even become a leading approach for physiologically increasing therapeutic effects, as knowledge from psychoneuroimmunology and related neuroscience areas is rapidly increasing. It is known that usually a third or so of people in placebo control groups in double-blind studies of pharmaceutical drugs obtain the same result that the drug being studied is meant to provide (Dienstfrey, 2005). This strongly suggests that clients' expectancies can deeply influence the outcome of medical treatments (Simonton, 2002). Also it looks like clients can develop healthy (favorable to fighting illness and increasing the immune response), as well as also illness-promoting (nocebo) beliefs. According to Pert, Dreher, and Ruff (2005), our bodies have a psychosomatic network of neuropeptides (small amino acid chains to be simultaneously found in brain and non-neuronal tissues), which "functions as a living processor of information-a means to transmit meaningful messages across organs, tissues, cells, and DNA" (p. 62). Neuropeptide receptors are everywhere in the body, allowing the same quoted authors to conclude that emotions are a "bridge between mind and body" (p. 63). So there is a basis to assert that conscious and unconscious emotions are influencing health, as immune cells are producing and receiving the same neuropeptides that are known to mediate emotional functioning and emotional information. These frontier areas can involve transpersonal psychotherapies. For example, Lancaster (2004) pointed out that dialogue between spiritual traditions and neurosciences can be very fruitful for the development of consciousness science, especially in the need to characterize consciousness states in their many varieties and subtleties.

Available knowledge about love and its effects on both mental and physical health, both at the individual and societal level, is also becoming more sophisticated (Rodrigues, 2008). This may change basic institutions, such as politics and education, as decision-makers and teachers may start noticing that love, if cultivated, promoted, and taught, can diminish crime (a societal disease), as well as mental and physical disease. Also, the view of humans characterized as transpersonal beings may change the main concepts about the goals of politics and education, shifting toward greater awareness, cultivating free will, expanding consciousness, and developing cultural co-operation. Last, values change, a normal by-product of the expansion of consciousness obtained in transpersonal psychotherapy (Maslow, 1968), and quite familiar to authors such as Roberts (1989) and Kasprow and Scotton (1999), may add to the concert. Specifically, changes in identity and values towards greater love and mental clarity may allow humanity to stop the limitless exploitation of resources (and competition for individual and corporate wealth) at all costs, which is depleting the planet and bringing environmental disasters closer and closer. In their place, we may find greater cooperation, solidarity, sharing, and recycling of goods, knowledge, all facilitated by transpersonal healing, such as through transpersonal psychotherapy broadly applied beyond just clinical work with individuals and families toward larger application to social systems. And in the clinical areas, transpersonal experiences may no longer be seen as synonymous with psychopathology, but rather a good starting point for individual growth and societal change.

References

American Psychiatric Association (1994). *Diagnostic and statistical manual of mental disorders IV-TR*. Washington, DC: Author.
Archambault, D. R. (2010). Inner work is the her's journey: Mythic interpretations of holotropic breathwork. *Dissertation Abstracts International, 72*(11) 1142b (UMI #3475554).
Armstrong, T. (2007). *The human odyssey*. New York, NY: Sterling Publishing.
Assagioli, R. (1970). *Psicossíntese*. São Paulo, Brazil: Editora Cultrix Ltda.

Atwater, P.M.H. (2011). *Near-death experiences: The rest of the story.* Charlottesville, VA: Hampton Roads.

Begley, S. (2008). *Train your mind, change your brain.* New York, NY: Ballantine Books.

Belschner, W. (2005). Die normalisierung des außergewöhnlichen. In P. Lengsfeld (Ed.), *Mystik - spiritualität der zukunft. erfahrung des ewigen* (pp. 299-309). Freiburg, Germany: Herder.

Binns, S. (1997). *Grof's basic perinatal matrix theory: Initial empirical validation* (Unpublished doctoral dissertation). Retrieved from http://www.grof-holotropic-breathwork.net/page/doctoral-dissertations

Blin, B., & Chavas, B. (2011). *Manuel de psychothérapie transpersonnelle.* Paris, France: InterEditions.

Bowman, C. (1997). *Children's past lives: How past-life memories affect your child.* New York, NY: Bantam Books.

Brouillette, G. (1997). Reported effects of Holotropic Breathwork®: An integrative technique for healing and personal change. *Dissertation Abstracts International, 67*(02) 0669B (UMI #DP14336).

Cardeña, E., Lynn, S., & Krippner, S. (Ed.). (2000): *Varieties of anomalous experience: Examining the scientific evidence.* Washington, DC: American Psychological Association.

Cardeña, E., & Winkelman, M. (Eds.). (2011). *Altering consciousness. Multidiscipinary perspectives* (Vols. 1 and 2). Santa Barbara, CA: Praeger.

Carpenter, J. (2002). The intrusion of anomalous communication in group and individual psychotherapy: Clinical observations and a research project. In Bial Foundation (Ed.), *Behind and beyond the brain* (pp. 255-274). Porto, Portugal: Bial Foundation.

Cervelli, R. L. (2009). An intuitive inquiry into experiences arising out of the Holotropic Breathwork™ technique and its integral mandala artwork: The potential for self-actualization. *Dissertation Abstracts International, 70*(12) 0669B (UMI #3380360).

Chamberlain, D. (1998). *The mind of your newborn baby.* Berkeley, CA: North Atlantic Books.

Clinton, A. (2006). Seemorg Matrix Work: A new transpersonal psychotherapy. *The Journal of Transpersonal Psychology, 38*(1), 95-116.

Comer, R. J. (2004). *Abnormal psychology* (5th ed.). New York, NY: Worth.

Cortright, B. (2007). *Integral psychology.* Albany, NY: State University of New York Press.

Davidson, R. (2004). Well-being and affective style: Neural substrates and biobehavioural correlates. *Philosophical Transactions of the Royal Society London, B, 359(1449)*, 1395-1411.

Davidson, R., Kabat-Zinn, J., Schumacher, J., Rosenkrantz, M., Muller, D., Santorelli, S., Urbanowski, F., ... & Sheridan, J. (2003). *Alterations in brain and immune function produced by mindfulness meditation. Psychosomatic Medicine, 65,* 564-570.

Deatherage, G. (1975). The clinical use of "mindfulness" meditation techniques in short-term psychotherapy. *Journal of Transpersonal Psychology, 7*(2), 133-143.

Descamps, M. (2006). Resistances. In the European Transpersonal Association (Ed.), *Methods of healing and awakening, transpersonal workbook 4* (pp. 31-44). Timisoara, Romania: Romanian Association for Transpersonal Psychology.

Dienstfrey, H. (2005). Mind and mindlessness in mind-body research. In M. Schlitz & T. Amorok (Eds.), *Consciousness and healing.* (pp. 51-60). St. Louis, MO: Elsevier Churchill Livingstone.

Donovan, S., Murphy, M., & Taylor, E. (1997). *The physical and psychological effects of meditation: A review of contemporary research.* Petaluma, CA: Institute of Noetic Sciences.

Ellsworth, P. C., Scherer, K. R., & Goldsmith, H. (2009). Appraisal processes in emotion. In R. Davidson, K. Scherer, & H. Goldsmith (Eds.) *Handbook of Affective Sciences* (pp. 572-95). New York, NY: Oxford University Press.

Everly, G., & Lating, J. (2002). *A clinical guide to the treatment of the human stress response* (2nd ed.). New York, NY: Kluwer Academic Publishers.

Friedman, H. (2006). The renewal of psychedelic research: Implications for humanistic and transpersonal psychology. *The Humanistic Psychologist, 34*(1), 39-58.

Friedman, H. (this volume). Transpersonal self-expansiveness as a scientific construct (Chapter 11).

Friedman, H. & MacDonald, D. (2002). Using transpersonal tests in humanistic psychological assessment. *The Humanistic Psychologist, 30,* 223-236.

Galegos, E. (1983). Animal imagery, the chakra system and psychotherapy. *The Journal of Transpersonal Psychology, 15*(2), 125-136.

Geels, A. (2011). Altered consciousness in religion. In E. Cardeña & M. Winkelman (Eds.), *Altering consciousness: A multidisplinary perspectives* (Vol. 1, pp. 255-276). Santa Barbara, CA: Praeger.

Grepmair, L., Mitterlehner, F., Loew, T., Bachler, E., Rother, W., & Nickel, M. (2007). Promoting mindfulness in psychotherapists in training influences the treatment results of their patients: A randomized, double-blind, controlled study. *Psychotherapy and Psychosomatics, 76*(6), 332-338.

Griffith, B. A., & Griggs, J. C. (2001). Religious identity status as a model to understand, assess, and interact with client spirituality. *Counseling & Values, 46,* 14-25.

Grof, C., & Grof, S. (1990). *The stormy search for the self: A guide to personal growth through transformational crisis.* Los Angeles, CA: Jeremy P. Tarcher.

Grof, C., & Grof, S. (2010). *Holotropic breathwork: A new approach to self-exploration and therapy.* Albany, NY: State University of New York Press.

Grof, S. (2000). *Psychology of the future.* Albany, NY: State University of New York Press.

Hanratty, P. M. (2002). Predicting the outcome of holotropic breathwork using the high-risk model of threat perception. *Dissertation Abstracts International, 63*(01) 0795B (UMI #3034572).

Hennezel, M., & Leloup, J. (1997). *L'art de mourir.* Paris, France: Éditions R. Laffont.

Hirai, T. (1989). *Zen meditation and psychotherapy.* Tokyo, Japan: Japan Publications.

Hitchcock, S. T., & Esposito, J. L. (2004). *Geografia da religiao.* Lisbon, Portugal: Lusomundo Editores.

Holmes, S. W., Morris, R., Clance, P. R., & Putney, R. T. (1996). Holotropic breathwork: An experiential approach to psychotherapy. *Psychotherapy, 33*(1), 114-120.

Huang, T., & Charyton, C. (2008). A comprehensive review of the psychological effects of brainwave entrainment. *Alternative Therapies in Health and Medicine, 14*(5), 38-50.

Johanson, G. (2006). A survey of the use of mindfulness in psychotherapy. *Annals of the American Psychotherapy Association, 9*(2), 15-24.

Johnson, C., & Friedman, H. (2008). Enlightened or delusional? Differentiating religious, spiritual, and transpersonal experience from psychopathology. *Journal of Humanistic Psychology, 48*(4), 505-527.

Jung, C. G. (1952): *Psychologie de l'inconscient.* Genève, Switzerland: Librairie de L'Université Georg & Cie.

Kasprow, M., & Scotton,B. (1999). A review of transpersonal theory and its application to the practice of psychotherapy. *Journal of Psychotherapy Practice and Research, 8*(1), 12-23.

Kjellgren, A., Lyden, F., & Norlander, T. (2008). Sensory isolation in flotation tanks: Altered states of consciousness and effects on well-being. *The Qualitative Report, 13*(4), 636-656. Retrieved from http://www.nova.edu/ssss/QR/QR13-4/kjellgren.pdf

Koenig, H. G., McCullough, M. E., & Larson, D. B. (2001). *Handbook of religion and health.* Oxford, UK: Oxford University Press.

Kolp, E., Krupitsky, E., Friedman, H., & Young, S. (2009). Entheogen-enhanced transpersonal psychotherapy of addictions: Focus on clinical applications of ketamine for treating alcoholism. In A. Browne-Miller (Ed.). *The Praeger International Collection on Addictions* (Vol. 3, pp. 403-417). Westport, CT: Praeger.

Korotkov, K. (2002). *Human energy field: Study with GDV bioelectrography.* New York, NY: Backbone Publishing.

Kubler-Ross, E. (1995). *Death is of vital importance.* New York, NY: Station Hill Press.

Lancaster, B. L. (2004). *Approaches to consciousness.* New York, NY: Palgrave MacMillan.

LeLoup, J. (2001). *Além da luz e da sombra.* Petrópolis, Brazil: Editora Vozes Ltda.

LeShan, L. (1984). *De Newton à percepção extra-sensorial.* São Paulo, Brazil: Summus Editorial Ltda.

Louchakova, O., & Lucas, M. (2007). Self as the clinical category: Reflections on culture, gender and phenomenology. *Journal of Transpersonal Psychology, 39,* 111-136.

MacDonald, D. A., & Friedman, H. (2002). Assessment of humanistic, transpersonal and spiritual constructs: State of the science. *Journal of Humanistic Psychology, 42,* 102-125.

MacDonald, D. A., Kuentzel, J., & Friedman, H. L. (1999a). A survey of measures of spiritual and transpersonal constructs: Part one-research update. *Journal of Transpersonal Psychology, 31*(2), 137-154.

MacDonald, D. A., Kuentzel, J., & Friedman, H. L. (1999b). A survey of measures of spiritual and transpersonal constructs: Part two-additional instruments. *Journal of Transpersonal Psychology, 31*(2), 155-177.

Mace, C. (2007). Mindfulness in psychotherapy: An introduction. *Advances in Psychiatric Treatment, 13,* 147-154.

Maslow, A. (1968). *Toward a psychology of being.* Princeton, NJ: Van Nostrand.

McCombs, B. L. (1989). Self-regulated learning and academic achievement: A phenomenological view. In D. J. Zimmerman & D. H. Schmeck (Eds.), *Self-regulated learning and academic achivement. Theory, research, and practice* (pp. 51-82). New York, NY: Springer-Verlag.

McCraty, R., Atkinson, M., & Tomasino, D. (Eds.). (2001). *Science of the heart. Exploring the role of the heart in human performance.* Boulder Creek, CA: HeartMath Research Center.

Miller, D. (2005). Mandala symbolism in psychotherapy: The potential utility of the Lowenfeld Mosaic Technique for enhancing the individuation process. *Journal of Transpersonal Psychology, 37*(2), 164-177.

Mishor, Z., McKenna, D., & Callaway, J. (2011). DMT and human consciousness. In E. Cardeña & M. Winkelman (Eds.), *Altering consciousness: Multidisplinary perspectives* (Vol. 2, pp. 85-120). Santa Barbara, CA: Praeger.

Nash, M., & Barnier, A. (2008). *The Oxford handbook of hypnosis.* New York, NY: Oxford University Press.

Netherton, M., & Shiffrin, N. (1979). *Past lives therapy.* New York, NY: Ace Books.

Nichols, D., & Chemel, B. (2011). LSD and the serotonin system's effects on human consciousness. In E. Cardeña & M. Winkelman (Eds.), *Altering consciousness: Multidisplinary perspectives* (Vol. 2, pp. 121-146). Santa Barbara, CA: Praeger.

Peres, J., & Nasello, A. (2007). Psychotherapy and neuroscience: Towards closer integration. *International Journal of Psychotherapy, 43*(6), 943-957.

Peres, J., Newberg, A., Mercante, J., Simao, M., Alberquerque, V., Peres, M., & Nasello, A. (2007). Cerebral blood flow changes during retrieval of traumatic memories before and after psychotherapy: A SPECT study. *Psychological Medicine, 32,* 1481-1491.

Peres, J., Simão, M., & Nasello, A. (2007). Espiritualidade, religiosidade e psicoterapia. *Revista de Psiquiatria Clínica, 34*(supl. 1), 136-145.

Pert, C., Dreher, H., & Ruff, M. (2005). The psychosomatic network: Foundations of mind-body medicine. In M. Schlitz & T. Amorok, *Consciousness & healing*, (pp. 61-92). St. Louis, MO: Elsevier Churchill Livingstone.

Pressman, T. E. (1993). The psychological and spiritual effects of Stanislav Grof's holotropic breathwork technique: An exploratory study. *Dissertation Abstracts International, 54*(08) 0795B (UMI #9335165).

Presti, D. E. (2011). Neurochemistry and altered consciousness. In E. Cardeña & M. Winkelman (Eds.), *Altering consciousness: A multidisplinary perspectives* (Vol. 2, pp. 20-41). Santa Barbara, CA: Praeger.

Roberts, T. (1989). Multistate education: Metacognitive implications of the mind/body psychotechnologies. *Journal of Transpersonal Psychology, 21*(1), 83-102.

Rodrigues, V. (2008). L'Amour, la santé et l'ethique. *Synodies, Automne*, 36-45.

Rodrigues, V. (2010). On consciousness-modifying (transpersonal) psychotherapy. *Journal of Transpersonal Research, 2*, 44-61.

Saldanha, V. (1997). *A psicoterapia transpessoal*. Campinas, Brazil: Editora Komedi.

Segall, S. R. (2005). Mindfulness and self-development in psychotherapy. *The Journal of Transpersonal Psychology, 37*(2), 143-163.

Simonton, C. O. (2002). *The healing journey*. Lincoln, NE: Authors Choice Press.

Stevenson, I. (1997). *Reincarnation and biology: A contribution to the etiology of birthmarks and birth defects* (Vol. 1: *Birthmarks;* Vol. 2: *Birth defects and other anomalies*). Santa Barbara, CA: Praeger.

TenDam, H. (1996). *Deep healing: A practical outline of past-life therapy*. Vinkenbuurt, The Netherlands: Tasso Publishing.

Travis, F. (2006). Are all meditations the same? Comparing the neural patterns of mindfulness meditation, tibetan buddhism practice "unconditional loving-kindness and compassion", and the transcendental meditation technique. Paper presented at the Science of Consciousness Conference, Tucson, AZ. Retrieved from http://drfredtravis.com/Other%20Meditations.html

Urbanowski, F. B., & Miler, J. L. (1996). Trauma, psychotherapy, and meditation. *Journal of Transpersonal Psychology, 28*(1), 31-48.

Walach, H. (2009). Spirituality: The legacy of parapsychology. *Archive for the Psychology of Religion, 31*, 277-308.

Wegela, K. (2003). Nurturing the seeds of sanity: A Buddhist approach to psychotherapy. In S. Mijares (Ed.) *Modern psychology and ancient wisdom*. (pp. 17-42). New York, NY: Haworth Integrative Healing Press.

Wells, A. (2000). *Emotional disorders and metacognition*. Hoboken, NJ: John Wiley & Sons.

Wilber, K. (2000). *Integral psychology*. Boston, MA: Shambhala.

Woolger, R. (2004). *Healing your past lives*. Boulder, CO: Sounds True.

Part VI
Transpersonal Studies

33

Ecopsychology and Transpersonal Psychology

John V. Davis and Jeanine M. Canty

Ecopsychology is one of the fields of study and practice focused on human-nature relationships. Although it shares much with environmental psychology, conservation psychology, deep ecology, environmental justice, and other fields that also focus on human-nature relationships, it is distinguished by its view of the fundamental inter-connection between humans and their environments, the use of concepts based on this relationship such as *ecological self* and *ecological unconscious*, the centrality of phenomenological and sensorial connections with the natural world, and the integration of practices based on the healing potential of direct contact with the natural world (i.e., ecotherapy) with practices oriented to environmental action and ecological, personal, and community sustainability. This chapter explores the historical roots and core themes of ecopsychology, its initial emergence as a radical psychology and further development as a more formal and inclusive field, and the role of spirituality and transpersonal concepts in ecopsychology.

As a radical pedagogy, ecopsychology encourages a critical analysis of globalized societies, particularly those within Western and "developed" nations, examining their common disconnection from, and domination of, the Earth and peoples who live in closer harmony with nature. Its pertinent critical analysis serves as a foundation for a fundamental worldview change and awakening, or rather reawakening, to inherent bonds with the natural world including those aspects of self-identity, body, emotion, and soul that are silenced within a mechanistic worldview and renewed by direct and immediate contact with nature. Revealing this disconnection with nature and a deeper self and reintegrating into healthy relationship with the natural world (including humans), ecopsychology provides a path of restoration between the small self of the individual and the larger Self of the world.

Ecopsychology's contributions include bringing more sophisticated psychological principles and practices to environmental education and action, developing psychotherapeutic and educational thinking and practices aligned with the values of

The Wiley Blackwell Handbook of Transpersonal Psychology, First Edition.
Edited by Harris L. Friedman and Glenn Hartelius.
© 2013 John Wiley & Sons, Ltd. Published 2015 by John Wiley & Sons, Ltd.

the natural world, and fostering lifestyles that are both ecologically and psychologically healthy (Doherty, 2009; Esbjörn-Hargens & Zimmerman, 2009; Roszak, 1992; Roszak, Gomes, & Kanner, 1995; Winter, 1996). A core theme is the broadening of self-identity to include other beings, the natural world, and the cosmos. It is here that ecopsychology and transpersonal psychology share common ground most visibly. To put it succinctly, humans and nature are both parts of a transpersonal whole. Deepening this identity promotes self-transcendence, self-realization, and optimal human maturity and at the same time, environmentally sustainable attitudes and behaviors.

Roots and History

There are three entwined roots of ecopsychology. In some respects, ecopsychology grew from observations about environmental action and the need for a more psychologically sophisticated approach to changing attitudes and behaviors toward the environment. Specifically, Roszak (1992) and others recognized that appealing to fear and shame, as he felt most environmental activists were doing, would not produce long-term change. Rather, appeals to love, devotion, and a "psycho-emotional bond" with nature (Swan, 1992) were needed. At the same time, the healing properties of direct contact with the natural world were being integrated into the human potential movement by Greenway (1991, 1995), Foster and Little (1980/1989a, 1989b), and others. Recognizing that this contact, itself, has psychological benefits for healing and human development led to practices for deepening this connection. A third contributing factor to the birth of ecopsychology was its call for deep cultural change among modern, industrialized cultures (Fisher, 2002; Roszak, 1992) and a corresponding recognition that most indigenous cultures already recognized a deep bond with the natural world (Gray, 1995).

While the views underlying ecopsychology are arguably ancient, the idea of ecopsychology first arose explicitly in the 1960s and 1970s as an awakening to the social and ecological crises of the time—including the first Earth Day and both the civil rights and feminist movements, a time marked by a general critical pedagogical analysis of systems and structures that were hierarchical and oppressive. A new narrative had emerged in which the personal was political, and many witnessing the destruction of ecological systems realized that this paralleled the rising psychological fears and disorders within themselves and others (Conn, 1995; Glendinning, 1994; Macy, 1983, 1995). The environmental movement was in full force, and alternative branches rooted in the critical analysis of the human domination of nature including peoples were emerging. These narratives include deep ecology, ecofeminism, and social ecology (Biehl & Bookchin, 2003; Chalquist, 2007). Although these areas of the environmental movement laid out our destructive relationship with the natural world, they did not address the psychological reasons behind destructive human behaviors, nor how to start healing.

The field of ecopsychology was developed explicitly in the 1990s most predominately with the work of Theodore Roszak, Mary Gomes, Allen Kanner, and Robert Greenway as a means to bridge the gap between ecology and psychology. These theorists saw a disconnection between environmentalists' overreliance on ecological science and political action in addressing the ecological crisis without considering its psychological dimensions. In contrast, mainstream psychology relegated anxieties, pathologies, and other forms of mental illness to the personal domain, rarely considering the effects of escalating planetary devastation or the benefits of direct contact with nature. Ecopsychology emerged as a response to these twin disconnections.

The first articulations of ecopsychology theory and practice concentrated on unraveling the reasons and consequences for this disconnection with nature and proposing avenues for restoration of an innate relationship with the natural world. For example, Fisher (2002) proposed ecopsychology as an evolving project for radical change toward serving the whole of life through the avenues of psychology, philosophy, critical evaluation, and healing practice. Ecopsychology sees the environmental crisis as rooted in a psychological crisis where humans of modern, industrialized, and technological civilizations have separated their identities from the rest of the natural world, which leads to seeing the planet as (merely) a material resource for human consumption. A major assumption is that *this crisis is embedded in the history and culture of modern, industrialized civilization that includes most of Western civilization.* The critical theory of ecopsychology looks at how Western civilization spurred the environmental crisis by creating this perceived disconnection ranging from the institutionalization of domestic agriculture, the role of language and abstract thought, the role of mechanistic science, and colonization (Abram, 1996; Anthony, 1995; Glendinning, 1994; Gomes & Kanner, 1995; Shepard, 1995). Ecopsychologists call for a shift in worldview and practice that will re-embed our individual human psyches into the natural world.

While the integration of the psyche of the individual with that of the earth may seem like a radical restructuring for humanity, this relationship has been a foundation of past and present indigenous peoples. According to Roszak (1995), "Once upon a time all psychology was 'ecopsychology'" (pp. 5-6). Ecopsychology seeks to restore this relationship, and some of its narrative focuses on what happened within the history of modern humans that obstructed this natural bond. In particular, the work of Paul Shepard (e.g., 1995, 1998) and Chellis Glendinning (1994) suggests that humans became arrested in their maturation with the invention of large-scale agriculture which resulted in a rift of our symbiosis with the natural world. Shepard labeled this *ontogenetic crippling* referring to a kind of developmental arrest in humans, while Glendinning went further with the concept of the *original trauma,* claiming this separation from nature has resulted in collective trauma. Doherty (2009) identified these views as representing ecopsychology's first generation focused in part on critiques of modern culture.

A second generation of ecopsychology has emerged with a stronger focus on research and therapeutic practice. The *Ecopsychology* journal was established in 2009, providing a forum for scholarly research and inquiry concentrated on the relationship of human and planetary well-being, the *European Journal of Ecopsychology* followed in 2010, and a number of innovative research projects on ecotherapy, nature-based models of human development, and integrations of environmental action and restoration with psychological healing and growth have appeared in recent years (Buzzell & Chalquist, 2007; Chalquist, 2007; Louv, 2005; Plotkin, 2003, 2007). This work is bringing ecopsychological concepts into tangible practice toward healing and reintegrating into a nature-based reality. Doherty (2009) has suggested that as ecopsychology moves into this second generation of research, theory, and application, it is becoming less defined by its countercultural, holistic, and romantic stance and more self-reflective, pluralistic, and pragmatic. Doherty called for an expansion from those early tenets of ecopsychology but not a rejection of them.

For some, this movement towards research and practice satisfies past concerns about the explicit spiritual and mystical flavor of early presentations of ecopsychology by Roszak and others. For example, Reser (1995) found cause for concern with the "quasi-religious—and often explicitly religious—character of the discourse" (p. 241), stating, "The rhetoric is of spiritual connecting and transformation, there is a clear quest for the sacred and use of ritual, frequent reference to earth magic and animism/transcendentalism, etc." (p. 242). Although Reser and others are skeptical about the value of an ongoing influence of transpersonalism in ecopsychology, its intersection with transpersonal psychology is an important aspect of ecopsychology's pluralism. As ecopsychology finds useful connections to ecotherapy, environmental psychology, conservation psychology, and other environmentally focused psychologies, it will also be fruitful to develop its connections with transpersonal psychology. While these recent developments have assisted in developing ecopsychology as a more formal field, there is danger that ecopsychology's radical critique of modern society and the transformative potential of the ecological self will be lost, replaced with a focus on nature as a useful therapeutic background.

Core Themes

Images of Human-Nature Relationships

Ecopsychology advocates certain images and concepts which reintegrate human identity with the natural world and which parallel those within transpersonal psychology. For the most part, ecopsychology presents two images for the relationship between humans and nature: (a) nature as home and its inhabitants as family (e.g., siblings or Mother Earth) and (b) nature as self, in which self-identifications are broadened and deepened to include the non-human world. These views stand in contrast to views that nature is dangerous and needs to be controlled and dominated or that nature is (merely) a useful resource to be exploited, protected, conserved, or stewarded. Jung made similar observations about the connections between the human psyche and nature (Jung & Sabini, 2002; Perluss, 2006). These images also parallel, to an extent, the concept of biophilia, the deep emotional bond humans have with nature (Kahn, 1999; Wilson, 1984).

Fox (1990) provided a useful outline of various positions on human-nature relationships leading to what he called *transpersonal ecology*, that is, that humans and the natural world are both parts of a more inclusive whole. A transpersonal view of human-nature relationships can include these images, and it can transcend them. Conceiving of nature as an expanded and more-inclusive self may be a necessary step in developing a more transpersonal view of the human-nature relationship. However, this broader self is not a final understanding. A transpersonal view goes beyond the nature-as-self image without invalidating it. Such a transpersonal view recognizes that both human and nature are expressions of the same ground of being. An understanding of unitive or nondual states and practices for developing this understanding is thus the foundation for an effective integration of transpersonal psychology and ecopsychology.

Ecological Unconscious, Self, and Identity

These terms refer to the understanding that, though they can be differentiated, humans and nature are not fundamentally separate. Roszak (1992) introduced the concept of the *ecological unconscious* which links the individual's psyche to that of the living world. In a holistic and transpersonal sense, ecopsychology is the story of our individual and collective souls within the context of the ecological crisis and our return to our innate relationship with all of life. The *ecological self* is a central concept related to the ecological unconscious. Coined by the late deep ecologist Arne Naess (1989) and further developed by ecopsychologists (Conn, 1995; Sewall, 1995), the ecological self is an identification of the individual with all of life in a manner that dissolves or transcends boundaries between *I* and *other* and between *I* and *nature,* paralleling the notion of Self in transpersonal psychology. A successful development of the ecological self through awareness, immersion in nature, and other forms of mindfulness and healing practices holds the key to reunification with the natural world and restoring human's untapped transpersonal capacities. Thomashow's (1996) work supports the ecological self by developing what he terms *ecological identity,* which uncovers one's personal stories with the natural places one has inhabited. This personalized approach fosters a deeper awareness of our intimate relationships with nature, prompting a resulting ecological ethos.

Trauma, Grief, and Healing

Critical ecopsychology recognizes that disconnection from, and resulting destruction of, nature manifests a collective trauma for all peoples living apart from the natural world. In essence, in separating from this home or larger self, these societies have supported a separation from their true nature. Glendinning (1994) described this process using the concepts of *the original trauma* (the point of disconnection) and *the primal matrix* (a healthy human state, prior to disconnection). The primal matrix is a fluid state of consciousness and being that includes "a sense of belonging and security in the world, trust, faith," "a sense of personal integrity, centeredness, capability," and "the capacity to draw vision and meaning from nonordinary states of consciousness" (pp. 20-21).

Emptiness, narcissism, and addiction are important themes within ecopsychology. Loss of relationship with nature parallels a loss of true self, replaced with a false self rooted in "narcissism ... that masks deep-seated but unacknowledged feelings of worthlessness and emptiness" (Kanner & Gomes, 1995, p. 79). In essence, separation from true nature results in woundedness and pathological behaviors including addictions ranging from excessive consumption, alcohol and substance addiction, eating disorders, codependency, technological addiction, and other forms of abuse and self-abuse. These addictions are relevant to ecopsychology inasmuch as they (a) arise, at least in part, from a disconnection from the natural world and (b) have severe negative environmental consequences.

Experiencing emotional pain and grief in order to start the healing process is another important ecopsychology theme. This process is spurred by seeing and accepting the realities of the ecological crisis and the collective and personal disconnections from nature. Joanna Macy (1983; Macy & Brown 1998) explicated the need to respond emotionally to the ecological crisis and the dangers of apathy and denial of this pain. Through feeling this pain, it is released as part of a larger system, and by exercising compassion toward it, despair can be transformed into empowerment. O'Connor (1995) pointed out that by accepting the crisis, it is possible to understand our human condition better including the reasons we allow the ecological crisis to occur. This process is paralleled by Conn (1995), who uses four practices with her ecologically oriented psychotherapy work: awareness, emotional responsiveness, understanding, and action (see pp. 166-170). Windle (1995) has argued that for environmentalists to be successful, they must engage nature across multiple dimensions including the emotional, relating the process of ecological despair to mourning the loss of a beloved. The impacts of environmental devastation on the human psyche and, more generally, the wounds and trauma of the disconnection of humans from the natural world are central to many ecopsychologists.

Practices

Ecopsychology is defined by its orientation to human-nature relationships rather than its practices, most of which can be found in other contexts. Ecopsychology calls for a reconnection between humans and the natural world, or more precisely, a reawakening and development of this connection, and its practices express this call. They may be identified as ecopsychological inasmuch as they reflect an integration of psychology and the natural world and promote environmental justice, ecological sustainability, and human development. Given such a broad approach, it is not surprising that a wide variety of practices have appeared in ecopsychological frameworks. Three broad themes may be discerned within this variety: awareness practices, environmental work, and ecotherapy.

Among the practices aimed at increasing awareness of the natural world and human-nature relationships are sensory awareness, mindfulness practices, mapping, and techniques for facilitating communications with the natural world, animals, plants, and landforms (e.g., Abram, 1996; Coleman, 2006; Devereux, 1996; Metzner, 1999; Plotkin, 2007, 2013; Sewall, 1999). Related to awareness practices, there are also methods for working with metaphor and symbol and methods for using nature as a means of expanding awareness, such as uses of nature as a projective device and mirroring. One might also include training in traditional ("primitive" or "survival") skills as a means of increasing awareness of, and in, the natural world. Ecopsychology has also contributed to a deeper understanding of the sources of environmental action. This has been reflected in environmental education; restoration and regeneration work; the promotion of attitudes and lifestyles which are environmentally, economically, socially, and psychologically sustainable; bioregionalism; and advocacy and demonstration of relocalization based on appropriate technology. Clear examples of these practices are found in environmental restoration work that aims simultaneously at psychological healing and development. Narrowly defined, ecotherapy integrates the natural world into counseling and psychotherapeutic settings by using nature as an element of psychological assessment (for example, including a person's history with and attitudes toward the natural world as part of a psychological assessment), using natural objects and metaphors for psychological healing, dealing with difficult emotions toward nature (including fears of nature and despair, grief, and anger about environmental devastation), and encouraging direct contact with nature. Broadly defined, ecotherapy includes other means of engaging nature as a therapeutic and developmental resource and promoting deeper bonds with the natural world. Such practices include gardening and horticultural therapy, animal-assisted therapy and education, place-bonding practices, wilderness therapy and outdoor adventure counseling, wilderness intensives such as wilderness-based rites of passage, and various kinds of nature-based, ritual-based shamanic work. As with any organization of such a rich collection, many practices cross the boundaries of these three categories. For example, earth-centered festivals and seasonal celebrations, expressive arts with a focus on human-nature relationships, and eco-theater might be used within an ecopsychological context.

With such a broad and inclusive list of practices, ecopsychology runs the risk of losing its focus and meaning. This is the reason for the crucial importance of an emphasis on promoting ecopsychological values such as ecocentrism and a view of human-nature relationships based on metaphors of family, home, or a more inclusive self. Nature-based mindfulness practices are ecopsychological when they are grounded in the fundamental interconnection of human consciousness and nature, learning traditional survival skills would be considered ecopsychological to the extent they promote a deeper bond between the learner and the natural world, and environmental restoration reflects ecopsychology when one's actions support a natural area and inner development as two aspects of one whole. As long as these values are kept in mind, ecopsychology's practices will be able to continue to expand in creative, coherent, and useful ways.

Transpersonal Dimensions of Ecopsychology

Common Theoretical Ground

A number of influential voices in ecopsychology have included a transpersonal view at its core most often through references to spirituality and nature mysticism. A recent edited volume on ecopsychology (Kahn & Hasbach, 2012) identified its transpersonal aspects as one of five core orientations of ecopsychology, that is, "interactions with nature that lead to optimal mental health and help to develop a sense of inner peace, compassion, and trust that pushes us forward into service and finally to the transpersonal" (Hasbach, Kahn, & Doherty, 2012, p. 2).

Although connections between ecopsychology and transpersonal psychology are not always acknowledged or accepted, it seems that a view of nonduality is shared by both fields (Davis, 2011). A self-identity that transcends the individual as a separate entity underlies transpersonal psychology. Although there are disagreements about the nature and extent of this transcendence, it is at the root of various core concepts in transpersonal psychology, including nonduality, holism, unitive consciousness, mystical experiences, peak experiences, self-transcendence, a collective unconscious, spiritual intelligence, and ego-transcendence (see, e.g., Caplan, Hartelius, & Rardin, 2003).

The role of nonduality in ecopsychology is generally articulated less explicitly, but it is central. At the focus of ecopsychology is a relationship between humans and nature characterized by seamless interconnection. While differentiations between humans and the non-human world are important, these relative differentiations are not fundamental any more than are differentiations between oaks and maples. Ecologically based images of different leaves on the same tree or individual waves on a single ocean are often used to portray ecopsychology's view of human-nature relationships. Concepts that are core to ecopsychology—such as *ecological self, ecological identity,* and *ecological unconscious*—point to a self-identity beyond the individual.

Theodore Roszak's *The Voice of the Earth* (1992), the seminal book in ecopsychology, connects it to nature mysticism, feminist spirituality, and in his conclusion, "the interplay between planetary and personal well-being, [phrasing which] is deliberately chosen for its traditional theological connotation" (p. 321). Snell, Simmonds, and Webster (2011) reviewed Roszak's work on ecopsychology and concluded that spiritual experience is an important theme in his presentation of ecopsychology. They also pointed out that Roszak avoided the term *spirituality* because he felt it would hinder acceptance of his argument. They concluded that "it would be prudent to account for Roszak's contribution and the significance of spiritual experience in his representation of ecopsychology" (p. 112). Warwick Fox's *Toward a Transpersonal Ecology* (1995) also articulated the intersection of ecopsychology and transpersonal psychology. Although the original 1990 publication of this book predates Roszak's (1992) major presentation of ecopsychology, Fox (1990) cited Roszak's earlier work at several points and includes Roszak in a list of writers who "see the cultivation of ecological consciousness in 'spiritual' or 'quasi-religious' terms" (p. 52). Robert Greenway (1995) pointed to dualism as "perhaps the source of our pervasive sense of being disconnected" from the natural world (p. 131) and suggested that such dualism (in contrast to nondual or unitive perspectives) is also at the root of Western culture's domination, exploitation, and destruction of human habitat, "the very basis of our survival as a species" (p. 131). Andy Fisher's *Radical Ecopsychology* (2002), another formative work for the field of ecopsychology, considered spirituality in some instances to be virtually synonymous with the reunion of humans and the rest of nature (p. 97), and a necessary foundation for encountering the depths of environmental suffering in order to engage in effective environmental action (pp. 190-191). Deborah Winter's *Ecological Psychology* (1996) is subtitled *Healing the Split Between Planet and Self,* suggesting this split is not fundamental, that it is a wound in need of healing, and that closing this split benefits both humans and the non-human planet. She cited Roszak's ecopsychology and Fox's transpersonal ecology as examples of a growing synthesis between ecopsychology and transpersonal psychology. Winter summarized her discussion of these fields this way:

The basic principle to be drawn from both gestalt and transpersonal psychology (and their recent forms of ecopsychology and transpersonal ecology) is that our ordinary experience of ourselves as separate autonomous beings is incomplete and inaccurate. [Recognizing this] will require … a shift in consciousness (the transpersonal emphasis) from the smaller, autonomous, ego-oriented self to the wider and deeper ecological self. Transpersonal psychologists, ecopsychologists, and transpersonal ecologists argue that such a shift is more than a cognitive event—it is also a directly perceptual and/or spiritual event. (p. 264)

Of particular interest to transpersonalists, Wilber (1996) referred to nature mysticism as a paradigm case for the first transpersonal level of development, he identified wilder places as "inviting places" to "relax egoic grasping" and seek optimal psychological health and transformation (p. 291), and he cited deep experiences of nature as examples of the mystical experience and extraordinarily healthy human development. Writing about the deep ecologists' (and presumably ecopsychologists') views of a transpersonal and ecological self, he called himself

a big fan of their work. They have an important message for the modern world: to find that deep Self that embraces all of nature, and thus to treat nature with the same reverence you would extend to your own being. (Wilber, 1996, p. 204)

It should also be noted that he considered deep ecologists (and again, presumably ecopsychologists) "basically half right and half wrong (or seriously incomplete)" (1996, p. 6). Responding to his criticisms is beyond the scope of this chapter, but they are worth noting in the relationship between transpersonal and ecopsychological thought (cf. Davis, 1998, see pp. 77-79).

Research on Transpersonal Experiences in Nature

Common ground between ecopsychology and transpersonal psychology can been seen in empirical research as well. Much research confirms the connection between nature experiences and various measures of psychological health including cognitive restoration, stress reduction, vitality, and altruism. Although these variables are not precisely or necessarily transpersonal, they are definitely of interest to ecopsychologists. More relevant to this discussion is the body of research demonstrating the spiritual or transpersonal aspects of nature experiences, corroborating and refining similar observations in a wide variety of nature, spiritual, and religious literatures.

Kaplan and Talbot (1983; see also Kaplan & Kaplan, 1989) evaluated a series of wilderness programs for inner-city youth and adults. Content analysis of participant's journals revealed the following impacts:

[During the backpacking trips] for many participants there is eventually a surprising sense of revelation, as both the environment and the self are newly perceived and seem newly wondrous. The wilderness inspires feelings of awe and wonder, and one's intimate contact with this environment leads to thoughts about spiritual meanings and eternal processes. Individuals feel better acquainted with their own thoughts and feelings, and they feel "different" in some way—calmer, at peace with themselves, "more beautiful on the inside and unstifled." (Kaplan & Talbot, 1983, p. 178)

[Immediately after the trip] there is a growing sense of wonder and a complex awareness of spiritual meanings as individuals feel at one with nature, yet they are aware of the transience of individual concerns when seen against the background of enduring natural rhythms. (pp. 179-180)

[At a follow-up] the wilderness is remembered as awesome, and is felt to have offered a compelling glimpse of a real world, and of a way of relating to one's surroundings and responding to one's daily opportunities and challenges, that was immensely satisfying. (p. 182)

Other empirical research also points to connections between nature experiences and concepts central to transpersonal psychology. Several empirical studies examined the relationship between nature experiences and peak experiences (for Maslow and others, a paradigm case of transpersonal experience). Wuthnow (1978) used three definitions of peak experiences in a large representative survey and asked respondents if they "ever had the feeling that you were in close contact with something *holy or sacred*," had "experienced the beauties of nature in a deeply moving way," or had the feeling of "being in harmony with the universe" (p. 61). Eighty-two percent of his sample reported being deeply moved by the beauty of nature, the most common of the three experiences, and 49% felt this experience had a lasting influence on their lives. Keutzer (1978) asked college students whether they had had a transcendent experience, 65% responded affirmatively, and of special interest here, the most common trigger was "beauties of nature such as sunset" (p. 78). In a cross-cultural confirmation of these findings, Hoffman and Muramoto (2007) found that samples of Japanese college students reported nature experiences as the first or second most common trigger for their peak experiences. Shiota, Keltner, and Mossman (2007) found nature to be the most common trigger for the experience of awe, a characteristic of peak and spiritual experiences. Rudd, Vohs, and Aaker (2012) found that experiences of awe, in comparison to other positive emotions such as happiness, brought people into the present moment and led to an expanded sense of time, greater willingness to engage in prosocial behavior, stronger preferences for experiences over material objects, and increased life satisfaction. Notably, this research used images of nature such as waterfalls and whales (among other techniques) to elicit awe.

In a survey of mental health services, Lukoff and Mancuso (2009) found that, among those surveyed throughout California, the spiritual practices most beneficial to mental health were, in order of frequency, prayer, meditation, attending religious services, and spending time in nature (out of 23 possible choices). Supporting the close relationship between nature experiences, spirituality, and mental health, 40.3% of respondents reported time in nature as a spiritual practice beneficial for mental health. Other empirical studies (e.g., Frederickson & Anderson, 1999; Stringer & McAvoy, 1992) have found spiritual experiences in the context of wilderness adventure activities. Overall, it seems that both the adventure element and the wilderness setting play a role in evoking transpersonal experiences and that one of the primary reasons people engage in wilderness experiences is to seek transpersonal experiences (Brown, 1989).

From its beginnings, ecopsychologists (and others) have proposed a relationship between feeling connected to nature and environmental behaviors, and while this connection is not yet well understood, research is now showing evidence of this. Empirical measures of "connectedness to nature" (Mayer & Frantz, 2004) and "relatedness to nature" (Nisbet, Zelenski, & Murphy, 2009) predict stronger valuing of non-human species, greater concern for the environment, and more proactive environmental action (Schultz, 2001). Although the concepts of *ecological self* and *ecological identity* suggest a deeper and more profound relationship to nature, a sense of emotional connectedness and being related to nature is still relevant to ecopsychology. Friedman (1983) showed that an expanded sense of self can come to include an identity with the entire world or universe, and using the Nature Inclusive Measure to operationalize *ecopsychological self,* St. John and MacDonald (2007) showed this expansion can come to include the natural world. This promising research directly addresses an important dimension of transpersonal development: a self-identity that has expanded to include the natural world and a sense of unity or oneness, representing empirical validation of core themes of ecopsychology.

Again, these experiences are foundational for transpersonal psychology and confirm the connections between ecopsychology and transpersonal psychology. In a poetic voice, Susan Griffin (1978) expressed the same transpersonally-laden insight:

> We know ourselves to be made from this earth. We know this earth is made from our bodies. For we see ourselves. And we are nature. We are nature seeing nature. We are nature with a concept of nature. Nature weeping. Nature speaking of nature to nature. (p. 226)

As humans, we are also nature caring for nature. This suggests the possibility of models of environmentally-responsible behavior which are rooted in nondual views of human-nature relationships and more successful techniques for developing proenvironment behaviors, which would be a useful direction for ecopsychology.

Conclusion

In many ways, ecopsychology began with a rejection of mainstream psychology and conventional culture—including technology—and the promotion of a romantic view of the natural world. The field's subsequent development has come to include more emphasis on ecotherapy and a broader view of environmental action. This welcome maturation seems useful as long as it continues to value thoughtful critiques of the cultural roots of environmental devastation and the centrality of the transpersonal dimensions of human-nature relationships. Distancing itself from these dimensions would deny the importance of mystical connections between humans and nature while replicating a mechanistic worldview and a human-nature duality. An inclusive ecopsychology will include cultural-political critique, conclusions grounded in a blend of quantitative and qualitative research, rich applications of ecotherapy, and psychologically mature approaches to environmental attitudes and action. In conclusion, these two fields share much common ground and a number of potential contributions to each other. Among transpersonal psychology's contributions to ecopsychology are conceptual frameworks and practices for exploring the spiritual dimensions of human-nature relationships in ways that are methodologically rigorous, conceptually sophisticated, and more effective. In turn, transpersonal psychology can benefit from ecopsychology's critique of those factors that lead to apathy, violence, and trauma (whether toward oneself, other people, or the environment) and its views and methods for realizing the natural world as a portal to the transpersonal.

References

Abram, D. (1996). *The spell of the sensuous: Perception and language in a more-than-human world*. New York, NY: Vintage Books.

Anthony, C. (1995). Ecopsychology and the deconstruction of whiteness. In T. Roszak, M. E. Gomes, & A. D. Kanner (Eds.), *Ecopsychology: Restoring the earth, healing the mind* (pp. 263-278). San Francisco, CA: Sierra Books.

Biehl, J., & Bookchin, M. (2003). Theses on social ecology and deep ecology. Retrieved from the Institute for Social Ecology, http://www.social-ecology.org/1995/08/theses-on-social-ecology-and-deep-ecology/

Brown, M. (1989). Transpersonal psychology: Facilitating transformation in outdoor experiential education. *Journal of Experiential Education, 12*, 14-21.

Buzzell, L., & Chalquist, C. (2007). *Ecotherapy: Healing with nature in mind*. San Francisco, CA: Sierra Club Books.

Caplan, M., Hartelius, G., & Rardin, M. A. (2003). Contemporary viewpoints on transpersonal psychology. *Journal of Transpersonal Psychology, 35*, 143-162.

Chalquist, C. (2007). *Terrapsychology: Reengaging the soul of place*. New Orleans, LA: Spring Journal.

Coleman, M. (2006). *Awake in the wild: Mindfulness in nature as a path of self-discovery*. Novato, CA: New World Library.

Conn, S. A. (1995). When the earth hurts, who responds? In T. Roszak, M. E. Gomes, & A. D. Kanner (Eds.), *Ecopsychology: Restoring the earth healing the mind* (pp. 156-171). San Francisco, CA: Sierra Books.

Davis, J. (1998). The transpersonal dimensions of ecopsychology: Nature, nonduality, and spiritual practice. *The Humanistic Psychologist, 26* (1-3), 69-100.

Davis, J. (2011). Ecopsychology, transpersonal psychology, and nonduality. *International Journal of Transpersonal Studies, 30* (1-2), 89-100.

Devereux, P. (1996). *Revisioning the earth: A guide to opening the healing channels between mind and nature*. New York, NY: Fireside.

Doherty, T. J. (2009). Editorial: Leading ecopsychology. *Ecopsychology, 1*(2), 53-56.

Esbjörn-Hargens, S., & Zimmerman, M. E. (2009). *Integral ecology: Uniting multiple perspectives on the natural world*. Boston, MA: Integral Books.

Fisher, A. (2002). *Radical ecopsychology: Psychology in the service of life*. Albany, NY: State University of New York Press.

Foster, S., & Little, M. (1989a). *The book of the vision quest: Personal transformation in the wilderness*. New York, NY: Simon & Schuster. (Original work published 1980)

Foster, S., & Little, M. (1989b). *The roaring of the sacred river: The wilderness quest for vision and self-healing*. New York, NY: Simon & Schuster.

Fox, W. (1990). *Toward a transpersonal ecology: Developing new foundations for environmentalism*. Boston, MA: Shambhala. (Also published 1995 by State University of New York Press, Albany, NY)

Frederickson, L., & Anderson, D. (1999). A qualitative exploration of the wilderness experience as a source of spiritual inspiration. *Journal of Environmental Psychology, 19*, 21-39.

Friedman, H. (1983). The Self-Expansiveness Level Form: A conceptualization and measurement of a transpersonal construct. *Journal of Transpersonal Psychology, 15,* 37-50.

Glendinning, C. (1994). *My name is Chellis and I'm in recovery from Western civilization.* Boston, MA: Shambhala.

Gomes, M. E., & Kanner, A. (1995). The rape of the well-maidens: Feminist psychology and the environmental crisis. In T. Roszak, M. E. Gomes, & A. D. Kanner (Eds.), *Ecopsychology: Restoring the earth healing the mind* (pp. 111-121). San Francisco, CA: Sierra Books.

Gray, L. (1995). Shamanic counseling and ecopsychology. In T. Roszak, M. E. Gomes, & A. D. Kanner (Eds.), *Ecopsychology: Restoring the earth healing the mind* (pp. 172-182). San Francisco, CA: Sierra Books.

Greenway, R. (1991). Mapping the wilderness experience. *Circles on the Mountain, 5,* 19-23.

Greenway, R. (1995). The wilderness effect. In T. Roszak, M. E. Gomes, & A. D. Kanner (Eds.), *Ecopsychology: Restoring the earth healing the mind* (pp .122-135). San Francisco, CA: Sierra Books.

Griffin, S. (1978). *Woman and nature: The roaring inside her.* New York, NY: HarperCollins.

Hasbach, P., Kahn, P., & Doherty, T. (2012). *Ecopsychology* roundtable: Patricia Hasbach and Peter Kahn. *Ecopsychology, 4*(1), 1-9.

Hoffman, E., & Muramoto, S. (2007). Peak experiences among Japanese youth. *Journal of Humanistic Psychology, 47,* 497-513.

Jung, C., & Sabini, M. (2002). *The Earth has a soul: C. G. Jung on nature, technology, and modern life.* Berkeley, CA: North Atlantic Books.

Kahn, P. (1999). *The human relationship with nature: Development and culture.* Cambridge, MA: MIT Press.

Kahn, P., & Hasbach, P. (Eds.). (2012). *Ecopsychology: Science, totems, and the technological species.* Cambridge, MA: MIT Press.

Kanner, A. D., & Gomes, M. E. (1995). The all consuming self. In T. Roszak, M. E. Gomes, & A. D. Kanner (Eds.), *Ecopsychology: Restoring the earth healing the mind* (pp. 77-91). San Francisco, CA: Sierra Books.

Kaplan, S., & Kaplan, R. (1989). *The experience of nature.* Cambridge, UK: Cambridge University Press.

Kaplan. S., & Talbot, J. (1983). Psychological benefits of a wilderness experience. In I. Altman & J. Wohlwill (Eds.), *Behavior and the natural environment* (pp. 163-203). New York, NY: Plenum Press.

Keutzer, C. (1978). Whatever turns you on: Triggers to transcendent experiences. *Journal of Humanistic Psychology, 18,* 77-80.

Louv, R. (2005). *Last child in the woods: Saving our children from nature-deficit disorder.* Chapel Hill, NC: Algonquin Books.

Lukoff, D., & Mancuso, L. (2009). Survey of individuals receiving mental health services and their families. Sacramento, CA: California Institute for Mental Health. Retrieved from http://www.mhspirit.org

Macy, J. (1983). *Despair and personal empowerment in a nuclear age.* Gabriola Island, BC: New Society.

Macy, J. (1995). Working through environmental despair. In Roszak, T., Gomes, M.E., & Kanner, A.D. (Eds.). *Ecopsychology: Restoring the earth healing the mind* (pp. 240-259). San Francisco, CA: Sierra Books.

Macy, J., & Brown, M. (1998) *Coming back to life: Practices to reconnect our lives, our world.* Gabriola Island, BC: New Society.

Macy, J., & Johnstone, C. (2012). *Active hope: How to face the mess we're in without going crazy.* Novato, CA: New World Library.

Mayer, F., & Frantz, C. (2004). The connectedness to nature scale: A measure of individuals' feeling in community with nature. *Journal of Environmental Psychology, 24*(4), 503-
515.

Metzner, R. (1999). *Green psychology: Transforming our relationship to the earth.* Rochester,
VT: Park Street Press.

Naess, A. (1989). *Ecology, community, and lifestyle* (D. Rothenberg, Trans.). New York, NY:
Cambridge University Press.

Nisbet, E., Zelenski, J., & Murphy, S. (2009). The nature relatedness scale: Linking individuals'
connection with nature in environmental behavior. *Environment and Behavior, 41*(5), 715-
740.

O'Connor, T. (1995). Therapy for a dying planet. In T. Roszak, M. E. Gomes, & A. D. Kanner
(Eds.), *Ecopsychology: Restoring the earth healing the mind* (pp. 149-155). San Francisco,
CA: Sierra Books.

Perluss, E. (2006). Touching Earth, finding spirit: A passage into the symbolic landscape. *Spring
Journal, 76*(2), 201-222.

Plotkin, B. (2003). *Soulcraft: Crossing into the mysteries of nature and psyche.* Novato, CA: New
World Library.

Plotkin, B. (2007). *Nature and human soul: Cultivating wholeness and community in a fragmented world.* Novato, CA: New World Library.

Plotkin, B. (2013). *Wild mind: A field guide to the human psyche.* Novato, CA: New World
Library.

Reser, J. (1995). Whither environmental psychology? The transpersonal ecopsychology crossroads. *Journal of Environmental Psychology, 15*(3), 235-257.

Roszak, T. (1992). *The voice of the earth: An exploration of ecopsychology.* New York, NY: Simon
& Schuster.

Roszak, T. (1995). Where psyche meets Gaia. In T. Roszak, M. E. Gomes, & A. D. Kanner
(Eds.), *Ecopsychology: Restoring the earth healing the mind* (pp. 1-17). San Francisco, CA:
Sierra Books.

Roszak, T., Gomes, M. E., & Kanner, A. D. (Eds.). (1995). *Ecopsychology: Restoring the earth
healing the mind.* San Francisco, CA: Sierra Books.

Rudd, M., Vohs, K., & Aaker, J. (2012). Awe expands people's perception of time, alters
decision-making, and enhances well-being. *Psychological Science, 23*(10), 1130-1136.

St. John, D., & MacDonald, D. (2007). Development and initial validation of a measure of
ecopsychological self. *Journal of Transpersonal Psychology, 39*(1), 48-67.

Schultz, P. (2001). The structure of environmental concern: Concern for self, other people,
and the biosphere. *Journal of Environmental Psychology, 21,* 327-339.

Sewall, L. (1995). The skill of ecological perception. In T. Roszak, M. E. Gomes, & A. D.
Kanner (Eds.), *Ecopsychology: Restoring the earth healing the mind* (pp. 201-215). San
Francisco, CA: Sierra Books.

Sewall, L. (1999). *Sight and sensibility: The ecopsychology of perception.* New York, NY: Penguin-
Putnam.

Shepard, P. (1995). Nature and madness. In T. Roszak, M. E. Gomes, & A. D. Kanner (Eds.),
Ecopsychology: Restoring the earth healing the mind (pp. 21-40). San Francisco, CA: Sierra
Books.

Shepard, P. (1998). *Coming home to the Pleistocene.* Washington, DC: Island Press.

Shiota, M., Keltner, D., & Mossman, A. (2007). The nature of awe: Elicitors, appraisals, and
effects on self-concept. *Cognition and Emotion, 21,* 944-963.

Snell, T., Simmonds, J., & Webster, R. S. (2011). Spirituality in the work of Theodore Roszak:
Implications for contemporary ecopsychology. *Ecopsychology, 3,* 105-113.

Stringer, L., & McAvoy, L. (1992). The need for something different: Spirituality and wilderness adventure. *Journal of Experiential Education, 15,* 13-20.

Swan, J. (1992) *Nature as teacher and healer. How to reawaken your connection to nature.* New York, NY: Villard Books.

Thomashow, M. (1996). *Ecological identity: Becoming a reflective environmentalist.* Boston, MA: MIT Press.

Wilber, K. (1996). *A brief history of everything.* Boston, MA: Shambhala.

Wilson, E. (1984). *Biophilia.* Cambridge, MA: Harvard University Press.

Windle. P. (1995). The ecology of grief. In T. Roszak, M. E. Gomes, & A. D. Kanner (Eds.), *Ecopsychology: Restoring the earth healing the mind* (pp. 136-145). San Francisco, CA: Sierra Books.

Winter, D. (1996). *Ecological psychology: Healing the split between planet and self.* Boston, MA: Allyn & Bacon.

Wuthnow, R. (1978). Peak experiences: Some empirical tests. *Journal of Humanistic Psychology, 18,* 59-75.

34

Feminist and Cultural Contributions to Transpersonal Psychology

Christine Brooks, Kendra Ford, and Anne Huffman

Transpersonal psychology has centrally focused on the psychospiritual development of the individual and the exploration of the technologies and practices that foster personal growth. Although Hartelius, Caplan, and Rardin (2007) noted that this personal growth often takes place in social contexts and may be undertaken for the sake of social as well as personal transformation, the contexts of these social frames and social impact have generally gone unexplored within the discipline of transpersonal psychology. Developments in schools of thought such as feminism (e.g., Brooks, 2010; Brooks & Crouch, 2010; see also other authors cited below), cultural psychology (e.g., Markus & Kitayama, 2003), and philosophies such as social constructionism (e.g., Gergen, 2008) have brought to the fore the necessity of exploring the situated nature of human experience and the need for contextualization of said experience within areas of transpersonal inquiry. The core concepts shared by the above-mentioned disciplines include the valuation of the subjective experiences of individuals and groups, a focus on relationality and the interconnected nature of human experience, and that identity is neither static nor singular but rather fluid, changing, and made up of a complex matrix of factors (e.g., biological sex, regionality, class, sexual orientation). The complexity of identity explored in these disciplines has contributed greatly to psychological literature in recent decades. Within transpersonal studies, personal identity has often been eschewed or viewed as a problem to transcend rather than an explicit area of inquiry, as often the concept of "trans" in transpersonal has been interpreted as beyond or above the ego rather than through the ego. As will be described below, this outmoded notion of personal identity has recently been questioned by transpersonally oriented scholars (e.g., Ferrer & Sherman, 2008).

The professional literature of transpersonal psychology is currently expanding through contributions from a greater diversity of authors and inclusion of diverse epistemological, methodological, and ontological frameworks. Notably the editors

The Wiley Blackwell Handbook of Transpersonal Psychology, First Edition.
Edited by Harris L. Friedman and Glenn Hartelius.
© 2013 John Wiley & Sons, Ltd. Published 2015 by John Wiley & Sons, Ltd.

for the *International Journal for Transpersonal Studies* have recently released special topic sections on feminism, relational spirituality, and ecopsychology (Brooks & Crouch, 2010; Hartelius & Harrahy, 2009; Schroll & Hartelius, 2011). As an example of a socially-situated transpersonal inquiry, feminist considerations of growth and transformation take a woman-centered approach:

> As a field of study, feminism, in its many forms, centers scholarship around the experiences of women and issues of vital importance to women's lives and well-being, such as economic justice, reproductive freedom, and freedom from harm and discrimination. With regard to areas of focus in much transpersonal scholarship, including states of consciousness, psychospiritual development, extraordinary human experiences, and psychological well-being, considerations of the differences men and women may experience are vastly underrepresented in the literature. Socio-cultural location and the influence of gendered identities on the daily lived experience of both individuals and groups are real factors in the differing ways women and men are treated as both subjects of research as well as authors of transpersonally-oriented scholarship. (Brooks & Crouch, 2010, pp. 28-29)

Building on the recent participatory turn (Ferrer, 2002; Ferrer & Sherman, 2008) influencing transpersonal studies, feminist (Fernandes, 2003), intersectional (Crenshaw, 1991), or cultural (Markus & Kitamaya, 2003) dialectical frames afford new vantage points through which spiritual and exceptional human experiences are viewed *in situ,* or within cultural contexts (Brooks, 2010). Such contextualization facilitates shifts from perennial or universalizing views of spirituality toward more inclusive and diverse perspectives on spiritual experiences and impacts interpretations of the meanings therein. In participatory philosophy, Ferrer and Sherman (2008), drawing on decades of feminist postmodern theological and religious studies scholarship, centralized embodied, immanent experience of the sacred and the divine. They noted that "postmodern feminism replaces a masculinized, discarnate, and supposedly universal and autonomous *Cartesian mental ego* with a gendered, embodied, situated, and participatory *intersubjective self* as the agent engaged in religious pursuits" (p. 13). In this view, locations of identity are taken as central to spiritual experiences, or *multilocal transpersonal events* (Ferrer, 2002). "This participation engages human beings in the activity I call *participatory knowing,* that is, a multidimensional access to reality that can involve not only the creative power of the mind, but also of the body, the heart, and the soul" (Ferrer, 2002, p. 3).

Chicana feminist, Anzaldua (2002) stated that "many are witnessing a major cultural shift in their understanding of knowledge . . . a shift from the kinds of knowledge valued now to the [spiritual] kinds that will be desired in the 21st century" (para. 16). Mainstream psychology as a whole, including feminist psychology, recently arrived at a juncture of readiness to address spiritual needs in psychological research and practice. However, the subfield of transpersonal psychology has over 40 years of documentation investigating different states of consciousness, psychospiritual processes, and transformative practices. This valuable material has been underutilized in psychology. Fernandes (2003) noted a "wariness" (p. 9) of mainstream feminists to embrace spirituality in public life and a lack of cross-pollination related to this subject area in women's studies and feminist psychology in both academia and practice.

Certainly a large majority of women value the "concepts of justice and equality and indeed of feminism [as] inextricably linked to notions of the sacred (Fernandes, 2003, pp. 9-10). However, a large proportion of mainstream feminists remain wary of embracing spirituality in public and political life. Feminist educator Fernandes (2003) commented on the apathy women's studies students displayed in the classroom. She also described a divide between feminists' personal lives and feminist's public lives, which she viewed as problematic for feminisms' future success in creating long lasting transformation in the world.

> [Feminism] misses the meaning and beliefs of a majority of the world's women who do not conceive of their relationship with their worlds, bodies and selves through modern notions of secularism; for such women, concepts of justice and equality and indeed of feminism are inextricably linked to notions of the sacred. (Fernandes, 2003, pp. 9-10)

This lack of integration of spiritual perspectives in feminist practices both in the academy and in social justice movements characterizes one of the challenges facing feminism at this time.

In an attempt to address this challenge, Fernandes (2003) introduced the possibility of a *spiritualized feminism* as a way for feminists to begin approaching their public and personal lives from a spiritual location to enhance sustainable social change. Fernandes urged feminists to develop more compassion and humility in their daily lives and establish a disidentified self in order to effectively create long lasting social transformation. Although introducing the concept of spiritualized feminism addressed a need in feminism, the author did not provide concrete examples of how to engage in such practices. Fernandes' oversight both confirms and perpetuates the lack of cross-pollination between feminist psychology and transpersonal psychology. The introduction of spirituality as a tool for social change may have been better understood had Fernandes included concrete spiritual practices based in compassion and self-inquiry practices (e.g., integral yoga or vipassana meditation). Some examples of such meditative practices, grounded in spiritual traditions (including Buddhist psychology, yoga philosophy, and esoteric practices) and transpersonal psychology can be found in works written by Walsh (1999), Metzner (1998), Durgananda (2002), Louchakova (2005), and Moore (1992). These authors among others contribute to the over 40 years of scientific psychological research based in spiritual and transpersonal philosophies.

Fernandes also neglected to include feminist spirituality scholars (Brooks, 2010) such as Plaskow and Christ (1989), Spretnak (1981), or feminist spirituality activists (e.g. Starhawk, 1987) in her book, which may have offered additional insights into framing a spiritualized feminist practice. A few examples of embodied spiritual practices inspired by feminist spirituality, which may have grounded Fernandes' approach in demonstrated practices include female shamanism (Noble, 1991); use of ritual (Starhawk; 1987); feminist research methods (Clements, Ettling, Jennett, & Shields, 1998); writing as a spiritual quest (Christ, 1986/1995); feminist approaches to religion (Plaskow & Christ, 1989); and the transformational qualities of the Dark Goddess (Woodman & Dickson, 1996).The lack of inclusion of feminist authors who have explored religion and spirituality further demonstrates the splitting within feminist camps with regard to this area of human experience and is a microscopic example of a macroscopic perspective in most mainstream disciplines including psychology, and a rich area of opportunity for transpersonal contributions to feminist dialogues.

Feminist spirituality authors address the diversity of women's transpersonal experiences and often ground these experiences in psychospiritual processes and earth-based concepts. One such approach to activism is through a consciousness of the interconnectedness of all things, which Starhawk (1982) called "*immanence*—the awareness of the world and everything in it as alive, dynamic, interdependent, and interacting, infused with the moving energies: a living being, a weaving dance" (p. 177). In addition, immanence is a philosophical underpinning that honors and respects the interdependence of all living things, maintaining a greater capacity for community and the ways in which one engages in activating social change.

Another concept strongly represented in contemporary feminist literature includes how the intersections of multiple identities within feminist spirituality allow for unique and complex perspectives. To articulate such intersections, a concrete example of a women-centered transpersonal perspective will be discussed later in his chapter. (e.g., Holiday's 2010).

As noted throughout this exploration of the intersections of feminism/cultural theory and transpersonalism, subjectivity is honored as a locus of knowing and development within both disciplines and serves as a specific locus of convergence in theory and praxis (Anderson & Braud, 2011; Jacob & Licona, 2005; Reinharz, 1992). To illustrate the lived, subjective experience as a means of example of such intersection, the following paragraphs contain an example of a personal narrative of feminist consciousness arising during one of the author's (Kendra Ford's) education in a transpersonal setting.

As one who identifies across feminist generations and was not raised with feminism but adopted a feminist identity in adulthood, I resonate with Kinser's (2004) description of "com[ing] to feminism *as feminism* on my own" (p. 127). I did not grow up in a feminist household, nor did I have exposure to women's studies while in undergraduate university in the United States. My deep plunge into feminism came in the past decade, during my late 20s when I was faced with a profound personal challenge that initiated a complete dismantling of my theretofore unexamined worldview, which when examined, was based on value structures fortified in patriarchy.

The reconfiguration process was instigated by a crisis of identity that caused me to question my foundational values and beliefs about myself as a woman living in American society. I realized during this experience that I had often viewed myself as an empowered woman, but through this time I began to identify the contradictions I was living. In one sense I was empowered; I was the first person (in addition to female) in my immediate family to graduate college and continue on to attend graduate school and I held respected jobs in my community, yet when it came to relationships with men I was crippled by insecurities enforced by patriarchal constructs about my body, how I should act, and the role of women in relationships. The lack of integration in my life heightened my understanding of how the constructs upon which I was basing my decisions, no longer applied to my actual identity. Learning this facilitated the urgency to decontextualize the patriarchal paradigm in which I was living and to develop a contextual language to help me consciously enter into the paradigm that I was creating.

My study of feminism, although supported via my graduate education, was initially a personal exploration, was practical, and practice oriented. For me, the practicality of studying feminism was to develop an understanding of what I was feeling and experiencing in my own life at a juncture of profound change. As I began to understand my own life via a feminist lens, I experienced a greater sense of freedom in making decisions, especially my body. I also developed a passion for engaging in social justice initiatives such as Eve Ensler's V-Day movement and felt it was important to incorporate practices (such as visualizations) to enhance my engagement in social justice work. My lifelong personal interest in spiritual matters had led me to a transpersonally oriented graduate program, and thus I had the natural tendency to assimilate feminism into spiritual and transpersonal psychology frameworks. Studying feminist theory through a transpersonal lens and a practice-centered orientation offered insight into the opportunities for convergence in both transpersonal and feminist practices.

As I had learned in my own practice as well as my education, I adopted an understanding of transpersonal psychology in terms of activism, the state of consciousness (as discussed earlier) in which one approaches social justice issues impacts the results of the action. For example, individuals driven to activism based on retributive action or selfish motivations may only perpetuate the forms of oppression that they desire to change (Fernandes, 2003). To create long lasting spiritual transformation, one must approach activism from a place of humility and compassion, and receptivity to the outcome of such activism. Fernandes (2003) stated, "compassion and humility must be understood not just as feelings or even ideas but as actual practices, practices that are a necessary component of this transformative social activism" (p. 59).

Such states of compassion and humility are functional components of Deikman's (2000) "receptive consciousness" (p. 306) and the mechanisms of a service-oriented (receptive) consciousness foster spirit "at a deeper level—with a reality much larger than our object selves" (p. 303). A receptive consciousness in direct comparison to an "instrumental consciousness" (Deikman, 2000, p. 303) is intentionally receptive to the surrounding environment, undifferentiated, open to spirit, connected with the intuitive self, and often communicates through the creative arts. A receptive consciousness is a state that must be cultivated on a daily basis so that every act permeates a level of consciousness, which encourages positive social change, both within the microcosm and macrocosm (Fernandes, 2003). Deikman described meditation as a viable practice for developing the capacity for receptive consciousness.

I adopted an understanding of transpersonal psychology as a scientific field of study concerned with human potential, and spiritual development, which can break down "egotistically-oriented portions of the self [in order] to accept the possible existence of other streams of awareness and perception" (Cunningham, 2007, p. 43). The integration of transpersonal psychology with feminist psychology prompted me to establish a deeper personal meaning within the two fields and ground the intersections within my own identity in order to heal myself and be of service to my community.

Holiday (2010), exploring the utility of intersecting transpersonalism and womanism, also insisted that psychospiritual models of health and healing must be situation, identity, and location specific. *Womanist* is a term coined by Alice Walker in 1979 and has blossomed into a movement dedicated to exploring and giving voice to the rich lived experience of women of color. Womanist psychological practice thus focuses on:

> three conduits to emotional healing that resonate with womanist values: the word, the body, and the kinfolk. These paths acknowledge the importance of using narrative and testimony, engaging the body as an ally, and remembering the individual in the context of her community in the development of more culturally competent therapeutic tools. (Holiday, 2010, p. 112)

A crucial component of womanist thought is that a womanist "loves the Spirit" (Holiday, 2010, p. 103). To this end, Holiday argued, transpersonalism and woman-ism have natural affinity as schools of thought since both disciplines value spirituality as a key component of human experience. In addition, she noted three other areas of intersection.

> Both womanist and transpersonal approaches (a) value lived experience as a valid source of data, (b) challenge paradigms that privilege mainstream assumptions (e.g., regarding the validity of including spirituality in psychology or the study of entheogens), and (c) offer empowering contexts for experiences that are often pathologized. (Holiday, 2010, p. 105)

Holiday also drew upon concepts of engaged spirituality and liberation psychol-ogy (Comas-Diaz, 2007; Martin-Baró, 1994) to inform her transpersonal womanist perspectives. It is through the spiritual life or via spiritual practice that personal trans-formation as well as social action and resistance to oppression can take place.

Such personal narratives as those above, are ways in which both transpersonal psychology and feminist philosophy and practice, have questioned the mechanistic-rationalistic thinking in science and technology that dominates current discourse (Haraway, 1985; King, 2002) and may occlude a clear view of situated spiritual experi-ence on both the individual and collective levels. As noted earlier, feminist and cultural lenses bring to the transpersonal context/situation specific markers for viewing spiri-tual and exceptional human experiences within socially constructed frameworks. Such a view invites opportunity for critical examinations of actions and experiences, such as a critique of the subordinate position held by women and the privileging of men within the hierarchy of the Catholic Church (Henold, 2008). This may create dialog that notices and names a social reality and fosters personal integration (Mustakova-Possardt, 1998) of potentially difficult material, while also opening up the conversation to the community at large.

René Descartes inaugurated the philosophy of the modern scientific age with his quests for truth and certainty. In Descartes' view, knowing the natural world required observation and reflection with the mind and reason. He did not rule out intuition or the senses, but rather felt that they had to be supported by some form of valida-tion so that one could know it as true (Ramazanoğlu & Holland, 2002). Descartes, among others, developed a way of viewing and understanding the natural world as part of a hierarchy that also held that there is a relationship between wholes and parts, and wholes are explained in terms of their parts (Fehr, 2004). This new scientific worldview produced an astounding amount of data that began to explain the natural world. Modern science further developed new ways of seeing order in the complexities and perceived chaos of nature, particularly through studying unpredictability in nature through the chaos theory (Fehr, 2004; Werndl, 2009). Thus the rational mind was prioritized and prized over the unconscious matter of the animal mind; the facilities of thinking and reasoning became the primary tools for making sense of the world rather than just responding to it. In the age of the Enlightenment and beyond the mind-body-spirit division became the accepted norm and domain of the rational and reductionist thinkers. Separating an event or experience from time and place produced a perceived objectivity; reduced to the space of subject and object, researcher and the observed, delivering a rational-mechanistic explanation. Empathy is then reduced as the observer investigates and explores with the mind, and not with the heart, losing rich data that may not be validated from an emotionally detached perspective. As Rosser (2002) pointed out, with regard to dysmenorrhea, that it was "only after prostaglandins were 'discovered' was there widespread acceptance among the male medical establishment that this experience reported by women had a biological component" (p. 231). Thus, even though women had been reporting on the bodily experiences of this phenomenon for quite some time (Fehr, 2004), it was seen as more of a *woman's complaint* rather than as something with a biological and hormonal basis. Little empathy was held for the women who were observed with this complaint and their lived experiences of it were invalidated, until it was proved that it was a valid scientific issue.

However, even science itself, or the idea of science, is a socially constructed reality, dependent on those who frame it empirically. This may result in a scientific authority becoming the social authority on valid forms of research in science and technology by granting them expert status. As Simone de Beauvoir (1949/1989) noted: "Representation of the world, like the world itself, is the work of men; they describe it from their own point of view, which they confuse with the absolute truth" (p. 143). This critique was echoed among feminist scholars in several disciplines, such as Sandra Harding (1986, 1991), Donna Haraway (1988), Evelyn Fox Keller (1982), and Helen E. Longino (1991), who in their writing on science and feminism pointed to the historical privileging of White males and the moderated presence of women and people of color. Further, feminist standpoint theories placed the relations between political and social power and knowledge on the center stage, particularly those that focused on the power relationships, noting that the power in science tended towards the privileged rather than the marginalized (Bowell, 2011). Those who have the power to name and decide what something is then wield the ultimate decision making power of whether or not the field is legitimate and comprises *real* science.

Therefore, if the cultural ground and specific lenses that transpersonal psychology uses, including an honoring of the subjective experience of spirituality and exceptional human experience are removed, the unique identity and narrative of the field is lost and rendered incoherent. Reclaiming the stance of site and culture, as well as gender, sex, ethnicity, and other locations of identity can reform and reinvigorate transpersonally-oriented research. One needs look no further than the research conducted by Mayoral, Laca, and Mejía (2010) on the daily spiritual experiences in Basques (Spain) and

Mexicans and life satisfaction. By studying the daily lived experiences of spirituality in two different countries and cultures, the authors were able to use the differences as variables in their research, and further, show that while culturally very different, daily spirituality for the respective participants was an experience relatively autonomous and independent of the objective conditions of life (Mayoral, Laca, & Mejía, 2010). Both Basques and Mexicans were studied in situ, affording a real time and place understanding of the country, culture, religion and/or spirituality, and gender of the participants. Removing these lenses would have detrimentally impacted this research.

Locating research in site and culture has been an important piece of feminist research, emancipating those studied from displacement, and allowing both researcher and those researched to claim their socially constructed realities. Feminists in the field of geography have led the way in reincorporating site and culture specific research as well as the need for empathy in working and researching others. Bondi (2003) argued that

> The concepts like introjection and projection, empathy and identification, can help us to reflect more productively on the richness of research relationships, including their unconscious dimensions. This is not about rendering the unconscious conscious, but about reframing issues of similarities and differences in order to use our ordinary experiences more fully, especially in our reflections on fieldwork interactions. (p. 73)

Nightingale (2003) gave voice to the concepts developed by Donna Haraway of partial and situated knowledges and the central idea that there is no one truth out there to be uncovered and, as a result, all knowledge is partial and situated, or linked to the contexts in which it is created. Therefore, as noted above in the consideration of participatory philosophy, the socially constructed assumptions of a psychospiritual event rest in the knowledge, culture, gender, race/ethnicity, and society in which it is situated, rendering attempts to divorce it from its context ill-advised. Scholars supporting the participatory view argue that when prised away from its moorings, spiritual experience is no longer the event it was when it was viewed in situ, and therefore no longer the thing or event about which knowledge can be sought. Rather, it becomes a new and different phenomenon now situated in a different and possibly incongruous or impoverished context that diminishes both researcher and researched (G. Hartelius, personal communication, April 30, 2012).

Efforts to relink mind-body-spirit via transpersonal theory and practice open the door for different ways of knowing. Feminist and cultural psychologies contribute to the transpersonal disciplines by creating a nexus of socially constructed views of spiritual experiences. When discussing transpersonal psychology, Daniels (2005) pointed to the various theoretical approaches that can be considered as predominantly immanent, with a horizontal or descendent path towards transformation; or a transcendent approach, which is viewed as a vertical or ascendant path. Within the descendent or horizontal path, transformation is sought out through connection to the natural world, the body, and the feminine (Daniels, 2005), in this case seen as a reclamation of historically female-associated things that were previously relegated to a lowly status, but now need to be restored in order to make a whole body of knowledge (Wilshire, 1989). Daniel's assertion, thus, further targets the ongoing dualism that informs the Cartesian logic of research and brings feminists forward as they reclaim the knowing that is inherent in the return of the mind-body-spirit connection. A valid critique by contemporary feminists points to the problems and pitfalls inherent in a generalized conflation of the feminine with the body, which often has more to do with concepts and qualities of maleness and femaleness, rather than being either a man or a woman (Wilshire, 1989). The subtle, and not so subtle, sexism that arises from this stance also gets attached to the value that society has weighted to the perceived desirability of the traits. This then becomes an often unexamined assumption within the field of science (Wilshire, 1989), which replicates a gender-binary theoretical construct that continues today in research.

With the introduction of feminist research methods that underscore the value of subjectivity and qualitative approaches in research, the researcher becomes both inside and outside the research, is included in the experiential, singular and plural, and within the construct of the intended research sees oneself and others, allowing fully for the contextual ideas of cultural and situation specific research as rich data rather than bias.

Organic inquiry (OI) is a qualitative, spiritually based, and feminist-oriented method of study which honors research as sacred and interconnected. OI is based upon the five principles of the sacred, the personal, the chthonic (in the earth), the relational, and the transformative (Clements et al., 1998). The intersections of feminist and cultural lenses are evident in OI. A core purpose of the method is to integrate psychological and spiritual understanding into research, honoring the processes of all the people involved: researcher, the researched, and the consumer of the research. OI emphasizes and invites transformation of heart and mind as well as providing information (Clements, 2011).

Bondi (2003), a therapist and Professor of Social Geography, spoke to the importance of observation and participation and the liminal space between them that "provides a way of understanding other people's experiences in the context of both similarities and differences between researchers and research subjects" (p. 64). Further, observation and participation relate to empathy and understanding as well as to the value of intuition in research methods such as OI.

> Empathy enables people to engage in the work of communicating and understanding aspects of their experiences across a multiplicity of differences. The similarities on which we draw reside primarily in our diverse experiences of this kind of interpersonal work: we know unconsciously if not consciously what it is like to feel similar to and different from others. We do not know what aspects of such similarities and differences will be salient in any particular interaction. Viewed in this way, our capacity to use our own experiences of interacting with others in the context of a whole panoply of similarities and differences is probably as important as attending to the particularities of similarities and differences of gender, class, race, age, sexuality and so on. (Bondi, 2003, p. 73)

The ontogeny of the researcher engaged in OI begins with one's topic and one's willingness to engage with the material in ways that requires the researcher to have developed an understanding of the strength and weaknesses of one's psyche (Clements, 2011). The researcher needs to be able to discern between subjective and objective, spiritual and material, and self and other (Clements, 2011) while staying present to what is arising and speaking to the researcher from the internal and external data in which one is immersed. The OI researcher's ability to take a perspective and engage in critical dialog with the social and cultural environment in which the research is located empowers the researcher who utilizes OI. In these forms of qualitative methods in which the researcher is the primary interpretive tool, socially constructed assumptions are made explicit and form a story arc that frames gender, time, place, and culture (among others), uniting personal and private aspects of meaning making (Mustakova-Possardt, 1998). Personal lived experience becomes the crux of the research and psychospiritual growth of not only the researcher and researched, but the readers as well, is a central goal of OI.

In this context spirituality, used here as the "deepest values and meanings by which people live" (Sheldrake, 2007, pp. 1-2) as well as transpersonal experiences, can refer to a potential dimension in all human beings, to the actualization of that capacity, and also to the study of that dimension via the research undertaken (King, 2002). Therefore the transpersonal events or moments can be explicit in the transformational effect or meaning it has on those involved (Daniels, 2005) and provide a wealth of data formerly ignored or discarded for not fitting a mechanistic model. The benefits of utilizing transpersonal material in research on human experience is threefold: (1) inquiry becomes a vehicle of transformation for self and others which may bring about social change; (2) social, political, and cultural contexts become part of the climate of the research, allowing for consideration of and acknowledgement of the impact of time and place (the lived realities of the researcher and those researched); and (3) the breakdown of certainty and rationality allow for the possibility of new research methods that hold the impossible as probable and welcomes the challenge to construct theory around transpersonal experiences, practices, or beliefs.

As Anderson and Braud (2011) noted,

> In addition to *information,* research can provide opportunities for *transformation.* Such transformation—in the form of important, meaningful, and sometimes profound changes in one's attitudes and views of oneself and of the world at large—can occur in the researcher or scholar; other participants, including colleagues and research participants; the readers or audience of the report; and even in the society or culture in which the research or scholar is situated. In the forms in which research is typically is conducted, transformative changes sometimes may occur as spontaneous, unintended side effects or aftereffects of a research project. (p. xv; emphasis in the original work)

Another research method developed within the transpersonal field and influenced by feminist concepts is Intuitive Inquiry (II). This method brings the compassionate heart to scientific inquiry and a renewed intentionality to the sciences (Anderson, 1998). II is a hermeneutic research approach that uses five cycles of iterative interpretation informed by intuition. The five cycles create an environment of inductive theory building that invites a deep commitment to the chosen topic and what it will reveal. Research becomes fluid and creative, and while the cycles here are iterative they do not reduce the material to one single causation at the smallest or lowest possible level. II is a deeply involved process that engages multiple aspects of the researcher as the topic is explored and moves from initial discovery of the topic to the final presentation of the data. The passion that informs the cycles leads to a unique form of inquiry and research that is intuitive and spiral, allowing ideas and materials to be revisited at certain specific points within the research process. Once again the specific cultural lenses of the researcher inform the what, how, and why of the research and also allows for a scope that is both deep and broad. The uses of "transpersonal skills such as intuition and alternative states of consciousness" (Braud & Anderson, 1998, p. 258) allow the researcher to (1) include data usually screened from conventional research, but here welcomed in; (2) assumptions in the case of II are made explicit and become part of the research itself, rather than being bracketed; and (3) the situational, the locational, and the specific are where the researcher resides and informs the decisions made in the process. Self-knowledge and outside knowledge become part of the whole of the knowledge discovered in the process of II.

In both OI and II passion is an important aspect of the researcher's choice of topic. Indeed, from a psychological interpretation of Hume, the faculty of reason (beliefs) cannot conflict with the passions (Phillips, 2005). Thus if one is following one's passion in the search of the psychospiritual it cannot conflict with one's beliefs, and is in itself worthy of research because it is connected to the researcher. In turn, this does not conflict with those invited to participate in the research, because they too become connected to the research and the researcher. Passion does not preclude science, but rather informs the inquiry, philosophical engagement, and method chosen. Passion further creates a dialog between researcher, topic, participants and ultimately the consumers of the research, which by the very nature of the cocreation of this dialectic, is socially constructed. Allowing passion to inform and invite the spiritual into consideration of a research topic broadens the available methods of scientific reasoning and pushes the known into the noetic without reducing it to a mechanistic model of a computer or robot.

As explicated above significant feminist and cultural contributions to the field of transpersonal psychology have emerged in research, theory, practice, and published literature. These movements incorporated into transpersonal studies, brought by a variety of contemporary scholars (as noted earlier), value and utilize personal voice and narrative in exploring and reporting on personal transformation, demand that research on experiences of transformation remain and be examined in situ, and foster greater diversity in understanding the nature and qualities of transformation. Transpersonal psychology is and will continue to be enriched by these many contributions. The work here is presented as a way to lead to a more useful discipline that adequately reflects the diversity of the world and allows the conversations that are necessary to ongoing growth and knowledge to continue.

References

Anderson, R. (1998). Intuitive inquiry: A transpersonal approach. In W. Braud & R. Anderson (Eds.), *Transpersonal research methods for the social sciences: Honoring human experience* (pp. 69-94). Thousand Oaks, CA: Sage.

Anderson, R., & Braud, W. (2011). *Transforming self and others through research: Transpersonal research methods and skills for the human sciences and humanities.* Albany, NY: State University of New York Press.

Anzaldua, G. E. (2002, October 11). Beyond traditional notions of identity. *The Chronicle of Higher Education Review: The Chronicle of Higher Education, 49*(7), B11-B13.

Bondi, L. (2003). Empathy and identification: Conceptual resource for feminist fieldwork. *ACME: An International E-Journal for Critical Geographies, 2*(2), 64-76.

Bowell, T. (2011). Feminist standpoint theory. In C. M. Bellon (Ed.), *Internet encyclopedia of philosophy*. Retrieved from http://www.iep.utm.edu/fem-stan/

Braud, W., & Anderson, R. (1998). *Transpersonal research methods for the social sciences: Honoring human experience*. Thousand Oaks, CA: Sage.

Brooks, C. (2010). Unidentified allies: Intersections of feminist and transpersonal thought and potential contributions to social change. *International Journal of Transpersonal Studies, 29*(2), 33-57.

Brooks, C., & Crouch, C. (2010). Transpersonal feminism: Introduction to special topic section [Special Issue]. *International Journal of Transpersonal Studies, 29*(2), 28-32.

Christ, C. (Ed.). (1995). *Diving deep and surfacing: Women writers on spiritual quest*. Boston, MA: Beacon Press. (Original work published 1986)

Clements, J. (2011). Organic inquiry: Research in partnership with spirit. In R. Anderson & W. Braud (Eds.), *Transforming self and others through research: Transpersonal research methods and skills for the human sciences and humanities* (pp. 131-159). Albany, NY: State University of New York Press.

Clements, J., Ettling, D., Jennett, D., & Shields, L. (1998). Organic research: Feminine spirituality meets transpersonal research. In W. Braud & R. Anderson (Eds.), *Transpersonal research methods for the social sciences: Honoring human experience* (pp. 114-127). Thousand Oaks, CA: Sage.

Comas-Diaz, L. (2007). Spirita: Reclaiming womanist sacredness into feminism. *Psychology of Women Quarterly, 32*, 13-21.

Crenshaw, K. W. (1991). Mapping the margins: Intersectionality, identity politics, and violence against women of color. *Stanford Law Review, 43*(6), 1241-1299. doi:10.2307/1229039

Cunningham, P. F. (2007). The challenges, prospects, and promise of transpersonal psychology. *International Journal of Transpersonal Studies, 26*, 41-55.

Daniels, M. (2005). *Shadow, self, spirit: Essays in transpersonal psychology*. Charlottesville, VA: Imprint Academic.

De Beauvoir, S. (1989). *The second sex* (H. M. Parshley, Trans.). New York, NY: Vintage Books. (Original work published 1949)

Deikman, A. J. (2000). Service as a way of knowing. In T. Hart, P. Nelson, & K. Puhakka (Eds.), *Transpersonal knowing: Exploring the horizon of consciousness* (pp. 303-318). Albany, NY: State University of New York Press.

Durgananda, S. (2002). *The heart of meditation*. South Fallsburg, NY: SYDA Foundation.

Fehr, C. (2004). Feminism and science: Mechanism without reductionism. *NWSA Journal, 16*(1), 136-156.

Fernandes, L. (2003). *Transforming feminist practice: Non-violence, social justice, and the possibilities of a spiritualized feminism*. San Francisco, CA: Aunt Lute Books.

Ferrer, J. N. (2002). *Revisioning transpersonal theory: A participatory vision of human spirituality*. Albany, NY: State University of New York Press.

Ferrer, J. N., & Sherman, J. H. (Eds.). (2008). Introduction. In *The participatory turn: Spirituality, mysticism, and religious studies* (pp. 1-80). Albany, NY: State University of New York Press.

Gergen, K. (2008). Social construction: Revolution in the making. Retrieved from: http://www.swarthmore.edu/x20607.xml

Haraway, D. (1985). Manifesto for cyborgs: Science, technology, and socialist feminism in the 1980s. *Socialist Review, 80*, 65-108.

Haraway, D. (1988). Situated knowledge: The science question in feminism and the privilege of partial perspectives. *Feminist Studies, 14,* 575-599.

Harding, S. G. (1986). *The science question in feminism.* Ithaca, NY: Cornell University Press.

Harding, S. G. (1991). *Whose science? Whose knowledge? Thinking from women's lives.* Ithaca, NY: Cornell University Press.

Hartelius, G., & Harrahy, M. (2009). Relational spirituality and developmental spirituality: Introduction to special topic section. *International Journal of Transpersonal Studies, 29*(1), 17-19.

Hartelius, G., Caplan, M., & Rardin, M. A. (2007). Transpersonal psychology: Defining the past, divining the future. *Humanist Psychologist, 35*(2), 1-26. Retrieved from http://www.informaworld.com/smpp/title~content=t775653705

Henold, M. J. (2008). *Catholic and feminist: The surprising history of the American Catholic feminist movement.* Chapel Hill, NC: University of North Carolina Press.

Holiday, J. M. (2010). The world, the body, and the kinfolk: The intersection of transpersonal thought with womanist approaches to psychology. *International Journal of Transpersonal Studies, 29*(2), 103-120.

Jacob, K., & Licona, A. (2005). Writing the waves: A dialogues on the tools, tactics, and tensions of feminisms and feminist practices over time and place. *NWSA Journal, 17*(1), 197-205.

Keller, E. F. (1982). Feminism and science. *Signs, 7*(3), 589-602.

King, U. (2002). Is there a future for religious studies as we know it? Some postmodern, feminist, and spiritual challenges. *Journal of the American Academy of Religion, 70*(2), 365-388.

Kinser, A. E. (2004). Negotiating spaces for/through third-wave feminism. *NWSA Journal, 16*(3), 124-153.

Longino, H. E. (1991). Multiplying subjects and the diffusion of power. *Journal of Philosophy, 88*(11), 666-674.

Louchakova, O. (2005). On advantages of the clear mind: Spiritual practices in the training of a phenomenological researcher. *Humanistic Psychologist, 33*(2), 87-112.

Markus, H. R., & Kitayama, S. (2003). Culture, self and the reality of the social. *Psychological Inquiry, 14*(3-4), 277-283.

Martín-Baró, I. (1994). *Writings for a liberation psychology* (A. Aron & S. Corne, Eds.). Cambridge, MA: Harvard University Press.

Mayoral, E. G., Laca, F., & Mejía, J. C. (2010). Daily spiritual experiences in Basques and Mexicans: A quantitative study. *Journal of Transpersonal Research, 2*(1), 10-25.

Metzner, R. (1998). *The unfolding self: Varieties of transformative experiences.* Novato, CA: Origin Press.

Moore, T. (1992). *Care of the soul: A guide for cultivating depth and sacredness in everyday life.* New York, NY: HarperCollins.

Mustakova-Possardt, E. (1998). Critical consciousness: An alternative pathway for positive personal and social development. *Journal of Adult Development, 5*(1), 13-30.

Nightingale, A. (2003). A feminist in the forest: Situated knowledges and mixing methods in natural resource management. *ACME: an International E-Journal for Critical Geographies, 2*(1), 77-90.

Noble, V. (1991). *Shakti woman: Feeling our fire, healing our world, the new female shamanism.* New York, NY: HarperCollins.

Phillips, D. (2005). Hume on practical reason: Normativity and psychology in *Treatise* 2.3.3. *Hume Studies, 31*(2), 299-316.

Plaskow, J., & Christ, C. (Eds.). (1989). *Weaving the visions: New patterns in feminist spirituality.* New York, NY: HarperCollins.

Ramazanoğlu, C., & Holland, J. (2002). *Feminist methodology: Challenges and choices*. London, UK: Sage.

Reinharz, S. (1992). *Feminist methods in social research*. New York, NY: Oxford University Press.

Rosser, S. (2002). Androcentric bias in clinical research. In J. A. Kourany (Ed.), *The gender of science* (pp. 228-236). Upper Saddle River, NJ: Prentice Hall.

Schroll, M., & Hartelius, G. (2011). Introduction to special topic section on ecopsychology. *International Journal of Transpersonal Studies, 30*(1-2), 82-88.

Sheldrake, R. (2007). *A brief history of spirituality*. Malden, MA: Blackwell Publishing.

Spretnak, C. (Ed.). (1981). *The politics of women's spirituality: Essays by founding mothers of the movement*. New York, NY: Anchor.

Starhawk. (1982). *Dreaming the dark: Magic, sex and politics*. Boston, MA: Beacon Press.

Starhawk. (1987). *Truth or dare: Encounters with power, authority, and mystery*. San Francisco, CA: Harper & Row.

Walsh, R. (1999). *Essential spirituality: Exercises from the world's religions to cultivate kindness, love, joy, peace, vision, wisdom, and generosity*. New York, NY: John Wiley & Sons.

Werndl, C. (2009). What are the new implications of chaos for unpredictability? *The British Journal for the Philosophy of Science, 60*(1), 195-220. doi:10.1093/bjps/axn053

Wilshire, D. (1989). The uses of myth, image, and the female body in re-visioning knowledge. In A. M. Jaggar & S. R. Bordo (Eds.), *Gender/body/knowledge: Feminist reconstructions of being and knowing* (pp. 92-114). New Brunswick, NJ: Rutgers University Press.

Woodman, M., & Dickson, E. (1996). *Dancing in the flames: The dark goddess in the transformation of consciousness*. Boston, MA: Shambhala.

35

Widening Circles

The Emergence of Transpersonal Social Engagement

Donald Rothberg and Katherine E. Coder

In 2007, Hartelius, Caplan, and Rardin defined the "psychology of transformation" (p. 1) as one of three critical components of transpersonal psychology. Further, they asserted that the growth of individuals and communities into "larger potentials" (p. 8) and applications, such as ethical thinking, service to humanity, right action, and compassionate social action, are aspects of the field. The emergent focus on the socially engaged dimensions of transpersonal psychology is especially crucial at this time of increasing economic, political, social, and ecological instability and crisis. Although some transpersonal theorists have made initial forays into connecting transpersonal psychology with collective transformation (Ferrer, 2008; Rothberg, 1986; Walsh, 1984; Wilber, 1995), this dimension of transpersonal psychology can best be described as *emergent* because a coherent body of knowledge has yet to be established. This chapter explores this emergent approach and includes sections on questions of definition and the use of various conceptual frameworks; the rationale for this approach; its psychological, social, and spiritual roots; some of the main examples and theories of transpersonal social engagement; research on the field; and critical questions regarding such an approach.

Defining and Situating Transpersonal Social Engagement

Transpersonal social engagement (TSE) is defined here as a form of inquiry and action connecting psychological, social, and spiritual dimensions. It is the inclusion and connection of all three of these dimensions that is distinctive. While many approaches exist that bridge two of these three dimensions—for example, one can think of social psychology, critical social theory grounded in depth psychology, socially engaged spirituality, and transpersonal psychology itself in its predominantly psychospiritual interpretations—TSE builds on such approaches, but goes further.

The Wiley Blackwell Handbook of Transpersonal Psychology, First Edition.
Edited by Harris L. Friedman and Glenn Hartelius.
© 2013 John Wiley & Sons, Ltd. Published 2015 by John Wiley & Sons, Ltd.

In this sense, TSE is concerned explicitly with psychospiritual development and its relationship with social engagement. Expressions of TSE are situated within a number of contemporary approaches that provide psychologically- and spiritually-grounded responses to social concerns. One can find versions of TSE rooted in more traditional religious or spiritual approaches, such as the nonviolence of Gandhi and King, liberation theology, socially engaged Buddhism, and various other interpretations of Judaism, Christianity, and Islam. In these versions, the psychological dimension may be rooted in a traditional spiritual psychology. One can also find expressions of TSE in which there is more of an incorporation of contemporary psychological, social, and spiritual approaches. Such examples of TSE are associated variously with feminism or women's spirituality; ecopsychology and ecologically grounded spirituality (Rothberg, 2011a); the integral, evolutionary approach of Ken Wilber and others; the participatory perspective of Jorge Ferrer and others; various more contemporary expressions of the world religions, notably the emancipatory spirituality of Michael Lerner and *Tikkun*; and various approaches grounded in other contemporary spiritually grounded psychologies, including somatic psychology (e.g., generative somatics), Jungian approaches, and transpersonal psychology itself.

TSE is distinctly different from fundamentalism. Fundamentalists, as with many exemplars of TSE, question modern secularization, desire an integrated spiritual life, and often analyze the spiritual roots of contemporary social problems (Rothberg, 1993). However, unlike most fundamentalists, the above exemplars of TSE generally place themselves in modern or postmodern frameworks and affirm (while often noting the limits of) the modern Western differentiation of science, democracy, and subjectivity out of dogmatic medieval religious worldviews.

The Rationale and Need for Transpersonal Social Engagement

TSE is particularly relevant as a response to a number of contemporary concerns including: the limitations and problems of modernity; a pervasive Western psychological and spiritual narcissism; the lack of well-developed connections between the psychological, social, and spiritual in mainstream psychology; and the necessity of psychological and spiritual development for those in social service and activism. In a sense, these concerns are all related to the importance of connecting the psychological, social, and spiritual dimensions—for psychologists, for those who are socially engaged in various ways, for spiritual practitioners, and for the general population.

The Limitations of Modernity

Modernity emerged in the 16th and 17th centuries, connected in the West with the rise of the sciences, capitalism and industrialism, democracy and individualism, and secularization; it can be understood, following Weber and Habermas, as based on a departure from the medieval religious framework in which all domains of life are unified. With modernity, there is a differentiation out of what Habermas called the objective world (studied by empirical science); the practical, intersubjective world (in which democracy develops); and the subjective world (especially explored in modern art, psychotherapy, intimate relationships, and modern expressions of spirituality). The differentiation of these worlds makes possible their autonomous development, separate from dogmatic religion, and the related projects mentioned above, what one might call the achievements of modernity (Rothberg, 1993, 2008).

Yet with modernity, there is also a lack of integration of these three worlds, and a generalized critique of all religion. The result is a marginalization of any remaining religion or spirituality as at best merely subjective, split off in various ways from all science and from social and political practice, including work for democracy and social justice. Furthermore, psychology is interpreted typically as a form of science, and, as such, separate from both the intersubjective world and the subjective world. In other words, with modernity, there is fragmentation—in this context, a split between the psychological (as scientific), the social, and the spiritual. In this light, TSE provides an approach that can support and integrate the achievements of modernity, while offering one way to develop the kind of integration that is lacking in modernity.

Global Crises of Modernity

TSE is also arguably one of the most powerful resources that might help us as humans respond with depth to the main *global practical concerns and crises* of our times—linked to a large extent with the systemic problems of modernity—such as ecological crisis, particularly global climate disruption; a high level of violent conflict; the increasing gap between rich and poor in the midst of globalization, with vast impoverishment (today approximately 1 billion people live "at the margins of survival"; United Nations Development Program, 2008, p. 25); and the weak state of global government and the need for further development of global justice and global civil society. TSE may help provide ways of developing postmodern ways of understanding ourselves and our world capable of going beyond the ineffective contemporary approaches—linked with hyperindividualism, and technical and capitalist responses to social ills (Kaplan, 1996; Loy, 2003).

Western Psychological and Spiritual Narcissism

Especially relevant to transpersonal psychology is the tendency of many Western spiritual aspirants to rest in middle-class enclaves separate from the vast suffering in other parts of the world (including places not far from such enclaves), in order to search for personal salvation or enlightenment through absorption in individualized quests and practices (Harvey, 2009; Nangle, 2008). For some, often interpreting Asian traditions, the world is seen as an illusion, a trap, a distraction, and a temptation (Woods, 1996). Spirituality in this light can be seen as narcissistic (Stanczak, 2006), rooted in the psychological narcissism of a hyperindividualistic culture (Lasch, 1979), distorted, and heretical (Rakoczy, 2006). TSE corrects such trends toward a narcissistic spirituality by highlighting the necessity of social engagement, and pointing to some of the psychological and spiritual roots of such narcissism, including what has come to be called "spiritual bypassing" (Masters, 2010).

The Limits of Mainstream Psychology

Watkins and Shulman (2010) explained that mainstream psychological models fail to place individuals and/or families in their sociocultural, economic, and environmental contexts. The authors argued that the role of psychology should not be "to help individuals and families adapt to the status quo when this present order contributes so massively to human misery, psychological and otherwise" (pp. 13-14). The pervasive positioning of much of mainstream psychology within the natural sciences, informed to a large extent by the so-called "medical model," according to which psychological problems are understood as analogous to medical problems, continues to block the field from incorporating information from "normalized power structures, gender relations, and ongoing cultural trauma" (p. 14) into its interpretations and treatments. TSE, as liberation psychology and other approaches, revisions psychological models and practices in the context of pressing social crises, while providing the further resources of spirituality.

The Importance of Psychological and Spiritual Development
for Social Engagement

Many of those socially engaged, including many operating from purely secular frameworks, have come to see the value and even necessity of connecting social service and social change work with personal, inner work, with various kinds of psychological and spiritual development (e.g., Zimmerman, Pathikonda, Salgado, & James, 2010). Such development is vital for a number of reasons. Such qualities as compassion, mindfulness, faith, and equanimity support the capacities for staying balanced with difficult circumstances. Working through "core wounds" and coming to greater psychological maturity and individuation similarly enhance the capacities of individuals and organizations to respond and function at higher levels.

Roots of Transpersonal Social Engagement

TSE finds its roots in psychological approaches linked with responses to social issues, traditions of progressive social transformation, and religious and/or spiritual traditions. Many of these traditions and approaches provide valuable resources, analytical frameworks, and practical tools, even if they do not themselves provide mature integrations of psychology, social engagement, and spirituality.

Psychological Traditions

Although lesser known today, some depth psychologies were formed with an "acute consciousness of social inequalities" (Watkins & Shulman, 2010) and their impact on psychological health and treatment. Many of the early psychoanalysts including Freud, Fromm, and Horney practiced depth psychology with "hopes of liberation on both social and psychological fronts" (p. 55) and saw the two similarly to profoundly intertwined (Jacoby, 1986). Critical social theorists associated with the Frankfurt School, including Fromm and Marcuse, linked depth psychology to social critique; the contemporary development of liberation psychologies, sometimes with spiritual dimensions, continues such an approach. Community psychology has similarly been concerned with community wellbeing and social justice (Nelson & Prilleltensky, 2010). Its central goal is to work at all levels and to accompany all in the quest for liberation and wellbeing. In addition, ecologically-minded psychology has often been developed in conjunction with transpersonal psychology (Esbjörn-Hargens & Zimmerman, 2009; Fox, 1990; Plotkin, 2003).

Movements of Social Transformation

Transpersonal social engagement has roots broadly in the Western traditions of social justice dating from the Jewish prophets, particularly the modern, secular expressions of movements for social change and social transformation, including democratic, socialist, anarchist, feminist, ecological, and civil rights movements, among others. In this context, social transformation refers to "intentional attempts to change a particular social group or some aspect of an entire society for the better according to some kind of shared norms" (Ruffing, 2001, p. 18). More recently, Hawken (2007) has asserted that we are in the midst of the "largest social movement in all of human history" (p. 4), which involves "tens of millions of people dedicated to change [and] ... willing to confront despair, power, and incalculable odds in an attempt to restore some semblance of grace, justice, and beauty to this world" (p. 4).

Religious and Spiritual Traditions

Religious and spiritual traditions at their best provide powerful resources for transpersonal social engagement. Out of such traditions have come the principles of justice, nonviolence, interdependence, and equality; visions of peace, reconciliation, and the beloved community; analyses of the roots of suffering and injustice; an emphasis on cultivating core virtues, such as love, ethical integrity, compassion, courage, patience, equanimity, wisdom, and awakening; and, the life stories of numerous exemplary figures (Rothberg, 2011b). In African and Native American indigenous traditions, a person can only become fully human and harmonized with the assistance of others in the context of the community (Mankiller, 2004). The individual and the collective in this sense are interdependent (Bangura, 2005). Although relatively unknown in Western and academic cultures, indigenous spiritual traditions have been teaching about and honoring peace and nonviolence centuries before Christian and/or Islamic missionaries arrived in indigenous homelands (Smith-Christopher, 2007).

Many of the world's religious and spiritual traditions began as social movements aiming to build compassionate societies and to address human suffering (Hawken, 2007). For example, following the Buddha's liberation under the bodhi tree, he eventually decided not to stay in his own private peace, as it were, but to enter the world to teach, counseling his followers: "Wander forth ... for the welfare of the multitude, for the happiness of the multitude, out of compassion for the world" (Bodhi, 2000, p. 198). This emphasis on compassionate action for the sake of others led to the development, in Mahayana Buddhism, of the bodhisattva, one who seeks enlightenment altruistically for the benefit of all beings (Śāntideva, 1997). In Hinduism, the model of karma yoga, particularly outlined in the *Bhagavad-Gita*, points to a path of real-ization through work and service. Karma yoga infuses its practitioners with courage, resilience, and calmness amid challenge, and was a key foundation for Gandhi's life and work.

In the monotheistic religious traditions of Judaism, Christianity, and Islam, ser-vice and social justice are mandated (DeYoung, 2007), often through prophecy, which combines contemplation with speech and action (Ruffing, 2001). The Jew-ish prophets, for instance, called for "society to realize God's will" (Armstrong, 1993, p. 352), and they forcefully voiced their disagreement with "what they saw as the transgression of basic ethical principles, self-centeredness, greed, a lack of compas-sion for those who were suffering, and moral and spiritual hypocrisy" (p. 353). Jesus, continuing the approach of the prophets, prescribed universal compassion and the "centrality of love in responding to the suffering of the world" (Rothberg, 2006, p. 100). Similarly, for most Muslims, the Prophet Muhammad is the archetypal exam-ple of a human being of highly developed character concerned with issues of morality, social justice, oppression, and humanitarianism. As a Prophet, he was considered a moral and social reformer, teaching justice and equality, and setting the example to be followed by all Muslims.

Some Main Approaches to Transpersonal Social Engagement

Those who have developed frameworks that can be identified, at least generally, with TSE include the following approaches: engaged spirituality (Stanczak, 2006); contemplation in action (Rohr, 2009); consciousness-in-action (Quiñones Rosado, 2007); liberation psychologies (Watkins & Shulman, 2010); deep ecology (e.g., Got-tlieb, 2001); ecofeminism (e.g., Diamond & Orenstein, 1990); the "work that recon-nects" (Macy & Johnstone, 2012); integral ecology (Esbjörn-Hargens & Zimmer-man, 2009); integral international development (Hochachka, 2007); mystic activism (DeYoung, 2004); sacred activism (Harvey, 2009); subtle activism (Nicol, 2010); socially engaged Buddhism and integrative spirituality (Rothberg, 2006, 2008); and spiritually advanced social change (Coder, 2011). A brief focus on several of these approaches will serve to illustrate the wider genre.

Liberation Psychologies

Watkins and Shulman (2010) defined liberation psychologies as "ideas, practices, and projects that nurture an imagination of alternative ways of thinking and acting together that can transform participation in social, economic, and ecological change and address psychological sufferings" (p. 3). Developing the concept of psychologies of liberation of liberation is based in the idea that psychological approaches must locate themselves in historical and cultural contexts and that much healing arises from "family, small group, and community-based dialogical approaches to psychological well-being" (p. 6). Liberation psychologists work from a paradigm of interdepen-dence and hope for "peaceful, just, and ecologically vibrant communities that support psychological well-being" (p. 10). The liberation of one is seen as integral to the liberation of all. Although liberation psychologies do not generally include an explicit foundation in spiritual teachings, the authors articulate a larger spiritual framing of this field combining both *"tikkun nefesh,* repair of our souls, and *tikkun olam,* repair of the world through our relations with others and nature" (p. 335).

Sacred Activism

Sacred activism, as articulated by Andrew Harvey (2009), is defined as "the joy of compassionate service ... married to a practical and pragmatic drive to transform all existing economic, social, and political institutions [in] a radical and potentially all-transforming holy force" (p. xviii). Sacred activism is oriented toward radical personal and collective transformation and is the marriage of "transcendent and immanent divine consciousness and bliss consciousness and peace, with actions of illumined compassion" (p. 70). Sacred activism is made possible through commitment to daily spiritual practices, surrendering to the divine, transforming anger, commitment to shadow work, and engaging in what Harvey has called "networks of grace" (p. 209). Networks of grace members commit to personal spiritual practices and group practice, strive to uplift one another, vow to commit to causes together, and find methods to handle shadow material.

The Work That Reconnects

One of the most influential approaches linking psychological, social, and spiritual perspectives has been the work of Joanna Macy and her colleagues, collected in recent years as "The Work that Reconnects" (Macy & Johnstone, 2012). Grounded in psychological insight into denial and repression in relationship to the pain of collective issues (initially the threat of nuclear war in the 1970s and 1980s), there are theories and practices to help access such pain, often allowing the surfacing of individual, community-related, and collective material that has long been stuck or inaccessible. This accessing of pain is situated in a larger framework offering numerous innovative practices, as well as an elegant theory of transformation that also includes invoking appreciation and gratitude before accessing painful realities, learning to see in a new way, and developing practical applications in the world.

Applications of Integral Theory

Integral theory is the result of almost 40 years of inter- and transdisciplinary scholarship in which Ken Wilber and others have integrated knowledge from a wide range of domains, including, spirituality, psychology, philosophy, anthropology, biology, and sociology (Brown, 2006). The integral framework is comprised of five major components—states, stages, lines, quadrants, and types—that can be examined in four major domains: interior-individual (e.g., psychological, spiritual); interior-collective (e.g., cultural); exterior-individual (e.g., behavioral); and exterior-collective (e.g., systemic, related to social structures). In addition, integral theory offers a multiperspectival framework for empirical investigation. One can find applications of integral theory connecting psychological, social, and spiritual dimensions in, for example, approaches

to consciousness-in-action (Quiñones Rosado, 2007); integral international development (Hochachka, 2007); integral ecology (Esbjörn-Hargens & Zimmerman, 2009);
and integral sustainability (Brown, 2006).

Socially Engaged Buddhism and Integrative Spirituality

Rothberg (2006, 2012) has outlined a model of socially engaged spirituality based on
Buddhism, with three domains of practice—individual, relational, and collective. He
outlined 10 core transformative areas, including ethical practice, developing mindfulness in action, clarifying and setting intentions, opening to suffering, balancing
taking care of self and helping others, working with "opponents," cultivating a sense
of interdependence, transforming anger, and acting with equanimity. Critical to spiritual practice is the understanding that each practice domain—individual, relational,
and collective—interpenetrates the other domains, producing a matrix of nine types
of spiritual practice, such that "our spiritual practice is increasingly *seamless*" (Rothberg, 2008, p. 362). For example, one might do purely "inner" practices focusing on
exploring sensations, emotions, and thoughts as such, or bring in practices to explore
how relational (e.g., family or community) and collective experiences and ideologies
(e.g., racism, sexism, or consumerism) influence inner experiences.

Spiritually Advanced Social Change

Coder (2011) has presented a potential form of transpersonal social engagement that
is based on her study of exemplars of what can be called "mystic activism." What
she called "spiritually advanced social change" is comprised of interdependent processes of interior-individuality, exterior-individuality, and sociocultural milieus that
potentiate healthy individual and sociocultural transformation. Coder's model highlights the importance of personal and spiritual development in social engagement, and
she noted its necessity in maintaining healthy interpersonal relationships, developing
resilience and stamina for challenging situations, and mitigating the effects of stress.
This model suggests that combining psychospiritual development with social activism
is synergistic, offering evidence for the validity of transpersonal social engagement as
an intervention.

Research Findings Regarding Transpersonal
Social Engagement

While empirical investigations in transpersonal social engagement are few (Coder,
2011), a number of studies reveal important findings for this emerging field. DeYoung
(2004), for example, used a combination of historical research, biography, and social
scientific portraiture to examine the lives of three mystic activists. He uncovered four
major themes:

> (1) They were motivated by their religious faith; (2) they had a worldview that emerged
> from the margins of society; (3) their identity was rooted in a belief that we share
> a common humanity; and (4) they embraced an ethics of revolution that demanded
> structural change. (p. 10)

The study revealed that the mystic-activists did not separate their faith from social justice or political action, remained hopeful, approached faiths outside their own, and found rest and renewal in spiritual practices.

Burdge (2006) studied four exemplary religious peace activists in Israel, utilizing psychological phenomenology to discern the essential experiences of spiritually-oriented peace activists working within a region of cross-cultural conflict. She looked for a relationship between peace activism and religious or spiritual experience. Results revealed a common phenomenological structure that included:

> a heart-centered open receptivity to experiences of self, others, and the Divine; an inability to psychically compartmentalize memories or experiences; a yearning to learn from differing others as a path towards deeper spiritual and self understanding; a deep inner awareness and connection with an internal sense of self that is experienced as divinely infused with universal human understandings; a consistently active spirituality-based moral filter through which actions are evaluated; an ability to sense similarities across apparent orientational divides; and a nearly continuous connection with love as a motivation for and appraiser of potential actions. (pp. iii-iv)

Walworth's (2008) research utilized biographical inquiry to study the lives of two contemporary "spiritually-based social activists" (p. iii) in order to understand the phenomenon of engaged spiritual life. Relevant to transpersonal social engagement are Walworth's findings that socially engaged spirituality is "an interconnected, multifaceted, cross-cultural movement" (p. 356) which points to the "indivisibility of spirituality and social transformation" (p. 357).

Coder (2011, 2012) studied three exemplary spiritually advanced social change agents using a hybrid methodology of constructivist grounded theory and multiple case studies. In addition to the findings aforementioned, the cross-case analysis suggested that personal change was being catalyzed as the individual experiences and personality traits of change agents met outward actions in social contexts. Catalyzing personal change was identified as an intrinsic process, which when combined with catalyzing sociocultural change, seemed to lead to a dynamic, living macroprocess that yielded ongoing individual and sociocultural transformations. The exemplars believed that combining spiritual and social engagement was critical for their own needs, and each supported this connection in the social movements in which they were involved. This analysis suggested that the exemplars mitigated stress and resisted experiences of compassion fatigue (and burnout) through resilience; committed, long-term spiritual practice was a key component in the development of such resilience.

Brenner and Homonoff (2004) utilized grounded theory to explore the influence of Zen Buddhist meditation practice on clinical social work and examined the practitioners' "practice framework, clinical practice, and interactions within larger systems" (p. 261). The data analysis revealed themes of increased awareness and attunement; acceptance of varied perspectives in clients and colleagues and a nonjudgmental stance; and responsibility, which involved seeing clearly and taking appropriate action.

Golden, Piedmont, Ciarrochi, and Rodgerson (2004) studied burnout in clergy using a composite index of three questionnaires and a hierarchical multiple regression analysis. Results showed that spirituality, particularly the "individual's perceived relationship with God" (p. 123), "showed incremental significance in predicting burnout even when controlling for personality and work environment" (p. 115). Their study supports the tenet that spirituality can help social change activists handle stress and develop resilience.

Spirit in Action (2005) evaluated their Circles of Change program, which yielded a thick description of the meaning of spirituality in activism and details of the barriers to its incorporation in social change work. The analysis revealed that connection to Spirit engenders an inclusive environment, shifts in individual consciousness that support connectedness, and access to inner supportive resources. The study found that many aspects of activist culture—the presence of limiting conceptions of Spirit, homophobic and/or sexist religious messaging, and religious persons' fear of harming others—served as barriers to the inclusion of spirituality in activism.

Stanczak and Miller's (2002) qualitative research identified and examined the connection between social change and spirituality, showing that the conversation about spirituality was beginning in academia, catalyzed by some of the most recent advances in psychotherapy, psychology, and business. The study concluded that engaged spirituality affects the "personal, local, and everyday" spheres as well as social networks, and exists as "a latent social resource among larger constituencies that do not have a viable outlet for this personal commitment" (Stanczak, 2006, p. 162). Spirituality and social change are determined to be synergistic, but spirituality must be "enacted through practice, through others, through institutions, through social structures, and through direct action to produce change" (p. 174).

Critical Questions Concerning Transpersonal Social Engagement

Given that TSE is an emerging phenomenon in a relatively early stage of development, most critical comments about it may relate to the degree to which the field has or has not met some of the lofty intentions mentioned above in terms of the rationale for TSE. For instance, practical paths of transformation are relatively undeveloped. Rothberg (2008) noted that most of the nine possible modes of spiritual practice identified in his matrix of integrative spirituality have yet to be clearly developed. Furthermore, most of the expressions of TSE mentioned above, including the approaches covered in more detail, do not fully integrate, theoretically and practically, the psychological, social, and spiritual dimensions. In many cases there may be more grounding in one of the three dimensions, with more rudimentary incorporation of the other two dimensions.

TSE has also been researched rather little. Only two of the aforementioned studies were situated in transpersonal psychology, and most of the research examining the nexus of social activism and spirituality were qualitative studies of exemplary figures. Overall, there is still very little scholarly study of social engagement and spirituality, and even less investigation of all three dimensions of TSE. Much more examination of this phenomenon is needed. There also remain methodological, theoretical, and practical challenges: How might one combine and integrate multiple methodologies (e.g., phenomenological and social analytical) to study *both* inner development and outer action, with attention as well to larger social structures and ideologies? Theoretically, how is it possible to connect psychological, social, and spiritual perspectives when there has often been a lack of clarity about how to understand the relationship between the psychological and the spiritual, the psychological and the social, and the social and the spiritual? Practically, however, there may have been more progress, with a great amount of innovation developing practices integrating the three dimensions, as is evident from the work of many of those mentioned as offering examples of TSE.

Another concern about TSE is whether it includes theories, findings, and practices generated from traditionally marginalized communities, and not just those from more privileged and/or Western academic locations. Although transpersonal psychology now embraces the use of feminist, critical, postmodern, and other non-traditional methodologies and studies marginalized communities, the field remains generally a place of privilege due to its lack of funding for scholarships and grants and the high cost of formal academic study (even as it is marginalized generally in academia). TSE is likely to remain relevant insofar as it continues to include dialogue and findings from a wide variety of global communities.

A further question concerns whether the integration of the psychological, social, and spiritual dimensions in TSE retains the *depth*—theoretical and practical—possible in each of these dimensions separately, at their best, or whether there is a tendency to provide more superficial expressions of each of these areas. How is the depth or developmental dimension articulated in TSE? Healthy forms of TSE will flourish if the resources from psychological forms of healing and inquiry, social analysis and action, and spiritual traditions, help practitioners of TSE to attain transformative depth.

Conclusion

In living its life in widening circles, transpersonal psychology is growing into broader social and collective applications, and the phenomenon of TSE is emerging, in part, from the transpersonal chrysalis of almost total attention to individually oriented psychospiritual development. Including social engagement and exploring aspects of the interdependence of psychology, social engagement, and spirituality, offers great promise for transpersonal psychology, as well as for social engagement, spirituality, and, indeed, for the world.

References

Armstrong, K. (1993). *A history of God: The 4,000-year quest of Judaism, Christianity, and Islam.* New York, NY: Ballantine Books.

Bangura, A. (2005). Ubuntogogy: An African educational paradigm that transcends pedagogy, androgogy, ergonagy, and heutagogy. *Journal of Third World Studies, 22*(2), 13-44. Retrieved from http://gsw.edu/~atws/journal.htm

Bodhi, Bhikkhu (Trans.) (2000). *The connected discourses of the Buddha: A new translation of the Samyutta Nikaya* (2 Vols.). Boston, MA: Wisdom.

Brenner, M. J., & Homonoff, E. (2004). Zen and clinical social work: A spiritual approach to practice. *Families in Society, 85*(2), 261-269.

Brown, B. (2006). Theory and practice of integral sustainable development: Part 1-Quadrants and the practitioner. *AQAL: Journal of Integral Theory and Practice, 1*(2), 366-405.

Brudge, S. (2006). The relationship between spirituality and peace activism: Phenomenological inquiry into the experience of peace activists in Israel. *Dissertation Abstracts International, 67*(02) 0669B (UMI #3207583).

Coder, K. E. (2011). "Shaking the world awake": An interfaith multiple case study of spiritually advanced social change agents. *Dissertation Abstracts International, 72*(11) 0669A (UMI #3468891).

Coder, K. E. (2012). "Shaking the world awake": A constructivist cross case analysis of the phenomenon of spiritually mature activism. *The Australian Community Psychologist, 2*(24), 111-132.

DeYoung, C. P. (2004). Mystic-activists: Faith-inspired leaders working for social justice and reconciliation. *Dissertation Abstracts International, 65*(10) 1064A (UMI #3149884).

DeYoung, C. P. (2007). *Living faith: How faith inspires social justice.* Minneapolis, MN: Fortress Press.

Diamond, I., & Orenstein, G. (Eds.) (1990). *Reweaving the world: The emergence of ecofeminism.* San Francisco, CA: Sierra Club Books.

Esbjörn-Hargens, S., & Zimmerman, M. (2009). *Integral ecology: Uniting multiple perspectives on the natural world.* New York, NY: Random House/Integral Books.

Ferrer, J. N. (2008). Spiritual knowing as participatory enaction: An answer to the question of religious pluralism. In J. N. Ferrer & J. H. Sherman (Eds.), *The participatory turn: Spirituality, mysticism, religious studies* (pp. 135-169). Albany, NY: State University of New York Press.

Fox, W. (1990). *Toward a transpersonal ecology.* Boston, MA: Shambhala.

Golden, J., Piedmont, R. L., Ciarrochi, J. W., & Rodgerson, T. (2004). Spirituality and burnout: An incremental validity study. *Journal of Psychology and Theology, 32*(2), 115-125. Retrieved from https://wisdom.biola.edu/jpt/

Gottlieb, R. S. (2001). The transcendence of justice and the justice of transcendence: Mysticism, deep ecology, and political life. In J. K. Ruffing (Ed.), *Mysticism and social transformation* (pp. 179-194). Syracuse, NY: Syracuse University Press.

Hartelius, G., Caplan, M., & Rardin, M. A. (2007). Transpersonal psychology: Defining the past, divining the future. *The Humanistic Psychologist, 35*(2), 1-26. doi:10.1080/08873260701274017

Harvey, A. (2009). *The hope: A guide to sacred activism.* New York, NY: Hay House.

Hawken, P. (2007). *Blessed unrest: How the largest social movement in history is restoring grace, justice, and beauty to the world.* New York, NY: Penguin.

Hochachka, G. (2007). An introduction to integral international development. *Journal of Integral Theory and Practice, 2*(1), 102-119.

Jacoby, R. (1986). *The repression of psychoanalysis.* Chicago, IL: University of Chicago Press.

Kaplan, A. (1996). *The development practitioner's handbook.* London, UK: Pluto.

Lasch, C. (1979). *The culture of narcissism: American life in an age of diminishing expectations.* New York, NY: Warner Books.

Loy, D. (2003). *The great awakening: A Buddhist social theory.* Boston, MA: Wisdom.

Macy, J., & Johnstone, C. (2012). *Active hope: How to face the mess we're in without going crazy.* Novato, CA: New World Library.

Mankiller, W. (2004). *Every day is a good day: Reflections by contemporary indigenous women.* Golden, CO: Fulcrum.

Masters, R. (2010). *Spiritual bypassing: When spirituality disconnects us from what really matters.* Berkeley, CA: North Atlantic.

Nangle, J. (2008). *Engaged spirituality: Faith life in the heart of empire.* Maryknoll, NY: Orbis.

Nelson, G., & Prilleltensky, I. (2010). *Community psychology: In pursuit of liberation and well-being* (2nd ed.). New York, NY: Palgrave Macmillan. (Original work published 2005)

Nicol, D. (2010). Subtle activism: The inner dimension of social transformation. *Dissertation Abstracts International, 72*(03) 0392A (UMI #3434800).

Plotkin, B. (2003). *Soulcraft: Crossing into the mysteries of nature and psyche.* Novato, CA: New World Library.

Quiñones Rosado, R. (2007). *Consciousness-in-action: Toward an integral psychology of liberation and transformation.* Caguas, Puerto Rico: ilé.

Rakoczy, S. (2006). *Great mystics and social justice: Walking on two feet of love.* New York, NY: Paulist Press.

Rohr, R. (2009). *The naked now: Learning to see as the mystics see.* New York, NY: Crossroad.

Rothberg, D. (1986). Philosophical foundations of transpersonal psychology: An introduction to some basic issues. *Journal of Transpersonal Psychology, 18*(1), 1-34.

Rothberg, D. (1993). The crisis of modernity and the emergence of socially engaged spirituality. *ReVision: A Journal of Consciousness and Transformation, 15*(3), 105-114.

Rothberg, D. (2006). *The engaged spiritual life: A Buddhist approach to transforming ourselves and the world.* Boston, MA: Beacon Press.

Rothberg, D. (2008). Connecting inner and outer transformation: Toward an expanded model of Buddhist practice. In J. N. Ferrer & J. H. Sherman (Eds.), *The participatory turn: Spirituality, mysticism, religious studies* (pp. 349-370). Albany, NY: State University of New York Press.

Rothberg, D. (2011a). The spirit of change: Spiritual and religious resources for peace and social justice movements. In M. Pilisuk & M. Nagler (Eds.), *Peace movements worldwide* (3 vols.)*: History and vitality of peace movements* (Vol. 1, pp. 113-128). Santa Barbara, CA: Praeger.

Rothberg, D. (2011b). Socially engaged Buddhist contemplative practices: Past and potential future contributions at a time of cultural transition and crisis. In M. Bush (Ed.), *Contemplation nation* (pp. 109-130). Kalamazoo, MI: Fetzer Institute.

Ruffing, J. K. (2001). Introduction. In J. K. Ruffing (Ed.), *Mysticism and social transformation* (pp. 1-25). Syracuse, NY: Syracuse University Press.

Śāntideva (1997). *A guide to the bodhisattva way of life* (V. A. Wallace & B. A. Wallace, Trans.). Ithaca, NY: Snow Lion. (Original work published in 8th century, CE)

Smith-Christopher, D. L. (2007). Indigenous traditions of peace: An interview with Lawrence Hart, Cheyenne peace chief. In D. L. Smith-Christopher (Ed.), *Subverting hatred: The challenge of nonviolence in religious traditions* (pp. 76-85). Maryknoll, NY: Orbis Books.

Spirit in Action (2005). Circles of change: Transforming the way we do change. [Report]. Retrieved from http://www.spiritinaction.net/Resources/circlesreport.pdf.

Stanczak, G. C. (2006). *Engaged spirituality: Social change and American religion.* New Brunswick, NJ: Rutgers University Press.

Stanczak, G. C., & Miller, D. E. (2002). *Engaged spirituality: Spirituality and social transformation in mainstream American religious traditions.* Los Angeles, CA: Center for Religion and Spiritual Culture, University of Southern California. Retrieved from http://crcc.usc.edu/resources/publications/engaged-spirituality-2002-spirituality-and-social-transformation-in-mainstream-american-religious-tr.html

United Nations Development Programme. (2008). *Fighting climate change: Human solidarity in a divided world. Human Development Report 2007/2008.* Retrieved from http://hdr.undp.org/en/reports/global/hdr2007-8/

Walsh, R. (1984). *Staying alive: The psychology of human survival.* Boulder, CO: Shambhala.

Walworth, C. L. (2008). Crossing borders with Elias Amidon and Elizabeth Roberts: A biography of engaged spiritual lives. *Dissertation Abstracts International, 69*(02) 1414A (UMI #3302966).

Watkins, M., & Shulman, H. (2010). *Toward psychologies of liberation*. Houndsmills, UK: Palgrave Macmillian.

Wilber, K. (1995). *Sex, ecology, spirituality: The spirit of evolution*. Boston, MA: Shambhala.

Woods, R. (1996). Mysticism and social action: The mystic's calling development, and social activity. *Journal of Consciousness Studies, 3*(2), 158-171.

Zimmerman, K., Pathikonda, N., Salgado, B., & James, T. (2010). *Out of the spiritual closet: Organizers transforming the practice of social justice*. Oakland, CA: Movement Strategy Center.

36

Modern Miracles from Ancient Medicine

Transpersonal Medicine Approaches

G. Frank Lawlis

As Joseph Campbell (1972) noted, people live according to their myths. Myths make life meaningful and make it possible to see life's challenges, including illness and disease, as events that communicate something about one's life and purpose. Western society currently has a set of myths governing the way that medicine is practiced and perceived that may well be contributing to less to good health than to its demise. At the same time, ancient healing myths that are often dismissed as absurd may hold the keystone to the future of health care.

Unfortunately, the myths that are refuted could potentially save lives and even souls. According to the World Health Organization's *World Health Statistics: 2011* (2012), the USA paid twice as much for health care per capita as any other nation in the world. They also reported that the USA ranked 39th in infant mortality, 43rd in adult female mortality and 42nd in adult male mortality, and 36th in life expectancy. It stands that although the health care system costs twice as much, the current set of healing protocols/myths enacted in the USA are not effectively caring for existing health needs. In fact, society will be losing ground at an increased rate if there is no change to the paradigm. The entrenched model has created a "pill" taking society which is not producing adequate results and which creates a whole new set of problems of its own. Drug side effects cause an estimated 770,000 injuries and deaths in the USA each year (Ehrenberg, 2012).

Only within the last century has the human spirit been left out of the equation of life transformation within the Western set of healing myths. Instead, one is left to believe solely in the mechanisms learned in labs and academic classrooms. Throughout the centuries past, various models of healing have been strained out from the acceptable societal norm by the dictates of authority, religion, or scientific-based rationality. The methodology inspired by today's health myths is to constrict care in such a way that the largest number of specialists can be involved; what might counterbalance this

The Wiley Blackwell Handbook of Transpersonal Psychology, First Edition.
Edited by Harris L. Friedman and Glenn Hartelius.
© 2013 John Wiley & Sons, Ltd. Published 2015 by John Wiley & Sons, Ltd.

approach would be to consider that healing factors are exponentially more powerful when integrated within a consideration of the whole person, instead of being isolated in a laboratory or classroom.

Two models are prevalent in the current health-care system. The first, and most relevant, is the biological model. The biological model maintains that a disease resides in the biological mechanisms of repair, and that healing resides in the body. The second model is a mental model in which the source of disease is separated out as a mental disorder. The mental models portray the disease as consisting of faulty mental processes.

This chapter deals with a model that has been a basis for healing from the first records of human history. It serves as a consistent basis in modern methodology for treating modern diseases. It is referred to here as the transpersonal medicine model (Lawlis, 1996). The ultimate goal of transpersonal medicine is realizing one's inherent completeness and divinity. There is an additional source—call it spiritual—which resides within each person and helps to unfold the capability to heal others and oneself if it can be cultivated and nurtured.

Ideally, medical treatment would allow the patient to heal drawing on natural internal sources designed to promote survival, and support these with well-designed external resources. It is sometimes quite difficult to break these two domains apart, and determine correctly which factor accounts for the beneficial result. For example, the positive results of taking a pill for a problem may be more dependent on who was administering the pill and how it was administered than the actual ingredients of the pill itself. Many times the administrator will take time to describe the actions of the pill in such a caring way as to build positive expectations. This, along with the power inherent in the ritual process of being administered the pill by a medical professional, may itself have a healing effect. In the book, *The Dairy of a Napoleonic Foot Soldier* (Walter, 1991), the author described a situation where he and two of this buddies were dying of a dreaded disease and the military officer explained that he had run out of medicine, but that he would write out the name of the medicine on a piece of paper and by eating the paper they would benefit. The next day they were well enough to continue their journey home.

Healing requires the will of the patient to change in the direction of potential wellbeing; it requires what might be called inspiration. From what sources can the human spirit be fed? The definition of transpersonal medicine is "trans" for "beyond," "personal" for "self," and "medicine" from "healing," or *healing from beyond self.* Perhaps the term could be extended to apply to healing beyond the ego of medicine as well.

Transpersonal Medicine/Transformation Pathway

Over a decade and half has passed since the publication of the book, Transpersonal Medicine (Lawlis, 1996), and new discoveries have been added with exciting components for the aspiring healer. One of the insights that has since emerged is referred to as the *initiation of intervention*. This is the critical decision to be healed and to embrace an action plan.

Generally, in medicine this is called the "diagnosis." Once there is a diagnosis, which is a conclusion of what mechanisms, physically or mentally, have gone wrong in the system, a plan or protocol is selected and followed. The practitioner creates a logical plan based on a conclusion as to what will correct the symptoms observed.

In transpersonal medicine, the "diagnosis" label is replaced by a "transformative charge" and the "protocol" is replaced by the steps or rituals that lead to transformation. The decision may be made by numerous avenues; however, the decision sets the person's single focus in life on the path of transformation. This transformation may or may not relate to a vulnerability to a disease per se, but it carries the urgency to change one's life. The catalyst for the transformation could be a vision, such as the burning bush through which God allegedly spoke to Moses to send him off to serve as a leader and guide to free slaves (Exodus 2-4). It could be a dream or a guide who leads one to perform curative acts, such as Dr. Phil and his "wake-up calls" to rebuild guests' lives.

The transpersonal moment may come in the form of a disease that serves as a catalyst for change, expressed through different thinking and perceptual patterns. When corrective behavior has been done, physiological changes have been reported, such as cancer tumors diminishing, the heart repairing itself and nerve regeneration (Doidge, 2007).

There is consciousness in every fiber of our human bodies. This consciousness is not just contained within our bodies, but also within everything around us. This consciousness can communicate to us through visions, dreams, other people or even such things as a "coincidence" that strikes you as significant, or even a medical professional that takes the time to listen, care, and provide an action plan toward health. Perhaps this is the essence or source of the "transpersonal moment."

In disease states, there appears to be a critical moment in which a person makes the decision to change, making available sources within and without. The decision itself is of enormous interest to transpersonal medicine because of its power to manifest changes in a disease. In alcoholism this moment of life-changing choice is often referred to as "hitting rock bottom." Conscious decision-making and the motivation to maintain the vigil of habitual change may not account for all the variance in recovery, but it is a major factor in all rehabilitation outcomes.

Antecedent Actions that Bring Transformative Moments

The antecedent conditions that lead to these transformative moments are categorized below, although many have co-factors:

Future prophet of things to come. As seen in movies or read in Charles Dickens's (1843) *A Christmas Carol,* The Spirit of Christmas Future frightens Scrooge into changing the way he hoards his riches, transforming him into a generous man capable of receiving and giving love. It is often a psychological strategy to give a future negative image to a person whose lifestyle is extremely unconstructive in order for them to see the damage they may do in their life and in others.

As the newest intern I was given the most difficult patient—as was traditional in the program. I administered the introductory tests to her as the usual ritual for beginning therapy—the fourth time in her stay with the program, because previous therapists had bailed in fear of her temper. Immediately following the evaluation I offered her my interpretation, if she wanted to know. She immediately responded affirmatively.

I ran through the called scores quickly and although the patient was a very bright woman, she asked for a summary. With a straight face I told her that the scores suggested that she was a spiteful woman full of anger and that if she continued to behave accordingly she would die without any friends at her funeral. (The scores did support this interpretation.) The patient was taken aback and looked worried. I reminded her that the test results could be wrong, and perhaps the outcome could be changed.

The next day she grasped my arm and asked for another appointment that day, if possible. She wanted to know what to do to change her future. We worked on her attitude and behavior around the hospital, including complimenting the staff for their support and using honest but supportive feedback. As she learned social skills, the staff naturally responded well to this patient who had given them such a bad time. I had not given the staff any feedback nor had I made any special reinforcement scheme. In ten days, the staff gave her a small farewell party for going from inpatient to outpatient status. The patient changed and gained several friends, and as things go, she learned to be happier. At year's end, I received a card from her saying that she had changed her life.

Potential seen from a higher source. Perhaps the most impressive moment came in my life when I was 15 years old, with a very bad case of defeat and acne, and a burning wish to make the varsity football team. My best showing thus far was as a substitute in the final moment of a game. A new coach came to me and told me that I could make the varsity football team if I wanted to. To me, it was like the impossible dream gone insane. But I believed, and buoyed by that choice, the inspiration of the coach, and hard work, three days later I made the team. Somehow, that coach was able to reach in and point me to the inner choice that I needed to make. For me, the experience was nothing short of miraculous.

A better-known story with the same point can be found in the gospel of John (5:1-8). In this story,

> Jesus went up to Jerusalem for a feast of the Jews. There in Jerusalem near the Sheep Gate was a pool, which in Aramaic is called Bethesda, and which is surrounded by five covered colonnades. Here a great number of disabled people used to lay—the blind, the lame, and the paralyzed. One who was there had been an invalid for thirty-eight years. When Jesus saw him lying there and learned that he had been in this condition for a long time, he asked him, "Do you want to get well?" "Sir," the invalid replied, "I have no one to help me into the pool when the water is stirred. While I am trying to get in, someone else goes down ahead of me." Then Jesus said to him, "Get up! Pick up your mat and walk." At once the man was cured; he picked up his mat and walked.

Christian tradition considers this to be a miraculous cure, yet regardless of how the innate powers of healing are brought forward, the results can be equally powerful.

Living another Self from within. It is a common ritual in many cultures, especially Native American tribes, to send an adolescent out to the unknown land beyond the village, draw a circle or drop a rope in a ten-foot diameter circle, and leave the would-be adult to wait there with a just a canteen of water until he or she has the vision of what he or she should have as their life mission (Harner, 1980). Whether it is in a dream, a vision, or some other mode of communication, the young adult arrives back in the camp with an answer. More often than not, the imagery or actual experience is with a totem animal, and it is that animal spirit and its attributes of strengths and talents that enable the individual to deal with challenges. For example, if a wolf visits and selects to become the animal spirit, it may point to the natural characteristics of a close team worker, family networker, compassionate caregiver, and powerful and clever hunter. The young tribesperson then dances the dance of the wolf and dresses in the costume in honor of the wolf in ritual.

Many cancer patients have taken a similar route in dealing with their diagnosis. The best example was a patient with Stage IV melanoma with weeks to live. He came to me with this explanation: In his dream "an old man appeared and told me if I wanted to live I was going to have to disappear and come back so differently that the cancer would not recognize me."

"How do I do that?" he asked. I told him that he could become his most mighty of animals, which I later found out was the tiger. He was to walk like a tiger, look like a tiger, feel like a tiger. This was going to be a challenge because he was a gentle man who was loved by everyone who met him, but he committed himself to this task.

After a bit of study he showed up with tiger shirt and walked on his toes in a very "tiger" way. He was friendly but not the way he had been before. He did not smile as broadly, and he chuckled without reason, as if he knew something we did not. He peered out through his half-closed eyes as if he was stalking something. He slept on the floor. And yes, his tumors disappeared.

Sensory deprivation. In this intervention, the patient is placed in an environment where he or she cannot listen to anyone or anything but themselves. The approach responds to the fact that most people develop their personalities and behaviors in sharp reaction, either dependent or rebellious, toward their parents and family. It is through interrupting the flow of information from outside the person that these patterns of reactivity may soften enough for them to become aware of their own destiny, and how they can serve the greatest good.

At the Origins Recovery Center in South Padre Island, Texas, where I spend a lot of my time, I built a sensory deprivation chamber based on my experience and needs. I have used a waterbed mattress with lamb's wool comforter for tactile deprivation. I pipe in underneath the chamber a drumming rhythm at a very low level to mask the touch and any noise from within. It is light proof and scent free.

For the addicted patients, I have seen remarkable results in what might be called their spirituality within just fifteen minutes duration. Many patients remarked that they discovered forgiveness for themselves and others, especially around Step Four for those involved in the Twelve Step process. However, the lasting impression is the discovery that they are aware of a personal self who gives them comfort and integrity throughout their days. Most important is they learn how to communicate with this internal wisdom and make decisions for life and change, even to the point of personal accountability.

Destruction of a damaging myth. Probably the most interesting of my observations have been in response to the moment when a person's cluster of myths are exposed and challenged. The television personality, Dr. Phil, seems to have the gift of enabling people to grasp the structure of their myths quickly. Of course, Dr. Phil's words do not exactly sound like those of a sage or monk. I remember one woman's face when she was talking about trying to control her husband's thoughts about sex and Phil interrupted her with a surprised look, "You can control someone's thoughts? That is really amazing." Then to her husband, "That would be so interesting if Robin could read your thoughts, especially if she could control them." The woman backed away from her statement, but as she did so, she reached the insight (with a little help) that she had a choice: She could insist on being right, and on believing she had control over her husband's thoughts, or she could enter the relationship based on an entirely new set of rules within their marriage. The latter would require that she shift her whole structure of beliefs and her whole way of being in the relationship.

Change in perspective through trauma. Trauma is a horrific shift from a positive life pattern, something one prays will never happen to their loved ones. When terrible things do happen, they can also be occasions for positive transformation (Wissler, 1921). Though the story may well be apocryphal, there is a tale that centuries ago the Egyptians develop a king-making ritual in which there could be a human-god transformation based on the shift in empathy with others (Knight & Lomas, 1998). According to this account, a potential Pharaoh would be held under water until he drowned, then resuscitated. Whatever the veracity of this popular account, Dr. August Reader (1995) has formulated how the brain reprioritizes blood pathways as survival preparation in cases of asphyxiation and drowning, which results in a permanent altruistic attitude toward life while changing behaviorally to be empathic and helpful to others in wise and unselfish ways.

There are accounts that various cultures have taken on physically challenging rituals in order to obtain similar results. For example, it is said that shamans in Ireland would tie a person suffering from depression to the back of a boat and drag them around the sea until they drowned. After the person was brought back (if they were), they would not be depressed anymore, and would be more than recovered (M. Harner, personal communication, September, 1990).

After the Transformative Moment of Decision, What Next?

Once the magic of the transformative moment of decision-making is done, there is an exploratory phase in which the new vista is brought into focus. What does it mean in lifestyle change? Where do I go to change my life? I have tried before and obviously did it wrong. Why is this different? These and other questions emerge as a person is brought to the edge of what may have been built from an early age. The question is: How do I start a new history? The following are transpersonal medicine avenues to a new life, as practiced from the most ancient of times to present.

Rituals. If you define rituals as habitual behavior, nearly everyone practices rituals every day; using transforming rituals is far from habitual. Transformative rituals are purposefully designed with transformation in mind (Lawlis, 1996): they have a form unique to their purpose. In the rituals I have employed, there is the initial phase that recognizes the universality of the need for transformation and the person is honored for their recognition for their insight and willingness to humble themselves to the ritual process. The second phase is when the individual makes the effort to change by verbal annunciation and action. To demonstrate they have accomplished the step and hence, their history, they show differences in their behaviors and even outward clothing.

At the Lawlis Peavey PsychoNeuroPlasticity Center (PNP Center) rituals are used a great deal, especially for people who have strong regrets that burden them with guilt and depressed thoughts. Participants use a shovel that I have painted gold and decorated with feathers—symbolizing flying over problems once relieved of the memories—to dig a small hole under a beautiful tree not far from the office. Before the ritual individuals are asked to write down and/or symbolize their regrets and fears in some way. The symbol may include a lock of hair or a small model of some fragment of the "mental baggage" to be left behind. As a group of support, the staff joins in a brief ceremony at what has come to be known as "Lost Hope Cemetery," to bury the small package. The participant fills in the dirt and says goodbye to his or her baggage and releases them to Mother Earth. There is always something that is changed in the clothing such as a bracelet of leather or a necklace. These rituals are important tools in enacting the life-altering decisions and insights that make up personal transformation.

Rehearsal imagery. Imagery is the basis for many transformative protocols, but in this application it is used as a path through the challenges of real change. The participant closes their eyes and focuses attention on (1) the problem or disease, and (2) the natural options one has in his or her personal situation, which includes personal strengths and environmental resources such as water, medicine, and so forth. Once these are exposed as options, the imagery begins with a typical scenario.

For example, suppose you are an addict to alcohol (the group most often researched with this technique), you would image a scenario in which you were tempted to take a drink. Suppose your trigger is being nagged by a person in authority; you would conjure up a scenario where you would be very tempted to go have a drink as an escape from that stress. The next step would be to think of at least three constructive ways to reduce the stress and not drink. For example, suppose you found ways to ignore the person through focusing on breathing until he or she went away. Or suppose you said something constructive, like "you are annoying me a lot and I can work harder and best alone." Or you might come up with singing or humming to yourself, making yourself better armed with each note or breath. Once you have a set of constructive options, you try playing each out in your mind through imagery and rate each as to how much you would use the strategy. Once there are good options, many people find that their confidence will increase significantly.

Sometimes the situation is a struggle against a disease. Drs. Carl Simonton and colleagues (1978) and Jeanne Achterberg (1985) developed powerful imagery exercises for cancer patients from their exceptional research in clinical studies. Achterberg and

Lawlis (1984) developed an imagery rating scale and found that for their 92 stage IV cancer patients those with high imagery were either in remission or their tumors were shrinking two months from the time of assessment, whereas, patients with low scores had deceased in the same time period.

Altered states of consciousness. One of the most ancient of healing methods is entering a different level of consciousness in order to find a new perspective on one's life. Certain types of altered states can offer unexpected imagery, helping the participant change his or her perception of the problem and come closer to a solution. For example, when dealing with chronic back pain, participants could meditate on their pain with the goal of finding at least one good thing from it that might be seen as a blessing. Success at this exercise has proven to be an effective discriminator of success in the program because ninety percent those who were unable to find one positive outcome of their condition failed to have a successful outcome. However, there were many who found some clue to relieve their suffering, such as forgiveness and developing new life goals.

Marriage conflicts are especially prone to resolution if altered states of consciousness are employed. After all, love is a state of consciousness that is different than crisis, and insight is certainly raised when a couple is able to discern issues from a different perspective. For a period of time, I used finger temperature monitors as a biofeedback device in order to confine the counseling to more of a meditative state. If one person became stressed a ringer on the biofeedback program would go off and the session would stop until the ringer ceased—which only happened when the person regained state of relaxation. I found that a ringer went off mostly when the person was lying, so counseling began to have a greater level of honesty that sped it to its conclusion.

I do not believe these processes of enhancing healing through the use of altered states are much different than those used in some pre-modern primitive cultures in their healing rituals. There are a number of ways of achieving an altered state of consciousness for constructive change, including those listed below:

- sensory deprivation (Leiderman, 1964);
- prolonged social deprivation and isolation (Byrd, 1938);
- extreme boredom (Heron, 1957);
- group trance (LaBarre, 1962);
- firewalkers' trance (Thomas, 1934);
- mystical and revelatory experiences (Wright, 1994);
- deep breathing experiences (Weil, 1999);
- sleep deprivation (Tart, 1977);
- dancing (Buzsuki, 2006); and
- listening to music (Levitin, 2006).

Old New Rhythms for Transpersonal Medicine

From the instant our hearts start a beat, our human lives and bodies run on rhythms. I have been captivated in the last ten years with the use of music and rhythm as avenues for healing. I have retold the story many times, but here is a summary of how I became aware of the power of song. During that time in my life I was newly appointed to head up a pain clinic as part of the orthopedic division at Southwestern Medical School and was very disappointed in my efforts to help these patients. By chance and desperation I attended a shamanic workshop directed by Michael Harner (1980), and he taught me a drum rhythm for pain management. I researched it under lab conditions and found the intervening processes involved the brain and stimulation of endorphin production. With clinical success, it became the cornerstone of my programs.

As I engaged myself in the study of acoustical factors that impacted healing, I visited and recorded hundreds of "healing songs" and chants, including some of the Native American songs, Hawaiian songs and rhythms, South American, Siberian, and African shamanic drumming. The complexity of the topic required me to divide my field of study to include frequencies and rhythm.

Life rhythms. In creating a program for Attention Deficit Disorder, my son and I developed a sound device (BioAcoustical Utilization Device—BAUD) that would stimulate the frontal lobes of the brain—imitating a signature of ADD (Lawlis, 2008). We showed that the people's brains were, indeed, stimulated and that they could perform higher levels of cognitive functions.

During a creative afternoon, I programmed my keyboard to integrate several rhythms and instruments with the same tempo to see if the result would help the ruminative depression of cancer patients with the thought that the brain might be trying to resolve some trigger worries and had lost its focus, much the way an orchestra might sound if they lost their conductor. I required that each person listen to the 22-minute recording at least two times a day. They could do anything they wanted while listening except watch television, which induces a different frequency. They could even dance to the music if desired. They usually had two therapy sessions during this period of time, in which they were assessed. The results were fascinating in that the positive outcomes were obvious but it took two to three weeks to see the differences. Even patients who would otherwise have been referred to the inpatient program blossomed with renewed energy and were very consistent in response. I have been recommending this recording for four years with tremendous success.

I later asked a group of psychologists who played instruments to come to my house to record various rhythms. One of these was a heart beat rhythm that lasted about 18 minutes. I reasoned that if this rhythm was the first one we ever hear in the beginning of our lives—the mother's heartbeat heard in the womb—then it must be powerful for creating relaxation and a sense of safety.

My perception of autism is that it is a brain development problem that can be worked with; however, what scares the parents are the "fits" and tantrums the child expresses when they are unhappy. Yet in my experience, over 90% of the time these children are acting that way out of fear or pain. As the parent tries to discipline, they only make the children more afraid and thus the child becomes extremely anxious. If parents could learn how to calm them, these tantrums might not be a problem. The autistic brain does have what is called sensory integration problems, which means they cannot process information as non-autistic individuals have learned to do. One ear may be faster or slower than the other; one eye may be slower than the other; one part of the body may be more sensitive than another. Their understanding of language may be slower, so you have to talk very slowly until their brain catches on. Basically they need a different pace to learning—and there are wonderful instructors who can do this.

A good example of how rhythm works for an autistic child can bee seen in what happened when Mary (not her real name) was being assessed, and something frightened her. She began to yell and run around frantically, pushing people out of the way. This was the typical behavior her mother described. We put her in a room with a bed that had speakers in the bottom of the mattress and started playing the heartbeat recording. As Mary heard the rhythm she became curious. She felt the bed and the vibration, crawled up, assumed the fetal position, and became very quiet. She had found a calm moment. As the assessments were processed the rest of the day, Mary would be taken to the bed whenever she became fearful—always with the same result. At the PNP Center we have given the CD to a number of parents with the similar instruction for calming the child down. Virtually all the parents reported success and said they were having a much better relationship.

My interest in rhythm continues, especially with the other rhythms designed for specific problems. For example, one recording uses marching rhythms with the thought that since this type of rhythm is used by the military to bring individuals into a community unity, it might be helpful for people who feel lonely and separated. When integrated with lyrics in rap songs, they led to some fascinating outcomes. Dr. Susan Franks (personal communication, January 2012) of the University of North Texas adopted the concept and we prepared three sets of lyrics to a nutritional program for 6th graders. This program was sponsored by Coca-Cola in its first year as a program to change children's eating behavior, and was called "Stomp for Life." The lyrics of the first song are in support of "Go Foods," the second is "No Foods," and the third is "Slow Foods." The *go* foods are healthy choices, the *no* foods are not healthy, and the *slow* foods are foods that should not be eaten every day. The children learned a short dance to each of the three sets of songs and beat out the rhythm with various forms of household appliances (toilet plungers, brooms, etc., or drum sticks.)

The results have been astonishing (S. Franks, personal communication, January 2012). The remarkable thing is that these children actually liked the class and voluntarily requested to take it again. Can you imagine children actually enjoying a class on the nutritional value of healthy food, when we are competing with a trillion-dollar fast-food industry every day? The second result was that these children learned the contents and could recite the intended content, and third, reports from the parents said that the children would start correcting them as to what food was best and asking for the good foods instead.

Frequencies of healing. In a sort of intuitive leaps that kept my interest in this aspect of the use of frequency in healing, the BAUD has emerged internationally as a device for treating fears, cravings, and pain. (Lawlis, 2010). The BAUD works on the basis of what is termed, neurohomeorhesis, for desensitization of cravings, pain, and anxiety issues. Homeorhesis is a term that means persistent pattern and/or same current, and in neurological terms would mean similar neurological patterns. As explained in psychology books, *homeostasis* refers to a pattern of balance to which the body and mind reverts when an event of arousal passes in order to restore healing/arousal activity cycles. For example, assume that a woman has been raped, tortured, or witnessed a very bad thing being done to her children. The event has been so terrible that the mind cannot comprehend such an event. She must deny it or distort it in order for her to go on. However, if her brain continues at the high frequency and cannot return to her state of balance, she will be in a homeorhesis state. Years can go by where she cannot do anything but struggle to stop this cycle. She will have nightmares, be under a reign of terror for fear things will happen again, and likely self medicate with anything that takes her mind elsewhere, such as alcohol or marijuana.

In essence the BAUD disrupts this homeorhesis pattern and allows the mind and body to resume in a balanced way. There are biofeedback readings that justify this interpretation and the quick resolution of anxiety states (such as post-traumatic stress disorder, PTSD) makes it clear that the return states are gratifying and well-learned. In 2010, at the International Society for Neurological Research in Denver, Colorado, I reported on 86 patients treated by 19 therapists in the USA, Switzerland, Portugal, and Denmark who underwent treatment with the BAUD for one or more sessions. A Likert rating of symptom severity was recorded before and after treatment for all patients, and three weeks after treatment in a subset of patients. All were significantly improved with most having no more symptoms in three sessions or less.

Ethics and the Journey Beyond

The journey of learning how to harness the power of transpersonal medicine goes on, and I will probably be questioned as to my choice of the word, "harnessed," in this context. If it is beyond the self, how can I harness it? And would I want to? In reality I cannot, but the myth of transpersonal medicine is that one can help to open the channel for this power to work. But there is a reaction to thinking one can possess its power. It takes discipline to understand the implications of the use of such power and how to use it with respect.

Some years ago I became entwined in the use of touch with my hands in the practice called Specific Human Emotional Nexus (Pavek, 1987). It is a system that calls for the use of human energy to help another person open up his or her energy flow to rebalance the body. I was very good at it. Tumors would disappear and pain would evaporate with the sensitivity of my hands. People would travel long distances to see me. It came to me that I possessed this power somehow. But I misused it many times for my ego. The myth occurred when it was clear that I never did "cure" anyone because they always came back. I would continue to see the same people for the same problems because I may have dealt with the symptom but the life dynamics were still there. The troublesome part is that I became part of the problem.

Because I was involved, many people refused to take responsibility for their own problem. When it dawned on me that one of the patients died because of this lack of responsibility that I should have insisted on, I backed out of the role of magician healer and into a more favored role as teacher.

The field of transpersonal medicine offers the basis for healing from within and it is often tempting to take responsibility for its outcome from use of the latest techniques. This can be the myth of specificity of healing acts. The secret is not in the single analysis of a single therapy but in the synergetic sum of all the parts of healing. This is the most profound statement of all: people heal in their own frame of reference and belief systems.

References

Achterberg, J. (1985). *Imagery in healing*. Boston, MA: Shambhala.

Achterberg, J., & Lawlis, G. F. (1984). *Imagery and disease*. Champaign, IL: IPAT.

Buzsuki, G. (2006). *Rhythms of the brain*. New York, NY: Oxford Press.

Byrd, R. (1938). *Alone*. New York, NY: G. P. Putnam Sons.

Campbell, J. (1972). *Myths to live by*. New York, NY: Penguin.

Dickens, C. (1843). *A Christmas carol*. Lexington, KY: SoHo Books.

Doidge, N. (2007). *The brain that changes itself*. New York, NY: Penguin Group.

Ehrenberg, R. (2012). Network analysis predicts drug side effects. *Science News, 181*(2), 12.

Harner, M. (1980). *The way of the shaman*. New York, NY: Harper & Row.

Heron, W. (1957). The pathology of boredom. *Scientific American, 196*, 52-56.

Knight, C., & Lomas, R. (1998). *The Hiram key*. New York, NY: Barnes & Noble.

LaBarre, N. (1962). *They shall take up serpents*. Minneapolis, MN: University of Minneapolis Press.

Lawlis, F. (1996). *Transpersonal medicine*. Boston, MA: Shambhala.

Lawlis, F. (2008). Using sonic stimulation to regulate symptoms of ADD. In *Proceedings of International Society for Neurofeedback and Research,* San Antonio, Texas.

Lawlis, F. (2010). An international study on effectiveness of sonic management (BAUD), *Proceedings of International Society for Neurofeedback and Research,* Denver, Colorado.

Leiderman, P. (1964). Imagery and sensory deprivation. *Proceedings of the Third World Congress in Psychiatry,* 227-231. Montreal, Canada.

Levitin, D. (2006). *This is your brain on music*. New York, NY: Plume.

Pavek, R. (1987). *The handbook of SHEN*. Sausalito, CA: SHEN Therapy Institute.

Reader, A. (1995). The internal mystery plays: The role and physiology of the visual system in contemplative practices. *Alternative Therapies, 1*(4), 54-63.

Simonton, C., Matthews-Simonton, S., & Creighton, J. (1978). *Getting well again*. New York, NY: Bantam.

Tart, C. (1977). Putting the pieces together: A conceptual framework for understanding discrete states of consciousness. In N. E. Zinberg (Ed.), *Alternate states of consciousness* (pp. 158-219). New York, NY: Macmilliam.

Thomas, E. (1934). The fire walk. *Proceedings of the Society for Psychological Research, 42*, 292-309.

World Health Organization. (2012). *World health statistics: 2011*. Geneva, Switzerland: WHO Press. Retrieved from: http://www.who.int/whosis/whostat/2011/en/index.html.

Walter, J. (1991). *The diary of a Napoleonic foot soldier*. New York, NY: Penguin.

Weil, A. (1999). *Breathing*. Boulder, CO: Sounds True.

Wissler, C. (1921). The Sun Dance of the Blackfoot Indians. *American Museum of Natural History Anthropology Papers, 16*, 437-444.

Wright, P. (1994). A psychobiological approach to shamanic altered states of consciousness. *ReVision, 16*(4), 164-172.

37

Transpersonal Experience and the Arts

From the Chauvet Cave to Occupy Wall Street

Lisa Herman

Music has an inexplicable way of elevating humankind to its noblest action. Music is the most durable of "cultural goods" and has stood the test of time. Art, like religion or other forms of cultural life, inspires and transforms—it elevates us above our "created" selves, our material, animal, worldly selves, and allows us to participate in the great adventure of Creation, not as partners with the Almighty, of course, but as His willing instrument. Everything a musician plays is an expression of Divine inspiration, and transformative for that very reason. Humankind yearns for the conscious connection to the Almighty which art affords us.

Youssou N'Dour (Cabinet Minister of Culture and Tourism, Senegal)

Humans from time immemorial have strived to open our body/minds to the transpersonal and share the extraordinary things that happen beyond pre-conceived possibilities. Through paint, music, words, and a host of other media we have made art, and thus helped manifest in the physical world images that arose after or while dwelling in the ineffable. Whether they are visual, audible, felt in our minds or any of the other ways we experience images, when we produce art we hope our work will evoke moments of extraordinary experience in others. We can be recipients of, or participants in, the creation of art, gazing at a sculpture or photo or participating in a dance or chorus. Through our engagement as creator or witness, we move beyond personal and cultural constructs and are allowed access to the transpersonal and what happens when we encounter phenomena beyond the everyday. Artwork as process or product acts as a change-agent when we are affected by it. We are moved to open to alternative states of consciousness as the different media allow us to engage with what we have previously not known. Often living on the edges of society, art-makers and their works challenge established notions of what is possible to be and do, and inspire us to increase our capacities, embrace more inclusive paradigms, and invent new ways

The Wiley Blackwell Handbook of Transpersonal Psychology, First Edition.
Edited by Harris L. Friedman and Glenn Hartelius.
© 2013 John Wiley & Sons, Ltd. Published 2015 by John Wiley & Sons, Ltd.

of living. Across time and cultures, the arts urge us to enter the transpersonal and redefine conceptions of who we are and who we can be.

Robert A. Hefner III, petroleum geologist and philanthropist, runs the Bradshaw Foundation and funded the filming of "Cave of Forgotten Dreams" (Herzog, 2010). This film helps make accessible art created 30,000 to 32,000 years ago, on the walls of the Chauvet cave. It was discovered in 1994 by cave explorers behind a wall of stone rubble. Few people are allowed into the cave as breath will destroy the work. Hefner (2005) has speculated that the paintings took their creators to superhuman feelings. Archeologist Jean Clottes (2010) has suggested there is magical, shamanic, or ritual significance to these paintings. In the movie, the filmmakers themselves testify about their own transformation in the cave, witnessing these paintings created millennia before the modern discovery. They are moved to the realm of the transpersonal as are many who watch the movie.

Making and witnessing art allows one to experience the transpersonal and also allows the sharing of that experience with others so they too can understand. Artists imaginatively construct sacred moments in the physical world and bring these moments to others so that they too can transcend the familiar, and perhaps move to constructing artful moments themselves; viewers, too, may become inspired.

Science, Language, and the Arts

As contemporary science and mathematics work to engage with what artists in the Chauvet cave seemed already able to express, some find they must use the language of the arts to describe what they know. As research generates data at an accelerating rate and theories to explain them become more complex, it is art and a transpersonal sensibility of meaningful connectedness to the whole that can inspire the elegance needed to make these explanations powerful. As the independent scholar Ellen Dissanyake has claimed, in her anthropological masterwork, *Homo Aestheticus: Where Art Comes From and Why* (1992), art makes things *special,* and is necessary for biological human change and evolution. Body/minds need to know that life as it has been assumed to be can be different. This is an important purpose of art.

Quantum physicists and chaos theoreticians perceive the physical universe artfully. We are living in a universe akin to a cosmic, vibrating symphony—in the words of mathematician, Brian Greene (1999): "According to string theory, the universe is made up of tiny strings whose resonant patterns of vibration are the microscopic origin of particle masses and force charges" (p. 206). He went on to say, "[The universe is] the epitome of poetic grace in which everything fits together with elegance, the multiverse and the anthropic principle paint a picture of a wildly excessive collection of universes with an insatiable appetite for variety" (p. 368). Science benefits from arts-based knowledge to describe the diversity of the cosmos and also the passion that shows through in the way artists express what they know.

Quantum physicists and theoretical mathematicians sometimes struggle to describe this felt-sense knowledge to others. They talk of that place of nonorder where order emerges. In their language they become poetic using names such as chaos, morphogenic and unified fields, web of life, whispering pond, quasitotal vision, and implicit order (Bohm, 1998; Briggs & Peat, 1999; Capra, 1996; Greene, 1999; Laszlo, 1996; Sheldrake, 1981). Transpersonal psychologists ironically use more prosaic terms and have called the transpersonal moving beyond the ego (Walsh & Vaughan, 1993); developmental psychologists have called it transitional space (Winnicott, 1971). Poets themselves may say the transpersonal is being inspired by a muse, and religions may call it faith (Carson, 1997; Eigen, 1993). Physicist David Bohm (1998) offered a reminder that scientific language "theory" and artistic language "theater" come from the same Greek root meaning "to view" or "spectacle" (p. 43).

Struggling to find language to represent what is known about the transpersonal through images in art and science, it is as if disciplines grow closer as they try to describe the indescribable. "It is no longer even appropriate to group biological, physicochemical, and energetic intensities on the one hand, and mathematical, aesthetic, linguistic, informational, semiotic intensities,... on the other" (Deleuze & Guattari, 1987, p. 109). We humans, in our multiplicity along with the entire multiverse, are made up of vibrating particles, each in our own otherness participating in the dance of becoming. The process of making art and witnessing it is the process of transformation.

> Perhaps there are two planes, or two ways of conceptualizing the plane. The plane can be a hidden principle, which makes visible what is seen and audible, what is heard, etc. which at every instant causes the given to be given, in this or that state, at this or that or that moment. But the plane itself is not given. It is by nature hidden. It can only be inferred, induced, concluded from that to which it gives rise....A plane of this kind is as much a plan(e), of organization as of development: it is structural or genetic, and both at once, structure and genesis, the structural plan(e) of formed organizations with their developments, the genetic plan(e) of evolutionary developments within their organizations....It is a plan(e) of transcendence....It may be in the mind of a god, or in the unconscious of life, of the soul, or of language: it is always concluded from its own effects. (Deleuze & Guattari, 1987, p. 265)

What is called the hidden transpersonal plan or plane as a location for transcendence, has parallel constructs in other fields. Some of these are: the tacit dimension (cf. Polyani, 1983), the implicate order (cf. Bohm, 1998), the quantum field (cf. Capra, 1996). What we as humans perceive in our lives is only a clue to what can be known. We, and everything that surrounds us, are particles and waves and "particles and waves are forms of abstraction from flowing wholeness" (Arnheim, 1966, p. 157). Particles and waves are the metaphors of scientists. Mathematicians speak in the metaphor of "chaos" (e.g., Li & Yorke, 1975), a formal term for a state of disorder. Artists know that states of disorder lead to creation and temporary equilibrium. Artists express this (dis)equilibrium in their work. This becoming/emergence of all things becomes art when the artist defines a boundary and presents a manifestation of what she or he knows. "A boundary is not that at which something stops but...from which something *begins its presencing*" (Heidegger, 1975, p. 154, emphasis supplied). Art is finding the right rhythm and the notes. It is order and disorder, particle and flow. Homeostasis alone does not account for evolutionary survival: We need to shake things up. As living systems, we need a "bewildering complexity" (Arnheim, 1966,

p. 183) of things: order and disorder. "The arts as a reflection of human existence at its highest have always and spontaneously lived up to this demand of plenitude" (Arnheim, 1971, p. 56).

Scientists and mathematicians are also describing the physically sensed world as artists might (e.g., Laszlo, 1996); physical reality can be seen as "a stupendous network of interaction and communication: a subtle but ever-present whispering pond" (p. xx). Artists often anticipate the discoveries of science: "Space and time, light and gravity, mass and energy are explored by physicists and artists, sometimes at the same time, sometimes one preceding the other, but seldom if ever in conscious knowledge of each other" (Shlain, 1991, p. 117).

Yet artists and scientists remain in relation to each other through their explorations of the transpersonal and together discover new ways for pursuing knowledge of who and where we are as humans. Bumping and jostling in transpersonal space, we encounter the images that create us. Our inquiring body/minds are vibrating structures engaged in vibrating structure with each other. "Human bodies ... are embedded in this ... field and are constantly interacting with it" (Laszlo, 1996, p. 211). There is connection "through a constant two-way *flow of images, thoughts, impressions and feelings,* and these shape (others') minds whether they realize it or not" (p. 221, emphasis supplied). The power of the arts is their capability to convey the images that unite us beyond our constructs of self and our present worldviews.

Fritzof Capra in his article, "The Dance of Shiva: The Hindu View of Matter in the Light of Modern Physics," (1972) and later in the *The Tao of Physics* (1991), beautifully related Nataraj's dance with modern physics. He said that "every subatomic particle not only performs an energy dance, but also is an energy dance; a pulsating process of creation and destruction .... without end .... For the modern physicists, then Shiva's dance is the dance of subatomic matter. As in Hindu mythology, it is a continual dance of creation and destruction involving the whole cosmos; the basis of all existence and of all natural phenomena" (p. 244). Yet Capra's comparison, although it draws on both science and Hindu spirituality, is itself neither science nor spirituality: It is an inspired vision of resonance between images from hard science and ancient tradition; it is transpersonal art.

Artists and the Experience of the Transpersonal

James e. Woody (n.d.), who has asserted that he is among the world's first proclaimed and recognized African-American transpersonal artists, offered this manifesto:

> I believe that paints and pigments can be approached as ritual objects, magical energetic substances, that we create a space for manifestation, we don't need to invent or devise from our minds. Painting or the ownership of them can be a meditative ritual, a ritual of affirmation and manifestation. When I am present with the actual reality of what I am doing, breathing, with a ritual object, my paint, paper or canvas in hand, only then am I clear what is before me. (n.p.)

This is his definition of transpersonal art:

> Transpersonal art is the symbolic reenactment of the abstract imagination, images of a timeless and internal universe, that are reflective in accordance with the knowledge of our time, organic expressions that demonstrate the eternal magic of the human condition. Transpersonal art is the modernism of the art movement, accurately reflecting the multiplicity of our reality, by expressing the realm of our primary meaning, a universal mode of consciousness that envisions life as sacred. These images may appear mystical, literal or conceptual, because the abstract elements vary as representation of the known, the less known, and the unknown. Whether you view Transpersonal art as simply a mirror of ordinary biological urges or as contact with other worlds filled with living beings, what is certain is they are our collective dreams and visions, the dramatic personae of our your own imagination realized as an independent entity with a life of its own. (Woody, n.d., n.p.)

The transpersonal, for art-makers as for scientists and mathematicians who imagine, is a way to understand there is more than conditioned physical experience of the world. This other knowing is sometimes called *intuitive,* accessed by a sixth sense or a muse: It is the sense that knows someone is standing behind you or that senses your lover will call at that very moment.

Mbuyiseni Oswald Mtshali (2008), speaking about oral tradition, suggested it is the poetic spirit that enables humans to rise above the level of other living organisms, and to use our mental, physical, and spiritual endowments to deal with the complexities of our universe. The poetic spirit can protect both the practitioner of poetics and the acolyte from even the most extreme of external pressures.

> [It] equips us with vital skills to deal with all types of conditions of life. A portrayal in words, sustained by the faculties of our five senses—as well as the sixth sense of balance and the seventh of imagination—sets us on an even keel, enabling us to face the demands of life and cope with the struggles of existence. Poetry brings us into unison with our surroundings, helping create a rhythm with the cosmos, so that we can live in harmony with other living beings in an ideal environment. We invoke the help of the sun, the moon, the stars, mountains and rivers. (n.p.)

Alex Grey, painter, sculpture and performance artist, provided this description of art and its relationship to the transpersonal in an interview with Steve Brooks (1999):

> I think the mission of art is to embrace some personal sense of the transpersonal. Sacred art crystallizes a kind of revelatory power that reinforces our own sense of the depth of the meaning of life and our predicament here. When art can do that, not just expressing the small self, but expressing the larger collective soul and helping to entrain people to a greater reality, it's beneficial. Art looks at the deepest level, which involves intensive self-examination and examination of the world, so that one can gear into spiritual domains. (n.p.)

The transpersonal may be where the mathematicians put imaginary numbers and it is the place where muses and their children, images, live. It is a creative field that does not exist in linear time, being ever-present, waiting for an artist/witness/scientist to manifest its products—the images—so they can present themselves as a theory or a painting or a dance. The transpersonal for the artist is a pulsating, living, evolving space that creates patterns and becomes chaotic to create new patterns. It is poetic space. The transpersonal is polyphony: noisy, exciting, surprising, dangerous, illogical/logical, loving, destroying, deeply engaging.

It is intense/dense in the transpersonal. It is boundless and can contain everything. Artists are "thus in the act of fitting an ever-changing reality so that there is no fixed or final goal to be attained. Rather, at each moment the end and the means are both to be described as the action of making every aspect fit" (Bohm, 1998, p. 86). The transpersonal for the artist is aesthetic space. It is a wild beauty

> that has no practical use: it never tells us what to do. It carries no directive action, but forces us to go beyond the useful, encounter the unexpected, and become aware of the unsolvable riddle of our existence. We lose mastery in the presence of beauty because there is no mastery to hold on to. The mastery is one of being there and acting. (Jacoby, 1999, p. 61)

In this space, where there are patterns, there is also chaos and disorder and images hurtle at us unbidden and we dance and sing and leap with them, in wonder and awe. Synchronistic events occur in the transpersonal; surprise connections in a highly charged level of experience (Hopke, 1991). Artists search for ways to express what they have felt, heard, seen, touched, smelled, tasted, and thought in the transpersonal because they seem to need to record and share what they experience. Inside and outside are less relevant in transpersonal space/time. "When one is most alive and real, can one locate experiencing as simply inside or outside?" (Eigen, 1991, p. 70).

The transpersonal space/state for the artist is where to access dramatic vision or unusual sensations. It is a state of readiness, of becoming. "Artistic skill is the combining of many levels of mind—unconscious, conscious, and external—to make a statement of their combination. It is not a matter of expressing a single level" (Bateson, 1972/2000, p. 470).

> *Between* things, where artists contact the transpersonal to receive their images, does not designate a localizable relation from one thing to the other and back again, but a perpendicular direction, a transversal movement that sweeps one *and* the other away, a stream without beginning or end that undermines its banks and picks up speed in the middle. (Deleuze & Guattari, 1987, p. 15)

"Where, exactly, is art?" asked philosopher, Ken Wilber (1997, p. 112). Art, for Wilber, is holonic like everything else in the universe. Every work of art is a holon, "which means that it is a whole that is simultaneously a part of numerous other wholes" (p. 112). Every human context imposes its own meaning on artwork, each context nested in another. What then if all these contexts were nested in beauty?

> What if one could somehow manage to see *everything* in the entire universe as being exquisitely beautiful, like the finest piece of great art? What if life could be experienced

with knowledge of the transpersonal? What if it were possible, right now, to see every single thing and event, without exception, as an object of extraordinary beauty (Wilber, 1997, p. 136)?

Paolo Knill, Barba, and Fuchs (1995), authors of *Minstrels of Soul,* reminded that beauty is not bound to the pleasantness of the theme or object presented. Beauty arrives when one is open to the transpersonal—the not knowing—to the surprise. Beauty can be horrific—it can be *in* the horrific in a way that makes it possible to bear the unbearable.

> Beauty radiates through the ways and means that the emergent is allowed to approach us. It moves us when we witness the painting, movements, sounds, rhythms, acts and words...in the artistic process, where pain is the subject that attracts our attention and empathic curiosity. The power of the artistic process allows us to approach the painful, the suffering, the ugly, the repulsive and the destructive. (p. 115)

In this way, the transpersonal is potentially omnipresent. Whenever a moment is witnessed as being/becoming art, then there is physical access to it. Whether the response is either as actor or spectator (Boal, 1995) one is actively invited into the space between the artistic creation and oneself (Gadamer, 1998), seized by beauty and engaged with it. It is "something required by every composition, graphic or musical, in drama or in reading. There is constant co-operative activity here" (p. 27). This kind of aesthetic response is not a removed state of being, a quiet contemplation of a timeless object. "Aesthetic drama compels a transformation of the spectators' view of the world by rubbing their senses against enactments of extreme events...(it is a) reflection in liminal time during which the transformation of consciousness takes place" (Schechner, 1988, p. 172). On the space/time continuum, the transpersonal is "now-time":

> a "space of time" of recognition and transformation. It doesn't carry us to a utopian or paradisal beyond, or to the "remove" of (traditional) aesthetic contemplation. Rather in now-time we are palpably, mimetically immersed in the unrecorded history of our social existence—in the conflicting loops, freeze-frames, vanishing, fragmented memories, in the very "accident and repetition"...that (traditional) aesthetic time banishes. (Diamond, 1997, p. 147)

Thought is based on perception and perception too is an artful pursuit. David Bohm (1994) compared perceiving to watching television:

> Clearly, there is a kind of imagination involved in looking at the tv image. If you were to look carefully you would see nothing but flashing lights. But you see people, trees, characters; you see emotional conflicts and danger; you see anger, fear, pleasure, but it's all yourself. It's all the imagination being infused into the picture on the screen—just as it gets infused into perception. So when you are looking at the tv set, what you experience must come from something like the imagination. Where else could it come from? (p. 160).

When thought is encountered imaginatively/poetically, one is in a transpersonal state and able to engage thinking itself as an image, consciously shaping what is uncovered in the transpersonal. Those images of thought, impressions, and feelings—those are what artists grope to engage with as data, from which they can present their discoveries. Yet seeking the transpersonal in this way is not a flight from reality. "Poetry does not fly above and surmount the earth in order to escape it and hover over it. Poetry is what first brings man onto the earth, making him belong to it, and thus brings him into dwelling" (Heidegger, 1975, p. 218).

Dorit Netzer (2008), transpersonal arts therapist, educator, and researcher described in her dissertation a study bringing new awareness and integration of knowledge in cognition beyond the personal as:

> the inspiration of transpersonal awareness of spiritual freedom through an imaginal response to selected mystical poetry. The imaginal was viewed as a bridge between spirit and cognition. The experience of transpersonal awareness of spiritual freedom was defined as recognition for that which extends infinitely beyond one's personal boundaries (including oneself, others, the visible and the invisible, known and unknown); a participatory, cocreative experience—intentionally enacted, cultivated, and lived. (p. iii)

In an artist's conception of the transpersonal we, as humans, are in our bodies, we feel, touch, smell, taste, see, and hear. The transpersonal exists in an interconnected intersubjective field, a space/time continuum where images ask to be concretized by humans in physical expression through the arts as they try to express to others what happens there. Artists often pay attention to their bodies as a source of knowledge of the transpersonal. They understand that spiritual knowing of the transpersonal source of inspiration is not divorced from the corporeal world or from their own sensing selves.

Artist/Dancer Louise Steinman (1995), in *The Knowing Body: The Artist as Storyteller in Contemporary Performance,* shared her ideas of the corporeal necessity for remaining in one's body to experience and express knowing through living everyday in one's proprioceptive system and its three main sources of input:

> *Kinesthesis* is the feeling of movement derived from all skeletal and muscular structure [and] includes the feeling of pain, our orientation in space, the passage of time, and rhythm. *Visceral* feedback consists of the miscellaneous impressions from our internal organs. *Labyrintine* or *vestibular* feedback, the feeling of our position in space, is provided by the cochlea, an organ of the inner ear. (p. 11)

Steinman (1995) emphasized that the arts are of this world and not a removal from it. As human beings we live here and now and we are obligated to live our present lives as well as experience the possibility of something else. We must cultivate ourselves to perceive both/and, to realize "the epiphanies, the unfamiliar and the wondrous, coexist with the familiarity of what we see everyday" (p. 71). Transpersonal inquiry into human concerns is performed through the arts. Artist/researchers (and all artists can be seen as researchers) are "citizens of primal cultures, cultivating the ability *to see* with the whole body, our whole body remembers, our whole body dreams" (p. 73). The actor/writer Spalding Gray described his experience of the transpersonal (though he did not use this term) as the process of improvisation:

> a flow of feeling that I could not name because the flow, which was directly connected to the physical flow of body movement, happened so quickly and in a continuum that it was more difficult to pin down and name. There was only direct unmediated expression . . . for the first time I experienced being held together with a group of performers by something other than words . . . At last I had room for internal reflection. I could think as I moved. I began to have a dialogue with myself. My thoughts were freer because they were not tied down to a psychological story line of a particular text. At first I was just moving and experiencing direct feeling . . . but as I did this more and more, and got familiar with it, there was more room for reflection. (interview in Steinman, 1995, p. 110)

Art that is capable not only of allowing transformative experiences for the artist, but of transmitting them to the spectator, is necessary to effect societal change in consciousness.

What is the world coming to?

The international art world itself recognizes the value of transpersonal art, art that leads to extraordinary experience and the recognition of greater human connection beyond individual and cultural constructs. Below is the description of a Venice exhibition in 2011 (Fondazione Musei Civici di Venezia, n.d.). The exhibition, TRA: Edge of Becoming

> presents 300 multi-media artists who explore "the transversal links between places, history, creative heritage and universal wisdom." About the title: TRA was chosen for its many meanings. Firstly, it can be read inversely to spell "art." In Italian it is a preposition that signifies "in-between" and "inside," and also connotes an action that goes "beyond" or "ahead of." TRA is also a common suffix in many Sanskrit words such as "mantra," "tantra," "yantra." Mantra is the literal translation of "instrument of thought," man—to think and tra—an instrument or tool. "Tantra" is the ancient system of knowledge that connects sexual and cosmic energy. "Yantras" are the signs and drawings that act like doors for energetic healing.

Educational institutes worldwide are honoring the arts as a lived pathway to the transpersonal. Sofia University (formerly the Institute of Transpersonal Psychology), in Palo Alto, California, has from its inception considered the expressive arts as one of its foundational pillars and requires almost all its students to take a course in creative expression as a way of knowing and expressing the transpersonal for themselves and for others whose lives they will affect. A course, "Music & Spirit," offered at the Community School of Michigan State University—an outreach arm of MSU School of Music—moves the arts beyond academic and clinical constrictions, to the community at large recognizing the transformative power of the arts to transcend both space and time. The course:

> offers a fresh approach to understanding and appreciating music by encouraging the practice of mindful listening. Learn how music affects body, mind, and spirit. Through a variety of guided listening experiences that focus attention on physical and emotional sensation, you will explore the intersections of musical perception and spiritual awareness. Musical selections presented will represent a wide variety of cultures and historical periods, from world folk music, Gregorian Chant, and Sufi masters to Gustav Mahler and Arvo Part. (Michigan State University, 2012)

A search on the Internet reveals a plethora of arts-based workshops, seminars, and courses for anyone who seeks a transformative experience and enlightenment beyond what they might consider the humdrum of their daily life.

Every culture has recognized the connection between the arts and the transpersonal, and has both honored and suppressed it. Artists have always pushed the edge of cultures advocating for creative transformation of self and society. Through making art, they are disturbers of the peace and predictors of what is to come. They can inspire others with access to the transpersonal so all can evolve into more inclusive ways of being and question what is. They can stir body/minds to action and into making this a better world. Transpersonal art seeks to find new ground, closer to the possibilities of what we can be as humanity.

Regaining Everyday Experience of Art and the Transpersonal

What is often called art in industrialized cultures has become separated from everyday experience and ensconced in art galleries, concert halls, theaters, movie houses, and museums where one pays top dollar to enter. Even when there is access, a look at attendees who peer at what the little cards next to the images say, perhaps remembering tasks not done or texting as they think they are taking in the artist's vision, suggests that many are no longer moved by witnessing art. Art in the Western world has become a commodity to be consumed, and only certain qualified people are expected to produce and appreciate it.

Sometimes, in religious settings, one is allowed to feel transcendence when hearing sacred music and joining in chanting. Here it is possible to experience images in movement, in the smell of incense and in the light pouring through stained glass or the swish of long robes draped gracefully on bodies, and one can feel the transpersonal. But the meaning of these images is prescribed. Art, whether in the gallery or church, has become codified by the dominant paradigm in society. People are not meant to look outside of their previous constructs of experience. In these cases art comes with an agenda for behavior and thought, or else is not allowed to exist.

Transpersonal art is meant to bring in the new. It is meant to disrupt and transgress and help one think/feel/know beyond the ordinary in oneself and in the world. Transpersonal art is also meant to help hold disturbing experience in the transpersonal, and from there return to the ordinary with ideas that coalesce into new forms that better serve one's communities and help them to change. Transpersonal art is meant to let one live for a while in the tension of not knowing while awaiting the emergence of new forms. In the experience of transpersonal art, a person learns to expand the world in which she or he lives.

Stanley Krippner (2002), humanistic psychologist, described the transformative potential of art from an experience of listening to music. He noted that if it is truly transpersonal, one's identity is changed by the experience.

> As students at the University of Wisconsin in the 1950s, and while hearing a recital by the great Chilean pianist, Claudio Arrau, a friend of mine and I had what I would now call "anomalies of personal experience of the peak experience type." I had never been "caught up" in music so intensely; my friend imagined that she was running toward the stage and prostrating herself at Arrau's feet! Other people in the audience might not have been so moved, but for the two of us the musical performance was uncommon and inexplicable in terms of our frames of reference at that time. From my perspective, many transpersonal experiences can be termed "anomalous" because they bring the cognized self into question. However, most anomalous experiences are not transpersonal; they may bring the experient's worldview into question (e.g., when someone who doubts the evidence for precognition has a dream that comes true) but leave the sense of identity fairly intact. (p. 3)

In the 21st century the creation of transpersonal art continues to evoke questioning of personal identity, thinking, and perspective. Perhaps in the spirit of artists who created paintings millennia ago in the Chauvet Cave, artists today challenge society's preexisting concepts. The powerful nature of transpersonal art, always understood as a path for awakening humans to the possibility of changing both self and the human world, provokes us to become more inclusive and diverse. Today transpersonal art, as always, opens humans to unimagined possibilities. It still creates gateways to recognizing and transgressing the normal. It is being reclaimed as a human birthright to challenge what is.

> The folk tradition in poetry goes back—I think you could say "forever." Because the power of the spoken word is the power that has always been available to everyone. It wasn't the privilege of the few, it has always been the words that have been available to all people to create something meaningful to share with everybody. Any time people are protesting and are calling out rhythmic or rhyming chants, there is the impetus of poetry behind it. (Wilder, 2008, n.p.)

Transpersonal art in the age of social media confronts society and is globally engaged. It can be threatening to established order. It is "artivism," social consciousness-raising proliferating in the environment of the Internet. The following is a statement by an artivist on the artivista website:

> Imagination is the most powerful force we have for liberation. Through theater, storytelling, and community engagement we can creatively address real-world issues and build spaces for interaction, dialogue and deeper engagement. My work offers a picture of human connection and solidarity through art-making. (Irani, n.d., n.p.)

Given the global crises we live in, it is imperative that humans connect with each other to transform present thinking and being. Transpersonal art provides this connection as well as connection to realms beyond present human knowing. In the second decade of this century images of the Occupy Wall Street movement regalvanized many worldwide with an expanded awareness of solidarity and the power of transcendence/transgression of the normal.

Michele Elam (2011), Martin Luther King Jr. Centennial Professor in the Department of English and past director of African and American Studies at Stanford University, has pointed powerfully to the transpersonal role of art. Inspired by a poster featuring a "young, black Angela Davis woman" she called for art that transforms under the title "How Art Propels Occupy Wall Street":

> In 1926, the renowned black intellectual, W. E. B. Du Bois, argued passionately that art should be used for social justice and that beauty can and must be marshaled for a larger good: "I am one who tells the truth and exposes evil and seeks with beauty and for beauty to set the world right.
>
> ... Let the Occupy movement's camps and protests and marches continue generating such art—art that inspires interracial unity where it may not yet exist, art that reminds us of the voices unheard, art that galvanizes practical social change when nothing seems to give, art that, in Du Bois' words, tries to make the world both beautiful and right. (Elam, 2011, n.p.)

References

Arnheim, R. (1966). *Toward a psychology of art*. Berkeley, CA: University of California Press.

Arnheim, R. (1971). *Entropy and art: An essay on disorder and order*. Berkeley, CA: University of California Press.

Bateson, G. (2000). *Steps to an ecology of mind*. Chicago, IL: University of Chicago Press. (Original work published 1972)

Boal, A. (1995). *The rainbow of desire: The Boal method of theatre and therapy*. London, UK: Routledge.

Bohm, D. (1994). *Thought as a system*. New York, NY: Routledge.

Bohm, D. (1998). *On creativity*. London, UK: Routledge.

Briggs, J., & Peat, D. F. (1999). *Seven life lessons of chaos: Timeless wisdom from the science of change*. New York, NY: HarperCollins.

Brooks, S. (1999). Alex Grey: The mission of a visionary artist. *Shambhala Sun* (July), n.p. Retrieved from http://alexgrey.com/press-media/articles/shambhala-sun-july-1999/

Capra, F. (1972). The dance of Shiva: The Hindu view of matter in the light of modern physics. *Main Currents in Modern Thought, 29*(1), 15.

Capra, F. (1991). *The tao of physics*. Boston, MA: Shambhala.

Capra, F. (1996). *The web of life: A new scientific understanding of living systems*. New York, NY: Anchor Books.

Carson, R. (1997). *Witness for nature*. New York NY: Henry Holt.

Clottes, J. (2010). *Cave art*. Paris, France: Phaidon Press.

Deleuze, G., & Guattari, F. (1987). *A thousand plateaus: Capitalism & schizophrenia*. Minneapolis, MI: University of Minnesota Press.

Diamond, E. (1997). *Unmaking mimesis.* London UK: Routledge.

Dissanyake, E. (1992). *Homo aestheticus: Where art comes from and why.* New York, NY: Free Press.

Eigen, M. (1991). Winnicott's area of freedom: The uncompromisable. In N. Schwarz-Salant & M. Stein (Eds.), *Liminality and transitional phenomena* (pp. 67-88). Wilmette, IL: Chiron.

Eigen, M. (1993). *The electrified tightrope.* Northvale, NJ: Jason Aronson.

Elam, M. (2011, November). How art propels Occupy Wall Street. CNN Opinion [Electronic Version]. Retrieved from http://www.cnn.com/2011/11/01/opinion/elam-occupy-art/index.html.

Fondazione Musei Civici di Venezia. (n.d.). TRA Edge of Becoming, Venice, Italy: Author. Retrieved from http://www.visitmuve.it/en/2011/07/1402/tra-edge-of-becoming-2

Gadamer, H. G. (1998). *Praise of theory: Speeches & essays.* (C. Dawson, Trans.). New Haven, CT: Yale University Press.

Greene, B. (1999). *The elegant universe: Superstrings, hidden dimensions, and the quest for the ultimate theory.* New York, NY: W. W. Norton.

Hefner, R. A. (2005). Art paintings of the Chauvet Cave. Retrieved from http://www.bradshawfoundation.com/chauvet/robert-hefner.php

Heidegger, M. (1975). *Poetry, language, thought.* (A. Hofstadter, Trans.). New York, NY: Harper & Row.

Herzog, W. (Dir.). (2010). *Cave of forgotten dreams* [Film].

Hopke, R. H. (1991). On the threshold of change: Symbolization and transitional space. In N. Schwarz-Salant & M. Stein (Eds.), *Liminality and transitional phenomena* (pp. 115-132). Wilmette, IL: Chiron.

Irani, K. (n.d.). *Artivista.org.* New York, NY: Author. Retrieved from http://www.artivista.org/tellingstories.php

Jacoby, M. (1999). The necessity of form: Expressive arts therapy in the light of the work of K. E. Logstrup. In S. K. Levine & E. G. Levine (Eds.), *Foundations of expressive arts therapy: Theoretical and clinical perspectives* (pp. 53-66). London, UK: Jessica Kingsley.

Knill, P., Barba, H. & Fuchs, M. (1995). *Minstrels of soul.* Toronto, ON, Canada: Palmerston Press.

Krippner, S. (2002) Dancing with the trickster: Notes for a transpersonal autobiography. *International Journal of Transpersonal Studies, 21,* 1-18.

Lazslo, E. (1996). *The whispering pond: A personal guide to the emerging version of science.* Boston, MA: Element Books.

Li, T. Y, & Yorke, J. A. (1975). Period three implies chaos. *American Mathematical Monthly, 82,* 985-992.

Michigan State University. (2012). *Music and spirit/sound and silence.* East Lansing, MI: Author.

Mtshali, O. M. (2008). The light of the poetic spirit. *SGI Quarterly: A Buddhist Forum for Peace, Culture and Education, 9*(1), n.p. [Electronic Version]. Retrieved from http://www.sgiquarterly.org/feature2008Jan-6.html

Netzer, D. (2008). Mystical poetry and imagination: Inspiring transpersonal awareness of spiritual freedom. *Dissertation Abstracts International, 69*(08) 0669B (UMI #3316128).

Polyani, M. (1983). *The tacit dimension.* Gloucester, MA: Doubleday.

Schechner, R. (1988). *Performance theory.* New York, NY: Routledge.

Sheldrake, R. (1981). *A new science of life.* London UK: Blond & Briggs.

Shlain, L. (1991). *Parallel visions in space, time and light.* New York, NY: Quill William Morrow.

Steinman, L. (1995). *The knowing body: The artist as storyteller in contemporary performance.* Berkeley, CA: North Atlantic Books.

Walsh, R. & Vaughn. (1993). *Paths beyond ego: The transpersonal vision*. New York, NY: G. P. Putnam's Sons.

Wilber, K. (1997). *The eye of spirit: An integral vision for a world gone slightly mad*. Boston, MA: Shambhala.

Wilder, S. (January, 2008). The Poetic Heart: Connecting Humanity. In *SGI Quarterly: A Buddhist Forum for Peace, Culture and Education*. *9*(1), n.p. [Electronic Version]. Retrieved from http://www.sgiquarterly.org/feature2008Jan-2.html

Winnicott, D. (1971). *Playing and reality*. London, UK: Tavistock Press.

Woody, J. e. (n.d.). Transpersonal artist, James e. Woody. Retrieved from http://www.besensitive.com

38

Transpersonal Education
Nancy Rowe[1] and William Braud

Education at its best—these profound human transactions called knowing, teaching, and learning—is not just about information, and they're not just about getting jobs. They are about healing. They are about wholeness. They are about empowerment, liberation, transcendence. They are about reclaiming the vitality of life.

(Palmer, 1997, p. 10)

As implied in Socrates' maxim that "the unexamined life is not worth living" (Plato, *Dialogues, Apology,* para. 38a), it is crucial that a person know themselves wholly and well in order to understand their true nature and in order to grow and develop. Careful examinations of outer and inner reality and of the world at large—as well as exploring such questions as who or what am I? Why am I here? What might I do next? What is the nature of life and consciousness and death? Is this physical world the only reality?—can help foster personal development and transformation while helping to fulfill some of the most crucial individual and collective needs.

Education that focuses on understanding self and transpersonal processes can facilitate learning that cultivates awareness, consciousness, and growth in both inner and outer realities as students explore academic subject matter. Transpersonal education includes practices and systems that have the potential to transform larger communities and the planet.

This chapter explores the concept of transpersonal education, the role of the educator, and process and practices that support transpersonal education at the school, classroom, and facilitator levels. The authors discuss process, obstacles, and challenges of transpersonal education and make suggestions for the future.

The Wiley Blackwell Handbook of Transpersonal Psychology, First Edition.
Edited by Harris L. Friedman and Glenn Hartelius.
© 2013 John Wiley & Sons, Ltd. Published 2015 by John Wiley & Sons, Ltd.

The Nature of Transpersonal Education

Etymologically, transpersonal education literally means *drawing out from beyond the mask*. Regarding education in its most general form, Plato suggested that "the power and capacity of learning exists in the soul already" and that true education could occur only when "the whole soul . . . turned from the world of becoming into that of being, and learn[ed] by degrees to endure the sight of being, and of the brightest and best of being, or in other words, of the good" (*The Republic*, VII, para. 518). Putting together these two observations, one might describe transpersonal education most succinctly as *the drawing out of the soul—the essential core of one's nature—from behind the ordinarily obscuring mask of ego*. The aim, in the remainder of this chapter, is to describe some of the ways in which this drawing out might be effectively accomplished.

Braud (2006) in his article on transpersonal holistic education described "the transpersonal" as

> ways in which individuals, societies, and disciplines might increase their ambit and become more inclusive and expansive in areas of sense of identity (including ways of being and ways of functioning beyond the typical egocentric mode), development and transformation, conditions of consciousness, ways of knowing, values, and service. The transpersonal also involves recognizing and honoring the spiritual aspects of our being, actions, and ways of thinking. (p. 135)

To understand the nature of transpersonal education, it is important to distinguish it from three other closely related but sufficiently different terms and concepts: *transpersonal psychology, transformative education*, and *spirituality/spiritual education*.

Transpersonal Psychology

Transpersonal psychology can be taken to mean an academic field that carefully explores transpersonal topics and integrates, embodies, and applies transpersonal processes. It might be characterized as a discipline that studies, researches, theorizes about, and applies information and findings relevant to, transpersonal material. Some transpersonal scholars have made a compelling case that transpersonal psychology be categorized as a science, one that relies on appropriate research methods, both conventional and transpersonal methods such as intuitive inquiry and hermeneutics (e.g., Daniels, 2005; Friedman, 2002). Such thinkers also distinguish transpersonal psychology from *transpersonal studies*, which is more general, including psychological as well as other approaches to its subject matter, and uses input from such areas as anthropology, sociology, philosophy, the other humanities, poetry, spiritual and folk traditions, and the arts (Boucouvalas, 1999; Daniels, 2005; Friedman, 2002). Friedman and Pappas (2006) recently suggested that if any transpersonal theory is to be considered valid in an ultimate and not merely relative sense, it must employ techniques that would be consistent with both conventional scientific approaches and, more broadly, approaches that are congruent with insights from other knowledge traditions and cultures (p. 48).

Through an extensive and careful content analysis of 160 previously proffered definitions of transpersonal psychology, Hartelius, Caplan, and Rardin (2007) found that these definitions tended to address three major themes: (a) transpersonal psychology offers something *beyond established ego psychology* (concerned with states, stages, paths, aspirations, capacities, perceptions, and realities beyond ego); (b) its practice is *integrative and holistic* (emphasizing embodiment, and social, ecological, and contextual factors); and (c) its aim and goal are the *transformation* of individuals and of society.

Anderson and Braud (2011) more recently offered another succinct characterization of transpersonal psychology: "Transpersonal psychology is the study and cultivation of the highest and most transformative human values and potentials—individual, communal, and global—that reflect the mystery and interconnectedness of life, including our human journey within the cosmos (p. 9)." Anderson and Braud's definition is a good example of Friedman and Pappas's (2006) cartography of a transpersonal psychology that blends transcendence, "highest and most transformative human values and potential," with immanence, a concept that suggests that transcendence is not necessarily expansive but can also "descend into the personal self through nature, the body, or the feminine" (Daniels, 2005; Friedman & Pappas, 2006) and be experienced through "awe, faith, mystery, or participative knowing" (p. 47). Immanence is reflected in the definition's reference to reflecting the mystery and interconnectedness of life (p. 48).

Transformative Education

Transformative education focuses on transformation within individuals, organizations, communities, society, and the planet (Markos & McWhinney, 2003; O'Sullivan, Morrell, & O'Connor, 2002). It fosters enhanced awareness of consciousness of being in the world and serves to create lasting change in a person's or community's frame of reference. Although transformation is an important aspect of transpersonal education, transformative education can be found in venues that may or may not be transpersonal in nature. Programs that may be transformative include (a) new career training, (b) humanitarian service, (c) spiritual renewal, (d) transformative learning, and (e) organizational implementation. By providing opportunities for people to examine and unlearn assumptions, ways of thinking, and ways of being that no longer serve them, learners can take on new purposes and perspectives (Markos & McWhinney, 2003), whether it be within cognitive processes or in the way that people are in the world (O'Sullivan et al., 2002).

Transformative learning, the area of transformative education most akin to transpersonal education, has many lenses. Mezirow (2003) first introduced the term transformative learning into educational discourse. He described it as "learning that transforms problematic frames of reference—sets of fixed assumptions and expectations (habits of mind, meaning perspectives, mindsets)—to make them more inclusive, discriminating, open, reflective, and emotionally able to change" (p. 58). Since that time, transformative educators have broadened the term to invite thinking around soul work (Dirkx, Mezirow, & Cranton, 2006), oppression (Schugurensky, 2002; Shahjahan, 2004), ecological consciousness (O'Sullivan & Taylor, 2004; Selby, 2002), feminist issues

(Miles, 2002), creative expression, and spirituality (Duerr, Zajonc, & Dana, 2003; O'Sullivan et al., 2002; Tisdell & Toliver 2003; Yorks & Kasl, 2006).

More recent definitions of transformative learning include the following:

> Transformative learning involves experiencing a deep, structural shift in the basic premises of thought, feeling, and actions. It is a shift of consciousness that dramatically and permanently alters our way of being in the world. Such a shift involves our understanding of ourselves and our self-locations; our relationships with other humans and with the natural world; our understanding of relations of power in interlocking structure of class, race, and gender; our body-awareness; our visions of alternative approaches to living; and our sense of the possibilities for social justice and peace and personal joy. (O'Sullivan, 2002, p. 11)

In an article highlighting a course in a transpersonal psychology program, Netzer and Rowe (2010) expanded on O'Sullivan's definition to include transpersonal experience:

> Whole-person, transformative learning [is] the process of experiencing meaningful and purposeful shifts in the ways learners perceive and process newly acquired knowledge and their own inner-knowing, by developing and integrating new awareness on personal and transpersonal levels, which is mindful, intuitive, embodied, and creatively informed. (p. 126)

Spirituality and Spiritual Education

What is spirit? The word is derived from a Latin word meaning "breathe" or "wind"—like respiration or inspiration . . . an invisible force—a life-giving essence that moves us deeply, or as a source that moves everything from within.

David Bohm (1993)

Spirituality. In order to understand what is meant by spiritual education, it is important to describe the concept of spirituality and to distinguish it from religion that denotes rituals, traditions, beliefs, and doctrine that are organized around rules and ceremony (Daniels, 2005). This discussion will focus only on the concept of spirituality.

Spirituality is associated with a great variety of meanings and viewed through a number of lenses. Transpersonal psychologist Frances Vaughan (2002) described the diversity of spiritual experience:

> Spirituality may also be described in terms of ultimate belonging or connection to the transcendental ground of being. Some people define spirituality in terms of relationship to God, to fellow humans, or to the earth. Others define it in terms of devotion and commitment to a particular faith or form of practice. To understand how spirituality can contribute to the good life, defined in humanistic terms as living authentically the full possibilities of being human . . . it seems necessary to differentiate healthy spirituality from beliefs and practices that may be detrimental to well-being. (p. 17)

Jennifer Lindholm and Helen Astin (2006) reflected on the spiritual process:

> At its core, spirituality involves the internal process of seeking personal authenticity, genuineness, and wholeness; transcending one's locus of centricity; developing a greater sense of connectedness to self and others through relationships and community; deriving meaning, purpose, and direction in life; being open to exploring a relationship with a higher power that transcends human existence and human knowing; and valuing the sacred. (p. 65)

Alluded to in the above definitions but perhaps not sufficiently emphasized are the relational, communal, interconnected, embodied, earth-based, and nature-related aspects that are important in feminine and indigenous forms of spirituality and in spirituality as lived in other cultures. Jorge Ferrer (2002) began to consider this in defining *embodied spirituality*: "Embodied spirituality... views all human dimensions—body, vital, heart, mind, and consciousness—as equal partners in bringing self, community, and world into a fuller alignment with the Mystery out of which everything arises" (Ferrer, 2008, p. 2).

Spirituality in schools, particularly secular education, has been called many names, including soul, soul/spirit, heart, heart-mind, "feelinged heart-body" (Miller, 2005).

Spiritual education. Spiritual education can be experienced in many forms. On one level, educators who claim spiritual education provide direct instruction on the content, processes and practices related to spirituality. This is often associated with a particular tradition or teacher such as Sri Aurobindo, Sai Baba, the Bahai religion, or Christianity. In these cases, spirituality is primarily concerned with beliefs, spiritual developments, and values of that particular teacher or faith.

Spirituality can also be incorporated into secular education (Glazer, 1999; Kessler, 2000; Miller, Karsten, Denton, Orr, & Kates, 2005; Tisdale & Toliver, 2003). Kessler (2005) described how to bring spirituality into the classroom without threatening religious beliefs. Her essay provides insight into ways that teachers can facilitate adolescent spiritual development in the following domains: (a) search for meaning and purpose, (b) longing for silence and solitude, (c) urge for transcendence, (d) hunger for joy and delight, (e) creative urge, (f) call for initiation, and (g) deep connection. She also explained that "Since we 'teach who are,' teachers who invite heart and soul into the classroom also find it essential to nurture their own spiritual development" (p. 102). Although transpersonal psychology is not technically "spiritual education," a large part of the transpersonal curriculum involves the cultivation of spiritual practice and the exploration of various spiritual traditions inform psychology.

Transpersonal Education

Transpersonal, transformative, and spiritual forms of education are interrelated. Each assumes that the seeker is on a journey of transformation (Baker, 2012; Braud, 2006; Dirkx et al., 2006; Markos & McWhinney, 2003) in which the ultimate goal is to bring personal authenticity, wholeness, a sense of relationship, and greater consciousness to self, community, and planet (Braud, 2006; Clark, 1974). Each discipline embraces uniqueness and meaningful content and incorporates multiple ways of knowing. Each path arrives at these goals through different doorways and lenses of understanding.

Indeed, transpersonal education can be considered a form of transformative education that includes components of spiritual education (Baker, 2012; Braud, 2006; Clark, 1974; Duerr et al., 2003; Miller, 2002, 2005; Rowe, 2011). What distinguishes transpersonal education from these other forms is its integration of *processes* and *practices* grounded in transpersonal theory and the world's wisdom psychologies and the inclusion of transpersonal ways of knowing (Braud, 2006; Clark, 1974; Duerr et al., 2003; Hart, Nelson, & Puhakka, 2000; Rowe, 2011; Sarath, 2003/2010a). It blends the epistemologies of the heart and intellect (Anderson & Braud, 2011; Braud, 2006; Clark, 1974; Duerr et al., 2003; Hart et al., 2000; Rowe, 2011; Sarath, 2010b).

In other words, transpersonal education includes essential *transpersonal content* and *qualities* that involve the *process and practice* through which these qualities might be discovered or re-discovered, identified, cultivated, integrated, and applied (Braud, 2006). The next section presents these processes and explores qualities associated with the transpersonal educator, which can be incorporated within any content area.

Transpersonal Processes and Ways of Knowing

Transpersonal education is a holistic, expansive, growthful, transformative process that involves a both/and rather than an either/or attitude; it is experiential and reflective, inclusive and integrated. It emphasizes not only conventional forms of intellectual functioning, critical thinking, analysis, and synthesis but also the many forms of intelligence (emotional intelligence, spiritual intelligence, and the multiple forms of intelligences), oral dialog, pluralistic ways of knowing, and the informative and educational value of personal experience, the wisdom of the body, the great spiritual and wisdom traditions (which are really world psychologies), "real philosophy, poetry, myth, story, the arts, contemplative inquiry, and all forms of creative expression. It advocates a form of experiential learning that is fully and deeply lived, immediate, embodied, particular, and concrete as well as community service and concrete. Its aim is to allow an individual to find his or her unique, authentic nature, potentials, and voice, and to express and apply this knowledge and wisdom to the greatest possible extent, for the benefit of self and others (Anderson & Braud, 2011; Braud, 2006; Gardner, 1999; Hart et al., 2000; Netzer & Rowe, 2010; O'Sullivan et al., 2002; Root-Bernstein & Root-Bernstein, 1999; Sarath, 2010b).

Cultivation of embodied spiritual or transpersonal values, qualities, and practices are key to transpersonal education (Baker, 2012; Braud, 2006; Clark, 1974; Frager, 1974; Netzer & Rowe, 2010; Sarath, 2010b). These qualities and values might include appreciation of differences, appreciation of others and of the Universe at large, attention, authenticity, compassion, creativity, deeper levels of meaning, discernment, empathy, expansiveness, gratitude, insight, inspiration, intention, interconnectedness, intuition, mindfulness, self-observation, spirituality, spontaneity, and wisdom (Baker, 2012; Braud, 2006; Brussat & Brussat, 1996; Clark, 1974; Hart et al., 2000).

Transpersonal practices not only facilitate awareness of self in relationship to a larger whole but often awaken learners to a sense of wonder and awe and can connect them to the cosmos (Miller, 2002, 2005). In transpersonal education, learners are encouraged to explore spiritual practices from diverse wisdom approaches, to inspire direct knowing and insight specific to their education and lives (Braud, 2006; Clark, 1974; Netzer & Rowe, 2010; Sarath, 2010b).

Ed Sarath (2010b), Music Professor at University of Michigan and founder of Students, Teachers, and Administrators for Transpersonal Education (STATE), an organization designed to bring transpersonal education into a variety of content areas, explained that

> Transpersonal education is rooted in processes that transcend the boundaries that separate the various spiritual pathways, and in so doing accesses common ground that invites a cross-traditional exploration, inquiry and analysis. By creating a bridge between diverse spiritual practices, and between spiritual/transpersonal experience and conventional forms of knowledge, we can begin to understand how these areas both unite and differ. An entirely new educational landscape emerges that promotes unprecedented kinds of transformation and development, and helps dissolve the boundaries between spiritual pathways and other fields of knowledge that are so problematic in our world. (section FAQ, para. 4)

Ultimately, transpersonal education incorporates self-discovery, self-cultivation, and transformation; its goal is to contribute to society and our planet:

> Virtually all of the challenges confronting modern society point to the need for foundational changes in how individuals think and act, which means a change in consciousness. It is not enough to define education solely in terms of practical mastery in one or more fields; internal mastery is also needed, where individuals transcend the sense of separateness that prevails in our times, and they experience more expansive and integrated modes of awareness. Our educational systems have both the capacity and the responsibility to provide this kind of development, providing they first undergo change in this direction within themselves. (Sarath, 2010b, section FAQ, para. 5)

Shared journey of discovery. Transpersonal educators are keenly aware of their own processes of awareness and inner change as they guide their students, protégés, and mentees (the seekers) on a journey of self-discovery, toward self-actualization and psychospiritual transformation (Partho, 2007). Whether through brief or long-term encounters, in one-on-one or group settings, educators and students share self-transformative paths, as the teacher emulates his or her lifelong experience and skillful guidance yet remains open to learning from the unique encounter with each student and the group dynamics at large. The circle of learners, teacher and students alike, interact and respond to one another in ways that facilitate connection to self, others, and Earth community, toward the integration of course content in ways relevant to each person's journey.

This reciprocity, which stems from the recognition of the sacred qualities and synchronicities in human encounters, values each person's unique nature, inner wisdom, and potential contribution. A soulful learning exchange amplifies individuals' authentic voices and movement toward change, to the greatest possible extent, toward the benefit of self and others. At the same time, all seekers are encouraged to challenge their own frames of reference and integrate their revised lenses into new awareness

(Anderson & Braud, 2011; Mezirow, 2003; Netzer & Rowe, 2010). As students serve each other through sympathetic resonance (Anderson, 2011), they are each asked to hold the tension between diverse perspectives and their own uniqueness and to live with contradiction and paradox (Duerr et al., 2003; Moore, 2005). They are given exercises that tap into their imaginal realm and empathic connection (Anderson & Braud, 2011; Netzer & Rowe, 2010), to hone their capacity to remain open to the innate nature of the transpersonal as both an experience of transcendence and immanence, where knowing emerges in unanticipated manners and wisdom is generated from weaving connections between the concrete and the ineffable.

The Process and Practice of Transpersonal Education

Aspects of transpersonal education can be found in many approaches. This section explores two cross-cultural approaches to education (one Eastern and one indigenous) as well as organizations and classrooms that fit well into the criteria of transpersonal education.

Cross-cultural Worldviews

Aurobindonian integral education, which includes characteristics of general forms of integral education (Esbojorn-Hargens, Reams, & Gunnlaughson, 2010), and traditional Pueblo education (Cajete, 1994, 2004) are two examples of education approaches that emulate transpersonal perspectives and qualities. These two approaches are grounded in specific spiritual and cultural perspectives. Integral education is based on the East Indian Yogic psychology that uses a map of transformation that primarily reflects transcendence, whereas Pueblo Education is grounded in indigenous cosmology and is a good example of an education system that reflects values of transmission and immanence.

Aurobindonian Integral Education.

> *Essentially there is but one single true reason for living: it is to know oneself. We are here to learn—to learn what we are, why we are here, and what we have to do. And if we don't know that, our life is altogether empty—for ourselves and for others.*
>
> The Mother (in Huppes, 2001, p. 205)

Integral education is an excellent example of transpersonal education; it is based on the spiritual teachings of Sri Aurobindo and Mirra Alfassa ("the Mother"; Center for Integral Education, n.d.; Partho, 2007) and grounded in Yogic psychology and practices that have a keen awareness of continuous spiritual transformation in a transcendent process (Cornelissen, Misra, & Varma, 2011). Two assumptions permeate this system: (a) Humans are evolutionary beings; they are in the process of evolving toward greater wholeness and eventually divinity, and (b) spiritual evolution is transformed into a creative force for the betterment of society as a whole (Partho, 2007).

Integral education is a whole person process that focuses on the development of the mind, body, emotions, soul, and spirit (Center for Integral Education, n.d.). Its major aim is psycho-spiritual transformation and the realization of one's true Self through self-mastery and movement toward a deepening and widening balance and harmony within self and community (Partho, 2007). Self-knowledge and world-knowledge are valued and considered essential for successful living (Center for Integral Education, n.d.). This approach assumes that students and teachers alike are lifelong learners who are willing to be part of an evolutionary spiritual journey and grow toward greater and greater consciousness in thought and action (Cornelissen et al., 2011; Center for Integral Education, n.d.; Partho, 2007). Learning includes reflection, contemplation and a continuous search for truth.

Integral teachers are expected to be guides, facilitators, and nurturers of the student's overall growth and development. The process is highly individualized according to the needs and abilities of the student; emphasizes processes of self-observation, self-reflection, self-awareness, and self-perfection; and has the dual purpose of providing both mundane and spiritual knowledge. The educational process can also be one of healing of mind, heart, and soul. For this reason, educators are expected to be on their own ongoing quest so that they might better understand the learner, the process of learning, and the ways of providing learning experiences and inspiration to help students embark on their inner journey (Center for Integral Education, n.d.; Cornelissen et al., 2011). "Thus, a teacher has to be a true *karma yogi* who engages in enjoined actions in the pursuit of knowledge, and is committed to the development of her self and her students" (Cornelissen et al., 2011, p. 104).

Integral educators help students to cultivate self-knowledge and have a clear understanding of their own true nature (Baveja, 2011; Partho, 2007) so that they can arrive at a more authentic and unique expression of self in the world. Authors of the website for the Center for Integral Education (n.d.) have suggested, "If everyone truly has a spark of the Divine as the center of his [or her] being, a comprehensive education must do more than ignore it or passively acknowledge it. Integral Education takes that spark, the soul, as the guiding principle for the education of each child" (n.p.).

As a reflection of this Aurobindian vision and integral education, the Center for Integral Education in San Diego County created the following mission statement for their preschool and elementary schools:

> The mission of the *Center for Integral Education* is to create beautiful and engaging educational environments where children can become aware of themselves and grow into conscious, creative and responsible individuals, participants in society, and contributors to the community of the future.
>
> Everything at the Center helps the students to: (a) Discover their unique and special aim in life; (b) Experience the joy of learning for its own sake; (c) Embody integrity, harmony, and beauty in every aspect of their lives. (Center for Integral Education, n.d., Mission, paras. 1-3)

Pueblo education. Gregory Cajete (2004), who introduced himself as an indigenous educator and Tewa Indian from the Santa Clara Pueblo, has described a number of principles and relationships that guide indigenous education in a chapter based on his keynote address at the Fourth International Conference on Transformative Education. These principles also guide transformative, transpersonal, and holistic education.

Cajete (2004) invited the reader to reflect upon the indigenous worldview as seen from the Pueblo people of New Mexico. He claimed that central to Pueblo education are the values of "interdependence, interconnection, and relationship with their history, their land, and with each other" (p. 103). Cajete began by describing the mountains and deserts of his homeland and refers to the guiding myth, a myth that gives his community a sense of perspective and also evokes responsibilities that are to be passed down from generation to generation, about living respectfully and sustainably on their land. The myth is a sacred story that can only to be told in its entirely in private ceremonies.

In general, the story speaks of humans as evolving beings within a landscape, people on a journey who are in the process of unfolding and becoming fully alive and human. This central teaching is shared, storied, sung, danced, and represented in various ways within indigenous communities. The myth illustrates an evolutionary process of relating to the world and shows that "how we view the world very much determines how we will treat it" (Cajete, 2004, p. 104). Pueblo spirituality and education is embedded in the ecological perspective that all things are interrelated and interconnected. Pueblo teachings "are coded within their stories, their designs and traditions of art and dance, within their languages, communities, and expressions of science and technology" (p. 105). Stories and storytelling are foundations of indigenous education and through archetypal images like Kokopelli, the archetype of creative spirit, help the seekers better understand how to create themselves.

Cajete (2004) described this education system as filled with story and meaning. He explained that stories teach about relationships with one another and with Earth, how to deal with issues related to social ecology, the importance for honoring plants and animals, and the interconnectedness of all life. Meaning is reflected in all things. He illustrated that an ear of corn is not merely sustenance; it is a symbol of life. Each kernel is individual as are humans, yet each is part of a collective or community, reflected in the corncob. Within a community there is a diversity of kernels and yet all are united expressing unity in diversity.

Cajete (2004) also reminded the audience that the Tewa language is very different from English. If Western concepts of education were translated into the Tewa language, there would be references to "pathways," "remembering to remember," "coming to know," or "breathing in" (p. 107).

Finally, Cajete spoke about the first light of the summer solstice and how it pierces through a window cut in the east side of the kiva. The first light on the longest day creates a column of light on the wall opposite the window and illuminates a strategically placed niche. This pattern is repeated throughout Chaco canyon during the solstice. For Cajete, it is an affirmation of indigenous ways of knowing and being in the world. He described it as a *sympathetic resonance* between self, Earth, Sun, and the whole Cosmos. It is a celebration of life set in place by the ancient ones.

Commentary. In the examples of Aurobindonian integral education and Pueblo education one can see parallels with transpersonal education. Both reflect an interest in educating the whole person and instilling values through specific practices. Both speak to the importance of a journey toward wholeness and how the individual is part of a larger community. Transpersonal psychology, Integral education, and Pueblo education are interested in spiritual growth and resonance with what is considered to be greater than self. All three are grounded in the deep philosophical belief that people are evolving in order to contribute to a better world.

Transpersonal Schools and Institutes

Research in transformative and spiritual education (Duerr et al., 2003) shows that although individual instructors incorporate spiritual and transformative aspects in their classrooms, few programs or schools are actually considered transformative. Of this group, even fewer transformative education programs consider themselves to be transpersonal. Indeed, transpersonal education at the school level is uncommon. Programs that are transpersonal do so with intention, with attention to transpersonal content and practice and related values, and this is seen in their mission/vision statements. Such statements ground the school or institute in their purposes.

This section highlights two institutions grounded in transpersonal education: Sofia University (formerly the Institute of Transpersonal Psychology), and the Center for Courage and Renewal. Following are descriptions of three courses that utilize transpersonal methods, and a strategy used by Rhea White that cultivates transpersonal ways of knowing as a self-educational process.

Sofia University. Commitment to transpersonal education is often built into founding principles of an institution and shows up in the mission/vision statement. These statements serve as a way to assess whether or not the institute has deviated from its original intention and to inform learning. Sofia University is an example of a school founded with the intention of embodying principles and practices of transpersonal education.

Sofia University, is a private, independent, non-profit graduate school in transpersonal psychology. It offers master's level and doctoral programs in transpersonal psychology, clinical psychology, and related topics in residential, hybrid, and online formats. Robert Frager and James Fadiman founded Sofia University under the name of the Institute of Transpersonal Psychology (ITP)[2] in 1975 to prepare students to study human nature from an approach that encompasses the whole person and incorporates the tenets of transpersonal psychology. They wanted to provide students with a solid intellectual foundation as well as an opportunity for deep personal growth and a lived experience of the subject matter. It was built on a founding principle that all aspects of human experience, including the spiritual dimension, are part of our human experience (Sophia University, n.d.). This original principle continues to be expressed, as can be seen within the 2012 mission statement:

> Through disciplined scholarly inquiry into the frontiers of psychology and spirituality, ITP [Sofia University] seeks to foster the development of individuals, organizations, and societies toward their fuller potential for wisdom, health and wholeness.... We value the qualities of mindfulness, discernment, compassion, and appreciation of differences, and

we embrace whole-person education that supports personal and community transformation. We value diversity and seek to impart knowledge and skills that empower people
to live together in peace within multicultural communities, the inherent unity of our
world and seek to foster a sense of the interconnectedness of all beings. We encourage
and promote service to local, national and international communities. We value all of life
and educate students in a way that treats all beings with respect and encourages living
in harmony with all of nature. We value consciousness and its evolution and engage in
rigorous research that includes multiple ways of knowing. (n.p.)

Tenets of transpersonal psychology, including personal growth, spirituality, being
of service to the world, expanding consciousness, and working toward wholeness,
originally intended as the school was being formed, are still reflected upon as the
school morphs and evolves today. Not only is this mission statement reflective of
the original intention, but the author, former president Thomas Potterfield, used a
transpersonal and inclusionary discernment process to arrive at the words. All faculty
and administrator voices were included and synthesized in the school's mission.

From 1995 to 2000, a six-faceted, longitudinal study assessed the transpersonal
nature of the program by examining the experiences and changes of students who
attended ITP (Braud, 2006; ITP is now Sofia University). The project's design
included complementary quantitative and qualitative research methods and honored both nomothetic and idiographic aims. Quantitative results indicated significant
changes in measures of the following qualities: decrements in egocentric grasping and
striving, increments in acceptance, greater self-transcendence, increased spiritual perspective, "thinner" and more permeable boundaries, increased present-centeredness,
and increased inner-directedness. Substantial positive changes also were reported in
areas of values, meaning, spirituality, attitudes, beliefs, intellect, body, emotions,
spirit, creative expression, community, openness, and connectedness. In the project's
qualitative components, the students reported increased awareness and changes in
personal growth, mindfulness, body-related areas, academic/scholarly areas, appreciation of interconnectedness, appreciation of differences, compassion, discernment, transformation, openness, surrender/acceptance, and professional areas; some
reported experiencing regression, cognitive dissonance, and disillusionment (Braud &
Schmitt, 2000).

Transformative, transpersonal education. Another mixed-methods study (Baker,
2012) explored the lived experience of transformation of students in the online master's program. Baker discovered that 92% of participants believed that they experienced
transformation, which was defined as "a profound and persistent shift toward greater
wholeness and authenticity" (p. iii). A thematic content analysis revealed that the
movement of transformation showed up in three forms: (a) from socially constructed
identity toward realization of the essential self; (b) from fragmentation toward greater
integration and wholeness of body, mind, and spirit; and (c) toward greater connection to self, others, and the natural world and was often accompanied by increased
awareness, gratitude, appreciation, and greater presence. The alchemical process of
transformation was described as a vessel that offered a combination of "tools" and
"conditions." "Conditions included experiences of *safety and love* which were created

by the curriculum and feeling of being held by their cohort of faculty, which sustained for a sufficient period of time" (p. iii). Students who experienced being seen, heard, and accepted for whom they were contributed to their ability to trust and consequently make significant shifts in their lives. Other educational components that participants suggested facilitated transformation included: experiential, creative, and embodied learning; spiritual practice; a focus on "being" along with "doing"; personal motivation and discipline; readiness; encouragement to be authentic and to bring gifts forward; acceptance; organic learning; earth-centered activities; core spiritual values made intentional by school; and learning diverse perspectives.

Center for Courage and Renewal. The Center for Courage and Renewal, a small non-profit organization, is another institute that embodies principles and practices of transpersonal education. It was started by Parker Palmer over a decade ago to foster both personal and professional renewal. The Center seeks to support participants as they create "positive change in their workplaces, professions, and communities, as well as in the lives of the people they serve" (Center for Courage and Renewal, 2006-2012).

This Center offers spiritual retreats and professional training. Facilitators utilize stories, contemplative solitude, deep listening, and poetry to open hearts so that participants may return to their workplaces with restored passion, commitment, and integrity. It uses the Clearness Committee (Palmer, 2006-2012), a strategy grounded in Quaker spirituality, as a means for decision-making and problem solving. This discernment process draws on inner and communal resources.

Programs and trainings offered through the Center for Courage and Renewal are transpersonal forms of education for a variety of reasons. The center's mission and philosophy draw on spiritual principles and values; they invite participants onto a journey of transformation where they eventually bring their understanding to their homeland community. Facilitators utilize transpersonal ways of opening to understanding, such as deep listening, contemplation, discernment, and dialog between the inner world and the outer world of action. Finally, their primary goal is to transform individuals, communities, and society, and this clearly has been accomplished: The Center has reached tens of thousands of people throughout the country.

Classrooms that Support Transpersonal Ways of Knowing

Transpersonal Education can also be found within individual classrooms. This section describes one class based on a curriculum model that is transpersonal and transformative and two examples where the teacher has integrated transpersonal ways of knowing into classes within traditional academic settings.

Inquiry into creative and innovative processes. Although courses on creativity can be taught in a variety of ways, the following transpersonal approach has been highly successful. In this class, creativity theory is taught using a learning structure that emulates intuitive inquiry (Anderson, 2011), in order to bring depth, transpersonal practice, and the potential for transformation.

"Inquiry into Creativity and Innovation" (Netzer & Rowe, 2010), a six-week online research course about creativity, creative process, creativity as spirituality, and a self-selected topic, was set into the five cycles of intuitive inquiry (Anderson, 2011). Intuitive inquiry invites the researcher into an exploration that balances scholarly research with transpersonal ways of knowing, including intuition, sympathetic resonance, imaginal learning, and creative exploration.

Students begin this course by participating in a contemplative activity that taps into their creativity and helps them notice topics potent within their psyche. From this place, they select a research topic that is moving them. In the second week, students delineate their preliminary lenses or preconceptions and become metacognitively aware (knowing about knowing) of how they have arrived at assumptions and understandings about this topic. Simultaneously, they read articles, books, and other sources of information related to creativity theory and their chosen topic. They create a set of questions and then interview a professional who can inform them about their topic. They continue using transpersonal and creative explorations to deepen their understanding about their research and allow their intuition to play a part in leading them down paths they might not otherwise consider. This dance between scholarship and intuitive exploration continues until the final week when papers are completed.

In the fourth week, students return to their preliminary lenses, discerning whether or not their understandings continue to hold true, and make a new list of lenses of awareness that weaves their combined insights from reading, interview, and experiential learning. They develop a creative synthesis project that integrates their learning and creatively expresses their new awareness. Students then write their papers.

This transpersonal approach to inquiry invites students into a journey of exploration and potential personal transformation as they move into their research, questioning their understanding and using the transpersonal values of discernment, radical honesty, and authenticity to transform their awareness and to note how this has happened. They explore their topics using transpersonal ways of knowing, such as imagination, dreams, contemplation, and connection with the earth, checking into their felt sense and intuitive awareness at each stage of the inquiry. The course structure invites a journey of transformation.

Integrating Transpersonal Ways of Knowing Into Conventional Classrooms

Educators in schools that teach transpersonal psychology have easily blended transpersonal material into various fields of study (Davis, 1998; Ferrer, 2002). This has helped advance transpersonal education. Other educators have found ways to incorporate transpersonal ways of knowing into conventional curricula. These initiatives make students aware of complimentary ways of studying a discipline. The following section profiles two such educators.

Integrated learning: teacher education. Sam Crowell, at California State University, San Bernardino, is a teacher educator in an integrative education program (Duerr et al., 2003). He has stated that he believes "we teach who we are" (p. 193) and that this assumption awakens students to a genuine exploration of self that leads to authentic teaching. He has described various ways that he has incorporated spiritual practice, self-exploration, and other transpersonal practices into his curriculum. He explained that he made room for a variety of spiritual practices and for reflection on spiritual topics, such as the sacredness of the experience and the need for quiet and stillness. He described co-teaching with a visual artist who was also a Zen monk. During that time his students learned to think through various art modalities, created a labyrinth as a way to show ancient participation in collective and individual consciousness, and explored the embodied notion of journeying to one's own center and "living within the question" (p. 193). He required his students to be authentic, reflect honestly, use introspection, and participate in contemplative activities.

Art history. Bowdoin College Associate Professor of Art History Susan Wegner incorporated contemplative practices into her art history seminars in direct relation to topics being studied even though she occasionally felt challenged in teaching a practice without demanding that there be a spiritual context for it (Duerr et al., 2003).

Specifically, Wegner incorporated the practices of *Lectio Divina* (divine reading), *Oratio* (prayer), walking the labyrinth, and contemplation practices from the *Cloud of Unknowing* as students read Medieval manuscripts and took in the art of the time (Duerr et al., 2003). In some of these practices she encouraged students to refrain from thinking and speaking and to be silent, open, and accepting of whatever comes. Students experienced what it means to sit in silence in a quiet place while saying a single word like "love" or "God." Wegner has expressed belief that experiencing contemplative practices is essential to the study of the devotional art of the Medieval period. As a result of these practices, students and the instructor experienced a closer connection to one another and a new way of learning.

Transpersonal Self-education

In addition to being helped and nurtured by a mentor, it is possible to self-educate oneself about the transpersonal. This can be done through readings, reflection, and engaging in regular spiritual practices, such as contemplation, meditation, and prayer. Another approach is to work with one's own *exceptional human experiences* (EHEs). EHEs are anomalous experiences, such as mystical/unitive, psychic, encounter, unusual death-related, and "exceptional normal" experiences, that, if worked with sufficiently, can foster transformative changes in the experiencer.

Of great relevance to transpersonal education is a model, proposed by Rhea White (1997), of how working with one's EHEs can have profound life impacts and can result in important transformative changes; she has called this the *EHE process*. This is essentially a *transpersonal self-education process*. The process begins by refusing to ignore, dismiss, or explain away one of these unusual experiences that cannot be explained in terms of conventionally recognized physical, biological, psychological, or sociological processes. Rather, one can attend more to the EHE and wish to learn its possible meaning. As people continue to work more deeply and extensively with their unusual experiences, they begin to uncover other similar experiences, their meaning and significance deepens, and the experiencers begins to discover and to actualize and express more of their true human potentials. Their self-schema, lifeview, and worldview begin to transform.

Experiencers begins to shift their prior self-narrative to a new one; they begin to disidentify with their earlier, limited, isolated, separate ego-self ("little self") and to re-identify with what White called a more inclusive "All-Self" (of a similar concept, William James (1902/1985 wrote, "[One] becomes conscious that this higher part is conterminous and continuous with a MORE of the same quality, which is operative in the universe outside of [one], and which [one] can keep in working touch with" (p. 508). One begins to live a new "project of transcendence," and develops a new way of being in the world. This new way includes a shift in one's self narrative from a *life-depotentiating* one in which unusual experiences are devalued, explained away, or viewed in a continuing anomalous or pathological context, to a *life-potentiating* one wherein exceptional experiences are affirmed and used in stories in which they have a more meaningful place. The new life-potentiating narrative is associated with a more productive, happier, healthier, zestier, and exciting life.

White (1997) suggested that one of the best ways to realize the benefits of EHEs is to prepare an extensive and ongoing journal of one's own EHEs in what she called the *EHE autobiography*. In an EHE autobiography, one attempts to tell the story of one's life, not in terms of the usual outer events of a typical autobiography, but in terms of one's inner life—the EHEs that one has had. In working on the EHE autobiography, one focuses increased attention on one's EHEs, allowing these to be better remembered and more fully integrated with each other and with the entirety of one's life. Working with EHEs in this systematic manner provides a catalyst for forms of growth and development that otherwise might not be possible. As in any transpersonal practice, it is important that one be psychologically ready to open to and integrate this new psychic material.

Future Directions

This chapter has attempted to bring together descriptions and examples of approaches to transpersonal education that might inspire greater dialogue and theory-building and perhaps address some of Cunningham's (2006) concerns about the need for research and support for scholarship in this field. The authors have attempted to clarify what is meant by transpersonal education without trying to bind it too tightly, yet at the same time differentiate it from other forms of education. The many ways that transpersonal education has been expressed and adapted have been highlighted. Transpersonal education is a lens into education, one that brings expansiveness, interconnection, exceptional human experiences, and psychospiritual transformation to the forefront, yet demanding that it adhere too tightly to definitional boundaries would limit its nature that tends to be dynamic, flexible, adaptive, spacious, visionary, and expansive. Moving toward the future, educators, scholars, and researchers need to continue the dialogue and improve upon ways that bring transpersonal education to all students from kindergarten to adulthood without holding it too tightly.

Already, some educators have offered concrete suggestions on ways to improve education that are closely aligned with the values and aims of transpersonal education and transformative education as discussed above. For example, writer, lecturer, editor, and educator David Lorimer (1990) has suggested 11 approaches that might be added to those currently existing in educational systems in order to help foster greater emotional, psychological, and spiritual growth and development in students. Some of these include placing human beings in a system context of interconnectedness, interdependence, and responsibility at the biological, ecological, social, psychological, and spiritual levels; cultivating reverence for all life; presenting comparative world-views to foster mutual tolerance and understanding; emphasizing the masculine and feminine qualities within each person; learning ways of acquiring inner peace as a result of silence and meditation; cultivating a sense of beauty that stimulates imagination and sympathies; and emphasizing the need to study in depth the nature of love in its widest sense and to work out how kindness, trust, and co-operation can best be fostered in the attempt to create a maximum of synergy within the world system (pp. 282-283).

Within transpersonal psychology, there have been many perspectives of the nature of transpersonal education. For example, in addressing transpersonal issues at the millennium, transpersonal philosopher and teacher of engaged spirituality Donald Rothberg (1999) has suggested seven possible future directions that transpersonal education might take, including focusing more on the link between study and action, between theory and praxis; guiding education by practice and the conscious sense that all experience in a given setting is relevant and related to learning and transformation; articulating various modes of disciplined spiritual inquiry, integrating these with other types of inquiry, and aiming at spiritual insight and wisdom as seriously as established modes of inquiry reach for empirical knowledge; emphasizing the connections between different levels of development and different disciplines; bringing together experiential, practical, intellectual, and spiritual dimensions of education; and recognizing that "ultimately the intention of transpersonal education is no less than spiritual transformation, the cultivation of wisdom and love, the opening of heart and mind, the deep communion with life" (p. 56).

The following statement serves as a conclusion that is well aligned with the nature and aims of transpersonal education:

> Education is meant to open many doors, leading to many rooms. Imagination thrives when sensual experience joins with reason, when Illusions link to Reality, when intuition couples with intellect, when the passions of the heart unite with those of the mind, when knowledge gained in one discipline opens doors to all the rest. The point of education must be to create whole people who, through their wholeness, can focus the accumulated wisdom of human experience into illuminated patches of splendor. (Root-Bernstein & Root-Bernstein, 1999, pp. 325-326)

Notes

1. I dedicate this chapter to my friend and colleague, William Braud, who crossed over weeks after we wrote this chapter. William's contribution to the field of transpersonal psychology was legendary. Even greater was his depth of spirituality. He showed us how teaching,

writing, and the sharing of scholarship can be a spiritual practice. He will be greatly missed by so many of his colleagues and students. (Nancy Rowe)
2. The name ITP (Institute of Transpersonal Psychology) will be used in research that was accomplished prior to the name change.

References

Anderson, R. (2011). Intuitive inquiry: The way of the heart in human science research. In R. Anderson & W. Braud, *Transforming self and others through research: Transpersonal research methods and skills for the human sciences and humanities* (pp. 15-70). Albany, NY: State University of New York Press.

Anderson, R., & Braud, W. (2011). *Transforming self and others through research: Transpersonal research methods and skills for the human sciences and humanities.* Albany, NY: State University of New York Press.

Baker, V. (2012). The alchemy of change: A mixed-methods study of transformation in an online master's program in transpersonal psychology. *Dissertation Abstracts International, 74*(02) 0669B (UMI #3522527).

Baveja, B. (2011). Situating teacher education in the Indian context: A paradigm shift. In R. M. M. Cornelissen, G. Misra, & S. Varma (Eds.), *Foundations of Indian psychology: Practical applications* (Vol. 2, pp. 132-146). New Delhi, India: Pearson.

Bohm, D. (1993). Science, spirituality, and the present world crisis. *Revision: A Journal of Consciousness and Transformation, 15*(4), 147-152.

Boucouvalas, M. (1999). Following the movement: From transpersonal psychology to a multi-disciplinary transpersonal orientation. *Journal of Transpersonal Psychology, 31*(1), 27-39.

Braud, W. (2006). Educating the "more" in holistic transpersonal higher education: A 30+ year perspective on the approach of the Institute of Transpersonal Psychology. *Journal of Transpersonal Psychology, 38*(2), 133-158.

Braud, W., & Schmitt, R. (2000, April). *Educating the whole person: Assessing student learning and transformative changes in an academic-experiential graduate psychology program.* Paper presented at the 76th Annual Meeting of the Association of Colleges and Universities, Western Association of Schools and Colleges, San Diego, CA.

Brussat, F., & Brussat, M. (1996). *Spiritual literacy: Reading the sacred in everyday life.* New York, NY: Simon & Schuster.

Cajete, G. (1994). *Look to the mountain: An ecology of indigenous education.* Skyland, NC: Kivaki Press.

Cajete, G. (2004). A Pueblo story for transformation. In E. O'Sullivan & M. Taylor (Eds.), *Learning toward an ecological consciousness: Selected transformative practices* (pp. 103-114). New York, NY: Palgrave.

Center for Courage and Renewal. (2006-2012) CourageRenewal.org. Retrieved from http://couragerenewal.org/about

Center for Integral Education. (n.d). Retrieved from http://www.integraleducation.org/vision_integral.htm

Clark, F. V. (1974). Rediscovering transpersonal education. *Journal of Transpersonal Psychology, 6*(1), 1-7.

Cornelissen, R. M. M., Misra, G., & Varma, S. (Eds.). (2011a). *Foundations of Indian psychology: Practical applications* (Vol. 2). New Delhi, India: Pearson.

Cunningham, P. F. (2006). Transpersonal education: Problems, prospects and challenges. *International Journal of Transpersonal Studies, 25,* 62-68.

Daniels, M. (2005). *Shadow, self, and spirit: Essays in transpersonal psychology.* Exeter, UK: Impact Academic.

Davis, J. V. (1998). The transpersonal dimensions of ecopsychology: Nature, nonduality, and spiritual practice. *The Humanistic Psychologist, 26*(1-3), 60-100.

Dirkx, J. M., Mezirow, J., & Cranton, P. (2006). Musings and reflections on the meaning, context, and process of transformative learning: A dialogue between John M. Dirkx and Jack Mezirow. *Journal of Transformative Education, 4*(2), 123-139.

Duerr, M., Zajonc, A., & Dana, D. (2003). Survey of transformative and spiritual dimensions of higher education. *Journal of Transformative Education, 1*(3), 177-211.

Esbjörn-Hargens, S., Reams, J., & Gunnlaughson, O. (2010). *Integral education: New directions for higher learning.* Albany, NY: State University of New York Press.

Ferrer, J. N. (2002), *Revisiting transpersonal theory: A participatory vision of human spirituality.* Albany, NY: State University of New York Press.

Ferrer, J. N. (2008). What does it mean to live a fully embodied spiritual life? *International Journal of Transpersonal Studies, 28*(1-2), 1-11.

Frager, R. (1974). A proposed model for a graduate program in transpersonal psychology. *Journal of Transpersonal Psychology, 6*(2), 163-166.

Friedman, H. L. (2002). Transpersonal psychology as a scientific field. *International Journal of Transpersonal Studies, 21*, 175-187.

Friedman, H. L., & Pappas, J. (2006). Self-expansiveness and self-contraction: Complementary processes of transcendence and immanence. *Journal of Transpersonal Psychology, 38*(1), 41-54.

Gardner, H. (1999). *Intelligence reframed: Multiple intelligences for the 21st century.* New York, NY: Basic Books.

Glazer, S. (Ed.). (1999). *The heart of learning: Spirituality in education.* New York, NY: Jeremy P. Tarcher/Putnam.

Hart, T., Nelson, P., & Puhakka, K. (Eds.). (2000). *Transpersonal knowing: Exploring the horizon of consciousness.* Albany, NY: State University of New York Press.

Hartelius, G., Caplan, M., & Rardin, M. A. (2007). Transpersonal psychology: Defining the past, divining the future. *The Humanistic Psychologist, 35*(2), 1-26.

Huppes, N. (2001). *Psychic education: A workbook.* Pondicherry, India: All India Press.

James, W. (1985). *The varieties of religious experience.* New York, NY: Penguin. (Original work published 1902)

Kessler, R. (2000). *Soul of education: Helping students find connection, compassion, and character at school.* Alexandria, VA: Association for Supervision and Curriculum Development.

Kessler, R. (2005). Nourishing adolescents' spirituality. In J. P. Miller, S. Karsten, D. Denton, D. Orr, & I. C. Kates (Eds.), *Holistic learning and spirituality in education: Breaking new ground* (pp. 101-108). Albany, NY: State University of New York Press.

Lindholm, J. A., & Astin, H. A. (2006). Understanding the "interior" life of faculty: How important is spirituality? *Religion & Education, 33*(2), 64-90.

Lorimer, D. (1990). *Whole in one: The near-death experience and the ethic of interconnectedness.* London, UK: Penguin/Arkana.

Markos, L., & McWhinney, W. (2003). Editor's perspective: Auspice. *Journal of Transformative Education, 1*(1), 16-37.

Mezirow, J. (2003). Transformative learning as discourse. *Journal of Transformative Education, 1*(1), 58-63.

Miles, A. (2002). Feminist perspectives on globalization and integrative transformative learning. In E. V. O'Sullivan, A. Morrell, & M. A. O'Connor (Eds.), *Expanding the boundaries of transformative learning: Essays on theory and praxis* (pp. 59-76). New York, NY: Palgrave.

Miller, J. P. (2002). Learning from a spiritual perspective. In E. V. O'Sullivan, A. Morrell, & M. A. O'Connor (Eds.), *Expanding the boundaries of transformative learning: Essays on theory and praxis* (pp. 95-102). New York, NY: Palgrave.

Miller, J. P. (2005). Conclusion: Seeking wholeness. In J. P. Miller, S. Karsten, D. Denton, D. Orr, & I. C. Kates (Eds.), *Holistic learning and spirituality in education: Breaking new ground*. Albany, NY: State University of New York Press.

Miller, J. P., Karsten, S., Denton, D., Orr, D., & Kates, I. C. (2005). (Eds.), *Holistic learning and spirituality in education: Breaking new ground*. Albany, NY: State University of New York Press.

Moore, T. (2005). Educating for the soul. In J. P. Miller, S. Karsten, D. Denton, D. Orr, & I. C. Kates (Eds.), *Holistic learning and spirituality in education: Breaking new ground* (pp. 9-16). Albany, NY: State University of New York Press.

Netzer, D., & Rowe, N. (2010). Inquiry into creative and innovative processes: An experiential, whole-person approach to teaching creativity. *Journal of Transformative Education, 8*(2), 124-145.

O'Sullivan, E. (2002). The project and vision of transformative education: Integral transformative learning. In E. V. O'Sullivan, A. Morrell, & M. A. O'Connor (Eds.), *Expanding the boundaries of transformative learning* (pp. 1-12). New York, NY: Palgrave.

O'Sullivan, E., Morrell, A., & O'Connor, M. A. (Eds.). (2002). *Expanding the boundaries of transformative learning*. New York, NY: Palgrave.

O'Sullivan, E., & Taylor, M. (2004). *Learning toward an ecological consciousness: Selected transformative practices*. New York, NY: Palgrave.

Palmer, P. (1997). The grace of great things: Reclaiming the sacred in knowing, teaching, and learning. *Holistic Education Review, 10*(3), 8-16.

Palmer, P. (2006-2012). *The Clearness Committee: A communal approach to discernment*. Seattle, WA: Center for Courage and Renewal. Retrieved from http://www.couragerenewal.org/parker/writings/clearness-committee

Partho (2007). *Integral education: A foundation for the future*. Pondicherry, India: Sri Aurobindo Society in association with UBSPD.

Root-Bernstein, R., & Root-Bernstein, M. (1999). *Sparks of genius: The thirteen thinking tools of the world's most creative people*. Boston, MA: Houghton Mifflin.

Rothberg, D. (1999). Transpersonal issues at the millennium. *Journal of Transpersonal Psychology, 31*(1), 41-67.

Rowe, N. (2011). *Comparison of the Master's of Transpersonal Psychology (MTP) program to characteristics of transpersonal psychology and transformative education*. Unpublished manuscript for the Program Review of Sofia University, Palo Alto, CA.

Sarath, E. (2010a). *Students, Teachers, and Administrators for Transpersonal Education (STATE): Integrating creativity, consciousness, & conventional academic studies*. Retrieved from http://state.edsarath.com/faq.html (Original work published 2003)

Sarath, E. (2010b). *Students, teachers, and administrators for transpersonal education* (Website). Ann Arbor, MI: Author. Retrieved from www.edsarath.com

Schugurensky, D. (2002). Transformative learning and transformative politics: The pedagogical dimensions of participatory democracy and social activism. In E. V. O'Sullivan, A. Morrell, & M. A. O'Connor (Eds.), *Expanding the boundaries of transformative learning: Essays on theory and praxis* (pp. 59-77). New York, NY: Palgrave.

Selby, D. (2002). The signature of the whole: Radical interconnectedness and its implications for global and environmental education. In E. V. O'Sullivan, A. Morrell, & M. A. O'Connor (Eds.), *Expanding the boundaries of transformative learning: Essays on theory and praxis* (pp. 77-94). New York, NY: Palgrave.

Shahjahan, R. A. (2004). Centering spirituality in the academy: Toward a transformative way of teaching and learning. *Journal of Transformative Education, 2*(4), 294-312.

Sofia University. (n.d.). History (n.p.). Author. Retrieved from http://www.sofia.edu/about/history.php

Tisdell, E. J., & Tolliver, D. E. (2003). Claiming a sacred face: The role of spirituality and cultural identity in transformative adult higher education. *Journal of Transformative Education, 1*(4), 368-392.

Vaughan, F. (2002). What is spiritual intelligence? *Journal of Humanistic Psychology, 42*(2), 16-33.

White, R. A. (1997). Dissociation, narrative, and exceptional human experience. In S. Krippner & S. Powers (Eds.), *Broken images, broken selves: Dissociative narratives in clinical practice* (pp. 88-121). Washington, DC: Brunner-Mazel.

Yorks, L., & Kasl, E. (2006). I know more than I can say: A taxonomy for using expressive ways of knowing to foster transformative learning. *Journal of Transformative Education, 4*(1), 43-64.

Appendix

Transpersonal Resources

This Appendix is organized into three categories: journals, degree-granting schools, and organizations. The resources listed are not inclusive of all possible listings, but provide a starting place for those seeking to learn more about, and participate with, transpersonal psychology.

Transpersonal Journals

International Journal of Transpersonal Studies

The *International Journal of Transpersonal Studies* (IJTS) is dedicated to publishing research that unites the global transpersonal community. The journal published semi-annually and is an open-access journal available free online (and is available in print upon request).

Website: http://www.transpersonalstudies.org (and to access free copies of the journal)
Contact information: Glenn Hartelius, Editor (Email: payattention1@mac.com)
Harris Friedman, Senior Editor (Email: harrisfriedman@hotmail.com)

Journal of Consciousness Studies

The *Journal of Consciousness Studies* is dedicated to publishing a broad array of articles and research on consciousness, including articles with transpersonal content. Since this is a fairly young area of research, the journal promotes spirited debates that encompass

The Wiley Blackwell Handbook of Transpersonal Psychology, First Edition.
Edited by Harris L. Friedman and Glenn Hartelius.
© 2013 John Wiley & Sons, Ltd. Published 2015 by John Wiley & Sons, Ltd.

Appendix

disciplines spanning the fields of philosophy, cognitive science, and biology, to name a few.

Website: http://www.imprint.co.uk/jcs.html
Contact information: Valerie Gray Hardcastle, Editor (Email: valerie.hardcastle@ uc.edu)

Journal of Humanistic Psychology

The *Journal of Humanistic Psychology* is dedicated to publishing a diverse array of topics associated with the field of humanistic psychology, including articles with transpersonal content.

Website: http://jhp.sagepub.com
Contact information: Shawn Rubin, Editor (Email: srubin@saybrook.edu)

Journal of Transpersonal Psychology

The *Journal of Transpersonal Psychology* is focused on the dissemination of information spanning the field of transpersonal psychology. The journal was founded following the development of the Association for Transpersonal Psychology in 1972, and fosters research in theory and application, while incorporating a values-oriented approach to human experience.

Website: http://www.atpweb.org/journal.aspx
Contact information: Marcie Boucouvalas, Editor (Email: jtpsych@vt.edu)

Journal of Transpersonal Research

The objective of the *Journal of Transpersonal Research* is to promote, bring together and disseminate the investigation of transpersonal psychology and psychotherapy, as well as other subjects related to this field.

Website: http://www.transpersonaljournal.com
Contact information: Roman Gonzalvo, Editor (Email: contact@transpersonaljour nal.com)

ReVision: A Journal of Consciousness and Transformation

ReVision focuses on the transformative dimensions of contemporary and traditional thought and praxis, and seeks to advance inquiry and reflection within fields such as philosophy, religion, psychology, social theory, science, anthropology, education, organizational transformation, and the arts. It is particularly interested in new models of transdisciplinary, interdisciplinary, multicultural, dialogical, socially engaged inquiry, and frontier science.

Website: http://www.revisionpublishing.org
Contact information: Jürgen Kremer, Editor (Email: editor@revisionpublishing.org or subscriptions@revisionpublishing.org)

The Humanistic Psychologist

The Humanistic Psychologist is the official journal of the Society for Humanistic Psychology, American Psychological Association Division 32. This peer-reviewed journal publishes a broad array of articles that span the field of humanistic psychology, including articles with transpersonal content.

Website: http://www.apadivisions.org/division-32/publications/journals/index.aspx
Contact information: Scott Churchill, Editor (Email: bonobo@udallas.edu)

Transpersonal Psychology Review

The *Transpersonal Psychology Review* is periodical associated with the Transpersonal Psychology Section of the British Psychological Society. This journal publishes a broad array of research pertaining to the field of transpersonal psychology.

Website: http://tps.bps.org.uk/tps/tpr.cfm
Contact information: Michael Daniels, Editor (Email: admin@transpersonalscience .org or enquiries@bps.org.uk)

Doctoral-Granting Schools Offering Transpersonal Programs

California Institute of Integral Studies

California Institute of Integral Studies offers a wide variety of courses and degrees related to transpersonal psychology, including Ph.D. programs in Philosophy and Religion, East-West Psychology, Anthropology and Social Change, and Transformative Studies. At the M.A. level the offerings include the topic areas of the listed Ph.D. programs, as well as Counseling Psychology with concentrations in Drama Therapy, Expressive Arts Therapy, and Somatic Psychology. In addition, there are MFA programs in Creative Inquiry and Writing and Consciousness.

Website: http://www.ciis.edu

ITA Professional (validated by Middlesex University)

ITA Professional is a not-for-profit enterprise based in the UK whose mission is to nurture human potential through the creation of courses, projects and initiatives which apply insights from transpersonal psychology in managerial, coaching, health and wellbeing, and artistic contexts. It offers an MSc in Professional Development in "Consciousness, Spirituality and Transpersonal Psychology," which is validated by

Middlesex University and provides accredited, practice-oriented routes for applying transpersonal perspectives in coaching, therapy, and/or management. Ph.D. opportunities are also available.

Website: http://www.transpersonalstudies.org.uk or PDF.net
Contact information: Professor B. Les Lancaster (Email: les.lancaster@ita-professional
.org)

Saybrook University

Saybrook University has a long tradition of in offering studies in humanistic and transpersonal psychology. Saybrook prepares students to be researchers, scholars/ teachers, and/or practitioners in transpersonal psychology.

Website: http://www.saybrook.edu
Contact information: Louis Hoffman (Email: lhoffman@saybrook.edu)

Sofia University

Sofia University, formerly the Institute of Transpersonal Psychology, is the oldest transpersonally-oriented institution of higher learning (founded 1975), and the largest center for transpersonal education and scholarship. The school currently offers a Ph.D. in Transpersonal Psychology, a transpersonally-oriented distance-learning Ph.D. in Psychology, a spiritually-oriented Psy.D. in Clinical Psychology, an M.A. in Transpersonal Psychology as either a distance-learning or low-residency program, an M.A., in Transpersonal Clinical Psychology, an M.A. in Spiritual Guidance, and an M.A. in Women's Spirituality. Sofia University emphasizes whole-person learning, including both intellectual, emotional, spiritual, physical, creative, and community aspects. The university is accredited by the Western Association of Schools and Colleges.

Website: http://www.sofia.edu

University of Northampton

The University of Northampton offers a postgraduate program in Transpersonal Psychology & Consciousness Studies that uses lectures, seminars and experiential workshops to critically reflect on current scientific understanding of the nature and properties of transpersonal states of consciousness and the experiences they elicit, and to apply that same critical scrutiny to a range of personal experiential practices that are introduced during the course. The program is nationally recognized and regularly audited by HEFCE and the BPS; faculty are closely involved with the Transpersonal Psychology Section of the British Psychological Society.

Website: http://www.northampton.ac.uk/courses/286/transpersonal-psychology-
and-consciousness-studies-msc/
Contact information: Professor Chris Roe (Email: chris.roe@northampton.ac.uk)

University of West Georgia

The University of West Georgia offers two graduate Psychology degrees: a Ph.D. in Consciousness and Society, and an M.A. in Humanistic/Transpersonal Psychology.

Website: http://www.westga.edu/psydept
Contact information: Donadrian Rice, Department Chair (Email: drice@westga.edu)

Transpersonal Organizations

International Transpersonal Association

The International Transpersonal Association (ITA) is an organization focused on bridging the global transpersonal community. As such, it is a global organization of organizations, and can serves as a starting point for searches for other transpersonal organizations. At last count, there were over twenty transpersonal associations representing national and regional constituencies, such as Alubrat (http://www.alubrat.org.br/), Association for Transpersonal Psychology (http://atpweb.org/), and EUROTAS (http://www.eurotas.org/), to name just a few. The ITA's vision encompasses promoting transpersonal perspectives through education, research, scholarship, and conferences, as well as to coordinate among the global transpersonal associations. It also provides a conduit for a wide range of transpersonal services, including coaching, consulting, and therapies conducted from a transpersonal orientation. Further information about ITA can be obtained at:

Website: http://www.transpersonalassociation.org
Contact information: itacontactpoint@gmail.com

Alternate Contacts:

Les Lancaster, President of ITA: (Email: les.lancaster@ita-professional.org)
Harris Friedman, President of the Board of ITA: (Email: harrisfriedman@hotmail.com)

Index

Figures and tables are listed in bold.

The Wiley Blackwell Handbook of Transpersonal Psychology, First Edition.
Edited by Harris L. Friedman and Glenn Hartelius.
© 2013 John Wiley & Sons, Ltd. Published 2015 by John Wiley & Sons, Ltd.

mind-body phenomena, 494, 495
mindfulness, 46, 215, 226, 443, 445,
548-9
meditation, 132, 436, 504, 556-7,
564-5
Mindfulness Based Stress Reduction, 69, 546,
548
mini-theories, 302-3, 304, 308, 310
modernism, 193-4, 195, 424
modernity, 627-8
monads, 180-81
Moody, Raymond, 367
Mormons, 422
motivation, 170, 188
M-R TPT, 203, 211, 212, 214, 218, 304,
305-6, 307, 308, 310
Mtshali, Mbuyiseni Oswald, 656
music therapy, 539-40, 647, 652
muslims, 631
Mystical Experiences Scale, 287
mysticism, 114-15, 126, 128, 132, 144,
168, 174, 189, 190, 228-9, 230,
233, 248, 321, 354, 422, 463-4,
471, 493, 495
activism, 633, 634
mythology, 25, 113, 176
comparative, 143-4
myths, 640, 645, 675

narcissism, 38, 197, 213, 575, 601, 628
Native America, 387
naturalism, 317, 318, 320, 321
natural language concept, 304-5
natural world, 598, 601-3, 607
nature, 33, 130, 175, 208, 390, 597, 601,
602, 603, 605
mysticism, 604-5
relationship with, 606-7
true, 568-9, 571, 573, 601
near-death experiences (NDEs), 75, 94, 97,
130, 133, 338-9, 347, 367, 368-9,
373, 374, 375-6, 411, 586
aftereffects, 370-72, 375
long-term therapeutic approaches,
376-8
post-integration issues, 371-2, 375, 378
research, 374, 375
Nelson, James, 420

neo-shamanism, 384
Neppe, V. M., 402, 411, 412
neurophenomenology, 261, 263, 264, 265,
273, 493, 504, 505, 506
cultural, 270-74
of lucid dreaming, 272-3
of time consiousness, 268-70, 271-2
neuroplasticity, 359, 360, 361-2, 556
neuropsychology, 556
neuroscience, 223-4, 229, 230-31, 233-5,
271, 493, 503, 504, 505
cognitive, 264-5
cultural, 264, 265
New Age, 174, 195, 306
New Testament, 47
noise-reduction model, 408
nomology, 289
nonduality, 390-91, 563, 574, 575, 576,
603-4
non-ordinary states of consciousness, 92-3,
94, 112, 326, 362, 419, 420, 422-3,
434, 496-7, 501-2
North America, 16, 52
now-point, 270, 272
numinosity, 113, 516

objectivism, 70-71, 189
objectivity, 289-90, 303
observations, 71, 92, 225
obsessive-compulsive disorders, 471
occult, 65, 67, 142, 144, 233
ontology, 34, 49, 56, 57, 73-4, 75, 77, 79,
104, 112, 114, 191, 196, 197, 206,
304, 316, 319, 321, 612
operationalizations, 283, 304, 305-6, 319,
323-4
organic inquiry, 251-3, 303, 620-21
original sin, 385-6
O'Sullivan, E., 669
Otto, R., 113
Otto, W. F., 124
out-of-body experiences (OBEs), 97, 102,
130, 335, 346-7, 370

pain, 506, 632, 648, 650
chronic, 548
emotional, 602
Palestine, 72

CPSIA information can be obtained
at www.ICGtesting.com
Printed in the USA
BVHW071214121219
566403BV00008B/65/P